Twentieth-Century Literary Criticism

Guide to Gale Literary Criticism Series

For criticism on	Consult these Gale series
Authors now living or who died after December 31, 1999	*CONTEMPORARY LITERARY CRITICISM (CLC)*
Authors who died between 1900 and 1999	*TWENTIETH-CENTURY LITERARY CRITICISM (TCLC)*
Authors who died between 1800 and 1899	*NINETEENTH-CENTURY LITERATURE CRITICISM (NCLC)*
Authors who died between 1400 and 1799	*LITERATURE CRITICISM FROM 1400 TO 1800 (LC)* *SHAKESPEAREAN CRITICISM (SC)*
Authors who died before 1400	*CLASSICAL AND MEDIEVAL LITERATURE CRITICISM (CMLC)*
Authors of books for children and young adults	*CHILDREN'S LITERATURE REVIEW (CLR)*
Dramatists	*DRAMA CRITICISM (DC)*
Poets	*POETRY CRITICISM (PC)*
Short story writers	*SHORT STORY CRITICISM (SSC)*
Literary topics and movements	*HARLEM RENAISSANCE: A GALE CRITICAL COMPANION (HR)* *THE BEAT GENERATION: A GALE CRITICAL COMPANION (BG)* *FEMINISM IN LITERATURE: A GALE CRITICAL COMPANION (FL)* *GOTHIC LITERATURE: A GALE CRITICAL COMPANION (GL)*
Asian American writers of the last two hundred years	*ASIAN AMERICAN LITERATURE (AAL)*
Black writers of the past two hundred years	*BLACK LITERATURE CRITICISM (BLC-1)* *BLACK LITERATURE CRITICISM SUPPLEMENT (BLCS)* *BLACK LITERATURE CRITICISM: CLASSIC AND EMERGING AUTHORS SINCE 1950 (BLC-2)*
Hispanic writers of the late nineteenth and twentieth centuries	*HISPANIC LITERATURE CRITICISM (HLC)* *HISPANIC LITERATURE CRITICISM SUPPLEMENT (HLCS)*
Native North American writers and orators of the eighteenth, nineteenth, and twentieth centuries	*NATIVE NORTH AMERICAN LITERATURE (NNAL)*
Major authors from the Renaissance to the present	*WORLD LITERATURE CRITICISM, 1500 TO THE PRESENT (WLC)* *WORLD LITERATURE CRITICISM SUPPLEMENT (WLCS)*

ISSN 0276-8178

Volume 212

Twentieth-Century Literary Criticism

**Criticism of the
Works of Novelists, Poets, Playwrights,
Short Story Writers, and Other Creative Writers
Who Lived between 1900 and 1999,
from the First Published Critical
Appraisals to Current Evaluations**

**Thomas J. Schoenberg
Lawrence J. Trudeau**
Project Editors

GALE
CENGAGE Learning

Detroit • New York • San Francisco • New Haven, Conn • Waterville, Maine • London

Twentieth-Century Literary Criticism, Vol. 212

Project Editors: Thomas J. Schoenberg and Lawrence J. Trudeau

Editorial: Dana Ramel Barnes, Tom Burns, Kathy D. Darrow, Kristen A. Dorsch, Jaclyn R. Hermesmeyer, Jeffrey W. Hunter, Jelena O. Krstović, Michelle Lee

Data Capture: Frances Monroe, Gwen Tucker

Indexing Services: Laurie Andriot

Rights and Acquisitions: Jennifer Altschul, Margaret Abendroth, Beth Beaufore

Composition and Electronic Capture: Gary Oudersluys

Manufacturing: Cynde Bishop

Associate Product Manager: Marc Cormier

For product information and technology assistance, contact us at **Gale Customer Support, 1-800-877-4253.**
For permission to use material from this text or product, submit all requests online at **www.cengage.com/permissions.**
Further permissions questions can be emailed to **permissionrequest@cengage.com**

Gale
27500 Drake Rd.
Farmington Hills, MI, 48331-3535

LIBRARY OF CONGRESS CATALOG CARD NUMBER 76-46132

ISBN-13: 978-0-7876-9987-1
ISBN-10: 0-7876-9987-X

ISSN 0276-8178

Printed in the United States of America
1 2 3 4 5 6 7 12 11 10 09 08

Contents

Preface vii

Acknowledgments xi

Literary Criticism Series Advisory Board xiii

Preface

Since its inception *Twentieth-Century Literary Criticism* (*TCLC*) has been purchased and used by some 10,000 school, public, and college or university libraries. *TCLC* has covered more than 1000 authors, representing over 60 nationalities and nearly 50,000 titles. No other reference source has surveyed the critical response to twentieth-century authors and literature as thoroughly as *TCLC*. In the words of one reviewer, "there is nothing comparable available." *TCLC* "is a gold mine of information—dates, pseudonyms, biographical information, and criticism from books and periodicals—which many librarians would have difficulty assembling on their own."

Scope of the Series

TCLC is designed to serve as an introduction to authors who died between 1900 and 1999 and to the most significant interpretations of these author's works. Volumes published from 1978 through 1999 included authors who died between 1900 and 1960. The great poets, novelists, short story writers, playwrights, and philosophers of the period are frequently studied in high school and college literature courses. In organizing and reprinting the vast amount of critical material written on these authors, *TCLC* helps students develop valuable insight into literary history, promotes a better understanding of the texts, and sparks ideas for papers and assignments. Each entry in *TCLC* presents a comprehensive survey on an author's career or an individual work of literature and provides the user with a multiplicity of interpretations and assessments. Such variety allows students to pursue their own interests; furthermore, it fosters an awareness that literature is dynamic and responsive to many different opinions.

Every fourth volume of *TCLC* is devoted to literary topics. These topics widen the focus of the series from the individual authors to such broader subjects as literary movements, prominent themes in twentieth-century literature, literary reaction to political and historical events, significant eras in literary history, prominent literary anniversaries, and the literatures of cultures that are often overlooked by English-speaking readers.

TCLC is designed as a companion series to Gale's *Contemporary Literary Criticism,* (*CLC*) which reprints commentary on authors who died after 1999. Because of the different time periods under consideration, there is no duplication of material between *CLC* and *TCLC*.

Organization of the Book

A *TCLC* entry consists of the following elements:

- The **Author Heading** cites the name under which the author most commonly wrote, followed by birth and death dates. Also located here are any name variations under which an author wrote, including transliterated forms for authors whose native languages use nonroman alphabets. If the author wrote consistently under a pseudonym, the pseudonym is listed in the author heading and the author's actual name is given in parenthesis on the first line of the biographical and critical information. Uncertain birth or death dates are indicated by question marks. Single-work entries are preceded by a heading that consists of the most common form of the title in English translation (if applicable) and the name of its author.

- The **Introduction** contains background information that introduces the reader to the author, work, or topic that is the subject of the entry.

- The list of **Principal Works** is ordered chronologically by date of first publication and lists the most important works by the author. The genre and publication date of each work is given. In the case of foreign authors whose works have been translated into English, the English-language version of the title follows in brackets. Unless otherwise indicated, dramas are dated by first performance, not first publication. Lists of **Representative Works** by different authors appear with topic entries.

- Reprinted **Criticism** is arranged chronologically in each entry to provide a useful perspective on changes in critical evaluation over time. The critic's name and the date of composition or publication of the critical work are given at the beginning of each piece of criticism. Unsigned criticism is preceded by the title of the source in which it originally appeared. All titles by the author featured in the text are printed in boldface type. Footnotes are reprinted at the end of each essay or excerpt. In the case of excerpted criticism, only those footnotes that pertain to the excerpted texts are included. Criticism in topic entries is arranged chronologically under a variety of subheadings to facilitate the study of different aspects of the topic.

- A complete **Bibliographical Citation** of the original essay or book precedes each piece of criticism. Source citations in the Literary Criticism Series follow University of Chicago Press style, as outlined in *The Chicago Manual of Style,* 15th ed. (Chicago: The University of Chicago Press, 2003).

- Critical essays are prefaced by brief **Annotations** explicating each piece.

- An annotated bibliography of **Further Reading** appears at the end of each entry and suggests resources for additional study. In some cases, significant essays for which the editors could not obtain reprint rights are included here. Boxed material following the further reading list provides references to other biographical and critical sources on the author in series published by Gale.

Indexes

A **Cumulative Author Index** lists all of the authors that appear in a wide variety of reference sources published by Gale, including *TCLC*. A complete list of these sources is found facing the first page of the Author Index. The index also includes birth and death dates and cross references between pseudonyms and actual names.

A **Cumulative Topic Index** lists the literary themes and topics treated in *TCLC* as well as other Literature Criticism series.

A **Cumulative Nationality Index** lists all authors featured in *TCLC* by nationality, followed by the numbers of the *TCLC* volumes in which their entries appear.

An alphabetical **Title Index** accompanies each volume of *TCLC*. Listings of titles by authors covered in the given volume are followed by the author's name and the corresponding page numbers where the titles are discussed. English translations of foreign titles and variations of titles are cross-referenced to the title under which a work was originally published. Titles of novels, dramas, nonfiction books, and poetry, short story, or essay collections are printed in italics, while individual poems, short stories, and essays are printed in roman type within quotation marks.

In response to numerous suggestions from librarians, Gale also produces a paperbound edition of the *TCLC* cumulative title index. This annual cumulation, which alphabetically lists all titles reviewed in the series, is available to all customers. Additional copies of this index are available upon request. Librarians and patrons will welcome this separate index; it saves shelf space, is easy to use, and is recyclable upon receipt of the next edition.

Citing *Twentieth-Century Literary Criticism*

When citing criticism reprinted in the Literary Criticism Series, students should provide complete bibliographic information so that the cited essay can be located in the original print or electronic source. Students who quote directly from reprinted criticism may use any accepted bibliographic format, such as University of Chicago Press style or Modern Language Association (MLA) style. Both the MLA and the University of Chicago formats are acceptable and recognized as being the current standards for citations. It is important, however, to choose one format for all citations; do not mix the two formats within a list of citations.

The examples below follow recommendations for preparing a bibliography set forth in *The Chicago Manual of Style,* 15th ed. (Chicago: The University of Chicago Press, (2003); the first example pertains to material drawn from periodicals, the second to material reprinted from books:

Cardone, Resha. "Reappearing Acts: Effigies and the Resurrection of Chilean Collective Memory in Marco Antonio de la Parra's *La tierra insomne o La puta madre.*" *Hispania* 88, no. 2 (May 2005): 284-93. Reprinted in *Twentieth-Century Literary Criticism.* Vol. 206, edited by Thomas J. Schoenberg and Lawrence J. Trudeau, 356-65. Detroit: Gale, 2008.

Kuester, Martin. "Myth and Postmodernist Turn in Canadian Short Fiction: Sheila Watson, 'Antigone' (1959)." In *The Canadian Short Story: Interpretations,* edited by Reginald M. Nischik, pp. 163-74. Rochester, N.Y.: Camden House, 2007. Reprinted in *Twentieth-Century Literary Criticism.* Vol. 206, edited by Thomas J. Schoenberg and Lawrence J. Trudeau, 227-32. Detroit: Gale, 2008.

The examples below follow recommendations for preparing a works cited list set forth in the *MLA Handbook for Writers of Research Papers,* 5th ed. (New York: The Modern Language Association of America, 1999); the first example pertains to material drawn from periodicals, the second to material reprinted from books:

Cardone, Resha. "Reappearing Acts: Effigies and the Resurrection of Chilean Collective Memory in Marco Antonio de la Parra's *La tierra insomne o La puta madre.*" *Hispania* 88.2 (May 2005): 284-93. Reprinted in *Twentieth-Century Literary Criticism.* Ed. Thomas J. Schoenberg and Lawrence J. Trudeau. Vol. 206. Detroit: Gale, 2008. 356-65.

Kuester, Martin. "Myth and Postmodernist Turn in Canadian Short Fiction: Sheila Watson, 'Antigone' (1959)." *The Canadian Short Story: Interpretations.* Ed. Reginald M. Nischik. Rochester, N.Y.: Camden House, 2007. 163-74. Reprinted in *Twentieth-Century Literary Criticism.* Ed. Thomas J. Schoenberg and Lawrence J. Trudeau. Vol. 206. Detroit: Gale, 2008. 227-32

Suggestions are Welcome

Readers who wish to suggest new features, topics, or authors to appear in future volumes, or who have other suggestions or comments are cordially invited to call, write, or fax the Associate Product Manager:

Associate Product Manager, Literary Criticism Series
Gale
27500 Drake Road
Farmington Hills, MI 48331-3535
1-800-347-4253 (GALE)
Fax: 248-699-8054

Acknowledgments

The editors wish to thank the copyright holders of the criticism included in this volume and the permissions managers of many book and magazine publishing companies for assisting us in securing reproduction rights. Following is a list of the copyright holders who have granted us permission to reproduce material in this volume of *TCLC*. Every effort has been made to trace copyright, but if omissions have been made, please let us know.

COPYRIGHTED MATERIAL IN *TCLC*, VOLUME 212, WAS REPRODUCED FROM THE FOLLOWING PERIODICALS:

American Literature, v. 69, March, 1997. Copyright © 1997 Duke University Press. All rights reserved. Used by permission of the publisher.—*Bulletin of Hispanic Studies,* v. 51, January, 1974 for "The Reality of Words in the Poetry of Pedro Salinas" by Robert G. Havard; v. 76, summer, 1999 for "Mirrors and Pedro Salinas' Doubled 'You'" by Vialla Hartfield-Méndez. Copyright © 1974, 1999 Liverpool University Press. Both reproduced by permission of Taylor & Francis, Ltd., http//:www.tandf.co.uk/journals, conveyed through Copyright Clearance Center, and the respective authors.—*CLA Journal,* v. 44, December, 2000. Copyright © 2000 by The College Language Association. All rights reserved. Used by permission of The College Language Association.—*Critique,* v. 7, spring, 1964. Copyright © 1964 by Helen Dwight Reid Educational Foundation. Reproduced with permission of the Helen Dwight Reid Educational Foundation, published by Heldref Publications, 1319 18th Street, NW, Washington, DC 20036-1802.—*Forum for Modern Language Studies,* v. 20, January, 1984 for "'Verdad de Mitos': Some Aspects of the Use of Classical Mythology in the Poetry of Pedro Salinas" by Sandra Price. Copyright © 1984 Oxford University Press. Reproduced by permission of the publisher and the author.—*French Forum,* v. 24, January, 1999. Copyright © 1999 by French Forum, Inc. All rights reserved. Reproduced by permission of the University of Nebraska Press.—*The French Review,* v. 43, February, 1970. Copyright © 1970 by the American Association of Teachers of French. Reproduced by permission.—*Frontiers,* v. 4, fall, 1979. Copyright © 1979 by the Frontiers Editorial Collective. All rights reserved. Reproduced by permission of the University of Nebraska Press.—*Journal of Modern Literature,* v. 29, fall, 2005. Copyright © 2005 Indiana University Press. Reproduced by permission.—*MLN,* v. 100, March, 1985. Copyright © 1985 by The Johns Hopkins University Press. Reproduced by permission.—*Orbis Litterarum,* v. 47, 1992. Copyright © 1992 Basil Blackwell Ltd. Reproduced by permission of Blackwell Publishers.—*Paragraph,* v. 24, March, 2001. Copyright © 2001 Edinburgh University Press Ltd. Reproduced by permission.—*Renascence,* v. 24, winter, 1972. Copyright © 1972 Marquette University Press. Reproduced by permission.—*The Review of Contemporary Fiction,* v. 13, fall, 1993. Copyright © 1993 *The Review of Contemporary Fiction.* Reproduced by permission.—*Revista de Estudios Hispánicos,* v. 20, May, 1986. Copyright © 1986 by Vassar College. Reproduced by permission.—*Romance Quarterly,* v. 35, May, 1988. Copyright © 1988 by The University Press of Kentucky. Reproduced with permission of the Helen Dwight Reid Educational Foundation, published by Heldref Publications, 1319 18th Street, NW, Washington, DC 20036-1802.—*The Southern Review,* v. 5 n.s., January, 1969 for "Djuna Barnes's Short Stories: An Estrangement of the Heart" by Suzanne C. Ferguson. Reproduced by permission of the author.—*Style,* v. 19, spring, 1985. Copyright © 1985 *Style.* All rights reserved. Reproduced by permission of the publisher.—*Symposium,* v. 25, spring, 1971. Copyright © 1971 by Helen Dwight Reid Educational Foundation. Reproduced with permission of the Helen Dwight Reid Educational Foundation, published by Heldref Publications, 1319 18th Street, NW, Washington, DC 20036-1802.

COPYRIGHTED MATERIAL IN *TCLC*, VOLUME 212, WAS REPRODUCED FROM THE FOLLOWING BOOKS:

Allen, Carolyn. From "Writing toward *Nightwood*: Djuna Barnes' Seduction Stories," in *Silence and Power: A Reevaluation of Djuna Barnes.* Edited by Mary Lynn Broe. Southern Illinois University Press, 1991. Copyright © 1991 by the Board of Trustees, Southern Illinois University. All rights reserved. Reproduced by permission of the publisher.—Antosh, Ruth B. From *Reality and Illusion in the Novels of J.-K. Huysmans.* Rodopi, 1986. Copyright © 1986 Editions Rodopi B.V., Amsterdam. Reproduced by permission.—Coffman, Christine E. From *Insane Passions: Lesbianism and Psychosis in Literature and Film.* Wesleyan University Press, 2006. Copyright © 2006 by Christine E. Coffman. All rights reserved. Reprinted by permission Wesleyan University Press.—Emery, Elizabeth. From *Romancing the Cathedral: Gothic Architecture in Fin-de-Siècle French Culture.* State University of New York Press, 2001. Copyright © 2001 State University of New York. Reprinted by permission of the State University of New York Press.—Frank, Joseph. From *The Widening Gyre:*

Gale Literature Product Advisory Board

The members of the Gale Literature Product Advisory Board—reference librarians from public and academic library systems—represent a cross-section of our customer base and offer a variety of informed perspectives on both the presentation and content of our literature products. Advisory board members assess and define such quality issues as the relevance, currency, and usefulness of the author coverage, critical content, and literary topics included in our series; evaluate the layout, presentation, and general quality of our printed volumes; provide feedback on the criteria used for selecting authors and topics covered in our series; provide suggestions for potential enhancements to our series; identify any gaps in our coverage of authors or literary topics, recommending authors or topics for inclusion; analyze the appropriateness of our content and presentation for various user audiences, such as high school students, undergraduates, graduate students, librarians, and educators; and offer feedback on any proposed changes/enhancements to our series. We wish to thank the following advisors for their advice throughout the year.

Djuna Barnes
1892-1982

(Also wrote under the pseudonym of Lydia Steptoe) American novelist, short story writer, playwright, poet, and journalist.

The following entry provides an overview of Barnes's life and works. For additional information on her career, see *CLC,* Volumes 3, 4, 8, 11, 29, and 127.

INTRODUCTION

Djuna Barnes is an enigmatic literary figure, most often associated with the "Lost Generation" of American expatriates living in Paris in the 1920s and 1930s. She produced a small but varied body of work spread throughout her lifetime, consisting of plays, poems, and short stories, as well as two novels. She was also a well-known journalist before she turned to writing literature. Barnes is primarily remembered, however, for the experimental novel *Nightwood,* published in 1936, which examines issues related to sexuality, identity, alienation, and the disintegration of civilization. Considered an innovator in style and form, Barnes is frequently linked with the modernists of the early twentieth century. She often employed a satirical and parodic manipulation of conventional literary modes and styles, blended genres within individual works, and ignored linear narrative, adopting instead a non-chronological depiction of time, often described as "symphonic" or "fugal." While Barnes's formal choices are considered modernist, her reliance on symbol and use of gothic, nightmarish imagery connect her work to symbolist and surrealist literary traditions. In recent years scholars have increasingly examined Barnes's literary contributions and asserted her importance as an early twentieth-century writer. As Phillip F. Herring has declared, Barnes "combined in a unique way some of the century's most biting satire with a view of the human condition that expressed profoundest gloom. In the best modernist tradition, her writing is idiosyncratic, original and full of enigmas, but it reminds the reader at times of predecessors." Herring concludes that "while comparisons might help us to place her in the modern tradition, ultimately, from the early journalism to her latest creative work, Djuna Barnes' artistic achievement was quite original."

BIOGRAPHICAL INFORMATION

Barnes was born on June 12, 1892, in Cornwall-on-Hudson, New York. Her father, Wald Barnes, an afflu-ent, visionary, and independent American, moved the family to a farm in Long Island in an effort to escape the trappings of society, which he greatly distrusted. Barnes's British-born mother, Elizabeth Chappell, suffered her husband's unconventional lifestyle, including his various adulterous affairs. She even allowed his mistress, Fanny Faulkner, to move into their home. Wald Barnes, who believed in polygamy, fathered five children with Elizabeth and four additional children with Fanny.

Barnes's father and her paternal grandmother, Zadel Barnes Gustafson, oversaw much of her education, which focused on literature, painting, and music. Barnes later claimed that her grandmother, who took part in early feminist campaigns, was a journalist, and once conducted a London salon, had the greatest influence on her early life. Few additional details regarding Barnes's childhood are known. Although some biographers have contended that the author was sexually abused by her father, Barnes never confirmed this during her lifetime. In 1912, when forced to choose between his two families, Wald left Elizabeth and their children and settled with Fanny, whom he later married.

Following this separation Barnes moved to New York City, where she studied art at Pratt Institute and the Art Students' League. She published poems in *Harper's Weekly* in 1911, and in 1913 began contributing stories and illustrated articles to the *Brooklyn Eagle.* She quickly established herself as a journalist and began writing articles and conducting interviews for some of New York's leading newspapers and magazines, including *New York Morning Telegraph, New York Herald,* and, under the pseudonym of Lydia Steptoe, *Vanity Fair.*

While living in New York Barnes became acquainted with Guido Bruno, who exhibited some of her artwork in his Greenwich Village garret. In 1915 Bruno published a chapbook of her poems and drawings, titled *The Book of Repulsive Women: 8 Rhythms and 5 Drawings.* Barnes began writing plays during this time, as well, including three one-act plays, which were produced by the Provincetown Playhouse in 1919 and 1920. Many of her poems and stories appeared in both literary and popular magazines, including the *Little Review,* the *Dial, Charm,* and *Smart Set.* While launching her literary career, Barnes continued to work as a journalist, a career which she maintained until the 1930s.

In 1919 Barnes moved to Paris as a correspondent for *McCall's* magazine. She remained there throughout the

1920s and 1930s, establishing relationships with many influential expatriate writers residing in the city, including Robert McAlmon, Ezra Pound, Gertrude Stein, and James Joyce, whom she interviewed for *Vanity Fair* magazine. In 1921 she met poet and critic T. S. Eliot, who helped to launch her literary career. During this time, Barnes became romantically involved with Thelma Wood, an American artist, who is generally considered the inspiration for the character of Robin Vote in *Nightwood*. Barnes also began socializing with Natalie Clifford Barney, an Ohio heiress who ran a Paris salon frequented by many important writers and artists. Barney was also openly homosexual and developed a circle of lesbian authors, activists, and socialites, including Barnes, during the years after World War I.

In 1923 Barnes published a collection of short stories, plays, poems, and drawings, which she simply titled *A Book*. A revised edition of the collection, which included additional stories but removed the drawings, was published in 1929 as *A Night among the Horses*. In 1928 Barnes published *Ladies Almanack,* a satirical portrait that chronicled the sexual escapades of Barney and her circle of lesbian intellectuals. That same year Barnes also published her first novel, *Ryder.*

While Barnes lived primarily in Paris during the 1920s and 1930s, she also traveled extensively throughout Europe and returned to New York on several occasions. Between 1929 and 1931 she moved to Greenwich Village to be with Thelma Wood and worked as a columnist for *Theatre Guild Magazine*. The relationship between Wood and Barnes was fraught with difficulties, however, and Barnes eventually left Wood, returning to Paris in the fall of 1931.

Over the next few years Barnes focused on her literary career and spent several summers writing while a guest of Peggy Guggenheim in England. Barnes's next novel, *Nightwood,* which is generally considered her masterpiece, was published in London in 1936, then in America the following year. The book was edited and introduced by T. S. Eliot, which helped it garner considerable critical interest and praise. Following the publication of *Nightwood,* Barnes spent several years in London. In 1940 she returned to New York, residing in Greenwich Village.

During the last decades of her life, Barnes lived a reclusive lifestyle, which she described as her "Trappist" period. After her return to the United States, she did not publish any work until 1958, when she produced a complex verse play titled *The Antiphon.* In the last years of her life, she continued writing and spent much of her time working on an unfinished volume of poetry. Barnes died on June 18, 1982, at the age of ninety.

MAJOR WORKS

Although not as well known as her later literary achievements, Barnes's early work has increasingly drawn critical attention. In her experimental first novel, *Ryder,* Barnes comically treats themes related to humanity's estrangement from the natural world and the disintegration of social order, while challenging the values of patriarchal society. Some critics have emphasized the autobiographical overtones of the novel, which revolves around the Ryder family, particularly the patriarch, Wendell Ryder. Wendell prides himself on being a free-thinker and champions polygamy, while causing pain in the lives of the women around him. Formally, the novel is comprised of fifty chapters and employs various literary and poetic modes, parodying scripture, fable, and the epic, while ignoring some of the cardinal conventions of traditional narrative, such as verisimilitude, standard dialogue, and chronological plot development.

While a number of critics have assessed the novel as an inferior forerunner to *Nightwood,* others have emphasized its formal and thematic accomplishments. Deborah Parsons has contended that *Ryder* "is at once a picaresque novel, social satire and eccentric family chronicle, but also a parable of the politics of sexual reproduction." Parsons further notes that in this early work, Barnes "eschews the conventional chronology and realist style of the family saga, which is told as if from hindsight, thus merging past, present and future. The stylized language and diction mimic earlier literary periods," while the "subtle juxtaposition and reworking of styles and genres," along with "breaks in conventional linearity of plot and narrative, indicate the strategies of modernism."

Ladies Almanack has also received renewed critical interest, particularly among feminist scholars. The book centers on the character of Evangeline Musset, modeled after Natalie Barney, who is described as a saint and the rescuer of young women. Throughout the narrative, Musset celebrates her lesbianism while she surrounds herself with a circle of lovers. *Ladies Almanack* borrows the almanac form, based on the twelve-month calendar, and employs religious imagery and Elizabethan language and style. Barnes's calendar, however, is based on moon and tide cycles, and is thus associated with the female experience of time through cycles of menstruation. The text, which is interspersed with parables, songs, and poems, is accompanied by over twenty original pen and ink drawings by the author.

While *Ladies Almanack* is considered a parody of Barney's circle, it employs an amiable tone, leading some scholars to maintain that the work's primary objective is to openly confront questions of sexual identity, by blurring distinctions between the genders, and to present a critique of patriarchal society from the often marginalized perspective of lesbian culture. Susan Sniader Lanser has described *Ladies Almanack* as "a linguistic and literary experiment, a dense and barely coherent discourse which spurns the conventions of realism, wanders far from the story it is supposed to tell, adopts a host of patriarchal forms and combines them in uneasy parody. The surface form of the text is the monthly chronicle, the almanac, but the book resembles the picaresque fable in structure, the mock epic in tone; it uses or parodies a host of forms including the saint's life, the ode, the prayer, the love song, the allegory, classical mythology, and Sacred Scripture itself." Lanser concludes that the book "creates a lesbian-feminist cultural mythology and even suggests a radical critique of patriarchy by recognizing the personal/sexual as political."

Barnes is best remembered for her novel *Nightwood,* which is generally considered her greatest artistic achievement. The novel is thematically structured, rather than driven by plot, and revolves around the character of Robin Vote, a magnetic American woman who refuses to attach herself to her surroundings or form lasting relations with others. In addition to examining themes related to sexuality and gender definition, the novel explores the effects of decaying civilization and the individual's disintegrating sense of personal identity.

The first chapter opens with the birth of Felix Volkbein, who is orphaned soon after entering the world. Born a Jew and a "Baron" with a fake pedigree, Felix inherits his father's wealth and grows up idealizing the past. Eventually he meets and marries Robin. They move to Vienna, and Robin gives birth to a son, Guido, named after Felix's father. Robin soon succumbs to her wanderlust, however, and leaves both her husband and her son behind in Vienna. In the second chapter, titled "La Somnambule," Barnes chronicles Robin's wanderings and introduces the character of Dr. Matthew O'Connor, whose commentary dominates much of the novel.

In the chapter "Night Watch," Robin meets Nora Flood, an American journalist in Europe. Robin and Nora become romantically involved, but Robin eventually leaves Nora for Jenny Petherbridge. Through much of the remainder of the novel Nora struggles to overcome her obsession with Robin, confiding in Dr. O'Connor and seeking his help as a sort of father-confessor. The controversial final chapter of the novel, titled "The Possessed," takes place in a rural area of the United States, where Nora owns a house. Disturbed by her dog's barking, Nora searches a small chapel on the property and discovers that Robin, now a ruined version of her former self, has been living there. The novel ends with Robin crawling along the ground, barking and snarling with Nora's dog.

Although desire and sexual expression are important themes in *Nightwood,* humanity's struggle with its basic animal nature is another central concern for Barnes. The author expresses this theme primarily through the character of Robin Vote, who wanders from lover to lover, and from place to place, satisfying her most basic urges without guilt or remorse. While Robin's amorality is a destructive force in the lives of the other characters, some critics have averred that by embracing her bestial nature, she is able to return to a state of innocence, beyond conscience and society's constraints. Formally *Nightwood,* like most of Barnes's work, defies categorization and subverts traditional literary conventions. Describing the effect of the novel's formal structure, Joseph Frank has suggested that "the eight chapters of *Nightwood* are like searchlights, probing the darkness each from a different direction yet ultimately illuminating the same entanglement of the human spirit."

Barnes eschews a linear depiction of time in the novel, as well, and in describing its narrative structure, many commentators have borrowed terminology from music, asserting that the book's form is fugal, contrapuntal, or symphonic. Donna Gerstenberger has observed that *Nightwood* demands "a reading against the dominant text of binary oppositions by which the Western world inscribes itself. It is a novel that rages against the imprisoning structures of the language and narratives of the 'day,' which create a history built on the oppositions of night/day, past/present, reason/madness, 'normal'/'abnormal,' truth/falsehood, gender, and origins (both historical and textual). It is a book that relentlessly undermines grounds for categorization. The ideal and the real, the beautiful and the ugly, subject and object become irrelevant distinctions; even the language of the novel works to slip the acculturated binary assumptions of signifier and signified, and the nature of narrative itself is destabilized as traditional categories are emptied of meaning."

Barnes's late work, *The Antiphon,* is often considered her most complex literary effort. Like many of her earlier publications, *The Antiphon* defies facile classifications. Bridging the genres of poetry and drama, it is most often described as a verse play. As in *Ryder,* Barnes seems to draw, once again, from her own childhood in her depiction of the Hobbses, an American family divided over the past actions of the patriarch, Titus Hobbs. The work is set at the beginning of World War II and takes place at the family's ancestral home in England, where the Hobbses have briefly gathered despite their differences. Exploring themes related to molestation, sexuality, power, and submission, Barnes abandons the comic tone she employed in *Ryder,* and ultimately rejects the possibility of reconciliation. Augusta and her daughter, Miranda, both victimized and betrayed by Titus, remain estranged from each other, despite their mutual suffering. *The Antiphon* ends tragically with both Augusta and Miranda dead on stage.

The play is written in blank verse and borrows from Elizabethan and Jacobean dramatic traditions, while utilizing modern elements of symbolism, absurdism, and surrealism. Although it is a respected work in the context of Barnes's oeuvre, the play has failed to attract a wide audience, partly, as some critics have argued, because of its obscure allusions, archaic diction, and difficult syntax. Louis F. Kannenstine has affirmed the play's importance, declaring that *The Antiphon* "taps the origin of modern drama in rituals of the medieval Christian church, suggests variations upon the forms of Greek tragedy and early closet drama, and most directly revives the tone of grandeur of Elizabethan drama with a nod at the Jacobean tradition as well. Also with the prominence of the set as a work of art and the multiple-level musicality of the verse, the play attempts to broaden the scope of dramatic form, to present new possibilities for modern theater." Kannenstine concludes, however, that *The Antiphon* "speaks out against the standards of the marketplace, the dominance of clock time, and the illusion of recorded history. Its effort to get back to a lost reality is intense enough to risk obscurity and ambiguity."

CRITICAL RECEPTION

Although Barnes was celebrated among her peers during the 1920s and 1930s, and achieved some success with her early literary efforts, she remains a marginal figure of the twentieth century. Her first novel, *Ryder,* which was reviewed widely, became a best-seller in the United States after its publication in 1928, but in the decades since has fallen into relative obscurity. Barnes is primarily remembered today for her single masterpiece, *Nightwood,* a work that continues to perplex and challenge critics and readers alike. In his introduction to the 1936 edition, T. S. Eliot commented that readers with "sensibilities trained on poetry" would be best suited to fully appreciate the novel. Eliot praised the novel's "great achievement of a style, the beauty of phrasing, the brilliance of wit and characterization" and asserted that it possessed "a quality of horror and doom very nearly related to that of Elizabethan tragedy."

Many critics since, while not always agreeing with Eliot's assessment, have recognized the book as an important and innovative contribution to American literature, comparable to the writings of James Joyce or Marcel Proust. In the words of Joseph Frank, *Nightwood* is an "amazing book, which combines the simple majesty of a medieval morality play with the verbal subtlety and refinement of a Symbolist poem." Some commentators, however, have argued that *Nightwood* is an odd and frustrating novel, unnecessarily difficult to decipher, and therefore limited in its importance. In fact, the esoteric

and overtly experimental nature of all of Barnes's writing, despite what many regard as her obvious literary talents, has ensured her relative obscurity and diminished status in American letters. Barnes herself was quoted as saying that she was "the most famous unknown of the century."

Commenting on this point in 1964, Alan Williamson observed that "Djuna Barnes, as a lesser member of the cluster of Lost Generation writers, has suffered from becoming the idol of an avant-garde cult while remaining unknown to the general public and deprecated by critics. On the one hand, she is justly praised for the strangeness and profundity of her psychological portraits, the eccentric keenness of her thought, the brilliant rendering of doom and decay, and a style which is at the same time precise and evocative. On the other hand, she is damned for the obscurity of her style and thought, for the morbidity and abnormality of her concerns, and for the unyielding pessimism with which she views man and his destiny." Williamson concludes that "the ultimate appraisal must fall closer to that of the cultist than to that of the philistine. Nonetheless, attempts in the heat of combat to exalt her into a major figure are unsound; she is clearly a writer of a very limited range and meager production, and as such must be relegated to the status of a brilliant minor writer."

In recent years Barnes scholarship has expanded to include lesser-known titles in her body of work. Whereas previous examinations focused on the author's formal and stylistic innovations, more recent studies have discussed the themes addressed in Barnes's work, as well as the author's commentary and stance on political, social, and sexual issues. For many scholars Barnes remains an inscrutable figure, who operated both in and out of literary, social, and political conventions. Discussing the author's use of satire and parody, Lissa Schneider has commented that "Barnes's satiric didacticism is both complex and unsettling in its ambiguities. Her satire is sharply double-edged. Through both structure and theme, her writings establish self-consciously structured oppositions between male and female, bourgeois and working class, artist and audience, only to parodically collapse or dissolve the bounds of those differences."

Barnes's treatment of sexuality and gender identity has prompted numerous debates among critics. During the 1970s some scholars, citing themes and characters from her work, championed Barnes as an important and inspirational lesbian writer. In the years that followed, however, other critics described Barnes as homophobic, noting that she denied her lesbianism later in her life. While some regarded her work as revolutionary, bringing the marginalized experience of homosexuals and other outcasts into focus, others countered that Barnes's often ambiguous renderings of lesbian and gay experience reinforced, rather than challenged, the prejudices of the dominant culture. Regardless, many critics continue to view *Nightwood* and *Ladies Almanack* as pioneering works of lesbian literature.

Writing in 1997 Dianne Chisholm suggested that "instead of viewing this author of American modernism as an unwitting agent in the production and legitimization of dominant culture, we might see her as the artificer of an obscene resistance, laboring in tacit solidarity with her Surrealist contemporaries. We might reconsider the view of *Nightwood* as a lesbian novel whose reception as such had to be deferred until it found an audience among lesbian and gay readers who knew how to recover its latent homosexual content." Two years later Mary E. Galvin praised Barnes's willingness to foreground homosexual experience in her work, asserting that she "consistently presents lesbian sexuality as central to her urban settings and her depictions of her times; the 'otherness' her characters experience is integral to the modernist scene." Galvin concluded that "Barnes consistently pushes at the boundaries of language, genre, and formal expectations with wit, humor, and exaggeration in order to make a space for lesbian existence in our literary heritage."

As many of Barnes's critics have noted, any one assessment of or approach to her work ultimately remains exclusive and incomplete. In the words of Margaret Bockting, Barnes could satirize "conventional expectations, religious and patriarchal tenets, and biased sociohistorical constructions (of public personalities, journalists, women, Jews, homosexuals)" while at the same time romanticize "solitude and privacy, flights of fancy, the 'simpler' pleasures of the past, 'quaint' personalities, ardent love, and relentless melancholy." Despite the varied opinions of Barnes's themes and her merits as a literary artist, most critics would concur with Galvin's appraisal: "In all her works, Barnes explores the real world of sexuality and creativity, human desire and consciousness, often, though not always, against the backdrop of repressive social structures and violence. The 'real story' behind her life choices and running continuously through her works is the story of a struggle for sexual and creative autonomy, the desire to enjoy the freedoms of modernism, against all personal, social, and cultural odds."

PRINCIPAL WORKS

The Book of Repulsive Women: 8 Rhythms and 5 Drawings (poetry and drawings) 1915
Kurzy of the Sea (play) 1920
*A Book (short stories, plays, poetry, and drawings) 1923; revised as *A Night among the Horses,* 1929, and *Spillway,* 1962

Ladies Almanack (prose) 1928
Ryder (novel) 1928
Nightwood (novel) 1936
The Antiphon (play) 1958
Vagaries Malicieux: Two Stories (short stories) 1974
Creatures in an Alphabet (poetry) 1982
Smoke, and Other Early Stories (short stories) 1982
Poe's Mother: Selected Drawings of Djuna Barnes (drawings) 1995
At the Roots of the Stars: The Short Plays (plays) 1995
Collected Stories (short stories) 1996
Collected Poems (poetry) 2005

*This work includes the plays *Three from the Earth, To the Dogs,* and *The Dove.*

CRITICISM

Joseph Frank (essay date 1963)

SOURCE: Frank, Joseph. "Djuna Barnes: *Nightwood.*" In *The Widening Gyre: Crisis and Mastery in Modern Literature,* pp. 25-49. New Brunswick, N.J.: Rutgers University Press, 1963.

[*In the following excerpt, Frank argues that* Nightwood *makes sense only when it is read not as a description of "an extra-artistic 'objective' world" but as "an autonomous structure."*]

The name of Djuna Barnes first became known to those readers who followed, with any care, the stream of pamphlets, books, magazines, and anthologies that poured forth to enlighten America in the feverish days of literary expatriation. Miss Barnes, it is true, must always have remained a somewhat enigmatic figure even to the most attentive reader. Born in New York State, she spent most of her time in England and France; and the glimpses one catches of her in the memoirs of the period are brief and unrevealing. She appears in *The Dial* from time to time with a drawing or a poem; she crops up now and again in some anthology of advance-guard writers—the usual agglomeration of people who are later to become famous or to sink into the melancholy oblivion of frustrated promise. Before the publication of *Nightwood,* indeed, one might have been inclined to place her name in the latter group. For while she had a book of short stories and an earlier novel to her credit, neither prepares one for the maturity of achievement so conspicuous in every line of this work.

Of the fantastical quality of her imagination; of the gift for imagery that, as T. S. Eliot has said in his preface to *Nightwood,* gives one a sense of horror and doom akin to Elizabethan tragedy; of the epigrammatic incisiveness of her phrasing and her penchant, also akin to the Elizabethans, for dealing with the more scabrous manifestations of human fallibility—of all these there is evidence in **Ryder,** Miss Barnes's first novel. But all this might well have resulted only in a momentary flare-up of capricious brilliance, whose radiance would have been as dazzling as it was insubstantial. **Ryder,** it must be confessed, is an anomalous creation from any point of view. Although Miss Barnes's unusual qualities gradually emerge from its kaleidoscope of moods and styles, these qualities are still, so to speak, held in solution or at best placed in the service of a literary *jeu d'esprit.* Only in **Nightwood** do they finally crystallize into a definitive and comprehensible pattern.

Many critics—not least among them T. S. Eliot—have paid tribute to **Nightwood**'s compelling intensity, its head-and-shoulders superiority, simply as a stylistic phenomenon, to most of the works that currently pass for literature. But **Nightwood**'s reputation is similar, in many respects, to that of *The Waste Land* in 1922—it is known as a collection of striking passages, some of breath-taking poetic quality, appealing chiefly to connoisseurs of somewhat gamy literary items. Such a reputation, it need hardly be remarked, is not conducive to intelligent appreciation or understanding. Thanks to a good many critics, we have become able to approach *The Waste Land* as a work of art rather than as a battleground for opposing poetic theories or as a curious piece of literary esoterica. It is time that we began to approach **Nightwood** in the same way.

Before dealing with **Nightwood** in detail, however, we must make certain broad distinctions between it and the novels already considered. While the structural principle of **Nightwood** is the same as of *Ulysses* and *A la recherche du temps perdu*—spatial form, obtained by means of reflexive reference—there are marked differences in technique that will be obvious to every reader. Taking an analogy from another art, we can say that these differences are similar to those between the work of Cézanne and the compositions of a later and more abstract painter like Braque. What characterizes the work of Cézanne, above all, is the tension between two conflicting but deeply rooted tendencies. On the one hand, there is the struggle to attain aesthetic form—conceived of by Cézanne as a self-enclosed unity of form-and-color harmonies—and, on the other, the desire to create this form through the recognizable depiction of natural objects. Later artists took over only Cézanne's preoccupation with formal harmonies, omitting natural objects altogether or presenting them in some distorted manner.

Like Cézanne, Proust and Joyce accept the naturalistic principle, presenting their characters in terms of those commonplace details, those descriptions of circumstance and environment, that we have come to regard as verisimilar. Their experiments with the novel form, it is true, were inspired by a desire to conform more closely to the experience of consciousness; but while the principle of verisimilitude was shifted from the external to the internal, it was far from being abandoned. At the same time, these writers intended to control the abundance of verisimilar detail reflected through consciousness by the unity of spatial apprehension. But in **Nightwood,** as in the work of Braque, the Fauves or the Cubists, the naturalistic principle has lost its dominance. We are asked only to accept the work of art as an autonomous structure giving us an individual vision of reality; and the question of the relation of this vision to an extra-artistic "objective" world has ceased to have any fundamental importance.

. . . . .

Ordinary novels, as T. S. Eliot justly observes, "obtain what reality they have largely from an accurate rendering of the noises that human beings currently make in their daily simple needs of communication; and what part of a novel is not composed of these noises consists of a prose which is no more alive than that of a competent newspaper writer or government official." Miss Barnes abandons any pretensions to this kind of verisimilitude, just as modern painters have abandoned any attempt at naturalistic representation; and the result is a world as strange to the reader, at first sight, as the world of Cubism was to its first spectators. Since the selection of detail in **Nightwood** is governed not by the logic of verisimilitude but by the demands of the décor necessary to enhance the symbolic significance of the characters, the novel has baffled even its most fascinated admirers. Let us attack the mystery by applying our method of reflexive reference, instead of approaching the book, as most of its readers have done, in terms of a coherent temporal pattern of narrative.

Since **Nightwood** lacks a narrative structure in the ordinary sense, it cannot be reduced to any sequence of action for purposes of explanation. One can, if one chooses, follow the narrator in Proust through the various stages of his social career; one can, with some difficulty, follow Leopold Bloom's epic journey through Dublin; but no such reduction is possible in **Nightwood.** As Dr. O'Connor remarks to Nora Flood, with his desperate gaiety: "I have a narrative, but you will be put to it to find it." Strictly speaking, the doctor is wrong—he has a static situation, not a narrative, and no matter how hard the reader looks he will find only the various facets of this situation explored from different angles. The eight chapters of **Nightwood** are like searchlights, probing the darkness each from a different direction yet ultimately illuminating the same entanglement of the human spirit.

In the first four chapters we are introduced to each of the important persons—Felix Volkbein, Nora Flood, Robin Vote, Jenny Petherbridge, and Dr. O'Connor. The next three chapters are, for the most part, long monologues by the doctor, through which the developments of the earlier chapters begin to take on meaning. The last chapter, only a few pages long, has the effect of a coda, giving us what we have already come to feel is the only possible termination. And these chapters are knit together, not by the progress of any action—either narrative action or, as in a stream-of-consciousness novel, the flow of experience—but by the continual reference and cross reference of images and symbols that must be referred to each other spatially throughout the time-act of reading.

At first sight, Dr. O'Connor's brilliant and fantastic monologues seem to dominate the book and overshadow the other characters; but the central figure—the figure around which the situation revolves—is in reality Robin Vote. This creation—it is impossible to call her a character, since character implies humanity and she has not yet attained the level of the human—is one of the most remarkable figures in contemporary literature. We meet her first when the doctor, sitting and drinking with Felix Volkbein in a Paris bar, is summoned by a bellboy from a nearby hotel to look after a lady who has fainted and cannot be awakened. "The perfume that her body exhaled," Miss Barnes writes of Robin,

> was of the quality of that earth-flesh, fungi, which smells of captured dampness and yet is so dry, overcast with the odor of oil of amber, which is an inner malady of the sea, making her seem as if she had invaded a sleep incautious and entire. Her flesh was the texture of plant life, and beneath it one sensed a frame, broad, porous and sleep-worn, as if sleep were a decay fishing her beneath the visible surface. About her head there was an effulgence as of phosphorus growing about the circumference of a body of water—as if her life lay through her in ungainly luminous deteriorations—the troubling structure of the born somnambule, who lives in two worlds—meet of child and desperado.

Taken by itself, this description is likely to prove more confusing than enlightening; but a few pages later another attempt is made to explain Robin's significance:

> Sometimes one meets a woman who is beast turning human. Such a person's every movement will reduce to an image of a forgotten experience; a mirage of an eternal wedding cast on the racial memory; as insupportable a joy as would be the vision of an eland coming down an aisle of trees, chapleted with orange blossoms and bridal veil, a hoof raised in the economy of fear, stepping in the trepidation of flesh that will become a myth.

It is significant that we first meet Robin—*la somnambule,* the sleepwalker—when she is being awakened; before that moment we have no knowledge of her life. Her life might be said to begin with that moment, and the act of awakening to be the act of birth.

From these descriptions we begin to realize that Robin symbolizes a state of existence which is before, rather than beyond, good and evil. She is both innocent and depraved—meet of child and desperado—precisely because she has not reached the human state where moral values become relevant. Lacking responsibility of any kind, abandoning herself to wayward and perverse passions, she yet has the innocence and purity of a child. (Nora tells the doctor in the seventh chapter that Robin played "with her toys, trains, and animals and cars to wind up, and dolls and marbles and toy soldiers.") Gliding through life like a sleepwalker, living in a dream from which she has not awakened—for awakening would imply a consciousness of moral value—Robin is at once completely egotistical and yet lacking in a sense of her own identity.

"And why does Robin feel innocent?" Dr. O'Connor asks, when Nora, Robin's lover, comes to him with her agonizing questions. "Every bed she leaves, without caring, fills her heart with peace and happiness. . . . She knows she is innocent because she can't do anything in relation to anyone but herself." But at the same time the doctor tells Felix, Robin's erstwhile husband, that Robin had written from America saying, "Remember me." "Probably," he remarks, "because she has difficulty in remembering herself." By taking these passages together, we can understand what the doctor means when he says that "Robin was outside the 'human type'—a wild thing caught in a woman's skin, monstrously alone, monstrously vain."

The situation of the novel, then, revolves around this extraordinary creature. Robin, Felix eagerly confides to the doctor, "always seemed to be looking for someone to tell her that she was innocent. . . . There are some people who must get permission to live, and if the Baronin [Robin] finds no one to give her that permission, she will make an innocence for herself; a fearful sort of primitive innocence." To be conscious of one's innocence, of course, implies a consciousness of moral value that, we have seen, Robin does not possess. If Robin could have found someone to tell her that she was innocent, she would have found someone who had raised her to the level of the human—someone who had given her "permission to live" as a human being, not merely to exist as an amorphous mass of moral possibility.

Once this fundamental problem is grasped, much of what we read in the rest of ***Nightwood*** becomes considerably clearer. At the beginning of the book we are introduced to Felix Volkbein, a Viennese half-Jew with a somewhat questionable title. What Miss Barnes says of Felix immediately gives him the same type of symbolic stature that Robin possesses:

> What had formed Felix from the date of his birth to his coming to thirty was unknown to the world, for the step of the wandering Jew is in every son. No matter where and when you meet him you feel that he has

come from . . . some secret land that he has been nourished on but cannot inherit, for the Jew seems to be everywhere from nowhere. When Felix's name was mentioned, three or more persons would swear to having seen him the week before in three different countries simultaneously.

Combined with this aspect of Felix is a curious "obsession for what he termed 'Old Europe': aristocracy, nobility, royalty. . . . He felt that the great past might mend a little if he bowed low enough, if he succumbed and gave homage." Immediately after seeing Robin, Felix confesses to the doctor that he "wished a son who would feel as he felt about the 'great past.'" "To pay homage to our past," he says, "is the only gesture that also includes the future." He pays court to Robin and, since her "life held no volition for refusal," they marry. Felix, then, makes the first effort to shape Robin, to give her permission to live by informing her with his own sense of moral values. He does so because he senses, almost instinctively, that with Robin "anything can be done."

Felix fails with Robin, just as do the others who try to provide her with a moral framework. But what exactly does Felix's failure imply? In other words, what is the sense of values that proves inadequate to lifting Robin to the level of the human? Because Felix is so astonishingly individual a creation, despite the broader significance of his role in the novel, this is a particularly difficult question to answer. Some clue may be found if we remind ourselves of another Wandering Jew in modern fiction, Leopold Bloom. Seeking for a character to typify *l'homme moyen sensuel,* not only of our own time but through all history, Joyce chose the figure of a Wandering Jew vainly trying to integrate himself into a culture to which he is essentially alien. And this predicament of the Jew is merely a magnification of the predicament of modern man himself, bewildered and homeless in a mechanical wilderness of his own creation. If Felix is viewed in this light, we may understand his dubious title, his abject reverence for the great tradition of the past, and his frantic desire to assimilate this tradition to himself, as so many examples of a basic need to feel at home in some cultural framework.

Until his meeting with Robin, Felix's relationship to what he considered the great traditions of the European past had been completely negative. The first chapter of the novel, dominated by Felix, is appropriately entitled "Bow Down"—for this phrase defines Felix's attitude toward the great tradition, even toward its trivial and unworthy modern representatives. "In restaurants he bowed slightly to anyone who looked as if he might be 'someone,' making the bow so imperceptible that the surprised person might think he was merely adjusting his stomach." The doctor links this blind, unthinking worship of the aristocratic traditions of the past with the attitude of the masses in general toward an aristocracy they have falsely deified; and he lights up in a flash the symbolic meaning of Felix's obsession.

"Nobility, very well, but what is it?" The Baron started to answer him, but the doctor held up his hand. "Wait a minute! I know—the few that the many have lied about well and long enough to make them deathless." Felix is in the position of the masses, the common men, desperately lying to themselves about an inherited sense of values which they know only by its external trappings. But by marrying Robin, the doctor realizes, Felix is staking his existence on the belief that these traditional values still have vitality—that they will succeed in shaping the primeval chaos of Robin into order. (On Felix's first visit to court Robin he carries two volumes on the life of the Bourbons.) Knowing that Felix's attempt is doomed to failure, the doctor makes an effort to warn him: "The last muscle of aristocracy is madness—remember that"—the doctor leaned forward—"the last child born to aristocracy is sometimes an idiot. . . . So I say beware! In the king's bed is always found, just before it becomes a museum piece, the droppings of the black sheep."

Robin does bear Felix a sickly, stunted, prematurely aged, possibly feeble-minded child—the droppings of the black sheep. And, after unwillingly conceiving the child "amid loud and frantic cries of affirmation and despair," Robin leaves Felix. The child had meant for Felix the creative reaffirmation of the great European aristocratic tradition; but Robin's flight reveals that this tradition is impotent. It contains nothing for the future except the wistful and precocious senility of Guido, Felix's child.

The next character to enter the lists with Robin is Nora Flood, who comes perhaps closest of all to giving Robin "permission to live." Nora, as a symbolic figure, is given meaning on a number of levels; but the title of the third chapter, "Night Watch," expresses the essence of her spiritual attitude. We are told that she keeps "a 'paupers' salon for poets, radicals, beggars, artists, and people in love; for Catholics, Protestants, Brahmins, dabblers in black magic and medicine"—this last, of course, being an allusion to the doctor. Nora was "by temperament an early Christian; she believed the word"; this meant that she "robbed herself for everyone. . . . Wandering people the world over found her profitable in that she could be sold for a price forever, for she carried her betrayal money in her own pocket."

It is significant that Nora is described in images of the American West: "Looking at her, foreigners remembered stories they had heard of covered wagons; animals going down to drink; children's heads, just as far as the eyes, looking in fright out of small windows, where in the dark another race crouched in ambush."

These images, Nora's paupers' salon, and her early Christian temperament all represent different crystallizations of the same spiritual attitude. Among the determinants of this attitude are a belief in the innate goodness of man (or at least in his capacity for moral improvement), a belief in progress, and an indiscriminate approbation of all forms of ethical and intellectual unconventionality—in short, the complete antithesis to the world of values represented by Felix. Irving Babbitt would have called Nora a hopeless Rousseauist, and he would have been right.

Characteristically, while Felix was drawn to Robin because he wished to use her, Nora is drawn to her through pity. The scene in which Nora meets Robin is important not only for what it reveals of their relationship, but also because there is a passage that confirms our interpretation of Robin. Both Robin and Nora are watching a circus performance when,

> . . . As one powerful lioness came to the turn of the bars, exactly opposite the girl [Robin], she turned her furious great head with its yellow eyes afire and went down, her paws thrust through the bars and, as she regarded the girl, as if a river were falling behind impassable heat, her eyes flowed in tears that never reached the surface.

Being neither animal nor human, Robin evokes pity from both species. Nora, intuitively understanding Robin's perturbation at the lioness's stare, takes her by the hand and leads her outside. And, although strangers until that moment, Robin is soon telling Nora "her wish for a home, as if she were afraid she would be lost again, as if she were aware, without conscious knowledge, that she belonged to Nora, and that if Nora did not make it permanent by her own strength, she would forget." What Robin would forget was where she belonged, her own identity, given to her at least for a while by the strength of Nora's love and pity.

Nora's failure with Robin is already foreshadowed in the first description of Nora as having "the face of all people who love the people—a face that would be evil when she found out that to love without criticism is to be betrayed." While Felix had deliberately tried to shape Robin, Nora simply envelops her in an all-embracing love that, because of Nora's belief in natural goodness, has no room for praise or blame. "In court," we read, Nora "would have been impossible; no one would have been hanged, reproached or forgiven because no one would have been accused." With a creature like Robin, the result was inevitable. Nora's self-sacrificing devotion does succeed for a time in giving Robin a sense of identity. Robin's unconditional acceptance by Nora, exactly as she is, eases the tension between the animal and the human that is tearing Robin's life apart; but in the end Nora is not able to give Robin "permission to live" any more than Felix could. Most of the third chapter of the novel is given over to an analysis of this slow estrangement between Robin and Nora, an estrangement all the more torturous because, while desired by neither, it is recognized as inevitable by both.

Yet the quality of Robin's relationship with Nora shows how much more closely Nora came to success than Felix. With Felix Robin had been passive, almost disinterested, in conformity with her somnambulistic nature. Although her life was a frenzy of activity, she never really acted in more than an animal sense; Robin's acts were always reactions to obscure impulses whose meaning she did not understand. With Nora, however, there are moments when Robin realizes the terror of their inevitable separation; and in these moments, clinging to Nora like a child, Robin becomes almost human because her terror reveals an implicit moral choice.

> Yet sometimes, going about the house, in passing each other, they would fall into an agonized embrace, looking into each other's face, their two heads in their four hands, so strained together that the space that divided them seemed to be thrusting them apart. Sometimes in these moments of insurmountable grief Robin would make some movement, use a peculiar turn of phrase not habitual to her, innocent of the betrayal, by which Nora was informed that Robin had come from a world to which she would return. To keep her (in Robin there was this tragic longing to be kept, knowing herself astray) Nora knew now that there was no way but death.

As usual, the appropriate comment on this situation is made by the doctor, seeing Nora out roaming the streets at night in search of Robin. "'There goes the dismantled—Love has fallen off her wall. A religious woman,' he thought to himself, 'without the joy and safety of the Catholic faith, which at a pinch covers up the spots on the wall when the family portraits take a slide; take that safety from a woman,' he said to himself, quickening his steps to follow her, 'and love gets loose and into the rafters. She sees her everywhere,' he added, glancing at Nora as she passed into the dark. 'Out looking for what she's afraid to find—Robin. There goes the mother of mischief, running about, trying to get the world home.'" Robin, it should be noticed, is identified with "the world"—which may mean that the world is really no better off than she is—and Nora's failure with Robin, or rather her derangement over this failure, is attributed to her lack of the Catholic faith.

The doctor does not say that the Catholic faith would have allowed Nora to control Robin by giving her a framework of moral values, but he does say that, if Nora had been a Catholic, the eccentricities of Robin's nature would not have plunged her into an abyss of self-torture and suffering. It is Nora's faith in natural goodness, her uncritical acceptance of Robin because of this faith, that has caused her to suffer. The doctor implies that as a Catholic she would have been able to rationalize Robin's nature in terms of the Catholic understanding of sin and evil; and while this would not have prevented the evil, it would certainly have eased the disillusionment and suffering. As we shall see later, this passage is crucial to an understanding of the book as a whole.

Nora realizes that Robin is lost to her when, at dawn, she looks out the window and sees another woman "her arms about Robin's neck, her body pressed to Robin's, her legs slackened in the hang of the embrace." This other woman, Jenny Petherbridge, is the only person in the novel without a trace of tragic grandeur—and this is not surprising, for she is depicted as the essence of mediocrity, the incarnation of the second-hand and the second-rate.

Chapter four, in which she makes her main appearance, is appropriately entitled "The Squatter." For her life is a continual infringement on the rights of other people, an infringement that becomes permanent merely by the power of persistence. "Her walls, her cupboards, her bureaux, were teeming with second-hand dealings with life. It takes a bold and authentic robber to get first-hand plunder. Someone else's marriage ring was on her finger; the photograph taken of Robin for Nora sat upon her table."

Jenny, again, is the only person in the novel who might be called bourgeois; and there is more than a touch of the *nouveau riche* in her ostentation and her lavishness with money. Wanting to possess anything that had importance, "she appropriated the most passionate love that she knew, Nora's for Robin." Jenny's relationship to Robin differs from those of Felix and Nora, for she has no intuition of Robin's pathetic moral emptiness; nor does she seize on Robin as a teeming chaos of vitality through which to realize her own values. She simply appropriates Robin as another acquisition to her collection of objects that other people have valued. Staking her claim to Robin immediately after Nora, Jenny's main function in the novel seems that of underlining the hopelessness of Robin's plight. To fall from Nora to Jenny—to exchange the moral world of one for the moral world of the other—is only too convincing a proof that Robin has still failed to acquire any standards of value.

At the conclusion of the fourth chapter, when we learn that Robin and Jenny have sailed for America, the novel definitely shifts its focus. Until this point Robin has been its center both spiritually and actually; but Robin now drops out of sight—though she is talked about at great length—and does not appear directly again until the brief concluding episode.

The next three chapters are completely dominated by the doctor, "Dr. Matthew-Mighty-grain-of-salt-Dante-O'Connor," whose dialogues with Felix and Nora—or rather his monologues, prompted by their questions—make up the bulk of these pages. The doctor serves as commentator on the events of the novel, if events they can be called; and as T. S. Eliot says of Tiresias in *The Waste Land,* what he sees, in fact, is the substance of the novel.

This comparison can bear closer application. There is an evident—and probably not accidental—similarity between the two figures. Like the man-woman Tiresias, symbol of universal experience, the doctor has homosexual inclinations; like Tiresias he has "fore-suffered all" by apparently being immortal (he claims to have a "prehistoric memory," and is always talking as if he had existed in other historical periods). Like Tiresias again, who "walked among the lowest of the dead," the doctor is father confessor to the creatures of the night world who inhabit the novel as well as being an inhabitant of that world himself. And in his role of commentator, the doctor "perceived the scene, and foretold the rest." For these reasons, Nora comes to him with the burning question—the title of the fifth chapter— "Watchman, What of the Night?"

It is impossible to give any exact idea of the doctor's monologues except by quoting them at length; and that would unduly prolong an already protracted analysis. But to find anything approaching their combination of ironic wit and religious humility, their emotional subtlety and profound human simplicity, their pathos, their terror, and their sophisticated self-consciousness, one has to go back to the religious sonnets of John Donne. It is these monologues that prove the main attraction of the novel at first reading, and their magnetic power has, no doubt, contributed to the misconception that *Nightwood* is only a collection of magnificent fragments. Moreover, since the doctor always speaks about himself *sub specie aeternitatis,* it is difficult at first to grasp the relations between his monologues and the central theme of the novel.

T. S. Eliot notes in his preface that he could place the doctor in proper focus only after a number of readings; and this is likely to be the experience of other readers as well. But as Eliot rightly emphasizes, the book cannot be understood unless the doctor is seen as part of the whole pattern, rather than as an overwhelming individual creation who throws the others into the background by the magnitude of his understanding and the depth of his insight. Now that the pattern has been sketched, we can safely approach the doctor a little more closely and explain his individual spiritual attitude. It is this attitude that, in the end, dominates the book and gives it a final focus.

"Man," the doctor tells Felix, "was born damned and innocent from the start, and wretchedly—as he must—on those two themes—whistles his tune." Robin, it will be remembered, was described as both child and desperado, that is, both damned and innocent; and since the doctor generalizes her spiritual predicament, we can infer that he views the condition of the other characters—and of himself—as in essentials no different. The doctor, who calls himself "the god of darkness," is a good illustration of his own statement. He is damned by his excess of the knowledge of evil, which condemns him to a living death. "You know what none of us know until we have died," Nora tells him. "You were dead in the beginning." But beyond the doctor's knowledge, beyond his twisted bitterness, is the pathos of abused innocence. "No matter what I may be doing," he cries, "in my heart is the wish for children and knitting. God, I never asked better than to boil some good man's potatoes and toss up a child for him every nine months by the calendar." And after the striking Tiny O'Toole episode, in which the doctor reveals all his saint-like simplicity (his attitude toward animals is reminiscent of St. Francis of Assisi) Nora says: "Sometimes I don't know why I talk to you. You're so like a child; then again I know well enough."

Because of his knowledge of man's nature, the doctor realizes that he himself, and the other people in the novel, differ from Robin only in degree; they are all involved to some extent in her desperate dualism, and in the end their doom is equally inescapable. "We are but skin about a wind," he says, "with muscles clenched against mortality. . . . Life, the permission to know death." Come to ask the "god of darkness" about that fabulous night-creature Robin, Nora draws the only possible conclusion from the doctor's harangues: "I'll never understand her—I'll always be miserable—just like this?" To which the doctor responds by one of his tirades that seems to be about nothing in particular, and yet turns out to be about everything.

The essential quality in the doctor that grows upon the reader is the practical futility of his knowledge, his own hopelessness and helplessness. In the early chapters he turns up occasionally, exhibiting an insight into the other people that they themselves do not possess and seeming to stand outside their dilemmas. But as the doctor comes to the foreground, we find this impression completely erroneous. He talks because he knows there is nothing else to do—and because to stop talking would be to think, and to think would be unbearable.

> "Look here," said the doctor. "Do you know what has made me the greatest liar this side of the moon, telling my stories to people like you to take the mortal agony out of their guts . . . to stop them from . . . staring over their knuckles with misery which they are trying to keep off, saying, 'Say something, Doctor, for the love of God!' And me talking away like mad. Well, that, and nothing else, has made me the liar I am."

And in another place he sums it up succinctly: "I talk too much because I have been made so miserable by what you're keeping hushed."

Still, the doctor cannot always maintain this role; he cannot always drown his own agony in a flood of talk for the benefit of others. And so, his own tension exacerbated by Nora's increasing hysteria, he bursts forth:

> "Do you think, for Christ's sweet sake, that I am so happy that you should cry down my neck? Do you think there is no lament in this world, but your own? . . . A broken heart have you! [he says scornfully, a few sentences later] "I have falling arches, flying dandruff, a floating kidney, shattered nerves and a broken heart! . . . Am I going forward screaming that it hurts . . . or holding my guts as if they were a coil of knives . . . ? Do I wail to the mountains of the trouble I have had in the valley, or to every stone of the way it broke my bones, or of every life, how it went down into my belly and built a nest to hatch me my death there?"

It is on this note that we take leave of the doctor, cursing "the people in my life who have made my life miserable, coming to me to learn of degradation and the night."

But, although the doctor as an individual ends on a note of complete negation, this is not his final judgment on the total pattern of the novel—it is only his final verdict on himself. His attitude toward Robin and the people surrounding her is somewhat more complex. We have already indicated the nature of this complexity by quoting the doctor's remark, when he sees Nora wandering through the streets in search of Robin, that she was a religious woman "without the joy and safety of the Catholic faith, which at a pinch covers up the spots on the wall when the family portraits take a slide." There may be nothing to do about Robin's situation—man's attempts to achieve a truly human existence have always ended in failure; but there is at least the consolation of what the doctor calls "the girl that you love so much that she can lie to you"—the Catholic Church. Discussing the confessional with Felix, the doctor describes it as the place where, although a person may lack genuine contrition, "mischief unravels and the fine high hand of Heaven proffers the skein again, combed and forgiven."

It would be unwise to bear down too heavily on this point and make the doctor's attitude more positive than it actually is. His Catholicism, although deeply rooted in his emotional nature, can offer consolation but not hope; and even its consolation is a puny thing compared to the realities of the human situation as the doctor knows it. "I, as good a Catholic as they make," he tells Nora, "have embraced every confection of hope, and yet I know well, for all our outcry and struggle, we shall be for the next generation not the massive dung fallen from the dinosaur, but the little speck left of the humming-bird."

If the doctor derives any consolation from his Catholicism, it is the consolation of Pascal contemplating the wretchedness and insignificance of man rather than that of Thomas Aquinas admiring an orderly and rational moral universe. "Be humble like the dust, as God intended, and crawl," he advises Nora, "and finally you'll crawl to the end of the gutter and not be missed and not much remembered." What the doctor would like to attain is the spiritual attitude that T. S. Eliot prays for in *Ash Wednesday:*

> Teach us to care and not to care
> Teach us to sit still.

The doctor cannot reach this state because he is too deeply involved in the sufferings of others ("I was doing well enough," he says to Nora, "until you came and kicked my stone over, and out I came, all moss and eyes"), but he recognizes it as the only attitude offering some measure of inner peace.

Since the doctor is not the center of the pattern in *Nightwood,* the novel cannot end merely with his last appearance. We know Robin's fate from his monologues, but we have not had it presented to us dramatically; all we know is that Robin has gone to America with Jenny. The brief last chapter fills this gap and furnishes, with the inevitability of great tragedy, the only possible conclusion.

Robin soon leaves Jenny in America, and, impelled by some animal instinct, makes her way to where Nora lives. Without Nora's knowledge she lives in the woods of Nora's estate—we are not told how, and it is of no importance—sleeping in a decaying chapel belonging to Nora's family. One night Nora's watchdog scents Robin, and Nora, hearing the dog bark, follows him to investigate. Entering the chapel, she is witness to this strange and horrible scene between Robin and the dog:

> Sliding down she [Robin] went . . . until her head swung against his [the dog's]; on all fours now, dragging her knees. The veins stood out in her neck, swelled in her arms, and wide and throbbing rose up on her fingers as she moved forward. . . . Then she began to bark also, crawling after him—barking in a fit of laughter, obscene and touching. The dog began to cry then . . . and she grinning and crying with him; crying in shorter and shorter spaces, moving head to head, until she gave up, lying out, her hands beside her, her face turned and weeping; and the dog too gave up then, his eyes bloodshot, his head flat along her knees.

What this indicates, clearly, is that Robin has abandoned her efforts to rise to the human and is returning to the animal state; the somnambule is re-entering her age-old sleep.

So ends this amazing book, which combines the simple majesty of a medieval morality play with the verbal subtlety and refinement of a Symbolist poem. This exposition, of course, has barely skimmed its surface; there are ramifications of the various characters that need a detailed exegesis far beyond the scope of my intention. But, limited as it is, the discussion should have proved one point. *Nightwood* does have a pattern—a pattern arising from the spatial interweaving of images and phrases independently of any time-sequence of narrative action. And, as in *The Waste Land,* the reader is simply bewildered if he assumes that, because language proceeds in time, *Nightwood* must be perceived as a narrative structure. We can now understand why T. S. Eliot wrote that "*Nightwood* will appeal primarily to readers of poetry," and that "it is so good a novel that only sensibilities trained on poetry can wholly appreciate it." Since the unit of meaning in *Nightwood* is usually a phrase or sequence of phrases—at most a long paragraph—it carries the evolution of spatial form in the novel forward to a point where it is practically indistinguishable from modern poetry.

Alan Williamson (essay date spring 1964)

SOURCE: Williamson, Alan. "The Divided Image: The Quest for Identity in the Works of Djuna Barnes." *Critique* 7, no. 1 (spring 1964): 58-74.

[*In the following essay, Williamson stresses the "Edenic vision" and the themes of the disoriented hero and the incestuous nature of love present in all of Barnes's work. He then offers a reading of* Nightwood *as a tragedy in which man's aspiration for love is both the means by which he "invests his existence with value and the main instrument through which his 'universal malady' works to destroy him."*]

I

Djuna Barnes, as a lesser member of the cluster of Lost Generation writers, has suffered from becoming the idol of an avant-garde cult while remaining unknown to the general public and deprecated by critics.[1] On the one hand, she is justly praised for the strangeness and profundity of her psychological portraits, the eccentric keenness of her thought, the brilliant rendering of doom and decay, and a style which is at the same time precise and evocative. On the other hand, she is damned for the obscurity of her style and thought, for the morbidity and abnormality of her concerns, and for the unyielding pessimism with which she views man and his destiny.

The ultimate appraisal must fall closer to that of the cultist than to that of the philistine. Nonetheless, attempts in the heat of combat to exalt her into a major figure are unsound; she is clearly a writer of very limited range and meager production, and as such must be relegated to the status of a brilliant minor writer. *Nightwood* is a masterpiece from any point of view; *The Antiphon,* a quasi-surrealist, quasi-Jacobean verse tragedy, is virtually unstageable but contains perhaps the best poetry written for the theater in our time. The early works, the stories, plays and poems in *A Book* (reissued, with additions, as *A Night Among the Horses*) and the early novel *Ryder* are highly original but stillborn, giving little suggestion of the brilliant if unprolific achievement of the later period.

Djuna Barnes' work is permeated by the dualism of day and night, which is expounded at length, if somewhat cryptically, in the great monologues of *Nightwood*. In the day, which is the world of everyday life, men behave as if they were immortal, as if a human being were a determinate, knowable and rational entity, and as if human communication, through language and, more profoundly, through love, were valid and satisfying. In the world of night, which underlies the day and which man enters through suffering, all these assumptions prove false. Man is "but a skin about a wind, with muscles clenched against mortality" (*Nightwood,* 83). Under man's rational consciousness lies the subconscious, an unfathomable jungle of dark forces which determine his life and which he cannot know or control. In his unconscious nature, any man is capable of every crime: "There is not one of us who, given an eternal incognito, a thumbprint nowhere set against our souls, would not commit rape, murder and all abominations" (88). Man is made aware of his unconscious self in dreams, in which his irrational impulses project themselves without fear of restraint or consequences. "We wake from our doings in a deep sweat for that they happened in a house without an address, in a street in no town, citizened with people with no names with which to deny them. Their very lack of identity makes them ourselves" (88).

Human communication is also a deceptive surface. Language, as a process of definition and abstraction, falsifies reality by denying the elements of change and mystery: it gives "a word (for a thing) . . . and not its alchemy" (83). Communication in love is equally unsatisfactory. Love is, for reasons that will be developed later, the direst need of the unconscious, and yet it is thwarted by the very nature of the unconscious as a sealed and impervious inner life unknown to the conscious selves which try to communicate.

> We swoon with the thickness of our own tongue when we say, 'I love you,' as in the eye of a child lost a long while will be found the contraction of that distance—a child going small in the claws of a beast, coming furiously up the furlongs of the iris.
>
> (83)

To paraphrase this typically intricate and economical simile, in trying to articulate love in language, as in the spectacle of a civilized child lost in the jungle who has reverted to an animal, we feel the magnitude of the distance between the rational consciousness and the animalistic forces of the unconscious.

Djuna Barnes' vision of love is thus in a sense Proustian: the torment of love lies in the knowledge that the beloved has a secret inner life in which the lover can never participate. The lover is jealous not of the known, but of the suspected rival. The emblem of love is the lover watching over the sleeping beloved, realizing that he can never know what is going on inside her at this moment, that she may be betraying or killing him in a dream, and at the same time knowing that he is equally capable of betraying or killing her in his dreams. The tragic paradox of love lies in the fact that the unconscious, which is the source of the desire for love, is incapable of possessing or of being possessed; it betrays the beloved in dreams, as it may force the conscious self to betray her in life. Love, in its stark futility, becomes, for the lover, a kind of death: "The night into which his beloved goes . . . destroys his heart" (87).

Thus man struggles in a world whose surface placidity is radically contingent on irrational hidden forces; he is isolated and constantly vulnerable to the destructive power of death, love and the darkness within himself. Djuna Barnes focuses the enigma of man's predicament and renders it significant in terms of a myth which bears a close kinship to the Christian myth of the Fall, but which offers little possibility of Christian redemption. The ecclesiastical tone which T. S. Eliot took in defending Djuna Barnes suggests strongly that he perceived a Christian habit of thought, if not doctrinal Christianity, in a writer who contended that "No man needs curing of his individual sickness; his universal malady is what he should look to" (32).

Djuna Barnes' Eden myth draws not on the orthodox Christian tradition, but on the Hermetic tradition, according to which man was created, in the union of conscious mind and animal matter, as a single hermaphroditic being, whose fragmentation into separate sexes occurred at the time of the Fall. This bisexual Adam was static and immortal, encompassing all human possibilities in potentiality; thus it was complete within itself, neither needing nor desiring anything in the external world. Translating from Christian into Darwinian terms, Djuna Barnes identifies this ideally unified identity with the moment in evolution of the "beast turning human" (37), when unconscious, passionate animal vitality took on rational consciousness. Man remembers and yearns for this moment through a kind of Jungian race memory: "a mirage of an eternal wedding cast on the racial memory" (37). On the individual level, this "eternal wedding" is identified with the half-forgotten period of early childhood when the personality is not fully formed and the child lives an existence impervious to the outside world, the period which Freud termed the source of the vision of paradise. In the post-Edenic world, the Hermetic Adam is incarnate in idiots and the insane, human beings who lack all "human" qualities, the capacity to feel emotion, to need and to become involved with the outside world. Robin Vote in *Nightwood* is such a person, and thus plays a pivotal role in the book and in Djuna Barnes' total vision; the quotations used to describe the Edenic vision have been taken from the passage in which Robin is introduced, which will subsequently be analyzed in detail.

The "universal malady" of the post-Edenic consciousness is the contradiction between its need for love and its intrinsic isolation, between its yearning for the remembered "eternal wedding" and its awareness of its fragmented and mortal nature. From this heretical Christian account of man's condition derive two of the most striking themes in the work of Djuna Barnes: the disoriented hero and the incestuous vision of love.

The typical hero in Djuna Barnes' work suffers from a radical split in his identity between what he aspires to be and what he psychologically or physically is. The extremes of this dissociation are found among the doomed figures of *Nightwood,* whose lives constitute a revolt against the very facts of their physical being: the Jew who has built his whole concept of the meaning of his life around his fraudulent pretenses to aristocracy, and the sexual inverts. In the early novel *Ryder,* Wendell's revolt is directed against his psychological identity; being essentially weak, shiftless and feminine, he creates and attempts to live by a false mask of strong, lusty, even brutal virility. The theme is echoed in the character of Miranda in *The Antiphon,* who is spiritually crippled by her inability to come to terms with her past and her family background, which are inescapably part of her.

This perpetual protagonist represents, in its most extreme form, the tragic encounter between an aspiring hero and a limiting universe, in that the antagonist is the protagonist's own nature rather than some external force pitted against him. This intensification is, however, also an internalization of the tragic process, and therefore non-dramatic. Comparing Djuna Barnes with other tragic writers, one discovers in her a curious repression of violence; introspective monologue is substituted for dramatic confrontation, and quiet acceptance of incurable suffering replaces the bloody catastrophe as a resolution. *The Antiphon* is an exception to this rule, and its situations are correspondingly more external; but even here there is, especially in comparison with the play's Jacobean models, a strange disparity between the depth of psychological horror and its expression in violence, which contributes greatly to the play's uncanny effect.

The one external involvement with which Djuna Barnes is passionately concerned is love; and her vision of love always contains an element of incest. The important love relationships in the later works are nearly always either familial or homosexual. Love, as the externalization of the disoriented hero's quest, arises from the fragmented individual's craving for Edenic completion; therefore the most perfect love is that in which the lovers are mirror-images, complementary to each other but sharing the same basis of identity in blood and/or sex. Thus Djuna Barnes writes in **"Six Songs of Khalidine,"** an early poem in the form of an elegy for a dead Lesbian lover:

> It is not gentleness but mad despair
> That sets us kissing mouths, O Khalidine,
> Your mouth and mine, and one sweet mouth unseen
> We call our soul . . .
>
> *(A Book,* 145)

In similar terms, Nora Flood in *Nightwood* describes her own Lesbianism: "A man is another person—a woman is yourself, caught as you turn in panic; on her mouth you kiss your own" (143). The Lesbian lover is "yourself," but "caught as you turn in panic," a turned, inverse, mirror image. This element of complementarity within an integral, shared identity is fundamental in the two most fully explored love-relationships in the work of Djuna Barnes: the Lesbian relationship between Nora and Robin in *Nightwood,* and the filial relationship between Miranda and her mother Augusta in *The Antiphon.* Both relationships clearly represent a union of separate and opposed halves of a single identity. All of Nora's spiritual faculties are directed outward, in an intense interaction with other individuals; she lacks understanding or even awareness of her own subconscious. Robin, on the other hand, is sealed in a kind of trance in which she has lost the ability to communicate with the outside world. Thus Robin looks to Nora for a love which can penetrate through her trance, make her capable of antiphonal love, and save her from insanity, while Nora, in loving Robin, is attempting to capture and understand her own subconscious. Similarly, for Miranda, to accept her mother despite her mother's guilt towards her is to accept her family background as a part of herself, and thus is the only way to attain self-knowledge and a complete identity. For Augusta, the only atonement which can restore the integrity she has lost by her marriage is to gain the acceptance and love of her daughter Miranda, her chief victim. It is Miranda who memorably celebrates the antiphonal love between two halves of the same identity as man's only possibility for salvation, for escape from the fragmentation and solitude which are the "universal malady:"

> As the high plucked banks
> Of the viola rend out the unplucked strings below—
> There is the antiphon.
> I've seen loves so eat each other's mouth

Till that the common clamour, co-intwined,
Wrung out the hidden singing in the tongue
Its chaste economy—there is the adoration.
So the day, day fit for dying in,
Is the plucked accord.

(The Antiphon, 119)

Djuna Barnes is, however, pessimistic about the possibility of such an escape; both the Nora-Robin and the Miranda-Augusta relationships end in mutual destruction.

The role of doctrinal Christianity, or, more precisely, Catholicism, in Djuna Barnes' vision is problematical. Churches, prayers, and apocalyptic imagery are ubiquitous, and Catholicism seems to be the ultimate, if unsatisfactory, source of strength for her saint, Matthew O'Connor in *Nightwood;* yet Christian salvation in its orthodox sense is clearly not even a conceivable solution to man's predicament. Djuna Barnes seems to be a radical Ockhamite fideistsceptic, for whom the disproportion between man and the total order renders any aspiration to knowledge of a divinity presumptuous and futile; only a blind appeal is possible. As Matthew puts it, "we all love in sizes, yet we all cry out in tiny voices to the great booming God, the older we get" (136). God is simply a name that man pronounces desperately when confronted with the ultimate contingency, precariousness and limitation of his position in this world. The Catholic Church, for Djuna Barnes, embodies this point of view because it interposes hierarchy, sacrament and the intercession of the saints between the believer and God; Protestantism presupposes a direct communication which, for her, resembles a negotiation between Lilliput and Brobdingnag. Her heretical theology is perfectly expressed in *Ryder:* "For some is the image, and for some the Thing, and for others the Thing that even the Thing knows naught of; and for one only the meaning of That beyond That" (2).

It is virtually impossible to speak of an ethic in Djuna Barnes' view of human situations, because that view rests on a total psychological determinism. Man is subject to the dictates of his unconscious nature even in his revolt against that nature itself. The courses of all the relationships in *Nightwood* are inevitable once chance has initially brought the characters together at certain particular places at certain particular times; the perception of this stark inevitability in human situations is the main cause of Matthew O'Connor's breakdown. No ethical principle can aid the hero who enters the world of the night through love or disorientation; the only dictum which can be directed to the ordinary person who is spared this suffering is a warning to pay homage to the dark gods for continued preservation from a destruction which it is finally beyond the individual's power to prevent: "think of the night the day long, and of the day the night through, or at some reprieve of the brain it will come upon you heavily" (*Nightwood,* 84).

Safety is the reward of moderation; but for man in his highest state of consciousness, which comes only in aspiration and revolt, destruction is inevitable. Pain increases in direct proportion to consciousness. Thus conscious life seems to be a mere freak of nature, or at most a register through whose tormented search for unity and permanence the inhuman universe is made aware of its own disorder and flux. Yet in this situation Djuna Barnes finds a basis for attaching a tragic value, which extends beyond stoicism, to human aspiration and suffering. Love, in that it seeks to heal fragmentation, to overcome solitude, and to deny mortality, is man's most perfect act of revolt; and in love man himself, by the force of his own suffering, of love as spiritual death, invests the loved object's existence with a value which it, as a meaningless freak of creation, did not possess before it was loved. "We were created that the earth might be made sensible of her inhuman taste; and love that the body might be so dear that even the earth should roar with it" (*Nightwood,* 83).

The apocalyptic imagery attached to love throughout the works of Djuna Barnes bears out the implications of this sentence. In the early elegy cited above, she refers to the pain of love as being in some strange way immortal, and preserving the identities of lover and beloved beyond death:

And now I say, has not the mountain's base
Here trembled long ago unto the cry
'I love you, ah, I love you!' Now we die
And lay, all silent, to the earth our face.
Shall that cast out the echo of this place?

(A Book, 146)

The same theme of a symbolic, if not literal, immortality echoes in Nora's cry when she realizes that her love for Robin is doomed. The speech could stand as emblem of the victory which man, in his love, as in religion, desperately affirms over the forces which destroy him.

In the resurrection, when we come up looking backward at each other, I shall know you only of all that company. My ear shall turn in the socket of my head; my eyeballs loosened where I am the whirlwind about that cashed expense, my foot stubborn on the cast of your grave.

(Nightwood, 58-9)

II

Djuna Barnes' short but intricate masterpiece, *Nightwood,* illustrates perfectly her muted and restrained variant of the Jacobean tradition, in which the tragic situation arises within a single person or between two people rather than on a larger social scale, the tragic doom operates through inner deterioration rather than through violence, and tragic revelation takes place in monologue rather than in confrontation. Her method is the direct opposite of that of the Jacobean dramatists, or of Faulkner, in which dark, inherently indefinable forces project themselves in a contorted, Gothic action which can never attain the status of a perfect objective correlative; in her work, style and action always suggest rather than define or project. The style of *Nightwood,* with its heavy reliance on metaphor and connotation, reflects this approach to content. Criticizing T. S. Eliot for his enthusiastic praise of *Nightwood,* Ezra Pound remarked in a limerick that "Her Blubbery prose had no fingers or toes," contrasting her with Marianne Moore, "scarce an exuberance, rather protagonist for the rights of vitrification and petrifaxis."[2] Yet style, for Djuna Barnes, must be oblique and suggestive rather than definitive, because the language of reality is irrational, and cannot be translated into rational vitrification; for her, the fingers and toes of style serve only to strangle reality.

The structure of *Nightwood* rests on the contrapuntal relationship between two distinct plots. The first centers around Robin Vote's strange and richly symbolic malady and its destructive effects on her and on the fragmented individuals for whom she exercises a magnetic attraction; the second traces the disintegration of Matthew O'Connor in the face of his inability to absolve this group, and especially Nora, of the exactions of their private dooms.

The somnambule is the controlling metaphor for Robin. She moves through the world in a dreamlike, self-contained inner existence, utterly impervious to any contact with the outside world. The perilous and unexplained trance into which she has fallen at her first introduction is emblematic of her terrible predicament; like Matthew in the emblem, Nora in actual life will cause her to awake for an instant, only to be plunged back into disintegration and insanity.

The realization of this character, which puzzled Eliot, is typical of Djuna Barnes' method of creating characters. She makes very little use of the orthodox realistic method of revealing character dramatically, through a copious and objective recording of action and dialogue, but rather concentrates on three techniques, in addition to monologue: the manipulation of decor, the emblematic use of a single gesture, and the self-conscious imposition of image and metaphor. An example of the latter, and dominant, method is the paragraph in which Robin is first described:

> The perfume that her body exhaled was of the quality of that earth-flesh, fungi, which smells of captured dampness and yet is so dry, overcast with the odour of oil of amber, which is an inner malady of the sea, making her seem as if she had invaded a sleep incautious and entire. Her flesh was the texture of plant life, and beneath it one sensed a frame, broad, porous and sleep-worn, as if sleep were a decay fishing her beneath the visible surface. About her head there was an effulgence as of phosphorus glowing about the circumference of a body of water—as if her life lay through her in ungainly luminous deteriorations—the troubling structure of the born somnambule, who lives in two worlds—meet of child and desperado.

> (34-5)

Images of unconscious life, of very old species low on the evolutionary scale, are used: "that earth-flesh, fungi," "plantlife." To these is connected the image of "oil of amber, which is an inner malady of the sea:" ambergris, beauty produced out of malady and decay ("luminous deteriorations"), and a product of the sea, symbol of flux and the unconscious, and primal origin of the evolution of life. By a play on words (ambergris is a waxy substance, and the word comes from the French *ambre gris*) ambergris becomes "oil of amber," fusing the connotations of oil, linked to sex, flux, and the irrational, and amber, a hard, impregnable case enclosing the fossil of a prehistoric animal, as the "dry" fungus holds "captured dampness," and as the somnambule's psychological shell immures her animal-like unconscious life from the outside world. The single phrase, "oil of amber," serves to reveal the intricate web of image and connotation which Djuna Barnes, in a technique more typical of poetry than of the novel, weaves into her descriptions. In the remainder of the paragraph, the rhetoric becomes more analytical: Robin is sealed in a "sleep incautious and entire," which is also a "decay" which "fishes" the depths of her unconscious. She lives entirely in the primordial world of the subconscious, and thus combines the innocence of the child, to whom good and evil are meaningless because he is unaware of the outside world, and the capacity to commit all crimes, since she is given over totally to the dominion of irrational forces: she is "meet of child and desperado."

Robin's decor echoes the same themes; her hotel room, with its jungle overtones, is patterned on Henri Rousseau's painting *The Dream,* in which a sleeping woman on a couch is transplanted from the real world of which she is oblivious to the middle of a jungle, the world of her dream. The room, in which Robin is "thrown in among the carnivorous flowers as their ration" (35), is sinister, suggesting the corrosion of Robin's human consciousness by the almost vegetable trance in which she is trapped.

Further on, the connection between Robin's sealed inner life and the myth of the Hermetic Adam becomes explicit:

> Sometimes one meets a woman who is beast turning human. Such a person's every movement will reduce to an image of a forgotten experience; a mirage of an eternal wedding cast on the racial memory; as insupportable a joy as would be the vision of an eland coming down an aisle of trees, chapleted with orange blos-

soms and bridal veil, a hoof raised in the economy of fear, stepping in the trepidation of flesh that will become myth; as the unicorn is neither man nor beast deprived, but human hunger pressing its breast to its prey.

(37)

She is the "eternal wedding" of consciousness and unconscious life, the evolutionary mid-kingdom which is also the "forgotten experience" of early childhood. Like the Hermetic Adam, she is imperviously sealed within herself, and hermaphroditic: she first appears wearing trousers, and the subsequent action confirms her bisexuality. She embodies the myths of creation and paradise and, for Djuna Barnes, the related myths of creatures half-animal and half-human; yet her transformation into myth is for her a source of "trepidation." The reason for this becomes clear when one realizes that this transformation takes place concretely in the eyes of the disoriented individuals who love her, in that her complete but indeterminate identity represents to each of them his particular mirror-image, his means of self-completion and salvation. Thus their love for her is an exploitation of her malady and lack of volition to transform her into a tool through which the lover can complete himself; it is a spider-like fusion of copulation and cannibalism, "human hunger pressing its breast to its prey." All her lovers, and especially Nora who understands and tries to save her, end by driving her deeper into solitude and madness, as she in turn destroys them by her inability to respond to their love and heal them.

Robin's transformation into the mirror image of the beholder is illustrated in the succeeding paragraphs, as the perspective changes from that of the author into that of the Baron.

The "Baron" is a Jew who passes himself off as an aristocrat. Out of a racial memory of the constant insecurity of the ghetto and the cultural rootlessness of a people who had neither a homeland nor a genuine participation in the cultures amid which they lived, he aspires to become part of an ancient tradition which will purge him of his sense of cultural lostness and give his posterity a patterned existence both physically and spiritually secure. To fulfill his design, he needs a suitable wife to give him children and bring them up in devotion to the aristocratic tradition; he sees Robin only in the light of her potentiality to fill this role.

Thus the Baron sees Robin's strange completeness only in the terms in which it offers salvation to his own fragmentation; he is aware only of her strange affinity for the past, her quality of seeming to be a dead spirit out of a past epoch reincarnate in a living being, a museum piece somehow endowed with life. The union of past and present in Robin represents to him the union of the separated halves of his own destiny, the spiritual aristocrat and the physical Jew: "as if this girl were the converging halves of a broken fate, setting face, in sleep, toward itself in time" (38).

Robin enters into marriage with the Baron with a somnambule's indifference. After the marriage, the Baron realizes that Robin can never be limited to the role he has conceived for her, that her attention is fixed not, as he had thought, on history but on "something not yet in history" (44). In revolt against the mold into which he tries to force her, she, "strangely aware of some lost land in herself" (45), takes to wandering. The Baron finally violates her sealed inner life not in copulation but by childbirth, through pain. She has been forced, by pain and violence, into an awareness of another being, in a kind of psychological rape; as a necessary consequence, she leaves the Baron.

This is the basic pattern for all of Robin's relationships. They begin in a quest for completion on the lover's side, and in indifference on hers; they break down as Robin revolts against the lover's attempt to force her into a mold and to compel a response from the depths of her being. Finally they end when the lover succeeds in wounding her to the point that her inner being is affected, and she must abandon him. This pattern appears most fully in the relationship between Robin and Nora Flood, which marks the crisis in Robin's development.

Nora Flood is a completely externalized personality, capable of unlimited sympathy and self-giving; she is equally incapable of selfishness and of introspection. Her spiritual life consists entirely in sympathy, in "recording . . . in a smaller but more intense orchestration" (52) the spiritual forces around her. In receiving the confessions of others she is capable of total understanding but not of moral judgment: "she recorded without reproach or accusation, being incapable of self-reproach or self-accusation" (53). For as staunch a believer in original sin as Djuna Barnes, the incapacity for self-accusation must indicate either a total obliviousness to the external world, as in Robin's case or a total lack of self-knowledge, as in Nora's.

Nora's memories and dreams are the primary key to the subconscious forces which are driving her. In her first dream, she is standing in her grandmother's room at the top of the house, looking down the stairwell at Robin, who is at the bottom, and calling to her to come up. As she calls, however, the stairway expands, carrying Robin farther and farther away from her. From Nora's memories we learn that her grandmother, whom she "loved more than anyone" (148), was a disturbed personality with Lesbian tendencies. This suggests that Nora's relationship with her grandmother established a primary pattern for her subsequent love-relationships. Her capacity for love, as she herself confesses, derives from her need for power, her need to possess and save a person who is in some way lost. Her sexual role is thus active and masculine, and her Lesbianism is its natural consequence. Her need for possession is the projection of a need for self-possession; the lost, irrational, inner-directed being whom she loves represents her own subconscious, the "night" half of herself of which she is oblivious. In the dream, thus, the grandmother represents the role into which Nora tries to draw Robin, "Robin disfigured and eternalized by the hieroglyphics of sleep and pain" (63). Nora's very attempt to make Robin her protected and saved love-object dooms the relationship, and drives the two farther apart, since Robin is unable to respond to or accept Nora Flood's possessive, protective flood of love.

Nora describes her love for Robin thus: "I tried to come between and save her, but I was like a shadow in her dream that could never reach her in time, as the cry of the sleeper has no echo, myself echo struggling to answer" (145). Robin consciously feels a "tragic longing to be kept, knowing herself astray" (58), yet, being psychologically unable to accept the role Nora tries to force on her, Robin Vote must regain revolt by wandering, in a series of drunken binges and Lesbian affairs. In this moral inferno, she retains her innocence by her imperviousness to contact with the outside world: "She knows she is innocent because she can't do anything in relation to anyone but herself." (146).

Robin finally loses her innocence as a result of Nora's efforts to penetrate the sealed depths of her being. Nora describes this psychological rape: "she was asleep and I struck her awake. I saw her come awake and turn befouled before me, she who had managed in that sleep to keep whole" (145). Nora forces Robin into an instant of intense contact, in which Robin becomes aware of Nora for the first time, and thus of her own guilt towards Nora, and of herself as seen through Nora's perspective. Thus Robin passes from static insanity to a state of fragmentation and perpetual torment, having gained a conscious perspective on her own madness and degradation, while remaining subconsciously trapped in her trancelike incapacity for responsive love. Nora represents to Robin the Madonna, both as inaccessible redeemer and as tacit accuser, since it is only through her that Robin possesses a vision of unattainable salvation and a sense of her own degradation; thus Robin must leave her, hoping to slip back into the sleep of insanity.

The ending contains the sinister suggestion that Nora herself is slipping into the trance of madness. This is hinted at in her second dream, in which her father (her masculine, protective sexual personality) attempts to rescue her dead grandmother (Robin) from a glass coffin, and, failing, dies himself. In the final interview with Matthew, in which Nora's behavior verges on hysteria, it becomes clear that a process of ingrowing is taking place in her which, in view of Robin's fate, is clearly sinister; her ability to feel and to become involved with the outside world is benumbed or even dead, while an intense awareness of her own subconscious appears in her for the first time. Matthew futilely warns her of

this: "You are . . . experiencing the inbreeding of pain. . . . But when you inbreed with suffering . . . you are destroyed back to your structure as an old master disappears beneath the knife of the scientist who would know how it was painted" (129-30). The failure of Matthew's attempt to purge Nora of her love for Robin and thus save her from incipient insanity is the immediate cause of his breakdown.

Matthew O'Connor, who acts as Greek Chorus to the tragedy of Robin and Nora, is a doctor practicing without a license, a sponger and petty thief, and a homosexual, and yet a saint in the traditional sense of the word. His vices render his sainthood credible, yet they serve a deeper function in elucidating the nature of that sainthood. Like Prince Myshkin's hypothesized impotence, Matthew's homosexuality, especially in view of the brief, mechanical, and purely physical nature of his homosexual liaisons, creates in him the ascetic negation of passion necessary for pure compassion and disinterestedness in dealing with human situations. Furthermore, his homosexuality, as a radical kind of disorientation, forces upon him a stark and unmitigated awareness of the desperate limitation and contingency of the human predicament. Matthew's plight recalls the myth of Philoctetes, of the wounded artist or saint who, through his wound, gains knowledge of the universal darkness underlying and threatening man's life, and a compulsion to creative or redemptive action as a defense against this destructive force.

Matthew appears at the beginning of the first great monologue in a woman's gown, symbol of his sexual disorientation; but in Nora's mind the gown soon becomes more pregnantly symbolic, as the "natural raiment of extremity" worn by "infants, angels, priests, the dead" (80). There is an implicit suggestion of Christ, the priest and victim; as a radically fragmented being, a man who should have been a woman, Matthew has suffered to the full the spiritual death of the night, and yet he is also the priest of the night, attempting to offer consolation and a sense of dignity on its victims. Matthew undergoes a genuine and Christlike agony in the face of human suffering; he combines a total self-consciousness, to the point of calculated deception, with respect to his methods, and a total lack of self-consciousness and pride with respect to his motives. This appears most clearly in the scene in the empty church.

Unlike Christ, however, Matthew realizes from the start that his function is merely palliative. His principal weapon against human suffering is talk, which he uses, not to show a way to salvation, but merely to distract, and to give the listener a sense of dignity which will make him more able to endure. Thus the great monologue spoken to Nora is not intended to tell her, as she wishes to be told, how to save her relationship with

Robin, but rather how to bear its loss, which is revealed as inevitable in the story which the doctor, after his long prologue, finally tells.

Matthew's talk, while seemingly mystical and abstract, undergoes subtle and self-conscious variation according to the person to whom it is addressed; the same concept, the limitation or "universal malady" of man, is expressed in terms of "the night" and "love" when Matthew speaks to Nora, in terms of "the past" when he speaks to the Baron. Like the traditional saint, Matthew is always concerned with the particular situation. However, he depends for his effect more on the distracting power and emotional tone of words than on their meaning. Nora, for instance, clearly is not intended to understand Matthew's monologue, nor does she; she remains silent, breaking in with desperate questions only when the illustrative examples the doctor uses wander, by chance, close to her own particular predicament.

Even in its limited purpose, however, the monologue is ultimately futile; it cannot finally alter in any way Nora's incapacity to endure her fate. The failure of Matthew's aspiration to sainthood is brutally clear in the supreme irony by which Matthew himself plays a decisive role in Robin's abandonment of Nora, the event which is the direct cause of his breakdown. It is Matthew who, out of pity for Jenny, introduces her to Robin and thus precipitates Robin's break with Nora. Matthew suffers under a tremendous burden of pity for others, who, by the "universal malady" inherent in their humanity must inevitably frustrate, maim and destroy each other; yet, perceiving the deterministic psychological forces by which they are driven, he knows he cannot blame, alter or save them. He is thus placed in a position which must ultimately become unbearable.

There are suggestions of deterioration in Matthew long before his final breakdown: "The Baron was shocked to observe, in the few seconds before the Doctor saw him, that he seemed old, older than his fifty odd years would account for" (110). Matthew's inability to save Nora is only the final straw in the accumulation of futility which destroys him. He is broken basically by the realization that he cannot be Christ, that he cannot transmute the perpetual crucifixion of his life into any kind of redeeming force. He has self-lessly assumed the burden of others' suffering in addition to his own, and has not even been able to palliate that suffering by his Christlike act. This is the root of his despair: "I love my neighbour. Like a rotten apple to a rotten apple's breast affixed we go down together. . . . I apply the breast the harder, that he may rot as quickly as I" (153). He is driven mad, not by the ingratitude of others, but by the realization that, after the enormity of his suffering, he is not "a good man doing wrong, but the wrong man doing nothing much" (162).

At the end of the book, Robin, in an act which represents simultaneously a disintegration into total animality and a masochistic atonement for her guilt towards Nora, attempts intercourse with Nora's dog as Nora looks on horror-stricken. The incident ironically fulfills Matthew's apocalyptic utterance on the immortality of Nora and Robin's love: "Nora will leave that girl some day; but though those two are buried at opposite ends of the earth, one dog will find them both" (106). The dramatic irony preserves the tension in which the two plots merge and which is the root of *Nightwood* as tragedy: that man's aspiration as crystallized in love, whether sexual or Christian, is both the means by which man invests his existence with value and the main instrument through which his "universal malady" works to destroy him.

Notes

1. All page references are to the following editions:

   A Book, Boni and Liveright, New York, 1923.

   Ryder, Horace Liveright, New York, 1928.

   Nightwood, Harcourt, Brace & Co., New York, 1937.

   The Antiphon, Farrar, Straus & Cudahy, New York, 1958.

2. *Letters of Ezra Pound* (New York, 1950), p. 286.

Suzanne C. Ferguson (essay date January 1969)

SOURCE: Ferguson, Suzanne C. "Djuna Barnes's Short Stories: An Estrangement of the Heart." *Southern Review* n.s. 5, no. 1 (January 1969): 26-41.

[*In the following essay, Ferguson analyzes the nine stories included in the* Selected Works of Djuna Barnes, *finding in them an economy of language, a skillful "fusing of experience and idea," and a "chilling precision" lacking in her works of longer fiction.*]

Included in the *Selected Works of Djuna Barnes* (1962), with *Nightwood* and the 1958 verse play, *The Antiphon,* are nine short stories carefully chosen and revised from a volume last printed in 1929.[1] These stories, along with perhaps two or three not reissued,[2] are striking not only as they reveal the development of the themes, characters, and techniques of Miss Barnes's most famous work, *Nightwood,* but as masterpieces of the kind of short story that, however severely limited in its vision, nonetheless presents with ferocious clarity those moments of recognition and illumination in which fallen man perceives his damnation. Moreover, they create in a special and powerful way the feeling of disestablishment and disintegration in the society and the individual so deeply experienced by Miss Barnes's generation.

Her world is a world of displaced persons—of an Armenian country boy on the lower east side of Manhattan, of Russian emigrés in Paris, Berlin, Spain, or New York, of Scandinavians or English in American farmland. They have abandoned national, racial, and ethical traditions; their human contacts are laceration. They lack even the integrity in isolation that comforts the characters of Hemingway or the early Faulkner, for they are estranged against themselves. Their aborted and ineffectual attempts to find meaning, order, or love are the subjects of the stories. Technique, as well as subject, marks the stories as extraordinary. Readers who find the verbal pyrotechnics of *Nightwood,* or of the 1927 novel, *Ryder,* or of *The Antiphon* too often merely talky and falsely rhetorical will discover in most of the stories a fusing of experience and idea. Economy is especially characteristic of the revised versions collected in the *Selected Works,* where verbal fat has been pared away, and objects, persons, and actions flash out with chilling precision. This is not to say, of course, that the stories are easy to read; on the contrary, like those of Katherine Mansfield and Katherine Anne Porter—which technically many of them resemble—they retain their meaning in a very dense texture, where each detail is significant and essential to the whole. And in spite of *Nightwood's* relatively wide circulation they are generally unknown today.

Overshadowed by the greater writers and literary showmen of her time, Djuna Barnes remains a lonely and obscure figure, one of the postwar exiles to Paris, where she contributed regularly from about 1918 to the *Little Review* and *The Smart Set,* and occasionally to *The Dial* and later to Ford's *transatlantic review.* A volume of poems, *A Book of Repulsive Women,* had appeared in 1915, and her first collection of short stories, *A Book,* was issued by Boni & Liveright in 1923. The intimate of only a few—E. E. Cummings and his wife, for instance—she is known to the literary world in general as the author of one work, *Nightwood,* an experimental novel published in 1937 and highly praised by T. S. Eliot and by Edwin Muir, among others.[3]

The rambling form of the novel—called fugal or symphonic by its admirers—in which the focus moves from one to another of the main characters, resting for a third of its bulk on the homosexual gynecologist, O'Connor, whose only experience is vicarious, in conjunction with the lavish symbolic settings, has invited comparison with Joyce's *Ulysses.* In her earlier novel, *Ryder,* which besides a shifting narrative focus and iconic settings has parodies of Chaucer, Sterne, and apparently the English Bible, the influence of Joyce is even more evident. It seems clear, however, that although Miss Barnes adopts some of Joyce's devices, her sense of organic function, or form, in a long work is simply insufficient to assimilate them. Instead of a carefully unfolded epiphany she presents a chain reaction of firecrackers popping, helter-skelter, in a dozen directions. Still, the encomiums of Eliot are not wholly unfounded. In parts of *Nightwood,* and even in some passages of *Ryder,* she exhibits truly remarkable gifts of imaginative projection and language. If her eloquence is occasionally specious, it is also at times powerful and accurate. Eliot saw in *Nightwood's* pervading burden of evil "a quality of horror and doom very nearly related to that of Elizabethan tragedy" (p. 231); more like, I should say, the vision of the Jacobean decadence: Ford, Tourneur, and some of Webster.

In the short stories, where there is less temptation to empty bombast, the vision of depersonalization, of loss of identity, of "horror and doom," comes through with greater clarity. Because the vision is not so extreme as in *Nightwood,* the characters are generally not so extremely psychopathic; repulsive as many of them are, they still retain enough of common humanity to awaken pity, if not full sympathy. The groom who is ironically trampled by his own horses in **"A Night among the Horses,"** for example, is foolish, even contemptible, yet he has the dignity not only of a victim but of one who can distinguish persons from things—a quality not shared by his persecutor. Taken up by his master's daughter, a "small fiery woman with a battery for a heart and the body of a toy, who ran everything, who purred, saturated with impudence, with a mechanical buzz that ticked away her humanity," (p. 30f.) he loses his simple identity even as she tells him: "You simply can't go on being a groom forever. . . . I'll make a gentleman out of you. I'll step you up from being a 'thing.'" (p. 31) She does not "step him up," but debases him. As he contemplates the possibility of marriage—she, it is plain, does not—he correctly perceives its consequences; "he'd be neither what he was nor what he had been; he'd be a thing, half standing, half crouching, like those figures under the roofs of historic buildings, the halt position of the damned." (p. 32)

Half drunk at a masked ball, where he is the only one in evening clothes though she has insultingly invited him to come dressed as a hostler, he makes his break for freedom, first drawing a magic circle about her in the rosin of the dance floor with his cane. Fleeing to the pasture, he slips between the fence rails determined to capture and mount one of his horses, then escape. "He was no longer afraid. He stood up, waving his hat and cane and shouting. They did not seem to know him . . ." (p. 34) Panicking, the horses run him down while he sobs "I *can* do it, damn everything, I can get on with it; I can make my mark!" (p. 35)

In a typically muted ending, the narrator continues:

> The upraised hooves of the first horse missed him, the second did not. Presently the horses drew apart, nibbling and swishing their tails, avoiding a patch of tall grass.
>
> (p. 35)

The grotesque mummery of the courtship is matched by the gruesome irony of death. The mistress, Freda Buckler, who "darted and bobbled about too much, and always with the mindless intensity of a mechanical toy kicking and raking about the floor," has indeed made him a thing—literally as well as figuratively. The horses, mindless too, instinctive, purposeless, perceive the monstrosity she has created and destroy it, but only by accident.

In addition to the bizarre and destructive relationship of man and woman, echoed in other stories and in *Nightwood,* "A Night among the Horses" introduces two interrelated motifs of estrangement that appear again and again in the writings of Djuna Barnes: the symbols of the doll and the mindless, peaceful animal.[4]

Of the two, the doll is least ambiguous, for it is one of the manifestations of human beings with the soul removed. Lifeless, mechanical, grotesque, the dolls buzz along spreading misery to those who mistake them for persons. Freda Buckler, Moydia of **"The Grande Malade,"** Addie in **"The Rabbit,"** the idiot child of **"Cassation,"** and Robin Vote, Jenny Petherbridge, and Frau Mann in *Nightwood* are all characteristically dolls. The sexlessness of the doll, as is evident in the activities of Miss Barnes's doll-women, is no warranty that the doll will not participate in sexual experience, but merely that the experience will not be meaningful.

Naturally enough, many of the doll-women also keep dolls and play with them. The lesbian Dusie in a story by that name[5] which is ultimately worked into *Nightwood,* plays with dolls at the home of her lover, Mme. K———. The context of her play is especially relevant:

> When she was ill it was sorrowful to see her, she suffered such shallow pain, as if her body were in the toils of a feeble and remorseless agony. Then she would lie over, her knees up, her head down, laughing and crying and saying, do you love me? to every woman, and every woman answered that they loved her. But it did not change her, and suddenly she would shout: Get out get out of my room! Something in her grew and died for her alone.

> When they were gone, thrown out, she would sit up in bed and amuse herself with the dolls they had brought her, wooden animals and tin soldiers, and again she would cast them from her with cunning energy.[6]

Her play and her life are sickeningly the same. In *The Antiphon* (1958), an enormous doll's house with its family is used by the aged materfamilias, Augusta, to reveal the secret of the hostility between her and her daughter Miranda. The doll play is apparently meant to be deeply symbolic of the true relationships of the family, but in the play, which has other unsatisfactory elements besides, it seems a crude satire of modern child psychotherapy. In the simpler contexts of **"Dusie"** and

"A Night among the Horses," as well as in the complex *Nightwood,* however, the doll and the evil it reflects are real and effective.

Animals and animal imagery are not so simply evil, and the ambivalence with which Miss Barnes treats her beasts (of whatever genus) indicates perhaps the most profound tension in all her writing. For although reviewers and commentators on all her books[7] dwell upon her "sympathy with the beasts" and her yearning to be absorbed into their simple world, this half-truth distorts more than it makes clear. While it is obvious in **"A Night among the Horses"** that the horses are a more noble choice of life than their mistress, it is also obvious that their life is an impossible life for the man. Trying to join them he is only monstrous.

A more subtle and extended treatment of the problem occurs in "The Rabbit," in which the bovine Armenian, Amietiev, "timid," "gentle," though he has always felt a kinship with the cows and ducks of his farm and has taken pleasure in contemplation of them, is goaded into killing "something" by the avaricious and cruel Addie. He strangles a rabbit stolen from a butcher shop near the inherited Manhattan tailoring business for which he left Armenia; prior to his decision to kill for Addie—to be masculine, heroic for her—he always found the butcher shop, with its rows of calves' heads, quarters of beef, and hanging carcasses of ducks "horribly sad; the colours were a very harvest of death." He does not wish to kill, yet he can think of no other way to be a hero. "He thought about this a long time, and finally came to the inevitable conclusion. All heroes were men who killed or got killed. Well, that was impossible; if he were killed he might as well have stayed in the country and never laid eyes on Addie—therefore he must kill—but what?" (p. 50) So he steals the rabbit; in reality, of course, absurd, but the vitality of the writing almost brings it off:

> Something moved in the box, breathing and kicking away from him; he uttered a cry, more grunt than cry, and the something in the box struck back with hard drumming fright.

> The tailor bent forward, hands out, then he shoved them in between the slats of the box opening, shutting them tight! tight! tighter! The terrible, the really terrible thing, the creature did not squeal, wail, cry: it panted, as if the wind were blunt; it thrashed its life, the frightful scuffling of the overwhelmed, in the last trifling enormity.

> (p. 52)

When Addie returns and looks in the box, she begins to laugh "harsh, back-bending laughter. 'Take it or leave it,' he shouted, and she stopped, her mouth open." (p. 52) She accepts the magnitude of his deed, and is in fact frightened by the change in him. In the early version of the story the final effect is blurred, equivocal. She pushes him out of the shop, where, dazed, "he looked up into the air, sniffing it and smiling. 'Come,' she said, 'we are going to have your boots shined.'" The implication is that he has entered her world and is at home there for the first time. The rabbit was after all only a rabbit. In the *Selected Works* version, however, when Amietiev emerges from the shop, he has forgotten her. "He was shaking, his head straight up, his heart wringing wet." (p. 53) Like Freda Buckler, Addie has ruined her man; no longer a happy beast, he is not able to enter the world on the other side of beasthood; his "harvest of death" is his own death.

The apparent longing for the freedom and peace of the beasts is nowhere more in evidence than in the novel *Ryder,* and Miss Barnes's inability to come to terms with its difficulties is one of the main causes of the novel's failure. In *Nightwood,* on the other hand, she attempts a full development of the person who lives in the beast world in her characterization of Robin Vote, "beast turning to human . . . the vision of an eland coming down an aisle of trees, chapleted with orange blossoms and bridal veil, a hoof raised in the economy of fear, stepping in the trepidation of flesh that will become myth." (p. 262)

Profoundly discontented in her halfway house, Robin tries, in the only ways she can devise, to enter fully the human world; when she accepts the fact that no depravity can give her conscience—make her human—she reverts to the beast world, no longer an eland but a dog, infinitely more degraded than the real dog whom she terrifies with her weeping, barking, and grovelling. Such treatment hardly indicates approval of or desire for the mindless freedom of beasthood. Like the doll, the beast represents an impasse in the individuation of Miss Barnes's characters. Because they are unable to reconcile their instinctive and violent revulsion against any intrusion upon the perfectly autonomous self with their equally strong and instinctive need for love, they remain outside human provenance, dangerous to themselves and to others, estranged.

This symbolism of animals and dolls, recurrent as it is in Miss Barnes's stories and novels, directs attention to her constant concern with the idea that becoming human is paradoxically all but impossible for people. This idea is also developed in other contexts. In the brilliant **"Aller et Retour,"** the vigorous Russian widow, Erling von Bartmann, returns from Paris to her daughter in Nice after the death of Herr von Bartmann, deserted by her seven years before. The character is fully drawn in the opening pages, which record her journey, by train, with stopover in Marseilles. Even her casual attention in the marketplace of Marseilles is occupied with sex and death, which come to surround her like an aura: a whore plucking a robin, postcards of mermaids and women bathing on display beside funeral wreaths. She enters a church, but her prayer is only to herself:

> She turned the stones of her rings out and put her hands together, the light shining between the little fingers; raising them she prayed, with all her vigorous understanding, to God, for a common redemption.
>
> She got up, peering about her, angry that there were no candles burning to the *Magnifique*—feeling the stuff of the altar-cloth.

> (p. 5)

Finding her daughter, Richter—"her father had wanted a boy"—grown up in body but still a child in mind, she prepares to stay home "for quite a while." (p. 6) After dinner, after playing Schubert waltzes "with effervescence" on the piano, she speaks to Richter about life.

> "[Life] is filthy; it is also frightful. There is everything in it: murder, pain, beauty, disease—death. . . . You must know *everything,* and then *begin.* . . . Man is rotten from the start. . . . Rotten with virtue and with vice. He is strangled by the two and made nothing; and God is the light the mortal insect kindled, to turn to, and to die by."

> (p. 9, my ellipses)

And so on. Then, in the darkness,

> "Are you thinking?" she said.
>
> "No," the child answered.
>
> "Then *think,*" Madame von Bartmann said loudly, turning to the child. Think everything, good, bad, indifferent; everything, and *do* everything, everything! Try to know what you are before you die."

> (p. 10)

A few days afterward Richter asks her mother's permission to announce her engagement to a government clerk chosen by her father. When the mother has ascertained that he has sufficient money, there appears "a look of pain and relief on Madame von Bartmann's face," and she directs Richter to invite Mr. Teal to dinner. Mr. Teal is hilariously true to type:

> "I shall do my best to make your daughter happy. I am a man of staid habits, no longer too young," he smiled. "I have a house on the outskirts of Nice. My income is assured—a little left me by my mother. My sister is my housekeeper, she is a maiden lady, but very cheerful and very good." He paused, holding a glass of wine to the light. "We hope to have children—Richter will be occupied. As she is delicate we shall travel, to Vichy, once a year. I have two very fine horses and a carriage with sound springs. She will drive in the afternoons, when she is indisposed—though I hope she will find her greatest happiness at home."

> (p. 11)

Two months later, her daughter married, Mme. von Bartmann is on her way back to Paris, saying to herself, simply, "'Ah, how unnecessary.'" (p. 11) The irony cuts both ways, of course, for although it is clear that Richter will never become a person, it is equally clear that for all her knowledge and wise counsel, Mme. von Bartmann is not a person, either. And considering the world Djuna Barnes has made for her, she is probably fortunate not to be.

The outrageous comedy of plot and character in **"Aller et Retour,"** combined with its simplicity and technical proficiency, result inevitably in a tour de force. In **"Spillway"**—titled more pompously **"Beyond the End"** in the 1923 volume—Miss Barnes's world view is presented in a more complex and psychologically realistic form. If not the best of the stories, it is at any rate the one having the most immediate appeal, partly because its realism is moving where the caricature of **"Aller et Retour"** is merely amusing, and partly because the fundamental problem of inner estrangement is so fully and effectively articulated.

The story of Julie Anspacher's return home, uncured, after five years at a tuberculosis sanitorium, it is set in a farmland apparently meant to be Scandinavian, in any case a place of well water and windlasses. The time is probably in the last years of the nineteenth century; one wonders if Mann's *Tristan* (1902) provided the *donnée*.

Mrs. Anspacher brings with her a daughter, not her husband's ("he was slightly surprised"). After some conversation about her health, he attempts to inquire about the child. When Julie readily admits that the girl is hers, he is nonplused:

> "What in the world is all this about?" he demanded, stopping in front of her. "What are you in this mood for—what have I done?"
>
> "Good heavens, what have *you* done! What a ridiculous man you are. Nothing of course, absolutely nothing." She waved her arm. "That's not it; why do you bring yourself in. I'm not blaming you, I'm not asking to be forgiven. I've been on my knees, I've beaten my head against the ground, I've abased myself, but—" she added in a terrible voice, "it's not low enough, the ground is not low enough; to bend down is not enough, to beg forgiveness is not enough, to receive?—it would not be enough. There just isn't the right kind of misery in the world for me to suffer, nor the right kind of pity for you to feel; there isn't a word in the world to heal me; penance cannot undo me—it is a thing beyond the end of everything—it's suffering without a consummation, it's like insufficient sleep; it's like anything that is without proportion. I am not asking for anything at all, because there is nothing that can be given or got—how primitive to be able to receive—"
>
> (p. 65)

Expecting to die, fearing death, "filled with fever and lust" Julie bore the child; its father died, but Julie, contrary to her anticipation, did not. Despite her own illness, neither did the child. And so Julie has come home,

she says, because "a thing should make a design; torment should have some meaning. I did not want to go beyond you, or to have anything beyond you—that was not the idea, not the idea at all." (p. 66) She hopes, knowing it is in vain, that he will have some understanding of her problem. She attempts to explain further:

> "I thought, Paytor may know—"
>
> "Know what?"
>
> "Division. I thought, he will be able to divide me against myself. Personally I don't feel divided; I seem to be a sane and balanced whole, but hopelessly mixed. So I said to myself, Paytor will see where the design divides and departs, though all the time I was making no bargain, I wasn't thinking of any system—well, in other words, I wanted to be set *wrong*. Do you understand?"
>
> (p. 67)

He doesn't, perhaps excusably, but as they talk on he begins to believe that he will understand "sometime later" and will then be able to help her. He leaves, and she hears him practicing with a pistol in his shooting loft.

Alone in the darkening downstairs, Julie hears the brook coming down the mountain; "she thought, water in the hand has no voice, but it really roars coming over the falls. It sings over small stones in brooks, but it only tastes of water when it's caught, struggling and running away in the hands." (p. 68) The passage culminates the imagery of water in the story; and like the rain that impinges on the earth in "Araby," its symbolic function is basically traditional. Julie herself associates the brook with memories of her childhood; by extension, it is life—her own and life in general. When it is flowing it has a voice, as life has meaning, audible but unintelligible. For Paytor, who is strong and whose family is all long-lived, the stream flows and sings unnoticed, but for Julie, whose life is perpetually ending, there is no song. "I am lost," she says, "in still water." When Paytor had asked her about her religion, she had replied that religion is "to carry me away, beyond," and she demands more than mere release, the spillway of the title. Even her habitual fight with death is only a determination to be "certain of something else first." (p. 69) Given time, she thinks she may find it.

Cold, feeling for her coat in the darkness, she tries to think:

> "All his family . . . long lives . . . and me too, me too," she murmured. She became dizzy. "It's because I must get down on my knees. But it isn't low enough," she contradicted herself, "But if I put my head down, way down—down, down, down, down . . ." She heard a shot. "He has quick warm blood—" Her forehead had not quite touched the boards, now it touched them, but she got up immediately, stumbling over her dress.
>
> (p. 70)

This is the end of the story: ironic, hopeless. Not only has she been denied the understanding she seeks; she has killed Paytor, who in spite of or perhaps because of his strength and logic has come to his conclusion "instantly," as is usual with him, but this time he has not been able to face the "fight to destroy" it. (p. 68)

The beginning of an answer to Julie's question, a provisional understanding—no matter how minimal—between her and Paytor, is quite out of the question. Julie's protestation that she loves Paytor is as meaningless as Mme. von Bartmann's prayer. This is the horror of Miss Barnes's world. That Julie cannot comprehend what we like to call the meaning of life and death is not entirely unbearable; where even *human* love is possible, men can endure without such comprehension. But in a world where religion is no more than release and love only a spillway, life itself is finally stopped off. The terrors of *Nightwood* are its last convulsion. The essential kindness, even good will, of both Julie and Paytor intensifies the horror; in the early version, **"Beyond the End,"** Paytor is merely a typical figure: the self-centered, imperceptive husband, one more than a little culpable in Julie's despair. The humanization of Paytor in **"Spillway"** hones the ironic edge much finer. If Paytor is not unkind, Julie's predicament cannot be simply a reaction to his boorishness or apathy; it must spring entirely from within herself. The total but involuntary estrangement of each human being from all others becomes more and more Miss Barnes's obsession, as her revisions of the early stories show.

In **"The Doctors,"** to me the most powerful of the stories, the threads of Katrina Silverstaff's quest for life in death and Rodkin's pitiful attempt to emerge into life twine and unravel without ever touching, insulated by the ironic fates that govern Djuna Barnes's universe. The story is typical of her writing in the vigorous conception of striking characters and situations, fully visualized scenes, and tense, even epigrammatic pointing of individual phrases, not to mention the unremitting pressure of nameless evil that seems to surround and imprison it with hydraulic force. It is typical, too, in the dissociation of its characters from their own pasts; the doctors Silverstaff, Otto and Katrina, are German Jews living on Second Avenue "in the early twenties" (they eat in a Hungarian grill); Rodkin is apparently from nowhere—in the first version of the story "[he] might have been of any nationality in the world." (*A Night among the Horses*, p. 109) The story is more extensively reworked than any of the others, testifying not only to Miss Barnes's continued interest in it, but to the real difficulty of embodying such a subject in a short story. Like the boy in Aiken's "Silent Snow, Secret Snow," Katrina can be diagnosed as schizophrenic, yet such classification is in itself meaningless. Both authors are concerned with the peculiar qualities of the individual experience, and the perspective this experience imposes upon the "normal." Moreover, Katrina's problem, like Julie Anspacher's, is essentially philosophical and religious. Here the attempt to establish a relationship to the "not-I" is clearly and desperately an attempt to reach God—or something acceptably like God. While the story is still not wholly satisfactory, its inexorable pessimism is haunting and depressingly persuasive.

While her husband Otto is a medical doctor, Katrina is a metaphysical one, though she is presented as treating animals and birds from the office she shares with her husband. "Both had started out for a doctorate in gynecology. Otto Silverstaff made it, as they say, but Katrina lost her way somewhere in vivisection, behaving as though she were aware of an impudence. . . . She never recovered her gaiety." (pp. 54, 55) She is not incapable, not squeamish, but she loses track of the purely medical; something complex, "an impudence," has entered her mind.[8] And so she is introverted, abstracted, "incomprehensible" to her husband, a kind, liberal man devoted to medicine and entirely outside her, though "inordinately pleased" with her. They have two children, a girl and a boy, one nine, the other eight, when the action takes place.

Katrina is given to announcing that "'We have fashioned ourselves against the Day of Judgment' . . . at the oddest moments seemingly without relevance to anything at all." And one day, for no apparent reason, she opens the door to an itinerant Bible peddler named Rodkin (who had, he said, "just missed it last year when he was selling Carlyle's *French Revolution*"). Rodkin is slight pale, fair, "so colourless as to seem ghostly." (p. 56) He is led like a somnambulist through an extraordinary encounter with Katrina, who says she "must have religion become out of the reach of the few; I mean out of reach for a few; something impossible again . . . at the moment religion is claimed by too many." (p. 57) She insists that she needs not his help, but *hindrance*; he is to be "only the means," and she is to be his mistress. "'But,' she added, 'do not intrude. Tomorrow you will come to see me, that is enough; that is all.'" (p. 57)

When he arrives, however, embarrassed and sheepish, "She sent word by the maid that she did not need him." It is not until the third time he calls that she is "in."

> She was quiet, almost gentle, as if she was preparing him for a disappointment, and he listened. "I have deliberately removed remorse from the forbidden; I hope you understand."
>
> He said "Yes" and understood nothing.
>
> She continued inexorably: "There will be no thorns for you. You will miss the thorns but do not presume to show it in my presence." Seeing his terror, she added: "And I do not permit you to suffer while I am in the room: Slowly and precisely she began unfastening her brooch. "I dislike all spiritual decay."

"Oh, oh!" he said under his breath.

"It is the will," she said, "that must attain complete estrangement."

Without expecting to, he barked out, "I expect so."

(p. 58)

The fantastic spiritual vivisection that Katrina performs upon herself and her action is among other things a complete reversal, an overturning, of Christ's symbolic action in his passion and sacrifice; it is willful, desperate denial of all that is human. She will cut away remorse, conscience, repentance, the will itself, and the leftover parts may flutter as they please on the operating table. She has chosen Rodkin as her means to death—"some people drink poison, some take the knife, others drown, I take you"—because she instinctively recognizes him as one of the living dead.

She wants no more to destroy him than Julie wants to destroy Paytor, but once he is let in on her predicament, his destruction is inevitable. His participation with her in her undertaking begins to call him into life. He wants to suffer, though she has forbidden him; he wants to follow her; and when his night with her is over, he feels that he has almost become "somebody." When she refuses to speak to him, he becomes nobody again. Leaving, he cries, "You are taking everything away. I can't feel—I don't suffer, nothing you know—I can't—" (p. 59) When he returns to look at the house a few days later he finds "a single length of crêpe" hung on the door. He becomes a drunkard, a nuisance, "and once, when he saw Doctor Otto Silverstaff sitting alone in a corner [of a café] with his two children, he laughed a loud laugh and burst into tears." (p. 60)

The nightmare world of Katrina Silverstaff is only partly the world of her deranged mind; there is just enough realistic circumstantial detail surrounding her—the seed cakes she carries home for tea, the barges hauling bright bricks to the islands, the furnishings of the office and the waiting room, the daughter's ballet lessons, the cigarette she lights for Rodkin—to retain a focus, however inverted and distorted, on the real world. Somewhere in vivisection, Katrina must have seen the overwhelming impudence, the overwhelming irony of existence. Her response is an overwhelming insult: the only way left to approach God. It is not very far from here to *Nightwood.*

Although most of the stories do not extend to the compass of **"Spillway"** and **"The Doctors,"** they all explore the estrangement and terror of life without love, and since none of the characters can accept traditional responses and relationships instead of love, only emptiness is left. Some die by a fiat of will, like Katrina Silverstaff. Others, like the Russian sisters of **"The Grande Malade,"** "move on." The world developed by

Djuna Barnes is a very full fictional realization of the desolate, depersonalized images of T. S. Eliot's *Preludes.* What is missing, significantly, is "The notion of some infinitely gentle/ Infinitely suffering thing." Suffering there is in plenty, gentleness, in nothing.

Most of the stories are told by a noncommittal omniscient narrator who shows herself only in the quality of her descriptions; she tells nothing directly; even summary is accomplished by skillful accumulation of details. In the few stories with a first-person narrator—**"Cassation," "The Grande Malade," "Dusie,"**—the narrator's detachment has the added horror of coming from one involved in the action. Shocking, remote, the stories nonetheless have all the power a unified vision and superbly controlled prose can give. When they fail it is often merely from overstrain.

Unlike the novels and the long play, where the writing, as Alfred Kazin observed in his review of *Nightwood,* "has occasionally . . . an intensity that is only verbal: long after the idea or emotion has been exhausted, the tone is sustained,"[10] the stories maintain correspondence between matter and manner. Along with the novels, they have their being outside society and historical milieu, and indeed the vacuum that surrounds them is responsible for not a little of their impact. While we may feel that Miss Barnes's conception of man is narrow and at times even shallow, the evidence of much contemporary history compels us to admit its appalling veracity. These stories, long out of print and out of sight, deserve a wider appreciation, not only as representative work of the modernist period, but as remarkable examples of their genre. Like the best stories by the best writers of her generation, the best stories of Djuna Barnes—I should pick **"Spillway," "The Doctors," "Aller et Retour,"** possibly one or two more—expand our ideas of what the short story can do, and in this way expand our awareness of life.

Notes

1. *Selected Words of Djuna Barnes* (New York: Farrar, Straus, and Cudahy, 1962). All quotations are from this edition, unless noted. Faber & Faber issued *The Short Stories of Djuna Barnes* in a separate edition in 1962. The 1929 volume is called *A Night Among the Horses* (New York: Horace Liveright); it is a reissue, with added materials, of *A Book* (Boni & Liveright, 1923).

2. The nine are: "Aller et Retour," "Cassation," "The Grande Malade," "A Night among the Horses," "The Valet," "The Rabbit," "The Doctors," "Spillway," "The Passion." Faber & Faber's edition of the short stories also contains "The Boy Asks a Question." Other interesting and valuable stories from the earlier volumes are "The Robin's House," "Mother," and "Indian Summer."

3. See Eliot's preface to *Nightwood* (all editions), and Edwin Muir, "The Present Age," in *Introductions to English Literature*, V (London, 1939), 150-51, 153-54.

4. See Ulrich Weisstein, "Beast, Doll, and Woman: Djuna Barnes' Human Bestiary," *Renaissance*, XV (Fall, 1962), 3-11, for discussion of the animal and doll symbols in *Nightwood* and *The Antiphon*. I cannot agree with many of Mr. Weisstein's interpretations.

5. "Dusie," *Americana Esoterica*, edited by Carl Van Doren (Macy Nasieu, 1927), pp. 75-82.

6. *Ibid.*, p. 78.

7. See Weisstein, *op. cit.*, and review article in *Nation*, CXVIII (Jan. 2, 1924), 14.

8. In the early version, "Katrina Silverstaff," she studied veterinary medicine and "smiled in a strange, hurt and sarcastic way when dissecting." This is a much cruder conception, and quite different.

9. I find this ending particularly pallid, and damaging to the story; the flattened out coda is typical of Djuna Barnes, no doubt under the influence of Chekhov, and sometimes it does work.

10. Alfred Kazin, *New York Times Book Review*, March 7, 1937, p. 6.

Louis F. Kannenstine (essay date 1977)

SOURCE: Kannenstine, Louis F. "Early Plays and *The Antiphon*." In *The Art of Djuna Barnes: Duality and Damnation*, pp. 128-60. New York: New York University Press, 1977.

[*In the following excerpt, Kannenstine explicates* The Antiphon, *focusing on its complex and often misunderstood language and form, as well as on its central themes of "divided being" and "the receding present."*]

A great deal has been said about the obscurity of [*The Antiphon*] since it appeared in 1958. One might have supposed that in revising it for inclusion in the 1962 volume of *The Selected Works,* Miss Barnes would have intended to clarify a number of passages for bewildered readers. Except for a few points at which the interruption or abridgement of dramatic monologues seems to alter meaning or to facilitate both readability and playability, this was not the case. Besides correcting printer's errors, she seems to have been trying to gain an even tighter compactness of blank verse with no reduction of its eccentric punctuation or abundant archaisms. Despite the diversity of critical opinion on

either published version of *The Antiphon,* no one denies that the play presents formidable difficulties for its readers. There is a story that Janet Flanner tells of how, when admitting to Miss Barnes her concordance with T. S. Eliot's admiration of its archaic language but inability to "make head or tail of its drama," Miss Barnes replied, "'I never expected to find that you were as stupid as Tom Eliot.'"[1] The language surely stands as a barrier to ready comprehension of much of the play's action and motives. One does not have to read far into the first act to discover a nearly forbidding richness of invention. Take, for instance, these early lines of Miranda's addressed to Jack Blow:

> It's true the webbed commune
> Trawls up a wrack one term was absolute;
> Yet corruption in its deft deploy
> Unbolts the caution, and the vesper mole
> Trots down the wintry pavement of the prophet's
> head.[2]

As often elsewhere, the context in which this is placed provides no direct illumination of its meaning, which is already concealed in archaisms, cramped syntax, and compound metaphors. Considering the abundance of such passages, John Wain reached a conclusion similar to that of many reviewers: that Miss Barnes had developed the "clotted" quality of Jacobean verse to such a degree that her language became too opaque for either stage performance or solitary reading.[3]

In language as well as form, *The Antiphon* is a reaction against the state of the contemporary theater. As a theatrical columnist, it will be recalled, Miss Barnes discovered that what was missing in modern drama was a sense of contemplation, the "'will-to-see-things-through with the mind'" that had been eventually sacrificed for action that was too often mere fumbling. "'If some character in the play of a hundred years ago was irresolute . . . ,'" she wrote, "'he probed that sickness with his wit, and came forth with a soliloquy or an argument that made of him, no matter how ludicrous his situation, a figure of ponderable value.'"[4] Although the theatrical "Almanack" columns cite numerous instances of the past recaptured in this respect, such moments are seldom found to be sustained and are usually the result of some particular actor's contribution to his role beyond the written play. Without mind, Miss Barnes perceived, the stage becomes an arena of noise and clatter, and the spectator is driven to the silence of the cinema for the experience of reflection that language once provided in the theater.

So *The Antiphon* is first of all an effort to recapture the oral grandeur that had once engaged the mind in dramatic spectacle. Its blank verse at once elevates its language above common speech. In addition, the play's action is so minimal, with so much of its length given to excavation into the pasts of the principal characters, that a static situation is created in which attention is drawn largely toward the language itself. It seems that Miss Barnes's early difficulty in creating and sustaining dramatic tension is transformed here into an asset. Disdain for traditional plot and structure again enables the author to create space in which to pursue the elusive aspects of human relationships. And it is precisely this factor which most disturbs critics, who time and time again raise doubts as to the play's suitability for stage performance.

It would be unwise to proceed to discuss this issue without first pausing to consider the plot of *The Antiphon* itself. For if the language becomes the main thing, and if that language is compact or opaque in a way that produces frequent obscurity, the coherence of the dramatic action as a whole is threatened. The reader or spectator is repeatedly brought to a *cul-de-sac* from which he must set out again toward some point of illumination or recognition, and the rise and fall of the action are thus radically affected. There is a "breaking-up of surfaces," according to Howard Nemerov, an abandonment of traditional plot sequence and coherence: ". . . allegory, moral and anagoge are made to emerge as if by a kind of Cubist handling from the shattered reflections of 'story.'"[5] This, he argues, is the direct result of the play's almost total lack of literal level of action. To be sure, Miss Barnes's "Cautionary Note" to the 1962 version of *The Antiphon* warns that "this play is more than merely literal,"[6] and the ironic jab of her remark is worthy of her aristocratic Augusta at her more imperious moments. When attempting to describe the concrete events of the play, one becomes aware of the author's extreme distrust of literal experience itself, of the reality of the present moment.

As in *Nightwood,* time and place are abruptly and specifically indicated at the beginning. The play opens in England during the war of 1939, as the stage directions state. Miranda, daughter of Augusta Burley Hobbs, returns to Burley Hall, a former "college of chantry priests" (*A*, p. 80) and the ancestral Beewick township home of the Burleys since the late seventeenth century. The manor is a ruin, open for refuge to travellers but still presided over by Miranda's Uncle Jonathan as surviving steward and custodian. Miranda, caught up in the flight of war refugees from the Continent, has been accompanied from Paris by Jack Blow. Although he appears in the dress and assumed role of coachman, he is in fact Miranda's brother Jeremy. This information is not disclosed until the final curtain, but one senses that Miranda has become aware of the disguise. At what point she actually perceives Jack's identity is a matter of ambiguity.[7] But it is clear, as the family past begins to unfold in act 1, that Jack Blow knows and presumes too much. "You talk too much, too much leave out,"[8] observes Miranda.

It is Jeremy himself, who had fled his American home some twenty years earlier, who has summoned Augusta as well as her daughter to her childhood home, fully aware that she would be accompanied by her mercenary sons Dudley and Elisha. These are the "merchants" that Miranda recurrently and apprehensively fears and, as they enter a momentarily empty stage while Augusta is still asleep in her car, it is clear that the daughter's vague terror is justified. In the presumed absence of the lost loved brother, Dudley and Elisha intend their mother and sister no good: "The ground they stand on, let's uncover it, / Let us pull their shadows out from under them!"[9] But the principals remain ignorant of their presence in this act. As Jack whispers in an aside, "I'm not too sure what's brewing hereabouts!" (*A* [*The Antiphon*], p. 111).

This first act serves as a prologue to the lengthy second, which resumes the exposition and is continuous in time with the first. Miranda, with Jack's encouragement, had already begun to visualize her mother's past by recalling the coming of her polygamous and freethinking American father, Titus Hobbs, to Beewick, and his own mother's engineering of the meeting with Augusta. Also, Jack had related at length to Burely his meeting with Miranda in Paris and their subsequent flight. Act 2 opens with Augusta's emphatic entrance. She does not recognize her brother at first, and Jeremy is of course disguised. Augusta's speculations on his whereabouts as well as on an altered Burley Hall lead to prolonged reflections upon past events: Augusta's departure for America with her husband, his subsequent treachery by adultery again with the connivance of Titus's mother Victoria, who "could cluck in anyone for daughter" (*A*, p. 154), and the childhood of Miranda, unprotected among "Procuress, procured, and bastard!" (*A*, p. 166). Mounting along with this is Augusta's profound sense of ambivalence toward her daughter, heightened by an intense identification with her. As Augusta says, "In short, I can't afford her / She's only me" (*A*, p. 162). Presently, with Jack and Uncle Jonathan offstage, Dudley and Elisha don animal masks and proceed to taunt and torment the women viciously. Their abuse is interrupted with Jack enters bearing a doll house. "Hobb's Ark, beast-box, doll's house," which reveals in miniature through its tiny windows the scene of ultimate betrayal by the father; the rape of Miranda by a travelling Cockney that had been arranged by Titus "for experiment."[10] This climactic revelation of Miranda's sacrifice—"'Do not let him—but if it will atone—'" (*A*, p. 186) she had cried—brings out her will to vindicate not only Augusta as woman and as victim, but also her father, raised as she had been to trust innocently in his faith.[11] At this point, with all "shaken by diminutive," the act closes.

The third act is a lamentation and Augusta's final agony, involving the specific antiphon of the title. Mother and daughter are alone onstage, the others having retired for the night. It is clear by this point that something has happened to the play's sense of time. With the intense absorption in the past that has come about, the present has become diffuse. The dread of the war of 1939 has become generalized, transformed into a timeless sense of holocaust, of the imminent collapse of civilization. The shift to an allegorical dimension has taken place. Now, upon the reunited halves of a gryphon, "once a car in a roundabout," Augusta and Miranda confront one another. As the play's "Cautionary Note" has forewarned, ". . . their familiarity is their estrangement, their duel is in hiatus, their weapons tempered" (*A,* p. 79). Augusta, failing to get Miranda to tell her of her life, loves, and adventures, turns to play. Exchanging shoes and hats, they begin an imaginary voyage together which becomes a quest for identity. Augusta, however, is torn and divided. "I think it's time I saw me as Augusta," she says, but she cannot resist for long her need to merge with, to become her daughter. In Miranda, however, she has "a daughter for inquisitor!" (*A,* p. 195). Miranda recalls her love for her mother in its Edenic phase:

> Before the tree was in the cross, the cradle, and the coffin,
> The tragic head-board, and the victim door,
> The weeper's bannister, the cunning pannel.

> (*A,* p. 194)

But, she accuses, "Titus Adam/Had at you with his raping hook," whereupon "A door slammed on Eden, and the Second Gate, / And I walked down your leg" (*A,* p. 195).

The antiphonal duel thus proceeds in phases of empathy and antagonism, oneness and duality. At one poignant moment, Miranda urges,

> Rebuke me less, for we are face to face
> With the fadged up ends of discontent:
> But tie and hold us in that dear estrangement
> That we may like before we too much lose us.

> (*A,* p. 213)

The crass world intrudes, however, and Augusta yields. As she hears Dudley and Elisha preparing to depart, she simultaneously senses that her longed-for Jeremy is near. Miranda attempts to hold her, to block her way as she tries to mount the stairs. Augusta brings a curfew bell down upon her daughter, and both collapse upon the gryphon. At the abrupt final curtain, Jack speaks of ". . . the hour of the uncreate; /The season of the sorrowless lamenting" (*A,* p. 223), and exits "with what appears to be indifference."

The movement of *The Antiphon* involves a gradual tapering off of plot momentum, a cessation of action. Its carefully timed *ralenti* accompanies the shift of the

work to a more purely allegorical level. Correspondingly, there is an increasing absorption in its language and even its visual or scenic element. In the hush of act 3, there is a notable change in the quality of the verse, of which Miranda's key lines offer evidence:

> Where the martyr'd wild fowl fly the portal
> High in the honey of cathedral walls,
> There is the purchase, governance and mercy.
> Where careful sorrow and observed compline
> Sweat their gums and mastics to the hive
> Of whatsoever stall the head's heaved in—
> There is the amber. As the high plucked banks
> Of the viola rend out the unplucked strings below—
> There is the antiphon.
> I've seen loves so eat each other's mouth
> Till that the common clamour, co-intwined,
> Wrung out the hidden singing in the tongue
> Its chaste economy—there is the adoration.
> So the day, day fit for dying in
> Is the plucked accord.

> (*A,* p. 214)

It is a "hidden singing" that is brought out here by means of chaste economy in the cathedral silence of the night. The tone of liturgical gravity of this passage had been introduced earlier by Miranda's admonition,

> Be not your own pathetic fallacy, but be
> Your own dark measure in the vein,
> For we're about a tragic business, mother.

> (*A,* p. 205)

And the singing quality is sustained throughout the act by lyric passages in which Augusta tries to approach her daughter by pretending, by turning their encounter into fairy tale and imaginary journey. But the chant is fated to end in discord, the women being too world-weary and old to undo the curse of the father. Their absurd death fulfills Miranda's warning, "He, who for fear, denies the called response / Denies the singing, and damns the congregation!" (*A,* p.209).

It is here in the final act that a musical motif is brought out in full degree in verse and supportive image. As in *Nightwood,* high and low themes have been in interplay throughout. On the one hand, bandstand instruments onstage reinforce Augusta's recollection of Kapellmeister Stack with his baton, conducting a trumpet voluntary to the approach of a major-general, "Miranda's first cadet" (*A,* p. 135). And there is a refrain that Jack Blow frequently hums: "Hey then, 'Who / Passes by this road so late,' Always gay?" (*A,* p.89), a line from the opening of "Compagnons de la Marjolaine," the song of the Chevalier du Guet Royal, which had been organized in the eighteenth century for night patrol of the streets of Paris. Besides its simple effectiveness in arousing apprehension, the refrain also extends the dimension of time beyond the present military threat on the Continent. But musical themes play upon a higher level in the final antiphon, where the sustained image of the viola in Miranda's lines quoted above lends an overtone of chamber music to the liturgical chant. Finally the hidden singing that is plucked out in the formal and resonant verse of the last agony is terminated by the cacophony of panic that precipitates the death blow, followed by Jack's flat coda at his exit.

Visual conception and design are functional too in *The Antiphon.* The set is an extremely important element. Superbly visualized down to the last prop—the brass curfew bell which becomes the death instrument that rings the antiphon to a close—the scene, the Great Hall of Burley, is so suggestive of the play's main themes that it stands as its symbolic core. The first cluster of objects introduced in the stage directions, the "flags, gonfalons, bonnets, ribbons and all manner of stage costumes" (*A,* p.81) which hang over the balustrade, immediately relates to Miranda, to her associations with the theatrical world, her international past, and her fondness for pageantry. A dressmaker's dummy in "regimentals," placed before a Gothic window, sustains the hint of pageant or military processional (while serving as a coy reminder that Miss Barnes's world is one in which fashion counts). Haphazardly arranged about this dummy are "music stands, horns, fiddles, guncases, bandboxes, masks, toys and broken statues, man and beast" (*A,* p.81). These evoke not only the father with his love of the hunt and of music-making, but also time past, childhood and the nursery,[12] elements to be echoed in numerous snatches from nursery rhymes. The masks of pig and ass are to be donned by the sons, bringing the recurrent man-beast dichotomy into focus in a crucial agon in act 2. And the broken statues, of course, suggest the wear of time as well as the fractured mother-daughter entity, Miranda and Augusta perceiving themselves in their intense empathy as a divided whole.

Little by little it becomes clear that the set incorporates things in the concrete present that represent occurrence in the historical past or altogether outside of chronological time. In the moment which brings present and past together, there is captured an explicit and ominous sense of ruin. The Gothic window is paneless, a ruined colonnade is visible through a crumbled wall, and Miranda's theatrical costume is "elegant but rusty" (*A,* p. 82). The decline of Western civilization which is one allegorical motif in the play is thus visualized before ever articulated. In effect, the compression or condensation noticeable in the play's language becomes evident in its visual scheme too. The set could bear strong comparison to the shadow boxes of Joseph Cornell, which evoke a past beyond chronology by juxtaposition of "found" objects: perhaps a clay soap bubble pipe, a fragment of an old map, a child's alphabet block or toy tin sun, all enclosed within a twilight blue box decked with astrological symbols on the interior walls. Similarly, individual concrete objects instantaneously assume universal and timeless dimension in Miss Barnes's set. The Great Hall of Burley is in line with the earlier visual collages in *Nightwood*: the rococo halls of Hedvig Volkbein, the jungle room of Robin, the American salon of Nora, and the squalid lodgings of the doctor, all memorable settings which suggest the accumulation of time.

Miss Barnes's principal themes of divided being and the receding present thus begin to emerge in *The Antiphon.* They are embodied together in one of the play's two key stage properties. At the end of a central table with an apt formal setting are the two halves of the gryphon which once had been a car in a carousel and thus once a part of childhood. But it is not the antiquity or the fantasticality of the piece alone that is significant. It was the father who once halved the gryphon with a saw. In act 3, it is upon the reunited halves that the mother and daughter "voyage" and become one being. It has been suggested that this mythic figure, half eagle, half lion, relates to Dante's encounter with the gryphon in canto 31 of the *Purgatorio,* "that beast/Which in two natures one sole person is,"[13] symbol of "incarnation, duality resolved, divine and human nature made one."[14] The allusion possibly extends to the car that the gryphon fastens to the barren tree in the subsequent canto, causing it to come to flower—which, in turn, might be taken to illuminate Augusta's frequent plea to Miranda to put her to a tree at her death.[15] Paradoxically, however, it is finally upon the gryphon that the two women fall to death after having become momentarily whole and again divided, a fulfillment of Augusta's utterance, "Love is death . . ." (*A,* p.196).

Equally important is the sinister toy, the doll's house called "beast-box" which Jack brings onstage in act 2, his motive being "to medecine contumely / With a doll's hutch—that catches villains!" (*A,* p.224). This bizarre object seems the equivalent of the supernatural machinery, the macabre masquerade often employed in Jacobean tragedy.[16] The device conforms to Aristotle's rule that "the supernatural should be used only in connection with events that lie outside the play itself, things that have happened long ago beyond the knowledge of men, or future events which need to be foretold and revealed. . . ."[17] But there are no gods to intervene in 1939. There is only Jack-Jeremy who has engineered the revelation, apparently hoping that his conjuring will have the purgative effect of bringing the family past into focus. In effect, the miniaturization of the manor with its doll inhabitants is the objective correlative of the act of memory which reduces the complexity of experience to manageable proportions. The trick evokes what Doctor O'Connor called "'the almost fossilized state of our recollection,'" making the doll house "'an accumulation, a way to lay hands on the shudder of a past that is still vibrating'" (*N* [*Nightwood*], pp. 118-19). So Augusta bawdily asks upon seeing Titus's effigy, "Was this the stick that leapt me, gentlemen?" (*A,* p. 182). But something undeniable appears before her through tiny windows. As Jack accuses,

> The crystal, like a pregnant girl, has hour
> When it delivers up its oracle,
> Leaving the chamber to the adversary.
> The eye-baby now you're pregnant with
> You'll carry in your iris to the grave.
> You made yourself a *madam* by submission. . . .
>
> (*A,* p. 185)

It may be true that in *The Antiphon* "the tragic flaw is neither more or less than life itself,"[18] considering that the play ultimately functions on an allegorical level. But in its specific past action it was Augusta's *hamartia* or error of judgement, followed by her moral weakness and submission, that was the source of the present tragedy of estrangement. The doll house indicts Augusta, its rape scene making it an "*abattoir.*"[19] As she can neither finally confront nor effectively deny its truth, it traps her in the halt position of the dammed.

All in all, the ornate and complex visual plan of *The Antiphon* is so highly developed that, beyond its symbolic significance, it nearly becomes something independent of the play itself. In other words, it exceeds the limits of basic dramatic necessity to such a degree that it almost seems a separate element. In addition, it has occurred to a number of critics that the language also detaches itself from the drama, taking on a life of its own extrinsic to the events of the play and the lives of its characters. It should be clear, however, that what is involved here is the trans-generic mode that has been noted as operative in all of Djuna Barnes's major work. The overall failure of her early one-act plays betrayed a restlessness, an impatience with the delimiting forms of modern theater and the deadening effect of so much activity without reflection. The consequence of all this was to look backward and create for this late and mature play a hybrid form evocative of major phases of historical drama. Thus *The Antiphon* taps the origin of modern drama in rituals of the medieval Christian church, suggests variations upon the forms of Greek tragedy and early closet drama, and most directly revives the tone and grandeur of Elizabethan drama with a nod at the Jacobean tradition as well. Also with the prominence of the set as a work of art and the multiple-level musicality of the verse, the play attempts to broaden the scope of dramatic form, to present new possibilities for modern theater.

As suggested earlier, this departure has aroused a widespread anxiety on the part of readers which has to do with the question of the work's performability. Lionel Abel is not alone in wondering how the most intelligent audience could possibly understand the play when hearing its difficult lines for the first time spoken on stage.

The sheer difficulty of its verse, he suggests, renders the play, doubtfully readable in the first place, virtually unplayable as well. The reviewer for the *Times Literary Supplement* concurs in the opinion that only an audience willing to devote much time to study of the text could get the gist of it from its performance. But the audience alienating difficulty of the language, he suggests, completes the author's "rejection of the normal experiential world which she begins by obliterating most conventional manifestations of character." So the real reason for Miss Barnes's use of dramatic form is "to create a formal complexity beyond the range of other verse forms, and complexity is integral to her vision.[20] This amounts to saying that *The Antiphon* is in no sense a conventional drama, that its deviation from the genre is deliberate, and that it has no business being subjected to the common standards of dramatic criticism.

Apart from a reading of *The Antiphon* given in Cambridge, Massachusetts, in 1958 by the Poet's Theatre as a result of Edwin Muir's admiration of the play, it has been put to the actual test of staging only once. In February 1961, the Royal Dramatic Theatre of Stockholm presented *The Antiphon* in a translation by Dag Hammarskjold and Karl Ragnar Gierow. The reviews that followed in the Swedish press seem to have been on the whole affirmative in response to Olaf Melander's ability to convey the nuances of such an "exclusive" drama in his production. While one reviewer claimed that the play was ultimately unfit for staging because "'it is as a lyrist rather than a dramatist that Djuna Barnes has created her mysterious world,'"[21] the response of Dr. Ivar Harrie was more typical:

> Yes, the audience really caught on—gradually. After the first act people were very awed—and a little afraid of showing how lost they felt. The second act has a bewildering—but unescapably exciting—effect. The third act . . . broke down all resistance: there was no alternative but to surrender to the dramatic poem.[22]

Although *The Antiphon* has yet to be presented in its own language on the stage, the overall success of the Stockholm effort casts doubt upon the pronouncements concerning its staging potential that greeted its publication in 1958.

The appropriateness of language to genre, however, comes into more serious question on another level. Kathleen Raine, although convinced that she is discussing a work of great distinction, feels that its speeches are not shaped by the active emotions of the characters: ". . . they are aggregates of fancy, not imaginative expressions proceeding from an inner unity of condition or thought."[23] Thus the play loses dramatic immediacy. Another critic, Donna Gerstenberger, comes to a similar conclusion but from the observation that "the passion and feeling of the play are lost in the intensity and difficulty of the verse, and what external action there is always carries with it the sense that it is an afterthought."[24] So beyond the problem of comprehension that the language presents to the reader, it is argued that the verse is essentially antidramatic, divorced from the feelings of its characters and the events that arouse them. Lionel Abel states the problem even more cogently. The reader as well as the presumed spectator, he argues, confronts characters who, rather than speaking from emotion, are writing poems onstage:

> . . . the characters scarcely talk to each other. Each one is intent on subtilizing and distilling his own thought and feeling into a verse expression adequate to the author's norms of rhetoric, and these are not at all dramatic norms. The result: there is no dialogue in any proper sense of the term . . . and the words spoken by any one character have scarcely any effect on the others.[25]

Most readers would allow that there is a certain justice in Abel's remarks. The characters do at times seem to be speaking in a kind of vacuum; the speech of one character frequently seems undifferentiated from that of another. If all voices are finally one and the same voice, the result is that the play indeed becomes static despite the aptness of overall effect for the author's theme of identity. Abel finally throws up his hands: "But I am judging *The Antiphon* as a play—I don't know if there are any categories for judging a closet-drama."[26]

The Antiphon exhibits Miss Barnes's characteristic impatience with familiar categories. Richard Eberhardt was prompt to call it "a poem, a verse play for reading"[27] rather than a play for acting. "This is Senecan drama, not for the public stage but the closet," wrote another reviewer. "Its chief effect is to reveal to us Djuna Barnes' romantic image of herself, and that is no small thing."[28] And Miss Barnes herself asserted that *The Antiphon* was written not for acting but primarily for the writer.[29] All in all, it would seem that it is as a closet drama that the work must finally be judged, even if this category has become an elusive one in the present age. True to its form, like Milton's *Samson Agonistes* and Browning's "Pippa Passes," it applies "the standards of one day to the art of a later day."[30] This fact in itself, of course, does not determine its category. The fact is that it is literary to such a degree that to read it as a poetic drama rather than as a dramatic poem is to create confusion.

Aside from the question of playability, it remains to determine what position *The Antiphon* takes in Djuna Barnes's collective work. Seemingly isolated in time from the main body of her writing and problematic in genre, it actually relates back to the concerns of the young playwright of the twenties whose work at that time had begun to take a turn more literary than dramatic. *The Antiphon* gives evidence of a mature aware-ness of dramatic form and of classical theater, while either ignoring inherited conventions or adapting them to its own purposes. Like *Nightwood* it is at once experimental and traditional: experimental in its radical departure from the standard generic modes, traditional in its use of past forms to delineate a modern landscape. That the author and her major works still remain difficult to classify late in a century of literary experimentation, is one indication of the success of her method.

The Antiphon is traditional in still another respect. It invites comparison with two other verse plays of the twentieth century that revive the ancient theme of a curse upon a house. A parallel with W. B. Yeats's *Purgatory* has been described as follows:

> As in *Purgatory,* the scene . . . is a compelled if somewhat unwilling return to the ancestral home, the place where many of the difficulties of the present were begot. And as in Yeats' play, much of the present action seems to be defined by a sexual conflict in the past arising from the indignation suffered by an aristocratic mother from a pleasure-loving father. . . . The past in both plays provides the source of a neurotic hatred in the present, and both end with death that falls short of resolution.[31]

Striking similarities also exist between *The Antiphon* and T. S. Eliot's *The Family Reunion*. The return in each becomes a drama of sin and attempted expiation that reaches into the ancestral past. From each conflict emerges an overbearing sense of time. The past dominates Burley Hall as much as it does Wishwood, as in Eliot's choral passage:

> In an old house there is always listening, and more is
>   heard than is spoken.
> And what is spoken remains in the room, waiting for
>   the future to hear it.
> And whatever happens began in the past, and presses
>   hard on the future.
> The agony in the curtained bedroom, whether of birth
>   or of dying,
> Gathers in to itself all the voices of the past, and projects them into the future.[32]

For Harry, Lord Monchensey, the present is a "loop in time,"[33] while in *The Antiphon* it exists as a dial without hours, allowing the hidden to be revealed, mystery to be manifest.

With such corresponding thematic overtones in mind, one might suppose that these two plays were directly influential upon *The Antiphon.* Both appeared in 1939, a time when Miss Barnes was involved in the initial phases of composition, and could have played a part in the formative process. Of course neither Yeats's one-act play nor Eliot's work fall into the category of closet drama. Yeats's devotion to a public theater remained constant in his later years, and his free verse possessed colloquial ease and flow. Eliot, moreover, sought to bridge the gap between everyday speech and rhetorical eloquence so that the one would merge into the other without impediment. For this reason *The Family Reunion* demanded to be staged, to become public. The difficulties of Miss Barnes's verse, for reasons mentioned earlier, create an immediate barrier to stage transition. The dramatic poem's full effects, if available at all, are at hand on the printed page.

What is clear, however, is the continuity between *The Antiphon* and Miss Barnes's earlier works, notably *Ryder.* As Marie Ponsot observes, *The Antiphon* continues, clarifies, and concludes the earlier story. In the later work, Wendell Ryder becomes Titus Hobbs and Amelia reappears as Augusta. Sophia is again present in Victoria, Augusta's mother-in-law, while Kate-Careless appears in passing as an ugly mistress of the father. Also, Miss Ponsot notes, "Julie of *Ryder,* Nora of *Nightwood* and Miranda are essentially one person, grown from girlhood into death."[34] Finally Miss Barnes's play provides "a clearer and wider view of the ancestral figures who stalk her work."[35] Along with the characters who are transfigured to greater or lesser degree evolve the themes which are prominent in *Ryder, Ladies Almanack,* and the short stories, and which accumulate in *Nightwood:* the post-Edenic condition of women, the middle condition as the measure of humanity, and the paradox of time which reveals the modern age as a shambles.

The Antiphon offers what is perhaps Djuna Barnes's strongest image of "the horror of what men do to women in making them mothers, and women to men in giving birth to them."[36] Again the cycle of procreation is seen to be unending, ceaselessly repeating the loss of Eden and terror of schism or division. Even more than before, the figure of father and procreator is presented as a suprahuman aggressive force. Like Ryder, Titus Hobbs is recalled as pliant, "an eager, timorous, faulty man" (*A,* p.144). But the feminine component, maternally affectionate and receptive to all nature as in O'Connor, has all but vanished in the new patriarch, "Titus! Self-appointed Holy Ghost and Father. / Prophet, Savior, out of Salem—brag of heaven; / Wived in righteous plenty—Solomon."[37] Wendell the free-thinker has become Titus the anarchist, bent upon principled destruction of social and familial order. Miranda's conception is rape, and it is rape that the father in turn eventually brings upon the daughter. Miranda and Augusta become co-sufferers, sacrifices to the Old Testament force of Original Sin. The sons all the while become either blind like the time-bound merchants Dudley and Elisha, or confused like Jack-Jeremy, ambivalent and unsure in his motives, and not at all unlike young Wendell. The women in turn become the victims of the next generation of men, of Dudley and Elisha's overt malice as well as Jack's uncertain intentions and machinations. For mother and daughter love is death. "Peram-

bulator rolling to the tomb; / Death with a baby in its mouth" (*A,* p.219).

Djuna Barnes's universe is one in which women find their very strength in submission. If the masculine principle of domination and imposition is indomitable, as generation after generation after the fall of Adam and Eve have demonstrated, then what recourse is left to women in the end? To rebel against or to try to destroy the male is to subvert the order of civilization and invite self-destruction, as shown by Julie Anspacher and Katrina Silverstaff in *Spillway.* To allow that all women have posed for the madonna, however, and to embrace the archetypal role of mother like Sophia can be a sort of victory. Alternately, there is the recourse of standing apart, of existing within the limits of a separate universe which excludes men or moves beyond the range of the masculine psyche. In *Ladies Almanack* and those one-act plays in which ladies take tea, men are ruled out altogether. The union of women draws a line at the threshold of masculine dominion.

Hence the bond between Augusta and Miranda. Alone in the third act in the night where waking distinctions dissolve and merge, the two reach the plane of metaphor where Augusta is Miranda and Miranda is Augusta, familiarity in estrangement. As women they are estranged from the universe as a totality. As mother and daughter, they are at the same time one and separate. As mother, Augusta perceives that "Miranda's all Augusta laid up in Miranda."[38] Yet when Miranda finally will not let Augusta know her, their oneness becomes torment. "In what pocket have you my identity?" asks Augusta. "I so disoccur in every quarter of myself / I cannot find me" (*A,* p.213). As the two stare upon each other "with unbuttoned eyes." the essential paradox of the middle condition is revealed.

To transcend the literal and mundane world of facts (that of the merchants) and confusion (that of Jack-Jeremy) is to attain the level of poetic vision or metaphor where dualisms vanish and everything is interrelated and significant. Augusta and Miranda share the suffered understanding, the tragic all-knowingness of Miss Barnes's superior women, from Madame von Bartmann to Nora Flood. Their distinction lies in their attainment of the middle vision which abolishes duality by making new connections: the plucked accord, the reunited gryphon, the rendered antiphonal response. But this is a tragic business. To be divided is to go down unknowing, while to be united is to suffer the loss of identity. The middle plane is the halt position of both total coherence and dissolution. The duel between Augusta and Miranda is one between "two beasts in chancery" (*A,* p.188). There can be no victory or resolution short of death, for mother and daughter are suspended, "Caught in the utmost meridian and parallel" (*A,* p.222). They are "the damned," Jack Blow says, "who won't capitulate!" (*A,* p. 86).

A condition of suspension dominates the entire play, and is in fact integral to its sense of time. Miranda first sees in Burley Hall "a rip in nature," a premonition seconded by Jack's opening lines: "There's no circulation in the theme, / The very fad of being's stopped" (*A*, p.82). The dial without hours measures the time of the play. Yet at the same time, the women are trapped in a "clocked encounter" (*A*, p.189) that cannot be stopped. The literal action advances by clock time, but its solidity or reality gradually diminishes. The antiphon of the third act is out of time. When Miranda says "Mother, there's no more time. All's done" (*A*, p.199), she announces that chronological time has been abolished, that the present is finished. The abrupt intrusion of clock time that the departure of the sons heralds promptly precipitates destruction as well.

The exhaustion of Augusta and Miranda sums up the world-weariness of a shopworn age. As in her earlier work, Miss Barnes sees history as recorded devaluation. The year 1939 is the age of the barbarian, of the merchant who tauntingly boasts, "We're timely" (*A*, p.150). Augusta is all too aware that in her time "Glory used to be the aim—now it's possessions" (*A*, p.172). Since "nothing now is wrought by hand / To give into the hand particular, / Nor pride of execution" (*A*, p.108), p.108), the apocalyptic moment is at hand. If, however, time has run out, there is the recurrence of the past to fill the gap. What the clock cannot measure of history cannot be abolished, nor can it be falsified or cheapened. "They say a snail from Caesar's grave / Crawled into Napoleon's snuff box" (*A*, p. 91), reflects Jack Blow, possibly hinting at a continuity beneath the broken surface of historical record. The stopped watch will then leave a void to be filled by the past rushing in, and the given present moment will be one of historical recession.

It is this sense of time that is a dominant subject of Djuna Barnes's later poems, from **"Transfiguration"** of 1938 to **"The Walking-Mort"** of 1971. These are so few in number to date, however, that *The Antiphon* stands out as Miss Barnes's major act of poetic expression so far. Its position in modern poetry is probably unique. It is anachronistic in its turn against the present, against its literary practices as well as its aesthetic standards. Up to a point it resembles the long poems of David Jones, *In Parenthesis* and *The Anathémata,* with their complex patterns of recondite allusions reaching back to the remotest areas of history. But its shape is that of a dramatic poem out of the tradition of closet drama, a conspicuous departure from a period where a verse play stands or falls as performed before the public. Furthermore, as a poet Miss Barnes would seem to hold with James Joyce on at least one point. Poetry, wrote Joyce, "speaks of that which seems unreal and fantastic to those who have lost the simple intuitions which are the test of reality. Poetry considers many of

the idols of the market place unimportant—the succession of the ages, the spirit of the age, the mission of the race."[39] *The Antiphon* speaks out against the standards of the marketplace, the dominance of clock time, and the illusion of recorded history. Its effort to get back to a lost reality is intense enough to risk obscurity and ambiguity. A reader might in the end wish indeed to direct Jack Blow's words to Miranda back against their author: "What a ferocious travel is your mind!" (*A*, p. 87). Yet upon successive readings *The Antiphon* becomes a quarry from which precious ore may be extracted. It is finally Djuna Barnes's most compact and definitive work.

Notes

1. Janet Flanner, *Paris Was Yesterday: 1925-1939,* ed. Irving Drutman (New York: Viking Press, 1972), pp. xvii-xviii.

2. Barnes *The Antiphon* (1958), p. 8.

3. John Wain, review of *The Antiphon* by Djuna Barnes, *Observer,* 2 February 1958. The Djuna Barnes Papers.

4. Barnes [Lydia Steptoe], "Hamlet's Custard Pie," p. 34.

5. Nemerov, p. 90.

6. Barnes, *The Antiphon* in *Selected Works,* p. 79.

7. In a four-page summary of the action of *The Antiphon,* evidently prepared for the assistance of translators of the work, Miss Barnes makes it clear that the ambiguity here is intentional. See "Notes Toward a Definition of *The Antiphon*" in the Djuna Barnes Papers.

8. Barnes, *The Antiphon* (1958), p. 13.

9. Ibid., p. 24.

10. Ibid., p. 95.

11. In view of frequent misreadings of this scene, Miss Barnes is particularly emphatic on this point in her "Notes Toward a Definition of *The Antiphon*" [in the Djuna Barnes Papers]. Stanley Edgar Hyman, for example, erroneously states that the father himself raped Miranda. See Hyman, p. 60.

12. Barnes, "Notes Toward a Definition of *The Antiphon*," p. 1.

13. Paola Milano, ed., *The Portable Dante* (New York: Viking Press, 1947), p. 352.

14. Nemerov, p. 90.

15. There is a note of martyrdom in the request which is unmistakable. But Miss Barnes may also have in mind the primitive belief that the souls of the dead animate trees, or that a tree planted upon a

grave will revive the spirit and protect the body from corruption. See chapter 9 of Sir James George Frazer, *The Golden Bough: A Study in Magic and Religion,* 1-vol., abridged ed. (New York: Macmillan, 1958), pp. 132-33.

16. Kathleen Raine, "Lutes and Lobsters," *New Statesman,* 8 February 1958, p. 174.

17. Aristotle, *On Poetry and Style,* trans. with an introduction by G. M. A. Grube (New York: Liberal Arts Press, 1958), p. 31.

18. Nemerov, p. 89.

19. Barnes, *The Antiphon* (1958), p. 95.

20. "A Daughter for Inquisitor," review of *The Antiphon* by Djuna Barnes, *Times Literary Supplement,* 4 April 1958, p. 182.

21. Nils Beyer in *Stockholms Tidingen,* 18 February 1961. From a sheet of excerpts of reviews of the Swedish production of *The Antiphon.* The Djuna Barnes Papers.

22. Dr. Ivar Harrie in *Expressen,* 18 February 1961.

23. Raine, p. 175.

24. Donna Gerstenberger, "Three Verse Playwrights and the American Fifties," in *Modern America Drama: Essays in Criticism,* ed. William E. Taylor (De Land, Florida: Everett, Edwards, 1968), p. 122.

25. Lionel Abel, "Bad by North and South," *Partisan Review* 25 (Summer 1958): 462.

26. Ibid., p. 465.

27. Richard Eberhardt, "Outer and Inner Verse Drama," *Virginia Quarterly Review* 34 (1958): 620.

28. Rudd Fleming, review of *The Antiphon* by Djuna Barnes, *Washington Post and Times Herald,* 16 March 1958. The Djuna Barnes Papers.

29. Letter to Willa Muir, 20 August 1962. The Djuna Barnes Papers.

30. T. H. Dickinson, quoted in William Flint Thrall and Addison Hibbard, *A Handbook to Literature* (New York: Odyssey Press, 1960), p. 92.

31. Gerstenberger, p. 120.

32. T. S. Eliot, *The Family Reunion* (New York: Harcourt, Brace & World, Harvest Books, 1967). p. 93.

33. Ibid., p. 18.

34. Ponsot, p. 48.

35. Ibid., p. 47.

36. Abel, p. 465.

37. Barnes, *The Antiphon* (1958), p. 114.

38. Ibid., p. 62.

39. James Joyce, "James Clarence Mangan," *Critical Writings,* ed. Ellsworth Mason and Richard Ellmann (New York, The Viking Press, 1959), p. 185.

Bibliography

The following bibliography is selective. It should be supplemented by Douglas Messerli's *Djuna Barnes: A Bibliography.* The reader is also referred to the Djuna Barnes Papers at the McKeldin Library at The University of Maryland at College Park, Maryland.

ABBREVIATIONS

The Antiphon (1962 version in *Selected Works of Djuna Barnes*): *A*

Nightwood: *N*

I. WORKS OF DJUNA BARNES

BOOKS

The Antiphon. New York: Farrar, Straus & Cudahy, 1958.

[A Lady of Fashion]. *Ladies Almanack.* Paris: the Author, 1928.

[A Lady of Fashion]. *Ladies Almanack.* New York: Harper & Row, 1972.

Nightwood. London: Faber & Faber, 1936.

Nightwood. Introduction by T. S. Eliot. New York: Harcourt, Brace & Co., 1937

Nightwood. Introduction by T. S. Eliot. New York: New Directions, New Directions Paperbooks, 1961.

Ryder. New York: Horace Liveright, 1928.

Selected Works of Djuna Barnes: Spillway, The Antiphon, Nightwood. New York: Farrar, Straus & Cudahy, 1962.

Spillway. London: Faber & Faber, 1962.

POEMS

"Transfiguration." *London Bulletin,* First Series, no. 3 (June 1938): 2.

"The Walking-Mort." *New Yorker,* 15 May 1971, p. 34.

NEWSPAPER AND MAGAZINE ARTICLES

[Steptoe, Lydia]. "Hamlet's Custard Pie." *Theatre Guild Magazine,* July 1930, pp. 34-35.

II. Works about Djuna Barnes

Books

Gerstenberger, Donna. "Three Verse Playwrights and the American Fifties." In *Modern American Drama: Essays in Criticism.* Edited by William E. Taylor. De Land, Florida: Everett, Edwards, 1968, pp. 117-28.

Hyman, Stanley Edgar. "The Wash of the World." In *Standards*: A Chronicle of Books for Our Time. New York: Horizon Press, 1966.

Periodicals

Abel, Lionel. "Bad by North and South." *Partisan Review* 25 (Summer 1958): 461-66.

[Anonymous]. "A Daughter for Inquisitor." *Times Literary Supplement,* 4 April 1958, p. 182.

Eberhardt, Richard. "Outer and Inner Verse Drama." *Virginia Quarterly Review,* 34 (1958): 618-23.

Nemerov, Howard. "A Response to *The Antiphon.*" *Northwest Review,* Summer 1958, pp. 88-91.

Ponsot, Marie. "Careful Sorrow and Observed Compline." *Poetry,* October 1959, pp. 47-50.

Raine, Kathleen. "Lutes and Lobsters." *New Statesman,* 8 February 1958, pp. 174-75.

Susan Sniader Lanser (essay date fall 1979)

SOURCE: Lanser, Susan Sniader. "Speaking in Tongues: *Ladies Almanack* and the Language of Celebration." *Frontiers* 4, no. 3 (fall 1979): 39-46.

[*In the following essay, Lanser investigates "some troubling questions for lesbian-feminist criticism" generated by* Ladies Almanack, *probing such issues as what defines a "lesbian text" or "lesbian writer," and what are "the implications of a work so ambiguous that some (male) critics have read it as anti-lesbian?"*]

What does it mean for lesbians to laugh, to rejoice, to celebrate? When the celebration is textual (public and verbal), what linguistic/aesthetic forms permit this profoundly radical act? What do patterns of lesbian humor and celebration, and the relationship between the two, tell us about the lesbian community? How has lesbian celebration changed during the past fifty years; do the artifacts of our foremothers nurture us or simply confuse? Is the humor of an alternative culture necessarily double-edged? And when we confront an ambiguous lesbian text, how can we be sure, to paraphrase Adrienne Rich, that it is the lesbian in us, and not the dutiful daughter, who laughs?[1]

These are some questions I bring to and from my readings of Djuna Barnes' *Ladies Almanack.* Published in 1928, which Jeannette Foster calls a "peak year" for lesbian literature (not only Barnes, but Radclyffe Hall, Colette, Elizabeth Bowen, Virginia Woolf, and Gertrude Stein were all writing lesbian that year), this cryptic and fascinating volume is, in the words of Bertha Harris, "in its way and for its time, a document of lesbian revolution"[2] and one of the most celebratory lesbian artifacts of the First Wave. Yet not everyone reads it as such—and few are willing to read it at all—so dense and obscure are its perspective and its prose. Like its more famous sister-text of the same year, Radclyffe Hall's *The Well of Loneliness,* *Ladies Almanack* raises some troubling questions for lesbian-feminist criticism: when is a text a "lesbian text" or its writer a "lesbian writer"? When is linguistic complexity an invitation to explore rather than a barrier to surmount? What are the implications of a work so ambiguous that some (male) critics have read it as anti-lesbian? Can satire be a vehicle for validation? Can an elusive and inaccessible text teach and please in ways that a conventionally clear discourse cannot?

These are difficult questions; I shall not so much answer as speculate on them through my reading of *Ladies Almanack.* Such a reading is perhaps best begun by distinguishing the vision of *Ladies Almanack* from the darkness of Barnes' more famous *Nightwood* (1936), where hope has died with the imminence of the fascist plague. *Ladies Almanack* strikes an almost light and playful note in contrast. It was written for the amusement of Barnes' (lesbian) friends who persuaded her to publish it, financed the venture, and printed it privately and anonymously (though its authorship was commonly known) in France. Its readers were its own cast of characters: the circle of Natalie Clifford Barney, *l'Amazone* whose Paris salon was the center of lesbian culture in Europe between the wars. The *Amazone* of *Ladies Almanack* is an audacious lesbian saint, and although the text is often confusing and elusive, it is also a bawdy discourse-à-clef which defines all women as potential lesbians, celebrates female sexuality and autonomy, and suggests that love between women is a subversive act.

Ladies Almanack is also a linguistic and literary experiment, a dense and barely coherent discourse which spurns the conventions of realism, wanders far from the story it is supposed to tell, adopts a host of patriarchal forms and combines them in uneasy parody. The surface form of the text is the monthly chronicle, the almanac, but the book resembles the picaresque fable in structure, the mock epic in tone; it uses or parodies a host of forms including the saint's life, the ode, the prayer, the love song, the allegory, classical mythology, and Sacred Scripture itself. Literary historians suggest that Barnes' idea for the form of *Ladies Almanack* was inspired by the rumor that James Joyce was never without his book of saints (Barnes' "ladies" are never to be without their "almanack"). Perhaps the source for the title was the journal published from 1704 to 1841 in England called, "LADIES Diary and Woman's ALMANACK," also having an elaborate subtitle, as does Barnes' 1928 book. Barnes herself suggests the motive for the substance of *Ladies Almanack* when she explains in its 1972 foreword that her book is "neap-tide" to the Proustian chronicle";[3] allegedly Barnes and her friends were dissatisfied with Proust's portrayal of Lesbos in *Sodome et Gomorrhe,* which had recently appeared.[4] The *Almanack* is illustrated by its author with baroque cherubs, ornate parodies of religious iconography, feminized zodiacs, and other emblems archaic and arcane. The result is a pastiche which defies generic classification. In the foreword Barnes calls the book a "slight satiric wigging"; perhaps this is classification enough.

The discourse of *Ladies Almanack* is a dense and highly metaphoric prose through which almost nothing is made clear; the text speaks indirectly, figurally, and evasively. Sentences are winding, inverted, impossibly long. Antecedents get misplaced, verbs dangle, pronouns lose their source. Key words are often elided from sentences, so that the meaning of a statement like

> "I, even I, came to it as other Women, and *I never a Woman* before nor since!"
>
> (p. 24, emphasis mine)

remains forever indeterminate. Archaicisms are common, neologisms crop up frequently, grammatical forms are resurrected from the Renaissance or invented on the spot. There is a mingling of registers and vocabularies that continually disturbs: plain modern English coexists with fancy Elizabethan; obscure terms are juxtaposed with blunt unpleasantries. The metaphors often make one strain desperately, and still end up not quite making sense—"the anomaly . . . that, affronted, eats its shadow" (foreword); "she thaws nothing but Facts" (p. 37); "Outrunners in the Thickets of prehistoric probability" (p. 43); "two Creatures sitting in Skull" (p. 51)—are all frustratingly typical. And enshrouding the whole are the Capital Letters: most nouns and a few adjectives and verbs are capitalized, so that the text seems at once ancient and fantastical.

The perspective and the tone of *Ladies Almanack* are sometimes equally indeterminate, clouded by indirect discourse, rhetorical questions, oxymorons, and maxims of uncertain intent. Lesbian lovemaking is called a "Distemper" and a "Beatitude" in the same passage; women loving women are like a "tree cut of Life," yet they make a "Garden of Ecstasy" (p. 12). "Love in Man is Fear of Fear," but "Love in Woman is Hope without Hope" (p. 23). In addition to these contradictory and coded messages, dozens of passages can be read as either literal or ironic. The result is a text whose decoding is highly dependent on the reader's own desires. In *Ladies Almanack,* the language of celebration is embedded in ambiguity, accounting for both the frustrations and the pleasures of the text.

There are plausible explanations for the ambiguity of language and perspective in *Ladies Almanack* in addition to the sheer delight Barnes and her friends took in innuendo and obscurity. The text itself gives us a coded rationale. A journalist, Barnes knew that lesbian material

> could be printed nowhere and in no Country, for Life is represented in no City by a Journal dedicated to the Undercurrents, or for that matter to any real Fact whatsoever.
>
> (p. 34)

If the intent of *Ladies Almanack* was to represent "Undercurrents," they had best be shrouded in obscurity. Another passage suggests that the inaccessible prose of *Ladies Almanack*

> would loom the bigger if stripped of its Jangle, but no, drugged such it must go. As foggy as a Mere, as drenched as a Pump; twittering so loud upon the wire that one cannot hear the message. And yet!
>
> (p. 46)

The complicated prose makes enough "noise" to put off the censors; if the "Jangle" were removed, the text would be more threatening.

The coded and elusive discourse of *Ladies Almanack* may also have served some protection for Djuna Barnes. Barnes has never publicly declared her sexual preference, nor has literary history revealed it; perhaps she did not want herself labeled even by the friends for whom she wrote. The narrative voice is evasive, devious, playfully indirect. There are moments when the narrator does say "I" or "we," but never in a context that totally commits her to a lesbian identity. Usually the narrative voice is carefully unclear. Perhaps she can indeed be linked with her character, Patience Scalpel, as James Scott claims, but Scott forgets that Patience Scalpel moves away from rigid heterosexuality during the course of the text. Perhaps, instead, she is like Maisie-Tuck-and-Frill (whose name is probably a salacious spoonerism), speaking "in that voice which has been accorded ever to those who go neither Hither nor Thither; the Voice of the Prophet" (p. 23); for Maisie, lesbianism is "a good place," but "a better when seen Indirectly" (p. 24). But however elusive and shifting the narrative perspective, and whatever the authorial relationship to lesbianism, the rhetorical stance of *Ladies Almanack* is an inside stance; if the narrator is an observer, she is also some sort of participant in this world.

Because *Ladies Almanack* is not totally coherent on either the ideological or the grammatical plane, and because writers are usually presumed heterosexual unless proven otherwise, it is not surprising that the two male critics who have written more than fleetingly of *Ladies Almanack* have declared it to be predominantly anti-lesbian. James Scott's reading of the text ignores all its lesbian affirmation and its ironic potential; he considers it a protest against "the absurdity of female promiscuity," "the sterility of the sisterhood," and "the absence of decent restraints of privacy," making the text a document of Victorian morality—perhaps the one thing it is not.[5] Louis Kannenstine, writing in a somewhat more enlightened vein, recognizes moments of "Sapphic manifesto" in the text, but claims that the book's humor is only "surface levity" concealing "a pain-racked comedy," and documenting the "horror" of "coming back upon oneself."[6] These readings fail to recognize that *Ladies Almanack* was written for a lesbian audience and presupposes a homocentric view of the world; as a result Kannenstine passes over and Scott grossly misreads the overriding lesbian pleasures of the book. The stance of *Ladies Almanack* may be clouded, but a careful (gynocentric) reading breaks through the fog: *Ladies Almanack* is an inside joke.

Recalling the nature of the group for whom Barnes was writing strengthens this reading of the text. As Bertha Harris explains, the international group of lesbians dwelling in Paris in the 1920's was complacently elitist, not only in its social class but in its homocentrism:

> The world, as they saw it, was quite naturally divided into rigid class systems and into gay and straight; and, in their extension of such logic, to be upper class was at its finest to be also gay. Even if she were raised by a washer-woman, as was the case with Romaine Brooks, her lesbianism gave her automatic rank as an aristocrat: to be lesbian was at its finest to be also upper class. In general, all that was heterosexual was "ugliness" and all that was lesbian, "beautiful"; and they spent their time in refined enactment of that which was beautiful and fleeing from that which they knew as ugliness. . . . They directed their energies toward the recreation of what they wanted to be their ancestry, an age of Sappho delightful with lyric paganism, attic abandonment.[7]

This class association with lesbianism pervades *Ladies Almanack*. As the title page proclaims, this book is for *ladies,* for women of the upper class, for presumably asexual Victorian madonnas. Its author is also a "lady"—even a "Lady of Fashion,"—and so is its hero, *Dame* Musset. But any "Maid" can become a member of this elite. *All* ladies should carry the almanack, "as the Priest his Breviary, as the Cook his Recipes, as the Doctor his Physic, as the Bride her Fears, and as the Lion his Roar!" (p. 9).

Another layer of coding permeates *Ladies Almanack* simply because it was written for a private readership.

The characters all represent members of Natalie Barney's circle, though each is presented in the typically "flattened" mode of fable and satire. The Duchesse de Clermont-Tonnerre becomes the Duchess Clitoressa; Radclyffe Hall and her lover, Una, Lady Troubridge, are called Tilly Tweed-in-Blood and Lady Buck-and-Balk; Janet Flanner is one half of a pair of journalists called Nip and Tuck; and Natalie Barney is Dame Evangeline Musset, *l'Amazone* herself. Though Natalie Barney's annotated copy of the text reportedly includes a key to the characters, I suspect that *Ladies Almanack* is filled with very private references and jokes whose meanings may never be known. Yet for all its privacy of intention and discourse, the *Almanack* creates a lesbian-feminist cultural mythology and even suggests a radical critique of patriarchy by recognizing the personal/sexual as political. As it rewrites scripture, documents lesbian rituals, muses about women's condition, and tells the mock-heroic story of its patron saint, Dame Musset, *Ladies Almanack* offers both a mockery of patriarchal values and institutions and a vision of women turning to women in pleasure and joy.

I read in *Ladies Almanack* at least three different modes of discourse, each with its own perspective, tone, and rhetorical stance. First, there are the passages which explore social and philosophical issues. These are the most ambivalent, and the least humorous segments of the text; they yield the book's few moments of gloom and much of its contradiction. The second set of sequences fashions a fanciful gynocentric lore, using song and poetry, parodic illustration, and androcentric myths turned upside-down. This material is celebratory, quietly humorous, and potentially the most exciting in terms of re-creating a woman-centered cultural history. The third mode of discourse in *Ladies Almanack* encompasses most of the narrative sequences which tell the story of Dame Musset and her coterie. This is the most overtly sexual, salacious, and satirical portion of the text, the most accessible, and the most blatantly lesbian. The three modes of discourse are interwoven and interspersed rather than sequential, and sometimes one mode slips directly into another: a myth about women's edenic origins slides into the story line, and the mythic Eve becomes Daisy Downpour; some of Dame Musset's friends take on the philosopher's role. Each chapter of the book is named for a month of the year and is headed by an illustration. The segments vary in length and formal composition: some tell the story of Dame Musset and her friends, others are essays, several are composites of poetry, narrative, and lore. The melange of modes and media permits an exploration of lesbian possibilities from multiple points of view, each form carrying another shade of difference in vision or tone. The interweaving of philosophic, mythic, and narrative modes of discourse each with its particular tendencies of mood, creates a sense of motion in the text: not a beeline, but an uneven journey, now meandering, now dashing, like one of Dame Musset's romps through the Bois. This movement progressively deepens the rationale for lesbianism at the same time that it defines more and more women as actual or potential lesbians.

The narrative discourse which holds *Ladies Almanack* together recounts the life of one Dame Evangeline Musset, lesbian crusader, savior, and saint. Her last name evokes the French romantic poet Alfred de Musset, who counted George Sand among his notorious liaisons; "Evangeline" recalls the religious evangelists as well as the saintly Longfellow heroine. Both names are appropriate: Dame Musset is an unrivaled lover and a tireless proselytizer for the lesbian cause. No ordinary lesbian, Musset is "one Grand Red Cross" for the relief of female sexual arousal. And though some women come to homosexuality after marriage, discarding "Duster, Offspring and Spouse" in middle age, Dame Musset was a lesbian from birth. She was intended by nature to be a boy; when she "came forth an Inch or so less than this, she paid no Heed to the Error" (p. 7) but went about doing just fine without the "Tools for the Trade" (p. 8); indeed, her "Slips of the Tongue" were more successful with women than any male prowess.

The preface that introduces Dame Musset also introduces the theme that female and lesbian sexuality are naturally and virtually synonymous. In the guise of a rhetorical question, an anonymous voice says that from time immemorial women have been one another's best lovers; no better remedy has been found "that will content that Part," nothing "so solaces it as other Parts as inflamed, or with the Consolation every woman has at her Finger Tips, or at the very Hang of her Tongue" (p. 6). Even Patience Scalpel, the stubbornly heterosexual damper on lesbian heat (appropriately introduced with the words "January" and "cold" framing her name), unwittingly acknowledges the superiority of lesbian love. Though she insists her own daughters "shall go a-marrying" (p. 13), she sees love between women as "a Garden of Ecstasy" (p. 12).

The playful oppositions of perspective presented early in the text in the persons of Dame Musset and Patience Scalpel form the poles within which the discourse circulates. In the "March" section these two figures confront one another again during a discussion of lesbian separatism. Lady Buck-and-Balk, one of a British couple who would legalize lesbian marriage in order that "Alimony might be Collected; and that Straying be nipped in the Bud" (p. 20), would do away with men altogether; her partner Tilly Tweed-in-Blood finds men useful for "carrying of Coals" and "lifting of Beams" (p. 24). Patience Scalpel, who since "January" has been trying to fathom the reason women become lesbians, accuses the group of preferring one another to men only from the lure of forbidden fruit. "Were it not for them," she scoffs, "you would not be half so pleased with

things as they are. Delight is always a little running of the Blood in Channels astray!" (p. 24). But Dame Musset emphatically rejects this interpretation, suggesting that women choose women for reasons more politically significant:

> "When I wish to contemplate the highest Pitch to which Irony has climbed, and when I really desire to *wallow* in impersonal Tragedy," said Dame Musset, "I think of that day, forty years ago, when I, a Child of ten, was deflowered by the Hand of a Surgeon!"
>
> (p. 24)

Evangeline's friends swear to take revenge. But Dame Musset stops them:

> "Peace!" said Dame Musset, putting a Hand upon her Wrist, "I am my Revenge!"
>
> "I had not thought of that," said Tilly happily, "You have, verily, hanged, cut down, and re-hung Judas a thousand times!"
>
> "And shall again, please God!" said Dame Musset.
>
> (p. 26)

The implications of symbolic castration are as clear as anything is clear in *Ladies Almanack*. And that Musset's tragedy is "impersonal" suggests that it is not unique.

While Patience Scalpel continues her dissenting stance in the "May" chapter, she is fast becoming a minority of one. This section is heralded by a picture of two women lying together bare-breasted under a benevolent sun while a third woman looks on in dismay. The text explains the picture: Patience Scalpel is holding forth "in the Voice of one whose Ankles are nibbled by the Cherubs" while "amid the Rugs Dame Musset brought Doll Furious to a certainty" (p. 30). Patience is still wondering what women see in one another, but Dame Musset lets us know that lesbianism is becoming increasingly popular:

> "In my day I was a Pioneer and a Menace, it was not then as it is now, *chic* and pointless to a degree, but as daring as a Crusade, for where now it leaves a woman talkative, so that we have not a Secret among us, then it left her in Tears and Trepidation. Then one had to lure them to the Breast, and now," she said, "You have to smack them, back and front to ween them at all! What joy has the missionary," she added . . . "when all the Heathen greet her with Glory Halleluja! before she opens her Mouth, and with an Amen! before she shuts it!"
>
> (34)

The mock-lament that all women are becoming lesbians marks another step in uniting the positions represented by Musset and Scalpel. This development on the narrative level is reinforced by philosophical and poetic passages such as the "July" entry, which claims that lesbian love language is richer and more intense than the heterosexual variety, and the poem presented in "June" which warns that when women are finished with their patriarchal obligation to reproduce they will turn to each other.

The "August" chapter marks a climactic point in the uniting of "woman" and "lesbian" on the narrative and philosophical planes. The essay that opens the chapter discourses about an unidentified "they" that seems to encompass both heterosexual women and lesbians. This sense is reinforced in the plot, for it is in August that Patience Scalpel begins to yield. With dry irony the narrator reveals:

> though it is sadly against me to report it of one so curing to the Wound as Patience Scalpel, yet did she . . . hint, then aver, and finally boast that she herself, though all Thumbs at the business and an Amateur, never having gone to so much as a Nose-length into the Matter, could mean as much to a Woman as another."

> (p. 50)

It appears that the lone renegade has come out. And for the rest of the *Almanack,* every woman is more or less a lesbian. By November Dame Musset is running about recruiting housewives, and though at first most of the young women do not listen, Musset can finally boast that "ten Girls I had tried vainly for but a Month gone, were all tearing at my shutters" (pp. 78-79).

Along with the extension of lesbianism to include all women comes an increased attention to woman's oppression in patriarchy. The "September" section is the most overt in this recognition; the narrator complains that woman's "very Condition" is "so subject to Hazard, so complex, and so grievous" (p. 55) that by middle age her body has been distorted and her mind "corrupt with the Cash of a pick-thank existence" (p. 56). She suggests that although a woman may spend "half her duration" "upon her Back" (p. 56), it will never be her preference. The message is reinforced by a poem called "Lists and Likelihoods," that catalogues the types of women likely to become lesbians. Virtually everyone is included: vixens, hussies, athletes, virgins, and even

> The Queen, who in the Night turned down
> The spikes of her Husband's Crown
> Therein to sit her Wench of Bliss.

> (p. 60)

The universe itself is female; lesbianism is the cosmic choice:

> . . . all the Planets, Stars and Zones
> Run girlish to their Marrow-bones!
> And all the Tides prognosticate
> Not much of any other state!

> (p. 60)

Supporting this textual movement to unite all women under the lesbian banner are a language rich in sexual imagery and a set of alternative, gynocentric myths. Many of the sexual terms in *Ladies Almanack*—furrow, nook, path, keyhole, whorl, crevice, conch shell—would be at home in Monique Wittig's *Les Guérillères*. Myriad passages offer the pleasure of sexual innuendo. A recipe for lesbian love potion that appears in "October," for example, is also an instruction for lovemaking that ends with a directive to "ride Luck's Mare at a Gallop a trot, and when the Mass bubbles and the River's lip quivers, call it dear Cyprian, and take her under your Wing on the warm side" (p. 72). The "July" discussion of lesbian love language says it is "more dripping, more lush, more lavender, more mid-mauve, more honeyed, more Flower-casting" (p. 46) than the narrator dare say; clearly it is not only the love language of lesbians that is dripping, lush, and lavender. Sexual double-entendres pervade *Ladies Almanack*: to speak in tongues is always to say two things at once.

Equally important are the alternative stories the text creates, especially as antidotes to patriarchal religious myth. The "February" section, for instance, presents a misproportioned icon of Saint Musset as a Virgin Mary figure; she stands upon a tasseled pillow with a heart in one hand and a rose in the other, a glowing crown on her head, angels surrounding, and supplicants kneeling at her feet. In the "June" entry Dame Musset tells Doll Furious about "the Fourth Great Moment of History," recasting the Old Testament to unite two infamous women, Sheba and Jezebel:

> "Jezebel, that flighty forthright, used to spend much of her Time in angling from her Window and crying 'Uoo Hoo!' to the Kings that way wending to War and to Death. And some turned in at her Door, and others went on, though not a many 'tis true. Thus was Jezebel employed, when the Queen of Sheba passed beneath her Window, and Jezebel leaning outward called 'Uoo Hoo!'

> *"And that was Jezebel's last 'Uoo Hoo!'"*

> (p. 41)

And the section ("March") where a community of friends raised the issue of lesbian separatism is juxtaposed on the same page as the story of another community:

> This is the part about Heaven that has never been told. After the Fall of Satan (and as he fell, Lucifer uttered a loud Cry, heard from one End of Forever-and-no-end to the other), all the Angels, Aries, Taurus, Gemini, Cancer, Leo, Virgo, Libra, Scorpio, Sagittarius, Capricornus, Aquarius, Pisces, all, all gathered together, so close that they were not recognizable, one from the other. And not nine Months later, there was heard under the Dome of Heaven a great Crowing, and from the Midst, an Egg, as incredible as a thing forgotten, fell to Earth,

and striking, split and hatched, and from out of it stepped one saying, "Pardon me, I must be going!" And this was the first Woman born with a Difference.

(pp. 25-26)

Here we have lesbian myth-making at its most basic: a fable of lesbian creation from angelic parthenogenesis within a paradise from which the last male angel has been cast.

The final entry of **Ladies Almanack,** "December," is the most ribald and audacious of all. All the major themes and strands of the text—the life of Dame Musset, the religious parody, the sexual play, the portrayal of sisterhood—come together most fascinatingly and salaciously in the final section of the text. By now Dame Musset has lived ninety-nine years as savior and evangelizer, and her missionary activities have outlived their need: "she had blossomed on Sap's need, and when need's Sap found such easy flowing in the Year of our Lord 19- what more was there for her to do?" (p. 81). On her deathbed Saint Musset asks her followers, who are "of many Races and many Tempers," to honor her death each in her own way, as each "loved me differently in Life." The funeral is a melange of rites, including a procession that resembles the Way of the Cross: "Women who had not told their Husbands everything, joined them" (p. 83).

Finally, lesbian sexuality itself emerges triumphant as Evangeline Musset proves her sainthood:

> They put her upon a great Pyre, and burned her to the Heart. . . . And when they came to the ash that was left of her, *all had burned but the Tongue,* and this flamed, and would not suffer Ash, and it played about upon the handful that had been she indeed.

(p. 84, emphasis mine)

Dame Musset is to be the same tireless and renowned lover in death as in life. The women rush to the urn of ashes for sexual communion:

> And seeing this, there was a great Commotion, and the sound of Skirts swirled in haste, and the Patter of much running in feet, but Senorita Fly-About came down upon that Urn first, and beatitude played and flickered upon her Face, and from under her Skirts a slow smoke issued, though no thing burned, and the Mourners barked about her covetously, and all the Night through, it was bruited abroad that the barking continued, like the mournful baying of Hounds in the Hills, though by Dawn there was no sound, And as the day came some hundred Women were seen bent in Prayer. And yet a little later between them in its Urn on high, they took the Ashes and the Fire, and placed it on the Altar in the Temple of Love. There is said, it flickers to this day, and one may still decipher the Line, beneath its Handles, "Oh ye of little Faith".

(p. 84)

This ending may seem lewdly patriarchal, in bad taste, irreverent, even grotesque; I confess to discomfort in reading it. But this wild finale of **Ladies Almanack** surely celebrates, proclaims, the gift of tongues. Whatever our own tastes in the matter, the text is an affirmation "in its way and for its time." The glorification of the tongue as the ultimate sexual instrument must surely have provided an antidote to the ethos of phallic supremacy and clitoral insufficiency of a newly Freudian age.

Today, when "documents of lesbian revolution" are more numerous and more accessible, and sexuality more speakable, it may be illuminating to set **Ladies Almanack** against its conventional and muted counterpart, *The Well of Loneliness.*[8] Together, these two texts—the best known and the most obscure lesbian writings of 1928—frame the borders of lesbian textuality in their moment of history. Radclyffe Hall cramped her lesbian consciousness inside the conventions of the mimetic novel and the Victorian mind in order to reach a vast conservative, heterosexual, middle-class audience, with the express purpose of explaining and defending lesbianism and pleading for "tolerance." It should not surprise us that a text as public as *The Well of Loneliness* would have to speak a different language from the private tongue of **Ladies Almanack.**

In keeping with its mandate, *The Well of Loneliness* is formally and structurally conventional, offering a clear, eventful, and moving narrative in the (by then conservative) nineteenth-century realistic mode. Its plot engages the reader in a mimesis of lesbian life, but it is otherwise conventional; the first part centers on the coming-of-age of its female hero, Stephen Gordon, and the second records a love relationship which becomes triangular and culminates in a boy-gets-girl denouement. Despite the pleas of Valerie Seymour, the book's Natalie Barney figure, Stephen deliberately destroys her relationship with Mary in order to "save" Mary from a lesbian life; in giving up her own happiness, Stephen reinforces notions of female sacrifice, the hegemony of institutionalized heterosexuality, and lesbian inferiority. The language of *The Well of Loneliness* is equally conservative. There is no challenge to androcentric discourse, no question of a lesbian-feminist linguistic consciousness. The prose is almost entirely literal and without irony or nuance except, significantly, when Stephen and Mary become lovers. Nothing is said literally about what women do in bed, but there are a few rapturous passages about turbulent rivers lying gentle and about a purple afterglow (pp. 359-60). Acquiescence to the heterosexual institution in *Well* takes us far from the subversion of **Ladies Almanack.** Stephen Gordon refuses the easy comfort with lesbian life that forms the premise for the **Almanack**; hers is to be the painful path of martyrdom, the grim fight for the "legions" of lesbians to follow her. There are moments of peace in

The Well of Loneliness, but the tone is generally heavy and the moments of joy are dutifully restrained. Nor is this surprising, given the text's mission to convert. To the heterosexual audience for which Hall was writing, lesbian celebration would surely have been offensive, if not a contradiction in terms; there was barely room for lesbian tolerance. *The Well of Loneliness* is a passionate plea, a cry of rage; audacious in the clarity with which it portrays lesbian living, it cannot afford to dare in structure, language, or tone. Celebration is a luxury for some future date, or for the safety of lesbian privacy.

It is, of course, precisely in privacy that *Ladies Almanack* is able to exist. But to understand the differences between the two texts it is not enough to know their divergent reasons for existence; one can also explore the close relationship between language and sexuality in the two texts. Just as restraint and sobriety are wedded to conventional narrative discourse in *The Well of Loneliness,* so are verbal and sexual openness joined in *Ladies Almanack.* Frederic Jameson suggests that every oppressed group begins its existence as object, "and learns itself in shame before it arrives at the stage of becoming a subject in turn."[9] As an oppressed people begins to learn its name, to break the silence that has enshrouded it, it can begin to move from shame to anger to celebration. As lesbians make this journey, we also move from silence to speech to a language of our own, for in the (phal)logocentric culture which is our Western heritage, our "shattering entry into history" requires us to seize language itself and, having seized it, create it anew.[10]

This theft and renewal of speech permits us to create a discourse in which we are present as subjects; a language which is dependent upon the words of the oppressors keeps us "locked against ourselves," and the culture which such language fosters is "intensive and painful."[11] It is this kind of culture which *The Well of Loneliness* represents. Radclyffe Hall broke a silence, and she broke it in the oppressor's own words. It is significant that the moments of joy in *The Well of Loneliness* are rare and subdued, and that sexuality appears in metaphor. Most of *The Well of Loneliness* is a learning in anger and pain, if not also in shame.

In the struggle for a lesbian language, we can begin by giving our meanings to their words: we can pirate patriarchal linguistic forms. Hélène Cixous and Claudine Hermann refer to women's piracy of language with the French verb "voler," which means both to fly and to steal: we become "voleuses de langue," robbing the patriarchy and flying off with its most sacred words and artifacts. As Julia Stanley and Susan Robbins note, much lesbian humor works through this kind of theft, "'playing off' heterosexist assumptions and institutions," taking patriarchal myths and subverting them to lesbian use.[12] Djuna Barnes performs this kind of "volée" in

creating *Ladies Almanack*; many of the humorous and celebratory lesbian artifacts of the 1970's operate in a similar mode.[13]

Linguistic reclamation is most free and most freeing when it encompasses the joyful reclamation of female sexuality. "Censor the body," says Cixous, "and you censor breath and speech at the same time."[14] "The exploration of our sexuality is a crucial factor," says Sheila Rowbotham, "in the creation of a revolutionary female consciousness."[15] Cixous recognizes that the suppression of our bodies and our speech is parallel: we have learned to speak and to desire in shame. She asks: "Why so few texts? Because so few women have as yet won back their body. Women must write through their bodies." Cixous goes further: women must write through one another's bodies as well: "It is necessary and sufficient that the best of herself be given to woman by another woman for her to be able to love herself and return in love the body that was 'born' to her."[16]

Ladies Almanack is one of the first modern texts (with some of Gertrude Stein's poetry) that writes through the lesbian body, celebrating not the abstraction of a sexual preference, but female sexuality and its lesbian expression. It is not only the linguistics of *Ladies Almanack* which separate it from *The Well of Loneliness,* but the book's relationship to the female body, to female pleasure, and to female bonding. By appropriating patriarchal forms, by taking androcentric language and imbuing it with lesbian significance, *Ladies Almanack* finds a way to celebrate by—all puns intended—speaking in tongues. One must, of course, be immensely grateful to *The Well of Loneliness*; one can also be glad to have the lighter vision of the *Almanack.* And both of these texts offer a historical perspective on the lesbian-feminist culture of the 1970's, which may be moving toward a new "linguistics of celebration" as surely as it has come to different conventions for lesbian mimesis.

It is a sign of the distance lesbian literature has traveled in fifty years that the conventional fiction of our time, Rita Mae Brown's *Rubyfruit Jungle,* embraces not only the clarity of discourse, readability of plot, and mass appeal of *The Well of Loneliness,* but the pride, humor, and sexual openness of *Ladies Almanack* as well. It is an equally important sign, I believe, that lesbian culture continues to create works which are linguistically and formally experimental, for these texts jar us into alternative worlds where our celebrations need not rely on the piracy of patriarchal modes, but lead us instead to discover riches and rituals of our own. The mythic passages of *Ladies Almanack,* its blending of woman and lesbian, its tentative gynocentrism, seem to me to lay groundwork for the radical lesbian discourses of Monique Wittig—*Les Guérillères* and *Le corps lesbien.* *Ladies Almanack* has reminded us that language is ours to steal and subvert; the celebrations of the Second

Wave reveal that language is also ours to reinvent. In the journey toward new forms of consciousness and unheard-of celebrations, *Ladies Almanack* signifies the pleasures and the perils of speaking in tongues.

Notes

1. See Adrienne Rich, "It is the lesbian in us . . ." *Sinister Wisdom,* No. 3 (1977), pp. 6-9. Rich's statement: "It is the lesbian in us who is creative, for the dutiful daughter of the fathers in us is only a hack."

2. Bertha Harris, "The More Profound Nationality of their Lesbianism: Lesbian Society in Paris in the 1920's," in *Amazon Expedition: A Lesbian Feminist Anthology,* ed. Phyllis Birkby, Bertha Harris, Jill Johnston, Esther Newton, and Jane O'Wyatt (New York: Times Change Press, 1973), p. 81.

3. Djuna Barnes, *LADIES ALMANACK showing their Signs and their tides; their Moons and their Changes; the Seasons as it is with them; their Eclipses and Equinoxes; as well as a full Record of diurnal and nocturnal Distempers, written and illustrated by a Lady of Fashion* (1928; rpt. New York: Harper & Row, 1972), foreword. All subsequent references will be cited by page number in the text. The 1972 edition is the first public printing of *Ladies Almanack*; the private edition of 1928 numbered only 550 copies.

4. See George Wickes, *The Amazon of Letters* (New York: Putnam's, 1976), p. 202.

5. James Scott, *Djuna Barnes* (Boston: Twayne, 1976), Chapter 5.

6. Louis Kannenstine, *The Art of Djuna Barnes: Duality and Damnation* (New York: New York Univ. Press, 1977), pp. 47-56.

7. Harris, p. 79.

8. Radclyffe Hall, *The Well of Loneliness* (Garden City, New York: Blue Ribbon Books, 1928).

9. Frederic Jameson, *Marxism and Form* (Princeton Univ. Press, 1971), p. 301.

10. Hélène Cixous, "The Laugh of the Medusa," trans. Keith Cohen and Paula Cohen, *Signs,* 1, 4 (Summer 1976), 880.

11. Sheila Rowbotham, *Woman's Consciousness, Man's World* (Baltimore: Penguin, 1973), pp. 32-33.

12. Julia Stanley and Susan Robbins, "Lesbian Humor," *Women: A Journal of Liberation,* May 1977, pp. 26-29.

13. For example, Alix Dobkin's song "A, You're an Amazon," Jan Oxenberg's film "A Comedy in Six Unnatural Acts," Judy Grahn's fable "The Psychoanalysis of Edward the Dyke," and Olga Broumas' poem "Little Red Riding Hood."

14. Cixous, 880.

15. Rowbotham, p. 36.

16. Cixous, 881-82.

Miriam Fuchs (essay date 1983)

SOURCE: Fuchs, Miriam. "Dr. Matthew O'Connor: The Unhealthy Healer of Djuna Barnes's *Nightwood.*" In *Images of Healers, Volume Two,* edited by Anne Hudson Jones, pp. 125-34. Albany: State University of New York Press, 1983.

[*In the following essay, Fuchs traces the transformation and deterioration of Dr. Matthew O'Connor, in* Nightwood, *from healer to a sufferer similar to the other characters in the novel, claiming that in his loss of the "sustaining powers to bring comfort" to others, Barnes suggests that "healing in the modern world is an impossible task."*]

Nearly fifty years after the publication of *Nightwood,* critics are still arguing over the merits of this strange and powerful novel. Many agree with T. S. Eliot, who was Djuna Barnes's editor at Faber and Faber, that "beauty of phrasing" and "brilliance of wit and characterisation" are two of the qualities that make *Nightwood* an important American novel.[1] Other critics tend to agree with Leslie Fiedler that "dislocated lyricism, hallucinated vision, and oddly skewed language" may be interesting, but not enough for *Nightwood* to be considered more than a curious example of modern fiction.[2] No doubt as readers continue to study the language, inscrutable characters, shifting points of view, and spatial organization, they will continue to disagree. However, one aspect of the novel is rarely disputed, and that is its focus on suffering and the need to be healed.

Each character's particular suffering is hard to analyze. Robin is afflicted with somnambulism; her son Guido is born with an unexplained mental deficiency; Matthew O'Connor seems schizophrenic. The first reader to discuss this focus on illness was perhaps T. S. Eliot, who wrote the well-known introduction to *Nightwood.* In it, he warned other readers to avoid thinking of the novel as "a psychopathic study," but rather to view it as a heightened dramatization of the degree of human misery that usually remains well hidden.[3] Eliot did not feel it was necessary to explain each mysterious illness rationally or to subject each character's behavior to meticulous analysis. Each affliction is instead an additional metaphor for the loss of control and predictability, and each method of healing serves as a metaphor for regaining control. When the healer himself, Dr. Matthew O'Connor, is overcome by illness and cannot effect a cure, Barnes's statement of twentieth-century civilization becomes clear. If she wants to suggest that healing in the modern world is an impossible task, a sentimental vestige from another age, she does so with unforgettable force. Whether *Nightwood* is merely a curious novel or, in fact, a highly significant novel, its ending is one of the most devastating scenes in all of modern literature.

Barnes accomplishes much of her message through the figure of Dr. Matthew-Mighty-grain-of-salt-Dante-O'Connor. Although he is larger than life, emerging from the realm of myth, O'Connor is also an American who practices medicine in Paris during the 1920s. His realistic qualities include being skilled, loquacious, and clever. His fantastic qualities include his ability to be everywhere at the right time (though later he insists it has been at the wrong time) and to know the motives and whereabouts of others. Somewhere between O'Connor's realistic and fantastic qualities fall his role-playing talents. He serves as general practitioner, seer, father confessor, psychologist, and all-around savior. In addition, he insists he was the doctor who delivered Nora Flood, Robin's first female lover. O'Connor manages to accomplish all this without a license to practice medicine in the first place. Gradually, though, the line between the healer and the healed becomes tenuous, and the healer is forced to realize that he is no longer immune to various afflictions. When O'Connor concentrates on himself, he decides that his personal disease has been a compulsion to play a life-long charade of falsehoods; he confesses to being a sham, a coward, a buffoon, a transvestite. Thus, for each of his public roles, this healer has possessed a private role, and when the metamorphoses become dizzying and debilitating, the healer collapses.

Dr. O'Connor neither develops nor deteriorates in a vacuum. Robin Vote is his patient, and when he is helping her or when he isn't, he is inextricably tied to her, even when they are on opposite sides of the Atlantic Ocean. For part of *Nightwood,* the dividing line between the healer and his patient is assured; we first meet Robin as O'Connor, like a magician, masterfully treats her disease during a house call; they seem antipodal in almost every way. As the chapters progress, O'Connor's suffering seems to resemble Robin's suffering. Soon their afflictions have some similarities, and finally their fates are identical; the antipodes become fused. The landscape of *Nightwood* is international, but nowhere in this panorama of New York, Berlin, Paris, and Vienna is there a lasting cure for the various illnesses of its inhabitants. Lacking sustaining powers to bring comfort, the savior begins to resemble the sufferer; the demarcation between them collapses to the regrettable common denominator of victim.

O'Connor is at his voluble best in the early chapters. He entertains guests at an aristocratic gathering in Berlin with bombastic tales. Almost instantly, he is back home in Paris, inviting a new friend, Baron Felix Volkbein, to accompany him to visit a patient. Felix agrees and is astonished at what he finds. Robin Vote has succumbed to an extraordinary somnambulistic condition. She is neither human nor bestial, childlike nor adult, conscious nor unconscious, but a creature hovering among all of these extremes.

O'Connor proves himself to be a remarkable healer in the face of this bizarre situation. Robin suffers from an atavistic disturbance, whose source reaches back to the realm of myth. Perhaps because of corresponding atavistic instincts, the doctor does not bother with modern treatments but relies on ancient ritual. As this scene becomes infused with myth, its eerie and timeless qualities evoke ceremonies of pagan priests and medicine men that Sir James G. Frazer described in *The Golden Bough: A Study of Magic and Religion,* a book that many authors, including Eliot, used for source materials. O'Connor's first metamorphosis or transformation takes place here. Not just a secular doctor, this volatile personality acquires the ageless dimension of healer as he uses methods derived from rituals in ancient Syria, Babylonia, and Greece. Frazer describes how in the spring flowers were placed in pots of soil, which were then thrown into the sea to promote new life. He adds that a variation of this ritual exists even in modern times where "The custom of drenching a leaf-clad person, who undoubtedly personifies vegetation, is still resorted to in Europe."[4] In fact, O'Connor's method of restoring Robin to consciousness is reminiscent of the symbolic resurrection of Adonis. Like the god, Robin is associated with fertility. Felix knows instantly that she will one day bear his child and he is overwhelmed by the excessive moisture and fecundity that permeate Robin's bedchamber. The decor is dominated by a "confusion of potted plants, exotic palms and cut flowers."[5] As a modern metamorphosis of Adonis, Robin's body exudes a perfume like that of "earthflesh, fungi, which smells of captured dampness. . . . Her flesh was the texture of plant life, and beneath it one sensed a frame, broad, porous and sleep-worn, as if sleep were a decay fishing her beneath the visible surface" (p. 259). Robin's white bedclothing suggests her sacred dimension while her later tendency to wear young men's clothing on the streets of Paris links her further to the youthful male god.

The point is that O'Connor is able to treat his patient successfully because he has a profound empathy that instinctively allows him to penetrate her mythical dimensions and bring her back to the twentieth century. Just as she oscillates between these two realms, so does he. O'Connor manages to revive Robin by flinging handfuls of water at her motionless body, re-enacting ritual and providing evidence of her odd vegetative associations:

A series of almost invisible shudders wrinkled her skin as the water dripped from her lashes, over her mouth and on to the bed. A spasm of waking moved upward from some deep-shocked realm, and she opened her eyes.

(p. 260)

Robin apparently returns to consciousness because O'Connor metamorphoses into a corresponding figure from myth. He seems at the height of his powers, but at this point his private, and more questionable, metamorphoses remain concealed.

O'Connor's ability to move from garrulous entertainer to mythical healer is followed by his talent to serve as an authentic clairvoyant. Robin Vote and Felix Volkbein marry, though her reasons for doing so are obscure. When she leaves her husband and baby boy, Felix has no idea of her whereabouts. Four months later she is seen with Nora Flood and apparently having an affair with her. Robin is "unable or unwilling to give an account of herself" during that time, and so Felix goes to O'Connor for information. The doctor knows all and tells Felix where his wife has been: "In America, that's where Nora lives. I brought her into the world and I should know" (p. 271). O'Connor's being an obstetrician at least twenty years earlier is surprising in itself, but why that should allow him to know where Robin has been for four months is unclear. O'Connor possesses psychic powers and later on confesses to knowing much more. In this situation, though, he functions again as a healer, able to provide what Felix needs and, in effect, to perform another miracle.

While O'Connor functions as a healer with salutary results, he moves in and out of the narrative. His position remains subordinate to the two protagonists Felix and Robin. This effect is created not just by the plot, but also by the fictional point of view. Throughout the first four chapters the doctor moves deftly and successfully, presented by an omniscient third-person point of view. This voice surveys all of the characters but concentrates only intermittently on O'Connor. But this changes when Robin Vote abandons all of her lovers, who then come to O'Connor for advice and solace. The fifth chapter, "Watchman, What of the Night?" is primarily dialogue between Nora and O'Connor. The sixth chapter, "Where the Tree Falls," consists of talk between Felix and O'Connor, and the seventh chapter, "Go Down, Matthew," is again talk between Nora and the doctor. These conversations may be introduced by a third-person voice, but in each chapter the first-person disquisitions of suffering and what to do about it take over. Moreover, the heightened drama and extreme passions seem to swell to huge proportions. What remains in the reader's mind is the obsessive talk—incessant monologues, ineffectual dialogues, and tormented lamentation of human intimacy and betrayal.

This formal change in point of view and intensity in emotion is matched by a slowdown in plot. These changes also indicate an important new aspect of O'Connor's role. He no longer triumphs as the healer and guardian of his patients' emotional and physical well being. His personal anguish seems equal to theirs, and his link to ancient traditions of healing is made to appear ludicrous and deceptive. His loss of humor and of sustaining medical treatment is followed by his literal collapse as he does not even have the strength to hold up his own body, much less that of a patient. At the end of *Nightwood,* he and Robin are no longer antipodes. O'Connor falls to the ground in "Go Down, Matthew," and in the next (and final) chapter, "The Possessed," Robin also falls to the ground in pathetic failure. O'Connor's whining represents the desperate nature of his last transformation, and Robin's actual barking represents a hideous and lasting metamorphosis.

Evidence of O'Connor's private tragedy can be found in "Watchman, What of the Night?" as Nora Flood arrives at the door of his chambers without having an appointment. She does not mind that it is three o'clock in the morning when she asks the concierge to let her in. Nora finds the doctor in a grotesque impersonation that is worthy of quotation:

A pile of medical books, and volumes of a miscellaneous order, reached almost to the ceiling, waterstained and covered with dust. Just above them was a very small barred window, the only ventilation. On a maple dresser, certainly not of European make, lay a rusty pair of forceps, a broken scalpel, half a dozen odd instruments that she could not place, a catheter, some twenty perfume bottles, almost empty, pomades, creams, rouges, powder boxes, and puffs. From the half-open drawers of this chiffonier hung laces, ribands, stockings, ladies' underclothing and an abdominal brace, which gave the impression that the feminine finery had suffered venery. A swill-pail stood at the head of the bed, brimming with abominations.

(pp. 294-95)

This passage suggests how anomalous the doctor's private life appears in comparison to his public image. The neglected medical books, rusty instruments, and disarray of female appurtenances reveal his disheveled psyche and his urges to be a transvestite. Together, they constitute a horrifying travesty of O'Connor's ability to fulfill whatever role his patients need, for the underside of his public personalities is this private charade: His "head . . . was framed in the golden semi-circle of a wig with long pendent curls that touched his shoulders, and falling back against the pillow, turned up the shadowy interior of their cylinders. He was heavily rouged and his lashes painted" (p. 295). Apparently O'Connor's secret habits repel even its primary actor, for the swill-pail near the bed is filled, but still O'Connor partakes in this isolated, obsessive performance.

This tableau shatters any notion the reader has concerning O'Connor as a safeguard against or healer of disease. He cannot hold together the fragmenting psyches of his patients, as they consult in despair with him in the second half of the novel, and he cannot prevent his own psyche from splitting in two genders and two personalities. In "Watchman, What of the Night?" he further tarnishes his mythical and healthful past by self-mockery. He insists that one of his early transformations, as well as his most enjoyable, was working as a female prostitute along the waterfront of Marseilles. He also insists that he maintained his male traits, for he recounts marrying his brother's wife and fathering children by her. When the reader is probably at a loss to explain precisely what gender O'Connor really is, the doctor again adds to the confusion by confessing: "It was more than a boy like me (who am the last woman left in this world, though I am the bearded lady) . . ." (p. 311). Finally he admits to Nora Flood, "no matter what I may be doing, in my heart is the wish for children and knitting. God, I never asked better than to boil some good man's potatoes and toss up a child for him every nine months by the calendar" (p. 304). Nora is accustomed to being in the role of patient, and the shock of this reversal causes her to respond with utter silence. She has come to visit, expecting constructive advice about Robin's betrayal of her love, but she discovers that her healer is also in dire need of his own physician and psychologist. The sexuality in *Nightwood* is often fluid and unpredictable. Lesbianism, adultery, and heterosexuality are part of its structure and thematic assumptions, but they do not seem to be Barnes's foremost concerns, which are wider in implication, extending to any kind of human intimacy and the decreasing ability of any one human to remain loyal or in control of his or her own life. But O'Connor's private transvestism is different. It comes as a surprise even to Nora, who has been Robin's lover, and certainly comes as a surprise to the reader. It is the first significant clue to his fantasy (and reality) of adultery with his brother's wife and desire to be perceived as a woman. The wig of long golden curls and his rouged cheeks make the doctor unmistakably grotesque.

As *Nightwood* progresses, O'Connor's speeches occupy more and more pages until the line between healer and patient is obliterated. In addition, similarities between Robin Vote, who is everyone's concern, and O'Connor begin to emerge. They are linked in profound ways. O'Connor knows mysteriously all of Robin's lovers and when and where she abandons them. In her absence, the lovers pursue O'Connor for information and comfort, realizing that he knows far more than they. Ironically perhaps, Robin is a female who often dresses in male clothing, and O'Connor is a male who privately dresses in female clothing. Also, both undergo identity variations. Along with those already mentioned, O'Connor describes himself as having been a "worn out lioness,"

"a coward in my corner," an "angel on all fours," a "god of darkness." Joseph Frank, in *The Widening Gyre*, points to the doctor's extra-human talents of "apparently being immortal (he claims to have a 'prehistoric memory' and is always talking as if he existed in other historical periods)."[6] Frank compares him to the Greek seer Tiresias, who also possessed powers of prescience and was said to have been both male and female. Robin Vote also experiences any number of identities. She is described as a "desperado," a "child," a "beast turning human," "an infected carrier of the past," a lesbian, and a heterosexual.

O'Connor's first-person monologues illustrate the extent to which this character has come to depend upon multiple transformations—despite each new one becoming a crucible for him. Louis F. Kannenstine describes the doctor's hovering among identities as "a middle state of painful unresolve or incompletion between the terminal points of his thought and activity."[7] The problem is that when O'Connor finally understands those terminal points, he is completely debilitated. Until his final collapse, O'Connor keeps exploring identity after identity and wishing for some of the old ones to return. Indeed, this roleplaying may have been his form of immunity to the afflictions of his patients. In the end, though, he does not know precisely what he is or what he would like to become. The doctor knows only that his protean talents have eradicated whatever original self or terminal point he might have had, and so he realizes that "the reason [he] knows everything is because he's been everywhere at the wrong time and has now become anonymous" (p. 297). Thus, too many identities and too much knowledge have cancelled out Dr. Matthew-Mighty-grain-of-salt-Dante-O'Connor.

The only absolute truth for this failed healer is the certainty that his life has been accursed. Once the beneficent bringer of comfort, he now lashes out at his patients:

> May they all be damned! The people in my life who have made my life miserable, coming to me to learn of degradation and the night.
>
>   . . . . .
>
> [S]o I stand here, beaten up and mauled and weeping, knowing I am not what I thought I was, a good man doing wrong, but the wrong man doing nothing much. . . .
>
> (pp. 358-59)

O'Connor confesses the failure of his profession as well as distinct misanthropy. He does this in the *Café de la Mairie du VIe*, his neighboring tavern, and his fellow patrons look on in astonishment at the dramatic monologue of a drunkard. And the drunkard declares that the elaborate masquerade that has been his life is over. There is nothing left—no good to be done, no single role for which he is suited, no strength in his body. Once he abdicates the role of physician, seer, magician, and mythical healer, his personal immunity vanishes. O'Connor relegates himself to mutability and ultimately to nothing—an actor without an audience, a creature without a cause. The more he relinquishes, the more his body is drained of strength, and he cannot stand on his own: "[O'Connor] tried to get to his feet, gave it up. 'Now,' he said, 'the end—mark my words—now *nothing but wrath and weeping!*'" (p. 362). In this final prophecy O'Connor insists on being let loose from all that he has pretended to be. His terminal disease is ignorance of who he really is, and his only release is anger and tears.

Since O'Connor and Robin are always related to each other, whether as antipodes or close reflections, it is not surprising that his words in the café predict precisely what happens to Robin in the next and last chapter, entitled "The Possessed." Always wandering from one city to another, from one continent to another, Robin has been what each lover has wanted her to be. She has been like "a wild thing caught in a woman's skin" (p. 347), following the sexuality of her current partner but inevitably wandering on again. Robin is like an animated surreal *objet trouvé*, acquiring character from each new environment in which she finds herself. Long after she leaves Nora Flood, she simply appears in America, near the private chapel on Nora's property in the Northeast woods.

The unnerving silence, broken only by Nora's dog who senses Robin's arrival and barks wildly, is a clue to the doom that Robin will suffer. The animal's instinct is a second clue. Directly reflecting O'Connor's collapse to the floor of the café and his prophecy, Robin crouches and loses the support of her legs. She falls to the floor near the altar. The dog comes close, imitating her movements, and Robin establishes a kinship between them by swinging her head against his—still another clue. Robin's human traits erode as her bestial ones surface. With her physician in no better shape than she, and thousands of miles away, there is no medicine man and no savior—only the howling dog: "Then [Robin] began to bark also, crawling after him—barking in a fit of laughter, obscene and touching" (p. 366). Robin's final metamorphosis is horrifying and repelling. She discovers a terminal point of being, but one without forgiveness, understanding, or salvation.

The unfolding of **Nightwood** may depend on fantasy and nightmare, making it hard for a reader to distinguish between the literal and the figurative. But the distinctions are hardly crucial, for Djuna Barnes's purpose is to create a dramatic and exaggerated construct with enough realistic details to be recognizable. Thus, the desires and needs, the frustrations and the cures are familiar, even if their specific contexts are not. Within this fictional construct are characters who need healing and a central figure who, for much of the novel, succeeds in providing it. But Dr. O'Connor and Robin Vote transcend the surface activity of the plot by possessing multiple identities from multiple epochs. O'Connor seems to be the archetypal healer while Robin seems to be the archetypal victim or sufferer. Dr. O'Connor especially survives his responsibilities by being so many personalities although his metamorphic existence is too heavy a burden. The unfathomable Robin Vote changes identity and sexual preferences until the last one is animalistic; the gregarious doctor is so haunted by his multifarious selves that he wills himself to a state of exhaustion and reclusiveness. Severing himself from the patients who have demanded that he help them, O'Connor abjures his long past, his loyalty, compassion, and use of knowledge to effect regeneration of body and spirit. If Robin's and O'Connor's final identities seem to be remissions from the uncertainty of multiple selfhood, those remissions guarantee nothing but degradation of their human qualities. The odds may not be in favor of finding a cure for maladies as Djuna Barnes perceives them, but utterly rejecting the role of healer, as O'Connor does, and utterly accepting one's bestial tendencies, as Robin does, assure absolute doom.

Notes

Djuna Barnes died at the age of ninety on June 18, 1982.

1. T. S. Eliot, "Introduction" [to *Nightwood*], in Djuna Barnes, *Selected Works of Djuna Barnes* (New York: Farrar, Straus and Cudahy, 1962), 231. The English edition of *Nightwood* was published in 1936, and Eliot's introduction appears there and in all subsequent editions of *Nightwood*.

2. Leslie Fiedler, *Love and Death in the American Novel,* rev. ed. (New York: Stein and Day, 1966), 490.

3. T. S. Eliot, "Introduction," in *Selected Works of Djuna Barnes,* 230.

4. Sir James G. Frazer, *The Golden Bough: A Study in Magic and Religion,* abr. ed. in 1 vol. (New York: Macmillan, 1958), 397.

5. Djuna Barnes, *Selected Works of Djuna Barnes* (New York: Farrar, Straus and Cudahy, 1962), 259. All subsequent quotations are from this edition and are cited parenthetically in the text.

6. Joseph Frank, *The Widening Gyre: Crisis and Mastery in Modern Literature* (Bloomington: University of Indiana Press, 1968), 43.

7. Louis F. Kannenstine, "Djuna Barnes and 'The Halt Position of the Damned,'" in *A Festschrift for Djuna Barnes on her 80th Birthday,* ed. Alex Gildzen (Kent, Ohio: Kent State University Libraries, 1972), n.p.

Lawrence R. Schehr (essay date spring 1985)

SOURCE: Schehr, Lawrence R. "Djuna Barnes's *Nightwood*: Dismantling the Folds." *Style* 19, no. 1 (spring 1985): 36-49.

[*In the following essay, Schehr contends that the first half of* Nightwood—*which is markedly different from the second half in its excessive narration and its concern with "diegesis" as opposed to "mimesis"—"is ultimately less the foundation of a plot than it is the deployment of the theories of its own textual production."*]

> Tyger! Tyger burning bright
> In the forests of the night
>
> 　　　　　　　　　　　　Blake
>
> I want to be alone.
>
> 　　　　　　　　　　　　Garbo

Djuna Barnes's recent death will undoubtedly provoke a spate of articles and perhaps a book or two lamenting the fact that Barnes refused to wear the mantles of celebrity that should have been hers after the critical success of *Nightwood* more than forty years ago.[1] Critics will surely attempt to unravel the enigma of this strange woman, a one-time member of the sacred circle of Americans in exile in Paris, who became the Greta Garbo of the literary world after having returned to the United States. She lived in her own exile for forty-one years, a recluse in an apartment in Greenwich Village, writing very little (*Antiphon,* being the only work of any significance) and no other sustained prose after *Nightwood.* If critics decide to become reinterested in Barnes, as a reevaluation of the first half of the century takes place, the novel will undoubtedly be subject to some sort of repeated thanatographical investigation in which clues of alienation will be sought in the novel to justify Barnes's subsequent odd, reclusive behavior.[2] Perhaps too, lamentations will follow: if only she had followed that masterpiece with others. We must, the critics will say, circumscribe her alienation (as has been done with Plath or Pound); we must interpret her silence (as has been done with Rimbaud). Such are the origins of literary myths and of many a doctoral dissertation. Perhaps we can attempt to preempt some of this thanatography by looking at the novel for its own writing, as the theorization, though implicit, of the production of this writing, and not as the reflection of its author's psychobiography.

T. S. Eliot wrote the introduction to *Nightwood* in quite laudatory tones. He praises the novel but he also issues a caveat: he warns the reader not to impose a restrictive morality on the work (xv-xvi). In so doing, the reader would totally mistake the work, miss its rich characterizations, patterns, and interweavings of real life. Eliot's vaguely apologetic preface is wholly understandable given both "Puritan morality," as Eliot puts it (xv) and the temperament of the critic in question. It is of course a protest against a moralizing, narrow-minded criticism that refused all novelty as aberrant, all different behavior as psychopathic: "And finally, it ought to be superfluous to observe . . . that the book is not a psychopathic study" (Eliot xv). And thus, ironically before the fact, it is written against those who will now attempt to normalize the text through psychobiography. This novel is not "a horrid sideshow of freaks" (Eliot xvi), but a rich interweaving of real lives, of "human misery and bondage" (xv). In underlining the amoral, as opposed to the immoral, nature of the novel, even despite some of the characters' individual proclivities (male and female homosexuality and transvestitism for example), Eliot certainly helped to avert condemnation and to facilitate critical acceptance of the work. Yet a problem still remains.

If the inevitably thanatographical reading seems to be erroneous, Eliot's reading is also inadequate. Half a century later, in these more "liberated" times, *Nightwood* does not shock in the slightest. More importantly, Eliot's reading does not take into account the first part of the novel. That is to say, his interpretation and apology are a function of the interrelationships among the characters, their various affairs and interests, and their workings as a group in the real (or verisimilar) world. Eliot views the novel as mimesis and pays no attention to the diegesis. There is, however, one brief indication: he notes that in his first reading of the novel, he found it to drag a bit before the presentation of Matthew O'Connor (xii). One can only conclude that the fact that a character is presented or introduced and is not just "there" in a wholly mimetic fashion would seem to raise questions about the manipulation of reader and text, questions with which Eliot chooses not to deal.

In fact, out of 170 pages (in this edition), fully the first seventy-nine are devoted to the introduction and presentation of the characters. It is not until after this extensive exposition that the part in which Eliot truly evinces interest is brought to the fore. Almost one half of the novel is taken up with the exposition, as if Barnes fully intended to insist on the construction, introduction, and presentation of the fiction. Hence, before reading *Nightwood* as a reflection, be it of a public (societal) or a private world, we should look at the ways in which the world has been constructed, not brought to life, but to writing. While the second part of the novel is certainly of major interest, it needs to be studied in its own right. The concern in this study will primarily be with the establishment of characters and semiosis through the theorization of modes of representation.

If we read the novel according to critical norms, it is hard at first to conceive of a reason for such lopsided construction. If, for example, *Nightwood* is a multicharacter study, as Eliot suggests it is, the novelistic canon—at least the post-Jamesian canon—would dictate that the bulk of character development occur in situation, by revelations that come out of the character interrelationships—illumination through "showing," not "telling." In such a light, the first half of this novel, with its barely integrated paths that are far too long for mere exposition in such a short novel, could only be seen as a clumsy attempt at verisimilitude to make it seem as if the characters just happened to come together, without any effort.[3] We are certainly meant to see the second half of the novel as being non-manipulative, but this feint can only be prepared by the machinations of the first half. As compared to the first half, with its scarcity of dialogue, the second is relatively devoid of narration, except for the totally diegetic last chapter, which circumscribes the novel's dialogue in a diegetic frame. The second half of the novel is filled with long monologues (mostly Matthew's) and dialogues, and there is the barest minimum of narratorial intervention. It is only after having read the whole text that one begins to wonder at the rather odd distribution of diegesis and mimesis (in the sense of dialogue).

In order to make sense of the beginning of the work, it must be taken on its own terms: it is neither the absence of dialogue as such nor is it precisely the background that supports the real events of the novel; the second half is not the entelechy toward which the beginning tends. The first half is rather a text followed by something that is, in part, an attempt to make sense of various strands and kinds of characterization and semiosis by means of the imposition of a plot—rationalization—on language. The beginning of *Nightwood* is ultimately less the foundation of a plot than it is the deployment of the theories of its own textual production.[4] Each of the first four chapters proposes a theory of fiction: of the production of the sign and of its implementation. But each theory also recursively covers up its arbitrary beginning, that is to say, the unquestionable axioms that serve as the ontological and epistemological bases for the theory. Each of the theories proposed seems then to be a natural, acceptable mode of semiosis, meaningfulness, and, of course, of representation.[5]

THE SIGN AS IDENTITY OF PRODUCTION

The first chapter of the novel rather overtly presents a theory of semiosis that depends on false and falsified origins of the sign. Felix Volkbein, about to become a "character," is born under the sign of the Hapsburgs: "the valance stamped with the bifurcated wings of the House of Hapsburg" (1). Yet the sign is neither his nor that of his parents: his father, Guido, is (was) an Italian Jew, his mother, Hedvig, is Viennese, but one cannot be certain that she is a Hapsburg. She, too, is only lying under the sign. As if to cover up the indeterminacy of

the mother's ancestry, the character is immediately killed off by the narrator: it little matters whether or not the Hapsburg emblem was hers, for it is not her son's birthright, as his is not a matrilineal society. But Felix is already an orphan as his father has died six months previously. The indefinite relation of sign to referent is also seen in the first reference to the father. Just as it is with the mother, there is an uncertainty in the relation between the sign and a referent: "never appearing in public without the ribbon of some quite unknown distinction tinging the buttonhole with a faint thread" (1). The parents are attached to signs by faint threads that may or may not denote a true relation. But the child is (always) already severed, without father or mother, with no lines of attachment. He is thrust into the world, cut off from all that gives sustenance and meaning: "she named him Felix, thrust him from her, and died" (1).

In order for the sign to be authorized as a character, in order for this name to have a referent so that it appears to be the simulacrum of a person, it is given a genesis. The point of origin and foundation is constantly moved back. To ground the text, Barnes develops what might be termed the semiotic equivalent of a third-man argument, in which a third position guarantees the existence of the first two, a fourth guarantees the third, and so forth. The reader's attention is focused on Guido, and Felix takes shape in the realm of verisimilitude. In a sort of metalanguage of genealogy, the text moves back to Guido, the father, in order to justify the existence of the son. But the father too, in retrospect, is seen to be as alone as the son:

> And childless he had died, save for the promise that hung at the Christian belt of Hedvig. Guido had lived as all Jews do, who, cut off from their people by accident or choice, find that they must inhabit a world whose constituents, being alien, force the mind to succumb to an imaginary populace.
>
> (3)

And an imaginary populace it is, to which our minds succumb, prey to what Klein calls "the Godelian dilemma . . . the aporetic contagion" (94).

To arrest the endless retrogressive movement from sign to sign and to make it seem a priori that we are dealing with truth and with people, the sign is grounded in an unimpeachable point of origin: "[h]e had adopted the sign of the cross" (Barnes 3). Sign and referent are unified in the cross: origin is resurrected and signs and referents exist in stable relations and configurations. Barnes, however, concomitantly undercuts the pretense, as she does throughout the novel:

> In life he had done everything to span the impossible gap; the saddest and most futile gesture of all had been his pretence to a barony. He had adopted the sign of the cross; he had said that he was an Austrian of an

old, almost extinct line, producing, to uphold his story, the most amazing and inaccurate proofs: a coat of arms that he had no right to and a list of progenitors (including their Christian names) who had never existed.

(3)

It is a story full of proofs that prove nothing and replete with supporting facts that are fictions. It does not matter, however, that the facts are fictions, for they are nonetheless the authorization for the story to continue.

At every point, the reader is only allowed to move one step back from a given position in the text. To ground Felix as a character, orphan alone in the world though he be, the text moves back to Guido. Yet Guido too must be grounded in some reality. Amidst all the lies, the attempts to bridge an impossible gap, is the sign-object that is fount and origin, beyond which the reader cannot go. From then on, the gap is bridged between signs and referents and Guido's legacy to his son is not only legitimized but also quite simply made possible as the word had been made flesh.

Guido continues to serve as a sign but is henceforth imbued with a power of augmentation, having spanned the impossible gap. He mediates between unanchored or transcendent signifiers, such as money and other sign-objects, which, like the cross, are both signs and objects at the same time: he buys and sells old masters and first editions (5) and, in the process, augments and solidifies his own position: "he had managed . . . to secure for Hedvig . . . a house, that, large, dark and imposing, became a fantastic museum of their encounter" (5). Hedvig, the mother, one of his acquisitions, is also the one who defines what will serve as sign-objects: "[i]f ever there was a massive *chic* she had personified it" (4). In sum, there is an amassed amount of power—the power of transformation of signs into objects or subjects and the power of signs to produce other signs.

At every moment, through its constant displacement of sense and meaning, through its eternal difference from itself, the text distracts the readers from the "level"— for lack of a better term that would denote the "deep structure," or the ontological and epistemological groundings of the text—of its production to the level of the veiling of this production. In other words, we are drawn away from the level at which arbitrary signs are fictionally transformed into objects, and we are asked instead to look at the genesis of a human being and the fictions of his life. But it is important to remember that every moment of the production of the plot is veiling the actual product of the text, the *mise-en-fiction* that is both the retroactive justification for writing and the protractive justification for the necessary fiction that the writing is real, lived, and experienced.

In terms of the continuation of the fiction, we can understand Felix as the product of the preceding sign sys-

tems and not as the inheritor, by some mysterious emanation and transmission, of the mystical nature of the Wandering Jew:

> No matter where and when you meet him you feel that he has come from some place—no matter from what place he has come—some country that he has devoured rather than resided in, some secret land that he has been nourished on but cannot inherit, for the Jew seems to be everywhere from nowhere.

(7)

Felix, subject, living character, retains the power of the unanchored signifier, the sign that is always displaced, deferred, and different from itself:

> Felix called himself Baron Volkbein, as his father had done before him. How Felix lived, how he came by his money—he knew figures as a dog knows the covey and as indefatigably he pointed and ran—how he mastered seven languages and served that knowledge well, no one knew.

(8)

Felix's parents, as was pointed out above, are formed as characters by a directed orientation of signs: Guido is formed by a process of authentification of signs; Hedvig, less fleshed out, to be sure, is oriented around what is *chic*, what is right, what signs are intertwined with power, all this despite the "common" nature of her surname. Felix is less the product of two (fictional) people than of the two sign-orientations that their characters thinly veil:

> His embarassment took the form of an obsession for what he termed "Old Europe": aristocracy, nobility, royalty. He spoke any given title with a pause before and after the name. . . .
>
> [. . .]Searching, with quick pendulous movements, for the correct thing to which to pay tribute: the right street, the right cafe, the right building, the right vista.

(9)

Felix is a character, tenuously manufactured, in search of a novel to be in: "In his search for the particular *Comédie humaine* Felix had come upon the odd" (9-10). As of this point in the text he has not found a novel in which he can participate, and Barnes is constantly threatening to return him to mere semiosis:

> . . . the slowly and tirelessly milling Jew once more becomes the "collector" of his own past. His undoing is never profitable until some *goy* has put it back into shape that it can again be offered as a "sign."

(10)

Barnes veils and unveils, veils and unveils again. But it is too soon for the text to come apart, demonstrating its own endlessly deferred position, showing the inevitable fiction of any fixed point of origin. To avoid a textual short-circuit, Barnes introduces an anecdotal interlude, heralded by a character whose very name is a contradictory sign: Frau Mann. Frau Mann (also known as the Duchess of Broadback) and a transvestite-as-character—that is to say, Matthew, who eventually begins the "telling" part of the novel (79)—help to save the text from constantly reinscribed self-de(con)structive veilings and unveilings. Searching for a novel, Felix finds travesty.

THE SIGN AS LIE

The second chapter gives us Doctor Matthew O'Connor, not as a *persona ex machina* but as the genesis of a character. The character of the doctor is produced by a simple operation of transformation, wherein one sign is replaced by a second one, which is perceived to be a lie. The equation of transformation is doubly notable. First, as the justification for the operation, there is Felix: "Felix thought to himself that undoubtedly the doctor was a great liar, but a valuable liar" (30). Since Felix is already authorized as a character (and as an "evaluator"), he alone can give credence to the *mise-en-fiction* of Matthew. The second point is that the perception of a sign-as-lie leads to the perception of the sign that the sign has supposedly replaced: The sign-of- or -as-truth. Thus the fact that there is a lie, which can be a prevarication, falsification, displacement, or deferral, means that there is a sign-as-truth covered up behind it. In both points here (Felix and the lie/truth), there is once again the idea that the reader is only permitted one step back: that is, Matthew is "authenticated" by Felix, but the reader does not go back to question the validity of Felix's existence. Or, more importantly, the sign-as-lie covers up the sign-as-truth, and the validity of the sign-as-truth—that is, whether or not a sign can be true or have truth (ontological and epistemological problems)—is not questioned:

> Even the doctor's favorite gesture—plucking hairs out of his nostrils—seemed the "vulgarization" of what was once a thoughtful plucking of the beard.
>
> (30)

If the truth be known, it is not that Matthew was once pensive; it only seems that way. Grammatically, there is a "thoughtful plucking," a structure that makes little (if any) sense. But that does not matter: the plucking of nostril hair *seems* to be the displacement of the plucking of the beard, a clichéd sign for thought. We go no further then in interrogating that point of the text.

If there is no truth, if the sign-as-truth does not exist, then the lie is not a lie, and the text falls apart: truth must precede and be valorized in the pair truth/lie. Moreover, Barnes must insist that the reader go no further back in his quest for a true zero-point of origin: Matthew's signs must have truth value. It is in fact Matthew who introduces the paradox of the Cretan liar,

thus bringing the problematic point well within sacralized tradition: "'All right, Jews meddle and we lie . . .'" (31). The Jew meddles, and thus he is within the system; but he is outside the system, so he cannot meddle. The Irishman tells the truth, and the truth is that he lies, but if he lies. . . .[6] The paradox, even at the level of sign production and orientation, stands as a limit to investigation. The paradox cannot even be perceived as such, and Matthew's statement, for purposes of comprehension, must be taken as a demonstration of two logical types. The higher-typed truth signals the lie but is replaced by it as well. The system functions because we are led to believe that the paradox is simply a limit and a differentiation, and not something that itself has to be taken into account.

In the first chapter, Barnes saves the system by the introduction of travesty; here, she does so by the introduction of paradox that poses as both truth and lie. Again, it must be stressed that this textual event does not occur merely at some superficial level of plot, but rather at a more fundamental level of textual production. Both the travesty and the paradox are kinds of "double-binds," not logically solvable as such. We can either accept the paradox or the travesty as the game of veiling and unveiling, or instead, we can avoid the paradox or travesty by rationalizing the text: this is not a fictional textual production but verisimilitude.

THE DEATH OF THE SIGN

Robin Vote is a sign born of death, of nonhuman matter, of otherness:

> The perfume that her body exhaled was of the quality of that earth-flesh, fungi. . . . Her flesh was the texture of plant life. . . . About her head there was an effulgence as of phosphorus glowing about the circumference of a body of water—as if her life lay though her in ungainly luminous deteriorations.
>
> (34)

If Matthew could become a character because Felix had already become one, then Robin can be born because Matthew has become a character. At the same time, Felix no longer matters in the production of Robin, just as his parents no longer mattered for Matthew:

> Experiencing a double confusion, Felix saw the doctor, partially hidden by the screen beside the bed, make the movements common to the "dumb-founder," or man of magic; the gestures of one who, in preparing the audience for a miracle, must pretend that there is nothing to hide; the whole purpose that of making the back and elbows move in a series of "honesties," while in reality the most flagrant part of the hoax is being prepared.
>
> (35-36)

Matthew prepares Robin for Felix as she too vacillates in a binary opposition, the opposition that is implied between life and death:

Such a woman is the infected carrier of the past: before the structure of our head and jaws ache—we feel that we could eat her, she who is eaten death returning, for only then do we put our face close to the blood on the lips of our forefathers.

(37)

But the opposition is not between life and death, but between life and life, referent and sign. Robin emerges on the other side of death, reconstituted, not as a sign masquerading as a character but as a character masquerading as a sign. She is no longer real but virtual: "Pricing a small tapestry in an antique shop facing the Seine, he saw Robin reflected in a door mirror of a back room . . ." (42). Death lies at the center, dividing, separating, joining referent and sign. Robin undergoes *sparagmos* to be reborn as sign. Death, an absence, a vacuum, is a countersign to the cross that is the consubstantiality of referent and sign: death is the total separation of sign and referent.

The metatextual relations in the development of Matthew and Felix show the artifice of creating a character by orienting a group of signs and by blocking investigation past a certain point given as a point of origin: paradox is given as difference and not for what it is, the coterminous opposition of mutually exclusive but interdependent terms. For Matthew, the terms take the form of truth and lie, for Felix, of heredity and non-heredity. For each there is an avoidance of the problem of the paradox. The first feint comes from the assumption that words like "truth" or "lie" can apply to a diegetic fiction in the same way they apply to an assertion in the real world.[7] We choose to make rational sense out of the distribution of signs and thus accord truth-values at every level. Matthew lies or tells the truth. Felix inherits or doesn't: we avoid the ambiguities of the text because we choose to believe, a priori, that we are dealing with characters. Robin, however, is the ultimate reduction to an absurdity of the situation: the presentation of Robin shows what price we pay for making the facile interconversion from semiosis (or diegesis) to mimesis and back again, as if the two processes were somehow equivalent. Death is at the center, and we cannot get from one to the other without passing through death. In other words, if we choose to ignore the mutually exclusive nature of sign and referent and choose, on the other hand, to make an equivalence or adequation between them, we must commit the ultimate violence. This violence produces death, which is both the founding point of origin of the equivalence and the absolute point past which we cannot go. In the crystallization of Robin, the stakes are at their highest, and the mechanism is at its barest: signs can be exchanged for character and character for signs, but only if there is a sacrifice.

After Felix and Matthew, the theory of the production of the character is understandable. Robin provides the turning point for the reversal of the construction of the character. Nora and Jenny are given as characters a priori, as Barnes tries to show the other side of the coin—the reduction of character into sign. Felix and Matthew are on one side, Nora and Jenny on the other, men are on one side, women, on the other, and Robin, the bisexual conjunction and disjunction, the figure with the epicene name, bridging a gap, astride a tomb, is at the center of the chiasmus, inscribed at the zero-point, which is also the point of death.

The Character as an Identity of Production

Nora exists a priori as a character; Barnes has no need to produce her by transforming signs into character. What is necessary is to make her readable. The character serves as a sign and specifically, as a deictic, self-referential one: "She was known instantly as a Westerner" (50). Nora signifies the identity of the sign with itself, both as deixis (the epistemology of comprehending the sign) and as fundamental nature (the deep ontological identity of the sign): "By temperament Nora was an early Christian; she believed the word" (51).

Barnes is aware, however, of the sacrifice to be made, for if the character is to serve as a sign, it cannot be identical to itself. The fundamental identity of the sign to itself is for Barnes as fictional as the self-identity of the character, the character as a fixed product. For the sign to be a sign, it must be disseminated as such, and in the dissemination, pieces are irretrievably lost as the sign fragments:

Nora robbed herself for everyone; incapable of giving herself warning, she was continually turning about to find herself diminished. Wandering people the world over found her profitable in that she could be sold for a price forever, for she carried her betrayal money in her own pocket.

(51-52)

As the bearer and distributor of disseminated signs, Nora is constantly moving about in order to try to (re)attach herself to an object:

Whenever she was met, at the opera, at a play, sitting alone and apart, the programme face down on her knees, one would discover in her eyes, large, protruding and clear, that mirrorless look of polished metals which report not so much the object as the movement of the object.

(52)

The sign constantly moves, disseminating its parts, but it constantly teeters on the edge of unveiling itself as a character: "She was once of those deviations by which man thinks to reconstruct himself" (52). If the signs turned characters (Felix and Matthew) are constantly on the point of unveiling themselves as the signs they are, then Nora is constantly on the point of being unveiled as the receiver of signs, as a subject:

One sensed in the way she held her head that her ears were recording Wagner or Scarlatti, Chopin, Palestrina, or the lighter songs of the Viennese school, in a smaller but more intense orchestration.

(52)

To "confess" to her was an act even more secret than the communication provided by a priest. There was no ignominy in her; she recorded without reproach or accusation. . . .

(53)

THE CHARACTER AS LIE

Jenny, last of the quintet, is given a priori just like Nora, and, just like Matthew, everything is a lie:

She had a beaked head and the body, small, feeble, and ferocious, that somehow made one associate her with Judy; they did not go together. Only severed could any part of her have been called "right."

(65)

The character is not a character but constantly moves toward being a sign: her own body signifies Judy, a puppet in a theatrical tradition of ritual, semiosis. Jenny emits signs as if they were hers: "She had a fancy for tiny ivory or jade elephants; she said they were luck; she left a trail of tiny elephants wherever she went" (65-66). As if to be(come) a sign, she emits truthless signs—charms as luck. But it is always "as if," the eternal lie of the sign which, at every moment, unveils the truth behind the lie:

Someone else's marriage ring was on her finger; the photograph taken of Robin for Nora sat upon her table. The books in her library were other people's selections.

(66)

Every sign of Jenny is an inauthentic one, but there is no purported sign-as-truth (as there is with Matthew) waiting to be uncovered. There is only the character posing as signs:

Hovering, trembling, tip-toeing, she would unwind anecdote after anecdote in a light rapid lisping voice which one always expected to change, to drop and to become the "every day" voice; but it never did.

(66-67)

She had a continual rapacity for other people's facts; absorbing time, she held herself responsible for historical characters.

(67)

The story teller is born. After all the fictions, veilings, and unveilings of the production of fiction, the story is almost an after-thought, but it is, most importantly, the covering up of all these theories of fiction. With one

more sign, the novel finally enters the realm of the mimetic, the world in which "telling" is the operative mode of textuality:

The doctor's head with its over-large black eyes, its full gun-metal cheeks and chin, was framed in the golden semi-circle of a wig with long pendent curls that touched his shoulders, and falling back against the pillow, turned up the shadowy interior of their cylinders. He was heavily rouged and his lashes painted. . . . [T]he doctor had snatched the wig from his head, and sinking down in the bed drew the sheets up over his breast. Nora said, as quickly as she could recover herself: "Doctor, I have come to ask you to tell me everything you know about the night."

(79)

DESTRUCTURING THE SIGN

The four characters/signs of Felix, Matthew, Nora, and Jenny can be grouped variously around Robin Vote at the center. Two men, two signs are opposed to two women, two characters; each side masquerades as the other. Two identities regroup, (Felix and Nora) are opposed to two differences—two lies (Matthew and Jenny). At every point there is a counterpoint to deconstruct a purported fixedness of position, and it is not merely a position of veiling of the truth. Unveiling *or* veiling, unveiling *and* veiling: none can escape the game of constantly deferred positions. Each position is a fiction, as is each veiling or unveiling of that position, as is the game of veiling and unveiling itself. The text exists in the playing out of the game.

Death then is still at the center, as Robin, the name of the messenger of the devil—and the devil's familiar finally appears at the end of the novel (169-70)—lies in epicene nomination. Even her family name says "yes"—"vote"—and "no"—"veto" through a fair exchange of positions. Death then is fixedness, avoided only by playing out the game of fictions, exchanging vote for veto, Robin as a man's name for Robin as a woman's name, lie for truth, identity for difference, sign for character, fiction for fiction.

Finally, the novel returns to diegesis. The characters are reabsorbed from the world of re-presentation and assumed verisimilitude into a narrative, where the only direct speech is fragmentary: "[s]he said a hotel was 'good enough'" (167) and "[s]he accused Robin of a 'sensuous communion with unclean spirits'" (168). And in this final chapter entitled "The Possessed," the narrator returns the characters to the narrative fold from which they first emerged in the first part of the novel, dehumanizing them, to be sure, and making them a part of the now neutral narrative that is no longer bound to represent or to create: ". . . in her speech and in her gestures there was a desperate anonymity" (168).

Closing the novel in a world where the characters no longer are distinct from the narrative out of which they first appeared, Barnes rejects spoken language itself:

Then she began to bark also, crawling after him—barking in a fit of laughter, obscene and touching. The dog began to cry then, running with her, head-on with her head, as if to circumvent her; soft and slow his feet went padding. He ran this way and that, low down in his throat crying, and she grinning and crying with him; crying in shorter and shorter spaces, moving head to head, until she gave up, lying out, her hands beside her, her face turned and weeping; and the dog too gave up then, and lay down, his eyes bloodshot, his head flat along her knees.

(170)

Perhaps the thanatographers will have been right after all. Perhaps like Robin who could be said to be the author's *alter ego* at the end of the text, Barnes too "gave up," having "lied out," so to speak, having created as many fictions as it was as humanly possible for her to create. No more speech, no more fictions. Like Greta Garbo, who, not long after having laughed in *Ninotchka,* becomes silent, Djuna Barnes barks, laughs, and cries, and then becomes silent as well.

Notes

1. There is remarkably little criticism of Barnes written from a modern theoretical perspective. Mention might be made however of two articles dealing with narrative: Elizabeth Pochoda, "Style's Hoax: A Reading of Djuna Barnes's *Nightwood,*" and Charles Baxter, "A Self-Consuming Light: *Nightwood* and the Crisis of Modernism." The most sustained recent study of Barnes is found in Alan Singer's *A Metaphorics of Fiction,* in a chapter entitled "The Horse Who Knew Too Much: Metaphor and the Narrative of Discontinuity in *Nightwood.*" Singer develops an interesting study of the rhetorical function of metaphors in Barnes's novel. For Singer, the conventions of the novels are rhetoricized through the play of language, and specifically through the rhetorical value of metaphor (52). Singer also discusses the function of the lie in Barnes's text, but focuses on the psychology of the lie (54ff) even though, as he points out through the development of his argument, such a "psychology/esthetic of the lie" (57) may reach an impasse; that is to say, the author is not successful in producing "a 'realistic' freestanding character" (60). Singer continues, nevertheless, to develop an argument that is based to a certain extent on a psychology of the characters, though a figurative one. The focus in this essay is somewhat different, as the concern is with the epistemology and ontology that are necessary presuppositions for semiosis to be produced in the narrative. Singer's study is a valuable contribution to work on Barnes, especially through its concerns with rhetorical figures and generic constraints in this rather aberrant novel.

2. A recent biography by Andrew Field seems to do just this. Quite an informative work, it makes much ado about Barnes's singular personal relations.

3. One could conceive of alternatives to the post-Jamesian model, but none would justify the lopsided development as such. For example, (without doing justice either to Proust or to Joyce), one could define a protocol for the development of the *Recherche* or *Ulysses* which would not only be a more integrated approach to mimesis and diegesis, but would, more importantly, be a means of novel writing that continually modifies the theorization of its own position. That is to say, in the works of Joyce and Proust, there is a continual reevaluation of the modes of production of the text, a continual theorization of position, and a *concomitant* undercutting of position. Barnes, on the other hand, presents what would seem to be an organic (perhaps Mann-like) view of the novel, in which exposition leads to development, but in which there is a sequence of theoretical positions. Although the theorizations of semiosis in Barnes's novel are mutually exclusive, they can truly only be undermined by the critic, for we are expected to maintain the verisimilitude of each of the characters as he/she is developed throughout the remainder of the novel.

4. Balzac's early work, *La Peau de Chagrin,* has a similar protocol. The first part of the novel is an extended theorization or anatomization of the production of meaning in the text, in which Balzac demonstrates how the introduction of an ideological (or metaphysical) position informs the production of meaning. The second part of the novel is an extended monologue. Of course, there is a major integration of material in the third part. In *Nightwood* however, the "third part"—that is to say, the last chapter—returns to pure diegesis and does not present a mixed or integrated mode of narrative.

5. Needless to say, the theories are also mutually exclusive. Opting for one as a generalized theory of semiosis would mean eliminating the others as viable modes. But this cannot be, for it would entirely undercut the production of most of the characters. The alternative is to consider each in turn, and to make the (arbitrary) leap of faith to verisimilitude for the second part of the novel. For an interesting discussion of mutually exclusive theorizations see Gasché (322-26).

6. Richard Klein has recently discussed the Cretan paradox in a most interesting article in which he also discusses the question of a semiotic view of the lie (93-98).

7. No attempt is being made here to dismiss the intensely complicated problem of referentiality. What is in question is the categorical assumption of rational referentiality both in the text and by the reader. But this novel precisely "undoes" the former; we should therefore not accept the latter so easily.

Works Cited

Barnes, Djuna. *Nightwood.* New York: New Directions, 1961.

Baxter, Charles. "A Self-Consuming Light: *Nightwood* and the Crisis of Modernism." *Journal of Modern Literature* 3 (1974): 1175-87.

Eliot, T. S. "Introduction," in Barnes xi-xvii.

Field, Andrew. *Djuna: The Life and Times of Djuna Barnes.* New York: Putnam, 1983.

Gasché, Rodolphe. "The Stelliferous Fold: On Villiers de l'Isles-Adam's *L'Eve Future.*" *Studies in Romanticism* 22 (1983): 293-327.

Klein, Richard. "Under 'Pragmatic' Paradoxes." *Yale French Studies* 66 (1984): 91-109.

Pochoda, Elizabeth. "Style's Hoax: A Reading of Djuna Barnes's *Nightwood.*" *Twentieth-Century Literature* 22 (1976): 179-91.

Singer, Alan. *A Metaphorics of Fiction: Discontinuity and Discourse in the Modern Novel.* Tallahassee: Florida State Univ. Press, 1983.

Cheryl J. Plumb (essay date 1986)

SOURCE: Plumb, Cheryl J. "The Vanity of Ryder's Race." In *Fancy's Craft: Art and Identity in the Early Works of Djuna Barnes,* pp. 75-89. Selinsgrove, Pa.: Susquehanna University Press, 1986.

[*In the following essay, Plumb studies Barnes's treatment of the protagonist Wendell Ryder in* Ryder, *claiming that in addition to his appealing qualities as a critic of "middle-class conformity and sexual repressiveness," he is an "outlaw" in his single-minded dedication to procreation, his fear of death, and "his denial of the life of the spirit."*]

Djuna Barnes's first novel, *Ryder,* perplexed its early reviewers. Responses ranged from the *American Mercury* view, "a piece of rubbish," to L. Calhoun's thoughtful summation, which, touching also upon Barnes's own character, points to *Ryder's* diversity:

> Now, in Paris, . . . Djuna Barnes has written a book that is all that she was, and must still be—vulgar, beautiful, defiant, witty, poetic, and a little mad—a bewil-

dering hodge-podge of the obscene and virginal, of satire and wistfulness, of the grossest humor and the most delicate sadness—a book that absolutely baffles classification, but that surely is a most amazing thing to have come from a woman's hand.[1]

Disparate elements are so pervasive in *Ryder* that reviewers and critics have questioned its thematic unity and the outcome of its action. Some reviewers found the book a good-humored portrayal of Wendell Ryder, who "loved all womankind and loved them well." C. Hartley Grattan observed, "She has written a highly sophisticated and amusing hymn to the inherent lustiness of mankind." L. B. wrote that *Ryder* "is really a tragedy of women."[2] However, a hymn "to the inherent lustiness of mankind" suggests a very different reading from one that views the book as a "tragedy of women." In the biography, *Djuna,* Andrew Field argued that the book is highly autobiographical and drew parallels between Wendell Ryder and Barnes's father, adding that "Miss Barnes hated her father."[3] The biographical information suggests that a reading which sees Wendell as an embodiment of heroic masculine principle may be a misreading—a result, perhaps, of overemphasizing the narrative line to the exclusion of the digressive material, which creates the effect of multiple chords. By exploiting juxtapositions of characters and themes, Barnes achieves double meanings. For example, the character of Wendell Ryder seems positive, yet as she had in the journalism, Barnes orchestrates criticism of Ryder's character.

Thus, even though the diversity of *Ryder* seemed new in comparison to the style and techniques of the short stories that had appeared in the decades before the publication of *Ryder,* the newness is a matter of degree rather than one of kind. For in *Ryder* Barnes relies on contrasting moods, styles, themes, and on an intricate structure built upon digressions and a series of debates. And all are familiar techniques in the journalism and fiction (though used more sparingly) to achieve double meaning or to undercut an apparent surface meaning. And in *Ryder* we find Barnes's ongoing exploitation of social satire and her concern with the human spirit.

Barnes's apparent aims in *Ryder* are twofold. The first level is social: she satirizes middle-class conformity and sexual repressiveness. At this level Wendell Ryder is a rather appealing nonconformist who challenges the orthodoxy of society. For example, Scott identifies the theme of *Ryder* as "a developing conflict between social 'propriety' and Wendell's unorthodox life style." He concludes: "The book argues, in effect, that, disjointed and peculiar as Ryder's life appears, it is closer to nature than more conventional lives; that such a life is more spontaneous, more joyous, and far more productive of beauty."[4] However, Barnes is also interested in human consciousness, and in *Ryder* her second aim is to present the perpetual conflict between physical nature and the human spirit in terms of the innocent, that is, unconscious, egotism of Wendell Ryder. Essentially, the organizing idea of the book is the sufficiency of Wendell Ryder, whose devotion to physical being is symbolized by his polygamist philosophy, a philosophy that also identifies him with procreation and death. However, the negative aspects of Ryder have not been generally recognized, partly because of *Ryder*'s elaborate structure and partly because of the surface charm of Wendell Ryder.

Irreverent and likeable, Ryder is an outlaw—opposed to the repressiveness of society. He goes about the neighborhood asserting a polygamist philosophy that mocks middle-class sexual beliefs. He wishes his children to grow up free of social and sexual repression; therefore, he educates his growing family at home. When he encounters objections from the school board, he meets their inquiries with an attack upon the conditions of the school and its well, pointing out that as a citizen he will demand a new well be dug and pure water supplied: "Ryder as an outlaw is less trouble than citizen Ryder," he warns.[5] He argues the similarity of animal nature and human nature with respect to sexuality: "What is this swims like dregs within the truth / That animal and man be set apart? / I hear not muchë difference in the heart / That beatës soft and constant under hide, / And this same hammer ticking in my side!" (p. 77). Both he and his mother Sophia represent a humorous and open acceptance of sexual nature, though she finds her son's devotion to procreation "past comprehension." When he asks, "What does one do with nature?" Sophia answers wryly, "A humane man would occasionally give it respite" (p. 226).

But if Ryder's character represents a criticism of the sexual attitudes of society, Barnes also undermines this character much as she had that of Wilson Mizner in her early *Telegraph* feature. Thus, even though Ryder's polygamist philosophy mocks middle-class reticence and sexual practice, his middle-class roots are apparent nevertheless. Ryder's sexuality is in the service of procreation, that ever present middle-class duty, though the exaggeration of his sexuality for comic effect initially obscures this fact. Chapter 10, for example, describes Wendell's dream of having as many children as the number of chess pieces, then as many as the number of cards in a deck. Readers may see this as merely comic, but Barnes turns the comedy to irony. While his extraordinary service to procreation is comic, more important is that this devotion masks his fear of death. As a begetter of children, Ryder is identified with the procreative principle, which, through various digressions, is associated with death. Thus, after initially leading a reader to share Ryder's perspective, Barnes calls Ryder's values into question.

The methods that Barnes uses to question Ryder's values derive from early practices of juxtaposing themes and characters, but in *Ryder* she extends the practice through her use of the anatomy form. In *Anatomy of Criticism* Northrop Frye discussed many of the features that are apparent in *Ryder*: a "digressing narrative"; symposium discussions, or dialogue forms; "mixtures of verse and prose"; catalogues; and a tendency to *melos,* or metrical elements in prose; "stylizing of characters along 'humor' lines; and ridicule of philosophers and pendants."[6] In *Ryder* Barnes uses these devices not only to question Ryder's life but also to question whether a life can adequately be represented in a linear fashion and whether there is value in such representation. As J.-K. Huysmans and Gourmont had declared, naturalistic depiction of a life seemed a dead end.

While one might hesitiate to suggest that all the disparate material can be successfully related to a single pattern, much of the disparate material of *Ryder* questions the values of Ryder. Wendell's conversation with the stiltsman, for example, seems an arbitrary interruption of the narrative, yet the dialogue relates to the underlying theme of identity, achievement, and betrayal, even as it complicates the surface level of the work. The stiltsman, playing on the idea that an arch honors the achievements of man, declares: "In like manner I, poor Tom, do erect myself to myself, as it is not likely that by other than my own achievements I shall reach that pinnacle of renown." And he adds, "Everything is true that is honoured" (p. 24). Ryder's curious response to this declaration, "I fled you down the arches of the years," is a misquote from Francis Thompson's "Hound of Heaven": I fled Him, down the arches of the years." The difference between the two passages is that one suggests secular identity, the other Christ as Hound of Heaven. Both contexts imply that Ryder's giving in to his nature is a flight from something—achievement, or perhaps the identity of self that the stiltsman asserts by "erecting himself to himself." On another level Ryder's allusion, whether conscious or not, points to his denial of the life of the spirit. A possible source for the stiltsman's allusion reinforces this theme: "Unless above himself he can Erect himself, how poor a thing is man."[7]

In *Ryder* Barnes uses a mixture of verse and prose to raise doubts about Wendell's ideas and conduct. For example, in Chapter 10, written in heroic couplets, Ryder is identified with sensuality and death; begetting children is seen as a kind of futile game: "Though all, alas, in time unto the tombs / The game must go . . ." (p. 69). The same chapter presents what seems an unrelated matter, Ryder's fastidiousness: "To this exceeding niceness had he groped / Out of a still small voice which said: 'No pains / Can be too cunning where dame nature reigns'" (p. 76). His fastidiousness is obsessive and comic, a sign of his refusal to accept mortality.

In the same chapter, Ryder's identification with animal nature to justify his unrestrained sexuality is drawn to its logical and ironic conclusion. Barnes shows that while Ryder identifies with animal nature to justify his sensuality, he nevertheless maintains, as did the middle class, his superiority to animal nature by virtue of reason. In this context a fairly perplexing digression becomes intelligible. Barnes, in presenting Ryder's attempt to teach animals to speak, particularly his horse Hisolodalgus, creates a comic situation that demonstrates Ryder's kinship with animal nature as well as his failure to understand the full implications of that identity. Ryder, having determined that "nothing so out-flares / And brings to speech, as flattery of breed," praises his animals so that they might speak and avoid slaughter. He reasons that man will hesitate to slaughter that which speaks in his own tongue. Barnes's humor here is fantastic and disconcerting. She has joined a humorous innocence in Wendell's character with a satiric thrust at human vulnerability to flattery. More biting is the irony that humankind indeed does not hesitate to take the lives of those humans who speak the same language. The final irony, of course, is that while Ryder identifies with animal nature with respect to sexuality, he fails to comprehend that mortality rides mankind as well.

The heroic verse of this chapter is particularly effective in undermining Ryder's heroic pretensions as father and philosopher. The verse increases Dan Wendell's stature, but only to undermine comically this "legendary" figure. While the verse implies Ryder's heroism, his deeds are not only comic but often ludicrous, such as the attempt to teach animals to speak. The heroic verses that refer to Ryder's fastidiousness are not only bawdy, but they reduce his stature to physical being. Thus, the disparity between the middle English verse form and the mundane details should warn readers that despite the humor there is an element of foolishness about this rather likeable character.

Important to the criticism of Ryder and his philosophy are various digressions that associate Ryder with procreation and death. The connections are implied rather than stated directly. By disrupting the story of Ryder's life and its satiric aim, these chapters create thematic echoes that insinuate Ryder's inadequacies.

Chapter 19, for example, "Amelia and Kate Taken to Bed," relates in a fairly straightforward fashion that both Kate-Careless and Amelia gave birth on the same day. Amelia's child is a boy, Kate's a girl. Wendell's elaborate dressing of a child is described in Chapter 21, "Wendell Dresses His Child." His elaborate care, the infant's stillness, and the repetition of the phrase, "that it knew not joy or sorrow separately, for that it was born feet first, amid wailing and crying and great lamentation, from the midst of its mother" warn that the infant may be stillborn. Only in Chapter 22, "And Amelia Sings a Lullaby," is the death of Kate's child confirmed indirectly by Amelia's reference to a lost child and a woman's sorrow. Her lullaby characterizes birth as passing through "the world's gate," which, as it can refer to death as well as birth, conflates the two.

The lullaby relates Amelia's feeling that life is a mixed blessing, given its trouble, and that death may not be a bitter thing. Though some readers have seen the lullaby as indicative of Amelia's hatred for Kate, details of the passage suggest the possibility that Amelia's song reflects her attitude about death in general. Furthermore, Amelia's basic decency is commended by Kate when she confronts Wendell and his mother.

A troublesome point, however, is Ryder's solicitous care for the dead (or dying) infant. Barnes's elaborate and heavily cadenced prose and the ritualistic manner in which Wendell dresses the child (p. 129) create a sense of confusion in the reader. Some of this confusion is generated by the conflicting moods: an understandable sorrow at the infant's early death, but also a sense of excessive sorrow created by the elaborate prose and by the contrast between Amelia's resignation and Wendell's attitude toward both infants. The dead child is Ryder's, as the chapter title indicates. He has, however, questioned the paternity of Amelia's son because of its dark color, until O'Connor observes, "Bile alone is father of its colour" (p. 121). In effect, because of the elaborate prose and the identification of Wendell with the dead child, Wendell is associated with death.

In these chapters Barnes explores Ryder's character in order not only to comment satirically on social taboos, particularly with respect to sexual conventions, but also to show the limited values of Ryder's views. On the surface, he is associated with a zesty love of live, but to the extent that he is identified with an exaggerated procreative principle, the pattern becomes complicated. Beneath the surface lust for life is the corollary connection with fear, indecisiveness, and death. He tells Dr. O'Connor that he breeds children so that he may come to memory from time to time. Lacking a belief in a transcendent God and the life of the spirit, he plans a sort of immortality through his children.

THE DEBATES OF RYDER

Qualification of Ryder's character and aims is carried out most humorously in a series of debates in which Ryder's character is measured against adversity and found wanting. The series begins with Chapter 8, "Pro and Con, or the Sisters Louise," which is an abstract statement of Wendell's suitability. This idea is then examined in the epistolary debate between Amelia and her sister Anne. Ryder's dialogues with Molly Dance, Laura Twelvetrees, Lady Bridesleep, and Dr. Connor conclude the series.

The sisters Louise play no active role in the narrative line; the purpose of the chapter is tangential commentary, establishing the universal context for the reader's acceptance of Ryder as representative of human nature. The sisters face each other, playing a piano duet, while they discuss the uses of adversity (p. 48). The subject of their rather ribald debate is Wendell Ryder. One sister, presumably Pro, offers "that never man before so thoroughly enjoyed his parts, so trusted to them, and so managed them that . . . others trust in like measure." Her sister, arguing the Con position, admits a "floating doubt as to the ultimate importance, shall I say, satisfaction, of man to the mass, when . . . the mass is female and the man is Wendell." The issue is then rephrased as whether the "nature in one man can be perpetual." Her sister, Pro concludes, "Hardly perpetual, but perhaps recurringly satisfactory" (p. 49).

Along with the sexual innuendoes run the themes of trust and the permanence of life itself in the individual. The sister, Con, who doubts man's "importance," and specifically Wendell's, tells a parable of a world order where women live in harmony until the appearance of Ryder sets them against one another: "Writhing, biting, tearing, scratching, screaming, crying, over and over they rolled, in blood and tears . . . and down, down into the valley's bottomless depth, now she on top, now she, now she under, now she, and into the ravine at last, where between tall rank grasses the rubbish blooms." The sister, ostensibly Pro, asks, "Do they return?" Con answers, "Does Hell spew out its damned? It does."

When her sister asks whether they should "encompass a return," the sister Con, who has created the parable of the fall, replies, "My dear, stir up the fire for tea, and remember that Hell is not for ladies" (p. 51). In short, the resolution is against the cycle of life represented by Ryder, namely, birth and death. The sister Con argues against this kind of adversity: "Hell is not for ladies."

In the following chapter a debate similar to that of the sisters Louise ends differently. Do what she can to dissuade Amelia, Anne loses her sister to Wendell. Anne and Amelia are interesting emotional counterpoints to the sisters Louise. Ann (Con) is a pessimist; she has jilted three men because none is worthy. Amelia (Pro) is the naive optimist, a willing believer, who suggests that Anne's wisdom is not wisdom, but fear: "'Tis because you are too fearful . . . and no sooner see a touch of green but do think the whole man a little game" (p. 64).

Amelia's name suggests the alternative she chooses, for "Amelia" literally means "diligent" and reaches back to the Germanic base, *amal*, meaning "work" or "trouble." In pulling Ryder off the wall and into her "inner courtyard," Amelia accepts adversity, the cycle of life, activity, and struggle. Those traits go with her throughout

Ryder, for she is the worker. Neither Kate-Careless nor Ryder shares her diligence.

These thematic strands—adversity and Ryder's suitability—are extended into his encounter with neighborhood women who challenge his assumption that he and his philosophy are able to meet adversity. In these affairs, the women willingly and humorously accept him as a lover, while simultaneously rejecting his procreative philosophy. In each situation, as in the meeting with Laura Twelvetrees, Ryder asserts his aim to father exceptional children who will grow up independent of the values of society and testify to his values in doing so. His encounters with Molly Dance and Lady Bridesleep, however, demonstrate not only the shortsightedness of his philosophy but, in a sense, its very commonness, its middle-class quality.

Perhaps only Molly Dance offers a genuine parallel to Wendell Ryder in terms of her procreative propensities. Molly Dance might well represent Rémy de Gourmont's principle that one has an "inalienable right to interpret the world in whatever way one pleased."[8] Her cosmology, to Ryder's consternation, is an inventive and irreverent takeoff on traditional middle-class beliefs. Original sin, for example, in Molly's understanding, was not woman's but man's: "It was an apple, surely, but man it was who snapped it up, scattering the seeds, and these he uses to this day to get his sons by" (p. 259). Revealing an enormous capacity for life, plus humor and imagination, Molly Dance is completely amoral. As a dog breeder, she exercises rare caution with respect to the mating of her dogs; however, as the narrator relates, "Molly, it must be writ, was no better than her dogs, and seldom as good, for she got her children where and when it pleased her" (p. 249). Wendell inquires if she knows who is the father of her last born. Molly replies, "who cares? He didn't, I don't, and the child won't have to, and that's simplification" (p. 260). Ryder offers to establish certainty in the matter by fathering her next child, and Molly agrees amiably enough. Afterward, however, she observes, "there's only one thing that might make something uncertain of this certainty." She explains that the issue is "whether the child shall know you for its father or no," adding that two nights ago the corner policeman had the same idea. And that, Molly muses, "only goes to show you that one man's thoughts are not worth much more than another's" (p. 261). On two levels Ryder's ideas are shaken: in his pride of fatherhood and in his estimation of his own personal importance.

Ryder's encounter with Lady Bridesleep is a variation of his encounter with Laura Twelvetrees, who has asserted the "aristocracy of no outcome." The difference between the two women is that Lady Bridesleep is well into her sixties and therefore past childbearing age, a fact that Ryder fails to notice. Characterized as an epicure and one who was "pleased by nature at its most natural," Lady Bridesleep embodies Gourmont's argument, in "Dissociation of Ideas," that all varieties of human sexuality are natural, denying the claims of religious moralists who argued that certain forms of sexuality were "against nature" and that sexual pleasure and procreation were necessarily linked. In Lady Bridesleep, we see the voluptuary, who, because of her age, represents the separation of carnal pleasure from the procreative duty.

When Ryder asks when they shall name the child he imagines Lady Bridesleep has conceived, she replies, "Nothing and Never. . . . He shall accomplish all the others leave undone. You need No Child also, my good man, all fathers have one. On him you shall hang that part of your ambition too heavy for mortal" (p. 279). Obliquely, the experience points toward the vanity of all mortal ambitions, though Ryder does not yet perceive the significance of Lady Bridesleep's message. Here Ryder is ridiculed not for his apparently unlimited sensuality, which is matched by that of Lady Bridesleep, but for the extravagant claims he makes for his own "satisfactoriness," which is to be exemplified by his children. Both encounters point to the futility of Ryder's procreative philosophy as a means of justifying his existence. What remains is his discovery of the vulnerability of the self he has created.

RYDER'S VULNERABILITY

Ryder's vulnerability is foreshadowed as he talks with his mother of his response to Oscar Wilde, whose fate anticipates Ryder's own. Though he regarded Wilde as a man of beauty and imagination, Ryder recalls seeing Wilde and turning away from him:

> The scandal had burst, and though he was the core, the fragrant centre of a rousing stench, in a month he was a changed man, not changing, sitting within his cell, weeping, writing, plotting "De Profundis," his fingers outside his mouth, shuddering in all his soft female body, direct suffering in his breasts; a bull caught and captured, sentenced, hamstrung, marauded, peered at, peeped upon, regarded and discovered to be a gentle sobbing cow, giving self-suck at the fountain of self, that he might die in his own image, a soft pain chartered she, a girl cast out of heaven, harnessed for a stallion's turn; tremolo to his own swan song. I turned away and was matchlessly damned.
>
> (p. 218)

This passage is interesting because its style is particularly appropriate to Ryder's narcissistic musing and because it implies a thematic parallel between Ryder and Wilde. Constructed on elaborate parallel phrases, the linear movement is held together loosely with semicolons. Identified as loose style by Morris W. Croll, in *"Attic" & Baroque Style,* the passage depends upon asymmetrical techniques, including length of phrases,

or movement by a series of metaphorical leaps. In this passage, Ryder, as speaker, moves through a series of predicate nouns, from "man" in the first series, through "bull," "pain-chartered she," "girl," to "tremolo." The progression of the sentence is not logical; rather the reader is forced to make imaginative connections between the items in the series."[9] In this process the reader recreates Ryder's imaginative perception of Wilde's changing self-concept.

The effect of such a style, in Croll's view, is to present the prose of an "animated talker"; its purpose, "to portray a mind thinking," not necessarily the reasoned and formally shaped thought itself. The series of adjectives, "caught and captured, sentenced, hamstrung, marauded, peered at, peeped upon . . ." expresses not only Ryder's latent fear of social scrutiny but equally the fear of self-scrutiny, leading to a self-image less pleasing than what he normally projects and enjoys; thus the animated talker conceals from himself and others an undesirable self—but ironically in talking betrays himself. The prose is strangely appropriate to Ryder's situation: that is, his talk simultaneously reveals and obscures himself to himself and to readers.

Ryder has created an image of himself as a father and enlightened social rebel, a role which justifies his existence in his own eyes and simultaneously feeds his vanity. However, the fragility of this self-shaped identity is illustrated by thematic ties between Ryder and Oscar Wilde. With the identification of Ryder and Wilde, two themes come together: physical nature and sexuality and the created self. The significance of these themes within the structure of the book is apparent if we consider *Ryder* from a symbolic perspective.

THE SYMBOLIC CONTEXT

The symbolic level of *Ryder* is set in the opening chapter, "Jesus Mundane," a puzzling chapter as it bears no apparent relationship to those that follow: the story of Sophia's parents, Sophia's chamberpots, and Wendell's birth. "Jesus Mundane" is a direct address, though the identities of who is addressed and who is speaking are never disclosed. The reader is forced to assume that some spirit is addressed by some Creator and the spirit descends to the world to be born. That much can be ascertained through the implied parallel with Jesus announced in the chapter's title. The spirit is advised, "Go not with fanatics," who are distracted with the end of life, but "Go, thou, then, to lesser men, who have for all things unfinished and uncertain, a great capacity. . . . Thy rendez-vous is not with the Last Station, but with small comforts, like to apples in the hand, and small cups quenching . . ." (p. 1). The speaker seems to imply that the business of humankind is with physical reality. Furthermore, uncertainty and ignorance are man's initial condition. What has gone before is unknown: "These things are as the back of thy band to three. Thou hast not seen them" (p. 5).

Despite its obscurity, the direct address establishes a context which indicates that at one level the character of Wendell Ryder is to be read symbolically as representative of mankind in general. The opening invites the reader to trace the progress of the spirit who descends to the trial of existence. If the opening establishes the context of a symbolic trial, then the repeated question of the conclusion—"And whom should he disappoint now?"—suggests the failure of Wendell Ryder. The nature of the failure is confirmed by the symbolic details of his unusual costume.

Ryder, who dresses in green and has white rats about him when Amelia first sees him, shares this rather eccentric trait and others with the father of the three boys in Barnes's early drama, *Three from the Earth.* In that drama, the father, alluded to by Kate and the three boys, is revealed to have a weak stomach and to have been a country philosopher of sorts; he has tried to be perfect, failed, and ended up by slitting his own throat because "everything"—a fat wife who has been a prostitute, Kate whom he has loved, and the three boys—has been "too much" for him.

Ryder shares with his prototype his polygamous household, his weak stomach, and his philosophical bent, but their common penchant for green clothing and white rats is perhaps the most striking similarity.[10] J. E. Cirlot notes in *A Dictionary of Symbols* that green, as associated with the sixth enigma of the tarot pack, The Lover, is identified with "indecision," "uncertainty and temptation."[11] The sixth enigma itself refers to the legend of Hercules who was given the choice of two women: "the one personifying Virtue (or decisive activity, vocation, sense of purpose, and struggle) and the other Vice (passive-ness, surrender to base impulses and to external pressures)." The dress of the tarot lover is particolored, red and green, red for activity and green for indecision; Ryder's red hair can be seen perhaps as substitute for the original parti-colored dress. The other significant detail of Ryder's dress, as it is described, is the presence of white rats. Again, Cirlot records that rats are associated with "infirmity and death . . . a phallic implication has been superimposed . . . but only in so far as it is dangerous or repugnant."

Thus, Ryder's green clothing and his subsequent choice of Kate-Careless are symbolic. Given Amelia's association with work and striving and the acceptance of adversity, Ryder's choice of the fleshy and passive Kate-Careless—indifference itself, a fact of her allegorical name—confirms his surrender to "base impulses and external pressures." His life is an evasion, for rather than cultivate a self-awareness adequate to accept mortality and the limitation of physical nature he has sur-

rendered to physical nature, evading spiritual potential. This is apparent when, confronted by the angry townspeople who demand that he choose between Kate and Amelia, he acknowledges to his mother Sophia: "I have unfathered myself" (p. 318). He has given up self-direction for social controls. In such a context, the possibilities that the stiltsman has offered in the beginning become comically relevant, for Ryder has operated at the level of the pun which the stiltsman offered, but in doing so he has, in another sense, failed to "erect himself to himself."

The final chapter concludes with repetitions of the phrase, "And whom should he disappoint now?" Ryder is sitting in a field surrounded by animals:

> And everything and its shape became clear in the dark, by tens and tens they ranged, and lifted their lids and looked at him; in the air and in the trees and on the earth and from under the earth, and regarded him long, and he forbore to hide his face. They seemed close ranged, and now they seem far ranged, and they moved now near, now far, as a wave comes and goes, and they lifted their lids and regarded him, and spoke not in their many tongues, and they went a far way, and there was a little rest, and they came close, and there was none. Closing in about him nearer, and swinging out wide and from him far, and came in near and near, and as a wave, closed over him, and he drowned, and arose while ye yet might go.
>
> And whom should he disappoint?

(p. 323)

Rich with ambiguity, the image identifies Ryder's character metaphorically with nature and self-consuming concern. He is surrounded by animals, that is, limited to natural, instinctual reality. The wavelike motion, apparent in the animals' eyes that advance, accusingly, and recede, giving rest, evokes the water image wherein Narcissus saw himself reflected. Significantly, drowning suggests a surrender to self. His capitulation to social demands represents his failure to forge truth and values for himself, just as his capitulation to physical desires represents a denial of the spirit.

Nevertheless, in Ryder's character, Barnes achieves an objectivity that does not condemn, for he remains an amiable character, though the series of debates necessarily qualify his views. Yet because he fails to create a truth that goes beyond simple rebellion against the restrictive codes of society, readers experience a feeling of disappointment and also sympathy. The mingling of moods that pervades the book achieves a distancing effect so that we recognize in Ryder the human condition: uncertain and beleaguered from within and without by conflicting desires.

THE ALTERNATIVE TO RYDER

In *Ryder* Barnes has created a work that dramatizes her concerns with morality, identity, and conscious awareness. In doing so, she has made these concerns the inconspicuous organizing principle of the work. On one level, *Ryder* appears to be a protest against a repressive middle-class ethic, yet on the symbolic level, the work conveys a considerably more complex idea. The principle of sensual reality is never denied; it is, however, presented as limited, yet powerful in distorting human nature. Barnes's point here is that human nature is not limited to physical reality. O'Connor, Julie, and Elisha testify to the spiritual dimension of human nature.

O'Connor, as a sensual being, is acutely aware of the pleasures of the flesh, and, as a physician, of human suffering and the fragility of human life. Subject to the conflicting claims of the senses and also aware of a desire not to be subject to the senses only, he represents the perpetual conflict between physical nature and the needs of the human spirit. He recognizes both the insufficiency and the necessity of the sensual reality. O'Connor's experience convinces him that one cannot trust nature, the sensual reality alone, though this is what Ryder has done, elevating his own physical nature to a philosophy.

While O'Connor never achieves the purity and serenity he desires, the strength of his sensual drive and its nature—O'Connor is a homosexual, a form of sexuality the middle-class considered "unnatural" and degenerate—convince him of his subjugation to the flesh, thereby providing the impetus that necessitates reasoned control, that is, manners, God, or moral behavior, something to regulate the instincts. He is, therefore, like Wendell Ryder in terms of instinctual nature, but while O'Connor recognizes the need for control (success is something else), Ryder rationalizes his nature through his philosophy extolling instinct.

In addition to the point of view represented by O'Connor, the perspectives of Ryder's children provide alternative views that qualify those of Wendell Ryder. Both Elisha and Julie reject Ryder's ways. Though our view of Julie is a series of glimpses, these disclosures show she is different and special. Julie attacks Kate for lying when Elisha strikes her brother Hannel, seeing her not as the disease, but as "the manifestation of such emanating directly from her father" (p. 183). Even though her grandmother loves Julie best, Sophia has a difficult relationship with her because of Julie's independence. Knowing that she herself is not as grand as she appears, Sophia lies, thinking: "the thing I've seemed will balance the account." It does—almost, for Julie, recognizing the lies, later sees them as the best of a "capacious soul." Yet Julie prefers truth.

Julie is a shadowy figure whose implications as a character are illuminated when one considers them in the context of O'Connor's discussion with one of Ryder's sons. In response to the boy's cynical belief that there is no point in any activity, O'Connor asserts the value of the activity for its own sake:

> You get no more good by diligent thought than another by no thought at all, saving the thought which you have, and he has not, and while 'tis true that you must give it up at death and loose it on the wind again, like a caged pigeon, it was yours once, and may go croaking of the difference, with somewhat of your voice, to be heard by yet another ear, for a remembrance.

(p. 307)

O'Connor's image describes the practice of generation by ideas, an activity that characterizes the role of the artist. Hence the importance of Julie's difference. As she stands apart from the family and as she recognizes her grandmother's willingness to put the best face on things as a betrayal and an achievement, she surpasses both Sophia and Wendell.

Elisha too stands outside the family and is identified as artistic because of his skill in playing the piano. He shares with Julie her respect for truth, having interrupted the fight among Kate, Amelia, and Julie to confess that he has "chiseled Hannel's head," and his mother is a liar for denying it. Now, years later, as he prepares to play for the townspeople, he "bends over . . . he is with himself alone, he has thrown off the people, a drowning mass about a drowning man's neck, and plays loud, and is liberated to himself, softly, softly for my soul's sake, says he, and plays softly" (p. 296). Elisha's way, "playing for his soul's sake," testifies to the human potential of the artist for liberating the soul from subjection to the physical being.

Through O'Connor, Julie, and Elisha, Barnes introduces a theme of the human spirit that balances physical nature. The comment of André Gide, a symbolist early in his career, is interesting in this context. In his *Journals* Gide wrote:

> I am torn by a conflict between the rules of morality and the rules of sincerity. Morality consists in substituting for the natural creature (the old Adam) a fiction that you prefer. But then you are no longer sincere. The old Adam is the sincere man.

> This occurs to me: the old Adam is the poet. The new man, whom you prefer, is the artist. The artist must take the place of the poet. From the struggle between the two is born the work of art. . . .[12]

The poet, then, represents experience, the realm of physical reality, but the artist, conscious decision. The work of art represents a precarious balance, a sacrifice of instinctual life but also a gain drawn from the conflict. A good is born from evil, in the sense that Baudelaire saw poetry as a redemptive act, the flowers that bloom from evil.

As in many of the short stories, the symbolic level is incorporated into the structure of *Ryder*. Beneath the surface complexity of *Ryder* and its level of social satire of middle-class values, the organizing principle of the work is the conflict between physical nature and the human spirit, an idea that has pervaded Barnes's early work from the interviews and one-acts, to the short stories of the Paris years.

In **Ryder** brief incidents used to vary the tone of the work and thematic parallels to qualify the character of Wendell Ryder produce a complicated texture that gives **Ryder** a sense of fullness—and a deceptive feeling of movement. A great many incidents are likely to create a feeling of activity as opposed to the slow, steady development of a single narrative line. In fact, the sense of activity belies the stasis at the heart of **Ryder**. The interaction of the household and Ryder's many affairs produces little in the way of crisis and denouement—repetitiveness is the primary fact of this world. The denouement comes from outside the basic action when Ryder is somewhat arbitrarily forced to choose between Kate and Amelia. Though Ryder fails to order his life, the reader confronts the disorder of Ryder's life. From the whirlpool of incidents, themes, parallel motifs, digressions, and debates, the reader provides the interpreting intelligence. Balance is necessary. The diversity of **Ryder** demands, in effect, that the reader achieve a balance, or understanding, through the complexity of **Ryder's** surface.

Notes

1. Calhoun, L., "A Woman's Hero," *The Argonaut* 104 (1 September 1928): 12. The *American Mercury* view is quoted in Messerli, 96.

2. These quotations appeared in Messerli, 97-100. The original reviews appeared in the following newspapers: *Toledo* (Ohio) *Times Magazine,* 21 October 1928, 12; New York *Sun,* 18 August 1928, 21; *New Republic* 55 (24 October 1928): 281-83.

3. Field, 31.

4. Scott, 63, 76.

5. Barnes, *Ryder* (New York: Boni & Liveright, 1928; rpt., New York: St. Martin's Press, 1979), 167. All further references are to the reprinted edition.

6. Northrop Frye, *Anatomy of Criticism: Four Essays* (Princeton: Princeton University Press, 1957; rpt. 1973), 309.

7. The source is Samuel Daniel's "Epistle to the Countess of Cumberland," stanza 12.

8. Burne, 24.

9. Morris W. Croll, *"Attic" & Baroque Style: Essays by Morris W. Croll,* ed. J. Max Patrick and Robert O. Evans, with John M. Wallace (Princeton: Princeton University Press, 1966; rpt. 1969), 213.

10. Elizabeth Chappel to Djuna Barnes, 9 May 192(4)? There is general critical agreement that Wendell Ryder is based on Barnes's father. Thus it is interesting that Barnes's mother, Elizabeth Chappell, writes to Djuna in London suggesting that Djuna have Aunt Sue show her the wall where she met Djuna's father. According to her letter, he wore pants patched with green cloth and had white rats about him.

11. Cirlot, 185-86, 259-60. The following summary is taken from Cirlot's commentary.

12. André Gide, "The Reflexive Image," *Journals 1889-1913,* 11 January 1892, excerpted in *The Modern Tradition,* ed. Richard Ellmann and Charles Feidelson, Jr. (New York: Oxford University Press, 1965), 189.

Works Cited

PRIMARY SOURCES

BOOKS

Ryder. New York: Boni & Liveright, 1928. Reprint. New York: St. Martin's Press, 1979.

MANUSCRIPTS: THE DJUNA BARNES PAPERS, MCKELDIN LIBRARY, UNIVERSITY OF MARYLAND, COLLEGE PARK

Chappell, Elizabeth. Letter to Djuna Barnes (9 May 192(4)).

SECONDARY SOURCES

Burne, Glenn S. *Remy de Gourmont: His Ideas and Influence in England and America.* Carbondale: University of Southern Illinois Press, 1963.

Calhoun, L. "A Woman's Hero." *The Argonaut* 104 (1 September 1928): 12.

Cirlot, J. E. *A Dictionary of Symbols.* Translated by Jack Sage. New York: Philosophical Library, 1962.

Croll, Morris W. *"Attic" & Baroque Style: Essays by Morris W. Croll.* Edited by J. Max Patrick and Robert O. Evans, with John M. Wallace. Princeton: Princeton University Press, 1966. Reprint. 1969.

Field, Andrew. *Djuna: The Life and Times of Djuna Barnes.* New York: G. P. Putnam's Sons, 1983.

Frye, Northrop. *Anatomy of Criticism: Four Essays.* Princeton: Princeton University Press, 1957. Reprint. 1973.

Gide, André. "The Reflexive Image," *The Journals of André Gide, 1889-1913.* In *The Modern Tradition.* Edited by Richard Ellman and Charles Feidelson, Jr. New York: Oxford University Press, 1965.

Gourmont, Rémy de. *The Natural Philosophy of Love.* Translated by Ezra Pound. New York: Liveright, 1922.

————. *Remy de Gourmont: Selected Writings.* Edited and translated by Glenn S. Burne. Ann Arbor: University of Michigan Press, 1966.

Huysmans, J.-K. *Against the Grain.* 1884. Reprint. New York: Illustrated Editions, 1931.

Messerli, Douglas. *Djuna Barnes: A Bibliography.* N.p.: David Lewis, 1975.

Scott, James B. *Djuna Barnes.* Boston: Twayne Publishers, 1976.

Donna Gerstenberger (essay date 1989)

SOURCE: Gerstenberger, Donna. "The Radical Narrative of Djuna Barnes's *Nightwood.*" In *Breaking the Sequence: Women's Experimental Fiction,* edited by Ellen G. Friedman and Miriam Fuchs, pp. 129-39. Princeton, N.J.: Princeton University Press, 1989.

[*In the following essay, Gerstenberger notes the flaws in T. S. Eliot's and Joseph Frank's respective readings of* Nightwood, *asserting that both critics fail to convey adequately how the narrative "constantly calls attention to itself as narrative," while it simultaneously "destabilizes, in almost every case, the explanatory power of narrative based on the notion of historical origins."*]

"Wir setzen an dieser Stelle uber den Fluss"

The critical reception of Djuna Barnes's *Nightwood* is marked by a history of readings that focus on everything except its radical narrative achievement. This is a fate that Barnes shared with Joyce, as critics spoke to subject matter and biographical inferences, noting only in passing that the narrative method itself seemed confused or confusing. For Joyce, however, subsequent critics came more quickly to view his narrative practice as significant in itself and there to acknowledge the radical nature of his achievement. Barnes's fate has been to wait until recent years for a recognition of her narrative achievement.[1]

Barnes's first critical reader was T. S. Eliot, and the reception of *Nightwood* was at once cursed and blessed by the high priest of modernism, whose proprietary anxiousness in his well-meaning introduction to the novel seems surprising from the man who had published 14 years earlier what was to become the most influential experimental poem of the first quarter of the century. Eliot, who had worked with Barnes's novel in its various stages of publication, had read *Nightwood* a number of times; yet he clearly misses the point of Barnes's narrative form, for in his introduction he still worries the question of a genre definition. Barnes's work is, he insists, a novel, even though he knows that his contemporaries will be primarily struck by its absence of realism. Having approached the question of genre by what *Nightwood* is not, Eliot finds that he must, as one who genuinely wishes to recommend *Nightwood* to the reader, make two caveats that ignore the issue of form: that the appeal of the book will be primarily to readers of poetry and that "the book is not a psychopathic study" (xv). We need to recall that these caveats come from the author of *The Waste Land,* who had welcomed Joyce's *Ulysses* with strong praise.

One thing that Eliot's convoluted introduction to *Nightwood* does not say is that the novel must have held for him a shock of recognition, for Barnes's novel shares aspects of content and form that the writer of *The Waste Land* cannot have missed. *Nightwood* belongs, on one level at least, to a kind of modernism exemplified by Eliot himself, for on a global level Barnes's novel stakes out the same territory as Eliot's poem, which is that of a civilization (particularly Western European) in decay, an aristocracy in disarray, a people estranged from a sense of identity. Moreover, each of these works seeks to embody the contemporary situation in its fragmentary, nonlinear form, which demands that the reader come to terms with a self-referential internal coherence. And there is the figure of Dr. Matthew-Mighty-grain-of-salt-Dante-O'Connor, a character Eliot may have seen as an impolite version of that other historically sanctified male-female figure who has "foresuffered all"—identified in Eliot's *Waste Land* notes as the place where "the two sexes meet." O'Connor, mirroring Tiresias, sheds no light for Eliot; only of his own work, does Eliot say, "What Tiresias *sees,* in fact, is the substance of the poem" (50). Not until 1963 in *The Widening Gyre* does Joseph Frank spell out the connection that Eliot could not have failed to see. Finally, Barnes's title echoes Dante's dark wood as much as Eliot's poem the world of *The Inferno,* with the important difference that only in Eliot's work does the historical voice offer any promise of normative meaning.

What Eliot does and does not say helped to seal the fate of *Nightwood* for many years. Eliot's resistance to the novel's relationship to the material of his own poem may be covertly acknowledged in his comment that readers trained to poetry are the only proper readers of Barnes's novel, but that advice helped to label Barnes's book as one of interest to writers only—a label that stuck for at least 40 years. Eliot's constricted praise may well have risen from a recognition that *Nightwood,* although working with the same cultural materials, was a more radically experimental work than *The Waste Land*—which it unquestionably is. For all of *Nightwood's* shared signatures with the avant-garde of its own time, it had, like much of Gertrude Stein's work, to wait for a period that could provide the comprehension it deserves.

For *Nightwood* demands, in a way that *The Waste Land* does not, a reading against the dominant text of binary oppositions by which the Western world inscribes itself. It is a novel that rages against the imprisoning structures of the language and narratives of the "day," which create a history built on the oppositions of night/day, past/present, reason/madness, "normal"/"abnormal," truth/falsehood, gender, and origins (both historical and textual). It is a book that relentlessly undermines grounds for categorization. The ideal and the real, the beautiful and the ugly, subject and object become irrelevant distinctions; even the language of the novel works to slip the acculturated binary assumptions of signifier and signified, and the nature of narrative itself is destabilized as traditional categories are emptied of meaning. The difficulties of confronting the totality of the experimental work called *Nightwood* must have been severe for the man who wrote "Tradition and the Individual Talent," and to argue that to fail to accept the novel's characters is to risk the "inveterate sin of pride" is to raise one more of the false trails that has kept subsequent readers from seeing the work in its totality. Monique Wittig speculates, correctly I think, that "Djuna Barnes dreaded that the lesbians should make her *their* writer, and that by doing this they should reduce her work to one dimension" (66).

As a novel, *Nightwood* asks with total commitment, how do we live outside the comfortable-because-known prison of "enlightenment" of the "day"? What narratives do we make when we acknowledge that their making is their sole existence, that there is no historical reality to validate them by? And finally, in what form can the novel exist when it destabilizes the traditional idea of narrative? For Barnes these are questions that can only be answered by a novel that proclaims itself by its process and by its refusal to rely on the old narrative assumptions of plot and character developed in servitude to a fixed way of reading and inscribing reality. To question traditional assumptions demands the abandonment of the fictions that both create and confirm them and a total reorientation toward the nature of narrative itself. Looking squarely at the radical scope of Barnes's novel sheds some light on Eliot's evasive, resistant introduction. Although *The Waste Land* predictably became the exhibition piece for the New Critics, a conspiracy of critical silence became Barnes's fate, and it is a telling irony that postmodern critics have to labor to rescue Eliot's poem from the prisoning binary readings of the New Criticism, whereas *Nightwood* offers itself to readers in the last quarter of the century without the weight of "enlightened" history to which the text refuses to bow down.

Even recent critics like Shari Benstock, who, in *Women of the Left Bank,* offers a feminist reading that understands the difficulty of female narrative in a male-constituted world, tend to read the novel in both the cultural and obligatory countercultural terms of Barnes's lesbianism and her biographical misfortunes in love. Benstock is right when she says what is culturally self-evident, that the "perversion *Nightwood* exposes is not the depravity of homosexuality, the horrors of transsexuality, or the ugliness of woman's hidden nature, but the tragic effect of woman's estrangement from her own self" (263); yet the very terms of her discourse—perversion, depravity, horrors, ugliness, estrangement—perpetuate the notions of their culturally created opposites. What may have been true about Barnes's own life is not necessarily true of the novel, which gives the lie through its narrative form to the idea that any language claims or cultural visions, patriarchal or other, can provide a grounding for "truth" or "knowledge." The claims of *Nightwood*'s narrative are too radical to admit meaning to such a reading. For this reason it is important to pay attention to the often neglected first chapter of the novel.

Barnes "opens" her novel with a mock-creation narrative, embedded in a larger narrative about the decline of Western Europe, invoking the labor of pretentious centuries that brings forth Felix, the wandering Jew of this work, who, mocked by his own name, is forever un-Felix, since his culturally inscribed goal is to find something to bow down to, the metaphysical homeland promised him by the enslaving idea of a continuous and linear historical past. The story of his birth is, in the opening paragraph of the novel, the story of his mother's death, for she gives birth, under the bifurcated wings of the Hapsburg crest, "seven days after her physician predicted that she would be taken" (1). In the biblically allotted time for making worlds, she dies toward Felix's creation, whose inheritance from his father, the Jew who has married his Valkyrie, is a phony coat of arms and two portraits of his grandparents, which turn out to be "reproductions of two intrepid and ancient actors" (7)—a version of reality neither more nor less useful for the world of the novel than any other construction of reality.

The reader learns more in detailed objective ("historical") terms about Felix's parents—the father who dies before his birth and the Austrian woman who lives seven days toward death—than about anyone else in the novel, an anti-introduction that concludes: "At this point [the acquisition of the phony ancestral portraits] exact history stopped for Felix who, thirty years later, turned up in the world with these facts, the two portraits and nothing more" (7). At this point the "present" of *Nightwood* begins for the reader who, like Felix, the wandering Jew, is abandoned by a creation narrative that gives the lie to itself, that offers only an untrustworthy grounding to hope for narrative stability. The labor of centuries has given us an un-baron seeking his nonexistent barony, clutching at the tatters of undifferentiated nobility, pomp, and pageantry. The price of Felix's obsession is the self, and he is a man so uninhabited by self that "three or more persons would swear to having seen him the week before in three different countries simultaneously" (7). His desperate desire for historical order attaches him finally to "the pagentry of the circus and the theatre," where at last he finds "a Princess Nadja, a Baron von Tink, a Principessa Stasera y Stasero, a King Buffo and a Duchess of Broadback" (11), who pander to the need for performed order in a world of flux in the same way that traditional fiction depends on characters who are fixed and fully determined in their roles so that the reader may track the "changes" they may undergo within narrative progression. Felix is willing to settle for whatever promises him a narrative order, totally unaware that, in this unconventional novel, he is one of the "empty" characters, who foolishly waits to be made full by an idealized external content, which *Nightwood* denies.

Trust in historical progression and in narrative as a means to a serviceable end has undergone its initial destabilization by the time Felix enters the "circus" present of the novel, and it is appropriate that at this point Matthew O'Connor, the doctor who is not a doctor, is introduced at a party given by a Count Altamonte, a nobleman who is probably not a nobleman. The party promises an evening's entertainment of living statues, which the count, who suspects he has "come upon his last erection," adores. The party does not take place; it is another of the promises of Barnes's narration that is canceled out. A pattern of desire and deferral, absence not filled by presence, is, ironically, an essential ingredient of *Nightwood*'s rich narrative presence.

While the guests wait for their host, O'Connor fills up absence with endless stories: "stories that do not amount to much . . . [to man] merely because they befell him without distinction of office or title—that's what we call legend and it's the best a poor man may do with his fate; the other . . . we call history, the best the high and mighty can do with theirs" (15). Felix is deeply distressed by O'Connor's definition of religion as "story," which answers in "Gothic echoes" the confessional tale of the "knotty, tangled soul" and merely fulfills the recognizable end of all traditional narratives: "Mischief unravels and the fine high hand of Heaven proffers the skein again, combed and forgiven!" (21).

Felix has fled from O'Connor before the doctor "tells" the story of Felix himself ("damned from the waist up") by recounting the story of Mlle Basquette, "damned from the waist down, a girl without legs, built like a medieval abuse" (26). Although this is one of O'Connor's many stories in which its author (not inter-

ested in unraveling the skein of narrative) seems to respond to the subject at hand by aiming in the opposite direction, it carries for the reader echoes of Felix's ancestral home with its halls "peopled with Roman fragments, white and disassociated; a runner's leg, the chilly half-turned head of a matron stricken at the bosom" (5), for Barnes's own narrative constantly calls attention to itself as narrative, validating its own existence as "story" at the same time that it destabilizes, in almost every case, the explanatory power of narrative based on the notion of historical origins. There are, for this novel, no fragments that can be shored up against our ruin.

Joseph Frank, in *The Widening Gyre,* the first serious attempt to come to terms with *Nightwood* as a radically experimental text, calls attention to this kind of "reflexive reference" as the method for approaching the novel that will solve the "mystery" of its form, a mystery that cannot be attacked by "approaching the book, as most of its readers have done, in terms of a coherent temporal pattern of narrative" (30). Although Frank's instincts about the radical nature of Barnes's narrative are sound, he seeks to solve the mystery of her experimental prose by substituting the concept of spatial form for linear narrative, a reading he comes to through Lessing and the examples of Eliot and Pound. As Alan Singer points out in his chapter on *Nightwood* in *A Metaphorics of Fiction,* although Frank understands that *Nightwood* is difficult because it abandons "the time continuum of the nineteenth-century plot paradigm," the new esthetic Frank provides only renames the problem without sufficiently accounting for the origin of the problem (48).

The substitution of spatial form for linear narrative cannot bring Frank to useful conclusions about the nature of Barnes's text. That Frank has failed to read the real intention of the first crucial chapter, "Bow Down" (which Barnes used as the working title of the novel), is made clear as he proceeds with a reading that works to reduce the whole to the story of Robin Vote and the devastating effects that follow for those who try to inscribe their own desires on her apparently blank tablet of self. Skipping to the emergence of Robin Vote and the extrapolation of conventional narrative that can be made from the "action" that follows results in a model of reading that necessarily undermines the radical integrity of the whole. The novel that Frank reads is not *Nightwood* but something that might be entitled *The Short Unhappy Life of Robin Vote and Her Lovers.*

After explaining that in *Nightwood,* "as in the work of Braque, the Fauves or the Cubists, the naturalistic principle has lost its dominance" and that "the question of the relation of this vision to an extra-artistic 'objective' world has ceased to have any fundamental importance" (28), Frank urges a narrative coherence not unlike those critical readings of Faulkner that center on Caddy Compson or Addy Bundren as "absent" characters, forgetting that the obsessions of the other characters can make equally blind the critic who prioritizes those obsessions at the expense of the language and narrative by which *they* are created. Frank's actual discussion of *Nightwood* betrays the esthetic he espouses and trivializes rather than frees the reader's sense of Barnes's narrative. Frank's problem begins in his idea that narrative must be expressed by the old notion of a *reduction* of the whole to something like the printed line of a map, which can show the journey separate from the experience of the journey itself. *Nightwood,* Frank has told us, resists such a reduction, but because Frank's ideas about narrative have not been rethought in a sufficiently radical way, he still needs to reduce Barnes's novel and in the process to destroy its narrative locus, which resides solely in the process of its telling.

Frank's limitations are evident when he takes Matthew O'Connor to task for telling Nora "'I have a narrative, but you will be hard put to find it'" (32). "Strictly speaking," the narrative moralist in Frank admonishes, "the doctor is wrong—he has a static situation, not a narrative . . ." (32). In spite of the courage Frank has displayed in trying to find an adequate way of reading *Nightwood,* he fails to recall that Barnes deals with stasis a number of times in the novel but never in relation to the doctor. In the first chapter there are the (absent) living statues of the lofty count whose probably assumed name means "high mountain," the poseur who puts himself above the flux. The concern with stasis runs throughout the novel, but Barnes examines the idea of stasis most consistently in writing out the relationship of Jenny Petherbridge and Robin. Jenny is "the squatter," who appropriates the objects of other people's feelings and the secondhand expressions of their lives much as Felix, also identified with statues and stasis, seizes every possible remnant of a lost tradition. On one occasion, Jenny and Robin become living statues, a double shadow to the actual statue in Nora's garden. And, again, shortly after the garden scene, in a passage that sounds a good deal like Faulkner, thinking of Keats's urn: "thus they presented the two halves of a movement that had, as in sculpture, the beauty and the absurdity of a desire that is in flower but that can have no burgeoning . . . ; they were like Greek runners, with lifted feet . . . eternally separated, in a cataleptic frozen gesture of abandon" (69). The static scene in the garden brings Nora to her first felt experience of evil, her first moment of passing judgment on the world—a moment unlike any other in the book—and Barnes makes it clear that stasis marks the absence of authentic feeling.

When Felix tells O'Connor that Robin, whom he never really knew, remains to him only as an image—"but that is not the same thing. An image is a stop the mind makes between uncertainties" (111)—he, aside from sounding for us like Robert Frost, unwittingly eluci-

dates Barnes's persistent metaphoric elaborations in the novel, which underwrite and become a part of her general narrative practice. Alan Singer's exhaustive and insightful examination of Barnes's use of tropes makes it unnecessary to repeat those observations here except to say that Barnes's refusal to rest in images, in the "stop the mind makes between uncertainties," confirms the narrative process and coherence of the novel. An image is also what Felix has of his family, "preserved," he says, "because I have it only from the memory of one single woman, my aunt; therefore it is single, clear and unalterable" (112). Precisely because it is single and unalterable it is static and inauthentic in the way the image must be for Barnes that claims in a single and unmediated act to capture the signified by the signifier.

Stasis clearly is a legitimate part of the narrative act in a theoretical sense, and for Frank to read O'Connor as static and therefore having no narrative is to be doubly wrong. One needs to recall O'Connor's narrative in "Bow Down" of the cow trembling as the bombs drop, her hide running with the water of terror, about which he says, "there are directions and speeds that no one has calculated, for believe it or not that cow had gone somewhere very fast that we didn't know of, and yet was still standing there" (23). The reader of *Nightwood* experiences O'Connor largely *as narrative*. The novel inscribes him by story and narrative act (i.e., not to be confused with Barnes or the implied narrator of the novel but as a creator within the larger narrative), whose stories often seem to exist for their own telling, glancing blows off the side of his real subjects but nonetheless inscribed within Barnes's narrative purpose. The attentive reader is surprised that the doctor is described as a "small" man at the beginning of the second chapter, "La Somnambule," because he has seemed as large as his language, as commanding as his fictions, as fertile as his imagination when first we see him in "Bow Down."

Felix, whose needs from the beginning have seemed closest to the expectations of the traditional reader, decides that "the doctor was a great liar, but a valuable liar. His fabrications seemed to be the framework of a forgotten but imposing plan . . ." (30). That Felix is no more an adequate guide than are his traditional readerly expectations should be clear. It is precisely that there is no plan and no framework but that imposed by human history and its institutions, the constructed "truths" that begin in desire and fear of extinction, that is the deepest knowledge and heaviest burden of O'Connor and his "lying" tales, which are "lies" only in the sense that they are tied to the necessities of a language, which both confirm and create the structures the "rationality" of the day has imposed.

Language, because it inscribes and is inscribed by convention, is a trap as reductive as narrative is for Joseph Frank, and one that Barnes seeks to escape in *Night-*

wood. In "Watchman, What of the Night?" Doctor-Priest-Shaman O'Connor tells Nora, "we who are full to the gorge with misery should look well around, doubting everything seen, done, spoken, precisely because we have a word for it, and not its alchemy. . . . To think of the acorn it is necessary to become the tree. And the tree of night is the hardest tree to mount . . ." (83). Nora has come to ask O'Connor to tell her everything he knows of the night, and he can only by indirection truthfully tell of the night, which the keepers of rationality destroy for the sake of the day. "The very constitution of twilight is a fabulous reconstruction of fear. . . . Every day is thought upon and calculated, but the night is not premeditated. The Bible lies the one way, but the night-gown the other" (80). Nora finally asks the painful question many readers of *Nightwood* have asked of it: "How do you live at all if this wisdom of yours is not only the truth, but also the price?" (90).

For O'Connor, a surplus of language and of stories is the only way to neutralize the lie of adequacy and possession inherent in the act of narrative, and his answer is a long time coming as he follows the glancing blows of endless stories by way of saying that all answers are equally true and lying, until finally he says, "I tuck myself in at night, well content because I am my own charlatan" (96). The cost of his contentment is great because of the unreasonable demands for absolute truth put on him as a narrator, but like O'Connor, the reader knows that in *Nightwood* the only text that does not lie is narrative conscious of its own fictionality. This text as "valuable liar" does not pretend to traditional truth even within the narrative convention. The reader who comes wholly to *Nightwood* must be willing to pay the same price O'Connor has paid for his, at best, contingent wisdom. And for many readers the price has been unthinkable.

Even those readers for whom contingency and the elaborate alchemy of uncertainty have explanatory power are brought up short by the brief, final chapter, "The Possessed," which has often been seen as a coda, for lack of a better term, to the novel. It follows the silencing of Matthew's great voice with his final acceptance that there is, in the end, *"nothing, but wrath and weeping!"* (166) for the inhabitants of *Nightwood.* Only the narrator's voice is heard in "The Possessed," and this voice is straightforward and declarative, the same voice that opens the novel with the outrageous tale of Felix's birth and heritage. It is the narrator's dispassionate voice that follows Robin's circuitous path through the fields, past the responsive animals, to Nora's family chapel, where the novel ends in a tableau—a wordless scene of Nora and Robin, the latter seemingly bereft of human consciousness. Even Nora's dog, so threatened by Robin's release of the little that had held her human, gives up and lies down beside her weeping figure. In a novel that has been dominated by voices

there remain only Robin and the dog, both making sounds that exist outside of (and perhaps, beyond) language. *"Wrath and weeping"* begin when the elaborating voice of contingency is silenced.

Barnes is not, however, in this last section, giving up on her narrative or speaking to its failure to sustain the "meaning" of its form as some critics have suggested.[2] She is, it seems to me, completing the novel in a way that makes clear that the narrative transaction has been between *Nightwood* and the reader. The probable failure of its characters to survive a world whose clear message is that "Thou shalt be one thing or another" within terms of established certainties is the final alchemy of a novel whose narrative has, by the very nature of its existence, demonstrated again and again that "Life is not to be told, call it as loud as you like, it will not tell itself" (129). All the conventional readings of experience, collective and individual, called history, philosophy, religion, can only create structures that substitute for a reading of life. They can only provide at best a rendering of agreements made by a collective desire for a realm of permanence and order, to which traditional narrative has become the handmaiden and language the pretender. Barnes, by questioning the narrative enterprise in the most radical way possible, has pushed her experiement further than all readers are willing to go, but those who can, those who do, no longer need a creation narrative, for all creation narratives predispose toward a desired end, one that limits and deceives. The indeterminant ending of *Nightwood* mocks the novel's already mocking beginning to remind the reader once again that, if the desire of *The Waste Land* is survival with meaning, the desire of Barnes's novel is freedom from the prison of meaning, and to accept this fact is to understand the radical experience of narrative that is *Nightwood.*

Notes

1. Melvin Friedman in *Stream of Consciousness* makes it clear that he understands Barnes's importance as an experimental writer, but it is Joseph Frank, in his essay on spatial form, who makes the first sustained attempt to come to terms with the form of *Nightwood,* an inquiry that is continued in Louis F. Kannenstine's *The Art of Djuna Barnes* and, most successfully, in Alan Singer's *A Metaphorics of Fiction.* In 1976, Elizabeth Pochada can still begin her article, "Style's Hoax," by saying, "Judging by its modest six or so appearances in the *MLA Bibliography,* Djuna Barnes's *Nightwood* has meant a good deal less to literary critics than it has to some contemporary novelists" (179).

2. A number of critics read the collapse of O'Connor as the collapse of the novel or of Barnes's sense of the novel. Pochada is one: "Perhaps this is why

'The Possessed,' the section that follows 'Go Down, Matthew' and concludes the novel, seems an anticlimax. The novel has already jettisoned language; O'Connor has exited . . ." (188). Charles Baxter, after having asserted that the "doctor's fine talk and Djuna Barnes's fine writing conclusively and inevitably merge" (1187), sees the book reaching a crisis from which it cannot recover.

Works Cited

Barnes, Djuna. *Nightwood*. 1936. Introd. T. S. Eliot. New York: New Directions, 1961.

Baxter, Charles. "A Self-Consuming Light: *Nightwood* and the Crisis of Modernism." *Journal of Modern Literature* 3 (1974): 1175-87.

Benstock, Shari. *Women of the Left Bank: Paris, 1900-1940*. Austin: U of Texas P, 1986.

Eliot, T. S. *The Waste Land and Other Poems*. New York: Harcourt, 1958.

Frank, Joseph. *The Widening Gyre: Crisis and Mastery in Modern Literature*. New Brunswick: Rutgers UP, 1963.

Friedman, Melvin. *Stream of Consciousness: A Study in Literary Method*. New Haven: Yale UP, 1955.

Kannenstine, Louis F. *The Art of Djuna Barnes: Duality and Damnation*. New York: New York UP, 1977.

Pochada, Elizabeth. "Style's Hoax: A Reading of Djuna Barnes's *Nightwood*." *Twentieth Century Literature* 22 (1976): 179-91.

Singer, Alan. *A Metaphorics of Fiction*. Tallahassee: Florida UP, 1983.

Wittig, Monique. "The Point of View: Universal or Particular?" *Feminist Issues* 3 (1983): 62-69.

Phillip F. Herring (essay date 1990)

SOURCE: Herring, Phillip F. "Djuna Barnes and the Narrative of Violation." In *Modes of Narrative: Approaches to American, Canadian and British Fiction Presented to Helmut Bonheim*, edited by Reingard M. Nischik and Barbara Korte, pp. 100-09. Würzburg, Germany: Königshausen & Neumann, 1990.

[*In the following essay, Herring argues against biographical readings of* Nightwood *as "a lesbian cry against patriarchy or an attack on fascism in defense of marginalized people," calling it instead a metaphysical work that depicts all of human nature as "perverted and grotesque."*]

Djuna Barnes (1892-1982), until recently undervalued as a major contributor to literary modernism, combined in a unique way some of the century's most biting satire with a view of the human condition that expressed profoundest gloom. In the best modernist tradition, her writing is idiosyncratic, original and full of enigmas, but it reminds the reader at times of predecessors: There is a saltiness in her comic descriptions associated with writers such as Rabelais, and an uncompromising dedication to her craft that suggests the tradition of Flaubert, Stein and Joyce. Add to this something of Joyce's technical virtuosity and his love for dictionaries, the occasional use of Nietzsche's aphoristic style, and the misanthropy of Swift. Barnes' bleak pessimism could be located somewhere between that of Schopenhauer and John Millington Synge. The style of some of her drawings and illustrations derives from Aubrey Beardsley. Among contemporaries, one is reminded of Flannery O'Connor's genius in creating comically grotesque misfits. At times her minimalist vision of a world in decay bears comparison with that of Samuel Beckett, who helped her financially in later years.[1] However, while comparisons might help us to place her in the modern tradition, ultimately, from the early journalism to her latest creative work, Djuna Barnes' artistic achievement was quite original.

Since the letters, manuscripts and other memorabilia of Djuna Barnes became available to scholars in 1970, when they were purchased by the University of Maryland, details of her very private life have begun to emerge. Controversy surrounds Barnes in death as it did in life. A biography by Andrew Field, published in 1983,[2] contains errors and important gaps, and it has rightfully been disparaged in reviews. Part of the current controversy centers on the possibility that Barnes was sexually abused as a girl. Barnes' play *The Antiphon* (1958),[3] and her novel *Ryder* (1928),[4] semiautobiographical in nature, and certain of her verbal statements, speak in varying ways of the heritage of rape—even incest. The correspondence I have seen fails to corroborate these allegations, but in Barnes' fiction the dominant voice speaks the narrative of violation.

Djuna Barnes' family was unusually talented, though eccentric. Her father Wald preached polygamy, but for financial reasons had to limit himself to bigamy. In 1889 he married Djuna's English mother, Elizabeth Chappell, and they had five children. In about 1897 he brought another woman into the household, Fanny Faulkner, and together they had four children. Djuna and her mother deeply resented Fanny and her brood, and in 1912 Djuna's mother divorced Wald and took the children to live in poverty in the New York area. Until the age of sixteen, Djuna had an extremely close relationship with her grandmother Zadel. Although there can be no doubt of Zadel's deep love for Djuna and all her talented grandchildren, her general encouragement of sexual permissiveness led to bizarre and unhappy consequences. She gave her blessing to Wald's bigamy, and in 1910 Zadel also coaxed Djuna (then seventeen) into a common-law marriage with the fifty-two-year-old Percy Faulkner, a brother of Fanny, the mistress Wald married after his divorce.

The years 1910-12 were probably traumatic for Djuna: first the dissolution of her own 'marriage' and then that of her parents. Bitterness produced a cynical wit that became her artistic trademark, evident even in the earliest work.[5] Field summarizes "an undated initial draft of *The Antiphon*," a play Barnes described as autobiographical, in which a farmer attempts to rape his sixteen-year-old daughter by the farm gate. Unsuccessful, he ties her up, hangs her from a barn rafter, and barters her to a farmhand for a goat. A graphic description of the rape follows, which is witnessed by a terror-stricken young brother.[6] T. S. Eliot, who helped edit the play, forced drastic cuts in those sections dealing specifically with incest.[7] Field's evidence is based on Barnes' fiction, and on her insistence that these works were semiautobiographical. However, one must always allow for artistic license, and it is probably too late for the truth of these allegations to be known with any certainty.

Evidence of Djuna's bitterness does exist in a letter of April 2, 1958 from her brother Thurn, who comments on *The Antiphon* by noting its revenge motif regarding events that took place long ago. In the margin Djuna noted that in writing *The Antiphon* she sought justice, not revenge, in evoking sexual abuse, a subject not dead for her and not to be forgotten. In *Ryder,* rape and the sexual exploitation of women are continually at issue.

Barnes' literary works strongly militate against the father.[8] James B. Scott says that Wald Barnes "trusted nature but distrusted society" and had a "messianic impulse to reform that society to the prototype of nature herself."[9] Wendell Ryder, Wald's counterpart in *Ryder,*[10] defends polygamy as he might have defended incest, as being nature's way in the animal world: "for polygamy is the only bed a man rolls out of, conditioned to meet the world."[11] At another point he says,

> 'See [. . .] the little girls stumbling to school; it's their future maternity that makes them stare into the hedges like that. Mark,' he says, 'the squirrels lifting their tails unabashed'; he calls that pure reason and unobstructed inner vision.[12]

Thus this composite father's argument for incest might run as follows: since sexuality is natural in humans, fathers may introduce daughters to this part of their nature, a common occurrence in the animal kingdom; nature serves as precedent. (Similar arguments are made today by child pornographers who wish to legitimate pedophilia.)

Yet another chapter of *Ryder* tells us something different: "Rape and Repining" seems a general lamentation with deeply personal implications that could, of course, point as easily to the Percy Faulkner fiasco as to her father:

> A Girl is gone! A Girl is lost! A simple Rustic Maiden but Yesterday swung upon the Pasture Gate, with Knowledge nowhere, yet is now, to-day, no better than her Mother, and her Mother's Mother before her! Soiled! Despoiled! Handled! Mauled! Rumpled! Rummaged! Ransacked! No purer than Fish in Sea, no sweeter than Bird on Wing, no better than Beasts of Earth![13]

Common to all of Barnes' work is this sense of personal outrage, anger and bitterness. As Scott says, for Djuna Barnes "the entire human enterprise is an atrocious but alluring mistake."[14] Consequently, the theme of death as preferable to violation is present early and late in her work. A story of the early 1920s, **"No-Man's-Mare,"** tells of a beautiful young wife on Cape Cod who wishes to perish and does; a wild mare is captured and burdened with the corpse, which it is to transport to the cemetery. At one point the mare plunges with the wife into the sea; both appear to swim out, thus escaping the corruption of society. At the end of *The Antiphon,* Miranda allows her mother, now made aware of her complicity in sexual abuse, to beat her to death with a bell.

In the 1920s and 1930s Barnes was a familiar figure in Left Bank circles in Paris, where she knew Joyce, Pound, Hemingway, Stein, and was especially close to Natalie Clifford Barney and other lesbian artists. During this period she began her lengthy love affair with Thelma Wood; Barnes' Novel *Nightwood* (1936), which is loosely based on her painful sundering with Wood, is considered to be her major artistic achievement.

THE PLOT OF NIGHTWOOD

Nightwood begins with the deathbed scene of Hedvig Volkbein, whose "military beauty"[15] suggests Austrian militarism in dance and gesture. She dies giving birth to Felix, whose fate will not be a happy one. Soon thereafter the father, Guido, dies, a Viennese Jew of Italian extraction who calls himself "Baron," having invented a phoney pedigree in "remorseless homage to nobility" (p. 2). So far we have an unmotherly mother who goose-steps through life to die at forty-five in childbirth and a father who makes absurd attempts to blot out his Jewish heritage in order to assimilate into an aristocracy that would have despised him. The strategy of inversion continues.

Orphaned Felix inherits his father's wealth and passion for noble lineage, so that he comes to live in a world of historical allusion and reference. This young Baron

Volkbein associates with circus performers who also falsify identities, and thus comes to meet the other major characters of *Nightwood*. With their phoney titles, they too have ludicrous surnames, reminiscent of those in the "Cyclops" episode of *Ulysses*.[16] We meet a masculine Frau Mann, i. e. the Duchess of Broadback, whose "coqueteries were muscular and localized," and Count Onatorio Altamonte, whose name suggests an onanistic oratory on a high mountain (p. 12).

If some are fools, others are grotesque, reminding one that Dr. O'Connor says, "'only the scorned and the ridiculous make good stories'" (p. 159). Pity is little in evidence. Nikka the Nigger is remembered, a tattooed black man who used to wrestle a circus bear, whose body has become a complex, highly allusive, erudite text (pp. 16f.); and there is the legless beauty of the Pyrenees, Mademoiselle Basquette, who wheels through the mountains on a board (p. 26).

Such beings are humorous digressions, comic *tours de force*; the novel's real interest lies in love entanglements and in Dr. O'Connor's hilarious commentary on them. Felix meets, woos and weds the American Robin Vote, for "he wished a son who would feel as he felt about 'the great past'" (p. 38). Back in Vienna, her behavior becomes stranger and stranger. She begins to wander, and eventually leaves Vienna, Felix and their baby Guido.

The first chapter's title (and the novel's original title) is "Bow Down," an act of obeisance impossible for Robin; the second chapter is "La Somnambule," with an ironic nod to Bellini, suggesting Robin's mindless wandering and metaphysical hollowness. In the chapter "Night Watch," Robin meets Nora Flood at a circus, and a great love affair begins that is *Nightwood*'s chief interest. Inevitably Robin begins to wander again, from bed to bed and pub to pub. In "The Squatter," Robin leaves Nora for Jenny Petherbridge, which becomes Nora's great tragedy, an obsession she attempts unsuccessfully to conquer during the rest of the novel. In the next three chapters ("Watchman, What of the Night," "Where the Tree Falls," and "Go Down, Matthew"), Dr. O'Connor becomes a clearing house of consolation for those who desire Robin: Felix, Nora and Jenny. Robin's magnetism, and what her life-style says about human nature, have a devastating effect on all concerned, not least of all on father-confessor Matthew O'Connor.

Nightwood's bizarre last chapter, "The Possessed," is located in a rural area (probably New York or Connecticut) where Nora has a house. Her dog barks excitedly as she seeks the cause of his disturbance in a small chapel. There Robin, now seemingly derelict and insane, apparently worshipping before a "contrived altar" (p. 169), slides down before the dog as if ready for another sexual conquest. Thus the novel ends.

Readers and critics have for long been puzzled about the ending. The entire chapter reads like a vivid dream such as Nora has of the grandmother (pp. 62f; 148f.). If the ending of *Nightwood* is also meant to be a revenge against Djuna Barnes' unfaithful lover Thelma Wood, then it is a terrible vengeance indeed.

The writing of this novel may have exorcized some of the pain Barnes felt at the breaking off of her relationship of long duration with Thelma, for it is about a love affair like theirs. But *Nightwood* resists classification: it is not precisely revengeful *roman à clef,* though there is some of that. To say that it defends marginalized people, portraying their lives of suffering and abuse, may be accurate, but the cause of marginalization seems to lie not in any overt political system or patriarchal structure or homophobia. *Nightwood* is neither a defense of homosexual life-style as preferable to heterosexuality, nor a condemnation of it. (Barnes does not judge on moral grounds; her quarrel is with life itself.) Thus *Nightwood* is not precisely a lesbian novel, as Lanser argues.[17] In fact, if there is one main culprit in the novel, it is the human need to express sexuality. *Nightwood* describes fictional worlds where all beauty has departed, where civilization is unspeakably corrupt, while nature is devoid of affirmation because of the universal urge to couple and procreate. Such a narrative struggles between repression and the need to cry out for understanding, as does the central narrator of *Nightwood,* Dr. Matthew O'Connor. In a Cartesian mutation, he says, "'to think is to be sick'" (p. 158). The plot of *Nightwood* seems to have been designed to keep the reader continually off balance—at once stunned by the technical virtuosity of the writing, sickened by the vision of despair, while amused at the malicious satire and comical grotesques.

PHILOSOPHICAL AFFINITIES

It is on the level of metaphysics that *Nightwood* transcends the autobiographical, where one sees its evasion of attempts to reduce it to a lesbian outcry against patriarchy[18] or an attack on fascism in defense of marginalized people,[19] for it argues that human nature itself is perverted and grotesque. In such an argument the margins disappear. Barnes would seem to agree with Schopenhauer and Nietzsche on the nature of human existence as suffering. One of the central metaphysical statements in the novel is: "'No man needs curing of his individual sickness; his universal malady is what he should look to'" (p. 32). Yet in *Nightwood* only Matthew O'Connor, who presents Barnes' own world view in the narrative style of his real-life counterpart, Daniel Mahoney, can sufficiently transcend individual suffering to construct a metaphysics of pessimism, which, for all its rambling, does make a coherent statement about life. Others are so locked into their personal misfortunes that they scarcely make sense. A more contemporary way to express the problem would be to say that at the core of all of *Nightwood*'s characters is desire—desire to change one's essence or, for most of the central figures, the essence of Robin, whose problems energize the plot.

Given that life is suffering, the greatest crime for this kind of pessimist would be procreation, and on this issue Barnes is consistent. Of the early stories, Scott says:

> Miss Barnes sees life and the perpetuation of life as a mistake; indeed, it is a mistake to be alive, and then by procreation, to compound that error and produce more tragedy and pain. She finds death, then, to be an affirmation and a triumph [. . .] she sees life as meaningless but as quite understandable.[20]

Barnes frequently returns to the question of procreation. In 1910 Zadel Barnes expressed her hope that Djuna and Percy would have children. In *Ryder,* however, Amelia's mother says "Never, never, have children. And God forgive me [. . .] for making you mortal; if you live you will be a fool. It takes a strong woman to die before she has been a fool."[21] In *The Antiphon* (Act 3), it is said that parents sin against the child in giving birth to it,[22] an injustice Barnes herself presumably avoided when she had an abortion in 1933. In *Nightwood,* in a particularly distraught mood, Robin is seen holding her baby "high in her hand as if she were about to dash it down," later confessing "'I didn't want him!'" (pp. 48f.).

Metaphysics, as Williamson suggests, is reflected by both Darwinian and Christian concerns.[23] Robin is "beast turning human" (p. 37); through her conversion to Roman Catholicism she aspires to transcend her beastly limitations (p. 46). Matthew O'Connor is a devout Catholic even if an insatiable pederast. Nora says, "'God laughs at me, but his laughter is my love'" (p. 143); Ignatius Loyola sounds the "deepest note" in Felix's existence (p. 10); Nora is described as "by temperament [. . .] an early Christian" (p. 51), and Dr. O'Connor spots her as Christian too (p. 60). Jenny is "a Christian with a wanderer's rump" (p. 97).

Djuna Barnes was, of course, not the first female writer to describe a wandering woman like Robin, who causes grief through her amoral actions. It does not seem to have been pointed out in the criticism of *Nightwood* that Gertrude Stein had, in 1909, published "Melanctha" in *Three Lives,* which portrays a black female who needs the stability of home, friendship and later a lover, but whose need for experience, especially sexual experience, causes her to "wander" (one of the story's key words). Melanctha is never able to overcome this paradox; she needs love and security, but the moral strictures of those who love her are oppressive. She must wander to experience life (for her this is instructive),

but then she is called immoral. Ultimately she is rejected by parents, friends and lovers. In *Nightwood,* Robin Vote's animal nature causes her similar problems, but unlike Melanctha she seeks transcendence in religious faith.

DESIRE

How does one then account for religious desire in this wasteland where one waits in vain for redemption?[24] The answer may be in the nature of desire itself, which in *Nightwood* is insatiable. Schopenhauer said that objects of desire, when attained, always become boring. According to Alan Singer, Barnes' point is that homoerotic desire, since ultimately narcissistic, will always be frustrated.[25] Schopenhauer, of course, would see no difference between this and other forms of desire, and Barnes' point is surely about desire itself rather than homoeroticism. (Felix and his son Guido are frustrated, as is Mlle. Basquette.)

The specific example, however, is homoerotic desire, the frustration of which is imaged in an erotic positioning of Jenny and Robin:

> Jenny leaning far over the table, Robin far back, her legs thrust under her, to balance the whole backward incline of the body, and Jenny so far forward that she had to catch her small legs in the back rung of the chair, ankle out and toe in, not to pitch forward on the table—thus they presented the two halves of a movement that had, as in sculpture, the beauty and absurdity of a desire that is in flower but that can have no burgeoning, unable to execute its destiny; [. . .]—eternally angry, eternally separated, in a cataleptic frozen gesture of abandon."
>
> (p. 69)

Such desire is narcissistic in *Nightwood.* Nora says, "'For Robin is incest too; that is one of her powers'" (p. 156) and "'Matthew, [. . .] have you ever loved someone and it became yourself?'" (p. 152) and, "'A man is another person—a woman is yourself, caught as you turn in panic; on her mouth you kiss your own'" (p. 143).

In *Nightwood,* the desire for transcendence from this world of suffering through religion seems the ultimate expression of narcissism; it simply reflects the intensity of human suffering in desire. For Samuel Beckett, mathematics seems to be the ultimate absurdity for, with it, one can solve numerical and logical problems within a larger frame of meaninglessness. *Nightwood* may show the absurdity of religious feeling within that same larger frame.

Narcissistic desire is what motivates plot and character, accounting also for the theme of inversion. From the circus performers to the Volkbeins, everyone belies his/her essence. Dr. Matthew O'Connor's single obsession is the desire to be a woman. He says, "'God, I never asked better than to boil some good man's potatoes and toss up a child for him every nine months by the calendar'" (p. 91). Nora, seeing him in bed dressed in a woman's nightgown, awaiting a customer, thinks, "'He dresses to lie beside himself'" (p. 80) as she has lain beside herself as Robin.

Felix realizes too late that "he was not sufficient to *make* her [Robin] what he had hoped" (p. 44 [my emphasis]), presumably believing that since she comes from the United States, a country with a short history, her essence can be readily changed: "'With an American anything can be done'" (p. 39). He desires Robin and a son (p. 38) to fulfill his desire for noble lineage, which will always remain beyond his reach.

Felix's son Guido will desire a mother; Nora and Jenny will desire their lover Robin. Robin, we have said, desires at the same time contradictory things: to have the stability of a monogamous relationship while wandering promiscuously; to be a Roman Catholic while having the moral nature of an animal.[26] Ultimately, she is a love object answering to the narcissistic needs of others, an insolvable mystery to all including herself. Every character in *Nightwood* has urgent desires that are blocked.

ANIMALITY AND INNOCENCE

The theme of animality in *Nightwood* is related to questions of morality and religion, and here we return to the paradigm of nature. For Barnes the central paradox of human existence seems to have been that we have lost our animal innocence and yet as humans can achieve neither forgiveness nor transcendence, though doomed to desire it in this vale of tears. Animal innocence means having no haunting consciousness, no disturbing memories of the past, no guilt. This is the positive side of animal behavior, and the attraction of Robin. Nora Flood says, "'Have I been simple like an animal or have I been thinking?'" (p. 133). It is consciousness, Scott says, that in Barnes' fiction alienates humans from the animal world.[27]

Yet for humans to act as subhumans is both to deny their moral nature and to bring misery to others. Despite the current trend to see Robin as a liberated woman and Nora as bound by puritanical values in wanting an exclusive relationship,[28] Barnes seems to condemn Robin's unselective promiscuity as destructive to one's self and others. Desiring the exclusive relationship that most people want, regardless of sexual orientation, Nora represents a norm in *Nightwood.* Alas, it is left to Dr. O'Connor to smash her illusions, to show her the impossibilty of stable human relationships in a Barnesian world that seems designed to make people suffer. If Robin is to be pitied as "a beast turning human" (p.

33), Nora is pitiful as the innocent romantic who believes that love is meant to last. Finally, it is Dr. O'Connor's cynicism that fills the vacuum of normality. This cynicism is a normal response to the ultimate frustration of all desire in the world of Djuna Barnes.

James Baird argues that *Nightwood* is "an allegory of the loss of innocence, not the innocence of Adam and Eve before the imposition of Scriptural Law, but the innocence of the jungle."[29] The novel "is but one more vision of the night wood in which human beings live and struggle backward in a search for the innocence of childhood."[30] The spirit of this idea seems captured in a lyrical section in *Ryder*[31] describing young Julie's discovery of human corruption.

The desire for return to the lost innocence of childhood is indeed a common theme in Barnes. Seen from this perspective, the enigmatic first poem **"From Fifth Avenue Up"** in *The Book of Repulsive Women,* which Barnes published at the age of twenty-three, can now be seen as a revelation of the violated self longing for infantile innocence. The first stanza reads:

> Someday beneath some hard
> Capricious star—
> Spreading its light a little
> Over far,
> We'll know you for the woman
> That you are.[32]

Her readers are beginning to know Djuna Barnes for the woman that she was, a woman whose trauma in girlhood created in her art brilliant wit intermingled with haunting cries of despair.[33]

Notes

1. That Irish writers predominate on this list is no accident; Barnes felt a kinship with them, especially Joyce and Synge.

2. Andrew Field, *Djuna: The Life and Times of Djuna Barnes* (rev. ed., Austin: University of Texas Press, 1985 [1983]).

3. Djuna Barnes, *The Antiphon: A Play* (New York/London: Farrar, Straus & Cudahy/Faber, 1958).

4. Djuna Barnes, *Ryder* (repr. New York: St. Martin's Press, 1979).

5. A photo in Field's biography (following p. 98) documents another instance of violation. As a reporter for the *New York World Magazine,* investigating the force-feeding of English suffragists, Djuna Barnes allowed herself to be force-fed and photographed (cf. *op. cit.,* pp. 53f.).

6. *Op. cit.,* p. 193.

7. Just as Ezra Pound made editorial suggestions for *The Waste Land,* so too did Eliot for *Nightwood* and later for *The Antiphon,* and his continual urg-

ing of Barnes to cut material from these works resulted in excessive cutting. There is need for a critical edition of the works which will address this problem. See Lynda Curry, "'Tom, Take Mercy': T. S. Eliot and *The Antiphon*," in Mary Lynn Broe (ed.), *Silence and Power: A Reevaluation of Djuna Barnes* (Carbondale: Southern Illinois Univ. Press). Yet *Books in Print* lists the Broe book as cancelled.

8. Field says: "Miss Barnes hated her father. All the rest followed from that" (*op. cit.,* p. 31). This is a simplistic statement that fails to reflect Barnes' very complex feelings about her father.

9. James B. Scott, *Djuna Barnes* (Boston: Twayne, 1976), p. 16.

10. Scott was told by Djuna Barnes that both Ryder and Titus in *The Antiphon* are modeled on her father (Field, *op. cit.,* p. 185). In a recent conversation with me, Scott elaborated on this point, saying that Barnes told him that her father convinced her to allow a neighboring man to deflower her. Barnes held both parents responsible for this sexual abuse, and this remained a grievance.

11. *Ryder,* p. 219.

12. *Op. cit.,* p. 211.

13. *Op. cit.,* pp. 26f.

14. Scott, *op. cit.,* p. 20.

15. Djuna Barnes, *Nightwood* (repr. New York: New Directions, 1946), p. 1. Page numbers in the text refer to this edition.

16. In *Ulysses* we find such monstrosities as "Archjoker Leopold Rudolph von Schwanzenbad-Hodenthaler" [U. 12.559-60] and "Herr Hurhausdirektorpresident Hans Chuechli-Steuerli" [U. 12.566-7]; James Joyce, *Ulysses* (New York: 1984 [1922]), p. 252.

17. Susan Sniader Lanser, "Speaking in Tongues: *Ladies Almanack* and the Language of Celebration," *Frontiers,* 4 (1979), 39-46.

18. Cf. Lanser, *op. cit.*; Shari Benstock, *Women of the Left Bank* (Austin: University of Texas Press, 1986), *passim.*

19. Cf. Jane Marcus, "Laughing at Leviticus: *Nightwood* as Woman's Circus Epic," *Cultural Critique,* 13 (Fall 1989).

20. Scott, *op. cit.,* p. 24.

21. *Ryder,* p. 40; also cf. p. 117.

22. For this idea also cf. *Ryder,* p. 34.

23. Cf. Alan Williamson, "The Divided Image: The Quest for Identity in the Works of Djuna Barnes," *Critique,* 7 (1964), 58-74.

24. Eliot must have seen the parallel; was this his meaning when he recommended the novel to readers of poetry? He may also have been hinting that Barnes had reiterated his themes of wasteland and religious redemption, which is rather wide of the mark since it implies a Christian perspective.

25. Alan Singer, "The Horse Who Knew Too Much: Metaphor and the Narrative of Discontinuity in *Nightwood*," *Contemporary Literature,* 25 (1984), 66-87, here 70.

26. The nuns understand Robin to be beyond the reach of religion: "that they were looking at someone who would never be able to ask for, or receive, mercy" (p. 46).

27. Scott, *op. cit.,* p. 70.

28. Cf. Marcus, *op. cit.*; Benstock, *op. cit.*

29. James Baird, "Djuna Barnes and Surrealism: 'Backward Grief,'" in Kenneth H. Baldwin/David K. Kirby (eds.), *Individual and Community: Variations on a Theme in American Fiction* (Durham, N.C.: Duke Univ. Press, 1975), pp. 160-81, here p. 175.

30. *Op. cit.,* p. 178.

31. Cf. *Ryder,* p. 137.

32. Djuna Barnes, *The Book of Repulsive Women: 8 Rhythms and 5 Drawings,* first published in *Bruno's Chap Books,* 2, No. 6 (Nov. 1915), pp. 89-111; a pirated edition was published in *The Outcast Chapbooks,* No. 14 (Yonkers, N.Y.: Alicat Bookshop, 1948).

33. I wish to express my appreciation to Cara Chell, Shari Benstock, and to the McKelden Library of the University of Maryland for allowing me to make use of unpublished work. An article that was consulted, but is not cited in my article, is Ulrich Weisstein, "Beast, Doll, and Woman: Djuna Barnes' Human Bestiary," *Renascence,* 15 (1962), 3-11.

Karen Kaivola (essay date 1991)

SOURCE: Kaivola, Karen. "Djuna Barnes and the Politics of the Night." In *All Contraries Confounded: The Lyrical Fiction of Virginia Woolf, Djuna Barnes, and Marguerite Duras,* pp. 59-100. Iowa City: University of Iowa Press, 1991.

[*In the following essay, Kaivola emphasizes what she describes as a "contradictory split" running through* Nightwood, *stating that whereas the novel "undermines social control in order to produce a textual terrain rela-*

tively free from constraint," the characters are driven by a desire "to constrain or control others" or "to be controlled themselves."]

For Virginia Woolf, rhythmic, lyrical prose was an ideal form. With such prose she could accomplish contradictory aims: she could write toward subjects she felt were transgressive, taboo, and dangerous (the force of the unconscious, women's experiences and vulnerability in the world, female desires and sexuality), while she could, with an aestheticizing diffuseness, retreat from some of the more frightening and violent aspects of subjectivity such explorations necessarily involve. She could put into her fiction a sense of the struggle between prosodic and symbolic properties in language—and in such a way as to suggest the force of a desire capable of destroying culture while achieving, paradoxically, in her own work a highly sophisticated form of cultural expression. She could reveal and conceal her subjects. By way of contrast, Djuna Barnes's *Nightwood,* although diffuse in the sense that it maps the irrational "night world," is anything but an aesthetic retreat from the violence of sexuality and desire. By delving into the "heart of darkness" without the limitations of the boundaries formed by Woolf's internalized restraints, Barnes produces a force fueled by conscious and unconscious desire, obsession, and violence. This force shatters any aestheticizing qualities characteristic of lyricism, though Barnes's work, like Woolf's, owes much of its intensity to contradictory impulses.

Nightwood maps regions of female subjectivity and desire much more explicitly than Woolf's fiction. Like Woolf, Barnes is interested in what has not been previously explored, but she takes the whole enterprise of mapping female subjectivity and desire further by writing directly of the power of unconscious forces in structuring desire. She uses desire as a force to exceed what is rational or contained. For Barnes, desire cannot be contained by definitions any more than it can be made to conform with socially legitimized ideals. Because to some extent demonic, it overturns such ideals and the discourses that sustain such ideals, including those with which Nora initially fashions herself. But Nora's way of seeing the world is severely curtailed and thus flawed, as we come to see given the ways *Nightwood* critiques and parodies the use of dominant discourses to territorialize and thus control feminine desire and subjectivity.

Nightwood shows that, inscribed by forms of power that structure society and sexuality, desire is formed in relation to and yet always exceeds such powers, including psychoanalysis, religion, ideas of what constitutes gendered subjects and gendered behavior, and institutionalized heterosexuality. It resists imperialistic discourses and impulses by refusing formulas or simplistic, reductive categories of human subjects; it subverts the powers that operate by classifying human subjects and experiences in order to define and privilege certain configurations of health, sexuality, gender, ethnicity, or religion. For all these reasons, the text is deeply disturbing. But even more unsettling are the ways the text seems strangely in collusion with what it ostensibly critiques. *Nightwood* takes shape along contradictory lines: not only does its fantastical prose explode dominant discourses with the force of desire, it to some extent reinscribes key components of fascistic discourses. The text's language seems at once subversive and complicit, comic and tragic, sexist and feminist, racist and not racist, ahistorical and historical. Cannot, Matthew asks, "a beastly thing be analogous to a fine thing if both are apprehensions?" (125). It would seem so: in *Nightwood* such oppositions collapse, producing a fearful force of unusual intensity.

While Barnes was more open than Woolf with respect to transgressive subjects, she was not free from all constraints. Whereas for the most part Woolf experienced what restrained her from writing what and as she liked as internal constrictions, the restraints Barnes experienced were largely external. She could and did write of the "night world" and the violence of desire as experienced by women. But unlike Woolf, she did not have the means to publish her own work. Her ostensible freedom was comparatively curtailed. To a greater extent she simply *had* to care at some point what others, particularly publishers, thought. The story of *Nightwood*'s publication, a story of such restraints, is a tale of male power and prerogative, of masculine cultural authority. What we have to work with is, as a result, a problematic text.

In 1935, after a frustrating and unsuccessful attempt to find an American publisher (a period of time, in Andrew Field's words, when the manuscript "did not even suffer the usual agonizing delays but shot in and out of the publishers' offices as though it were being ejected from a greased revolving door in an old silent movie" [207]), Barnes's manuscript reached T. S. Eliot at Faber and Faber in London. Like some of the American editors, Eliot told Barnes that in order for the manuscript to be published sections would have to be cut. So Barnes gave Eliot the freedom to edit as he wished. Critics report variously about the extent to which he exercised this privilege. Field claims Barnes had written 190,000 words and that she herself cut it to 65,000 before the manuscript reached Eliot. (The published version is roughly 50,000 words.) According to Field, Eliot "concentrated mainly on paring down the part of the doctor who he was anxious should not be allowed to steal the main attention in the novel" (212). But recent feminist analyses interpret the evidence in Barnes's manuscripts differently. Shari Benstock claims Eliot reduced the manuscript by more than two-thirds and eliminated—"among other things—scenes that expressed explicit lesbian rage and virulent anticlerical sentiment" (428).[1] If the extent of Eliot's role is for the moment somewhat controversial, even mysterious, still it is certain that he influenced the final form of Barnes's major literary text.[2]

The title *Nightwood* was Eliot's idea. It is a rich and resonant title for this text, and Barnes apparently accepted it quickly and easily. As Field points out, it is easy to imagine Barnes's delight at Eliot's proposal "with its unwitting secret watermark of Thelma's name in it" (212). For it has been supposed by many that Thelma Wood, Barnes's lover in Paris, inspired the fictional figure of Robin Vote, the strange, nocturnal, and haunting presence around which other figures circulate.[3] At the same time, *Nightwood* suggests Nora Flood: in her "there could be seen coming, early in her life, the design that was to be the weather-beaten grain of her face, that wood in the work; the tree coming forward in her, an undocumented record of time" (50). The title thus links Nora and Robin, who are in fact intimately connected since, for Nora, Robin comes to symbolize her own unacknowledged and unconscious desires.

In yet another sense the title resonates with the Night Town episode in Joyce's *Ulysses,* for *Nightwood* rewrites Night Town's withdrawal of rationality. Leopold Bloom's experience in Night Town is episodic—it's just a temporary excursion into the world of the night; Bloom returns to the rational world empowered and renewed by his experience. *Nightwood*'s withdrawal from rationality is not episodic but virtually entire: it ventures further away from the meaningful constructs of culture throughout the entire text. But however appropriate the title, a feminist critic is likely to feel, as I do, somewhat uneasy about Eliot's involvement with *Nightwood*. Although he and Barnes maintained a connection over the years following its publication and although he admired *Nightwood* more and more, as Jane Marcus puts it, "Like Djuna herself, [one] feels ambivalent about Eliot's role in her life, and has a perverse desire to see the publication of the whole manuscript of *Nightwood,* to find out what it was like before the editorial red pencils cut it down to size" ("Carnival" 6).[4]

The story of *Nightwood*'s publication reads as Barnes's struggle to have her expression made public against considerable odds. Likewise, the text itself maps Nora's fight to find her own voice despite all the forces, including social and cultural conditions, that conspire to prevent her from finding it. Nora's love for Robin, a woman who is both different from and the same as herself, is intimately connected to her effort to articulate and know herself in ways not previously charted by culture or in its texts. A product of an American heritage and its puritanical values, Nora admits only to rational qualities, which, in combination with her attempts at self-justification, make her largely unknown to herself. We are all, to some extent, unknown to ourselves: *Nightwood* writes toward this unknown, toward those aspects of ourselves that we cannot know because they cannot be put into language or given a final, fixed form. But Nora's situation is different, for a woman who loves and desires another woman would not, especially in the early twentieth century, find many cultural texts or artifacts to help her articulate her own experience and difference from the heterosexual norm.

Given Nora's struggle to articulate her own version of her identity and experience and to speak of these things to Matthew O'Connor, a male whose compulsive need to speak is overwhelming and often threatens to drown Nora's voice entirely, Eliot's influential involvement with *Nightwood*'s publication seems eerily prefigured in the text itself. That is the case, however, with an important qualification: Matthew's authority is effectively undermined, whereas Eliot's authority to determine the shape of *Nightwood* was definitive. Matthew does not prevent Nora from speaking her own truths. Little about Matthew is legitimate or powerful, though he is sought after by the marginal figures in the text. In contrast, Eliot was a person of considerable influence and cultural power. We read Eliot's edited version, and some even argue that it is only owing to Eliot's endorsement that Barnes's work is recognized at all.

Many voices speak in *Nightwood,* undermining the authority of any one position and producing a contradictory and heterogeneous discourse composed of an amalgam of styles and perspectives. Some are fascistic, some are not. What Jane Marcus has called its "carnival of voices" represents the strength of social authority as well as resistance to it, the constructed nature of that authority along with the desire for a more authentic "natural" authority, and subjects produced by and in social configurations in such ways that they resist and desire their own captivity, subjection, and purification. That is to say, they perpetuate and thus are in collusion with structures that produce dominance and subordination. Whereas on the one hand *Nightwood* undermines social control in order to produce a textual terrain relatively free from constraint, on the other the figures who populate this terrain are anything but free from a will to power: they want to constrain or control others—or to be controlled themselves. This radical split runs throughout the text like a geological fault line under its performative surface.

Nora is a good example of this contradictory split, for she is in collusion with the repressive structures she ostensibly opposes. She wants power, but when she goes to Matthew to learn of the night, for she has been unwilling or unable to risk experiencing it directly, she grants him what the text denies him: the authority of a doctor, priest, or prophet. Her intent is self-serving. She wants him to somehow validate the unique intensity of her own pain, as well as her desire to set limits on Robin (who mirrors unacknowledged parts of herself), in ways that will return power to herself. Her will is voracious. She insists upon the difference of her relationship with Robin, and yet she perpetuates heterosexual structures and ways of being in that relationship. She wants to control Robin, to possess her. She wants to believe they are precisely the same, even as she recognizes their differences.

Robin too is contradictory. Although she rejects Nora's possessiveness, she also wants to be protected by Nora's love, as is illustrated when she pleads, "You have got to stay with me or I can't live" (143). To some extent complicit with the possessive mechanisms operating between them, Robin also wants to destroy these mechanisms in order to be "free." When Nora tries to keep strangers' hands off Robin, Robin lashes out at her, running behind her for blocks accusing "with a furious panting breath, 'You are a devil! You make everything dirty! . . . You make me feel dirty and tired and old'" (143).

With Robin, Barnes provides an alternate way of seeing Nora's puritanical and controlling impulses and finds a way to symbolize what exists beyond a culture that produces subjects so desperate and needy. This antithesis to culture, Barnes seems to suggest by linking Robin with both, is our future as well as our past. What makes Robin such a haunting and terrifying figure is that she embodies the antithesis of culture. Although she keeps "repeating in one way or another her wish for a home" (55), she cannot stay fixed within the confining architecture of any cultural construct. Perhaps she seems very much "alive" because always moving and compelling because she moves at the very limits of what the other characters dare to imagine, but she is tormented, an alarming creature who, because racked with pain, "sleepwalks" through life so that she will only half suffer.

Nora's life with Robin provides a temporary and tenuous escape from society and thus from history, which is impossible to escape absolutely or authentically. But for a time she is able to withdraw from the world into the more thrilling private place they construct together. This private world, like the text itself, is filled with signs of theater and spectacle: "circus chairs, wooden horses bought from a ring of an old merry-go-round, venetian chandeliers from the Flea Fair, stage-drops from Munich, cherubim from Vienna, ecclesiastical hangings from Rome, a spinet from England, and a miscellaneous collection of music boxes from many countries" (55-56). Their home is fantastical, eccentric, and theatrical, thrilling in its difference. These theatrical accoutrements and circus props indicate that their life together is all at once an escape from history, a retreat from life into art, something of a dramatic performance,

and a struggle to find a new form for a new relationship. Robin's speech is also linked with dramatic performance: "In the tones of this girl's voice was the pitch of one enchanted with the gift of postponed abandon: the low drawling 'aside' voice of the actor who, in the soft usury of his speech, withholds a vocabulary until the profitable moment when he shall be facing his audience" (38). The language is highly stylized and theatrical: Robin is described as "enchanted with the gift of postponed abandon" (38), a curious way to suggest that she withholds conversation and connection. Robin stages herself and keeps herself from being known apart from the way she chooses to present herself. The theatricality implies mystery, because what lies beyond Robin's guarded persona is unknown.

Like the house that Robin and Nora inhabit together and like Robin herself, the language of the text is theatrical, a performance. Robin and Nora's ambivalent relation to history and society is mirrored by the language of the text, which shares in the desire to be free from confinement. It frees customary symbolic restraints as it points toward the unknown. By fracturing syntax and sense it produces a certain intuitive but not literal sense. The language follows not *a* rhythm but many rhythms. It shapes without entirely containing its subject, as in the following passage describing Robin:

> The woman who presents herself to the spectator as a "picture" forever arranged is, for the contemplative mind, the chiefest danger. Sometimes one meets a woman who is beast turning human. Such a person's every movement will reduce to an image of a forgotten experience; a mirage of an eternal wedding cast on the racial memory; as insupportable a joy as would be the vision of an eland coming down an aisle of trees, chapleted with orange blossoms and a bridal veil, a hoof raised in the economy of fear, stepping in the trepidation of flesh that will become myth; as the unicorn is neither man nor beast deprived, but human hunger pressing its breast to its prey.

> Such a woman is the infected carrier of the past: before her the structure of our head and jaws ache—we feel that we could eat her, she who is eaten death returning, for only then do we put our face close to the blood on the lips of our forefathers.

> (37)

The passage begins by stating that the woman who turns herself into an image to be contemplated is the chief danger, but rather than explaining or elaborating this idea, it jumps to the very different idea of "beast turning human." A reader is immediately thrown off balance. The rest of the paragraph accumulates clauses without any kind of break. The effect is as disconcerting as the images described: "a mirage of an eternal wedding"; a cannibalism that includes us—"we feel that we could eat her"—collapses the structures of culture that separate us from prehistory. It is not possible,

Barnes suggests, to be radically different from our "barbarian" ancestors. Barnes challenges our sense of ourselves as rational individuals in the world, for the beast forces the retreat of both rationality and individuality. To deny this is to be like Nora, who is blind to the beast in herself but can sense it in Robin. And Barnes's point is more ahistorical than historical: this desire to "put our face close to the blood on the lips of our forefathers" transcends space and time. It is not explicitly linked to a particular historical context; its danger (arrived at through women like Robin) is universal.

In the final chapter, it is the language as much as it is what actually happens that gives the encounter between Robin and Nora's dog sexual overtones and thus positions it absolutely outside "normal" human behavior, producing a spectacle of transgression. More precisely, it is the rhythm of the language, which quickens with increasing intensity as Robin "goes down" in the chapel, approaches the dog, and, worse, against its will backs it into a corner:

> Then she began to bark also, crawling after him—barking in a fit of laughter, obscene and touching. The dog began to cry then, running with her, head-on with her head, as if to circumvent her; soft and slow his feet went padding. He ran this way and that, low down in his throat crying, and she grinning and crying with him; crying in shorter and shorter spaces, moving head to head, until she gave up, lying out, her hands beside her, her face turned and weeping; and the dog too gave up then, and lay down, his eyes bloodshot, his head flat along her knees.

> (170)

This prose depends upon and foregrounds rhythm and cadence: these nonsignifying properties, paradoxically enough, *do* signify. As the passage describes "shorter and shorter spaces" so too do its own clauses become shorter and shorter to produce a sense of sexual intensity. What occurs between Robin and the dog is alarming, frightening, a spectacle produced by a warp in the representational fabric of language.

With all its theatricality, language offers in *Nightwood* the alluring if ultimately illusive possibility of an escape from the materiality of history. This is one of the central contradictions that runs through *Nightwood,* cutting across a number of fields. Barnes's language may not offer the sometimes diffuse, aesthetic retreat of Virginia Woolf's, but it offers a different kind of escape into a spectacular shattering of discourse that is at once theatrical, performative, comic, and alarming. Its theatricality produces a sense of a more vivid reality, even as it destroys the notion that language is a transparent medium. It leaves us with a signifying surface that, because so transgressive and astonishing, fractures our expectations of how language represents the world. By making language theatrical—a performance or spec-

tacle—Barnes constructs a rift between language and experience, although this rift is not as self-conscious or explicit as it is in the writing of Marguerite Duras. Given what Barnes represents, in addition to the split between language and experience she also produces a dramatic gap between culture and its destruction, as Woolf will do (five years later) in *Between the Acts.* Here, as in *Between the Acts,* the split between culture and its destruction results in textual "erotics," language that moves along the line of fault formed by such a rift.[5]

In *Ariel and the Police,* Frank Lentricchia maintains that the desire for lyricism is a contradictory impulse. On the one hand, it responds to the cartography of imperialistic structures of containment and domination. The desire for lyricism—a "politics of lyricism"—produces writing without plot or historical subject, writing that does not conform to the structures of any philosophical system. On the other hand, it satisfies desires stimulated by consumer capitalism; such writing is an "improvisational song of desire, a writing about itself in the sense that the 'itself' is a longing as language eking itself out, each phrase a kind of blind adventure going nowhere, an infinite and exquisite foreplay" (202). Despite the Derridean overtones of his language, Lentricchia's point is more Marxist than deconstructionist: for Lentricchia, such writing reinscribes "the epic of bourgeois interiority, wherein the life of the spirit is hard to distinguish from the special sort of desire stimulated in the time and place of first-world consumer capitalism" (204). Our longing for lyricism, from this point of view, is a longing for an escape from the quotidian, the highly structured routines and rituals of our lives that leave so little room for play or spontaneity. What we want most, Lentricchia notes, is to be thrilled and captivated by such writing.

Barnes's longing to escape from history is expressed in *Nightwood* as a longing for the destruction of culture, and the language is indeed thrilling and captivating. The text provides for a reader something like the escape from the quotidian and the historical that Robin and Nora find in the theatricality of their own passion. Individual passions and pleasures take precedence over any kind of larger context or community. They and we withdraw into a space that is unusually complex, for in their relationship each plays the part of lover, mother, and daughter—and, for us as we read, other kinds of boundaries, such as those separating culture and its destruction, become blurred. Concomitant with this use of prose and retreat from society, however, is Barnes's insistence on the historical, on the concrete, undeniable, atrocious results of material conditions on subjectivities within larger cultural configurations. These are impulses Barnes links with culture as effects of culture, inseparable from it and especially from its horrors and atrocities. Therefore, the text is profoundly contradictory for the reader, who experiences the split between ahistorical impulses and historical imperatives.

When in 1932 and 1933 Barnes was writing what would eventually become *Nightwood,* she planned to call it "Bow Down: Anatomy of Night." Her use of "Bow Down" as a working title indicates that power, embodied either in individuals or social institutions, was central to her design. To bow down is to become humble to external authority, to collapse under the weight of overwhelming, insupportable grief. Field argues that the phrase "bow down" does not imply becoming humble to external authorities but instead points to "man's descent back into the kingdom of the animal, which is something both preferable to his human captivity and yet obscene" (183). In a sense he is right: the animal world does exert an extraordinary force here as a realm uninscribed by cultural forms of power and domination. It is a region unmapped and forgotten—or better yet, repressed—by culture; it is dangerous because it cannot be articulated and thus tamed by discourse and consciousness. It is fitting that Barnes chose the chapter title "Watchman, What of the Night" from Isaiah 21, for there the oracle cries: "My heart flutters, dread makes me tremble, the twilight I longed for has become my horror" (21:4). *Nightwood* explores the horror of the twilight—the loss of consciousness, the destruction—we long for. To descend back into the animal kingdom is to move toward a place uninscribed by history—it is prehistory brought into the present and thus made ahistoric. Because it preexists language, it cannot be known through language. It is a place unstructured by hierarchy: difference is horizontal, not vertical. Therefore there are no clear distinctions between good and evil, humans and beasts, or masculine and feminine. For all these reasons it is alluring, terrifying, and distinctly not human.

At the same time that it is ahistorical, the text records events with historical specificity. It, like Isaiah, links degradation, destruction, and bowing down to the painful survival of the Jewish community, a particular group of marginalized people. This connection is perhaps most apparent in Guido and his son Felix, although all of *Nightwood*'s figures are constantly bowing down or "going down." The effects of exclusion, subjection, and vulnerability are personally and socially devastating, as we see in the initial portraits of Guido. This evidence of pain produced by historical circumstances contradicts those aspects of the text that seem ahistorical or universal.

Nightwood begins in 1880 with the birth of Felix Volkbein, Guido's son, "in spite of a well-founded suspicion as to the advisability of perpetuating that race which has the sanction of the Lord and the disapproval of the people" (1). The narrative voice is ambivalent. What are we to make of the narrator's claim that such a sus-

picion is "well-founded"? Written in the 1930s during a period of increasing political fascism in which Hitler rose to power, the context for such language was anything but politically neutral. If the passage is glossed as a general negation of human life by making "that race" include all races, if it is made into a metaphorical expression of modernist despair about culture and humanity, then the specificity of the passage, its particular form of anti-Semitism, is lost. Embedded in such a reading is a naturalizing, ahistorical view of human pain and despair: it claims that social, political, and economic contexts have no place in the production of human subjectivity, happiness, or suffering. Although *Nightwood* was read in the socially and politically conscious 1930s as aesthetically apolitical and even self-indulgent in its *exclusion* of relevant social and political commentary, the ways that conflicting voices in the text articulate sexual difference and Jewishness are very much political, though contradictory and disturbing because supportive of anti-Semitic impulses. At the same time, the politics of Barnes's life and art, while highly individualistic and not always consistent, shows signs of a sensitivity to institutions or individuals taking control of others' bodies and minds.[6]

Regardless of evidence from Barnes's life that demonstrates her resistance to fascistic forms of control, it is often quite difficult to determine her attitudes toward power and violence from her writing, and not just in *Nightwood.* In *Ladies Almanack* the question gets formulated in terms of her attitude toward the female body and lesbian love, which critics read not only in divergent but diametrically opposing ways and which is of interest given Barnes's own willingness to cross a cultural taboo and love another woman. (Even here, her attitude is contradictory: Barnes would say later in her life, "I'm not a lesbian. I just loved Thelma" [Field 37].) Many readers (myself included) read the *Almanack* as a celebration of the female body and lesbian love, while others have proposed that it is instead a fierce attack on lesbianism.[7] Since the book was written for the private amusement of those very women (Natalie Barney and company) it caricatures, whom Barnes knew in Paris, the latter reading is less plausible.

But the text is playful, satiric, and perhaps ambiguous enough to support opposing interpretations: it provides an especially vivid example of how a reader's own values and perspectives work to influence the positions she or he assumes. Even among those whose readings are more or less similar, reactions to particular scenes differ for complex and subtle reasons. Susan Sniader Lanser, for instance, who also reads the text as a private celebration, admits to discomfort with the final scene, which I find much more humorous than disturbing.[8] In this scene, Evangeline Musset (who is modeled on Natalie Barney) dies and her body is burned; only her tongue survives. The women rush to the ashes with a "great Commotion, and the sound of Skirts swirled in haste . . . but Seniorita Fly-About came down upon that urn first, and beatitude played and flickered upon her Face, and from under her Skirts a slow smoke issued, though no thing burned. . . . And as the day came some hundred Women were seen bent in Prayer" (84). As Lanser notes, the "glorification of the tongue as the ultimate sexual instrument must surely have provided an antidote to the ethos of phallic supremacy and clitoral insufficiency of a newly Freudian age" (44).

Here women are reduced to their genitals, and the reduction both mirrors and becomes strangely subversive of modern patriarchal culture's fetishization of the female body. Since the women's pleasure is not heterosexual, Barnes does not simply reflect patriarchal structures, and so she makes room for a position outside those structures, a position capable of subverting the authority of masculine discourses. In *Nightwood,* Barnes comments on the sort of comic attitude she uses in both texts as a defense against vulnerability and painful exposure. The passage describes Nora: "Cynicism, laughter, the second husk into which the shucked man crawls, she seemed to know little or nothing about" (53). (And if Nora is often read as a portrayal of Djuna Barnes, at least in this area Barnes was not at all like her character. Given the dark comedy of Barnes's writing and the stories of her quick wit, guarded privacy, and distance, this second husk seems to have been something she knew well.)

When the narrative voice in *Nightwood* seems to share the perspective of fascistic ideologies, it is more disturbing than Barnes's ambivalence in *Ladies Almanack.* It is even more troubling since Barnes refused to admit any connection between politics and the text, which suggests that any inscriptions of fascistic ideologies were politically unconscious on her part. Field reports that in later years Barnes "reacted violently to suggestions that the 'decadence' of *Nightwood* had anything at all to do with the spirit of Nazism" (15). She insisted on its separation from the most significant political events of its context. It is not surprising that Barnes's refusal to grant any connection between her art and the political contexts that surrounded it deeply troubles her critics who oppose fascism. Shari Benstock notes that Barnes's claims notwithstanding, the figures who populate *Nightwood* are precisely those who would be targeted by Hitler (426). She's right; against the "superior race" that would build the new society, these groups were defined as antisocial, undesirable elements and categorized in precise groups—for example, Jews, homosexuals, and transsexuals—or simply as inferior because physically weak or mentally different, like Felix and Robin's son Guido. More precisely, however, it is Barnes's treatment of these groups in the text that unravels the fixity and authority of fascistic discourses and positions; such treatment contradicts and ultimately

subverts whatever fascistic traces remain. Without disputing that *Nightwood* seems at times strangely in collusion with discourses that contain and exclude and without attempting to apologize for this tendency, I would argue that the text, despite contradictions which have not been adequately addressed in the criticism, also attempts to subvert fascism. For example, its refusal of discourses that categorize and purify is apparent in the ways it represents marginality.

Jews, like lesbians, are made marginal by the dominant culture: whatever seems damning about either is produced in relation to a different norm established by that culture. Guido suffers from his sense of Jewish marginality and his haunting memories of how Christians have persecuted his ancestors. The yellow-and-black handkerchief he carries symbolizes the ordinance of 1468 which decreed that

> with a rope about its neck, Guido's race should run in the Corso for the amusement of the Christian populace, while ladies of noble birth, sitting upon spines too refined for rest, arose from their seats, and, with the red-gowned cardinals and the *Monsignori,* applauded with that cold yet hysterical abandon of a people that is at once unjust and happy, the very Pope himself shaken down from his hold on heaven with the laughter of a man who forgoes his angels that he may recapture the beast. This memory and the handkerchief that accompanied it had wrought in Guido . . . the sum total of what is the Jew. He had walked, hot, incautious and damned, his eyelids quivering over the thick eyeballs, black with the pain of a participation that, four centuries later, made him a victim, as he felt the echo in his own throat of that cry running the *Piazza Montanara* long ago . . . the degradation by which his people had survived.
>
> (2)

Guido possesses concrete historical evidence of the persecutions Jews have been subjected to, of his own marginality. In the present, such formerly public symbols are private and isolating: they cannot be read by Guido's Christian wife, Hedvig, whose demeanor is militaristic and foreboding. His knowledge of the past separates him psychologically and emotionally from the dominant Christian world. Even though far removed from the run in the Corso, Guido can still feel "the echo in his own throat of that cry . . . the degradation." Because he internalizes his culture's definitions, he is to himself always an outsider, always on the margin. His options are curtailed by having been produced by that culture, and his choice—perhaps a poor one—to attempt to span this impossible gap with various pretenses is alienating as well as sad and futile. If, as the narrator claims, "the saddest and most futile gesture of all [was] his pretence to a barony" (3), this is because he attempts to become absorbed into the dominant culture and complicit with his persecutors.

His attempt to fashion a new identity is not particularly successful. It forces him to pretend to be radically different—with respect to ethnicity, class, and religious origins—from what he is. In addition, Guido adopts the sign of the cross—a symbol of the very group that oppresses him—and produces various signs to support his pretense to be a Christian baron: a coat of arms, a list of Christian progenitors, even portraits of Gentiles he claims are his parents. These portraits bear a superficial physical resemblance to him but are in fact "reproductions of two intrepid and ancient actors. Guido had found them in some forgotten and dusty corner and had purchased them when he had been sure that he would need an alibi for the blood" (7). But the most profound resemblance is that he is just as much an actor as they. However paranoid Guido's purchase of the portraits as an alibi for his heritage may seem, it can hardly be considered such, given what the years following the publication of *Nightwood* would demonstrate in the most unimaginable and horrible terms.

If Guido's acquisitions are attempts to be part of the dominant culture, one of the most powerful ways Barnes subverts that culture is through a refusal of the labels and titles that reproduce an oppressive status quo. Initially, Guido is described by the narrative voice with very little compassion as "mentally deficient and emotionally excessive, an addict to death; at ten, barely as tall as a child of six, wearing spectacles, stumbling when he tried to run, with cold hands and anxious face . . . trembling with an excitement that was a precocious ecstasy" (107). Guido becomes from this point of view "deficient" because he is different. But "deficient" and "excessive" are not value-free terms: they inscribe hierarchy, not just difference. Guido can be "deficient" and "excessive" only in relation to some preconceived ideal. In this case the ideal seems to be one of mental and physical strength, competence, and control. Guido does not meet these standards, and the narrator judges harshly his failure to do so.

Felix takes a different stance: as he says to Matthew O'Connor, Guido "is not like other children, not cruel, or savage. For this very reason he is called 'strange.' A child who is mature, in the sense that the heart is mature, is always, I have observed, called deficient" (115). Felix treats Guido kindly: he is, astonishingly enough given his hopes for a son like himself, able to put aside his wishes in an effort to accept Guido as he is and, more, as someone different from himself whom he cannot understand. So, although Felix is "startled out of himself" when Guido speaks of wanting to enter the church, Felix buys him a metal Virgin and learns more about Catholicism: he does not insist on shaping his son into an image of himself, which is precisely what one expects will happen when he tells Matthew of his desire for a son "who would feel as he felt about the 'great past'" (38). Although Guido's preoccupation with Catholicism does suggest a fascination with a continuous tradition that links the past to the present, he is not

obsessed with the same kind of cultural and aristocratic past that haunts Felix. His religious tendencies connect him with his mother and thus, ironically, since Catholicism is powerful in modern European culture, with her exteriority, for his actions echo Robin's earlier—if less successful—attempts at conversion. Thus, he is displaced by his associations with both mother and father.

Curiously, Matthew appears to use language reminiscent of the narrative voice but manages to shift the way that language signifies. When he says that "with Guido, you are in the presence of the 'maladjusted,'" he quickly adds tha he is not "using that word in the derogatory sense at all" (116). With such a qualification he separates himself from the narrator and the tendency to write others off by labeling them in simplistic ways. Unlike the narrator, he does not intend "maladjusted" to be understood as a clinical, confining term. Both Felix and Matthew attempt to articulate Guido's value, even though they acknowledge their inability to understand him completely and even though Felix is troubled and anxious because other people say Guido is "not sound of mind" and because he "does not grow up" (120). Matthew's response connects (in a rather wonderful way) Guido with the text's more general affirmation of the possibilities in the unknown:

> The excess of his sensibilities may preclude his mind. His sanity is an unknown room: a known room is always smaller than an unknown. If I were you . . . I would carry that boy's mind like a bowl picked up in the dark; you do not know what's in it. He feeds on odd remnants that we have not priced; he eats a sleep that is not our sleep. There is more in sickness than the name of that sickness. In the average person is the peculiar that has been scuttled, and in the peculiar the ordinary that has been sunk; people always fear what requires watching.
>
> (120)

Through his "excessive" feelings, Guido is linked with the feminine and thought to be mentally unstable. In order to alleviate Felix's discomfort with Guido's difference, Matthew produces the wonderful image of Guido's mind as a bowl whose contents, though unknown, may be valuable nevertheless. He points out that much is not contained by the signs people use in order to make sense of the world: word and thing are not identical, and for some things we have no words at all. He warns that we must proceed cautiously and refuse to rob others of their subjectivity with clinical labels constructed in what Michel Foucault has called the discourses and disciplines of knowledge and the will to truth.[9]

In "The Discourse on Language," Foucault proposes that "in every society the production of discourse is at once controlled, selected, organised and redistributed according to a certain number of procedures, whose role is to avert its powers and its dangers, to cope with chance events, to evade its ponderous, awesome materiality" (216). For example, not every topic can be spoken of, and not everyone can speak of subjects not forbidden. As a culture we set up various procedures to qualify or authorize members of society to use specialized discourses. In this way, the "danger spots" of politics and sexuality are controlled and brought into discourse in particular ways, so that it is actually *in discourse* that they exercise their power. For Foucault, discourse is not just the "verbalisation of conflicts and systems of domination, but . . . the very object of man's conflicts" (216).

There are serious problems, however, with imagining discourse more material than actual social conditions. To emphasize the power of language to the exclusion of material social conditions or, worse, to equate language with those conditions and suppose that a change in language will improve oppressive social conditions are finally conservative gestures. As Hal Foster insists, however seduced we may be by "ideas of historical ruptures and epistemological breaks, cultural forms and economic modes do not simply *die,* and the apocalypticism of the present is finally complicit with a repressive status quo" (*Recodings* 1). *Nightwood* breaks with the conventional language and subjects of fiction, but as I've noted previously, it doesn't follow that Barnes was an activist. And as Benstock states, the living and writing patterns not only of Barnes but of other women writers such as Jean Rhys and Anaïs Nin reveal "complex reactions *against* the call to social and political involvement in the period. In a political climate that demanded social relevance in literature, these women writers . . . seem to exploit an entirely private, even secret, female experience" (424). Similarly, to make discourse the "very object of man's conflicts" can be a way to retreat from social exigencies.

Yet discourse has some material effects, and it can be a site of resistance. Foucault also maintains that the West uses discourse as a vehicle for power in the form of a will to truth. The use of labels and the containment of subjectivities are two manifestations of this will to truth. Barnes refuses to let the language of *Nightwood* serve as a vehicle for power: labels are suspect and subjectivities exceed categorization and purification (which provides, perhaps, some indication why she refused to use the term "lesbian" to describe herself). Similarly, Matthew disrupts and subverts the use of such a discourse for the workings of disciplinary power: his credentials are suspect; he refuses to sustain the illusion of a transparent relationship between word and thing.

But Matthew's sensitivity is not mirrored by the world at large (figured to a great extent by the narrative voice itself), and so his words seem, according to that more conventional world and its attitudes, misguided. In his attempts to find a language capable of providing comfort and solace in a painful world, he does not care how hyperbolic he becomes in the process or even if he lies. Truth is not his intent, and he questions its relevance to a more humane and human-centered discourse. From normative perspectives, the "remedies" he offers come at the price of "true" knowledge. But from another, Matthew's discourse is antithetical to a fascist rhetoric that would crush difference and territorialize whatever threatens its control, whether explicitly or implicitly through the power of the unknown.

Matthew embraces the indeterminacy of the unknown. When he walks out on Nora, he encounters an expriest who wants to know "whether you were ever *really* married or not" (159). Matthew refuses the terms of the question:

> Should I know that? . . . I've *said* I was married and I gave the girl a name and had children by her, then, presto! I killed her off as lightly as the death of swans. And I was reproached for that story! I was. Because even your friends regret weeping for a myth, as if that were not practically the fate of all the tears in the world! What if the girl *was* the wife of my brother and the children my brother's children? . . . Who says she might not have been mine, and the children also? Who for that matter . . . says they are not mine?
>
> (159-160)

It is hard to tell whether the woman Matthew claimed he married and loved is really the wife of his brother or whether that is yet another fiction built upon a fiction. The expriest pressures Matthew to be definitive about fact and fiction because he wants to know, once and for all, "what is what." For Matthew, that kind of truth is irrelevant if not impossible to know conclusively. He implies that those we grieve for are products of our own fantasies and idealizations rather than "real" subjects as they might exist apart from our imaginings. Most of the weeping in the world is, therefore, just for one myth or another. Ultimately it makes no difference what is real and what is fantasy—at least with respect to human suffering and pain. To care too much about what is fact and what is fiction is to be "right down in the mud without a feather to fly with" (160).

If categories such as "the maladjusted" are attempts to fix identity in ways that not only can be articulated but also organized according to principles of exclusion and thus known and controlled, then Matthew's attempt to change how we use such terms mirrors the text's larger project of questioning human knowledge by propelling what we think we know into the unknown. It undermines individuals' efforts to produce, fix, and define identity with titles. When figures in the text use such categories or titles, their efforts to make sense or give shape express what they intend inadequately. Their efforts simultaneously suggest their desire to be what they are not, to be persons of social significance and power, and make them as well as their so-called legitimate counterparts in mainstream culture seem ludicrous. These counterparts, such as the Count, are exposed as just as dependent upon arbitrary constructs as are their "debased" reflections. Neither the powerful nor the powerless are immune to Barnes's critique.

Like his father, Felix calls himself Baron, but his attempt to attach himself with words to the aristocracy merely makes his exclusion from it more radical and absolute. The title provides no real clue to his identity but instead obscures it, putting more distance between word and thing, making his public self inauthentic. The imagined private self that would by contrast be authentic is so radically inaccessible as to be beyond articulation and knowledge, to be virtually nonexistent. Some, like Felix, attempt to redefine and thus subvert the categories into which they fall, but if Felix can hide his Jewishness and Matthew can hide his transvestism, others cannot hide and are persecuted simply because they are different or disabled. The weak are especially vulnerable, as we see most painfully when Matthew tells the story of Mademoiselle Basquette, a girl without legs who wheeled herself through the Pyrenees on a board. Her difference and disability are constantly apparent, and because her vulnerability is so visible she is prey to the likes of the sailor who rapes her and then puts her back on her board miles away from town.

Titles promise an escape from identity and vulnerability because they construct an artificial self for the subject, a wall between the person and the world. Significant human contact or community among the circus people is minimal, but Felix feels most at home with these people who have adopted estranging titles similar to his own. Like him, they have "seized on titles for a purpose. . . . They [take] titles merely to dazzle boys about town, to make their public life (and it was all they had) mysterious and perplexing" (11). Titles work to distance individuals from each other and from themselves and make them feel less vulnerable. When Felix clings to his title to "dazzle his own estrangement" (11), he makes a spectacle of his lack of identity.

Like Felix, Frau Mann takes a title (the Duchess of Broadback) to mask her lack of identity and produces an image or spectacle of herself instead. Her desire to see the living statues and the Count is an ironic comment on her own objectification and estrangement, for she fails to recognize the extent to which she is like them. Frau Mann describes the Count as "*something that must be seen*" (13, emphasis mine). Her discourse objectifies him, unconsciously reflecting the way she herself has been objectified and perpetuating oppressive structures. To look at objectified others is, for her, to gaze into a mirror:

> In her face was the tense expression of an organism surviving in an alien element. She seemed to have a

skin that was the pattern of her costume: a bodice of lozenges, red and yellow . . . red tights, laced boots—one somehow felt they ran through her as the design runs through hard holiday candies, and the bulge in the groin where she took the bar, one foot caught in the flex of the calf, was as solid, specialized, and as polished as oak. The stuff of her tights was no longer a covering, it was herself; the span of the tightly stitched crotch was so much her own flesh that she was as unsexed as a doll. The needle that had made one the property of the child made the other the property of no man.

(13)

Felix is intrigued by the notion that Frau Mann could have at one time been involved with the Count because she seems so utterly asexual. And she seems asexual because she has become dehumanized, identical with her work. Her trapeze costume *is* her skin; it runs through her tissue like the design that continues on the inside of hard candies; her crotch is covered over and sealed. Although "the property of no man," Frau Mann is still objectified, a commodity. It's her defining characteristic. Sewn into a form as rigid as a doll, there's no life, no desire, left. She escapes being contained and controlled as the property of some man, but subjection, Barnes suggests, is more complex than this.

Titles and labels signify not only the circumscription and control of consciousness but of the body as well. Perhaps to a greater extent than any other woman of her time, Barnes was able to write the body into language, and she did so in ways that expose and critique inscriptions of power on human subjects. Foucault links such an inscription of power to the development of capitalism. In order to analyze the signifying power of the body, *Discipline and Punish* traces transformations in the ways criminals have been treated in the West. Under the monarchies that preceded capitalism, punishment was directed against the offender's body in public, theatrical rites of torture orchestrated by the sovereign—all offenses were understood to be offenses against the sovereign. With the increasingly important status of property, the emerging capitalist state required new forms of punishment and control. At this time, Foucault argues, the implementation of social control shifted from directly controlling bodies through pain to controlling bodies through their minds with representations (such as the idea of pain and the mental torture produced by such an idea). In this appropriation of minds, the mind is inscribed upon as if it were a tablet. The shift occurred because modern capitalist society requires subjects who will respect not the authority of the sovereign but the authority of property. It requires subjects who will police themselves and who will, seemingly of their own accord, choose subjection.

In **Nightwood,** the effects of power on the body and consciousness are circular, for while one form of power controls the body through the inscription of consciousness, another controls consciousness by writing on the body. This interrelationship is apparent in Matthew's use of the black body to signify sexuality and depravity: he describes Nikka, who "used to fight the bear in the Cirque de Paris" crouched naked except for an "ill-concealed loincloth all abulge as if with a deep-sea catch, tattooed from head to heel with all the *ameublement* of depravity" (16). Written on Nikka's body are words and images of Western culture, a culture not his own but which has nonetheless inscribed his body and structured his mind: he is willing to fight the beast for the pleasure of white European audiences. By gazing at the spectacle of Nikka and the beast, such audiences can distance themselves from nonhuman qualities they project onto Nikka, from aspects of their own sexuality and their capacity for depravity. In their racism they are like the pope and the so-called refined Christian populace who witnessed the run in the Corso that haunts Guido's memory and significantly informs his understanding of what it means to be a Jew. Both instances are examples of how the irrational and demonic components of the unconscious are given legitimate, if horrible and indefensible, cultural expression.

That Nikka's body is literally inscribed emphasizes his subjection to white male culture and separates Barnes's portrayal from Matthew's. For she comments, however indirectly, on his signifying power and undermines it as natural or given by exposing it as culturally determined, whereas Matthew's discourse fails to suggest any such awareness. Although Nikka is made to signify sexuality, the writing on his body robs him of his own capacity for sexual pleasure. What he signifies is not equivalent to the fact of his situation. Matthew claims that despite this representation of virility, Nikka himself is impotent: "He couldn't have done a thing (and I know what I am talking about in spite of all that has been said about the black boys) . . . though (it's said) at a stretch it spelled Desdemona" (16). Matthew's discourse ("black boys") is racist. "Desdemona" suggests miscegenation and violence: what makes Nikka impotent may in fact be that his penis has been tattooed. That it is tattooed with a word that can only be read "at a stretch" (when erect) makes the word into an implicit warning and Nikka's impotence a form of punishment, a sign of the violence white male culture can inflict on the black man if he desires a white woman. In this way Nikka is dehumanized in order that he may produce cultural significance. He is like the living statues that Felix and Frau Mann come to see at Count Onatorio Altamonte's. Moreover, he consents to this use of his body: he performs willingly.

But by having Matthew use such language, Barnes runs the risk of seeming to adopt Matthew's dehumanizing stance herself. This portrayal produces an extraordinarily difficult and complex dilemma. The dilemma is similar to issues related to radical forms of performance art or film, which raise questions about whether the female (black) body can be used to deconstruct sexist (racist) representations or whether the mere fact of using the body perpetuates sexism (racism). Denaturalizing what seems natural or given is to intervene in the ideological work that such images perform in cultural contexts. And as Hal Foster notes, complicity is necessarily a part of any deconstructive enterprise. In a discussion of feminist art involved with Lacanian psychoanalysis, Foster argues that "if this work elicits our desire for an image of woman, truth, certainty, closure, it does so only to draw it out from its traditional captures (e.g. voyeurism, narcissism, scopophilia, fetishism), to reflect back the (masculine) gaze to the point of selconsciousness" (*Recodings* 8). A similar principle is at work in Barnes's portrayal of Matthew portraying Nikka. And yet this principle remains disturbing because it is in collusion with what it seeks to disrupt. It makes readers and viewers confront their own complicity and contradictory responses.

Barnes's treatment of male sexuality subverts conventional notions of masculinity, male power, and authority—and typical female responses to these notions. Those who at least initially seem more viril, Nikka and the Count, are impotent whereas Felix is "not sufficient to make [Robin] what he had hoped" (44). At the top of *Nightwood*'s social hierarchy, and thus its most socially and politically powerful figure, Count Onatorio Altamonte is titled, wealthy, white, heterosexual, and male. Felix's first encounter with a "gentleman of quality" is with the Count (12). But, although he hasn't given up the idea of sexual desire, the Count fears that he will become impotent. When he returns to the crowded house with a young girl in a riding habit, he immediately throws them all out. Matthew explains that it is "for one of those hopes that is about to be defeated. . . . Count Onatorio Altamonte . . . suspected he had come upon his last erection" (25). If this hope is "about to be defeated," the Count is already impotent.

In the most explicit rejection of masculinity and male sexuality, a rejection at once comic and poignant, the text's central male figure, Matthew O'Connor, takes out his penis and speaks to it, subjecting it to humiliation:

> I spoke to Tiny O'Toole because it was his turn; I had tried everything else. There was nothing for it this time but to make him face the mystery so it could see him clear as it saw me. So then I whispered, "What is this thing, Lord?" And I began to cry; the tears went like rain goes down on the world without touching the face of Heaven. Suddenly I realized that it was the first time in my life my tears were strange to me because they went straight forward out of my eyes; I was crying because I had to embarrass Tiny like that for the good it might do him.
>
> (132)

Given the phallocratic culture of the West, such an undoing of the sign of male power and privilege is rather delightful and liberating. At the same time, Matthew's pain is awful and heart wrenching.

The text's representation of differences in sexuality is its most effective undermining of oppressive cultural structures and of its tendency to seem strangely in collusion with such structures. The text's vanishing point is its undoing of institutionalized heterosexuality: it insists not only on Matthew's difference as a transvestite but on the difference of lesbian passion and love. In both cases the clinical labels attached to difference are subverted. And in both the feminine is privileged—heterosexuality is refused. It is when Robin's thoughts have wandered to other women that Felix finds her asleep after reading the memoirs of the Marquis de Sade. Initially a sign of indifference or boredom, her sleep turns to fear when she awakens to find Felix. She rejects his attempts to comfort her and pushes him away. It is as if her encounter with masculine rituals of sadistic sexuality and violence influences, perhaps even in part causes, her rejection of heterosexual marriage (something she seems to have drifted into more than chosen). Robin's initial indifference and subsequent fear make an important point: one cannot merely ignore oppressive structures or imagine them away. Robin's reasons for fear are justified. Even if Barnes's text subverts the dominant culture's phallocentric bias, other cultural texts (including Sade) do not, and, more important, a subversive text cannot in itself alter its cultural context (though it may contribute to such a project). *Nightwood*'s difference from that cultural context works most effectively against the traces of collusion with oppressive forces that riddle the text.

Like Guido, Robin is outside mainstream culture; even more, she is, like the beggar woman in Duras's *The Vice Consul,* antithetical to culture itself. An enigma more unreal than human, she is projected on the screen of the others' desires. Like Caddy Compson in Faulkner's *The Sound and the Fury,* she has no voice and functions as the object of others' desires: they create her. Unlike Caddy, however, Robin is not constructed as the product of masculine imaginings and projections, for, apart from her early marriage to Felix, she is desired by women or explained by a man who experiences himself as a woman. Although Robin's difference in sexuality propels Barnes's representations into an alternative textual space, at the same time Nora's and Jenny's possessive forms of love are not all that different from heterosexual forms.

Robin's difference from any human norm is established immediately through her connections with nature—with plants and animals—and her radical separation from what is enduring and traditional is established by her inability to convert to Catholicism, perhaps even to take it seriously. She prays in church, unable to "offer herself up," unable to be anything but what she is, unable,

too, to be anything but miserable. She is troubled by her "preoccupation that was its own predicament" (47). The exact nature of the preoccupation is never elaborated, which gives it the effect of being all the more powerful, like Robin herself, because so mysterious and undefined. Yet, in the midst of her misery, out of "some hidden capacity, some lost subterranean humour," when bowing down in church she laughs (47). Barnes does not attempt to explicate this hidden capacity for laughter, which is unmapped by consciousness or volition. But as Hélène Cixous suggests, women's capacity for laughter is a disrupting and disturbing force; it can be a refusal of patriarchal institutions such as the church, a refusal to march in line.[10] Although Barnes is not as utopian as Cixous, whose work is most valuable for its capacity to inspire rather than for its ability to be put to pragmatic uses, Robin's difference is underscored by her laughter, which shatters the silence of the church. Laughter may be dangerous and subversive but if it liberates her at all, it does so only in passing, for at the next moment she is sleepwalking once again.

As figures who subvert conventional gender roles, Robin Vote and Matthew O'Connor are not simply feminine and masculine respectively but are instead the "third sex." Robin, the "tall girl with the body of a boy," produces an androgynous image in her white flannel trousers and lacquered pumps. Biologically male, Matthew is "the last woman left in this world . . . the bearded lady" (100), "the other woman that God forgot" (143). Strangely enough, although literally bearded he is also more conventionally feminine, more defined by patriarchal discourses—which he internalizes in order to shape his femininity—than any biological female in the text. Unlike the women, his desires are shaped by what it has traditionally meant to be a woman: "No matter what I may be doing, in my heart is the wish for children and knitting. God, I never asked better than to boil some good man's potatoes and toss up a child for him every nine months" (91). No woman in the text has such desires—they do not knit, take care of men, or produce children. There is no Mrs. Dalloway or Mrs. Ramsey in Barnes's textual world. To some extent, then, Matthew's forms of femininity actually reconstruct cultural definitions of gender rather than subvert them.

To undo gender as it is constructed by culture is to move toward what culture represses. In this respect *Nightwood* echoes the Night Town of Joyce's *Ulysses* but with a twist, substituting in its title the natural image of wood for the cultural image of the town. The title suggests Joyce but points toward the differences between Barnes's and Joyce's treatment of the irrational and surreal, taboo desires, and what is so repressed by society that it can be approached only in the night, if indeed psychic structures will allow it to be experienced at all. For both, cross-dressing and gender inversions figure the absence of rationality and cultural order, as Sandra Gilbert and Susan Gubar have noted, though the significance of that absence is different in each.[11] Barnes and Joyce see the maintenance of dichotomized gender difference as essential to social order; in *Nightwood,* clothing articulates the limitations of equating gender with biological sex as part of a more general critique of "dressing the unknowable in the garments of the known." As representatives of the third sex, Robin and Matthew are more than simply feminine and masculine members of a particular social order. There is something *right* about the third sex, which, like the doll, is "sacred *and* profane" (142, emphasis mine).

In a review of Brenda Maddox's *Nora: The Real Life of Molly Bloom,* Carolyn Heilbrun writes that although Leopold Bloom is androgynous, "it is arguable whether or not Joyce could have allowed any woman, in or out of literature, to be so" (5). In Night Town, the inversion of masculine and feminine roles is not sacred and profane, it is simply profane. There is nothing sacred about Bella transforming into Bello, and Bloom's transformation into a woman signifies his maladjustment and the dangers of pushing androgyny too far. It thus plays into male fears of becoming too feminine and is instructive about what will happen as a result. As a woman, Bloom is exposed to a public spectacle of degradation, pain, and humiliation that eventually restores the rational, as symbolized by the male's assertion of his masculine sexual "rights" and priorities. The sadomasochistic ritual is Bloom's punishment for succumbing to what Bella, or Bello, calls "petticoat government" and for being dangerously "feminine" himself. It is a punishment and degradation that he (or his feminine self) desires.

Bloom's "femininity" is linked to a masochistic desire to be controlled, in both mind and body. He assumes femininity as a role; he plays out a fantasy that is but a part of who he is and that is radically different from his ordinary appearance in society. Bello responds in the anticipated and predictable sadistic manner demanded by the dichotomous structure Joyce puts into operation. Bello promises to make Bloom like one of his whores, a process that he will control by transforming Bloom's body: "As they are now, so will you be, wigged, singed, perfumesprayed, ricepowdered, with smoothshaven armpits. Tape measurements will be taken next your skin. You will be laced with cruel force into vicelike corsets of soft dove coutille, with whalebone busk, to the diamond trimmed pelvis . . . while your figure, plumper than when at large, will be restrained in nettight frocks" (535). As the female Bella becomes the male Bello, what emerges is a parodic expression of how modern patriarchal culture imagines, despises, and fears the female who assumes the male position of privilege and power. Bello puts his heel on Bloom's neck and commands: "Feel my entire weight. Bow, bond-slave, before the throne of your despot's glorious heels, so glis-

tening in their proud erectness" (531). In this episode Joyce asserts that in males feminine characteristics are twisted and skewed, as are masculine characteristics in females. Unlike *Nightwood,* the bowing down in Night Town is sadomasochistic; it is exclusively to the power embodied in an individual who is able to exercise that power over others' minds and bodies. The significance of bowing down is therefore much more limited and less heterogeneous than in *Nightwood,* where bowing down simultaneously signifies a number of contradictory actions, from bowing down to cultural authority to bowing down before the more overwhelming magnitude of the indeterminable to bowing down from the weight of insupportable grief.

Although the Night Town episode is surrealistic, it partakes of and remains within culturally constructed gender hierarchies. To be feminine here is to be degraded because women's minds and bodies are restricted and dominated by men. While in this presentation there is an implicit critique of such domination, Joyce does not explore the subversive potential of the victim or outsider: he instead explores the territorialization of those others, including the production of their own taboo desires. It is taboo for a man to express, as Bloom does, submissive, demeaning, degrading qualities that the culture defines as feminine. In this culture, as John Berger's analysis of Western art has shown, we are only comfortable when women express such qualities.[12]

Such degradation is very different from what we find in *Nightwood.* When Matthew dons women's gowns, it is not to engage in sadomasochistic, ritualized behaviors. In fact, as Nora describes it, the image becomes one of considerable power and strength: "Is not the gown the natural raiment of extremity? What nation, what religion, what ghost, what dream, has not worn it—infants, angels, priests, the dead; why should not the doctor, in the grave dilemma of his alchemy, wear his dress?" (80) If the gown empowers Matthew by giving public form to what he experiences as a private and unconventional reality, Bloom's temporary movement toward his own repressed desires and fantasies—irrational from the perspective of the dominant culture—empowers him in a very different, more conventional way. For it is after the Night Town episode that Bloom is able to restore heterosexual order by returning to a more assertive, conventionally masculine position: he is able to reassert himself sexually with Molly and resume their disrupted sexual relations.

As radical as its representations of differences in sexuality are, however, Barnes's text finally fails to escape oppressive cultural structures because of the ways such structures have always already influenced consciousness. For instance, by "wandering away" from heterosexuality, Robin does not simply walk into a lesbian utopia: her relationships with women are marked by violence, pain, and possessiveness. Her difference in sexual orientation is not liberating: it is women, not men, who seek to control her. By hopping from bed to bed she refuses to be possessed but leads a tortured life that precludes real intimacy.

One of the reasons for the failure of lesbian love to achieve a desirable alternative to heterosexuality in the text is that these women have internalized the violence toward and hatred of women in Western culture. Matthew describes the curses he's heard women scream at one another in the public toilets at night. Their anger is violent, and it is marked by self-loathing: "May you be damned to hell! May you die standing upright! May you be damned upward! May this be damned, terrible and damned spot! May it wither into the grin of the dead, may this draw back, low riding mouth in an empty snarl of the groin! May this be your torment, may this be your damnation!" (95). By damning the clitoris these women damn their own sexual pleasure as well as that of other women. They have been inscribed by the violence of Western society in ways that structure subjectivity and desire.

Nora's and Jenny's attempts to possess and dominate Robin are marked by violence that is especially acute when they are insecure about the extent or effectiveness of their control. They mimic the worst kinds of aggressive masculine behavior. After a desperate attempt to manipulate Robin during the carriage ride with Matthew, the English girl, and the child, Jenny proclaims that while men know nothing about love, women "should know—they are finer, more sacred; my love is sacred and my love is great" (75). Robin rejects this position of sameness and superiority simply due to gender and tells Jenny to shut up, that she doesn't know what she's talking about. Jenny embraces sexual difference in loving Robin but not Robin's difference from herself (or, more accurately, Jenny's idealized version of herself). In a desperate attempt to deny and control this latter difference, Jenny attacks, scratching and hitting Robin with a violence that the child, who watches the entire spectacle, finds intolerable.

It is from women, not men, that Robin receives her blows. Though she shies away from Felix after reading Sade, when she is struck by women it is as if she has no strength or will with which to protect herself. When Nora fears she cannot possess Robin, that "it is over," she strikes Robin as she sleeps, forcibly waking her. The horrible reality of her action torments Nora: "I saw her come awake and turn befouled before me, she who had managed in that sleep to keep whole. . . . I didn't know, I didn't know it was to be me who was to do the terrible thing! No rot had touched her until then, and there before my eyes I saw her corrupt all at once" (145). The change seems to occur entirely within Nora. She first idealizes Robin and then in her anger imagines

that she has the power to make Robin corrupt. Robin, however, is not pure or immune to violent impulses. Felix sees her holding their child Guido as if she were to dash him down to the floor. Nora finds her holding the doll that is their symbolic child in an identical posture. Although Robin brings her son down gently, she will later smash the doll, an act that challenges, symbolically, the way culture constructs the mother as unambivalently loving, devoted, and self-sacrificing.

Despite her rejection of motherhood and her attempt to destroy the symbol of the child she cannot have with Nora, Robin herself is frequently associated with childhood. Therefore, it seems fitting that she speaks most loquaciously with the child at Jenny's party and then later with a young English woman, for it is as if her more natural and comfortable connections are with the very young. Nora's belief that Robin was somehow unsullied and innocent until she, Nora, struck her awake reinforces this image. Similarly, Nora notices how childlike Matthew seems when she visits him in the night. She again casts herself as more experienced and knowing, even though she goes to him (at least at first) for what she thinks he can teach her. "You're so like a child," she says to Matthew (133); in reference to Robin she remarks, "I saw her always like a tall child who had grown up the length of the infant's gown, walking and needing help and safety" (145).

But Matthew is skeptical about childhood as a time of innocence, free from pain and cultural conditioning. And he reminds Nora that she herself knows better: "You know as well as I do that we were born twelve, and brought up thirteen, and that some of us lived" (152). Matthew asserts that childhood is an adult fantasy, that as a time of innocence and freedom it is largely imaginary. External pressures and cultural shaping are already at work. Still, childlike qualities reveal aspects of the self that have not been completely territorialized and produced by the dominant culture. To be childlike is to be toward the "other side" of how one will eventually be positioned and will position oneself according to the various categories of race, gender, and class.

Nora's dreams map the early conflict between unconscious desires and cultural taboos that in part produce contradictory impulses and show that such conflict and contradiction continue, assuming different forms in one's psychic life. Nora's dreams figure what desires remain too taboo to acknowledge; they also eclipse the emotional importance of the mother and suggest that the contradictory impulses of love and hate coexist. The first dream brings out the emotional importance of other women in her life, and re-creates the original moment of traumatic loss, the separation from her mother. It is a dream she has dreamt before but never before dreamt well. As if the original moment of separation from her mother were too painful even for a dream, her grandmother stands in for her absent mother. Nora confides that in her childhood she loved her grandmother more than anyone, but even if her relationship with her grandmother is so close, it does not account for the complete absence of her mother. After Nora's second dream Matthew notes her mother's absence and, projecting himself into her situation, responds with the cry, "It's my mother without argument I want" (149).

In the first dream, Nora is standing in a room that both seems and does not seem to be her grandmother's. Although her grandmother's belongings—portraits of her husband and writing instruments—are in the room, it nevertheless has the feel of the "nest of a bird which will not return" (62). Nora is left behind. Nora's desire to recover the lost closeness with her grandmother is an impossible desire: the complete connection she longs for with the woman she loved most cannot be realized, as her grandmother's absence—as well as her mother's—from the dream suggests. Robin takes the grandmother's place: it is the entry of Robin that makes it a dream that Nora knows she is dreaming for the last time. Yet, despite Robin's presence, she remains as inaccessible as the absent grandmother. Nora wants Robin to come into the room with her, "knowing it was impossible because the room was taboo. The louder she cried the farther away went the floor below, as if Robin and she, in their extremity, were a pair of opera glasses turned to the wrong end, diminishing in their painful love" (62).

Without this other, Nora fears she will cease to exist. Her grandmother is absent from the room Nora has constructed, and in this room Nora doubts her own existence. She longs to "put her hands on something in this room to prove it; [but] the dream had never permitted her to do so" (63). Nora does not specify what she wants to put her hands on, but if, as Jane Marcus maintains, she wants to touch the plume and inkwell, the dream points toward a belief that it is through language that she can produce a self.[13] At the same time, though, she recognizes that this enterprise involves doing something to Robin and to her grandmother, making them both "disfigured and eternalized by the hieroglyphics of sleep and pain" (63). To write is to disfigure and to eternalize, as Robin is disfigured and eternalized by the dreams and by Nora's conscious representations.

In the dream, triangles form between Robin, the grandmother, and Nora, but the identity of each merges with the others in a series of shifting and disfiguring substitutions. Nora seems indistinguishable from the grandmother in drag because it is Nora who orchestrates the dream and symbolizes Robin, who does something to her; Robin thus becomes like the child Nora, seduced by the grandmother; Robin and the grandmother are figured as cross-dressers and as women who are continually in the process of leaving the space that Nora has constructed for them. Nora's construction of a room that is not really her grandmother's mirrors what she does in constructing a space for Robin in which Robin cannot live. Thus it is hardly surprising that Robin is rarely there, even though they arrange their physical space together, for the psychic architecture that fits Nora simply doesn't work with her grandmother or Robin, no matter how close her bond with either one of them.

Nora's love is both homoerotic and incestuous: Robin—the forbidden whom she can't understand and who thus has the power to produce terror—is to Nora at once lover, mother, and child. Unable to admit the incestuous element in her love or determined to forget it, Nora represses it from consciousness but dreams it in the form of her grandmother. It is fitting that Robin, the new love, enters into this dream, making it "complete" even in its fragmented and disjointed quality, its series of substitutions.

The dream leads not to another dream but rather to a childhood memory of the grandmother encountered in a corner of the house, pointing to the basis of dreams in the material conditions and contexts of individual lives and the dreamlike quality of memory. Nora is not only abandoned, she is betrayed. Dressed as a man, Nora's grandmother approaches her with a "leer of love [and says] 'My little sweetheart'" (63). Two forbidden loves converge, one homosexual, the other incestuous. Her beloved grandmother, "for some unknown reason" in tight trousers and red waistcoat, suddenly betrays her by seeming unfamiliar, strange, and theatrical. That this image of her grandmother as a circus performer should appear to her after this particular dream suggests a symbolic connection between the events of the dream and memory. In addition, the image incorporates the love of Nora's adult life: a woman who dresses as a man, a woman she meets at the circus (hence her grandmother's outlandish outfit), and a woman whose love she cannot absolutely count on (like her grandmother who frightens her with a leer, awakens her sexually, and then betrays her by dying).

The image of the grandmother is, in addition, extraordinarily significant in the context of Barnes's own life. As Mary Lynn Broe notes in "My Art Belongs to Daddy," Barnes's relationship with her own grandmother, Zadel Barnes, was extremely complex. Broe examines letters Zadel sent to Djuna—letters that are explicitly erotic—and argues that Zadel seems to have both protected Djuna from her father (in the sense that she offered her an alternative, female-centered world) and violated her (by denying her "access to knowledge, to power, and her own voice. . . . At work is a seduction into family fantasies. . . . Boundaries are transgressed; the duty to protect and the right to use get irrevocably confused"

[48]). If in Woolf's *Between the Acts* incest is shaped to a great extent through allusion, in **Nightwood**'s dream scene Barnes more explicitly portrays a relationship with incestuous overtones. And she represents her experience of it as essentially ambivalent and contradictory. The grandmother is loved and hated, desired and feared. Barnes offers an experience of love that cannot be understood within existing cultural discourses on family structures and relationships but one that makes emotional sense within this particular family. For Woolf and Barnes, the dynamics of incest are represented in language that struggles against itself. While their language works to reveal an experience unshaped by existing "official" discourses, it simultaneously struggles to conceal what is transgressive and shameful.

When Nora awakens from the first dream, she must face the reality of Robin's betrayal. She looks out the window into the garden, where she is unable to distinguish Robin and Jenny, who are locked together in an embrace, from the lines and shadows of the statue of the "tall granite woman bending forward with lifted head" (55). In the ensuing moments of extremity, standing motionless like a statue herself, Nora peers into the "faint light of dawn" until her eyes meet Robin's and they stare at one another—each as if the other were a living statue. By bringing her lover into the garden outside Nora's window, Robin stages a spectacle for Nora's gaze—a spectacle that will make Nora a child whose trust is finally completely shattered. The horrifying and incontrovertible fact of Robin's betrayal seems not only quite literally evil but of sufficient magnitude to destroy Nora. She imagines that the force of her emotions will change this awful reality, that "the design would break and melt back into Robin alone" (64). Needless to say, though, her wishing for it does not make it so, and shortly thereafter Robin sails with Jenny for America.

After Robin leaves, Nora has to admit that the material and psychic spaces she has constructed for Robin don't work. She therefore seeks Robin on Robin's own ground, in the night at cafes, in Marseilles, Tangier, and Naples. It is when she sees a young girl who strikes a pose similar to Robin's, of half sleeping and half suffering, that she realizes what she has been to Robin: "Looking from her to the Madonna behind the candles, I knew that the image, to her, was what I had been to Robin, not a saint at all, but a fixed dismay, the space between the human and the holy head, the arena of the 'indecent' eternal. At that moment I stood in the centre of eroticism and death" (157-158). By getting outside herself and seeing herself from Robin's point of view, as a "fixed dismay" or a contradictory subject, Nora begins the painful process of deidealization. She sees herself not as pure, spiritual, and disembodied but in the split between body and spirit. She describes the place of this realization as the "centre of eroticism and death."

It is a place where desire connects not only with the annihilation of the ego and individuality but with the desire to destroy the other, the beloved. Robin flees from death, as Matthew suggests, by engaging in a succession of encounters to escape the kind of serious attachment that would force her to be aware of the inevitability of death and the hostilities that coexist with love.

Nora's second dream explicitly links eroticism and death and provides another way of understanding the seriousness and the terror of her involvement with Robin. In Nora's second dream her grandmother is dead, her father living, and she herself a figure in the dream who is asleep and unable to act. But the dreaming self observes what the dreamed self does not. This is a powerful image, for it suggests a nascent awareness of herself as unseeing and the beginning of a new understanding of that unaware self. What the Nora who sleeps in the dream cannot see the dreaming Nora does:

> There in my sleep was my grandmother, whom I loved more than anyone, tangled in the grave grass, and flowers blowing about and between her; lying there in the grave, in the forest, in a coffin of glass, and flying low, my father who is still living; low going and into the grave beside her, his head thrown back and his curls lying out, struggling with her death terribly, and me, stepping about its edges, walking and wailing without a sound; round and round, seeing them struggling with that death as if they were struggling with the sea and my life; I was weeping and unable to do anything or take myself out of it. . . . It went on forever, though it had stopped, my father stopped beating and just lay there floating beside her, immovable, yet drifting in a tight place. And I woke up and still it was going on; it went down into the dark earth of my waking as if I were burying them with the earth of my lost sleep.

> (149)

There is an unusual intimacy in this dream between Nora's father and grandmother. Together they are visible to the world, especially to Nora, and yet insulated from it. Nora is unable to make her presence known to them, and when she awakes she wants to repress or bury the image of her father drifting in that tight place with his mother. Moreover, Nora recognizes his rage as something that *she* has done to her grandmother (after all, it is her dream), dreaming through her father. And it is something she has done to Robin as well. The violent impulse is her own, though she fears and disowns it by projecting it onto her father. Within the context of what we know of the Barnes family's particular erotic arrangements, it is perhaps also indicative of Barnes's rage at both her father and grandmother, as well as her recognition of the complexities of the relationship between her father and his mother.

Nora's love for Robin becomes a figurative act of murder, which is something that Nora recognizes only gradually and with great difficulty. As soon as Robin is loved and inscribed on Nora's heart, Nora "kills her" in order to possess her and preclude change. Robin ceases to exist, except ideally: "In Nora's heart lay the fossil of Robin, intaglio of her identity, and about it for its maintenance ran Nora's blood. Thus the body of Robin could never be unloved, corrupt or put away. Robin was now beyond timely changes, except in the blood that animated her" (56). The blood that animates Robin is Nora's, not her own. Thus, although Nora thinks she wants greater intimacy with Robin, her way of loving actually imposes an unbridgeable distance between them. This inscription of Robin is both beyond change and unreal, and as such it denies the constantly moving contours of what we call identity.

It is, as Nora's dreams demonstrate, in the night world that one most directly encounters the instability and contradictions of identity. Nora's refusal to admit Robin's difference despite and within the similarity of their female bodies speaks to a desire to confirm her own identity through an external love object of the same gender. It is a confirmation of their difference as a couple from the rest of the world. When Nora says, "She is myself. What am I to do?" (127) she means to suggest what she elaborates only later, that for a woman to love another woman is to break with institutionalized heterosexuality and the cultural narratives that produce it: "There's nothing to go by. . . . You do not know which way to go. A man is another person—a woman is yourself, caught as you turn in panic, on her mouth you kiss your own. If she is taken you cry that you have been robbed of yourself" (143). But Nora's language imitates the language of heterosexuality, itself an attempt to articulate similarity despite difference within the heterosexual tradition of romantic love, even while she tries to articulate her and Robin's separation from all that. As in *Wuthering Heights* when Catherine Earnshaw proclaims, "I am Heathcliff," Nora desires a similarity that transcends all external difference, sexual or otherwise—a likeness that implies her love includes a form of self-love that excludes difference and otherness.

Through these dreams Nora glimpses and thus gains access to herself in new ways. When she dreams of herself as asleep, she produces a figure of herself that is much like Robin. Robin is "la somnambule," the sleepwalker who is aware that she "belongs" to Nora, but it is also true that "if Nora did not make it permanent by her own strength, she would forget" (55). But whereas Robin half sleepwalks in order to half suffer, Nora struggles to be more awake regardless of the pain in the perhaps misguided belief that the history of her relationship to Robin can be changed, that a new story can be told. She both succeeds and fails, for part of what she must learn is that no matter how wide awake one becomes, there are limits to what one can know and what language can express—what one knows is always askew because of the imperfect correspondence be-

tween word and thing. What seems like truth to one is but a strange perspective to another, and the imposition of one's truths on others is a dangerous, violent, and ultimately unsuccessful enterprise. We cannot—and should not attempt to—control others' desires and behavior. Still, there are things Nora can and does learn: not everything is unknowable. For her to gain knowledge necessitates giving up the fantasy of herself as innocent. As Matthew says, "To be utterly innocent . . . would be to be utterly unknown, particularly to oneself" (138).

The power of the unknown is alluring. But to pursue it exclusively is to pursue perpetual innocence: it is to choose, by rejecting knowledge itself, to remain unknown to oneself in important ways. Perhaps the central contradiction in *Nightwood* rests here, in the power of the unknown to overturn virtually every form of knowledge—even epistemology as a human activity. This is ultimately a dangerous and repressive move. Matthew's discourse, because an infinite eking out of language, leads to confusion, to the compelling attraction of language as an embodiment of desire, to just this kind of embracing of the unknown. But Nora's goals are more pragmatic.

There is no end to the confusion in *Nightwood,* no final solution to the difficult questions the text asks about the possibilities available for subjects who resist oppressive and repressive cultural configurations with tremendous ambivalence and pain. It is as if the representations of differences in sexuality are constructed around a vortex which constantly threatens to suck all forms of human significance into its own emptiness. Nora resists its pressure, and in order to do so she must paradoxically rely on certain cultural forms that the text deconstructs, including psychoanalysis. Nora seeks to understand Robin's night world and to learn to speak her own story. "I'm so miserable," she tells Matthew. "I don't know how to talk, and I've got to. I've got to talk to somebody. I can't live this way" (129). Matthew does not, however, play the classical analyst to Nora's patient or priest to her confessor. Unlike the analyst who listens but rarely speaks, becoming essentially a blank screen upon which the patient projects fantasies, or the priest who listens in silence, Matthew fills up the text with his own monologues, believing that Nora and others will find comfort, if nothing else, in the distraction his speech offers. But even if his intentions are good, it is Matthew who is thus comforted, though it may be more accurate to say that like the others he is merely momentarily diverted. That his speech relieves his own suffering is especially apparent when his pain intensifies as Nora begins to discover her voice and insist upon more space for herself in their exchanges. Clearly this is the scene of neither analysis nor confession. Rather, these exchanges parody both psychoanalysis and confession. As Marcus points out, in *Nightwood* the doctor's womb envy is so strong that it parodies Freudian penis envy:

> The psychoanalyst's office is a filthy bedroom with a reeking chamber pot. Freud's famous totems, the sacred objects from ancient cultures that people his shelves and tables in H. D.'s famous tribute, are mocked by O'Connor's rusty forceps, broken scalpel, perfume bottles, ladies' underclothing and abdominal brace. The psychoanalytic structure is ruptured as the patient asks the question and the doctor answers. The doctor is in bed in a granny nightgown and wig, powdered and rouged, and the patient stands by his bed; it is three in the morning, not three in the afternoon. The patient is rational, Puritanical and analytical and the doctor is mad.
>
> ("Laughing" 233)

But madness is a concept to use with care here, and in some ways the result of their exchanges mirrors the desired result of analysis. Nora does learn how to speak and begins to give shape to what she has hitherto been unable to put into words. If she is not "cured"—for perhaps no cure is possible—she takes the authority of her own experience more seriously.

Early portraits of Nora describe her as one whose need to control her environment keeps her aloof. She is entirely nonjudgmental of others; she neither reproaches nor accuses. But this is because she keeps herself distant and different. While these qualities draw others to her, they also frighten them, for she merely reflects their own images back to themselves. Unable to insult her or hold anything against her, they are embittered at having to "take back injustice that in her found no foothold" (53). Her eyes are unseeing in that they impose a predetermined design on the chaos of experience: to others they are like "that mirrorless look of polished metals which report not so much the object as the movement of the object" (52). The world is as inaccessible to her as she is to it, for like the plays she attends it is "contracted and fortified . . . in her own unconscious terms" (52). As Nora herself is unconscious of the design she imposes on the world, she is unaware that it is a design at all. But in fact the "world and its history [are] to Nora like a ship in a bottle; she herself [is] outside and unidentified, endlessly embroiled in a preoccupation without a problem" (53).

Like Robin, Nora's preoccupation is her predicament, a predicament that seems to get resolved—or more accurately, turn into a different kind of predicament—by their contact with one another. Because their love exists beyond the prescribed categories of heterosexual culture, beyond the known and opposed to cultural prescription, it provides an impetus for change. Still, Nora and Robin are different as women and as lovers. Unlike Robin, Nora wants power and control. As she asserts,

"And I, who want power, chose a girl who resembles a boy" (136). They each play a part that for a time locks them together in a circular psychological drama. Robin's distance and self-sufficiency produce in Nora a desire for more closeness and make her neediness more intense, which makes Robin even more distant.

Yet Robin is not altogether distant from her surroundings. In marked contrast to Nora's aloof distance at the events of high culture—at plays and operas—is Robin's proximity to the circus, the opposite of high culture. Here, animals all but climb out of the ring at the spot where she sits. The caged lioness makes the connection between Robin and the animals even more pronounced: she bows down and regards Robin "as if a river were falling behind impassible heat; her eyes flowed in tears that never reached the surface" (54). Not only does the lioness acknowledge some painful bond between them, the image of Robin and the lioness is the inverse reflection of Nora at the theater. The former is incomprehensible but made powerfully alive and poignant in the language Barnes uses to describe it. The latter is understandable but dead.

Shari Benstock argues that in "mapping the inversions and subversions of sexual difference under the law that would enforce heterosexuality, Barnes's work anticipates (and simultaneously puts into question) the Lacanian notion that heterosexuality unwrites the very law of difference it would seem to put into place. That is, heterosexuality in Western culture is really a form of what has previously been defined as homosexuality: as a search for an image of the self, a search for the twin, a search for confirmation of one's identity through the double, a reinforcement of *sameness* under the guise of difference" (247). Nora is unable to distinguish Robin from herself. And yet, as Benstock notes, Barnes questions the way homosexuality is defined by traditional psychoanalytic theory. Nora's desire is to a great extent structured and influenced by patriarchal, heterosexual law—it is impossible for her to step outside culture to attain an ahistorical homosexual love. At the same time, her experience takes her outside the known, to what has not yet been written (though the text itself makes a contribution to getting it written). Unlike her grief, the forms for which she can borrow from theater, her sexual contact with Robin has no public form to appropriate, leaving her entirely on her own.

In psychoanalytic terms Nora's love—like all love—originates in narcissism but is transferred to an overvalued love object. This puts her in a "masculine" position, for women, Freud argues, generally love only themselves. It is roughly in these terms that Matthew reads Robin's narcissism. For Matthew, the narcissistic woman is characterized by the need to be loved rather than to love, by self-sufficiency, and by beauty. According to Matthew, "Every bed [Robin] leaves, without caring, fills her heart with peace and happiness. She has made her 'escape' again. That's why she can't 'put herself in another's place,' she herself is the only 'position'; so she resents it when you reproach her with what she has done. She knows she is innocent because she can't do anything in relation to anyone but herself. You almost caught hold of her, but she put you cleverly away by making you the Madonna" (146). Here Robin seems characteristic of Freud's narcissistic woman, who is frightening in her self-contentment and self-sufficiency. For Freud, such a woman does not need man's desire to please and desire herself. What is attractive about such women is their ability to maintain a primary narcissism that men give up but remain nostalgic for. However, Nora challenges the authority of Matthew's interpretation, as in the passage previously quoted when Nora realizes she was not for Robin the Madonna (as Matthew suggests she was) but rather a "fixed dismay . . . the 'indecent' eternal" (157).

Along similar lines, Sarah Kofman challenges Freud's interpretation of the narcissistic woman. Kofman points out that Freud does not pursue what his analysis in "On Narcissism" opens up: the possibility of conceptualizing women as criminal outsiders rather than as hysterics. As a criminal, "woman is the only one who knows her own secret, knows the solution to the riddle and is determined not to share it, since she is self-sufficient, or thinks she is, and has no need for complicity" (66). Instead he chooses a way of thinking that soothes male egos, that says that a woman is "completely ignorant of her own secret, [but is] disposed to help the investigator, to collaborate with him, persuaded that she is 'ill,' that she cannot get along without man if she is to be 'cured'" (66). Kofman states that at some level Freud knew otherwise, that women were—or conceivably could be—great criminals, not hysterics, but strove to "pass them off as hysterics, for it is very much in men's interest that women should share their own convictions, should make themselves accomplices to men's crimes, in exchange for a pseudo-cure, a poison-remedy, a 'solution' that cannot help being pernicious since it restores speech to women only in order to model it on men's, only in order to condemn their 'demands' to silence" (66-67).

In her proximity to the beast, her flagrant disregard of patriarchal, heterosexual values, and her "narcissism," Robin is a criminal outsider. She does not fit into psychoanalytic or other cultural categories, which is her disruptive strength. If she at times seems in collusion with oppressive social structures, she manages to break away—yet what she breaks away to seems alternately alluring and horrifying. If, as Kofman suggests, in a heterosexual society the demands put on female subjects to transfer their erogenous impulses from the primary love object (the mother) to the father produce the conditions that predispose women to neuroses and hys-

teria, such qualities are most evident in Robin when she's married to Felix and in Nora before she meets Robin. For it is then that the greatest repression is required by each. All this supports the idea that heterosexuality is a social but not a psychic norm. Robin and Nora are dissatisfied with the restrictive feminine sexuality that society encourages and sanctions; neither is neurotic nor hysterical in her playing of both "masculine" and "feminine" roles. In order to be neurotic or hysterical, one must operate within the social contract and according to the rules where such terms apply, and with *Nightwood* Barnes produces a context that displaces that social contract. To the extent that either Robin or Nora is neurotic or hysterical, it is owing to being trapped between the confines of culture and the destruction of that culture—to being in collusion, whether consciously or unconsciously, with it.

With *Nightwood,* Barnes works to find a language capable of breaking through to the other side of culture, to its destruction. Despite the contradictions and collusions in the text, to a great extent she succeeds. But what *Nightwood* simultaneously demonstrates is that it is virtually impossible to use language to represent an alternative that is not utopian without partaking in existing, sometimes oppressive cultural configurations.

Notes

1. Benstock's notes suggest she has drawn her own analysis from Jane Marcus's work with the original manuscripts, and she writes that Marcus's "preliminary findings suggest that Eliot was particularly uncomfortable with the connections Barnes drew between the expression of lesbian anger and societal institutions, particularly the church" (476n9).

2. The manuscripts for *Nightwood* are part of the Djuna Barnes collection in the Porter Room of McKeldin Library at the University of Maryland, College Park. There are various edited versions, which is perhaps why it is hard to separate changes Barnes initiated from changes initiated by Eliot. Given the rejection of the manuscript by so many publishers, it no doubt must have seemed preferable to Barnes to have it published in a reduced, altered form than not published at all. The library also holds a collection of correspondence between Barnes and Eliot, some of which discusses changes made to *Nightwood* and which may help in sorting all this out.

3. Like many modernists, Barnes drew on her life in Paris to create the context and atmosphere of *Nightwood*. Although it can be reductive to read a literary text strictly in terms of its author's life, in addition to more recent critics, many of Barnes's contemporaries and even Thelma Wood herself

apparently took Robin Vote as a portrayal of Thelma. One notable exception is Lynn DeVore, who demonstrates the similarity between the language Barnes used to describe Robin and her descriptions of her close friend Baroness Elsa Von-Freytag. In some cases the language is identical, which suggests at the very least that Robin is not just a portrait of Thelma.

4. The letters Barnes and Eliot exchanged over the years include discussions of Barnes's later work. One of the reasons Eliot's involvement elicits the desire to see the entire manuscript is his ambivalent attitude toward Barnes's work. He praised *Nightwood* but wrote mixed praise for the jacket of *The Antiphon*: "From the point of view of the conventionally minded *The Antiphon* would be still more shocking—or would be if they could understand it—and still more tedious—because they will not understand it—than *Nightwood*. It might be said of Miss Barnes, who is incontestably one of the most original writers of our time, that never has so much genius been combined with so little talent" (Field 222).

5. See the discussion of *Between the Acts* in the previous chapter for an extended treatment of this kind of postmodern textual erotics.

6. Before her expatriation, if she was not exactly politically active, Barnes's activities and journalistic writing indicate that she was politically aware. Field points out that in 1914 "she did some anti-war drawings for the Pacifist movement prior to America's entry into the First World War" (15). And during this period her journalistic writing and interviews of various people, are informed by strong personal and social views. In these interviews, even as she makes the personalities central and vivid, Barnes herself emerges as a distinctive presence (see Douglas Messerli's *Djuna Barnes Interviews*). Although she didn't follow her grandmother's lead and join the women's suffrage movement, Barnes's sympathy with the suffragists is suggested by her willingness in 1914 to undergo the kind of force-feeding that was then being inflicted on the English suffragists. She found it an "anguish beyond description" (Field 53):

> If I, play acting, felt my being burning with revolt at this brutal usurpation of my own functions, how they who actually suffered the ordeal in its acutest horror must have flamed at the violation of the sanctuaries of their spirit? I saw in my hysteria a vision of a hundred women in grim prison hospitals, bound and shrouded on tables just like this, held in the rough grip of callous warders, while white-robed doctors thrust rubber

> tubing into the delicate interstices of their nostrils and forced into their helpless bodies the crude fuel to sustain the life they longed to sacrifice.
>
> (Field 54)

Barnes knew from this rather dramatic experience the demoralization of having her will and body blatantly overpowered and violated—albeit by her own consent—by official and "legitimate" custodians of social order and control. But despite this early political involvement, Barnes later claimed to be apolitical, a position she maintained "through the decades of depression, communism, fascism, war, and McCarthyism" (Field 15).

7. James Scott and Louis Kannenstine are two early critics who argue that *Ladies Almanack* is actually an attack on lesbian love.

8. Lanser writes that "this ending may seem lewdly patriarchal, in bad taste, irreverent, even grotesque; I confess to discomfort in reading it," but adds "this wild finale of *Ladies Almanack* surely celebrates, proclaims, the gift of tongues" (44). A revised version of Lanser's essay appears in *Silence and Power*. Although published too late to be of use here, the essays in *Silence and Power* promise to be influential in Barnes scholarship.

9. See Foucault's "The Discourse on Language" in *The Archeaology of Knowledge*.

10. See Hélène Cixous, "Castration or Decapitation" and "The Laugh of the Medusa."

11. For a more complete discussion of cross-dressing in *Nightwood* and in other modernist texts see Sandra Gilbert, "Costumes of the Mind: Transvestism as Metaphor in Modern Literature," and Susan Gubar, "Blessings in Disguise: Cross-Dressing as Re-Dressing for Female Modernists."

12. John Berger, *Ways of Seeing*.

13. In "Laughing at Leviticus," Marcus writes that "Robin is in fear because she is being written about. Nora experiences the dream as 'something being done to Robin, Robin disfigured and eternalized by the hierglyphics of sleep and pain' (*N* 63)—that is, being made into La Somnambule. As publicist for the circus, Nora is dreaming herself into the male role of master of ceremonies, Djuna Barnes writing this novel as circus" (246).

Bibliography

Barnes, Djuna. *The Antiphon*. London: Faber and Faber, 1958.

———. *Ladies Almanack*. New York: Harper and Row, 1972. Privately printed Robert McAlmon, 1928.

————. *Nightwood.* London: Faber and Faber, 1936. New York: Harcourt, Brace, 1937.

Benstock, Shari. *Women of the Left Bank: Paris, 1900-1940.* Austin: University of Texas Press, 1986.

Berger, John. *Ways of Seeing.* New York: Viking Press, 1973.

Broe, Mary Lynn. "My Art Belongs to Daddy." In *Women's Writing in Exile.* Ed. Mary Lynn Broe and Angela Ingram. Chapel Hill: University of North Carolina Press, 1989.

————, ed. *Silence and Power: Djuna Barnes: A Reevaluation.* Carbondale: Southern Illinois University Press, 1991.

Cixous, Hélène. "Castration or Decapitation?" Trans. Annette Kuhn. *Signs* 7 (1981): 41-55.

————. "The Laugh of the Medusa." Trans. Keith Cohen and Paula Cohen. *Signs* 2 (1976): 39-54.

DeVore, Lynn. "The Backgrounds of *Nightwood*: Robin, Felix, and Nora." *Journal of Modern Literature* 10 (1983): 71-90.

Duras, Marguerite. *The Vice-Consul.* Trans. Eileen Ellenbogen. New York: Pantheon, 1987. Originally published as *Le vice-consul.* Paris: Editions Gallimard, 1966.

Field, Andrew. *Djuna: The Life and Times of Djuna Barnes.* New York: G. P. Putman's Sons, 1983.

Foster, Hal. *Recodings: Art, Spectacle, Cultural Politics.* Port Townsend, Washington: Bay Press, 1985.

Foucault, Michel. *Discipline and Punish: The Birth of the Prison.* Trans. Alan Sheridan. New York: Vintage, 1977. Originally published as *Surveiller et punir; naissance de la prison.* Paris: Editions Gallimard, 1975.

————. "The Discourse on Language." In *The Archeology of Knowledge.* New York: Pantheon, 1972. Originally published as *L'Ordre du discours.* Paris: Editions Gallimard, 1971.

Freud, Sigmund. "On Narcissism: An Introduction." In *The Standard Edition of the Complete Psychological Works.* Ed. James Strachey. London: Hogarth Press, 1953.

Gilbert, Sandra. "Costumes of the Mind: Transvestism as Metaphor in Modern Literature." *Critical Inquiry* 7 (1980): 391-418.

Gilbert, Sandra, and Susan Gubar. *No Man's Land: The Place of the Woman Writer in the Twentieth Century,* vol. 1. New Haven: Yale University Press, 1987.

Gubar, Susan. "Blessings in Disguise: Cross-Dressing as Re-Dressing for Female Modernists." *Massachusetts Review* 22 (1981): 477-508.

Heilbrun, Carolyn. "Sacrificed to Art." Review of *Nora: The Real Life of Molly Bloom* by Brenda Maddox. *Women's Review of Books* 12 (1988): 5.

Kannenstine, Louis. *The Art of Djuna Barnes: Duality and Damnation.* New York: New York University Press, 1977.

Kofman, Sara. *The Enigma of Woman.* Trans. Catherine Porter. Ithaca: Cornell University Press, 1985. Originally published as *L'Enigme de la femme: La femme dans les textes de Freud.* Paris: Editions Galilée, 1980.

Lanser, Susan Sniader. "Speaking in Tongues: *Ladies Almanack* and the Language of Celebration." *Frontiers: A Journal of Women's Studies* 4 (1979): 39-46.

Lentricchia, Frank. *Ariel and the Police.* Madison: University of Wisconsin Press, 1988.

Marcus, Jane. "Carnival of the Animals." *Women's Review of Books* 8 (1984): 6-7.

————. "Laughing at Leviticus: *Nightwood* as Woman's Circus Epic." In *Silence and Power: Djuna Barnes: A Reevaluation.* Ed. Mary Lynn Broe. Carbondale: Southern Illinois University Press, 1991.

Messerli, Douglas. *Djuna Barnes Interviews.* Washington, D.C.: Sun and Moon Press, 1985.

Scott, James. *Djuna Barnes.* Boston: Twayne Publishers, 1976.

Woolf, Virginia. *Between the Acts.* London: Hogarth, 1969.

Carolyn Allen (essay date 1991)

SOURCE: Allen, Carolyn. "Writing toward *Nightwood*: Djuna Barnes' Seduction Stories." In *Silence and Power: A Reevaluation of Djuna Barnes,* edited by Mary Lynn Broe, pp. 54-65. Carbondale: Southern Illinois University Press, 1991.

[*In the following essay, Allen interprets three early short stories by Barnes—"Cassation," "The Grande Malade," and "Dusie"—in light of recent feminist theory that questions the validity of sexual difference.*]

Djuna Barnes' status as a lesbian culture hero has shifted dramatically over the last decade. In 1973 Bertha Harris lovingly celebrated Barnes and her Paris circle as models for Harris' own life as a lesbian; in 1984 Tee Corinne characterized Barnes as homophobic.[1] There is, of course, evidence for both positions. Barnes herself said she was not a lesbian, that she "just loved Thelma,"[2] and as she grew older and more isolated, she had a low tolerance for her female admirers.[3] Nevertheless, Harris is right to honor her as a representative of "practically the only available expressions of lesbian culture we have in the modern western world" since Sappho.[4] Even though Barnes' denial of her lesbianism, reinforced as it was by a homophobic dominant culture and a new literature of sexology,[5] emerges in what little biographical information we now have, *Nightwood* and *Ladies Almanack* remain classics of lesbian imagination. I will argue further that three of her stories, linked by the "little girl" who narrates them, also belong to that imaginative tradition.

While *Nightwood* may be what Catharine Stimpson calls a lesbian narrative of damnation,[6] it portrays in Robin and Nora's relationship currents of lesbian sexuality still being debated in recent feminist work. Both its references to mother-daughter dynamics and its mixing of "pleasure and danger" anticipate recent discussion.[7] In less overt but equally powerful ways, Barnes' "little girl" stories have in their textual shadows these same configurations. These stories—called "little girl" stories because of the original titles of two, **"A Little Girl Tells a Story to a Lady"** and **"The Little Girl Continues"**—culminate in a third that is a direct precursor to *Nightwood,* **"Dusie."** All three interrogate gender identity and homosexuality. In my reading of them I look to shadows rather than to surfaces, and I read in the context of recent work on "difference," work which provides the light necessary for the play of these shadows.

The history of feminism's "second wave" is in part a history of the shifting value placed on difference. Beginning with a realization that the stress on difference between men and women has resulted in unequal separate spheres, feminist thinkers moved first against sexual difference toward a stress on abilities and talents shared by women and men. In the 1970s the tenets of liberal feminism came under attack by radical feminists who celebrated woman as different from—and superior to—men. Recently many feminists have argued from a position that stresses differences among women, in recognition of the danger inherent in obliterating factors of race and class in discussions of oppression.[8]

Alongside this feminist dialogue on difference and oppression developed another on difference and repression,[9] growing primarily out of Freudian and neo-Freudian psychoanalysis and centered on the oedipal/castration crisis in the formation of sexuality. In this novel, especially as it is reformulated by Lacan reading back through Lévi-Strauss and Saussure, woman is Other, lack, the means by which man knows what he is. French feminist scholars have criticized this theory because it does not permit woman to have difference of her own, to occupy anything more than a negative space. A growing number of feminists revising these models are focusing on possibilities for investigating the preoedipal, and thus the role of the mother rather than the father. In different revisionist ways, French psychoanalysts Julia Kristeva and Luce Irigaray both make the mother prominent in their work, though both still write with the father of psychoanalysis and his son, Lacan, looming over them.[10] Others acknowledge directly that the model is simply inadequate for understanding the construction of the female subject. In her reinterpretation of object-relations theory, American sociologist Nancy Chodorow argues further that the stress on sexual difference by male psychoanalysts demonstrates their own male need to remain as differentiated as possible from the feminine in light of the problematics of separation from the mother as first caretaker.[11]

Both *Nightwood* and the "little girl" stories explode the binary structure underlying Western thought from Plato forward that recent feminist theorists like Irigaray and Chodorow so radically question. By refusing the categories male and female, by shifting terms of sexual difference, Barnes' texts become radical examinations of dichotomous difference. By refusing to take maleness and the phallus as the norm, by questioning the construction of gender and the nature of sexuality, they rupture the surface of convention and illuminate the world of night. While Barnes may have denied her lesbian relationships, her texts question the dichotomous presence of sameness and difference in their presentation of lesbian sexuality.

Nightwood's seventh chapter, "Go Down Matthew," contains the novel's most extended discussion of gender and sexuality. Together Nora and Matthew give us a portrait of the invert, the third sex. In that portrait we recognize the boy in the girl, the girl in the Prince; not a mixing of gendered behaviors, but the creation of a new gender, "neither one and half the other" (*N* [*Nightwood*], 136). A woman loving someone of the third sex loves her as herself and her child. It is clear throughout the chapter that both these dynamics are at work in Nora's relation to Robin. Thus the Lacanian insistence on sexual difference is overturned here in favor of likeness: "she is myself" (*N,* 127). Here there is no Other; there is only oneself: "A man is another person—a woman is yourself caught as you turn in panic; on her mouth you kiss your own" (*N,* 143). The lover is not only like the self; she is the self.

But the chapter takes up difference as well. A man lies bejeweled in a velvet-lined box staring into a mirror to contemplate his own difference. Here he sees not a recognition of himself as differentiated subject, but himself as like the figure in the mirror and unlike the rest of the world. He celebrates his nonconformity. As such he resembles Matthew, Nora, and Robin, whose sexuality is "an honorific reappropriation of sexual difference."[12] That is, in their love of the same sex, they, like the man in the box, admire their nonconformity, their sexual difference from the rest of the world. Barnes is particularly clear about this difference in *Ladies Almanack*:

This is the part about Heaven that has never been told. After the fall of Satan . . . all the Angels . . . gathered together, so close that they were not recognizable, one from the other. And not nine Months later, there was heard under the Dome of Heaven a great Crowing, and from the Midst, an Egg, as incredible as a thing forgotten, fell to the Earth, and striking, split and hatched, and from out of it stepped one saying, "Pardon me, I must be going!" and this was the first Woman born with a Difference.

After this the Angels parted, and on the Face of each was the Mother look.

(*LA* [*Ladies Almanack*], 26)

The angels merge and give birth to the woman with a difference, the lesbian whose manners and mores as seen in the Natalie Barney circle are the subject of the book's fond wit.

So, although Robin and Nora are alike because they are both women, they are also lesbians, women with a Difference. And even in their likeness, they are different people, a differentiation marked especially in the text's casting of Nora as mother, Robin as child. Here is the second dynamic in **Nightwood**'s lesbian relationships—one's lover is not only one's self but also one's child: "Robin is incest too" (*N*, 156), a girl-child dressed as a boy who plays with toy trains and soldiers. The lovers' relationship is infused with an imbalance of power of mother to child righted when Robin the lover expresses her adult autonomy by leaving Nora to sleep with other women. At the same time the mother-child relationship is shot through with eroticism since mother and child are also lovers. As lovers they cannot conceive, so they share a doll to mark their union. Here is another turn on sameness and difference, for the doll resembles the child, yet is not alive: "The doll and the immature have something right about them, the doll because it resembles but does not contain life, and the third sex because it contains life but resembles the doll" (*N*, 148). Robin is like the doll, but different from it, just as Nora is like Robin, but different from her, just as Matthew, Nora, and Robin are like each other in their sexuality, but different from the world at large.

Neither of these currents is startlingly new in lesbian fiction; Barnes' French contemporary Colette, for example, also focused on the mother-daughter dynamics in lesbianism. Nor is either unexplored by psychoanalysis. Recent work, however, leaves aside nineteenth-century sexology's emphasis on sickness to celebrate the same kind of ambiguities that emerge in Barnes' novel. This recent work directly or indirectly attacks the phallocentric insistence on sexual difference and opens the way for alternative theorizing.

Luce Irigaray's two companion essays, "Quand nos levres se parlent" ("When Our Lips Speak Together") and "Et l'une ne bouge pas sans l'autre" ("And the One

Doesn't Stir without the Other"), both rupture the Lacanian model of sexual difference and provide a text against which to read Barnes' "little girl" stories.[13] The first essay is, among other things, a dialogue between two women lovers who acknowledge their likeness ("When you say I love you . . . you also say I love myself").[14] What earlier psychoanalysts dismiss as narcissism becomes self-affirming because it is not an embrace of sameness and closure, which Irigaray identifies with maleness, but a lyric of multiplicity. Like Barnes' texts, Irigaray's undermines what she calls the "currency of alternatives and oppositions." She writes in the shadow of Lacan and, without naming him, disputes his view of sexual difference that negates woman.

The second essay, as its translator notes, echoes the first in its continuing meditation on woman-to-woman relationships, now shifted from lovers to mother and daughter. The daughter speaks to the mother from her undifferentiated state (in male psychoanalytic terms, the preoedipal): "I would like us to play together at being the same and different. You/I echoing endlessly and each staying herself." Here as in the earlier essay, the question of sameness and difference has parameters quite removed from standard models that pass over the preoedipal to concentrate on the role of the Father in the construction of sexual difference. It allows for difference in the context of resemblance, just as lesbian discourse does. Irigaray's essay fills a descriptive gap in male theory, then deliberates on the damage done when the woman is "trapped in a single function—mothering."[15] She both stresses the complexities and the sensuality of the mother-daughter connection and acknowledges the limiting dichotomy, mother-woman, in the referential world.

Chodorow also ruptures the Freudian/Lacanian insistence on the primacy of the father's role in structuring female sexuality. Unlike Irigaray, however, she is less interested in reformulating difference than in delineating differentiation. She connects difference with a model that reduces the mother to the "not-me," thus obliterating her as a subject. She stresses instead the process of the daughter's struggle to differentiate herself from the mother, the fluidity rather than the fixity of gender difference, and the potential slippage in heterosexual orientation for women because of their bonds with the mother.

Beneath the surface of their conventional prose, the three "little girl" stories anticipate a number of these contemporary feminist currents. The stories are held together not only by their common narrator, but also by the common interrogation of gender and sexuality that shadows the text. In all three stories a young woman tells a story to a lady. The narratives themselves are stories of one kind of seduction or another, seductions that have one younger and one older participant. The stories about seduction imprint on the narrative situation a forbidden atmosphere—the seduction of female by female, by older or younger, with incest shadowing the shadows. The narrator herself has the absolute autonomy usually reserved for men. She travels all over Europe, alone or with her sister; she decides how long she will stay, how she will live, when she wants to leave one place and move on to another. We know less about the auditor, the mysterious "Madame." But the narrator wants her to listen. *"Nicht wahr,"* she says; *"n'est-ce pas,"* "is it not so?" always seeking confirmation, looking for assent. Even in the midst of the stories themselves, the narrator intrudes with direct addresses or little asides to her listener so that we never forget she is a "little girl" telling her stories to "a lady": "Then this last autumn, before the last winter set in (you were not here then, Madame)," or "Sometimes it is beautiful in Berlin, Madame, *nicht wahr?*"[16] Of course the narrator is not a little girl at all, but a precocious young woman who implicates herself and her sexuality even as she seems with innocent nonchalance to be recounting some other woman's story to the presumably attentive "Madame." Her three stories, increasingly overt in their sexual content, are themselves a fictional seduction of the older "Madame" by the younger narrator, Katya.

In **"Cassation"** a mysterious older woman tries to convince Katya to come and live with her and take care of her child. Literally, that is—sexually, it is not a seduction story, yet there hangs over it an atmosphere of eroticism not unlike that of *Nightwood*. Originally titled **"A Little Girl Tells a Story to a Lady"** and first published in 1925, the story was revised and retitled **"Cassation"** for *Spillway*. The new title, come upon long after Barnes' Paris days and her denial of her own involvement with women, stresses what is now the standard reading of all the *Spillway* stories: the fascination with the void, with negativity, with the abyss at the heart of the world. Such a reading also connects **"Cassation"** to *Nightwood,* but it misses the radical nature of the text's questioning of conventional gender difference and sexuality. As usual in Barnes' fiction, plot is a minimal pretext. Several times Katya sees a mysterious and dramatic woman in a café; one day they are drawn together, and the woman invites the girl home. After they have lived together for a year, the woman, Gaya, asks Katya to stay forever to care for her mentally vacant child. Katya refuses, leaves, returns to say goodbye, and finds Gaya in bed with the child, both making the same wordless sound of vacancy.

The plot operates in a world of unconventionally marked gender and sexual likeness. The only man in the story is Gaya's husband, a sort of feminized ghost. He is little, dainty, dreamy, uncertain, appears infrequently, and does not participate in the action. Gaya does attribute to him what several generations later would be called "the power of the weak," the mark of woman. Conversely, the women, both Katya and Gaya, are independent and autonomous. In their year together they walk out, admire military cannons, hold intellectual conversations about philosophy and the state of civilization. During these brief scenes in the first half of the story, the women generally occupy masculine rather than feminine positions. But within this reversed gender structure, there are still differences in power. The older woman has the active/male role, the younger the passive/female role. Katya does what Gaya asks.

Halfway through the story, however, there is a shift in power. In the first half of the story Gaya has been the stronger force, leading the girl home, ensconcing her in a bedroom for a year, treating her in part as a child, in part as an intellectual equal. When in the story's second half Gaya must finally become a mother to her vacant child because of the child's growing need for care, the power shifts to the participant narrator. Katya exercises a masculine power of refusal in ignoring Gaya's pleas for her to stay, and Gaya, in turn, is reduced to child-like helplessness.

This then is the gendered structure of the story: the women marked by traditional masculine traits, the man by traditional feminine ones; the women present, the man absent. The reversal that drives the narrative comes when the older woman must assume the "trap" that Irigaray describes, the most institutionalized female role possible—the role of the mother. When she does so, the power dynamic shifts and with it the positions both filled by the two women. The "little girl" now controls the action. The mother cannot prevent her going and collapses into madness. This gendered narrative is written in language charged with sexual meaning that complements and complicates the structure. Throughout the story the two women, though never lovers, act out child-mother relationships like those referenced in the passages of "Go Down Matthew." Reading particular scenes and particular turns of phrase in the light of that chapter illuminates the sexual subtext of the narrative.

Early in the story, the women go home together:

> Then one evening we came into the garden at the same moment. It was late and the fiddles were already playing. We sat together without speaking, just listening to the music, and admiring the playing of the only woman member of the orchestra. She was very intent on the movements of her fingers, and seemed to be leaning over her chin to watch. Then suddenly the lady got up, leaving a small rain of coin, and I followed her until we came to a big house and she let herself in with a key. She turned to the left and went into a dark room and switched on the lights and sat down and said: "This is where we sleep; this is how it is."
>
> (*SW* [*Selected Works of Djuna Barnes*], 14)

This scene resembles one in *Nightwood* when Robin and Nora first meet, brought wordlessly together at a circus with a lioness bowing in recognition. In **"Cassa-**

tion" the women's first meeting begins with Katya walking elsewhere, looking at the statues of emperors (who look like widows, in keeping with the story's gender reversals), when she suddenly thinks of the café and the tall woman she has seen there. She returns; Gaya is there and speaks to her for the first time in a "voice that touched the heart" about her home with its Venetian paintings "where young girls lie dreaming of the Virgin" (*SW*, 13). The narrator sums up for Madame: "I said I would meet her again some day in the garden, and we could go 'home' together, and she seemed pleased, but did not show surprise" (*SW*, 14). Then follows the passage quoted above. Like the *Nightwood* scene, the two women come together silently; one leaves suddenly, and the other follows. In between, they focus not on a lioness but on the intensity of the only woman member of the orchestra. Here it is not the recognition of the animal appropriate to Robin's beast-self, but sexual difference, that only woman musician, that sends them home to the bedroom. Once there, the narrator takes time to describe the massive dimensions and great disorder of the room but saves her most lavish description for a great war painting which runs together "in encounter" with the bed. In it "generals, with foreign helmets and dripping swords, raging through rolling smoke and the bleeding ranks of the dying, seemed to be charging the bed, so large, so rumpled, so devastated" (*SW*, 14). So much for men in the bedroom.

In this narrative preparation, the two women have been drawn together by the repetitions of chance and the power of a woman's music; conventional expectations lead the reader to expect a sexual encounter. Here they are in front of the bed; the narrative action has been stopped to point to male violence and then? In any throwaway lesbian novel they might fall onto the bed, overwhelmed by Destiny. In **"Cassation"** they are prevented from so doing; a child lies in the center of the pillows, "making a thin noise, like the buzzing of a fly" (*SW*, 14). The charged atmosphere shifts from incipient sexuality to the needs of the child. But Gaya does nothing except drink a little wine, insist that Katya stay, throw herself on the bed, her hair spread around her, and fall asleep. Later that night she puts Katya to bed as she might a child or a young lover, loosening and braiding her hair. Katya stays a year.

After that year together, when the condition of Gaya's child worsens, Gaya, in the central monologue of the story, tries to convince Katya to stay and care for the child. She promises to be like her mother, her servant, she denies their previously intellectual sharing:

> Now you will stay here safely, and you will see. You will like it, you will learn to like to the very best of all. I will bring you breakfast, and luncheon, and supper. I will bring it to you both, myself. I will hold you on my lap, I will feed you like the birds. I will rock you to sleep. You must not argue with me—above all we must have not arguments, no talk about man and his destiny.
>
> (*SW*, 18)

The sexual undercurrents of their coming together have earlier been bound up with Gaya's playing at the mother's role. Faced with actually mothering her own helpless child, the woman of power has become the suppliant who wishes to make her friend into her child's caretaker. As she continues her plea, she literally confuses her own child with Katya; friend and child become the same, as if Katya could fill in the vacancy of Gaya's daughter. Her actual daughter cannot provide the companionship that both Chodorow and Irigaray stress is basic to the mother-daughter relation; instead, the child's mental absence calls only for the mother's caretaking role. Not only is Gaya confronted with the institution of motherhood, but experientially she must mother a child who can never be her companion.[17] To avoid such mothering, Gaya tries to convince Katya to become her child's caretaker; in her speech, she merges Katya as caretaker with Katya as daughter-substitute. Were she successful, she, like Nora in **Nightwood**, could have her intimate as her child and be both her companion and her caretaker. Her independence threatened by Gaya's attempt to make her a dependent "daughter" rather than a playful intimate, Katya refuses. Her need for differentiation, as Chodorow might say, is as great as Gaya's confusion between her desire not to mother at all and her need for a daughter-companion. Their parting, like their meeting, is shadowed by longing:

> Then Madame, I got up. It was very cold in the room. I went to the window and pulled the curtains, it was a bright and starry night, and I stood leaning my head against the frame, saying nothing. When I turned around, she was regarding me, her hands held apart, and I knew that I had to go away and leave her. So I came up to her and said, "Good-bye my Lady." And I went and put on my street clothes, and when I came back she was leaning against the battle picture, her hands hanging. I said to her, without approaching her, "Good-bye my love" and went away.
>
> (*SW*, 19)

Katya now has the power that initially was Gaya's. In the final scene, Gaya is no longer differentiated from her vacant daughter. She sits beside her child, imitating her mad sound, the seductive woman-turned-mother-turned-child fallen into the void.

Read in the context of "Go Down Matthew," this story confirms its configuration both of difference in likeness and mother-child dynamics between women intimates. Of course the story is "about" cassation, as Gaya's long monologue and the ending indicate. But it is also about a little girl telling a story to a lady, one woman speaking to another about attraction, the power of women, the devastation of motherhood, and the conflation of child and intimate. It assumes a female world, then gives up the shifts in power, conventionally marked masculine and feminine, as a comment on the consequence of the ultimate female role—mothering.

The second story in the sequence, **"The Grande Malade"** continues the subtexts of gender and of sexuality/nurturance. Its original title, **"The Little Girl Continues,"** connects it to **"The Little Girl Tells a Story to a Lady,"** just as its revised *Spillway* title, **"The Grande Malade,"** is linked to **"Cassation"** in its implication of annulment by disease. Unlike the earlier story, however, its unconventional structuring of gender implicates the male as well as the female characters. Again the story involves pairs of the same sex. Significantly, although the plot purports to be about a heterosexual couple, Moydia and Monsieur X, we never see them alone as a couple or hear anything of their relationship. Instead, the narrative construction subverts the ostensible focus of the plot by concentrating on the couples, Moydia and her sister Katya, and Monsieur X and his patron, the Baron. Katya, here again active and autonomous, is both narrator and participant. The story is of a cap, a cape, and a pair of boots, all marking transgression of gender and blurring of lines of difference. Katya has given up flowered hats in favor of a cap like her father's and Chinese trousers. Only the women listen to her, whereas men adore her sister Moydia. Moydia is feminine difference in this pair marked by female likeness. If **"Cassation"** is shadowed by the incestuous potential between women intimates, **"The Grande Malade"** suggests instead the sexuality of father-daughter couples. Moydia chooses as her lover Monsieur X, who himself is paired with the Baron, a man of "aged immaturity" who taps around after Moydia with his cane. With the Baron she is a gamine, teasing him in her childlikeness, sitting in his lap, playing either "the kitten or the great lady as occasion demanded" (*SW,* 24). He plays the passive but receptive older "father" to her spoiled child-flirt.

The story opens with Katya's description of Moydia's physical beauty. Its first half establishes them as a pair, always together, walking in the Tuilleries, hanging lace curtains over their beds to smoke and talk of lovers. They differ in their appearance; Moydia is clearly feminine, while Katya has her trousers and her cap. The sisters are like, an inseparable "we," but different not only in their appearance, but in their relation to father figures. Katya wants to be her absent father; Moydia wants to take him as a lover, substituting for him the available presence of the old Baron.

The males in the story, however, spend more time with each other than with the sisters. Monsieur X seems particularly unsuited as a lover for Moydia: "He was the protege of a Baron. The Baron liked him very much

and called him his *'Poupon prodigieux,'* and they played farces together for the amusement of the Fauborg. That was the way it was with Monsieur X, at least in his season when he was, shall we say, the *belle-d'un-jour* and was occupied in writing fables on mice and men, but he always ended the stories with paragraphs *très acre* against women" (*SW,* 24). Moydia leaves town to visit her actual father, the one who lives so strongly in the imagination of Katya. During her absence Monsieur X dies with the Baron at his side. The narrative's only repeated passage, its doubling appropriate in a story where likeness defeats conventions of sexual difference, recounts Monsieur X's death and refers obliquely to the unconventional strains of the story. Katya tells Madame of Monsieur X's death: "When the Baron saw that Monsieur X was truly going to die, he made him drink. They drank together all night and into the morning. The Baron wanted it that way. 'For that,' he said, 'he might die as he was born, without knowing'" (*SW,* 27). A page later, Katya repeats the scene and the quote for Moydia when she returns from her visit. What is it that Monsieur X doesn't know? Among other things, surely, that his ties to the Baron were greater than those to Moydia.

Katya asked the Baron for something belonging to Monsieur X to give as a remembrance to Moydia. He gives her Monsieur X's cape. Given the fame of Djuna Barnes' own cape, familiar to all who knew her in Paris at the time of the story's publication in *This Quarter,* it is difficult not to see the story's cape as something of a private joke. But more than that, it marks a further transgression of gender identity, passing from a man of uncertain sexuality to a woman who in wearing it, as the story tells us, comes to resemble her dead lover. By wearing his cape, she becomes not only a masculinized woman who replaces the feminized man but also the "protege" of the old Baron-father with whom she earlier has had such a sexually coy relationship. Meanwhile, the boots that Monsieur X had earlier promised Katya are quite forgotten. So while Moydia puts on a man's cape, Katya must forego her man's boots; for both, clothes mark their move away from boundaries of gender identity toward an ambiguous center, "neither one and half the other," as Matthew O'Connor says. The matrix of gender and sexuality in "The Grande Malade" is not that of "Cassation," yet both stories are shadowed by outlawed transgression of difference boundaries. In their undercurrent of incest and their fascination with likeness and difference within that likeness, they anticipate the overt emergence of these ideas in *Nightwood.*

"Dusie," like *Nightwood,* brings the undercurrents to the surface. Published in a collection called *American Esoterica* and not included in *Spillway,* perhaps because of its unambiguous lesbian subject matter, **"Dusie"** directly anticipates many of *Nightwood*'s preoccupations. Like other homosexual texts, the story's very existence challenges theories of sexual difference. Within its theoretical structure of sameness, difference appears at the textual level in the variety of women presented, but particularly in the condemnation of one who commits an act of violence. Like *Nightwood*'s Jenny, Clarissa disappears before the narrative closes. The women who remain, like Nora and Robin, participate in the familiar mother-daughter-lover configuration.

The story is set entirely in a world of likeness. In Madame K's lesbian salon there are no men, only women with different roles. Questions of conventional gender give way to an explicit focus on sexuality. Dusie is the prototype of *Nightwood*'s Robin. She dresses in trousers, plays with dolls and toy soldiers, has many women lovers who call her pet or beast "according to their feelings."[18] In a description that looks forward to Matthew's *Nightwood* speech on the third sex as "uninhabited angels," the narrator says, "You felt that you must talk to Dusie, tell her everything, because all her beauty was there, but uninhabited, like a church, *n'est-ce pas*, Madame?" ("**Dusie**," 78). Like Robin she has brief outbursts of temper coupled with an unheeding absence. She has a "strong bodily odor" not yet elaborated as the earth-flesh, fungi perfume of *Nightwood*. Her movements are "like vines growing over a ruin" just as Robin recalls the "way back" of prehistory ("**Dusie**," 78). Others talk in front of her about her death. But she doesn't notice and "that made it sorrowful and ridiculous, as if they were anticipating a doom that had fallen already a hundred years" ("**Dusie**," 79). Other descriptions look forward just as directly both to the character and the language of *Nightwood*.

Clarissa anticipates Jenny just as Dusie does Robin. Both Clarissa and Jenny are thieves of others' lovers. Both mark difference in their female worlds; they counterpoint the other pairs of women lovers by their acts of violence and their narrative disappearances. Both are completely dependent on everyone they know. Jenny, the squatter, lives by appropriating others' words and loves. Clarissa seems "as if she lived only because so many people had seen and spoken to her and of her. If she had been forgotten for a month, entirely by everyone, I'm sure she would have died" ("**Dusie**," 77). She knows how to teach evil, just as Jenny does, and the story's brief action, Clarissa's mutilation of Dusie's foot, shares the power of physical violence with *Nightwood*'s carriage scene in which Jenny attacks Robin, making bloody scratches on her face. In both scenes the violence has a sexual context: after the carriage ride, Robin goes with Jenny as lover to America. Clarissa says to Dusie, "You must think, too, about the most terrible virtue, which is to be undefiled because one has no way for it; there are women like that, grown women, there should be an end . . ." ("**Dusie**," 81). These are the last words "the little girl" overhears before she falls

asleep. When she awakes, Dusie is asking her to leave the bedroom. When she returns, Clarissa is gone and Dusie's foot is crushed. In this context, it is difficult not to hear the sexual implications of "defiled."

Set against this violence, the mother-daughter-lover dynamic in Dusie's relation with Madame K is warmer, but no less problematic. Though the story does not address the dynamic as directly as *Nightwood* does, it shares the novel's ambivalence about mothering one's lover. Dusie's dolls and tin soldiers, her vulnerability, and her self-absorbed absence signal her childlikeness. She clings to her lover, Madame K, as "the only reality." Madame K is mistress of the house, a large, very full blonde Frenchwoman who, the narrator reminds us, is childless. When she is with Dusie, she looks "like a precaution all at once" ("**Dusie**," 77). The narrator says she does not fear for either of them because of the way they "were with each other always" ("**Dusie**," 81). In the final moments of the story when Madame K returns from a visit to her own mother[19] and finds Dusie with her foot crushed, she takes the foot in her lap and says to the narrator: "You see how it is, she can think no evil for others, she can only hurt herself. You must go away now" ("**Dusie**," 82). Her maternal protectiveness, like Nora's of Robin, is unable to prevent Dusie's defilement. Despite this failure, this story, like "**Cassation**" before it and *Nightwood* after, makes clear how bound up with sexuality women's attempts to nurture are in Barnes' work.

With its discourse on the third sex as uninhabited angels, "Go Down Matthew" works out more elaborately what we see in Dusie as a character just as *Nightwood* contains the story of Dusie, Clarissa, and Madame K writ large. What is missing in *Nightwood* is the "little girl" as narrator. Indeed, the little girl's role in "**Dusie**" is considerably reduced from what it was in her first story, "**Cassation**," where she is half of the pair central to the story, and in "**The Grand Malade**," where she puts the story of Moydia in relief by her difference from her. In "**Dusie**" she is more strictly a narrator and less a participant, though she does consent to stay with Dusie when Madame K goes off and thus can report something of the goings-on between Dusie and Clarissa. But clearly her role is fading. In "**Dusie**" she no longer has a name; in *Nightwood* she disappears altogether. The novel's narrative voice sounds like that of the unseen birds in Robin's hotel room—present but not assigned to a character.

"**Dusie**" has a related figure for its narrative and that of the other "little girl" stories. In Dusie's room are two canaries, "the one who sang and the one who listened" ("**Dusie**," 76). As the "little girl," the one who is only a year younger than Dusie, sings her stories to "Madame," she becomes increasingly explicit in the sexual nature of her tales. We never learn how Madame responds, but we listen as Barnes works her way toward the exploration of gender and sexuality that is most fully presented in "Go Down Matthew." From **"Cassation"** with its shadow story about mothering through **"The Grande Malade"** and its sexual uncertainty to **"Dusie"** and *Nightwood,* in which lesbianism and meditation on inversion preoccupy the central characters, Barnes puzzles over likeness and difference, self and other, sexuality and gender. That these same puzzles are now crucial to feminist theory makes Barnes' place in a lesbian canon less important than her prescient raising of issues still hotly debated sixty years after she wrote her stories of seduction.

Notes

1. Harris, "The More Profound Nationality of Their Lesbianism: Lesbian Society in Paris in the 1920s," in *Amazon Expedition,* ed. Phyllis Birkby et al. (New York: Times Change Press, 1973), 77-88; Corinne, in a slide show on lesbian images in art at a panel, "Old Dyke Tales: The Diversity of Feminist Experience," National Women Studies Association Conference, Douglass College, June 1984. Not all recent assessments by lesbians have been negative, however. See, for example, Monique Wittig, "The Point of View," *Feminist Issues* 3 (Fall 1983): 63-69.

2. Andrew Field, *Djuna: The Life and Times of Djuna Barnes* (New York: Putnam's, 1983), 37. Since Field rarely documents the sources of information in this, to date the only book-length biography of Barnes, its scholarly usefulness is limited.

3. Field, *Djuna,* 233. For example, Anaïs Nin wrote her admiringly about how Nin's own work had been influenced by *Nightwood,* but Barnes didn't answer her letter.

4. Harris, "Profound Nationality," 87.

5. For a delineation of that literature in connection with Barnes' contemporary, Radclyffe Hall, see Esther Newton, "The Mythic Mannish Lesbian: Radclyffe Hall and the New Woman," *Signs* 9 (Summer 1984): 557-75.

6. Stimpson, "Zero Degree Deviancy: The Lesbian Novel in English," in *Writing and Sexual Difference,* ed. Elizabeth Abel (Chicago: Univ. of Chicago Press, 1982), 244.

7. For discussion of "pleasure and danger" in lesbian sexuality see Carole Vance, *Pleasure and Danger* (London: Routledge & Kegan Paul, 1984), especially essays by Gayle Rubin and Alice Echols. For mother-daughter dynamics, see below.

8. For details of this history see Hester Eisenstein, "Introduction," in *The Future of Difference,* ed. Hester Eisenstein and Alice Jardine (Boston: G.

K. Hall, 1980) xvi-xxiv; Hester Eisenstein, *Contemporary Feminist Thought* (Boston: G. K. Hall, 1983); and Alison Jaggar, *Feminist Politics and Human Nature* (Totowa, NJ: Rowman and Allanheld, 1983).

9. This distinction between oppression and repression has become shorthand for contrasts between recent American and French feminisms. See, for example, Alice Jardine, "Prelude: The Future of Difference," in *The Future of Difference,* xxv-xxvii; and Margaret Homans, "Her Very Own Howl," *Signs* 9 (Winter 1983): 186-205.

10. For a discussion of Kristeva and Irigaray in the context of French feminist theory, see Josette Feral, "Antigone or the Irony of the Tribe," *Diacritics* (Fall 1978): 2-14.

11. Chodorow, "Gender, Relation, and Difference in Psychoanalytic Perspective," in *The Future of Difference,* 3-19. For a full discussion of her ideas see *The Reproduction of Mothering* (Berkeley: Univ. of California Press, 1978).

12. Herbert Blau, "Disseminating Sodom," *Salmagundi* no. 58-59 (Fall 1982-Winter 1983), 237.

13. "When Our Lips Speak Together," trans. Carolyn Burke, *Signs* 6 (Autumn 1980): 66-79; "And One Doesn't Speak without the Other," translated and with an introduction by Helene Vivienne Wenzel, *Signs* 7 (Autumn 1981): 56-67. Both of these essays are very subtly wrought and deserve a full reading which space does not permit here. Irigaray's work also stresses woman and language and thus is a particularly promising intertext for Barnes.

14. Irigaray, "When Our Lips Speak Together," 70.

15. Irigaray, "And the One Doesn't Stir without the Other," 61, 66.

16. "The Grande Malade," *SW,* 25; "Cassation," *SW,* 19.

17. For a full delineation of the difference between mothering as "institution" and as "experience," see Adrienne Rich, *Of Women Born* (New York: Norton, 1976).

18. "Dusie," in *American Esoterica,* (New York: Macy-Masius, 1927), 78. Hereafter cited in text.

19. As in "The Grande Malade," actual parents are absent from the story proper. Barnes saved parental confrontation for *Ryder* and *The Antiphon.*

Selected Bibliography

This bibliography can serve as a supplement/update to Douglas Messerli's *Djuna Barnes: A Bibliography* published in 1975. Indeed, Messerli's bibliography should be consulted when references are made to certain original Barnes publications.

Barnes, Djuna. *Ryder.* New York: St. Martin's Press, 1979.

———. *Ryder.* New York: St. Martin's Press, 1981.

———. *Ryder.* With an Afterword by Paul West. Lisle, Illinois: Dalkey Press, 1990.

Field, Andrew. *Djuna: The Life and Times of Djuna Barnes.* New York: Putnam's, 1983.

Gilbert, Sandra M. "Costumes of the Mind: Transvestism as Metaphor in Modern Literature." In *Writing and Sexual Difference,* ed. Elizabeth Abel, 193-219. Chicago: University of Chicago Press, 1982.

Harris, Bertha. "The More Profound Nationality of Their Lesbianism: Lesbian Society in Paris in the 1920's." In *Amazon Expedition: A Lesbian Feminist Anthology,* ed. Phyllis Birkby, Bertha Harris, Jill Johnston, Esther Newton, and Jane O'Wyatt, 77-88. New York: Times Change Press, 1973.

Messerli, Douglas John. *Djuna Barnes: A Bibliography.* New York: David Lewis, 1975.

ABBREVIATIONS

Unless otherwise indicated, all quotations from the works of Djuna Barnes derive from the following editions:

LA: Ladies Almanack, showing their Signs and their tides; their moons and their Changes; the Seasons as it is with them; their Eclipses and Equinoxes; as well as a full Record of diurnal and nocturnal Distempers. Written and illustrated by a Lady of Fashion. 1928. Reprint. New York: Harper & Row, 1972.

N: Nightwood, 1936. Reprint. New York: New Directions, 1961, 1977.

R: Ryder, 1923. Reprint. New York: St. Martin's Press, 1956, 1979.

SW: Selected Works of Djuna Barnes: Spillway, The Antiphon, Nightwood. New York: Farrar, Straus and Cudahy, 1962.

Jane Marcus (essay date 1991)

SOURCE: Marcus, Jane. "Laughing at Leviticus: *Nightwood* as Woman's Circus Epic." In *Silence and Power: A Reevaluation of Djuna Barnes,* edited by Mary Lynn Broe, pp. 221-50. Carbondale: Southern Illinois University Press, 1991.

[*In the following essay, Marcus highlights the "Rabelaisian," grotesque, and circus-like qualities of* Nightwood *in an effort to rescue the work from its status "as a lesbian novel or a cult text of high modernism," positioning it instead as "a brilliant and hilarious feminist critique of Freudian psychoanalysis," and ultimately of fascism.*]

Lion and woman and the Lord knows what

—W. B. Yeats

O monsters, do not leave me alone. . . . I do not confide in you except to tell you about my fear of being alone, you are the most human people I know, the most reassuring in the world. If I call you monsters, then what name can I give to the so-called normal conditions that were foisted upon me? Look there, on the wall, the shadow of that frightful shoulder, the expression of that vast back and neck swollen with blood. . . . O monsters, do not leave me alone. . . .

—Colette, *The Pure and the Impure*

Djuna Barnes' great Rabelaisian comic epic novel, *Nightwood* (1936), is beginning to excite the critical attention it deserves. As a contribution to that effort this essay is a feminist interpretation that argues, among other readings, that *Nightwood* is a brilliant and hilarious feminist critique of Freudian psychoanalysis and a parody of the discourse of diagnosis of female hysteria. Using Julia Kristeva's *Powers of Horror,* I argue that *Nightwood,* in its original title of "Bow Down" and its continual reference to submission and bowing or lowering of the self, is a study in *abjection,* and that by its concentration on the figure of The One Who Is Slapped, the downtrodden victim, it figures by absence the authoritarian dominators of Europe in the 1930s, the sexual and political fascists. While Kristeva studies abjection as a pathology, I maintain that Barnes' portraits of the abject constitute a political case, a kind of feminist-anarchist call for freedom from fascism. Looking at Nikka's tattoo as a defiance of the Levitical taboo against writing on the body, I see the body of the Other—the black, lesbian, transvestite, or Jew—presented as a text in the novel, a book of communal resistances of underworld outsiders to domination. Its weapon is laughter, a form of folk grotesque derived from Rabelais and surviving in circus.

With Bakhtin's *Rabelais* as model methodology, I see *Nightwood*'s extravagant language and imagery as a direct descendant of medieval "grotesque realism" (as *Ladies Almanack* is certainly a descendant of the Rabelaisian almanac hawked about in Paris street fairs). In this "reversible world" or "world turned upside down," Barnes moves from high to low culture, from opera to circus, and even expands Bakhtin's categories from their base in the material to include the mystical and mental grotesqueries that he excluded.

I would also argue that the status of *Nightwood* as a lesbian novel or a cult text of high modernism has obscured the ways in which it is a French novel, indebted as much to Victor Hugo and Eugène Sue as it is to Rabelais. My purpose in reviving *Nightwood* is political. Strangely canonized and unread, it cannot function as a critique of fascism. The revision of modernism in which this essay participates is an effort to read race, class, and gender back into the discussion. Unlike most expatriate writing from this period, *Nightwood* paints the Paris underworld and demimonde with its own colors, not a specifically American palette. Its characters are Barnes' modern "misérables," brothers and sisters to the hunchback of Notre Dame. *Nightwood,* like modernism itself, begins in Vienna in the 1880s. Freud, fascism, Hitler, "high art," and the lumpen proletariat haunt the text as a potent "political unconscious." *Nightwood*'s hysterical heteroglossia is a perverse and almost postmodern folk-text in which language and its possibility for figuration is as potent and explosive as it is in Shakespeare or Joyce.

TATTOO AS TABOO

Ye shall not make any cuttings in your flesh for the dead, nor print any marks upon you . . .

—Leviticus 19:27-28

In order to be pure and symbolic, Kristeva argues, the patriarchal body may have only one mark, the circumcision, a cut that duplicates in the symbolic order the natural cut of the umbilical cord that separates mother and son. The ritual cut replaces the natural cut: "the identity of the speaking being (with his God) is based on the separation of the son from the mother.'"[1] In political terms, patriarchal identity is established by marking the body to distinguish it not only from the unclean mother, but from the polytheistic worshippers of the mother goddess who threaten the tribe. The establishment of marked sexual difference with rigid boundaries differentiates the people of the Bible from those of other religious cults, such as the worshippers of Dionysius in Greece, for whom the erasure of sexual difference is the point of ritual activity. (The Jews were neither the first nor the only people to use circumcision, a practice some anthropologists see as a form of menstruation envy.)

Writing on the body, I would argue, is breaking a powerful patriarchal taboo for the inheritors of the Judeo-Christian ethos in which the possession of the Logos is indicated by writing on the holy tablets. Making human skin into a page or a text violates the symbolic order. A body covered with marks is too close to the natural "unclean" state of the newborn's body, which bears the marks of the "unclean" placenta, the traces of its mother's blood. A tattoo, then, is not only taboo; it is also the birthmark of the born-again—the self-created person who denies his or her birth identity. This "monster" is a carnivalesque figure who reveals in the taboo-shattering act of making the body a book, dissolving the difference between spirit and matter.[2] (The Levitical

taboos include incest and homosexuality and mark out any aberrant or physically blemished person as unpleasing to God. While the prohibition extends to prevent the union of same and same or human and animal, it also extends to the mixing of things: seeds should not be mingled, nor breeds of cattle; clothing should not be made of both linen and wool.)

In this context, Djuna Barnes' *Nightwood* might be called "The Lamentations of the Levitically Impure." Leviticus is about separation; *Nightwood* is about merging, dissolution, and, above all, hybridization—mixed metaphors, mixed genres, mixed levels of discourse from the lofty to the low, mixed "languages" from medical practice, circus argot, church dogma, and homosexual slang. Barnes' revision of the Old Testament parallels Joyce's revision of Homer in *Ulysses*. By making hybrids of the sacred texts of Western culture, both writers revitalize "high" culture, carnivalizing the dead bodies of the old texts, engorging them in a sacred/profane cannibalism. *Nightwood* is also a dangerous novel, if we use Mary Douglas' concept of "purity and danger," for the whole social order of this novel is "impure."[3] The world is turned upside down for carnival; it is the reversible world of the circus, the night world of lesbian, homosexual, and transvestite Paris. Leviticus writes the rules for purity of blood. Ironically, it is Felix, the wandering Jew, marked as impure by a world that has incorporated his culture's ethic of purity and named Jews themselves as impure, who searches hopelessly for a "pure" aristocratic European bloodline: "With the fury of a fanatic, he hunted down his own disqualification" (*N* [*Nightwood*], 9). *Nightwood* makes a modernism of marginality. Its "danger" is that the excluded object of its rage, the white Christian male, might read it. The Aryan Superman is absent from the text, but his "uprightness" is the ethic that the characters' abjection opposes.

At a party in Vienna in the 1920s echoing act 2 of *Die Fledermaus* the characters of *Nightwood* meet. Count Ontario Altamonte is entertaining "the living statues," collecting for his amusement—as some European aristocrats did—circus people, Jews, transvestites, exiled Americans. I take one passage as my example here, but the whole novel encourages close reading. Dr. Matthew O'Connor tells Felix the story of "Nikka the nigger," whose name not only mimics the obscenity of the word, like a Middle European mispronunciation of the racist epithet, but has a feminine ending. He "used to fight the bear at the Cirque de Paris." His role is that of the savage male battling the beast for the thrill of an effete audience. But O'Connor exposes the myth of the fascist projection of savage sexuality on to the black man:

"There he was, crouching all over the arena without a stitch on, except an ill-concealed loin-cloth all abulge as if with a deep-sea catch, tattooed from head to heel with all the *ameublement* of depravity! Garlanded with rosebuds and hack-word of the devils—was he a sight to see! Though he couldn't have done a thing (and I know what I am talking about in spite of all that has been said about the black boys) if you had stood him in a gig-mill for a week, though (it's said) at a stretch it spelled Desdemona. Well, then, over his belly was an angel from Chartres; on each buttock, half public, half private, a quotation from the book of magic, a confirmation of the Jansenist theory, I'm sorry to say and here to say it. Across his knees, I give you my word, 'I' on one and on the other, 'can,' put those together! Across his chest, beneath a beautiful caravel in full sail, two clasped hands, the wrist bones fretted with point lace. On each bosom an arrow-speared heart, each with different initials but with equal drops of blood. . . .

"The legs," said Doctor O'Connor, "were devoted to vine work, topped by the swart rambler rose copied from the coping of the Hamburg house of Rothschild. Over his *dos,* believe it or not and I shouldn't, a terse account in early monkish script—called by some people indecent, by others Gothic—of the really deplorable condition of Paris before hygiene was introduced, and nature had its way up to the knees. And just above what you mustn't mention, a bird flew carrying a streamer on which was incised, '*Garde tout!*' I asked him why all this barbarity; he answered he loved beauty and would have it about him."

(*N,* 16-17)

O'Connor exposes in his tale ("at a stretch it spelled Desdemona") the white man's projection of desire for the white woman on to the black man, the white's naming of the black's genitals as "rapist," the white man's desire to rape and kill woman. The pun on the word "spell" suggests that his penis is *named* Desdemona, as O'Connor's penis is *named* Tiny O'Toole, but "spell" could also be read sexually as "to satisfy" Desdemona or, in another meaning, to take someone's place. The name concealed by Nikka's knickers is Verdi's Desdemona more than Shakespeare's, as Nikka acts an operatic Othello. The miscegenation and murder suggested by "Desdemona" are also in the tattoo's "confirmation of the Jansenist theory," defined by the *Oxford English Dictionary* as the heresy of belief in the eternal battle of good and evil, the belief in the "perverseness and inability for good of the natural human will." Nikka's tattooed body is like one of Lambroso's drawings of criminals or Djuna Barnes' drawings for *Ryder* or *Ladies Almanack.* There are no margins; the text and illustrations devour the page; every inch of space is covered with drawings and writings, breaking both the Levitical taboo of writing on the body and the taboo on mixing objects, for text and drawings clash with each other, mixing the sacred and profane, the vulgar and the reverenced, the popular and the learned. The texts of each breast and buttock contradict each other as the ferociously oxymoronic frenzy of Barnes' prose style, like

her painting style, continually yokes opposites in violent opposition, mocking Levitical prohibitions in an endless play at dissolving and reconstituting difference.

The length of the name, Desdemona, suggests a gigantic penis and is part of an age-old tradition of sexual jokes. But it also suggests Othello and "savage" jealousy and murder. Victor Hugo's *Notre Dame de Paris,* with its famous digression on the criminal underworld and the sewers, is invoked in the line "Paris before hygiene was introduced."[4] Hugo's earlier novel *Bug-Jargal* (1818 and 1826) was, like Aphra Behn's *Oronooko,* a study of a figure of "the royal slave."[5] This figure, a projection of a "phallic negro," is the white man's archetypal erotic animalization of the black. The white's spelling of desire on the black's penis, the pricking of the "prick" in what must have been a very painful operation, renders him impotent as a man while it mythologizes him as savage maleness. The black man's body is a text of Western culture's historical projections and myths about race. The angel from Chartres represents the myth of the black as angelic, innocent, and childlike during the early days of slavery; the book of magic refers to Europeans' fears of African religions. The Rothschild rose from Hamburg may suggest money made in the slave trade. The caravel suggests a slave ship, and the elegant wrists the ladies who benefited from slavery. In a further description of the tattoo, O'Connor claims that an obscene word runs down one side into the armpit, a word uttered by Prince Arthur Tudor on his wedding night, "one word so wholly epigrammatic and in no way befitting the great and noble British Empire" (*N,* 16). We may assume that that word, *merde,* is the Doctor's favorite and the author's too, since the text is as full of references to bird droppings as Paris itself is.

We know from Barnes' long response to Emily Coleman's essay on *Nightwood* that she expected readers to understand the references to Victor Hugo in the novel and to see it as part of the comic tradition of grotesque realism reaching back through Hugo to Rabelais.[6] In *Les Misérables,* Jean Valjean's fellow convict Cochepaille is tattooed with the date of the defeat at Waterloo, 1815. In *Nightwood,* Robin wanders from church "monstrously unfulfilled" with her large monk's feet, and the nuns at the convent of Perpetual Adoration give her a sprig from their rosebush and show her "where Jean Valjean had kept his rakes" (*N,* 46). Hugo describes the way in which the basest word in the French language, *merde,* became the finest word, as General Cambronne hurled it at his enemy on the battlefield. Hugo says that the expression of the excremental equals the soul, and in a note about the novel he claims that *merde* was the "misérable de mot," the outcast word, as his *misérables* were outcast people.[7] The fecal motif in Hugo's sewer chapters is continued in Barnes' *pissoir* passages and in her description of O'Connor's chamber pot.[8] For Hugo, the person who says *merde* is Prometheus, expressing the obscene laughter of the oppressed. The language of the latrine, which O'Connor speaks in the novel, is regenerative and Rabelaisian, as voiding is cleansing. Gutter language, *fex urbis,* is the voice of outcast people. In these chapters Hugo explores the argot of the underworld, its special culture, and defines it as "verbe devenu forçat," the word becomes a convict.[9]

Similar convict words are chained together in Dr. O'Connor's speeches, his stories of grotesque and painful suffering, the intensely overdetermined figures banging against the bars of the prison-house of language. His swearing, the mixture of prayer, oath, and profanity, the inclusion of the Virgin Mary and shit in the same sentence—all this goes back to Rabelais, reminding us of Gargantua arriving in Paris and drenching the crowd with urine, his "Mère de . . . merde . . . shit, Mother of God." Dung and defecation, in the Rabelaisian tradition described by Bakhtin, are part of carnival's reversal of authoritarian values, the eruption of folk humor in a bawdy acceptance of decay as renewal, of death as part of life. The language of this irrepressible force, as Bakhtin says, privileges the lower parts of the body. Critics who have described *Nightwood* as modernist decadence or the product of perversity have missed its deep roots in folk culture via Hugo and Rabelais. For Barnes is the female Rabelais, the articulator of woman's body/bawdy language. Like Hugo and Rabelais before her, Barnes writes scatology as ontology. She affirms being by celebrating the Below, the belly, the bowels, the big feet of Robin Vote and Nikka, who is a natural black man only to the knees.

Nikka's tattooed body, to return to the text, is a cabalistic ritual object put on display at the circus. Fighting the bear, he reminds us of Eugène Sue's Morok and Hugo's bizarre *L'homme qui rit,* whose monstrous and maimed characters resemble those of *Nightwood.* The friendship between the bearlike man Ursus and the civilized wolf Homo reminds us of Robin Vote as "the beast turning human" and the novel's controversial last scene with the dog; and Hugo's circus wagon as a universe of human, animal, and divine monsters is an earlier version of the circus world of *Nightwood.* "Garlanded with rosebuds and hack-work of the devil," Nikka's body is also a journalist's page (hack; Barnes as a brilliant journalist and "hack" writer; printer's devil). The tattoos, with their combination of text, vines, flowers, gothic script, and so forth, are an exact version of the early definition of the grotesque. In *Rabelais,* Bakhtin describes the bold infringement of borders in early grotesque art, in which forms "seemed to be interwoven as if giving birth to each other," animal, vegetable, and human passing uncannily one into another (*Rabelais,* 32). Nikka's body is like one of Djuna Barnes' drawings for *Ryder,* which I describe as "Pennsylvania Dutch surrealism" to capture their combination of folk naïveté and vitality with mythical beasts, texts, human figures, and grotesque vines.

But the art of tattooing is also a kind of bloody needlework. Thelma Wood, Djuna Barnes' lover and the model for Robin Vote, was an artist who did silverpoint etchings, a genre that one might call, with its dangerous, uncorrectable pinpricks, a "high art" form of tattoo. These etchings are also tabooed objects, studies of cannibalistic flowers and fetishistic shoes. (Thelma Wood's Berlin sketchbook is in the McKeldin Library.)

In the body of Nikka, Barnes creates an aesthetic of the Modernist Grotesque, a delicate and exotic refinement of the gross Rabelaisian realistic grotesque and the romantic intellectual grotesque of E. T. A. Hoffmann. Nikka's body as ritual object asserts the real and unalterable grotesquerie of the human body. In *The Painted Body,* Michel Thévoz follows Lacan in seeing the marking of the body as primitive human grappling with the mirror stage of development and identity formation, so that human skin is humanity's "first ground and surface of sign-making."[10] In other words, the body is our first book, the primal blank page on which our ancestors wrote. Anthropological evidence places the most ancient tattoos on the genitals, a tattooed or decorated phallus or voluptuous female body decorated on breast, buttocks, and genital areas being among the first human artifacts. Our own bodies were our first works of art, a remaking of the self. *Nightwood's* project is a remaking of gender and race categories of selfhood, and it is preoccupied with skin as a blank page. In Nikka's case, the tattoo so graphically described is another of Barnes' reversals: Africans seldom tattoo the body, preferring scarification or body painting, while light-skinned peoples, notably Asians, use tattoos. Marking the body seems to enact opposite meanings, suggesting first a symbolic separation from the mother as in Kristeva's use of the terms "semiotic" and "symbolic," where "semiotic" means all that Plato excluded from art— circus, carnival, festival, music, laughter, and dance. But it also marks the return of the repressed savage and unconscious desire. *Nightwood's* language is a perfect example of this "semiotic" in practice.

Thévoz sees the original tattoo as a symbolic mark of the human being's social relation to culture and circumcision as a representation of the taboo against incest with the mother. In Western culture, tattoo has been used to mark the subject as a slave or convict and has lost its ritual social origins in inclusion rather than exclusion from culture. The modern tattoo is like the mark of Cain, a sign of exclusion. But it also identifies the body with a certain class or group. The meaning of tattoo has changed historically from embodying symbolic law in "primitive" societies to marking the outlaw in modern societies—hence the figure in the modern novel of the lesbian feels that she has the mark of Cain on her forehead. (Cain seems to survive as a figure for the pre-patriarchal, driven out because he will not slaughter an animal for a patriarchal god.) Nikka in *Nightwood* is like the convicts in Kafka's *The Penal Colony,* their bodies tattooed by the infernal machine that inscribes each criminal with the text of the law he has infringed. French soldiers in the nineteenth century often tattooed the side of the hand with the word "merde" so that it would deliver a message when they saluted their superiors.

Djuna Barnes was fascinated with *maquillage.* Body painting, makeup, extravagant costuming, and cross-dressing are part of the style of what Shari Benstock calls "Sapphic Modernism."[11] Figuring Nikka as abjection, his skin a text on which the dominant culture writes him as other, Barnes writes from the place of exclusion as woman, exile, and lesbian, juggling the double message of the memory of body marking as beautiful and social and its present meaning as sinister and shameful. Thévoz relates the angry or erotic tattoos of modern convicts and mental patients as the outcasts' defiance of logocentric society's exclusion of them—hence the body and hair painting of contemporary "punk" culture. The answer to the question raised by Nikka's tattoos in *Nightwood* may be found in Ilse Koch's barbaric collection of tattoos cut from the skin of victims of Nazi persecutions at Buchenwald. Given the Levitical prohibition against writing on the body, these "works of art" were taken not from the bodies of Jews but from other outsiders; they represent the moment when culture ceases to laugh at Leviticus and begins to shudder.

Since so many readings of *Nightwood* situate the reader as "normal" and the characters as perverse and "damned," reading against the grain of the text's privileging of the oppressed as "us," I propose this reading as a sisterhood under the skin with the victimized, as the "fluid blue" under Robin's skin allies her with Nikka. In a similar way, many studies of the Nazis (aside from the brilliant film *Our Hitler*) emphasize the perversity of individual sadists rather than the complicity of a whole nation in genocide. Such readings deny not only history and reality but also the power of art, expressed in fiction like *Nightwood,* to change us.

Modernism, then, if we take *Nightwood* as its most representative text, is a tattoo on the backside of a black homosexual circus performer. The non-Aryan, nonheterosexual body is a book inscribed with the modern failure to understand or assimilate the difference of race, class, and gender. Sexuality, liminality, and color are textualities written on the body in thousands of pinpricks, little dots that make a language of bloody ellipses, a dot-dot-dot or code of absences as presence. The representation of taboo in tattoo is a fierce example of the display of the body as other, a ritual hieroglyphic of pleasure and pain, an invitation to read the body of the Other as a book. What is absent is the Nazi who will burn this book.

If Joyce in *Ulysses* writes ancient and modern patriarchy, mythologizes woman and Others the mother, Djuna Barnes in *Nightwood* laughs at Leviticus, bringing all the wandering Jews, blacks, lesbians, outsiders, and transvestites together in a narrative that mothers the Other. While Joyce privileges the fertility of the modern mother-goddess and her private parts, Barnes privileges the penis. But she celebrates the nonphallic penis, the limp member of the transvestite Dr. O'Connor—who masturbates in church like the Jongleur of Notre Dame doing tricks for the Virgin Mary—and the black man's impotent genitals that bear the white man's sexual burden.

The symbolic phallus as law is absent from *Nightwood,* replaced by the wayward penis of outlaw and transvestite. But its presence is brilliantly conveyed in the person of a woman, Hedvig Volkbein, Felix's mother, who dies in childbirth, not quite convinced by Guido, an Italian Jew masquerading as a German aristocrat, that his blood is untainted. Hedvig is German militarism. With her "massive chic," her goose step, her "hand, patterned on seizure," she dances in "a tactical manoeuvre" with shoulders conscious of braid and a turn of head that holds "the cold vigilance of a sentry." Like Lina Wertmüller's daring representation of a Nazi concentration camp commandant as a woman in her powerful film *Seven Beauties,* Barnes breaks taboo by representing absent Aryan patriarchal power in the person of a woman. In the film, Italy is to Germany as woman is to man, the Other. So the Italian male is Other to the German woman, feminized by fascism.

Kenneth Burke says *Nightwood* is not political, that it has nothing to do with the Nazis.[12] Burke's discomfort with the seeming anti-Semitism of *Nightwood* is understandable. The scholar working on the text is confronted with T. S. Eliot's editorial cuts of passages that seem overtly homosexual or questionably anti-Semitic. But Djuna Barnes identifies with all outsiders. She was originally named Djalma, after Eugène Sue's *Wandering Jew.* Sue's Djalma is tattooed by a "thug" in Java during his sleep, and his killing of the panther onstage in chapter 14 is surely a source for Robin's scene with the lion in *Nightwood.*[13] But I would argue that the "political unconscious" of *Nightwood* is located in its supposedly irrelevant first chapter, meant to disguise its existence as a lesbian novel.

As *Nightwood* is not only a lesbian novel, its antifascism is apparent only when its triumphs over its own anit-Semitism, when we realize that its characters—Jews, homosexuals, lesbians, transvestites, gypsies, blacks, and circus performers—were all to perish in the Holocaust. Felix Volkbein is named for his role as wandering Jew (and the Yiddish Theatre in New York?), his middle European sadness contradicting the happiness of the Italian "Felix." As "Volkbein" he is the foot soldier of history, the portable slave, the legman of disaster, the unofficial "advance man" of the Paris circus, as Nora Flood is in reality the legwoman of the Denckman Circus. Like the Roman fragment of a runner's leg in his parent's plush Vienna flat, Felix is "disassociated" from his past. As his ancestor's black-and-yellow handkerchief reminds him of the medieval Roman circus in which Jews were forced to run around the arena with ropes around their necks, his restless search for "pure" racial nobility to which to "bow down" signifies his internalization of racial difference while underscoring the reality of a Europe in which racial purity has been obscured by mixed marriages and false credentials. The dismemberment and fragmentation of the Roman statues, the runner's leg, and the "chilly half-turned head of matron stricken at the bosom" recall early Roman circuses that sacrificed outcast Christians to the lions and medieval circuses in which outcast Jews were terrorized and prophesy with chilling accuracy the Nazi destruction of millions of Jews and other outcasts, devoured by their modern technological lions, the gas chambers and ovens of the concentration camps.

The blond Aryan beast slouching toward Buchenwald is present in this novel only in Hedvig's resemblance to him in 1880, but Felix's uneasiness, his attraction to the Catholic church, his scholarly labors, and his devotion to the past, to his sick child, and to the topsy-turvy world of the circus are reminders of what was destroyed by fascism's ugly fist. Felix is literally the foot of the folk, the embodiment of Bakhtin's carnivalesque, the preserver of circus culture and history.

Joyce's Night Town with cross-dressed Bella-Bello played against Bloom in a corset, like Tiresias in Eliot's *Waste Land,* suggests emasculation, not the ancient and powerful life-force of mythical transvestite figures. Barnes' doctor-transvestite is only posing as a gynecologist, and he identifies with the maternal principle. He lampoons all of the male sex doctors whose own sexual identity was so troubled, from the mad Otto Weininger to Havelock Ellis (who was aroused only by women urinating) to the Freud of the Fleiss letters. Unlike Joyce's Night Town, Barnes' *Nightwood* privileges the female world of night, magic, and ritual in the last scene in the chapel in the forest (Dante's darkwood), suggesting that "culture," in the primitive figure of Robin as racial memory, survives in America as Europe is destroyed by fascism.

The exiled Felix with his monocle reminds one of Djuna Barnes' sketch of Joyce (plate 13), as *Nightwood* in its static structure reflects Stephen Dedalus' aesthetic of

stasis and proves it wrong, for fiction can be just as "impure" standing still as it can be while wandering. Joyce is recalled in O'Connor's chamber pot, in the naming of Nora, and in Nora's flat in the rue de Cherche-Midi, the home of the eye clinic where Barnes visited Joyce after his many operations. Did he give the printer's copy of *Ulysses* with hand corrections to the author of *Nightwood* in tribute to a writer of one of the few modernist texts to rival his phallogocentrism? Or, by giving the logos to a woman-identified man, does Barnes rob it of patriarchal privilege? Since O'Connor, "the Old Woman who lives in the closet," defines the female as only the maternal and womb-centered, his is a matriarchal phallogocentrism, a gynologos, not a cliterologos. Molly's "yes" is answered by Robin Vote's "no" to marriage, "no" to motherhood, "no" to monogamous lesbianism. Robin's "no" is a preverbal, prepatriarchal, primitive bark—as the novel ends in America and she ritually acts the bear before her Madonna-Artemis, goddess of autonomous sexuality, owner of her body and her self. As Europe bows down to fascism, O'Connor asks, "Why doesn't anyone know when everything is over, except me? . . . I've not only lived my life for nothing, but I've told it for nothing—abominable among the filthy people" (*N,* 165).

Despite Burke's denial of its political awareness, I believe *Nightwood* is the representative modernist text, a prose poem of abjection, tracing the political unconscious of the rise of fascism, as lesbians, blacks, circus people, Jews, and transvestites—outsiders all—*bow down* before Hitler's truly perverted Levitical prescriptions for racial purity.

We might also see the "political unconscious" at work in the other meanings of "tattoo."[14] After the Doctor finishes telling the story of Nikka, Felix asks him about Vienna's "military superiority." For a tattoo is also a military drum signal or call to alarm, as well as a symbolic drama or masque performed by soldiers by torchlight to act out the victory of valor over the forces of the night. The rosy-faced German boys the doctor recalls will soon be at the gates of the night world of Paris. The drumbeats of racial "purity" will sound against Nikka, O'Connor, and Volkbein. The evening of the "living statues" and outcasts at the Count's is a museum of soon-to-be-exterminated human types, like Hitler's Jewish Museum at Prague, meant to be all that was left of Jewish culture after the Holocaust. As Hugo's *Notre Dame de Paris* is an antihistorical novel prefiguring the Revolution, *Nightwood* is an ahistorical novel anticipating the Holocaust.

When the "living statues" are expelled from the party, the scene anticipates uncannily all the Expulsions from the Party of modern European history. Their refuge is a café in Unter den Linden, the traditional meeting place of homosexuals and political aliens. O'Connor explains the Count's action as fear of impotence: he "suspected that he had come upon his last erection" (*N,* 25). The erection is a signifier of order and uprightness. And the remark is uncanny in the light of subsequent political events, as in Frau Mann's lament, "I've an album of my own . . . and everyone in it looks like a soldier—even though they are dead" (*N,* 27). The narrator may say with Doctor O'Connor: "Oh, *papalero,* have I not summed up my time! I shall rest myself someday by the brim of Saxon-les-Bains and drink it dry, or go to pieces in Hamburg at the gambling table, or end up like Madame de Staël—with an affinity for Germany" (*N,* 126).

RITUAL AS INSTRUCTION: BARNES CRITIQUES FREUD

My voice cracked on the word "difference"; soaring up divinely. . . .

(*N,* 92)

Nightwood is problematic for the woman reader and unusual for modernism because it is such a tightly closed text and because the narration is so distant and detached. Its heteroglossia resides in the doctor's multivoices stories of abjection; its carnivalesque is not open to the audience but stylized and ritualized in the performative mode. *Nightwood* avoids the intimacy of a Colette or Woolf novel in which narration is shared with the reader so that she feels cocreative in the making of the text. The narrative voice here seems to have no gender except in the vitriolic description of Jenny Petherbridge, which privileges Nora's pain. Jenny, as the most abject character (because her author hates her), might be Barnes' portrait of the voyeuristic reader or literary critic, collecting other women's clothes and discarded loves. Strictly cast in the role of "audience," the reader is forced to "bow down" to the text, to replicate the anxiety of abjection. The reader reads at the site of what Naomi Schor calls the "bisextuality" of female fetishism. As a lesbian novel *Nightwood* dramatizes illicit love in a patriarchy, and some readers may find Nora's possessive infantilization of Robin as patriarchal as Hedvig's militarism or Felix's fixation on Germany. Despite the fact that its plot is a lesbian love story, *Nightwood* does not write the lesbian body as *Ladies Almanack* does, nor does it dramatize female desire, except insofar as it voices victimization, sets the alienated subjectivity of all outsiders, and flouts bourgeois concepts of normality by privileging the private pain of a panoply of "monsters." The indeterminate desire of transvestite, Jew, lesbian, and black makes the forbidden erotic into a political cry for freedom. Racism, sexism, anti-Semitism, and homophobia are challenged by this text. Mademoiselle Basquette, raped on her wheeled board, is the archetypal sexual victim as "basket case," humiliated and used by male sadism as Nikka is abused by male masochism. The desire of the disabled like

Mademoiselle Basquette, "a girl without legs, built like a medieval abuse" (*N,* 26), for love and freedom *as they are,* rather than to be made "normal," cannot be made into a universal principle of natural law. As Hans Mayer writes in *Outsiders,* "The light of the categorical imperative does not shine for them,"[15] and O'Connor says, "even the greatest generality has a little particular" (*N,* 89). Mademoiselle Basquette, who looks like the figurehead of a ship and is raped by a sailor, is the disabled woman, hostage to men, of Hans Christian Andersen's "The Little Mermaid," as brilliantly analyzed by Nina Auerbach in *Women and the Demon.* There is always another Other.

By centering the marginal, *Nightwood* provides a spectacle of human bondage that articulates the angst of the abject so well that the absent upright, the pillars of society, are experienced unconsciously by the reader as the enemies of the human spirit. Figuring plot as plight in the tradition of the great nineteenth-century French realist fictions of Victor Hugo and Eugène Sue, Barnes modernizes the story of the oppressed hunchback or Jew to include sexual outcasts. As a melodrama of beset "perverts," *Nightwood* transcends its models by its refusal to play on the reader's pity. The human dignity of the aberrant is maintained by the narrator's objectivity, the irrepressible comic carnivalesque tone, and the exuberant vitality of obscene language.

The linguistic richness of *Nightwood*—its choked abundance of puns and plays on words, its fierce allusiveness to medieval and Jacobean high and low art, the extraordinary range of its learned reach across the history of Western culture—marks it as the logos-loving match of *Ulysses.* We are not accustomed to thinking of Djuna Barnes as a learned woman, a scholar as well as a writer. Nor does *Nightwood* arrange itself neatly next to other modernist, experimental works by women in an antilogocentric act. Gertrude Stein robs words of meaning, objectifies them, empties them, and fills them again out of her own ego. Woolf and Colette experiment with an intimate and flexible female sentence. The narratives of Jean Rhys, H. D., or Elizabeth Bowen are inescabably women's novels. If we place *Nightwood* among female antifascist fiction of the 1930s—Christina Stead's *The House of All Nations,* Virginia Woolf's *The Years,* and Marguerite Yourçenar's *Coup de Grâce*—it fits thematically. Woolf's novel traces the rise of fascism from the 1880s to the 1930s by concentrating on its origin in the patriarchal family. Stead condemns capitalism for its collaboration with fascism. Yourçenar brilliantly exposes German militarism and its patriarchal code of honor by privileging the ruthless and ethically bankrupt officer-narrator, leaving the reader the work of judging his self-serving narrative. In light of these antifascist texts, *Nightwood*'s project is to expose the collaboration of Freudian psychoanalysis with fascism in its desire to "civilize" and make "normal" the sexually aberrant misfit. *Nightwood* asserts that the outcast is normal and truly human. Freud and fascism, by labeling deviance medically and politically, expose the inhumanity of the madness for order in every denial of difference from Leviticus to the sex doctors, Kraft-Ebbing, Havelock Ellis, Otto Weininger, and even Freud himself. Barnes makes us all misfits, claiming that in human misery we can find the animal and the divine in ourselves.

In this reading Nora is the archetypal Dora or female hysteric, and Dr. Freud is brilliantly parodied in the figure of Dr. Matthew-Mighty-grain-of-salt-Dante-O'Connor. The lesbian patient chooses as doctor a transvestite whose most passionate desire is to be a woman, whose womb envy is so strong that it parodies Freudian penis envy mercilessly. The psychoanalyst's office is a filthy bedroom with a reeking chamber pot. Freud's famous totems, the sacred objects from ancient cultures that people his shelves and tables in H. D.'s famous tribute, are mocked by O'Connor's rusty forceps, broken scalpel, perfume bottles, ladies' underclothing, and abdominal brace. The psychoanalytic structure is ruptured as the patient asks the question and the doctor answers. The doctor is in bed in a granny nightgown and wig, powdered and rouged, and the patient stands by his bed; it is three in the morning, not three in the afternoon. The patient is rational, puritanical, and analytical; the doctor is mad. When Nora complains of heartbreak at the loss of Robin, Matthew mocks her: "A broken heart have you! I have falling arches, flying dandruff, a floating kidney, shattered nerves *and* a broken heart! But do I scream that an eagle has me by the balls or has dropped his oyster on my heart?" (*N*, 154).

But he proves to be a brilliant feminist psychoanalyst and he devastatingly deconstructs her dream. Floating in a Chagall-like dreamscape, her grandmother, "whom I loved more than anyone," is in a glass coffin with her father circling the grave struggling with her death. In the dream she watches, unable to do anything; then her father's body stops circling and drifts immobile beside the grandmother's body.

O'Connor detects the absence of the mother in Nora's dream. "'It's my mother without argument I want!' And then in his loudest voice he roared: 'Mother of God! I wanted to be your son—the unknown beloved second would have done!'" (*N*, 149-50). The two grandmother incest dreams constitute a revisionary psychological constitution of the female self, which we may call a *nonology*. The *nona* or grandmother may well become a young woman's role model and beloved in cases of real or imagined incest, when the mother has not protected the daughter from the father's assaults. Nora refuses to deal with the relationship between her love for Robin and her own role as daughter in the family. She begs the doctor to tell Robin never to forget her. O'Connor's

psychological advice to the upright Nora is that she must bend, bow down, experience the body and get out of herself in ritual or carnival, let herself go, deal with the animal in herself:

> "Tell her yourself," said the doctor, "or sit in your own trouble silently if you like; it's the same with ermines—those fine yellow ermines that women pay such a great price for—how did they get that valuable colour? By sitting in bed and pissing the sheets, or weeping in their own way. It's the same with persons; they are only of value when they have laid themselves open to 'nuisance'—their own and the world's. *Ritual itself constitutes an instruction.* So we come back to the place from which I set out; pray to the good God; she will keep you. Personally, I call her 'she' because of the way she made me; it somehow balances the mistake. . . . That priceless galaxy of misinformation called the mind, harnessed to that stupendous and threadbare glomerate compulsion called the soul, ambling down the almost obliterated bridle path of Well and Ill, fortuitously planned—is the holy Habeus Corpus, the manner in which the body is brought before the judge. . . ."
>
> (*N*, 150; emphasis added)

The doctor continually points out to Nora that the rigidity of her American Protestant consciousness, her fear of the body, of drink, promiscuity, and dirt, make her love for Robin destructive, possessive, patriarchal in its insistence on monogamy and control of the beloved. He mocks her romantic possessiveness: "there you were sitting up high and fine, with a rose-bush up your arse" (*N*, 151).

Like Freud, O'Connor has an inexhaustible fund of case histories of aberrant behaviour, and he has a great deal to say about the art of writing. "I have a narrative, but you will be put to it to find it" (*N*, 97), he tells his "patient." He begs Nora to stop writing letters tormenting Robin: "Can't you rest now, lay down the pen?" Since he has no one to write to, he takes in "a little light laundry known as the Wash of the World" (*N*, 126), the psychoanalyst as Irish washerwoman, the writer as producer of dirty linen. "Haven't I eaten a book too? Like the angels and prophets? And wasn't it a bitter book to eat? . . . And didn't I eat a page and tear a page and stamp on others and flay some and toss some into the toilet for relief's sake—then think of Jenny without a comma to eat, and Robin with nothing but a pet name—your pet name to sustain her . . ." (*N*, 127). Telling one of his homosexual stories in which he claims that he can tell the district and nationality of every penis he encounters like a gourmet, he asks, "Must I, perchance, like careful writers, guard myself against the conclusions of my readers?" (*N*, 94). He rails against American cleanliness, praising "the good dirt"; because a European bathes in "true dust," he can trace the history of his actions. His body is his page. "*L'Echo de Paris* and his bed sheets were run off the same press.

One may read in both the travail life has had with him—he reeks with the essential wit necessary to the 'sale' of both editions, night edition and day" (*N*, 89). Nora's problem is the body/mind split. "The Anglo-Saxon has made the literal error; using water, he has washed away his page" (*N*, 90). The doctor wants Nora to recognize her animality, to face her desire for Robin as physical, and to stop seeing herself as "saving" a lost soul.

The great writer writes from the body. The dirty bed-sheet is the writer's page. Patriarchal culture has traditionally seen women as a blank page on which to write. So Nora sees Robin, and projects herself on to that page. Djuna Barnes' genius lies in her ability to overcome Nora's anxieties, and she is one of the few women writers whose novel was run off the same press as her bed sheets. Contemporary novels such as Gabriel Garcia Marquez' *A Hundred Years of Solitude* or Günter Grass' *The Flounder* owe a great deal to the fantastic realism of *Nightwood*. Feminist fantastic realism has its own as yet critically uncharted history, but certainly *Nightwood* may be read in the context of Sylvia Townsend Warner's *Lolly Willowes*, Rebecca West's *Harriet Hume*, Joanna Russ' *The Female Man*, and their brilliant successor, Angela Carter's *Night at the Circus*. I have argued in "A Wilderness of One's Own" that these novels often appear after a period of realism in fiction reflecting political activism on the part of women, like Woolf's *Orlando* and *Flush*, where the writer is frustrated at the failure of struggle to change the power structure.[16]

Nightwood differs from its sister texts in its anticipation of historical horror, its proleptic impulse. Women writers have traditionally been forced to wash away from their page any mention of desire. It is as if Djuna Barnes had decided to include in *Nightwood* every word, image, and story that women have never been able to tell, to flout every possible taboo from the excretory to the sexual, and to invent, in Nora's grandmother incest dreams, her *nonology*, taboos uncatalogued even by Freud. Her boldness is remarkable. Even H. D., in her *Tribute to Freud*, was sly and subtle in her critique of "the master." She undermines his authority by greeting his dog first, by getting him to complain that she won't love him, by pretending that he treats her as an equal, by claiming that he approves of her relationship with Bryher, by describing him as a fellow student of myth and the collective unconscious. In short, H. D. fictionalizes Freud as Jung. Her "tribute" is really to woman's power to make the analyst collaborate with her, to save her "abnormality" for her art.

Djuna Barnes' critique of Freud is less directly personal than H. D.'s, but both are part of a modernist feminist insistence on woman-centeredness and partnership between doctor and patient. *Nightwood* challenges not only Freud, but the whole history of the treatment of female hysteria. Dr. O'Connor's lies seem to Felix "to be the framework of a forgotten but imposing plan"; "the great doctor, he's a divine idiot and a wise man" (*N*, 30, 31). Matthew says, "the only people who really *know* anything about medical science are the nurses, and they never tell; they'd get slapped if they did" (*N*, 31). (The nurse is a major icon of European modernism. See the brilliant story by Barnes' friend Antonia White, "The House of Clouds," and one of many novels about nursing in World War I, Irene Rathbone's *We That Were Young*.)

O'Connor claims that he is not neurasthenic and pronounces, "No man needs curing of his individual sickness; his universal malady is what he should look to" (*N*, 32). These remarks are part of the slapstick dialogue, with Felix as "straight man," which introduces "La Somnambule." Stage Irishman and stage Jew mock each other's racial traits as liars and meddlers and make fun of doctors. The comic pair then wake Sleeping Beauty, in the person of Robin Vote, "meet of child and desperado" (*N*, 35). In keeping with the carnival spirit of their "act," O'Connor plays magician or "dumb-founder" at a street fair and turns his back on the patient to make up his hairy face with her powder and rouge and steal a hundred-franc note. The reader "watches" this scene as a cabaret act and "reads" it as a pantomine of Sleeping Beauty woken by the wrong prince as well as a classic joke about a crooked apothecary or quack doctor.

The narrator tells us that "the woman who presents herself to the spectator as a 'picture' forever arranged is, for the contemplative mind, the chiefest danger" (*N*, 37). The "picture" of the disheveled Robin flung like a dancer on the bed, in a scene like Rousseau's "jungle trapped in a drawing room," emphasizes her legs and feet in men's white flannel trousers and dancing pumps. Extraordinarily cinematic, the scene reverses the reader's picture of Marlene Dietrich in 1930s vamp films such as *The Blue Angel* or *Blonde Venus* (which even has a gorilla, a "beast turning human"). We remember Dietrich "transvested" from the waist up in top hat and tails, pointing the contrast to very feminine legs. In a famous essay Kenneth Tynan wrote of Dietrich what might be said of Robin Vote: "She has sex but no particular gender. They say . . . that she was the only woman allowed to attend the annual ball for male transvestites in pre-Hitler Berlin. . . . [T]his Marlene lives in a sexual no man's land—and no-woman's either. . . . [S]he is every man's mistress and mother, every woman's lover and aunt. . . ."[17] In the context of *Nightwood*, one would say, "Every woman's lover and grandmother."

Lesbian subculture in Paris in the 1920s and 1930s affords many examples of the woman in a tuxedo. (Rebecca West once described Radclyffe Hall and Una

Troubridge as looking in their male attire and cropped hair like "a distant prospect of Eton College.")[18] As tattoo is a form of the general Levitical taboo against transvestism, Robin's appearance in men's trousers is another version of writing on the body, or rewriting the body. The carnival of cross-dressing destabilizes identity, keeping bisexuality from being anchored to one pole and acting out a "female fetishism," denying Freud's assumption that fetishism is exclusively male. Naomi Schor's argument—"that ultimately *female travesty,* in the sense of women dressing up as or impersonating other women, constitutes by far the most disruptive form of *bisextuality*"—applies more fully to **Nightwood** than to any other novel I can think of, though it is characteristic of the lives and work of the whole movement of "Sapphic Modernism." If "female fetishism is an oxymoron," then one may argue that Djuna Barnes' style itself is a form of fetishism which allows the reader free play in the riddle of sexuality.

Even Robin's skin participates in tattoo and links her to Nikka and to Nora's obsession with her as "purity's black backside." Consoling Felix for the loss of Robin, O'Connor later compares her to a horse whose "hide was a river of sorrow. . . . Her eyelashes were gray-black, like the eyelashes of a nigger, and at her buttocks' soft centre a pulse throbbed like a fiddle. . . . Yes, oh God, Robin was beautiful. . . . Sort of fluid blue under her skin, as if the hide of time had been stripped from her." Robin's "hide," her "flayed body," is "the infected carrier of the past"; she is "eaten death returning" (*N,* 37), exactly Bakhtin's construction of the material body as the memory of culture. The "fluid blue" under Robin's skin is like Nikka's tattoo. The scene at the circus when Robin is lionized by the lion's eyes reminds us of Mae West's brilliant articulation of female animal desire in the classic 1930s film *I'm No Angel.* As a heroine, Robin rescues libido from the exclusive possession of men. The agency of her desire and its refusal to be fixed as the desired object of lesbian lovers or husband, contained in motherhood, or controlled by T. S. Eliot's or other critics' reading of her as doomed, damned, or pathologically placed as a medical case study is a textual triumph. Even Robin's voice (reported, for she only speaks twice) resembles Marlene Dietrich's: "In the tones of this girl's voice was the pitch of one enchanted with the gift of postponed abandon: the low drawling 'aside' voice of the actor who, in the soft usury of his speech, withholds a vocabulary until the profitable moment when he shall be facing his audience" (*N,* 38). It is precisely that pitch of postponed abandon that characterizes the art of Dietrich: the "low drawl," the slight catch in the phrasing, the way she sang the sensual as if it were a lullaby, and, above all, the sense that every song was sung as if she were remembering it from a long time ago—these are the things that constitute her appeal. So Robin's "soft usury" of speech is related to her archetypal resemblance to the ancient past. There is a nonthreatening animal growl to this voice; O'Connor would call it the voice of the dream prince, the "uninhabited angel," the genderless or empty sign of her body in which child and desperado meet. Robin is a speechless picture for much of the novel, but her outburst at Nora (the fetish talks back?) when she is drunk in the street is telling: "You are a devil! You make everything dirty! . . . You make me feel dirty and tired and old!" (*N,* 143). She makes Nora give money to an old prostitute: "'These women—they are all like her,' she said with fury. 'They are all good—they want to save us!'" (*N,* 144). Robin's sisterhood with the downtrodden, crawling in the gutter with outcasts, is the way in which "ritual constitutes an instruction for her. Her abjection is the reverse of Nora's uprightness, and it is privileged in the novel as the more *humane condition.* She doesn't want to be saved; she wants to be free.

There is an ironic message for Nora in Matthew's tale of the London "Tupenny Upright": "ladies of the *haute sewer* . . . holding up their badgered flounces, or standing still, letting you do it, silent and indifferent as the dead. . . . [T]heir poor damned dresses hiked up and falling away over the rump, all gathers and braid, like a Crusader's mount, with all the trappings gone sideways with misery" (*N,* 130-31).

At the very heart of the novel the twin *pissoir* passages condemn the upright. A woman curses her lover in the toilet: "May you die standing upright! May you be damned upward!" She curses her lover's genitals: "May this be damned, terrible and damned spot! May it wither into the grin of the dead, may this draw back, low riding mouth in an empty snarl of the groin" (*N,* 95). The rest of this passage anticipates Robin on all fours at the end of the novel. "For what do you know of me, man's meat? I'm an angel on all fours, with a child's feet behind me, *seeking my people that have never been made,* going down face foremost, drinking the waters of night at the water hole of the damned . . ." (*N,* 95; emphasis added). The lesbian curse on the clitoris in the *pissoir* is terrifying. Why does Barnes set it next to the rollicking tales of happy homosexual cruising ("cottaging") and O'Connor's domestication of the Parisian *pissoir* as his cottage ("my only fireside is the outhouse" [*N,* 91])? What is missing from the casual sex of the men is the possessiveness of "love." (These passages couldn't be written after AIDS.) Yet when Nora seeks solace in the arms of other women she misses Robin even more. Barnes seems to suggest that the dynamics of lesbian sexuality are different from those of homosexuality. Matthew longs to be someone's wife while Robin rejects Nora's wifely domestic ways and her infantalization of her. In Latin "infans" means speechless, and **Nightwood** creates the sex object as the silent subject.

Between them, O'Connor and Nora try to analyze lesbianism, though she cannot give up her posture, derived from patriarchal conceptions of love, of the abandoned wife. The discussion centers on the figure of the doll as the lesbian's child, Robin's smashing the doll, Jenny Petherbridge's gift of another doll to Robin and the figure of the prince. Robin says she chose a girl who resembles a boy as a lover from the figures of the prince and princess in romances. "We were impaled in our childhood upon them as they rose through our primers, the sweetest lie of all . . ." (*N,* 137). When the love that one has been told to expect never arrives, one chooses the androgynous figure of the prince.

Nora tells the doctor that the doll she shared with Robin was "their child," but she also says, "We give death to a child when we give it a doll—it's the effigy and the shroud" (*N,* 142). O'Connor tells Nora that she really wanted Robin to *be* a doll, an "uninhabited angel," an object onto which she could project "sexless misgiving." But she does not really listen to him or respond to his analysis.

> Do you think that Robin had no right to fight you with her only weapon? She saw in you the fearful eye that would make her a target forever. Have not girls done as much for the doll? The last doll, given to age, is the girl who should have been a boy, and the boy who should have been a girl! The love of that last doll was foreshadowed in the love of the first. The doll and the immature have something right about them, the doll because it resembles but does not contain life, and the third sex because it contains life but resembles the doll.
>
> (*N,* 148)

So sleeping Robin is not really the princess but the prince.[19]

The scene in which Robin raises her child over her head as if to smash it, but doesn't, and the later scene in which she smashes and kicks the doll—her "child"—with Nora have an element of the uncanny in them. We may compare the treatment of the doll figure in *Nightwood* to Freud's essay "The Uncanny."[20] When O'Connor tells Nora that she has "dressed the unknowable in the garments of the known" (*N,* 136), he is giving a definition of the uncanny much like Freud's definition of a species of the horrifying that is also very familiar. Freud's essay is a peculiar example of the analyst as literary critic, or rather, as father of patriarchal aesthetic theory. Like some contemporary theorists, he begins, "I have not made a very thorough examination of the bibliography" ("Uncanny," 123). He then claims that he himself is not susceptible to the uncanny but will nevertheless write the essay since most aesthetic theory deals only with "the sublime." Freud fills the gap with several pages from dictionaries in various languages defining *unheimlich.* *Heimlich* comes to mean not only *homely* in some cases, but its opposite, and magic is associated with it as well as the secret parts of the body. It never occurs to Freud that *heimlich* refers

to the female world of the home with safety and comfort provided by woman. The transition of the word's meaning from holy to unholy, from the domestic to the horrific, clearly marks the historical change from male pleasure in the female to his fear of woman, her body and her space. Freud, albeit unwittingly, is one of the best examples of this ideological reversal. While Freud's definition is a workable one, there is a great discrepancy between his definition and his examples, most of which come from E. T. A. Hoffmann's *Tales.*

I maintain that Freud's notion of the uncanny, as developed in his examples, is gender-biased: only certain men would experience the uncanny in the cases he cites, and women do not find these situations uncanny. Therefore, they are not universal. It seems perfectly reasonable to suppose that male and female versions of the uncanny should be different from each other and to examine the female versions of the uncanny offered by *Nightwood* in contrast to Freud's analysis. Since women have been the providers of *heimlichkeit* or domestic bliss, it is obvious that their experiences of the uncanny will be different. Freud, quoting Jentsch, starts his inquiry by finding the uncanny in our doubt as to whether something that appears animate is really alive or whether a lifeless object might really be alive ("Uncanny," 132), as in waxwork figures or dolls.[21] Freud is at some pains to deny the importance of the figure of the doll, Olympia, in the uncanny effect of Hoffmann's "The Sand-Man," the first act of Offenbach's opera *Tales of Hoffmann.*[22] (I wonder if one could read Manet's famous painting *Olimpia* as another participant in the Freud-Hoffmann doll-making paradigm, the reduction of women to the passive object of the male gaze. The painting seems to invoke an order of objecthood: white woman—doll, black woman—dog.)

Hoffmann's fantastic realism and grotesquerie were a direct influence on Djuna Barnes. While Bakhtin regards Hoffmann as too alienated and morbid to participate in the Rabelaisian folk tradition of grotesque, Djuna Barnes was influenced by and participates in both traditions. The romantic concern with the sick self, the move of fairy-tale fantasy from pastoral forest to metropolitan café, the concern with night and dream and with Mesmer's experiments with hypnotism, "the science of the soul," as proof of the existence of the supernatural—these concerns come from Hoffmann to Barnes and are part of the intellectual origins of *Nightwood.* "The Sand-Man" was originally published in *Night Pieces,* and Hoffmann shared Barnes' love of Callot, the seventeenth-century grotesque engraver of creatures part beast and part human. Like Barnes, Hoffmann had an amazon grandmother, and he enjoyed disfiguring the margins of her Bible with images of satyrs and hell. His portrait of Olympia seems to have come from his mother, described as rigid, cold, hysterical, and given to staring vacantly into space (*Tales,* 18, 19).

Nathaniel's obsession with Olympia, the automaton, is based on her passivity: "Never before had he such a splendid listener. She neither embroidered nor knitted; she did not look out of the window nor feed a bird nor play with a lapdog or kitten . . . she sat for hours on end without moving, staring directly into his eyes, and her gaze grew ever more ardent and animated" (*Tales*, 162). Through the spyglass he buys from Coppelius, Nathaniel sees his real lover, Clara, as a doll and tries to kill her. Eyes are the heart of the story, and Freud insists on reading through men's eyes a tale of fear of castration in the loss of eyes and the hero's relation with his father and Coppelius as a good father/bad father drama.

I suggest that Freud's analysis represses his own interest in the collaboration of Professor Spalanzini with the mysterious charlatan Dr. Coppelius/Coppola (Italian for "eye-socket") in which he may have seen his own collaboration with the eventually discredited Fliess, though the part of the body in question was the nose. The two doctors "create" a woman. (The womb envy of the Freud-Fliess letters is obvious; Fliess believed that men had cycles like women, and Freud appeared to accept this idea.)[23] What is at issue in the story is the male doctors' creation and destruction of the woman patient. Hoffmann's Olympia is mechanical, "La Somnambule." The intellectual history of "somnambulism," which meant hypnotism (not merely sleepwalking), is the direct forerunner of Freud's definition of the unconscious. In this history the line between science and charlatanism was very thin. For Fourier, Eugène Sue, Victor Hugo, Mesmer, and Hoffmann, somnambulism proved the existence of the human spirit, the collective unconscious, or God. This antienlightenment, antimaterialist doctrine of "illuminism" was also the mother of modern socialism; metempsychosis (Joyce's "met him pike hoses") and animal magnetism were some of its tenets, as were an adrogynous god, a sexed universe, and a division of the world into animal, human, and angel.[24] Since so many of these ideas animate the world of *Nightwood*, I suspect that Djuna Barnes' intellectual origins are to be found here.[25]

When she labels Robin Vote "La Somnambule," Djuna Barnes is not aligning her with Lady Macbeth but with the innocent heroine of Bellini's opera *La somnambula*, whose romantic story was written to prove the existence of the soul to atheists and rationalists. People are not simply "living statues," material automatons, it was argued, but animated by spirit. The count in the opera was a "scientist" who proved to the unbelieving folk that the heroine's unconscious spirit caused her to walk in her sleep and that her rational self had no control over her actions. Unlike *Tales of Hoffmann, La somnambula* no longer commands the immense popularity it had in the nineteenth century, largely because intellectual historians have not been willing to see the roots

of modern thought, either socialism or psychoanalysis, in these romantic, irrational experiments. At a production of *La somnambula* in Washington, D.C. (December 1984), the audience laughed through the scene in which the heroine sings of her love for her fiancé while sleepwalking to the count's bed. The unconscious power of her desire is the point of the opera, as it is the point of Robin's nightwalks into promiscuity in *Nightwood*: she retains her innocence, her association with the virgin Diana of Epheseus. We interpret Robin's virginity as control over her own sexuality; as a sleepwalker she is the collective unconscious of undifferentiated female desire. Felix says she has the "odour of memory"; her speech is "heavy and unclarified"; "there was in her every movement a slight drag, as if the past were a web about her" (*N*, 118, 119).

Nightwood plays operatic allusions against circus allusions in a dialectic between folk and highbrow art on the subject of desire. O'Connor introduces Robin to Jenny Petherbridge at the opera, the powerful *Rigoletto* (also based on a Victor Hugo plot), in which the father murders his daughter while trying to avenge her rape, refusing to accept the fact that she loves the count who raped her. O'Connor mocks the Diva: "there's something wrong with any art that makes a woman all bust!" (*N*, 103).

Though Felix asks for Wagner's music to be played in cafés, O'Connor turns Wagner's heroic chaste male ideal of brotherhood, as well as the medieval patriarchal theme of the quest (used to great effect by the Nazis), into a joke and a feminist critique of Wagner: "one woman went down through the ages for sitting through *Parsifal* up to the point where the swan got his death, whereupon she screamed out, 'Godamercy, they have shot the Holy Grail!'" (*N*, 96). Barnes is taking potshots at the repressive ideal of male celibacy articulated by Wagner, an ideal that displaces desire onto evil figures of seductive females. The operatic *motives* are also "answered" in the dialogue of the novel with lines from music-hall and popular songs. This pastiche of fragmented pieces from the past of Western culture that we now associate with the postmodern is also practiced by Barnes in her painting and drawing: *faux* woodcuts, parodies of the Beardsleyesque, copies of folk-art cartoons in which the faces are made into realistic portraits while the rest of the drawing is derivative, oil paintings on cardboard.

The doctor tells the story of Don Anticolo, the tenor from Beirut, who mourns his dead son while drinking with a dozen sailors and throwing up and down the box of his ashes "no bigger than a doll's crate" in a scene that recalls Robin smashing the doll. The whole of the chapter "The Squatter" mimics the opera as well as a commedia dell'arte Punch and Judy show. When Jenny dresses up in costume and takes Robin and her guests in old-fashioned carriages to the Bois, the grand masquerade scene is an abduction from the lesbian seraglio; the fighting and scratching of the lovers are like a puppet show at a fair where Punch and Judy are both women; and the child Sylvia, who is caught in the quarrel, adds a melodramatic *frisson*. Djuna Barnes' father composed operas, including the comic and melodramatic "Allan Castle," whose heroine is stabbed as she poses inside a picture frame, anticipating Nora's "framing" in the window as she observes Robin with another woman and in the doorway of the chapel in the last scene.[26]

To return to Freud, Hoffmann, and the uncanny, one may say that the (woman) reader (though "woman" is not a universal category) does not experience a chill when the mechanical doll is smashed and the eyes roll on the floor, whereas some women do have such a response to Robin smashing the doll in **Nightwood**. The (woman) reader of "The Sand-Man" knows that Nathaniel will reject Clara precisely because she is not a doll, because she has a mind and uses it to analyze his obsessions as well as to criticize the poem in which he predicts that he will kill her. Hoffmann pictures the patriarchy in the persons of the two doctors, constructing "woman" as a passive, mindless doll and passing on this "ideal" to a young man who accepts the image, sees through the patriarchy's lens, its dark glass, and cannot relate to a real woman. "The Sand-Man" is, in fact, about the construction of the male gaze and the oedipal initiation of the son into the father's dominating I/Eye. Coppola's doll does not move the reader because she is so patently not of woman born, so clearly a creature of male science and male desire. When Robin smashes the doll the horror is caused by the erasure of the difference between sign and signified. Western culture has socialized girls by giving them dolls to develop their maternal instincts. A doll *is* a baby, they are told. It is precious and must not be broken. The uncanny moment is caused by Robin killing her and Nora's baby, the symbol of their union. The doll signifies as well the unnatural and illegitimate in their relationship.

The smashing of the doll is a recurrent scene in women's writing. The mathematician Sophie Kovalevsky tells in *A Russian Childhood* of her pathological fear of dolls; in *Smile Please* Jean Rhys almost defines her writing self as the doll breaker. Fear of objectification and abjection seem to be at work here, as well as fear of motherhood. The classic story is that of Maggie, deliberately working out her anger on a doll in George Eliot's *The Mill on the Floss*. Eliot calls the doll "a fetish which she punished for all her misfortunes." She has banged three nails into the doll's head in her fury, and the trunk is "defaced by a long career of vicarious suffering." What is interesting is that Maggie never really destroys the doll, for in order to go through her ritual of comforting it after she has beaten it, she has to

leave it some semblance of likeness to herself. The doll as a toy or "baby" is a relatively recent cultural phenomenon, but there is a long history of the doll as a magical ritual object. In the Russian version of Cinderella, it is the doll that brings Baba Yaga to save the heroine.

Freud claims that the doll Olympia is "nothing else but a personification of Nathaniel's feminine attitude toward his father in infancy" and "a dissociated complex of Nathaniel's which confronts him as a person" ("Uncanny," 139). I suggest that she is Freud's patient, the female hysteric, who is hypnotized and forced into "good" and wooden behavior and eventually destroyed by quarreling male "doctors." Freud claims that one of his patients believed that her dolls would come to life if she looked at them with enough concentration, but that "the idea of the living doll excites no fear at all" ("Uncanny," 140).[27] For a woman who is socialized to be looked at, who even objectifies herself in the mirror, the uncanny is not figured in symbolic castration of the eyes—for she is the object being gazed at—but in the fear of becoming a living doll or statue, of becoming only an object. Robin and Nora act as *kores* (in Greek, *kore* means "pupil of the eye") or "living statues" of the lesbian as eternal maiden while looking at a representation of such abjection in the statue with the blank, protruding eyes; as pupils (in the other meaning of the word) of the eye, they deconstruct the process of objectification/abjection of woman. Felix, with his monocle and false portraits of ancestors as blank-eyed actors, returns the gaze of the Aryan at the Jew.

Djuna Barnes' articulation of the female uncanny and its relation to writing in a complex of signs around images of dolls and eyeless statues participates in female modernism's larger interrogation of gender and the writing self under the male gaze, which also includes the problem of the struggle between the needle and the pen. (In "Il vole," set to music by Poulenc in "Fiancailles pour rire" [1939], French poet Louise de Vilmorin writes, "I should like to sew but a magnet/Attracts all my needles.") Jean Rhys uncannily suggests in *Smile Please* the relation of the woman's eye to her "I."

> Before I could read, almost a baby, I imagined that God, this strange thing or person I had heard about, was a book. Sometimes it was a large book standing upright and half open and I could see the print inside but it made no sense to me. Other times the book was smaller and inside were sharp flashing things. The smaller book was, I am sure now, my mother's needle book, and the sharp flashing things were her needles with the sun on them.

Her nurse forbade her to read and told her a version of the sand-man story:

> "If all you read so much, you know what will happen to you? Your eyes will drop out and they will look at you from the page."

"If my eyes dropped out I wouldn't see," I argued.

She said, "They drop out except the little black points you see with."

I half believed her and imagined my pupils like heads of black pins and all the rest gone. But I went on reading.[28]

The relationship between the woman reader and the woman writer often reproduces the uncanny feeling of your own eyes looking up at you from the page. God/father/book is indecipherable, but in reading a sympathetic writer and in writing for a sympathetic reader, the woman can look at herself and be looked at without fear. The eye of God is the big book, but in the little book the needles (pens) connect with the eyes of the mother as the daughter's mirror. When the book is the mother's eye, the daughter writing finds her "I."

Freud asks, "Who would be so bold as to call it an uncanny moment, for instance, when Snow-White opens her eyes once more?" ("Uncanny," 154). Many women would be so bold. Certainly we may read Nora's dream of her dead grandmother in a glass coffin as her wish to be the prince who wakes Sleeping Beauty or Snow White. Her anxiety is caused by her wish to kill her father, who is already playing that role and standing in her way in the dream. The dream, with its absent mother and hovering father, also enacts the struggle to maintain female connection within the patriarchy, the desire to remove the possessive father and incorporate the magic grandmother, to erase the boundaries imposed by patriarchal culture. Robin, lying prone on the bed, acting as a "picture" for others to look at in the chapter "La Somnambule," is the proverbial woman patient. By exposing the erotics of the doctor-patient relationship, its voyeurism and quackery, Barnes brilliantly parodies the famous scene in which Charcot and a group of upright doctors hypnotize the horizontal female hysteric. We see psychoanalysis as circus in Matthew "I am my own charlatan" O'Connor, whose womb envy is openly expressed: "it was a high soprano I wanted, and deep corn curls to my bum, with a womb as big as the King's Kettle. . . . [I]n my heart is the wish for children and knitting. God, I never asked better than to boil some good man's potatoes and toss up a child for him every nine months by the calendar" (*N*, 91). As transvestite-shaman, O'Connor knows by vicarious experience what certain women want. His analysis of Nora and his advice that "ritual constitutes an instruction" amount to a feminist critique of patriarchal psychoanalysis. "And do you need a doctor to tell you that it is a bad strange hour for a woman? If all women could have it all at once, you could beat them in flocks like a school of scorpions; but they come eternally, one after the other . . ." (*N*, 101). He recognizes female desire as different from men's and urges difference on Nora. He claims to be "the last woman left in this world" (*N*, 100), though

he is "the bearded lady." O'Connor's transvestism is a positive force in *Nightwood*. The most powerful representation of the uncanny in the novel occurs when Nora sees him in bed in his flannel nightgown and curly wig and says, "God, children know something they can't tell; they like Red Riding Hood and the wolf in bed" (*N*, 79). In the typescript of the novel the following lines are crossed out: "with what cunning had his brain directed not only the womanly, but the incestuous garment? For a flannel night dress is our mother."[29] In fragments from the chapter "Go Down, Matthew" Barnes wrote: "What sense is there in saying the girl went wrong at twenty, that she wore a bowler hat by preference when but eight months old and showed a liking for kissing her grandmother's left elbow; it's not that she did so that needs explanation, its what it seemed like while she was about it."

Children liking Red Riding Hood and the wolf in bed is uncanny because O'Connor is acting the role of Nora's grandmother in the other dream, the version that is "well-dreamt" because Robin enters it "like a relative found in another generation." Nora is looking down into the house "as if from a scaffold" at her grandmother's high room "bereft as the nest of a bird which will not return" (Nora is mocked by O'Connor as "Turdus musicus," or The European singing thrush); Robin is lying below in fear with a disk of light (obviously a spotlight) on her. Nora keeps calling her to come into the "taboo" room, but "the louder she cried out the farther away went the floor below, as if Robin and she, in their extremity, were a pair of opera glasses turned to the wrong end, diminishing in their painful love" (*N*, 62).

The house is *unheimlich* because, though it has all her grandmother's things, it is the opposite of her real room and "is saturated with the lost presence of her grandmother, who seemed in the continual process of leaving it." It is a house of incest, and if Robin enters it she joins the incestuous family. There are two grandmothers, a beautiful feminine one and one "dressed as a man, wearing a billy cock and a corked moustache, ridiculous and plump in tight trousers and a red waistcoat, her arms spread saying with a leer of love 'My little sweetheart.'" Nora had wanted to put her hands on something in this room but in the past "the dream had never permitted her to do so." I suggest that she wants to put her hands on "the plume and the inkwell" and the pictures of her ancestors mentioned in the beginning of the dream: that is, she wants to take up her grandmother's profession of writing.

The costume her grandmother wears is that of the master of ceremonies at the circus, precisely the role of the narrator of *Nightwood*. Robin is in fear because she is being written about. Nora experiences the dream as "something being done to Robin, Robin disfigured and eternalized by the hieroglyphics of sleep and pain" (*N,* 63)—that is, being made into La Somnambule. As publicist for the circus, Nora is dreaming herself into the male role of master of ceremonies, Djuna Barnes writing this novel as circus. Her grandmother is herself in drag. The grandmother is cross-dressed as herself, the writer. This role of narrator as master of ceremonies at the circus is spelled out in "La Somnambule" in the description of Robin's room as like a jungle trapped in a drawing room: "the set, the property of an unseen *dompteur,* half lord, half promoter, over which one expects to hear the strains of an orchestra of wood-winds render a serenade which will popularize the wilderness" (*N,* 35).

The performative structure of *Nightwood* is like an eight-ring circus, brilliantly controlled by the grandmother-narrator-*dompteur* as each "act" is performed and the living statues speak their lines. As Paul Bouissac argues in *Circus and Culture,* circus acts progress in a dialectic of control and disturbance, culminating in a triumphant assertion of the performer's mastery. The reader is never allowed to play a participatory role but is eternally cast as "audience" at the circus or cabaret.[30]

In her dream Nora sees her grandmother as a "wolf," in both senses, and recognizes the ill-fitting male costume she must don as granddaughter-writer; when she constructs the doctor as her grandmother, a fine feminist transference for a workable psychoanalysis begins. Like Felix watching O'Connor's tricks at Robin's bedside, the reader experiences "a double confusion" (*N,* 35) as the narrator alternates between *dompteur* and "dumbfounder," providing a sideshow and "preparing the audience for a miracle" (*N,* 35). Barnes' rhetorical tricks are like the magician's feints with back and elbows, "honesties" to distract the audience from his hoax. Is *Nightwood* a hoax or a profoundly humanistic and political novel? When the woman acts the beast and the beast turns human in the last scene, do we laugh or weep?[31]

Bakhtin would argue that Barnes, like Rabelais, does not reverse the world for carnival as political therapy or release, in the steam-engine model of social behavior; but that Barnes' characters represent the revolutionary potential in folk culture.[32] That is, *Nightwood* reveals that gays and outcasts *have* a culture, a linguistically and philosophically rich culture, encompassing high and low art, opera and circus, psychoanalysis and religion, and that this culture is a vital political force.

Inversion reveals the essence of the particular historical moment that we construct as the "rise of fascism" in the "upright" defining their differences from the abject by race, gender, or sexual practice. At this historical moment the outcasts constitute the essence of human culture. Fascism chooses to eliminate from "civiliza-

tion" those very figures who are the "symbolic forms" of humanity in ancient traditions: circus folk, lesbians, homosexuals, transvestites, and the Jew who is the recorder of history and culture.

The "splendid and reeking falsification" of the world of carnival and circus in *Nightwood's* reversals is redemptive. As in Rabelais, the circus folk take royal titles: Princess Nadja, Baron von Tink, Principessa Stasera y Stasero, King Buffo, and the Duchess of Broadback. In carnival, enthronement of the fool implies dethronement of hierarchy. They are "gaudy, cheap cuts from the beast life" (*N,* 11) as the butcher is a stock figure in old European carnival. (O'Connor compares penises to mortadellas, and carnival parades often featured enormous phallic salamis.) Nadja's spine curves like a lion's, and Frau Mann's costume is like Nikka's tattoo:

> She seemed to have a skin that was the pattern of her costume: a bodice of lozenges, red and yellow . . . one felt they ran through her as the design runs through hard holiday candies, and the bulge in the groin where she took the bar, one foot caught in the flex of the calf, was as solid, specialized and as polished as oak. The stuff of the tights was no longer a covering, it was herself; the span of the tightly-stitched crotch was so much her own flesh that she was as unsexed as a doll. The needle that had made one the property of the child made the other the property of no man.
>
> (*N,* 13)

Here the novel's themes converge: circus performer = doll = lesbian. In *Fires* Marguerite Yourçenar imagines Sappho as an aging lesbian trapeze artist, in a mode described by Susan Gubar as preserving "the utopian grandeur of the lesbian aesthetic project in the modernist period."[33] Memoirs of Paris in the 1920s and 1930s recall the circus, the elegant trapeze act of Barbette, the Texas Transvestite, the human gorilla.[34] In *Nightwood* the lovers meet at the circus and mix circus figurines with ecclesiastical hangings in their flat, continuing carnival's tradition of mixing the sacred and the profane. Robin laughs in church and goes home to read de Sade on the day she gives birth, and O'Connor masturbates in church as the Transvestite of Notre Dame in one of the novel's most hilarious scenes. Bouissac defines circus as a *language,* "a set of rules for cultural transformations, displayed in a ritualistic manner that tempers this transgressive aspect." It enacts freedom from culture and inverts the ordinary. He claims that "individuals who have not been fully integrated into a culture find it more acceptable to enjoy this type of performance, as do individuals with a marginal or unique status, such as poets and artists."[35] As Lévi-Strauss says, we see the circus as supernatural, a place where human beings can still communicate with animals and with our own "higher powers." One of *Nightwood's* most fascinating aspects is that it has more animal characters than people, from lions to mouse-meat, cows, horses, fish, and an extraordinary number of birds, adding to its archetypal qualities.

Like the circus, *Nightwood* is polycentric; it makes the reader uneasy with time and history for political purposes. Robin Vote, Nora Flood, and O'Connor (whose names intersect in their *o*'s, *r*'s, and *n*'s) are performers of archetypal roles. The hybrid form of the fiction reinforces the hybrid experience of the characters. O'Connor says, "Take away a man's conformity and you take away his remedy," and tells of the paralyzed man in a velvet box at Coney Island: "suspended over him where he could never take his eyes off, a sky-blue mounted mirror, for he wanted to enjoy his own difference" (*N*, 146). Robin is the androgynous ideal, the archetype of the savage virgin Diana, a feminist version of the Noble Savage; *Nightwood* is her "sacred grove." The name "Vote" signifies the suffragettes, often martyrs and victims of police and government brutality. As a young reporter, Barnes investigated the violent force-feeding of hunger-striking suffragettes by having herself forcibly fed: "If I, play-acting, felt my being burning with revolt at this brute usuparation of my own functions, how they who actually suffered the ordeal in its acutest horror must have flamed at the violation of the sanctuaries of their spirit?"[36] The accompanying photograph, which shows Barnes, the prone victim, being violated by a group of doctors (plate 1), echoes the picture of the hysterical woman being hypnotized by Charcot and the French doctors. The image conflates the subordination of the politically independent woman with that of the medical model of the aberrant woman. Barnes experienced force-feeding as a kind of rape, as did many of the brave women of the movement. Christabel Pankhurst was figured as Joan of Arc on the front page of *The Suffragette*. Martyrdom, sainthood, and the androgynous militant figure of the woman in men's clothes were part of the mythology of this feminist modernism, and Barnes draws on its culture for Robin.

But *Nightwood*'s uniqueness lies in its language, its billingsgate and—to use a phrase Freud coined for the analysis of dreams in his letters to Fleiss, a nice combination of Yiddish and Greek—its "dreckology," the continual use of animal and human excremental imagery, from "whale shit" to "dinosaur droppings" to bird turds. Djuna Barnes is the female Rabelais. Only ribaldry is powerful enough to carry *Nightwood*'s political vision. For she was writing, like Nora in the dream of her grandmother, at what Victor Hugo calls "noir ceur sublime de l'écritoire," the sublime blackness of the inkstand.[37] Despite fascism or political repression, folk art survives among the marginal and in the circus: "Clowns in red, white and yellow, with the traditional smears on their faces, were rolling over the sawdust as if they were in the belly of a great mother where there was yet room to play" (*N*, 54).

If I am right in reading *Nightwood* as a prophecy of the Holocaust, an attack on the doctors and politicians who defined deviance and set up a world view of us and them, the normal and abnormal, in political, racial, and sexual terms, a world that was divided into the upright and the downcast, the horror that in fact took place is still very difficult for us to contemplate. In *Colette: A Taste for Life*, Yvonne Mitchell describes Sarassani, the "great circus king" who invited the European press to performances in Berlin in the early 1930s in order to get bookings in France for his troupe of five hundred animals. Djuna Barnes and Thelma Wood may well have been there with Colette and other journalists. Because the circus performers were Jews, Yugoslavs, and blacks, and because Sarassini chose expatriation over firing his crew, they were scapegoated by the Nazis. The night before he left Antwerp for South America, "the tent housing his twenty-two elephants caught fire, and most of them were burned to death."[38]

The abjection Barnes figured in *Nightwood* is mild compared to the murder and dehumanization (including medical experimentation) of the Nazi concentration camps. When American soldiers liberated the camps, the stench of excrement and death overpowered them. They could not identify with the tortured, starved prisoners as fellow human beings. One soldier wrote of them as a "horde of gnomes and trolls. . . . Some hop on crutches. Some hobble on stumps of feet. Some run with angular movements. Some glide like Oriental genies." Another described the emaciated victims as "huge, lethargic spiders," and others described the "absent-minded apes" of Buchenwald, while many said the scenes were like a bestial circus nightmare.[39] While the soldiers had difficulty identifying with the humanity of the Nazi's victims, civilians refused to believe the newsreel evidence of the massacres. Eventually the press began to focus on individual perverse Germans as perpetrators of the crimes, since people could not deal with the idea of sadism on such an immense scale, involving an entire nation. Interestingly, the press focused on two women, "Irme Grese, the Bitch of Belsen," and "Ilse Koch, the Beast of Buchenwald." It seems to me immensely significant, though it has not been noted before, that the press singled out individual women as symbols of Nazi sadism and cruelty, as objects of hate, when nazism itself was such a patriarchal ideology and the crimes were committed almost entirely by men. Ilse Koch is significant for us, for she collected pieces of tattooed human skin from camp prisoners. Did she write on the skin as a direct challenge to Leviticus? Were Felix and Guido among her victims? Certainly Nikka's body as the black backside of Western culture and the mutilated body of Mademoiselle Basquette challenge us to remember the inexpressible horror of the Holocaust. *Nightwood* reminds us that the human condition is a sister- and brotherhood of difference, and that ideologies that seek to erase those differences and define only themselves as human are indescribably dangerous.

Notes

1. Julia Kristeva, *Powers of Horror: An Essay on Abjection* (New York: Columbia Univ. Press, 1982), 100.

2. See Mikhail Bakhtin, *Rabelais and his World,* trans. Hélène Iswolsky (Bloomington: Indiana Univ. Press, 1984). Hereafter cited in text as *Rabelais.*

3. Mary Douglas, *Purity and Danger* (London: Routledge and Kegan Paul, 1966).

4. See Victor Brombert, *Victor Hugo and the Visionary Novel* (Cambridge: Harvard Univ. Press, 1984).

5. Aphra Behn is one of the few precursors to Barnes whose work survives. Most women's bawdy humor available to us is oral, as in Bessie Smith and black women's music; but see Regina Barreca, ed., *Last Laughs: Perspectives on Women and Humor* (London and New York: Gordon and Breach, 1988).

6. Emily Coleman's essay with Djuna Barnes' comments and objections is in the McKeldin Library, University of Maryland, College Park. The Emily Coleman papers are at the University of Delaware.

7. Brombert, *Victor Hugo,* 109.

8. For another analysis of Barnes' excremental imagination, see Louise De Salvo, "'To Make Her Mutton at Sixteen': Rape, Incest and Child Abuse in *The Antiphon,*" in this volume.

9. Bombert, *Victor Hugo,* 116.

10. Michel Thévoz, *The Painted Body* (New York: Rizzoli, 1984).

11. Shari Benstock, *Women of the Left Bank* (Austin: Univ. of Texas Press, 1986).

12. Kenneth Burke, *Language as Symbolic Action* (Berkeley: Univ. of California Press, 1968). Burke notes the God/dog reversal in the last scene of *Nightwood.*

13. Eugène Sue, *The Wandering Jew* (New York: Random House, 1940). A full study of the influence of Eugène Sue on Djuna Barnes remains to be done. It is clear that Sue's career as doctor-sailor-writer is a major source for the character of Matthew O'Connor. The description of Morok the lion-tamer—with his beasts, Judas, Cain, and Death—in chapter 1 of *The Wandering Jew* begins

with a three-sided chapbook illustration of his conversion from beast to human, a savage fleeing from wild animals, transformed to their tamer in the last picture. It is not difficult to imagine the young Djuna Barnes' identification with outsiders deriving from the novel after which she was named. Her early journalism produced memorable portraits of misfits and outsiders, and the chapbook or broadsheet is an important motif in her writing and drawing.

14. See Fredric Jameson, *The Political Unconscious* (Ithaca: Cornell Univ. Press, 1981). While I find Jameson's categories valuable for this analysis, one must point out that he does not count feminism as part of the political nor does gender appear in his system. For a good discussion of these issues, see Judith Gardiner's review, *In These Times,* 28 October 1981.

15. Hans Mayer, *Outsiders: A Study in Life and Letters* (Cambridge: MIT Press, 1984). Naomi Schor's essay is in *The Female Body in Western Culture,* ed. Susan Suleiman (Cambridge: Harvard Univ. Press, 1986), 363-72.

16. Jane Marcus, "A Wilderness of One's Own," in *Woman Writers and the City,* ed. Susan Silverman (Cambridge: Harvard Univ. Press, 1986), 363-72.

17. See "Berlin in Person," *TLS,* 28 December 1984, 1507. Heinrich Mann, from whose novel the script of *The Blue Angel* was taken, was surely an influence on Barnes in *Unrath* and *Der Untertak.*

18. For feminist discussions of the importance of transvestism to women artists, see Susan Gubar, "Blessings in Disguise: Cross-Dressing as Re-Dressing for Female Modernists," and Sandra Gilbert, "Costumes of the Mind," both in *No Man's Land* (New Haven: Yale Univ. Press, 1988-89); and Shari Benstock's response to and revision of their arguments in *Women of the Left Bank.* To this debate among feminist critics on the function of transvestism in women's culture, I would add that Barnes' presentation of a male transvestite as hero is a very clever way of privileging the female. Radclyffe Hall's *The Well of Loneliness* (New York: Covici and Friede, 1928) was clearly an influence on *Nightwood,* and I maintain that the structure of *Nightwood* is based on cabaret "acts." *The Well of Loneliness* also gives a guided tour of gay bars in Paris in the 1920s. I believe that the novel's title is a play on the name of a well-known homosexual and lesbian club in London in the 1920s, called the Cave of Harmony after the club in Thackeray's *The Newcomes,* famous for impersonations, improvisations, and dirty songs. Radclyffe Hall's tour includes Monsieur Pujol of the Ideal, who "collected inverts" and en-

tertained his straight clients with photographs of his customers and a sinister locked leather notebook in which he catalogued his "collection" (Hall, *Well,* 441-42). He tells stories like Dr. O'Connor, but their object is not the same. At Le Narcisse the patron is a transvestite who sings both sentimental and lewd songs. At Alec's the whole "miserable army" of inverts is gathered. He sells cocaine to his "fillies" and Stephen is called "Ma Soeur" by a dying young addict of whom she thinks, "It's looking for God who made it" (Hall, *Well,* 449). The contrast between Hall's tragic, despairing vision and Barnes' comic approach is instructive. Barnes never reifies her outcast figure into an "it." Yet Angela Ingram points out that Hall's line repeats the earlier scene where the fox is hounded to death as "scapegoat," and she is referring to all outcasts as hounded beasts, a view she and Barnes might have shared.

19. The figure of the lesbian lover as a fairy-tale prince or page is common in women's writing. In Antonia White's *Frost in May* (1933; rpt. New York: Dial, 1982), the heroine's adored friend in a Catholic girls' school in England, Léonie, is seen as "a young prince, pale and weary from a day's ride, with his lovelocks carelessly tied in a frayed ribbon. . . . Her feeling for Léonie was one of pure admiration, the feeling of page for prince, too cold and absolute to be called love" (79, 80). Antonia White was part of the Peggy Guggenheim circle at Hayford Hall where Djuna Barnes wrote part of *Nightwood*. For another reading of this novel and of the gender configurations at Hayford Hall, see Broe "Incest as Exile," in *Women's Writing in Exile.*

20. Sigmund Freud, "The Uncanny" (1919), in *On Creativity and the Unconscious* (New York: Harper & Row, 1958), 122-61. Hereafter cited in text as "Uncanny."

21. See Nancy Harrison, "Jean Rhys and the Novel as Women's Text," Ph.D. diss., University of Texas, Austin, 1983.

22. For "The Sand-Man," see *Selected Writings of E. T. A. Hoffmann,* ed. and trans. Leonard J. Kent and Elizabeth C. Knight (Chicago: Univ. of Chicago Press, 1969), vol. 1. Hereafter cited in text as *Tales.*

23. See the review of the Freud-Fleiss letters in the *New York Times Magazine,* 17 March 1985. As Freud repressed physical evidence of father-daughter incest to write his seduction theory, so Marx rejected earlier nonrational socialisms to create Marxism as a science. Consequently, in each ordering and theorizing of self and history an important component is left out and made Other.

After Freud, the real incest victims were neglected until quite recently. "Other" socialisms were denied by Marxists. See Barbara Taylor, *Eve and the New Jerusalem* (New York: Pantheon, 1983), for feminist socialisms in pre-Marx English history.

24. I am indebted here to a paper read by Gareth Stedman Jones at Texas in March 1985 on the nonrational origins of socialism in French thought. In a typescript of *Nightwood* in the McKeldin Library, after Robin is called "the infected carrier of the past," the phrase "the *magnetized* beastly" is crossed out; clearly it is a reference to the magnetic theory of somnambulism of Mesmer. Bernard Benstock points out that Marx discusses these thinkers in *Capital*; see "Making Capital Out of Vampires," *Times Higher Education Supplement,* 15 June 1984.

25. As I write, the Barnes family papers at Maryland have been opened to scholars. [The Barnes papers were opened in June, 1985. Ed.] I suspect that both her father, Wald Barnes, and her grandmother, Zadel Barnes, were deeply interested in Fourier, Mesmer, Hugo, and Sue, and that the family experiments in living on their farm owed much to the influence of Fourier's ideas.

26. This information was supplied by Nancy Levine; Wald Barnes' novels and musical compositions are in the possession of Kerron Barnes and Duane Barnes.

27. Freud says that the mother of a girl he had cured regarded psychoanalysis itself as "uncanny." Helplessness causes one to feel "uncanny," he argues, and tells the story of being lost in the streets of a town in Italy on a hot afternoon. Three times, while trying to get out, he returns to the same place, a street where "nothing but painted women were to be seen at the windows" ("Uncanny," 143). This hardly needs a feminist analysis. Though Freud says that he "drifted into this field of research half involuntarily" ("Uncanny," 160), I suggest he was writing the male fear of being castrated by the father as a cover for his own guilt at having mishandled his women patients. For a brilliant analysis of the power of the mesmerized woman and of Freud's relation to hysterical women patients, see Nina Auerbach, *Woman and the Demon: The Life of a Victorian Myth* (Cambridge: Harvard Univ. Press, 1982).

28. Jean Rhys, *Smile Please: The Letters of Jean Rhys,* ed. Francis Wyndham and Diana Melly (New York: Viking, 1984), 20-21.

29. The typescripts of "Bow Down" and *Nightwood* are in the McKeldin Library, University of Maryland, College Park. When it is possible to quote

from T. S. Eliot's letters, a full study of his cuts and corrections to *Nightwood* should be made with the aim of restoring and publishing the text as Barnes wanted it. While Eliot did have to think of the censor, many passages could be restored. He corrected her French and German and marked out many passages on Jews, one on King Ludwig, and a scene with the doctor in jail, as well as passages that might be considered obscene. He crossed out, "You can lay a hundred bricks and not be called a bricklayer, but lay one boy and you are a bugger" (202). He told her to think over whether she wanted to say of Jenny, "when she fell in love it was with a perfect fury of accumulated dishonesty," and he told her to take out Matthew calling himself a faggot, a fairy, and a queen in the scene in the carriage. He crossed out "and the finger of our own right hand placed where it best pleases" and the McClusky passages on a girlish boy in the war. In the description of the "Tuppenny Upright" he crossed out "letting you do it," but she restored it in 1949. He wanted to change "obscene" to "unclean" on the last page and said he couldn't understand why Robin had candles in the chapel at night. Barnes' penciled note says, "Sample of T. S. E.'s 'lack of imagination' (as he said)." Also cut is a homosexual courtroom joke in which the judge asks, "What do I give a man of this sort?" and the clerk replies, "A dollar, a dollar and a half, two dollars." The whole of Matthew's circumcising the regiment scene is cut. The collection also includes Barnes' library. Inside her copy of Eliot's *Collected Poems* she wrote, "He said 'Someday they will say I copied you,'" and in his *On Poetry and Poets* she wrote in 1981, "Mr. E. said of the last act of *The Antiphon* that it was one of the greatest last acts he had ever read. But he did not so write of it."

30. I have discussed this aspect of *Nightwood* in a review of Andrew Field's *Djuna* in *The Women's Review of Books* 1, no. 8 (May 1984). See also Paul Bouissac, *Circus and Culture: A Semiotic Approach* (Bloomington: Indiana Univ. Press, 1976).

31. Note the resemblance of Robin as a beast to the description of Charlotte Brontë's Bertha in chapter 26 of *Jane Eyre*: "What it was, whether beast or human being, one could not, at first sight, tell; it grovelled, seemingly, on all fours; it snatched and growled like some wild animal. . . ."

32. For discussions of carnival, see Barbara A. Babcock, ed. *The Reversible World: Symbolic Inversion in Art and Society* (Ithaca: Cornell Univ. Press, 1978); see in particular David Kunzles, "World Upside Down: The Iconography of a European Broadsheet Type"; and Natalie Zemon

Davis, "Women on Top: Symbolic Sexual Inversion and Political Disorder in Early Modern Europe."

33. Marguerite Yourçenar, *Fires* (1935; rpt. New York: Farrar, Strauss, Giroux, 1981); Susan Gubar, "Sapphistries," *Signs* 10, no. 1 (1984). See also Colette, *The Pure and the Impure,* for further connections between woman, circus, cabaret, and lesbianism.

34. For a modern version of Barbette's story see Albert Goldbarth's prose poem, *Different Fleshes* (Geneva, NY: Hobart and William Smith Colleges Press, 1979). Writing of the painter Soutine, Goldbarth says, "No one had ever prayed before in Meat Cathedral," which also recalls Barnes' Rabelaisian use of the butcher motif.

35. Bouissac, *Circus and Culture,* 8.

36. "How It Feels to Be Forcibly Fed," *New York World Magazine,* 6 September 1914, sec. 5, p. 17.

37. Brombert, *Victor Hugo,* 202.

38. Yvonne Mitchell, *Colette: A Taste for Life* (New York: Harcourt, 1975), 177.

39. See Robert H. Abzug, *Inside the Vicious Heart: Americans and the Liberation of Nazi Concentration Camps* (New York: Oxford, 1985), 56, 128-29, 132.

Selected Bibliography

This bibliography can serve as a supplement/update to Douglas Messerli's *Djuna Barnes: A Bibliography* published in 1975. Indeed, Messerli's bibliography should be consulted when references are made to certain original Barnes publications.

Benstock, Shari. *Women of the Left Bank: Paris, 1900-1940.* Austin, Texas: University of Texas Press, 1986.

Broe, Mary Lynn. "My Art Belongs to Daddy: Incest as Exile—The Textual Economics of Hayford Hall." In *Women's Writing in Exile,* ed. Mary Lynn Broe and Angela Ingram, 41-86. Chapel Hill, North Carolina: University of North Carolina Press, 1989.

Burke, Kenneth. "Version, Con-, Per-, and In- (Thoughts on Djuna Barnes' Novel *Nightwood*)." In *Language As Symbolic Action; Essays on Life, Literature, and Method,* 240-53. Berkeley, California: University of California Press, 1968.

Gilbert, Sandra M. "Costumes of the Mind: Transvestism as Metaphor in Modern Literature." *Critical Inquiry* 7 (Winter 1980): 391-417.

Gubar, Susan. "Blessings in Disguise: Cross-Dressing as Re-Dressing for Female Modernists." *Massachusetts Review* 22 (Autumn 1981): 477-508.

Marcus, Jane. "Carnival of the Animals." Review of *Djuna: The Life and Times of Djuna Barnes,* by Andrew Field. In *Women's Review of Books* 1 (April 1984): 6-7.

ABBREVIATIONS

Unless otherwise indicated, all quotations from the works of Djuna Barnes derive from the following editions:

A: *The Antiphon.* 1958. Reprint in *Selected Works,* 79-224.

LA: *Ladies Almanack, showing their Signs and their tides; their moons and their Changes; the Seasons as it is with them; their Eclipses and Equinoxes; as well as a full Record of diurnal and nocturnal Distempers.* Written and illustrated by a Lady of Fashion. 1928. Reprint. New York: Harper & Row, 1972.

N: *Nightwood,* 1936. Reprint. New York: New Directions, 1961, 1977.

R: *Ryder,* 1923. Reprint. New York: St. Martin's Press, 1956, 1979.

Lissa Schneider (essay date fall 1993)

SOURCE: Schneider, Lissa. "'This Mysterious and Migratory Jewelry': Satire and the Feminine in Djuna Barnes's 'The Terrorists.'" *Review of Contemporary Fiction* 13, no. 3 (fall 1993): 62-9.

[*In the following essay, Schneider analyzes "The Terrorists," a satiric newspaper tale Barnes wrote early in her career, claiming that this "marginalized story" serves "as a particularly intriguing locus for examining the status of the feminine in patriarchy," as well as the "subversive complexities" of Barnes's satire.*]

Djuna Barnes has said, "We would teach man with a joke."[1] Barnes's "jokes," however, catch everyone in their psychosexual-textual crossfire, leaving no social or psychic position unchallenged. While the humor in her writings often displays an affinity with the broad, physical comedy of vaudeville, a humor keyed to the visual register through stereotypic contrasts in her characters' appearance and behavior, Barnes's satiric didacticism is both complex and unsettling in its ambiguities. Her satire is sharply double-edged. Through both structure and theme, her writings establish self-consciously structured oppositions between male and female, bourgeois and working class, artist and audience, only to parodically collapse or dissolve the bounds of those differences. Thus, that which she would "teach" can be read only in the implied margins of her many "parodic inversions".[2]

Barnes's representations of gender and class structures lie at the heart of her work. Her characters, as others have remarked, "are often types,"[3] representative of a given social or psychic position. Yet these stereotypical positions often prove unstable or illusory when taken to their exaggerated extremes.[4] Her satiric writings thus function to critique rather than support the ideology of difference articulated through the binarisms of Western metaphysical thought. Whether or not the diffuse implications of her parodic inversions were fully considered, her satiric writings intimate what Lacanian-Derridean discourses have identified as the fraudulent workings of the phallocracy through which, nevertheless, our individual—and always gendered—subjectivities are constituted. Reading these sites of rupture or disorder, those places where differences break down and parodic oppositions dissolve—in other words, reading the feminine—provides a broader understanding of the subversive complexities of her satire.

This essay focuses on one of Barnes's satiric newspaper tales of 1913-1919, **"The Terrorists,"** reprinted in the collection ***Smoke and Other Early Stories*** (1982). Journalistic writings—perhaps due to associations with sensationalism and quick cash—are notorious for their exclusion from the literary canon, and Barnes's newspaper tales prove no exception. Yet these ambiguous early fictions, written in Barnes's youth for financial remuneration when first on her own in New York City, contain much of interest for those concerned with exploring the gender/genre divide. Indeed, as a marginalized story within a marginalized genre of a marginalized writer, **"The Terrorists"** serves as a particularly intriguing locus for examining the status of the feminine in patriarchy.

The feminine can be understood as the subjugated second term of any binary opposition in a symbolic system that takes the phallus as its primary signifier. **"The Terrorists"** satirizes the subjugated status of the feminine through its themes and structuring devices even as its (non) status in the modernist canon repeats this marginalization. **"The Terrorists"** textually apposes Pilaat Korb, a drunken poet and would-be revolutionary, with a nameless woman of bourgeois origins designated simply as "Pilaat's wife."[5] The story employs third-person narration to describe their bohemian life together in Greenwich Village. Korb agitates against middle-class oppression while his wife, who appears to be the sole wage-earner, clears tables at a local café for "'the pigs,' the smug and respectable who brought their wives and children to dine" (161).

In this brief and formally sophisticated tale, the two characters superficially adhere to stereotypically discrete masculine and feminine positions, both through a narrative structure that grants Korb first appearance in the text, more and significantly longer speeches, and a proper name, and through a narrative content that consistently represents "Pilaat's wife" as the physical and intellectual diminutive of her husband. Yet despite her deferred appearance in the text, a description of her thoughts and behavior concludes the story; although Korb's speech heavily dominates the dialogue, ultimately more is revealed about her history and inner nature than his. If she imitates her husband, he, "thinking that she was expressing herself" (162), parodically imitates her imitation of him.

Yet it would be misleading to suggest that the feminine position supersedes that of the masculine in this ambiguous story; both positions are satirized through the odd mirroring relation that binds these two characters even as it signals their exaggerated differences. Thus the gap-toothed smile of the chain-smoking wife is as comically parodic as Korb's red-veined and watering eyes (159-160). The parodic inversions function so that neither position carries implied authority. At the same time, although narrative structure and content initially suggest that Pilaat and "Pilaat's wife" adhere to discrete masculine and feminine positions, ultimately Barnes subverts this apparent representation of absolute sexual difference to provide a striking example, not of the subjugation of the feminine under phallic law, but rather of the tacit and necessary failure of that law. Like the "mysterious and migratory jewelry" described in **"The Terrorists"** as possessing a will of its own, beyond the control of either Korb, his wife, or his wife's bourgeois family, the feminine proves elusively and disruptively indeterminate.

"The Terrorists" possesses a crystalline structure that underscores the dyadic imaginary relation that binds Pilaat Korb and his wife. The opening, which focuses exclusively on Korb, mirrors the conclusion, which focuses on Korb's wife. They parodically mirror one another in their opposing physical characteristics as well. Thus she is "frail" (160) and "delicate" (161)—the "little wife" (163)—and he, "robust" (159) with an "indomitable digestion" (159); she is "very young" (160), and he, "a man of fifty odd" (159). His hair is "long" (159), while hers is "cut short" (161); he loves "clean shirts" (160), and she wears "loose and dirty blouses smeared with paint and oil" (161).

These polarities, which signal her subordinated status by making her the physical diminutive of her husband, are further reinforced by the narrator's pointed omission of her given name. Without a name, she stereotypically stands in for all women, who lose their name through marriage and thus possess no authorized speaking position within the symbolic. While Korb is a published poet, his wife partakes of this authority only by carrying his poems with her and "reading them aloud or studying them nonchalantly" (161). When she reads the poems, it is then Korb who speaks through her. Even when "Pilaat's wife" is given her own rare lines of dialogue, the narrator suggests that her words mimic the learned rhetoric of her revolutionist husband: "She said

'we' with that intonation used by agitators" (162). Thus she, a parodic mirror for all female subjects in patriarchy, equivocally speaks "in a mode of masquerade, in imitation of the masculine, phallic subject."[6]

Yet if the self-consciously structured oppositions in **"The Terrorists"** suggest that Korb and his wife double one another as two halves of one whole or unified self, as complementary masculine and feminine polarities, other textual details surface that subvert this illusive complementarity predicated on feminine lack. In **"The Terrorists,"** absolute sexual difference, as well as any concept of absolute class difference, constantly threatens to dissolve upon close examination. For if hers is the voice of masquerade, his voice threatens to disappear altogether: "He no longer wrote poetry or plays, nor did he keep up his connection with a paper which he had started, and which spoke harshly of all things" (163). In this story, the artist figure is a fraud; the macho working-class terrorist, a man domesticated by "too many clean shirts in youth" (160), is unable to free himself from bourgeois desires. Insofar as the (illusion of) masculine speaking subjectivity, as many have argued, is predicated upon the power to control or direct the gaze via pen or camera, his inability to continue writing suggests his symbolic castration.

While she imitates her husband in both speech and gesture, he, when inciting his working-class companions to revolutionary action, "would then end up leaning far back as his wife did when she copied him, thinking that she was expressing herself" (162). Unwittingly, they imitate each other as they pursue the illusions of gendered speaking subjectivity. For both men and women, entry into the symbolic and language through the mirror stage entails tacit acceptance of those illusions—to do otherwise, as Shari Benstock explains, is "to risk exclusion from language in psychosis."[7] Nevertheless, while the masculine subject inherits the authority to speak and act with the father's name, it is after all an empty or false inheritance. In actuality, the masculine subject has received nothing tangible. Consequently, Korb comically looks to his wife for guidance in self-expression even as she occupies herself in copying him.

Barnes's parodic and destabilizing inversions continue. Thus, from "his early love of the people" (159), Pilaat Korb comes to despise the "sad, shabby hearts" of the working class as "pitifully weak" (160): "Had Pilaat come from a less cleanly family, he would have loved [the people] very strongly and gently to the end. But he had been *comforted and maimed in his conceptions and his fellow love by too many clean shirts in youth*. He still longed to correct things, but he wanted to correct them as one cleans up a floor" (160; italics mine). Indeed, his nickname "Terrorist" derives not from revolutionary activities in support of the working class, but rather from the shouting that "began to awe those of his own group" and led them "when he made a gesture of pity" to raise "their arms to protect themselves" (160).

All of Korb's shouting only serves to underscore his fear of his own powerlessness and feminization, a fear any recognition of which he must repress and displace by terrorizing his working-class peers and dominating his wife. He cannot outshout, however, the castrating implications of the narrator's reminder that he has been "maimed" in his "conceptions and fellow love by too many clean shirts in youth." The reader sees what Korb cannot: that Korb's "maimed" and castrated status indirectly equals the diminished position of his wife within the social order. Despite the apparent absence of a middle ground between his "clean shirts" and her "dirty blouses," those "clean shirts" link him to bourgeois attitudes beyond his conscious control, and are themselves strikingly associated with the domestic and the feminine.

Just as Korb desperately feigns the masculine position, his wife "deliberately set[s] about annihilating her own soul and her own delicate, sensitive, and keen insight" (161) in stereotypic complicity with the demands of the feminine. Still, insofar as "Pilaat's wife" possesses something to "annihilate" that is indefinable and outside observable reality—"insight," a "soul"—her characterization resists patriarchy's construction of woman as image. Her compliance with the feminine role, moreover, is always marked by an underlying current of comic resistance. She reads Korb's obscure poems aloud not because she enjoys them, but because "she wanted to puzzle the strangers" (161). Her efforts at self-erasure are equally calculated: "She liked to be the center of whispers, for then she could be impersonal and forget herself without any danger of falling into obscurity" (161).

The narrator mentions that the townspeople nicknamed Pilaat's wife "Joan d'Arc" (160). Although this nickname is dismissively attributed to "a certain pale loveliness about the frail oblong of her face" (160), the allusion recalls a revolutionary female military genius who—albeit with grim reprisal—defies the limits of gender and class to effect social change. The townspeople's nickname stands in marked contrast to the pet diminutives through which Korb effects to contain her: he calls her "Little One" and "Sniffle Snuffle" (164).

Her character lies somewhere between the "unresolved clash"[8] of alternatives suggested by her various nicknames. Even the narrator is confused by her ambiguous status. On the one hand, the narrator says of this twenty-seven-year-old: "After all, she was only a little girl who, because she was interested, thought that she must assume fury, and because she was too lazy to dress her hair after the fashion, cut it off" (164). This suggests that her revolutionary "fury" and masculine affects—the

"heavy boots" (161), the cropped hair—are but the masquerading of a "little girl." On the other hand, in the succeeding line the narrator adds: "Yet there was something strange about Pilaat's wife. She did not like the society of silly and vain women, and she did turn most naturally to such men as her husband moved among" (164).

If there is "something strange" about Pilaat's wife, something unfixed and undefinable, there is something equally strange about the "mysterious and migratory jewelry" (165) she inherits from her bourgeois parents. A traditional symbol of the feminine, these "gems and silvers" (165) also represent the shackles of the dominant social order from which she has affected to escape. Her parents, "respectable people" with "vain ideas" of "a marriage of money" (164) for their daughter, recall the "smug and respectable" "pigs" she waits on at the café. The jewelry, however, which they had given to their daughter "when they had their first ambitions in the way of a well-to-do doctor" (164) as a future son-in-law, appears to possess its possessors, rather than the other way around. For it is they "who had been dropped in successive generations into the midst of old and tarnished jewelry comprising the family splendor" (164). In a manner that parallels Korb's (failed) efforts to master and displace "feminine" weakness, Barnes's use of passive voice indicates that the family has little control over the jewelry, which, inverting the usual order of things, appears to have inherited *them*.

Pilaat's wife attempts to thwart the constraints of gender and class by refusing the "marriage of money" of her parent's ambition and immediately pawning the family jewelry. But just as her pawned jewels inexplicably keep returning to her in the text, the demands of the symbolic register are not something she can escape. As Jacqueline Rose explains in *Feminine Sexuality,* the symbolic demands that the subject line up under the door marked "Gentlemen" or the door marked "Ladies"—even though this positioning is temporary, constantly renegotiated within the psyche, subjectivity is always gendered.[9] Thus, in one scene, when she tosses the jewels aside saying, "I'm tired of supporting them" (165)—and with them, the constraints of the feminine position—it is Korb who fatefully returns them to her, in effect pressuring her back under the sign for the ladies' room door. An earlier passage, however, emphasizes the unconscious aspect of her relation to the jewels through that recurrent use of passive voice: "this jewelry would come back, piece by piece, and appear on her wrist or about her neck or upon her ears, and at such times she drew a little aside from her husband and his friends, and would sit dreaming in a corner" (164-65).

Korb also exhibits ambivalence about the jewels, the sight of which "always put him into a passion either of avarice or contempt" (165). Again recalling the manner in which the feminine becomes "the site of disorder that the system must posit and repudiate in order to achieve its (illusion of) coherence" (Benstock 6), Korb concurrently both desires and despises that which he can neither control nor entirely eschew. The jewels invoke his ambiguous relation to the bourgeoisie, whom he despises and yet, occasionally, emulates, as well as his ambiguous relation to the feminine. Hence his distress. In one moment he "demand[s] that the jewels be cleared away with the rest of the 'rubbish'" only, in the next, to lay claim to them again, "swearing . . . that he was being treated like a man 'who had not come honestly by his decorations'" (165). His need to repress recognition of this contradictory, fraudulent position then sends him "off into a melancholy reverie," speechless, to drink "innumerable bottles of wine" (165).

Korb's conflict becomes most explicit when, in a drunken rage, this self-described "man of force" (166) genders nature female and then fantasizes her rape and ultimate annihilation: "How she would shiver, how she would implore. But I should have no mercy. No, not even when she got upon her knees and wept at my feet and covered them with her insufferable tears. . . . I would laugh aloud, and shake her by those horrible, ample shoulders of hers, and would cry out to her, 'Now die, die; we do not care!'" (167). Longing for a sense of control over feminine disorder, he rails against time itself, which demands—against his masculinist desire to uphold the law of the phallus and see the world and his relation to it in terms of simple oppositions—that life be lived "on the prescribed gradual plan" (163).

The passage of time serves as the continual reminder of his own feminizing weakness, of his own mortality. As he says, "we are weak, miserable creatures, and we leave to nature all the tearing down of the scenery, and to her we leave all the building up of the same scenery next year and the year after for interminable and tireless and wearisome years" (167). If the feminized "plan of nature" can be ripped to pieces (167), then, as he says, "We shall never be connected with you any longer as the outcome of your whims. *We are set free—thus*" (168; italics mine).

His conception, however, of what it would mean to be "set free" from nature's "whims" falls far short of this (impossible) desire to tear the veil of the symbolic with "the Imaginary fictions it constructs" (Benstock 195), and enter the Real. Perhaps recognizing the impossibility, perhaps just too drunk to notice, in lieu of the absolute destruction of nature, and with "her," time and death itself, Korb and his friends settle for the decision to attack the town's bourgeoisie. To this end, they "collect things that would do as missiles" (168)—comic symbols of supplementary phallic power in the form of chair legs and paperweights—and plan their onslaught for dawn.

Through all this masculine mayhem, Pilaat's wife sleeps, "her hand over her bracelets" (169), which have mysteriously appeared encircling her wrist once again, rather like manacles binding her to "The Law that declares . . . woman must submit to the phallic order, fraudulent though it may be" (Benstock 7). When she awakes, it is midday, and the men lie asleep about her on the floor, having "moved away from those things that they had collected as weapons. They had rolled onto them, and they found that they hurt and were uncomfortable" (169). While the men lie in their drunken stupor, the picture of passive impotence, the story concludes with Pilaat's wife as she smiles, "contemplates one or two new phrases she would use in relation to life," and places "Pilaat's book in her pocket" (170), preparing to go out. A moment rife with unresolved contradictions, it suggests that while she continues to exist only "in relation" to the masculinist order, unable to escape the symbolic, with "its dream of a totalizing structure, which goes by the name of patriarchy" (Benstock 194), she nevertheless puts language, masculine discourse, in her pocket and carries it away with her, for an instant the "thief of language."[10] Meanwhile, the men's illusion of phallic power and control is shown to be just that, a hilarious illusion—and an illusion that hurts and is uncomfortable when conscious boundaries are momentarily collapsed in sleep.

Notes

1. Djuna Barnes, "Just Getting the Breaks: Donald Ogden Stewart Confides the Secret of World Success," *Theatre Guild Magazine* 7 (April 1930), 36.

2. Frank Palmeri, *Satire in Narrative: Petronius, Swift, Gibbon, Melville, and Pynchon* (Austin: University of Texas Press, 1990), 4. Palmeri's excellent discussion of narrative satire, while focusing only on male satirists, takes a Bakhtinian approach and contributes many new insights on the genre.

3. Cheryl Plumb, *Fancy's Craft: Art and Identity in the Early Works of Djuna Barnes* (Selinsgrove: Susquehanna University Press, 1986), 13. See also Douglas Messerli's introduction to *Smoke and Other Early Stories* (College Park, MD: Sun & Moon, 1982), 10.

4. In this vein, Nancy J. Levine says that in Barnes's early writings she "clearly itches to force the complacent to acknowledge their affinity with anomalous, marginal people." See "'Bringing Milkshakes to Bulldogs': The Early Journalism of Djuna Barnes," in *Silence and Power: A Reevaluation of Djuna Barnes,* ed. Mary Lynn Broe (Carbondale: Southern Illinois University Press, 1991), 34. To extrapolate further, however, insofar as Barnes underscores the complacent's affinity with the marginal, she also portrays the marginal as bound by

the psycho-social structures and attitudes of the dominant or complacent.

5. Djuna Barnes, "The Terrorists," in *Smoke and Other Early Stories,* 164. All further references will be included in the text. ("The Terrorists" first appeared in the *New York Sunday Morning Telegraph,* 30 September 1917.)

6. Elizabeth A. Grosz, *Jacques Lacan: A Feminist Introduction* (London: Routledge, 1990), 72.

7. Shari Benstock, *Textualizing the Feminine: On the Limits of Genre* (Norman: University of Oklahoma Press, 1991), 7; hereafter cited parenthetically.

8. Palmeri, 8.

9. Jacqueline Rose and Juliet Mitchell, eds. *Feminine Sexuality: Jacques Lacan and the école freudienne* (New York: Norton, 1982), 42.

10. Alicia Ostriker, "The Thieves of Language: Women Poets and Revisionist Mythmaking," in *The New Feminist Criticism: Essays on Women, Literature, and Theory,* ed. Elaine Showalter (New York: Pantheon Books, 1985), 315.

Andrea L. Harris (essay date 1994)

SOURCE: Harris, Andrea L. "The Third Sex: Figures of Inversion in Djuna Barnes's *Nightwood.*" In *Eroticism and Containment: Notes from the Flood Plain,* edited by Carol Siegel and Ann Kibbey, pp. 233-59. New York: New York University Press, 1994.

[*In the following essay, Harris studies the inversion of gender identity and sexuality in* Nightwood, *focusing especially on the figure of Dr. Matthew O'Connor, whom she claims not only shows that "the gender of the invert is left undecideable and indeterminate" but that all gender identity is "constructed and ambiguous."*]

Dr. Matthew O'Connor, the voluble storyteller of Djuna Barnes's 1937 novel, **Nightwood,** spins tales on the subjects of woman's sexuality, homosexuality, desire, and love, spouting wild anecdotes, bitter laments, and intricate theories in a series of densely metaphorical monologues addressed primarily to a woman. By means of the figure of the doctor, a transvestite gynecologist, and his theories, the novel conceives of gender identity as an open-ended range of possibilities rather than a strict choice between masculine or feminine. Matthew bases his theories of gender and sexuality on two ambiguously gendered characters—Robin Vote, "a girl who resembles a boy," and himself.[1]

Matthew's gender ambiguity has a strong impact on his position as a storyteller and on his narrative authority. On the one hand, Matthew is an authoritative male speaker who aims to explain the intricacies of inversion to Nora Flood, Robin's lover. That is, Matthew speaks with the authority of his masculine subjectivity and his status as a doctor. Yet these traditional bases of authority are blatantly undercut by the fact that he is a would-be woman and an unlicensed quack.[2] By portraying Matthew as a transvestite gynecologist/theorist, Barnes creates a biting parody of the figure of the sexologist whose aim is to define the nature of female inversion. The theorist's interest, however, is found to be more than theoretical: Matthew studies women in order to satisfy his desire to be a woman. Matthew's own ambiguous gender position allows him to question the gender binary and to construct more complex models of fluid gender identifications on the wide-ranging gender spectrum.

Matthew devises several theoretical models for inversion or homosexuality that throw both masculine and feminine radically into question. The gender of "the third sex" or the homosexual consists of a vacillation between masculine and feminine, regardless of her or his biological sex. By making the relation between sex and gender asymmetrical and indeterminate, the text denaturalizes the supposed congruence between sex and gender that is promoted by means of the gender binary. The invert thus provides a way of breaking open the closed and symmetrical binary opposition between masculine and feminine and challenging the idea of the binary opposition on which gender has been understood to rest. In a textual doubling of sexual inversion, the invert is inscribed in the text by means of the rhetorical figure of the chiasmus, a figure that consists of a double inversion.[3] Matthew attempts to determine the truth of inversion in these formulae, but the shifting, unstable nature of his own formulae undoes his quest for the truth. What happens to gender in this process? Matthew's figures of inversion rely to some extent on the gender binary at the same time that they question and undo it, an ambiguity that I will explore below. Matthew thus becomes a kind of deconstructive theorist of inversion, but at the same time he is a parody of the sexologist whose discourse relies upon and confirms the gender binary. This ambiguity can be seen especially in Matthew's transvestism. While on the one hand Matthew is sophisticated in his reading of gender ambiguity, particularly its manifestations in inversion, on the other hand he is very literal in his use of transvestism as a means of arriving at an end—being a woman. Other strands of the text also work to question this reliance upon the masculine/feminine opposition. First, Robin Vote, as a representation of the feminine, escapes any attempt to pin her down.[4] Finally and most importantly, not only do Matthew's own figures for inversion undermine the truth of inversion, in that the gender of the invert is left undecidable and indeterminate, but they also render undecidable the truth of gender—the simple binary scheme upon which gender is based. The con-

structed nature of gender in the invert is not just a special case of gender ambiguity; instead, it points to the
constructed and ambiguous nature of all gender identity.

DISCONNECTING GENDER FROM SEX

In *Nightwood,* gender is a free-floating range of possibilities: one is neither masculine nor feminine, but both
masculine and feminine to varying degrees and in various combinations. This sounds like a utopian description of androgyny, which is hardly the situation sketched
by the novel. When gender is conceived not as fixed,
certain, and consistent with sex and desire but as unstable, shifting, and inconsistent with sex, this situation
sometimes causes conflict and pain, as it does for Robin
and Matthew.[5] In *Nightwood,* Matthew and Robin, who
typify the difficulties of those whose gender identities
are compound and multiple, are seen struggling against
the culturally constructed meanings attached to their
sexed bodies, which are in conflict with their gender
identifications. Their conflict is caused by the act of
disconnecting gender from sex. This is the first, necessary step in refiguring the relation between masculine
and feminine. If anatomy (or sex) is not seen as destiny,
then gender need no longer be conceived as equivalent
to sex; in other words, femaleness does not presuppose
femininity. This allows the body to be cut loose from
culturally prescribed meanings, yet this does not result
in the return to a precultural, natural, and, therefore,
nongendered state, for that would be impossible. Once
cut loose from these prescribed meanings, newly gendered meanings may be devised for the body. Some of
these new inscriptions of gender are embodied in Matthew's figures of inversion.

Several passages typify the divide between sex and
gender that predominates in the novel, one being Robin's experience of pregnancy. When Robin becomes
pregnant early in the novel, she thinks of her pregnancy
as "some lost land in herself" (45). At this point, she
begins to wander far from home, a habit that becomes
characteristic over the course of the novel and that underlines her similarity to animals. When Robin gives
birth, the event is described in this way:

> Shuddering in the double pains of birth and fury, curs-
> ing like a sailor, she rose up on her elbow in her bloody
> gown, looking about her in the bed *as if she had lost
> something.* . . .
>
> A week out of bed *she was lost,* as if she had done
> something irreparable, as if this act had caught her at-
> tention for the first time.
>
> One night, Felix, having come in unheard, found her
> standing in the centre of the floor holding the child
> high in her hand as if she were about to dash it down,
> but she brought it down gently.
>
> (48; my emphasis)

At first, the child she is about to have is represented as
"a lost land" within her, in the sense that it occupies a
body that had formerly been hers entirely. Robin then

experiences giving birth as the loss of "something": the
"land" within her that was lost to the child (in other
words, her uterus, which held the fetus) now seems
doubly lost since she has given birth. This double loss
is then further compounded: it becomes the loss of herself ("a week out of bed she was lost"). The "fury" and
"despair" that mark Robin's feelings about having a
child lead to her "cursing like a sailor" during childbirth, an act that underscores her masculinity even during this most feminine of acts. Her despair is then transmuted into the rage that nearly leads her to kill the
child. Threatening to dash the child to the floor is a gesture she repeats with the doll that she gives to Nora; in
the second instance, she actually does throw the doll/
child to the floor. Robin's pregnancy is figured as a loss
rather than as a gain or a "gift" of life, and this indicates her refusal of motherhood as an intrinsic trait of
femininity and even of femaleness. Robin rejects the
necessity of the link between motherhood and femaleness because maternity is not an expression of her gender identity. Robin does not possess the intrinsic femininity that is supposed to follow from her sex. Rather,
maternity becomes a means by which Robin understands her distance from femininity.[6]

The refusal to be constrained by anatomical sex is
shared by Matthew, the novel's other invert. Inversion
in Matthew's case involves the desire to possess a different sex in order to possess a different gender. Since
Barnes does not see anatomy as a constraint upon gender, however, Matthew can mime women and thereby
become a woman in a man's body. While Robin rejects
motherhood, Matthew longs for it, in an inversion of
traditional gender roles that is typical of the novel.[7]
Matthew often refers to himself as a girl or a woman
("am I not the girl to know of what I speak?" [90]) and
bemoans the fact that although he is anatomically male,
he is psychically feminine. Matthew explains the dilemma of his gender that is at odds with his sex in this
way:

> No matter what I may be doing, in my heart is the wish
> for children and knitting. God, I never asked better
> than to boil some good man's potatoes and toss up a
> child for him every nine months by the calendar. Is it
> my fault that my only fireside is the outhouse?
>
> (91)

Matthew longs to have the body of a woman and a
woman's capacity to reproduce, but instead he must
dress as a woman and mime the sex that he can never
possess "naturally." Matthew is unable to have a home
or a "fireside," which is something that he sees as a
luxury attained only by those with a legitimate sexuality. His only home is the outhouse or kiosk, a place for
cruising men.

Although Barnes trumps up Matthew's authority and
uses him to mock the male fascination with women, his
"gender trouble," to use Judith Butler's term, is not

mocked. Rather, his gender trouble actually makes his theories of the invert or "the third sex" more believable because these theories are informed by experience. Matthew's love for men has been thwarted because he was born a man. He tells his tale of thwarted desire in terms of past lives:

> In the old days I was possibly a girl in Marseilles thumping the dock with a sailor, and perhaps it's that memory that haunts me . . . am I to be blamed if I've turned up this time as I shouldn't have been, when it was a high soprano I wanted, and deep corn curls to my bum, with a womb as big as the king's kettle, and a bosom as high as the bowsprit of a fishing schooner? And what do I get but a face on me like an old child's bottom—is that a happiness, do you think?

(90-91)

Matthew's image of the woman he was meant to be is a transvestite's fantasy. She is a hyperbole: he/she would have the highest voice, the longest hair, the deepest womb, and the highest bosom. Transvestism involves taking the prominent features of one sex and inflating them with hyperbole. These features are then put into even sharper relief by their appearance on a person of the opposite sex. The result is that Matthew's fantasy of himself as the "real" woman he was meant to be is an exaggeration of the features of stereotypical femininity. Femininity seems less natural as a result of the transvestite's image of it: drag makes evident the cultural construction of all gender roles.[8]

The shifting, unstable nature of Matthew's gender emerges clearly in his many asides on himself. In "Watchman," winding up for his account of the first meeting of Robin and Jenny, Matthew explains to Nora, "It was more than a boy like me (who am the last woman left in the world, though I am the bearded lady) could bear, and I went into a lather of misery watching them and thinking of you" (100). Matthew's gender is put into question the moment it is established by virtue of the way in which the subject of speech in these remarks is predicated: the "boy" underscores his undeveloped masculinity and his helplessness as a witness of this fateful meeting; the "last woman" suggests that he alone retains some vestige of true femininity compared to those who are anatomically female. And perhaps the most apt description is the "bearded lady," for he is an anomaly, a strange confusion of masculine and feminine. Matthew's misery is caused by the thought of Nora's pain, and his close identification with her may lead in part to his identification of himself as a woman in these remarks. In another instance where his ambiguous gender comes to the fore, Matthew refers to himself as "the other woman that God forgot" (143). He explains Nora's confession to him in this way—naturally she would come to him, for he is the woman that God forgot, or "the girl that God forgot," as he also calls himself (73). Not only is he a woman in a man's body (and

thus God has forgotten him), but also he is an exceptional woman, the most womanly of women, as he establishes in the passages mentioned above. This endows him with a knowledge of the love of woman for woman, and of another special case like Robin, who may be, in a similar way, the last boy that God forgot. Just as Matthew, a man, is "the girl that God forgot" precisely in that he is a man and yet a girl, Robin is "the boy that God forgot" in that she is a woman and yet a boy. These complex formulations indicate the complexity of the relations among sex, gender, sexual practice, and desire in the novel. A question that arises about Matthew's gender ambiguity is, if Matthew is "the girl that God forgot," what does this mean for his role as the theoretician of sexuality and gender?

THE THEORETICIAN OF SEX AS BEARDED LADY: DR. MATTHEW O'CONNOR

Before we examine **Nightwood**'s theories of homosexuality, the theorist behind the theories should be discussed. "Dr. Matthew-Mighty-grain-of-salt-Dante-O'Connor" is a theorist as well as a priest figure who hears confessions (80). As a storyteller and theorist, Matthew carries great weight in the novel, but his full title (he is "mighty" but not worth "a grain of salt") seems to suggest that he is a mockery. Matthew is a figure of masculine discursive authority in the novel, and his monologues occupy so much of the novel that he sometimes seems a second narrator. But his apparent discursive authority in the text should be questioned, not taken at face value. To question Matthew's authority is to question the masculine prerogative to know in general, and to know in particular the truth of woman. Nora approaches Matthew with questions—"What is Robin?" and "What is the love of woman for woman?"—that are versions of the age-old question—"What is woman?" Men have always attempted to answer this question, but have always "knocked their heads against it," as Freud complained.[9] Matthew is a figure of Freud, of Ulrichs and other sexologists, and also of the male modernist artist who seeks to usurp the place of the feminine subject for his own.[10] By questioning Matthew's apparent discursive authority, we are merely following Barnes's lead, for she has made him a mockery of the authoritative male theorist: he is a frustrated transvestite and a quack doctor who envies women bitterly because he is not and cannot be one.

One way to question his authority in the novel is by considering his "profession"—gynecology. Many critics note that Matthew is a quack, but few find his specialty worth mentioning, though it is significant. Matthew is a gynecologist, and an "unlicensed practitioner" who practices with license at that (35). Throughout the novel, the only occasion on which he "practices medicine" is when he makes his house call on Robin in "La Somnambule," if throwing water on a woman who has fainted can be called medicine. The other references to his profession in the text are some details about his medical instruments. Matthew's oath, "May my dilator burst and my speculum rust, may panic seize my index finger before I point out my man" (32), seems to have come true by the time Nora goes to see him in his rooms in "Watchman, What of the Night?" for his tools are rusted and he, if not his index finger, is in a panic about being discovered in drag by Nora. In this passage, while Nora takes in the sight of Matthew in gown and curls, the narrator describes his surroundings, dwelling on the assortment of objects on Matthew's dresser:

> On a maple dresser . . . lay a rusty pair of forceps, a broken scalpel, half a dozen odd instruments that she could not place, a catheter, some twenty perfume bottles, almost empty, pomades, creams, rouges, powder boxes and puffs. From the half-open drawers of this chiffonnier hung laces, ribands, stockings, ladies' underclothing and an abdominal brace which gave the impression that the feminine finery had suffered venery.
>
> (78-79)

The reader's shock is as great as Nora's when she makes this house call. The tools of Matthew's medical arts are sure to maim any woman who comes under them: the forceps are rusty and the scalpel broken. It is difficult not to see Matthew as a misogynist after reading this passage. Why does the text provide this exhaustive catalogue of objects? First, this description provides a backdrop for the heavily rouged man lying in bed in his nightgown. The specific objects on the dresser are significant, however.

The description of Matthew's dresser top is a catalogue of mismatched objects: women's makeup bottles lie next to rusty medical instruments; lacy "ladies' underclothing" lies next to a man's abdominal brace. Just as Matthew's sex, gender, and sexuality are incongruent—they form no logical, intelligible order—so is the assortment of objects in his private space incongruent. The result of this confusion of objects—feminine/masculine, cosmetic/medical, whole/broken—is that the privileged objects are contaminated by the very nearness of the others. And what is privileged here is the feminine finery, for it corresponds with the rouged and wigged man lying in bed. In private, Matthew plays at being a woman, and these objects enable him to carry out his fantasy. Although the masculine objects correspond to Matthew's "real" gender and his public persona, for Matthew, these are not real, but a false and inescapable condition. We can see this tension between the privileged feminine objects and the loathed masculine objects in the description of the masculine brace whose proximity sexually taints the women's lingerie: it "gave the impression that the feminine finery had suffered venery." Matthew's collection of feminine adornments constructs femininity as a pose, a facade created by the application to a blank surface (the woman) of a series of coverings: rouge, powder, perfume, hair combs, clothing, and so on. Matthew is deprived of a "natural" femininity, yet Barnes suggests through this concept of femininity as a facade or a masquerade that femininity does not exist in a natural state. Thus, it is available to Matthew to the same degree that it is available to any woman.

Through this description of objects, the text not only constructs femininity as a masquerade, but it also brings together Matthew's public persona and his private persona.[11] In private, Matthew is a transvestite, and the perfume, pomade, stockings, and lace indicate his attempt to play a woman since he is not one. In public, on the other hand, Matthew is Dr. O'Connor, the great storyteller and unlicensed but skilled doctor. His choice of gynecology seems arbitrary until we discover that Matthew longs to be a woman, for being a gynecologist helps relieve Matthew's frustration at being a man. Since he cannot be a woman, he can at least attempt to control women by means of his authority as a doctor. Since his desire to be a woman is thwarted and impossible to realize actually, he cultivates and studies women's bodies—both their internal parts and their diseases—as well as the external finery used to adorn their bodies. What is the effect of this characterization of Matthew—as a quack who practices gynecology because of his envy of women—on his position as the authority on sexuality in the novel?

Some critics see Matthew as the narrative foundation of the novel. Elizabeth Pochoda, for example, asserts that Matthew controls the novel's language, as if he, rather than Barnes, has written the novel. For this reason, she claims that the chapter entitled "The Possessed" is a stylistic failure and an "anticlimax" because it is not propelled by Matthew's storytelling abilities.[12] Pochoda does not consider that Barnes has silenced him; rather, she insists that his silence is Barnes's silence. By displacing the female author and replacing her with a male character, Pochoda blocks a feminist reading of the gender ambiguity that Barnes has put into play in her portrayal of Matthew. Although Pochoda denies Barnes authorial control, in a gesture suggestive of the poststructuralist notion of "the death of the author," she grants it fully to Matthew. Charles Baxter also attributes the control of the novel to Matthew, suggesting that "the novelist continues to write as long as O'Connor can talk."[13] For Alan Singer, the monologues bear such weight that he mistakenly attributes certain passages in the novel to the doctor when in fact it is the narrator speaking.[14] This tendency to privilege Matthew to the point of erasing the actual narrator is a common feature of the criticism up until the feminist revival of Barnes in the 1980s. In recent criticism, Matthew's ambiguous authority is noted by Jane Marcus, for example, who also sees him as a parody of Freud. Donna Gerstenberger sees his narrative power as contained by that of

Barnes. She is correct to note that although his "stories often seem to exist for their own telling," they are "nonetheless inscribed within Barnes's narrative purpose."[15] In a text that does much to undermine all hierarchies, it is difficult to maintain that a figure such as Matthew holds such overwhelming discursive authority that he usurps the actual narrator's position.

Through these details of Matthew's portrayal—his quackery, his falling silent in a drunken heap in "Go Down, Matthew," his envy of women, and his self-mockery—Barnes creates a ridiculous figure, one who evokes laughter more than reverence. Yet some critics see in Matthew a masterful prophet, a reading that is possible only when his sexuality is misread, as Baxter misreads him in his equation of homosexuality with narcissism.[16] Baxter's traditional view of masculine authority would be undercut completely were the critic to acknowledge Matthew's femininity. Ignoring this, Baxter depicts him as a figure of monolithic authority—a prophet, a character who steals the novel. Yet, if the surface of this character is scratched, one sees that Barnes trumps up his authority and undercuts it at every turn. In doing so, she inscribes a male figure who tries to usurp the feminine role but who nevertheless holds on tight to his masculine prerogatives. The nod to nineteenth-century sexologists only makes the parody more biting. Through her transvestite gynecologist/priest/psychoanalyst, Barnes reveals some very interested motives behind the masculine discursive fascination with women. Matthew devises his theories of "the third sex" in order to explain Robin to Nora, but also to come closer to an understanding of woman for himself. The undecidability of both of these figures—the invert and woman—undermines Matthew's own authority, making him a still more ambiguous figure. Yet this ambiguity may better qualify him as an authority on subjects that by their questionable status undermine authority.

SEXUAL/TEXTUAL INVERSIONS: THE "PRINCE-PRINCESS"

Matthew responds to Nora's questions about the night and about Robin with a series of compelling rhetorical figures for the invert, figures that operate by means of syntactical inversion. What is the status of masculine and feminine before inversion takes place? Barnes is writing both within and against a dominant tradition in which discourse is organized around binary oppositions rooted in the man/woman couple. *Nightwood* centers around a series of privileged terms that are traditionally associated with the feminine in the history of Western culture: the night, the irrational, and the unconscious.[17] Although the feminine is privileged rather than the masculine, the gender binary prevails, for the hierarchy has simply been overturned. Barnes goes further in questioning this hierarchy, however, with her figures of in-

version. Because of the complex, shifting nature of gender in the invert, neither masculine nor feminine can be said to predominate, as in a hierarchical binary structure. Matthew uses the term "invert" to describe a state of vacillation—a blurring and confusion of genders within the subject—not a simple predominance of feminine over masculine or masculine over feminine. Since masculinity and femininity are not eradicated but proliferated through inversion, the gender binary is at the same time assumed in these figures and questioned and disrupted through them. Inversion involves the figuring and refiguring of gender, for inversion consists of a merging and confusion of genders within the subject. For example, when female sex is joined to masculine gender identity and desire for women, to simply name the gender of this subject "feminine" or "masculine" is inadequate and misleading. This complex gender identity cannot be designated by these terms, yet it does not exist outside this binary; rather, it is an offshoot of the binary.[18] Masculine and feminine are propagated and proliferated in such a subject, one that *Nightwood* designates variously as the third sex, the invert, the prince, and the doll.

Matthew's first theory of the origin of homosexuality is prompted by Nora's remark about Robin's masculine appearance: "I, who want power, chose a girl who resembles a boy" (136). Matthew picks up this thread of androgyny and weaves a tale about love for the "same" sex, but this is clearly not love for the "same" sex, pure and simple, for Robin's resemblance to a boy is the mark of her difference.[19] According to Matthew, the love for the "invert" arises from childhood, specifically from childhood reading of romances and "fairy" tales. The passage reads:

> What is this love we have for the invert, boy or girl? It was they who were spoken of in every romance that we ever read. *The girl lost, what is she but the Prince found?* The Prince on the white horse that we have always been seeking. *And the pretty lad who is a girl, what but the prince-princess in point lace*—neither one and half the other, the painting on the fan! We love them for that reason.
>
> (136; my emphasis)

What we find in this discussion of inverts is a series of inversions, both syntactical and logical. The figure for female homosexuality is the prince: "the girl lost," the lesbian, is "the Prince found." The term for the female homosexual is the prince, which is also the term for the male homosexual in the rest of the passage, which will be discussed below. It seems at first that the figure for the female invert is based upon the male and derived from it secondarily. This is a familiar scheme, common in Freudian theory. But when we turn to the discussion of the male invert, we find that there is no stable referent in the passage whatsoever—no referent that is primary. The only referents for the male homosexual are the girl (he is "the pretty lad who is a girl"), yet the girl is the prince. The second referent for the male homosexual is the prince-princess: the male invert—"the pretty lad who is a girl"—is "the prince-princess in point lace." In other words, the figure for the male invert refers to the figure for the female invert, and vice versa. There is no way out of this closed circle of reference, for we are never told exactly what the prince is. This figure becomes still more mysterious in this description: "The girl lost, what is she but the Prince found? The Prince on the white horse that we have always been seeking." We have always sought the prince, for he is a desirable object, but once we find him, it is only to discover that the prince is female—he is "the girl lost." This type of young masculinity and bravado turns out to be a boyish woman in drag, and "the girl lost," when we find her, is a feminine and boyish prince. In each case, our expectations are confounded by gender ambiguity, so we must continue our search, for what we have found is not what we were looking for. This search is also endless because these fairy-tale figures are fictional and therefore elusive. We may search the world over, but we will not find them, for they imprinted themselves upon our imaginations in childhood, and this childhood realm is their only locus.

To return to the figure for the male invert: he is described early in the passage not just as the prince but as "the prince-princess." This formulation suggests an androgyny that the male invert possesses but not the female invert. This figure is adorned in "point lace," a detail that calls to mind Matthew's feminine finery, spilling lavishly out of his dresser drawer when Nora arrives at his room at the beginning of "Watchman, What of the Night?" Why is the gender ambiguity of the female invert apparently captured by the comparison to the prince ("the girl lost" is "the Prince found"), while that of the male invert is not adequately described by the comparison to the prince? In other words, why the asymmetry in the figures for the two inverts, while other parts of the passage suggest that inversion is inversion, regardless of the invert's sex? Matthew seems to need to use a bigendered term to convey male inversion. As a male invert, Matthew has a stake in the formulation of this figure. What his dual term does is to assert both the masculinity and the femininity of the male invert while the femininity of the female invert is completely eradicated: she is simply a prince. The result is that masculinity is predominant over femininity in the invert. As an authoritative male speaker, Matthew wants to retain his masculine privilege, a privilege outside the domain of princesses. As we will see in the continuation of this passage, the invert is more prince than princess. Although the princess enters the scheme here, she does so only in the composite figure of the "prince-princess," and she is absent from the rest of Matthew's musings.

Yet what are the implications of the absence of the princess from the rest of the passage on the prince as the invert? Perhaps the pertinent question is not why the princess is omitted later in the passage but why it is added early in the passage. The "prince-princess in point lace" may be read as an intrusion into the text of the mark of transvestism—Matthew's mark. Just as Matthew's lacy lingerie peeks from his drawer in "Watchman," further exposing him for what he is or longs to be, so this distinctly feminine image of the princess peeks through and bursts in upon his otherwise predominantly masculine figures of princes. In other words, femininity, excessive with respect to discourse, as Irigaray has shown, shows its face here.[20] And this femininity is the mark of Matthew—the invert of inverts—that overt transgressor of the gender binary, the transvestite. Yet if transvestism entails a transgression of the gender binary, how is it that Matthew believes he can capture femininity by means of transvestism? Matthew fails to see that because the trappings of womanhood are transferable—they may be worn on men as well as women—they do not convey stable, essential femininity, but instead they point to unstable, constructed femininity—femininity as masquerade. Although he is well aware of the instability of gender identity and the incongruence between sex and gender in himself, Matthew regards cross-dressing not as the subversion of the gender binary, which it is, but as a means to capturing and claiming true femininity for himself.[21]

Despite the one conspicuous appearance of the princess, the overall emphasis of the passage is on princes. This emphasis on masculinity escalates when the princess is dropped from the rest of Matthew's musings. Matthew goes on at first to stress the origin of desire in childhood reading and fantasy: "We were impaled in our childhood upon them as they rode through our primers, the sweetest lie of all, now come to be in boy or girl" (136-37). The basis of object choice in childhood reading shows the grounding of desire in fantasy. Barnes has chosen the sort of fairy-tale figures that usually form the basis for heterosexual fantasies. Yet the gallant prince on the white charger is not only the rescuer of Sleeping Beauty and Cinderella but also the desirable object for the male invert and the model for both the male and female invert. Matthew calls this childhood fixation on the characters of children's storybooks "the sweetest lie of all." Why is the love for these characters a lie? Since these characters are fictional, they are ideal creatures whom we seek, but never find. This love is the "sweetest" lie of all in part because Matthew is a lover of princes himself. But more importantly, this lie is "sweetest" because desire in *Nightwood* is firmly rooted in the imagination and is best kept there—desire, once realized, is no longer desire but failed love.

This passage about inversion employs a rhetorical figure based on syntactical inversion; thus, textual inversion doubles sexual inversion. The last phrase in the passage contains a chiasmus, typically a symmetrical structure, although this one is asymmetrical: "In the girl it is the *prince,* and in the boy it is the *girl* that makes a prince a prince and not a *man*" (137; my emphasis).[22] If this were a symmetrical chiasmic reversal, the phrase would read, "In the girl it is the *prince,* and in the boy it is the *princess.*" Yet this version of the phrase is impossible because Matthew has removed the princess from the model entirely because the princess signifies not just femininity but the transvestite's version of femininity, and transvestites are a special case of inverts. Another symmetrical variation of the phrase is, "In the girl it is the *boy* and in the boy it is the *girl.*" The girlish aspect of the boy makes him a prince, but the princely aspect rather than the boyish aspect of the girl makes her a prince in Matthew's version of the model.[23] The prince is also the model for the invert, male or female, for the girl and the boy are treated as one here: "In the girl it is the prince, and in the boy it is the girl that makes a prince a prince and not a man." The statement explains what causes *both* boy and girl to become princes. In other words, the female invert and the male invert are described by means of the same figure—that of the prince. Another asymmetry in the text involves the girl again. Matthew states that it is the prince in the girl and the girl in the boy that creates inversion or "makes a prince a prince and not a man." The male invert (prince) is "not a man," as stated by the text; by the same token, the female invert (prince) is not a woman. Yet the text only implies that the female invert is not a woman; it does not state it. The asymmetry here is so great that it is as if the conclusion of the phrase were lopped off: the fact that the female invert is not a woman is simply omitted from the passage. But perhaps this asymmetry is not the result of Matthew's privileging of the masculine model. Barnes may be suggesting that a female homosexual is still a woman in a way that a male homosexual cannot be a man. "Womanhood" is not threatened by homosexuality as "manhood" is, because of the historical privilege and status of the latter. The omission of the statement that the female invert is not a woman may also suggest that women have a fundamental bisexuality, as Freud argued.

Why is the male the primary referent in Matthew's discussion of the invert? There are two factors that cause the text's blind spot concerning the girl. First, a boy who is like a girl and a girl who is like a boy are essentially the same creatures—androgynous, "third-sexed" creatures. Second, an androgyny in which masculinity is slightly more predominant seems to be privileged in *Nightwood* by means of Matthew's focus on Robin; therefore, the prince is the predominant model, not the "prince-princess." We see this in Robin's un-self-conscious androgyny (she is "a girl who resembles a boy" [136]), which is privileged in the novel, whereas Matthew's transvestism, which rests on a belief that he is truly a woman, makes him a parodic figure.[24] Because both male and female inverts have the same origin (in childhood fixations on androgynous characters) and because they have the same qualities (an androgyny in which masculinity is slightly more pronounced and same-sex love), Matthew uses the same term to refer to both female and male homosexuals—they are "the third sex" or "the invert." The use of the same term for female and male homosexuals also works to undo the binary opposition between male and female: "the third sex" questions the hierarchy between the first and second sex.

The asymmetry of the syntax in the passages describing the prince is not merely an aberration of a classically symmetrical figure of speech. The symmetrical versions described above are dependent upon the diametrical or binary opposition between masculine and feminine. To posit the male and female homosexual as diametrical opposites would be in effect to recreate the masculine/feminine opposition that the text is attempting to undo by means of the figure of "the third sex." This figure is inscribed as a third term precisely in order to question the legitimacy of a strict opposition between masculine and feminine. In *Nightwood,* the masculine is inhabited by the feminine, and vice versa: all of the text's inverts are not merely inverted; rather, they live out the tension between masculine and feminine and are in some way both masculine and feminine. Their state is not one of the simple inversion of gender positions, but rather of the constant vacillation between them (or among them).

Take, for example, Robin's complex gender identity. "She" is not simply a woman who, seeing herself as masculine, wants to be a man, which would imply a resolution of the conflicts among sex, gender, and desire. Rather, Robin is, in the terms of the novel, a girl/prince: a female (her sex) who resembles a feminine male—the prince (her gender)—and who loves women (her desire). These incongruous identifications exist side by side, and the tension among them is never resolved in a simple formula such as, "Robin is a man in a woman's body."[25] Robin is *not* a man in a woman's body, but a woman who loves women, who seems masculine, and whose very body and self-presentation also seem masculine. A passage from Butler describes the kind of intricately gendered being that Robin is:

> It is possible to become a being whom neither *man* nor *woman* truly describes. This is not the figure of the androgyne nor some hypothetical "third gender," nor is it a *transcendence* of the binary. Instead, it is an internal subversion in which the binary is both presupposed and proliferated to the point where it no longer makes sense.[26]

Robin is indeed a being whom neither "man" nor "woman" describes adequately Yet, while I have followed Barnes in describing Robin as a member of the third sex," Butler cautions that this type of gendered being is something other than the androgyne or the "hypothetical 'third gender.'" While the notion of "the third sex" was first coined to describe the idea of the man trapped in a woman's body and has also been understood as an androgynous state beyond gender, Barnes's "third sex" is a radical reconceptualization of this idea.[27] Her vision of "the third sex" is much closer to contemporary notions of the socially constructed, performative nature of gender. By means of this third term, which would undermine the binary opposition between masculine and feminine, Barnes's text refuses simple binary opposition or symmetry in its articulation of gender. This third term will be more explicitly theorized in Matthew's other model for inversion, discussed in the next section, where Matthew names this third term "the third sex."

"The Third Sex"

Matthew's second model for homosexuality—the doll—is similar to that based on the prince: it is lifeless, yet lifelike; it derives from childhood; and it is androgynous. Matthew offers his second theory in response to Nora's story of the doll that Robin has given to her. Nora regards a doll given to a woman by her lover as a replacement for, or a representation of, the child they cannot have: "We give death to a child when we give it a doll—it's the effigy and the shroud; when a woman gives it to a woman, it is the life they cannot have, it is their child, sacred and profane" (142). As a gift from a woman to her lover, the doll is a stand-in for the child the women cannot have, indicating the attempt to model their life after a heterosexual relationship, an attempt that necessarily fails. In a sense, the doll is a sign of this failure, yet Nora is nevertheless attached to the doll as a gift from Robin.[28] Thus, when Robin throws and "kills" the doll in a fit of rage, the action devastates Nora. This incident takes place when Robin returns home after wandering the night streets, a habit that underscores the distance between the lovers. Nora attributes Robin's violent treatment of the doll to the fact that "she was angry because for once I had not been there all the time, waiting" (148). For Nora, the doll is a mediator between Robin and herself: it is a replacement for the connection that is lacking between them.

The doll resembles the figure of the prince as invert not only in its relation to childhood fantasy but also in the way that it is inscribed in the text: both models appear as chiasmic reversals. After discussing Robin's sense of herself as the doll, Matthew likens the doll explicitly to the invert:

The last doll, given to age, is the girl who should have been a boy, and the boy who should have been a girl.

The love of that last doll was foreshadowed in that love of the first. The doll and the immature have something right about them, *the doll because it resembles but does not contain life, and the third sex because it contains life but resembles the doll.*

(148; my emphasis)

In this passage, the origin of homosexuality is located again in childhood, or rather in a regression to childhood ("the last doll given to age" is the doll that an adult might give to another adult, as Robin gives Nora a doll and Felix a baby). More important, the "last doll" is a metaphor for the homosexual: "the girl who should have been a boy and the boy who should have been a girl." The love that they inspire was "foreshadowed" in the love of the first doll of childhood, just as the love of the prince was foreshadowed, or actually inspired by, the love of the figure of the prince in fairy tales. The model for homosexuality is again a replica of a person that children endow with a name, a character, and so on, like the princes of childhood readers. Children may project their desires onto such figures; they may perceive them as doubles of themselves. In short, the doll and the prince may be transformed into whatever the child wants them to be because they are purely fictional. Similar to the function of the doll for Nora, the prince is also a beloved yet lost object that is introjected and incorporated through melancholia. In the same way, Nora loves Robin because Robin's lack of identity at first allows her to be transformed into anything. In this sense, the doll and the invert are both inanimate figures that can be animated.

Again, the structure of the passage is that of a chiasmus—this time, a double chiasmus. The first sentence contains a simple symmetrical chiasmus: "the girl who should have been a boy, and the boy who should have been a girl." The sentence beginning "the doll and the immature" forms another symmetrical chiasmus: "the doll because it resembles but does not contain life, and the third sex because it contains life but resembles the doll." As in the passage on the prince, the text construes sexual "inversion" as syntactical inversion. The symmetry of these inversions at first seems to imply a simple acceptance of a binary scheme for gender: homosexuality is the result of being misplaced in one's anatomical sex. But this simple inversion—the invert is the girl who should have been a boy and the boy who should have been a girl—is subverted by the language of the rest of the passage.

There Matthew describes the doll's face as a composite of two sexless beings: "The blessed face! It should be seen only *in profile*, otherwise it is observed to be the conjunction of the identical *cleaved halves* of sexless misgiving!" (148; my emphasis). In other words, the doll's face is neither n asculine nor feminine, and for this reason in particular he uses the metaphor of the doll for the homosexual. Matthew's image relies on the idea of the splitting in two (as implied by "cleaved," "halves," and "profile") of something that we expect to be whole (the face). Yet "cleave" also refers to a joining together, as in the biblical reference to marriage. The face is that part of the body traditionally thought to convey identity, a concept that implies wholeness and unity. The face of the invert, however, is divided, torn asunder, and therefore the only way to convey the impression of the whole (an idea that is implicit in the meaning of the face) is to look at only one half—the profile.

One word stands out in this passage that seems to work against the predominant note of division and disunity. That word is "identical": the face is "observed to be the *conjunction* of the *identical* cleaved halves of sexless misgiving." Though the face of the doll/invert is divided, its parts are identical to each other. The two identical halves of the doll's face could be read as masculine and feminine, conjoined: each half consists of a blend of masculine and feminine.[29] Thus, gender confusion is conceived not as a simple case of a man trapped in a woman's body (or a woman trapped in a man's body) but as a complex case of both genders inflecting one body.[30] The halves referred to in the passage are not only the parts of the face; they are also the "cleaved halves of sexless misgiving." That is, the division is caused by the uncertainty of the doll/invert about its sex, which results in a state of "sexless misgiving." On the other hand, the sex of the invert has been "misgiven," or given wrongly: Matthew's image also implies that inversion is the result of an incorrect assignment of sex. Since the conjunction of masculine and feminine in one person is perceived as gender uncertainty in our culture, the invert seems a sexless creature, suspended in a state of uncertainty or misgiving. The text's careful delineation of the self-division of the doll/invert is what works against the seemingly simple binary scheme of these particular chiasmi. The self-division indicates that the doll/invert is made up of both masculine and feminine characteristics: so the formula "the girl who should have been a boy" then represents a girl/boy, not a boy in spirit and in sexuality who is at war with her female body.

These analogies between the invert and lifeless dolls or fairy-tale figures emphasize on one level the idea that gender and sexuality are not necessarily consistent with anatomical sex, because the connections between them are constructed through the psyche, language, and culture, and are not natural. Although homosexuality is often construed as a false miming of the "natural" genders found in heterosexuality, what Barnes is trying to get at here is the way in which "the third sex" makes explicit the performative nature of all gendered behavior.[31] A glance at a passage on "the third sex" as the "Sodomite" reveals that this is one of the reasons for

the placement of the invert in the realm of the fictional as opposed to the real. In "Watchman," Matthew turns to the subject of loving a "Sodomite" after introducing the night to Nora.

> "And do I know my Sodomites?" the doctor said unhappily, "and what the heart goes bang up against if it loves one of them, especially if it's a woman loving one of them. What do they find then, *that this lover has committed the unpardonable error of not being able to exist—and they come down with a dummy in their arms.* God's last round, shadow-boxing, that the heart may be murdered and swept into that still quiet place where it can sit and say: 'Once I was, now I can rest.'"
>
> (93; my emphasis)

Although the term "Sodomite" historically refers to male inverts, Matthew is clearly using it to refer to female inverts as well, since he speaks of what happens when a woman loves one of them, and Nora clearly loves a female invert. Just as he merges male and female homosexuals under the terms "prince" and "invert," so he uses the masculine term "Sodomite" to refer to both sexes. While Matthew's aim in describing the prince and the doll was theoretical, his aim in describing the sodomite here is existential. The doll and the prince were devised to show the origin of homosexuality in childhood and to describe the qualities of this other sexuality. These figures were also devised in order to theorize the complex gender identity of the invert. Here, on the other hand, he explains to Nora what *happens* when one loves a sodomite. He speaks, that is, of his painful experience: "And do I know my Sodomites?" refers not to his encyclopedic knowledge of the species invert but to the basis of his knowledge— his own life as an invert and his frustrated desires. His subject, as he goes on to say, is "what the heart goes bang up against if it loves one of them."

The invert's inability to exist causes pain and anguish to those who love inverts. But why does Matthew claim that the invert is "not able to exist"? Once again, the novel likens the invert or "Sodomite" to that which is lifeless—in this case, a "dummy," which, like the doll, is an imitation of life. Matthew's prince similarly was "a lie"—a desirable object that was always sought but never found, because it did not exist in the real. Although the prince exists, at least in the imagination, he/she is unattainable because he/she is absent from the real. But the lifelessness of the sodomite as dummy seems more dramatic than that of the prince or the doll: the doll "does not contain life," according to Matthew, while the sodomite is "*not able to exist.*" The invert's habitat is the night, and consequently, the invert is associated with the novel's central terms—the anonymous, the unconscious, nonreason—which are associated with death and nothingness.[32] For this reason, in part, the invert "is not able to exist." The invert is also one of the many abject, outcast characters that populate this novel:

as Marcus argues, *Nightwood* is a tale of Jews, blacks, lesbians, and transvestites, oppressed others who resisted the authoritarian domination that typified European politics in the 1930s.[33] The invert, like other oppressed people—like other "others"—lives on the margins of society, which is figured as the night in this novel, a space that is privileged yet still marked as outside. In other words, "the third sex" is a term that subverts binary oppositions by being a conjunction of masculine and feminine: the very term "the third sex" poses a challenge to the structure of binary opposition that shores up the world of the day, discourse, and structures of power.

"THERE IS NO TRUTH" OF GENDER

In attempting to resolve the question of the degree to which *Nightwood*'s figures of inversion rely upon the gender binary even as they deconstruct the truth of inversion, I will close by considering a remark of Matthew's that may be read as a self-reflexive comment on his own status as a speaker. Matthew describes to Nora the mistake involved in imposing a formula on love: "There is no truth, and you have set it between you; you have been unwise enough to make a formula; you have dressed the unknowable in the garments of the known" (136). In order to understand her love for Robin, Nora goes to Matthew for an explanation of the truth about Robin, the truth about homosexuality, and the truth about the night. But these truths—or formulae—do not exist and this is something that Matthew also tries to teach Nora. Although Matthew's voice in the novel is endowed with authority, his authority is also ambiguous: while admitting that there is no truth and that he only tells lies, he nevertheless presents Nora with several accounts of inversion that sound like attempts to speak the truth. Yet rather than reveal the truth, as Matthew sets out to do, he only reveals the inadequacy of his own formulae.

While focusing on Nora's desire for the truth, this remark of Matthew's is also self-reflexive in that he is aware that he himself has "dressed the unknowable in the garments of the known." As a self-professed theorist of sexuality, Matthew has devised models for the invert that do precisely this: they take an unknowable entity and explain it by means of familiar terms that the invert itself puts seriously into question. Matthew has taken the person whose gender is an indeterminable amalgamation of masculinity and femininity and given it a name (or several names), an origin, and a history. But for Barnes, "the third sex" is fundamentally undecidable, and any attempt to formulate it is bound to miss its mark. The characters Robin and Matthew, as well as Matthew's theories of the invert, have shown that masculine and feminine are not easily distinguishable, do not neatly coincide with male and female, and that gender is not a simple choice between two options.

Although *Nightwood* has ventured a theory of "the third sex," it undoes its own attempt precisely to show that there is no certain truth of either inversion or gender. "The third sex" is the mark of this uncertainty.

Matthew's metaphor of "dressing the unknowable in the garments of the known," as formulaic as it may seem, brings together all the uncertainty and undecidability surrounding gender in this text. First, it is a self-conscious remark in that it refers to his own transvestism in an almost literal way. Although Matthew claims that it is an error to "dress the unknowable in the garments of the known," isn't this what he himself attempts to do by means of his transvestism? In his desire to be a woman, he takes the costumes and cosmetics that are cultural markers of femininity—"the garments of the known"—and uses them to "dress the unknowable." But what is the unknowable in this instance—the woman Matthew longs to be or the ambiguous gender that he possesses? In his eagerness to be a true woman, or a woman in truth, Matthew has mistaken the feminine masquerade for the essence of woman. Removing the "garments" of femininity from Matthew would simply reveal an aging man, not the beautiful young woman he longs to be. In a similar way, his ambiguous gender, "the third sex," is unknowable (in the sense of being indeterminate and in flux) and undecidable, and no garment could ever take the shape of its strange contours. The text seems to suggest then that "the third sex" is fundamentally "unknowable." Although via Robin the text also represents the feminine as mysterious, enigmatic, and unknowable—and in this way, she resembles an essential feminine—it also moves toward a recognition of femininity as construct or masquerade. The scene in which Nora finds Matthew in drag, surrounded by "feminine finery," indicates the impulse in the text toward this other view of transvestism: instead of garments failing to convey the truth of woman, garments—the masquerade—themselves constitute femininity. In this sense, Matthew may be read both as a parody of the nineteenth-century sexologist and as a prescient sketch of a contemporary gender theorist. While *Nightwood* anticipates the theorization of gender as performance, there still lingers in this rich text a belief in an essential, fundamental gender difference lurking beneath, as it were, the garments of culturally constructed, multiple gender differences.

Notes

1. Djuna Barnes, *Nightwood* (1937; rpt. New York: New Directions, 1961), 136. Further references to this work will appear in the text.

2. Given the fact that *Nightwood* is a modernist text, it may be that Matthew's femininity actually provides, rather than undercuts, his narrative authority. Gayatri Chakravorty Spivak writes that the masculine displacement of the feminine subject

position provides deconstruction with its discursive power ("Displacement and the Discourse of Woman," in *Displacement: Derrida and After,* ed. Mark Krupnick [Bloomington: Indiana University Press, 1983], 169-72). Alice Jardine has also examined the valorization of the feminine as a means of exploring the meaning of modernity in twentieth-century male-authored writing (*Gynesis: Configurations of Woman and Modernity* [Ithaca, N.Y.: Cornell University Press, 1985], 25). I read Matthew similarly, as a male theorist who masquerades as a woman in order to displace his own subjectivity.

3. These figures must be read both thematically and stylistically, for issues of gender and style cannot be separated in the study of women modernists' texts, where gender experimentation is tied closely to stylistic experimentation. Style was the primary focus of criticism on Barnes until the late 1980s, when Sandra M. Gilbert and Susan Gubar, Shari Benstock, and Frann Michel brought attention to the centrality of gender within Barnes's texts, while also examining style. See Gilbert and Gubar, *Sexchanges,* Vol. 2 of *No Man's Land: The Place of the Woman Writer in the Twentieth Century,* 2 vols. to date (New Haven, Conn.: Yale University Press, 1989); Shari Benstock, *Women of the Left Bank: Paris, 1900-1940* (Austin: University of Texas Press, 1986); and Frann Michel, "Displacing Castration: *Nightwood, Ladies Almanack,* and Feminine Writing," *Contemporary Literature* 30, no. 1 (1989): 33-58. One notable early study of gender and style in *Nightwood* is Carolyn Allen's 1978 essay, "'Dressing the Unknowable in the Garments of the Known': The Style of Djuna Barnes's *Nightwood,*" in *Women's Language and Style,* ed. Douglas Butturf and Edmund L. Epstein (Akron, Ohio: University of Akron Press, 1978), 106-18. Recent feminist readings of the novel that continue the study of gender and style and that I will discuss below are essays by Judith Lee and Jane Marcus in Mary Lynn Broe's *Silence and Power: A Reevaluation of Djuna Barnes* (Carbondale: Southern Illinois University Press, 1991). See Lee, "*Nightwood*: 'The Sweetest Lie,'" 207-18; and Marcus, "Laughing at Leviticus: *Nightwood* as Woman's Circus Epic," 221-50. In my focus on Matthew as a storyteller/theorist, I am returning to one of the tendencies of 1970s and early 1980s Barnes criticism. The critics Charles Baxter, Elizabeth Pochoda, and Alan Singer, whose work I will examine below, tended to emphasize Matthew's discursive power and narrative authority, which they saw as eclipsing Barnes's authorial power. I would like to reread Matthew's narrative authority and the focus of his narrative—inversion and gender—in light of some of the insights of feminist Barnes studies on the text's inscription of gender.

4. For convincing readings of Robin as a representation of the feminine, see Michel, "Displacing Castration," 41-42, and Lee, "*Nightwood,*" 210-11.

5. I am using Judith Butler's definition of gender identity as "a relationship among sex, gender, sexual practice, and desire" (*Gender Trouble: Feminism and the Subversion of Identity* [New York: Routledge, 1990], 18).

6. While Robin rebels against both pregnancy and motherhood, and thus in some sense she rejects her gender role, her possibilities for complete rejection are more limited than those of Matthew, who rebels against masculinity through dressing as a woman. Matthew can refuse to engage in masculine sexual behavior, while Robin's reproductive capacity is a constant fact of life.

7. Gender role is defined as "a set of expectations about what behaviors are appropriate for people of one gender" (Suzanne J. Kessler and Wendy McKenna, *Gender: An Ethnomethodological Approach* [New York: Wiley, 1978], 11).

8. On the denaturalization of gender in drag performance, see Esther Newton, *Mother Camp: Female Impersonators in America* (Chicago: University of Chicago Press, 1979), 103, 107.

9. Sigmund Freud, "Femininity," *The Standard Edition of the Complete Psychological Works of Freud,* trans. James Strachey, 28 vols. (London: Hogarth, 1964), 22:113.

10. Marcus comments on Matthew as a scathing parody of Freud, or of sexologists in general. See "Laughing at Leviticus," 233-34, 245. For discussions of the masculine displacement of the feminine subject position, see note 2 above.

11. The masquerade of femininity, first theorized by Joan Riviere, designates the deliberate putting on of femininity—according to Luce Irigaray, the "affirmation" of traditional connotations of the feminine. See Riviere, "Womanliness as a Masquerade," in *Psychoanalysis and Female Sexuality,* ed. Hendrik M. Ruitenbeek (New Haven, Conn.: College and University Press, 1966), 209-20; and Irigaray, *This Sex Which Is Not One,* trans. Catherine Porter (Ithaca, N.Y.: Cornell University Press, 1985), 76. This affirmation allows for a transformation, or a "transvaluation," of the feminine itself because it is the feminine's potentially subversive qualities that are privileged. See Naomi Schor, "This Essentialism Which Is Not One: Coming to Grips with Irigaray," *differences* 1, no. 2 (1989): 48. The feminine's multiplicity, unde-

cidability, and excess are self-consciously emphasized as a way of setting loose their subversive potential. For other feminist discussions of masquerade and the related term "mimesis," see Mary Ann Doane, "Film and the Masquerade: Theorising the Female Spectator," *Screen* 23, nos. 3-4 (1982): 81-82; and Butler, *Gender Trouble,* 47-53.

12. Pochoda writes, "The novel has already jettisoned language; O'Connor has exited, and really there is no way to rescue the end of the story from the melodrama it has eschewed so far" ("Style's Hoax: A Reading of Djuna Barnes's *Nightwood,*" *Twentieth Century Literature* 22 [1976]: 188). The style of "The Possessed" is spare and monosyllabic not because Barnes has reached her limit in previous chapters, but because language has been such an obstacle to Robin and Nora that they attempt silence as a last resort. Moreover, the novel's resources are not depleted; rather, Matthew's resources are depleted because the misery that he experiences in telling stories on subjects that others are "keeping hushed" leads him to choose silence over speech as well. See *Nightwood,* 162-63.

13. Charles Baxter, "A Self-Consuming Light: *Nightwood* and the Crisis of Modernism," *Journal of Modern Literature* 3 (1974): 1177.

14. Alan Singer, "The Horse Who Knew Too Much: Metaphor and the Narrative of Discontinuity in *Nightwood,*" *Contemporary Literature* 25, no. 1 (1984): 75, 82.

15. Donna Gerstenberger, "The Radical Narrative of Djuna Barnes's *Nightwood,*" in *Breaking the Sequence: Women's Experimental Fiction,* ed. Ellen G. Friedman and Miriam Fuchs (Princeton, N.J.: Princeton University Press, 1989), 136.

16. Baxter, "A Self-Consuming Light," 1180.

17. For a discussion of the masculine/feminine hierarchy, see Hélène Cixous, "Sorties," in *New French Feminisms,* ed. Elaine Marks and Isabelle de Courtivron (New York: Schocken, 1981), 90-91. My discussion of the status of the masculine/feminine opposition in *Nightwood* is informed by Michel's convincing argument that the feminine in Barnes's texts closely resembles the feminine within the work of Hélène Cixous, Luce Irigaray, and Julia Kristeva. See Michel, "Displacing Castration," 34-39. For the connection between the night and the destabilization of identity, an issue too involved to be addressed adequately here, see *Nightwood,* 81-83, 88.

18. Butler's notion of the relation between stable and destabilizing gender provides a clear framework for Barnes's notion of the third sex as I am for-

mulating it, and I am indebted to Butler here: gender is destabilized "through the mobilization, subversive confusion, and proliferation of precisely those constitutive categories that seek to keep gender in its place by posturing as the foundational illusions of identity" (*Gender Trouble,* 34).

19. Pamela L. Caughie critiques the tendency to read androgyny as a transcendence of gender in criticism on Virginia Woolf. For example, in Gilbert and Gubar's reading of androgyny in women's modernist fiction, they negate the very gender categories they seek to maintain by construing androgyny as a state "beyond gender." See Gilbert and Gubar, *Sexchanges,* 332, 361-62. Following Caughie, I argue that the ambiguously gendered "third sex" enacts or deploys gender, rather than transcends it. See Caughie, "Virginia Woolf's Double Discourse," in *Discontented Discourses: Feminism/Textual Intervention/Psychoanalysis,* ed. Marleen S. Barr and Richard Feldstein (Urbana: University of Illinois Press, 1989), 46, 51.

20. Irigaray, *This Sex,* 78.

21. See Butler, *Gender Trouble,* 136-38, for a reading of drag as a subversive practice that creates gender confusion and proliferation.

22. My reading owes much to Andrzej Warminski's reading of an asymmetrical chiasmus in Nietzsche's *Birth of Tragedy.* The metaphor in question that undergoes a chiasmic reversal involves the opposition of Apollo and Dionysos, light and dark, blinding and healing. Warminski's text dwells on this figure for some thirty pages and cannot be paraphrased here. However, the thrust of his reading is that Apollonian light is found to result in the same nothingness that the Dionysian night presents to the senses. And this nothing is "radically unknowable" in terms of binary opposition. This is the reason for the figure's bursting the boundaries of a tidy symmetrical reversal. I would suggest that similarly, for Barnes, gender and sexuality cannot be contained or even suggested within the confines of a scheme of thinking based on binary opposition. See *Readings in Interpretation: Holderlin, Hegel, Heidegger* (Minneapolis: University of Minnesota Press, 1986), xxxv-lxi.

23. For a convincing gloss on this passage, see Michel, "Displacing Castration," 42. She points out that the female invert "contains the difference that she is"—the difference of inversion—while the male invert "becomes an invert by containing the difference of the feminine." According to Michel, Matthew's figures of inversion thus reaffirm the gender binary in that difference is located "on the side of Woman" in these figures. Yet

Michel argues that another of Matthew's descriptions of the invert "disrupt[s]" the "binary structure of gender." She reads the description of the invert as "neither one and half the other" as stressing otherness and difference and thus disrupting the gender binary (*Nightwood*, 136). While I agree that Matthew's figures rely on the gender binary to a certain degree, I argue that the asymmetry of the figures, as well as the complex interplay among all components of gender identity in the text's inverts—sex, gender, sexual practice, and desire—result in the disruption rather than the reaffirmation of the gender binary.

24. While Robin's androgyny is described as a natural trait, it is also deliberate in that she dresses like a boy, perhaps to enhance her masculinity.

25. The idea of a woman trapped in a man's body is put forward by Gilbert and Gubar, an idea that the language of the text does not bear out. See their *Sexchanges,* 216-17.

26. Butler, *Gender Trouble,* 127. Emphasis in original.

27. "The third sex," the term that best conveys *Nightwood*'s inscription of inversion, is a term coined by the nineteenth-century sexologist Karl Heinrich Ulrichs to designate the concept of the homosexual as a man trapped in a woman's body. This concept, also known as the "man-woman," was further theorized and popularized by better-known sexologists such as Richard von Krafft-Ebing and Havelock Ellis. See J. E. Rivers, "The Myth and Science of Homosexuality in *A la recherche du temps perdu,*" in *Homosexualities and French Literature,* ed. George Stambolian and Elaine Marks (Ithaca, N. Y.: Cornell University Press, 1979), 265-66. Benstock provides important commentary on the effects of such theories in the sociocultural realm for women writers of the 1920s and 1930s (*Women of the Left Bank,* 49-52).

28. The doll stands in for the loss of Robin: in a response to Robin's refusal of love, Nora displaces her love onto a stand-in, the doll. Nora in this way resembles the melancholiac of Sigmund Freud's "Mourning and Melancholia." See *General Psychological Theory,* ed. Philip Rieff (New York: Collier, 1963), 164-66. Butler's reading of the incorporative structure of melancholy in the formation of gender identity is also suggestive in relation to Nora, but this issue is too involved to take up adequately in this essay. See Butler, *Gender Trouble,* 48-53.

29. This is but one of a series of metaphors in *Nightwood* that involve the joining and merging of halves and that indicate the overcoming of opposition. See 38, 69, 138.

30. Not only does Barnes subvert the opposition of masculine and feminine by means of this metaphor of the face, but she also subverts the opposition of spirit and body an opposition that is congruent with the masculine/feminine opposition. The face is seen as conveying identity and yet it is a part of the body: it conjoins the internal (the soul) and the external (the body) on the level of the body.

31. Butler's theorization of gender as performative and constructed sheds new light on gender in *Nightwood.* On the question of the relation of heterosexuality and homosexuality to gender identity, Butler writes that "the replication of heterosexual constructs in non-heterosexual frames brings into relief the utterly constructed status of the so-called heterosexual original. Thus, gay is to straight *not* as copy is to original, but, rather, as copy is to copy. The parodic repetition of 'the original' . . . reveals the original to be nothing other than a parody of the *idea* of the natural and the original" (*Gender Trouble,* 31). This denaturalization of the so-called natural basis of gender and sexuality (their supposed basis in anatomical sex) through parody and mimicry is what is behind the placement of the prince, the doll, and the invert in the realm of fiction. Fiction, like mimicry and parody, is in the register of rhetoric and performance.

32. Allen was the first critic to recognize the subjects of *Nightwood* as "the power of the night, of irrationality and the unconscious; and the nature of love, particularly love between women," and to suggest the connection between the night and inversion ("'Dressing the Unknowable,'" 107).

33. Marcus, "Laughing at Leviticus," 221.

Deborah Tyler-Bennett (essay date 1995)

SOURCE: Tyler-Bennett, Deborah. "'Her Wench of Bliss': Gender and the Language of Djuna Barnes' *Ladies Almanack.*" In *Language and Gender: Interdisciplinary Perspectives,* edited by Sara Mills, pp. 95-103. London: Longman, 1995.

[*In the following essay, Tyler-Bennett asserts that* Ladies Almanack *creates "a picture of lesbian history" in almanac form, and she explores the ways in which Barnes "deliberately inverts known devices from the sixteenth and seventeenth centuries" in the novel in order to "re-evaluate the almanac form in terms of gender."*]

This essay does not represent a close linguistic reading of Djuna Barnes' text, **Ladies Almanack** (Barnes 1928b) but considers the way in which the text engages gender archetypes, and thus subverts and explores older verbal and visual forms, such as ballads, almanacs and chapbooks. Barnes was born in Cornwall-on-Hudson, New York State, in 1892, and died at Patchin Place, Greenwich Village, in 1982. She is chiefly remembered for her novel *Nightwood* (Barnes 1936) and for the increasingly reclusive lifestyle which has been represented as typifying her old age. Barnes occurs as an 'exotic' figure in many memoirs of the 'modernist' period, and *Ladies Almanack* has come to be regarded as a who's who of the lesbian salon of Natalie Clifford Barney. Barnes' use of language, it will be argued here, deliberately inverts known devices from the sixteenth and seventeenth centuries, thus allowing borders (chronological, historical and between genres) to be crossed. Barnes' usage of historical phrases (both 'legitimate' and 'underground'), her use of verbal listings and elliptical and rhythmical line structures, create an almanac which is difficult to fit in to current definitions of 'modernism', a term which remains, itself, problematic, as Bonnie Kime Scott notes (Scott 1990: 10-11). This essay demonstrates how Barnes' use of language enables her to re-evaluate the almanac form in terms of gender.

Indeed, in engaging with the almanac form, a form, with exceptions, most often used by men, Barnes both reconsidered and transmuted that form. By so doing, she was writing into the past whilst creating a picture of lesbian history which did not depend on *fin-de-siècle* stereotypes. In 1927, one year before the publication of *Ladies Almanack,* Barnes wrote a preface to the posthumous 'selected letters' of her friend, the poet Elsa, Baroness Von Freytag Loringhoven, published in *transition* magazine (Barnes [**"Introduction to the selected letters of Elsa von Freytag Loringhoven"**] 1928a: 19). In her preface, Barnes stated: 'such of her things as are in my possession, letters written in her time of agony . . . I now give parts, as they make a monument to this her inappropriate end, in the only fitting language which could reveal it, her own' (Barnes 1928a: 19). Freytag Loringhoven, a German exile, had constantly written of her struggle with the English language and this difficulty with grammar and syntax has also been applied by certain critics to Barnes herself (Field 1985). Barnes had little formal schooling and thus her emphasis on the Baroness's 'own' language is important, firmly linking language to the concept of self outside academic constraints. In moving and desperate letters, written shortly before her suicide, the Baroness outlined the difficulties of being a woman writer. It might be argued that, like her, Barnes suffered from a horror of being categorised and thus created works which fitted into many literary and artistic categories. Therefore, when Marianne Moore commented that 'reading Djuna Barnes is like reading a foreign language, which you understand' (Broe 1991: 155), she outlined a vital part of Barnes' aesthetic.

Moore's comment might be applied to a reading of *Ladies Almanack,* a text which has, until recently, been dismissed as a comic 'diversion' amongst Barnes' serious works (Field 1985: 124-5). Despite new readings of the text by Susan Snaider Lanser (Lanser 1992: xv-xlv), Karla Jay (Jay 1991: 184-91), and Fran Michel (Michel 1991: 170-83), *Ladies Almanack* remains the least discussed of all Barnes' works. Yet it is a vital work, as Lanser suggests, not merely in terms of Barnes' career as a whole, but in histories of the lesbian novel (Lanser 1992: xv-xlv).

Ladies Almanack was privately printed in Paris in 1928, by Maurice Darrantière on behalf of Djuna Barnes (Field 1985: 124-5). It was published under a pseudonym which had an eighteenth-century ring to it, 'a Lady of Fashion'. This may have also referred to a private joke as Natalie Barney's lover, Romaine Brooks (Cynic Sal in the text), had been photographed as 'a Lady of Fashion' in 1908 (Secrest 1974: 163). The original print-run consisted of 1,050 copies, the first fifty of which possessed illustrations hand-tinted by Barnes herself. It was to have been distributed by Edward Titus, who lost confidence in the volume when he saw its lesbian content, and was thus privately distributed among friends (Field 1985: 124-4). Thus the text became notorious, both for what it contained and for the way in which it was sold. As a satire on Barney's circle, the text was also both a public and a private work.

As the study by Karla Jay reveals, the text is usually discussed more in terms of who it satirized than in terms of its form (Jay 1991: 184-94). However, it could be argued that a discussion of form is crucial to an understanding of the piece as a whole. A cast-list, including Barney, has been applied to the text from Barney's annotated copy (Field 1985: 124-5). Yet, by applying this type of literary 'who's who' to the piece, ideas concerning the text's exploration of gender are omitted. Essentially, the text is a pastiche which employs terminology from sixteenth- and seventeenth-century popular literature—ballads, chapbooks, almanacs, hagiographies, conduct-books and bestiaries—as well as containing private jokes which refer to Barney's own circle. In *Border Traffic,* Maggie Humm quotes Frederic Jameson's description of pastiche as a product of postmodernism, 'each group comes to speak an "idiolect", a curious private language of its own which is spoken at the moment when pastiche appears and parody has become impossible. Pastiche is blank parody that has lost its sense of humour . . . this is a condition of marginality' (Humm 1991: 15). Humm rightly discusses the problems of relating statements such as this to writings by women. The pastiche of the *Ladies Almanack* is one which very definitely retains its bawdy and irreverent sense of humour. Using pastiche, the text quite clearly effects the type of border crossing which Humm describes as issuing 'a profound challenge to the literary canon, and to the very process of criticism as an exercise in gender proprieties' (*ibid.*: 9). By means of an eclectic blend of secular and religious imagery, Barnes' text crosses several borders, including those of gender, class and history.

When asking about the sources of the work, Barnes' biographer, Andrew Field, was given an evasive reference to 'some old French albums which' she had 'picked up in the bookstalls of Paris' (Field 1985: 125). The text, which begins in the style of a conduct-book, is referred to as 'the book which all ladies should carry' and is a lesbian re-working of several antique forms (Barnes 1928b: 5). By deliberately imitating both chapbook conventions and the almanac tradition, Barnes is not only re-working male-dominated conventions but also acknowledging the way in which many of these forms covertly refer to women's history. In the past, as work by Elaine Hobby reveals, texts which suggested that 'all ladies' should carry them were often instructive manuals, a good example of this being the conduct-books of the seventeenth and eighteenth centuries (Hobby 1988: 8). In rewriting the instruction book, a work intended for a young female audience, Barnes re-evaluates a past form in terms of lesbianism. The title page, which is famous more for its parodic element than for the gender implications with which it presents the reader, is concerned with outlining all aspects of the female condition. If this is compared with the headings of tracts from the seventeenth-century, such as *Mundus Muliebris* by John and Mary Evelyn (Evelyn and Evelyn 1690), both the quality and clarity of the parody become obvious.[1] The introduction to **Ladies Almanack** describes a cycle of moons and tides associated with femininity, which re-writes the traditionally male calendar of the almanac. Thus Barnes creates an idea of woman's time connected to birth, menstruation, pregnancy and menopause. This can be contextualised historically for, as with the seventeenth-century almanac-maker Sarah Jinner, Barnes can be regarded as placing a new context upon a yearly calendar of times, thus privileging the 'moons and tides' of women above conventional time-scales (Hobby 1988: 181-2). Barnes' text reminds the reader that women, such as Sarah Jinner and Mary Holden, both of whom created women's almanacs, are able to alter time-scales and, by so doing, creates a female calendar in which her heroine (Evangeline Musset) and her heroine's circle can exist.

Musset, 'as fine a wench as ever wet bed', celebrates her lesbianism over the seasons of her life (Barnes 1928b: 6). She and her countless lovers are watched by the almanac's one heterosexual character, Patience Scalpel. Scalpel, whose very name is emblematic of her critical nature, wonders at these women who are transmuted by Barnes into figures from baroque art: 'she saw them gamboling on the Greensward, heard them pitch and moan within the Gloom of many a stately mansion; she beheld them floating across the Ceilings, (for such was art in the Old Days) diapered in *Toile de Jouy* and welded without Flame, in one incalculable embrace' (*ibid.*: 11). In making a linguistic reference to the 'cherubs' which filled Renaissance and Baroque art works, Barnes combines both the religious and the secular, as the cherubs (divine children) are replaced by Musset's friends (secular figures). Thus an angelic hierarchy is secularized (as it becomes one with Musset's lesbian circle), as secular women form a kind of celestial tableau, or lesbian heavenly chorus. Quite often, at the conclusion of certain passages, the women are frozen in tableaux. The 'incalculable embrace' is typical of this use of language: the tableau, taken as it is from visual art and transmuted into verbal art, implies that Musset's type of sexuality will remain for eternity. Patience Scalpel does not deny this sexuality but neither does she understand it.

As Dame Musset remains surrounded by seraphic women for much of the text, it is perhaps inevitable that she will be beatified at the work's conclusion. Even her birth re-writes the biblical concept of creation:

> There was heard from under the dome of heaven a great crowing, and, from the midst, an egg fell to earth and striking, split and hatched and from out of it stepped one saying 'Pardon me, I must be going!' And this was the first Woman born with a difference. After this the angels parted, and on the face of each was the Mother look. Why was that?
>
> (Barnes 1928b: 26)

This biblical pastiche combines the ornate phraseology of biblical texts with commonplace speech; for example, after the 'great crowing' and the egg falling majestically to earth, one expects a miraculous and mysterious birth, but the commonplace statement 'Pardon me, I must be going!', totally undercuts this. The angels, who, it is implied, have created the egg, re-write a portion of the Bible for themselves, becoming active creators rather than passive spectators. This is birth without male participation and Barnes' angels appear to be androgynous. Yet it is not only the Bible which is parodied skilfully by Barnes. In her ballad 'Lists and Likelihoods', she re-writes the misogyny of sixteenth- and seventeenth-century ballads by creating a list of lesbian archetypes which poke fun at early ballad depictions of women as either shrill viragos or the victims of male cruelty. Barnes replaces misogynistic archetypes:

> The Vixen in the coat of red,
> The Hussy with the honey head,
> Her frontal Bone soft lapped up,
> With hempen ringlets like the Tup,
> The Doxy in the Vest of kid,
> Rustling like the Katie-did,
> With Panther's eyen dark and wan,
> And dove's feet to walk upon.
>
> (Barnes 1928b: 60)

At first glance, this listing appears to invoke a selection of female archetypes, but it also hints at the lesbian possibilities behind such stereotypical images. Words such as 'Vixen', 'Hussy', and 'Doxy' were, as Salgado and others have noted, traditionally linked to prostitution (Salgado 1972). Yet here, Barnes uses them in a more positive light, as the women possess a type of fierce aloofness which enables them to transcend the stereotypical language allotted to them. The animals and birds listed link them to the medieval bestiary, where animals and humans merge to form fantastic beasts, such as the Siren (Benton 1992: 36). As Barnes herself created a bestiary, *Creatures in an Alphabet* (Barnes 1981), the use of linguistic devices from the form in other texts is not surprising.

In the verse which follows, Barnes lists archetypes of lesbianism: the feminine lesbian: the mythic 'mannish' lesbian (defined by Esther Newton (Newton 1984: 557-75) and the Lesbian History Group amongst others (Lesbian History Group 1989: 217-18), described here as the 'starry Jade with Mannish stride' (Barnes 1928b: 60); and the 'masculine' sportswoman. Here, Barnes employs myriad terms which were deployed in caricatures of lesbian life but undercuts them, revealing the humour which many previous writers failed to recognise. In late nineteenth-century writings, such as those by Louys and Gautier, lesbianism, as Lillian Faderman has pointed out, was presented as a diseased state, evil and exotic (Faderman 1985: 369). Such nineteenth-century symbolist writers defined the lesbian body by deploying a discourse of disease. Faderman perceives these *fin-de-siècle* notions as also occurring in Barnes' work but this can be strongly contested (Faderman 1985: 369). In parodying these verbal representations of the female body, Barnes reveals that works on lesbian sexuality could be both humorous and celebratory. As Lanser notes, Dame Musset's name could be seen as parodic, as Alfred de Musset was one such symbolist writer (Lanser 1992: xxix). Likewise, Barnes' ballads run counter to symbolist prose, as they provide positive female images. For example, women described in the ballad vary from a trapeze artist to a queen who seeks out her own 'wench of bliss' (Barnes 1928b: 60). This makes the point that there is no such thing as a 'typical' lesbian, as lesbians can come from all walks of life and all class groups. Stereotypical doxies, hussies and viragos, who previously inhabited misogynistic ballads, chapbooks and, later, novels, are transmuted into amazonian and liberated figures. Thus the discourse of desire, as the women are depicted as both strong and active and thus oppose the 'decadent' image of the passive, invalided woman.

As is obvious, naming is very important to the text as a whole. Many of the names used are doubly emblematic, redolent both of actual members of Barney's circle and of female archetypes. Lady Buck-and-Balk and Tilly Tweed-in-blood are archetypes meant to refer to Radclyffe Hall and her lover, Lady Una Troubridge (Field 1985: 124). Buck-and-Balk and Tweed-in-Blood employ language similar to that used in Hall's *The Well of Loneliness* (Hall 1928) to describe their ideas on marriage between women. As with women listed in the ballad, they are defined by their basic characteristics: 'Lady Buck-and-Balk sported a monocle and believed in spirits. Tilly Tweed-in-Blood sported a stetson and believed in marriage' (Barnes 1928b: 18). Unlike Dame Musset, the two are pacifists who plead for tolerance. Musset dismisses their gentle discourse, scorning their delicacy and innate seriousness and responding with a violent discourse of her own. The two plead for lesbianism to be sanctioned by marriage, and for monogamy, which, if bound by law, should only be nullified by the courts. Their language includes words such as 'love', 'hearts', 'pity', 'dear', 'need' and 'poignancy' (Barnes, 1928b: 19), whereas Musset's discourse (which suggests that differences are best settled by duels) is full of terms such as 'struck', 'fowling-piece' and 'terror' (*ibid.*). Musset's discourse is one of strength, whereas Buck-and-Balk speaks of 'morals' (*ibid.*).

Such differentiations between discourses (whether between Musset and the two Englishwomen or between Musset and Scalpel) fill the text. Also typical is the way in which Barnes carefully adhered to the almanac form, making the cycle of Dame Musset's life appear to be inevitable. Each month comes to represent a period of Dame Musset's life and each ends on a different note. For example, June ends with a positive couplet:

> Of such is high and gaming pride,
> of Woman by a Woman's girlish side.
>
> (Barnes 1928b: 40)

This note is then carried through July, where women are shown to be ideal partners for each other (Barnes 1928b: 43). However, as the cycle continues, it becomes clear that this affirmation cannot last as Dame Musset is growing older (*ibid.*: 68). August brings 'distempers' and concludes in confusion with the rattle of 'memory bones' (*ibid.*: 54). Such confusion creates a class border crossing, as it affects both high and low alike and is composed in true almanac form: 'some dropping Tea-pots and Linens, Some Caddies and Cambric, some Sea-weed and saffron, some with Trophy Skulls and Memory Bones, gleanings from Love's Labour lost' (*ibid.*). As has been indicated earlier, these portions of the text, with their complex couplings of words, reflect Musset's life cycle, as they describe the motions of the tides and seasons traditionally connected with femininity. Thus, the discord of August is followed by the displacement of September. In the text, Barnes makes a statement which might be used as a coda for the work as a whole: 'the very condition of Woman is so subject to Hazard, so complex, and so grievous, that to place her at one moment is but to displace her at the next' (*ibid.*: 55). This could also be applied to Barnes' aesthetic as a whole.

The shifting boundaries of femininity are also charted in the various 'border crossings' effected by the language of the text. By the time that the last seasons of the year are reached, Dame Musset is old and dying. Dame Musset will die in December when it is 'right' for her to die, thus completing the text's cycle. She is buried by a troop of mourning women, and her tongue, a parody of Shelley's heart perhaps, refuses to burn in the funeral pyre (*ibid.*: 84). This might also recall an inversion of the traditional image of the scold's tongue, creating a symbol of the undeniable power of women's language.

What I wish to suggest in this essay is that by using a language appropriated from old texts, frequently texts of a misogynistic nature, Barnes places the lesbian woman at the centre of the picture rather than at its margins. Thus, she foregrounds the sense of a lesbian past. Just as Janet Todd suggests that in works by Aphra Behn 'the wit is in the appropriation' of themes and linguistic tropes from earlier works (Todd 1989: 12-36), this might also be said to be true of Barnes, whose plural text uses many forms, but remains peculiarly difficult to categorise. In other words, **Ladies Almanack** is a text where use of pastiche enabled Barnes to place the lesbian self at the centre of history. This placing is achieved by a use of language which invokes opposition, combining the religious with the secular, the human with the animal, the violent with the passive, and the woman with the saint. Dame Musset's tongue, which 'would not suffer ash' (Barnes 1928b: 84), might therefore stand as a metaphor for the power of her speech and the strength of her image. If Barnes' Musset is, at the text's conclusion, beatified, then she also provides a secular symbol as she reverses the misogynistic archetype of the scold and remains 'unbridled' to the last.

Note

1. The title pages of *Ladies Almanack* reads: 'Ladies Almanack; showing their Signs and their Tides, their Moons and their Changes; the Seasons as it is with them; their Eclipses and Equinoxes; as well as a full Record of diurnal and nocturnal Distempers'. *Mundus Muleibris* reads: 'Mundus Muleibris; or the Ladies Dressing-Room Unlocked and her Toilette Spread in Burlesque, Together with the Fop's Dictionary'.

Bibliography

Barnes, D. (1928a) Introduction to the selected letters of Elsa von Freytag Loringhoven, *transition*, 11, 19-20.

Barnes, D. (1928b) *The Ladies Almanack,* Darrantière, Dijon.

Barnes, D. (1936) *Nightwood,* Faber and Faber, London.

Barnes, D. (1971) Language in the secondary classroom, pp. 11-77 in Barnes, Britton and Rosen 1971.

Barnes, D. (1981) *Creatures in an Alphabet,* Dial, New York.

Benton, J. R. (1992) *The Medieval Menagerie: Animals in Art in the Middle Ages,* Abbeville, New York.

Broe, M. L. (1991) (ed.) *Silence and Power: Djuna Barnes, a Re-evaluation,* Southern Illinois University Press, Carbondale.

Eveleyn, J. and M. (1690) *Mundus Muliebris,* London.

Faderman, L. (1985) *Surpassing the Love of Men,* Women's Press, London.

Field, A. (1985) *Djuna: The Formidable Miss Barnes,* Texas University Press, TX.

Hall, R. (1928) *The Well of Loneliness,* Cape, London.

Hobby, E. (1988) *Virtue of Necessity,* Virago, London.

Humm, M. (1991) *Border Traffic: Strategies of Contemporary Women Writers,* Manchester University Press, Manchester.

Jay, K. (1991) The outsider among the expatriates: Djuna Barnes and the ladies of the Almanac, in L. Broe (ed.) *Silence and Power: Djuna Barnes, a Re-evaluation,* Southern Illinois University Press, Carbondale.

Lanser, S. S. (1991) 'Speaking in tongues': Ladies Almanack and the discourse of desire, pp. 156-69 in Broe 1991.

Lesbian History Group (1989) *Not a Passing Phase: Lesbians in History 1840-1985,* Women's Press, London.

Michel, F. (1991) All women are not women all: Ladies Almanack and women's writing, in Broe 1991.

Newton, E. (1984) The mythic, mannish lesbian: Radclyffe Hall and the New Woman, *Signs,* 9, 557-75.

Salgado G. (ed.) (1972) *Coney Catchers and Bawdy Baskets,* Penguin, Harmondsworth.

Scott, B. K. (ed.) (1990) *The Gender of Modernism,* Indiana University Press, Bloomington.

Secrest, M. (1974) *Between Me and Life: A Biography of Romaine Brooks,* Macdonald and Janes, New York.

Todd, J. (1989) *The Sign of Angellica: Women, Writing and Fiction 1660-1800,* Women's Press, London.

Dianne Chisholm (essay date March 1997)

SOURCE: Chisholm, Dianne. "Obscene Modernism: *Eros Noir* and the Profane Illumination of Djuna Barnes." *American Literature* 69, no. 1 (March 1997): 167-206.

[*In the following essay, Chisholm offers a re-reading of* Nightwood *in order to ascertain "the specific materials and techniques" of its "obscenity" and "the transgressive function it has played in the history of modern culture."*]

> From the moment that Sade delivered its first words and marked out, in a single discourse, the boundaries of what suddenly became its kingdom, the language of sexuality has lifted us into the night where God is absent, and where all of our actions are addressed to this absence in a profanation which at once identifies it, exhausts itself in it, and restores it to the empty purity of its transgression.
>
> —Michel Foucault, "Preface to Transgression"

> But the true, creative overcoming of religious illumination . . . resides in a *profane illumination,* a materialistic, anthropological inspiration.
>
> —Walter Benjamin, "Surrealism"

The question of obscenity challenges the bounds of legal discourse by prompting inquiry into the nature of transgression. The transgressivity of "obscene art" does not derive from its illegality alone. Drawing upon a tradition of avant-garde practice, obscene artistry is engaged with but different from obscenity as defined under the law. Obscene art may be legalized by new court rulings and/or legitimized by a body of liberal taste and still retain the power to shock. Questions concerning the artistry of obscenity and the reading of art for non-discursive modes of transgression are often lost in the discussion of the strategies and effects of legalization.

Modernist art is produced at the same historical moment and in the same social space as "obscene" art. When we think of the provocative work of Anglo-American literary modernism, the famous trials of James Joyce's *Ulysses*, D. H. Lawrence's *Lady Chatterley's Lover,* Radclyffe Hall's *Well of Loneliness,* Henry Miller's *Tropic of Cancer,* and William Burrough's *Naked Lunch* come immediately to mind. Their transgression was made visible through the legal spectacularization of "obscene" sexuality.[1] Or, to put it another way, modernist sexuality became generally recognizable through the law's censorious focus on "corruptive" speech and verbal image.[2] Legal prosecutions led the way in shaping public knowledge about the obscene practices of modernist art; through legal mediation, the reader was directed to construe modernist transgression, favorably or unfavorably, as outlawed sexual representation.

Opposing censorship, libertarians argued for the "artistic merit" of banned or confiscated work that the law had judged obscene. The claim of artistic merit became the principal tactic of legitimization deployed in the struggle to define and extend the limits of social value and acceptability. Champions of the outlaw, libertarians nevertheless collaborated with the law by attempting to contain the shock of avant-garde sexualities within an aesthetics of pornography, forging a discourse and pedagogy of, and eventually a market for, "modernist erotics."[3] Through the "liberation" of taste, society's dominant ideal ironically prevails. The argument of artistic merit has repeatedly been used to ground the campaign to legalize or even canonize obscene productions where the obscenity in question is believed sufficiently artistic and centrally heterosexual, and where misogyny and homophobia are the implied subtexts of the work's poetic license.[4] Such a liberal strategy may eventually accommodate tasteful, counter-cultural (and even homosexual) representation, but it brandishes an epistemology that excludes an obscenity which is critically aberrant and unrepresentative or dialectically antisocial.

In the United States obscene art won the right to protection under the First Amendment provided it could demonstrate sufficient artistic merit—or the supposed equivalent, "social value"—to justify its obscenity.[5] Based on a modernist standard of artistic sufficiency, such legislation places an impossible burden on postmodern transgression. The legalization of obscene modernism sets a precedent for the aestheticization of the political—the disciplining and neutralizing of shock through public training in literary appreciation. The avant-garde assault on bourgeois culture and the aesthetics of commodity consumption is, to a great extent, authoritatively recuperated by the legal and canonical strategies of the liberal arts.

How does art forge obscenity? What materials and techniques does art obscenely assemble to subvert the codes of social domination? How does the legal view of obscenity, including the perception of exceptional artistic merit, obscure and arrest a radical artistic practice? How does the legalization of obscene modernism serve a dialectic of false social "progress" that secures a liberal appreciation of its symbolic capital, while managing modernism's transgression through tasteful misrecognition?

The French philosopher Michel Foucault saw something other than legal obscenity in the pornography of Georges Bataille, to which he pays homage in his "Preface to Transgression." He points to a Sadean "language of sexuality" that, since it is self-referential, profanes neither divine nor secular social codes and suffers no transgressive limit. Against the absolute illumination of Enlightenment morality, Bataille circumscribes a carnality of unfathomable night. But Foucault, after locating this "single discourse" beyond the domain of God and Law, has little more to say about Bataille's subversive capacity. Ultimately, Foucault loses faith in the negative capability of avant-garde obscenity. He retires his project of transgressive modernism and initiates a critique of quotidian space, abandoning the esoteric language of Sadean nihilism for the public and popular discourse of sexual hygienics, the communications of everyday regimen and routine.[6]

The introductory volume of *The History of Sexuality,* in which Foucault outlines his sober departure from Bataille's "subversive" *Histoire de l'érotisme,* clinically assesses the disciplinary space produced by technological modernity.[7] Specifying both the macro- and microscopic range of these technologies, from the formal strategies of state surveillance to the daily operations of sexual self-administration, he leaves little or no room for avant-garde intervention. For the disenchanted Foucault, there is no space for obscene practices that are not criminal, insane, or pathological under social, medical, or legal rubrics. Artists who create an obscene work do so, he implies, under the imperceptibly ubiquitous gaze of panoptic power and at the risk of conforming to an authority—imaginary or material—or disqualifying themselves as rational, social beings.

Foucault's dystopic recoil from the revolutionary aims of modernist transgression is troubling, but it contributes substantially to an understanding of how the question of obscenity may be framed. From a genealogical point of view, the question is rhetorical, since it is bound to be posed in the terms of a discourse that delimits and hypostatizes all forms of sexual deviance in categories of criminal and/or pathological perversity. The later volumes of *The History of Sexuality* trace Foucault's return to transgression as a practical problem for the aesthetics of everyday existence. His project detours through the *ars erotica* of antiquity as a prolegomena to understanding how the space of sexual modernity might be recovered and practiced by today's marginal selves and communities. But in the course of reorienting his critique from panoptic space to marginal practices (for example, the S/M practices of gay leathermen), he never returns to the practices of obscene modernism to elaborate his "preface" to transgression.[8] The genealogist's postscript to obscene modernism is missing.

To open the question of obscenity to a fuller dialectical inquiry, I urge that we avoid both the pretensions of liberal strategy and the digressions of Foucaultian cynicism. Like a line of avant-garde theorists and critics before me (Peter Bürger, for instance, and Julia Kristeva), I suggest that we think of transgression as an explosive interaction of heterogeneous material, lawful and artful, discursive and nondiscursive, eccentric and quotidian. In addition, I urge that we think of artistic obscenity as a particular practice of transgression that shocks and

disperses the reactive forces of the sexual status quo while mobilizing radical, historical, and political insight. We might further reevaluate obscene modernism as a specific mode of artistic transgression, one that employs language to forge a textual space within sexual discourse and sexual modernity where we can see simultaneously the eloquent suppression of erotic possibility and the profane limit of bourgeois decency.

We might also consider a more overdetermined case of obscene modernism than Bataille's pornographic extremism. The art of Djuna Barnes both attracts and eludes the censor. Her modernist classic *Nightwood* (1937) helps set the aesthetic standard of legal obscenity in the same moment that it subverts the legal understanding of artistic transgression, conveying a shock that has yet to be received. Constituting what Gilles Deleuze and Felix Guattari might call a "nomadic assemblage," the novel traverses, combines, and juxtaposes American puritanism and French pornography, French surrealism and American realism. The novel displays the prudent (aesthetic, legal, marketing) orientation of Barnes's editor, T. S. Eliot, then working for the English publisher Faber, as well as the impetus to mimic Joycean profanity after the lifting of the ban on *Ulysses* in 1933. Written mostly in England in the thirties, but situated in Paris in the twenties and between the bohemias of Paris, New York, Vienna, and Berlin, *Nightwood* also articulates the distance between "flâneur realism" and "lesbian realism,"[9] between the city of surrealist revolution and the state of lesbian exiile: a queer space.[10]

What makes *Nightwood* an especially interesting case is that it points to its own obscenity, to obscene speech and acts, even after Barnes revised the manuscript in response to Emily Coleman's friendly emendations and Eliot's editorial advice. The manuscript was first brought to Eliot's attention as a bold exploration into the wilderness of human eroticism. "'Can you read that and not see that something new has been said about the very heart of sex?—going beyond sex, to that world where there is no marriage or giving in marriage— *where no modern writer ever goes?*'"[11] wrote Coleman to Eliot, arguing for the text's publication on the grounds of its transgressive originality. Eliot was persuaded, but it took Barnes's further insistence on the necessity of obscenity to overrule his censorial omissions. The new critical edition of *Nightwood* from Dalkey Archive Press indicates the cuts and changes made by Eliot that Barnes did not always condone. We have evidence that Barnes convinced Eliot to retain the novel's most shocking passage, which he strongly recommended deleting but she foregrounded by moving to the last chapter. Moreover, to make explicit the character of her transgression, she persisted in using the word "obscene," which he had changed to "unclean."[12]

Yet as a device of artistic transgression *Nightwood*'s obscenity goes unnoticed, even where its sexual "decadence" continues to fascinate and trouble. Directed by Eliot's introductory remarks to regard its offensive language as an eccentric poetics, censors overlook it. Conversely, determined to recover what has been hidden behind the legitimizing veil of aesthetics, critics—particularly feminist critics—read Barnes's obscenity for signs of forbidden being; they "out" a whole carnival of transgressive and/or abject sexualities—lesbianism, homosexuality, sadomasochism, vampirism, transvestism, bestiality, pederasty, incest.[13] Some of these critics go so far as to lobby for what they have outed, calling for celebration or condemnation depending on how they identify their evidence.[14] The recuperation of *Nightwood*'s sexual outlawry by a politics of representation tends, however, to be rhetorical, not because there are no lesbians or sadomasochists or incest survivors or practitioners of bestiality in the text, nor because Barnes shows no sympathy for the sexually disqualified,[15] but because her narration does not voice the struggle of an emerging subculture so much as foreground the duplicitous—"obscene"—frame of speech in which any unbecoming sexuality must be lived and thought.[16] Instead of speaking out on lesbianism in cryptic modernism, *Nightwood* seriously challenges the epistemological and ontological claims of sexual discourse in general and the category of "inversion" in particular. Discursivity, as much as prudery, is the target of her transgression. What, then, are the specific materials and techniques of *Nightwood*'s obscenity?

To answer this question I draw on a theory of transgression that takes the art of profanation, not the law of obscenity, as its point of departure. And since I need a theory that does more than point to the dark, as does Foucault's preface to Bataille, I refer my reading of *Nightwood* to Walter Benjamin's "profane illumination." As a contemporary of Barnes, as a foreigner living and writing in Paris, and as an astute reader of modernity and the French avant-garde, Benjamin shares Barnes's cultural geography and artistic orientation. His writing on French surrealism presents a particularly timely conjunction of avant-garde shock tactics, Baudelairean erontology, and critical theory for throwing dialectical light on Barnes's mystifying obscenity. This is the light of the historical materialist—ultimately, a political illumination that derives its tactics of engagement from the technique of the art it theorizes.[17]

For Benjamin, the Surrealist method of profanation is not merely an aesthetic or erotic matter. Its trick is to document a case of "esoteric love" and capture its uncanny drift against the city's industrial wasteland, recasting the "outmoded" Paris passages and arcades of nineteenth-century splendor with an aura of degraded experience so as to shock readerly consciousness into a "nihilistic" awareness of capitalism's devastating

progress.[18] Surrealism is not the first artistic movement to deploy a subversive eroticism, but it outdoes its Romantic and Sadean precursors by using eros to invoke and release the revolutionary energies concealed in the detritus of industrialist-capitalist society.

In considering the critical difference that art brings to the question of obscenity, I make it my primary purpose to understand the obscene technique of Djuna Barnes's *Nightwood* and the transgressive function it has played in the history of modern culture. Towards this end, I distinguish my reading from those that examine the discursive and disciplinary effects of *Nightwood*'s legalization. I work with Walter Benjamin's modernism, but rather than oppose it to Michel Foucault's postmodernism, I seek a fruitful conjunction. Rereading *Nightwood* between the insights of Benjamin's "Surrealism" and those of the first volume of Foucault's *History of Sexuality* affords a rapprochement between the historical materialist and the genealogist, a method of advancing sexual politics that combines dialectical image with discursive critique. Privileging the tradition of avant-garde nihilism, in particular the *eros noir* of surrealism in whose shadow glows the defeat of revolutionary libertinage, my reading will be more *queer* than lesbian.[19]

The "Non-case" of Nightwood

Though her best-known work was neither seized nor banned, Barnes was no stranger to obscenity action. In 1928 *Ryder* was published in expurgated form, and in the same year Barnes and friends hawked copies of *Ladies Almanack* on the streets of Paris and eventually smuggled it into America after her European distributor, Edward Titus, backed out of their agreement for fear of the book's confiscation. *Nightwood* was edited and published nearly ten years later with the threat of censorship still in the air. In spite of Judge Woolsey's 1933 ruling that ended the ban on Joyce's *Ulysses* in the U.S., the campaign against obscenity in literature continued. In fact, the focus was intensified on American (rather than foreign) works, specifically those that presented themes of homosexuality, incest, and prostitution.[20]

Nightwood reacts tacitly to legal obscenity's jurisdiction, switching dramatically from the up-front tactics Barnes used to protest the expurgation of *Ryder*. As she explains in her foreword to the earlier work, Barnes was forced to delete several passages, which she replaced with asterisks to indicate where the text had been corrupted.[21] *Nightwood,* on the other hand, suffers no omissions to which the author did not agree. But with this later text Barnes does not resign her protest so much as avoid legal proceedings with tactics of a different, not readily identifiable, not clearly predictable obscenity. In place of a hortatory foreword denouncing the law's barbaric intrusion, and in place of boldly flagged editorial cuts—self-conscious tactics that alert the reader to the impotence of the creative writer confronted by public power—there appears at the climactic ending of *Nightwood* a convulsive and disturbing image that the narrator quixotically describes as "obscene and touching."[22] Whereas *Ryder*'s obscenity is purged and marked to reflect and accommodate the socially dominant discursive order, *Nightwood*'s obscenity resists the proprieties of speech with an uncanny declaration of "touching" profanation. In legal terms, *Nightwood* is a "non-case"; yet it is defiantly obscene.

A Foucaultian reader might argue that in presenting a "non-case" of legal obscenity, *Nightwood* functions all the more effectively as an undercover agent in the production and policing of modern identities. In a recent article, Leigh Gilmour astutely argues that *Nightwood* is the artful issue not merely of talented craftsmanship but, more importantly, of editorial manipulation designed to circumvent legal action.[23] She contends that this manipulation has had a hand in instituting and safeguarding the heterosexual identity of high modernism. Editorial steps taken to ensure that *Nightwood* would escape legal condemnation can be shown to deploy an aestheticizing strategy that purges the more realist and populist homosexual content that threatens to abuse poetic license, while legitimizing the more rarified inscriptions of homosexuality as literary eccentricity. The shapers of *Nightwood*'s reception are thus instrumental in producing a category of literariness that formally distinguishes "high" from "low" modernism and that legitimizes erotic poeticizing at the expense of homosexual politicizing and the push for representation.

In explaining the process by which modernist (sexual) identities are formed and disciplined, Gilmour follows an argument developed by Foucault in *The History of Sexuality*. According to Foucault, the medical and legal discourses that compose the body of knowledge of *scientia sexualis* assume an ontological foundation on which administrative powers rely for classifying, regimenting, and disciplining what are only epistemological typologies of deviance, pathology, and criminality. Thus sexual types and behaviors acquire the "reality" of sexual identity, which occasions in turn a "real" need for medical, juridical, and pedagogical regard and regulation. The example Foucault outlines is the procedure by which the medieval sodomite, for whom sodomy was only a sin or breach of conduct, is displaced by the modern homosexual, for whom deviance constitutes the core of being.[24] By the 1920s the regime of *scientia sexualis* expanded its capacity to recognize, pathologize, and criminalize sexual types through the instrumentation of obscenity law and, in particular, the *Hicklin* doctrine.[25] Radclyffe Hall's *Well of Loneliness* (1929), having been pronounced obscene under *Hicklin* for its unrepentant lesbianism, became the *cause célèbre* of "lesbian writing":[26] "when *The Well of Loneliness*

was banned it was hypostatized as an obscene and lesbian novel."[27] Gilmour argues that, in view of these and other legal precedents,[28] Barnes's editor, T. S. Eliot, took care to script an introduction and make editorial cuts that foregrounded the "poetic" instead of the "psychopathic" features of the novel (*Nightwood*, xv). In colluding with the law, Eliot produces a "modernist" (as opposed to a realist) text, and he legitimizes a "modernist" (as opposed to a homosexual) identity.[29] Eliot's Barnes is a "modernist writer" whose treatment of perverse material is literary—not deviant.[30]

Gilmour is convincing on the point that *Nightwood*, even as a "non-case" of legal obscenity, still has a constitutive role to play in the production and legitimization of modernism. But her claim that legalizing forces obscure and delay the recognition of what, decades later, is now being received as a lesbian novel begs the question of *Nightwood*'s status as a homosexual text. Why, she asks, was the formally less adventurous *Well of Loneliness* able to cultivate a lesbian identity when the artistically more radical *Nightwood* was not? Why did the criminalization of *Well* instantly prompt a lesbian following instead of the legally sanctioned *Nightwood*, "which was not banned" and "would have to wait for a later generation of readers"? Gilmour contends that "Barnes's readers did not 'see' the lesbianism of Nora and Robin [*Nightwood*'s primary lovers] . . . because it was presented neither through a medical discourse nor in terms of narrative realism." The lesbianism is evidenced in the text, but its visibility is allegedly obscured by the deployment of "the category of the literary" to avoid prosecution.[31]

But if Barnes's lesbianism is not legible under available, pathologizing rubrics, if it bears no identifying signs of medical taxonomy or narrative realism, how then is it to be recognized as such? What is lesbianism if not a discursive category or operation? How does Gilmour "see" the lesbianism behind this strategic literary/legalizing obscurity? Why does she insist on reading the characters of *Nightwood* as lesbian (or as representing sexual identity) when she concedes that the writing departs from the practice of narrative realism?[32] Why read erotic realism back into an avant-garde text to imply that the author, in collaboration with the editor, intended to represent lesbianism surreptitiously? Is the function of avant-garde literariness limited—in this or any other writing—to obscuring the art of representation, that is, of making visible and identifiable, hence real, the discursive categories of *scientia sexualis*?

The claim that *Nightwood* should be perceived as the tortured and muted expression of a lesbian relationship is critically misleading. Barnes's novel does not voice the cause of the maligned invert, and it displays none of the sentimental plotting of forbidden love that distinguishes the narratives of Radclyffe Hall.[33] On the other hand, the novel does bear traces of the Beardsleyesque decadence of Barnes's *Book of Repulsive Women* (1915), the Elizabethan bawdiness of *Ladies Almanack* (1928), and the bohemian pandemonium of *Ryder* (1928). Each of these books is an example of the extravagant, hard-edged writing that Barnes had been perfecting since her days as a Greenwich Village journalist. But there is a darkness in *Nightwood* that combines Barnes's affection for Burton's *Anatomy of Melancholia* (1621) with a flirtatious appreciation of Surrealism's De Sade. I propose that, far from writing a "narrative of lesbianism,"[34] whether poetic or psychopathic, Barnes strongly resists the tendency that animated her amazonian contemporaries to elaborate and glorify "inversion"; instead, she flaunts a queer scepticism concerning sexual liberation and its bohemian milieux, profaning the illusions of their "reverse discourse."[35] Barnes does tackle obscenity law but not with a proclamation, latent or implicit, of homosexual rights.

One of Barnes's more extravagant tactics is the use she makes of the notorious Doctor Matthew O'Connor, whose garrulity is peppered with enough "Irish" to have in itself been sufficient reason for the book to fail the *Hicklin* test. "Am I the golden-mouthed St. John Chrysostom, the Greek who said it with the other cheek?" she has the Doctor ask rhetorically; "No, I'm a fart in a gale of wind, an humble violet under a cow pad" (96). The Doctor's specialization is gynecology and obstetrics, and yet his dilatory meditations on the nature of erotic suffering omit or defy the implementation of diagnostic categories: "may my dilator burst and my speculum rust, may panic seize my index finger before I point out my man" (*Nightwood*, 32). Instead of availing himself of one of the most powerful strategies of his profession, the Doctor panics at the thought of actually deploying his authority to name, categorize, and pathologize. The term "lesbian" never appears in his speech (or anywhere else in the text), although the category "invert" is subject to much riddling and demystifying speculation. His musings reveal that the truth of inversion is to be found not in the rites of confession or the diagnoses of sexology but in the archives of fantasy, where it enthralls with the aura of a romantic lie: "what is this love we have for the invert, boy or girl? It was they who were spoken of in every romance that we ever read. . . . They are our answer to what our grandmothers were told love was, and what it never came to be; they the living lie of our centuries. When a long lie comes up, sometimes it is a beauty; when it drops into dissolution, into drugs and drink, into disease and death, it has a singular and terrible attraction" (*Nightwood*, 136-37). It is the Doctor's unwitting fate to be interminably engaged in relieving his friends of a romantic religiosity they suffer as a form of enlightenment. His primary tactic of demystification is his shocking use of obscenity. It is has a limited effect on Baron Felix von

Volkbein, a figure of the *ressentiment* of decaying European aristocracy, and even less on Nora, a chimera of new womanhood, bohemia, and frontier puritanism. The Baron is "troubled by obscenity" but interprets the Doctor's disgustingness as a projection of melancholia. The struggle to resist the Doctor's voluble and prolific profanity is more drawn out in Nora's case, but the stubborn piety that characterizes her quest to know and confess the truth about sexuality vanquishes even the most brilliant dialogical maneuvering in his pornological investigations. She is consequently unprepared for the climactic "obscene and touching" encounter and collapses from the shock.

What is this obscenity that is unobtrusive yet crucial to the erotic play and plot of Barnes's text? What is the art of Barnes's obscenity and what are the politics of her erotics? How does she affect the reader's, if not the character's, moral sensibility? These are questions that Gilmour overlooks, since her focus is on the legalization of *Nightwood* and its effects. For the critic who focuses on the productive alliances of legality, sexuality, and poetry, *Nightwood* presents a case of artistic complicity with legitimizing forces. But Gilmour misses the technique the artist uses to historicize and expose the social reproduction of discursive sexuality.

That *Nightwood* does not deploy the tactic of reverse discourse, voicing and celebrating homosexuality with the same scientific vocabulary used to condemn it, is no more proof that Barnes colluded with Eliot in censoring obscene—which is to say, homosexual—passages than that she had difficulty expressing her lesbianism. The targets of Barnes's obscene doctor(ing) are precisely the categories of inversion and perversion that comprise the sexological confession, categories that narrative realism so richly elaborates and that both European decadence and American bohemianism readily absorb—despite their conscientious liberalism. Though Eliot's editorial actions anticipate (and perhaps advance) the interaction of law and literature in the United States—they do not purge *Nightwood* or its modernist legacy of antisocial transgression. Barnes may have endorsed Eliot's editorial cuts not because she shared his prescient prudence or aesthetic taste but because the cuts sharpened her text without weakening her obscene device. To get to the heart of this device, I turn to Walter Benjamin.

"Profane Illumination"

In an attempt to theorize the practice of Surrealism, Benjamin explains and defends its artistic method as a political strategy. His "Surrealism" appeared in 1929,[36] when the movement was entering a crucial phase of its history, "a moment when the original tension of the secret society must either explode in a matter-of-fact, profane struggle for power and domination or decay as a public demonstration and be transformed."[37] Benjamin forges reflections that catalyze artistic self-recognition, as if by clarifying the technique of Surrealist activism he could also catalyze its transformation. Chief among these is his notion of "profane illumination."[38]

The Surrealists took up the "passionate revolt against Catholicism" led by Rimbaud, Lautréamont, and Apollinaire (Benjamin, 179). They aimed to overcome the narcosis of "religious illumination" by dispensing a more potent and dangerous intoxicant, a "profane illumination" whose sources of "inspiration" were "materialistic, anthropological." Hashish, opium, and other hallucinogenic drugs facilitate an "introductory lesson" to this "profane illumination," since the "loosening of the self by intoxication is at the same time, precisely the fruitful, living experience that allowed [the surrealists] to step outside the domain of intoxication." Profane illumination is a visionary demystification, "but the true, creative overcoming of religious illumination certainly does not lie in narcotics." The active agency is not mystery, ecstasy, or any of the inducements of religiosity; it is an uncanny trompe l'oeil, a "dialectical optic" (Benjamin, 190) displayed against a backdrop of spiritual enlightenment and industrial progress that throws into luminous relief the wreckage and obsolescence of material life.

The intoxicant in Breton's *Nadja,* the central text of Benjamin's meditation on profane illumination, is "esoteric love," but the lady herself is not intoxicating. Eros loosens the structure of bourgeois perspective, allowing narrator and reader to behold a shockingly degraded world. Abandoning lovemaking to the strange automatism of the unconscious, Breton follows Nadja on her somnambulent excursions about Paris. He is carried by their erotic drift into what first strikes him as a shady sideshow of dereliction and madness but what turns out to be (as he and we are shocked to discover) just the everyday street life that Nadja navigates with the ingenuity of the homeless. How bizarre that esoteric love should be the galvanizing vehicle of dialectical materialism. And yet, it is an erotic transport that mediates the passage from aesthetic nostalgia to "revolutionary nihilism": "Breton and Nadja are the lovers who convert everything that we have experienced on mournful railway journeys (railways are beginning to age), on godforsaken Sunday afternoons in the proletarian quarters of the great cities, in the first glance through the rain-blurred window of a new apartment, into revolutionary experience, if not action. They bring the immense forces of 'atmosphere' concealed in these things to the point of explosion" (Benjamin, 182).

The "trick" of this conversion, Benjamin speculates, "consists in the substitution of a political for a historical view of the past."[39] Breton uses esoteric love as a device to distract the senses from their utilitarian preoccupations and to induce an experiential break with the

commercial present. He charts, with intimate familiarity, the venues and artifacts of pre-industrial Paris to which he and Nadja unconsciously gravitate, witnessing his own convulsive horror at the transmutation of once vibrant and cultivated life into the rubble and routine of today's mechanical metropolis. He is overwhelmed by the image of material destitution, which capitalism, because of its progressivism, fails to recognize but which the experience of degraded love makes devastatingly clear.

The profane illumination relies on the devices of esoteric love to effect its "conversion" without glorifying erotic mystique. It is the interpenetration of the mysterious and the everyday that distinguishes Surrealism from Romanticism. Benjamin cautions serious readers not to place "histrionic or fanatical stress on the mysterious side of the mysterious" since it "takes us no further": "we penetrate the mystery only to the degree that we recognize it in the everyday world, by virtue of a dialectical optic that perceives the everyday as impenetrable, the impenetrable as everyday" (Benjamin, 189-90). The profane illumination deploys, moreover, a "moral exhibitionism, which we badly need." *Nadja* demonstrates that "to live in a glass house is a revolutionary virtue par excellence" (Benjamin, 180). Finally, Breton's esoteric love affords us a revelation not of a sublime psychology but of a moral structure that binds creativity to an oppressive political economy. Instead of the optimism that enthralls the poets of bourgeois reform, the images of the profane illumination organize the affective energies of an uncompromising pessimism.[40]

Benjamin tells us that Breton thought of *Nadja* as "'a book with a banging door'" (Benjamin, 180). We could say the same of *Nightwood*: with Barnes's omniscient third-person narrator we enter the various *chambres à coucher* of her characters, tuning into their most intimate negotiations as if playing the role of *voyeur-voyants*. We are over(t)ly exposed to the erotic life of private beings and granted more than a keyhole (but less than a panopticon) to view their nocturnal haunts and habits.

Nightwood parades a "moral exhibitionism" with more scope and intensity than *Nadja*. We follow the night-walk of Nadja-clone Robin Vote through the *pissoirs* of Paris, the slums of Marseilles, the waterfront of Tangier, and the *porto basso* of Naples. The technique by which she, or rather the phantasmagoria of modern sexual commerce, is exposed compares with Surrealism's dialectical optic. We "see" the Janus-faced morality that structures Robin's domestic interiors and public stages but only as illuminated by the profane Doctor in dialogical conflict with Robin's disenchanted lover, the "progressive" Nora Wood. Much of the novel is set in a bohemia where a classless society parades itself with a boundless decadence that is indeed intoxicating, especially as distilled in Barnes's descriptive opulence. But revolutionary nihilism gathers greatest force in the private, sacred, and ruinous domains of bedroom and chapel, where we see eros struggle uncannily with a state of destitution.

The narrative and dialogues of *Nightwood* focus on the mysterious affair between Nora and Robin. Their "esoteric love" animates their everyday lives with a troubling incommensurability that derives from a difference not of class, race, gender, or sexual orientation but of mode of sexuality. Robin sleep(walk)s her way through the streets and slums of Europe's great commercial cities and, for more than one enlightened character, exists as a romantic cipher of what Nadja personified for Breton: "the great living, sonorous unconscious that inspires [his] only convincing acts" (Breton, quoted in Benjamin, 176). For Nora, who meets her at a circus, Robin signals a primeval animism that Nora had not known she was missing and that she tries obsessively to domesticate and possess. For the Baron, who meets her with the Doctor during one of her narcoleptic seizures,[41] Robin recalls a figure straight from the jungles of Henri Rousseau (35). Both visions are erotically mesmerizing, and both lend themselves to profane illumination.

The Baron is so enchanted by his initial image of Robin that he aspires to marry her, believing her sleeping fits to be a divine enigma and her American impressionability an ideal remedy for an exhausted European aristocracy, whose patrilineage he fraudulently assumes. Bourgeois pretentiousness, propped up by religious illumination and moral optimism, blinds him to the wreckage that "progress" bestows upon history, including the acceleration of fascist nationalism. But his aspirations are upset when his romantic projections are obscenely shattered by another, more potent image.

A year into their marriage and the night before she is due to deliver her child, the Baron returns to their Paris home to find Robin asleep in a chair, her hand on a book lying open on the floor. To his astonishment, he notes she has been reading De Sade's memoirs and has underscored the following passage: "*Et lui rendit pendant sa captivité les milles services qu'un amour dévoué est seul capable de rendre*" (47).[42] While she may be drugged with a Sadean dream, the Baron suffers the termination of his eugenic illusions: "and suddenly into his mind came the question, what is wrong?" (47).[43]

It is not the passage from De Sade as such but the image of Robin "sleeping with" De Sade that momentarily rouses the Baron from his romantic stupor. The image accomplishes what a simple recitation of De Sade could not: an anachronistic coupling of the most antithetical moments of European modernity. Appearing before the Baron as a ghost of history past and seeming to impreg-

nate the Baroness with notions of revolutionary libertinage, De Sade darkens the Baron's genealogical phantasy of aristocratic restoration. The "moral exhibitionism" of this image alerts us not merely to the repressed sexual restlessness of the new-woman-cum-nouvelle-noblesse but more particularly to the survival of the *ancien régime,* whose sense of propriety lives on, despite De Sade, in the virulent *ressentiment* of the bourgeoisie.

The progressively reactionary modern turns to the most primeval sources of inspiration, believing them to be forward-looking. The Baron is such a modern. He finds solace in the *ancien régime,* but since it is not a tangible reality, he frequents the salons and circuses of bohemia, the only places left where he can still recover a semblance of nobility to which he can "bow down."[44] His other source of inspiration is erotic mysticism, found abundantly in Catholicism and symbolist painting, which he "sees" in Robin. Capitalism affords the middle classes the chance to flirt with aristocracy and allows them to forget the work still to be done to complete the revolution. The Sadean image of Robin does not awaken the Baron to his responsibility to political history, but it does shock his regressive sense of progress, altering his perception of her (the modern American woman's) role in cultural reproduction, making him "see" her differently—as a problematic agent and moral obstacle rather than an impressionable vessel.

There are other instances where bourgeois sentiment and false consciousness are exposed, but not quite with the effect of the profane illumination. The Doctor's "obscenity" at times upsets the Baron's pretension to claims of nobility,[45] but it has none of the power of the image to shock an enterprising moral unconscious. The most potent instance of profane illumination occurs at the close of *Nightwood.* The entire narrative seems to lead up to it, though the way is indirect. Much space is given to the Doctor's queer meditation on the nature of erotic affliction, just as *Nadja* gives space to Breton's musings on desire and madness. But the brutal image at the end of *Nightwood* is all the more climactic for the detours that precede it.

How does profane illumination work? What is the play of "esoteric love"? The climactic image has an instantaneous impact, but its effect has a history: the chronicle of *amour fou entre deux femmes.* After Robin gives birth to the Baron's feeble-minded son, she is delivered of her role as Baroness; but she is less a free spirit than a haunted soul, driven destructively towards the irrational, the mysterious, and the ecstatic, which she finds in frenzied bouts with booze, women, Catholicism, and beasts. A cipher of unconscious automatism, Robin possesses as little communicative agency as Nadja. She slums about, though she has no obvious economic reason to do so. Her erotic drift is strangely anchored in Nora. We are deprived of a pornographic account of their lovemaking but spared no details of their sordid estrangement. There are many banging doors, and most open onto the night. Nora follows Robin into dimly lit streets and shadowy interiors, hoping to see her and save her from the dark thing that drives her but losing her in a penumbra of wantonness. Nora believes Robin is possessed, knowing no other way to explain Robin's compulsion to profane their romance at every turn, to express joy at rare moments of domestic peace in "songs like a practiced whore who turns away from no one but the one who loves her" (57).

Despite her progressive leanings, Nora sees Robin in the mystifying light of religious illumination. Nora hosts the "strangest 'salon' in America"[46] and frequents the bohemian circles of Europe. Nora is a freelance journalist and a full-time *flâneur*, but she also shares roots with Seventh-Day Adventists (52) and the brand of American puritanism that forged the western frontier (50-51). Such occupations and beliefs are strange bedfellows for bohemia but not unlikely soulmates for the ecumenical spirit of capitalism. Like the Baron, Nora conjures up sources of primeval inspiration to satisfy bourgeois longings for moral reassurance. She "sees" in Robin a natural and exotic animality but only in blind reaction to the industrial bleakness of everyday life. She cultivates her romantic illusions in bohemia, a retreat from "progress" masquerading as ultramodern. At the same time, she draws on the repositories of her religious memory. The space for hysterical conflict is great, but the embattled ideologies (romanticism, puritanism) are mobilized by the same moral optimism of bourgeois self-deception.

Nora is attracted by Robin's wildness, which she is tempted to domesticate like an enterprising circus manager. She follows Robin through the gutters, dogged as much by her need to know Robin's "shame" as by her desire to recover their relationship. Her pursuit drives Robin away. Robin resists these colonizing affections with abject beastliness, which Nora, in turn, tries to recuperate with pity. Robin escapes into reckless vagrancy, finding homelessness more dignifying than the demoralization of domesticity. It is only Nora's pious hounding that makes Robin feel filthy (143).

So the story goes. *Nightwood* presents many instances of moral exhibitionism, but where is the profane illumination? Benjamin finds it in the way Surrealism casts light on the "outmoded" objects and buildings of capitalism. Barnes also casts such a light. Things that stand out with uncanny emotional value expose the moral impoverishment of political economy. One of these things is the doll that Robin gives to Nora: a lifeless fetish of aborted desire (147) but not an icon, as Nora supposes, of the devilry of inversion (148). The doll, like the Bar-

on's feeble-minded son, allegorizes the barrenness of bourgeois cultural reproduction, for which bohemian perversity offers no cure. New women, no less than decadent aristocrats, are haunted by modernity's destruction of past forms of life and its failure to create new ones. Robin and Nora harbor nightmarish dreams of the antiquated family (149) while pursuing the marginal freedoms of a modern "lesbian" lifestyle.

Seeing one of Robin's dolls in another woman's bed is what finally breaks Nora's heart.[47] At the same time, the incident intensifies her reliance on a moral delusion that the Doctor attempts to treat with obscene provocations: "'Stop it! You were a "good woman," and so a bitch on a high plane, the only one able to kill Robin and yourself'" (146). But the shock of profane speech has none of the power of the image in the final scene. To recall the situation: Nora is at her country home in upstate New York when she is alerted by the barking of her dog to something in the night outside. She follows the dog, running and breathless, to the "decaying chapel" on the top of the hill. Plunging into the jamb of the door she beholds Robin, dressed in boys' trousers, in a frozen pose of worship before a "contrived altar" (169). At "the moment that Nora's body struck the wood, Robin began going down" (169). "Sliding down she went; down, her hair swinging, her arms held out. . . . And down she went" (169) until she has sunk to all fours, and turned on Nora's bewitched hound: "then head down, dragging her forelocks in the dust, she struck against his side. He let loose one howl of misery and bit at her, dashing about her, barking. . . . Then she began to bark also, crawling after him—barking in a fit of laughter, obscene and touching" (170).

We do not know how Nora experiences this scene, or even if she remains conscious. (Has she knocked herself out, striking the wood? Does she faint from the shock of seeing Robin and strike the wood as she falls?) In any case, she is a vehicle of uncanny perception; physically and emotionally tormented by something at the limit of her conscience, she leads us to the site of a grotesque epiphany. We might not be surprised that her hounding piety should lead to a chapel, that she should be dogged by her own doggedness, or that the final scene should reveal the jam(b) they are in. But we are shocked by Robin's conversion and the sacred and profane architectonics. Like Breton and Nadja, Nora and Robin move through the space of a historical moment where the present frame of past life is made luminously decrepit. It is not just the deterioration of buildings that we see but the degradation of the human subject as well. From the door jamb we witness the impact of exterior, objective forces—the material decline of social life (embodied in the decaying chapel)—on the subjective interior (Robin's psychosis), and the haunting dereliction of both (the chapel, Nora, and Robin are all falling apart).

The image of Robin "going down" on her knees before the altar, but down so far as to surpass all limits of religious supplication, devolving into a species of the lowest moral order (more beastly than Nora's dog, and more hounded) is a surreal profanation. The surreal presents the invisibly real in an all-too-literal image. Just as the chapel falls into ruin, so too does the human subject. It is the corporeal and emotional ruination of the human that makes us see the ruinous progress of social and psychological life from a materialist point of view. A gothic or naturalist presentation would use the devices of symbol and metaphor to imply a fall from grace or a return of the repressed. The surreal image, however, deploys a dialectical optic which keeps the political and the psychotic simultaneously in view. A psychoanalytic focus would obscure the political component by highlighting the symptomatology that signifies the transhistorical war between civilization and libido.

Nightwood's chapel is not gothic; its most terrible feature is that it is a "weather-beaten white" (169). It sits on a hill above the house where Nora hosts her bohemian salons but, unlike the house, has not held a congregation for ages. It has not been torn down but left to rot. The chapel and the conjugal bedroom (the other ruined site of *Nightwood*) look back to an age of construction when society was organized by the Church and an aristocracy of blood. They have been eroded by revolutionary progress, especially industrial revolutionary progress; the bourgeoisie, especially the bohemian bourgeoisie, treat them as outmoded without, however, constructing something new. Robin occupies this antique architecture with the savagery of a homeless nomad. Modernism breeds barbarism: behind the liberal façade, it is literally going to the dogs.

Eros Noir

Nightwood unleashes feelings that are so incommensurable ("obscene and touching") that they test the limit of rational perception. It is between narrator and reader, not between characters, that this riot of sensibility is communicated. Exposed to the violent collapse that Barnes's estranged lovers unconsciously and uncannily embody, we participate in a negative transference whose primal scene is less tragic than nihilistic. The profane illumination is the political technique of this transference, and it is not intended as catharsis. Dispelling any liberal illusions we may have cultivated about modern sexuality and progressive society, it is deployed as the wrench that jams the works of social reproduction.

The image of Robin and Nora's "going down" (sadly, not on each other) is provocative but hardly titillating. More pessimistic and more obscene than Breton's *amour fou*, Barnes's eroticism shares Bataille's vulgar materialism. But *Nightwood* is not pornographic. Nor does Barnes produce what some Foucaultian critics refer to as "erotic literature,"[48] the narrative of reverse discourse in which a scandalized homosexuality attempts to speak and act in its own name.

It is possible to read Radclyffe Hall as the producer of a reverse discourse. Critics have demonstrated that her *Well of Loneliness* uses erotic realism to affirm and "authenticize" the category "lesbian" and thus to overrule the pejorative taxonomy of medical, judirical, and theological discourses from which it derives.[49] But Barnes's erotic *sur*realism deploys techniques more complex than those of reverse discourse. *Nightwood* neither names nor celebrates lesbianism. Instead, it articulates a queer antidiscourse, which, voiced by the melancholic Doctor, confounds the confessions of modern sexology with ejaculations of libertine gourmandise.

Nor does Barnes react to the discourse of obscenity by producing, like D. H. Lawrence, a literature that claims to be erotically healthy. If Lawrence sought to purge modern love of "pornography and obscenity" with a redeeming vitalism and wholesome heterosexuality,[50] Barnes imagines an erotic decrepitude beyond good and evil. Lawrence rallies against obscenity in the guise of sexual liberation, but with his charismatic reversal of the tactics of prohibition he in fact advances the hygienic regime.[51] His erotic exhibitionism conceals and reproduces his sexual conservatism.[52] That is why the author of *Lady Chatterley's Lover* is so easily co-opted by public education: the program of sexual self-enlightenment in Lawrence's didactic fiction is a ready tool for elite consumption, as it is later for a populist pedagogy.[53] Ministries of health and welfare discover that teaching, instead of banning, Lawrence is by far the more effective method of managing bodies in a modern liberal democracy.

Nightwood offers poor material for the consultant of sexual hygiene, and with respect to erotic fulfilment it teaches nothing, not even how *not* to proceed. Against Lawrence's phallic optimism, Barnes's eroticism is grotesquely pessimistic: he guides his reader through dionysiac passages to ecstatic sexual self-understanding, whereas she riddles and shocks with excremental speech and unconsumable images. Despite editorial care, *Nightwood* functions as an obscene aberration in "progressive" culture.

Barnes uses a tactic different from Lawrence's to protest obscenity. Instead of purging sexuality, she magnifies its aura of profanity. *Nightwood* reorganizes the devices of "obscene" literature. There are literary antecedents as well as legal precedents for her avant-garde obscenity. Critics frequently point out that the garrulity of Doctor "Mighty-grain-of-salt-Dante-Matthew-O'Connor" (80) owes its punch to James Joyce's four-letter "Irish." Barnes also peppers her narrative with the imagery and scenography of Flaubert,

Boccaccio, and De Sade, authors who, like Joyce, were banned in America in the twenties and thirties. For instance, there is a passage in *Nightwood* that adapts the famous carriage scene in *Madame Bovary* for which Flaubert was arraigned by the French courts. *Nightwood*'s chapter 4, "The Squatter," also features seduction in a horse-drawn carriage, though Flaubert's lovers are hidden behind tightly sealed blinds as the carriage circles Rouen in broad daylight, while Barnes's ride in an open hack as they circumnavigate the woods and lower quarters of Paris at night (*Nightwood,* 71-76).

The scene in *Nightwood* is as erotically charged, as mysterious and intoxicating as Flaubert's. But what scandalizes the reader of the nineteenth century—the public adultery of a bourgeois wife—has been replaced by a blasphemy more appropriate to the twentieth: deranged love. The scene follows an evening of entertainment hosted by Jenny Petherbridge, one of the nouveaux riches who suffers from creative poverty. She conspires to seduce Robin and take for herself the object of Nora's desire and inspiration. Her plan of a midnight ride through the Paris woods in antique carriages is a lavish, if clichéd, tactic of avaricious romancing. Robin, however, disdainfully ignores Jenny's attentions until Jenny, crazed with frustration, attacks her. Bleeding and battered, Robin falls forward, "her knees on the floor . . . so that when the whole of the gesture was completed, Robin's hands were covered by Jenny's slight and bending breast, caught in between the bosom and the knees" (76). Intoxicated with their own histrionics, they are profane dervishes who stage an unfulfilling whirl of seduction and supplication.

We have seen this gesture of Robin's before: it is the gesture of "going down." She makes it when she kneels to pray on the prie-dieu, troubling the truly penitent with her physical intensity "as if some inscrutable wish for salvation, something yet more monstrously unfulfilled than they had suffered, had thrown a shadow" (46). We see it again in the final scene in the chapel. In each case, this gesture circumscribes a motion that is paradoxically sacred and profane, obscene and touching. But the trick of profane illumination is the optic of historical materialism, not moral conundrum.

For all its sophisticated construction, bohemia is a collapsible façade. The architecture of the scene between Robin and Jenny is designed to show the erotics of destitution. The carriage is a fashionable prop in an outmoded dream of courtship. To get to the enchanted woods, it must be driven through the squalor of working-class suburbs. Jenny is rich enough to hire hacks and horses but she must highjack desire, having none of her own. Her attraction to Robin is a simulacrum of passion. Moving in on Robin while Robin is still being accommodated by Nora but no longer anywhere at home, Jenny takes possession not of a woman but of an abandoned residence, a dereliction. Behind the classy romancer we see the sordid artifices of "the squatter."

Nightwood is set in the Paris of Surrealism, not Flaubert's provincial nineteenth-century France. Barnes's characters are the street-addicted "paupers" of modern urban life, "the *détraqés,*"[54] as are those of *Nadja* and Aragon's *Paysan de Paris* (1924/25). While the arcades of the previous century supply the material conditions for the flourishing of the *flâneur,* the industrial postwar recovery of the 1920s and 1930s sets the scene for the *détraqué.* The *flâneur* and the *détraqué* are late developments of the *bohème,* whom Benjamin describes as one who conspires against the status quo but merely as an *agent provocateur* lacking political conviction and likely to swing in any "revolutionary" direction for love of spectacle.[55] They are also paupers in that they resist the industriousness of the modern megapolis but not its intoxication. What distinguishes the *détraqué* as an even later development of the *bohème* is the means of intoxication: the *flâneur* gets drunk on the commodity, the *détraqué* on refuse. The *flâneur* strolls through the merchandise that fills the arcades, enraptured with the same "aura" of commodity fetishism that enraptures the crowd, though it is the crowd from which he remains heroically and poetically detached.[56] The *détraqué* retreats from the commercial spotlight to poorly lit districts where he spends his libidinal economy on the depreciated arts of the circus and the theater.[57] The *flâneur* embodies the perspective of the commodity itself, or so we might, with Benjamin, understand Baudelaire's reference to "the holy prostitution of the soul."[58] The *détraqué* is likewise objectified, but he is intoxicated with the process of degradation by which he becomes "incommunicable" (*Nightwood,* 52) and unconsumable. "The *Détraqué*" could be the last chapter in the history of bohemian conspiracy. It would outline the failure of abject resistance to market forces despite Surrealism's attempt to convert abjection into revolutionary nihilism.

The novels of Surrealism are guides to Paris's demimonde, to the obscure salons, theaters, and circuses where the *détraqués* cultivate and circulate their esoteric arts.[59] At the outset of *Nadja,* Breton describes the passage he takes to the demimonde, where he discovers the latest haunts of Parisian phantasmagoria. His first step is to follow a method of exposure to any chance event that alerts the public censor. This takes him to the *Théâtre des Deux Masques,* where he watches a "nearly banned" production of *Les Détraquées* with "unbounded admiration."[60] Featuring a strange entanglement between the headmistress of a girls' school, a fashionable mademoiselle, a student, and her grandmother, the play prepares him to meet Nadja, a true *détraquée* with whom he proceeds to have a mad affair. He follows her through the city, documenting her clandestine streetwalker's habits and amusements with the inspired detail of a distracted physician.[61]

Nora is already a *détraquée,* but she falls for Robin like an addict seeking a more powerful narcotic. She takes Robin in large doses but, like Breton, she has a limit. When Robin begins strolling the streets at night instead of coming home, Nora pursues her with dread and shame. A worldly American, she flirts with French decadence in bad faith. Unlike Breton, she is unprepared to be exposed to the seedier side of the city and its nocturnal transfiguration. To dispel the nightmare she has entered, she seeks the Doctor's enlightenment. But of all the *détraquées* the Doctor is the most extravagant. He opens his door onto another view of the city, more wasted and degraded than the slums through which Robin drags Nora.

Late one night Nora calls on the Doctor for an emergency tête-à-tête, but what transpires is a profane illumination. The location and size of his residence come as a shock to Nora, "who had not known that the Doctor was so poor" (78). He occupies a single room that would impress any visitor with its disconcerting coupling of interior and exterior and its queer assemblage of bedchamber, surgery, and closet. We can see the grave state of modernity in the disorder and decay of the things that fill this room:

> A pile of medical books, and volumes of a miscellaneous order, reached almost to the ceiling, water-stained and covered with dust. Just above them was a very small barred window, the only ventilation. On a maple dresser, certainly not of European make, lay a rusty pair of forceps, a broken scalpel, half a dozen odd instruments that [Nora] could not place, a catheter, some twenty perfume bottles, almost empty, pomades, creams, rouges, powder boxes and puffs. From the half-open drawers of this chiffonier hung laces, ribands, stockings, ladies' undergarments and an abdominal brace, which gave the impression that the feminine finery had suffered venery. A swill-pail stood at the head of the bed, brimming with abominations. There was something appallingly degraded about the room, like the rooms in brothels, which give even the most innocent a sensation of having been an accomplice.
>
> (78-79)

It is specifically the destitution of *sexual* modernity that is revealed in the Doctor's private and professional wrack and ruin. A flamboyant cross-dresser and *gourmet* sodomite (91-94), he is reduced to entertaining in the muck of his *boudoir-urinoir.* The confusion of "forceps" and "feminine finery" imply that he has been forced to choose gynecology as the only legitimate conduit to the pleasure he takes in playing the woman's part. But, as the "rusty" and "broken" tools of his trade also testify, gynecology is a poor instrument for servicing eros. A survivor of this political economy, his practice of everynight life bears witness to the perversion of sodomy and the wreckage of libertinage. In the clutter we can see the material waste of scientific progress.

The profane illumination, Benjamin observes, "brings the immense forces of 'atmosphere' concealed in these things to the point of explosion." Barnes brings the immense forces of atmosphere concealed in this room to the point of explosion, not only in this one devastating image but again and again in the ensuing dialogue between the Doctor and Nora. Though "dismayed" (79) by the Doctor's "extremity" (80), Nora persists in her quest for guidance. But instead of doctrine or knowledge, the Doctor dispenses a radical heterodoxy, compiled of a multitude of folk wisdoms—Irish blarney, queenly drollery, anecdotal gossip—mixed with loose allusions to Burton's *Anatomy of Melancholy* (1621)[62] and other textual sources, most of them "obscene." Nora wrestles with the Doctor's implications, contesting his "alchemical" (80) erudition with sources of her own in New World puritanism. It is a match made in hell.

The dialogue between the Doctor and Nora that takes up the entire chapter of "Watchman, What of the Night?" and much of "Go Down, Matthew" has often been read as a parody of the scene between Freud and Dora.[63] But it might also be viewed as a modern adaptation of the indoctrinating dialogues played out in De Sade's *Philosophy of the Bedroom.* The dialogue in **Nightwood** literally takes place in the Doctor's *"chambre à coucher"* (79). Nora's request that he tell her everything he knows about the night (79) cues him to take up such incendiary Sadean themes as the liberty of sodomy, the enslavement of love, and the promiscuous Nature of the she-beast.[64]

The Doctor takes Nora's cue in a direction different from the one she expects. He prompts her to imagine another way of life—a "night life"—using intoxicating and provocative devices reminiscent of those deployed by revolutionary Surrealism. When she turns her thoughts obsessively to Robin, he tells her to think of "French nights" specifically, cueing her in turn to dream of what she, in harboring a puritan imaginary, finds impossible to conceive.[65] In doing so he follows the Surrealists, who with their sleeping fits, automatic writing, seductive dreaming, and round-table *recherches sur la sexualité* contrive to experience life beyond the limits of bourgeois anthropology. His directing her to conjure up "the night" is itself a surrealist tactic,[66] which he embellishes with the mesmerizing excrementality of a Boccaccio or Pasolini:

> "Have you thought of the night, now, in other times, in foreign countries—in Paris? When the streets were gall high with things you wouldn't have done for a dare's sake, and the way it was then; with the pheasants' necks and the goslings' beaks dangling against the hocks of

gallants, and not a pavement in the place, and everything gutters for miles and miles, and a stench to it that plucked you by the nostrils and you were twenty leagues out! The criers telling the price of wine to such effect that the dawn saw good clerks full of piss and vinegar, and blood-letting in side streets where some wild princess in a night-shift of velvet howled under a leech; not to mention the palaces of Nymphenburg echoing back to Vienna with the night trip of late kings letting water into plush cans and fine woodwork! No," he said, looking at her sharply, "I can see you have not!"

(81-82)

The Doctor's dialogical doctoring of their repartee undercuts Nora's moral inquisition into Robin's inexplicable vagrancy. He acquaints her with a carnivalesque body politic and its shameless corporeality. "The French," he says, "have made a detour of filthiness—Oh, good the dirt! Whereas you are of a clean race, of a too eagerly washing people. . . . Be like the Frenchman . . .—he can trace himself back by his sediment, vegetable and animal, and so finds himself in the odour of wine in its two travels, in and out, packed down beneath an air that has not changed its position during that strategy" (84-85). The Doctor also introduces what Georges Bataille in 1929 heralds as "the heterological"—the waste products of the intellectual process[67]—into Nora's whitewashed liberalism. Like Bataille's heterology, the Doctor's most shocking intervention makes use of De Sade's libertine manifestos.

Between Barnes's interlocutors a libertine wisdom of the past battles with a Protestant sexology of the present. Against the pathologizing discourse of inversion, which affects the Doctor no less than Nora, the Doctor observes the naturalness of sodomy in both sexes: "I haunt the *pissoirs* as naturally as Highland Mary her cows down by the Dee—and by the Hobs of Hell, I've seen the same at work in a girl" (91). He recalls De Sade's demagogic Dolmance, who, reeducating the naive Eugénie, exclaims, "Ah! far from outraging Nature, on the contrary—and let us be well persuaded of it—, the sodomite and Lesbian serve her stubbornly from a conjunction whose resultant progeniture can be nothing but irksome to her."[68] An epicurean, like Dolmance, the Doctor can distinguish one fuck from another in the dark, declaring his taste for democratic variation: "Do I know my Sodomites? . . . And though your normal fellow will say all are alike in the dark, negro or white, I say you can tell them, and where they came from, and what quarter they frequent, by the size and excellence—" (94). Furthermore, the Doctor can readily identify the "best port" for cruising—the "*Place de la Bastille*" (92), naming the site from which De Sade launched his revolution.

But the Doctor does not, like Dolmance, hail women's libertinage to be the principal weapon against universal enslavement to Enlightenment morality,[69] though he insists that under the present regime women, just as men, are damned for their pleasure in same-sex coupling. Of the city's *détraqués,* the "sodomites" are the most down and out. Once model republicans of the French Revolution, they are now "excommunicated" specters of post-Revolutionary decadence.[70] Since it is religious illumination Nora so earnestly and so blindly solicits, the Doctor obliges her with a blast of Sadean blasphemy:

> look for the girls also in the toilets at night, and you will find them kneeling in that great secret confessional crying between tongues, the terrible excommunication:
>
> "May you be damned to hell! May you die standing upright! May you be damned upward! May this be damned, terrible and damned spot! May it wither into the grin of the dead, may this draw back, low riding mouth in an empty snarl of the groin! May this be your torment, may this be your damnation! God damned me before you, and after me you shall be damned, kneeling and standing away till we vanish! For what do you know of me, man's meat? . . . May you pass from me, damned girl! Damned and betraying!"

(95)[71]

In the dark light of melancholic reason, we see pleasure's disciples betray themselves in the act of consummation. These are the descendants of the first sexual revolution and contemporized versions of Baudelaire's lesbians, those *femmes damnées,* who, having no revolutionary context for their transgression, manage only to burn themselves. Through a spiral of moral progress and bourgeois liberation, they become today's most abject heretics.

Just as Dolmance impresses upon Eugénie his observation that "love . . . devours, consumes us, without affording us other than metaphysical joys, which bear such a likeness to the effects of madness,"[72] the Doctor tries to impress upon Nora that no sacrifice of love will save her and Robin from the fetters of pleasure. Love, in this post-Revolutionary age, is the progenitor and guardian of vice. Sade's sodomite embodies the creed of pleasure for pleasure's sake, but in this political economy his nonreproductive embraces are indulged with moral despair. He survives by going underground, taking anguish for his ecstasy, trapped in his escape from the sentiments of desire. "'And do I know my Sodomites?' the Doctor said unhappily, 'and when the heart goes bang up against it if it loves one of them, especially if it's a woman loving one of them?'" (93). But Nora makes a poor Eugénie. She resists the Doctor's provocations and accepts her estrangement with suffering devotion. "Love," she concludes, "is death, come upon with passion; I know, that is why love is wisdom. I love her as one condemned to it" (137).

Barnes deploys De Sade without revolutionary optimism. Nora succumbs to sentimenal slavishness. The Doctor reaches his wits' end trying to find the right device to effect Nora's de-indoctrination. Robin is lost to the night. In her we see not the residue of the Sadean libertine but the failure of the Sadean revolution. That she makes her way back to the decaying chapel suggests her "excommunication" is not yet complete. Is not her final transfiguration a reiteration of the Sadean wisdom that the history of sexual liberation has so savagely twisted?: "Woman's destiny is to be wanton, like the bitch, the she-wolf; she must belong to all who claim her. Clearly, it is to outrage the fate Nature imposes upon women to fetter them by the absurdities of a solitary marriage."[73]

* * *

Benjamin's formulation of the "profane illumination" helps us understand how Barnes's obscene device works. It works as a "dialectical optic" that reveals the things of the present in a politicized historical light so that we can see the progressive decay of modernization. We see the deterioration of church and conjugal household in the age of bourgeois secularization, and we see an appalling resurrection of these ruins in the bohemian reaction to the spirit of capitalism. We also see the degradation of sodomy in the age of sexological confession and sexual liberation. Barnes's obscene device works most poignantly as "moral exhibitionism," illuminating, behind the façade of erotic liberalism, the failure of the French Revolution to destroy the shackles of sentimental humanism. Using Benjamin's optic to reread *Nightwood,* we can see a crack in Foucault's panopticon, placed there by the pressures of a revolutionary nihilism. Nothing should be more revolting to progressive culture than to see De Sade still in chains: Barnes's obscene insight is inciteful profanation.

Far from colluding with the mechanisms of legitimization which aestheticize and neutralize the radical elements of her writing, Barnes aligns herself with writers, past and present, whose works had been banned, and she forges her offensive language and imagery into a collective technique of social negation. *Nightwood* works like a Trojan horse, constructed out of a vast battery of obscene materials and inserted into juridical, sexological, and theological discourse where it clears explosive queer space for radically rethinking the history of sexuality.

Instead of viewing this author of American modernism as an unwitting agent in the production and legitimization of dominant culture, we might see her as the artificer of an obscene resistance, laboring in tacit solidarity with her Surrealist contemporaries. We might reconsider the view of *Nightwood* as a lesbian novel whose reception as such had to be deferred until it found an audience among lesbian and gay readers who knew how to recover its latent homosexual content. We might read *Nightwood* as a minor, instead of minority, eroti-

cism, an *eros noir* that spotlights the limbo of sexual community shared between bourgeois culture and sapphic bohemia in an advanced stage of capitalism. Whatever gaiety Barnes signifies, it is not easily recuperated.[74] *Nightwood*'s erotics deploys an ethics of pessimism. Its politics is not the politics of identity. The carnival of characters, the *détraqués* who haunt this novel, is a heterogeneous figure of abjection in the final front against rationalization and *embourgeoisment*. That this front is presented as the last dismal cycle of *la comédie humaine* is not to be taken as encouragement by gay radicals. What Barnes provokes is the realization that if the progressive destruction of modernity is to be diverted, a different set of techniques and tactics must be practiced in place of reverse discourse and other foibles of *ressentiment*.

Notes

1. See Felice Flanery Lewis, *Literature, Obscenity, and Law* (Carbondale: Southern Illinois Univ. Press, 1976).

2. See Robert A. Jacobs, "Dirty Words, Dirty Thoughts and Censorship: Obscenity Law and Non-Pictorial Works," *Southwestern University Law Review* 21 (1992): 155-83. For recent discussions of literary obscenity in the United States, see Susan Stewart, *Crimes of Writing: Problems in the Containment of Representation* (New York: Oxford Univ. Press, 1991); and Edward de Grazia, *Girls Lean Back Everywhere: The Law of Obscenity and the Assault on Genius* (New York: Random House, 1992).

3. See Ian Hunter, David Saunders, and Dugald Williamson, *On Pornography: Literature, Sexuality and Obscenity Law* (New York: St. Martin's Press, 1993).

4. See Richard Easton, "Canonical Criminalizations: Homosexuality, Art History, Surrealism and Abjection," *differences* 4 (fall 1992): 133-75; Carolyn Dean, "Pornography, Literature, and the Redemption of Virility in France, 1880-1930," *differences* 5 (summer 1993): 62-91; Lindsay F. Watton, "Constructs of Sin and Sodom in Russian Modernism, 1906-1909," *Journal of the History of Sexuality* 4 (January 1994): 369-94.

5. Obscenity in itself has never qualified for constitutional protection; see Amy N. Adler, "Why Art Is On Trial," *Journal of Arts Management, Law and Society* 22 (winter 1993): 322-34.

6. Foucault's commitment to the textual strategies of avant-garde eroticism peaked in the early sixties, most notably in his *Homage à Georges Bataille* (Michel Foucault, "Preface to Transgression," in *Language, Counter-Memory, Practice,* ed. Donald F. Bourchard, trans. Donald F. Bourchard and

Sherry Simon [Ithaca, N.Y.: Cornell Univ. Press, 1977]). By the seventies Foucault rejected the project of modernist negation that *Tel Quel's* revolution in poetic language had revived, turning his attention instead to the positive, discursive mechanisms of social order. *Volonté de savoir,* the first volume of *Histoire de la sexualité,* examines the production and management of erotic subjects through the medico-juridical authorization and distribution of sexual (self)knowledge. The critique of power poses a categorical imperative for the genealogist: "We must define the strategies of power that are immanent in this will to knowledge. As far as sexuality is concerned, we shall attempt to constitute the 'political economy' of a will to knowledge" (Michel Foucault, *History of Sexuality,* vol. 1, trans. Robert Hurley [New York: Vintage, 1990], 73). For a superb account of this transition, see John Rajchman, "The Ends of Modernism," in his *Michel Foucault: The Freedom of Philosophy* (New York: Columbia Univ. Press, 1985), 9-42.

7. "To conceive the category of the sexual in terms of the law, death, blood and sovereignty—whatever the references to Sade and Bataille, and however one might gauge their 'subversive' influence," Foucault writes, "is in the last analysis a historical 'retro-version.' We must conceptualize the deployment of sexuality on the basis of the techniques of power that are contemporary with it" (*History of Sexuality,* 150).

8. See Michel Foucault, "Sexual Choice, Sexual Act," in *Foucault Live (Interviews, 1966-84),* ed. Sylvère Lotringer, trans. John Johnston (New York: Semiotext[e], 1989), 211-32.

9. French literary critics recognize "flâneur realism" to be one of the genres of oppositionality available to nineteenth-century middle-class Bohemia, while lesbian (and) feminist literary critics recognize "lesbian realism" to be a twentieth-century genre of counter-disciplinary narrative, citing Radclyffe Hall's *Well of Loneliness* as the groundbreaking text.

10. In this essay I use the term *queer* to distinguish Barnes's antagonistic sexuality and sexual nihilism from "lesbian" sexuality and its positive historical and utopian instances of identity and solidarity. That is to say, while Barnes's primary lovers are indeed two women whose chief entanglement is erotic and sexual and therefore "lesbian" in the most banal sense, the focus of *Nightwood's* gaze falls on the dark, unsymbolizble thing or the unbridgeable void that negates and devastates their affair.

11. Emily Coleman, quoted in the introduction to Djuna Barnes, *Nightwood: The Original Version*

and Related Drafts, ed. Cheryl J. Plumb (Normal, Ill.: Dalkey Archive Press, 1995), xxi.

12. *Nightwood: The Original Version and Related Drafts,* 210.

13. In her retrospective of Barnes, Mary Lynn Broe points to Jane Marcus's revolutionary rereading of *Nightwood,* which brings to light Barnes's rendering of the modern political unconscious, including the repressed differences of race, class, gender, and sexuality. In line with Marcus's findings, Broe adds that "Barnes's plays, stories, and early newspaper essays interrogate conventional or public sexual ideologies," and that "Barnes alone among the 'new women' playwrights dared to introduce vampirism ('The Dove'), incest ('Three From Earth'), and various radical sexual ideologies in her work." Broe also notes without elaborating that Barnes "examines the failures of representational reality and also the asymmetries of age and power and the contradictions inherent in gender definitions that undercut family intimacies, encoding complex modes of eroticism for which we as yet have no literary typology" ("Djuna Barnes [1892-1982]," in *The Gender of Modernism,* ed. Bonnie Kime Scott [Bloomington: Indiana Univ. Press, 1990], 19-45). See also *Silence and Power: A Reevaluation of Djuna Barnes,* ed. Mary Lynn Broe (Carbondale, Ill.: Southern Illinois Univ. Press, 1991).

14. See, for example, Ann B. Dalton, "'This is *obscene*': Female Voyeurism, Sexual Abuse, and Maternal Power in *The Dove*," *Review of Contemporary Fiction* 33 (fall 1993): 117-39. Dalton identifies the strange erotic interaction between female characters in Barnes's one-act play "The Dove" as cryptic testimony, but the clearest literary evidence we have of the sexual abuse Barnes allegedly endured as a young woman. She traces biographical evidence of grandmother-granddaughter incest in Barnes's early correspondence, arguing it to be the projected latent content of *Nightwood's* symptomatic obscenity. See conversely, Bonnie Kime Scott's chapter "Beasts Turning into Humans" in *Refiguring Modernism: Postmodern Feminist Readings of Woolf, West, and Barnes* (Bloomington: Indiana Univ. Press, 1995), 71-122. Scott uncovers the bestiality of *Nightwood,* urging that the final shocking scene between dog and woman be hailed as therapeutic: "the extended actions of dog and woman are suggestive of ritual healing. Both beast and human have a therapeutic run through the emotions, full of gesture, movement, and even pain" (117).

15. *Nightwood: The Original Version and Related Drafts,* xviii.

16. I take particular exception to the argument put forward by Jodey Castricano in "Rude Awakenings: or What Happens When a Lesbian Reads the 'Hieroglyphics of Sleep' in Djuna Barnes's *Nightwood*," *West Coast Line* 15 (winter 1994-95): 106-16. Presupposing that "since *Nightwood* confronts and engages the reader with a lesbian point of view, and since that view is marked by lesbian desire," Castricano urges us to decode the "lesbian Imaginary" of the shocking last chapter (106, 112). In her focus on the "hieroglyphics" of this "Imaginary," she overlooks Barnes's avant-garde arsenal of obscene artistic devices. In fact, she overlooks *Nightwood*'s legal, historical, artistic, and modernist texts and contexts altogether, reading exclusively in light of deconstructive and psychoanalytic theories.

17. In turning from Foucault to Benjamin, I do not mean to imply that no one comes after Foucault to take up the literary art of sexual transgression. Gilles Deleuze, for instance, develops a "pornological" method of analysis for reading and distinguishing the obscene maneuvers of De Sade, Von Sacher-Masoch, and Pierre Klossowski. But pornology focuses on the transgressive techniques specific to pornographic literature or philosophy. Benjamin's "profane illumination" is more appropriate to Barnes's obscure transgression, which lies somewhere between the obscene and the profane; unlike pornology, it also sheds light on her tactic of historical pessimism.

18. Walter Benjamin, "Surrealism," *Reflections: Essays, Aphorisms, Autobiographical Writings,* ed. Peter Demetz, trans. Edmund Jephcott (New York: Schocken, 1978), 181-92.

19. It will quickly become apparent that my method of queer reading is one of reading for minor, as distinct from marginal or minority, literary practice. I emphasize Barnes's "deterritorialization of," or nomadic exodus from, traditional and urban social spaces, her making visible (through dialectical imaging) the society of impoverishment shared by bourgeois culture and sapphic bohemia. Hence my approach is closer to Gilles Deleuze and Félix Guattari's "minor literature" than to Eve Kosofsky Sedgwick's or Judith Butler's "queer theory" and its tactical, deconstructive focus on the double binds and duplicitious framing of sexual minority and marginality.

20. See Lewis, 126-28.

21. "This book, owing to censorship, which has a vogue in America as indiscriminate as all such enforcements of law must be, has been expurgated. Where such measures have been thought necessary, asterisks have been employed, thus making it matter for no speculation where sense, continuity, and beauty have been damaged" (Djuna Barnes, *Ryder* [New York: Boni and Liveright, 1928], xi).

22. Djuna Barnes, *Nightwood* (New York: New Directions Press, 1937), 170. This is the second American edition, the one restored by Dalkey Archives Press. Quotations from *Nightwood* are taken from this edition and will hereafter be indicated parenthetically in the text.

23. Leigh Gilmour, "Obscenity, Modernity, Identity: Legalizing *The Well of Loneliness* and *Nightwood*," *Journal of the History of Sexuality* 4 (April 1994): 603-24.

24. Foucault, *History of Sexuality,* 43.

25. The *Hicklin* doctrine, fashioned in 1868 by the Queen's Bench, became the legal standard by which the freedom of authors and publishers in the United States was measured until 1933, when it was temporarily but not definitively overruled. The doctrine set out to judge "whether the tendency of the matter charged as obscenity is to deprave and corrupt those whose minds are open to such immoral influences, and into whose hands a publication of this sort may fall" (Quoted in Jacobs, 164).

26. Employing the *Hicklin* test, the English magistrate, Sir Charles Biron, found Hall's *Well of Loneliness* criminally obscene, pronouncing the book as one "which would tend to corrupt those into hands it might fall." He decided that "acts of the most horrible, unnatural and disgusting obscenity are described in the most alluring terms in this book and that none of the women involved are treated as in the least blameworthy. Characters living in filthy sin are treated as attractive people and put forward with admiration. Indeed, the result is described by the authoress as giving these women extraordinary rest, contentment and pleasure; and not only that, but it is actually put forward that it improves their mental balance and capacity" (Quoted in De Grazia, 191-92).

27. Gilmour, 614.

28. In addition to the ruling on Radclyffe Hall's *Well of Loneliness,* Gilmour cites the ban on Havelock Ellis's *Sexual Inversion* as a "legal precedent" motivating the editorial transmutation of *Nightwood.*

29. In her introduction to *Nightwood: The Original Version and Related Drafts,* Plumb observes that "all in all, the editorial hand was light; certainly because he anticipated potential difficulty with censors, Eliot blurred sexual, particularly homosexual, references and a few points that put reli-

gion in an unsavory light. However, meaning was not changed substantially, though the character of the work was adjusted, the language softened." Still, she concurs with Gilmour in adding that "Eliot used the preface for the first American edition to set the work as a philosophical examination of universal human nature, leading attention away from its homosexual theme" (xxiii-xxiv).

30. "Whereas Barnes's 'deviance' was strictly a matter of literary style, Radclyffe Hall was perceived as both the lesbian in the text and the lesbian writing the text. . . . Because Barnes's legal identity was primarily literary, her novel was not subject in the same way as Hall's to the intersection of literary and lesbian that identifies obscenity" (Gilmour, 623).

31. Gilmour, 614, 623.

32. Gilmour welcomes Donna Gerstenberger's argument that "*Nightwood*'s complexity has been consistently evaded, its thematics puzzled over but its narrative experimentalism neglected," and that Eliot was "the inaugurator of this trend," but she concludes that "the critical response is comprehensible as the proliferation of an interpretation of invisibility, a reproduction of Eliot's early, strategic evasion of the obscene on behalf of *Nightwood*" (Gilmour, 617).

33. Barnes resisted identifying herself and her writing as lesbian. Susan Sniader Lanser reports that Barnes "apparently feared her lesbian admirers would make her famous for *Ladies Almanack* rather than for *Nightwood,* which she considered her great book" and that she didn't "want to make a lot of little lesbians" (Susan Lanser, introduction to *Ladies Almanac* [New York: New York Univ. Press, 1992], xv). Despite disappointment that *Nightwood* was not better known, Barnes "nonetheless seems to have resented the intrusion of critics ('idiots') and disparaged the feminist, lesbian, and gay scholars who were helping to secure her place in modern literature. She claimed to be shocked by the sexual mores of the seventies and insisted repeatedly, 'I'm not a lesbian, I just loved Thelma'" (xvii-xviii).

34. Gilmour, 616.

35. The term "reverse discourse" is Foucault's: "There is no question that the appearance in nineteenth-century psychiatry, jurisprudence, and literature of a whole series of discourses on the species and subspecies of homosexuality, inversion, pederasty, and 'psychic hermaphroditism' made possible a strong advance of social controls into this area of 'perversity'; but it also made possible the formation of a 'reverse' discourse; homosexuality began

to speak on its own behalf, to demand that its legitimacy or 'naturality' be acknowledged, often in the same vocabulary, using the same categories by which it was medically disqualified" (*History of Sexuality,* 101).

36. This essay was originally published as three installments in *Die Literarische Welt* in the late winter of 1929.

37. Benjamin, "Surrealism," 173. Subsequent references to this essay will appear in the text.

38. Peter Demetz observes that Benjamin's essay is "among his most cryptic and important texts" and that "the key concept of the 'profane illumination,' which emerges here to characterize Surrealist vision, suggests Benjamin's own way of unveiling, in his materialist hermeneutics, how history resides in some of the things of the world and institutions of society" (introduction to Walter Benjamin, *Reflections: Essays, Aphorisms, Autobiographical Writings,* vii-xliii, xxx-xxxi). For a detailed study of this concept and its centrality to Benjamin's engagement with Surrealism, see Margaret Cohen, *Profane Illumination: Walter Benjamin and the Paris of Surrealist Revolution* (Berkeley and Los Angeles: Univ. of California Press, 1993).

39. "It is more proper to speak of a trick than a method" (Benjamin, "Surrealism," 182).

40. "What is the program of the bourgeois parties? A bad poem on springtime, filled to bursting with metaphors. . . . And the stock imagery of these poets of the social-democratic associations? Their *gradus ad parnassum*? Optimism. . . . Surrealism has come ever closer to the Communist answer. And that means pessimism all along the line. Absolutely. Mistrust in the fate of literature, mistrust in the fate of freedom, mistrust in the fate of European humanity, but three times mistrust in all reconciliation: between classes, between nations, between individuals" (Benjamin, "Surrealism," 190-91).

41. Robin arrives in Paris from America in 1920. According to André Breton, the Paris twenties hosted that phase of Surrealism known as the "sleeping fits" or "Nap Period"; see Breton, *Nadja,* trans. Richard Howard (New York: Grove Weidenfeld, 1960), 31.

42. That Robin should be reading De Sade in Paris in the early 1920s is not surprising given that De Sade was enjoying a revival among literary circles at that time. Apollinaire spearheaded this revival by publishing a selection of De Sade's work, proclaiming him to be "the freest spirit that ever lived"; see the publisher's preface to *Justine, Phi-*

losophy in the Bedroom and Other Writings, ed. and trans. Richard Seaver and Austryn Wainhouse (New York: Grove Weidenfeld, 1965), xix. Between 1926 and 1935, Maurice Heine edited for publication four of De Sade's manuscripts, including *Les Infortunes de la Vertu* (the original draft of *Justine*) and *Les 120 Journées de Sodome, ou l'Ecole du Libertinage* (the "lost manuscript" of the Bastille). Barnes would also have had access to *La Philosophie dans le boudoir,* which De Sade saw published in his lifetime, and *Correspondance inédit du Marquis de Sade de ses proches et ses familiers* published in 1929 (perhaps the "memoirs" to which *Nightwood* alludes). De Sade was not as fashionable among English modernists, though Swinburne printed an *Apologie de Sade* for private circulation in 1906. *Justine* and *Juliette* were the first of De Sade's writings to be published in translation in the United States, in 1965 and 1968, respectively.

43. The Baron had been "wrecking himself and his peace of mind in an effort to acquaint her with the destiny for which he had chosen her—that she might bear sons who would recognize and honour the past. For without such love, the past as he understood it, would die away from the world" (45).

44. See the first chapter of *Nightwood,* "Bow Down." Barnes initially used *Bow Down* as a working title for the novel; see Paul Bowles, *Without Stopping: An Autobiography* (New York: Ecco Press, 1972), 167.

45. "'Nobility, very well, but what is it?' The Baron started to answer him, but the doctor held up his hand. 'Wait a minute! I know—the few that the many have lied about well and long enough to make them deathless. So you must have a son,' he paused. 'A king is the peasant's actor, who becomes so scandalous that he has to be bowed down to—scandalous in the higher sense naturally. And why must he be bowed down to? Because he has been set apart as the one dog who need not regard the rules of the house, they are so high that they can defame God and foul their rafters! but the people—that's different—they are church-broken, nation-broken—they drink and pray and piss in the one pot. Every man has a house-broken heart except the great man. The people love their church and know it, as a dog knows where he has to conform, and there he returns by instinct. But to the graver permission, the king, the tsar, the emperor, who may relieve themselves on high heaven—to them they bow down only'" (39).

46. "It was the 'paupers' salon for poets, radicals, beggars, artists, and people in love; for Catholics,

Protestants, Brahmins, dabblers in black magic and medicine" (*Nightwood,* 50).

47. "'We give death to a child when we give it a doll—it's the effigy and the shroud,'" Nora confesses to the Doctor. "'When a woman gives it to a woman, it is the life they cannot have, it is their child, sacred and profane; so when I saw that other doll—'" (*Nightwood,* 142).

48. See Hunter et al., 92-134.

49. See Jonathan Dollimore, "From Inversion to Authenticity: *The Well of Loneliness,*" in his *Sexual Dissidence: Augustine to Wilde, Freud to Foucault* (Oxford: Oxford Univ. Press, 1991), 48-52.

50. In 1929, Lawrence published an article on "Pornography and Obscenity" that "was to become a definitive statement for proponents of liberal and libertarian positions on obscenity law and literature" (Hunter, 97). See D. H. Lawrence, "Pornography and Obscenity," in *Phoenix: The Posthumous Papers,* ed. Edward D. McDonald (1936; reprint, Harmondsworth, U.K.: Penguin, 1980), 170-87. Using a duplicitous argument, Lawrence deplores *both* pornographic obscenity *and* obscenity law for their "attempt to insult sex, to dirt on it" (175). He attacks "emancipated bohemians who swank most about sex" for being "still utterly self-conscious and enclosed within the narcissus-masturbation circle" and contends that "the French, who are supposed to be so open about sex, will perhaps be the last to kill the dirty little secret" (184).

51. He calls for an end to the "insult . . . to sex and the human spirit" ("Pornography," 175) and for "freedom from lies . . . the lie of purity and the dirty little secret" (185). Denouncing the "sneaking masturbation pornography of the press, the film, and present-day literature," he celebrates instead "the creative portrayals of the sexual impulse that we have in Bocaccio or the Greek vase-paintings . . . which are necessary for the fulfilment of our consciousness" (187).

52. "Lawrence and [Theodore] Van Velde who, in writing, respectively, *Lady Chatterley's Lover* and *Ideal Marriage: Its Physiology and Technique* (1928) can both be viewed as marriage reformers. . . . Literary erotics provided the means whereby those individuals equipped with the apropriate cultural abilities could construct themselves, through a detailed, continuous problematising of pleasures, as the subjects of their own sexuality" (Hunter et al., 124).

53. Lawrence's literary and didactic recuperation of pornography follows a process that began with the Romantics. "In this process, on the one hand, lit-

erary aesthetics annexed various techniques of pornographic writing and . . . on the other hand, employed a critical and moralising strategy, by submitting the erotic materials to aesthetic interpretation and judgment. In so doing, it transformed the techniques of pornography by combining them with literary devices used in the serious novel. This balancing act depended on the 'dialectical ability of the writer and reader'—that is, the ability to treat autoerotic excitation as a necessary moment of derepression and at the same time to reconcile it with the intellectual and moral imperatives of educative literature" (Hunter et al., 109).

54. "Those who love a city, in its profoundest sense, become the shame of that city, the *détraqués,* the paupers; their good is incommunicable, outwitted, being the rudiment of a life that has developed, as in man's body are found evidences of lost needs. This condition had struck even into Nora's house" (52).

55. Walter Benjamin, "The *Bohème,*" in *Charles Baudelaire: A Lyric Poet in the Era of High Capitalism,* trans. Harry Zohn (1973; reprint, London: Verso, 1983), 11-34.

56. Benjamin, "The *Flâneur*" in *Charles Baudelaire,* 35-66.

57. The last half of *Nightwood*'s first chapter is set in the bohemian circus of an androgynous trapeze artist, the Duchess of Broadback (Frau Mann), where the Baron and the Doctor first meet. (Nora meets Robin at the Denckman circus in New York in the fall of 1923.) Among the actresses, acrobats, and sword-swallowers are classless bands of nomads who, like "Princess Nadja," seize on titles "merely to dazzle the boys in town, to make their public life (and it was all they had) mysterious and perplexing" (*Nightwood,* 11).

58. Benjamin, "The *Flâneur,*" in *Charles Baudelaire,* 56.

59. "The trajectory of Breton's *Nadja* is . . . among the promenade routes that the *Guides to Mysterious Paris* recommends" (Cohen, 3).

60. Breton, 40.

61. Breton originally trained as a physician. His medical studies were interrupted by World War I, during which he "found himself working in the latter half of 1916 at the neuropsychiatric center of Saint-Dizier under Raoul Leroy, one of Charcot's former assistants," from whom he learned of Freud and for whom he felt "'an extra-medical admiration'" (Cohen, 57).

62. Allegedly Barnes's favorite book; see Lanser, xxxi.

63. Gilmour, 616. Gilmour argues that Nora's "effort to articulate a recognizable narrative of lesbianism, so reminiscent of Dora's own circumvented therapeutic project," is repeatedly, persistently thwarted by the Doctor.

64. The Surrealists carried De Sade's incendiary ideas into the twentieth century. "Everything remains to be done, every means must be worth trying, in order to lay waste the ideas of family, country, religion," Breton declares in the *Second Manifesto.* "[The Surrealists] intend to savour fully the profound sorrow, so well acted, with which the bourgeois public—inevitably prepared in their base way to forgive them a few 'youthful' errors—greets the steadfast and unyielding need they display to laugh like savages in the presence of the French flag, to vomit their disgust in the face of every priest, and to level at the breed of 'basic duties' the long-range weapon of sexual cynicism"; quoted in Dawn Ades, afterword to *Investigating Sex: Surrealist Discussions 1928-1932,* ed. José Pierre, trans. Malcolm Imrie (London: Verso, 1992), 192-93. Unfortunately, they fall short of his ideas concerning sodomy; see *Investigating Sex,* 5.

65. "'But,' Nora said, 'I've never thought of the night as a life at all—I've never lived it—why did she?' 'I'm telling you of French nights at the moment,' the Doctor went on, 'and why we all go into them'" (82).

66. *Nightwood* may allude to the distraction that so preoccupies Breton: "I have always, beyond belief, hoped to meet, at night and in a woods, a beautiful naked woman. . . . I adore this situation which of all situation is the one where I am most likely to have lacked a *presence of mind*" (Breton, 39). The Paris night is a prominent motif of Philippe Soupault, one of the founders of the Surrealist movement (see his *Last Nights of Paris,* 1928) and of Robert Desnos, the Surrealist famed for his sleeping fits. Desnos prefaces his *Liberty or Love* (1927) with Rimbaud's "Night-Watch" and includes a chapter on "Depths of the Night." (Barnes's chapters "Nightwatch" and "Watchman, What of the Night" invite comparison.) His chapter "Roll, Drums of Santerre" resurrects De Sade as "hero of love, of generosity and of liberty" with "eyes shining in the darkness, face barely lit but visible in the clear night of Paris," whom Desnos proposes to follow into the abyss; see Robert Desnos, *Liberty or Love,* trans. Terry Hale (London: Atlas, 1993).

67. Dialogism and heterology are different movements in critical materialism that target homogenous systems of social domination. Like Benjamin, Bataille locates revolutionary forces in the detritus of

capitalism's imperialist progress and launches an anti-Hegelian dialectic: "Above all, heterology is opposed to any homogeneous representation of the world, in other words, to any philosophical system. The goal of such representations is always the deprivation of our universe's sources of excitation and the development of a servile human species, fit only for the fabrication, radical consumption, and conservation of products. But the intellectual process automatically limits itself by producing of its own accord its own waste products, thus liberating in a disordered way the heterogeneous excremental element. Heterology is restricted to taking up again, consciously and resolutely, this terminal process, which up to now has been seen as the abortion and the shame of human thought" (Georges Bataille, "The Use Value of D. A. F. De Sade," in *Visions of Excess: Selected Writings, 1927-1939,* ed. Allan Stoekl, trans. Allan Stoekl et al. (Minneapolis: Univ. of Minnesota Press, 1985), 91-104, 96.

68. De Sade, "Philosophy in the Bedroom," *Justine, Philosophy in the Bedroom, and Other Writings,* 276.

69. De Sade, 322.

70. The Doctor expounds on this point in a passage Eliot deleted that tells the story of his obscenity trial. He recalls "the night I popped Tiny out to relieve him of his drinking, when something with dark hands closed over him as if to strangle the life's breath out of him and suddenly the other, less pleasing hand, the hand of the law, was on my shoulder and I was hurled into jail, into Marie Antoinette's very cell" (Barnes, *Nightwood: The Original Version and Related Drafts,* 26). Caught in a double-vise, the doctor is groped by the sodomite's "dark hands" only to be gripped by the "less pleasing" strong-arm of the law which he likens to the heavy-handed sector of Marat's revolutionary rearguard; his tiny, natural, nobility being flung into a prison fit for a queen.

71. An earlier draft of this passage reads: "*Look for the girls also, in the toilets of the night, and you will find them kneeling in that great* second *confessional,* the one the Catholic church forgot—over the door "Dames," a girl standing before her, her skirts flung back one on one, while between the columns the handsome head of the girl made boy by God, bends back, the posture of that head volts forth the difference between one woman and another—crying softly between tongues, *the terrible excommunication* of the toilet" (*Nightwood: The Original Version and Related Drafts,* 262 [deletions in roman]). Barnes cuts the butch-femme scenography and heightens the drama of profanation. It is no less clear in the final version that it is

the women's toilet "*Dames,*" not the *Notre Dame,* where this nocturnal love is "confessed," and that the mode of confession, "crying between tongues," is cunnilingus. What is even more clear is that it is the women themselves who, excommunicated first by the Church and again by progressive, post-Revolutionary society, damn and betray each other with brute, irredeemable pleasure.

72. De Sade, 285.

73. De Sade, 219.

74. The word "gay" appears near the end of the dialogue between Nora and the Doctor. Nora uses it in recalling one of the few verbal exchanges she has had with Robin. But in wishing "'everyone to be gay, gay'" except Nora, thus "driving [Nora] insane with misery and fright" (155), Robin wields the word vindictively, acting out a ferocious *ressentiment.*

Margaret Bockting (essay date December 2000)

SOURCE: Bockting, Margaret. "Satire and Romanticism in the Work of Djuna Barnes." *CLA Journal* 44, no. 2 (December 2000): 204-30.

[*In the following essay, Bockting explores Barnes's creation of "a dialogue between two discourses," that of satire and that of romanticism, in her early works of journalism and her novels* Ryder *and* Nightwood.]

"You made a beautiful fable, then put Voltaire to bed with it," Matthew O'Connor tells Nora Flood in *Nightwood.*[1] Combining seemingly discordant discourses is a consistent feature of Djuna Barnes's prose style throughout her career. In her early newspaper articles, her best-seller *Ryder,* and her later, more famous novel *Nightwood,* she sets up dialogues between different points of view, particularly the satirical and the Romantic. As Sherrill Grace remarks, close attention to the newspaper pieces yield a better understanding of Barnes's narrative techniques.[2] Carl Herzig notes that Barnes's journalism, like her fiction, is characterized by a tension between sensuous description and abstract commentary. Barbara Green and Nancy Levine point out, in Barnes's articles, a mixing of modes and an interplay between the positions of participant and spectator, elements that Louis Kannenstine and Marie Ponsot discern in *Ryder* and that Charles Baxter and Alan Singer perceive in *Nightwood.*[3] What repeatedly holds these elements together, though, in the journalism and the novels, is the counterpoint between satire and Romanticism.

In her interview with David Belasco[4] and her articles on local New York attractions and popular entertainment, Barnes satirizes typical journalistic expectations and offers Romantic flights of imagination, creating a dialogue between two discourses—one that fetishizes data and another that values personal memory, psychological association, and stylistic embellishment. She dramatizes the tension between her official task of discovering previously unknown facts about famous figures and her own self-consciousness about intruding on personal privacy. Not content with simply satirizing social attitudes and behaviors, she sometimes waxes nostalgic about the "simple" or "vanishing" pleasures that she discovers by diverging from her prescribed responsibilities as a reporter. Her journalism, in other words, reveals her attempt to succeed as a reporter (for this was her source of income) and at the same time re-script the role of journalist, making it more self-reflective and flexible.

For instance, the narrator of **"David Belasco Dreams"** (1916) comments self-consciously on the journalistic conventions that require her to disregard individual predilections or the mood of the moment if either might interfere with the relentless pursuit of information. When Belasco emerges from "the inner room of the studio," she decides that to ask him "idiotic questions about the stage and the stars that he had made, as though he were nothing more nor less than a profitable patch of sky," would be "an unpardonable error" (187-88). In an earlier interview, facing a similar dilemma about how to respect privacy, she mocks the expectations of sensationalist journalism: "It is the usual and natural thing, the cornering of a man: the pelting with impertinent questions, of going away and telling the world. . . ."[5]

Her pronounced anxiety about the journalist's job is related to a cultural climate that had, since the late nineteenth century, made privacy an issue of intense debate. By the early twentieth century, this debate focused on the threat to "personality and feelings" posed by Kodak cameras, advertising practices, and sensationalist journalism.[6] Assuming the high value of privacy, Barnes foregrounds her discomfort concerning the moral ambiguity of her position. When she first encounters Belasco, she perceives him as

> no longer just the public man that men of genius must inevitably be, but that more inaccessible thing—the hermit of that same publicity. One hides behind the hat with which one bows to the world. It is through these things that we come by our solitude at all.
>
> (187-88)

She romanticizes privacy as something so endangered that is must be guarded or hidden, and she presents herself, paradoxically, as an interviewer determined to protect his privacy while at the same time revealing to the public a glimpse of the "real" (i.e., genuine or authentic) personality of her subject. She asks readers to accept her story as a respectful disclosure of an individual's personal ideas, feelings, opinions. In other words, she does not pry into his private life, but she evokes a sense of his temperament.

Using the description of material objects, not to provide backdrop for the conversation but as manifestation of the producer-playwright's "inner" life, she notes,

> [I]n this studio there are almost too many beautiful things—a room overcrowded with emotion, as a heart is overcrowded with heartbeats, . . . as Belasco's brain is with new emotions.
>
> (188)

As the interview progresses, it becomes a catalogue of Barnes's and Belasco's musings on the significance of his various antiques and artifacts. The portrait that emerges eschews the purely literal. Barnes insists on the subjectivity of both interviewer and subject, and she implies that subjective experiences, rather than supposedly objective "facts," constitute what is worth reporting. (This, of course, leads to the omission of certain kinds of observations. For instance, neither Belasco nor Barnes cares to discuss the fact that he participates in and benefits from the commerce, excitement, and haste that he so deplores, even though box office success is what enables him to continue practicing the arts of playwrighting, directing, and producing, just as it allows him to purchase the rare objects that constitute his opulent private sanctuary.)

At the end of the article, Barnes remarks that only after having spent an hour with her does Belasco put himself "in the attitude of a man who is going to be interviewed" (198). At this point she describes her own assumption of the role of newspaper reporter: "'Oh, yes,' I said, as if remembering also, 'I came to ask you about the stars you have made . . .'" (198). The phrase "as if" suggests that they have never actually forgotten their professional identities. In spite of the kindred spirit that they have found in one another, these figures have met, the framing scenes remind us, because they both can earn their livings by entertaining the public. Nevertheless, their meditative comments on Belasco's religious icons and ancient armaments create a world seemingly remote from the "cold, commonplace day" (198) of a famous man faced with a woman trying to make money by writing about him. As they drift through antique-cluttered rooms, they sound less like interviewer and interviewee than like comrades who share a deep appreciation for the past and a keen sympathy for the plight of the artist in a technological age. At one point he even claims that the proliferation of lunch counters and the existence of rapid transportation (i.e., fast food, automobiles, and the elevated train) have precluded America's chance for poetic development:

> "A man who might otherwise be a thinking man, rushes into lunch, grabs a sandwich, a glass of milk, a piece of pie, and presto—he has killed a Hamlet. . . . Do you think that it is simply accident that has made all the great names of Europe 'loungers,' as we call them?"
>
> (195)

Through the dialogue of the interviewer and her subject, Barnes's article idealizes the past and the exotic while satirizing both the frantic pace of modern life and the public's craving for sensational disclosure.

"David Belasco Dreams" alludes to an investigative style of reporting only to reject it. As Nancy Levine notes, however, Barnes, in most of her articles, fulfills the reporter's "obligation to tell [who,] how, when, and where," though supplementing those elements with "marginal, concealed" details that allow her "to respond" to the "psychological environment."[7] Furthermore, Barnes's approach shares the features that Margaret Higonnet has attributed to feminist history: it includes not only the "exceptional, marked event," which takes place in public or "institutionally defined arenas," but also the "landscape of the mind" and the "interplay of memory and social fictions."[8] Barnes, though, does more than just sustain both documentary and poetic sensibilities. In **"Three Days Out"** and in two articles on Coney Island and two on New York City, she simultaneously satirizes popular, supposedly objective discourses and valorizes associational, subjective perspectives.

In **"Three Days Out"** (1917), Barnes accompanies members of a New York drama company to a town where they perform an unnamed play. She emphasizes that the actors' lives are characterized by monotony, routine, and exhaustion: they rehearse and then perform the same scenes over and over again; repeatedly, they pack and unpack, ride trains, put on and remove makeup, and find yet "another hotel passable enough for three days' existence."[9] The actors' schedules allow them almost no rest and little time or inclination for thinking or for venturing away from theater or hotel.

In addition to exposing and regretting the unceasing demands of an actor's life, she faults the play and the playwright's ideas, and she mocks the director's style, disparaging all of them for their allegiance to "the soul of everything American, the hurry, the ostentation and the vulgarity." During a rehearsal of this melodrama about the New York "fast set," the director insists that a particular scene must move rapidly: "please remember," he says, "that a man can be killed twice as quick as that in these days. Snap it up a bit, snap it up!"

Counterpointing this satire is Barnes's amused but admiring characterization of her friend Helen Wesley. Barnes's use of odd juxtapositions and numerous references to the past make this woman appear both enigmatic and anachronistic. She describes Helen as

> a woman who might have been ten or ten hundred, but who had made the irrevocable mistake of being but thirty odd, a woman who might have enjoyed life on a steady, immaculate and tidy plane, but who had lapsed

into that dingy delicacy observed in ancient prints. A woman like the resurrected spindle of a mid-Victorian chair, a woman with the soul of a Cleopatra and the yearnings of a George Eliot, who, lounging among yellow art-craft cushions, yearned for the melancholy plushes and austere carvings of an age long gone.

Here the figure of Helen embodies cyclical time: she is the most recent version of particular recurrent types (Cleopatras and George Eliots); she signifies the resurrection of the past. The narrator of **"Three Days Out"** obviously prefers Helen's reflectiveness and evocation of the past to the thoughtless haste which she attributes to the modern world and to the modern view of life epitomized in the play.

Barnes's alienation (from "the hurry, the ostentation and the vulgarity" of the play and the "the monotony" of the actors' existence) persuades her to leave hotel and theater and to explore a religious encampment at Ocean Grove. In this unpretentious place, she encounters the re-enactment of an old ritual and becomes attentive to, rather than distracted from, time and mortality. At this point in the article, she highlights sensuous experience and suspends the disillusioned, critical tone that she had used earlier. When she peers through a crack into an auditorium, she sees "small unreal children skipping about a Maypole. . . . They turned and danced, their vague, small faces coming around and disappearing again in a mist of floating hair." The change in tone, the visionary quality of the images, and a final image of old couples being helped into chairs make the Ocean Grove episode resemble a Romantic moment of transport from what Keats describes as "the weariness, the fever, and the fret" of modern commerce, to the realm of poetry and imagination, where one may contemplate "shapes of delight, of mystery, and fear" ("Ode to a Nightingale" line 23, "Sleep and Poetry" line 1).[10] Like the earlier passages that establish Helen's affinity with the past, the images of Ocean Grove both counter the unnamed playwright's vision of life and mark a detour from the journalistic enterprise of reporting on a drama company's latest tour.

Similarly, in two articles on Coney Island, Barnes fulfills her obligation to report on major features of the amusement parks, but seems more inclined to create images of the past and of the ordinary that represent refuge from the hectic pace and sensationalism of modern entertainment as personified by park rides and gimmicks. **"If Noise Were Forbidden at Coney Island, a Lot of People Would Lose Their Jobs"** (1914) suggests that "perhaps the best of Coney is not its showy side," but "that little dim, ivy-grown beer garden with its sedate squares of cheese . . . and the papa and mama eating a quiet lunch from an egg basket."[11] In **"Surcease in Hurry and Whirl—On the Restless Surf at Coney"** (1917), "the sound of a dance" leads her to peer "into the darkness of a long shed" where "an old man [is] executing an Irish jig" and "faces . . . dip in and emerge from foaming mugs of beer." Compared to the main attractions, this scene "is less pretentious, it is even dirty, but it is not afraid to be natural."[12] Perceived unnaturalness or gimmickry (the emphasis on size, mechanism, and distortion) alienates this persona from the most modern parts of Coney, while relatively familiar subjects (people eating and drinking) reassure and comfort her.

Like the Coney Island articles and **"Three Days Out,"** **"Seeing New York with the Soldiers"** (1918) also creates an interplay between competing perspectives—one that relishes data and another that prefers the psychological and poetic. To fulfill the project of reporting the contents and describing the route of a bus tour, she quotes the tour guide (or "'educated lecturer'")[13] whom she repeatedly refers to as "the megaphone man." His identifications of places and his terse bits of historical and factual information appear throughout the article in brief flashes, almost as narrative going on in the background; meanwhile, several rather different vignettes engage most of the reader's attention: Barnes counterpoints the standardized tour guide with impressionistic rendering, personal anecdote, fabrication, and memory.

The impressionistic approach begins early in the article as Barnes selects various details about the tourists on the bus and about the scents, sounds, and sights that pass the moving window. While gathering these impressions, she adds that the lecturer "began shouting: 'On the near left-hand corner, midway of the block, you see the spot where Hoimen Rosenthal was murdered'" (325). As the bus moves through town, he points out "'the biggest church in New York taking up four city blocks and holding thirty-six hundred praise-givers'" (326), "'the house with solid onyx steps'" (327), "'the highest point in the elevated tracks, called Dead Man's Curve'" (331), and similar sites. At the end of the tour, advertising "another trip" available to the public, he recommends seeing "'the Bowery, with its endless procession of human wrecks, old and young'" (334).

The quotations from the megaphone man indicate that the tour style (and news reporting style?) call for "objective" precision regarding extraordinary or sensational things and events (murder, wealth, danger), a stance that Barnes parodies again in a later work, **"On Returning from Abroad"** (1928):

> The rubbish in the streets and along the gutters spoke of a greater, better descent. Cigarette butts are tossed from casements the world over . . . , but can any country on earth point to a single butt that has fallen as far, as, say this, from the roof of the Woolworth building? It can not.[14]

In **"Seeing New York with the Soldiers,"** she juxtaposes the tour-guide/advertising style with the expression of a sensibility interested in the significance of small and familiar details and in the play of memory and imagination. Instead of displaying monumental or shocking items, such passages focus on ordinary people and activities. Including the megaphone man's "informative" style, however, enables Barnes to fulfill the newspaper reporter's role while at the same time managing to assume a poetic persona.

This double perspective becomes particularly evident when she juxtaposes the tour guide's statistics about the size of the church (that holds "'thirty-six hundred praise-givers'" (326)) with her own description of its mysterious atmosphere:

> The great doors were ajar. A woman in a red skirt and plume stood in its shadow. Far away a stained-glass window shed little drops of holy colors upon the drab backs of supplicants. For a moment before we were gone, the white hands of some statue reached out of the darkness, folded, lifted.
>
> (326)

In addition to the interplay between megaphoned data and poetic impressions, the article includes a contrast between the lecturer's perspective and that of a story Barnes elicits from a French officer on the bus. By temporarily suspending references to the tour, she immerses the reader in an extended fabrication as the French officer answers her query, "'What do you think of New York?'" After carefully describing what he once saw through an Eleventh Street window, he surmises, "'Now, Balzac would have known what to do with that,'" and then proceeds to weave a story based on the setting and its two figures (328-29).

While the tourists listen to the megaphone man and gape at New York sights, Barnes becomes the Frenchman's audience. He not only proposes that these figures are mother and son, but that she must pawn her possessions to appease her son's desire to have "'a manner'" which "'he cannot have'" without "'sufficient money in his pockets'" (329). His account is very suggestive: it leaves much unsaid, many things open to speculation. Is the son profligate or simply a dilettante or perhaps an artist? Why must he ask his mother for money? Why does he sleep until she gives him the money and leave immediately afterward?

Moreover, the Frenchman self-consciously draws attention to his act of inventing these characters and their private lives. As he begins his interpretation, he uses the word "'probably'" three times, thus sounding self-conscious about the fact that he is guessing, surmising. At the end of his story, he asks Barnes, "'Is that not it?'"—suggesting that his audience's participation will grant credibility to his interpretation (329-30). The closing question also provides a transition from the story of the anonymous figures on Eleventh Street, back to the tour which, seemingly coincidentally, at this very moment enters an exchange between lecturer and soldiers about another son and mother (in this case Hetty Green, once reputedly the wealthiest woman in America). No story develops, however, for the megaphone man continues his job of labeling the buildings as they pass.

By juxtaposing the tour-guide's narrow devotion to data with the Frenchman's interest in psychological import, Barnes indicates her disenchantment with the journalistic enterprise of **"Seeing New York with the Soldiers."** The soldiers, she says, do not hear her (when she turns to them after speaking to the Canadians and the French officer) because they are absorbed in "looking at the home of the famous, dead Hetty" (330). To see the City with them would be to glance hurriedly at whatever the megaphone man designates, but to miss the Frenchman's attempt to emulate Balzac. She both fulfills her task, however, and, like the Romantic, offers "'imaginative creation'" as an alternative to and criticism of "rationalist or empiricist" discourse.[15]

She more overtly engages in revising and refuting "cultural and discursive frameworks"[16] in **"There's Something Besides the Cocktail in the Bronx"** (1919). Instead of including an alter ego such as the Frenchman, she herself assumes the role of oppositional identity in relation to an anonymous male figure who strongly resembles the "educated lecturer" of **"Seeing New York."** This male figure, who harps on the reporter's obligation to amass facts and omit personal associations, represents "the existing structure of authority"[17] that Barnes challenges.

The article's opening lines mock "'fact absorbers'" as those who dole "'out statements that it [the Bronx] is sixty-four miles square and that it is the city of babies.'"[18] Yet awareness that this purely "objective" perspective may be expected of her makes Barnes self-conscious about including her personal memories. After each brief recollection, she wonders if it helps establish the appropriate or acceptable meaning of the Bronx. Later, a "fact absorber" appears in person. He denies the legitimacy of her memories. According to him, personal associations should not be part of the picture of the Bronx. He says that only "facts" are relevant (350-52).

The narrator, however, adopts a Romantic persona. She describes how she once was delighted by the quaint personalities and antics of "some suburban society of bug hunters" whom she had accompanied from the Bronx Botanical Gardens to Clason Point (347-49). She also recalls that when she "was quite young," she had "sneaked into Poe's house," where, finding a shoe in the attic, she had "shuddered with unbecoming pleasure, thinking, This is the shoe of that man who made my brother scream in his sleep last night" (349).

In contrast to the Romantic persona, which Barnes has adopted, the man who accompanies her seems Utilitarian. He authoritatively insists (without a trace of the uncertainty that Barnes admits regarding *her* vision) that the Bronx is properly defined as "'the 'Hub'" or "'the great transfer point'" (350). As he and the narrator converse, a dialectic occurs between this Advocate of Hard Facts and the Romantic Idealist (a dialectic that resembles the one between tour guide and French officer in **"Seeing New York"**). To him Barnes assigns all the lines about the modern, industrialized, technologized, fast-paced, mass-entertainment-oriented, urban environment. He believes that she should give the newspaper audience the names, numbers, sizes, and precise locations of places, but not any of the associations which they might evoke for someone who once lived there. He explains that to depict the Bronx properly, one must catalogue the bridges, theaters, and civic centers. Appearing after Barnes's engaging personal memories, his lists seem dull; his information lacks the emotional reverberation and psychological suggestiveness of her stories. Eventually she refuses the self-righteous man's advice that she "'must not overlook the banks'" and "'must write something about schools—about the Hall of Fame'" (351-52). By including his voice and message as well as her own, she manages to have it both ways—to provide a standardized, factual report as well as a series of Romantic meditations—and, in addition, to display a debate between a poetic narrator and a data monger.

Despite the self-doubt expressed early in the article, Barnes allows herself (as narrator) a partial victory in the struggle between perspectives. While the Romantic is only slightly susceptible to advice from the information junkie, he, though "scornful" of the personal angle, unwittingly becomes caught up in a tale she weaves about a beautiful, melancholy girl brought up in a convent school. When she reaches the point of saying that she would gaze at the school when her friend was "'no longer there,'" he wonders, "in an awed voice," "'Where was she?'" (352). Thus Barnes implies that he temporarily forgets his disapproval of story-telling. (This scene resembles the situation that occurs in *Ryder* (1928) when Wendell, skeptical about Molly's understanding of the Bible, becomes so entranced by her story that, "forgetting himself," he eagerly asks how Jonah enticed the Hound of Heaven to earth.[19]) Like the Frenchman's narrative (in **"Seeing New York with the Soldiers"**), and like Barnes's escape to Ocean Grove or her vision of Helen as nymph (in **"Three Days Out"**), the memories included in **"The Bronx"** resist the fact-fetishizing perspective which she, as journalist, ostensibly must (and does) provide.

Building on strategies which she had developed in her earlier work, in *Ryder* Barnes satirizes both religious and secular discourses about reality and meaning.[20] By mimicking Biblical language and, at the same time, subverting Christian dogma, **Ryder** provides a feminist critique of "both the scribes of Genesis and the pontificate" of Paul the Apostle.[21] Sheryl Stevenson and Marie Ponsot concur that this novel incorporates and mocks a variety of stylistic and generic forms. Cheryl Plumb adds that the plot reveals "the futility of [Wendell] Ryder's procreative philosophy as a means of justifying his existence."[22]

Although the members of the Ryder family are central to the plot, a figure outside the family most effectively mocks patriarch Wendell Ryder's profligacy and disregards his egotistical claims to authority. This female character, Molly Dance, accepts motherhood with neither the sentimental fervor which Wendell intends to inspire in women nor the dread which his wife Amelia expresses, but rather with nonchalance. Contentedly self-sufficient, she remains unwed and claims that she cannot be sure of the identity of the father (or fathers) of her ten children. Furthermore, like Elizabeth Cady Stanton (an admired acquaintance of Barnes's grandmother), Molly has the audacity to revise the Scriptures that underpin the oppression of women.

The historical figure, Stanton, launched a "sustained ideological assault on religious orthodoxy" in the 1890s.[23] With the help of twenty-three women (including three ordained ministers), she compiled *The Woman's Bible,* in which some chapters are "presented as proof that Scripture was sexist; others to show that, if reinterpreted, men and women were indeed equals in the Bible."[24] Like *The Woman's Bible,* Molly's stories offer a feminist reimagining of scripture. Her creation myth begins not in the the Garden of Eden nor with a divine command for light, but with water and a whale. The "First Man" in her story is not Adam but Jonah, who is shaped not from dust or clay nor by the hand of God, but comes from a womb-like space—out of a whale's mouth.[25] The hand of God, the voice of God—indeed any evidence of Him—is conspicuously absent from the opening section of Molly's account. When the first reference to deity finally does appear, it is indirect: "'Jonah had the wick of the Lord running in the midst of him like a candle.'" (256).

Molly proceeds to depict, not the Old Testament Yahweh, but a stagehand or juggler: "'God [was] tossing up the sun every minute, which was a day, and it falling back again, which was a night, because things moved swiftly, that the nations might get started'" (256). Her version of Genesis focuses not on a Superior Being's rules and judgments, but on an angel's delivery of land, Jonah's experiences, the birth of poetry, and the arrival of animals—all of which occur in an unorthodox manner (though perhaps not in a manner any more fantastic than some Biblical events, for, as Stanton points out, scripture "is full of contradictions, absurdities and impossibilities" (213)).

The appeal of Molly's story, however, lies not only in its eclectic quality, but also in her elaborate description of Jonah, a symbolic portrait in which she mingles allusions to evolutionary theory with emblems associated with Noah, Christ, and mermen:

> ". . . and he was a sight, for he was the First Man, all decked out in olive branches and briars, and a crown of thorns, and his underneath all scaled, for everything was fish in that time."
>
> (255)

Molly's audience, Wendell Ryder, who at first listens with a condescending attitude, becomes intrigued by Jonah's dilemma—how to catch the Hound of Heaven:

> "And did he [snare the Hound]?" asked Wendell eagerly, forgetting himself.
>
> "How is it that you do not know?" cried Molly, "for wasn't it by the discovery of the miracle of fire?"
>
> (258)

Wendell's self-forgetfulness is significant because it is highly uncharacteristic of him. Throughout the novel, he repeatedly assumes his own self-importance and rarely questions the rightness or righteousness of his values and actions. In confronting Molly, he takes the stance of authority or paternalism; he expresses bewildered concern about (what he sees as) the inaccuracy and disorder of her thoughts (254-55, 260). To Wendell, she is in error, and his own knowledge is irrefutably the correct and only knowledge. Molly has a rather different notion of epistemology. Although like him "she could not be got, on any account, to see what was wrong with her information," unlike him "she would have been the last to cry . . . down" someone else's account simply because it did not match her own (254). She points out that narratives are not disinterested: while acknowledging that "'what you think is fine,'" she also knows that "'what I think is fine, and better suited to my purpose'" (254).

Her respect for subjectivity (her own and others') enables her to remain undaunted by Wendell's judgmental attitude. For a moment she even eludes his critical perspective and engages his curiosity. As her tale progresses, however, he notices that she has not introduced the problem of "original sin," which, in the Biblical account, was Eve's fault. In response, and claiming midwife Mary Flynn as her dependable source (for Mary "'was right up to the ears in vision'"), Molly avers that "'the original sin was not a woman's'" (259). Because this is not the story he approves (i.e., the male-authored/authorized story), Wendell dismisses the narrative as well as the story-teller, exclaiming, "'You are all manners of mixed up in all things! . . . You are as mixed as a pack of cards!'" (260). Disliking her revision, he labels it as further evidence of her failure to think properly. In fact, he objects not only to Molly's subjectivity in particular, but to any female subjectivity that does not complement man's. He wants to know how "'a man'" is "'to have pride of his ways in you, when he cannot find them ten minutes later?'" (260). His question assumes that woman's purpose is to bolster man's sense of self-worth by mirroring and revering him, his ideas, and his beliefs; she is not supposed to think for herself nor to deviate nor dissent.

Molly parodies the modes and materials of conventional narratives, refutes scriptural definitions of "woman," and mocks masculine self-importance. In addition, her adoption of a non-condemning, sometimes satirical, sometimes romanticizing subject position in relation to everything and everyone—including dog thieves and blasphemous children (253)—and her "liking" for "all things, of all kinds, all at once, in the same place" (252) suggest, albeit through extreme example, the possibility of alternatives to typical, restrictive conceptions of order and beauty. Through the hyperbolic figure of Molly Dance, Barnes again attempts what she had accomplished in her articles and interviews: through satire and Romanticism, to challenge accepted notions of what constitutes knowledge.

Molly Dance is a descendent of the feminist Romantic of the articles: the latter contends with authoritarian, "modern" males while the former confounds the egotistical patriarch, Wendell Ryder. Which figure carries on this role in *Nightwood*? Actually, three figures in Barnes's last novel perform the roles of satirist and Romantic: the third-person narrator, Doctor Matthew O'Connor, and Nora Flood. The third-person narrator satirizes Christian dogma regarding Jews and romanticizes the relationship between Matthew O'Connor and Felix Volkbein. O'Connor had already appeared in *Ryder,* where he resembles Molly Dance in his garrulity and iconoclasm. In *Nightwood* he continues to take liberties with scripture, engage in inventive digression, and express sympathy for animals. He also romanticizes and satirizes himself as well as the relationship between Nora Flood and Robin Vote. The Romantic persona of her early articles prefigures Nora. Diane Chisolm's description of Nora—as one who cultivates "romantic illusions" and regrets "modernity's destruction of past forms of life" (183-84)—applies perfectly to the narrators of **"There's Something Besides the Cocktail in the Bronx," "David Belasco Dreams," "Seeing New York with the Soldiers," "Three Days Out,"** and the articles on Coney Island. Nora becomes the narrator of "a lover's discourse" ("a beautiful fable") about herself as Robin's madonna and savior, and then discloses and mocks Robin's and her own selfishness (puts Voltaire to bed with the beautiful fable).

Paying attention to the continuity of the satirical tone in Barnes's work, from her early journalism through *Nightwood,* may help readers address questions raised by

critics such as Meryl Altman and Karen Kaivola, who suggest that the narrator of this novel essentializes Jewishness and condones ethnic prejudice and discrimination.[26] As Jane Marcus and Julie Abraham observe, however, "the story of [the Jewish characters] Felix Volkbein [and his father] functions as a paradigm of Barnes's understanding of the relation of the powerless" to the records of the "'high and mighty'"[27]; the novel is engaged in a struggle with normative versions of history and identity.[28]

In other words, the narrator satirizes the arrogance of those who appropriate Jewish culture to validate Christianity:

> It takes a Christian, standing eternally in the Jew's salvation, to blame himself and to bring up from that depth charming and fantastic superstitions through which the slowly and tirelessly milling Jew once more becomes the "collector" of his own past. His undoing is never profitable until some *goy* has put it back into such shape that it can again be offered as a "sign." A Jew's undoing is never his own, it is God's; his rehabilitation is never his own, it is a Christian's. The Christian traffic in retribution has made the Jew's history a commodity; it is the medium through which he receives, at the necessary moment, the serum of his own past that he may offer it again as his blood.
>
> (*NW* [*Nightwood*] 10)

The tone of the prose parodies the languages of religious and eugenic discourses, satirizing the mentality that treats Jewish history as a commodity that can be made part of a commerce controlled by the Christian production and marketing of meaning(s). Just as Molly, in *Ryder,* mocks biblical claims about the Creation and Fall of Man, so the narrator of *Nightwood* satirizes Christian claims regarding the "true" meaning of events depicted in the Old Testament, and ridicules Christian insistence that the stories of Abraham, Jonah, and Moses have significance only insomuch as they prefigure the story of Christ and Christian salvation. In a telling reversal of the Christian accusation that Jews were responsible for Christ's death, *Nightwood* asserts that Christianity has been responsible for the "crucifixion" of Jewish ideas, sacrificing them for its own ends (*NW* 10). Christianity assimilates the Old Testament by insisting that it is intelligible solely as a precursor to the New Testament. Labeling this process exploitative, referring to it as "the Christian traffic in retribution" (*NW* 10), the narrator indicts the traffickers for their failure to respect difference, for their self-gratifying sense of entitlement, and for their self-serving distortion of the meaning of Judaism and Jewishness. How, then, can Altman wonder if the narrator fails to disapprove of a situation in which "Jewish culture is doomed to be sold and resold"?[29]

And why, then, does Kaivola argue that *Nightwood* uses Jews to represent a "degeneration" that is "figured as primitive and that culminates with the younger

Guido," Felix's son (*NW* 180)? Actually, the Baron's child (who is one quarter Jewish and never referred to as a Jew) is linked more closely to the representation of Robin (who is not Jewish) than to any other character: Guido's neck reminds Felix of his former wife (*NW* 91); the Baron claims that "'she [Robin] is with me in Guido, they are inseparable'" (*NW* 99); and throughout the chapter "Where the Tree Falls," Felix repeatedly associates mother and son with one another. Donna Gerstenberger also disregards the fact that throughout Barnes's short stories, children are for the most part depicted as sickly: "physically weak or suffering some kind of dementia," they are "not so distant cousins to Guido."[30] Barnes repeatedly rejects—in *Ryder*, "Cassation," "Aller et Retour," "Oscar," "Spillway," and "Smoke"—popular, sentimental representations of children, childhood, and parenting. Guido represents a continuation of this pattern, not an attempt to construe Jewishness as primitive or degenerate.

Kaivola, like Altman, disregards the sardonic tone used to describe Christian arrogance and self-righteousness. When Felix's father, the elder Guido, envisions the past, he sees

> ladies of noble birth, sitting upon spines too refined for rest, [who] arose from their seats, and, with the red-gowned cardinals and the *Monsignori*, applauded with that cold yet hysterical abandon of a people that is at once unjust and happy, the very Pope himself shaken down from his hold on heaven with the laughter of a man who forgoes his angels that he may recapture the beast.
>
> (*NW* 4)

Kaivola thinks that the phrase "hold on Heaven" "inscribes a privileging of Christianity,"[31] but the phrase is sarcastic: it appears in the same sentence that labels the Christian audience "unjust" and describes their mental state as one of "cold yet hysterical abandon." In this context, reference to a pope's "hold on heaven" parodies the notion of papal infallibility, mocks and denounces Catholicism's claim to be the only true religion. This narrator neither admires nor condones, much less privileges the Christians' attitude or behavior.

Whereas she uses satire in the first part of the novel and in the account of Felix and Robin,[32] in the depiction of the relationship between Felix and Matthew, Barnes employs a Romantic discourse (which she sustains, with modifications, in the story of Robin and Nora). (This is not to say that there is no humor in these accounts.) Several passages establish the Baron's strong emotional response to Matthew. When they first meet at Count Altamonte's party, the doctor's description of a tattooed male body and his reference to the "'damp rosy mouths'" of Austrian schoolboys (*NW* 15) make Felix uncomfortable. The host's long absence and Matthew's suggestive remarks provoke the Baron to "uncontrol-lable laughter," which "he was never able to explain to himself," and to "a notion that he was doing . . . something much worse than laughing" (*NW* 16). At one point he is "waving his arms in distress and saying 'Please, please!' staring at the floor, feeling deeply embarrassed to find himself doing so" (*NW* 16). Besides creating for readers an obscurity that reflects Felix's own uncertainty, this passage establishes that he is ashamed to find himself overcome by emotion. Emotional excess or lack of control is generally associated with the feminine; his "distress" at the party registers his fear of feminization and prefigures his upcoming struggle with his feelings for the doctor.

After establishing that the Baron next meets O'Connor in Paris and accompanies him to a bar, the narrator describes Felix's imaginative interpretations of the doctor's verbal and physical gestures:

> Felix thought to himself that undoubtedly the doctor was a great liar, but a valuable liar. His fabrications seemed to be the framework of a forgotten but imposing plan; some condition of life of which he was the sole surviving retainer. His manner was that of a servant of a defunct noble family, whose movements recall, though in a degraded form, those of a late master.
>
> (*NW* 31)

By envisioning O'Connor as a mystical link to the past (which Felix reveres), the Baron rationalizes/explains his desire to be in the company of one whom he had at first regarded simply as a "volatile person who called himself a doctor" (*NW* 16).

The narrator describes Felix's ongoing attempt to accept his attachment to O'Connor as the process "by which what we must love is made into what we can love" (*NW* 36). The narrator underlines the Baron's initial innocence/ignorance regarding the personal significance of his friendship with O'Connor and emphasizes the dilemma that Felix's love and denial create for the doctor: "Felix was astonished to find that the most touching flowers laid on the altar he had raised to his imagination were placed there by the people of the underworld, and that the reddest was to be the rose of the doctor" (*NW* 31). This final phrase—"the rose of the doctor"—concludes a long sentence devoted primarily to an extended metaphor that compares the Baron's "astonishment" to the way "the *corsage* of a woman is made suddenly martial and sorrowful by the rose thrust among the more decorous blooms by the hand of a lover suffering the violence of the overlapping of the permission to bestow a last embrace, and its withdrawal" (*NW* 31). By linking O'Connor with an anonymous lover caught in the paradoxical condition of being granted and denied permission to embrace his beloved, the metaphor offers a figurative image of the doctor's position in relation to Felix: he both can and cannot declare his love. O'Connor is caught in the lover's role—as created in and through Romantic literary convention; thus he resembles Cyrano de Bergerac, who simultaneously conceals and reveals his love for Roxanne, or Heloise, who feels compelled to repress and express her desire for Abelard.

As Roland Barthes remarks in *A Lover's Discourse,* "to impose upon . . . passion the mask of discretion: this is a strictly heroic value." Yet "to hide passion totally . . . is inconceivable: not because the human subject is too weak," but because passion is "made to be seen: the hiding must be seen. . . . [I]t must be known and not known."[33] The doctor tells the Baron, "'May my dilator burst and my speculum rust, may panic seize my index finger before I point out my man'" (*NW* 33). Saying that he withholds a declaration draws attention to the fact that he has such feelings; his remark serves as disguised admission. The speaker in *A Lover's Discourse* both echoes O'Connor's remark and indicates the function of his "denial": "I want you to know that I don't want to show my feelings. . . . I set a mask upon my passion, but . . . I designate this mask" (Barthes 43).

The last time *Nightwood* brings together the Baron and the doctor, the reader witnesses yet one more ambiguous exchange:

> Felix ordered a *fine.* The doctor smiled. "I said you would come to it," he said, and emptied his own glass at a gulp.
>
> "I know," Felix answered, "but I did not understand. I thought you meant something else."
>
> "What?"
>
> Felix paused, turning the small glass around in his trembling hand. "I thought," he said, "that you meant that I would give up."
>
> The doctor lowered his eyes. "Perhaps that is what I meant—but sometimes I am mistaken."
>
> (*NW* 102)

In conjunction with the dialogue, the descriptive details in this passage (Felix's trembling hand, O'Connor's lowering of his eyes) suggest that the characters are experiencing the strain of holding strong emotions in check. Ultimately, it is easier for the Baron to accept the "maternal" fate of devoting his life to his sickly child (*NW* 99) than for him to embrace the idea of loving O'Connor.

In contrast to the doctor's self-restraint in expressing his feelings for Felix, Nora repeatedly declaims her feelings for Robin Vote, bewails her loss, glorifies and laments the experience of love. She mythologizes Robin as "the beloved" and herself as "the lover." In conversations with Matthew, she "speaks the conventions which define the conduct of the lover" (Barthes 3). She

adopts the role of lover by weaving an amorous discourse from "an exhausting memory [which] forbids voluntarily escaping love; in short, forbids inhabiting it discreetly, reasonably" (Barthes 51).

One chapter in particular, "Go Down, Matthew," emphasizes the performative element of love and of the lover's identity: Nora's remarks draw on literary precedents—especially *Wuthering Heights,* by Emily Bronte[34]—for the portrayal of passion, and she and O'Connor become audiences for each other's sadness. Thus this chapter manifests Barthes's contention that "enamoration is a *drama,* if we restore to this word the archaic meaning Nietzsche gives it: 'Ancient drama envisioned great declamatory scenes, which excluded action'" (Barthes 94). Composed of a conversation between Nora and the doctor, "Go Down, Matthew" places Nora in the position of suffering lover, but also emphasizes O'Connor's identification with that role. He takes up her story as if he has lived through the same experience—or as if the "lost love" plot is so powerful or predictable that he can accurately reconstruct both events and the feelings (*NW* 119). (At any rate, Nora does not contradict his version of her story.)

Accompanied only by a few terse references to tone, gesture, and setting, Nora's prolonged lament constitutes an "episode of language which stages the absence of the loved object" and transforms "this absence into an ordeal of abandonment," giving "shape to absence," elaborating its meaning (Barthes 13-14). The text's self-consciousness about this process occurs when O'Connor points out that Nora has made her beloved into a legend, a myth, and that the memory of someone loved is an appealing fiction (*NW* 106, 117). His comment draws attention to the fabricators/lovers themselves, who imbue the trivial with magnitude, charge "the infinitesimal event" with "huge reverberation" (Barthes 93). Nora's intense and sustained performance of the lover's discourse ultimately overwhelms O'Connor, reminds him of his own experience, stirs his own misery (*NW* 126-8). After she finishes talking, he stands in "confused and unhappy silence" and then leaves without a word (*NW* 130).

Nightwood dramatizes the Romantic effect: Nora's melancholy and her imagery of excessive feeling evoke O'Connor's melancholy; her unmitigated expression of longing and loss disturbs the equilibrium he usually maintains through wit, epigram, obscenity, and extended metaphor. By devoting so much of *Nightwood* to a lesbian lover's discourse and by having this discourse listened to and participated in by a homosexual man who has had to conceal his feelings, Barnes defies the modern stricture against the sentimental and unsettles the theory of "abnormal" desire. As in her journalism, so in her novels, Barnes satirizes conventional expectations, religious and patriarchal tenets, and biased sociohistorical constructions (of public personalities, journalists, women, Jews, homosexuals). At the same time she romanticizes solitude and privacy, flights of fancy, the "simpler" pleasures of the past, "quaint" personalities, ardent love, and relentless melancholy.

Notes

1. Djuna Barnes, *Nightwood, the Original Version and Related Drafts,* ed. Cheryl Plumb (Normal, IL: Dalkey Archive Press, 1995) 117. Hereafter cited parenthetically as *NW* in the text. See, also, Barnes' *Collected Stories,* ed. Phillip Herring (Los Angeles: Sun and Moon, 1996).

2. Sherrill E. Grace, review of *Interviews: Resources for American Literary Study* 16 (Special Book Review Issue, 1986-89): 168.

3. See Carl Herzig, "Roots of Night: Emerging Style and Vision in the Early Journalism of Djuna Barnes," *Centennial Review* 31 (Summer 1987): 255-69; Barbara Green, "Spectacular Confessions: 'How It Feels to Be Forcibly Fed,'" *Review of Contemporary Fiction* 13.3 (Fall 1993): 70-88; Nancy J. Levine, "'Bringing Milkshakes to Bulldogs,'" *Silence and Power: A Reevaluation of Djuna Barnes,* ed. Mary Lynn Broe (Carbondale: Southern Illinois UP, 1991) 27-34; Louis F. Kannenstine, *The Art of Djuna Barnes: Duality and Damnation* (New York: New York UP, 1977); Marie Ponsot, "A Reader's *Ryder,"* *Silence and Power* 94-112; Charles Baxter, "A Self-Consuming Light: *Nightwood* and the Crisis of Modernism," *Journal of Modern Literature* 3.5 (July 1974): 1175-87; and Alan Singer, "The Horse Who Knew Too Much: Metaphor and the Narrative of Discontinuity in *Nightwood,"* *Contemporary Literature* 25.1 (1984): 66-87.

4. Djuna Barnes, "David Belasco Dreams," *Interviews,* ed. Alyce Barry (Washington, DC: Sun and Moon, 1985) 187-88. Hereafter cited parenthetically in the text.

5. Djuna Barnes, "Charles Rann Kennedy Explains the Meaning of Tangoism" (1914), *Interviews,* 30-31.

6. Robert E. Mensel, "'Kodakers Lying in Wait': Amateur Photography and the Right of Privacy in New York, 1885-1915," *American Quarterly* 43 (1991): 27.

7. Nancy Levine 31-32.

8. Margaret R. Higonnet and Patrice Higonnet, "The Double Helix," *Behind the Lines: Gender and the Two World Wars,* ed. Margaret Higonnet, et al. (New Haven: Yale UP, 1987) 46-47.

9. Djuna Barnes, "Three Days Out," *New York Morning Telegraph Magazine* 12 August 1917: 4. Hereafter cited in the text without pagination since the entire article is on page 4.

10. In *The Norton Anthology of English Literature,* vol 2, ed. M. H. Abrams, George H. Ford, and David Daiches (New York: Norton, 1979) 823-25 and 799-800, respectively. See also Keats's letter to Benjamin Bailey, *Norton Anthology* 864-66.

11. "If Noise Were Forbidden at Coney Island, a Lot of People Would Lose Their Jobs" (1914), *New York,* ed. Alyce Barry (Los Angeles: Sun and Moon Press, 1989) 145.

12. "Surcease in Hurry and Whirl—On the Restless Surf at Coney" (1917), *New York* 280-81.

13. "Seeing New York with the Soldiers" (1918), *New York* 325. Hereafter cited parenthetically in the text.

14. "On Returning from Abroad," *Charm* 10 (October 1928): 28. Hereafter cited parenthetically in the text.

15. Terry Eagleton, *Literary Theory* (Minneapolis: U of Minnesota P, 1983) 18-19.

16. Rita Felski, *Beyond Feminist Aesthetics: Feminist Literature and Social Change* (Cambridge: Harvard UP, 1989) 167-68.

17. Felski 168.

18. See "There's Something Besides the Cocktail in the Bronx" (1919), *New York* 346. Hereafter cited parenthetically in the text.

19. *Ryder* (1928; New York: St. Martin's, 1979) 258. Hereafter cited parenthetically in the text.

20. See Kannenstine 38, 49, 52, and James Baird, "Djuna Barnes and Surrealism: 'Backward Grief,'" *Individual and Community: Variation on a Theme in American Fiction,* ed. Kenneth H. Baldwin and David K. Kirby (Durham: Duke UP, 1975) 160-81.

21. Baird 170.

22. Cheryl J. Plumb, *Fancy's Craft: Art and Identity in the Early Works of Djuna Barnes* (London & Toronto: Associated University Presses, 1986) 83.

23. Maureen Fitzgerald, foreword, *The Woman's Bible,* by Elizabeth Cady Stanton (Boston: Northeastern UP, 1993) viii.

24. Judith Hole and Ellen Levine, "The First Feminists," *Women: A Feminist Perspective,* ed. Jo Freeman (Palo Alto: Mayfield, 1979) 553.

25. Elizabeth Cady Stanton, *The Woman's Bible* (1895; Boston: Northeastern UP, 1993) 255. Hereafter cited parenthetically in the text.

26. See Meryl Altman, "A Book of Repulsive Jews? Rereading *Nightwood*," *Review of Contemporary Fiction* 13.3 (Fall 1993): 160-71, and Karen Kaivola, "The 'beast turning human': Constructions of the 'Primitive' in *Nightwood*," *Review of Contemporary Fiction* 13.3 (Fall 1993): 172-85.

27. Julie L. Abraham, "'Woman, Remember You': Djuna Barnes and History," *Silence and Power* 255.

28. Jane Marcus, "Laughing at Leviticus: *Nightwood* as Woman's Circus Epic," *Silence and Power* 228, 249; Abraham 255-56.

29. Altman 167-68.

30. Donna Gerstenberger, "Modern (Post) Modern: Djuna Barnes among the Others," *Review of Contemporary Fiction* 13.3 (Fall 1993): 33-40.

31. Kaivola 173.

32. *See* Judith Lee, "*Nightwood*: 'The Sweetest Lie,'" *Silence and Power* 209-11.

33. Roland Barthes, *A Lover's Discourse*, trans. Richard Howard (New York: Hill and Wang, 1978) 42. Hereafter cited parenthetically in the text.

34. Sanra Gilbert and Susan Gubar, *No Man's Land*, vol. 2, *Sexchanges* (New Haven: Yale UP, 1988) 237.

Mairéad Hanrahan, (essay date March 2001)

SOURCE: Hanrahan, Mairéad. "Djuna Barnes's *Nightwood*: The Cruci-Fiction of the Jew." *Paragraph* 24, no. 1 (March 2001): 32-49.

[*In the following essay, Hanrahan investigates how* Nightwood *"undermines the very distinction between Jew and non-Jew" and notes that, for Barnes, "the Jew's condition crystallizes a predicament she considers general: the failure of representation itself."*]

Djuna Barnes's self-attributed status as 'the most famous unknown in the world' can claim some support from the publishing history of **Nightwood**. Since its appearance to critical acclaim in 1936, this extraordinary novel, whose 'quality of horror and doom' T. S. Eliot compared to that of Elizabethan tragedy in his Introduction to the first American edition, has retained a limited but constant readership. The main reason for the text's failure to reach a broader public is almost certainly its impenetrability at both syntactical and narrative levels. One of the most puzzling enigmas in this tale of an intense passion between two women is the importance given the figure of the Jew at the outset of the novel. Although the beginning features both prominent Jewish characters and an extensive narrative discussion of Jewishness, neither the narrative discussion, after the first chapter, nor the main Jewish character, Felix, after the second, features largely. A number of different interpretations have been advanced in explanation, generally elaborating a parallel of some kind between the Jew and the homosexual.[1] While the parallel is beyond dispute, I would like to suggest that the relationship Barnes envisages between the Jew and other figures of the Other is more complex than a simple analogy establishing a resemblance between two separate and separable analogues. Close reading of the section of **Nightwood** which focusses on Jews shows that it especially calls 'the' Jew into question. While Barnes adopts the classic image of the Jew as Other, outcast, pariah, she adds a twist in that this image does not suffice to provide him with a distinct identity; the Jew features only in his relationship to the Other, his relationship *as* Other, so Other that even his Otherness does not belong to him.[2] As far as we know, Barnes only ever knew Judaism superficially, from the outside; it was a religion to which she did not belong, a religion which for her symbolized not belonging. This essay aims to show that the Barnesian Jew suffers from so total a lack of identity, so unredeemable a confusion that any attempt to redeem his condition only aggravates it. Most notably, any attempt to *represent* it is portrayed by Barnes as a step towards its Christianization (and thus its debasement). In contrast with readings of the novel as an analysis of a uniquely Jewish condition,[3] I would argue that Barnes's writing undermines the very distinction between Jew and non-Jew it proposes. For Barnes, the 'Jew's condition crystallizes a predicament she considers general: the failure of representation itself. Detailed examination of a number of key passages reveals that the difficulty of defining the Jew opens onto the wider epistemological impossibility of achieving any definition whatsoever. Both insofar as the text conveys a meaning, and even more radically insofar as the practice of writing it embodies operates against meaning being conveyed, Barnes's Jew's message is that the only story possible is an excruciatingly meaningless concoction, a *cruci-fiction*.

The impossibility of isolating the question of the Jew is already evident in the opening paragraphs describing Felix's birth:

> Early in 1880, in spite of a well-founded suspicion as to the advisability of perpetuating that race which has the sanction of the Lord and the disapproval of the people, Hedvig Volkbein—a Viennese woman of great strength and military beauty, lying upon a canopied bed of a rich spectacular crimson, the valance stamped with the bifurcated wings of the House of Hapsburg, the feather coverlet an envelope of satin on which, in massive and tarnished gold threads, stood the Volkbein arms—gave birth, at the age of forty-five, to an only child, a son, seven days after her physician predicted that she would be taken.

Turning upon this field, which shook to the clatter of morning horses in the street beyond, with the gross splendour of a general saluting the flag, she named him Felix, thrust him from her, and died.[4]

The Jew's suffering is closely linked to that of woman becoming a mother. Hedvig dies in giving birth both to her son and to his name; the mother has no place in the symbolic order, the sphere of nomination (subsequently, Hedvig plays practically no further role in the book). However, her effacement leaves the ironically named Felix with only the dubious felicity of completing his orphanage, as his father had died six months previously. The access to the domain of the father which psychoanalysis suggests is achieved in compensation for the loss of the mother's body is thus uncertain. Furthermore, the father's dominace in the symbolic order is immediately problematized: 'Guido Volkbein, a Jew of Italian descent, had been both a gourmet and a dandy, never appearing in public without the ribbon of some quite unknown distinction tinging his buttonhole with a faint thread' (1). Guido appears to have a 'distinction', an honour, something that sets apart, differentiates; the 'thread' with which his ribbon marks his clothes is the classic means of escaping from the labyrinth, *guid*ing oneself out of confusion. But the ribbon is a 'faint' thread, nearly indistinguishable, which only 'tinges' his buttonhole. Moreover, it is 'quite unknown': Guido's distinction is utterly undistinguished. Finally, according to Barnes's much-loved *Oxford English Dictionary*, 'gourmetism' can also mean daintiness in eating. Insofar as the syntax invites us to relate the distinction as much to the gourmet as the dandy, it becomes the visible trace of Guido's love for good food, conferring on him only the total lack of discrimination of both a gourmet and a dandy.

The confusion which Felix inherits from both sides is also sexual: Hedvig is a 'woman of great strength and military beauty', while Guido's stomach protrudes, 'marking the exact centre of his body with the obstetric line seen on fruits' (1). The roles are also reversed in that the German-sounding 'Volkbein', which is first given as Hedvig's surname, would seem to belong more obviously to someone Viennese than to a 'Jew of Italian descent'. The fact that traditionally only a woman's first name was proper to her suggests that the Jew's condition corresponds to a woman's, a suggestion which moreover echoes powerfully in the author's own—extremely unusual—first name, a deformation of Eugène Sue's 'Djalma': *Jew*na.

To what extent, then, does Felix carry on Hedvig, or the question of 'race'[5] carry on that of sex? Which exactly is the 'race which has the sanction of the Lord and the disapproval of the people', that Hedvig perpetuates by giving birth to Felix: her own, or that of her husband? In spite of the periphrastic detail, the race remains un-

clear. Is the 'sanction' positive or negative? What 'people' disapproves of it? Is it one race in particular or the human race in general? Felix's birth on the seventh day makes the novel's opening scene a parody of the opening of the Book of Genesis, the book which relates both the creation of humanity and the emergence of the Jews as God's chosen people. Although subsequent paragraphs invite us to read the race Felix continues as that of the Jews, Barnes presents it initially as a race which cannot be clearly distinguished.[6] Being a Jew means being fallen—*like everybody else*.

The instability of the Jew's emergent identity is immediately emphasized by the repetition of the word 'race' in a context describing its homonym, a race which is run:

> The autumn, binding him about, as no other season, with racial memories, a season of longing and of horror, he had called his weather. Then walking in the Prater he had been seen carrying in a conspicuously clenched fist the exquisite handkerchief of yellow and black linen that cried aloud of the ordinance of 1468, issued by one Pietro Barbo, demanding that, with a rope about its neck, Guido's race should run in the Corso for the amusement of the Christian populace, while ladies of noble birth, sitting upon spines too refined for rest, arose from their seats, and, with the red-gowned cardinals and the *Monsignori*, applauded with that cold yet hysterical abandon of a people that is at once unjust and happy, the very Pope himself shaken down from his hold on heaven with the laughter of a man who forgoes his angels that he may recapture the beast. This memory and the handkerchief that accompanied it had wrought in Guido (as certain flowers brought to a pitch of florid ecstasy no sooner attain their specific type than they fall into its decay) the sum total of what is the Jew. He had walked, hot, incautious and damned, his eyelids quivering over the thick eyeballs, black with the pain of a participation that, four centuries later, made him a victim, as he felt the echo in his own throat of that cry running the *Piazza Montanara* long ago, '*Roba vecchia!*'—the degradation by which his people had survived.
>
> (2)

Not only is race—in the sense of those who are connected by common descent, bound together ('with a cord about its neck')—confused with running—in the 'Corso', whose name etymologically means a race—but the line between race and religion—from the latin *religare*, to bind—is blurred. The entire passage plays on the tension between movement and attachment. The autumn 'binds' Guido about, with 'racial memories', but equally he adopts the autumn by calling it 'his' weather, naming the season as one names a son. Autumn's other name, which appears later on in the novel (53), is the fall, reminiscent of the expulsion from paradise: the question is why Guido should attach himself to such a 'season of longing and of horror'. The expression suggests a contrastive allusion to Keats's 'season of mists and yellow fruitfulness'; Barnes's Jew (like her homosexual?) knows only fruit*less*ness. Childless, Guido invents a genealogy; at issue is his attempt to re-call the past, create a Jewish history. Unlike Hedvig, nomination seems to afford him some degree of appro-priation. Yet, as we shall see, he seems more 'bound' to the Christians than to his fellow Jews. The word 'weather' also astonishes, especially as the passage deals rather with time (translated by the same word as weather in French, the foreign language Barnes knew best), and the comma placing 'the autumn' in apposition makes the syntax awkward. The strangeness of the sentence indicates a foreignness in the relationship to language, as though Guido's history were possible only in the Other's terms.

The details of Guido's walk confirm the difficulty of constituting a history of his 'race'. 'Then walking in the Prater he had been seen carrying': the series of parti-ciples makes it impossible to situate the walk tempo-rally. Did he walk in the autumn or afterwards ('then' could mean either)? Was it during or before his walk that he was seen? The handkerchief seems to com-memorate a past moment of importance to the Jews, but by carrying it in a 'conspicuously clenched' fist does he exhibit or hide it? The audible is as questionable as the visible: in what sense of the verb can a handkerchief, used to wipe away tears, '[cry] aloud' of 1468?

No explanation has ever been proposed for the enig-matic date of the ordinance, which corresponds to no recognizable historical referent. One reading may how-ever provide a clue to Guido's desire to commemorate such a deplorable scene. In his analysis of the poetry of the Jewish poet, Paul Celan, Jacques Derrida argues that a date—like a signature, or a proper noun—is a 'spectre' of the 'non-repeatable' singularity which it nonetheless repeats. A date is both decipherable, be-cause of its inscription in a code, the calendar, and in-decipherable, because of its uniqueness.[7] As such, a date shares the same structure as circumcision,[8] another event which only happens once and which inaugurates a Jew into his community. In the light of Derrida's analysis, it is interesting that the autumn should 'bind' Guido about with racial memories: bondage serves him as a bandage. The colours of the handkerchief are the yellow and black into which primordial chaos was first differentiated; yellow is also the colour of the Star of David, with which the Nazis were beginning to mark out the Jews at the time of writing *Nightwood.* In Guido's gesture can be read the desire to preserve the memory of a singular event by which his people were set apart, circumscribed, a symbolic circumcision of the race rather than of the individual.

This distinction of the Jews as a people does not, how-ever, separate them from others. The ordinance demands their *sub*-ordination; if they gain recognition as a race,

it is only at the price of their subjection to the Christian 'populace', i.e. to the low-born, the commoners. The more the Jews are fallen, degraded, the higher the Chris-tians rise; the text shifts upwards along both the social hierarchy (from the populace to 'ladies of noble birth', who 'ar[i]se from their seats') and the ecclesiastical (from the cardinals and the Monsignori to 'the very Pope himself). Yet this Christian ascendancy over the Jews in no way betokens a spiritual elevation. It carries rather the overtones of a sexual crescendo. The ladies arise from 'sitting upon spines too refined for rest': by calling attention to the word *spine* (how does one sit 'upon' a spine?), the text invites a paragrammatical reading, as its anagram *penis.*[9] The ladies have erec-tions, the male prelates wear gowns, both applaud with a 'hysterical abandon': the scene is orgiastic in its de-tail. Moreover, the Christians are at once 'unjust and happy'; in an ironic twist, their surpassing of the *lex talionis* means that they act worse than justice requires, not better, distinguishing themselves from the Jews only by behaving both unfairly and uncharitably, failing in the very virtue which should in principle characterize them. Barnes represents the Pope, the pinnacle of the Church, in markedly Luciferian terms as a man 'shaken down from his hold on heaven' who 'forgoes his angels that he may recapture the beast'. The mention of a beast sounds echoes of the Great Beast of the Apocalypse, suggesting blasphemously that the cult of the Antichrist is what tells the Christians from the Jews.

For Barnes, then, what defines the Jews is their subju-gation by the Christians, i.e. their subjugation by a people itself distinguished by its degeneracy. Further-more, her writing *reproduces* this subjugation, in that the Jew in effect disappears in the second part of the long sentence describing his 'race', after the conjunc-tion 'while' marking a shift to the indicative mode. Whereas the order that Guido's race 'should' run does not specify if the race ever took place or not, the ac-tions of the Christians are presented in positive terms, as matters of fact; indeed, if the sentence is read in strict accordance with the rules of grammar, the ladies arise and applaud not while Guido's race is running, but when the ordinance is issued. Barnes's writing thus suggests that the Jew's past is only anchored in time, becomes history, insofar as it is mediated by the Chris-tians.[10]

Not only does the Jew depend for his identity on a scene involving his degradation, but that identity, origi-nating in a spectacle, is in turn subject to degradation. Guido becomes a Jew by identifying with the Jews, his walk had 'wrought' in him a sense of his identity; yet the identity he thus acquires has none of the toughness which the verb 'wrought', used especially in relation to metals, might indicate; the comparison with 'certain flowers' gives it an organic aspect, liable to decay. The flowers attain a pitch of 'florid ecstasy' (from the Greek *ekstasis,* literally beside oneself, out of place): they blossom to such an extent that they reach the limit of being flowers. And no sooner do they attain their 'specific type' than they 'fall into its decay': no sooner does the particular border on the universal than it loses its representative capacity. Even more astonishing, the fall, which is paralleled at the level of the signifier in the sequence *flowers-florid-fall,* and in the etymology of the word 'decay' (from the Latin *decadere*), affects the 'type', the category, as much as the individual flowers: they fall into 'its' decay. The text offers a parodic allusion to Mallarmé's famous ideal flower, 'l'absente de tous bouquets'; for Barnes, the abstraction, the idea is as susceptible to decay as the contingent forms which embody it. Similarly, the Jew's identity is disaggregated in the very process which constitutes it. The unusual use of the singular in the ordinance decreeing that Guido's race should run with a rope about 'its' neck earlier indicated that the target is the Jews as an (id)entity, rather than the individuals who comprise the race. Guido's commemorative gestures then wrought in him 'the sum total of what is the Jew', fashioned, defined in him 'the' Jew. But what the Jew is—or more precisely, 'what is the Jew'—is never specified; the unusually awkward, arrhythmical syntax, causing the reader to stumble over the pronoun (which can be an indirect interrogative as well as a relative), further undermines its referential function. The sentence which registers the possibility of a Jewish identity defines it in indefinite, imprecise terms, as though its only attribute was imprecision. Guido thus both changes himself and problematizes the very notion of 'the' Jew by his attempt to perpetuate it.

The entire paragraph is in fact summarized in the last words: 'the degradation by which his people had survived'. This degradation refers in the first instance to pawnbroking, the Jews' traditional livelihood, as reflected in their cry 'running' the Piazza Montanara long before ('*Roba vecchia*' means second-hand clothes). But the passage also suggests that their degradation enabled the Jews to survive not only as individuals, by providing them with an income, but *as a people,* by providing them with an identity, that of the degraded. Guido's repetition of his people's degradation thus both affords him a communal identity (his 'participation' makes him a 'victim') and affords that identity survival. Yet that survival in turn is not immune from decay. The word 'degradation' derives from the Latin *gradus,* step or degree; Guido's walk is, literally, a step down, a degradation of the 'race' he is trying to recall, just as the tears evoked by the handkerchief are reduced to his quivering eyelids, or his ancestors' cry finds in him only an echo which gets no further than his throat. The tragedy in *Nightwood* is that there are degrees only of degradation; the Jew's identity is even further degraded by being represented.

For Barnes, then, 'what is the Jew' remains untellable; any attempt to represent it is a distortion. Even the one characteristic she associates with the Jew, that of having no stable characteristic, does not clearly single him out; in *Nightwood,* Jewishness is universal. *Who* is a Jew seems as uncertain as *what* is a Jew:

> And childless he had died, save for the promise that hung at the Christian belt of Hedvig. Guido had lived as all Jews do, who, cut off from their people by accident or choice, find that they must inhabit a world whose constituents, being alien, force the mind to succumb to an imaginary populace. When a Jew dies on a Christian bosom he dies impaled. Hedvig, in spite of her agony, wept upon an outcast. Her body at that moment became the barrier and Guido died against that wall, troubled and alone. In life he had done everything to span the impossible gap; the saddest and most futile gesture of all had been his pretence to a barony.
>
> (3)

'Guido had lived as all Jews do, who, (. . .)': the amphibology created by the comma after 'do' makes it impossible to know if Guido lived as all Jews, or merely as those Jews who are cut off from their people. Is the alienation the text attributes to the Jews common to all or only to some of them? And, if not a determining feature of Jewishness, could it not also be common to non-Jews? Moreover, before the text elaborates on the insurmountable barrier cutting Guido off from his Christian wife, it tells us that those Jews of which he is one are 'cut off from their people'. It is because they are cut off from their *own,* 'by accident or choice', that they are forced to mix with the Other, inhabit a world of alien 'constituents'. Besides component parts, 'constituents' means the electors in a constituency, those who decide. God's chosen people have no power to choose;[11] Barnes sees them in a position to relate only to whose to whom they cannot relate; in the event, Guido is as cut off from his own blood, Felix, whom he never sees, as he is from Hedvig, against whose body he dies, 'troubled and alone'. He is fated to suffer from an unmitigated confusion,[12] without however the consolation of losing himself totally; even in death, fusion with the Other eludes him. 'He had died (. . .) Guido had lived (. . .) Guido died (. . .) In life he had (. . .)': the textual sequence presents Guido's death as a continuation of his life as an unhappy 'outcast', his ceaseless efforts to 'span the impossible gap'. The *bar*rier which Hedvig's body represents echoes Guido's most futile gesture, his 'pretence to a *bar*ony'. His distinction is both false and fruitless: *baron* is a homophone of *barren.* The consonants of the word are furthermore those of the author's surname,[13] confirming on yet another level the existence of a parallel between Jew and homosexual. Djuna Barnes, or *barren Jew*?

Yet is the 'gap' which Guido strives in vain to span not redolent also of the *generation gap,* given the emphasis at the opening of the quotation on the lapse of time between his death and his child's birth? The bar between the religions is also a gap between the generations. Felix's dispossession is more extreme than his father's both because he is bereft of his two parents at birth and because, as the son of a Jewish father and a Christian mother, he inherits an even greater degree of religious indistinctness. Through Felix, Barnes suggests not only that the Jew's condition degenerates with the passing of every generation, but that being born is a sufficient condition for being an 'outcast'. The *Oxford English Dictionary* defines generation in terms similar to degradation as a 'step in descent'; every generation, of every race or *genus,* shares for Barnes in what it is to be a Jew.

In the first seven pages of **Nightwood,** the description of Felix's mother and father is immediately followed by a description of portraits of his paternal grandparents, which turn out to be 'reproductions of two intrepid and ancient actors' (7).[14] His ancestors, then, are revealed to be only portraits. But the reader further learns that the description of his parents has no more historical validity than the faked portraits of his grandparents:

> At this point exact history stopped for Felix who, thirty years later, turned up in the world with these facts, the two portraits and nothing more. His aunt, combing her long braids with an amber comb, told him what she knew, and this had been her only knowledge of his past. What had formed Felix from the date of his birth to his coming to thirty was unknown to the world, for the step of the wandering Jew is in every son. No matter where and when you meet him you feel that he has come from some place—no matter from what place he has come—some country that he has devoured rather than resided in, some secret land that he has been nourished on but cannot inherit, for the Jew seems to be everywhere from nowhere.
>
> (7)

The 'facts' about Hedvig and Guido presented in the opening pages by a third-person, seemingly extradiegetical narrator, are in fact the creation of Felix's aunt, described in terms strongly evoking a siren, with all the seductive illusion such a figure entails, and whose memory, as well as her knowledge, is bound to be unreliable thirty years on. 'Exact history' thus not only stops for Felix at his birth but its 'exactness'—like that of the narrative itself, for why should the second (seemingly) extradiegetical narrator be any more reliable than the first?—is irremediably problematized.

It is highly significant that the revelation of (the falseness of) Felix's history is accompanied by his emergence as a Christlike figure, a Jew about whose life little is known until his appearance in the world at thirty. The exemplary Christian is—was—a Jew. The world in which Felix appears is one where this time all the 'constituents' could be Jews. The Barnesian equivalent

to Marina Tsvetaëva's much-quoted epigraph that 'all poets are Yids' is that all *sons* are Jews; Felix's absence from history seems as much due to his being a son as to his being a Jew. 'No matter where and when you meet *him*': the pronoun's antecedent can be read as either 'the wandering Jew' or 'every son'.[15] Both here represent a figure whose spatial and temporal imprecision reflects the uncertainty of his country of origin. For the reference to a geographical exile applies as forcefully to the 'son' as to the 'Jew' in that the 'country that he has *devoured*', the 'secret land that he has been *nourished* on', carries strong connotations of the mother's body.[16] 'No *matter* where (. . .) no *matter* from what place': the mother, *mater,* even resonates in the sentence. Everyone who is born, cast out from/by the mother, shares the exile of the Jew.

The quotation suggests that every son is a Jew insofar as he is 'unknown', having lost the paradise of maternal indifferenciation yet unable to appropriate his loss by casting it in a (hi)story. A Jew who has become 'known', then, is a Christian. This double bind in which the Jew is caught, between distinction and indistinction, is the focus of the longest narrative disquisition on Jewishness in the text:

> In his search for the particular *Comédie humaine* Felix had come upon the odd. Conversant with edicts and laws, folk story and heresy, taster of rare wines, thumber of rarer books and old wives' tales—tales of men who became holy and of beasts that became damned—read in all plans for fortifications and bridges, given pause by all graveyards on all roads, a pedant of many churches and castles, his mind dimly and reverently reverberated to Madame de Sévigné, Goethe, Loyola and Brantôme. But Loyola sounded the deepest note; he was alone, apart and single. A race that has fled its generations from city to city has not found the necessary time for the accumulation of that toughness which produces ribaldry, nor, after the crucifixion of its ideas, enough forgetfulness in twenty centuries to create legend. It takes a Christian, standing eternally in the Jew's salvation, to blame himself and to bring up from that depth charming and fantastic superstitions through which the slowly and tirelessly milling Jew once more becomes the 'collector' of his own past. His undoing is never profitable until some *goy* has put it back into such shape that it can again be offered as a 'sign'. A Jew's undoing is never his own, it is God's; his rehabilitation is never his own, it is a Christian's. The Christian traffic in retribution has made the Jew's history a commodity; it is the medium through which he receives, at the necessary moment, the serum of his own past that he may offer it again as his blood. In this manner the Jew participates in the two conditions; and in like manner Felix took the breast of this wet nurse whose milk was his being but which could never be his birthright.
>
> (10)

From the beginning, the text produces a tension between the particular and the universal. Whereas Balzac dreamed of encapsulating humanity in its entirety in his work, Felix seeks 'the particular *Comédie humaine*', a concept which defies all interpretation. The word 'particular' is at odds both with the generality associated with the human, and with the definite article, a marker of the recognisable, the translatable. How can a special case represent the type? Furthermore, is the 'odd' a variant of the particular Felix seeks, or at variance with it, the result rather than the object of his quest? It is never clear which of the 'odd' meanings of odd—peculiar, motley, unmatched, uneven, etc.—is to the fore, just as to 'come upon' may mean to discover by chance or to have an orgasm. In the search to make sense of the particular details of the text, the reader is placed in a position similar to that of Felix of 'coming upon the odd', encountering a collection of words which seem totally incongruous. The extraordinary (and disorderly) assortment of Felix's attributes described in the long second sentence of the quotation is reflected in its syntactical confusion: the many appositions at the beginning make the meandering sentence extremely hard to follow, especially as the proliferation of nouns has the effect of blurring the boundaries between the various syntagms. Felix is 'conversant' with so many things, a connoisseur in so many areas, that his discernment, his capacity to distinguish is called into question. The inappropriate appearance of the universal ('read in *all* plans for fortifications and bridges, given pause by *all* graveyards on *all* roads') paradoxically suggests an inability—or a refusal—to generalize from the particular, as though no graveyard was in any way representative of another. Equally bewilderingly, his mind 'dimly and reverently reverberated to Madame de Sévignée, Goethe, Loyola and Brantôme', four figures with neither language, sex, century nor theme in common. Does the list have any significance other than the fact that these are historical figures, in other words, that their names have left an imprint on Western culture? That is, on Christian culture? The 'reverberation' of Felix's mind from singularity to singularity picks up on the word 'conversant' which derives from the Latin *convertere,* to turn about;[17] his turning to these Christian figures can be read as a form of *conversion*. Loyola evokes the deepest response in Felix, being 'alone, apart and single', three attributes which all reinforce the idea of the Jesuit's distinctness. In contrast, the Jew is paradoxically dependent on the Christian for a sense of his separateness.

'A race that has fled its generations from city to city' is one of the principal images which have provided support for the reading of the Jew as a metaphor for the homosexual. But metaphor functions as much through the play of difference of tenor and vehicle, as through their identification.[18] The race in question, introduced only by an indefinite article, is not identified by Barnes: it carefully evokes *both* the Diaspora of the Jews *and* the 'fruitlessness' of the homosexual. The reference to the 'crucifixion' of its ideas and the 'twenty centuries'

which have since elapsed is specific enough to impose a particular religious interpretation, while the fact that it has 'not found the necessary time for the accumulation of that toughness which produces ribaldry' suggests on the contrary a sexual vulnerability. The very sentence which elaborates on the Jew's suspension between the particular and the general thus blurs the boundaries between the Jews and another *race maudite*. Such a race, in fact, *has not found the necessary time*: it has managed to become neither history nor legend.[19]

The 'crucifixion of its ideas' indicates a reference to Christ's Crucifixion, an event which inaugurated a new era, a new ideology. But the expression can also be read literally, as the constitution of the race's ideas, the fixing of its state in a form or image capable of rendering its confusion and dispossession, its agonising cruciformity. This suggests that for Barnes the Jew's condition can only enter history as a cruciform fiction, a *cruci-fiction,* which emerges indistinctly, between history and legend, thanks to the Christian image par excellence, a fiction utterly dependent on Christian intervention. For a Jew to gain access to his past, 'it takes a Christian, standing eternally in the Jew's salvation, to blame himself and to bring up from that depth charming and fantastic superstitions'. But what does it mean for a Christian to 'stand in' the Jew's salvation: to advance it or to block it (as in to stand in the way)? The expression implies an impure interiority; the Christian is neither external nor internal to the other's salvation, but eternally, irremediably involved in it. The spatial undecidability increases: a Christian must blame himself, abase himself, in order to 'bring up' from that 'depth' the means by which the Jew can reclaim his past. The high and the low are further subject to exchange: the 'depth' could refer to the Jew's salvation in which the Christian stands as much as to the latter's culpability, and 'to bring up', in the sense of to vomit, connotes abjection as well as elevation. Moreover, not only are superstitions—beliefs or practices based on fear and ignorance—generally considered a degradation of religion, but their qualification as 'charming', or magical (from the Latin *carmen,* a charm or spell), and 'fantastic', produced by the imagination, removes them even further from the religious faith which is indispensable to salvation. The word superstition derives from the Latin *superstare,* to stand over; there is thus a textual shift from standing *in* to standing *over,* from interlocking to separation, suggesting that the superstitions 'brought up' by the Christian paradoxically save the Jew by damning him.

Through these superstitions the Jew 'once more becomes the "collector" of his own past', reassembles, reappropriates his scattered past. The use of inverted commas highlights the strangeness of this appropriation; one more usually collects the past of others, not one's own. The past the Jew collects seems never to have belonged to him, even in the past: he 'once more' becomes its collector. All he can appropriate, or more precisely all that can be appropriated from his past by a Christian, is his original decomposition or dispersal, his 'undoing': 'His undoing is never profitable until some *goy* has put it back into such shape that it can again be offered as a "sign".' And not only the Jew has no past other than his undoing; not only he needs a Christian for this undoing to take form; but it is never clear that he in fact profits from either his original undoing or the form given it: 'A Jew's undoing is never his own, it is God's; his rehabilitation is never his own, it is a Christian's.' To the extent that for Barnes every form is foreign to the Jew, perhaps only the foreignness of all form is proper to him? Italics draw attention to the word *goy* in the text, the Jews' term for a non-Jew, deriving from the Hebrew; the only quality Barnes's writing ascribes to the Jews is the otherness or foreignness of all form, all property, all definition.[20]

The shape given the Jew's condition is unmistakably reminiscent of Christian liturgy. His 'undoing' is transformed in such a way that 'it can again be offered as a "sign"', just as in the Offertory of the Mass the bread and wine are offered to God to be transformed in the Consecration into the 'signs' of the body and blood of Christ. The Jew's past only becomes a sign, exchangeable, by becoming the property of the other: 'The Christian traffic in retribution has made the Jew's history a commodity.' The use of the word 'retribution' in this context evokes both the Last Judgment, the moment when one's salvation or damnation is decided in accordance with the life one has led, and the justification advanced for pogroms that they were in punishment of the Jews for having put Christ to death. As such, especially linked with the word 'traffic', it introduces the question of recompense, of exchange (it derives from the Latin *retribuere,* to give in return). The Christian redeems the Jew's history, but this redemption resembles less the pure offering or gift of Christ's sacrifice than redemption in the sense of an economic transaction, a 'traffic', a shameful, clandestine commerce. The Christian traffic is in *signs*: by making the Jew's history possible, exchangeable, the Christian commercialises it, makes it a 'commodity', the object of a purchase or sale. And the agent or subject of this exchange, to whom the profit (an old meaning of *commodity,* according to the *OED*) accrues, is the Christian.

However, insofar as the Christian traffic constitutes the Jew's history as an object, it also suits the Jew. Felix's search for the 'particular *Comédie humaine*' as described in this long passage seems precisely an attempt to reify flux, confusion, i.e. to transform into a *commodity* the *odd* on which he had *come*. Insofar as the Christian makes the Jew's past exchangeable, he renders it appropriable: the Christian traffic 'is the medium through which he receives, at the necessary moment,

the serum of his own past'. This commodification is the means of the Jew's salvation, the transfusion which saves him. 'Medium' also means an intermediary, especially with the dead; it is by means of a Christian intermediary that the Jew receives, without ever being able to make it his, his (own) middle condition.

He receives the 'serum' of his past, his past already ordered, distilled by the Other. Like any form, this serum represents a selection, a separation; the serum is the liquid which separates from the clot when blood coagulates. The history with which the Christian presents the Jew is an isolation of the non-isolatable, the non-separable, the liquid. As such, it is a distortion of the reality it seeks to recall; the process it opens up to the Jew further aggravates the distortion. He receives the serum 'that he may offer it again as his blood': the moment at which the Jew gains access to his past is the moment at which the echoes of the Consecration, the transubstantiation of the bread and wine into the body and blood of Christ, are the strongest. The Eucharist is the sacramental representation of Christ's sacrifice on the cross; it is meant to abolish historical time, the twenty centuries since the Crucifixion, by making really present the Redeemer's body and blood. The Jew's history thus depends on the celebration of the event which inaugurated the downfall of his people. But the inscription of the Eucharist raises the question of representation itself. A number of expressions stress the repetitive nature of the Christian traffic: 'once more', 'put back into shape', 'again', 'again'. Christianity features in the text as the religion which *re-presents* salvation, as the religion of representation. The Jew's predicament is that the only salvation available is the Christian illusion that representation can somehow redeem the past, restore its presence. For Barnes, the Jew's history depends on Christian mediation because there is no representation other than Christian. Being represented, named, even as a Jew, is equivalent to a baptism, the sacrament which purges original sin with the attribution of a name. The serum, a beneficial remedy intervening 'at the necessary moment', saves the Jew by giving him access to representation, but this representation remains fundamentally Christian. To the extent, then, that the Jew gains access to representation, he becomes Christianized. 'In this manner the Jew participates in the two conditions': representation enables him to participate in his own condition, but his very participation at the same time places him at a remove from it. Participation 'in the two conditions' evokes communion in both species—and the one who receives communion thus, who receives the Offertory gifts and is the mediator of the sacrifice of the Mass, is the Christian priest. In an ultimate ironic twist, the Jew himself participates in representation like a Christian intermediary.

Moreover, by representing his condition, the Jew does not mitigate his alienation. 'In like manner Felix took the breast of this wet nurse whose milk was his being but which could never be his birthright': the milk (or whey? 'serum' is the watery part left when milk curdles) Felix takes at the breast of a maternal substitute gives him a 'being', invests him with a certain ontological status which will always however remain unsure. His dispossession is absolute; he has no right even to the milk of a wet nurse; being born gives him no rights at all.

The image of maternal loss at the end of the narration's discourse on the Jew invites us to read the 'two conditions' in which Felix participates as two states of dispossession which in *Nightwood* are inextricably entangled: that of the Jew and that of the son. The 'wet nurse' at whose breast both Jew and son suck, and which offers only a substitute for mother's milk—a substitute which, proclaiming itself as such, underlines rather than abolishes the loss it aims to relieve—operates as a metaphor of representation itself. Barnes's use of the image of the Jew as absolute outsider in effect proclaims as futile the belief that representation can 'really' make present the past, play a redemptive role. Thus, by virtue of the slippage they inscribe from the particular situation of the Jew to the more general inadequacy of representation, the opening pages of the novel place the text as a whole under the sign of the Jew's hopeless search for a (hi)story which will consolidate his identity. The uncertainty of the distinction between Jew and non-Jew which is elaborated there carries its effects through into the subsequent narrative development: *Nightwood* can be read both as an illustration of the Jew's particular failure to enter history (Felix not only becomes Christianized but also virtually disappears from the text: the shift in narrative focus makes his disappearance manifest) and as a generalisation from that particular. Barnes precisely sees the Jew as crucified *between the particular and the general.*

It could be argued that to some extent *Nightwood* repeats the 'crucifixion' it describes, that reinventing images of the Jew as absolute outsider can contribute to perpetuating them.[21] Moreover, the question can be asked whether by using the Jews' dispossession as a metaphor of a general condition of lack of identity, Barnes elides their specificity, is in turn guilty of consigning them to oblivion. These concerns are all the more legitimate given the place of enunciation; the politics of a non-Jew's pronouncements on Jewish identity are obviously different from those of a Jew. Indeed, our analysis throws into relief how radically the way such a gesture would be perceived (and thus its politics) has changed since Barnes wrote her text: the freedom with which she borrowed the classic image of the Jew then would be characterized today, after the Holocaust, as an unacceptable liberty. But the non-exteriority of Jew and non-Jew she evokes so powerfully can also be marshalled in her defence. Her novel makes clear that it is

impossible to categorize her *at the level of her identifications* as a 'non-Jew'. Far from distancing herself from the total lack of identity she attributes to the Jews, she identified with it so powerfully that she adopted it as the keynote for the work which was her passion for so many years. At the beginning of *The Blacks*, Genet asks: 'But what is a Black? and first of all, what colour is he?' Decades earlier, Barnes in effect asked in *Nightwood*: But what is a Jew? and first of all, what religion is he?

Notes

1. See especially Jane Marcus, 'Laughing at Leviticus: *Nightwood* as Woman's Circus Epic', Julie L. Abraham, '"Woman, Remember You": Djuna Barnes and History', *Silence and Power: A Reevaluation of Djuna Barnes,* edited by Mary Lynn Broe (Carbondale and Edwardsville, Southern Illinois University Press, 1991) pp. 221-50 and 252-68, and Meryl Altman, 'A Book of Repulsive Jews?: Rereading *Nightwood*', *Review of Contemporary Fiction,* 13:3 (1992), pp. 160-71.

2. The question of the Jew as 'Other' has been the subject of much theoretical debate over the last fifty years. In France, for example, Jean-Paul Sartre offered the first systematic analysis of antisemitism in *Réflexions sur la question juive* (Paris, Gallimard, 1954). More recently, the question of the relationship to the Other which is central to the thinking of both Jacques Derrida and Emmanuel Lévinas is closely linked in the work of both philosophers to their experience as Jews (see especially Emmanuel Lévinas, *Totalité et Infini: Essai sur l'extériorité* (La Haye, Martinus Nijhoff, 1961) and *Difficile Liberté* (Paris, Albin Michel, 1963); Jacques Derrida, 'Circonfession', in Geoffrey Bennington and Jacques Derrida, *Jacques Derrida* (Paris, Seuil, 1991) and *Le Monolinguisme de l'autre* (Paris, Galilée, 1996)). Barnes's writing foreshadows these writers' emphasis on identity as a relational construct; what is unusual in her case is how strongly she identifies with an Otherness to which, as a non-Jew, nothing attached her and which she represents not positively, as an alterity to be respected in its irreducible singularity, but in the most pessimistic terms possible, as a condition of utmost alienation.

3. Jane Marcus, for example, reads *Nightwood* as a 'prophecy of the Holocaust' (*op. cit.,* p. 249).

4. Djuna Barnes, *Nightwood* (New York, New Directions, 1937), p. 1. Future page references will be given in the text.

5. For a modern reader, the historicity of Barnes's borrowing of the figure of the Jew comes across most strongly in her use of the term 'race'. Today,

it would be impossible to use the word in order to suggest (as I am arguing Barnes did) the *non-*exteriority of Jew and Gentile, given that in the wake of the Holocaust, the mere use of the term in relation to the Jews runs the danger of implying an acceptance of the biological and genetic doctrines which Nazism put to such appalling effect.

6. National, as well as sexual and racial, identity is uncertain from the outset. The opening of the novel is set in fin-de-siécle Vienna, during the decline of the Hapsburg dynasty, whose wings are stamped on Hedvig's bed, beside the 'tarnished gold threads' of the Volkbein arms. Hedvig names Felix 'with the gross splendour of a general saluting the flag'—but which nation's flag? When Barnes was writing *Nightwood,* Israel did not yet exist; the Jews had no national emblem. Is Hedvig's gesture that of a general saluting a flag which does or does not represent him?

7. Jacques Derrida, *Schibboleth* (Paris, Editions Galilée, 1986), p. 37.

8. *Ibid.,* p. 97.

9. The only other inscription of the word in *Nightwood* lends itself compellingly to such a reading: 'the spine on her sprung up' (125).

10. For Julie Abraham also, the Jew's history only exists in relation to Christianity. But whereas Abraham posits the Jew in relation to a dominant discourse, seeing in his marginality a metaphor for the lesbian's exclusion from male, heterosexist history (*op. cit.,* pp. 257-9), I am suggesting that Barnes exploits the uncertainty of the Jew's history to question the very possibility of *any* record which could adequately retrace the past.

11. Like his father, Felix will marry a Christian wife, whose name is Robin *Vote.*

12. His confusion is echoed in the reversal of sexual roles: 'When a Jew dies on a Christian bosom he dies impaled.' The (masculine) Jew is penetrated on/by a (feminine) bosom.

13. Elizabeth Béranger has shown how names circulate within the text: 'Baronin' contains both 'Robin' and 'Baron' as well as 'Nora', which in turn is a displacement of 'O'Connor'. See *Une Epoque de transe* (Lille, Presses Universitaires de Lille, 1977), p. 420.

14. For a discussion of these portraits, see Béranger, *op. cit.,* pp. 496 *et seq.*

15. For a discussion of the fact that the Jew in *Nightwood* is a masculine figure, see my doctoral thesis, *Djuna Barnes, Jean Genet et la différence des sexes, des sexualités: Pour une poétique du désir* (Université de Paris VIII, May 1994).

16. See Freud's argument that the *unheimlich* or uncanny place is 'the former *Heim* [home] of all human beings, (. . .) the place where each one of us lived once upon a time and in the beginning. There is a joking saying that "Love is home-sickness"; and whenever a man dreams of a place or a country and says to himself, while he is still dreaming: "this place is familiar to me, I've been here before", we may interpret the place as being his mother's genitals or her body' (*The 'Uncanny', Pelican Freud Library 14,* edited by Albert Dickson, Penguin, 1985, p. 368).

17. See also one of the earliest and most valuable contributions to Barnes criticism, Kenneth Burke's 'Version, con-, per- and in-: thoughts on Djuna Barnes's novel *Nightwood*', *Southern Review* 2 (1966-7), pp. 329-46.

18. See for example Paul de Man's study of metaphor's resistance to the recuperation of stable meaning in *Allegories of Reading: Figural Language in Rousseau, Nietzsche, Rilke, and Proust* (New Haven and London, Yale University Press, 1979).

19. O'Connor later relates the difference between Jew and Christian to that between legend and history: 'Legend is unexpurgated, but history, because of its actors, is deflowered—every nation with a sense of humour is a lost nation, and every woman with a sense of humour is a lost woman. The Jews are the only people who have sense enough to keep humour in the family; a Christian scatters it all over the world' (15).

20. Here there is a striking similarity with Celan: 'for the Jew, as you know well, what does he own that really belongs to him, that is not lent, borrowed, never restored to him' ('Conversation on a mountain', *Strette,* Mercure de France, 1971, p. 171; my translation). For Celan, as for Barnes, the essence of the Jew is to have no definable essence, no property; even his name is 'unpronounceable' (*ibid.,* p.)

21. Meryl Altman has voiced unease at the way *Nightwood* may repeat rather than subvert Western representation of the Jews. See 'A Book of Repulsive Jews?: Rereading *Nightwood*', *art. cit.,* p. 167.

Deborah Parsons (essay date 2003)

SOURCE: Parsons, Deborah. "A Female Comic Epic: *Ryder.*" In *Djuna Barnes,* pp. 28-43. Horndon, England: Northcote House, 2003.

[*In the following essay, Parsons describes* Ryder *as "Barnes's most overtly autobiographical work," highlighting its central themes of the conflict between nature and culture, "the politics of sexual reproduction," and the mutual relationship "between man and beast."*]

'I am writing the female Tom Jones'[1]

One of Barnes's early assignments in Paris was her interview with James Joyce for *Vanity Fair* in 1922, in which she described *Ulysses* as 'that great Rabelaisian flower'.[2] Her first novel, *Ryder* (1928), offered her own tribute to Rabelais, a modern parody by a *female* writer of the bawdy and satiric style of the eighteenth-century comic epic. It rather surprisingly became a brief best-seller on its publication in New York, securing Barnes's reputation within the expatriate modernist circle and relieving her financial dependency on magazine work. Some degree of *Ryder*'s initial success might be put down to public curiosity, aroused by its censorship and consequent reputation as dangerously risqué. *Ryder* was just one of a number of works that famously fell foul of literary censorship in the 1920s, including Joyce's *Ulysses*, Radclyffe Hall's *The Well of Loneliness* and D. H. Lawrence's *Lady Chatterley's Lover*. When the novel was seized by the New York Post Office, Barnes was forced to remove passages referring to bodily fluids or religious blasphemy, along with several of her illustrations.[3] The final published version included a defiant foreword written by Barnes from Paris:

> This book, owing to censorship, which has a vogue in America as indiscriminate as all such enforcements of law must be, has been expurgated. Where such measures have been thought necessary, asterisks have been employed, thus making it matter for no speculation where sense, continuity, and beauty have been damaged.
>
> That the public may, in our time, see at least a part of the face of creation (which it is not allowed to view as a whole) it has been thought the better part of valour, by both author and publisher, to make this departure, showing plainly where the war, so blindly waged on the written word, has left its mark.
>
> Hithertofore the public has been offered literature only after it was no longer literature. Or so murdered and so discreetly bound in linens that those regarding it have seldom, if ever, been aware, or discovered, that that which they took for an original was indeed a reconstruction.
>
> In the case of Ryder they are permitted to see the havoc of this nicety, and what its effects are on the work of the imagination.
>
> (*R* [*Ryder*] vii)

What remained, however, was far from prudish, and instead remained so shockingly frank that one reviewer in the *New York Evening Sun*, referring to the expurgations, commented that, 'In spite of this cautiousness, I doubt that the book is sold openly in Boston'.[4] Described by the *Evening Post* as, 'the very backlash of Puritanism', it upturned literary, religious and sexual orthodoxy through linguistic and thematic misrule.

THE FAMILY TREE

Ryder is at once a picaresque novel, social satire and eccentric family chronicle, but also a parable of the politics of sexual reproduction. Barnes's style, however, in the words of one recent reviewer, 'honors no boundaries and makes no concessions'.[5] In *Ryder* she eschews the conventional chronology and realist style of the family saga, which is told as if from hindsight, thus merging past, present and future. The stylized language and diction mimic earlier literary periods, notably that of Chaucerian verse and the Restoration drama which expressed the tone of a post-Puritan age through bawdy frivolity and unrestrained blasphemy. The subtle juxtaposition and reworking of styles and genres, however, along with breaks in the conventional linearity of plot and narrative, indicate the strategies of modernism. The plot, as much as there is one, is based closely on Barnes's childhood on Storm Mountain and tells the story of Wendell Ryder, an instinctive polygamist who lives on a homestead with his mother, his wife and his mistress, along with their eight children.

The early chapters of the book present a brief history of the family, introducing Sophia Ryder, her son Wendell and his future wife Amelia, their life in England and relocation to America, and the arrival of Kate Careless, a friend of Sophia's from London who becomes Wendell's mistress. The focus then turns to accounts of Wendell's repeated infidelities, his evergrowing family, and the peculiar domestic events of the Ryder household. Refusing to conform to the dictates of puritan mores, Wendell houses his two families, one by Amelia and one by Kate, in attempted harmony under one roof, rejecting the rigidity of the local school, and insisting on the children being educated at home. After increasingly threatening demands by Church and school that Wendell submit to their social law, he is accused of immorality and told to sacrifice his lifestyle or face prosecution.

Ryder is Barnes's most overtly autobiographical work, and both Andrew Field and Phillip Herring in their biographies emphasize the context of Barnes's childhood on the Long Island farm and the direct parallels between Wendell and Sophia Ryder and Barnes's father and grandmother. Wald Barnes's beliefs and lifestyle, abetted by his doting and equally free-thinking mother, resulted in an unusual domestic environment in which his two families lived under one roof. Neither Djuna nor her brothers attended school, receiving a creative and artistic education at home. In *Ryder,* Barnes offers a largely sympathetic portrayal of her father, which celebrates his social nonconformism even though it also expresses her resentment at his constant adultery. In her later work, however, notably Nora's dream of her leering grandmother in *Nightwood,* and the family hatred and tragedy of *The Antiphon,* she would reveal a more emotionally abusive family history and the memory of sexual advances by both her father and grandmother. Angry at her father's unfaithfulness and what she perceived as her mother's bias towards her sons, Barnes certainly formed her closest family attachment with her grandmother, one that the teasingly erotic letters from Zadel to Djuna in the Barnes archive suggest may have been incestuous. In *Ryder,* Wendell's daughter Julie, the character who can be equated with Barnes herself, is described as Sophia's 'favourite child' (*R* 143).

Zadel, with her stories of her life as a journalist and her literary salon in London, was undoubtedly an influence on her granddaughter. In Barnes's fictional version of her family history, she recalls Zadel's varied interests and vibrant imagination in an image of the walls of Sophia's bedroom, onto which are repeatedly pasted pictures that fascinate her, forming a palimpsestic scrapbook of history and identity, from which no picture or clipping is ever removed:

> Sophia's wall, like the telltale rings of the oak, gave up her conditions, as anyone might have discovered an they had taken a bucket of water to it, for she never removed, she covered over. [. . .] the originals were, as she herself was, nothing erased but much submerged.
>
> (*R* 13)

She admires self-reliant women, including 'George Eliot, Brontë, Elizabeth Stanton, Ouida, the great Catherine, Beatrice Cenci, Lotta Crabtree, and the great whore of the spirit, the procuress of the dead, the madame of the Bawdy-house-of-the-Shades, the miracle worker—"Caddy-Catch-Can"' (*R* 13). The mix is eclectic but all are marked by determination or unconventionality. One or both of these qualities is evident in each woman: the writers George Eliot and Emily Brontë (Barnes pointedly referring to the pagan-orientated Emily as *the* Brontë); leading suffragist Elizabeth Stanton; Catherine, Empress of Russia; sensation writer Ouida; Lotta Crabtree, a hugely popular nineteenth-century variety actress; and Beatrice Cenci, a young Roman noblewoman sentenced to death by the Pope in 1599 for the murder of her cruel father, whose story was turned into a verse tragedy by Percy Bysshe Shelley in 1819. 'Caddy-Catch-Can' is possibly Madame Helena Blavatsky, the Russian spiritualist and co-founder of Theosophy, who Phillip Herring suggests Zadel Barnes may have known in London.[6] The male figures pictured on the wall are more divergent in their appeal, 'men she admired for this and that' (*R* 13), but include Dante, Oscar Wilde and Savonarola, the ascetic Dominican preacher who denounced the corruption of the Medici dynasty in Florence and was excommunicated and sentenced to death for heresy in 1498. All hold the status of quasi-prophet or divine celebrity. Following down the wall from the portraits are prints of 'all she abhorred', various forms of human and animal torture, and a picture of capital punishment by pregnancy, 'the filling of the belly, known as the Extreme Agony' (*R* 13), in which reproduction is again portrayed as torturous and unnatural.

Sophia is described as coming from

a great and a humorous stock. By 'great' is meant hardy, hardy in life and hardy in death—the early Puritan. [. . .] By 'humorous' is meant ability to round out the inevitable ever-recurring meanness of life, to push the ridiculous into the very arms of the sublime.

(*R* 9)

Barnes viewed the American puritan past with a consistent hatred, but, for her too, humour provided a means of relief from the adversity of human existence, and 'to push the ridiculous into the very arms of the sublime' offers a succinct summary of her constant aim in both life and literature. The strategy is epitomized in the story of the series of five chamber-pots that are ordered by Sophia when she comes of age, embellished in gold lettering with the phrases 'Needs there are many', 'Comforts are few', 'Do what you will', 'Tis no more than I do', 'Amen' (*R* 11). Ten years later, two of the pots have been broken and thus the lines 'Comforts are Few' and 'Tis no more than I do' have been lost. Shortly after, 'Do what you will' suffers a similar fate, and after another ten months 'Needs there are many'. Only 'Amen' is left, and 'Sophia looked upon this catastrophe with something of fear' (*R* 12). Representing different stages in life, the pots mark the early loss of any comfort and sense of autonomy, followed later by indifference. Man is left only with needs, which disappear when he prays for death. The theme is Barnes's black vision of existence, but the manner of telling is an example of the coexistent wit that provides the repartee to her despair and characterizes the mock-epic style of the novel.

JESUS MUNDANE

Ryder opens with the introduction of Wendell as 'Jesus Mundane', accompanied by a drawing in which he sits astride his horse on a cloud, surrounded by adoring women in puritan dress. In a parody of the Bible, the text informs the reader of his divine calling as a fleshly saviour:

> Go not with fanatics who see beyond thee and thine [. . .] for such need thee not, nor see thee, nor know thy lamenting, so confounded are they with thy damnation and the damnation of thy offspring, and the multiple damnation of those multitudes that shall be of thy race begotten [. . .]. Alike are they distracted with thy salvation and the salvation of thy people. Go thou, then, to lesser men, who have for all things unfinished and uncertain, a great capacity, for these shall not repulse thee, thy physical body and thy temporal agony, thy weeping and thy laughing and thy lamenting.
>
> (*R* 3)

Wendell's role on Earth, as he imagines it, is not to conform to the religious 'fanatics' who aim for salvation through the rejection and damnation of material pleasures and the denial of the physical body, but to promote a doctrine of superabundant procreation. The prodigal son, his vain desire is to become the 'Father of All Things' (**R** 210), a philosophy that he passes on to his son Timothy. His boast is to create a race in which all aspects of beast and human will be combined and 'No heart will beat with a difference' (**R** 211), and to achieve this aim he pursues a plan of 'bedding in all beds' (**R** 211) and encouraging free love amongst all things. An underlying theme of the novel is thus the exploration of the differentiation of nature and culture, focusing on the clash between Wendell's lustiness and the society within which he lives. Barnes's perspective is ambiguous, implying support of Wendell's lifestyle as an act of resistance against an austere Protestant morality, and yet critiquing the denigration of women by his arrogant masculinity. In part his unorthodox lifestyle suggests an alternative to the social hegemony of middle-class conservatism and sexual repression, and as such Wendell is an appealing character, with an instinctive and vital approach to life, his insistence on the naturalness of sexual activity, and his recognition of female sexual desire, for example, radically denying the strict religious and moral doctrine of provincial American puritanism. At the same time, however, Wendell remains firmly entrenched within a gendered account of sexuality, in which the purpose of intercourse is procreation and women's sensual pleasure only of importance as a boost to his male vanity.

The tension between these accounts is debated in chapter eight by two unmarried sisters 'Pro and Con', whose role seems to be that of a chorus, breaking the flow of the narrative to provide commentary on Wendell's character. While Pro contemplates the possible truth of his claim that 'no woman, however fanciful, however given to speculation and to trial, to coquetry and to gorging, can be happy without his peculiar kind of collusion' (**R** 39), Con argues tartly that he 'paints a rosy picture of polygamy' only for 'the *man*' (**R** 40-41). Contemplating the choice of fleshly sexuality or spinster gentility, they decide to opt for the latter. A similar comparison pervades the discussion between Amelia, as she is about to leave for America and marriage with Wendell, and her sister Ann, who chooses to remain unmarried and live as a female companion. Despite the calm and rational arguments that are made against Wendell, however, the life of the spinster is empty and sterile when compared with the passion and vitality of his sexual activity. Pro and Con, for example, indulging in discussion of Wendell's exploits as a titillating diversion from the polite decorum of their everyday life, recall Vera and Amelia Burgson from Barnes's play **The Dove,** frustrated by their repressed desires. Barnes does briefly hint at an alternative, in the description of six women who satisfy their sexual desires amongst themselves in lesbian foreplay, 'snatching at their companions' individual herbage and soft spots' (**R** 41). With the arrival of Wendell and

his 'thundering male parts' (**R** 42), however, this non-procreative sexual activity is quickly abandoned and the women instead fight each other in jealousy.

Throughout **Ryder** Barnes voices a dark underside to Wendell's philosophy of procreation by calling attention to the pain and destructiveness of childbirth. Written against the socio-political background of the birth control movement of the 1910s and 1920s, which attempted to counter disease, high maternal death rates and excessive family size, the novel reflects not only the argument for contraception by campaigners such as Margaret Sanger in the US and Marie Stopes in England, but also a cultural backlash and re-emphasis by patriarchal Western society of women's fundamental role as child-bearer. Wendell, for example, argues that free love is a natural and therefore moral act, but his continual promiscuity without any use of contraception results in the frequent pregnancies of both Amelia and Kate, and the financial burden of an ever-increasing family. By the end of the novel, when the 60-year-old Sophia is forced into begging and he attempts to economize on the household expenses by feeding the children with bread made from cow feed, his wife and mistress have little sympathy. Their long obligation to satisfy his sexual demands is now counterbalanced by Wendell's responsibility to support them and their children. Overhearing Wendell and Sophia discussing what they are to do, for example, Kate screams in fury that he has brought his troubles upon himself:

> 'I'll have my children, as many as I like, and that for you! [. . .] you've taken me, you've brought me to your house, you've bred with me, and I've got the taste.' Here she laughed. 'I've become infatuated with the flavour of motherhood; you poked it under my nose, and I've learned to like it. It makes me ill, and there's no pleasure at either end, but I'm addicted, and it's your fault, keeper of the shop, and madame of the keeper!'

> (**R** 170)

When he pleads to Sophia 'Mother, what does one do with nature?', even she turns away, recognizing Kate's suffering in pregnancy and responding wearily that 'A humane man would occasionally give it respite' (**R** 172).

If Barnes's relish of the humorous bawdy and romping pace of language in **Ryder** endorses sexual activity as natural and pleasurable, her representation of pregnancy as a condition that weakens the female body and can even prove fatal expresses angry support of the need for women's sexual emancipation through birth control. Chapter thirteen, 'Midwives' Lament, or the Horrid Outcome of Wendell's First Infidelity', is a brief and sombre verse that commemorates the death of one of his sexual conquests,

> Who died as women die, unequally
> Impaled upon a death that crawls within;

> For men die otherwise, of man unsheathed
> But women on a sword they scabbard to.
> And so this girl, untimely to the point,
> Pricked herself upon her son and passed
> Like any Roman bleeding on the blade—
>
> (*R* 77)

The euphemisms are unmistakably transparent and the woman dies as a result of Wendell's penetrating penis, 'pricked' by his 'sword' and 'impaled' on the child within her. Such a disaster seems impossible to prevent, however, as man is locked into a cycle of reproduction. The chapter 'Rape and Repining', for example, sets a more general context for Wendell's sexual roving. Bemoaning women's inevitable fall—

> A Girl is gone! A Girl is lost! A simple Rustic Maiden but Yesterday swung upon the Pasture Gate, with Knowledge nowhere, yet is now, to-day, no better than her Mother, and her Mother's Mother before her! Soiled! Despoiled! Handled! Mauled! Rumpled! Rummaged! Ransacked!
>
> (*R* 21)

—the narrator despairingly mourns the rapid loss of virginity, venting an angry diatribe against such easy capitulation to male seduction:

> Can Hounds track her down to Original Approval: the Law frame her Maidenly again; the not-of-occurring-particular-Popish dispensation reset her Virginal? Can Conclaves and Hosts, Mob and Rabble, Stone her back into that sweet and lost condition? Nay, nor one Nun going down before the down going Candle, pray her Neat.
>
> (*R* 21)

The tone is exaggerated, and the chapter at first a parody of moralistic dismay at such abandoned behaviour from the liberal perspective of the 1920s. As it continues, however, the reason for the narrator's passion—which is that heterosexual coupling extends and continues the torturous existence that human beings must endure before death—becomes apparent. A similar notion of the painful mortality of mankind is found in Dr Matthew O'Connor's alternative account of the Genesis myth, in which 'Sorrow burst and the seeds fell and took root, and climbed about the stations of the cross and bore Him down to earth, and climbed on and on and bore Matthew and Nora and Jason down to earth, [. . .] and climbed on and bore their children and their children's children down to earth' (*R* 140). Wendell's philosophy of procreation, intended to endow his name with immortality, is thus ironically also associated with the death wish. 'Man is born to die', the narrator informs the woman reader, 'and we, with Fortitude, have made the Farthest Outposts of Death a Lawful Goal, but you, in this Wanton Act, have advanced that Mark' (*R* 27). Women are thus made as responsible as Ryder himself for the perpetuation of the human race, and the chapter ends in frustration at the inevitability of male and female coupling: 'It is Spring again [. . .] It is Girls' Weather and Boys' Luck' (*R* 29).

This negative representation of the inevitability of reproduction and motherhood is immediately followed by the chapter introducing Amelia de Grier, Wendell's future wife. When Amelia is 17, her mother tells her to 'Never, never, have children', but, resigned to the futility of her warning, predicts: 'It takes a strong woman to die before she has been a fool. No one has the imagination; I did not, you will not' (*R* 32). Amelia in turn later tells her own daughter, Julie, 'Once I was safe enough and I could not let well enough alone, but must get myself in the way of doom and damnation by being natural. So take warning by my size and don't let a man touch you, for their touching never ends, and screaming oneself into a mother is no pleasure at all' (*R* 95). As she goes into labour, however, the 10-year-old Julie lies on her bed, clutching a doll to her stomach and screaming in mock childbirth. Pregnancy seems impossible to avoid, but it makes of women little other than self-destructive breeding machines. Sophia's mother, Cynthia, after years of continual child-bearing, lies on her deathbed with her fourteenth, 'a terrible suffering centre without extremities' (*R* 7).

DENYING THE FATHER

Despite Wendell's mission to become the progenitor of an entire 'Ryder' race, the novel actually constantly undercuts the patrilineal, notably through women who confound the male act of fathering and deny the otherwise inevitability of women's reproductive role. Sophia Ryder, although herself a mother, and a woman who gains the devotion of single women and appeases the jealousy of wives by demanding 'Call me mother!' (*R* 12), refuses men any status as the father of her children. Her own conception is never described, the novel stating only that 'she had hatched on every side' (*R* 9). Moreover, contriving to remain aloof from woman's guilt and complicity in procreation, she denies having intercourse with Wendell's father, the Latin tutor John Peel, after her first fall. Telling Wendell that he was conceived in a dream in which she was visited by the spirit of Beethoven, she claims: 'You know well enough how thoroughly I hated your father. Would it be conceivable then, that I, of some mettlesome quality, should give him access to that place that so heartily complained upon the first intrusion?' (*R* 37). Refusing her husband's name for both herself and her children, it is thus Sophia who stands at the head of the Ryder family tree, as matriarch and the main financial provider for the family. By the age of 70, when her son has reduced his family to penury, she turns her talents to 'superbly conceived letters of beggary' (*R* 14), always signed 'Mother', to wealthy men that she had known in earlier days. 'Dressing in irreproachable linen, wrapping her pauper's cloak about her' (*R* 15), she resourcefully manages to keep the family in comfort.

Two other women, Molly Dance and Lady Bridesleep, oppose male sexual authority by directly repudiating Wendell's claim of fatherhood. As her name suggests, Molly Dance is a woman who has enjoyed sexual promiscuity as much as Wendell himself, and who has 'got her children where and when it pleased her' (*R* 191). Unaware of who her father is, she is as unconcerned about the fact that she does not know who the various fathers of her own children might be as she is about their illegitimacy. Wendell's masculine pride, by contrast, is bewildered by her indifference, as she asks him, 'who cares? He didn't, I don't, and the child won't have to, and that's simplification' (*R* 198). To 'simplify' men out of the reproductive equation is unbelievable to Wendell, however, who offers to father the next child, seemingly naïvely unaware of Molly's mocking agreement and her power to easily undercut his patriarchal authority. After intercourse he is thus confounded when she slyly teases, 'there's only one thing that might make something uncertain of this certainty' (*R* 199), telling him that a policeman had had the same idea two nights before. Refusing Wendell's phallocentric suggestion, moreover, that whereas his promiscuity is a divine act, her own is damned and will lead her to hell, she asserts that 'Original sin was not at all as your biographers make it [. . .] original sin was not a woman's' (*R* 197).

Lady Bridesleep, an older woman who has past her menopause, also determines to ridicule Wendell's conviction of his role as primogenitor. Like Molly Dance, Lady Bridesleep too enjoys the sensual pleasures of the sexual act, yet as a result of her sterility is able to indulge without fear of pregnancy. Realizing that Wendell is ignorant of her age, she welcomes his flatteries and knowingly allows him to seduce her. The following morning however, when Wendell asks her what they should name their child, she laughs at his presumption, replying, 'Nothing and Never [. . .] No child'. Explaining that his seed has been wasted within a barren body, she tells him that this 'non-child' proves his fallibility, and that 'On him you shall hang that part of your ambition too heavy for mortal' (*R* 211).

One other figure who stands in contrast to Wendell's virile, procreative philosophy is the homosexual Dr Matthew O'Connor, the physician who attends the pregnancies of Amelia, Kate and Molly Dance and will reappear, older, more bitter and more verbose in *Nightwood*. O'Connor's occupation as a physician places him in alliance with natural science, dealing with the physical body and its growth and degeneration. Despite thus accepting the body as animal, however, he contemplates the mortality of the body with despair. Refusing to deny the desires of his flesh, he is yet also desperate for

some meaning and spiritual life beyond it, which he seeks in the rites of the Catholic Church. Unlike Wendell, who is agnostic and attempts to detach himself from the authority of the Church, O'Connor turns to the church in order to articulate as a sin at the confessional his otherwise 'unspeakable' homosexuality, and to cry in blasphemous prayer at the altar: 'who am I that I should be damned forever and forever, Amen?' (*R* 139). At his words however, he experiences a vision in which the church burns in flames around a black mass:

> The candles took root and grew and rose toward the ceiling, and bloomed and wilted and died, and the ceiling grew and mounted and bloomed and wilted and died, and came down. And the stars came out on the great pillars of the candelaburm, and slid with them and dwindled and flickered and stood once more about the bier, the soft bodies of mourners in woolly clothing kneeling. [. . .] The figures at the altar blurred, crossed, melted into each other; fornication of the mass, parted and bred Death, Death's wailing child in wax, lying in a pool of wine, mouth open for the gushing breast of grief, pouring forth the Word in an even belt of wrath. The sacred cow swam the shallow chancel, a garland on his brow, lowing, In peace let him rest! The church turned upside down.'
>
> (*R* 140)

The scene is one of profane spiritual inversion. Although it upturns religious doctrine, however, it does not negate adoration of, or supplication to, the mystical. As a more degenerate O'Connor will explain in *Nightwood*, the opulent Catholicism of an ancient Europe, rather than the austere Puritanism of new and progressive America, holds solace for the damned in its sensuous spirituality. For it is with the decoration of the Catholic church, its candelabra, wine and garlands, that he envisions a material worship and erotic ecstasy, one that depends on the acknowledgement of faith and divinity even within a profane communion.

MYSTICISM AND THE BEAST

Wendell spurns the Church, in jealousy over the status of God as the supreme father. Denying the spirit, he justifies his doctrine of polygamy by identifying his actions with those of the animal world, claiming that his promiscuity is natural and bestial. He is sensitive to the natural world and recognizes an affinity with the animal in the sensual and instinctive aspects of the human organism; man's beating heart and physical needs and desires. In the verse summary of the novel in chapter ten, 'The Occupations of Wendell', for example, he questions the difference between his own instinctive desires and those of the animal world:

> Eft Wendell pondered, and he say him 'Sooth!
> What is this swims like dregs within the truth
> That animal and man be set apart?
> I hear not much difference in the heart

That beats soft and constant under hide,
And this same hammer ticking in my side!'

(*R* 61)

Although the equation is select and ultimately superficial, Wendell associating himself predominantly with the stud, in a hierarchy of beasts in which women are viewed merely as breeding stock for his valuable seed, he nevertheless disrupts the binary divisions of nature/culture and beast/human by refusing to distinguish himself from nature or to differentiate his family from his animals.

In *Beasts of the Modern Imagination* (1985), Margot Norris identifies a brief period, lasting from roughly the last decade of the nineteenth century to the 1930s, in which the cultural and biological uncertainty that resulted from evolutionary theory brought about a new fascination with the instinctual and the bodily, temporarily binding what she describes as 'the great cleft produced in our human being by the repression of the animal and the living body'.[7] This perspective, the blurring of the categories of man and beast, is a marked feature of Barnes's work. A primary source for *Ryder,* for example, was *L'Imagerie imaginaire* (1926), a collection of images of human-animal hybrids from the fifteenth century in which animals take on human roles and vice versa in an upturned hierarchy of the human and bestial, and a carnivalesque prediction of the nineteenth-century Darwinian collapse of man and animal that shook the anthropocentric assumptions of Western civilization. Images of animal and human morphology occur, moreover, in Barnes's Beardsleyesque illustrations for the poems of *The Book of Repulsive Women,* and continue in *Nightwood, The Antiphon* and the unfinished *Creatures in an Alphabet.*

What fascinates Barnes in all these texts, including *Ryder,* is the animal heritage within man's prehistory, the vestiges of animal spirit that remain embedded within the human memory and influence a connection and mutual recognition between man and beast, 'something recognized, forgotten, and yet insistent still in affects, instincts and dreams, like a faint nostalgia for our own infantile and presocial past'.[8] Wendell does not fully realize this connection until the closing chapter of the book. When, after capitulating to social demand and telling Amelia that he has chosen Kate over her as his wife, he escapes the house and sits helplessly pondering the future in a field, the animals surround him:

> And everything and its shape became clear in the dark, by tens and tens they ranged, and lifted their lids and looked at him; in the air and in the trees and on the earth and from under the earth, and regarded him long, and he forbore to hide his face. They seemed close ranged, and now they seemed far ranged, and they moved now near, now far, as a wave comes and goes, and they lifted their lids and regarded him, and spoke

> not in their many tongues, and they went a far way, and there was a little rest, and they came close, and there was none.

(*R* 242)

For Barnes then it is not so much in his carnal instincts that Wendell approaches true connection with the animal, but in this recognition of their dumb appeal when he has surrendered them to the forces of social authority and convention.

Ryder portrays a semi-mystical, cultural memory of the bestial that prefigures that of Robin Vote in *Nightwood,* perhaps one reason for Barnes's dedication of the novel to Thelma Wood. In the story of Beast Thingumbob, for example, which Wendell tells to his children Julie and Timothy, the natural world is presented as a realm of folklore or fairytale, the Beast himself being part bird, part lion and part ram. The Beast falls in love with a woman-like creature with no face, ten breasts, and hoofs instead of feet. The female beast has lived for hundreds of years without love but is 'not virgin as other women are' (*R* 119), by which Wendell seems to mean that she has been contented with her single existence, as although 'she had a greater share than any mortal woman could bear or possibly see to put up with, [. . .] to her the putting up was no great business' (*R* 120). Now, however, 'fettered to the earth for a season of harvesting, after which she was to return to the gods' (*R* 119), her time has come for sexual consummation. The physical act of love is her ultimate purpose on earth but will result in her death, and she calls the Beast to her, telling him 'I shall die beneath you, yet from my body you shall garner ten sons' (*R* 121).

The story is in part a further example of Wendell's own idealistic vision of himself as a natural beast with a spiritual purpose to deliver women from the asexual state of virginity, and a commentary on the destructive effects of his constant siring on his wife and mistress. It is also a mystical allegory of the fertility cycle of birth and death, however, that hints at an earlier, prehistorical state in which the cycle of time has no relevance. The story confounds not only social and religious but also evolutionary hypotheses of man identity and genealogy, and the illustration that accompanies the story, which depicts Beast Thingumbob in mourning next to his dying mate, was significantly one of those censored from the original edition for its 'unnatural' subject matter.

'And what does it mean?' asks Timothy as he contemplates the story of Beast Thingumbob. A similar question was silently posed by *Ryder*'s appreciative but perplexed contemporary reviewers, who drew attention to the novel's broad humour and presentation of a grotesque comedy of the human body, but avoided commentary on plot and meaning by focusing on Barnes's deft parodies of her bawdy influences, which by general consent were regarded as Rabelais, Sterne, Fielding and Joyce. With the colourful characters, witty eighteenth-century dialogue and complex formal style of **Ryder,** Barnes certainly proclaimed her status within Paris-based modernism, yet perhaps this very association also resulted in a simultaneous diversion of attention from the gender perspective of her narrative, her attempt to write the *'female* Tom Jones'. On the republication of **Ryder** in 1980, the *San Francisco Review of Books* commented:

> Perhaps language, however elaborately deployed, cannot gain human beings, particularly women, much purchase against their sexuality, against whatever combination of desire, obsession, trust, and despair binds them to torment at the hands of another. It may, however, provide a temporary reprieve, especially when the readily available alternative—isolation and sterility—begins to exert its fascination.[9]

The reviewer had the benefit of speaking from hindsight. Three months after the publication of **Ryder,** Barnes's pseudonymous **Ladies Almanack** became available on the streets of Paris, a chapbook in which language again battles against male authority, through the teasing tongue of a lesbian saint.

Notes

1. Quoted in Andrew Field, *Djuna: The Life and Times of Djuna Barnes* (New York: Putnam's, 1983), 127.

2. Djuna Barnes, 'James Joyce', *Vanity Fair,* April 1922, 104.

3. The illustrations, one depicting 'Beast Thingumbob' and another a soprano urinating in the street, are reprinted in the 1990 edition of *Ryder* published by the Dalkey Archive Press.

4. C. Hartley Grattan, 'A Lusty Book', *New York Evening Sun,* 1 August 1928.

5. Review of *Ryder* (St Martin's Press, 1980), *San Francisco Review of Books,* 7 April 1980, 6.

6. Herring, *Djuna,* 43.

7. Margot Norris, *Beasts of the Modern Imagination* (Baltimore: Johns Hopkins University Press, 1985), 3.

8. Ibid.

9. Review of *Ryder, San Francisco Review of Books,* March 1980 (Djuna Barnes archive, McKeldin Library, University of Maryland).

Select Bibliography

Works by Djuna Barnes

The Book of Repulsive Women: Eight Rhythms and Five Drawings (New York: Bruno's Chapbooks II, no. 6, 1915; Los Angeles: Sun & Moon Press, 1989).

Ryder (New York: Boni & Liveright, 1928; Illinois: Dalkey Archive, 1990).

Ladies Almanack (Dijon, France: Darantière, 1928; New York: Harper & Row, 1972; Illinois: Dalkey Archive, 1992).

Nightwood (London: Faber & Faber, 1936, 1950; New York: Harcourt Brace, 1937).

The Antiphon (London: Faber & Faber, 1958; New York: Farrar, Straus, 1958).

Creatures in an Alphabet (New York: Dial Press, 1982).

Biographical and Critical Studies

Field, Andrew, *Djuna: The Life and Times of Djuna Barnes* (Austin, TX: University of Texas Press, 1985). An interesting biographical study, although poorly documented and less accurate than that of Herring (see below).

Herring, Phillip, *Djuna: The Life and Work of Djuna Barnes* (New York: Viking, 1995). The best recent biography, extensively researched and documented.

Background Reading

Hall, Radclyffe, *The Well of Loneliness* (London: Virago, 1982).

Norris, Margot, *Beasts of the Modern Imagination* (Baltimore, MD: Johns Hopkins University Press, 1985).

Melissa Jane Hardie (essay date fall 2005)

SOURCE: Hardie, Melissa Jane. "'Repulsive Modernism': Djuna Barnes' *The Book of Repulsive Women*." *Journal of Modern Literature* 29, no. 1 (fall 2005): 118-32.

[*In the following essay, Hardie equates the 1949 republication of* The Book of Repulsive Women *by the Alicat Bookshop, which was done against Barnes's wishes, to the "notion of a textual return" thematized in the poems themselves, which "employ figures associated with modernity in a diction borrowed from the writings of the* fin-de-siècle."]

> "The only exact knowledge there is," said Anatole France, "is the knowledge of the date of publication and the format of books." And indeed, if there is a counterpart to the confusion of a library, it is the order of its catalogue.
>
> (Benjamin, "Unpacking my Library," *Illuminations* 60)

In 1952, Djuna Barnes wrote to Margaret Anderson, who had asked to reprint some early work of hers:

I feel it is a grave disservice to letters to reissue merely because one may have a name for later work or for the unfortunately praised earlier work,—*or for the purpose of nostalgia or "history" which might more happily be left interred.*

(Djuna Barnes to Margaret Anderson, 30.4.52)[1]

As one of the more famous shut-ins of the modernist movement, Barnes sometimes wished a similar fate for her early publications. She interprets the function of re-issue as a doubly negative one: "to reissue merely because one may have a name for later work or for the unfortunately praised earlier work"; the authorial name becomes in Barnes's words "a name for later work", a prolepsis. Reissue suggests "merely" the fortuity of a lack of symmetry between text and its author, a relationship whose negotiation is routed through and thus collapsed with the principle of textual intermediation variously embodied by the publisher, editor, and public.

Barnes opts, with irony, for the language of death; the "grave disservice" puns on the trope of text as corpse, an abject object which can only speak of history as vicissitude. The metaphorics of the dead text charge the lack of symmetry of the relationship between author and text with the profitable function of instituting the agency of the "living" author. Textual desuetude is re-read to instantiate authorial vitality: a useful institution of agency for the author whose texts threaten to have a healthier life in the public sphere than she does.[2] In fact, in her own practice Barnes was singularly adept at creating and perpetuating texts whose bodies spoke of change, and she was responsible for the republication of numerous texts which charted the diversity of history through careful rewriting; Barnes preferred the reissue of texts she had herself sedulously revised.[3] Barnes's notorious labor of revision, which provided the occupation of her post-expatriate years in New York, structurally stands to her writing, and in particular her poetry, as an attempt to erase the degree zero of the moment of publication.[4] This erasure was effected through two principal strategies: the total revision that resists any abiding resemblance between drafts and the act of revision as an act of endless deferral, a structure perhaps more familiar to any writer. If the pseudo-historical proposition embedded in Anderson's request is that the disinterred text resemble its earlier public sphere manifestation—look the same as it used to—Barnes is at odds, in various ways, with this proposition. In her work, as it were, nothing looks the same as it used to.

Barnes's sharp note to Anderson mentions "the unfortunately praised earlier work," an oblique aside that may be traced to a similar moment of disinterment which had occurred three years previously: the republication of her 1915 chapbook, *The Book of Repulsive Women,* in 1949. In Barnes's sixteen pages of vita, prepared for Who's Who, she simply leaves *The Book of Repulsive*

Women out of her list of publications (Series 1, Box 1, Djuna Barnes-vita). Barnes wrote to its new publisher, Oscar Baron:

you do not have my permission for this publication [. . .] I categorically forbid you to make such publication, and [. . .] if you proceed with such publication it will be at your own risk and peril.

(Djuna Barnes to Alicat Bookshop 13.10.48)

The republication of *The Book of Repulsive Women,* a text Barnes specifically wished to repress within her writing career, is a return of the repressed that mimics in the sphere of publication the text's own representations of literary history and its figurative returns, a representation that poses such returns as deadening.

Barnes wrote:

[. . .] I most certainly do not want any republication of that book of Repulsive Women [sic]. I hope no other person will ever get the unhappy idea.

(Djuna Barnes to Oscar Baron 29.1.48)

The edition was printed, to Barnes's "horror."[5] Ironically, a number of people have had that same idea, leading to a series of republications of Barnes's earliest book, which make it the most reprinted, with the exception of *Nightwood.*[6]

Agitating against the reappearance of the chapbook, Barnes characterized the reissue as an "[. . .] act of piracy" (Djuna Barnes to Oscar Baron, Alicat Bookshop 13.10.48). Oscar Baron argued to Barnes that *The Book of Repulsive Women* was "[. . .] intrinsically a very fine collection of verse, not at all dated by the transition of 33 years" (Oscar Baron to Djuna Barnes 13.10.48). He described his desire to reprint as "[. . .] the desire of a bibliophile to communicate a good piece of writing to another" (Oscar Baron to Djuna Barnes 13.10.48).

Baron aligns his publication with a connoisseurship that contingently disenfranchises the author as her text's "owner" in favor of an exchange of property between bibliophiles. Baron's letter signifies precisely how *The Book of Repulsive Women* may be "dated" by virtue of such an act, which precisely isolates and establishes the book's status as an "object" or "piece of writing" to be circulated among fetishist-connoisseurs; in this case such an identification is particularly marked given the text's status as a *livre composé.* This discourse of connoisseurship curiously mingles with Baron's desire to republish an arcane text in a modern edition. Baron's edition, in which the poems and illustrations are reproduced in white print on murky colored and coarse-weave paper, without page numbers, announces its own eccentricity as a boutique publication. Similarly, its republication as an "Outcast Chapbook" (Kannenstine 17) already coded it as marginal, "cast out," at once situating the text as an exemplar of the (now) dispersed field of modernist practice and marking its strangeness or estrangement from modernist canons. In Baron's edition, it joins a collection of bibliophile curiosities. Barnes's wish, that the "ancient" text remain ancient and forgotten, is proleptically coded in its status as a chapbook, an ancient or recondite textual offering.[7] In all her references to the volume, Barnes rarely gets the title right, calling it "that book of repulsive women," as if by doing so she limits the possibilities of its position within her own vita. In one letter describing the reissue, Barnes wishfully suggests that the book as material object had vanished: "I did not know that it still existed, and so did nothing about the copyright" (Djuna Barnes to Erich Linder, 18.11.48). Barnes comprehensively represses the existence of the text as object, referring here not to the historical existence of the text, but to the enduring existence of copies of the publication. Postulating or fantasizing its non-existence in this way—as an extreme exercise of copyright protection—mimics her repression of the historical, published text implicit in sequestering it from her vita and continuously misstating the title revisions: an elaboration of her writerly principle that nothing looks the same as it used to.[8]

Barnes's use of the metaphor of the dead text is echoed by critics of *The Book of Repulsive Women,* even as they pursue disparate analyses of the text. Carolyn Burke, in a reading of *The Book of Repulsive Women* as a generative text for women's modernist writing, suggests that "*The Book of Repulsive Women* reveals its author's awareness that she has, in fact, reached a dead end in the New York of 1915" (Burke 71). Louis Kannenstine, in an unremittingly unfavorable account of the poems, places the question of their survival firmly within a discourse on modernism as a practice of supercession and improvement: he suggests that "[i]t is doubtful that most of the early poems could survive by modern standards" (Kannenstine 18).

Kannenstine, in his negative account of the text, suggests that

[t]he tapering off of Djuna Barnes's productivity as a poet corresponds more or less to the decline in her output of essays and commercial writing.

(Kannenstine 18)

For Kannenstine there is a curious relationship between Barnes's early poetry, her least commercially oriented practice during her pre-expatriate career, and her journalism of that period.[9] Barnes worked as a successful journalist during the period in which *The Book of Repulsive Women* was first published, although its contents are only distantly (though I will suggest significantly) allied to that practice. This oxymoronic match between a commercial quotidian prose and ersatz decadent verse can be theorized through an understand-

ing of their dialectical relationship signalled in Kannenstine's use of the term "productivity." This was certainly the period in which Barnes published the most poetry, though not necessarily the occasion of her most sustained work with poetic genres, which more probably occurred during her post expatriate "exile" in Manhattan.[10] Kannenstine's model of productivity, then, returns us to the problematic relationship between the marketplace and the writer, and publication as the moment of textual and authorial production.

Baron's introduction of the ancient text into a modern marketplace, subtended by the discourse of the book connoisseur, represents a moment in the cultural life of Barnes's poetry which reproduces precisely those tensions between modernity and its history, publication, and privacy, which feature throughout her texts. In linking the title of *The Book of Repulsive Women* to its publishing history, and to its figurative strategies, the notion of a textual return can be extended to the way in which Barnes's verses employ figures associated with modernity in a diction borrowed from the writings of the *fin-de-siècle*. Both the verses and the illustrations that accompany them are clearly derivative of *fin-de-siècle* styles (Kannenstine 19-20), although Scott reads them as "Imagist" (Djuna Barnes 132). Guido Bruno, the original publisher of the chapbook, describes Barnes through the paradox of such an association in an interview published in 1919:

She is only one of many: a new school sprung up during the years of the war. Followers of the decadents of France and of England's famous 1890s, in vigorous, ambitious America.

(Barnes Interviews 388)[11]

Bruno's title for the interview, "Fleur du Mal à la Mode de New York." captures the intriguing association made by him between "vigorous, ambitious America" and the 1890s, and does so in part by doing it in French, mixing his citation of Baudelaire with an expression *au courant* precisely because it is in French.

Bruno's macaronic epithet represents modernity in or as an act of translation. It also marks another central issue in the analysis of Barnes's writing, the question of stylistic atavism and derivation. The "return" of *The Book of Repulsive Women,* despite Barnes's efforts to repress it in her vita, is matched by the return in her texts of a symptomatic recourse to the diction and style of earlier generations of writers in English. One of the most consistent features of Barnes's work is her manipulation of old genres and styles, a feature that has led to her perception as an oddity within modernism.[12] Accounts of Barnes as an historical oddity or "throwback" haunted her career.[13] Barnes's use of traditional verse structures and a diction usually associated with decadent writing is one demonstration of the text's manipulation of the overdetermined relationship between modernism and decadence, a relationship explored at length by Calinescu (151-221).[14]

The process of cultural "salvage" in Barnes's work may be aligned with one of Calinescu's defining parameters of kitsch; he quotes Wedekind's contention that kitsch is "the contemporary form of the Gothic, Rococo, Baroque" (225).[15] This is a series of styles with which Barnes is frequently associated: Barnes's writing is frequently characterized as Elizabethan, Restoration, Rococo, Augustan, Gothic, Decadent, either thematically, stylistically or generically. Barnes's use of archaism in her texts similarly figures the tension between modernism as a practice of cleansing (Benstock) and a practice of salvage (Ross).[16] In particular, Barnes's use of both literary antiquities and the work of her contemporaries marks the dialectical relationship between modernity and history as its returned repressed, if we accept the interpellation of stylistic atavism within poetry under the rubric nothing looks the same as it used to.

Barnes's process of reclamation may be allied with definitions of kitsch such as Calinescu's and with definitions of camp such as Ross offers in *No Respect* as "a rediscovery of history's waste, the re-creation of surplus value from forgotten forms of labor." (151). By this definition, the reissue-as-resurrection of *The Book of Repulsive Women* in 1949 figures a "camp liberation" of the collectible "piece of writing." Baron's reissue of the text in a form that figured archaism was nonetheless a new edition and as such may be read as a prophylactic modernizing: an old text but a new commodity. In this sense, Baron's piracy, as Barnes chose to describe it, is a return of her own textual piracy throughout the volume, and perhaps Barnes's displeasure with Baron sprang in part from her sense of ambivalent identification with the project. In particular, the piracy of copyright, interpellated as a discourse of material textuality, translates the plagiaristic piracy of the ersatz—or immaterial—decadent text precisely as expatriation, for Barnes, will become a trope of historicity, "translating" the modernity of Paris, "Capital of the Nineteenth Century" (Benjamin Baudelaire 155) as a nascent, twentieth-century American modernism.

The problem of return for modernism is thematized through both the subject matter and the disposition of poems in *The Book of Repulsive Women*. The poems describe the antics and practices of the "repulsive women," who are variously in homage to decadence, lesbians, and corpses, and they do so through a protocol of rehearsal. Poems are referred to each other both through subject matter and placement in the volume: **"From Fifth Avenue Up"** is followed by **"From Third Avenue On"**; **"In General,"** the second poem, is followed some pages later by **"In Particular."** "Corpse A" is matched by "Corpse B," and so on. Similarly, the

poems' movement or oscillation between the figure of the lesbian as a meta-woman, or discourse on woman, and the female corpse, a figuration of the stasis or immobility of poetic femininity, describes the text's shuttling between imitation or plagiarism as embodied discourses and critique, inverting the logic of disinterment or reissue to suggest instead that where generational critique takes place, nothing looks the same as it used to.

The title of *The Book of Repulsive Women* offers a reading of its women which the poems explore through the figurative manifestation of female corporeality. It was a title Barnes was to refer to in later years as "idiotic" (Djuna Barnes to Wolfgang Hildesheimer 19.1.69), but it succinctly demarcates the tropological investigations of the volume. Repulsion figures the trope as a "turn" or repulsion, but also figures the "repulsive" women as corporeal representatives in the text of a troping that is also a repulsion or anti-troping. In this sense, the effect of repulsive woman is in dialectical relationship to the function of the figure as tropism, as a form of inclination or attraction. They both participate in, and are differentiated from, a reading of the trope that relies upon the phallus as its transcendental signified, the subject of inclination or desire. The "repulsive" women are turned, but also turn away, their bodies acting as both the ground of representation and as apotropaic, a "turn off," guarding against the very figurative strategies through which they are described. Repulsive women also figure the unpredictability of the rhyme, as it works to discern resemblance or attraction or similarity between words, proposing an attraction or resemblance between them, whilst instituting their semantic, if not phonetic difference. Rhyme instantiates revision. For Burke, Barnes's use of rhyme is "satiric" (71), and her poetry manifests "verse patterns whose repetitions mock the very subject matter that they are in the process of unfolding "(71). Mocking imitation between poems—Barnes's and others'—is subordinated to the oscillations of rhyme necessarily located within the text; *The Book of Repulsive Women* employs parodic rhyme not merely to satirize the model, but more importantly to investigate the aural logic of rhyming. The dependence, in other words, of her texts upon some never-specified decadent "original" is negotiated through a thematized interest in the structure of rhyme as an internal system of derivation. Rhymes, insofar as they are always similarly dissimilar, operate to attract and repulse words from each other, proposing a poetic logic in which nothing looks (sounds) the same as it used to.

Not surprisingly, this process is most trenchantly formulated in the pair of poems titled **"In General"** and **"In Particular."** These poems exemplify the complex rhetorical work offered throughout the sequence, but curiously enough they avoid entirely the question of a gendered body, speaking instead of, or to, cloths and rags. With an elliptical and complex form of address, they each ask two questions of an unmarked addressee.

> What altar cloth, what rag of worth
>   Unpriced?
> What turn of card, what trick of game
> Undiced?
> And you we valued still a little more than Christ.
>
> ("**In General**" 11, ll. 1-6)[17]

"**In Particular**" follows the structure of "**In General**" almost exactly.

> What loin-cloth, what rag of wrong
>   Unpriced?
> What turn of body, what of lust
> Undiced?
> So we've worshipped you a little
> More than Christ.
>
> (15, ll. 1-6)

The poems are abrupt, even peremptory, apostrophes; each operates as much as an interruption as an interlocution. This shared address, from "we" to "you," hypostatizes the paradox of each poem's content. Each poem is abrupt and seemingly random, apparently at odds with the contextual material of the collection. And yet, in their specificity and directness, as in their titles, which suggest elaboration, demonstration, pointedness—each is overdetermined in terms of address; Each addresses a "you" who is both "general" and "particular," both ultimately ambiguous, "general," and pointedly specific, "particular." Rather than forming a pattern of enhanced detail, from general to particular, both are equally general, equally particular, shifting detail only as a matter of repetition. The title of the collection alone suggests that the poems are addressed to, and speak of, "repulsive women." And yet, in each of these two poems, the logic of their tropological operations produces an apostrophic address whose subject (without agency) is consistently repulsed; insofar as the address presumes intimacy, its rehearsal promotes repulsion.

Both poems thematize value, chance, and random effect; rather than offer the figure of Christ as a point of ideological reference, it becomes a trope of pure value, functioning here as much to structure the preceding rhymes as to suggest any question of spirituality. The movement charted from "general" to "particular" proceeds principally as sheer antithesis: "altar cloth" becomes "loin cloth," "worth" becomes "wrong." The metaphorical movement from "altar" to "loin," or from "worth" to "wrong," could hardly be described as from general to particular; each seems to depend upon aural similarities that override precise semantic functions. This antipodean model of revision is made more problematic by the retention of the same rhyme in both poems: in demonstrating the "turn" from "altar" to "loin,"

from "worth" to "wrong," the poems remain identical in their rhymes, which link "unpriced" "undiced" and "Christ." If the move from general to particular implies a teleological direction from rule to exemplar, or from abstraction to concrete entity, from wide angle to microscopic, the two poems suggest instead that such a movement finds in similarity—the overriding premise of such a formulation—sheer difference, or sheer repulsion. The move from a fairly usual use of the prefix "un" in "unpriced" to a more novel "undiced" marks the migration of a principle of negativity and negation, which is the work the repulsive women will do throughout the sequence, simultaneously as (in general) the corporeal representatives of revulsion (repulsive feminine corporeality) and (in particular) the principle of negation within these representations, negativity as the mark of a supplementary inscription of corporeality.

The rhymed shift from "undiced" to "unpriced" in each poem is paralleled by a shift in the use of each word between the two; "unpriced worth," which figures both worthlessness and pricelessness, degenerates into a "trick of game." Asking "What trick of game/Undiced?" points to a future calibrated only through its potential for more "dicing," which stands here equally for a practice of random iteration (iteration of the particular to ramify the general) and for a principle of infinite examination, calibration, "dicing" become division and dissection. These two meanings are in turn antithetical, as they equally figure accident and destination. Shifting from "undiced" to "unpriced" transfers the usual locating of rhyme from the beginning to the end of the word, a shift whose catachrestic novelty, indexed by the novelty of the prefix "un," proposes another motion of the repulsive turn from the end to the beginning of the line. Rhyme is inverted, another movement that structurally instates the repulsive potential of the "invert" woman.

By locating two poems in such obvious and yet opaque dialogue, the collection situates a series of problematics congruent with the "problem" of the historical status of the text discussed earlier. On the one hand, it raises the question of the collection per se: what logic, or at least *post hoc* formulation, might be adequate to formally and contextually relate diverse poems once they are collected? How might one address the paradox of a collection of repulsive items, each moving against the other even as propinquity highlights resemblance, repetition, closeness? On the other, it raises an ancillary issue that becomes fundamental to an historical reading of the tropological investments of the collection: given the premise of an intertextuality that implicates material both internal to the collection and external to it (the issue of derivativeness), how might the idea of movement or migration between texts be formally analyzed? In the case of these poems these issues are adduced through those morphological shifts noted above, and more specifically through their incorporation with a semantic shift from questions of chance to questions of the body. An analysis of these metatextual concerns with location and iteration shows that the question of repetition and divergence that I am suggesting is a formal registration of "repulsion," is enumerated, or exemplified, in "particular," perhaps, through a return to a discourse of the body. The renovation of "turn of card [. . .] trick of game/Undiced?" as "turn of body, what of lust/Undiced?" suggests both caprice and a foreclosure of meaning. Returning to the body is a "trick of game" and yet an inexorable turn, in which the physical gesture of a turned card is "turned" to turn the body. "Lust" as the index par excellence of the physical and its powers of attraction and repulsion, stands alone, unmodified and "undiced".

In the same way that repulsion offers a suggestive account of the syntactical and structural work of poetry, it offers direction for the reader, oriented to the text. The irony of the title could not be lost for a project of republication—what made this "repulsive" book so attractive to Baron and others? Perhaps it remained attractive at least partly because repulsion, irrespective of its valence, does suggest the positionality of reader; it is an orienting term even in its antipathy. Barnes dedicated the chapbook to her mother:

> To Mother
> Who was more or
> less like all mothers,
> but she was mine,
> —and so—
> She excelled.
>
>   (7)

"More or less," an equivocation that tropes oscillation as neutral effect, translates the simultaneous ascription of motherhood as a singular and plural category. If Barnes's dedication ironizes the singularity of any category, her play with the address of her poems—singular and plural—is uncannily matched by Kannenstine's conflation of subject and object as he turns to discuss the poem **"In General"**:

> Since the point of view of the narrative "we" in these poems is unvarying, it does not matter whether these women are taken individually or **"In General,"** as this brief poem is titled [. . .]"
>
>   (Kannenstine 22)

Kannenstine is correct in noting the unvarying use of a first person plural as the voice of the poems; his collapse of this voice with the subjects of the poems is more unusual, displacing the kinds of complex relays in evidence in the poems discussed above as a sheer translation of subject and object. Barnes's dedication figures above all the syntax of the shift from general to particular and its relevance to the topoi of the poems. The dedication provides orientation for one of the collec-

tion's most explicit thematizations of its own project. "Twilight of the Illicit" addresses its apostrophes to an immaterial, metaphorized lesbianism, an "illicit" practice, matched by the "illicitness" of addressing an immaterial bodily practice. It does so through tropes of maternity, suggesting both a genealogical relationship between tropes of self-sufficient feminine sexual practices and the fecund female body, a familiar convergence, and the genealogical routing of lesbianism as a generative custom:

> You, the twilight powder of
> a fire-wet dawn;
> You, the massive mother of
> Illicit spawn;
> While the others shrink in virtue
> You have borne.
>
>   (17 ll. 25-30)

This poem suggests the oxymoronic practice of decadent modernism through the trope of a "fire-wet dawn"; dawn and twilight chiastically link modernism and decadence to figures of maternal and lesbian corporeality in a scheme that perversely reconfigures the liaison of modernism and decadence—"twilight" and "dawn"—through this corporeal catachresis: an impregnating lesbian practice.

Barnes offers two lines of figuration for the bodies of the women she describes: figures of stillness, which are themselves repulsive to an account of the trope as a "turning" movement, and figures of repulsion, a turning away to be contrasted with the trope as a figure of inclination or desire. The logic of these poems is intricate: they argue both the difference of action and inaction and the difference between actions in their figurative register. Acts of figuration produce an instance of the gendered nature of figurative description, offering a representation of differences between tropes of action and inaction—masculine and feminine—which is subtended by an account of differences within representations of tropological action, thematized as feminine in the text. This simultaneity of reference instantiates a simultaneity that is also at work in repression; repression and its return are simultaneous (Freud, "Repression" 154). The figure of the repulsive woman simultaneously tropes inclination, desire, and apotropaic repulsion. The effect of these poems in describing an oscillation between the function of trope and anti-trope limns the text's deictic and figurative strategies, a relationship foregrounded throughout Barnes's writing. The "turning" of the trope may be seen as a turning towards and away, in other words, as a metaphorization of action. One way to figure the movement antithetical to tropism is through stillness: a stillness that features in Barnes's descriptions of women in the book. In **"Suicide"** (21), she writes of two women's corpses identified as "Corpse A" (l.1) and "Corpse B" (l.7). The movement of these bodies to a morgue is described as antithetical to their stillness:

> Corpse B
> They gave her hurried shoves this way
>   And that.
> Her body shock-abbreviated
> As a city cat.
> She lay out listlessly like some small mug
> Of beer gone flat.
>
> (21 ll.-13)

Barnes's figure resembles the famously bathetic simile that opens "The Love Song of J. Alfred Prufrock" to offer a similar effect of inaction:

> Let us go then, you and I,
> When the evening is spread out against the sky
> Like a patient etherised upon a table. [. . .]
>
> (1-3)

In **"Suicide,"** however, it closes the poem, with a figuration of stillness that, like Eliot's, guards against figurative "fancy" even as it is perversely figurative. The still, "flat" beer "flattens" the body of the woman as a consumable with a use-by date. This figure relies upon the "repulsive" body of the corpse as marker of temporality; repulsion, here figured as stillness, closes the poem which describes the body of the dead woman.

Barnes's figures of stillness are indebted particularly to the tradition of ekphrasis and in particular to Keats's "Ode on a Grecian Urn":

> Though her lips are vague as fancy
> In her youth—
> They bloom vivid and repulsive
> As the truth.
> Even vases in the making
>   Are uncouth.
>
> ("Seen From the 'L,'" 14 ll.21-26)

Barnes relies upon the point of view offered by the "L" to describe her woman-turning-vase. The "L," an elevated train line that bisected Manhattan, is the place where stillness and movement meet, in the body of the journalist-*voyeur* moved, but not moving, through the city streets. Barnes's text orients us to the bodies of her women by orienting us to the poems as observers whose "general" and "particular," singular and plural vision of them is panoramic. Bruno described the poems as singular, and their audience as plural; the poems become the vehicle which, in exchange, offers transportation between these two positions. He suggests that the chapbook is

> a chant which could be sung by those who are in the daily procession through the streets and highways of our metropolis but which could also be sung by those who are on balconies and house-tops viewing the eternal show of daily life.
>
> (Bruno in Kannenstine 20)

Barnes makes use of the "L" as the locomotive site of spectatorship, the place where the city is observed by the *flâneur*.[18] The *flâneur*, the solitary male figure of high modernity who strolls and gazes, is automated as the passenger, whose prospect is topographical, not cultural: a point of view described by transit, the passage of time, rather than voyeurism, the act above all of stillness.[19] Locomotion institutes the passive orientation of the erstwhile strolling voyeur. The spectatorship of Barnes's anonymous *flâneur* is represented as a process reproduced in the turning of the woman into a vase, as the vagueness of "fancy" is contrasted with the "vivid" and "repulsive" nature of "truth" before the transformation enacted by observation.

Barnes returns to the *flâneur* his locomotion through the anachronism and misposition of the "L." The point of stationary observation is nevertheless always also a point of transport; the *flâneur*, like the suicide, is motionless and moving. The stillness of the voyeur, whether figured through the act of voyeurism itself or through the implication of the locomotive as a mechanical representative of modernism, is ultimately the agent positioned by the giddying turns of the repulsive women, whose logic of antithesis collects him as its delayed referent. This move proleptically forestalls the bibliophile—1949's simulacrum of the *flâneur*—and his appreciation of the "object" of poetry. Her transformation of observation reproduces one of the key topoi of modernism—the flâneur—as the representative of a gendered logic of surveillance, and in positioning him on the "L" she ironizes his ambulatory stretch. As their historical movement is circumscribed by the logic of their own positions, the position of stillness is transposed from the repulsive women, whose bodies even when still are turning, to the *flâneur*, bibliophile, erstwhile publisher, Baron, and Bruno alike. Barnes's figures suggest that what is never possible is the reproduction of the text: the stationary position of the *flâneur*-cum-bibliophile is indexical to the rotations of the text which render it unreproducible even, or especially, in facsimile. To reissue is not to reproduce. This historical disarticulation lies at the heart of Baron's reissue of the boutique chapbook, under the auspices of dilettantism, and through the mechanism of late capitalism's fetish of the reproducible text. This failure of reproduction is chiastically structured by the text's original boutique publication and its piracy of decadence. Barnes's move to suppress the text was her failed tactic in a disengagement from Baron; the text's own figurative strategies do the work in any case. Precisely because, like a corpse, Barnes' unrevised chapbook lay "still," "repulsive" for all those years, its reissue as a self-similar artifact of early modernism "merely" showed that nothing looks the same as it used to.

Notes

1. The analysis offered in this paper is based in part upon material held as the Djuna Barnes Collection, University of Maryland at College Park. I thank the Authors League Fund for permission to quote from this material. All references to unpublished letters and typescripts will be given parenthetically in the text. A directory of unpublished materials will be found in the bibliography. Part of this letter is quoted in Broe, *Silence and Power* 251.

2. With the exception of her last book, *Creatures in an Alphabet* (1982), Barnes's publications after 1958 to her death in 1982 were all republished earlier work.

3. Her short story, "Aller et Retour" (which, in reply to the request that opened this paper, she offered to Anderson in place of the story Anderson wished to reprint) is emblematic. It was published in four versions over nearly forty years, from 1924 to 1962.

4. For a somewhat grudging account of Barnes's labor of revision, see in particular O'Neal (1990).

5. In 1949, Barnes wrote to her Italian agent at the Agenzia Letteraria Internazionale:

   > Yes, unfortunately, and to my horror, and against protests, one Oscar Baron has re-printed a booklet of ancient origin (1915 to be exact) called "The Book of Repulsive Women". I did not know that it still existed, and so did nothing about the copyright.

   (Djuna Barnes to Erich Linder, 18.11.48)

6. Most recently republished by the Sun and Moon Press, and Bern Boyle Books (both 1989), *The Book of Repulsive Women* was also, according to the copyright data, included in the Bern Boyle edition republished in 1976 by Rob Doll (8).

7. For "ancient," see Barnes's letter to Linder, n4.

8. One other consequence of the reprint was registered some twenty-five years later in the form of a 1972 edition of *Ladies Almanack,* for which Barnes gave approval, according to Susan Sniader Lanser, "allegedly fearing the kind of literary piracy that had already occurred with *The Book of Repulsive Women*" (Lanser 165). Barnes's permission to reprint *Ladies Almanack* represented an abstraction of the ideas of prophylaxis and consent; it implied these principles only through the case of their transgression.

9. For a summary of Barnes's career during this period, see Field (1983). Barnes worked as a journalist through the early teens to the late twenties, although her journalism shifted significantly during this period. Selected journalism is collected in *Interviews* (1985) and in *New York* (1989).

10. Barnes's last book, *Creatures in an Alphabet* (1982), as noted above, was her only one new publication after 1958. Suggestively, it was a collection of verse and illustrations at least superficially similar to *The Book of Repulsive Women.*

11. Kannenstine traces the *fin-de-siècle* effect of these poems directly to Guido Bruno, their publisher, "a champion of aestheticism" (19); as Barnes feared, with the republication of the book the publisher becomes the locus of the aesthetics of the text.

12. Schenck states this problem most cogently in her outline of a polemic for her analysis of genre in modernism:

    > My polemic throughout this essay is the dismantling of a monolithic modernism defined by its iconoclastic irreverence for convention and form, a difference that has contributed to the marginalisation of women poets during the period and even division among them [. . .].

    (244)

13. This is particularly well demonstrated in Messerli's descriptive bibliography (1975).

14. See also Cassandra Laity in "H. D and A. C. Swinburne: Decadence and Sapphic Modernism" (1990) and Marilyn Gaddis Rose in "Decadence and Modernism: Defining by Default" (1982) for analyses of this relationship sensitive to issues of gender.

15. Calinescu's quotation, his translation, is from Frank Wedekind *Gesammelte Werke* (Munich: George Muller, 1924) 9: 210.

16. Benstock writes: "Fear of contamination is the founding premise of modernism" (186-187).

17. All references are to the 1989 Ben Boyle edition of *The Book of Repulsive Women*; the 1989 Sun and Moon edition is un-paginated.

18. See Orvell (1989) on William Dean Howells, the "el" and spectatorship (36). See Buck-Morss (1989) on Benjamin's complex theorizations of these relationships.

19. See Wolff (1985) on the gender specificity of the historical and tropological *flâneur.*

Works Cited

Unpublished Materials All unpublished materials are part of the Djuna Barnes Collection at the University of Maryland at College Park. References follow the McKeldin Library catalogue data.

Barnes's letters are catalogued under the name of the recipient. Letters are carbon copies of typescript.

Series I, Box 1: Djuna Barnes—daybooks; Djuna Barnes—vita.

Series I, Box 1: Agenzia Letteraria Internazionale (Erich Linder); Alicat Bookshop (Oscar Baron); Margaret Anderson.

Series I, Box 9: Wolfgang Hildesheimer 1959-1970.

Barnes, Djuna. "Aller et Retour." *Transatlantic Review* 1 (April 1924): 159-67. Rpt in *A Night Among the Horses, Selected Works of Djuna Barnes,* and *Spillway.*

———. *A Night Among the Horses.* New York: Liveright, 1929.

———. *Creatures in an Alphabet.* New York: The Dial Press, 1982.

———. *Interviews.* Ed. Alyce Barry. Foreword and Commentary by Douglas Messerli. Washington: Sun and Moon Press, 1985.

———. *Ladies Almanack.* 1928. New York: Harper and Row, 1972.

———. *New York.* Ed. with commentary by Alyce Barry. Foreword by Douglas Messerli. Los Angeles: Sun and Moon Press, 1989.

———. *Selected Works of Djuna Barnes: Spillway/The Antiphon/Nightwood.* 1962. London and Boston: Faber and Faber, 1980.

———. *Spillway.* London: Faber and Faber, 1962.

———. *The Book of Repulsive Women.* 1915. Los Angeles: Sun & Moon Press, 1989.

———. *The Book of Repulsive Women.* 1915. New York: Alicat Bookshop, 1949.

———. *The Book of Repulsive Women.* 1915. New York: Ben Boyle Books, 1989.

Benjamin, Walter. *Charles Baudelaire. A Lyric Poet in the Era of High Capitalism.* Trans. Harry Zohn. 1973. London: Verso, 1985.

———. *Illuminations.* Ed. Hannah Arendt. Trans. Harry Zohn. New York: Schocken Books, 1969.

Benstock, Shari. "Expatriate Sapphic Modernism: Entering Literary History." Jay and Glasgow 183-203.

Broe, Mary Lynn and Angela Ingram, eds. *Women's Writing in Exile.* Chapel Hill and London: U of North Carolina P, 1989.

Broe, Mary Lynn ed. *Silence and Power: A Reevaluation of Djuna Barnes.* Carbondale and Edwardsville: Southern Illinois UP, 1991.

Bruno, Guido. "Fleurs du Mal à la Mode de New York—An Interview with Djuna Barnes by Guido Bruno." 1919. Reprinted in Barnes *Interviews* 383-388.

Buck-Morss, Susan. *The Dialectics of Seeing: Walter Benjamin and the Arcades Project.* Cambridge, Mass.: The MIT Press, 1989.

Burke, Carolyn. "'Accidental Aloofness': Barnes, Loy, and Modernism." Broe, *Silence and Power* 67-79.

Calinescu, Matei. *Five Faces of Modernity: Modernism Avant-Garde Decadence Kitsch Postmodernism.* Durham: Duke UP, 1987.

Eliot, T. S. [Thomas Stearns]. *Collected Poems 1909-1962.* London: Faber and Faber, 1974.

Field, Andrew. *Djuna: the Life and Times of Djuna Barnes.* New York: G. P. Putnam's, 1983. Published as *The Formidable Miss Barnes.* London: Martin, Secker & Warburg, 1983. Rpt. with new material as *Djuna: The Formidable Miss Barnes.* Austin: U of Texas P, 1985.

Freud, Sigmund. "Repression." 1915. *On Metapsychology* 139-158.

———. *On Metapsychology: The Theory of Psychoanalysis.* Trans. James Strachey. Ed. Angela Richards. Harmondsworth: Penguin, 1984. The Pelican Freud Library 11.

Gaddis Rose, Marilyn. "Decadence and Modernism: Defining by Default." *Modernist Studies* 4 (1982): 195-206.

Jay, Karla and Joanne Glasgow, eds. *Lesbian Texts and Contexts: Radical Revisions.* New York and London: New York UP, 1990.

Kannenstine, Louis F. *The Art of Djuna Barnes: Duality and Damnation.* New York: New York UP, 1977.

Laity, Cassandra. "H. D. and A. C. Swinburne: Decadence and Sapphic Modernism." Jay and Glasgow 217-240.

Lanser, Susan Snaider. "Speaking in Tongues: Ladies Almanack and the Discourse of Desire." Broe *Silence and Power* 156-168. Revised version of "Speaking in Tongues: Ladies Almanack and the Language of Celebration." *Frontiers* 4 (Fall 1979): 39-46.

Messerli, Douglas. *Djuna Barnes: A Bibliography.* Rhinebeck, NY.: David Lewis, 1975.

O'Neal, Hank. *"Life is painful, nasty, and short - in my case it has only been painful and nasty": Djuna Barnes, 1978-1981: an Informal Memoir.* New York: Paragon House, 1990.

Orvell, Miles. *The Real Thing: Imitation and Authenticity in American Culture, 1880-1940.* Chapel Hill & London: The U of North Carolina P, 1989.

Schenck, Celeste M. "Exiled by Genre: Modernism, Canonicity, and the Politics of Exclusion." Broe and Ingram 225-250.

Scott, James B. *Djuna Barnes.* Boston: Twayne, 1976

Wolff, Janet. "The Invisible *Flâneuse*: Women and the Literature of Modernity." *Theory Culture and Society* 2 (1985): 37-46.

Christine E. Coffman (essay date 2006)

SOURCE: Coffman, Christine E. "'What Insane Passion': Djuna Barnes's *Nightwood.*" In *Insane Passions: Lesbianism and Psychosis in Literature and Film,* pp. 103-36. Middletown, Conn.: Wesleyan University Press, 2006.

[*In the following essay, Coffman maintains that* Nightwood *should not be described as a "lesbian novel," suggesting instead that the book, mainly through the dominant voice of Dr. Matthew O'Connor, employs the trope of "purportedly psychotic queer women" as "screens for the madness at the heart of the Western symbolic."*]

> Freud's entire elaboration of the theory of identification works ceaselessly to negotiate a traumatic perception installed at the very heart of modernity: the fear of a fundamental and irretrievable loss of connection to the Other.
>
> —Diana Fuss, *Identification Papers*

In his now infamous introduction to the first edition of Djuna Barnes's 1936 *Nightwood,* T. S. Eliot invokes the opposition between sanity and insanity with the aim of insisting that the novel is not merely a "psychopathic study" (xv). Obliquely referencing both the queerness and the misery of Barnes's characters, Eliot attempts to dissuade readers from believing that the novel has no bearing on the lives of "normal" people (xv). For Eliot, the "abnormalities of temperament" shown by Barnes's queer characters are part of the novel's "deeper design": that of illustrating "the human misery and bondage that are universal." Eliot's introduction insists on the misery of "normal lives," striving to preempt readers from smugly dismissing *Nightwood* as a "horrid sideshow of freaks" (xvi). Yet ironically, in thus staking claim to the universality of the novel's plot, Eliot mimics the denial he presumes to characterize the reader. He does not claim that "normal" people *misrecognize* their own misery by refusing to see themselves in *Nightwood,* but rather that their misery "is mostly concealed." Refusing the possibility that the misery of some "normal lives" might be just as visible as that of Barnes's queer characters, Eliot reenacts rather than critiques the paranoid cultural logic through which queers' plights come to stand in for, and thereby mask, the problems of the people and the world around them.

Moreover, as Tyrus Miller observes, Eliot's rhetoric assumes that readers' misrecognitions of texts are "purely privative" rather than potentially productive—or indeed an inescapable feature of reading (122). If Eliot engages in a classically paranoid preemptive strike, striving to fend off interpretations whose consequences he finds potentially damaging, he in turn misrecognizes the extent to which Barnes's book *does* engage with the topic of psychopathology. *Nightwood,* much as do Lacan's "Motifs" and Breton's *Nadja,* figures love between women as a mother fixation that takes the form of a quasi-psychotic merger, an "insane passion for unmitigated anguish and motherhood" in which the women appear to have no agency in their desperate acts (75). *Nightwood* does not, however, present a diagnosis of its characters' insanity that we should take at face value; rather, it performs an "immanent critique" of the Western symbolic through which lesbianism would appear as an "insane passion." As Monica Kaup notes, the novel performs a "deconstruction of discursive authority" that "uncovers the fallacies of functional-scientific discourse" ("The Neobaroque" 102, 101).[1] Barnes stages a clash between the narrator's voice and the commentary of a fascinated male "clinician," Matthew O'Connor. Unlike Lacan and Breton, however, Barnes refuses to grant patriarchal authority to its doctor: O'Connor is not only a "quack" gynecologist but also both queer and (arguably) psychotic himself.[2] Functioning as a queer theorist *avant la lettre,* O'Connor does not believe in the neutrality of medicine, but rather questions the stability of the diagnostic framework within which lesbianism appears as psychosis. His mockery challenges the heterosexist assumptions at work in the figures of psychosis through which he represents passion between women, and thereby suggests that their pain is but a symptom of a larger social ailment. With O'Connor its most dominant voice, *Nightwood* as a whole suggests that purportedly psychotic queer women appear as screens for the madness at the heart of the Western symbolic, whose pretense to normalcy and cultural dominance was made all the more tenuous in the rapidly changing climate of the early twentieth century. Redeploying the terms through which queerness could be construed as madness, Barnes's novel launches an attack on the paranoid cultural logic through which women who desire other women are presented as threatening psychosis at the individual level and collapse at the cultural level.

If this chapter focuses on a specific strain of passion between women within one of what in a larger sense are Barnes's "queer texts," it does not do so to assert that *Nightwood* "organizes itself under the sign of same-sex love," as Joseph Boone would describe it (Allen 17; Boone 234-235). Barnes's novel does not seek an ontology of "homosexuality," "lesbianism," or "lesbian identity"; instead, its departure from the conventions of narrative realism (those so crucial to Radclyffe Hall's identity-based pleas for tolerance, for example) defies any attempt to pin it down as providing a specific representation of "lesbianism" as such.[3] Barnes's text thus cannot in any simple sense be described as a "lesbian novel," despite the claims that have been made of it in the past.[4] And while a number of scholars have begun the important work of critiquing the reduction of *Nightwood* to a commentary on lesbianism, conceived as an ontologically stable identity, they have stumbled on the question of how to acknowledge the text's "queer" undercutting of categories of identity while also delineating the specific modes of passion it traces out.[5] So if, like Carolyn Allen, I select for discussion here a strain of eroticism between women from what in a larger sense are Barnes's "queer texts," I do so to assert neither that female same-sex desire should be taken as an organizing principle for the novel nor that its female characters should be interpreted as navigating the vicissitudes of a "lesbian" identity that precludes their experiencing other kinds of passion. Rather, I do so to track the implications of the novel's persistent association of passion between women with psychosis, primitivism, and degeneration. Embedded as these discourses are in the politically charged question of the terms that are used to draw the line between delusion and reality, madness and sanity, Barnes's characters' struggles with madness are—contra Allen—both "psychic" *and* "sociopolitical" (Allen 17).[6]

PSYCHOSIS, NARRATIVE FRAGMENTATION, AND QUEER CRITIQUE

The style of *Nightwood* opens up a space for its critique of the patriarchal terms of the Western symbolic through which early twentieth-century psychoanalysis figured lesbian passion as psychosis. While the narrator of *Nadja* flirts with yet is ultimately unable to embrace wholly the psychosis that is embodied in Nadja and enacted in the text's own fragmentation, *Nightwood* comes much closer to inhabiting madness, both at the stylistic and characterological levels. Viewed in light of the psychoanalytic theories of lesbianism and psychosis that *Nightwood* invokes, T. S. Eliot's famous pronouncement that Barnes's novel would "appeal primarily to readers of poetry" calls quickly to mind Terry Eagleton's observation of affinities between poetic and schizophrenic language: both depend on "riddling associations and affective rather than conceptual links between ideas" (Eliot xi; Eagleton 159). Writing of these similarities, Elizabeth Meese describes the novel's poetic bent as a "crisis of style" similar to the linguistic and perceptual distortions of schizophrenia (Meese 56).[7] Barnes's textual practice, then, goes beyond what numerous critics describe as an imitation of the mechanisms of the unconscious, and instead mimics those of madness.[8] *Nightwood* tracks the psychical and stylistic ravages of psychosis, both representing it in its characters and reproducing its mechanisms through its poetic style and departure from linear narrative.

By miming the distortions of schizophrenia, Barnes's novel interrogates at the level of language the psycho-analytic accounts of the psyche whose casting of lesbianism as psychosis is a source of its characters' psychical pain.[9] By the 1950s, Lacan would formalize the ideology that underpins such theories. In Lacan's account, the unconscious arises through the repression of the Name of the Father that institutes paternal law. In psychosis, that signifier is not available for repression because it has been foreclosed, and materials remain at the surface that might otherwise have been consigned to the unconscious and made available for representation only obliquely in dreams (Fink, *The Lacanian Subject,* 74-76).[10] Lacan's presentation of the *paternal* signifier as the ground of the symbolic renders some (though not all) instances of homosexuality and transgendered identification as symptoms of psychosis. *Nightwood* both anticipates and questions such theories by implicating the reader in the text's madness. Drawing on Jacqueline Rose's argument that "a confusion at the level of sexuality brings with it a disturbance in the visual field," Jean Gallagher highlights moments in the novel at which the reader's perception is destabilized because it is focalized through a character confused by an "image of gender ambiguity," such as that of Robin Vote or Matthew O'Connor (Rose 226; Gallagher 287). This disturbance in perception creates the effect of madness. As the text shifts from one scene of gender ambiguity to the next, the visual field vacillates, making the reader complicit in the madness the text represents. Unable to distinguish between reality and delusion, the reader is jarred out of the position of clearheaded diagnostician that the stability of a realist text might have encouraged.

Meese also asserts that *Nightwood* "writes against" Lacan, but her argument needs rearticulation. She claims that the "schizophrenia" of both "*Nightwood* and lesbianism" demonstrate that "Barnes never bought the buoyancy of the illusion (or allusion to wholeness, Identity)" conjured in the mirror stage (56). Yet for Lacan, it is not resistance to the imaginary via the refusal of the mirror stage but instead the foreclosure of the Name-of-the-Father that precipitates psychosis. While Meese conflates the symbolic and the imaginary by explaining the mirror stage as formative both of "the illusion of identity" and of "access to language," one might emphasize instead Lacan's assertion that it is at the "moment in which the mirror-stage *comes to an end*" that the "dialectic that will henceforth link the *I* to socially elaborated situations" begins (Meese 56; Lacan, "The mirror stage," 5; emphasis added). The "symbolic matrix" that governs the social is immanent in the mirror stage, yet there is a temporal gap between the child's "jubilant assumption of his specular image" and his or her articulation as subject within the linguistic structure that determines that matrix (2). The possibility for foreclosure of the Name-of-the-Father arises precisely in the *gap* between mirror-stage identification and the entrance into language. Because it enables the psychotic to bypass subjection to symbolic strictures, the mechanism of foreclosure refuses the privilege ordinarily granted to the symbolic.

In mimicking the mechanisms of schizophrenia, *Nightwood* challenges those symbolic mandates that at the mirror stage are immanent but not yet articulated in language, and thereby questions the hegemonic reality whose acceptance would be required for entrance into the symbolic order.[11] As Jane Marcus argues, *Nightwood* sends up the psychoanalytic symbolic, diminishing the phallus by emphasizing the "Tiny O'Toole" possessed by Matthew O'Connor, the quack physician who serves as a parody of a psychoanalyst in his role as confessor to the other characters (Barnes, *Nightwood,* 132).[12] Marked as Schreberian both in his apparent schizophrenia and in his sexual inversion, O'Connor lives every day in a world that for Schreber is only one of psychotic delusion: he characterizes his activity as "the contemplation of the mad strip of the inappropriate that runs through creation" (105). A dominant feature of the narration, O'Connor's tirades undercut the heterosexist terms of symbolic law (Fuchs 125).[13]

While the diminution of O'Connor's penis is also a diminution of the symbolic phallus, neither it nor his incisive commentary offer a means of rearticulating the symbolic, however. Simply challenging symbolic mandates does not ensure their transformation: we can never be assured that a text's dismantling and reconstituting of the symbolic necessarily involves the progressive transformation of its imperatives, as the varied torments of psychotic patients often illustrate so clearly.[14] Though Matthew O'Connor's tirades perform a critique of psychoanalysis's assumptions about the perilously psychotic aspects of female homosexuality, they nonetheless offer only limited revisions to psychoanalysis's bleak account of lesbian desire.

As Chisholm argues, the story of Nora's love for Robin, a "Nadja-clone," might be compared to surrealist accounts of the "mad" fascination provoked in artists by the abjection of the *détraquée*. Much as does *Nadja* in its account of "Breton's" embrace of the *détraquée* through "mad love," *Nightwood* chronicles an "*amour fou*"—yet one "*entre deux femmes*"—through which Nora and Robin are "intoxicated with the process of degradation" that renders them "'incommunicable' (Barnes, *Nightwood,* 52) and unconsumable" (Chisholm, "Obscene Modernism," 182, 189). And much as in the play by Palau that fascinates Breton, the derangement of the female *détraquée* in *Nightwood* is marked by her "perverse" desire for other women. Barnes's novel, however, revises surrealist accounts of *l'amour fou* by making explicit the "perverse" desire of the *détraquée* and by making *l'amour fou* structurally available to two women within the symbolic.[15] Nonetheless, by detailing Robin's and Nora's spectacular unraveling in its concluding chapter, *Nightwood* shows that its psychoanalytically informed construct of lesbian *amour fou* is ultimately doomed, made untenable by the phallogocentric premises on which it is founded.

An Undocumented Record of Time

If *Nightwood* ultimately suggests that psychosis is ill-suited to rearticulating the terms of the symbolic, it nonetheless criticizes the logic through which Western civilization projects fears about its transformation onto its primitive others. Barnes's characters' descents into madness represent not only their own unraveling but also, more important, that of the Western symbolic that construes their passion as insanity. Though *Nightwood* does not effect a wholesale transformation of the symbolic, it does offer a trenchant examination of the implications of patriarchal ideology for efforts to write about queer subjectivities and desires. The tropes of mourning, melancholia, and psychosis the novel invokes to track the precipitous beginning and gradual "ruin" of Nora's and Robin's "insane passion" exhume the residue of the larger crisis of Western civilization of which their failed relationship is a symptom (142, 75). Nora's grief over Robin's departure allegorizes "the fear of a fundamental and irretrievable loss of connection to the Other" that Diana Fuss presents as "the very heart of modernity" (39). Characterized as "an early Christian" who "believe[s] the word," Nora is associated with logocentrism and the metaphysics of presence. Yet she mourns a larger loss of stability and narrative coherence through her grief over Robin's sexual wanderings, having lost "the joy and safety of the Catholic faith" (51, 60). In so doing, she courts the very madness approximated by the text. The novel's invocation of Nora's place within history is thus paradoxical. She is characterized both as a Puritan from "early American history" and as an "unidentified" being who is radically "outside" of history (51, 53). This paradox is a function of the logic of primitivism at work in the novel. Just as Freud, in a notorious example of Western retrospective projection, casts racial primitives as having no history, so does *Nightwood* position Nora as a queer primitive.[16] This projection maintains Nora not without but within discourse, though barely at the margins of the visible: what Butler calls the "abject," a "radically uninterrogated . . . shadowy countless figure for something that is not yet made real" ("How Bodies Come to Matter" 281). Moreover, if Laplanche and Pontalis are correct in describing projection as "a defence of very primitive origins," then the logic of projection through which queers and non-Westerners appear as abject works to cover over the elements of primitivism at work in the Western symbolic and to displace them onto its racial and sexual others (349). *Nightwood,* filled with imagery not only of individual but also of cultural dissolution, exposes the mechanism of projection through which the Western symbolic misrecognizes its own dissolution by insisting on the insanity of its queers.

The novel suggests an imperialist strain of Christianity to be the source of a literal and epistemic violence against queers and non-Westerners in which Western queers are sometimes themselves complicit.[17] In characterizing Nora as a Westerner, for example, the narrator identifies her with colonizers for whom God is "so ponderous in their minds that they could stamp out the world with him in seven days" (50-51). While Nora does not practice any religion, O'Connor cites her residually Christian mind-set as the reason for the strong sense of betrayal that made her mourning for Robin painfully intense: he considers Nora a "religious woman . . . without the joy and safety of the Catholic faith" (60-61).

O'Connor terrifies her by offering a mythological account of the genesis of lesbian self-hatred that is also an allegory for her and Robin's failed relationship. He evokes the presence, within a larger array of hardened creatures of the night, of "girls" cursing each other during sex in public toilets. While the final version of *Nightwood* uses only allusion to invoke the women's sexual acts, an early draft, reproduced in Cheryl J. Plumb's volume containing the original version of *Nightwood,* depicts two women engaged in cunnilingus in the public toilets. In Plumb's reproduction of what Barnes has marked as "discarded pages from early copy of *Nightwood,*" the phrase "that great secret confessional"—which invokes the toilet stalls in the 1937 edition—is followed by the following text that is omitted from the final version: "the one the Catholic church forgot—over the door *Dames,* a girl standing before her, her skirts flung back one on one, while between the columns the handsome head of the girl made boy by God, bends back, the posture of that head volts forth the difference between one woman and another" (Barnes, "Watchman" ["Watchman, What of the Night?"], 262). In the margin to the left of the excised passage lies an *X* that Barnes's notes attribute to Eliot (Plumb 242). The revision to this passage elides not only the overt depiction of public sex but also the "difference" in gender between the girl with the "skirts flung back one on one" and the "girl made boy by God."[18]

The final version presents all lesbians as "girls" who share a collective voice. Drinking of each other at the public toilets, "the water hole of the damned," the girls damn each other to hell and curse the "terrible and damned spot" of their pleasure, exhorting it to "wither into the grin of the dead . . . draw back, low riding mouth in an empty snarl of the groin" (Barnes, *Nightwood,* 95). The frequent repetition of "damned" within this passage reinforces the narrative of damnation performed as the imagined "girl" asserts to her lover that

"God damned me before you, and after me you shall be damned, kneeling and standing away till we vanish!" (95). Through her tirade, the girl reanimates the discourse that both produces lesbian desire and causes its own destruction as the girls' bodies, "kneeling and standing" in a pose both religious and sexual, vanish into nothingness through desiccation.

O'Connor sets this scene in a public toilet, a venue used not only for the radical queer practice of public sex to which he alludes here and elsewhere, but also, more commonly, for defecation. Catherine Whitley reads *Nightwood* as a novel that construes history as "human filth" that one must accept as a part of "human identity" rather than "expunge" (96-97). Published in 1936, during the rise of a fascist state that strove to make excrement of those people who threatened Germany's sense of racial purity—particularly the Jews and queers that populate Barnes's novel—*Nightwood* uses O'Connor's tirade to offer a counterdiscourse in which a toilet that symbolizes queers' threatened expulsion from history becomes instead the site of the queer woman's emergence as a subject integrated into history. As Victoria Smith argues, O'Connor emphasizes "the arbitrary and constructed nature of legend and history" by implying "that the stories of the disempowered only get remembered in legend, which has the valence of fiction or myth, whereas the stories of the powerful get remembered as history, which has the valence of fact" (197).

Striving to reconstruct the narrative of queers' history, O'Connor's tirade not only excavates the process of damnation through which lesbians are produced as abject, but also opens up a space in which to construct the narratives, however fragmentary, that might remedy their lack of subjectivity and history. His story of the cursing girls in the public toilet offers an alternative to the dominant narrative of their history. On the one hand, it suggests that lesbians have no written history but that of the damnation that conditions their curses; on the other, it counters their abjection by reversing the myth of the fall from grace. Whereas in the passage that was excised from the final edition, the "girl made boy" was made both lesbian and mannish "by God" (Barnes, "Watchman," 262), in the revised passage, the collective voice rapidly shifts position from that of the damned to that of the innocent, insisting that in the toilets, she is "an angel on all fours . . . seeking my people that have never been made" (95). Because they involve "going down," both girls' poses invoke what Dana Seitler calls the "bestial devolution" common to "all the characters who populate" the novel's "degenerating landscape" (550). Rather than capitulating to the sexological narrative of degeneration, however, the girl's statement creates a fantasy of queer prelapsarian innocence that positions a certain kind of Christian dogma, rather than queer sexuality, as the cause of damnation and then suggests the possibility of narratives—animated by a "God" who makes girls into boys—that might counter the Christian one.

The novel's use of paradox similarly works not to reinforce but instead to expose and critique the violence that produces bodies that seem to have no histories. O'Connor classifies the cursing lesbians in the toilet among other *détraquées* who, used to the night, "have an unrecorded look" (94). Their stories "unrecorded," their angelic queer bodies "uninhabited" by narrative, members of the third sex nonetheless enter into discourse as future inhabitants of a "kingdom . . . without precedent" (148). Describing Nora as "an undocumented record of time," the narrator suggests that she does have a place within history, though one that has yet to be recorded (50). Moreover, she is posed as "one of those deviations by which man thinks to reconstruct himself" (53). In these instances, the text uses the future anterior to intimate a new symbolic, longingly holding out an image that has yet to come to be. If, as Victoria Smith asserts, *Nightwood* tracks the "(non)inscription" into history of its socially marginalized characters, confronting the problem of representing those whose narratives "fall outside the purview of official history," its use of the future anterior holds out the possibility that their histories might one day be written (197). The text's temporality, in other words, is that of the mirror stage: it presents an image in which one jubilantly thinks one recognizes one's self and that, though remaining forever a misrecognition, provides the illusion of stability and coherence in which the symbolic—here, a new queer symbolic—is immanent, if not actualized.[19]

Viewing *Nightwood* as performing a queer symbolic in the future anterior rather than in the present allows one to nuance Sarah Henstra's argument that O'Connor's "monologues . . . operate as a *mimesis of subjection*" that "imitate[s] the process by which subjects are located in society" (135), tracing "the symbolic boundaries dividing sanctioned and unsanctioned, central and marginal, day and night" in order to underscore the ways in which they are "relational, unstable, and vulnerable to the possibility of imaginative redrawing" (144). In the space of the future anterior, the commentary provided by the narrator and O'Connor begins to write the history of the erasure of lesbianism that subtends Nora's mourning, even though she will eventually unravel rather than rearticulate the symbolic whose terms oppress her. The larger circumstance in which the narrator and O'Connor situate Nora's predicament—the emergence of the modern queer whose history has yet to be written and whose assertion of subjectivity is presented under the sign of insanity—renders her grief the mourning of a loss that is not a loss (their relationship plays out in the realm of an ostensibly primitive identification presented as predating history and subjectivity)

to a rival who is not a rival (the relentlessly mimetic Jenny Petherbridge, in snatching away Robin, imitates in Nora a subject of desire that has yet to come to be).

If, in this sense, Nora's and Robin's breach exemplifies what Lacan has asserted to be the phantasmatic nature of all relationships, the novel's use of the narrator and O'Connor to situate Nora's grief historically nonetheless maintains an edge of political critique. As Victoria Smith argues, *Nightwood* "paradoxically performs unspeakable loss and demands that we recognize loss (of history, of a lover), as well as recognize the subject who speaks" (195). Nora's fragmented narrative of her rupture with Robin endows both women with an affectional history and seeks to maintain the belief that their relationship still is real. The narrative fragmentation that results thus is not, *pace* Nancy Hartsock, a suspect tactic that undermines the emergent minority subject. Instead, it is particularly well suited for providing an account of the cultural positioning of queers whose history has yet to be written, and for constructing a narrative, however fractured, of their struggles to emerge as subjects. Though in *Nightwood,* this struggle does not transform the symbolic and only hints at the possibility of its rearticulation (as I shall show at the end of this chapter), the novel nonetheless positions their fates not as instances of innate queer pathology but as the effects of the Western symbolic through whose logic of paranoid projection their passion is construed as primitive and as madness.

What Insane Passion

Nightwood not only subversively mimes the mechanisms of psychosis in order to perform a trenchant attack on the paranoid cultural logic that conflates lesbianism with madness, but also cites and critiques that construct at the characterological level. Much as in Breton's *Nadja*, in *Nightwood* lesbianism stands in for psychical dissolution in its larger manifestation. Characterized by an undifferentiation from others and a lack of deliberate agency that parallel the workings of the primary processes, Robin Vote is frequently held up by critics as a "simulacrum" for the unconscious or for psychosis (Gilmore 615).[20] Meese, for example, argues that in *Nightwood* lesbianism is experienced as a schizophrenic "horror . . . of the subject and object both being oneself" (56). Her account of lesbianism as schizophrenia parallels Lacan's "Motives of Paranoid Crime": while the psychoanalyst does not cast the Papin sisters' dilemma as that of being both subject and object to each other, his assertion that they never emerged from narcissistic undifferentiation places them at the same state of psychosexual development that Meese invokes. Similarly, commenting on the "insistent fury" with which "the squatter," Jenny Petherbridge, weepingly pursues Robin Vote in an effort to wrest her from the arms and home of Nora Flood, the mad doctor O'Connor declares that "[l]ove of woman for woman" is an "insane passion for unmitigated anguish and motherhood" (75). What is most striking about O'Connor's oft-quoted phrase is the conflation of "anguish" and "motherhood" through which his generalization about lesbian passion both gains and loses meaning, with regard both to the coupling of Jenny and Robin that is his immediate object, and to the larger field of lesbian passions to which his generalization would extend. O'Connor's declaration anticipates Kristeva's description of the aggressive fusion of the "homosexualmaternal": he pathologizes lesbianism qua "motherhood" as "insane" and in need of mitigation, assuming, as do certain psychoanalysts, that the mother-daughter dyad is dangerous by definition, and must be interrupted by the paternal third term (Michel, "Displacing Castration," 43).[21]

Yet *Nightwood,* in distinction from Lacan and Kristeva, complicates and ultimately critiques the construal of lesbianism as psychotic. Unlike *Nadja,* Barnes's novel is not governed by one character's overriding phantasy, but instead is an open-ended narration that takes up and rearticulates psychoanalytic constructions of lesbianism, splitting tropes of psychosis between several characters. However much O'Connor's oracular declarations attempt to provide a totalizing characterization of lesbianism as a passion for "anguish" and "motherhood," by virtue of their discursive excess they fail to do so; instead, the intersections of his performatives with other discourses on lesbian passion render Jenny's form of "insanity" distinct from that of either Nora or Robin."[22] While the "perfect fury of accumulated dishonesty" with which Jenny falls in love with Robin might be described as an "insane passion" that traffics in "secondhand . . . emotions" plundered from Nora, the "insistent fury" of Jenny's appropriative love is structurally different from Nora's "insane" merger with Robin (67, 75). And while an openly vicious, "unmitigated anguish" provokes Robin's affair with Jenny, the anguish of "unmitigated . . . motherhood" would most aptly be said to characterize Nora's bond to Robin.[23] Robin's romantic involvements, by contrast, entail a violent repudiation of motherhood, from her abandonment of her son Guido to her destruction of the doll that symbolizes her and Nora's child.

Much as Robin furiously shatters the doll, *Nightwood* assaults the homophobic construct of the psychotic lesbian, scattering its shards into fragmented narratives. And though the doll is initially presented as a symbol for lesbian sterility—Nora asserts that "when a woman gives [a doll] to a woman, it is the life they cannot have, it is their child, sacred and profane"—O'Connor resignifies it by endowing it with the ambiguous ontology of the (Butlerian) abject, much as he does for the "angels on all fours" who curse each others' desires in the public toilets (142, 95). Including himself as "one of them," an "uninhabited angel," he declares: "The last

doll, given to age, is the girl who should have been a boy, and the boy who should have been a girl. . . . The doll and the immature have something right about them, the doll because it resembles but does not contain life, and the third sex because it contains life but resembles the doll" (148). Thus described, the "third sex" is paradoxical not only for being so easily misrecognized as only a simulacrum of a human being, but also for being "the *last* doll," the last in a line of simulacra, rather than the original being of which the doll would be a copy (emphasis added). As do the "angels on all fours" in the toilets, the "uninhabited angel[s]" who resemble dolls reign in a "kingdom . . . without precedent": one that exists in the future anterior of the mirror stage, that immanent symbolic in which the copy could become the original, the last could become the first, the sterile could become the fruitful, the socially dead could become the socially viable.[24] Though Barnes's fractured narratives are those of queer misery rather than of queer joy (O'Connor laments that he has "spent near fifty years weeping over bars" because of his life as an "uninhabited angel") Barnes's novel gains its power by stripping them of the ahistorical, individualistic, and totalizing force of clinical case studies and presenting them instead as consequences of early twentieth-century homophobia.

A Beast Turning Human

Robin is the character on whose persistent absence, both physical or psychical, all of the fractured narratives of Barnes's novel focus. To the extent that *Nightwood* can be said to have a narrative (O'Connor declares that "I have a narrative, but you will be put to it to find it") Robin is its absent center: the novel tracks in excruciating detail the way in which her lovers' attempts to understand and thereby master her come to naught while she herself remains elusive (97). She is positioned as such through a logic of projection. As Elisabeth Bronfen observes, the other characters' "attraction to Robin . . . centers on a misapprehension of her": figuring her as what Lacan would call the *objet a,* they "succeed in making Robin the emblem of their own desires," yet "fail to signify her" (174).[25] While she "invites the transferences of others," she "is also always more than [their] projections" (174).[26] Thus while we hear much from other characters—especially O'Connor—of the psychical primitivism that ostensibly renders her incapable of assimilating into the human world, we hear little from Robin herself of her motives and desires. Thus "spoken for and seen through the consciousness of others, Robin is never represented through psychological realism," as Kaup observes ("The Neobaroque" 98).[27]

Frequently positioned as a "simulacrum" for psychosis, that most primitive of psychical states, Robin is both a figure for language's inability to reflect reality and the point at which the novel's treatment of the association of lesbianism with madness at the level of character intersects with its deployment of the characteristics of psychosis at the level of its textual practice (Gilmore 615). This characterization of Robin suggests that the novel positions lesbianism and psychosis within discourse as sharing certain elements while not being reducible to one another. Even though Robin's lesbian passions occupy much of the narration, her undifferentiation extends beyond those moments in which she merges with Nora and Jenny, and characterizes her relationships with men as well. Whereas Nora is portrayed as having narcissistically merged with Robin in a quasi-psychotic manner, Robin's lack of agency and direction is attributed to a psychical primitivism that is linked to psychosis but that is not equivalent to lesbianism.[28] Robin's repeated refusal to be interpellated into her lovers' worlds is her most consistent characteristic, and socially constructed identities simply seem not to take hold on her psyche: she abandons her roles as Felix's wife and Guido's mother; she wanders away from Nora and Jenny.[29] Jean Gallagher rightfully suggests that in leaving Nora, Robin strives to break from the "narcissistic model of homosexual desire" promulgated by early twentieth-century psychoanalysis, fleeing the claustrophobic circularity of the circus performance at which she meets Nora and then the "continuing physical enclosures of lesbian desire" (294-295). However, Robin neither engages in a process of "[b]ecoming lesbian," as Meese claims, nor rescripts psychoanalysis to make desire between women viable (61). Rather, she refuses all attempts—lesbian or otherwise—to contain her.

As such, she is presented as psychotic, as a psychical "primitive" who rejects all symbolic inscription. As Ernst van Alphen argues, Robin "is always the addressed" and "does not speak herself"; she appears not to be inscribed into the symbolic order, which "generates desire," but to stand only as the "object of the desire of others" (157). Robin is not fascinating to her lovers, however, because she represents "the once-experienced unity of the imaginary stage" (157). Rather, the fascination she exerts on others stems from her seemingly primitive, presymbolic existence. Both Robin's husband, Felix Volkbein, and her lover, Nora Flood, are attracted precisely by her ostensibly primitive qualities. Her bond with Nora, for example, is formed in a synchronic moment of identification with the primitive world of the beast: the two women first meet at the circus, where a fearful moment of recognition between Robin and a "powerful," "furious" lioness immediately cements the two women's bond and inspires their cohabitation (54).

It is no coincidence that Barnes's narrative places such a heavy emphasis on the role of identification in precipitating Nora and Robin's union. As Diana Fuss notes,

"[i]dentification, the first and most 'primitive' of psychical mechanisms, provides Freud with a ready conceptual relay linking 'invert' and 'savage'": much like the "primitive" psychical process of identification, "[b]oth 'invert' and 'savage' are represented in temporal terms, placed within a static ontology that constructs each figure as representative of a primordial phase of human development" (36). *Nightwood* repeats this confluence in the scene at the circus, which is striking for its evocation of the incommensurability of the body and the psyche. This evocation produces the effect of psychical synchrony, indeed psychical automatism, that characterizes the compelling identification that leads to the two women's immediate cohabitation.[30] This automatism is strongly linked to both women's psyches throughout the novel: Nora's mind is "endlessly embroiled in a preoccupation without a problem"; Robin's "thoughts were in themselves a form of locomotion" (53; 59-60).[31]

Like *Nadja,* then, *Nightwood* turns on the apparent "enigma" posed by the psyche of the queer woman, on the construction of her motives as unavailable for rational account (Barnes, *Nightwood,* 44). While Lacan and Breton position her as the limit of "civilization," as the socially and psychically "primitive," *Nightwood* illustrates the way in which that positioning takes place through the mediation of identification. If, in its dependence upon the slide between subject and object, identification is fundamentally a primitive psychical mechanism that is experienced by normal subjects and psychotics alike, it must be understood as always threatening a slide into that most primitive of psychical states: the psychotic undifferentiation in which the distinction between subject and object irremediably breaks down. *Nightwood* makes precise the threat of psychosis the lesbian is understood to pose to civilization: that of the unraveling of the civilized subject, indeed of the social order itself. The automatic identification spectacularized in the scene at the circus is not, after all, solely a function of psychosis. In Lacanian theory, an incommensurability between action and psychical motivation characterizes all modes of subjectivity. In that Nora and Robin themselves are functions of the constructions of "civilization" deployed in the novel—even Robin's apparent primitivism is a retroactive construction perpetrated by civilization—the automatisms made apparent in their startling identification might be said to mark civilization and its supposedly normal subjects as well. The counterpoint between Nora and Robin further underscores the fine and often mobile line between the civilized and the primitive. While Robin is more strongly linked to primitivism throughout the novel, Nora, too, is consistently marked by the primitive: both "savage and refined," she maintains property and attends the opera, yet also is drawn to the circus, that debased world of the *détraquée* (50). This simultaneous presence of elements of civilization and barbarism in

Nora and in Robin's other admirers recalls the juridical construction of the Papin sisters, whose acts of "refined torture" the prosecution decried as "barbaric" in order to suture over the crisis in the meaning of civilization signaled by the murders (Houlière, qtd. in Dupré 95).

Nightwood, however, takes up the dialectic of civilization versus barbarism more explicitly than did the Papins' prosecutor, renegotiating it in order to underscore the way in which constructs of primitivism are a function of civilization. The novel's characterization of Robin as primitive and "innocent" of all human laws is a function of this projective logic. In *Nightwood,* after all, the innocent never lives in an unadulterated state of bliss; instead, she enters into discourse as always already condemned. As O'Connor paradoxically asserts, "man was born damned and innocent from the start, and wretchedly—as he must—on those two themes—whistles his tune" (212). O'Connor does not here oppose "innocence" to guilt, but rather to the damning speech act to whose interpellation one must respond. Even when, wandering away from her husband and child, she takes "the Catholic vow," Robin, unlike Nora, refuses to be interpellated into the Judeo-Christian symbolic that would damn her (51, 45). When Robin prayed, "her prayer was monstrous"; she could not "conceive a bargain"—accept the "forced choice" of inscription into the Western symbolic in exchange for subjectification—and therefore could neither "be saved [n]or damned" (47).

However, Robin does not experience her body in bits and pieces, returning to a primordial state that precedes narcissism and that allows her temporarily to relive "the blameless innocence of childhood prior to the moment of the *Spaltung* or splitting that, in Lacanian terms, enunciates the gendered subject in the patriarchal register of language," as Suzette Henke claims (335). Such an argument positions Robin as the "prelapsarian self" of the novel's other characters, especially Nora (Benstock, *Women,* 262).[32] In so doing, it misses the constructed nature of the primitive. In Lacan's essay "The mirror stage," on which Henke bases her argument, the ostensible temporal priority, or primitivism, of the *corps morcelé* is a retrospective construct produced by the symbolic order; the "violently unorganized *image*" of the body-in-pieces with which Henke associates Robin *only comes after* the mirror stage so as to *represent what came before*" (Gallop, *Reading Lacan,* 80). Thus, even as much as Robin's refusal of interpellation constitutes her primitive "innocence," her rejection of symbolic inscription can only be represented to us through the symbolic's terms: to figure Robin as presymbolic or "outside the human type" requires one to presuppose the symbolic and specific "human type[s]" (146).

Therefore if Robin is a figure for what Kenneth Burke calls the "temporally primal," it is an illusory primacy that is phantasmatically constructed from within the symbolic order (251). Even though Robin seems to elude the symbolic, she nonetheless can be represented only through its terms; indeed, she actively takes up the role of the "primitive innocen[t]" (117). While O'Connor notes that she is the type of person "who must get permission to live" from some outside authority, from some representative of the symbolic, he also says that at the same time, she is always "looking for someone to tell her that she [is] innocent," and that if she does not find such a person "she will make an innocence for herself; a fearful sort of primitive innocence" (117). Thus if Robin is positioned as the fascinatingly primitive other of Nora and Felix, it is not as an utopian figure who experiences unmediated access to a state of "blameless innocence" that purportedly precedes symbolic law. Rather, it is an "innocence" whose contours are drawn through the act of attempting to evade the terms of the symbolic. Those who love Robin imagine her "every movement" to be "an image of a forgotten experience": an image that, through the distortional process of recollection, represents an earlier time in life through the terms of the present (Barnes, *Nightwood,* 37). As such, Robin's "primitive innocence" can only be accessed by those around her through the symbolic, and they find in her not an unmediated connection to an authentically primitive state that precedes civilization, but rather a reflection of the primitive elements at the core of their own, seemingly civilized, subjectivity. As Sharla Hutchison notes, Robin first appears in the narration in surroundings whose primitivism is coded not as natural but as artificially constructed: "the plants are 'potted,' and the so-called jungle is 'trapped in a drawing room'" (218). Moreover, as Susana S. Martins observes, Robin is "framed for her spectators" as both the subject of a painting and an elaborate theatrical set (116). Explicitly staged as civilization's phantasmatic construction of its origins, Robin "does not serve the role of erotic muse in the same way Nadja did for Breton," who fetishized the madwoman's seemingly primitive innocence of the terms of the symbolic (Hutchison 218).

Instead, as "beast turning human," caught between civilization and that which it construes as primitive, Robin experiences what Julia Kristeva would come to call "abjection": the struggle, at the borderline between the pre-Oedipal and the paternal symbolic, with the terms through which symbolic mandates open up possibilities for psychical life (Barnes, *Nightwood,* 37).[33] Kristeva explains that "Even before being *like,* 'I' am not but do *separate, reject, ab-ject*" (*Powers* 13). And as Elizabeth Grosz notes, the abject "is neither subject nor object, neither image nor 'reality'"; instead, it "is a consequence of recognizing the impossibility of the identity of either subject or object, and yet the necessary dependence of each on the other" ("Body" 87). In her refusal of identification, Robin behaves as the subject-in-process of abjection: she "can't 'Put herself in another's place'" because "she herself is the only 'position'" (146). "[O]utside the 'human type'—a wild thing caught in a woman's skin," she appears within the narration in the liminal state of being torn between beastliness and humanity (146). If, having fainted, she appears to O'Connor as a "beast turning human," at key moments of reversal—in her immediate identification with Nora at the circus, in her fraught embrace of Nora in their apartment, in her final struggle with the dog in the country chapel—it is as if she is a human turning beast (37). Her abjection, then, marks a more complicated relation to symbolic law than that of "primitive innocence": she simultaneously seeks and evades the symbolic.

The paradox through which Robin is simultaneously figured as representing primitive innocence and worldly corruption—as being the "infected carrier of the past" through which "we put our face close to the blood on the lips of our forefathers"—is a function of the logic of retrospective projection through which she can be represented as presymbolic only by invoking the symbolic's terms (37). Through this logic, she appears both as the innocent, presymbolic primitive and as the corrupt degenerate: the figure of decline that appears as threatening precisely because it projects onto a figure from the seeming "past" a vivid and disturbingly corporeal image of the present symbolic's own unraveling.[34] The imagery of the bloody and infectious kiss forms the emblem of this retrospective projection. Its invocation of a person pressing her face to that of her ancestors signals the collapse of distance between past and present, and its focus on physical connection to the "forefather's" bloody lips tinges this gesture to the past with the erotic threat represented by the psychotic woman. Moreover, the projection at work in the construction of Robin accounts for the paradoxical notion of degeneration. The simultaneously threatening and appealing primitive is not a throwback to the authentic innocence of a presymbolic realm, but rather is an image of the past projected from within the symbolic's virtual theater. It is not the singular degenerate that causes the symbolic to be in decline, but rather the symbolic itself that projects her image so as to misrecognize its internal movement of decay.

In calling our attention to this retrospective projection, O'Connor's commentary highlights the psychical and social consequences of Robin's refusal to be interpellated as "damned." One such result, of course, is psychosis. Her refusal to accept the foundational condemnation through which the Western symbolic would instill guilt is, in psychoanalytic terms, a refusal of subjectification through the refusal to form the superego. Yet the brilliance of *Nightwood* is that both the narrator and O'Connor emphasize the constructed nature of Robin's madness: it is only through the terms of the symbolic that she appears as "mad," and the novel holds out the possibility that she might, within another symbolic, be otherwise—perhaps in that "life that [Nora] had no part in," set in a "foreign land" whose harmonies "rang clear" in the French, German, and Italian songs that Robin sang as she cleaved from Nora in their home (57). Yet the "company" that Robin keeps through these songs is one of which both she and Nora remain "unaware," for its "people . . . have never been made": they dwell in a future symbolic of which one can hear only the longing echoes (57, 95).

LOVE HAS FALLEN OFF HER WALL

Though *Nightwood* cries out for a symbolic in which queers will have a history, it is one that has yet to be made; the dominant strain in the novel tracks the way in which the current order causes queers to unravel. If Robin Vote is the figure onto whom civilization's phantasies about the attractions and dangers of primitivism are projected, Nora Flood, in her devastation, represents the unraveling of the Western symbolic and the concomitant failure of a model of love based on domestic confinement. The same imagery of degeneration that marks the entrance of Robin's body into the narrative also marks the description of Nora's home in New York. Overrun by weeds and frequented by bohemian intellectuals, her home is an index of the emergence of the primitive within an ostensibly civilized human dwelling. And it is no coincidence that the scene of Nora and Robin's primitive recognition is the circus, that spectacle of *tamed* animality, for Nora and Robin take a Parisian flat that one critic calls a "psychic prison," and that Nora herself describes as "this house I took that Robin's mind and mine might go together" (Henke 334; Barnes, *Nightwood,* 139). Fusing figures of shared domestic space with figures of shared psychical space, *Nightwood* represents the women's mutual psyche through the household objects chosen during their time together: their flat is decorated with items that, as the objectification of and material support of their shared psychical space, attest to "the combining of their humours" (55). As feminist scholars have pointed out, the regulation of the female body and psyche often has operated through her confinement within the domestic sphere, through what Kristina Deffenbacher memorably calls the "housing of wandering minds." In Barnes's novel, the collective "personality" objectified in the women's belongings gradually becomes the instrument of their punishment: Nora eventually "suffered from the personality of the house," fearing that "if she disarranged anything Robin might become confused—might lose the scent of a home" (56). The fixity of the household objects paradoxically works as a force upon Nora, conditioning the "soft and careful movements" to which her fear of disturbing the house confines her (56). The very immobility of the women's shared unconscious, then, both propels and constrains Nora's physical and psychical trajectory. Implied as well by Nora's fear that her lover "might lose the scent of a home" is the effect of Robin's continuing beastliness—of her instinctual propulsion by "scents"—on the "psychic prison" of their relationship. As Nora's home in New York bears on its exterior the signs of "degeneration," so the flat in Paris becomes an interior space of psychical primitivism.

Nora and Robin's household initially appears, then, as the specific "psychic prison" to which certain psychoanalytic theorists assume lesbians to be confined in their ostensibly psychotic, primitive undifferentiation. This narcissism is associated especially strongly with Nora, who asks Matthew O'Connor if "you ever loved someone and it became yourself," signaling the way in which she has appropriated Robin's image for her own narcissistic purposes (152). She then generalizes that all lesbian love is narcissistic, contrasting the distance presumably inscribed in the heterosexual relation to the narcissistic overidentification that characterizes her love for Robin: she declares that "[a] man is another person—a woman is yourself, caught as you turn in panic; on her mouth you kiss your own" (143). Psychoanalytically informed criticism on the novel has been dominated by readings that parallel Nora's latter declaration. Henke, for example, asserts that Nora and Robin are imprisoned in a mutually narcissistic embrace. She describes Nora and Robin's world as a "self-sufficient microcosm *à deux*" and asserts that

> Each tries, unsuccessfully, to valorize the other through a process of perfect reflection. Inhabiting the same subject position, they cannot engage in speech or dialogue; nor can they work through the Hegelian dialectic necessary to relationship. Meaning has been cut, split, externally fixed in a setting that demands the perfect completion of an ever-elusive transcendental signifier.[35]
>
> (335)

Presenting the two women as perilously doubling each other, Henke aligns herself with Lacan's claims about the Papin sisters' purportedly perilous narcissism. Though Lacan's article diverges from Henke's account of Nora and Robin by emphasizing the violent dialectic ostensibly at work in the Papins' passion, both critics present a female same-sex relationship as narcissistic imprisonment caused by the lack of mediation.[36] This similarity perhaps arises because *Nightwood* itself mimes Lacan's phallogocentric logic in its use of death as a figure for lesbian passion. Tormented by Robin's wanderings, Nora finally realizes that only "[i]n death Robin would belong to her," be an object completely under her control (58). For Nora, the roles of lover and beloved are permanently unfixed. She does not distinguish between herself and Robin, avoiding singular pronouns altogether by insisting that "*we* love each other like death" and by declaring that *all* "[l]ove is death, come upon with passion" (139; emphasis added; 137).

Indeed, while Nora strives symbolically to kill Robin by possessing her, she also perceives herself as symbolically imprisoned and finally murdered by her lover. Nora claims that at home, Robin "was watching me, to see that no one called, that the bell did not ring, that I got no mail, nor anyone hallooing in the court, though she knew that none of these things could happen. My life was hers" (147). Upon finally discovering Robin's betrayal, Nora gasps as if "at the moment of [her] final breath" (64). If an ideologically vehement critical divide has arisen over the question of whether Nora, through her "masculine" possessiveness, or Robin, through her "immoral" infidelities, is the "true" victimizer, both sides ignore the slippery reversals of victim and victimizer, prisoner and jailer, that characterize Nora's and Robin's domestic dynamic.[37] In so doing, they miss the way in which any attempt definitively to adjudicate the women's household disputes—whether by Nora, Robin, O'Connor, or the literary critic—is thwarted by the novel's own troping of lesbian passion as a mysterious, automatic drive that cannot definitively be located in one woman or the other.

Though *Nightwood* represents love as a violently passionate yielding through which the beloved is taken as an object and reanimated by the lover, the novel also suggests that its ravages are not always undesirable. Nora's use of simile in her assertion that "we love each other like death" implies that their passion is not only for one another but also for death itself. That is, while their "[l]ove is death" in the intensity of its destructive impulse, that death also is itself something passionately loved: one might say that Nora is "passionately attached" to her own destruction.[38] This link between lesbian passion and death appears frequently in late nineteenth- and early twentieth-century Western literature, from the destructive passions of Baudelaire's "femmes damnées" to the fatal vampirism of Swinburne's "Faustine" to the treacherous kisses of Vivien's "Undine." Scholars such as Lillian Faderman claim that in using violent images of lesbian passion, women writers such as Barnes and Vivien show that they have "internalized completely the puerile and self-dramatizing aspects of aesthete-decadent literature" by men (*Surpassing* 362-363). A Lacanian interpretation of aggression, however, provides us with a different way of understanding its significance in literary constructs of lesbian desire. For Lacan, specular aggressivity is constitutive of subjectivity itself; it is a primitive relation that continues to mark normal subjectivity as well.[39] One might view the frequent association of lesbian passion with violence and self-destruction in fin de siècle and early twentieth-century literature as a displacement of the primitive aggressivity subtending all subjectivity onto the socially marginalized, supposedly underdeveloped figure of the lesbian.

Aggressivity between women has been a focus of discussion for feminist critics of Barnes, who, taking as their cue Nora's remark that Robin is both "my lover and my child," "a tall child who had grown up the length of the infant's gown" to need help and security from a mother, have often argued that *Nightwood* textualizes the ministrations of what Kristeva would call the pre-Oedipal mother ("Motherhood," 156, 145). Calling Nora "the mother of mischief" for her frantic pursuit of the wandering Robin, O'Connor casts lesbianism as a perilously violent undifferentiation between mother and daughter, as a dangerous mode of domestic confinement: he reminds Nora that "Donne says: 'We are all conceived in close prison, in our mothers' wombs we are close prisoners all'" (97). Read within the context of psychoanalysis, Donne's words recall Kristeva's account of the "homosexual-maternal," of the imprisoning and aggressive space of the mother-daughter dyad. Crossing *Nightwood* with Kristeva, Henke asserts that in playing "the role of (M)Other/Lover" in a relationship that lacks mediation, Nora "perpetually confirm[s] Robin's misrecognition of wholeness and plenitude in the phallic (M)Other who centers her destabilized personality" (335).[40]

Barnes scholars who buy into Kristeva's framework, however, miss the irreducibility of *Nightwood* to psychoanalytic claims about the "homosexual-maternal." First, the novel presents two divergent accounts of Nora's desire, positioning her both as the quintessential feminine narcissist (the overidentifying mother) and as the jealous, "masculine" lover. This double presentation echoes the contradiction whereby Lacan presents Christine Papin's psychosis both as a prototypically feminine narcissism and a dangerous appropriation of masculinity. Second, and more important, Nora and Robin's relationship is represented through a renegotiation rather than an uncritical acceptance of psychoanalytic accounts of same-sex desire, as Allen, Benstock, and Lee suggest.[41] If Nora indeed plays the role of "phallic mother," she is remarkably unsuccessful in "centering" Robin, as Henke acknowledges (335). Nora meticulously maintains their apartment, afraid that her partner might "lose the scent of home," yet Robin wanders out night after night, prowling the bars and cafés for partners both male and female (56).

Indeed, while Nora and Robin occupy the same physical space, the Paris flat, they do not always inhabit the same psychical space. In contrast to Nora, Robin represents the radical refusal to be housed; her mind does not "get loose and into the rafters," but instead pursues liaisons that extend beyond her and Nora's "psychic prison." Moreover, the novel suggests that Robin experiences a psychical division through which "[t]wo spirits were working in her, love and anonymity," creating distance between herself and Nora despite the intensity of their passion (55). Indeed, the much-cited passage that describes Nora and Robin as "so 'haunted' of each other that separation was impossible" suggests not complete fusion but instead distanced attachment (55). The trope of haunting suggests that the two women occupy the same physical place, yet at the same time are not quite "there." As if driven by an automatism that eludes conscious mastery, when "there entered with Robin a company unaware" she would sing "haunting" songs whose "foreign harmonies" intimate to Nora that Robin is "singing of a life that she herself had no part in" (57). Likewise, certain movements and turns of phrase informed her "that Robin had come from a world" entirely foreign to that of their Paris flat (58). By casting Robin as a foreigner, these metaphors of place and national identity signal the psychical division that propels her and Nora's "haunting" of one another. Much as a home would be possessed by the spirit of the ghost who haunts it, Robin is possessed by songs that hint at another life—perhaps even another symbolic—and Nora, in turn, is "haunted" by the enigmatic universe intimated by that music. It is significant that Terry Castle, in her study on the longstanding tradition of literary representations of lesbians as specters, mimes the novel's logic of primitivism by concluding from *Nightwood* that "[t]o be possessed of an apparition is to feel her within, like some primitive disorder" (54). Nora and Robin's passion is not an unmediated merger but an attachment that, experienced as haunting, is ever elusive: they slide uneasily in and out of the same subject position with a mysterious, primitive automatism, neither fusing nor separating entirely. While they strive toward fusion, their torment is defined precisely by their failure to accomplish it completely: sometimes "they would fall into an agonized embrace, looking into each other's face, their two heads in their four hands, so strained together that the space that divided them seemed to be thrusting them apart" (55-58). Nora later declares that "Robin's love and mine was always impossible," paradoxically implying that their love is a singular entity (it "was" always impossible) that takes divergent paths (those of "Robin's love" and "mine") (139). Instead of repeating psychoanalysis's narrative of lesbians' narcissistic reflection in each other's image, then, *Nightwood* emphasizes the way in which Nora's narcissism is *not* mirrored by Robin, whose refusal to be captured ensures only Nora's own psychical imprisonment.

Nora's narcissistic overidentification with Robin is facilitated by her retrospective construction of Robin as primitive. Nora remains bound by Robin's apparent proximity to the primitive world of the beast; she is driven mad precisely by her harkening to a sense of the "primitive" she senses in herself and finds confirmed in Robin. At one point, Nora asks O'Connor if "you ever loved someone and it became yourself" (Barnes, *Nightwood,* 152). The slippery nature of the agrammatical "it" that "became" Nora confounds the distinction between loving subject and beloved object, figuring her narcissism and ultimately her madness at the level of the sentence. A reader willing to ignore the peculiar reference to a person as "it" might reasonably interpret "it" as referring to "someone": to Robin who "became" Nora. Yet in another reading, "it" might be read as an agrammatical and free-floating pronoun that attempts to signify the general condition of loving. In this second reading, "yourself" becomes the structure of love itself, and not just the subject position of a lover structurally differentiated from the beloved in whom she loses herself. This second reading figures the primary narcissism that vehiculates Nora's automatic, seemingly magical identification with the "primitive" Robin (Barnes, *Nightwood,* 53). Even in the "secondary narcissism" of her attraction and eventual psychical bondage to the errant Robin, Nora's subjectivity bears the trace of this primitive state. Nora's eventual return to a state of primary narcissism mirrors that of the psychotic, whose return to a condition of preobjectal undifferentiation precludes the assumption of a subject position. Driven "insane with misery and fright" by Robin's wanderings, Nora experiences what some scholars call "incipient insanity" as she frantically pursues her lover through the cafés and nightclubs of Paris in a futile attempt to draw her back and rehouse her mind (Barnes, *Nightwood,* 129; Williamson 72).

Just as the imprisoning nature of Nora and Robin's household is rendered through a figurative play between domestic and psychical space, the ravages of Nora's narcissism are performed through domestic metaphors even as she literally leaves her home in search of Robin. Observing Nora's nocturnal pursuits, O'Connor comments:

> "Love has fallen off her wall. A religious woman," he thought to himself, "without the joy and safety of the Catholic faith, which at a pinch covers up the spots on the wall when the family portraits take a slide; take that safety from a woman," he said to himself . . . "and love gets loose and into the rafters. She sees her everywhere."
>
> (60-61)

If we read the word "[l]love" as referring to Nora, O'Connor's expression can be interpreted as a conflation of Nora the physical being with Nora the subject of desire: she is reduced to her love for Robin. O'Connor's imagery thus has the same effect as the linguistic slippage of the self-interrogation through which Nora asks herself if "you ever loved someone and it became yourself" (152). It underscores the quasi-psychotic undifferentiation at work in Nora's loss of herself in the primitive Robin. The two passages differ, however, in that Nora's query conflates both herself and Robin with "love," while O'Connor's remark conflates only Nora with "it." O'Connor's remarks highlight the pure narcissism of Nora's pursuit, her maintenance of the structure of love in the absence of its object.

Moreover, O'Connor's declaration that "love has fallen off her wall" underscores the way in which Nora's literal attempt to bring her lover home is a response to the figurative unsettling of her psychical "home" by Robin's departure. The doctor's domestic imagery implies a parallel between the "family portraits" that "take a slide" and Nora's fallen "[l]ove" for Robin: if one reads the passage backward, O'Connor's rhetorical sleight of hand can be seen to paint Nora and Robin's love as a stable image that can be installed on the wall of the patriarchal mansion to mark them as its rightful lesbian heirs. Yet the portrait is neither of Nora nor of Robin but of "love," so as a decorative domestication it fails to suppress the mobility of desire, thereby precipitating its own fall. Nora's is a love always already fallen, always already "off its wall." Furthermore, this phrase implies the paradox marked by the women's "queering" of domestic space, indeed by the limit-setting paradox that characterizes queerness itself. Nora and Robin are not compliant with the traditional arrangements of patriarchal domesticity, yet their love is also off "*its*" wall, the wall that *is* theirs to the extent that it is the necessary point of departure for their refusals. Potentially progressive in its appropriation and rearticulation of the terms of normative heterosexuality, Nora and Robin's love nonetheless is represented, through the imagery of the fallen portraits, as destructive: the doctor's rhetorical slide between falling "love" and falling "family portraits" suggests that their passion is a form of psychical unraveling that precipitates a collapse in the patriarchal family whose (symbolic) portraits hung on the wall before Nora's and Robin's.

At the same time as O'Connor figures Nora's madness as a fall, as a form of degeneration heralding the collapse of the patriarchal family, he also represents it as a foiled flight, as a failed attempt to transcend the constraints of the patriarchal home: let "loose," Nora's mad love for Robin would allow her to escape, to fly up and away as if unfettered; instead, her desire is blocked by the "rafters," closed in by the patriarchal space that collapses around her and that even follows her into the streets. This paradoxical space of restricted liberty characterizes the domestic topographies of *Nightwood*: quoting Donne, O'Connor declares that "'[w]hen we are born, we are but born to the liberty of the house—all our life is but a going out to the place of execution and death'" (97). The novel associates liberty with animality: when she enters the narration in a faint, Robin seems "to lie in a jungle trapped in a drawing room" (35). This household is the bastion of a patriarchal civilization whose failure in its project of domesticating the beast leaves society ever prone to what it perceives as degeneration.

The course taken by Nora's madness, then, does not so much illustrate the way in which lesbianism is especially conducive to overidentification as it points out the way in which the representation of Nora's love as jealous, narcissistic delusion is conditioned by a phallogocentric cultural frame. This phallogocentrism sets the stage for the representation of Nora's grief, at its furthest limit, as a hallucinatory attempt to suture the gap arising from the loss of "the joy and safety of the Catholic faith" (60). O'Connor presents Catholicism as a desirable symbolic replacement for the patriarchal family whose destruction is signaled by the fallen portraits: religion "covers up the spots on the wall when the family portraits take a slide" (60). Lacking the support of patriarchal institutions, lacking grounding in the symbolic order by the phallic signifier, Nora sees Robin "everywhere" in a hallucinatory attempt to sustain her desire in the absence of its object (61). Nora's lesbianism thus is figured as an attempt at suture, yet one that fails to repair the unraveling of patriarchal religion. Taken as a whole, then, O'Connor's discourse on how "[l]ove has fallen off her wall" traces out the way in which lesbianism appears both as cause and symptom of the unraveling of the symbolic order of the Catholic faith: as destructive of the patriarchal symbolic and, in turn, as impossible to sustain with sanity in the absence of the symbolic.

THE INBREEDING OF PAIN

Miming the logic of "psychical memorialization" through which the "murdered Other" is "entombed inside the subject" in introjective psychical processes such as mourning, the novel figures Nora's psyche as a tomb in which the petrified trace of the wayward Robin is preserved (Fuss 34). *Nightwood* uses the spatial confinement of the grave as a metaphor for the psyche:

> Love becomes the deposit of the heart, analogous in all degrees to the "findings" in a tomb. As in one will be charted the taken place of the body, the raiment, the utensils necessary to its other life, so in the heart of the lover will be traced, as an indelible shadow, that which he loves. In Nora's heart lay the fossil of Robin, intaglio of her identity, and about it for its maintenance ran Nora's blood. Thus the body of Robin could never be unloved, corrupt, or put away. Robin was now beyond timely changes, except in the blood that animated her.
>
> (56)

Nightwood uses figures of bodily incorporation to invoke Nora's psychical introjection of Robin. Moving from a literal to a figurative meaning of the word "heart," Barnes conveys Nora's psychical attachment as a physical attachment: not merely her desire, but also her very blood sustains the life of the relationship. This image of physical inseparability suggests the dual nature of identification as well. In introjecting and sustaining the object called "Robin," Nora herself is marked by and therefore unable to escape it, at the same time as her psychical processes continue to perpetuate it. Robin is traced into her lover's heart as a

"fossil," an "intaglio," "an indelible shadow," yet also is sustained only by "Nora's blood." This paradoxical image reflects the dual impulse that drives introjection itself. For Freud, a subject's introjection of a vanished object is always an attempt to preserve the libidinal link to that object in the face of a contradictory reality—to attempt, that is, to reanimate a dead object.

As a process in which the subject (re)appropriates the object for her own libidinal purposes, introjection also is marked by aggressivity. Even at its outset, Nora and Robin's relationship has a ghostly quality that marks them as always already dead: their narcissistic "haunting" of one another renders "separation . . . impossible" and their bonds eventually perilous (55). Later, by presenting Nora's love as "analogous . . . to the 'findings' in a tomb," Barnes figures it as presupposing the death of its object: Nora's love for Robin is legible only through the traces left in the ravages around them. By drawing an analogy between love and the remnants of the dead, this passage also implies that love itself is a graveyard into which the murdered love-object is buried, the place where one finds not the living and breathing flesh of the beloved but only her lifeless skeleton and decaying possessions. Nora's sense of inseparability from her lover depends precisely on the obliteration of Robin accomplished through her introjection: the only trace of Robin that remains is the "fossil" reanimated by "Nora's blood." Thus, paradoxically, Nora must (figuratively) kill off and fossilize Robin to propel her frantic drive "to bring Robin back by the very velocity of the beating of her heart" (61). Just as ancient civilizations only can be brought back to life through the constructions of archaeologists, so can the dead only be reanimated in their mourners' imaginings. Nora's hope that her heartbeat would suffice to reincarnate Robin as faithful lover thus signals, too, her embroilment in the narcissism of an Imaginary aggressivity that must kill Robin in order to keep her animate. Maintained not by Robin's but by "Nora's blood," the phantasmatic "body of Robin" is permanently preserved in Nora's animation as a lifeless puppet, "beyond timely changes" outside of Nora's control.

In Lacanian theory, however, imaginary aggressivity is not peculiar to Nora's extreme narcissism but instead is constitutive of subjectivity itself.[42] Nora's example illustrates how lesbian desire, qua pathological narcissism, appears within some psychoanalytically informed discourses as the most extreme limit of subjectivity—as the illustration of the perils of the narcissistic dialectic. These dangers are shown most clearly in the breakdown between subject and object in the novel's figuration of Nora's psyche. A consequence of Nora's incorporation of Robin is her decreased ability to distinguish herself from the lover she has animated in her own image. If "[i]n Nora's heart lay the fossil of Robin, intaglio of her identity, and about it for its maintenance ran Nora's blood," it is unclear precisely whose identity is marked by the "intaglio:" the pronoun "her" could refer to either of its female antecedents (56). Because the "fossil of Robin" serves as the "intaglio," on the one hand it is Robin's identity; on the other, however, it has also marked Nora's identity as an "indelible shadow," and indeed is animated by Nora herself. Nora's identity is constituted, then, by the abolition of the boundary between subject and object that characterizes her introjection of Robin.

Nora's confusion of her identity with that of Robin later is figured as comparable to a confusion of her very body with her lover's: during Robin's evenings out, Nora feels her absence as

> a physical removal, insupportable and irreparable. As an amputated hand cannot be disowned because it is experiencing a futurity, of which the victim is its forebear, so Robin was an amputation that Nora could not renounce. As the wrist longs, so her heart longed, and dressing she would go out into the night that she might be "beside herself," skirting the café in which she could catch a glimpse of Robin.
>
> (59)

During Robin's escapes, at the painful limit of the women's "haunting" of each other, Robin appears as "an amputated hand," as a phantom limb whose painful pull drives Nora mad by exacerbating their "insupportable and irreparable" breach (55). Observing that "[i]n the phantom limb, the diseased limb that has been surgically removed continues to induce sensations of pain in the location that the limb used to occupy," Grosz notes that "the absence of a limb is as psychically invested as its presence" (*Volatile* 41). Analogously, Nora's psychical investiture in Robin persists despite her escapes. Yet *Nightwood* does not simply deploy the category of the psychical to account for bodily sensation. Instead, renegotiating the tenacious mind/body split by figuring the psyche as body, the novel uses the notion of the "phantom limb" to do exactly the opposite: to evoke Nora's psychical state. Nora's heart longs for Robin "just as" the bloody "wrist longs" for the severed hand. Moreover, by reminding us through corporeal imagery of the physicality of Nora and Robin's former union, the conceptual reversal performed by this passage complicates, rather than outright rejects, standard accounts of the "phantom limb." Nora's psyche itself is represented as a bodily organ, the heart, whose identity is marked by the "intaglio" both of herself and Robin. Nora's heart necessarily divides in mourning her lover: through the analogy to the wrist, her heart's longing is figured as both the physical and the psychical pain of having lost a part of itself.

"Beside herself"—split from the very object she has incorporated—Nora not only feels Robin's absence as an "amputation," but also hallucinates her reappearance:

she "sees her everywhere" in a hallucinatory attempt to suture the split through reunion with Robin (61). While the confusion of subject and object suggested by this passage is characteristic of the mourner's incorporation of the lost object into the self, it also is characteristic of psychosis. Similarly crying to O'Connor that "I can't live without my heart!" Nora eventually represents Robin as her heart itself, transferring agency from herself to her phantasmatic incarnation of the absent lover she is unable to live without (156). The novel's presentation of Nora as hallucinating in response to separation from Robin is another point at which it crosses with accounts of the Papin sisters: Christine Papin, too, was described by Lacan and others as prone to violent delusion during her separation in prison from Léa.[43] That these two women's hallucinations of their absent loved ones are presented through what are conventionally construed as two separate but related ailments—Nora's as mourning and Christine's as melancholia—suggests that the distinction between the two states is less clear than the conventional understanding of melancholia as psychotic, "pathological mourning" would allow (Freud, "Mourning and Melancholia," 250).

Freud himself begs the question of the distinction between melancholic psychosis and the "hallucinatory wishful psychosis" that he claims to accompany mourning, even as he insists that only the latter is a normal, nonpathological experience because the possibility of its being otherwise "never occurs to us" ("Mourning and Melancholia" 243).[44] In so doing, he makes a rhetorical move that is similar to the one through which Lacan positions Christine and Léa Papin as having transgressed the limits of "the human community" in the violent culmination of their narcissistic psychosis. In both analysts' arguments, "psychosis" appears not as an objective diagnosis but as a construct that is invested both with the force of the author's medical authority and with his unexamined biases. By contrast, the much-noted mockery of medical authority in *Nightwood,* accomplished through the privileging of the pseudodiagnostic voice of the "quack" gynecologist, Matthew O'Connor, foregrounds precisely the politics of medical authority that render questionable the diagnosis of "psychosis," and, in turn, the construction of the "psychotic lesbian."[45] Nora's reports of her "hallucinations" of the absent Robin's reappearance are offered in dialogue with O'Connor, a figure well positioned to question the biases often invoked to distinguish the normal from the pathological.

The novel's openness to criticism of psychoanalytic biases allows it to break down the distinction between mourning and melancholia in its invocation of Nora's grief. Freud asserts that while identification is the psychical mechanism that propels both mourning and melancholia, the predisposition to the "pathological mourning" that is melancholia "lies in the predominance of the narcissistic type of object-choice" (248-250).[46] *Nightwood*, however, calls this distinction into question by emphasizing Nora's narcissism and by figuring her increasingly intense mourning as a slide into melancholia as her increasingly vehement self-reproaches and narcissistic identification with Robin develop into what O'Connor calls the "inbreeding of pain" (129). His phrase highlights the way in which the cause of Nora's pain gradually has moved from outside to inside: from the torment of Robin's repeated disappearances to the ravages of the self-reproaches to which Nora subjects herself in her eventual assumption of blame for their love's unraveling. Berating herself for having made Robin "bitter" and evasive by having "dashed . . . down" the "shadow" of innocence with which she veiled the implications of "her life at night," Nora cries, "I can't live without my heart!" (156). What appeared earlier as a "fossil of Robin" incorporated into and maintained by Nora's heart here appears as a phantom limb, as a hallucinatory rendering of the very organ from which separation would mean death. Indeed, melancholia is the form of mourning most strongly marked by the extreme aggressivity of psychosis, by the imminent possibility that the melancholic's death (by suicide) will follow her identification with the "dead" object.[47] We might recall that Nora's sudden awareness of her and Robin's imminent separation is represented as a figurative death: upon finding Robin clinging to Jenny in the courtyard, Nora gasps "with the intolerable automatism of the last 'Ah!' in a body struck at the moment of its final breath" (58, 64).

O'Connor represents Nora's "inbreeding of pain" as caused by an internal division in which one part of her psyche levels accusations against the other. In drunken frustration, he describes Nora as "beating her head against her heart, sprung over, her mind closing her life up like a heel on a fan, rotten to the bone for love of Robin" (161). However, he also tells her that "you are the only one strong enough to have listened to the prosecution, your life; and to have built back the amazing defence, your heart!" (153). Just as the narrator slides between metaphors of the body and the psyche in figuring Nora's heart as animating the "fossil" of Robin, so does O'Connor in his representation of Nora's psychical split as a battle between two parts of the body: "her head" represents the realm of reason, and repeatedly beats upon "the heart" that stands in for her emotional bond to her lover. Moreover, combining metaphors of law, body, and psyche in a series of rhetorical equivalencies, O'Connor equates Nora's "life" with the "mind" that "clos[es] her life up" through a rationalistic "prosecution"; he contrasts it with the "heart" whose emotional logic conflicts with the reasoning of the "mind" yet provides a strong "defense" against the claims of the prosecution. "Amazing" in its defense of itself, Nora's heart makes claims that are unusual, yet also implicitly superior to those made by her "mind." Her singularity, indeed superiority, as a human being lies in her being "the only one strong enough" to have allowed her "heart" to prevail against charges of its irrationality.

The triumph of Nora's "heart" has important consequences for the novel's deployment of psychoanalysis's conventional linking of female same-sex desire to psychosis. It recalls the Hegelian *belle âme* (beautiful soul), whose commitment to the "law of the heart" Lacan presents as psychotic in his 1946 essay "Remarks on Psychical Causality" ("Propos sur la causalité psychique"). If, as I argued in the introduction, Lacan's attempt to distinguish ordinary subjects' *méconnaissance* from that of psychotics founders on his assumption of a world of "actuality" that he refuses to consider to be ideologically circumscribed, O'Connor's presentation of Nora's "triumph" insists on the law of her queer heart over and against the putative reality that the world is grounded in (hetero)sexual difference (Lacan, "Propos," 172). He thereby displaces the idea that her insistence on her love for Robin makes her psychotic; instead, he renders it socially valid by representing her "heart" as prevailing over reason in legal battle. While elsewhere O'Connor presents "love of woman for woman" as an "insane passion," as the limit of the social, in this moment of reversal he reconfigures it—through the very "defense" mounted by Nora's refusal to cede her lesbian passion—not as madness, but as an alternate form of reason, as the founding principle of an alternate social order (75). Thus, instead of proposing her lesbianism as the cause of her madness, as did Lacan's interpretation of the Papin sisters, O'Connor's rhetorical reversal instead suggests that the conflation of her insanity with her desire for Robin is conditioned by a phallogocentric representational frame whose purchase on subjectivity is historically and ideologically contingent, rather than transhistorically necessary. What a misogynist interpretation would present as her irrationality, as the index of her social and psychical primitivism, appears as the hallmark of rationality, of civilization, in this alternate universe. O'Connor's "great virtue," after all, is that he never uses "the derogatory in the usual sense" (116-117).

A Fine and Terrifying Spectacle

However important it is for us to view Nora's insistence on the law of her heart as a brave refusal to cede a desire that the heterosexist symbolic would render an "insane passion," her reverse discourse has its limits. It involves a repudiation, rather than a rearticulation, of the dubious claim that the symbolic must necessarily be structured through "sexual difference."[48] While at one moment O'Connor elevates Nora as a queer heroine, as "the only one" able to fortify her heart against the ravages of patriarchy, in another instance he describes her frantic pursuit of Robin not as the triumphant establishment of a new civilization but instead as "the demolishing of a great ruin" (153, 142). The larger narrative trajectory of *Nightwood* traces out the demolition to which O'Connor refers, suggesting that his positing of an alternative symbolic order does little to halt the destructive path paved for Nora by a patriarchal society that renders her lesbianism an "insane passion" (142). Her refusal to cede her desire does not successfully rearticulate symbolic law, but instead leads to the "fine and terrifying spectacle" of her destruction in the scene of failed reunion tracked in the novel's final chapter, "The Possessed" (142-143). Alerted by the barking of her dog, Nora follows it from her upstate New York home to a chapel at the top of a hill. "[C]ursing and crying" for no apparent reason, she runs in pursuit of her dog, only to plunge "blindly" into the chapel door (169). Felled, her enraged passion thwarted by the patriarchal structure of the chapel—by the very social order that produced her lesbianism as insanity—Nora disappears from the narration, never to witness the scene that compelled her. All that remains of Nora is her dog, its beastliness standing in for the primitivism that subtends her own subjectivity and that of the social order whose unraveling she represents.

Through a process of automatic, primitive identification with an animal that recalls the women's initial meeting at the circus, the narrative then substitutes Robin for the felled Nora: in what Dana Seitler calls a "moment of 'becoming animal,'" Robin comes to identify with Nora's dog (554). Completing the descent into animality that began when she "circled closer and closer" to Nora while wandering through the woods and engaging in specular identifications with animals—speaking to them, grasping them, "straining their fur back until their eyes were narrowed and their teeth bare, her own teeth showing as if her hand were upon her own neck"—Robin goes down on all fours before the altar at the moment Nora strikes the doorframe, and begins an eroticized struggle with the dog (168). If at first, Robin's status as a person is ambiguous (she is "someone" Nora loved "and it became" herself), and if she eventually becomes an "it" (she is "something strange" that had loved Nora but later had "forgotten" her), in "The Possessed" she finally descends to animality in her identification with the dog, another "it" (152, 156). In this instance, she is not a "beast turning human," but instead a human turning beast: the site onto which the primitivism at the heart of the symbolic is displaced (152). By identifying with the dog, Robin identifies with Nora's "primitive" core, an act that can be fully accomplished only through Nora's destruction.

Taking place in a chapel, and prompted by the felling of Nora, the "Madonna" upon whom Robin depends and against whom she rebels, Robin's descent into animality tracks the unraveling of patriarchal religion and of the gendered and sexual regime upon which patriarchal society is founded. Her descent not only undoes the complex network of ideologies from which the figure of the psychotic lesbian has emerged, but also clears

the space for the rearticulation of the terms on which they are founded (146). As Jane Marcus suggests, Robin's descent is anticipated in O'Connor's invocation of the "angel on all fours" in the public toilet ("Laughing at Leviticus" 238). The association of the "possessed" Robin with the queer girl "seeking [her] people that have never been made" suggests that what might seem to be the penultimate example of psychotic foreclosure of symbolic mandates represents instead a longing for a new symbolic order on whose threshold Robin might be said to be poised with her canine partner (Barnes, *Nightwood,* 95). Seitler suggests that the process of "becoming animal" could make such a rearticulation of the foundational terms of the symbolic possible. She asserts that

> As the degeneration narrative increasingly sinks into the excess of its own interpretive frames, the bestialized and otherwise degraded body emerges to reconsolidate and realign meanings [by] ironiz[ing] the relations between woman and animal, pervert and beast, and bestiality and raciality, reformulating these terms into unpredictable combinations capable of transforming what each one means.
>
> (555, 554)

Yet if such a rearticulation—a progressive outcome of which is so longed for in O'Connor's story of a queer "kingdom without precedent"—might be made possible by Robin's "becoming-animal," its future is by no means set in advance. It is, as Seitler concedes, "unpredictable." Barnes unravels the Western symbolic in its own decaying chapel and opens up a space for its displacement, but does not offer us a subject whose life such a rearticulation has made more livable.[49] Instead, Barnes leaves us, through the future anterior of our memory of a kingdom that has yet to come to be, longing for the moment of the mirror stage: for that point at which one jubilantly assumes the specular image whose coordinates determine the "fictional direction" of one's "asymptotic" way of "coming-into-being"; for that point at which the "symbolic matrix," however it might come to be defined, is immanent, if not yet actualized (Lacan, "The mirror stage," 2).

Notes

1. Kaup's emphasis is on the way in which Barnes's neobaroque proliferation of signifiers undercuts "the reader's belief in the power of naming through singular, exclusive analytical concepts" ("The Neobaroque" 101).

2. For arguments that O'Connor's function is to mock the psychoanalyst's role, see Kautz; Martins; and Jane Marcus, "Laughing at Leviticus." Focusing on similarities between the interpersonal dynamics displayed in *Nightwood,* those of pedagogy, and those of Freud's analysis of Dora, Wilson offers an extended discussion of O'Connor's quasi-psychoanalytic sessions with Nora. For an argument that he mocks the function of the sexologist, see Andrea Harris, 63.

3. Radclyffe Hall's *The Well of Loneliness* is arguably the most famous "lesbian novel" in the Western literary tradition. Barnes scholars have a particular fondness for contrasting *Nightwood* to *The Well of Loneliness* because of the two novels' diametrically opposed representational strategies; my own remarks about the contrast between Barnes and Hall are indebted to the work of Allen, Boone, Chisholm ("Obscene Modernism"), and Gilmore.

4. For discussions of *Nightwood* as a "lesbian novel," see Julie Abraham, Castricano, Gilmore, Bertha Harris, Lee, and Marcus ("Laughing at Leviticus"); for a discussion of its inflection of what now is called bisexual identity, see Michel, "I just loved Thelma." For complications of such claims, see Allen, Boone, Chisholm ("Obscene Modernism"), Fleischer, Andrea Harris, and Meese.

5. Diane Chisholm, for example, critiques the "recuperation of *Nightwood*'s sexual outlawry by a politics of representation"; she argues that "instead of speaking out on lesbianism in cryptic modernism, *Nightwood* seriously challenges the epistemological and ontological claims of sexual discourse" ("Obscene Modernism" 171-172). According to Chisholm, *Nightwood* "flaunts a queer skepticism concerning sexual liberation and its bohemian milieux, profaning the illusions of their 'reverse discourse'" (176). This formulation incisively points out that *Nightwood* cannot be reduced to a "reverse discourse" advocating the rights of oppressed minorities by voicing "the struggle of an emerging subculture" (172). Chisholm's argument, however, proceeds as if debunking naïve claims to identity-based liberation necessarily requires the wholesale abandonment of any consideration of sexual specificity.

Joseph Boone, on the other hand, provides a helpfully sophisticated account of how one might read the way in which the novel traces out a range of "queer" sexualities at the same time as it places heavy emphasis on specifically same-sex love. He begins by arguing against "reifying same-sex love as *the* lens through which to read its narrative" and by insisting that it instead figures a "polymorphous desire" that would most aptly be termed "queer"; he goes on to assert that nonetheless, "the novel's representation of its underworld of aliens and outcasts organizes itself under the sign of same-sex love" (234-235). Boone's formulation is problematic, however, in its elevation of same-sex love as an organizing principle, if not a "lens," for the novel: the umbrella-principle he proposes inevitably leaves many threads of *Nightwood* uncovered. Matthew O'Connor's transvestism and professed desire to be a woman, for example, cannot so simply be assimilated into what we now call "homosexuality" or "same-sex love." Boone's

curious choice of support for his privileging of the "sign of same-sex love"—O'Connor's query, "What is this love we have for the invert, boy or girl?"—betrays the conceptual difficulty on which his reading founders (qtd. in Boone 235). The novel's persistent use of a rhetoric of "sexual inversion" can hardly be said to be subordinate to a homosexual, or even same-sex "sign," for the polarizing logic that ascribes to one partner the desire to be the opposite-sex partner of the other might be read retroactively as an anticipation either of contemporary "homosexual" identities *or* of "transgendered" and "transsexual" identities—the latter of which might (but do not necessarily) involve the explicit repudiation of an identity based on "same-sex" object-choice. The category of "inversion" is more successful in signaling the impasse in sexual ontology created by dualistic thinking than in successfully describing either the sense of bodily belonging or the desired object-choice of those persons to whom it would refer, and should be maintained as a site of undecidability irreducible to subsequent attempts to enlist it in the service of "homosexual," "transgendered," or "transsexual" identity.

If *Nightwood* might be described as a "queer" novel, then it is not, as Boone claims, because its deployment of sexological theory anticipates a contemporary use of "queer" that retains homosexuality as its definitional center at the same time as it undoes false dichotomies supporting the "hetero/homo" divide, but instead because, as Andrea Harris demonstrates through close reading, its rhetorical "inversions" produce the sexological figure of "'the third sex'" as "fundamentally undecidable" (Boone 235; Harris 94). I would modify Harris's argument only slightly by suggesting that this undecidability is not merely a function of Barnes's "biting parody" of sexological discourse but is inherent in the sexologists' conceptualization of "inversion" itself (233).

6. Here I follow psychoanalytically informed writers such as Cixous and Kristeva, whose work undermines the false dichotomy between the "psychical" and the "sociopolitical."

7. For an implicit comparison of Barnes's text to the mechanisms of psychosis, see Bock.

8. For readings that focus on the unconscious, see Baird, Boone, Carlston, Castricano, Henke, Kannenstine, Marcus ("Laughing at Leviticus"), and Robert Nadeau.

9. For discussions of the novel's undermining of linear narrative—one of the ways in which its style mimes madness—see Béranger ("La femme invisible"), Bock, Boone, Burke, Gerstenberger, Kalfopoulou, Meese, and Schehr.

10. To understand the novel's mechanism as mimicking that of "psychosis" carries somewhat different implications for a politicized reading of psychoanalysis than do recent and highly influential efforts, by Jane Marcus and many after her, to read it as a textualization of the "political unconscious" of Barnes's era (231). While the political gesture animating Marcus's argument provides a helpful means of approaching the novel's figurations of lesbian primitivism and psychosis, her claims about the political valences of the "unconscious" require further scrutiny. Only by allowing Bakhtin's account of the carnivalesque as "reversal of authoritarian values" to stand in for the Freudian unconscious is Marcus able to insist that the novel performs a purely progressive mocking of fascist fears of degeneration (Marcus, "Laughing," 226). Moreover, if Marcus is correct in asserting of *Nightwood* that "Freud, fascism, Hitler, 'high art,' and the lumpen proletariat [*sic*] haunt the text as a potent 'political unconscious,'" we nonetheless must recall that the unconscious is the field in which the most elusive and sometimes even the most reprehensible of human motives can play out (Marcus, "Laughing," 222). We are by no means assured that the resistances of a text qua unconscious will correspond to the radical political resistances we most desire to read into it.

11. See Kaup, *Mad Intertextuality,* 39-62, for a differently formulated argument that *Nightwood* performas a "destructing of paternal creation" (44). Kaup is persuasive in arguing that Robin's madness "topple[s] the entire symbolic edifice of filiation," though her claim that O'Connor stands as her Frankenstein-like father is a stretch (46).

12. Marcus argues that O'Connor is a "mad" parody of Freud whose "womb envy" parodies Freud's concept of "penis envy"; while I agree with her reading of O'Connor, I dispute her identification of Nora as "the archetypical Dora or female hysteric" (who somehow is also "rational . . . and analytical") ("Laughing" 233).

13. For discussion of insanity at the characterological level, see in addition to Fuchs the 17 October 1936 review of *Nightwood* in the *Newstatesman and Nation* (reprinted in Marcus, "Mousemeat," 197-199); Béranger; Chisholm, "Obscene Modernism"; Fadiman, review of *Nightwood* in the *New Yorker,* 13 March 1936 (reprinted in Marcus, "Mousemeat," 203-204); Herring, *Djuna,* 203-217; Kaup, *Mad Intertextuality,* 39-62; and Williamson. Contrasting with my focus on parallels between O'Connor and Schreber, Kautz, Marcus ("Laughing at Leviticus"), and Wilson emphasize his similarities to and departures from the persona Freud took on while analyzing hysterics.

14. As Elaine Showalter's study of *The Female Malady* implies, psychiatric institutions themselves often serve to reproduce, in the guise of a "cure," the symbolic imperatives contested by the mechanisms of mental illness. And as Sander Gilman (*Freud, Race, and Gender*) and Eric Santner illustrate in their work on the Schreber memoir, a psychotic's delusions can trace out reactionary as well as progressive political identifications.

15. Here we must recall, from chapter 2, both the heterosexism of the surrealist theory of *l'amour fou* and the way in which a presumption of heterosexuality conditions the disavowal through which the "Breton" of *Nadja* articulates his fascination with Palau's lesbian "détraquées." In "Obscene Modernism," however, Chisholm neither remarks on Palau's marking of the *détraquée* as sexually perverse nor comments on Barnes's important revision of the sexual politics of surrealism. For other discussions of Nora and Robin as *détraquées* or as "deranged," see Boone, Herring ("Djuna Barnes and Thelma Wood"), and Reizbaum.

16. See Fuss, 32-40, for a discussion of Freud's racializing and sexualizing of the "primitive."

17. By no means am I suggesting that all forms of Christianity or that all Christians participate in the homophobia attributed to Puritanism by *Nightwood*. While in the present day, different Christian denominations and the individuals within them vary in their acceptance or rejection of homosexuality, what I speak of here is a conservative strain, bound up in the legacy of Puritanism, that is invoked in *Nightwood*.

18. The cutting of this passage, with its open depiction of lesbian sexuality and what now would be called butch-femme gender, calls into question Gilmore's claim that "Eliot's cuts and Barnes' acceptance of them have more to do with obscuring gay male sexuality than with lesbian sexuality" (621). I am grateful to Therese Paetschow for pointing out the differences between the New Directions edition of *Nightwood* and the manuscript pages of "Watchman, What of the Night?" that appear in facsimile in the Plumb edition.

19. Victoria Smith also points out the parallel *Nightwood* draws between the erasures of history experienced by queers and Jews, the latter of whose historical circumstances are evoked in the story of the Volkbeins. For Barnes, Smith asserts, "[t]he figure of the Jew and Jews' relation to history become . . . ways in which to represent how history is constructed, who gets written in and who gets written out" (197).

20. For discussions of Robin as the "unconscious," see also Backus, Baird, Benstock (*Women of the Left Bank*), Boone, Carlston, Henke, Kalfopoulou,

Jane Marcus ("Laughing at Leviticus"), and Bonnie Kime Scott. For Robin as mad or as psychotic, see above. For Robin as primitive, see Baird, Benstock (*Women*), Béranger, Boone, Burke, Carlston, Castricano, Fleischer, Fuchs, Henke, Levine, and Robert Nadeau.

21. In "Motherhood According to Giovanni Bellini," Kristeva perpetuates Lacan's assumption of the structural necessity of the "third term" for a subject's entrance into the symbolic order, yet diverges from it in her positive valuation of the child's quasi-psychotic experience of pre-Oedipality.

22. Here I refer to critical debates on the role of O'Connor in the narration. While early commentators on the novel tended to read the discursively dominant O'Connor as providing a totalizing commentary on the novel's events, more recent scholars have criticized such estimations as overvaluations that unduly credit the male O'Connor with an authority that the structure of the novel itself does not grant him. While these latter critics have emphasized the distinction between O'Connor and the narrator, and have drawn attention to other characters whose pronouncements have import for the larger novel, I add to their critiques the assertion that O'Connor's very attempt to assert discursive authority inevitably fails.

23. See Allen, 21-45, for one treatment of Nora's maternal stance toward Robin.

24. Here I reference Orlando Patterson's notion of "social death," which describes the way in which slaves have been "alienated from all 'rights' or claims of birth" and barred from inclusion in "any legitimate social order" (5). I invoke "social death" in this context not to draw false parallels between the social exclusion of queers and the bondage of slaves—forms of oppression that have markedly different histories and structures—but to highlight the ambiguous ontology assigned to the queers of *Nightwood*. My thanks to Christopher Peterson for calling my attention to Patterson's work.

25. See Lacan's *The Four Fundamental Concepts of Psycho-Analysis* for a discussion of the *objet a.*

26. See Roof, *Come As You Are,* 141, for another discussion of the projections at work in the characters' figuration of Robin.

27. Kaup makes a compelling argument that neobaroque style enables *Nightwood* to depart from certain techniques frequently associated with high modernist experimentalism: the use of stream of consciousness to render realistic depictions of the fragmented psyche; and the use of what Eliot called the "mythical method" to bring unity to the fragments of modernity ("The Neobaroque").

28. I am by no means taking the stance of a clinician whose primary task is to diagnose Nora and Robin as "psychotic"; as should be clear, I find the terms of such a diagnosis to be highly problematic. Instead, I trace out the way in which psychoanalysis and sexology, as two available sources for Barnes's representations of desire between women, condition the way in which *Nightwood* portrays the lesbian psyche through the same tropes used by clinicians to characterize the mental structure of psychotics.

29. Seitler similarly points out that "Robin's endless migrations . . . frustrate identitarian notions of sexuality" (549).

30. If all of the texts featured in this book might be read as paradigmatic of the figure of the psychotic lesbian who continues to appear even in contemporary lesbian popular culture in the guise of the "psycho ex-girlfriend," Barnes's *Nightwood* might be said as well to contain, in its story of Nora's and Robin's near immediate domestic union, the paradigmatic example of what now is called the "lesbian U-Haul syndrome" of immediate cohabitation.

31. See page 57 especially for a figuration of Robin's and Nora's commingled voices and identities.

32. Backus similarly claims that Robin's "unconsciousness is 'born' rather than acquired," and "resembles the Lacanian Imaginary" in its status as temporally prior to symbolic law (426). These perspectives elide the way in which the symbolic is immanent even in the imaginary, as well as the way in which those states purportedly "prior" to the symbolic are produced, through negation, by the terms of the symbolic itself.

33. Kristeva uses "abject" in a somewhat different manner than Butler. For Kristeva, who situates her definition within the framework of Lacanian psychoanalysis, "abjection" refers to the process of separating from the pre-Oedipal mother and finding a foothold in the symbolic; for Butler, who presents her definition through a Hegelian logic, the term indicates that which is excluded through dialectical opposition. See *Powers of Horror* for Kristeva's theory of abjection; see Butler's "Gender As Performance" and "How Bodies Come To Matter" for an overview of her arguments.

34. See Seitler for an excellent discussion of *Nightwood* as a text that "dramatize[s]" and unsettles the logic through which "the human-beast hybrid" serves as "a persistent and threatening reminder of how far society could fall if perverse sexuality is allowed to continue unhindered" (530). Much as I do, Seitler concludes that the novel presents "a

world in a state of ruination for which there is no outside" and in which "everyone is degenerate" (556).

35. As neither Barnes nor Henke provide any indication that they were familiar with the Papin affair or with Lacan's commentary on it, I do not argue for any *direct* influence of his work in the 1930s either on *Nightwood* or on Henke's reading. Both of them, however, are clearly familiar with the wider sphere of psychoanalytic discourse from which Lacan's analysis of the Papin sisters emerged. Barnes's deployment of tropes that intersect with Lacan's underscores the presence, within 1930s quasi-medical discourse, of the figure of the "lesbian psychotic." Moreover, the similarities between Lacan's and Henke's texts suggest the way in which conclusions about psychotic lesbianism easily follow from the psychoanalytic paradigm I critique throughout this book: the phallogocentric teleology that renders lesbianism representable as narcissistic undifferentiation.

36. Charles Baxter similarly notes that Nora's "difficulty is engendered by her own narcissism, which drives her to love her own image at one remove and which makes her unable to forget that approximation (Robin Vote) when it is taken away" (1179). Nora's is the delusional pursuit of an ideal, the incessant attempt to transform the world according to her own image, to make Robin cease her refusal to inhabit Nora's construct—an act only possible through the obliteration of Robin herself. However, Baxter misses *Nightwood*'s force as a *critique* of psychoanalysis when he earnestly takes up the diagnostic role of the clinician and juxtaposes himself to Doctor O'Connor, the quack whom he charges with the inability to identify Nora's true ailment.

37. Feminist critics such as Benstock, Kennedy, and Jane Marcus ("Laughing at Leviticus") emphasize that Nora's possessiveness makes her "the unknowing instrument of the patriarchy" by attempting to "make Robin conform to a moral code based on patriarchal self-interest and misogyny" (Benstock, *Women,* 263).

38. In *The Psychic Life of Power,* Judith Butler explores the dynamic of "passionate attachment" through which one clings to the workings of power that condition one's subjection. Her account is a rejoinder to those who, like Faderman, "presume a subject who performs an internalization" of the oppressive effects of power, rather than a subject who is constituted through the workings of power (4). Butler's account is useful in displacing the assumption that queer representation would be devoid of all violence were it not for the influence of so-called negative representations of murderous queers.

39. See Lacan, "Aggressivity in psychoanalysis."

40. See also Boone, Carlston, Castricano, Guthrie, Jane Marcus ("Laughing at Leviticus"), and Michel for discussions of pre-Oedipality.

41. Allen insists that in *Nightwood,* "difference precedes sameness," leading Nora "not [to] self-annihilating *sameness* but [to] crucial *resemblance,* a relation of identity layered with figures of alterity" (32); Lee argues that the novel presents "an insurmountable difference" between its lovers (212). Benstock makes the similarly grounded argument that *Nightwood,* along with several other of Barnes's works, "examine[s] the difference *within* sexual difference" (*Women of the Left Bank* 247). These influential arguments nonetheless remain problematic. Casting the women's turbulent relationship as a "struggle to establish difference," Lee ascribes a psychical maturity to Robin that is belied by the consistency of the novel's rhetorical linking of her to primitivism and degeneration, yet she overlooks the way in which *Nightwood*'s casting of Robin as a "beast turning human" might be just as problematic as its inflection of figures of lesbian narcissism (212).

42. See Lacan, "The mirror stage" and "Aggressivity in psychoanalysis."

43. In "Motives of Paranoid Crime," Lacan notes Christine's hallucinatory states and eventually links them to what he views as pathologically narcissistic lesbianism; however, he makes less of the role of her separation from Léa in the genesis of her delusions than does Dupré.

44. Freud's distinction between mourning and melancholia is less than clear. Though Laplanche and Pontalis would later categorize melancholia as a psychosis distinct from both paranoia and schizophrenia, in "Mourning and Melancholia," Freud neither elucidates the psychotic aspects of mourning nor explores their relation to melancholia (Laplanche and Pontalis 370). Instead, he symptomatically refuses explicitly to explore the very commonalities his own discussion of mourning as a "hallucinatory wishful psychosis" suggests to exist between the psychotic state of melancholia and the psychotic form taken by mourning in its most extreme moments. Implicitly constructing the mourner as normal, he asserts that, in contrast, the extreme reaction of the melancholic renders her "suspect." As a result, the melancholic becomes the subject of a clinical investigation that is

intended to ferret out signs of her "pathological disposition," and that is conducted not only by Freud the clinician but also by "us," the reader-assistants whose presumed normalcy and consensus are sufficient proof that mourning is not "a pathological condition" because that possibility "never occurs to us" ("Mourning and Melancholia" 243). He makes a similarly tautological appeal to a commonsense understanding of "normalcy" in his claim that melancholia arises when the loss of an object does not lead to the "*normal . . . withdrawal of the libido from [the] object and a displacement of it on to a new one,*" as in mourning (249; emphasis added). Yet if, as Fuss suggests, this formulation indeed suggests that melancholia is "not the opposing of mourning but its most violent continuation"—that it is "pathological mourning"—then we might ask not what distinguishes melancholia from the ordinary experience of mourning, but instead what similarities it shares with those extreme instances of mourning that culminate in a "hallucinatory wishful psychosis" that allows the bereaved to turn "away from reality" in order to *avoid* withdrawing her libido from the absent object (Fuss 38; Freud, "Mourning and Melancholia," 250, 244). The psychotic turn taken by this especially "intense" form of mourning implicitly differentiates it from the "normal" process of displacement and recathexis later assumed by Freud in his hasty opposition of mourning to melancholia. Freud's failure to account for this progression from a "normal" into a "psychotic" mode of mourning, however, elides the question of the difference between "normalcy" and "psychosis." In so doing, Freud opens up two not entirely incompatible lines of speculation: (1) that mourning itself may have variants that parallel melancholia not only in their initial provocation by loss but also in their later manifestation in a flight from "reality"; and (2) that mourning, in carrying the potential for "hallucinatory wishful psychosis," itself might be a socially acceptable (and therefore "normal") means of entering into that same psychical territory of the psychotic (244, 249).

Even "A Metapsychological Supplement to the Theory of Dreams," the essay that immediately precedes "Mourning and Melancholia" in the *Standard Edition* and that engages differences between "normal" and "psychotic" modes of hallucination more explicitly, does not point to a clear distinction between the two. Exploring the various ways in which subjects are able to flee "reality," this essay sketches out some differences between the "topographical" and "temporal" regressions operative in "normal" processes such as dreaming and grieving and in those presumably pathological

mechanisms propelling the psychoses ("Metapsychological" 222). Though Freud opens the paper by presenting "grief" as one of the "*normal* prototypes of *pathological* affections" under consideration, by the end of the essay mourning nonetheless gives way to the dreamwork as the exemplary instance of a "normal" regressive process (222; emphasis added). Through this rhetorical effacement of mourning, Freud tacitly questions its status as "normal," but nonetheless continues to uphold a distinction between "normalcy" and "pathology" by opposing the dreamwork to the mechanisms of psychosis.

This refusal to complicate the distinction between sanity and insanity leads to an explicitly paranoid preemptive strike in the section that examines the implications of "hallucinatory wishful psychosis." Freud explains that hallucinatory psychosis "achieves two by no means identical results": that of bringing "hidden or repressed wishes into consciousness," and that of representing them, "with the subject's entire belief, as fulfilled" (230). His conclusion that the hallucinating subject entirely believes in "the reality" of the fulfillment of his wish is accompanied, however, by a sense that he is entering into theoretical terrain that is dangerous: he cautions that his speculations reveal "the gravest" kind of "uncertainties" about the distinctions between normalcy and pathology (229). The rest of the essay is devoted to an attempt to explain the absolute nature of the binary between "normal" and "pathological" hallucinations in terms of their divergent topographical effects. Freud defensively states that his aim in comparing "dreams with pathological states akin to them" is not to explore the way in which the universality of hallucination might allow us to rethink definitions of sanity and insanity, but instead to "clear up" (orig. "Klärung") a feared infection of normal subjectivity by the hallucinatory process of the dream-work ("A Metapsychological Supplement" 229; 420). This claim strives to reorient the reader to a clinical viewpoint in which the hallucinations of "normal" subjects are not seen as symptoms of pathology (229).

Freud fails, however, to distinguish successfully between pathological and non-pathological modes of hallucination. Arguing that all hallucinations are caused by a "withdrawal of cathexis" propelled by a psychical regression that allows the subject to evade reality-testing, Freud notes that this regression can be accomplished at various topographical sites: "[i]n dreams the withdrawal of cathexis (libido or interest) affects all systems equally; in the transference neuroses, the *Pcs.* cathexis is withdrawn; in schizophrenia, the cathexis of the *Ucs.*; in amentia, that of the *Cs.*" (232-

235). The pathological or nonpathological nature of hallucination, then, depends upon the site from which cathexis has been withdrawn in regression. Yet Freud presents the very fact of topographical distinctions between the dreamwork and the psychoses as proof that the former can be seen as uncontaminated by the latter. In so doing, he continues to beg the question of the distinction between sanity and insanity, providing nothing more than his initial assumption of the normalcy of the dreamwork to uphold the claim that it is absolutely distinct from psychosis.

If we turn Freud's argument on its head, however, and look carefully at the topographical distinctions he proposes, the line between psychosis and normalcy blurs significantly. If in the three "pathological" states—"the transference neuroses," "schizophrenia," and "amentia"—cathexis is withdrawn from specific topographical sites, in the purportedly normal state, the dreamwork, all of these sites are affected equally by regression. Furthermore, in the latter process, regression is accomplished the most thoroughly of all, and in fact includes multiple regressions that in themselves are identified as "pathological." This commonality of regression to psychosis and the dreamwork makes it difficult to understand Freud's insistence that his topographical analysis proves that the dreamwork is any more "normal" than the mechanisms of psychosis.

In *The Shell and the Kernel,* Nicolas Abraham and Maria Torok take a different approach than mine to the project of complicating the distinction between mourning and melancholia. Garry Sherbert brings Abraham and Torok's work on "cryptic mourning" to bear on the theme of incest in *Nightwood.*

45. Critical invocations of Barnes's use of O'Connor to mock masculinity and psychoanalytic discourse are many: see Benstock (*Women of the Left Bank*), Boone, Henke, Gilbert and Gubar, Kautz, and Jane Marcus ("Laughing at Leviticus").

46. In her account of melancholia as the "violent continuation" of mourning, Fuss suggests that the two processes are similar not only because they are propelled by an initial loss, but also because they are accomplished through identification. The melancholic, she explains, fails to introject the lost object, and instead takes "the ego itself as its object of incorporation, . . . [t]urning identification's violent impulses completely inward" and consuming "itself in an act of auto-cannibalism" (37). For Freud, although in melancholia the lost object is "withdrawn from consciousness," the self-reproaching melancholic nonetheless harbors a secret identification with the object she has re-

fused to incorporate: she takes its qualities as her own, citing its faults as cause for self-flagellation (Freud, "Mourning and Melancholia," 245).

47. Laplanche and Pontalis identify "melancholia and mania" as psychoses structurally distinct from paranoia and schizophrenia (370).

48. Despite its problematic resistance to subjecting "sexual difference" to the same critique applied to other "ideological formations" (Butler, *Bodies,* 196), the work of Slavoj Zizek is nonetheless useful in distinguishing the inefficacy of psychosis, which is characterized by the refusal of symbolic mandates, from the "Real of an act" that could change the *point de capiton* and therefore prompt an overhaul of the symbolic's coordinates. See especially Zizek's contributions to Butler et al., *Contingency, Hegemony, Universality.*

49. Although Catherine Guthrie also presents an account, derived differently than my own, of the way in which *Nightwood* reconfigures the symbolic order, I hesitate to concur with her presentation of the novel as a wholly successful "refounding" of "the symbolic on the basis of lesbianism" (54). Even though O'Connor's remarks reconfigure social law to render lesbianism sane and viable, they do not necessarily suggest lesbianism to be the foundational principle of the social order.

Works Cited

Abraham, Julie. "'Woman, Remember You': Djuna Barnes and History." In *Silence and Power: A Reevaluation of Djuna Barnes,* edited by Mary Lynn Broe, 252-268. Carbondale: Southern Illinois University Press, 1991.

Abraham, Nicolas, and Maria Torok. *The Shell and the Kernel: Renewals of Psychoanalysis.* Vol. 1. Edited and translated by Nicholas T. Rand. Chicago: University of Chicago Press, 1994.

Allen, Carolyn. *Following Djuna: Women Lovers and the Erotics of Loss.* Bloomington: Indiana University Press, 1996.

Backus, Margot Gayle. "'Looking for the Dead Girl:' Incest, Pornography, and the Capitalist Family Romance in *Nightwood, The Years,* and *Tar Baby.*" *American Imago: Studies in Psychoanalysis and Culture* 51, no. 4 (1994): 521-545.

Baird, James. "Djuna Barnes and Surrealism: 'Backward Grief.'" In *Individual and Community: Variations on a Theme in American Fiction,* edited by Kenneth H. Baldwin and David K. Kirby, 160-181. Durham: Duke University Press, 1975.

Barnes, Djuna. *Nightwood.* New York: New Directions, 1937.

————. "Watchman, What of the Night?" Facsimile. In *Nightwood: The Original Version and Related Drafts,* edited by Cheryl J. Plumb, 261-265. Normal, Ill.: Dalkey Archive Press, 1995.

Baxter, Charles. "A Self-Consuming Light: *Nightwood* and the Crisis of Modernism." *Journal of Modern Literature* 3 (1974): 1175-1187.

Benstock, Shari. *Women of the Left Bank: Paris, 1900-1940.* Austin: University of Texas Press, 1986.

Béranger, Elisabeth. "La femme invisible: Introduction à l'écriture de Djuna Barnes." *Caliban* 17 (1980): 99-110.

Bock, Martin. "The Nocturnal Visions of Joyce and Barnes." In *Crossing the Shadow-Line: The Literature of Estrangement,* 65-84. Columbus: Ohio State University Press, 1989.

Boone, Joseph Allen. *Libidinal Currents: Sexuality and the Shaping of Modernism.* Chicago: University of Chicago Press, 1998.

Breton, André. *Nadja.* Translated by Richard Howard. New York: Grove, 1960.

Bronfen, Elisabeth. "Wandering in Mind or Body. Death, Narration and Gender in Djuna Barnes' Novel *Nightwood.*" *Amerikastudien/American Studies* 33, no. 2 (1988): 167-177.

Burke, Kenneth. "Version, Con—, Per—, and In— (Thoughts on Djuna Barnes's Novel *Nightwood*)." *Language As Symbolic Action: Essays on Life, Literature, and Method.* Berkeley and Los Angeles: University of California Press, 1968. 240-53.

Butler, Judith. "Gender as Performance: An Interview with Judith Butler." Interview with Peter Osborne and Lynne Segal. *Radical Philosophy* 67 (Summer 1994): 32-39.

————. "How Bodies Come to Matter: An Interview with Judith Butler." Interview with Irene Costera Meijer and Baukje Prins. *Signs* 23, no. 2 (Winter 1998): 275-286.

————. *The Psychic Life of Power: Theories in Subjection.* Stanford: Stanford University Press, 1997.

Butler, Judith, Ernesto Laclau, and Slavoj Zizek. *Contingency, Hegemony, Universality: Contemporary Dialogues on the Left.* London: Verso, 2000.

Carlston, Erin. *Thinking Fascism: Sapphic Modernity and Fascist Modernism.* Stanford: Stanford University Press, 1998.

Castle, Terry. *The Apparitional Lesbian: Female Homosexuality and Modern Culture.* New York: Columbia University Press, 1993.

Castricano, Jodey. "Rude Awakenings: or What Happens When a Lesbian Reads the 'Hieroglyphics of Sleep' in Djuna Barnes' *Nightwood.*" *West Coast Line* 28, no. 3 (1994-1995 Winter): 106-16.

Chisholm, Dianne. "Obscene Modernism: *Eros Noir* and the Profane Illumination of Djuna Barnes." *American Literature* 69, no. 1 (1997): 167-206.

Coffman, Christine. "The Papin Enigma." *GLQ* 5, no. 3 (1999): 331-359.

Deffenbacher, Kristina Kathleen. "The Housing of Wandering Minds in Victorian Cultural Discourses." Ph.D. diss., University of Southern California, 1998.

Dupré, Francis. *La "solution" du passage à l'acte: le double crime des soeurs Papin.* Toulouse: Erès, 1984.

Eagleton, Terry. *Literary Theory: An Introduction.* Oxford: Basil Blackwell, 1983.

Eliot, T. S. Introduction to *Nightwood,* by Djuna Barnes. New York: New Directions, 1937.

Faderman, Lillian, ed. *Surpassing the Love of Men: Romantic Friendship and Love between Women from the Renaissance to the Present.* New York: Morrow, 1981.

Fink, Bruce. *The Lacanian Subject: Between Language and Jouissance.* Princeton: Princeton University Press, 1995.

Fleischer, Georgette. "Djuna Barnes and T. S. Eliot: The Politics and Poetics of *Nightwood.*" *Studies in the Novel* 30, no. 3 (Fall 1998): 405-437.

Freud, Sigmund. "A Metapsychological Supplement to the Theory of Dreams." In *The Standard Edition of the Complete Psychological Works of Sigmund Freud,* translated and edited by James Strachey, 14:222-235. 24 vols. London: The Hogarth Press, 1958.

————. "Mourning and Melancholia." 1917. In *The Standard Edition of the Complete Psychological Works of Sigmund Freud,* translated and edited by James Strachey, 14:239-260. 24 vols. London: The Hogarth Press, 1958.

Fuchs, Miriam. "Dr. Matthew O'Connor: The Unhealthy Healer of Djuna Barnes' *Nightwood.*" *Literature and Medicine* 2 (1983): 125-134.

Fuss, Diana. *Identification Papers.* New York: Routledge, 1995.

Gallagher, Jean. "Vision and Inversion in Nightwood." *Modern Fiction Studies* 47, no. 2 (2001): 279-305.

Gallop, Jane. *Reading Lacan.* Ithaca: Cornell University Press, 1985.

Gerstenberger, Donna. "Modern (Post) Modern: Djuna Barnes among the Others." *Review of Contemporary Fiction* 13, no. 3 (1993): 33-40.

Gilbert, Sandra, and Susan Gubar. *No Man's Land: The Place of the Woman Writer in the Twentieth Century.* Vol. 2. New Haven: Yale University Press, 1989.

Gilman, Sander. *Freud, Race, and Gender.* Princeton: Princeton University Press, 1993.

Gilmore, Leigh. "Obscenity, Modernity, Identity: Legalizing *The Well of Loneliness* and *Nightwood.*" *Journal of the History of Sexuality* 4, no. 4 (1994): 603-624.

Grosz, Elizabeth. "The Body of Signification." In *Abjection, Melancholia, and Love: The Work of Julia Kristeva,* edited by John Fletcher and Andrew Benjamin, 80-103. New York: Routledge, 1990.

———. *Volatile Bodies: Toward a Corporeal Feminism.* Bloomington: Indiana University Press, 1994.

Guthrie, Catherine. "Refiguring the Sacred: Surreal Theater as the Space of Alterity in the Works of Leonora Carrington, Djuna Barnes, Angela Carter, and Audre Lorde." Ph.D. diss., Washington State University, 1996.

Hall, Radclyffe. *The Well of Loneliness.* 1928. Reprint, New York: Anchor, 1990.

Harris, Andrea. *Other Sexes: Rewriting Difference from Woolf to Winterson.* Albany: State University of New York Press, 2000.

Harris, Bertha. "The More Profound Nationality of their Lesbianism: Lesbian Society in Paris in the 1920's." In *Amazon Expedition: A Lesbian Feminist Anthology,* edited by Phyllis Birkby, Bertha Harris, Jill Johnston, Esther Newton, and Jane O'Wyatt, 77-88. Washington, D.C.: Times Change Press, 1973.

Hartsock, Nancy. "Rethinking Modernism: Minority vs. Majority Theories." In *The Nature and Context of Minority Discourse,* edited by Abdul JanMohamed and David Lloyd, 17-36. New York: Oxford University Press, 1990.

Henke, Suzette A. "(En)Gendering Modernism: Virginia Woolf and Djuna Barnes." In *Rereading the New: A Backward Glance at Modernism,* 325-342. Ann Arbor: University of Michigan Press, 1992.

Henstra, Sarah. "Looking the Part: Performative Narration in Djuna Barnes' *Nightwood* and Katherine Mansfield's "Je Ne Parle Pas Français." *Twentieth Century Literature* 46, no. 2 (2000): 125-149.

Herring, Phillip. "Djuna Barnes and Thelma Wood: The Vengeance of *Nightwood.*" *Journal of Modern Literature* 18, no. 1 (1992): 5-18.

———. *Djuna: The Life and Work of Djuna Barnes.* New York: Viking, 1995.

Hutchison, Sharla. "Convulsive Beauty: Images of Hysteria and Transgressive Sexuality: Claude Cahun and Djuna Barnes." *Symploke: A Journal for the Intermingling of Literary, Cultural, and Theoretical Scholarship* 11, nos. 1-2 (2003): 212-226.

Kalpofoulou, Adrianne. "Fractured Selves and Created Unities in Djuna Barnes' *Nightwood.*" In *Women, Creators of Culture,* edited by Ekaterini Georgoudaki and Domna Pastourmatzi, 273-281. Thessaloniki: Hellenic Association of American Studies, 1997.

Kannenstine, Louis F. *The Art of Djuna Barnes: Duality and Damnation.* New York: New York University Press, 1977.

Kaup, Monika. *Mad Intertextuality: Madness in Twentieth-Century Women's Writing.* Trier: Wissenschaftlicher Verlag Trier, 1993.

———. "The Neobaroque in Djuna Barnes." *Modernism/Modernity* 12, no. 1 (2005): 85-110.

Kautz, Elizabeth Dolan. "Gynecologists, Power, and Sexuality in Modernist Texts." *Journal of Popular Culture* 28, no. 4 (1995): 81-91.

Kennedy, Ann. "Inappropriate and Dazzling Sideshadows: Interpellating Narratives in Djuna Barnes's *Nightwood.*" *Post Identity* 1, no. 1 (1997): 94-112.

Kristeva, Julia. "Motherhood According to Giovanni Bellini." In *Desire in Language: A Semiotic Approach to Literature and Art,* edited by Leon S. Roudiez, 237-270. New York: Columbia University Press, 1980.

———. *Powers of Horror: An Essay on Abjection.* Translated by Leon S. Roudiez. New York: Columbia University Press, 1982.

Lacan, Jacques. "Aggressivity in Psychoanalysis." In *Ecrits: A Selection,* translated by Alan Sheican, 8-29. New York: Norton, 1977.

———. *The Four Fundamental Concepts of Psycho-Analysis.* Translated Alan Sheridan. New York: Norton, 1977.

———. "The Mirror Stage as Formative of the Function of the I." In *Ecrits: A Selection,* translated by Alan Sheridan, 1-7. New York: Norton, 1977.

———. "Motifs du Crime Paranoïaque: le crime des soeurs Papin." *Minotaure* 3/4 (December 1933): 25-28.

———. "Motives of Paranoid Crime: The Crime of the Papin Sisters." Translated by Jon Anderson. *Critical Texts* 5, no. 3 (1988): 7-11.

———. "Propos sur la causalité psychique." In his *Ecrits,* 151-193. Paris: Seuil, 1966.

Laplanche, Jean, and J.-B. Pontalis. *The Language of Psycho-Analysis.* Translated by John Nicholson-Smith. New York: Norton, 1973.

Lee, Judith. *"Nightwood:* The Sweetest Lie." In *Silence and Power: A Reevaluation of Djuna Barnes,* edited by Mary Lynn Broe, 207-218. Carbondale: Southern Illinois University Press, 1991.

Levine, Nancy J. "'I've always suffered from sirens': The cinema vamp and Djuna Barnes' *Nightwood.*" *Women's Studies* 16 (1989): 271-281.

Marcus, Jane. "Laughing at Leviticus: *Nightwood* as Woman's Circus Epic." In *Silence and Power: A Reevaluation of Djuna Barnes,* edited by Mary Lynn Broe, 221-250. Carbondale: Southern Illinois University Press, 1991.

———. "Mousemeat: Contemporary Reviews of *Nightwood*." In *Silence and Power: A Reevaluation of Djuna Barnes,* edited by Mary Lynn Broe, 195-204. Carbondale: Southern Illinois University Press, 1991.

Martins, Susana S. "Gender Trouble and Lesbian Desire in Djuna Barnes' *Nightwood*." *Frontiers: A Journal of Women Studies* 20, no. 3 (1999): 108-26.

Meese, Elizabeth. *(Sem)erotics: Theorizing Lesbian: Writing.* New York: New York University Press, 1992.

Michel, Frann. "Displacing Castration: *Nightwood, Ladies Almanack,* and Feminine Writing." *Contemporary Literature* 30, no. 1 (1989): 33-58.

———. "'I just loved Thelma': Djuna Barnes and the Construction of Bisexuality." *Review of Contemporary Fiction* 13, no. 3 (1993): 53-61.

Miller, Tyrus. *Late Modernism: Politics, Fiction, and the Arts Between the World Wars.* Berkeley and Los Angeles: University of California Press, 1999.

Nadeau, Robert. "*Nightwood* and the Freudian Unconscious." *International Fiction Review* 2 (1975): 159-163.

O'Connor, Noreen. *Wild Desires and Mistaken Identities: Lesbianism and Psychoanalysis.* New York: Columbia University Press, 1998.

Palau, P. L. *Les Détraquées.* [Paris?]: n.p., n.d.

Patterson, Orlando. *Slavery and Social Death: A Comparative Study.* Cambridge, Mass.: Harvard University Press, 1982.

Plumb, Cheryl J. *Nightwood: The Original Version and Related Drafts.* By Djuna Barnes. Normal, Ill.: Dalkey Archive Press, 1995.

Reizbaum, Marilyn. "A Modernism of Marginality: The Links Between James Joyce and Djuna Barnes." In *New Alliances in Joyce Studies: when it's aped to foul a delfian,* edited by Bonnie Kime Scott, 179-192. Newark: University of Delaware Press, 1988.

Roof, Judith. *Come As You Are: Sexuality and Narrative.* New York: Columbia University Press, 1996.

Rose, Jacqueline. *Sexuality in the Field of Vision.* London: Verso, 1986.

Santner, Eric. *My Own Private Germany: Daniel Paul Schreber's Secret History of Modernity.* Princeton: Princeton University Press, 1996.

Schehr, Lawrence. "Dismantling the Folds: Djuna Barnes' *Nightwood*." *Style* 19, no. 1 (1985): 36-49.

Scott, Bonnie Kime. *Refiguring Modernism.* 2 vols. Bloomington: Indiana University Press, 1995.

Seitler, Dana. "Down on All Fours: Atavistic Perversions and the Science of Desire from Frank Norris to Djuna Barnes." *American Literature* 73, no. 3 (2001): 525-562.

Sherbert, Garry. "'Hieroglyphics of Sleep and Pain': Djuna Barnes' Anatomy of Melancholy." *Canadian Review of Comparative Literature* 30, no. 1 (2003): 117-144.

Showalter, Elaine. *The Female Malady: Women, Madness, and Culture in England, 1830-1980.* New York: Pantheon Books, 1985.

Smith, Victoria L. "A Story beside(s) Itself: The Language of Loss in Djuna Barnes' *Nightwood*." *PMLA* 114, no. 2 (1999): 194-206.

van Alphen, Ernst. "Affective Reading: Less of Self in Djuna Barnes' *Nightwood*." In *The Practice of Cultural Analysis: Exposing Interdisciplinary Interpretation,* edited by Mieke Bal, 151-170. Stanford: Stanford University Press, 1999.

Whitley, Catherine. "Nations and the Night: Excremental History in James Joyce's Finnegan's Wake and Djuna Barnes' *Nightwood*." *Journal of Modern Literature* 24, no. 1 (2000): 81-98.

Williamson, Alan. "The Divided Image: The Quest for Identity in the Works of Djuna Barnes." *Critique: Studies in Contemporary Fiction* 7 (1964): 58-74.

Wilson, Deborah S. "Dora, Nora, and Their Professor: The 'Talking Cure,' *Nightwood,* and Feminist Pedagogy." *Literature and Psychology* 42, no. 3 (1996): 48-71.

Ann Martin (essay date 2006)

SOURCE: Martin, Ann. "Djuna Barnes: Wolves in Sheep's Clothing." In *Red Riding Hood and the Wolf in Bed: Modernism's Fairy Tales,* pp. 115-53. Toronto: University of Toronto Press, 2006.

[*In the following excerpt, Martin comments on Barnes's "manipulation of source texts and language," such as the fairy tale, in her works.*]

Very well—what is this love we have for the invert, boy or girl? It was they who were spoken of in every romance that we ever read. The girl lost, what is she but the Prince found? The Prince on the white horse that we have always been seeking. And the pretty lad who is a girl, what but the prince-princess in point lace—neither one and half the other, the painting on the fan! We love them for that reason. We were impaled in our childhood upon them as they rode through our primers, the sweetest lie of all, now come to be in boy or girl, for in the girl it is the prince, and in the boy it is the girl that makes the prince a prince—and not a man. They go far back in our lost distance where what we never had stands waiting; it was inevitable that we should come upon them, for our miscalculated longing has created them. They are our answer to what our grandmothers were told love was, and what it never came to be; they, the living lie of our centuries.

Djuna Barnes, *Nightwood*

In one of his lengthy monologues from *Nightwood,* Matthew O'Connor discusses 'this love we have for the invert,' identifying the fairy tale as a narrative axis around which sexuality turns (D. Barnes 1937, 136). The stories that Matthew has read and been read are 'primers' introducing him to traditional gender roles (136). But the transformation of the child into the adult in accordance with inherited stories of heterosexuality has been undercut in Matthew's case. Though he has been 'impaled' upon the lessons contained in these childhood books, there is a gap between the text and the body for whom that story's version of love 'never came to be' (137). David Copeland suggests that Matthew's is the modernist's recognition of fairy tales as 'romantic delusions' (1997, 7); Judith Lee argues that Barnes depicts the 'inadequacy' of the 'fairytale romance' in the setting of the Left Bank (1991, 208). I suggest that it is the very disjunction between the lesson and the lived experience that leads to Matthew's enabling interpretation of the source texts. For Matthew, the heterosexual characters of the fairy tales have been transgendered all along: it is not the bride or the groom, but the 'invert' that has been 'spoken of in every romance that we ever read' (D. Barnes 1937, 136). As Leigh Gilmore writes, 'the doctor has read in fairy tales the permanently perverse codes of gender, sexuality, and desire' (1994, 617). The hero is thus 'the sweetest lie,' for though he appears to be the representative of heterosexuality in the texts, Matthew's penetrating eye places him as a 'prince-princess in point-lace' (D. Barnes 1937, 136). Matthew reads the tales twice, then: first by focusing on what his Victorian 'grandmothers were told love was,' and second, by acknowledging his own 'answer' or response to nineteenth-century visions of gender and marriage (137). The fairy tale is turned into a palimpsest in Matthew's doubled view of its depiction of sexuality, as his 'miscalculated longing' for the 'Prince on a white horse' whom he has 'always been seeking' changes but retains traces of the original narrative (137, 136).

Matthew's manipulation of fairy tales reflects Barnes's own manipulation of source texts and of language. Like Joyce and Woolf, her modernist experimentations with diction, with narrative structure, and with intertextuality produce interpretative possibilities rather than stable points of reference for the reader. In the epigraph to this chapter, for instance, Barnes's repetition of the word 'come' draws attention to its multiple meanings: to move towards and reach a destination; to become perceptible; to descend from; to occupy spatially; to achieve orgasm (OED). Matthew's discussion of 'what our grandmothers were told love was, and what it never *came* to be' plays with these shades of significance (D. Barnes 1937, 137; emphasis mine). The definition of love has not been achieved, has not come to pass, has not come into sight. As a result, Matthew's interpretation has not descended from it, but instead from another source. Ultimately, Matthew suggests that the Victorian figuration of love lacks for him, as for his grandmothers, meaning and potency, and that it leads to a disappointment that is both emotional and sexual: neither Matthew nor the grandmothers 'came' to orgasm through it. Matthew has, however, arrived at an alternative reading of the love portrayed in fairy tales. Though he has been 'impaled [. . .] upon' the narratives, or penetrated by the messages of the texts, he has also 'come upon them' (136, 137). He has discovered a different meaning of the tales according to his own sense of sexual identity and has experienced an orgasmic pleasure by asserting (and inserting) his own interpretations. The Prince is thus 'the sweetest lie' in several senses: he indicates the deceptive nature of the heterosexual narrative, he represents Matthew's sweet discovery of inversion within the text, and he becomes a more fulfilling alternative, or a good 'lay.' Interpretation becomes copulation in Matthew's reading of the fairy tales, a moment of intercourse in which the adult who has internalized or been ridden by the stories of childhood is also able to ride them to a climax that is at once narrative and sexual, painful and pleasurable.

Djuna Barnes, like Joyce and Woolf, presents characters who exercise their authority as readers by acknowledging the lessons they have been taught and using those inherited visions of class, gender, and sexuality for their own ends. Allusions to fairy tales are sites where such readings are made evident. But the relationship between the source text and the reader, or between the ideology encoded in the fairy tale and the reader's response to that ideology, is complicated by the various social structures that Barnes depicts in *Ladies Almanack, Ryder, Nightwood,* and *The Antiphon.* Like Woolf's uses of 'Cinderella' in *Orlando,* where Lady Ritchie's version of the fairy tale is combined with other variants, Barnes's characters are involved in networks of power where authority arises from many different locations: mainstream and marginal, sexual and intellectual, familial and political. The different communities and spaces that are the settings for Barnes's works affect cultural interactions differently. Thus, though Barnes addresses the effects of a patriarchal order, such as the one suggested in the primers that Matthew encounters as a child, she also explores the hierarchies of the margins, including those positions of strength that Matthew himself occupies. Though he may defy the lessons of his childhood and assert an alternative vision of sexuality or desire, Matthew teaches lessons of his own to Nora, who must in turn deal with the control that Matthew wields in his Left Bank apartment. While Barnes presents the productive relationships that can occur between readers and texts, authors and audiences, and speakers and listeners, power is not necessarily decentred or diluted; rather, it is exerted by all parties. Interpretative certainty is foiled in this dynamic, not by an absence of authority but by the presence of multiple positions from which different forms of control can be exercised and resisted.

In reading Barnes in relation to the various social networks that she presents instead of according to a stable structure of dominance and opposition, I take a slightly different tack from other trends in Barnes criticism. In part, this is a response to some feminist reconsiderations of modernism, in which Barnes and other women writers of the era, such as Virginia Woolf, are seen to participate in a reaction against 'the men of 1914'—T. S. Eliot, Ezra Pound, Wyndham Lewis, and James Joyce—and the 'confining paternal, avuncular, and male modernist relationships and literary patterns' connected with those men (B. Scott 1995, 1:xxxvii). For instance, Mary Lynn Broe critiques Eliot's editing or 'text-bashing' of Barnes's play *The Antiphon,* and reads his influence as a 'suppression' of Barnes's feminist modernist project (1990, 22). Shari Benstock suggests that Barnes's invocation of 'disjointed, grotesque, and abstract' female figures in her early poetry is 'part of a developing critique of women's place in modern society' that shows the negative effects of the patriarchal culture on the female body and mind (1986, 241). Along similar lines, Sandra Gilbert and Susan Gubar assert that Barnes counters the norms of her society by 'compos[ing] in an English that predates the emergence of women writers, as if to reclaim lost dictions for her sex' (1987, 246). Jane Marcus also examines Barnes's response to patriarchal authority and emphasizes the liberatory potential of the transgressions against the Law of the Father that are depicted in *Nightwood.* In 'Laughing at Leviticus: *Nightwood* as Woman's Circus Epic'—one of the more influential works contained in Broe's 1991 collection of essays on Barnes, *Silence and Power*—Marcus argues that Barnes's novel includes 'a brilliant and hilarious feminist critique of Freudian psychoanalysis,' which undermines the foundations of the medical and political discourses that marginalize the characters of the novel (1991, 221). She reads *Nightwood* as an indictment of the dominant forces in society that have 'defined deviance and set up a world view of us and them, the normal and abnormal' (249). Barnes draws upon the carnivalesque traditions of Rabelais and the circus in this view to rebel against the divisive prohibitions of Leviticus and Hitler, as the 'grotesqueries'

or the bodies that Barnes presents indicate the author's celebration of difference and her rejection of hierarchical purity (222).

Such approaches have led to an invaluable re-evaluation of the political nature of Barnes's work, which, as Marcus points out, had been dismissed to a large extent by previous critics (1991, 229). At the same time, this strand of critical inquiry regarding the 'outsiders' of the patriarchal order has had the paradoxical effect of privileging the mainstream and downplaying the complicated politics of the margins, or of those communities associated with the carnival, the circus, and the Parisian Left Bank (221). Power can be exerted in a range of contexts and according to a number of ideologies, and while Marcus and other critics emphasize the liberatory potential of violating traditional social laws, Barnes depicts also the negative aspects of boundary crossings. In texts such as *Ryder, Nightwood,* and *The Antiphon,* where authority is invoked in unpredictable and often disturbing ways, systems predicated on the rejection of mainstream values are often abusive themselves. What Barnes indicates in these texts is the fluidity of power and its presence in a range of different communities.

The pluralistic nature of Barnes's work, which features multiple interactions rather than binary oppositions, is reflected in the formal aspects of her writing. Her irony, wordplay, and literary allusions produce many possible interpretations through which she troubles notions of textual authority and prompts the reader to participate in the creation of meaning. Her references to the Bible, to Chaucer's poetry, to Elizabethan literature, and to the texts of her contemporaries are fascinating examples of her engagement with sources and traditions. In her references to fairy tales, the same kinds of combinations take place, often in the same allusion, as different versions and interpretations of the stories overlap and, at times, come into conflict. Her descriptions of characters involve the same sense of combination and contradiction where, like the 'prince-princess in point lace' (D. Barnes 1937, 136), clothes, bodies, and sexualities are layered to produce an amalgam that is more than the sum of its parts. The over-determination of the body echoes the overdetermination of the text and the fairy-tale intertext, as the characters' incongruous uses of fashion and Barnes's multilevel use of language hint at a range of potential identities and meanings.[1]

For example, Matthew O'Connor's cross-dressing aligns him with the Wolf from 'Little Red Riding Hood,' who disguises himself as the Grandmother. The Wolf's position in the fairy tale, like Matthew's place in the novel, indicates the enabling aspects of drag, where both figures use clothing in a socially prohibited way for their own pleasure. Dame Musset in *Ladies Almanack,* Barnes's roman-à-clef based upon Natalie Barney's 1920s lesbian salon, is a similar figure. Like Matthew and the

Wolf, her body is ostensibly at odds with the clothes she wears, but in the context of the Parisian Lesbos that is the setting of the text, she represents the promise of sexual and social freedom. Indeed, Dame Musset is presented as a kind of Fairy Godmother, who turns the speaker into a successful Cinderella. But her role in the piece, like Natalie Barney's role in Barnes's life, points to other restrictions, especially financial, which complicate the sense of liberation depicted in *Ladies Almanack*. While the different meanings that are combined in her name and her appearance undermine the fiction of a singular identity, they also signal a nexus of authority that has very real effects on the speaker and the author of the text.

The communities that Barnes explores often exist at the margins of 'normal' society, and while they represent spaces that are liberating in many ways, they too involve some significant costs to the individual. Nora's epiphany regarding 'Red Riding Hood and the wolf in bed,' for instance, speaks to the desire but also the anxiety that the child experiences in his or her confrontation with the composite, gender-bending figure of the Wolf-as-Grandmother (D. Barnes 1937, 79). Nora's dreams connect this highly sexual image from 'Little Red Riding Hood' to other fairy-tale scenarios in Barnes's works that feature an older, wolfish female figure. The Grandmother's cross-dressed body is both fascinating and frightening for the granddaughters whom she haunts in Barnes's fiction. Like Dame Musset, the Grandmother comes to represent a web of control—sexual, professional, literary, and familial—and one that is very much involved with Djuna Barnes's own grandmother, Zadel Barnes Budington Gustafson. Given Barnes's probable experiences with incest or sexual abuse within her unconventional family unit, this association is deeply disturbing. If there is a freedom that comes from breaking the laws of a patriarchal society, the family politics that are presented in *Ryder* and in Barnes's play *The Antiphon* suggest that there are abuses that can arise as a result.

Barnes explores the limitations and possibilities not just of social transgression, however, but of narrative control. If, as Judith Butler suggests, an incongruous citation of a sexed position is 'at once an interpretation of the norm and an occasion to expose the norm itself as a privileged interpretation' (1993, 108), allusions to fairy tales expose the provisionality of the writer's authority. This is enabling for Barnes, who is able to react against previous encodings of fairy tales or other intertexts and use them to respond to her past and present situations. But her temporary authority is also double-edged, since any reformulation can also be critiqued. The figure of the Grandmother has added significance for this reason. Zadel Barnes's story of 1875, 'The Children's Night,' features a range of fairy tales, and in her own uses of the texts, Barnes confronts not just the familial but the narrative control that the older storyteller wields. Barnes echoes Woolf's approach here by combining variants and by using the tales and their dramatis personae in different ways throughout her texts, thus asserting the place and potential power of the reader and the child. Zadel Barnes, the Mother Goose figure, is transformed into a character in Barnes's novels, and where the Grandmother is a loving maternal figure, she is also depicted as the Evil Stepmother or the disguised Wolf. Even so, she remains a traumatic as well as a chaotic figure who continues to haunt Barnes's protagonists. The issue that Barnes raises in her references to fairy tales, then, is not just what they mean, but whether authorial control is possible, desirable, and feasible in relation to the history of the tales and the settings in which they are and have been used.

Note

1. As David Copeland suggests, in *Nightwood* 'images are reappropriated from [. . .] fairy-tales and redeployed as intimations, rather than revelations' (1997, 2).

References

Barnes, Djuna. (A Lady of Fashion, pseud.) 1928. *Ladies Almanack*. Normal, IL: Dalkey, 1992.

———1937. *Nightwood*. New York: New Directions, 1961.

———1962. *The Antiphon*. In *The Selected Works of Djuna Barnes: Spillway / The Antiphon / Nightwood*, 77-224. London: Faber, 1998.

———1995. *Ryder*. Normal, IL: Dalkey. (Orig. pub. 1928; rev. 1990.)

Barnes, Zadel. 1875. 'The Children's Night.' *Harper's New Monthly Magazine* 50 (296): 153-64.

Benstock, Shari. 1986. *Women of the Left Bank: Paris, 1900-1940*. Austin: University of Texas Press, 1988.

Broe, Mary Lynn. 1990. 'Djuna Barnes (1892-1982).' In *The Gender of Modernism: A Critical Anthology*, ed. Bonnie Kime Scott, 19-29. Bloomington: Indiana University Press.

———ed. 1991. *Silence and Power: A Reevaluation of Djuna Barnes*. Carbondale: Southern Illinois University Press.

Butler, Judith. 1993. *Bodies That Matter: On the Discursive Limits of 'Sex.'* New York: Routledge.

Copeland, David. 1997. 'A Fairy-Tale Undressed?: Little Red, Children, and Narrative Revelation in *Nightwood*.' Paper presented at the annual meeting of the Modern Languages Association, Toronto.

Gilbert, Sandra M., and Susan Gubar. 1987. *The War of the Words*. Vol. 1 of *No Man's Land: The Place of the Woman Writer in the Twentieth Century*. New Haven, CT: Yale University Press.

Gilmore, Leigh. 1994. 'Obscenity, Modernity, Identity: Legalizing *The Well of Loneliness* and *Nightwood*.' *Journal of the History of Sexuality* 4 (4): 603-24.

Lee, Judith. 1991. '*Nightwood*: 'The Sweetest Lie.'' In Broe 1991, 207-18.

Marcus, Jane. 1991. 'Laughing at Leviticus: *Nightwood* as Woman's Circus Epic.' In Broe 1991, 221-50.

Scott, Bonnie Kime. 1995. *Refiguring Modernism.* 2 vols. Bloomington: Indiana University Press.

Woolf, Virginia. 1928b. *Orlando.* Ed. J. H. Stape. London: Blackwell, 1998.

FURTHER READING

Bibliographies

Messerli, Douglas. *Djuna Barnes: A Bibliography,* New York: David Lewis, 1976, 131 p.
> Book-length bibliography of works written by Barnes as well as books, periodical essays, reviews, dissertations, and non-English studies about the author and her literature.

Stevens, Jamie. "Djuna Barnes: An Updated Bibliography." *Review of Contemporary Fiction* 13, no. 3 (fall 1993): 201-04.
> Bibliography of works by and about Barnes that supplements the book-length bibliography by Douglas Messerli.

Biographies

Field, Andrew. *Djuna: The Formidable Miss Barnes,* Austin: University of Texas Press, 1985, 287 p.
> Book-length biography of Barnes that is frequently cited by later critics.

Herring, Phillip. *Djuna: The Life and Work of Djuna Barnes,* New York: Viking, 1995, 386 p.
> Biography of Barnes that attempts to provide more detail about the woman and the writer than what is presented in previous works.

Criticism

Allen, Carolyn. "The Erotics of Nora's Narrative in Djuna Barnes's *Nightwood*." *Signs* 19, no. 1 (autumn 1993): 177-200.
> Suggests how Nora's experiences in *Nightwood* "may be read as a narrative of lesbian erotics," then attempts to show "how such an erotics critiques Freud's influential writings on narcissism and desire."

Alphen, Ernst van. "Affective Reading: Loss of Self in Djuna Barnes's 'Nightwood.'" In *The Practice of Cultural Analysis: Exposing Interdisciplinary Interpretation,* edited by Mieke Bal and Bryan Gonzales, pp. 151-70. Stanford, Calif.: Stanford University Press, 1999.
> Explicates the theme of "the loss of self" in *Nightwood* while underscoring that the affect of the novel on the reader is also a loss of self.

Benstock, Shari. "Djuna Barnes: Rue St.-Romain." In *Women of the Left Bank: Paris, 1900-1940,* pp. 230-67. Austin: University of Texas Press, 1986.
> Surveys Barnes's career as a writer and expatriate in Paris, attempting to separate her works, both in terms of content and style, from the dominant modernist and patriarchal criticism that has distorted their meanings and minimized their contributions to feminist literature.

Berni, Christine. "'A Nose-Length into the Matter': Sexology and Lesbian Desire in Djuna Barnes's *Ladies Almanack*." *Frontiers* 20, no. 3 (1999): 83-107.
> Traces Barnes's "interpretation of sexual desire" in *Ladies Almanack,* maintaining that "the lesbian bodies that populate" the novel "resist sexological and socially hegemonic" classifications of lesbianism as "an inversion" and "as regression to infantile relations."

Biers, Katherine. "Djuna Barnes Makes a Specialty of Crime: Violence and the Visual in Her Early Journalism." In *Women's Experience of Modernity, 1875-1945,* edited by Ann L. Ardis and Leslie W. Lewis, pp. 237-53. Baltimore: Johns Hopkins University Press, 2003.
> Relates Barnes's early newspaper writing to the advent of sensational journalism at the beginning of the twentieth century, which was made possible by new technologies in the production of newspapers.

Bloomberg, Kristin and M. Mapel. "Hekate's Queendom of the Damned: Djuna Barnes's *Nightwood*." In *Tracing Arachne's Web: Myth and Feminist Fiction,* pp. 87-105. Gainesville: University Press of Florida, 2001.
> Studies "the interpretive thread of occult witchcraft" in *Nightwood,* proposing that by viewing the novel and its central character, Robin Vote, through the mythic figure of Hekate, "it is possible to unravel additional complexities from the threads of this perplexing text."

Bockting, Margaret. "The Great War and Modern Gender Consciousness: The Subversive Tactics of Djuna Barnes." *Mosaic* 30, no. 3 (September 1997): 21-38.
> Investigates the ways in which Barnes's work exposes the brutalization and suffering caused by World War I and thereby questions conventional ideas about masculine heroism and feminine tenderness.

Bombaci, Nancy. "'Well of Course, I *Used* to Be Absolutely Gorgeous *Dear*': The Female Interviewer as Subject/Object in Djuna Barnes's Journalism." *Criticism* 44, no. 2 (spring 2002): 161-85.

Maintains that in her early journalistic work Barnes occupied the paradoxical position of the "female fetishist," attempting "to experience the roles of both the feminized spectacle" and "the masculinized gaze that tries to control it."

Burke, Kenneth. "Version, Con-, Per-, and In- (Thoughts on Djuna Barnes's Novel, *Nightwood*)." *Southern Review* n.s. 2, no. 2 (April 1966): 329-46.

Studies what Burke calls the "terministic tactics" Barnes employs in *Nightwood* and contends that the novel finds its "stylistic fulfillment in the accents of lamentation," the subject of which is "the sorrows of unrequited love."

Carlston, Erin G. "'The Learned Corruption of Language': *Nightwood*'s Failed Flirtation with Fascism." In *Thinking Fascism: Sapphic Modernism and Fascist Modernity,* pp. 42-85. Stanford, Calif.: Stanford University Press, 1998.

Offers a detailed examination of the influence of nineteenth-century decadence on Barnes's style as a writer. Carlston then equates figures of aestheticism and decadence in *Nightwood,* such as lesbianism, decay, suffering, and death, with Barnes's antifascist ideology.

Caselli, Daniela. "'Tendency to Precocity' and 'Childish Uncertainties' of a 'Virago at Fourteen': Djuna Barnes's 'The Diary of a Dangerous Child.'" *Yearbook of English Studies* 32 (2002): 186-204.

Explains how the notion of the child has shaped the criticism of Barnes's short stories, enabling critics to construct a biographical basis for both the "murkiness" of Barnes's most complex stories and the simplicity of her more material works.

Eliot, T. S. Introduction to *Nightwood,* by Djuna Barnes, pp. i-viii. New York: Harcourt, Brace & Company, 1937.

Emphasizes the poetic force of Barnes's writing, saying that *Nightwood* "will appeal primarily to readers of poetry." In a frequently quoted remark, Eliot also asserts that "the book is not a psychopathic study," since the "particular abnormalities" of the characters are meant to reflect a "deeper design," namely that "human misery and bondage" are universal.

Galvin, Mary E. "'Dropping Crooked into Rhyme': Djuna Barnes' Use of Form and the Liminal Space of Gender." In *Queer Poetics: Five Modernist Women Writers,* pp. 83-103. Westport, Conn.: Praeger, 1999.

Analyzes the poems in *The Book of Repulsive Women,* proposing that the central idea of the collection is not the repulsiveness of the women it depicts but "the cultural attitudes heaped on these figures of scorn."

Gerstenberger, Donna. "Modern (Post) Modern: Djuna Barnes among the Others." *Review of Contemporary Fiction* 13, no. 3 (fall 1993): 33-40.

Argues that Barnes's writings, even her early short stories and plays, attack the underlying "assumptions of the narrative cultural exchange in which knowledge . . . is presumed to be the reasonable and predictable product of the right combinations of desire, presence, and epistemology."

Gildzen, Alex, ed. *A Festschrift for Djuna Barnes on Her 80th Birthday,* Kent, Ohio: Kent State University Libraries, 1972, 20 p.

Collection of poems, tributes, and essays devoted to Barnes and her work.

Goody, Alex. *Modernist Articulations: A Cultural Study of Djuna Barnes, Mina Loy, and Gertrude Stein,* Basingstoke, England: Palgrave Macmillan, 2007, 242 p.

Studies the work of Barnes, Mina Loy, and Gertrude Stein within the context of modernism.

Grobbel, Michaela M. "In Memory of the Lost Body: Performance of Resistance in Djuna Barnes's *Nightwood*." In *Enacting the Past and Present: The Memory Theaters of Djuna Barnes, Ingeborg Bachmann, and Marguerite Duras,* pp. 19-72. Lanham, Md.: Lexington Books, 2004.

Provides a reading of *Nightwood* that focuses on "the crucial relationship between history, representation, and memory" in the novel.

Hanrahan, Mairéad. "Djuna Barnes' *Nightwood*: Where Man Is with Wo(e)." In *Writing Differences: Readings from the Seminar of Hélèn Cixous,* edited by Susan Sellers, pp. 81-94. Milton Keynes, England: Open University Press, 1988.

Focuses on the sorrow, confusion, and misery "encountered at every level" of *Nightwood,* stating that all of the novel's characters evince "a passionate desire for an impossible 'end,'" namely death.

Henke, Suzette A. "(En)Gendering Modernism: Virginia Woolf and Djuna Barnes." In *Rereading the New: A Backward Glance at Modernism,* edited by Kevin J. H. Dettmar, pp. 325-41. Ann Arbor: University of Michigan Press, 1992.

Describes Barnes and Virginia Woolf as two writers who wrote from "marginal subject positions" within the "dominant phallocentric hegemony" of modernism yet "nevertheless succeeded in mapping revolutionary strategies for the avant-garde disruption of logocentric narrative."

Herzig, Carl. "Roots of Night: Emerging Style and Vision in the Early Journalism of Djuna Barnes." *Centennial Review* 31, no. 3 (summer 1987): 255-69.

Maintains that "Barnes's major themes, images and linguistic techniques" displayed in *Nightwood* can be discerned in her journalistic work.

Jay, Karla. "The Outsider among the Expatriates: Djuna Barnes's Satire on the Ladies of the *Almanack*." In *Lesbian Texts and Contexts: Radical Revisions*, edited by Karla Jay and Joanne Glasgow, pp. 204-16. New York: New York University Press, 1990.

Discusses Barnes's satire of a number of the wealthy patrons in Paris who supported her work, especially Natalie Clifford Barney, in *Ladies of the Almanack*.

Levine, Nancy J. "'I've Always Suffered from Sirens': The Cinema Vamp and Djuna Barnes' *Nightwood*." *Women's Studies* 16, nos. 3-4 (1989): 271-81.

Contends that Barnes used the popular image of "the cinema vamp" as her model of female power when she created the character of Robin Vote in *Nightwood*.

Loncraine, Rebecca. "*The Book of Repulsive Women*: Djuna Barnes' Unknown Poetry." *PN Review* 29, no. 6 (summer 2003): 40-5.

Critiques *The Book of Repulsive Women*, stating that the author's "unknown poetry throws new light on her development as a writer, provides a further dimension to her oeuvre, and brings to the public a distinctive voice that is witty and dark, repellent and compelling."

Martins, Susana S. "Gender Trouble and Lesbian Desire in Djuna Barnes's *Nightwood*." *Frontiers* 20, no. 3 (1999): 108-26.

Contends that in *Nightwood* Barnes seeks to upset predetermined classifications of lesbianism, especially homosexual desire "as it was defined in Freudian terms."

Martyniuk, Irene. "Troubling the 'Master's Voice': Djuna Barnes's Pictorial Strategies." *Mosaic* 31, no. 3 (September 1998): 61-81.

Argues that the interaction between the texts of *The Book of Repulsive Women* and *Ryder*, on the one hand, and the illustrations Barnes drew and included in each work, on the other, "is a central component of Barnes's radical feminism."

Rupprecht, Caroline. "Between Birth and Death: The Image of the Other in Djuna Barnes's *Nightwood*." In *Subject to Delusions: Narcissism, Modernism, Gender*, pp. 93-131. Evanston, Ill.: Northwestern University Press, 2006.

Asserts that the "discrepancy between different modes of representation" in *Nightwood*, one being "performative," the other "referential," "is due to the narcissistic structure of the novel itself."

Sánchez-Pardo, Esther. "Melancholia Reborn: Djuna Barnes's Style of Grief." In *Cultures of the Death Drive: Melanie Klein and Modernist Melancholia*, pp. 306-42. Durham, N.C.: Duke University Press, 2003.

Focusing mainly on the novel *Ryder*, assesses the melancholic nature of Barnes's work.

Scott, Bonnie Kime. "Djuna Barnes's Migratory Modernism." In *American Modernism across the Arts*, edited by Jay Bochner and Justin D. Edwards, pp. 218-33. New York: Peter Lang, 1999.

Offers a biocritical assessment of Barnes as a "migrant writer," placing her in the context of "migratory modernism" in order "to take Modernist study toward a more complex understanding of the physical and mental movements and rhythms of Barnes, and perhaps a whole set of American Modernists."

Smith, Victoria L. "A Story beside(s) Itself: The Language of Loss in Djuna Barnes's *Nightwood*." *PMLA* 114, no. 2 (March 1999): 194-206.

Focuses on the theme of "unspeakable loss" in *Nightwood*, highlighting the "textual and psychic strategies" Barnes employs in the novel "for speaking unspeakable losses and desires."

Stange, Martina. "'Melancholia, Melancholia': Changing Black Bile into Black Ink in Djuna Barnes's *Nightwood*." In *Hayford Hall: Hangovers, Erotics, and Modernist Aesthetics*, edited by Elizabeth Podnieks and Sandra Chait, pp. 133-49. Carbondale: Southern Illinois University Press, 2005.

Emphasizes the concept of melancholy in *Nightwood*, arguing that the novel conveys "a marked tension" between "the will towards expression and the pained realization of the inadequacy of words to make that expression," as well as Barnes's recognition "that language is an insufficient medium for portraying the truth, an insight that is profoundly melancholic."

Trubowitz, Lara. "In Search of 'the Jew' in Djuna Barnes's *Nightwood*: Jewishness, Antisemitism, Structure, and Style." *Modern Fiction Studies* 51, no. 2 (summer 2005): 311-34.

Postulates that the character of Felix Volkbein is an essential figure in *Nightwood*, maintaining that the novel's "shape and style are both intricately linked to Felix or, more precisely, linked to the Jew that Felix, and his father Guido, represent."

Veltman, Laura J. "'The Bible Lies the One Way, but the Night-Gown the Other': Dr. Matthew O'Connor, Confession, and Gender in Djuna Barnes's *Nightwood*." *Modern Fiction Studies* 49, no. 2 (summer 2003): 204-27.

Contends that Barnes's placement of the character of Dr. Matthew O'Connor in *Nightwood* within the Roman Catholic church, as well as her "invocation of the confessional," not only "complicate patriar- chal notions of sex and gender" in the novel, but also question "the ability of language (the word) and religion (the Word) to make either known—or, indeed, to make meaning at all."

Additional coverage of Barnes's life and career is contained in the following sources published by Gale: *American Writers Supplement*, Vol. 3; *Contemporary American Dramatists*; *Contemporary Authors*, Vols. 9-12R, 107; *Contemporary Authors New Revision Series*, Vols. 16, 55; *Contemporary Literary Criticism*, Vols. 3, 4, 8, 11, 29, 127; *Contemporary Novelists*, Eds. 1, 2, 3; *Contemporary Women Dramatists*; *Dictionary of Literary Biography*, Vols. 4, 9, 45; *Encyclopedia of World Literature in the 20th Century*, Ed. 3; *Gay & Lesbian Literature*, Ed. 1; *Literature Resource Center*; *Major 20th-Century Writers*, Eds. 1, 2; *Major 21st-Century Writers*; *Modern American Literature*, Ed. 5; *Reference Guide to American Literature*, Ed. 4; *Short Story Criticism*, Vol. 3; *Twayne Companion to Contemporary Literature in English*, Ed. 1; and *Twayne's United States Authors*.

Là-bas

Joris-Karl Huysmans

The following entry presents criticism of Huysmans' novel *Là-bas* (1891; *Down There*). For discussion of Huysmans' complete career, see *TCLC,* Volumes 7 and 69.

INTRODUCTION

Là-bas is a leading example of Decadent and *fin de siècle* fiction, as well as an important milestone in the development of French literature. The novel addresses a variety of themes, including mysticism, redemption, literary production, and moral decay, but it is best known for its examination of Satanism and the occult practices of both fifteenth- and nineteenth-century France. *Là-bas* is considered a transitional book within Huysmans' body of work, marking the end of his Decadent literary period and his rejection of naturalism for a more spiritually inspired style, which he called "spiritualistic naturalism." Although *Là-bas* has inspired mixed reactions from readers and critics in the years since it first appeared, it is generally regarded as one of Huysmans' most important books, which prepared the way for his major novels on Catholicism, such as *En route* (1895) and *La cathédrale* (1898; *The Cathedral*), and which stylistically anticipated a number of tenets of modern and postmodern fiction. Brendan King has asserted that "if *Là-Bas* is firmly rooted in its time, it is also a remarkably contemporary novel: its concerns are still our concerns." King concludes that *Là-bas* "reminds us that we have always been capable of gross acts of violence that challenge our notion of what it means to be human, and that one of the functions of art in a civilised society is to find new metaphors to help us assimilate those aspects of humanity we find most problematic. *Là-Bas* is a book to make us look again at what we are and what we believe, and to decide whether we are on the road to heaven, *là-haut,* or on the road to hell, *là-bas.*"

PLOT AND MAJOR CHARACTERS

Là-bas is an episodic, descriptive novel, set in Paris in 1888 and 1889, which centers on the protagonist Durtal, a novelist-historian who is writing a fictional biography of the fifteenth-century murderer and Satanist Gilles de Rais (also referred to as "de Retz"). The novel begins with a philosophical discussion, in which Durtal, generally regarded as Huysmans' alter ego, declares that naturalism, focused on the outer world of the physical, is inadequate to convey the full scope of human experience, particularly in matters of the mind and soul. Frustration with this inadequacy, as well as his disgust with the state of contemporary society, together prompt Durtal to conduct his study of de Rais and the occult.

Gilles de Rais's exploits are presented in explicit detail in several chapters, which are interspersed throughout the book. Gilles de Rais, a model for the figure of Bluebeard, served in the French military and rode with Joan of Arc against the English at Rouen. After retiring to his castle at Tiffauges he lived extravagantly, squandering his fortune and embracing necromancy in an effort to recoup his financial losses. Gilles de Rais studied alchemy, but his studies required ritual sacrifices, and he later admitted to kidnapping, torturing, and murdering hundreds of children, most of whom were young boys. In 1440, after evidence of his crimes was uncovered, Gilles de Rais was convicted of murder, rape, sodomy, and heresy and was excommunicated from the Catholic Church. He was sentenced to execution, and though he repented his crimes in Confession, he was hanged in October of 1440. At one point in the narrative, Durtal visits the castle at Tiffauges to supplement his research.

While conducting research into occult practices of the fifteenth century Durtal also investigates the practice of black arts in his own time. He becomes involved with Hyacinthe Chantelouve, a lady of society and a practicing Satanist, who declares that she is visited nightly by incubi. Chantelouve introduces Durtal to Canon Docre, a defrocked priest who now practices satanic rituals and celebrates the Black Mass. At the climax of the novel Chantelouve arranges for Durtal to attend a Black Mass led by Docre, which Huysmans documents in graphic detail. The event features sexual rituals and culminates in the desecration of the Host, or sacramental bread, through the use of various bodily fluids. Ultimately it is this desecration that drives Durtal to flee from the Black Mass. He is followed, and eventually seduced, by Chantelouve. After they have sexual intercourse, Durtal is repulsed when he notices the desecrated Host sprinkled in the bed. He finally abandons Chantelouve.

Other important characters in the novel are a doctor named des Hermies, who distrusts modern medicine and promotes the use of herbs and folk remedies, and Louis Carhaix, a poor bell-ringer who lives in the tower of Saint-Sulpice. Durtal also learns about occult lore from Gévingey, an astrologer, and Dr. Johannès, a defrocked priest who formerly practiced Satanism. When Docre curses Gévingey, it is the efforts of Dr. Johannès that preserve Gévingey's salvation. At the close of the novel Durtal, des Hermies, and Carhaix gather in the tower of Saint-Sulpice to discuss the dismal state of their society. In the background, they hear crowds cheering for General Boulanger, who has just been elected a deputy in Paris.

MAJOR THEMES

For some scholars, literary production, or the writing process itself, is a significant theme in *Là-bas*. Richard Bales has declared that "*Là-bas* is a book about a person writing a book. And as we see Durtal struggling with the problems of creating his book, so we simultaneously witness the various methods which Huysmans employs in creating *his*. Put another way, *Là-bas* is at the same time a story of textual production and textual production itself." Bales also has noted that the novel is "rich in linguistic features which call attention to themselves, and thus keep the reader constantly aware of the ongoing process of literary construction."

Huysmans, whose subject matter often closely resembled his personal life, frequently blurred the lines between fiction and nonfiction, between narrative and autobiography, and most scholars generally agree that Durtal's experiences closely mirror those of Huysmans himself in writing his novel. As a result, *Là-bas,* as some commentators have suggested, is highly self-referential, and in this respect it anticipates the self-reflexive, metafictional forms found in modernist and postmodernist literature.

Huysmans' focus on literary production also raises questions about the role of art and its effect on audiences, as well as the artist. Some scholars have suggested that Durtal, and consequently Huysmans, develops spiritually through the writing process. According to others, Durtal employs literary production as a means of escape from reality. Emphasizing this latter point, Ruth B. Antosh has asserted that Durtal "displays a desire to escape reality and transcend time," and he "succeeds in prolonging reveries and atavistic memories by writing them down and transforming them into a permanent document, into a work of art. The process of artistic creation enables Durtal to *become* the character he is describing." Antosh argues that while Durtal "finds a temporary release from himself through the process of artistic creation, he is forced to recognize that art is at best an imperfect refuge."

The conflict of opposing spiritual forces, Christian mysticism and Satanism, is another important theme in *Là-bas*. Huysmans exposes satanic practices of both fifteenth-century and nineteenth-century France, through the characterization of Gilles de Rais, Canon Docre, and Mme. Chantelouve, while the bell-ringer Carhaix, a devout Catholic, represents Christian mysticism. Primarily, however, Huysmans examines these opposing spiritual forces by charting the internal struggles of the major characters.

Gilles de Rais, a once-pious member of society and companion of Joan of Arc, is the most extreme example of this struggle. After committing the most heinous of crimes, he confesses, repents, and returns to the Catholic faith, presumably receiving forgiveness in the process. Similarly, Canon Docre undergoes an extreme conversion. Serving once as a priest, he abandons the Catholic faith and embraces Satanism. Many of the satanic rituals in which Docre participates involve a defilement or desecration of sacraments and Christian symbols. The Black Mass, designed as an inversion of the Catholic Mass, specifically involves the violation of the sacramental Host. Docre is so devoted to his Satanist tenets that he tattoos a cross on the sole of each foot.

According to some critics, the primary battleground of the opposing forces of Christian mysticism and Satanism is within the protagonist, Durtal, who embarks on a spiritual quest as he researches and writes his book. At the beginning of the novel Durtal searches for an approach to life that accounts for matters of the human soul. While immersed in his studies of Gilles de Rais, he is briefly drawn to Chantelouve but is eventually repulsed by her practices. Although he cannot devote himself to the ritual of the black arts, the supernatural aspect of Satanism, nevertheless, becomes a reality for him. After abandoning Chantelouve and rejecting Satanism, Durtal closes the novel in Carhaix's tower, poised to embrace Christian mysticism as his spiritual faith, reflecting Huysmans' own conversion to the Catholic Church. In this respect, as Brendan King has noted, *Là-bas* was instrumental in Huysmans' conversion to Christianity, "for having become convinced of the reality of the supernatural through his dealings with the occult, it was only logical that Huysmans should accept the reality of the supernatural in the shape of a Christian God."

Another important theme in *Là-bas* is "spiritual naturalism," an aesthetic approach developed by Huysmans as he wrote his novel. In a letter to art critic Jules Destrée, Huysmans described spiritual naturalism, or what he also referred to as "supranaturalism," as realism combined with "flights of the soul." Prior to the publication of *Là-bas*, Huysmans had produced several works that reflected naturalistic tenets, as espoused by French writer Emile Zola. Eventually he was accepted into Zola's inner circle of naturalist writers. At the beginning of *Là-bas,* however, Huysmans refutes naturalism as a literary philosophy. In the debate between Durtal and des Hermies, the two characters outline the insufficiencies of the naturalist approach, concluding that it is reductionist and fails to account for the spiritual aspect of human life.

To overcome these inadequacies, Huysmans developed the idea of spiritual naturalism, which was inspired by his visit to a museum in Kassel, Germany, in 1888 and his first exposure to the *Crucifixion,* a painting by the German Renaissance artist Matthias Grünewald. While Grünewald's technique was naturalistic, realistically depicting Christ's death on the cross in graphic detail, Huysmans believed that the artist had also managed to transcend realism and convey Christ's spiritual nature through the very brutality of his suffering, without the use of halos or other religious iconography. A lengthy description of the painting, as well as Durtal's reaction to it, is included in the novel.

Durtal laments that his late nineteenth-century society seems disconnected from spiritual concerns. In contrast, however, fifteenth-century France embraces the supernatural, actively pursuing and participating in spiritual matters. In the study of alchemy, for instance, practitioners experiment with natural elements in order to reveal their latent supernatural attributes. The acceptance of transubstantiation, a Catholic doctrine stating that Communion bread and wine become the body and blood of Christ, is another example of the commingling of the natural and spiritual. According to some scholars, Huysmans' exploration of spiritual naturalism is more than a thematic preoccupation in *Là-bas*; it also reflects the author's attempt to change the direction of French literature. Robert Ziegler has declared that *Là-bas* "is a novel undertaken in the hope of burying the decomposing text of nineteenth-century realism, whose transfigured body could be resurrected in the form of 'un naturalisme spiritualiste.'"

CRITICAL RECEPTION

When the serial version of *Là-bas* first appeared in the French newspaper *Écho de Paris,* many readers were outraged and threatened to cancel their subscriptions. A few months later the novel was published in book form but was banned from sale in kiosks at railway stations. Nevertheless *Là-bas* attracted a considerable number of readers, partly because it addressed many of the concerns of late nineteenth-century French society and reflected the public's interest in mysticism and occult practices. Indeed, the novel developed a significant cult following and became Huysmans' first bestseller. Initial

critical responses, however, expressed ambivalence toward the novel's subject matter. In 1892, Arthur Symons described *Là-bas* as an "interesting," and "disquieting" experiment. While Symons praised the book's "dexterous interweaving of the history of Gilles de Retz (the traditional Bluebeard) with the contemporary manifestations of the Black Art," he argued that as a novel it was not entirely successful.

In the years following, *Là-bas* earned notoriety for its frank treatment of Satanism but received little critical attention, mainly because most commentators deemed its themes and subject matter unworthy of serious scholarship. Publishers however faced a difficult task of translating and keeping the book in print. Thirty years after its initial publication an American publisher attempted to produce an English translation. Although the most shocking passages were excised from the edition, the publishing firm was forced to withdraw the novel, after the Society for the Suppression of Vice complained that it was an affront to public morality. Readers nevertheless were able to obtain pirated copies of the book, as well as special limited editions catering to collectors.

It wasn't until the second half of the twentieth century that critics rediscovered *Là-bas,* many of whom confirmed its importance, not only to French literature, but to modern fiction generally. According to George Ross Ridge, writing in 1968, "*Là-bas* is not the very summation of Decadence," or "a great *tour de force*." but is, nonetheless, "a powerful and important novel." Ridge concluded that "its characterization of individuals, rather than types, is memorable. Its prose scintillates. The plot structure carries the reader on. Its subject matter of diabolism, or mysticism, versus the mundane reality of the nineteenth century is worthy of interest."

In more recent scholarship critics have studied the formal innovations of *Là-bas* and emphasized themes other than Satanism and occultism in the novel. Alain Toumayan has called *Là-bas* "a very complex novel," which "chronicles several major investigations, the principal contexts of which are epistemological, aesthetic, and metaphysical." Frustrated by the narrow focus of much of the criticism of the work, Robert Ziegler has argued that "Huysmans addresses a range of esoteric subjects: spiritualism, devil worship, campanology, homeopathic medicine, astrology. Yet because of the focus on Durtal's research into the history of Gilles de Rais and turn-of-the-century satanic ritual, the preponderance of critical attention has been directed to Huysmans' study of supernatural evil." Other scholars have noted the significance of *Là-bas* within the context of Huysmans' oeuvre. Richard Bales has declared that "*Là-bas* is an exceptionally 'readable' text ('lisible' in Barthes' sense), of a high degree of narrative sophistication. In my view, it is [Huysmans'] masterpiece."

As *Là-bas* has benefited from increasing critical study, scholars have begun to acknowledge its importance to the evolution of the novel-form in the twentieth century. Brendan King has remarked that "the journey taken by Durtal in *Là-Bas* constitutes a different order of experience, one that privileges subjectivity over the objectivity of science. Durtal's obsession with his own state of mind—and with the state of his soul—anticipates Modernism's fascination with the ego and with the unconscious." *Là-bas* has also attracted new readers with the recent publication of a reliable English translation, and as a result has garnered renewed critical interest. Rather than recoil over its subject matter, commentators today praise the book as an imaginative and original work, one in which Huysmans blurs the distinctions between subject and text and, in his concern with authorship and art, anticipates some of the cardinal issues of postmodern literature. As Ziegler has declared, "*Là-bas* remains arguably the author's greatest masterpiece, a pivotal work in which a new course for the novel is charted."

PRINCIPAL WORKS

Le drageoir à épices [*A Dish of Spices*] (prose poetry) 1874

Marthe, histoire d'une fille [*Marthe*] (novel) 1876

Sac au dos ["Sac au dos"] (short story) 1878

Les soeurs Vatard [*The Vatard Sisters*] (novel) 1879

Croquis Parisiens [*Parisian Sketches*] (prose poetry) 1880

En ménage [*Living Together*] (novel) 1881

A vau-l'eau [*Down Stream*] (novel) 1882

L'art moderne (criticism) 1883

A rebours [*Against the Grain*] (novel) 1884

Un dilemme (novella) 1887

En rade [*Becalmed*] (novel) 1887

Certains (criticism) 1889

Là-bas [*Down There*] (novel) 1891

En route [*En Route*] (novel) 1895

La cathédrale [*The Cathedral*] (novel) 1898

Sainte Lydwine de Schiedam [*St. Lydwine of Schiedam*] (biography) 1901

De tout (essays) 1902

L'oblat [*The Oblate*] (novel) 1903

Trois primitifs (criticism) 1905

Les foules de Lourdes [*Crowds of Lourdes*] (nonfiction) 1906

Down Stream (A vau-l'eau), and Other Works (prose poems, novels, and criticism) 1927

Œuvres complètes de J.-K. Huysmans. 23 vols. (novels, short stories, poetry, essays, and criticism) 1928-34

The Road from Decadence, from Brothel to Cloister: Selected Letters of J.-K. Huysmans (letters) 1989

CRITICISM

Arthur Symons (essay date 1892)

SOURCE: Symons, Arthur. "Joris-Karl Huysmans." In *The Symbolist Movement in Literature*, pp. 230-61. New York: E. P. Dutton & Company, 1919.

[*In the following excerpt, taken from a study of Huysmans originally published in 1892, Symons briefly critiques the novels* En rade *and* Là-bas, *praising the latter work as "a study of Satanism, a dexterous interweaving of the history of Gilles de Retz . . . with the contemporary manifestations of the Black Art."*]

A Rebours is a book that can only be written once, and since that date Huysmans has published a short story, *Un Dilemme* (1887), which is merely a somewhat lengthy anecdote; two novels, *En Rade* (1887) and *Là-Bas* (1891), both of which are interesting experiments, but neither of them an entire success; and a volume of art criticism, *Certains* (1890), notable for a single splendid essay, that on Félicien Rops, the etcher of the fantastically erotic. *En Rade* is a sort of deliberately exaggerated record—vision of the disillusions of a country sojourn, as they affect the disordered nerves of a town *névrose*. The narrative is punctuated by nightmares, marvellously woven out of nothing, and with no psychological value—the human part of the book being a sort of picturesque pathology at best, the representation of a series of states of nerves, sharpened by the tragic ennui of the country. There is a cat which becomes interesting in its agonies; but the long boredom of the man and woman is only too faithfully shared with the reader. *Là-Bas* is a more artistic creation, on a more solid foundation. It is a study of Satanism, a dexterous interweaving of the history of Gilles de Retz (the traditional Bluebeard) with the contemporary manifestations of the Black Art. "The execration of impotence, the hate of the mediocre—that is perhaps one of the most indulgent definitions of Diabolism," says Huysmans, somewhere in the book, and it is on this side that one finds the link of connection with the others of that series of pessimist studies in life. *Un naturalisme spiritualiste,* he defines his own art at this point in its development; and it is in somewhat the "documentary" manner that he applies himself to the study of these strange problems, half of hysteria, half of a real mystical corruption that does actually exist in our midst. I do not know whether the monstrous tableau of the Black Mass—so marvellously, so revoltingly described in the central episode of the book—is still enacted in our days, but I do know that all but the most horrible practices of the sacrilegious magic of the Middle Ages are yet performed, from time to time, in a secrecy which is all but absolute. The character of Madame Chantelouve is an attempt, probably the first in literature, to diagnose a case of Sadism in a woman. To say that it is successful would be to assume that the thing is possible, which one hesitates to do. The book is even more disquieting, to the normal mind, than *A Rebours*. But it is not, like that, the study of an exception which has become a type. It is the study of an exception which does not profess to be anything but a disease.

John D. Erickson (essay date February 1970)

SOURCE: Erickson, John D. "Huysmans' *Là-Bas*: A Metaphor of Search." *French Review* 43, no. 3 (February 1970): 418-25.

[*In the following essay, Erickson argues that the central idea in* Là-bas *is "an unresolved search," depicted primarily through the protagonist, Durtal, and his quest to find "the spiritual ideal" that exists within "the base materialism of his fellow men."*]

Subsequent to the appearance of the extravagant *A Rebours* in 1884, Barbey d'Aurevilly gave, in the *Roman contemporain,* his sensational opinion that, "Après un tel livre, il ne reste plus à l'auteur à choisir qu'entre la bouche d'un pistolet et les pieds de la Croix." Huysmans made his choice—of both the mouth of a pistol and the foot of the cross. In a paradoxical fashion reminiful of Baudelaire, Huysmans in his works to come sought the Divine presence through the pistol barrel, through the Infernal presence. After the appearance of *En Rade* in 1887 and after his encounter with the Abbé Mugnier, Huysmans said to the Abbé, "Je vais . . . publier un livre satanique, plein de messes noires. Je veux en faire un autre qui sera *blanc*. Mais il est nécessaire que je me blanchisse moi-même. Avez-vous du chlore pour mon âme?" And he murmured to the Abbé: "J'ai des atavismes religieux."[1] *Là-bas,* Huysmans' "satanic book," appeared in 1891.

The title of *Là-bas* indicates the dominant tendency of its subject matter. The narrator says at one point: ". . . si l'au-delà du Bien, si le là-bas de l'Amour est accessible à certaines âmes, l'au-delà du Mal ne s'atteint pas."[2] The "là-bas de l'Amour" would presumably be the subject of the "white book" which Huysmans proposed to the Abbé Mugnier, the realm of the ideal "accessible to certain souls"—in contrast to the "au-delà du Mal" which is unattainable, which leaves the seeker of evil, as he goes on to say, gasping and insatiable before the void. It is the pistol's mouth, but also a difficult and unfamiliar path that paradoxically leads through the Infernal to the Divine. This path, or at least the part of it that leads to the Infernal, is the subject of Huysmans' novel.

The book is about search, and no other character in it quests in greater frenzy than the hero, Durtal. Huysmans uses a particular image to convey the sense of his character torn by the conflict between bodily and spiritual needs. Durtal is suspended between the pure mechanism of sensation and the pure void of spirit. He is described as not being able to "décider son âme à faire le saut, alors qu'elle se trouvait, au bord de la raison, dans le vide" (I, 25). And in the bell tower with the bellkeep, Carhaix, "il se sentait mal à l'aise dans ce vide, attiré par ce trou béant d'où s'échappait, en de lointaines bouffées, le tintement moribond de la cloche qui oscillait sans doute encore, avant que de rentrer immobile, dans un complet repos" (I, 52). The bell which swings between furious activity and complete repose represents the state of Durtal. The void is that of pure spirit.

Durtal suffers from this limbo he inhabits, from this state in which he rejects the base materialism of his fellow men, but has not yet succeeded in replacing it with the spiritual ideal he longs for. He suffers from a vertigo of the soul. His condition does not appear to offer improvement, and in this sense the novel consists in an enduring crisis that refuses to unravel—the Chantelouve episode is over, the life of Gilles de Rais is past history, but the story of Durtal bids fair to continue forever. Durtal appears immobilized at the end of the novel, despite his furious activity, despite his desperate quest for a solution to the enigma contained in the character of the person whose history he has undertaken to write, Gilles de Rais, and in the character of the woman he has undertaken to know, Mme Chantelouve. Durtal's life, such as we see it here, resembles an unresolved search. Indeed, it *is* an unresolved search.

A complex metaphor underlies Durtal's search in *Làbas,* and provides the novel with the basis for its elaborate development. The life of Durtal on a metaphoric level is nothing other than the search of the medieval alchemist for the elusive philosopher's stone. The love Mme Chantelouve inspires in him, like the fascination which he feels for Gilles de Rais, evolves on an analogy with the obsession of the alchemist for his Stone. The alchemist of former times sought restlessly to decipher the enigma of the ancients, lost to them for several centuries. Durtal faces enigmas just as obdurate—the first of these lies in the character of Gilles de Rais (or Retz) who became a Marshal of France at the age of twenty-five, who was a retainer of Charles VII, who served as the guarantor of Jeanne d'Arc and rode with her entourage against the English at Rouen. After Gilles de Rais' service with the king, he retired to his domains, where, following a period of incredible extravagance, he tried to recoup his fortunes by the practice of necromancy and black magic. Durtal is fascinated by the bizarre mixture of goodness represented in his character and in his relations with the Maid of Orléans and the proclivity to evil found in his alleged torture and murder of several hundred children.[3]

How is it that a personality like that of Gilles de Rais could have existed? How can a woman like Mme Chantelouve incorporate two natures (her spiritual side and her carnal side) so antithetical? Durtal relentlessly pursues a formula. The medieval alchemists entertained the notion of a Golden Age—the time of the ancients when the formula for the discovery of gold was known—and Durtal equally looks back upon an age of gold. For it is the Medieval Age that holds the secret formula sought by Durtal, the age when the gold of the spirit was known, when the formula existed to find in the dross of the body the most precious metal of all—faith, goodness. In the conversation between Durval's friend, des Hermies, and Carhaix, des Hermies suggests that Carhaix prepare "un compendieux recueil d'hagiographie." Carhaix, more than anyone, would be capable of such a work,

> parce que vous êtes, Dieu merci! si loin de votre époque, si fervent des choses qu'elle ignore ou qu'elle exècre, que cela vous exhausserait encore! Vous êtes, bon ami, l'homme à jamais inintelligible pour ces générations qui viennent. Sonner les cloches en les adorant, et se livrant aux besognes désuètes de l'art féodal ou à des labeurs monastiques de vies de Saints, ce serait complet, si bien hors de Paris, si bien dans les là-bas, si loin dans les vieux ages!
>
> (II, 227)

The "là-bas" are "les vieux âges," the Middle Ages, the time Carhaix calls "le bon temps." And we can easily discern, on a temporal level, the antipodes of the novel: the present as against the Middle Ages which, for Carhaix, as well as for des Hermies, Durtal and Gévingey, represent the Golden Age, the time when there existed a profound unity between man's soul and body, between the spiritual and carnal. That unity, which Huysmans calls "spiritual naturalism," was known to the fifteenth century, with its platonic notion of the individual as a reflection of the Divine, and of all things of this world as incarnating the idea of a divine counterpart.

The Middle Ages offer a way to the "là-bas" of love, of human compassion. We recall the primitive artists described in *Là-bas,* who depicted the Christ of the poor, the very human Christ of Saint Justin, Saint Basil, Saint Cyril, of Tertullian, the Christ beset by doubt, who suffered very real fleshly agony. These artists presented matter, the flesh, transfigured by the spirit, just as in Huysmans' life of Gilles de Rais the great and horror-inspiring criminal will become transfigured by faith, by a humility greater than his criminality, or again, just as the parents of Rais' victims are transfigured by such sublime spirit that they weep out of pity for the monster who has violated and massacred their children.

The Middle Ages for Huysmans allowed of such a conjunction of spirit and flesh. It was the time when the safe conduct of a little peasant girl who was destined to become the savioress of France might be assured by a Gilles de Rais. Such a remarkable event might appear ironic in the extreme to us, but it is a paradox understood without difficulty by a man of the Middle Ages, or by a Huysmans, for the Saint and the great criminal after the fashion of Gilles de Rais are not without relationship. The narrator tells us, "Dans l'au-delà, tout se touche" (I, 82). On one occasion, des Hermies compares the Saint and the Satanic (I, 85). In the "Age d'or" all roads lead to God, or return to the spirit. There is only the "au-delà"—which we find after an arduous passage through evil. Ultimately it is the Saint or the saintly that prevails, as we see in Gilles de Rais who is touched finally by Divine Grace, or as symbolized by the figure of the saint in the "tableaux sur bois" which hang in the quarters of Durtal, who disappears only to reappear elsewhere in the picture (I, 121). In both cases it is the saintly which dominates in the end. But the unity of the Middle Ages is reflected not only in what we today think of as religious subjects; rather, it is a unity found in the interrelation of all the sciences, religion, and mysticism (for example, the medical and divine virtues attributed to stones, see II, 214-215). In contrast, in Huysmans' time, things signify nothing but themselves. The philosopher's stone for Huysmans stands in contrast to the positivist spirit of the modern age. The secrets of the ancients are lost to us.

It is those lost secrets that Durtal seeks. His brute matter is Gilles de Rais and Mme Chantelouve. His progress, if he were able to understand and accept the unity which they exemplify, would not be the material progress of his age, but spiritual progress, the capacity to undergo a transformation of faith and to believe. But for Durtal all effort leads in the end only to failure.

Let us look more closely at the stone metaphor which underlies the structure of the novel. Gilles de Rais represents at once two different things to Durtal. First of all, he incarnates the notion of unity which Durtal seeks to elucidate. In this sense, he represents the enigma of the philosopher's stone. But, on the other hand, Gilles de Rais is the alchemist type who himself seeks the Stone and, consequently, he serves as a model for the character of Durtal. Therefore, Rais is at once the alchemist and the philosopher's stone, the model and the enigma for Durtal.

Mme Chantelouve serves a similar purpose. She also is in search of the spiritual, of the diabolic, but her character is enigmatic. Like Rais she is torn by this dual tendency to good and to evil. She possesses both the cold body of the woman who is visited by incubuses and the warm passion and mind of a very human woman. Durtal consciously ponders the resemblance between Gilles de Rais and Mme Chantelouve:

> Ce qui est bizarre, se dit-il soudain, après un silence de réflexions, c'est que, toutes proportions gardées, Gilles de Rais se divise comme elle en trois êtres qui diffèrent.

D'abord le soudard brave et pieux.

Puis l'artiste raffiné et criminel.

Enfin, le pécheur qui se repent, le mystique

(II, 96)

There are as well many other details which call forth a comparison. The name Chantelouve suggests a nature at the same time tender and ferocious. And at the moment when Rais is stricken with the realization of the enormity of his crime, he also is described as a wolf (*loup*). Moreover, his ravenous nature stands in stark contrast to the solicitude he displayed toward Jeanne d'Arc.

But Mme Chantelouve does not only represent the enigma of the philosopher's stone. She also resembles the alchemist in search of it. In her love for Durtal she aspires after the ideal. In her letters, for instance, she speaks of "ma fiévreuse envie de vous connaître" (I, 144), or of experiencing "le troublant désir de vous connaître et me défendant de toucher à ce rêve de peur de le voir s'évanouir" (I, 145-146).

Everything is marvelously related in this enchanting novel. Durtal tries to resolve the enigma of Mme Chantelouve and Gilles de Rais and in doing so he comes to resemble them. Before his meeting with Mme Chantelouve he forms the idea of an unknown woman who incarnates all he longs for. At their first encounter she tells him, "comprenez donc que la réalité tuera le rêve" (I, 196)—words which suggest to us an enduring human verity. He is at first disappointed by her, but he seeks further, until little by little he becomes captivated by her:

> Celle-là [l'inconnue, la femme idéale] s'était complètement évanouie, il ne se rappelait même plus sa physionomie; Mme Chantelouve, telle qu'elle était réellement, sans fusion, sans emprunt de traits, le tenait tout entier, lui chauffait à blanc la cervelle et les sens.
>
> (I, 204-205)

The image which attaches to the description of this episode is subtle. Durtal, who seeks the ideal in Mme Chantelouve, is described as "un paladin bien triste" (I, 205)—which could be an allusion to no other than Gilles de Rais, the profoundly sad paladin who unceasingly seeks an ideal. After that first meeting, Mme Chantelouve appears indeed to be the philosopher's stone. Durtal's emotions are subsequently described in this manner: "Toute une bouffée de jeunesse l'enivrait . . . ; ses yeux fatigués éclairaient; sa face lui semblait plus juvénile, moins usée . . ." (I, 201). One must remember that the philosopher's stone has several attributes, among them the power to restore youth. The description here as elsewhere (I, 242, for example) suggests a rejuvenation. Moreover, the philosopher's stone is also called "le lion vert," while Mme Chantelouve and Gilles

de Rais are symbolically wolves. One also recalls "l'écriture d'un vert myrte" of Mme Chantelouve. Furthermore, the undecipherable nature of Mme Chantelouve resembles the cabalistic emblems of Nicolas Flamel, who recovers the secret of the philosopher's stone (I, 127). It is hardly surprising that the preparations of Durtal for the seduction of Mme Chantelouve closely parallel the vain attempts of Gilles de Rais as he experiments with different metals (II, 17). The failure of Gilles de Rais prefigures the outcome of the quest of Durval. Nor is it co-incidental that, just after having considered how he will seduce Mme Chantelouve, Durtal glances at the last chapter he has written on the life of Gilles de Rais—"au moment où les expériences d'alchimie, où les évocations diaboliques ratent" (II, 17). His seduction will fail also.

After Gilles de Rais' unsuccessful attempt to find the ideal, what is left to him? "Tous les souffleurs et les sorciers qui entourent le maréchal avouent que pour amorcer Satan, il faudrait que Gilles lui cédât son âme et sa vie ou qu'il commît des crimes" (II, 7). Gilles de Rais' life is history to Durtal. It is the story of a man who, when all efforts to find the secret of the Stone fail, sells his soul to Satan. He turns to an infernal black magic that will claim the lives of innocent children (I, 128). Durtal knows this. He knows too that "l'au-delà du Mal ne s'atteint pas."

> Excédé de stupres et de meurtres, le Maréchal ne pouvait aller dans cette voie plus loin. Il avait beau rêver à des viols uniques, à des tortures plus studieuses et plus lentes, c'en était fait; les limites de l'imagination humaine prenaient fin; il les avait diaboliquement dépassées même. Il haletait, insatiable, devant le vide; il pouvait vérifier cet axiome des démonographes, que le Malin dupe tous les gens qui se donnent ou veulent se livrer à lui.
>
> (II, 17)

And later Durtal will experience a similar inability to steep himself deeper in evil, to participate in a black mass.

What Durtal seeks in this strange couple is the ideal, or rather the springboard which will catapult him to the ideal. And therein lies his tragic flaw, for he is incapable of the power of faith needed to lift him beyond. He has tarried too long in the muck of reality—the reality that, as he finds out, kills the dream of perfection.

> . . . le tremplin s'était cassé; il demeurait les pieds dans la crotte, rivés au sol. Il n'y avait donc pas moyen de sortir de son être, de s'évader de son cloaque, d'atteindre les régions où l'âme chavire, ravie, en ses abîmes?
>
> . . . la réalité ne pardonne pas qu'on la méprise; elle se venge en effondrant le rêve, en le piétinant, en le jetant en loques dans un tas de boue!
>
> (II, 47-48)[4]

It is well for critics to see in such statements by Huysmans a condemnation of the naturalist school. But on a larger scale, is it not a condemnation of the society and age in which Huysmans found himself?

What has happened to the beliefs of man? The Golden Age eventually deteriorated into the Silver Age. The forces that influenced medieval man originated in the realm of divine spirit. But in the age depicted by Huysmans, the "fin de siècle," those forces originate in the society of men. There exists one force more lasting in its effect than any other. It is capital. It is silver. "Il change, en une seconde, toutes les habitudes, bouleverse toutes les idées, métamorphose les passions les plus têtues en un clin d'œil" (I, 24). Huysmans in *Là-bas* presents a paean of medieval times in such a way that he exposes at the same time the corruption of the modern world. The moderns have lost their energy, they have regulated their lives according to the fluctuations of the market, they have become crushed in the mill-wheel of capital (I, 188). In relation to the past, Huysmans appears to be a mystic, whereas in relation to the present he echoes Marxist doctrine.

At the time when the narrator speaks of Durtal as being mired in the reality of this world, it is still a question whether there is not still a means to attain the ideal. Durtal explores the world in search of just such means, but when all is done he has found none. At the novel's end, Durtal, Carhaix and des Hermies hear the shouts in the streets for the new "savior" of humanity, General Boulanger. But for des Hermies and Durtal, Boulanger represents the democracy and mediocrity they execrate. His very nickname, Boulange, suggests that we live in an age when angels are dragged in mud. But for Carhaix, the simple believer, faith in the future remains unshaken:

> Ici-bas, tout est décomposé, tout est mort, mais là-haut! Ah! je l'avoue, l'effusion de l'Esprit-Saint, la venue du Divin Paraclet se fait attendre! mais les textes qui l'annoncent sont inspirés; l'avenir est donc crédité, l'aube sera claire!

And Carhaix prays. Des Hermies is less optimistic:

> . . . ce siècle se fiche absolument de Christ en gloire; il contamine le surnaturel et vomit l'au-delà. Alors, comment espérer en l'avenir, comment s'imaginer qu'ils seront propres, les gosses issus des fétides bourgeois de ce sale temps? Elevés de la sorte, je me demande ce qu'ils feront dans la vie, ceux-là?

Durtal has the final word. They will do as their fathers and mothers did: "ils s'empliront les tripes et ils se vidangeront l'âme par le bas-ventre" (II, 235).

Thus ends the satanic book Huysmans proposed to write. It is the story of Durtal, the eternal alchemist, who rejects the way to evil but who cannot find the way to good. He suffers from the satiation of the material present and from the insatiability of his thirst for the ideal future he cannot attain. All that is necessary is a leap, but Durtal stands too deep in the mire of his time.

Notes

1. *J.-K. Huysmans à la Trappe,* cited by Pierre Cogny, *Le Naturalisme* (Paris: Presses Universitaires de France, 1963), p. 78.

2. J.-K. Huysmans, *Œuvres complètes* (Paris: Les Editions G. Crès et Cie, 1930), II, 17. Succeeding references to *Là-bas* in the text will be to this two-volume edition.

3. The historical personage is not the less legendary for having been connected, justifiably or not, with Perrault's story of *Bluebeard,* nor for having provided posterity with the materials for a sensational *Life.* Huysmans' history of Rais, though remarkably accurate in detail, is not to be taken for history, which it is not. Huysmans' personage is of novelistic, not historical, substance.

4. For a discussion of this recurrent image of the springboard, see "The 'Springboards' of Joris-Karl Huysmans" by Sister Lucy Tinsley, S.N.D. de N., *L'Esprit Créateur,* IV, 2 (Summer 1964), 94-101.

Joyce O. Lowrie (essay date 1974)

SOURCE: Lowrie, Joyce O. "Joris-Karl Huysmans: From Satanism to Mysticism." In *The Violent Mystique: Thematics of Retribution and Expiation in Balzac, Barbey d'Aurevilly, Bloy, and Huysmans,* pp. 131-55. Geneva: Librairie Droz, 1974.

[*In the following excerpt, drawn from her essay tracing Huysmans' transition from Satanism to mysticism in his fiction, Lowrie examines the author's depiction of evil and physical violence in* Là-bas *and notes the novel's "parallel or dual structure in which satanism is opposed to mysticism"—a conflict reflected in the spiritual struggles of the protagonist, Durtal.*]

> La pensée de Huysmans s'exprime à contrecourant, non sans courage. Si elle bénéficie d'une large audience, c'est que très rapidement se dessine un vaste mouvement de renaissance d'une pensée catholique française prête à s'imposer au XXe siècle.
>
> Jean-Laurent Prévost

Upon the publication of Huysmans' *A Rebours,* Barbey d'Aurevilly made the following statement in *Le Constitutionnel* (July 24, 1884): "Après un tel livre, il ne reste plus à l'auteur qu'à choisir entre la bouche d'un pistolet et les pieds de la croix."[1] Des Esseintes, the decadent hero of *A Rebours* (1884), had indeed gone "against the grain," and had found himself in an impasse at the conclusion of the novel. So, after *A Rebours,* Huysmans did, indeed, take one of the options predicted by Barbey, "les pieds de la croix." But he took the mystical route by way of the "back door," that is, by way of satanism. First came *Là-Bas* (1891), with its perusal of the lower realms; and then came *En Route* (1895) as the first step of the mystical trilogy of which the second and third steps were *La Cathédrale* (1898) and *L'Oblat* (1903).

Gilles de Rais, the 15th-century Bluebeard whose life is depicted in *Là-Bas,* embodies the Manichean duality conspicuous in most of the works studied so far. Gilles de Rais went from mysticism to satanism in one step: "Or, du mysticisme exalté au Satanisme exaspéré, il n'y a qu'un pas. Dans l'au-delà, tout se touche."[2] Huysmans' own aesthetic and religious trajectory is similar. In commenting on the fact that *En Route* follows *Là-Bas,* Huysmans said: "The one derived from the other. With his hooked claw, the devil drew me towards God."[3]

The extremes of violence and mysticism present in Barbey and Bloy are also present in Huysmans. Gilles de Rais indulged in "saintly orgies" at first and then in "criminal orgies." An examination of the criminal orgies of *Là-Bas* will carry us further in our definition of the violent mystique.

SATANISM EQUALS SADISM AND SACRILEGE

The structure of *Là-Bas* is based upon a parallel examination of satanism in the Middle Ages (specifically in the 15th century) and satanism in the present (the late 19th century). Durtal (the central character in the novel) is writing a book on Gilles de Rais and the facts he learns about his villain form one of the threads that is woven intermittently but consistently throughout the book. Satanism in the present revolves around Durtal's relationship with a satanic woman, Hyacinthe Chantelouve.[4]

Gilles de Rais is the character who represents the extreme limits of sadism and cruelty. His exploits equal those described by the Marquis de Sade. He managed to do this on two accounts: he chose children to be his victims, and secondly, he raped and brutalized them in almost unimaginable ways. The records show that his victims numbered in the seven or eight hundreds, but even then, "the number is insufficient and seems to be inexact."[5] In Chapter XI Durtal describes the horrible details of the crimes. After kidnapping the children of the villages surrounding the chateau de Tiffauges, in Brittany,

> Gilles et ses amis se retirent dans une chambre éloignée du château. C'est là que les petits garçons enfermés dans les caves sont amenés. On les déshabille, on

les bâillonne; le maréchal les palpes et les force, puis il les taillade, à coups de dague, se complaît à les démembrer, pièces à pièces. D'autre fois, il leur fend la poitrine, et il boit le souffle des poumons; il leur ouvre aussi le ventre, le flaire, élargit de ses mains la plaie et s'assied dedans. Alors, tandis qu'il se macère dans la boue détrempée des entrailles tièdes, il se retourne un peu et regarde pardessus son épaule, afin de contempler les suprêmes convulsions, les derniers spasmes. Lui-même a dit: "J'étais plus content de jouïr des tortures, des larmes, de l'effroi et du sang que de tout autre plaisir."[6]

He then tires of enjoying moribund victims and turns to vampirism and necrophilia:

> Artiste passioné, il baisait avec des cris d'enthousiasme les membres bien faits de ses victimes; il établissait un concours de beauté sépulcrale;—et, alors que, de ces têtes coupées, l'une obtenait le prix—il la soulevait par les cheveux et passionément, il embrassait ses lèvres froides.[7]

One day, when his supply of victims diminishes, he kills a pregnant woman so as to mangle the foetus.[8]

Gilles de Rais managed to distinguish himself from the common run of sadistic criminals by virtue of one particular trait: not only did he indulge in "carnal" rape, but also in what Durtal calls "spiritual" rape. He would have his accomplices slowly hang a child, and just before the child suffocated he would come in and "rescue" him. He would caress him and console him, and promise to return the child to his mother. The child, overcome with gratitude and joy, would love him and caress him in return. At that very moment "il lui incisait doucement le cou par derrière, le rendait, suivant son expression, 'languissant,' et lorsque la tête un peu détachée, saluait, dans les flots de sang, il pétrissait le corps, le retournait, le violait, en rugissant."[9] The violation, in these cases, was not only of the child's body but also of the child's entire being.

It is precisely this "spiritual rape" that interests Durtal, because satanism, to him, is a malady of the soul. The most vivid writing in Chapter XI of *Là-Bas* is in keeping with the above descriptions. The violation of childrens' bodies is a prelude to the almost surreal visions that Durtal lends to Gilles de Rais as the latter convulsively gropes, in horror, through the forests surrounding Tiffauges. The movement goes from carnage to visionary perversion. First, Gilles de Rais pierces the eyes of one of his victims and fingers "the milky blood" of the pupils. He grabs a spiked rod and strikes the victim's head until the brains spurt out. As the blood gushes forth and he is splattered with particles of brains, he grits his teeth, laughs wildly, and runs out into the forest. All of nature is transformed in his eyes. All he sees is perversion and obscenity. He witnesses the "immutable salaciousness" of the woods, discovers "the priapism of the trees":

Ici, l'arbre lui apparaît comme un être vivant, debout, la tête en bas, enfouie dans la chevelure de ses racines, dressant des jambes en l'air, les écartant, puis se subdivisant en de nouvelles cuisses qui s'ouvrent, à leur tour, deviennent de plus en plus petites, à mesure qu'elles s'éloignent du tronc; là, entre ces jambes, une autre branche est enfoncée, en une immobile fornication qui se répète et diminue, de rameaux en rameaux, jusqu'à la cime; là encore, le fût lui semble être un phallus qui monte et disparaît sous une jupe de feuilles, ou bien il sort au contraire d'une toison verte et plonge dans le ventre velouté du sol. . . . Puis, auprès les bifurcations des branches, des trous bâillent, des orifices où l'écorce fait bourrelet sur des entailles en ovale, des hiatus plissés qui simulent d'immondes émonctoires ou des natures béantes des bêtes. . . . Partout les formes obscènes montent de la terre, jaillissent en désordre dans le firmament qui se satanise; les nuages se gonflent en mamelons, se fendent en croupes, s'arrondissent en des outres fécondes; ils s'accordent avec la bombance sombre de la futaie où ce ne sont plus qu'images de cuisses géantes ou naines, que triangles féminins, que grands V, que bouches de Sodome, que cicatrices qui s'ébrasent, qu'issues humides.[10]

He returns, beside himself, to the chateau where he collapses and falls into a deep sleep, and the bodies of his victims return to haunt his dreams: "Les corps qu'il a massacrés et dont il a fait jeter les cendres dans les douves ressuscitent à l'état de larves et l'attaquent aux parties basses. Il se débat, clapote dans le sang, se dresse en sursaut, et accroupi, il se traîne à quatre pattes, tel qu'un loup, jusqu'au crucifix dont il mord les pieds, en rugissant."[11]

Huysmans shows, once again, that "s'il ne comportait pas un sacrilège, le sadisme n'aurait de raison d'être." Perhaps it is for this reason that he has Durtal imagine Gilles de Rais bite the foot of the cross at the conclusion of this chapter. This is also a prefiguration of Gilles' return to mysticism and of his repentance and desire to expiate his crimes. Huysmans considers the essence of satanism to be manifest in sexual violence; but he goes further. Violence equals violation, and Gilles de Rais violated not only that which was created by God, but creation at its most innocent: children. To violate children is to push the satanic impulse to its most terrible limit. Not only are children incapable of defending themselves, but in that they "trail clouds of glory" they represent the purity that is identified with God himself. Violation means the profanation of that which is holy. The violation of children is, then, even more specifically satanic or diabolical than the willful participation in evil exemplified in Barbey's *Diaboliques.*

In his analysis of Gilles de Rais, Durtal was quick to point out the insatiability of evil: "Si l'au-delà du Bien, si le là-bas de l'Amour est accessible à certaines âmes, l'au-delà du Mal ne s'atteint pas. . . . [Gilles de Rais] avait beau rêver à des viols uniques, à des tortures plus

studieuses et plus lentes, c'en était fait. . . . Il haletait, insatiable, devant le vide; il pouvait vérifier cet axiome des démonographes, que le Malin dupe tous les gens qui se donnent ou veulent se livrer à lui."[12] For Gilles de Rais, Satan becomes a manifestation of the cosmic void.

But the objective study of violence in the Middle Ages in the person of Gilles de Rais is not sufficient for Durtal. He must experience satanism in the present, and he does this through Hyacinthe Chantelouve. Durtal is struck by the fact that his mistress laughs, wildly, at times, over nothing. She also has small, pointed teeth. When Durtal goes to bed with her the first time he is acutely aware of the coldness of her body. She attests to nightly visitations by incubi, and when Durtal asks his friend Des Hermies about this he is told: "Autrefois, les femmes atteintes d'incubat avaient les chairs frigides, même au mois d'août."[13]

She had been the defrocked Canon Docre's mistress for a while, and although she claims to have put satanism behind her, it is through her that Durtal manages to meet Docre and to attend a Black Mass.

Docre is the evil satanist who officiates at Black Masses and who casts mortal spells upon his enemies. These spells are counteracted by the workings of a "good" occultist, Dr. Johannès. We recall (*supra.,* Chapter IV, section IV, "Bloy and the occultists of his time"), that Docre's model was the Abbé Louis Van Haecke, Chaplain of the Sacred Blood at Bruges. Information about him was furnished to Huysmans by Mme Berthe Courrière, who, with Henriette Maillat, provided the inspiration for Mme Chantelouve in *Là-Bas.* But Huysmans gathered, or surmised, most of his information on occultism from another defrocked priest, the Abbé Boullan (who becomes "Dr. Johannès" in the novel). Huysmans knew Boullan personally and liked him. He took many notes on what the latter told him about satanic practices of the day. What Huysmans did not realize, however, was that Boullan attributed to others (namely, to Van Haecke) practices in which he himself indulged. In the novel, thus, "Dr. Johannès," who was modeled after Boullan, is a hero, while "Canon Docre," who was modeled after Van Haecke, is a villain.

Boullan (his full name was Jean-Antoine Boullan and he lived from 1824 to 1893) founded a sect which is said to have had around 600,000 members. Norman Cohn, in *The Pursuit of the Millennium,* tells us that "this man regarded himself as the 'sword of God,' charged with the task of cleansing the earth of that impurity, the Church of Rome, and of saving mankind in the Last Days."[14] Cohn interprets Boullan's doctrines as being in direct continuity with the heresy of the Brethren of the Free Spirit. This heretical movement had been intimately associated with the flagellant sects in medieval Germany which indulged in "militant and bloodthirsty pursuits of the Millennium," various movements of which were peopled with "an elite of self-immolating redeemers."[15] What is striking are the similarities between the doctrines and interpretations of the flagellants and adepts of the Free Spirit and the violent and expiatory principles exhibited in Bloy's and Huysmans' works. Both Bloy and Huysmans researched these doctrines. Bloy did so because of his belief that the end of the world was imminent, and that he would have a hand in announcing to the world the cataclysms that were to precede the millennium. Huysmans did so out of curiosity, as well as from his desire to find meaning in a world which seemed, to him, to be dominated by materialism.

Boullan claimed to be the successor of Vintras, the prophet from Lyon who proclaimed the coming of "the glorious reign of Christ." Most of the ideas contained in Chapter XX of *Là-Bas* are ideas that Vintras preached, that Boullan adopted, and that Bloy claimed to be his own. In the novel, they are attributed to Dr. Johannès.

In Chapter XIX of *Là-Bas,* the chapter that precedes the elaboration of Vintras' and Boullan's ideas on the "coming of the Paraclette," Huysmans describes Canon Docre's Black Mass. It is said that Huysmans himself attended, in all likelihood, only one such Mass. His information, therefore, derives as much from his research into the subject as from firsthand knowledge. One of the main parts of the Mass was the sexual denigration of the sacramental Hosts. By describing the Mass and Durtal's experiences which follow the ceremony, Huysmans joins Mme Chantelouve, Canon Docre, and his followers into an integral picture of what satanism was in his day. Part of Hyacinthe Chantelouve's satanism had involved being the mistress of a priest. She defined this as incest (for the priest was her spiritual father) and as sacrilege as well.[16] It was from Canon Docre that she had learned to summon the incubi who possessed her nightly.[17] Interestingly enough, one of the prime doctrines of the Free Spirit heresy was that promiscuity was practiced on principle. Cohn tells us: "What emerges [from the adepts of the Free Spirit] is an entirely convincing picture of an eroticism which, far from springing from a carefree sensuality, possessed above all a symbolic value as a sign of spiritual emancipation—which incidentally is the value which 'free love' has often possessed in our own times."[18]

In *Là-Bas,* the Black Mass is described by Durtal as a ceremony that takes place in the abandoned chapel of an Ursuline convent. The congregation is composed of nymphomaniacs, painted male and female prostitutes, pederasts, and sodomites of all types. On the altar is a naked statue of Christ whose enormous phallus is visible and erect. Canon Docre himself is naked under his ecclesiastical vestments. The liturgy is composed of long invocations to Satan, who is called "maître des Esclandres, Dispensateur des bienfaits du crime, Intendant des sompueux péchés et des grands vices," and of blasphematory incantations against God and Christ.[19] The incantations drive the congregation to ecstatic hysteria, and at the moment of consecration, Canon Docre, upon saying, "Hoc est enim corpus meum," soils the Host with his own ejaculation. He distributes unleavened bread, and the women violate it in their own fashion. Durtal escapes, nauseated, and drags Mme Chantelouve with him. She tricks him into a sordid bar and into an even more sordid bed upstairs. After Durtal tears himself away from her, after having been aroused despite himself, he sees on the bed fragments of the Host which Docre had consecrated. Completely disgusted, he terminates his relationship with Mme Chantelouve.

Although Huysmans juxtaposes the evil Docre's activities (in Chapter XIX) to the "good" practices and beliefs of Dr. Johannès (in Chapter XX), it seems quite clear that both men held many things in common (as was probably the case with their real counterparts, Boullan and Van Haecke). "Evil" satanism and "good" occultism share the same background. Although the stresses are different, both White and Black magic are rooted in occultist beliefs and practices. Both Docre and Johannès, therefore, contribute to the satanic and occultist background of *Là-Bas.* The incorporation of Johannès' (or Boullan's) beliefs in the coming of the Paraclete and of the millennium and Docre's beliefs in "religious" promiscuity into *Là-Bas* adds to the esoteric background we are tracing and situates the themes under consideration well within an occultist framework.

By comparing Mme Chantelouve to Gilles de Rais, Huysmans creates, even further, a unified structural matrix in *Là-Bas.* Durtal sees three distinct beings in Mme Chantelouve, "la femme réservée et hautaine," "la femme couchée," and "une impitoyable mâtine, vraiment satanique." He sees the same number of distinctions in Gilles de Rais, "le soudard brave et pieux," "l'artiste raffiné et criminel," and "le pécheur qui se repent, le mystique."[20] By having Durtal make this comparison, Huysmans joins the medieval and the modern expressions of satanism and makes of them a symbolic whole against which he sets the other side of the novel. The other side is symbolized by the churchtower in which Durtal's friends, the Carhaix, live, and of which Carhaix is the bell ringer. Carhaix is an orthodox recluse whose passion is the maintenance, care, and symbolism of church bells. He is acquainted with a few of the satanists of his day and discusses, with Durtal, many of their beliefs, but generally, he decries their practices. He is more interested in mystical philosophy and ecclesiastical symbolism. By making the juxtaposition of Mme Chantelouve and her circle to the Carhaix, Huysmans creates a parallel or dual structure in which satanism is opposed to mysticism. Durtal's study of Gilles de Rais is thereby relegated to a position of much greater significance than that of merely fulfilling Durtal's intellectual curiosity or of presenting shocking details to spice up the novel. Gilles de Rais becomes a symbol of the tension that Durtal finds within himself and which he resolves, at least partly, by abandoning Mme Chantelouve and retreating, more and more, to the church tower situated high above the streets of Paris, "si bien hors de Paris, si loin dans les vieux âges!"[21]

This movement away from satanism and towards mysticism, from the somber caverns of the Black Mass to the high bell-tower, from an examination of physical violence, sadism, and satanism to a depiction of the spiritual violence involved in the "dark night of the soul" is precisely the movement that is inherent in *Là-Bas* but that occurs with greater precision in the transition from *Là-Bas* to *En Route.* The titles of the novels themselves reflect the shift.

Notes

1. Quoted by Jean-Laurent Prévost, *Le Roman Catholique a cent ans,* Paris, Librairie Arthème Fayard, 1958, p. 36.

2. Joris-Karl Huysmans, *Là-Bas,* Paris, Plon, 1966, p. 50.

3. Quoted by Henry R. T. Brandreth, *Huysmans,* New York, Hillary House, 1963, p. 82

4. Cf. Chapter IV for a full elaboration of Huysmans' sources. One of the models for Hyacinthe Chantelouve was Henriette Maillat, the mistress Huysmans shared with Péladan and with Bloy.

5. Joris-Karl Huysmans, *op. cit.,* p. 154.

6. *Ibid.,* p. 155.

7. *Ibid.,* p. 156.

8. *Loc. cit.*

9. *Ibid.,* p. 157.

10. *Ibid.,* pp. 158-159.

11. *Ibid.,* pp. 159-160.

12. *Ibid.,* p. 157.

13. *Ibid.,* p. 183.

14. Norman Cohn, *The Pursuit of the Millennium,* New York, Harper Torchbooks, p. 185.

15. *Ibid.,* cf. Chapter VI, "An Elite of Self-Immolating Redeemers," and Chapter VII, "An Elite of Amoral Supermen."

16. Joris-Karl Huysmans, *op. cit.,* p. 197.

17. *Ibid.,* p. 198.

18. Norman Cohn, *op. cit.,* p. 152.

19. Joris-Karl Huysmans, *op. cit.,* p. 240.

20. *Ibid.,* pp. 201-202.

21. *Ibid.,* p. 278.

A Selected Bibliography

GENERAL WORKS

Cohn, Norman *The Pursuit of the Millennium.* New York, Harper Torchbooks, 1960.

Prévost, Jean Laurent *Le Roman catholique a cent ans.* Paris, Librairie Arthème Fayard, 1958.

JORIS-KARL HUYSMANS: FROM SATANISM TO MYSTICISM

Brandreth, R. T. *Huysmans.* New York, Hillary House, 1963.

Huysmans, Joris-Karl *A Rebours, Oeuvres complètes,* VII. Paris, Crès et Cie., 1928.

La Cathédrale, Oeuvres complètes, XIV, 2pts. Paris, Crès et Cie., 1928.

En Route, Oeuvres complètes, XIII, 2 pts. Paris, Crès et Cie., 1928.

Là-Bas, Oeuvres complètes, XII, 2 pts. Paris, Crès et Cie., 1928.

L'Oblat. Paris, P. V. Stock, 1903.

Ruth B. Antosh (essay date 1986)

SOURCE: Antosh, Ruth B. "Memories and Reveries." In *Reality and Illusion in the Novels of J.-K. Huysmans,* pp. 52-80. Amsterdam: Rodopi, 1986.

[*In the following excerpt, Antosh notes that a central concern in* Là-bas *is Durtal's desire to "explore various avenues of escape through art and fantasy," concluding that although the protagonist experiences "a temporary release" through "the process of artistic creation, he is forced to recognize that art is at best an imperfect refuge."*]

The fading of the demarcation line between reality and fantasy, between the material world and the world of the imagination, is even more pronounced in Huysmans' next novel, *Là-Bas.* In this work, the writer-protagonist Durtal displays a desire to escape reality and transcend time which is similar to that of Des Esseintes and Jacques, but in contrast to them, he succeeds in prolonging reveries and atavistic memories by writing them down and transforming them into a permanent document, into a work of art. The process of artistic creation enables Durtal to *become* the character he is describing, although only while he is actually writing the book.

Ostensibly, Durtal, a well-known novelist, is merely writing a fictionalized history of Gilles de Rais, a fifteenth-century religious mystic and murderer; but his reasons for embarking on this project go far deeper than the desire to publish a historical novel. Like Des Esseintes and Jacques, he does not feel at home in the society of his time; like them, he longs to "s'écrouer dans le passé, revivre au loin . . ." ([*Oeuvres complètes,* 23 volumes] XII, 1, 29-30). The era to which he feels drawn spiritually and artistically is the late Middle Ages, and his research and writings on Gilles de Rais have been undertaken with a therapeutic aim in mind as well as an artistic one: "Le jour où Dutal s'était plongé dans l'effrayante et délicieuse fin du Moyen Age, il s'était senti renaître" (XII, 1, 29).

As might be expected of a writer whose main interest in his work is personal and spiritual, Durtal has little concern for accurate documentation. Such research as he does is aimed at gathering details which will stimulate his imagination and serve as "un tremplin d'idées et de style," not as a solid historical foundation (XII, 1, 30). He has little faith in the so-called science of history based on careful examination of documents and prefers to rely instead on his own innate feelings for the period and characters he describes. Thus, he believes, "Il ne reste . . . qu'à se fabriquer sa vision, s'imaginer avec soi-même les créatures d'un autre temps, s'incarner en elles, . . . se forger enfin, avec des détails adroitement triés, de fallacieux ensembles" (XII, 1, 31).

While Jacques' memory of the Marquise de Saint-Phal and Des Esseintes' escapist imaginings before the paintings of Salome are quite impersonal, Durtal enters into his fantasy (which is also a novel) by identifying with his subject, Gilles de Rais. The respectable Durtal's feeling of kinship for a man who was both a sexual pervert and a murderer may at first seem incongruous, but the two are in fact spiritual brothers. Both have dual leanings toward Satanism and Christianity, and both share a fondness for rare books and manuscripts, alchemy, and exotic food and drink. Lest the reader overlook the fact that the two also resemble Des Esseintes, Huysmans has Durtal remark that Gilles de Rais was "le Des Esseintes du quinzième siecle" (XII, 1, 77).

Just as the bell tower of Saint-Sulpice, far above the corruption of Paris, provides a physical and temporal refuge for Durtal, so his imaginary retreat to the late Middle Ages and to Gilles de Rais' castle of Tiffauges provides a similar haven on a psychological level: "Il . . . se cloîtra mentalement, pour tout dire, dans le château de Tiffauges" (XII, 1, 30). Furthermore, just as Jacques' revery of an imaginary apartment decorated

according to his tastes parallels Des Esseintes' decoration of an actual house in the preceding novel, so Durtal's mental flight to an imaginary castle refuge parallels Jacques' flight to an actual castle. In both cases the "reality" of one novel becomes the fantasy of the following novel. For the reader who reads *A Rebours, En Rade,* and *Là-Bas* successively, the effect is, ultimately, one of utter uncertainty concerning what is fact and what is fantasy; for the fantasy of one novel is just as convincing as the reality of another.

Durtal's fantasies concerning Gilles de Rais make up a large part of *Là-Bas* and take the form of something akin to interior monologues. It is often quite impossible to determine whether he is in fact in the process of writing his own book or merely daydreaming. The two processes—the workings of his imagination and the actual writing of the book—are thus merged into one creative act:

> . . . j'en étais, se dit-il, en parcourant son dernier chapitre, au moment où les évocations diaboliques ratent. . . .
>
> Gilles refuse d'aliéner son existence et d'abandonner son âme, mais il songe sans horreur aux meurtres. . . . Et il en est de même de ses complices . . . il leur fait jurer sur les Saints Evangiles le secret certain qu'aucun d'eux n'enfreindra le serment, car, au Moyen Age, le plus impavide des bandits n'oserait assumer l'irrémissible méfait de tromper Dieu!
>
> (XII, 2, 7)

The words "se dit-il" and the exclamation point at the end of the excerpt suggest that all this is going on in Durtal's mind. The verbs in the present are at this point, perhaps, merely examples of the historical present, and there appears to be a clear separation between the narrator or author (Durtal) and his subject (Gilles de Rais). As Durtal continues to meditate on Gilles, however, his personality begins to merge with that of his subject. In keeping with his previously mentioned theory that a writer of historical fiction must ". . . s'imaginer avec soi-même les créatures d'un autre temps, s'incarner en elles, . . . se forger enfin, . . . de fallacieux ensembles" (XII, 2, 13), Durtal begins to draw on his own "atavistic memory" for many of the gruesome details, and the verbs in the present become the remembered present of recollection:

> A la brune, alors que leurs sens sont phosphorés, comme meurtris par le suc puissant de venaisons, embrasés par de combustibles breuvages semés d'épices, Gilles et ses amis se retirent dans une chambre éloignée du château. C'est là que les petits garçons enfermés dans les caves sont amenés. On les déshabille, on les baillonne; le Maréchal les palpe et les force, puis il les taillade à coups de dagues, se complaît à les démembrer, pièces à pièces.
>
> (XII, 2, 13-14)

Although it is difficult to be certain, it would seem that Durtal is actually writing his novel only when he calls on his atavistic memory. At the end of this passage, which is fifteen pages long, Durtal closes his notebook, leaving the reader with the impression that he has also been writing. Durtal's reluctance to finish his book is evidence that he views the act of literary creation as an escape route far superior to mere daydreaming. When asked when he will complete the work, he replies: ". . . je ne désire pas qu'il se termine. Que deviendrai-je alors? . . . Vraiment, quand j'y songe, la littérature n'a qu'une raison d'être, sauver celui qui la fait du dégoût de vivre!" (XII, 2, 108).

Despite Durtal's desire to prolong the writing of his book indefinitely, the work progresses steadily, and at the end of *Là-Bas* it is nearly completed. The fact that the work will actually be finished seems at first puzzling, for most of Huysmans' protagonists fail in their artistic endeavors. The explanation of this apparent success on Durtal's part is, paradoxically, that it is in fact a failure; for once the novel is completed, Durtal will be deprived of his means of escape and thrown back into reality. While Leó, André, and Cyprien fail in their attempts at artistic creation because daydreams and memories interfere with their work, Durtal's novel succeeds precisely because it is made up of his own fantasies. Since his novel and his escape route are one and the same, the completion of the book represents an inevitable return to reality. The triumph of reality over Durtal's physical retreat in the tower of Saint-Sulpice occurs almost simultaneously with the completion of his novel; thus, as in earlier novels, the protagonist is deprived of both his physical and mental havens, although in *Là-Bas* he seems to have come closer to a definitive escape through Art.

Thus in the middle novels, the protagonists explore various avenues of escape through art and fantasy: Des Esseintes finds that fantasies inspired by the art of others (Moreau, Redon, Flaubert, Baudelaire, etc.) lead him inevitably back to himself; Jacques discovers that attempts to escape via the imagination to another era are always short-lived, and although in *Là-Bas* Durtal finds a temporary release from himself through the process of artistic creation, he is forced to recognize that art is at best an imperfect refuge.

Selected Bibliography

Oeuvres complètes. Ed. Lucien Descaves. Paris: Crès, 1928-1934. 23 vols.

Alain Toumayan (essay date May 1988)

SOURCE: Toumayan, Alain. "Huysmans and the Study of Crime." *Romance Quarterly* 35, no. 2 (May 1988): 131-38.

[*In the following essay, Toumayan demonstrates how Huysmans structures* Là-bas *as a debate between the doctrine of the Catholic church and Positivist scientific inquiry.*]

In an interview, first published in 1975, Michel Foucault notes that the interest in the criminal *per se* first appears during the early part of the 19th century. In connection with his presentation of the case study of Pierre Rivière, Foucault says: "Cette curiosité pour le criminel n'existait absolument pas au XVIIIe siècle où il s'agissait simplement de savoir si l'inculpé avait réellement fait ce qu'on lui reprochait. Ceci établi, le tarif était fixe. La question: quel est cet individu qui a commis ce crime? est une question nouvelle."[1] Louis Chevalier's major study of crime in Paris in the first half of the 19th century corroborates, in a broader perspective, Foucault's remarks. This work, *Classes laborieuses et classes dangereuses à Paris pendant la première moitié du XIXe siècle,* usefully combines the facts of criminal and demographic statistics during the period with the popular and aesthetic representation of crime in 19th-century Paris. Chevalier notes, for example: "Criminel, ce Paris de la première moitié du XIXe siècle l'est d'abord par l'accroissement du nombre de faits criminels qu'enregistrent les statistiques. . . . Criminel aussi par la marque du crime sur l'ensemble du paysage urbain. . . . Criminel, ce Paris l'est surtout par la place du crime dans les préoccupations quotidiennes des gens."[2] The fact that crime was a prime concern to the people of the period, to the social historians and to the writers and artists of the 19th century, is a thesis amply developed and extensively documented by Chevalier. The latter's study of 19th-century writers whose representation of crime is noteworthy will tend to focus on Balzac, Hugo, Sue, Daudet, and Zola, "pour ne citer que les plus grands,"[3] as Chevalier says. The presence of Balzac, Sue, and Hugo in his thesis is understandable given Chevalier's emphasis on the first half of the century—then again, *Les Misérables* was not published until 1862. Yet Chevalier's mention of Daudet and Zola, both born in 1840, makes all the more striking his omission of Huysmans (born in 1848), whose name does not figure in *Classes laborieuses et classes dangereuses.*

The purpose of this essay will be to add the name of Huysmans to the list of major 19th-century French writers for whom the questions of crime and criminality were an important concern. To that end I shall propose, in this essay, a reading of the novel *Là-Bas.*

Huysmans's *Là-Bas* is a very complex novel which delves into the spheres of satanism, madness, and crime and which chronicles several major investigations, the principal contexts of which are epistemological, aesthetic, and metaphysical. Among other things, *Là-Bas* is principally, I will argue, a case study of the 15th-century criminal baron, Gilles de Rais.[4] Indeed, between 1896 and 1899, Huysmans will excerpt verbatim the chapters of *Là-Bas* devoted to the case of Gilles de Rais and publish them separately as a case history, first presented in the acts of the "Congrès d'Ethnographie et d'Art Populaire" held in Niort in 1896, and entitled

"La Magie en Poitou: Gilles de Rais."[5] It is typical of Huysmans, moreover, to enter the 19th-century debate on crime and criminality with the case which was without doubt considered, during the 19th century, the most extreme criminal case in the history of France and one that in 20-century French letters would continue to inspire writers and thinkers in various genres: Artaud in 1933, Bataille in the early sixties, Roger Planchon in 1975, and Michel Tournier as recently as 1983, to name but a few.[6]

In its structure, *Là-Bas* is essentially a series of debates. These are punctuated by the protagonist Durtal's research into the case of Gilles de Rais and a brief affair with an enigmatic satanic woman who arranges Durtal's witnessing of a black mass. The application of a forensic model to *Là-Bas* seems especially appropriate for two reasons. On the one hand, the major portion of the novel is comprised, as noted previously, of discussions and debates on a whole range of subjects between Durtal, the doctor des Hermies, the Catholic Carhaix and his wife, and, on some occasions, the astrologer Gévingey. It is clear that, on this level, each character functions as the representative of a specific 19th-century ideology. In a more fundamental way, however, the novel, especially the study of Gilles de Rais in particular and of crime in general, is structured as a debate, the focus and moderator of which is Durtal; the principals of which are, on the one hand, the doctrine of the Catholic church which will interpret these cases in the context of possession and satanism and, on the other hand, the doctrines of Positivist scientific inquiry which will interpret them in the context of various models of madness and criminal behavior. Thus the principal thematic scenario of *Là-Bas* will consist in Durtal's critical investigation of the manner in which the two positions described above attempt to integrate the givens of the case into a plausible, coherent system. In general, Durtal's approach will be to challenge the legitimacy of the scientific approaches to this problem while maintaining the plausibility of various supernatural or paranormal interpretations of the phenomena in question. Of course the case of Gilles de Rais, by its excessive nature, lends itself quite readily to such a strategy.

Among the elements Durtal will underscore in the satanic argument are the following: Gilles de Rais's proximity to Joan of Arc during the One Hundred Years War, his alchemical and daemonic experimentations, the outrageous perversity of his crimes and the sheer number of his victims, his incomprehensible arrest, and his penance prior to his execution. However, Durtal will not accept at face value the traditional beliefs which call for the devil to manifest himself in accordance with a fairly specific morphological code: notably in a combination of certain animal and human forms. Durtal will outline another manifestation of diabolical influence: a crime committed in and for itself is a real, tangible attestation of the devil. Durtal writes: "le Démon n'a pas besoin de s'exhiber sous des traits humains ou bestiaux afin d'attester sa présence; il suffit, pour qu'il s'affirme, qu'il élise domicile en des âmes qu'il exulcère et incite à d'inexplicables crimes. . . . La volonté seule de faire paction avec lui doit pouvoir quelque-fois amener son effusion en nous."[7] Huysmans, in fact, seems to have shared this belief. In his preface to Jules Bois's book *Le Satanisme et la magie* (published in 1895, thus subsequent to Huysmans's conversion), Huysmans, noting various contemporary criminal proceedings, states: "l'on discernerait, en se donnant la peine de lire entre les lignes des dépositions, l'influence, l'intercession même du Très-Bas, dans ces affaires."[8]

As he maintains the plausibility of the interpretation of the Church, Durtal will challenge the presuppositions, methods, and conclusions of Positivist inquiry. His principal targets, at least the better known ones, are the Italian criminologist Cesare Lombroso, the British doctor Henry Maudsley, and the French specialist of neuroses, Jean Martin Charcot. First he challenges the apparent mastery which a specialized medical terminology implies:

> Toutes les théories modernes des Lombroso et des Maudsley ne rendent pas, en effet, compréhensibles les singuliers abus du maréchal. Le classer dans la série des monomanes, rien de plus juste, car il l'était, si par le mot de monomane l'on désigne tout homme que domine une idée fixe. Et alors chacun de nous l'est plus ou moins, depuis le commerçant dont toutes les idées convergent sur une pensée de gain, jusqu'aux artistes absorbés dans l'enfantement d'une oeuvre. Mais pourquoi le maréchal fut-il monomane, comment le devint-il? C'est ce que tous les Lombroso de la terre ignorent.
>
> (p. 104)

Next, Durtal goes right to the heart of the materialist method, which consists in attributing all phenomena to a material cause or principle. Specifically, Durtal challenges Lombroso's model of criminal behavior which ascribes such behavior to a cerebral lesion. In the following passage, Durtal reverses the causal relationship established by Lombroso between such a lesion and criminality.

> Les lésions de l'encéphale, l'adhérence au cerveau de la pie-mère ne signifient absolument rien dans ces questions. Ce sont de simples résultantes, des effets dérivés d'une cause qu'il faudrait expliquer et qu'aucun matérialiste n'explique. Il est vraiment trop facile de déclarer qu'une perturbation des lobes cérébraux produit des assassins et des sacrilèges; les fameux aliénistes de notre temps prétendent que l'analyse du cerveau d'une folle décèle une lésion ou une altération de la substance grise. Et quand même cela serait! il resterait à savoir, pour une femme atteinte de démonomanie par exemple, si la lésion s'est produite parce qu'elle est démonomane ou si elle est devenue démonomane par suite de

cette lésion,—en admettant qu'il y en ait une! Les Comprachicos spirituels ne s'adressent point encore à la chirurgie, n'amputent pas des lobes soi-disant connus, après de studieux trépans; ils se bornent à agir sur l'élève, à lui inculquer des idées ignobles, à développer ses mauvais instincts, à le pousser peu à peu dans la voie du vice, c'est plus sûr; et si cette gymnastique de la persuasion altère chez le patient les tissus de la cervelle, cela prouve justement que la lésion n'est que le dérivé et non la cause d'un état d'âme!

(pp. 104-105)

Then, in the *va et vient* between the 15th and the 19th centuries which is characteristic of *Là-Bas,* Durtal cites the contemporary case of a child who commits a particularly perverse and unmotivated murder. "Il ne témoigne d'aucun repentir, se révèle, dans l'interrogatoire qu'il subit, intelligent et atroce. Le docteur Legrand du Saulle, d'autres spécialistes l'ont surveillé patiemment pendant des mois, jamais ils n'ont pu constater chez lui un symptôme de folie, un semblant de manie même. Et celui-là avait été presque bien élevé, n'avait même pas été perverti par d'autres!" (p. 105). The case is cited precisely because it exceeds the criteria of science and medicine as well as the models of criminality proposed by Lombroso. It resists the causal models which would ascribe crime to a mental disorder (the child is intelligent), a mental illness (he has no symptoms of madness or mania), or to nefarious influences (he has not been corrupted by others).

From the debate between the two positions outlined above on the case of Gilles de Rais, and on various 19th-century criminal cases, Durtal will raise several other points of contention between these two perspectives. One of the specific questions is the problem of contagion, several instances of which the astrologer Gévingey attributes to systems of spirits, by analogy to contagion by bacterial and microscopic organisms.

> L'espace est peuplé de microbes; est-il plus surprenant qu'il regorge aussi d'esprits et de larves? L'eau, le vinaigre foisonnent d'animal-cules, le microscope nous les montre; pourquoi l'air, inaccessible à la vue et aux instruments de l'homme, ne fourmillerait-il pas, comme les autres éléments, d'êtres plus ou moins corporels, d'embryons plus ou moins mûrs?

(p. 129)

The fact that such a proposition is put forth by the eccentric and somewhat ludicrous Gévingey might suggest a certain skepticism with respect to the argument. Yet several chapters later, Durtal appropriates this argument and repeats it almost verbatim:

> Et pourtant! quand on y réfléchit, ne retrouve-t-on pas, aujourd'hui inexpliqués et se survivant sous d'autres noms, les mystères que l'on attribua si longtemps à la crédulité du Moyen Age? A l'hôpital de la Charité, le docteur Luys transfère d'une femme hypnotisée à une

autre des maladies. En quoi cela est-il moins surprenant que les artifices de la goétie, que les sorts jetés par des magiciens ou des bergers? Une larve, un esprit volant, n'est pas, en somme, plus extraordinaire qu'un microbe venu de loin et qui vous empoisonne, sans qu'on s'en doute; l'atmosphère peut tout aussi bien charier des Esprits que des bacilles.

(pp. 190-91)

On each of the points described above, Durtal's strategy consists in opposing two interpretative systems on a series of topics, and each time, as has been noted, Durtal will explicitly seek to demonstrate the viability of the religious interpretation and overtly challenge the scientific or Positivist interpretations. One should not, however, jump to conclusions too quickly regarding this strategy. It is, at this point, more of a heuristic or polemical gesture than an ideological one. Durtal's strategy is, again, that of a moderator, not that of an apologist for the Church's position. Indeed, Durtal's intention is not to simply prove or sanction the position of the Church, but to maintain the duality of positions which the scientific or Positivist interpretations precisely seek to reduce. (This is very clearly Henry Maudsley's project. His book, *Natural Causes and Supernatural Seemings* (1886) attempts deconstructions, based on medical models, of such apparently supernatural phenomena as Mary Magdalene's testimony of the resurrection of Christ, attributed by Maudsley to hallucinations due to an epileptic condition.[9])

If Durtal will not, in *Là-Bas,* explicitly side with one or the other of the positions which inform the argument, the question of the resolution of the debate is raised. (Some passages of *Là-Bas* leave little doubt as to which position has Huysmans's tacit approval, as his conversion to Catholicism, subsequent to the publication of *Là-Bas,* makes clear in retrospect.) Yet within the confines of the debate as it is presented in *Là-Bas,* the tension between the two arguments is not reduced dialectically or by other means, but it is resolved. How does this happen?

Là-Bas presents, among other things, the chronicle of its own genesis, specifically, the chronicle of Durtal's research on the case of Gilles de Rais. One such episode which Durtal recounts is a trip to the Vendée to visit the ruins of the fortresses which were the setting of Gilles de Rais's crimes. While there, Durtal experiences the persistence of the events of the 15th century in the popular imagination, in the form of the legend of Blue-Beard.

> Il s'était installé dans le petit hameau qui s'étend au bas de l'ancien donjon et il constatait combien la légende de Barbe-Bleue était restée vivace, dans ce pays isolé en Vendée, sur les confins bretons. C'est un jeune homme qui a mal fini, disaient les jeunes femmes; plus peureuses, les aïeules se signaient, en longeant, le soir,

le pied des murs; le souvenir des enfants égorgés persistait; le maréchal, connu seulement par son surnom, épouvantait encore.

(pp. 105-06)

This episode seems to suggest a different debate, though one which is related to the first one we have identified and discussed. Indeed, the act of the "aïeules peureuses" who make the sign of the cross, reinscribes the story within the conceptual sphere of religion, presupposing the explanation of daemonic possession. The younger women, no doubt free of certain prejudices (in accordance with the stereotype of the "aïeules dévotes"), articulate an alternative. Their phrase "C'est un jeune homme qui a mal fini," in its admirable economy, outlines a narrative: making no epistemological claims, it simply tells a story and thus founds the legend.

Such an alternative solution to the principal debate which organizes and structures *Là-Bas* defines Durtal's/Huysmans's aesthetic project in this novel. *Là-Bas* begins with a rather violent rejection of Naturalism on the grounds, precisely, of its reductive Positivist assumptions[10] (a rejection, which, incidentally, quite offended Zola). This is followed by Durtal's formulation of a new aesthetic of the novel, one derived from the aesthetic revealed to Durtal by the painting of the *Crucifixion* by Mattheus Grüne-wald, in Durtal's words, "le prototype exaspéré de l'art" (pp. 16-17). Such an aesthetic receives the apparently paradoxical description of "un naturalisme spiritualiste":

> Il faudrait, se disait-il, garder la véracité du document, la précision du détail, la langue étoffée et nerveuse du réalisme, mais il faudrait aussi se faire puisatier d'âme et ne pas vouloir expliquer le mystère par les maladies des sens; le roman, si cela se pouvait, devrait se diviser de lui-même en deux parts, néanmoins soudées ou plutôt confondues, comme elles le sont dans la vie, celle de l'âme, celle du corps, et s'occuper de leurs réactifs, de leurs conflits, de leur entente. Il faudrait, en un mot, suivre la grande voie si profondément creusée par Zola, mais il serait nécessaire aussi de tracer en l'air un chemin parallèle, une autre route, d'atteindre les en deça et les après, de faire, en un mot, un naturalisme spiritualiste; ce serait autrement fier, autrement complet, autrement fort!

(p. 8)

One will note, moreover, that each of the terms of the above formulation corresponds to one of the principals of the debate on the question of crime: *naturalisme,* of course, being the analogue, in aesthetic terms, of the Positivist, scientific methods and intentions; *spiritualiste,* on the other hand, corresponding to the doctrine and the interpretation of the Church. Hence, on the metatextual level of Durtal's writing of a novel about Gilles de Rais,[11] *Là-Bas* chronicles an aesthetic investigation which is a direct corollary to the primary ideological debate between Catholicism and Positivism which informs and structures the novel.

Thus the epistemological claims and assumptions of each position in the debate are modified, and it is resolved in aesthetic terms in accordance with the model suggested by the women Durtal encounters in his field research. This is a narrative/fictive model whose basis is as old as discourse itself: popular culture, legends, stories. *Là-Bas,* thus, in its attempt to renew the genre of the novel, situates itself in a discursive tradition as a repetition, a retelling, a recreation of the legend. And, as a retelling of the Gilles de Rais legend, but also as the story of Durtal's writing of the story, *Là-Bas* will present the process and the result of the aesthetic model which resolves the ideological debate on the case of Gilles de Rais and on the question of crime. Thus does the question of crime as it is studied, yea debated, in *Là-Bas* play a critical role in the development of Huysmans's aesthetic of the novel as well as in his spiritual destiny.

Notes

1. Michel Foucault, "Les Jeux du Pouvoir: (Entretien)," in *Politiques de la philosophie* (Paris: Editions Grasset & Fasquelle, 1976), p. 169.

2. Louis Chevalier, *Classes laborieuses et classes dangereuses à Paris pendant la première moitié du XIXe siècle* (Paris: Librairie Plon, 1958), pp. iv-v.

3. Ibid, p. 5.

4. As a case study of Gilles de Rais, *Là-Bas* is in large part inspired by Abbot Bossard's book which first appeared in 1885. See Abbé Eugène Bossard, *Gilles de Rais, Maréchal de France* (Paris: Champion, 1886, 2e édition).

5. Pierre James, "*Là-Bas,* Gilles de Rais et la Bibliographie," *Bulletin de la Société J.-K. Huysmans,* No. 25 (1952), pp. 225-28.

6. In his program for his theatre of cruelty, Artaud lists among other items the following: "4° L'histoire de Barbe-Bleue reconstituée selon les archives, et avec une idée nouvelle de l'érotisme et de la cruauté." See *Le Théâtre et son double* (Paris: Editions Gallimard, 1964), p. 151. Roger Planchon's *Gilles de Rais: Miracle en dix tableaux* (Paris: Editions Gallimard, 1975) seems to have been inspired by Artaud's note in *Le Théâtre et son double.* See also Georges Bataille, *Le Procès de Gilles de Rais* (Paris: Jean-Jacques Pauvert, 1965). Denis Hollier has an interesting article in which he relates Bataille's book to Artaud's theatre of cruelty: "La Tragédie de Gilles de Rais au 'Théâtre de la Cruauté,'" *L'Arc* No. 44 (1971), pp. 77-86. Finally, see Michel Tournier, *Gilles et Jeanne* (Paris: Editions Gallimard, 1983).

7. Joris-Karl Huysmans, *Là-Bas* (Paris: Plon, 1908), p. 104. All subsequent quotations from the text of *Là-Bas* will refer to this edition.

8. Jules Bois, *Le Satanisme et la magie* (Paris: Léon Chailley, 1895), p. x.

9. Henry Maudsley, *Natural Causes and Supernatural Seemings* (London: Kegan Paul, Trench and Co., 1886).

10. "Tu lèves les épaules, mais voyons, qu'a-t-il donc vu, ton naturalisme, dans tous ces décourageants mystères qui nous entourent? Rien.—Quand il s'est agi d'expliquer une passion quelconque, quand il a fallu sonder une plaie, déterger même le plus benin des bobos de l'âme, il a tout mis sur le compte des appétits et des instincts. Rut et coup de folie, ce sont là ses seules diathèses. En somme, il n'a fouillé que des dessous de nombril et banalement divagué dès qu'il s'approchait des aines; c'est un herniaire de sentiments, un bandagiste d'âme et voilà tout!" (pp. 5-6).

11. On the question of the "mise en abyme" structure of *Là-Bas,* see Max Milner, "*Là-Bas*: L'écriture dans le roman," in *Revue des sciences humaines: Joris-Karl Huysmans,* No. 170-171, 1978, pp. 9-20.

Christopher Lloyd (essay date 1990)

SOURCE: Lloyd, Christopher. "Monsters." In *J.-K. Huysmans and the* Fin-de-siècle *Novel*, pp. 83-113. Edinburgh: Edinburgh University Press, 1990.

[*In the following excerpt, Lloyd explains Huysmans' treatment of the satanic and mystical figure of Gilles de Rais in* Là-bas, *as well as the spiritual world of good and evil in the novel, concluding that whereas the author created in this work "powerful, memorably monstrous characters and visions," he failed to depict "true mysticism."*]

Good and Evil

It is in *Là-bas,* of course, that Huysmans produced his most notorious and engaging blend of mysticism, mystery and mystification and attempted to raise the natural and unnatural monstrosities of *En rade* and *A rebours* to a supernatural dimension. Alone of Huysmans' books, *Là-bas* is actually an adventure novel. (It has appeared in English in the series 'The Dennis Wheatley Library of the Occult', Sphere Books, 1974.) For once Huysmans manages to create the pulse of narrative excitement which is a feature of Maupassant and Zola at their best, a quality barely present in, say, Flaubert, whose massively sculpted descriptions and undermining of action create a peculiarly static sort of fiction. *Là-bas* has been compared to Gide's *Les Faux-Monnayeurs* thirty-five years later, in the sense that both works rather narcissistically strive to embody a theory of fiction which is proposed within their texts (e.g. by R. Kanters, *CTSJ,* 1963). But in addition, unlike more recent versions of experimental fiction, both novels manage to capture the reader's imagination on the level of incident, deftly interweaving different events and characters without lapsing into gratuitousness or incoherence.

Là-bas recounts three interlocking sets of adventures. The novelist turned historian Durtal studying the life of Gilles de Rais, the infamous fifteenth-century murderer and satanist. Durtal becomes entangled with a society lady, Mme Chantelouve, who turns out to be herself a practising satanist and associate of the notorious Canon Docre (this canon is fired by such blasphematory zeal that he has the Cross tattooed on the soles of his feet). Thirdly, Durtal is further initiated into occult lore by his friend Dr des Hermies and the astrologer Gévingey at the home of the bell-ringer Carhaix, who lives in the tower of Saint-Sulpice. To this cast list may be added the thaumaturge Dr Johannès, like Docre a defrocked priest. When Gévingey is bewitched by Docre, Johannès successfully engages in an epic battle for the astrologer's salvation. Meantime Durtal is introduced by Mme Chantelouve to the ritual of the Black Mass, and six intercalated episodes retail in explicit detail the atrocities, trials and repentance of Gilles de Rais.

Apart from Durtal and des Hermies, all these characters clearly exceed the bounds of normality, unlike the 'cupides bourgeois' and 'abominables mufles' (ch.2) who were Durtal's acquaintances as a man of letters. Gilles de Rais, erroneously nicknamed Barbe-Bleue by folk memory, is a 'monstre' (ch.2), an ogre on a massive scale. As Durtal proudly announces, 'le marquis de Sade n'est qu'un timide bourgeois, qu'un piètre fantaisiste à côté de lui!' (ch.4). Canon Docre too is a 'monstre authentique' (ch.5), though he usually satisfies his homicidal instincts by casting spells from a safe distance, breeding a menagerie of white mice for this purpose. He is 'le Gilles de Rais moderne' nevertheless (ch.9). Mme Hyacinthe Chantelouve, who claims the power to enjoy carnally any man, dead or living, at her will, and who has driven her first husband to suicide, is aptly named, as a flower of evil, a vampirical she-wolf. She presents herself as a 'monstre d'égoïsme' (ch.10). Carhaix, a former seminarist now defending the lost art of campanology, is an orthodox Catholic, but with his ghastly pallor, his avoidance of 'les rues d'en bas', he is 'en dehors de l'humanité, dans une aérienne tombe' (ch.3). Furthermore, Docre's Black Mass is presided over by an obscene Christ; for the Canon, Jesus too is a 'monstre', a sly hypocrite (ch.19). The first chapter of the book presents Grünewald's crucified Christ as a 'charogne éployée', a monstrously degraded redeemer. Finally, the novel is set in Paris in 1888-89: parallel to these excursions into the marvellous, it charts the rise to fame of another *monstre sacré*, General Boulanger, whose short-lived electoral success in January 1889 closes the novel (he committed suicide in September 1891, five months after **Là-bas** was published).

Huysmans' account of Gilles de Rais is indebted to the abbé Bossard's biography of 1885 (as he effectively admits in chapters two and twelve). But Huysmans insists much more on what he calls Gilles's mysticism (whereas a modern commentator like Georges Bataille labels him a 'dévot superstitieux' and emphasises the social causes of his crimes (1965:95)). Huysmans also seems to have invented an episode such as Gilles's delirious vision in the forest (ch.11) for his own purposes. None the less, a comment by Bossard offers a useful opening perspective on Huysmans' Gilles de Rais: 'tout dans sa vie peut se résumer en ces deux mots qui le caractérisent, spectacle et sensation' (1885:183). When Durtal jokingly calls him 'le des Esseintes du quinzième siècle!' (ch.4), a bolder explorer of 'le territoire des à Rebours', he is depicting Gilles as an aesthete, a bibliophile and man of culture in an age when few of his peers were even literate, but also stressing the excessiveness of his ventures, which reduce the neurotic Duke as much as the divine Marquis to a 'piètre fantaisiste' in comparison. Not only is Gilles de Rais a dandy on a grand scale, spending his entire fortune in eight years on extravagant displays, he is also able to conduct his quest for the absolute in spheres forbidden to the nineteenth century with its materialistic, humanitarian considerations. Unlike des Esseintes, who is foiled by moral and physical weaknesses, Gilles de Rais, at one with his time, is able to enjoy the limits of good and evil, of self-indulgence and degradation.

Huysmans' gleeful enthusiasm for this horrific figure can be rather disturbing. Visiting Tiffauges in 1889, he writes jubilantly to Odilon Redon: 'Les ruines de son château sont formidables et chacune des oubliettes qu'on ouvre, renferme encore les ossements des enfants qu'il violait et égorgeait, en invoquant le Diable!' (quoted in *BSH,* 1957:96). While a recent biographer, Michel Bataille, prudently refuses to describe Gilles's atrocities, Huysmans on the contrary goes to it with sadistic gusto, lingering on the aesthetics of torture rather in the fashion of Mirbeau's *Le Jardin des supplices*— when, for instance, the Marshal holds a macabre beauty contest with the decapitated heads of his victims (ch.11). Colin Wilson assesses this manner unsympathetically:

> One senses a curious immaturity in Huysmans' interest in Gilles; when he describes him disembowelling children and masturbating on their intestines, he is not really aware of the horror of the subject; it strikes him as bizarre, freakish and therefore fascinating.
>
> (1979:448)

What Wilson fails to see, however, is that this cruelty is more than an example of *fin-de-siècle* sadism. Huysmans is attracted to the Middle Ages precisely because of the period's 'immaturity'; or rather, it is 'plus naïf et moins bête' than modernity (ch.22). In this brutal, Christian society, suffering need not be seen in complicated humanitarian terms, but as part of a pure metaphysical spectacle. Once Gilles's soul is purified, his crimes count for nothing; he can pass from an extreme of evil to good and sincerely expect, without presumption, to be received into Paradise. As Max Milner argues (*BSH,* 1979), Huysmans attempts to show that evil for the Christian is a mystical rather than an ethical concept; sin is not the infraction of a law, but the refusal of love, of God or of one's neighbour.

All the same, a reader who fails to share the extreme 'Catholic' viewpoint displayed in the treatment of Gilles de Rais may have difficulty in taking Huysmans' interpretation very seriously. I cannot help thinking, in this context, of the mocking *reductio ad absurdum* of the Catholic notion of repentance in 'Le Juif latin', Apollinaire's story about a penitent sadist in *L'Hérésiarque et cie.* Having divided Mme Chantelouve into three separate characters (a salon lady, a whore, a satanist), Durtal makes a similar tripartite division in the case of Gilles de Rais (pious soldier, artist in crime, penitent). In other words, he prefers to emphasise the extremes of his behaviour rather than look for a rational pattern of motivation and continuity. Huysmans never ceases to tell us that Gilles is 'un homme dont l'âme était saturée d'idées mystiques' (ch.4), and makes Gilles's confession (on which most of the evidence against him is based) the mainstay of his demonstration of Gilles's transition from evil to good, sacrilege to piety. In fact, his actions might equally be said to be all of a piece: the excess of his remorse matches the excess of his sadistic frenzy; more sinisterly, the appallingly detailed confession of his atrocities enables him to relive them, exchanging the voluptuousness of torture for that of repentance, and enjoying in addition the 'spectacle et sensation' he produces before his dumbstruck audience. Re-enacting his crimes verbally, he is doubly their author. He orchestrates his penitence and execution, as Hyatte suggests, staging his own martyrdom in the fashion of medieval hagiology. Thus he actually gains public sanction for his pleasures and dies in glory. For the Middle Ages, good and evil seem to be virtually interchangeable.

Psychological analysis is, then, subordinated to a theological demonstration of supposedly medieval virtues. Huysmans wants to see Gilles de Rais in terms of absolutes, not as a social deviant or psychopath. This leads to an apparent contradiction in his presentation of good and evil. Sometimes, they are almost identical: 'du Mysticisme exalté au Satanisme exaspéré, il n'y a qu'un pas. Dans l'au-delà, tout se touche' (ch.4). But elsewhere they are 'aux deux pôles opposés de l'âme' (ch.8) and still more irrevocably opposed to 'la bourgeoisie de l'âme' of the nineteenth century (ch.8). The explanation is that, along the horizontal axis, so to speak, good and evil are at opposite ends; whereas on the vertical axis, which separates modern materialistic mediocrity from the medieval 'au-delà', they merge. This outlook may well seem to be antihumanitarian, irrational, and excessive; both good and evil come to depend on extremes of behaviour more than anything else.

Pierre Cogny points out, in his edition of *Là-bas,* that there are actually two spectacles of horror in *Là-bas*: the atrocities which Gilles de Rais inflicts on his victims are matched by the agony endured by the expiatory victim, Grünewald's Christ. Whether, as Cogny claims, one illustrates 'la mystique blanche' and the other 'la mystique noire' or not (ed. 1978:27), the initial impression made on the reader in each case is identical: an anguished display of physical torment, described in complaisant detail. The hideous Christ of the first chapter has been reduced to the state of a putrescent piece of meat: 'L'heure des sanies était venue; la plaie fluviale du flanc ruisselait plus épaisse, inondait la hanche d'un sang pareil au jus foncé des mûres; des sérosités rosâtres, des petits-laits, des eaux semblables à des vins de Moselle gris, suintaient de la poitrine . . .' (ch.1). The culinary images in particular (blood as blackberry juice, pus as whey or Moselle) make this spectacle of a Christ crucified like 'le boeuf écorché' of *Le Drageoir aux épices* far more disturbing than Canon Docre's intentionally blasphemous, leering, ithyphallic Christ. Yet this passage is meant, not as decadent blasphemy, but as a demonstration of the integration of spirit and flesh, of the validity of the Passion and Incarnation.

Huysmans' insistence on intensity and excess in his presentation of the 'au-delà' is not uncommon among authors who subscribe to a decadent Catholicism. One thinks of Baudelaire's 'Enfer ou Ciel, qu'importe?', or Barbey d'Aurevilly in *Les Diaboliques*: 'l'enfer, c'est le ciel en creux. Le mot *diabolique* ou *divin,* appliqué à l'intensité des jouissances, exprime la même chose, c'est-à-dire des sensations qui vont jusqu'au surnaturel' ('Le Dessous de cartes d'une partie de whist'). Both Grünewald's Christ and Gilles de Rais's crimes certainly show extremes of sensation, and both seek to enact a mystical transmutation. G.E. Kaiser argues that Grünewald's Christ illustrates the notion in Christian exegesis of the 'Folly of the Cross'. Christ redeems both human baseness and the inhuman monster of madness in man: 'Le Christ, par son incarnation et par la démesure de sa chute jusqu'à la déraison animale et folle, transforme la dégradation en acte de gloire et d'ascension' (1983:108). As for Gilles de Rais, having sought and failed to find the philosopher's stone, the key to the universe, he carries out his murders in part as an attempt to make contact with Satan, offering human sacrifices to the spirit of evil, his frenzy ever increasing as these experiments again fail to produce supernatural manifestations (though all the while he may be possessed unwittingly by the Devil).

Huysmans does not allow for this sort of ambiguity in his version of the Karlsruhe Crucifixion (Durtal actually sees the painting in Cassel). He insists relentlessly on the physical agony and moral ignominy of Christ ('crever ainsi qu'un bandit, ainsi qu'un chien', ch.1). What strikes Durtal when he first cries with astonishment on seeing the painting (and most art critics agree it is a deeply disturbing work) is its heightened, blood-curdling realism ('Grünewald était le plus forcené des réalistes'), which makes the transformation and revelation of the spiritual, of the 'céleste Superessence', all the more startling. 'Dans cette toile, se révélait le chef-d'oeuvre de l'art acculé, sommé de rendre l'invisible et le tangible, de manifester l'immondice éplorée du corps, de sublimer la détresse infinie de l'âme.' The invisible, by definition, can only be rendered symbolically. Yet Huysmans' transformation seems to be meant literally. The invisible and the tangible exist on equal terms; it is as though the body, when driven to its limits, quite literally forces the soul to emerge, as though substance when squeezed sufficiently produces spirit. Thus is seen in all the Primitives 'une transformation de la matière détendue ou comprimée, une échappée hors des sens, sur d'infinis lointains.'

Grünewald and the Primitives, of course, are meant to offer not only a mystic revelation but also an aesthetic model for a new spiritual realism. Although Gilles de Rais's atrocities are also seen in aesthetic, spiritual terms, these paroxysms of cruelty lead nowhere: 'l'au-delà du Mal ne s'atteint pas. [. . .] Il haletait, insatiable, devant le vide' (ch.11). Suffering has to be freely accepted by the expiatory victim to have a positive spiritual value; thus Gilles himself, after his repentance, can also be presented as a sort of mystic. In other words, what ultimately counts is an act of faith—on the part of the participants in the Passion depicted by Grünewald, but also, perhaps, on the part of the reader of *Là-bas*. Gilles's experience surely does show that matter alone, however much it is 'comprimée', produces nothing. Mysticism stems from an acceptance of Christian mystery, not from artistic form or from intensified naturalism.

Gilles de Rais's excesses are a final, extreme statement of the exploration of the material world—the world literally reduced to material for the ogre devouring his 'souper charnel' (ch.11)—which forms the basis of naturalism. His destruction of human 'material' is not merely intended to reduce his victims to objects for sexual or aesthetic pleasure, but to be a quest for spirit, for a means of escape, via God or Satan. But while Satan remains absent, the world Gilles tries to liquidate finally overwhelms him in his hallucinatory visions in the forest of Tiffauges—visions which take up the succession from the nightmares in *A rebours* and *En rade,* since, once again, the character is assailed by a nature presented in the form of obscene sexuality (the phallic, vaginal shapes of the trees, the swollen breasts and but-tocks of the clouds), a sexuality which is hideously dis-eased ('une maladrerie de la terre, une clinique véneri-enne d'arbres', ch.11).

Gilles de Rais fails in his enterprise to conquer the goods of this world (the philosopher's stone which he seeks not only transmutes base metals, thus granting endless riches, but cures all ills, giving eternal life). Sa-tan is the evil force behind the material world (in chap-ter one it is suggested that money or capital, the moti-vating forces of the modern world, are the work of the Devil), but he remains enticingly elusive—mysteriously beating two of the Marshal's associates, but refusing to appear to Gilles. In fact, as Max Milner argues (*BSH*, 1979), Satan is not simply absent in person, but an ab-sence in *Là-bas*: lack of love or compassion (hence Gilles's unimaginable cruelty), an intangible force which possesses Gilles without his knowledge or even manipulates the economy of capitalist society. At the same time, however, one notes a similar absence of positive forces for good in *Là-bas*: Huysmans' Christ does not appear as a glorious Saviour, enhancing man-kind through the power of his charity, but as a degraded, rejected figure, physically defiled by taking on the sins of the world. One might argue that the spiritual plane as a whole exists as an absence in *Là-bas*; what is con-stantly presented amounts to a series of highly physical spectacles—the torments of the Crucifixion, the roll-call of Gilles de Rais's crimes, the hysterical erotomania of the Black Mass, all depicted in lurid sensual detail. In Milner's view, the novel expresses 'l'angoisse d'un *manque* fondamental, la conviction que si la littérature manque le réel, c'est parce que le réel [. . .] ne peut être présent dans la littérature et dans l'art en général que comme manque' (*RSH*, 1978:19).

The objects of Huysmans' fictional world are the oppo-site of 'real' used in this sense. Steaks turn out to be il-lusory under the fork; in *A vau-l'eau* the adulteration of food metaphorically suggests a universal loss of val-ues—'tout fiche le camp' (ch.3), everything collapses when probed. In *Là-bas,* normally the real is either flawed (and thus unreal) or unattainable—as the title it-self indicates. The nineteenth century has managed to falsify even manure, as Durtal notes (ch.8), in its inces-sant adulteration of substances. What is most real, most authentically valued, is often what is most removed from the reality of everyday experience. Thus a 'real' love affair would be free from all sensual contact, ac-cording to Durtal: 'Il n'y a que ces amours réelles et in-tangibles, ces amours faites de mélancolies éloignées et de regrets qui valent!' (ch.13). Constantly, in fact, he prefers imaginary experience to the actuality of his day and age (whose inescapable presence prevails with the cries of the electioneering mob at the end of the novel, though perhaps only in the short term; their cardboard hero General Boulanger, set against the valiant if bloody

Maréchal de Rais, would flee the country within a few months). Durtal approaches both Gilles de Rais and Mme Chantelouve through writing, vicariously enjoying Gilles's experience of evil and becoming infatuated with his unknown correspondent through an exchange of letters when fictitious sentiments become genuine. While Durtal seems at best indifferent to the real, non-symbolic suffering of Gilles's victims, he is able to transmute a painting of the Passion into a mystical state-ment—for Grünewald's message is perceived through, or rather created by, an aesthetic filter. Hence too his fascination with the sin of 'Pygmalionism'—the artist committing incest with a creature of his imagination (ch.12). The physical presence of Mme Chantelouve, on the other hand, or personal participation in a Black Mass, are seen as degrading and disgusting.

Thus, paradoxical as it may seem, what is 'absent' is felt to be most real—be it the Middle Ages as opposed to modernity, idealised love as opposed to sexual con-gress, or in Grünewald's painting, the possibility of re-demption beyond a frenzied image of degradation. But mystery remains more important than true mysticism in *Là-bas.* Huysmans may well have peopled this novel, like *A rebours* and *En rade* before it, with powerful, memorably monstrous characters and visions, and cre-ated his own peculiarly hybrid form of fiction, but the success of his spiritual endeavours is another matter, as the next chapter of this study will show.

Bibliography

Abbreviations used in this bibliography are given at the end of the preface above. Works in English are pub-lished in London, and works in French in Paris, unless otherwise stated.

Works by J.-K. Huysmans

A vau-l'eau, Brussels, Kistemaeckers, 1882

A rebours, Charpentier, 1884

En rade, Tresse et Stock, 1887

Là-bas, Tresse et Stock, 1891

Other Works Cited or Consulted

Apollinaire, Guillaume, 1973: *L'Hérésiarque et Cie,* Le Livre de poche

Bossard, Abbé E., 1885: *Gilles de Rais,* Champion

Cogny, Pierre, 1979: 'Un projet avorté de roman: *La Faim* de J.-K. Huysmans', *RHLF,* 79, 835-46

———, 1987: *J.-K. Huysmans: de l'écriture à l'Ecriture,* Editions Téqui

Colin, René-Pierre, 1978: 'Huysmans et les saluts du "vieux garçon"', in *La Femme au XIXe siècle,* ed. R. Bellet, Lyon, Presses Universitaires, 113-21

Huysmans, J.-K., MS: Manuscript of *A rebours,* Bibliothèque Nationale, n.a.fr. 15761

————, 1977: *A rebours,* ed. M. Fumaroli, Gallimard, Folio

————, 1978: *A rebours,* ed. P. Waldner, Garnier-Flammarion

————, 1981: *A rebours,* ed. Rose Fortassier, Imprimerie Nationale

————, 1956: *A vau-l'eau,* ed. I. Gotta, Rome, Signorelli

————, 1984: *En rade,* ed. Jean Borie, Gallimard, Folio

————, 1978: *Là-bas,* ed. Pierre Cogny, Garnier-Flammarion

————, 1985: *Là-bas,* ed. Yves Hersant, Gallimard, Folio

Kraiser, Grant E., 1983: 'Descendre pour monter: la tête en bas de *Là-bas*', *Mosaic,* 16, 97-111

Milner, Max, 1979: 'Allocution sous le cloître Saint-Séverin', *BSH,* no 70

Mirbeau, Octave, 1957: *Le Jardin des supplices,* Fasquelle

Wilson, Colin, 1979: *The Occult,* Panther, Granada Publishing

References have been given in abbreviated form within the text. For works of fiction, divisions by part and/or chapter are cited, as appropriate (e.g. *Germinal,* part 2, ch. 4). For journals and editions of correspondence, the date of writing is cited (e.g. Goncourt, *Journal,* 2 March 1872). For critical and other secondary works, date of publication and page reference are given after the author's name (e.g. Cogny, 1953: 29). Full details of publication will be found in the bibliography for all works quoted.

The following abbreviations are used for periodicals:

BSH: Bulletin de la Société J.-K. Huysmans

CTSJ: Cahiers de la Tour Saint-Jacques

RHLF: Revue d'histoire littéraire de la France

RSH: Revue des sciences humaines

Richard Bales (essay date 1992)

SOURCE: Bales, Richard. "Huysmans' *Là-bas*: The Apotheosis of the Word." *Orbis Litterarum* 47, no. 5 (1992): 209-25.

[*In the following essay, Bales argues that the author's self-conscious manner of textual production is a major theme of* Là-bas, *which he describes as a highly sophisticated narrative and Huysmans' masterpiece.*]

By any standards, Huysmans' novels are curious affairs. Never totally fictional, yet never entirely autobiographical, they have exercised generations of critics with their obstinate refusal to settle down within a single comfortable genre definition. The early works are admittedly relatively straightforward and capable of satisfactory pigeon-holing: to all intents and purposes, the Naturalist label is accurate enough for **Marthe, Les Sœurs Vatard** and **En ménage.** But with the appearance of **A rebours** in 1884 a change in subject-matter and technique occurs, one which at a single blow questions the very genre of 'novel' itself. As Christopher Lloyd says in his recent study of Huysmans' novels, 'critics have struggled to interpret **A rebours** either as parody or autobiography.'[1] Evidently the desire to label is a strong priority, one which Lloyd dismisses in his continuation: 'in fact, des Esseintes [the main character] is a deliberately ambiguous figure, both the individual whose biography the novel recounts [. . .] and, on the other hand, a pretext or reflector for speculations which encompass wide areas of experience and culture.' (ibid.)

The fact is, the word 'novel' is a *pis-aller* when applied to **A rebours**: there is no one readily available label which would accurately describe such a heterogeneous work. 'Novel' is a label of convenience. And such will be the case with the rest of Huysmans' prose works—we call them novels for want of a better appellation. Indeed, they fail to perform one function which is taken for granted in normal novels - they no longer exist as discrete units. On the contrary, there is a 'flow', an interdependence, in the sequence of **Là-bas, En route, La Cathédrale** and **L'Oblat.** Barriers are broken down, not just in the traditional conceptions of novelistic subject-matter, but between novels themselves.[2]

There is a straightforward reason for these facts, of course: the heavily autobiographical nature of the major preoccupations in each novel, signalled by the invention of Huysmans' *alter ego,* Durtal. Further focused by conversion to Catholicism, the story of Huysmans/Durtal becomes virtually an autobiographical chronicle transposed into a seemingly more objective biographical mode (the last three novels). Looked at from the standpoint of normal critical expectations, these works are bound to be labelled failures by those who look for such novelistic prerequisites as intrigue or plot.[3] But this is not to say they are no good: they address different matters from those one normally encounters in novels—more esoteric, no doubt, and the form reflects this.

Là-bas is a slightly different case, it seems to me, lying as it does between Huysmans' earlier phase, where each work is clearly conceived as a discrete unit, and the later phase, where divisions are blurred and continuity is privileged. The brand new invention of Durtal, too, betokens a freshness which will evaporate in the later works. Finally, there are overlapping plots which, however unorthodox, do genuinely provide areas of tension and unpredictability rare in Huysmans' output. In short, *Là-bas* is an exceptionally 'readable' text ('lisible' in Barthes' sense), of a high degree of narrative sophistication. In my view, it is his masterpiece.

DOCUMENTATION

Là-bas is above all a compendium of information, compiled through the accumulation of documents. The novel is itself a document, of course; so there is a twofold action here. On the one hand, within the story of *Là-bas,* Durtal never ceases to gather together material relevant to his study of Gilles de Rais, along with the ancillary interest in present-day diabolism. And on the other, Huysmans, as author, displays an impressive rigour in assembling his novel along documentary lines (clearly the legacy of his Naturalist period).[4]

As far as Durtal's *modus operandi* is concerned, he is clearly a methodical soul, and is never happier than when surrounded by the tools of his trade: 'Il se leva, se promena dans sa petite pièce; les manuscrits qui s'entassaient sur la table, ses notes sur le maréchal de Rais dit Barbe-Bleue, le déridèrent.'[5] He places the greatest trust in documentary material, so much so that when, typically, an appreciation such as 'les documents sont précis' is proffered (139) its very brevity bespeaks authority. And, in Zolaesque fashion, he undertakes the obligatory trip to the place where much of the action he is studying occurred:

> [I]l a dû se passer de terribles nuits dans cette forteresse, se dit Durtal, revenant à ce château de Tiffauges qu'il avait visité, l'an dernier, alors qu'il voulait, pour son travail, vivre dans le paysage où vécut de Rais et humer les ruines.
>
> Il s'était installé dans le petit hameau qui s'étend au bas de l'ancien donjon et il constatait combien la légende de Barbe-Bleue était restée vivace, dans ce pays isolé en Vendée, sur les confins bretons.
>
> (135)

Nothing could better characterize the spirit of Durtal's literary venture than this brief episode where he recalls his visit to Tiffauges: the act of being in close contact with one's material, of somehow *witnessing* past events by virtue of this proximity, carries with it a sort of truth to fact which Durtal relishes.

More often than not, this truth resides in books, and in seeking out what might have been Gilles de Rais' reading matter, Durtal makes an implicit comment on his own professional bias towards the printed (or manuscript) word. Thus, Gilles' alchemical readings are tracked down:

> L'alchimie était déja très développée, un siècle avant qu'il [Gilles] ne naquît. Les écrits d'Albert le Grand, d'Arnaud de Villeneuve, de Raymond Lulle, étaient en-

tre les mains des hermétiques. Les manuscrits de Nicolas Flamel circulaient; nul doute que Gilles, qui raffolait des volumes étranges, des pièces rares, ne les ait acquis. [. . .] Ces œuvres étaient [. . .] défendues et par conséquent enviables; il est certain que Gilles les a longuement étudiées, mais de là à les comprendre, il y a loin!

> Ces livres constituaient, en effet, le plus incroyable des galimatias, le plus inintelligible des grimoires. Tout était en allégories, en métaphores cocasses et obscures, en emblèmes incohérents, en paraboles embrouillées, en énigmes bourrées de chiffres!

> (98)

The infectious delight with which Durtal dips into the chaotic world of alchemical manuscripts is all the more validated by being consonant with the spirit of Gilles de Rais himself, and with that of a singularly chaotic age, the incomprehensibility of which is celebrated in suitably emphatic style with exotic vocabulary and well-placed exclamation-marks. Such is Durtal's obsession with detail that it finds a fulfilment in the study of these curious texts, a study which can only result in an assertion of inscrutability.

This obsession is carried a stage further in the excursion into present-day diabolism which Durtal unexpectedly finds himself engaged upon. By a curious turn of events, he discovers that Madame Chantelouve, whose aim in life seems to be to seduce him, knows the infamous diabolist chanoine Docre—indeed she had at one time had him as confessor. In the face of her reluctance to tell him anything, Durtal no fewer than three times in the space of eight pages ponders on the 'renseignements qu'elle devait posséder sur le chanoine Docre' (241).[6] Such repetition speaks eloquently of Durtal's thirst for documentation.

The reader even has at his disposal a form of external corroboration of Durtal's documentary bent, in the shape of notations attributable to the narrator. It is as if the latter provides the occasional snapshot of Durtal as he goes about his task of gleaning information. Sentences such as 'puis il inspecta les pièces' (176) abound, underlining as they do Durtal's essentially visual process of perception. Any newcomer to the scene is subjected to a thorough visual examination—here, for example, the astrologer Gévingey:

> Tandis que la femme du sonneur achevait de mettre la table, Durtal examina le nouveau venu.
>
> C'était un petit homme, coiffé d'un feutre noir et mou, enveloppé de même qu'un conducteur d'omnibus dans un caban à capuchon de drap bleu.
>
> (157)[7]

A lengthy description ensues. In this manner, a sort of inward-moving dynamic is presented: first we see Durtal in the process of observing, then we move into his mind and share his observation. Nothing extraordinary in this, of course; yet it does stress the way in which the visual component is of vital importance to the construction of **Là-bas,** both on the level of authorial presentation and on that of the main character's habitual mode of perception and registration of events.

This dual process is most clearly visible in the Black Mass episode (ch. XIX). Significantly prefaced by yet another document, in the shape of an advance disavowal which Durtal is forced to write (286), the chapter is a welter of horrendous images and sounds. As the most intense part of the novel, it fittingly displays Durtal hard at 'work':

> Il la dévisagea [Mme Chantelouve]; elle était pâle; la bouche était serrée, les yeux pluvieux battaient.
>
> —Le voici, murmura-t-elle, tout à coup, pendant que les femmes couraient devant eux, allaient s'agenouiller sur des chaises.
>
> Précédé des deux enfants de chœur, coiffé d'un bonnet écarlate sur lequel se dressaient deux cornes de bison en étoffe rouge, le chanoine entra.
>
> Durtal l'examina, tandis qu'il marchait à l'autel.
>
> (298)[8]

The expected description follows.

This close interweaving of Durtal perceived and Durtal perceiving constitutes a sort of composite narrative feature, what I have called a 'snapshot'. But it is important to remember that a snapshot is only the artificial arresting of continuous movement: it is clearly mandatory to bear in mind the dynamic context of any given episode. And what emerges from this reflection is that, for such a dynamics to be maintained, the dual process of author/narrator observing Durtal observing others must be kept in play: the fluidity of interrelationships which this method permits is a guarantee of forward motion.

DIALOGUE

The principle of duality does not stop here, however. On the contrary, it finds a very full extension in the shape of one of the most basic elements of any storytelling enterprise: the manner in which the story is mediated. Here in **Là-bas,** the dialogic principle is evident right from the beginning, and with a vengeance.[9] The opening sentences plunge us *in medias res,* cutting into the middle of a conversation:

> —Tu y crois si bien à ces idées-là, mon cher, que tu as abandonné l'adultère, l'amour, l'ambition, tous les sujets apprivoisés du roman moderne, pour écrire l'histoire de Gilles de Rais—et, après un silence, il ajouta:—Je ne reproche au naturalisme ni ses termes de pontons, ni son vocabulaire de latrines et d'hospices,

> car ce serait injuste et ce serait absurde; [. . .] ce que je lui reproche, c'est d'avoir incarné le matérialisme dans la littérature, d'avoir glorifié la démocratie de l'art!
>
> (15)

This fulsome harangue from des Hermies (whose identity will not be revealed for a few pages yet) lasts in all for a good page and a half, maintaining a lecture-like tone throughout; yet we are clearly in a conversational situation, as the opening gambit indicates, and as the response from Durtal confirms:

> —Mâtin, tu y vas, toi, répondit Durtal, d'un ton piqué. Il ralluma sa cigarette, puis: le matérialisme me répugne tout autant qu'à toi, mais ce n'est pas une raison pour nier les inoubliables services que les naturalistes ont rendus à l'art; car enfin ce sont eux qui nous ont débarrassés des inhumains fantoches du romantisme et qui ont extrait la littérature d'un idéalisme de ganache et d'une inanition de vieille fille exaltée par le célibat!
>
> (16)

The character is clearly a different one from that of the speaker of the opening paragraphs; but the high-profile manner and recherché vocabulary are common currency. Even constructionally, similarities abound: the opening formula, the pause for effect, the building to a climax. Everything points to a deep fraternity of the two individuals who engage in dialogue. Yves Hersant neatly sums up the relationship:

> A la fin d'**A Rebours,** des Esseintes appelait de ses vœux «un esprit jumeau, un esprit détaché des lieux communs». Tel est des Hermies pour Durtal: *alter ego* du protagoniste, il apparaît du même coup comme l'*alter alter ego* de l'auteur, dans un roman où les acteurs vont par paires ou se dédoublent (après **Là-bas,** sa mission dialogique accomplie, des Hermies mourra et Durtal poursuivra seul sa carrière romanesque.)[10]

This is certainly true: des Hermies seems to be a necessary self-projection of Durtal himself, a sort of active sounding-board created for the purpose of articulating thoughts and ideas which would otherwise have remained trapped within the confines of one sensibility. Des Hermies is useful, in that Durtal—experimenting as he is with new material for a new book—can 'try out' his ideas on a friend before committing himself to paper. So the dialogic situation engineered by Huysmans seems ingenious enough.

Yet any reader of **Là-bas** will rapidly testify to the artificiality of the process in action. Many will have agreed with Pierre Cogny when he speaks of 'la gaucherie de la discussion entre les deux amis qui ne donne, à aucun moment, l'impression d'une conversation spontanée.[11] This gaucheness is so universally apparent that one finds examples in abundance; this, for example, from Durtal:

Si nous récapitulons les pièces qui nous furent trans-
mises, nous trouvons ceci:

Gilles de Rais, dont l'enfance est inconnue, naquit vers
1404, sur les confins de la Bretagne et de l'Anjou, dans
le château de Machecoul. Son père meurt à la fin
d'octobre 1415; sa mère se remarie presque aussitôt
avec un sieur d'Estouville et l'abandonne, lui et René
de Rais, son frère.

(59-60)

Des Hermies must surely already be in possession of
this elementary information: the justification that Durtal
is recapitulating on the surviving 'pièces' is perfunctory
in the extreme, and is the bare minimum necessary for
maintaining the illusion of dialogue.

Illusion, yes, for what we witness in such passages is
less the simple desire to convey information to the
reader (though this is of course the case) than the massive presence of supposed dialogue which constantly
aspires to the state of monologue. Of many instances,
the following passage shows how des Hermies too is
capable of delivering a lecture:

A la fin du quinzième siècle, c'est-à-dire au temps de
Gilles de Rais,—pour ne pas remonter plus haut—le
Satanisme prit les proportions que tu sais; au XVIe
siècle, ce fut peut-être pis encore. Il est inutile de te
rappeler, je pense, les pactions démoniaques de Catherine de Médicis et des Valois, le procès du moine Jean
de Vaulx, les enquêtes de Sprenger et des Lancre, de
ces doctes inquisiteurs qui firent cuire à grand feu des
milliers de nécromants et de sorcières.

(80)

This time there is not even an opening formula; and the
token gestures at dialogism ('que tu sais', 'il est inutile
de te rappeler') are so feeble as to be almost laughable.

Yet this constant provision of detail—the documentary
obsession we have already looked at—takes on a new
colour once one has transcended the artificiality of the
supposed dialogue form. What is really happening is
that dialogue is constantly converging into monologue,
and that monologue rejoins, whenever it can, the ever
precious document. There is a delectation in detail, an
accumulation of facts for their own sake, an autonomy
of documentation—all adding up to a literary configuration different from that of the basic dialogue form,
but which requires the preliminary stage of dialogue in
order to come into being. When Durtal exclaims of
Gilles de Rais, 'Il était le des Esseintes du quinzième
siècle! (66), he seems to sum up his whole literary enterprise, one which will privilege the hoarding of facts,
and by extension the literary enterprise which is *Là-bas*
itself: a book composed largely by accumulation, accre-
tion, and listing—a thoroughgoing celebration of the
word.[12]

Nevertheless, this celebration has its sinister side, where
the dialogic principle established at the outset of the
novel becomes parodied to such an extent that its validity becomes even more dubious. The artificiality of the
'conversations' between Durtal and des Hermies is mild
in comparison. I refer of course to the proceedings related in chapter XIX of *Là-bas,* notably the account of
the Black Mass which is its central feature. The dialogic form is clearly at work, but the perverse manner
in which it is employed is all too apparent: '—«Maître
des Esclandres, Dispensateur des bienfaits du crime, Intendant des somptueux péchés et des grands vices, Satan, c'est toi que nous adorons, Dieu logique, Dieu
juste!»' (299). This invocation to the Devil (there are
six paragraphs of it, complete with the inescapable
exclamation-marks) seems to be a genuinely applied
case of the dialogic principle, since the utterer of the
words—Docre—is an avowed diabolist; true dialogue
therefore seems possible. But there is soon a move away
from such dialogism when Docre begins to address
Christ in a parodic litany:

—«Et toi, toi, qu'en ma qualité de prêtre, je force que
tu le veuilles ou non, à descendre dans cette hostie, à
t'incarner dans ce pain, Jésus, Artisan des super-cheries,
Larron d'hommages, Voleur d'affection, écoute! Depuis
le jour où tu sortis des entrailles ambassadrices d'une
Vierge, tu as failli à tes engagements, menti à tes
promesses; des siècles ont sangloté, en t'attendant,
Dieu fuyard, Dieu muet!»

(300)

'Dieu muet' indeed. For Christ cannot but be silent in
the face of such an abuse of the dialogic principle, a
principle which Docre is manipulating under false pre-
tences. From being a potentially true dialogue with Satan, the verbal form can only pretend to be a dialogue
here; in fact, it is a monologue masquerading as dialogue. Further, even monologue is dispensed with as the
profanatory 'consecration' is reached ('un silence succéda à ces hurlements' (301)), when, instead of the customary genuflection, Docre masturbates on the host—
mute gesture speaking more eloquently than words, and
effectively abolishing even notional verbal communication. The rejection of true dialogue is underlined in this
non-verbal, physical act, when 'l'hostie, qu'il ramenait
devant lui, sautait, atteinte et souillée, sur les marches'
(303).

So, whether it is in Durtal's and des Hermies' anodine
conversations, or in the more sulphurous world of Docre's diabolism, there seems to be a tendency for the
dialogic form to disintegrate in a series of abolitions
which arise from a basically unfaithful dialogism. Yet
the yearning for an audience—and a responsive one—
remains as a guiding feature in all cases. Even if the
engineering of a dialogic situation is patently artificial,
one can see why Huysmans felt the need for such a
procedure: the story of *Là-bas* is largely one of the
freeing from silence of hidden words, words which
could not be known unless openly expressed for the
reader's benefit. Hence their verbal articulation.

CURIOUS LANGUAGE

While the Black Mass displays a malevolent celebration of the power of the word, there is in **Là-bas** a constant deployment of less harmful, indeed trivial, aspects of language. They are of an altogether different order, but are so recurrent that they register with a force equal to, perhaps greater than, Docre's blasphemies. For the most part they occur as tiny asides, barely perceptible at a first reading. Thus when, in the very first sentence of the novel, des Hermies pauses ('et, après un silence, il ajouta' (15)), one would scarcely notice it, were it not for the fact that almost identical notations occur with great regularity throughout **Là-bas**. A typical example occurs during the first meal which Durtal and des Hermies have in the Carhaix' abode; des Hermies is discoursing about Manicheism: 'Ici, je ne suis plus avec eux, poursuivit-il [des Hermies] doucement, après un silence, attendant que Mme Carhaix, qui s'était levée pour emporter les assiettes, allât chercher le bœuf.' (78) The context seems to offer little reason why des Hermies should fall silent at this particular point rather than at any other—or at all. True, Mme Carhaix's presence is functional in so far as she is the purveyor of domestic comforts which facilitate the dialogue in the first place; on the other hand, certain conversations can only be carried on in her absence. The fact is that silences such as these represent less a contribution to the sense of what is being discussed, or even a trait of character, than a stylistic *tic* on the part of Huysmans. For the state of silence affects all characters in the novel:

> Gévingey se tut, puis:—Le sujet est trop grave [. . .].
>
> (169)

> —Mais, dites donc, vous devez brasser à pleins bras le Satanisme avec votre Gilles de Rais, reprit Chantelouve, après un silence.
>
> (206)

> Durtal comprit que Chantelouve se refusait à parler de ses relations avec le chanoine Docre. Il garda le silence, un peu embarrassé.
>
> (207)

> Des Hermies remplissait les verres; ils mangèrent, en silence, le fromage.
>
> (228)

> Puis il se tut [Durtal].
>
> (220)

The device is everywhere.[13] Why? Does this quirk of Huysmans' represent a paucity of invention on his part? Or perhaps a lack of expertise at forward propulsion? (It seems that the placing of these silences might be intended to fulfil that function.) Perhaps so; for one is definitely aware of a certain degree of gaucheness. But I would argue that this pattern of silences draws attention—in a modest way—to the fact that literary language is an assemblage of words, and indeed underlines the work of assemblage, leading us back to the ever-present concept of the document, and the stress on precision.

So, when a silence occurs at the height of the Black Mass, it seems to represent a point of stepping-back for Durtal, an assessment of the horrors he has just witnessed: 'Durtal écoutait ce torrent de blasphèmes et d'insultes; l'immondice de ce prêtre le stupéfiait; un silence succéda à ces hurlements; la chapelle fumait dans la brume des encensoirs.' (301-2) Everything seems to be put into perspective, and here most notably the vile language uttered by Docre. As elsewhere, silence appears to be a prerequisite for the adequate shaping of language and a response to it: these little notations denoting silence thus, I would argue, offer an important check on the uncontrolled proliferation of language—a rigour analogous to that which Durtal seeks in accurate documentation.

There is another closely-allied thematic feature of **Là-bas,** but this time it is a *tic* of Durtal's alone. We see it here in immediate juxtaposition to a typical silence: '—Ah! dit Durtal, en allumant une cigarette, après un silence, ça vaut mieux que de causer de politique ou de courses [. . .]!' (340) Durtal is a heavy smoker, and indications of his rolling or smoking a cigarette seem to fulfil much the same function as the silences which we have just studied. They aid in the process of putting things into perspective, and perhaps go a stage further in facilitating concentration of thought on work in hand:

> —Mâtin, tu y vas, toi, répondit Durtal, d'un ton piqué. Il ralluma sa cigarette, puis: le matérialisme me répugne tout autant qu'à toi, mais ce n'est pas une raison pour nier les inoubliables services que les naturalistes ont rendus à l'art.
>
> (16)

> A n'en pas douter, ce fut une singulière époque que ce Moyen Age, reprit-il, en allumant une cigarette.
>
> (142)

> —Voyons, se dit-il, en roulant une cigarette, nous en sommes au moment où cet excellent Gilles de Rais commence la recherche du grand œuvre.
>
> (98)

These three examples[14] show, I think convincingly, that the cigarette motif, like the recourse to silence, is not just a decorative feature employed by Huysmans from time to time. It appears to be a strictly patterned element which bears a close relationship first to Durtal's research and by extension to the way in which **Là-bas** as a whole is a work which constantly displays a hyperawareness of language, its uses and abuses, even at this minimal level.

A final narrative device, but one which ties in closely with the two just studied, gives additional weight to the thesis that Huysmans is constantly making tiny adjustments to normal language, sufficient to jog the reader into an enhanced state of awareness at unlikely moments. When, for example, des Hermies says: 'dix heures sonnent et ton concierge va, dans l'escalier, éteindre le gaz' (18), one is immediately struck by the eccentric position (especially in speech) of 'dans l'escalier'; similarly in the following examples:

> Le père Rateau n'aura certainement pas fait, ainsi que je l'en ai prié, mon ménage à fond.
>
> (176)

> —Oh, voulez-vous me faire croire que vous n'avez jamais, ici, reçu des femmes?
>
> (181)[15]

These little syntactic displacements of innocuous words are of no great significance in themselves; yet they contribute to the thoroughgoing 'mise en question' of language itself as a means of communication. If adjustments on such a tiny scale can register, how much greater can larger aspects of textual production.

TEXTUAL PRODUCTION

Là-bas is a book about a person writing a book. And as we see Durtal struggling with the problems of creating his book, so we simultaneously witness the various methods which Huysmans employs in creating *his*. Put another way, *Là-bas* is at the same time a story of textual production and textual production itself. As we have already seen, the novel is especially rich in linguistic features which call attention to themselves, and thus keep the reader constantly aware of the ongoing process of literary construction. What I want to examine now are broader areas of textuality where Durtal and Huysmans overlap, and where the status of 'the text' is itself addressed.

Durtal, for all his professionalism as a writer, rarely theorises; there are, however, some elements of an *ars poetica,* generally regarding the place of the artist in society:

> [. . .] les rares artistes qui restent n'ont plus à s'occuper du public; ils vivent et travaillent loin des salons, loin de la cohue des couturiers de lettres; le seul dépit qu'ils puissent honnêtement ressentir, c'est, quand leur œuvre est imprimée, de la voir exposée aux salissantes curiosités des foules!
>
> (260)

And more particularly, concerning Durtal's own conception of his artistic role (it is important to quote the relevant section in its entirety):

> L'histoire supplanta chez lui [Durtal] le roman dont l'affabulation, ficelée dans des chapitres, empaquetée à la grosse, forcément banale et convenue, le blessait. Et cependant, l'histoire ne semblait être qu'un pis-aller, car il ne croyait pas à la réalité de cette science; les événements, se disait-il, ne sont pour un homme de talent qu'un tremplin d'idées et de style, puisque tous se mitigent ou s'aggravent, suivant les besoins d'une cause ou selon le tempérament de l'écrivain qui les manie.

> Quant aux documents qui les étayent, c'est pis encore! car aucun d'eux n'est irréductible et tous sont révisables. S'ils ne sont pas apocryphes; d'autres, non moins certains, se déterrent plus tard qui les controuvent, en attendant qu'eux-mêmes soient démonétisés par l'exhumation d'archives non moins sûres.
>
> (33)

So we return to the document, the concept with which we started. Durtal is all too aware that the seeming stability which documents provide is illusory, and history as a genre is no less at the mercy of the individual writer's hand than the more obviously personal genre of the novel. Little help here, then. But worse still, in the second paragraph, nothing can be taken for granted about the documents themselves: as individual items, they none of them can ever lay claim to absolute truth, and taken together they demonstrate a relativity which effectively cancels out any potential authority.

We can never, of course, pronounce on the way in which Durtal uses documentary material in his book on Gilles de Rais, for the simple reason that that book will always remain an invisible fiction. What we do, however, witness with fascination is the way in which Durtal's researches lead him into unexpected areas of experience which *will* become textual material—not in the book on Gilles de Rais, but in *Là-bas* itself. For there are points of intersection between the two books, the one potential, the other actual, notably when Durtal's interest in Gilles de Rais finds itself curiously updated by his contacts with present-day demonism:

> Durtal n'écoutait plus. Mme Chantelouve connaissait le chanoine Docre! Ah, ça, est-ce qu'elle aussi était une satanique!
>
> (172)

> —Vous connaissez le chanoine Docre?
>
> —Eh bien oui! [. . .] je l'ai même eu pour confesseur.
>
> (246-7)

It seems to Durtal as if the demonic practices which he assumed were long dead have now come to life; the material he is studying is indeed very alive, and he eloquently registers his astonishment when he exclaims of Docre that he is 'le Gilles de Rais moderne!' (170).

This overlapping of the two evolving texts—Durtal's study of Gilles and Huysmans' story of Durtal—is a constant, and clearly very conscious, feature of *Là-bas.*

Thus, a sort of 'textual contamination' frequently takes place, as, for example, when Durtal describes the books of alchemy he has to consult: 'Ces livres constituaient, en effet, le plus incroyable des galimatias, le plus inintelligible des grimoires. Tout était en allégories, en métaphores cocasses et obscures, en emblèmes incohérents, en paraboles embrouillées, en énigmes bourrées de chiffres!' (98) Many a reader might well find these comments a very accurate description of *Là-bas* itself!

The process of parallelism is at its clearest at the end of the novel. With a sigh of relief, Durtal greets the ending of his affair with Mme Chantelouve with the words 'Enfin, ce petit roman est terminé' (330); but for the reader, the word 'roman' also means *Là-bas,* whose end is very close. Then Durtal turns his attention to his work on Gilles de Rais: 'Au fond, ce que Gilles de Rais est plus intéressant que Mme Chantelouve; malheureusement mes relations avec lui tirent à leur fin aussi; encore quelques pages et le livre est achevé.' (330) Here the association is even closer: the 'invisible fiction' is a few pages from its end, just as, for the reader holding *Là-bas* in his hands, that book is, by virtue of the diminishing number of pages left, itself about to conclude.

This self-consciousness of closure inescapably invites a reassessment of *Là-bas* as a whole, for, as the end of the novel approaches, so the tying-together of ends prompts a following-back of the threads which lead to them. A summary of the novel undertaken at this point might read as follows: The enterprise is for Durtal to produce a documentary study; we witness this taking place via a series of conversations, in dialogic form; these conversations present local bizarreries of language; finally, the whole text appears to the reader as a supremely *visual* assemblage.

This last point is, it seems to me, the essential one, the element which binds the whole of *Là-bas* together. Put simply, Durtal's most acute sense, the one he uses preferentially, is the sense of sight, most lovingly exercised on the written word. And since Durtal is so close to Huysmans himself, it is not surprising that visual predilections should be constantly present in the overall organisation of the novel.

We have seen clearly enough, in the 'Documentation' section above, how the possession and the reading of texts is central to Durtal's task. The erudition thus acquired is articulated in the dialogues I dealt with in the following section. But a notable feature of the 'conversations' between Durtal and des Hermies is their artificiality as dialogues: in short, they are texts meant to be read, whose appeal is visual. The same is true of the odd turns of language which punctuate the novel—they represent so many little visual features, the writerly equivalent of brushstrokes. In every case, these lin-

guistic elements serve to *localize* events—the Gilles de Rais story; its thinking-out and retelling; the *tics* of language of the characters and of the author; the construction of *Là-bas* itself. Taken together, they all add up to the creation of a veritable mosaic, or, to borrow a famous title, a 'verbal icon'.[16]

In the true spirit of the novel, there is even a parody of this 'total visualization' at the end of the story:

> —Et voilà pourtant la panacée qui va tout guérir, fit des Hermies, en riant. Et il désigna du doigt, sur les murs, d'enormes affiches dans lesquelles le Général Boulanger objurguait les Parisiens de voter, aux prochaines élections, pour lui. [. . .]
>
> C'était une véritable débauche de placards; partout sur des papiers de couleur, s'étalaient, en grosses capitales, les noms de Boulanger et de Jacques.
>
> (327, 332)

So the ever-visual component makes its impact in an area—politics—very far from the taste of Durtal/ Huysmans, and apparently distant from the major preoccupations of *Là-bas.* In a sense, the modern election campaign is a rude shock of awakening from the intellectual, almost literally ivory-tower, pursuits of Durtal and des Hermies.[17] But it is not just a parody of the obsession with what is visual: the 'real' history of Boulanger provides a strange parallel with the rest of *Là-bas.*

Boulanger's election triumph dates to 1889, but it was short-lived, since he vacillated and didn't launch the expected coup d'état. Having fled to Brussels, he committed suicide on his mistress's grave there in 1891. This history of failure would have been fresh in the minds of the first readers of *Là-bas,*[18] so that the elation of the election campaign, as it is pictured in the novel, would have taken on a distinctly ironic hue. And for latter-day readers, for whom the Boulanger story means less and less, the whole episode can only appear ephemeral.

In effect, the proliferation of election posters at the end of the novel represents a debasement of what for Durtal is a sacrosanct area—the domain of the written word in its iconic aspect. For in this area Durtal is an out-and-out idealist, and will harbour no downgrading of the authority of the word in mediating truth. Right at the beginning of the novel, the tone had been set in uncompromising language: 'En s'acculant ainsi à ces pensées, il finissait, pour se rapprocher de cet idéal qu'il voulait quand même joindre, par louvoyer, par bifurquer et s'arrêter à un autre art, à la peinture. Là, il le trouvait pleinement réalisé par les Primitifs, cet idéal!' (20) What follows is the famous meditation on Grünewald's *Crucifixion,* one of the most detailed and penetrating descriptions of art even by Huysmans' standards. More than a description, it is perhaps better termed an adaptation in words of states of mind which contemplation of the painting arouses. So vivid is Durtal's pictorial recollection that he 'frissonna dans son fauteuil' (21), and the ensuing description is so detailed that it comes as no surprise when Durtal claims that 'Grünewald était le plus forcené des réalistes' (24). But a few lines further on—articulating the duality which is the cause of disagreement between himself and des Hermies—we read that the artist 'était le plus forcené des idéalistes' (ibid.). In effect, Durtal says, Grünewald 'était allé aux deux extrêmes' (25) and his art was 'sommé de rendre l'invisible et le tangible' (ibid.). In the face of what seems to be a uniquely pictorial field of perception and mediation, Durtal concludes: 'Non, cela n'avait d'équivalent dans aucune langue.' (ibid.)

Yet all the while, for the last four pages, what the reader has been witnessing is precisely that—an equivalent of one artistic medium in terms of another. Remembrance of Grünewald's painting has provided visual impetus for Durtal's creative faculties, and the latter proceeds to 'read' the painting, in the process turning it, for the reader, into a verbal icon. Put another way, since all forms of documentation are grist to Durtal's mill, Grünewald's *Crucifixion* is tantamount to text for him; he gives it verbal form in his mind; and this in turn becomes *real* text for the reader.

The Grünewald episode hovers over the whole of *Là-bas,* so forceful—and thematically pertinent—is its impact. Recapitulation of it within the text would be superfluous, for its implications regarding the coexistence of naturalism and mysticism will be acted out in Durtal's story as it unfolds. Study of Grünewald's painting permits the transition from visual to verbal icon, so that when the pathetic parody represented by Boulanger's posters is reached at the end of the novel, it serves as a reminder that a more genuine, fruitful visual stimulus has been available all along, and has led to the production of a novel which shares a common programme with it. Only now, the enterprise has been undertaken in a supremely verbal field of activity, one where the autonomy of the printed word permits its own organisation and orders everything into a closely integrated matrix. In short, *Là-bas* embodies the apotheosis of the word.

Notes

1. Christopher Lloyd, *J.-K. Huysmans and the Fin-de-siècle Novel,* Edinburgh, Edinburgh University Press, 1990, p. 87.

2. In this sense, it seems legitimate to see Huysmans as a precursor of Proust. On Proust and Huysmans, see Yves Clogenson, 'Proust et Huysmans,' in: *Entretiens sur Marcel Proust,* G. Cattaui and P. Kolb (Eds.) (Paris/The Hague, Mouton, 1966), pp. 15-34. More recently, R. Bales, 'Proust, Huysmans et la forme dialogique,' in: *Bulletin de la Société des Amis de Marcel Proust,* 39 (1989), 68-75.

3. Denis Saurat provides an extreme reaction: "Huysmans [. . .] has had many admirers; probably his conversion to Catholicism is the real cause of his pseudo-importance; nothing in his writings is of any note. His realism is out of date, and his mysticism a fake.' In: *Modern French Literature, 1870-1940* (London, J. M. Dent, 1946), p. 33.

4. Huysmans' letters to Arij Prins are littered with the word 'document' in connection with work on *Là-bas.* For example, 'O les documents!! il y en a tant dans ce livre qu'il n'y a pas moyen d'y faire d'art!'; 'Je connais du monde si étrange, et *Là-bas* m'en a tant fait connaître, que je souris un peu maintenant de ce qu'on nomme le document vrai, alors que l'invraisemblable ne l'est pas moins.' In: J.-K. Huysmans, *Lettres inédites à Arij Prins,* (Geneva, Droz, 1977), pp. 192, 228.

5. J.-K. Huysmans, *Là-bas,* Ed. A. Buisine (Paris, Le Livre de Poche, 1988), p. 29. All subsequent references are to this edition, except where otherwise noted.

6. The other references, couched in almost identical terms, are on pp. 243 and 249.

7. The same sort of scrutiny is applied later on in the novel: 'Durtal regardait l'astrologue. Il avait toujours sa tête en pain de sucre, ses cheveux de ce brun tourné, sale, qu'ont les poudres d'hydroquinone et d'ipéca, ses yeux effarés d'oiseau,' etc. (p. 309).

8. Cf. the following sentence, which displays in its baldest form Durtal's clear bent for observation: 'Du coup, Durtal se leva pour mieux voir, et distinctement, il entendit et il aperçut le chanoine Docre' (p. 302).

9. In employing the term 'dialogic principle' I am of course alluding to the work of M. M. Bakhtin (see especially *The Dialogic Imagination* (Austin and London, University of Texas Press, 1981)). However, most of what I have to say here addresses itself to true (or supposed) situations of dialogue, and less to the wider textural quality which preoccupies Bakhtin. Nevertheless, being constantly alerted to the many-strandedness of language is no bad thing in studying *Là-bas.* On Bakhtin, a useful guide is Tzvetan Todorov, *Mikhaïl Bakhtine: le principe dialogique* (Paris, Seuil, 1981). See also Michael Holquist, *Dialogism: Bakhtin and his World* (London and New York, Routledge, 1990), and David Lodge, *After Bakhtin* (London and New York, Routledge, 1990).

10. *Là-bas,* Ed. Y. Hersant (Paris, Folio, 1985), p. 386.

11. *Là-bas,* Ed. P. Cogny (Paris, Garnier-Flammarion, 1978), p. 14.

12. Des Esseintes is, of course, the aesthetic 'hero' of Huysmans' own *A rebours.* The intertextual reference, whilst humorous in effect, serves the serious purpose of underlining the very heavy textualisation of *Là-bas.*

13. Other examples of silence: pp. 43, 159, 165, 184, 260, 277, 301, 340, 344. The list is far from exhaustive.

14. Others: pp. 37, 51, 64, 90, 109, 164, 232, 237, 286, 317, 319, 332, 342, 347.

15. Further examples of eccentric phrase-positions: pp. 95, 129, 149, 205, 228, 235, 293, 347. On this topic, see Marcel Cressot, *La Phrase et le vocabulaire de J.-K. Huysmans* (Paris, Droz, 1938), pp. 99-100.

16. See A. K. Wimsatt, *The Verbal Icon: Studies in the Meaning of Poetry* (Lexington, University of Kentucky Press, 1954).

17. Because Carhaix, who is frequently visited by Durtal and des Hermies, lives in a (clearly symbolic) tower of Saint-Sulpice.

18. Boulanger's political power, that is. As Lloyd points out, his suicide dates from five months after the publication of *Là-bas* (Lloyd, p. 108).

Robert Ziegler (essay date January 1999)

SOURCE: Ziegler, Robert. "The Holy Sepulcher and the Resurrected Text in Huysmans's *Là-bas.*" *French Forum* 24, no. 1 (January 1999): 33-45.

[*In the following essay, Ziegler regards* Là-bas *as one of the earliest texts by Huysmans that thematizes "the absence of the literary subject" and postulates, through the image of Christ's crucified body and its "reconversion into spirit," a new possibility for literature, one not based on materialism but "on the transformation of the real into nothing."*]

Published in 1891, Huysmans's sensational novel about satanism, **Là-bas,** has often been regarded as a transitional work signaling the author's emancipation from the influence of Emile Zola and his progression toward his eventual conversion to Catholicism. As Huysmans came to discredit Zola's belief in biological determinism, the focus of his texts shifted away from the body and its appetites, and yet his hero, Durtal, remained unable to express with certainty what the future subject of

writing would be. It is not coincidental that Huysmans first problematized the status of literature at the same time that his interest in metaphysics was intensifying, when he was pursuing more deeply his study of what he considered the most vexing of Catholic dogma: the physical death and resurrection of Christ, the miracle of transubstantiation, and the sacrament of communion. As the body relinquished its central position in the fiction of the time, as the epistemological certainty afforded by Naturalism's embrace of scientific methodology was abandoned, Huysmans's texts began to thematize the issue of loss itself. Yet as **Là-bas** shows, the absence of the literary subject that Durtal deplores could seemingly be compensated for by the supernatural fullness of the religion toward which Huysmans was turning.

Because of its concern with these issues, recent psychoanalytic theory on mourning may be profitably applied to Huysmans's controversial novel since it can help to explain both the genesis of his conception of spiritual Naturalism and his association of the body that vanishes from literature with the transfigured body of the risen Christ. It is significant that in the beginning of **Là-bas,** the writer Durtal is already grieving over the prospect of his professional obsolescence. Thus, even in its opening chapter, Huysmans's book casts doubt on the future viability of literature and, in so doing, calls into question the reason for its being written. Indeed, although Huysmans's audience holds in their hands his finished volume, they are encouraged to wonder why they should continue reading if, as Durtal and des Hermies contend, literature has exhausted itself and now lies languishing in the cloacal vulgarity of Naturalism, the thin-blooded post-Romanticism of the novels of George Sand, or in the elitist impenetrability of the writings of the Decadents. "Alors quoi?" Durtal muses. "Et [il] se butait, mis au pied du mur, contre des théories confuses, des postulations incertaines."[1]

Remarking on the dismal teleology of Huysmans's embedded narratives, Max Milner argues that the monstrous stature of Gilles de Rais, the subject of Durtal's biography-in-progress, only underscores the puniness of the nineteenth-century devil worshipers that Huysmans's protagonist so ardently wishes to study and observe. The fire from the alchemist's retorts, the white corpses of the little boys Gilles disembowels, the crimson and purple of the sacerdotal robes Gilles collects: all the opulence, grotesqueness, and somber pageantry of the Middle Ages highlight the perfunctoriness of the Black Mass that Durtal sees celebrated by rouged choirboys amidst the smoke of dried datura and the blasphemous imprecations of Chanoine Docre. As the fullness of historical conjecture contrasts with the emptiness of modern-day experience, the story of Gilles serves as "une sorte de *répondant* qui permet au lecteur de mesurer la veulerie de son époque, en la confrontant avec un 'modèle' qui le dépasse dans toutes les dimensions."[2] If the richness of a fictionalized past can be drawn on only to emphasize the nullity of present life, if, as Milner claims, "le réel . . . ne peut être présent dans la littérature et dans l'art en général que comme manque" (19), Huysmans shows that the barrenness of Durtal's era disallows its use as the stuff of future art and thereby calls into question the justification of Huysmans's own novel.

While *Là-bas* centers on absences, what is everywhere present in the book are human bodies and their appetites: from the intertextual coupling of "Lisa, la charcutière du *Ventre de Paris,* et de Homais" ([*Oeuvres complètes*] 1: 7), to the joyless coitus of Durtal and Madame Chantelouve—from the savory bouillons served piping hot by Madame Carhaix in the belltower to the adulterated dinners that slowly poison the patrons of a local restaurant frequented by des Hermies. Indeed, the flesh and its abjection become tainted food causing the novel to waste away into Naturalist commonplaces about adultery and gluttony, and are themselves experiential somethings turned into literary nothing.

While expressing a longing for the insubstantiality of the sublime, Huysmans's early texts betray a gloomy fixation on meals and sex: as in the account of André Jayant's marital woes and Folantin's gastronomic wanderings in search of a decent place to eat. The hypostatized Christ turned into the Eucharist eaten by communicants at Mass reverses the spiritualization of the body that Durtal hopes religion can accomplish. So, instead of there being a purifying ascension, the Word is made flesh that is consumed, and Naturalism is faulted for having "incarné le matérialisme dans la littérature" (1: 6). The eschatological view of the pessimist Durtal is that all organisms hungering for transcendence are foredoomed to become carrion that is eaten again, as fat people's corpses provide nutrients for specialized worms, "les rhizophages," and thin people's corpses are devoured by "des phorias . . . les aristos de la vermine" (1: 45). Rather than promising redemption and escape from the corporeal plane, the sacrament of communion foreshadows the martyrdom of the writer, whose work is "broken, divided, passed around, consumed by the critics."[3] The circular itinerary of dust to dust is repeated in literature, since the dead are not pulverized and dispersed into eternity, but are reembodied as comestibles and texts, having "un goût de très ancien biscuit et une odeur de très vieux livre" (1: 44).

As Huysmans's novel privileges the archival graveyard that is desecrated by historical researchers like Gilles, it focuses on the crypt containing the nutrients they require. Corresponding to the real, which is represented in fiction as its deficiency, the *suprasensible* and the *supraterrestre,* toward which post-Naturalist literature reaches in vain, are figured in the text as Christ's empty sepulcher. The most exalted artists and criminals are the gravediggers, the earthworms, and ghouls that plumb the mystery of a body whose mortification leaves it lightened and cleansed. They are the geniuses like Grunewald, "[qui] avait brassé le charnier divin" and who, from "une triomphale ordure" had extracted "les menthes les plus fines des dilections" (1: 19).

Hanging distended on Grunewald's buckling cross, Christ's body is also defiled by the followers of Docre, becoming a ubiquitous signifier for a divinity corrupted by its transformation into art. It is because the Word is made flesh that it can be reconverted into artistic imagery, either as the leering, priapic Jesus displayed at the Black Mass, or as the Redeemer in Grunewald's canvas, whose physical suffering is so intense that it anticipates the obliteration of matter, its rarefaction and reconversion into spirit. As this essay argues, Huysmans sees the future possibility of literature's existence as dependent on the transformation of the real into nothing. Since Christ's crucified body, having been buried, is then risen, it leaves only what is unmentioned and missing as insurance of a later literary presence, as indemnification of the mystical text that Huysmans intuits but is unable to write.

In *Là-bas,* the significance of Christ's sepulcher as repository of the unwritable text may be explained through recourse to Abraham and Torok's study of the phenomenon of incorporation. Interring the lost object in "le caveau intrapsychique," the grieving subject is incapable of introjection in the Ferenczian sense of an internalization effecting an "élargissement du Moi."[4] Instead of acknowledging a loss compensated for by the object's recreation in artistic imagery,[5] the object is represented as denial, silence, and absence of the adaptive language of mourning. Triggered by the infant's original experience of distress caused by the mother's absence, vocalization succeeds consumption, and speech is precipitated by a frustrated impulse to eat. Thus, there is a gradual substitution of oral satisfactions, so that, in place of the mouth "pleine de l'objet maternel," there is "la bouche vide du même objet mais remplie de mots à l'adresse du sujet" (262).

In a Winnicottian analysis of the phenomenon of object use in the crucifixion narrative, Brooke Hopkins observes that, in addition to being "a maternal imago" representing "certain strikingly . . . feminized qualities: patience, nurturance, the ability to love,"[6] Jesus is also the object of fantasies of oral aggression recalling "the infant's incorporation of the mother, her breast, the nourishment from her body" (257). Because he vacates his tomb on the third day, Christ's disappearance is a reminder of the mother's unavailability and so explains Huysmans's sadistic fixation on the Passion and the Eucharist that is broken apart and devoured. The same Christ who is vilified by Docre for failing to discharge his role as "le Truchement de nos plaintes, le Chambellan de nos pleurs" (2: 164) is punished in Durtal's interpretation of Grunewald's painting by being himself assigned the position of the helpless child calling out in vain to a mother whose unresponsiveness renders her derelict and guilty: "le Christ assisté seulement de sa Mère qu'il avait dû, ainsi que tous ceux que l'on torture, appeler dans des cris d'enfant, de sa Mère, impuissante alors et inutile" (1: 18).

The production of Huysmans's text depends on the presence of the degraded, purulent, sanious, abscessed, bleeding body liquefied as infants' tears, as well as on the deodorized asepsis of the undescribed crypt. Both Huysmans's narrative and Durtal's history of Gilles are motivated by a desire to reach an end to matter and literature and by a simultaneous realization that the illusion of an epistemological lack compels it to be filled with superfluous new writing. "[L]e plus enfantin des leurres" (1: 31), history cheats Durtal's hunger for certainty since, as spurious science, it is also unreal nourishment. But it is because of its undependability that it encourages the introjection of the past as fiction. The creative energy of the historian is assured by the unknowability of the object of his research, and so the absence of the real guarantees the presence of its falsified reconstruction. Durtal's project to excavate evidence about Gilles's life is one whose success is a function of its unproductiveness. Each crypt that is opened contains fraudulent documents, unreliable maps indicating the location of other, older crypts nesting in an archeological *mise en abyme* that replicates the structure of Huysmans's novel. As for such source works, Durtal says: "S'ils ne sont pas apochryphes, d'autres, non moins certains, se déterrent plus tard qui les controuvent, en attendant qu'eux-mêmes soient démonétisés par l'exhumation d'archives non moins sûres" (1: 30).

Extending Milner's axiom that the vitality of art exists in inverse relation to the real that art encloses as absence, Huysmans's work implies that an empty crypt calls for a textual body, and that Christ's transfigured corpse presupposes a supernatural language to express it. Paralleling the construction of Durtal's book is the progressive collapse of Gilles's ruined castle at Tiffauges. Even in Durtal's visit to the site, he descends from the lichen-covered tower to the dungeons, from the chapel to the crypt (1: 181). The homology of container and contents turns the tomb into a cadaver, making the structural remains of the castle where so many had been murdered into "le squelette d'un donjon mort" (1: 182). Durtal's resurrective quest to flesh out the historical *dépouille* makes him imagine stone walls covered with gold tapestry and wainscoting of Irish wood, to visualize an earthen floor paved with black flagstones and green and yellow bricks. Setting aside his manuscript, Durtal daydreams of the castle's musculature and tegument, supplying the ornament of leather-covered linen chests and high-backed chairs. Confusing the cha-

teau with its residents, he fills both with the incendiary foodstuffs favored by Gilles, roast heron and squab, "plats parfumés, acides, talonnant l'estomac," fermented mulberry juice, "boissons affolantes qui fouettaient la luxure" (1: 185). Durtal peoples the "donjon sans châtelaines" with the women fantasized by drink-enflamed lords, dressing them in fur-lined robes, synthesizing them into "un idéal mannequin" (1: 186) that he drapes with precious stones and purple crystals, as the bones of history are reanimated by the revelry of fiction. Fed and clothed by the imagination of the dead whom Durtal's imagination brings to life, the nothingness dispersed by the centuries is gathered together, given form, focused in the hallucinated image of Madame Chantelouve, the missing mother momentarily restored as a creative mirage. "Et il la regardait, ravi, sans même s'apercevoir que c'était elle, lorsque son chat, sautant sur ses genoux, dériva le ru de ses pensées, le ramena dans sa chambre" (1: 186).

It is beneath the level of religion, under the chapel in the crypt of Tiffauges that the novelist begins his work, changing the skeleton into imagery, satisfying his hunger for beauty with an illusion before he is again left sickened by the body of the real. Unlike the tortured Christ who vanishes into the inexpressible, nineteenth-century matter, distilled into capital, increases, becoming an absence of the tangible goods that money replaces and a surfeit of the acquisitiveness and egotism that money engenders. Durtal's Manicheism causes him to regard Mammon-worship as the first satanic principle,[7] to see the amassing of wealth as "une loi organique atroce, édictée et appliquée depuis que le monde existe" (1: 23). Whereas the piety of Gilles is corroded by profligacy, driving him to alchemy in an attempt to obtain the gold he needs to liquidate his virtue as expensive debauchery, Durtal sees investment as a form of alchemy that makes existing funds self-begetting at the same time it corrupts the just man with thanklessness, lechery, insolence, and greed. Capital is language in mourning, Huysmans says, in its hiding "l'éclat de son nom sous le voile noir d'un mot" (1: 24). As the death of the real revitalizes fiction, an overabundance of matter condensed into a system of exchange that replaces words can only herald the end of art and the enthronement of the Anti-Christ, before whom "les Deux Mondes . . . meurent de désirs . . . comme devant un Dieu" (1: 24-25).

Shared by Docre and Durtal, Huysmans's antipathy for banks stems from a perception of capital as a medium rivaling with language, a signifying system that seizes reality, "accapare les substances" (1: 24), and buries referents in vaults in order to initiate a circulation of symbols that impoverishes the spirit and enriches the material world it destroys and brings back as abstraction. Those who visit Jesus's tomb find it empty, while buried capital (like the archaic fantasy of the omnipotent child who is himself and his mother, his mouth and her breast) is self-engendering: "[il] se nourrit, s'engraisse, s'enfante tout seul, dans une caisse" (1: 24).

In fact, the novel's only allusion to Christ's burial comes when Durtal equates the vacancy of "le Saint Sépulchre" (1: 187) with emptying the coffers of the medieval crusaders who sacrificed everything to liberate it. The Passion of the Savior is therefore linked to the ascesis of Christ's soldiers, "[qui] apportaient leurs richesses, abandonnaient leurs maisons, leurs enfants, leur femmes, acceptaient . . . des souffrances extraordinaires" (1: 187). Significantly, it is Docre who most explicitly describes the economics of the Redemption, as he ridicules the idea that the crucifixion could liquidate humanity's moral debt. Mocking Jesus as the "Vassal enamouré des Banques" (2: 164), Docre's satanic apostrophe taxes the Church with profiting from the despair of the disinherited, with defaulting on its duty to buy back mankind's iniquity with the pain of its martyrs and the prayers of its saints. In Docre's words, the Church becomes "la Chancellerie des Simoniaques" and God himself "le Dieu d'affaires" (2: 165).

Huysmans's insistence on contrasting Catholicism and capitalism, mysticism and Satanism, the Stock Market and the Church ("la forteresse du Bien opposée à la forteresse du Mal")[8] suggests a collapsing of these antitheses and a commercialization of faith that would turn the empty tomb into a full cash depository. Huysmans implies a conflation of Docre's bank god—deaf to the cries of the indigent—and Grunewald's "Christ des Pauvres" (1: 17), as Jesus's metonymization as his "chair triste et faible" (1: 17) recalls the tortured bodies of the poor, and the death cries of the forsaken Son echo "les râles des timides perclus par les famines, des femmes éventrées pour un peu de pain" (2: 164-65).

Crediting the "law of substitution," whereby saints "consume the moral dirt . . . their peers discharge and, in so doing, transmute the stuff of damnation . . . into the saving grace that affords the sinner eternal life,"[9] Huysmans cites the imminent disappearance of Christ's body as the potential nothingness that counterbalances the ugly, proliferating excess of human bodies. It is because Grunewald's Christ has gangrenous flesh that he redeems the corruption of the wicked, because his crypt is empty that it can hold the sins of the world.

If the purpose of art is to effect "une transformation de la matière détendue" (1: 13), the greatest saints are, like Lydwine, "gloutonne[s] de maux,"[10] weeping, suppurating, self-destroying apparatuses that digest the excrement of evil in order to turn it and themselves into nothing. A literature of aggression comes into being when mouths empty of the mother's breast become mouths filled with words of lamentation and fury, when

the missing body becomes the object of disappointment and rage. But then Christ and his Elect reembody the language of mourning as the mother's crucified limbs, and the child's verbal violence is inscribed onto the ignominious yet vanishing bodies of the Blessed, whose suffering turns words back into flesh. Sublimating "la détresse infinie de l'âme" means manifesting "l'immondice éplorée du corps" (1: 19), so that the great art Durtal imagines exists only to capture the instant that the full horror of the Incarnation is achieved and transcended. Disciple of Christ, the coprophagous Maria Alacoque "ramassa avec sa langue les déjections d'une malade" (1: 27), making the tongue that takes away the feces of guilt the tongue that strikes the writer dumb. Of Grunewald, Durtal writes: "Non, cela n'avait d'équivalent dans aucune langue" (1: 19). But before incorporation takes place, sin becomes offal that is eaten and annihilated by saints who waste away into diaphanous envelopes of immaculate invisibility. They are the almost perfect, like Saint Luce, whose body was so transparent, as Madame Chantelouve says, "qu'il voyait au travers de sa poitrine des ordures dans son cœur" (2: 28).

As the text of sin is erased from the page of the body, the martyr's luminous flesh contrasts with the stinking carrion of literature which rots in the wake of Naturalism's exhaustion. Durtal notes the pointlessness of aesthetic debate, the untenability of his theories of fiction, which disintegrate in the crypt of his mind "comme de décombres" (1: 10). Different from the reborn Christ, society is likened to the textual matter it expels, corpses without hope of resurrection: "je pense qu'elle est putréfiée, que ses os se carient, que ses chairs tombent," as Carhaix remarks. "Il est donc nécessaire qu'on l'inhume et qu'une autre naisse. Dieu seul peut accomplir un tel miracle!" (2: 198).

At the end of the novel, there is heard in the street the drunken cheering of people greeting the news of General Boulanger's election. Drowning out discussion of the dawning of the age of the glorious Paraclete, the clamor arrests a narrative which ends with a comment on its own supersession by a continued closing of the alimentary and excretory circuit. Offering itself as a model of literature that cannot finish, *Là-bas* proposes the blankness of its last half page as the clean tomb which becomes a cesspit filled with the cries of the "fétides bourgeois" (2: 235) who do not die but reproduce in order to stuff their guts and drain their soul's sludge "par le bas-ventre" (2: 235).

Underscoring the final impossibility of emptiness or silence, *Là-bas* is nonetheless a novel undertaken in the hope of burying the decomposing text of nineteenth-century realism whose transfigured body could be resurrected in the form of "un naturalisme spiritualiste." The unspoken thing interred in the novel is not the Eucharist, symbol of a reversal of introjection whereby food becomes words. The process that compensates for object loss by initiating discourse "au sein d'une 'communauté de bouches vides'" (Abraham and Torok 263) in fact resubstitutes communion for communication and denies the finality of loss, since the breast is restored as the host collectively consumed by a community that refuses to mourn. But as an unbeliever, Durtal cannot accept the mystery of the transubstantiated body, and his psychic inhumation of Christ's corpse as its empty receptacle assumes the secret, private, clandestine quality of incorporation in the clinical sense. Topologically represented by the vacated sepulcher, the textual lacuna refers to what cannot be eaten or expressed, since *"la perte soudaine d'un objet narcissiquement indispensable"* is also *"de nature à en interdire la communication"* (264).

In his biography of the author, Robert Baldick points to the writing of *Là-bas* as a pivotal moment in Huysmans's gradual progression toward conversion to Catholicism. Durtal's inability to believe, Baldick says, signals Huysmans's dawning realization "that only through faith in Christ could he satisfy the yearning for spiritual tranquillity which possessed his questing and weary soul."[11] Whereas Folantin at the end of *À vau-l'eau* had embraced the pessimism of Schopenhauer, by 1891, the year of the publication of *Là-bas,* Huysmans had already begun to turn away from a philosophy which offered no consolation to the disheartened: "the emptiness of [Schopenhauer's] conclusions repels me," he writes in a letter to an unidentified critic. "In the unintelligible abomination which is life, there simply cannot be nothing at all" (cit. in Baldick 181).

Despite this formulation, it is clear that, for Huysmans, an excess of corporeal existence, experienced as an intolerable everything, requires that its spiritual complement be defined as "nothing at all." It is because the incarnated Christ is miraculously changed into bread and wine of the kind with which fetid bourgeois stuff themselves that the lost object is incorporated as absence.

In Huysmans's novel, Durtal repeatedly insists on the literary separation of the material and spiritual. So while he acknowledges the terrestrial rut dug by Zola, Durtal stresses the need "de tracer en l'air un chemin parallèle, une autre route" (1: 11). Yet, the main portion of *Là-bas* is devoted to cataloguing incomprehensible or diabolical efforts to intermingle the sacred and the profane, the celestial and the earthly—attempts made by practitioners of the occult sciences Huysmans had begun to research prior to beginning his book. The knowledge of astral projection, the casting of spells, the apotelesmatic erudition of Gévingey, the invocation of the dead are dismissed, not as charlatanism, but as an affront to art. Horrified at the notion that the corner grocer could call up at a seance the ghost of Victor Hugo, Durtal regards

necromancers, satanists, Rosicrucian thaumaturgists as threatening the purity of the immaterial. So when Durtal sees the statue of a tumescent Christ at Docre's Black Mass, it represents for him a literalizing of the Incarnation which denies the divinity that Christ should embody.

Whereas scientific positivism is faulted for trying to explain the unexplainable, the occultists Durtal encounters impoverish the spiritual realm by lowering it to the level of the material. The demonic possession of the Ursuline sisters of Loudun is assimilated to symptoms of the hysteria Charcot diagnoses in his patients at La Salpêtrière (I, 233).[12] Accorded by medicine a certain statutory reality, evil is still banalized as pathology and therefore loses its prestige once it is diagnostically reduced to being "nothing at all." Saturating the invisible world with microbes, germs, *larves,* and *esprits volants,* science and satanism do not destroy matter but, by making it infinitesimally small, succeed only in magnifying its toxicity: "l'atmosphère peut, tout aussi bien charrier des Esprits que des bacilles," Durtal muses (1: 76).

As empty space is not really empty but seethes with microscopic agents of malevolence and disease, death does not bring an end to the corporeal but perpetuates an aggressive cycle of eating that begins with the infant nursing at the breast, continues with consuming the Eucharistic wafer, and starts over again with maggots digesting the digestive organs of overstuffed bourgeois cadavers in a sepulchral banquet of "ragoût de bon gros ventres" (1: 45). As Huysmans's revulsion for matter and food leads to a rejection of the Incarnation, des Hermies embraces the Manichean belief in the coequal principles of Good and Evil, invoking the memory of the twelfth-century heretics of Albi who were exterminated for repudiating the doctrine of Christ's humanity (1: 96).

Abraham and Torok maintain that, in incorporation, the object whose loss cannot be mourned once played the role of ego ideal. Yet the death of the object does not set in motion a mourning process that culminates in introjection whereby the loss can be expressed ("les *mots* de la bouche . . . venant . . . combler le vide du sujet" [264]). Instead, there is imputed to the object some secret shame that forbids recourse to language and results in swallowing the "objet honni," whose sullied status leaves it "fécalisé" and triggers fantasies of scatophagia of the kind associated with Huysmans's saints. The dead object can be preserved in the crypt of disavowal only if the subject euphemizes the loved one's imperfections and internalizes them as virtues—only if, as Abraham and Torok write, "le cryptophore . . . neutralise . . . les instruments . . . de la flétrissure, les métaphores issues de la déjection, de l'excrément, en posant ceux-ci comme comestibles, voire appétissants" (268).

Here one finds reasons for Durtal's parting company with the faithful, who celebrate the sacrament and accept the miraculous transformation of the abject body of Grunewald's Christ into ambrosial nourishment that assures the spirit eternal life. Despite regression from speech to consumption, Christ's interment for the Catholic is not a true instance of incorporation, since communion is a public, communal, joyous event intended to "exorciser le penchant . . . d'une incorporation psychique" (265).

As for literature, there is consensus among Huysmans's critics that the author was first drawn to Catholicism by the majesty of religious art: the beauty of the liturgy, the simplicity of plainchant, the soaring architecture of Chartres, the rich symbolism of medieval iconography described with such passion in Huysmans's post-conversion novels. Subsuming what is individual in art to analysis of anonymous art-as-worship, Huysmans begins in *En route* to exalt the doxological function of creation over the purely self-expressive.

It is the end of literature in this regard that is effected by incorporation, not of Christ's fecalized body, but of the Christ whose disappearance from the tomb and text recapitulates the loss caused by his death. As corruption teems with life and dead bourgeois bellies provide nourishment for worms, the rot of history fertilizes fiction, enabling verminous Naturalism to thrive on a diet of social decay. But if the Incarnation is rejected and Christ is removed from the cycle of alimentation, the repression of God's physicality becomes what is incorporated and makes emptiness the contents of the crypt. The narcissistic wound suffered when an idealized object is soiled need not be healed if the object has no material reality. Indeed, Durtal's inability to accept Christianity logically proceeds from a denial of Christ's body, since there can be no degradation of what does not exist to begin with.

It is easy to understand, then, why Durtal should be reluctant to publish his work on Gilles, as finished books themselves become edible corpses that slowly disintegrate into the biscuit-flavored dust blanketing library shelves. But if it is not an object of oral aggression, what is literature's purpose? "Alors quoi," Durtal asks about the future of his craft. In suggesting a way to resolve Durtal's perplexity, *Là-bas* stipulates that the production of the mystical text should follow the destruction of its antecedents. From the baby's cries over the mother's absence, language, which had always aimed at restoration of the body, finally moves toward its suppression, enshrining in the crypt the lost object as loss itself. As Christ's body ensures communion, his disappearance signals a transcendence of the material and guarantees the possibility of creating a text whose sole purpose is to bear witness. When there is nothing left to taste—no more excrement to scoop up—the tongue is

stilled, and the Resurrection that justified the writer's work also mutes him. Because it incorporates nothing as the potential for unlimited new creation, Huysmans's novel can express its hunger for the inexpressible only by describing an impossible dialectic: of the emptiness of the Sepulcher and the inexhaustibility of its riches, and the unwritability of the holy text and its proof that God is God.

Notes

1. Joris-Karl Huysmans, *Là-bas, Œuvres complètes XII* (Geneva: Slatkine, 1972) 1: 10.

2. Max Milner, "*Là-bas*: l'écriture dans le roman," *Revue des Sciences Humaines* 43.170-171 (April-September 1978): 11.

3. J. Hillis Miller, "The Critic as Host," in *Deconstruction and Criticism,* ed. Harold Bloom et al. (New York: Seabury P, 1987) 225.

4. Nicolas Abraham and Maria Torok, *L'Écorce et le Noyau* (Paris: Aubier Flammarion, 1978) 235.

5. Joseph Smith also sees the impulse to create as arising from the process of mourning: "the work of art," he suggests, "ultimately recapitulates original loss and celebrates the original imagistic recreation of the mother." "Mourning, Art, and Human Historicity," in *Telling Facts: History and Narration in Psychoanalysis,* ed. Joseph Smith (Baltimore: Johns Hopkins UP, 1982) 138.

6. "Jesus and Object-Use: A Winnicottian Account of the Resurrection Myth," in *Transitional Objects and Potential Spaces,* ed. Peter L. Rudnytsky (New York: Columbia UP, 1993) 258.

7. "Eh bien!" Durtal concludes, "ou l'argent qui est ainsi maître des âmes, est diabolique, ou il est impossible à expliquer" (1: 25).

8. Joris-Karl Huysmans, *Saint-Séverin, Œuvres complètes X* (Geneva: Slatkine, 1972) 14.

9. Robert Ziegler, "From Body Magic to 'Divine Alchemy': Anality and Sublimation in J.-K. Huysmans," *Orbis Litterarum* 4 (1989): 321.

10. Joris-Karl Huysmans, *Sainte Lydwine de Schiedam, Œuvres complètes* XV (Geneva: Slatkine, 1972) 2: 115.

11. Robert Baldick, *The Life of J.-K. Huysmans* (Oxford: Oxford at Clarendon P, 1955) 179.

12. For Jean Lorrain, it is the aesthetic and not the metaphysical consequences of this medicalization of the supernatural that matter. Patterned closely on Huysmans's text is a discussion between two theater-goers in Lorrain's "Lanterne Magique." Deploring the fact that science has killed the fan-

tastic, one says: "Oui, je sais, l'hypnotisme, le magnétisme, la suggestion et l'hystérie, les expériences de Charcot à la Salpêtrière, les demoiselles échevelées qui s'arc-boutent sur les mains et font aimablement cerceau sous le fallacieux prétexte qu'on leur a passé dans l'œil un reflet de cuiller, les actes de somnambulisme à tant l'heure, et les grands écarts de Mmes Donato. Moi, j'aime mieux les possédées, les religieuses de Loudun et les convulsionnaires de Saint-Médard; du moins le décor y était." *Histoires de masques* (Paris: Ollendorff, 1900) 51.

Elizabeth Emery (essay date 2001)

SOURCE: Emery, Elizabeth. "'The Soul of Arches': Huysmans and the Medieval Church." In *Romancing the Cathedral: Gothic Architecture in Fin-de-Siècle French Culture*, pp. 89-128. Albany: State University of New York Press, 2001.

[*In the following excerpt, Emery discusses Durtal's fascination with the Satanist Gilles de Rais in* Là-bas, *as well as his interest in the Middle Ages and medieval religious architecture.*]

> [Des Esseintes] may have been drawn toward the priesthood because the Church alone had collected art, the lost form of the centuries [. . .] the majority of the precious objects catalogued in the Musée de Cluny, having miraculously escaped the vile brutality of the sans-culottes, are from the old abbeys of France. Just as the Church preserved philosophy, history and literature from barbarism in the Middle Ages, so it has saved the plastic arts, protected until now those wonderful models of fabric and jewelry that manufacturers of holy objects spoil as much as they can even though they are unable to alter their initial, exquisite form. It was not thus surprising that he had sought out these antique bibelots, that he had, like many other collectors, taken these relics away from the antique stores and the secondhand country shops.
>
> —Huysmans, *A rebours* (1884)

Zola and Huysmans were fundamentally unhappy with their time. Jean Jaurès, in an 1895 article for *La Petite République Française,* commented on the sense of dissatisfaction that permeated fin-de-siècle life: "Some throw themselves into the socialist fray to finish with the ignominious world that no longer knows how to atone for the pain of the exploited with the joy of the exploiter. Others, like Huysmans, disdainful and wounded, take mental and emotional refuge in cloisters, in the deep fervent peace of the mystical Middle Ages."[1] Jaurès sums up the public perception of Zola's and Huysmans's differing reactions to the 1890s. While Zola seemed to reform society through his political activity, Huysmans appeared to withdraw: he converted to

Catholicism and began writing books about the symbolism, mysticism, and hagiography of the Middle Ages. By using the phrase "mystical Middle Ages," Jaurès capitalizes on a term made popular by the otherworldliness of Huysmans's *Là-Bas,* and applied by contemporaries to visions, apparitions, and dreams. Jean Lorrain, for example, distinguished mysticism from religion in an article for *Le Courrier français*: "[Mysticism] is fabulous poetry, the exaltation of imaginations that take offense at the harshness and rationalism of dogma."[2] This popular definition, which concentrates on conflicts between reality and fantasy, differed both from Huysmans's use of the word mysticism—an attempt to "articulate the inexpressible"—and from that of the Middle Ages—a way of speaking about using and understanding religious terms.[3] Although contemporaries perceived Huysmans as an escapist who hid from the problems of his time by fleeing into a neomedieval dreamworld of saints, cloisters, and cathedrals, part of this misconception developed from their incomprehension of his relationship to mysticism. His characters did not take solace in the darkened interiors of medieval houses of worship on a whim; like Zola, Huysmans used an idealized image of the cathedral in his novels in order to bring moral equilibrium to a society he perceived as corrupted by materialism and individualism. Where Zola claimed the cathedral for a secular religion of the future, Huysmans used it promote Catholicism. This chapter questions the ways in which Huysmans capitalized upon his contemporaries' fondness for museums, medieval art, and music to encourage them to treasure the cathedral and the religion it harbored.

. . . . .

THE CATHEDRAL AND THE PILGRIM

In *Là-Bas,* the first novel of the Durtal cycle, the narrator describes a medieval Dutch painting that hangs on the wall of Durtal's apartment. The painting portrays a hermit, crouched under a hut of branches, who, in a series of scenes, travels by boat and foot from a village to the Orient. The unknown saint's quest comes to an end as he climbs a hill toward an unfinished cathedral. As Ruth Antosh has noted, Huysmans probably intended this painting to prefigure Durtal's spiritual quest, which also ends with a cathedral. In his description of Durtal's apartment, the narrator mentions that this painting hangs over the fireplace in the space generally filled by a mirror. In fact, Huysmans owned this painting and knew the identity of the saint. It was Jerome, the translator of the Bible, a scholar who gave up worldly literature to study religious texts. Huysmans's decision to leave the holy man of the painting nameless thus invites a link with Durtal, who has no given name, no family, and is also a hermit who abandons secular literature for that of the Church.[4] Durtal and the saint make a physical journey that parallels their spiritual quest.

The relationship between Huysmans and his pilgrim character is complex: Huysmans, too, converted to Catholicism after writing a work about satanism. Through contacts with priests and through research into the alchemy, medicine, and hagiography of the Middle Ages, both men were drawn to the mysticism and symbolism of the Church. Both were enamored of the history and aesthetics of Catholicism, and both managed to tear themselves painfully from carnal desires in order to convert. After long struggles, they both become Benedictine oblates, thereby officially attaching themselves to religious communities. Both were forced back to Paris after their congregations fled to Belgium. Because of these similarities, the Durtal cycle is often interpreted as a thinly veiled autobiography.[5] But as Michel Viegnes has suggested, Huysmans uses Durtal to play a game of "hide and show": Durtal allows him to rewrite his life more positively than an autobiography.[6] Huysmans did, in fact, borrow from his own experience to portray Durtal's struggles to convert, but Durtal is not a true reflection of Huysmans.

Durtal, the hermit and pilgrim was free from social attachments, while Huysmans could never distance himself from them. For thirty years (until his retirement in 1898), Huysmans worked as a government employee, notably at the Ministry of the Interior (he was named *Chevalier* then *Officier de l'ordre de la légion d'honneur* for his achievements in administration); he ran his mother's book bindery once she died; he went on trips and corresponded regularly with his friends; and he took care of his sick mistress, Anna Meunier, his stepsisters, and his friends, Bloy, Verlaine, and Villiers de l'Isle-Adam. He was the executor of the estates of both Villiers and his friend Edmond de Goncourt, and became the first president of L'Académie Goncourt. Remy de Gourmont summed up Huysmans's tendency to complain bitterly about his job, his family, and social obligations while upholding them all to the best of his abilities when he said: "Until the end he remained vicious in words and kind in deeds."[7] It is ironic that Huysmans, who, for years, routinely dealt with problems caused by the Panama Canal scandal, the anarchist attacks of 1892-94, and the Dreyfus Affair while at work,[8] should be thought an escapist, while Zola, who spent half the year writing in Médan or Aixen-Provence—in what he called "my hole"—should be praised as a social activist.[9]

Huysmans wrote at work and during vacations; Durtal lives from his writing and has no other obligations. Huysmans went to churches accompanied by his friends George Landry and Gustave Boucher; Durtal is always alone in *En Route,* a solitary observer of church art and ceremony. While Huysmans shared a house with a married couple, the Leclaires, during his time as a Benedictine oblate at Ligugé, in *L'Oblat* Durtal lives with no one but his housekeeper. Durtal is a purified, simplified

version of Huysmans, with no responsibilities. Although the outline of their conversion is similar, Durtal is not Huysmans, but an idealized alter ego from which all complications except the spiritual have been removed.

In many ways, Durtal was the instigator of his author's quest. Huysmans conceived of *En Route* as a way of capitalizing on the novelty of satanism and mysticism. He saw it as a "white book"—the sequel and opposite ("à rebours") of *Là-Bas.*[10] It began as *Là-Haut,* a study of Christian mysticism and the writings of Teresa of Avila and Mary of Agreda. But as Huysmans frequented churches to gather information about Durtal's studies, he himself converted to Catholicism.[11] Reading *Là-Haut,* which was rediscovered in 1965, gives one the impression that Huysmans was practicing in fiction what he would go on to do in reality, as if his future crystallized as he wrote his novels.[12] There is a constant interplay between Huysmans's documentation for the Durtal cycle and his self-transformation as he wrote about Durtal.

The murky give-and-take between autobiography and fiction in the Durtal cycle can be clarified in light of the numerous late-nineteenth-century French conversions to Catholicism. Huysmans's novels are less autobiography, per se, than "conversion narrative," a genre that derives from the great Christian tradition of Augustine's *Confessions.* In his study of the 160 conversions of intellectuals that took place in France from 1885 to 1935, Frédéric Gugelot proves that the sheer volume of spiritual chronicles published at this time allows us to set this genre apart from other kinds of personal narrative. Accounts of conversion took many different forms (journals, essays, stories, novels) and differed in length, but like the Durtal cycle, all focus on the spiritual evolution of the principle character. Written at a distance from the actual event (hindsight was crucial for the analysis of the steps leading to conversion), the author's primary allegiance was to psychology.

Such accounts, written by intellectuals as varied as Léon Bloy, Adolphe Retté, François Coppée, Henri Ghéon, Paul Claudel, and Francis Jammes, sought to understand a unique conversion experience and to present it to others. Conversion was thus not only a private act between a believer and God, but also a public act of social and religious engagement for the Church. A confession narrative could edify unbelievers by demonstrating to them the rocky but rewarding path from loneliness and isolation to spiritual fulfillment. This journey is one step in the two-part dynamic of religious practice that Michel de Certeau breaks into "the act" and "the place." The "act" involves accepting faith and attempting to embrace the difficult and unending journey it entails, while the "place" is the destination, the longed for infinite experience. Because it is impossible to be assured of arriving at the final term of this journey—that is to say the exchanges and sharing that take place in a religious community—"community practice" is, for all intents and purposes, the "*real* place of religious life." "There is no longer any room for individualism."[13] The conversion narrative, which illustrates the ways in which an individual embraces faith and attempts to leave egotistical practices for spiritual completion at the heart of a community, provides a message that appealed to a society anxious about fragmentation and isolation. By proposing model itineraries and by naming welcoming communities, this genre was an extremely successful way of bringing people to the Church.[14] The Durtal novels should be considered within this Catholic context; the entire series takes shape and meaning in light of Durtal's spiritual journey.

Durtal is a simple figure; Huysmans's brilliance was to turn his own conversion narrative into a fictional product in which his everyman character provides a model for contemporaries. In his well-known review of *A rebours,* Barbey d'Aurevilly had remarked on the symbolic nature of Des Esseintes, whose spiritual torment served as an allegory of the soul of materialistic modern society: "In writing the biography of his hero, [Huysmans] not only presents the peculiar confession of a depraved and solitary character, but, simultaneously writes a case study of a society putrefied by materialism."[15] Durtal's bourgeois background makes him an even better reflection of modern society's spiritual illness than the flamboyant Des Esseintes. They both long to escape from the modern world and the *ennui* it inspires, but where Des Esseintes is the last of a degenerate race, Durtal is destined to evolve. His name implies both aridity and the possibility of change, as Huysmans told a friend: "In the languages of the North, [Durtal] signifies 'Valley of aridity' or 'Valley of the door.'"[16] Durtal wanders the wasteland of modern society seeking spiritual refreshment. Not unlike Zola's Pierre Froment, he is a figure of compromise who wants to believe. He visits all the churches of Paris, stays in a Trappist monastery, goes to Notre-Dame de la Salette, studies Notre-Dame de Chartres, visits the monastic community of Solesmes, and finally becomes an oblate attached to a Benedictine community.

How does the cathedral become a recurring motif and an emblem that helps his character along his journey? Durtal's spiritual adviser, l'abbé Gévresin, often tells Durtal that change in environment is necessary to gauging spiritual progress. In the Durtal cycle (as in *Les Trois Villes* and *A la recherche du temps perdu*), descriptions of cathedrals at stages of his journey reflect the character's spiritual evolution. They reveal his psychological state by externalizing his point of view. In *Là-Bas,* Durtal admires churches as does Des Esseintes; he considers them medieval museums that have preserved intriguing art from the past. As he learns more about the Church and its traditions in *En Route* and *La*

Cathédrale, however, he begins to see cathedrals in a spiritual dimension. He is horrified by those who (like Des Esseintes), buy altarpieces, tapestries, and lamps that used to belong in churches. Durtal begins to feel that a church's soul is dependent on the continuation of music, ornamentation, and ceremony. Yet at the end of *La Cathédrale* and in *L'Oblat,* he realizes that the art's material pales in comparison with its role in disseminating a spiritual message. In the Durtal cycle, descriptions of the cathedral accompany Durtal's shifting attitude toward public and private space, aesthetic and commercial production, didacticism and intuition.[17]

Second, as Huysmans developed the Durtal cycle as a conversion narrative, he adopted the cathedral as a model that reflected the form and content of his novels. Like Victor Hugo, he represented the cathedral as the foremost example of medieval art—"the most magnificent expression of art that the Middle Ages left us"—while describing literature as the pinnacle of modern art: "the most complicated, the most interlocking, the most haughty of all the arts."[18] Huysmans saw the cathedral as way for the Church to teach the uninitiated about the Christian community; similarly, he saw the novel as a way of educating his contemporaries about the communal values an increasingly secular and materialistic society had neglected. The cathedral's ability to link a seemingly infinite variety of art forms, theological messages, and social functions by subordinating them to a central value—Catholicism—also provided Huysmans with a model for his novels, in which description, dialogue, didactic messages, and plot were subordinated to Durtal's evolving consciousness.

THE CATHEDRAL AS MUSEUM

At the beginning of *Là-Bas,* Durtal incarnates the spiritual exhaustion of the fin de siècle. He is a former naturalist who has stopped writing novels because he is tired of elaborating fiction to surround his research and he can no longer bear the pettiness of literary squabbles. He is barely able to leave his Paris apartment because he so despises other people. In order to occupy himself, he has begun writing a study of Gilles de Rais, the marshal who assisted Joan of Arc before becoming a mass murderer, the diabolical model for Bluebeard.[19] Durtal is fascinated by Gilles de Rais's sudden shifts between Catholicism and satanism. But above all, he enjoys his project because it allows him to escape from the real world: "He had plunged into the terrifying and delicious late Middle Ages [. . .] he began to live in cool contempt for his surroundings and created for himself an existence far from the hubbub of literature, mentally cloistering himself, when all was said, in the castle of Tiffauges."[20] His research shuts him off from his problems and serves as therapy for the depression that ruins his health.

Like his contemporaries, Durtal has great admiration for bibelots. In fact, Durtal is fascinated by Gilles de Rais's conspicuous consumption. In an interesting act of self-referentiality, Huysmans describes Gilles de Rais—"the Des Esseintes of the fifteenth century"—as a writer, an artist, a musician, and a collector who isolated himself in the castle of Tiffauges in order to indulge his exotic tastes:

> The luxury of his chapel and collegiate church was practically demented. A complete metropolis of clergy—deans, vicars, treasurers, canons, clerks, deacons, school boys, and choir boys—was in residence at Tiffauges; an inventory remains of surplices, stoles, and amices, and fur choir hats lined with vair. Sacerdotal ornaments abound; here, one finds altar coverings of vermilion cloth, curtains of emerald silk, a cope of crimson and violet with gold trimmed borders, another of rose damask, satin dalmatics for the deacons, canopies embroidered, engraved with Cyprus gold; there, dishes, chalices and ciboria hammered and encrusted with uncut jewels, set with gems, reliquaries, including a silver head of Saint Honoré, a mass of incandescent treasures that an artist, installed in the castle, cuts to order.[21]

Durtal's rapture with Gilles de Rais's material possessions is striking in the three pages of this passage, which is less a description than an illustrated catalog of bibelots that he has elaborated for his friend, Des Hermies. Durtal is fascinated by Gilles de Rais as collector. The chapel explodes with color and light: from the red, green, purple, and blue fabrics to the reflections emanating from the gold, silver, and gem-encrusted artwork. Durtal revels in the opulence of the chapel without commenting on it. He makes no judgments about the ceremonies that might have been performed in such a radiant chapel, nor does he consider Gilles de Rais's beliefs or actions. He relishes the simple pleasure of rolling the names off his tongue. His enthusiastic enumerations of events in Gilles de Rais's life continue in this vein: he describes medieval documents pertaining to the Hundred Years War, alchemy and satanism, hagiography and hygiene, dress and interior design, and legal records with similar litanies of objects.[22] His appreciation of the Middle Ages and medieval religious architecture derives from the pleasure he takes in appropriating information and coveting rare objects from the past.

Durtal's fascination for collecting the dispersed documents recounting Gilles de Rais's life and reassembling them in his own work strikingly resembles the process by which Des Esseintes constructs his private cloister or chapel in *A rebours*. Durtal chooses only those documents that most interest him, thus turning his own writing into a thematic space in which he re-creates Gilles de Rais as a reflection of his own perverse imagination. He delights in the inanimate excesses of Gilles de Rais's collecting habits, yet he also lingers over the grisly details of the satanic rites—"litanies of lust"—practiced by the Marshal. Gilles de Rais raped his altar boys and dismembered over 800 children in what could be called his chapel *à rebours*, the bloody chamber in which he practiced his diabolical activities:

> Once their senses are phosporized, dazed by the powerful venison juices, kindled by inflammatory beverages laced with spices, Gilles and his friends retire into a distant chamber of the castle. The little boys locked up in the cellar are brought there. They are undressed, they are gagged; the marshal fondles them and forces them, then he gashes them with a dagger, taking great pleasure in dismembering them, piece by piece. At other times he splits their chest and he drinks the breath of their lungs; sometimes he opens up their belly, sniffs it, enlarges the wound with his hands and sits inside. Then, while he macerates in the mud softened by warm entrails, he turns himself around to look over his shoulder, so as to watch the supreme convulsions, the last spasms.[23]

Huysmans listed precious articles to evoke Durtal's materialistic fascination with Gilles de Rais's sumptuous chapel. But here the profusion of body parts—"chest," "lungs," "belly," "hands," "entrails"—coupled with the violence of the rapidly succeeding verbs—"fondle," "force," "gash," "dismember," "split"—creates a dizzying effect of mass butchery. The immediacy of the present tense places Durtal at the scene of the crime and exposes his vicarious enjoyment of the sacrilegious activities that take place in the bloody chamber. Unlike the chapel, which Huysmans described using archaic names and adjectives of color linked by a profusion of commas and semicolons, here the power of the spectacle derives primarily from the barrage of simple clauses in which verbs violate nouns.

How are we to interpret Durtal's perverse pleasure in recreating the decadent chapel and torture chamber of Gilles de Rais? Does Huysmans, too, delight in such grisly enumeration? Or is Durtal, like Des Esseintes, intended as a tongue-in-cheek mockery of contemporary excess?[24] The most likely answer, as for *A rebours,* is both. With Gilles de Rais, "the Des Esseintes of the fifteenth century," Huysmans pushes the caricatured collector of *A rebours* one step further in his continued psychological study of the lengths to which a desperately bored person will go in search of excitement. Such parallels between medieval and modern are constant throughout the novel, especially as Durtal discovers satanism in modern Paris. He participates in a similar—though slightly less bloody—scene near the end of the novel, when he attends a black mass with Hyacinthe Chantelouve, a married woman with whom he has an affair. What seems, at first glance, a normal low mass held in a chapel, becomes, by the end, a ceremony that completely violates the Eucharistic adoration with words, gestures, and bodily fluids. The mass culminates in a wild and obscene orgy in which the priest—a practicing Catholic priest—debauches choir boys, women, and men in equal numbers while they desecrate statues, the host, and people around them.[25]

As an antidote to such dissipation, Huysmans creates an alternate group that meets at the top of Saint Sulpice church in the lodgings of Carhaix, the bell ringer. Durtal discusses his adventures and tells his friends that he is not surprised that fin-de-siècle society is in such disarray when even spiritual counselors desecrate their vows by becoming degenerate agents of corruption. He insists that the nineteenth century is no worse than the Middle Ages; his time simply lacks moral direction. Gilles de Rais was able to repent and was forgiven by the victims' families, who prayed for him—"the soul of the Middle Ages shone in all its candid splendor"—but his modern ancestors continue to degenerate.[26] Carhaix believes that Catholicism will improve contemporaries, but Durtal and Des Hermies are less confident. Because they feel that belief in the supernatural has vanished, they fear that the children of the future will continue to worship their individual interests and consumerism, thus sinking further into the morass: "They will stuff their guts and flush souls through their loins."[27] The book closes with these words.

The sheer invective Durtal and his friends spew at nearly every sphere of society—politics, religion, science, literature, art—often make this work uncomfortable to read. In fact, Huysmans had intended to disturb his public by pointing out their superficiality and materialism.[28] The last thing he expected, however, was a resounding commercial success. Not only did the novel inflame the literary battles of the Huret interviews, but it was also banned in train stations, became a bestseller, and was labeled "the breviary of satanism," thus turning it into a vogue.[29] Two years later, Huysmans was still flabbergasted by the impact of the novel: "The strange thing about all of this—is that in spite of Panama [. . .] people talk about nothing but enchantment, black magic [. . .] I really shook things up."[30] Though Huysmans's violence was meant to disturb his contemporaries by showing them the dark side of modern France, his emphasis on communal spirituality introduces a solution. The book is not a unilateral condemnation of contemporary values, but suggests (albeit rather grudgingly) good morals as the basis for social renewal. Durtal is too attached to reason and materialism to abandon himself to faith, yet he senses that he must do so in order to end his spleen.

Durtal, a figure who so clearly encapsulates contemporary fascination for the unusual and the rare, provides Huysmans with a way of commenting on society's unhealthy obsession with materialism. He opens the door to what he calls "spiritual naturalism." *Là-Bas* begins with an extended commentary on this concept, which he illustrates by studying the ways in which the

Karlsruhe Crucifixion of Mattheus Grünewald carefully represents material elements (naturalism) while commenting on the way they represent religious exaltation (spiritual). Huysmans's literary tableaux—from dazzling chapel to bloody chamber to Gothic courtroom—reflect this technique as the art itself reveals Durtal's spiritual state. By the end of the novel he has changed. We find the inveterate loner and shut-in of the first pages at the top of Saint-Sulpice, philosophizing with a group of friends about how to save society. In this warm, cozy space, high above Paris, Durtal learns to appreciate the company of others.

Notes

1. Cited in Griffiths, 254-255.

2. In this article, which discusses a "bal mystique" inspired by *Là-Bas,* he added that mysticism was "grafted" upon religion, but was not a "synonym." *Le Courrier français* (22 February 1891).

3. See De Certeau. *The Mystic Fable,* vol. 1 (Trans. Michael B. Smith. Chicago: University of Chicago Press, 1992): 76. In chapters two and three, he defines the fifteenth-century concept of the mystic sciences as a *modus loquendi* that evolved into a "new science" in the sixteenth and seventeenth centuries.

4. The painting appears in *OC* [*Oeuvres complètes*] XII, 1, 121-122. See Ruth B. Antosh, "The Role of Paintings in Three Novels by J.-K. Huysmans."

5. While Robert Baldick's seminal biography, *The Life of J.-K. Huysmans,* gives a detailed account of Huysmans's life, the author often refers to the Durtal cycle as "autobiographical" and uses Durtal's experiences to describe Huysmans's. He also borrows liberally from literary works to describe the author's childhood, of which little is known. Most subsequent biographers have used Baldick's work extensively.

6. "Durtal et Huysmans: le jeu du montré et du caché," 181-82.

7. Cited in Lloyd, 10. See Baldick's biography for examples of Huysmans's kindness. Despite his outward grumpiness, he supported many people, both materially and psychologically. Christopher Lloyd sketches one of the most accurate and complex pictures of Huysmans's life in the first chapter of *Huysmans and the Fin-de-Siècle Novel,* 1-18.

8. In 1886 Huysmans was promoted to "sous-chef" in the Director's office of the Sûreté générale. He was in charge of expulsing immigrants and administering the pension plans of coup d'état victims. His correspondence with Arij Prins often

evokes the effects political and social troubles had on his job. Pierre Froment's visit to the Ministry of Finance in *Paris* gives an impression of the hectic atmosphere of such an environment.

9. Almost every letter from Huysmans to Hannon, Destrée, Prins or Goncourt focuses on Zola's absence, and emphasizes Huysmans's jealousy of his situation. The persistent myth about Zola's social activism developed in the 1890s when Zola threw himself into the Dreyfus Affair.

10. Letters to Arij Prins. 27 April 1891 (letter 108): 219; 23 May 1891 (letter 109): 222.

11. Madeleine Ortoleva summarizes the transformations of this project (22-40).

12. Examples of Huysmans's tendency to follow his character include his conversion, Durtal's research on Sainte Lydwine de Schiedam (which Huysmans would publish in 1901) and Durtal's desire to become a Benedictine oblate (Huysmans would do so in 1899).

13. *La Faiblesse de croire*, 8-9.

14. Gugelot, 227-268.

15. Cited in Descaves, "Notice," *OC* VII, 351-52.

16. Huysmans did not generally attach a great deal of importance to character names: he tended to use the names of places he had seen in train timetables. Durtal's name was special. When a friend mentioned Durtal as the name of a town, Huysmans latched on its northern etymologies, then used the word to name Durtal. See Baldick, 165, for this story. See also Viegnes, *Le Milieu*, 140-41, for a reading of the "door" symbolism in Durtal's name.

17. Although Michel Viegnes has written two very good chapters about Durtal's penchant for Gothic and Romanesque sanctuaries in *Le Milieu et l'individu dans la triologie de Joris-Karl Huysmans*, he considers them all on the same level. He does not explore Durtal's changing perception of these spaces throughout his quest. Durtal is progressively able to loosen his fixation on their material values in favor of the spiritual.

18. *Certains, OC* X, 8-9.

19. Durtal explains that a King Cômor was the true model for Perrault's tale, but regional legends continued to link Gilles de Rais's butchery of small children to the Bluebeard story (*OC*, XII, 2, 30).

20. *OC* XII, 1, 29.

21. *OC* XII, 1, 76-78

22. *OC* XII, 1, 124-137; *OC* XII, 2, 26-29; *OC* XII, 1, 177-187.

23. *OC* XII, 2, 14

24. See Baldick for the genesis of the novel as well as for various acquaintances Huysmans praised and mocked through Des Esseintes, 78-81.

25. *OC* XII, 2, 198.

26. *OC* XII, 2, 141. He is similarly impressed by the crowd's forgiveness before Gilles de Rais's execution (*OC* XII, 2, 232). This is, of course, a grossly idealized vision of medieval action, but Durtal's fascination with the positive aspects of the crowd is interesting for a character who is also so passionately interested in evil.

27. "Ils s'empliront les tripes et vidangeront l'âme par le bas-ventre" (*OC* XII, 2, 235). Thanks to Anthony Taylor Rischard for translation suggestions.

28. Nearly every letter from this period emphasizes the glee with which Huysmans anticipated the outrage of naturalists, mystics, Catholics, and those who practiced the occult sciences. See especially the correspondence with Arij Prins, letters 93-105.

29. See Baldick, 166, Issacharoff, 82-91, and Weber, 32-35.

30. 12 February 1893, letter 122 to Prins: 249.

Selected Bibliography

PRIMARY SOURCES

Huysmans, J.-K. *Lettres à Théodore Hannon (1876-1886)*. Ed. Pierre Cogny and Christian Berg. Saint-Cyr-sur-Loire: Christian Pirot, 1985.

———. *Lettres inédites à Arij Prins*. Annotated by Louis Gillet. Geneva: Librairie Droz, 1977.

———. *Lettre inédites à Edmond de Goncourt*. Ed. Pierre Lambert and Pierre Cogny. Paris: Librairie Nizet, 1956.

———. *Lettres inédites à Jules Destrée*. Ed. Gustave Wanwelkenhuyzen. Textes Littéraires Français. Geneva: Librairie Droz, 1967.

———. *Oeuvres complètes de J.-K. Huysmans*. Ed. Lucien Descaves. Geneva: Slatkine Reprints, 1972.

SECONDARY SOURCES

Antosh, Ruth B. "The Role of Paintings in Three Novels by J.-K. Huysmans." *Nineteenth-Century French Studies* 1984 (Summer-Fall 12-13:4-1): 131-46.

Baldick, Robert. *The Life of J.-K. Huysmans*. Oxford: Clarendon Press, 1955.

De Certeau, Michel. *La Faiblesse de Croire.* Paris: Editions du Seuil, 1987.

Griffiths, Richard. *The Reactionary Revolution. The Catholic Revival in French Literature, 1870-1914.* New York: Frederick Ungar Publishing Co., 1965.

Gugelot, Frédéric. *La Conversion des intellectuels au catholicisme en France 1885-1935.* Paris: CNRS Editions, 1998.

Issacharoff, Michael. *J.-K. Huysmans devant la critique en France.* Paris: Editions Klincksieck, 1970.

Lloyd, Christopher. *Huysmans and the Fin-de-siècle Novel.* Edinburgh: Edinburgh University Press, 1990.

Ortoleva, Madeleine Y. *Joris-Karl Huysmans: Romancier du Salut.* Sherbrooke, Québec: Editions Naaman, 1981.

Viegnes, Michel J. *Le Milieu et l'individu dans la trilogie de Joris-Karl Huysmans.* Paris: A. G. Nizet, 1986.

Weber, Eugen. *France Fin de Siècle.* Cambridge, MA: The Belknap Press of Harvard University Press, 1986.

Brendan King (essay date 2001)

SOURCE: King, Brendan. Introduction to *Là Bas: A Journey into the Self,* by J.-K. Huysmans, translated by Brendan King, pp. 7-15. Cambs, England: Dedalus, 2001.

[*In the following excerpt, King describes* Là-bas *as "a remarkably contemporary novel," a book "to make us look again at what we are and what we believe, and to decide whether we are on the road to heaven,* là-haut, *or on the road to hell,* là-bas."]

Ever since its publication in 1891, J. K. Huysmans' *Là-Bas* has provoked controversy. On its first appearance in print—it was serialised in the newspaper *Écho de Paris*—irate readers complained to the editor and threatened to cancel their subscriptions. When it was published in book form a few months later, it was banned from sale in railway station kiosks, which only had the effect of whetting the public's appetite for it. The book's subject matter was so daring that an English translation wasn't even attempted until thirty years afterwards, and when it was, its American publisher was politely asked to withdraw it, following a complaint from the Society for the Suppression of Vice that it constituted an outrage on public morals. And this despite the fact that the translation had been toned down and some of its most controversial passages excised. Indeed, *Là-Bas* has never, until now, been publicly available in a complete and unexpurgated English translation.

But though there have been attempts to suppress *Là-Bas,* the book has never suffered from a shortage of readers. Even during periods when English translations

of the book have been denied the usual channels of distribution, *Là-Bas* has still managed to find an audience through pirated editions (including an edition illustrated with Félicien Rops' darkly Satanic etchings) and through special limited editions aimed at the bibliophile and the collector. Although there are numerous contenders, not least among them Huysmans' earlier novel *A Rebours* (1884), *Là-Bas* surely has a claim to be the cult novel of the nineteenth century.

With its uncompromising depiction of acts of sexual intercourse, its graphic account of an orgiastic Black Mass, its equally graphic and repellent descriptions of child murder and mutilation, it is easy to see why the book became so notorious. Notoriety, however, isn't always good for a book's long-term reputation. *Là-Bas'* subject matter may have ensured it a place in the canon of cult books dealing with Satanism, but it has also had the effect of preventing it from being taken seriously as a work of literature, and as a result it rarely finds its way onto college reading lists. The only work by Huysmans to have attained this status is *A Rebours,* which, validated by its influence on Oscar Wilde's *The Picture of Dorian Gray,* has become required reading for students of the *fin de siècle* period. At the time of its publication, however, *A Rebours* had a relatively small readership and the ideas it contained appealed to an equally small number of aesthetes. By contrast, *Là-Bas* was Huysmans' first bestseller, capturing the public imagination and capitalising on a renewed interest in mysticism and the occult. With its allusions to, and fierce polemical discussions about, the occult, conspiracy theories, cultural imperialism in the shape of creeping Americanisation, mass murderers, female promiscuity, Satanic abuse, the shortcomings of materialism, hysteria, alchemy, alternative religions, homeopathy, mysticism and hypnotism, the novel is a compendium of the anxieties, fears and delusions of the late nineteenth century.

What is clear from this list is that if *Là-Bas* is firmly rooted in its time, it is also a remarkably contemporary novel: its concerns are still our concerns. Today, as in the 1890s, the authority of conventional religion is being undermined and alternative spiritualities are thriving; orthodox medicine is under attack from a flood of alternative or complementary therapies; and the issue of violence dominates our consciousness of ourselves and the society we live in. Reading *Là-Bas,* we are inevitably reminded of recent cases of juvenile murder and serial killing, or the seemingly endemic outbreaks of sexual abuse that are reported almost daily in the media. *Là-Bas* reminds us that we have always been capable of gross acts of violence that challenge our notion of what it means to be human, and that one of the functions of art in a civilised society is to find new metaphors to help us assimilate those aspects of humanity we find most problematic. *Là-Bas* is a book to make us look again at what we are and what we believe, and to decide whether we are on the road to heaven, *là-haut*, or on the road to hell, *là-bas.*

. . . . .

Huysmans published his first book *Le Drageoir à épices,* a collection of prose poems and sketches, at his own expense in 1874. It sold very few copies, but attracted the attention of a number of influential critics. From then on, Huysmans quickly established himself in the Parisian literary scene, and by the end of the 1870s he was a frequent guest at Flaubert's Sunday afternoon salons, had visited Goncourt's exotic *grenier* at Auteuil, and had become an integral part of Zola's Médan group, alongside writers such as Guy de Maupassant, Henry Céard and Léon Hennique.

During this period, Huysmans produced some of the blackest, most unrelentingly cynical works in the Naturalist canon. His first novel, *Marthe, histoire d'une fille* (1876), was a remarkable low-life portrait of a working class prostitute and her middle class lover. It anticipated Edmond de Goncourt's novel of the same subject, *La Fille Elisa* (1877), and was the first in what seemed to be a new genre of eponymously-titled novels about prostitutes that culminated in Zola's *Nana* (1881). *Les Soeurs Vatard* (1879), Huysmans' next novel, was a bleak portrayal of two women working in a printing factory, and was followed in 1881 by *En Ménage,* a bitterly ironic tirade against the bourgeois institution of marriage.

By the early 1880s, however, Huysmans was becoming increasingly dissatisfied with Naturalism, not so much in terms of form or style—Huysmans employed the same Naturalist techniques throughout his career, whether he was writing about Parisian prostitutes or saints in the Middle Ages—but as an intellectual, emotional and spiritual philosophy. Frustrated by Naturalism's limitations, Huysmans began to push back the boundaries of what constituted the subject of a work of fiction. *A Rebours* (1884), like Flaubert's *Bouvard et Pecuchet* (1881), was a novel without a plot, a compendium or encyclopaedia of sensation, which reflected, and arguably invented, the contemporary aesthetics of decadence. With *En Rade* (1887), Huysmans' anomalous position as a Naturalist reached its breaking point, the book being unequally divided between Naturalist-style descriptions of the grim realities of rural life, and three highly-stylised dream sequences in which the erotic and the fabulous seem to have free play.

It was not, however, until the publication of *Là-Bas* (1891) that Huysmans made his break with the Naturalists public. The novel begins with a debate between two of its leading characters, Durtal and des Hermies, on the failures of Naturalism, a debate which can be seen as a specific refutation of the very ideas that Zola had

outlined in his 1868 preface to the second edition of *Thérèse Raquin* (1867). Zola had famously written that in his novel he had "simply applied to two living bodies the analytical method that surgeons apply to corpses". Huysmans felt that this kind of analysis, in which the remorse of his characters "really amounts to a simple organic disorder", was grossly reductionist and took no account of the human soul or its aspirations. What Huysmans was searching for was a new aesthetic form, one that could synthesise the mundane and the transcendent, and he found it not by looking to the modern literary avant-garde, but to the Flemish Primitive painters of the sixteenth century. In 1888, Huysmans had visited a little museum gallery in Cassel where he saw Matthias Grünewald's stunning *Crucifixion*. What captivated him was how Grünewald had managed not only to be completely Naturalistic in his technique, painting one of the most uncompromising, unromanticised views of Christ in the whole of Christian iconography, but also to infuse his paintings with a sense of transcendence, of the life of the soul to which Huysmans felt himself drawn. Inspired by Grünewald's painting, Huysmans' broke through the impasse of Naturalism to formulate a new aesthetic theory, "spiritual Naturalism", which, in a letter to the art critic Jules Destrée, he defined as "absolute realism combined with flights of the soul".

From one of his unpublished notebooks, it is clear that Huysmans intended his new book, which he entitled "*Là-Bas,* voyager en soi-même" (*Là-Bas,* a journey into the self), to be an exploration of Durtal's state of consciousness. In contrast to des Esseintes in *A Rebours,* who tries to alter his state of mind by changing his surroundings, and Jacques Marles in *En Rade,* who tries to find an antidote to his mood of depression in the French countryside, Durtal's existential discontent leads him to try to change the conditions of his life from within. In this sense, Huysmans' novel of contemporary Satanism can be seen as a spiritual or psychological parallel to the novels of Jules Verne (1828-1905), whose "journeys" round the world or to the centre of the earth had captured the imagination of his generation. While Verne's exploratory novels can be seen as symbols of capitalist expansionism, and seem to embody a positivist ethic of discovery and exploration of the outside world, the journey taken by Durtal in *Là-Bas* constitutes a different order of experience, one that privileges subjectivity over the objectivity of science. Durtal's obsession with his own state of mind—and with the state of his soul—anticipates Modernism's fascination with the ego and with the unconscious.

For Huysmans, the step from materialism to Christian mysticism was a large one, and it could only be bridged indirectly—and unconventionally—through his investigations into contemporary Satanism. Of course Huysmans was not alone in his interest in the occult. If *Là-*

Bas is a reflection of a personal "search for the absolute", it is also a reflection of the general explosion of interest in mysticism, spiritualism and the occult that was such a prominent feature of the 1880s and 1890s. As Joanny Bricaud, the author of *J.-K. Huysmans et le satanisme* (1912), said of the period, "hardly a month goes by without the press informing us about magic spells or Black Masses celebrated by sacrilegious maniacs who are secretly perpetrating the filthy rites of Satanism". Huysmans himself kept a scrapbook of clippings from newspapers and journals of the day dealing with instances of vampirism, the Black Mass and the theft of Eucharists from Parisian churches.

Là-Bas is often described as one of the classic novels of the occult, but with hindsight it is clear that the book prefigures Huysmans' later conversion. Indeed, it was instrumental in it, for having become convinced of the reality of the supernatural through his dealings with the occult, it was only logical that Huysmans should accept the reality of the supernatural in the shape of a Christian God. It is also apparent that what Huysmans had uncovered in the course of his researches for *Là-Bas* so disgusted and distressed him that he suffered a violent reaction against the book's subject matter. He later described *Là-Bas* as a "black book" which he had attempted to exorcise by writing his "white book", *En Route* (1895). This was the first of Huysmans' ostensibly pro-Catholic works and took Durtal on to the next stage of his development, recounting his experiences during a retreat to a monastery. The remaining two volumes of this "spiritual autobiography" were *La Cathédrale* (1898), which established Huysmans firmly in the Catholic revival with its extended explorations of the aesthetics of Catholic symbolism, and *L'Oblat* (1901), which outlined Huysmans' views on human suffering and introduced the doctrine of mystical substitution, the belief that through religious devotion, it is possible to take on the sufferings of those too weak to bear them.

Robert Ziegler (essay date 2004)

SOURCE: Ziegler, Robert. "Nigredo: *Là-bas*." In *The Mirror of Divinity: The World and Creation in J.-K. Huysmans*, pp. 213-37. Newark: University of Delaware Press, 2004.

[*In the following essay, Ziegler demonstrates how Huysmans "uses his text, not to reflect, but to transform," stating that* Là-bas *becomes a crucible in which the "animalistic nature" of humankind is refined into "a spiritually transformed essence."*]

The publication, in 1891, of *Là-bas* (*Là-bas*), a novel "dont le succès" [whose success], as Jean-Marie Seillan says, was "environné d'un fumet de scandale" [sur-

rounded by a scent of scandal],[1] brought an abrupt end to Huysmans's quiet existence as a government functionary and as a serious fiction writer able to devote himself in private to the practice of his craft. The sensational subject matter of the novel and the mysterious circumstances surrounding the death of Abbé Boullan, the model for the character of Doctor Johannès, provoked a tempest in the press. Besieged by reporters pounding on his door, demanding he disclose information on the secrets of Black Masses, elemental spirits, satanic spells, the profanation of consecrated Hosts, Masonic ritual, and Rosicrucianism, Huysmans—virtually overnight—was turned into a public figure whose opinion was sought on a variety of contemporary issues.

Hounded by the media, Huysmans complained to Arij Prins about this new and unwanted attention: "Toute la presse parle d'envoûtements, je suis assailli d'interviews." [Everyone in the press is talking about spells. I'm overwhelmed with demands for interviews.][2] Both in newspaper stories and the novel, Huysmans alternates between crediting the dangerous authenticity of certain occult practices and dismissing most satanists as delusional hysterics. On the one hand, he describes a seemingly genuine séance at which the spirit of a deceased sailor had been summoned by participants, and, when told to manifest itself, had set in motion a table "se met à danser la gigue" [started doing a jig]. On the other hand, he explains away most cases of bewitchment, saying of the alleged victims: "[J]e les tiendrai presque tous pour des monomanes." [I consider almost all of them monomaniacs.][3]

Regardless of the notoriety brought Huysmans by his lurid tale, *Là-bas* remains arguably the author's greatest masterpiece, a pivotal work in which a new course for the novel is charted. In the book, Huysmans addresses a range of esoteric subjects: spiritualism, devil worship, campanology, homeopathic medicine, astrology. Yet because of the focus on Durtal's research into the history of Gilles de Rais and turn-of-the century satanic ritual, the preponderance of critical attention has been directed to Huysmans's study of supernatural evil.

The central conflict in the novel may not, however, be the one between Christian thaumaturges and satanic renegades, but the one between materialists and alchemists who transmute base matter into gold. A transitional work in Huysmans's literary development, *Là-bas* no longer offers the text as a mirror reproducing the real. Nor does it yet propose itself as a devotional instrument meant to image the divine majesty of Creation. For the first time, Huysmans uses his text, not to reflect, but to transform, so that the model for the literary work is the crucible instead of the mirror.

In *Là-bas*, Huysmans's characters air the question whether—on the level of science, art, and metaphysics—human life is inevitably governed by lust, cupidity, corporeity, and instinct, or whether, through study, sacrifice, and self-purification, man can sublimate the *materia prima* of his animalistic nature and refine it into the *ultima materia* of a spiritually transformed essence. For Huysmans, it is not only the soul but also the body and the book that are the battlefield on which opposing forces clash, struggling to degrade humanity by focusing it on the genitals, the intestines, and the pocketbook, or trying to direct its gaze upward by teaching nobility, love, and service.

Beginning with Durtal and des Hermies's debate over the uncertain future of literature, *Là-bas* is structured on an axis of high and low, past and future. Jean Descottignies observes that the topology of the novel mirrors both the verticality of man's posture and the stratified image of the Christian cosmos. As Descottignies says, the architecture of the novel "oppose, distribue et finalement hiérarchise les trois scènes de l'action: le logis de Durtal, abri de la vie quotidienne et de ses péchés mesquins, le château de Gilles de Rais, lieu du surhumain et de ses crimes, la tour de Saint-Sulpice, univers supra-terrestre où se réfugie la vertu. Terre, enfer, ciel: image de la structure que le dogme catholique assigne à l'ensemble de l'univers" [opposes, distributes, and finally hierarchically structures the three scenes where the action unfolds: Durtal's lodging, where he is sheltered from daily life and his little sins; Gilles de Rais's castle, the locus of the superhuman and the criminal; and the tower of Saint-Sulpice, the superterrestrial universe where virtue reigns. Earth, hell, heaven: it is the image assigned by Catholic dogma to the whole of the universe].[4]

Corresponding to Descottignies's schema for the three-fold setting of the action is Durtal's image of the planes on which the artwork is created. Initially, as suggested by the directional adverb with which Huysmans titles his book, naturalism's preoccupation with food and fornication guides the writer downward, toward a *là-bas* of biological determinism. Confining man (as Huysmans himself had done) to a netherworld of chophouses and brothels, naturalists situate their stories in a dungeon of working-class slums, alcoholism, hereditary ineluctability, animal lust, hopelessness, violence, and poverty. "Rut et coup de folie," as des Hermies complains, "ce sont là ses seules diathèses." [Rutting and madness, those are its only diatheses.][5] For both Durtal and des Hermies, hell has already been located in the naturalist world of bodies and instincts. Yet they also believe that an aesthetic of evil entails the possibility of an aesthetic of good. Only if there exists a subterranean realm seething with incubi, larvae, and evil spirits can its corresponding celestial kingdom be discovered and mapped out.

In des Hermies' pleonastic complaint, Zola's naturalism is attacked for having "incarné le matérialisme dans la littérature" [embodied materialism in literature].[6] By materializing matter, incarnating the body, and democratizing popular art, naturalism hypostatizes man's lowly physicality, plowing the same ground as Zola did in his fiction. But it is only from the body that transcendence can occur, only through transmuting the physical that spiritual perfection can be achieved. In his alchemical economy, Huysmans turns the despised body into an alembic in which suffering effects a purifying transformation.

With its embrace of scientific positivism and its adoption of the reductive methods of explanatory sociology, naturalism had led Durtal into a cul-de-sac where the creative wonder of inspiration had dried up, leaving him unsure how to proceed. Himself a physician versed in the experimental homeopathy of Caesar Matteï, des Hermies also criticized the depersonalizing techniques of modern medicine, with its mass-produced pharmaceuticals, its all-purpose diagnoses of hysteria, and its resistance to acknowledging the unexplained or the supernatural. According to Paracelsus, whom des Hermies calls "[l]'un des plus extraordinaires praticiens de la médecine occulte" [one of the most extraordinary practitioners of occult medicine],[7] "There is no field on earth in which heavenly medicine grows or lies hidden, other than the resurrected flesh or the 'new body' of man."[8]

For disciples of Zola's Doctor Pascal, however, curative power comes, not from God, but from books. Patients are metonymized as disorders caused by lesions that can be diagnostically identified and surgically removed. With their limited vision, the doctors of des Hermies's time saw no mystery below and no enchantment above. At first, it is Durtal's aesthetic dissatisfaction with the analytical aridity of the modern scientific world that enables him to believe in an invisible realm filled with astral bodies and elemental spirits as imperceptible as microbes. Whereas in naturalist fiction, only stomachs and penises talk, Durtal gradually comes to hear the voice of Carhaix's bells, the gibbering of demons, the language of the stars. In place of the sterile hermeneutic of science and commerce, Durtal discovers the hieroglyphs of astrologers and the spagyric sigils of wizards. When he looks straight ahead, all Durtal sees is advertising plastered on the walls of public urinals. But when he looks down at the reflections of electric signs shining on the sidewalk, "[I]l y a des signaux, des blasons d'alchimiste en relief sur ces rondelles, des roues à cran, des caractères talismaniques, des pentacles bizarres avec des soleils, des marteaux et des ancres" [there are symbols, the armorial bearings of alchemists on raised plinths, cogwheels, talismanic characters, strange pentacles with suns, hammers, and anchors].[9] Suffocating in an atmosphere of clarity and fact, Durtal rejects the evidence of science in favor of the mysteries of the occult, choosing the evocativeness of the past over the transparency of the present.

Durtal similarly dismisses the epistemological value of naturalism, with its pretension to scientific objectivity and its system of hypotheses, tests, and validations. Considering satanism as potentially enriching material for literature, Durtal is both open-minded and skeptical, receptive to Gévingey's stories of demonic infestations yet tempted to respond to them with deflating facetiousness. Supported by the devalued currency of unreliable records, history, in Durtal's view, is also a pseudoscience, one less creatively stimulating than astrology or chiromancy. "[L]e plus solennel des mensonges" [The most solemn of lies],[10] history assembles from the *materia confusa* of archival information an ordering theory that does not explain the remote events it treats but rather illuminates "le tempérament de l'écrivain qui les manie" [the temperament of the writer who is handling them].[11] Working with firsthand reports and dusty manuscripts, the historian is an artifex closeted in the laboratory of his imagination, burning away the dross of irrelevant detail and turning history, not into truth, but into art.

In the world of Durtal's contemporaries, knowledge had been enshrined as a false god, creating a cult of empiricism transmitted by a priesthood of scientists. Collectively ratified theories coined by science are money circulated by dirty hands, never purifying those who touch them, never ennobling those who store them up. In place of the counterfeit tender of debatable facts, Durtal proposes the introduction of ideas polished by style and gilded as art. In its incipient stages, Huysmans's religion of creative intelligence subordinates science to beauty as what inspires humanity and raises it up. From this perspective, experimental data and observable events are the impure metal in which gold lies sleeping, awaiting the initiate to awaken and extract it.

In *Là-bas*, Durtal's first allusion to satanism comes, not in the context of Canon Docre's obscene Sabbaths, but at the end of Durtal's meditation on the nefarious influence of money. A perversion of mystical alchemy which, as Manly Hall asserts, "is the science of multiplication . . . based upon the natural phenomenon of growth,"[12] capitalism promotes an unnatural contagion of selfishness, acquisitiveness, lovelessness, and sin. The principle of iconolatrous materialism, money is worshiped like Mammon or the Golden Calf—"[L]'argent qui est ainsi maître des âmes, est diabolique," as Durtal theorizes, "ou il est impossible à expliquer." [Either money, which is the master of the soul, is diabolical, or it is impossible to explain.][13] Excrementalizing everything it is exchanged for, money communicates the Midas touch that abolishes substances and transforms gold into death. As such, money is the corpse of the alchemist's gold.

Instead of activating, heating, healing, and quickening, it only numbs, immobilizes, and murders. "Here on earth," as Paracelsus says, "the celestial fire is a cold, rigid, and frozen fire. And this fire is the body of gold."[14]

According to the alchemist's axiom: "As it is above, so it is below." Yet for the speculator, the transmutation of lead into gold, feces into ambrosia, is not reenacted on a higher plane with the decay of the body and its resurrection as the spirit. For Durtal, money operates in the opposite way. Unlike the philosopher's stone, it debases matter and those who touch it, turning satisfaction into desire, and abundance into hunger. An instrument of magical transformation like the mystical *lapis*, "il change, en une seconde, toutes les habitudes, bouleverse toutes les idées, métamorphose les passions les plus têtues, en un clin d'œil" [it changes, in an instant, every habit, upsets every idea, transforms the most stubborn passion in the twinkling of an eye].[15]

In Huysmans's alchemical aesthetic, the noblest operation is the conversion of life's ugly randomness and existential contingency into the order and beauty of the work of art. Like events reworked as their meaning, authors die and are reborn as their textual children. Matter, treated with fire, is changed in an essential way, becoming lighter, finer, more rarefied—spiritualized as the future text that Durtal dreams of writing. On the other hand, capital, as the naturalists' exchange medium, oppresses and stupefies, increasing the gravity of the things in which capitalists invest libido, as they invest capital in the promise of things. Like the writer who sires his work "sans le concours d'un autre sang" [without the contribution of another's blood],[16] capital begets itself, reproducing in the dark belly of the cash box. Unlike alchemy, it is a force that brings increase without improvement. As food that no alchemical operation converts into gold, salt, excrement, or medicine, capital nourishes only inequity. "Il est l'aliment le plus nutritif des importants péchés" [It is the most important nutrient for serious sins],[17] changing generosity into miserliness, modesty into wantonness, disinterestedness into "un bas égoisme, un ignoble orgueil" [base egotism, ignoble pride].[18] Having destroyed the objects that it restores as their value, it becomes exponentially more virulent, concealing the glitter of gold behind "the black veil of a word."[19]

The subject of Durtal's fictional biography, Gilles de Rais, is himself a sinner who was nourished by money. Depleted by the expenses of war, by ruinous extravagance, and the pomp of his court, the maréchal's fortune had been further compromised by usury. It compelled him to sell off land and mortgage property, and drove him to black magic and attempts to fathom the secrets of alchemical transformations. Durtal's research leads him to suggest a possible link between Gilles's profligacy and his fascination with the spagyrical arts, associating the money that corrupts with the gold that sublimates. A vertical being in flight from the platitudinous banality of the quotidian, Gilles was first an ally of Joan of Arc, aspiring to the heights of spiritual heroism, before falling into an abyss of sacrilege and depravity. "Or, du Mysticisme exalté au Satanisme exaspéré, il n'y a qu'un pas" [From exalted Mysticism to cynical satanism, there is only a small step], as Durtal soberly intones.[20] Fired by greed, Gilles's quest for the philosopher's stone directed him, not "à la recherche de *l'or subtil*" [not in search of *subtle gold*], as Marie-Laure Colonna writes, but instead "à la production d'or sonnant et trébuchant" [to the production of hard cash, money that can be weighed].[21]

A man of extremes, collector of rare books, consumer of incendiary dishes, and student of arcane sciences, Gilles is a romanticized, Promethean projection of the sedentary, moderate, middle-class scholar/novelist Durtal, *bec fin* fond of Madame Carhaix's savory beef stews. Like Gilles, Durtal is uninterested in deciphering the cryptic formulas and mysterious recipes of alchemical experiments; he dismisses them as "le plus incroyable des galimatias, le plus inintelligible des grimoires" [the most incredible rigmarole, the most unintelligible grimoires].[22] But whereas Gilles aspired to the omnipotence conferred by limitless wealth and knowledge, Durtal is concerned with alchemy as a transformative principle as it is applied to art.

In his research on Gilles, Durtal learns the fundamental principles of medieval alchemy. Thus, Mercury is identified with life-giving language, with the tongue of fire that ignited the prophets, and with electrifying snakes that were turned into lightning bolts. Beyond the sphere of the stars, writes Hall, "is the Divine fiery water, the first outflow of the Word of God, the flaming river pouring from the presence of the Eternal. . . . [U]niversal mercury," Hall summarizes, "[is] the measureless spirit of life."[23]

Like Lucifer, Gilles had tried to control the original substance that supported life. And, like Lucifer, Gilles had been cast down and punished for his hubris. Different from the fallen angel—different even from des Esseintes, an illegitimate ventriloquist god requiring others to speak in his own voice—the true artist is a priest faithfully transmitting God's message, trying to puzzle out Creation's secrets, seeking to know Mercurius, who, as Jung says, is "the Logos become world."[24]

In their occult dabbling, Gilles's alchemist hirelings sift through elemental substances charged with archetypal meaning and magical power: arsenic, tin, menstrual blood, saltpeter, breast milk, human urine, the flesh of toads. It is important that Durtal's aesthetic of spiritual naturalism—modeled on the alchemical processes of circulation, elevation, and descent—does not repress the body or deny the activities of the digestive or reproductive organs. By fashioning himself as "[un] puisatier d'âme" [a well-digger of the soul],[25] the future novelist will illuminate the interactions of spirit and body, dream and reason, the base and the sublime. Revitalized by absorbing the solar light of intelligence, the body is transformed. The alchemical operation therefore serves as a model for the analytic process: it identifies unconscious conflicts somatically articulated by the appearance of symptoms, symptoms that can then be alleviated through understanding, leaving a healed body like the transformed substance at the bottom of the alembic. By converting the heaviness of the toad into the volatility of the eagle, psychic insight culminates with the spiritual aurefaction of the physical being. As Hall writes of the operation described in Hermes's *Emerald Tablet,* Mercury ascends from the vessel and then descends again from the heavens, until the "Earth has sucked it all in, when it must become the black, pitchy matter, the *Toad,*" which, Hall says, represents "the substances in the alchemical retort . . . and the lower elements in the body of man."[26]

Durtal's conception of a balanced literature encompassing both medicine and religion would explore the trail of the body that Zola had blazed while opening a parallel route leading to the realm of the human mind and spirit. While noble alchemy intends, not the material enrichment of adepts capable of turning lead into gold, but an elevation of their consciousness and a raising of their moral purpose, it also respects base matter which can potentially be freed of ignorance and impurity. Historical fact is primary material, valuable only if transformed into the higher knowledge afforded by art. The archivist who transmits the raw information contained in original manuscripts performs no transformative operation but instead values the stuff of history simply for itself. Like Gilles, who covets gold as material wealth—like the speculator accumulating the capital entitling him to the things that money eclipses—the historian who does not utilize his sources as "un tremplin d'idées et de style" [a springboard for ideas and style][27] is condemned to paralysis by his failure to transform. Durtal, on the other hand, takes the contradictory figure of Gilles as he emerges from a welter of primary documents, introduces him into the retort of his narrative, and refines him into a quasi-fictional character, one made intelligible, coherent, illuminated.

Significantly, it is only through fictional experimentation that meaning, order, and resolution are provided, while in the plot of Durtal's book and life, the parallel stories of satanic activity lead to his growing horror and bewilderment. Much of Huysmans's novel is devoted to examining secret and overt forces dedicated to the anti-alchemical goal of debasing the pure and rematerializing the sublime. Positional and symbolic inversions characterize the ceremonies conducted by Canon Docre and the fraudulent practices of corrupt businessmen who traffic in inferior merchandise.

After spending an evening in Carhaix's aerie, taking part in conversation ranging from Manichaeism to succubacy, Durtal descends to the street, goes back home, and dreams. Transposing the incommensurability of moral extremes—the loftiness of the bell-ringer's faith and the infernal sorcery of infanticides—Saint Sulpice represents the "double puits" [double shaft] that the well-digger of the soul must plumb. Standing on the threshold of Carhaix's apartment, des Hermies invites Durtal to look and "montra, d'un geste, les deux abîmes" [pointed at the twin abysses].[28]

Uprooted from the horizontal familiarity of his library, Durtal climbs into the tower, rising up into a thin atmosphere of rarefied discourse. Thus, when he returns to the world, he converts his metaphysical vertigo into dream imagery whose frightening content is neutralized by his defensive skepticism. In a hypnopompic vision that Durtal registers upon waking, he sees "la sarabande des sociétés démoniaques dont des Hermies avait parlé" [the saraband of satanic societies about which des Hermies had spoken][29] as a gaggle of female clowns that pass, parading on their hands, praying with their feet joined in a mock devotional gesture. From the image of the cross tattooed on the sole of Docre's foot, to the picture of the Hanged Man in the Tarot deck Arcanum, to the inverted cross of Melchizedek embroidered on the chasuble of Dr. Johannès, to Gilles's fornicating trees, whose coital ramification ends with their heads in the soil and their spread legs in the clouds, Durtal is introduced to a world where high and low are interchanged. In their rituals and invocations, as Huysmans observes, the worshippers of Lucifer adopt similar inversions. For them, "Lucifer est l'égal d'Adonai, il est le Dieu de lumière, le Principe du bien, tandis qu'Adonai est le Dieu de ténèbres, le Principe du mal. . . . C'est donc le christianisme retourné, le catholicisme à rebours." [Lucifer is the equal of Adonai; he is the God of light, the Principle of good, while Adonai is the God of darkness, the Principle of evil. Thus, it is Christianity turned on its head, Catholicism à rebours.][30]

On the terrestrial plane of everyday life, alchemical operations are performed by merchants who enrich themselves by converting the genuine into the meretricious. In *A rebours,* des Esseintes had already railed against those who falsified the material species of the Host, substituting cheap potato starch for real wheat used to make Communion wafers. The commercial transformation of gold back into lead generates profits for the tradesmen who defraud their customers. Using progress as their watchword, the positivists of Durtal's time had, in his view, produced nothing, improved nothing, discovered nothing. Familiar to the ancients, electricity was not a new phenomenon, nor was hypnotism, a sci-

ence practiced for centuries in India and Egypt. Rather than leading mankind down the road toward greater wisdom and self-mastery, businessmen had perfected the science of counterfeiting and pollution. Unlike alchemy, which removed contaminants, commerce introduced impurities, practicing "la falsification des denrées, la sophistication des produits" [the adulteration of foodstuffs, the contamination of manufactured goods].[31] In a case epitomizing the commercial impoverishment of reality, Durtal recalls how, in 1888, the chamber had been forced to enact a law forbidding the dilution of manure.

Like the philosopher's stone that multiplies the vitality of substances, fertilizer promotes growth, unlocks energy, and increases yields. In the prescientific imagination, as in psychoanalytic theory, gold and excrement are linked as end products of the process of transformation. "Graisse du monde" [Fat of the world], gold is a concentrate and a preservative, like the pitch deposited in the base of the alchemist's retort. As the crowning phase of the purification described in Hermes's *Emerald Tablet,* the "Last Digestion" ends when the nutrient rots and the substance is destroyed, precipitating black matter aurefied by absorbing the fire of heaven. For the capitalist, gold is excrement rendered useless by being accumulated. For the alchemist, excrement is gold that is valued for inseminating and effecting change. It was Victor Hugo who, in *Les Misérables* intuited the spagyric dimension of farming—the moving from sun to soil to wheat, from burial to sprouting, from the death of the seed to the birth of the fruit: "Si notre or est fumier," Hugo writes, "notre fumier est or" [If our gold is manure, our manure is gold].[32]

With his chronic digestive complaints, Huysmans also considered not only alchemy as alimentation, but also alimentation as art. After consuming the real, the writer could not simply evacuate it, unchanged, as text. Having destroyed it in its physical aspect, the writer expels material purified of contingency and enriched with meaning. It is in this respect that the writer assumes his hierophantic role, investing greater reality in the real by raising the text from its naturalist rut and setting it on its course in the sky. "Tout alimentation est transubstantiation" [All feeding is transubstantiation], as Durand affirms, a view shared by alchemists who "utilisent la communion alimentaire et ses symboles" [use the symbols of alimentary communion].[33]

It is no surprise that Huysmans's dyspeptic pessimists feel creatively blocked, sexually impotent, and spiritually starved. As exiles incapable of swallowing life, they are also unable to assimilate God. Like the reckless alchemist who takes no precaution before introducing material into the crucible and then releases fire and vapors that cause an explosion that blows up his laboratory, André Jayant is unprepared for the discovery of his wife's infidelity, and so reacts by succumbing to a gastric attack of flatulence and diarrhea. For Huysmans's fastidious aesthetes, the real must be preliminarily aestheticized and rid of the fatty excess of popular opinion, so that the discourse of fools is neutralized by the palliative application of style. After Jean Folantin's suggestion of a restaurant conspiracy to poison food, des Hermies advances a similar theory of murderous public refection, likening satanists to cooks who work at cheap diners and adulterate the manure of their meals. Subjects of des Hermies's toxicology study, the patrons at a particular establishment become bloated or wither away, their sallow, greenish complexions highlighting the violet cavities of their sunken eyes. In the course of his research, des Hermies identifies the ingredients used to mask rotten fish, spoiled meat, sewage-colored sauces—detecting the presence of tannin, coal dust, and plaster. While nutrients should die to revitalize consumers, here consumers are poisoned to extend the artificial life of food. As in all of Huysmans's fiction, eating is accorded pride of place in *Là-bas,* where the brilliance of intellectual debate is fostered by the culinary artistry of Madame Carhaix, the hostess-chef whose pot-au-feu serves simultaneously as food for thought.

Like the Eucharist, alchemical substances heated in the retort provide nourishment that transforms the person who prepares and ingests it. Unlike investment capital, which endlessly reproduces the filth of itself, the body of Christ is food that sanctifies those who partake of it. Yet on earth, in the grave, or on restaurant tables, the activity of the food chain continues uninterrupted, as gluttons die and their bellies rot, providing meals for rhizophagous maggots, while the trim cadavers of abstemious eaters are devoured by discerning phorias, worms that des Hermies praises as being "les aristos de la vermine" [the aristocrats of maggots].[34]

Inevitably, Huysmans's interest in transcendental nutrition leads him to a reflection on death as refrigerative and immobilizing or as liberating and resurrective. Precisely because decomposition of a substance must precede its regeneration, Grünewald's graphic portrayal of Christ's death in the body is able to suggest his imminent reappearance as the risen Savior. "What is it," Hall asks, "that dies on the cross, is buried in the tomb of the Mysteries, and that also dies in the retort and becomes black with putrefaction?"[35] Whereas money is excrement that does not fertilize, the noble body is susceptible to purification precisely because of its corruptibility.

In *Là-bas,* Huysmans explores the many ways in which artists perish in order to be transformed into their work, burning away the futile dross of their existences and leaving behind only the gold of their creations. An erstwhile naturalist, Huysmans had been used to reporting the body's uncensored language—messages issuing from the lower organs, words issuing from every orifice. The squelching of bitter eructations, the thunder of intestinal rumbling, and the gunfire of gas and wind, expressions that are democratic in their origin, meaning, and audience, were the antithesis of the chiseled phrases of des Esseintes's favorite prose poems. A cacograph, Huysmans's naturalist text transmits the noises of a disorderly reality, symphonies of discord like the sounds of the orchestra and the tumult of the book bindery in *Marthe* and *Les Sœurs Vatard.* But in Grünewald's canvas, the transmutation of Christ's crucified body had allowed "les menthes les plus fines des dilections" [the finest essence of charity] to be extracted from "une triomphale ordure" [a triumphal squalor].[36] Likewise, the naturalist sublimates the physical, elevating and preserving what, at the same time, is suppressed.

Forbidding Ouija boards and astrological charts, and all divinatory ritual and paraphernalia, the church identifies even the most popular and commercialized of occult practices as inherently satanic. As a writer himself, Durtal is appalled by the idea of popular invocations of the noble dead: "Quant à l'évocation des morts, la pensée seule que le charcutier du coin peut forcer l'âme d'Hugo, de Balzac, de Baudelaire, à converser avec lui, me mettrait hors de moi, si j'y croyais." [As for calling up the dead, the mere thought that the corner pork-butcher could compel the soul of Hugo, Balzac, or Baudelaire to converse with him would drive me out of my mind, if I believed it were possible.][37] By dying, Baudelaire escapes the allocutions of pork-butchers, replacing his body with the eloquent cadaver of his poetry. Unavailable to the nagging editors, witless mistresses, and transparent window-glass vendors he despised in life, he is sublimated into the gospel of his books.

To Durtal, communion with the spirits of departed artists has a necrophilic quality, as fools too uncultured to speak to Hugo through the medium of his books try to violate his grave and "force the soul" of its occupant. By denying death's transcendence, séances express a materialist ideology that refuses to acknowledge the elevated discourse between authors and audiences. A systematic alchemical conversion of experience into plot and life into meaning, art is completed by death. Efforts to compel Balzac to communicate with living illiterates debase the gold of his works, replacing art with corruption and literature with babble.

It is Durtal's horror at the necromantic quality of satanism—the use of the dead to carry spells, the predatory ghoulishness of succubacy—that tempers his fascination with devil worship and dampens his interest in complementing his research on Gilles with firsthand observation of Canon Docre's diabolical activities. What is the most disturbing to Huysmans's character is the fecundity of sameness, the inescapability of corporeity. With its directional indication of lowness, decadence, and ignobility, *Là-bas* chronicles the failure of ascensional urges, the checking of soaring motion, the fall back into the body.

J.-M. Wittmann notes that, in his relationship with Madame Chantelouve, Durtal moves from the prurience of fantasy to the disappointment of consummation: "[I]l est significatif que Hyacinthe puisse entrer dans la vie de Durtal et dans le roman sous la forme idéale d'une épistolière inconnue." [It is significant that Hyacinthe can enter into Durtal's life and into the novel in the ideal form of an unknown letter-writer.] "Personnage d'encre et de papier" [A character of ink and paper], as Wittmann calls her, she is not accorded "l'épaisseur d'un être de chair et d'os" [the substance of a flesh-and-blood being].[38] Another inversion of a sacred model, Madame Chantelouve is "chair faite Verbe" [the flesh made Word], letters rich in ambiguity. It is the elusiveness of mystery, the paucity of information, and the fragmentariness of documents that fire Durtal's passion for women and his love of historical research. Having burned away the impurities of immodesty and commonness present in a real sexual partner, Durtal creates a woman refined into green ink, delicate handwriting, and the scent of heliotrope lingering on her stationery.

As a letter writer, Madame Chantelouve enjoys the dignified inaccessibility of the dead and resembles Hugo and Baudelaire in being artistically redeemed by an evocative phrasing and careful style. A documentary shell, she is a loved one brought to life by the man who mourns her absence. The same erotic speculation informs Durtal's fantasy of Madame Chantelouve and his image of the splendor of life at Gilles's court. Like Madame Chantelouve's letters, the records of Gilles's pageantry and perversion are the skeleton that the researcher fits together and then utilizes as a springboard for his daydreaming. Similar to the pleasure Durtal derives from imagining the firm flesh of a mistress undilapidated by childbearing, his historical reverie leads him to take "le squelette d'un dongeon mort" [the skeleton of a dead fortress][39] and dress its sandstone frame with rich fabrics. He covers walls with Irish wainscoting; carpets floors with tapestry; furnishes the great halls with dressers and trunks covered in boarskin; fills the dining rooms with high-backed chairs; positions tables arrayed with steaming platters of roast heron, peacock, and bittern; and partakes in banquets copiously irrigated by fermented mulberry juice, thick red wine, and cinnamon cordials, plunging Gilles, his guests, and Durtal all together into "de monstrueux rêves" [monstrous dreams].[40]

Passing imperceptibly from the chimera of Madame Chantelouve to the ruins at Tiffauges, Durtal, like an incubus coupling with a being visited in dreams, indulges in the *délectation morose* of hypothetical lusts.[41] Identifying with Gilles's intoxicated friends—men aroused by spices, meats, and beer, yet confined to the womanless castle of their minds—Durtal first outfits the male guests who had been present at Gilles's feasts, then clothes their absent female counterparts, projecting a beauty he qualifies as "un idéal mannequin" [an ideal mannequin].[42] Given a gown with a train of white fur and adorned with emerald cabochons and purple crystals, she is the perfect form, needing only detail, flesh, and breath. It is the confluence of sensual musing and Durtal's historical research that animates the image, swells the bodice of the dress, fills the clothes, and lights the face with the smile of Madame Chantelouve. Merging the scholar and seducer, the fantasy builds to a climax, until Durtal's cat jumps on his lap and returns him to the ordinariness of his room.

Wittmann uses an alchemical image to compare the parallel development of Durtal's relationship and his book, describing his mistress and his sources as "une sorte de maitère brute" [a kind of raw material].[43] Unlike the alchemist, intent on completing the transmutation's final stage, Durtal is reluctant to bed the woman, write the novel, fulfill his dream. Pleased with the inchoateness of a project whose completion he delays, he enjoys "[une] écriture [qui] se fait alors délibérément lacunaire" [writing left deliberately incomplete].[44] Transposed as a flawed work, the artist fears discovering in it a reflection of his imposture. Incapable of removing the infelicities of diction, the impurities of style, and the dross of implausibility, he suspects he is no magus awakening an "idéal mannequin," but a charlatan whose creations are plodding automatons.

Originating in **Marthe,** Huysmans's early novel about an alcoholic prostitute, is the notion of the sin that Durtal refers to as Pygmalionism. With his fatuousness, a man sees mistresses as raw material refined in the crucible of his love. However, Durtal, who describes his liaison with Madame Chantelouve as "a novel," still worries that he will botch the relationship's final chapter. Not animated by their lovers' fiery touch, women revert to being matter, becoming marble when they are kissed, as Marthe had complained. No more proficient than the poet Léo in performing the role played by Pygmalion, Durtal struggles with the refractoriness of literature and love.

In moving from the transcriptive servility of the naturalist observer to the lucidity of the well-digger of the soul—skilled in deciphering dreams and mapping the unconscious—Huysmans's character might be expected to acquire deeper analytic acumen. Spatially organized according to the verticality of novel's setting, Durtal's life is crowned by the lofty discussions in Carhaix's tower, divided in the middle by the horizontality of the street with its pedestrian concerns, and underpinned by the subterranean world of his research into satanism, where the corpses of murdered boys piled up in the dungeons of oblivion.

While systematically applying to romance and art the alchemical principles of sublimation and division, Durtal also explores the countervailing impulse to collapse opposites and return to a state of pure materiality. Beginning with Durtal's reflection on the homogenizing influence of money, the novel examines sinister engines of hybridization, the forces of anarchy and confusion that obliterate distinctions between spirit and body, high and low, meaning and nonsense. A self-referential anatomy of the processes of its own construction, *Là-bas* is a work-in-progress mirrored in Durtal's project on Gilles de Rais. Yet while Huysmans suggests that authors are transmuted into the gold of their works, he also disparages the completed text by comparing it to a streetwalker—unclean meat indifferently handled by an audience of vulgarians. In imitation of Christ, the author may become his word made flesh, inspiration given voice, ideas turned into food shared among his readers. But as Christ was spat on, scourged, reviled, mocked, and tormented, literature is also "exposée aux salissantes curiosités des foules" [exposed to the degrading curiosity of the masses].[45] Objectified, displayed, sold to the first comer, the published volume is subjected to "une véritable prostitution" [a veritable prostitution].[46] The only way to guarantee its untarnished purity is for the writer to ensure it goes unread, preserving its integrity by keeping it, "ainsi que la femme qu'on aime, hors de portée, dans l'espace" [like the woman one loves, inaccessible and distant].[47]

From hypersensitivity to criticism to incestuous union with the work is only a small step for the writer to take. As the alchemical process of purification occurs by subjecting base material to the active agent that transforms it, the text acquires value through invigorating intercourse with its appraisers. The only difference between the narcissism of des Esseintes, in love with himself as an aesthete, and the incestuousness of the Pygmalionist, in love with his creations, is that the former is more infantile in his inability to produce anything. In the protectiveness of a writer who keeps his beloved work to himself, at home on a shelf, there is at least a recognition that the work possesses a certain independence and maturity. But in the Pygmalionist's insistence on his right to dominate a work that Durtal characterizes as "the daughter of his soul,"[48] the subordination of the creation serves to blur the separate status of the author and his objects.

There is a substantive difference between the sin of Pygmalionism and the delusional pleasure artists often take in the exercise of their talent. Captivated by the play of their imagination, they operate in what Winnicott calls the realm of potential space, as storytelling becomes a transitional activity seen as both truthful and imaginary. In his blundering invention of pretexts for breaking with Madame Chantelouve, Durtal performs an exemplary act of Pygmalionism, claiming to have fathered an illegitimate child, a six-year-old blonde whose fragile health requires his constant care. He grows progressively enamored of the little girl as he embellishes on the lies he tells about her history and condition: "Il s'emballa, finit par croire à l'existence de l'enfant, s'attendrit sur la mère et sur elle; sa voix trembla; des larmes lui vinrent presque aux yeux." [He got carried away, ended up believing in the child's existence, felt sorry for her and the mother; his voice trembled; tears almost came to his eyes.][49]

Succumbing to the autosuggestive power of the writer's narrative virtuosity is not the same as raping "sa fille d'âme," compromising the autonomy of the text, subverting the relationship between parent and offspring, forbidding exogamy, or violating an object endowed with the appearance of life. As Durtal realizes, Pygmalionism does not involve incest so much as autoeroticism; it is a cerebral onanism that excludes Galatea as a figment or illusion. Eliminating the difference between the writer, his material, and the audience causes a return to an earlier state of undifferentiated subjectivity.

Wittmann perceptively notes that, figuring prominently among the demonic characters appearing in *Là-bas* is Durtal's concierge, the dust-magician Rateau, who overturns furniture, terrifies Durtal's cat, and sows chaos. Transforming "la matière noble en matière vile" [noble matter into base matter],[50] Rateau dilutes the deep amber of a bottle of cognac, which mysteriously remains full while its contents grow more pale.

In an article entitled "The Devil Religion," Janine Chasseguet-Smirgel identifies the similar aims of alchemy and satanism. Emphasizing anal self-sufficiency, man's ability to produce enough to render God superfluous, devil worship also stresses Luciferian hubris, the fallen angel's pretension to displace the Creator. Whereas Judeo-Christian law forbids incest, homosexuality, bestiality, and human sacrifice, devil religions sanction the violation of these taboos.

In *La Retraite de Monsieur Bougran,* Huysmans had presented a neurotic culture fixated on legalistic formulas, governed by arcane protocols codified by a closed bureaucracy articulating rules in an obscure and secret language. A ministry clerk forced into retirement, Bougran had been taken from the world of productivity and self-respect and exiled to a realm of paralysis and guilt. With its images of metaphysical transgression, satanism offers the supernatural as an antidote to the suffocating effects of a civilization tyrannized by recondite laws, political opportunism, economic injustice, and soul-destroying science. Just as the sacrifice of Melchizedek counteracted Docre's evil spells, so a belief in the occult offers an alexipharmic cure for the disease of common sense.

According to Chasseguet-Smirgel, subversion of the paternal law that names, divides, and classifies "aims at reconstituting chaos from which a new kind of reality will be brought forth."[51] While the goal of noble alchemy is to sublimate and transmute, satanism moves toward depreciation and debasement, overturning the structured model of Christian dogma and restoring a primitive state of license, lawlessness, and confusion.[52] Violating divine and natural law, satanic practices, predicated on blasphemy and perversion, seek the recovery of freedoms surrendered to a punishing father and result, not in the elevation of a spiritually improved individual, but in his accession to a state of limitless power and pleasure. From this standpoint, the satanist's reversion to the anal stage affords mastery of the fear of castration and promotes fantasies of self-regeneration, a belief in magic feces, which are "constantly renewable."[53] Perhaps rejection of the nominative authority of the father even intends regression to an earlier state of indivisibility and self-sufficiency, where the unorganized material of the child's body was already gold.

Respecting the importance of the substance on which his operation is performed, the alchemist returns to the primordial matter he hopes to convert into its final form. Chasseguet-Smirgel argues that the devil worshipper and alchemist are motivated by the same objective: "to return to a state of homogeneous, undifferentiated matter from which a new reality . . . can be created."[54] In his archival research and his firsthand observations, Durtal distinguishes between the squalid, unimaginative ceremonies at which Canon Docre officiates and the truly Luciferian experiments undertaken by Gilles centuries earlier. At Docre's Black Mass, there had been a predictable inversion of familiar Christian symbols and standard rituals. Rouged pederast choirboys assisted Docre, naked under his bloodred chasuble embroidered with the image of a goat. Incense burners wafted the smoke of henbane, nightshade, and dried datura, while, in front of an altar surmounted by a priapic Jesus, Docre spewed blasphemous apostrophes to the God of Big Business, the Profaner of Vices. The hysterical outbursts marking the end of the ceremony—women straddling the crucifix, tearing their hair, desecrating the Host, barking like dogs—enact a parody of genuine transports of mystical ecstasy, violating the orderliness of liturgy and plunging participants into the fertility of anarchy.

Still, Docre's Sabbath is nothing compared to Gilles's psychotic holocausts, the slaughter of children disemboweled and violated in their intestinal wounds. Sodomy, vampirism, congress with the dead—Gilles's abominations are all committed as part of a satanic

campaign to overthrow nature, undo Creation, and restore the disorder that preceded it. Gilles not only invokes the devil but also strives to become a new Lucifer, a superhuman monster whose criminality is divine. As Chasseguet-Smirgel points out: "[T]he word *hybrid* comes from the Greek *hubris,* which means excess, extremism, outrageousness."[55]

Explaining Pygmalionism to Chantelouve, Durtal elaborates on the nature of the sin he claims to have invented. He denies that it merely involves the coupling of artists and their works; instead, he describes it as the expression of a totalizing ambition to be, to create, and to possess all at once, translating into art "un hermaphroditisme cérébral" [a cerebral hermaphrodism].[56] The pansexual, sadist god who, in raping his creatures, disallows their separateness as independent objects is the model for the Luciferian demiurge incorporating everything into himself, becoming the maker and his work, the origin and the end, the mirror and the image. According to Mircea Eliade, such symbolic hermaphrodism seeks "a reinstatement of chaos," "a return to confusion," resulting in "*a supreme act of regeneration* and an enormous increase in power."[57]

Huysmans's investigation into the occult world was itself prompted by a wish to revitalize literature languishing in the death throes of naturalism. In the diabolical practices of Canon Docre, Durtal had found more than an exasperated expression of the carnality prevalent among his contemporaries. Desecration of the Host by couples copulating on dirty sheets in cheap hotels, the long-distance murder of enemies executed by evil spirits delivering poisonous decoctions of toad flesh and menstrual blood: the satanic rituals that Durtal learns about depend on using bodily secretions, exploiting bodily weakness, and obstructing spiritual aspirations by capitalizing on bodily appetites.

The alchemical figure that best represents Durtal's idea of spiritual naturalism is the griffon. With the body of a lion and the head of an eagle, it is a mythical creature combining the aggressive physicality of the noblest of predators with the keen eyes and lofty station of a denizen of the skies. Gévingey remarks that hawks and falcons are instruments of white magicians, messengers from heaven, and symbols of elevation. For the alchemist, these birds of prey are endowed with rich significance: "Faire voler l'aigle, selon l'expression hermétique, c'est faire sortir la lumière du tombeau et la porter à la surface, ce qui est le propre de toute 'véritable sublimation'." [Making the eagle fly, according to the Hermetic expression, means bringing light out of the tomb, raising it to the surface. This is the characteristic of genuine sublimation.][58]

In the literary transmutation that Huysmans's hero undertakes, there is a rehabilitation of the body as sanctified "materia prima." *Là-bas* concludes with a grotesque image describing the ignominious crash of Durtal's soaring vision. Following the characters' discussion of the dawning of the Kingdom of the Holy Paraclete, they commiserate over the cynical atheism pervasive in their era, complain about the neglect of the wisdom of Paracelsus, and remark on the distance between the piety of the Middle Ages and the triumph of materialism celebrated by the election of General Boulanger. The fall from the occult realm back into the gray world of the quotidian, the collapse of the opposition between spiritual longing and physical appetite, is announced by Durtal in his final, most disgusting divinatory prophesy, in which he predicts that clamorous voters, destined to become a carrion feast for maggots, will forever stuff their guts and purge their souls "par le bas-ventre" [through their bowels].[59]

Evacuated as waste by ignoramuses, the spirit is gold locked inside the lead of their bodies. With the reversal of the transubstantiation of divinity into nourishment, there seems to be a culmination of a derisory eschatology, whereby the end of time is signaled by an ascendancy of the scatological. Unclean linen, lustful thoughts, rutting money, profaned altars—the nadir of man's journey toward transfigurative redemption is the moment when flesh is torn and matter is fired in the crucible, turning black before its final purification can begin. Like the earth in the retort that the alchemists called "the Toad," Christ's body and Gilles's soul were initially cleansed by torture in preparation for their final sublimation and ascension. As with the recent convert passing through the Dark Night of the Soul before he is embraced again by Christ and brought by Him back to the light, the alchemist's material is subjected to the fire in order to become imperishable and precious. It is like the white Host, which, in human hands, as Marie-Claire Bancquart says, "représente une incarnation souffrante, au sens le plus fort du terme 'incarnation'" [represents a suffering "incarnation," in the strongest sense of the term].[60]

Jung cites a philosopher who addresses a group of sages, saying: "The tortured thing, when it is immersed in the body, changes into an unalterable and indestructible nature."[61] Modeled on Christ's crucifixion, the substance is broken down to permit its elevation and attainment of higher form. Eliade says that this belief informed the operations of the alchemists, in which, "corresponding to the tortures, death, and resurrection of the initiate, the substance is transmuted, . . . attains a transcendental mode of being," becoming gold,—which, Eliade adds, is "the symbol of immortality."[62]

In Durtal's account of Gilles's arrest and trial, his punishment and execution, the latter was excommunicated first for offences falling within the church's jurisdiction, then sentenced to be burned alive for crimes against the state. In order to guarantee the truthfulness of Gilles's confession, Durtal claims Gilles was subjected "à la question canonique, c'est-à-dire à la torture" [to canonical interrogation, namely, to torture].[63] From the vociferous blasphemer who first appeared before the tribunal to the haggard, stricken penitent who confessed to unspeakable transgressions, Gilles had been transmuted by torture, purified by repentance: "[I]l s'était subitement renversé l'âme; il l'avait lavée de ses pleurs, séchée au feu des prières torrentielles, aux flammes des élans fous." [His soul has been overturned, washed by his tears, dried in the fire of torrential prayer, in the flames of his mad exaltation.][64]

Produced by pain, tears are the secretion that brings man absolution, lifting him above his degraded corporeity. In their laboratory at Tiffauges, Gilles's confraternity of alchemists had sought the secret of the philosopher's stone that changed the impure to the pure, "cette pierre des Sages . . . flexible . . . sentant le sel marin calciné" [that malleable . . . philosopher's stone . . . smelling of calcined sea salt].[65] Manly Hall quotes a letter by a seventeenth-century Rosicrucian who identifies the *lapis* as "the purest and cleanest . . . sea salt, so as it is made by the sun itself," salt dissolved in the "*Dew-water* . . . to be had in the months of May or June."[66] A distillate of rays, solar salt, and lunar water, it is suffering made substance, liquid fire, *aqua ardens,* that revolutionizes the soul and resurrects the fallen, whose black sins are converted into the gold of God's forgiveness.

The transformative medium of tears, if applied to tortured flesh, ensures the successful outcome of the spagyrical experiment. It is this alchemy of pain that Durtal sees in Grünewald's painting, as Christ's crucified body is volatilized, becoming a spirit that ascends to heaven. Suffering in Huysmans is both the essence of naturalist art and the operative principle that brings about its own transcendence. In Grünewald's picture, Christ is shown dissolving into blood and pus, the tears of wounds that presage the putrefaction of the substance. It is "l'ignominie de la pourriture" [the ignominy of corruption][67] that brings a radiant transformation, and bodily abjection that propels the soul into the firmament. Spiritual naturalism assumes the full weight of crude materiality, plumbing a cloacal netherworld of ugliness and horror, washing the tortured subject clean in "les essences les plus acérées des pleurs" [the sharpest essence of tears],[68] before his transmutation places him beyond images and words.

In the alembic of his novel, Huysmans puts literature to the question, breaking down old preconceptions about art's respectability and purpose. With Grünewald, he stirs the cauldron, bringing tormented matter to ebullition, following the recipe for changing heaviness into ether, the toad into the eagle, imprisonment into flight. Revealing "une expression surhumaine" [a superhuman expression] in "l'effervescence des chairs" [the fermentation of flesh],[69] Grünewald draws from physical destruction a sign of the regeneration of the spirit.

In *Là-bas,* there is an oscillation between the necromancer's rictus and the smile of the bell-ringer who is supported by his faith. Bodies that are disintegrated by the imagination or by time's passage are reconstructed by the visionary who sees beauty beneath the ruins. From history's wreckage, Durtal builds a castle paved with colored bricks and flagstones; he fills the upper rooms with luxury and the subterranean chambers with cadavers. An alchemist, he changes women into secret, sphinx-like mistresses, and dispels the maddening chatter of crowds with the ringing of church bells. Historical facts, accepted truths, are the base matter he treats with fire, black pitch from which he extracts the rare and precious stuff of fiction.

The dualistic theory that had structured Durtal's view of spiritual naturalism is first inverted, as high and low are symbolically interchanged, then collapsed as matter is reworked and transmuted into divine essence. Carhaix, Durtal, and des Hermies may await the Kingdom of the Holy Paraclete, when God sanctifies man's organs so that only the blessed will be fruitful. But at present, as des Hermies affirms, the heart retains the same form as the penis, ensuring that "tout amour de cœur finit par l'organe qui lui ressemble" [all love of the heart ends with the organ that it resembles].[70] Unredeemed, the terrestrial world is the alchemist's nigredo, made of matter, food, intestines, excrement, and chaos. The mortal plane of bodies is therefore identical to the body, the only site where art promotes the transmutation of the physical. As Huysmans writes in *Lydwine,* "cette divine alchimie . . . est la Douleur" [this divine alchemy . . . is Suffering],[71] the torment of the substance, the firing of base matter, the twisting of the limbs, the encircling thorns that pierce the forehead. The discovery of the philosopher's stone, which Huysmans identifies as love,[72] will make it applicable to humankind and thereby render art superfluous. But for now the text must chart the course of people set in motion by their suffering—journeying downward toward aggressiveness, sacrilege, and hatred, or rising upward through humility, obedience, and study, until they complete their transformation and attain the flawlessness of gold.

Notes

1. Jean-Marie Seillan, introduction to *Interviews,* by J.-K. Huysmans (Paris: Champion, 2002), 57.

2. Huysmans, *Lettres inédites à Arij Prins,* 248.

3. J.-K. Huysmans, "Chez J.-K. Huysmans—Le Satanisme dévoilé," interview with Austin de Croze, *La Cocarde,* March 8, 1893, reprinted in Huysmans, *Interviews,* 137.

4. Jean Descottignies, "*Là-bas* ou la phase démoniaque de l'écriture," *Revue des Sciences Humaines* 43, nos. 170-71 (April-September 1978): 70.

5. Huysmans, *Là-bas,* pt. 1, 6.

6. Ibid.

7. Ibid., pt. 2, 230.

8. Paracelsus, *Selected Writings* (Princeton, NJ: Princeton University Press, 1969), 83.

9. Huysmans, *Là-bas,* pt. 2, 210.

10. Ibid., pt. 1, 31.

11. Ibid., pt. 1, 30.

12. Manly Hall, *The Secret Teachings of All Ages* (Los Angeles: Philosophical Research Association, 1977), 156.

13. Huysmans, *Là-bas,* pt. 1, 25.

14. Paracelsus, *Selected Writings,* 148.

15. Huysmans, *Là-bas,* pt. 1, 24.

16. Ibid., pt. 2, 35.

17. Ibid., pt. 1, 24

18. Ibid., pt. 1, 23.

19. Ibid., pt. 1, 24.

20. Ibid., pt. 1, 82.

21. Marie-Laure Colonna, "L'Attitude alchimique," *Cahiers Jungiens de Psychanalyse* 88 (Spring 1997): 15.

22. Huysmans, *Là-bas,* pt. 1, 124.

23. Hall, *Secret Teachings of All Ages,* 155.

24. C. G. Jung, *Alchemical Studies,* trans. R. F. C. Hull, in vol. 13 of *The Collected Works C. G. Jung* (Princeton, NJ: Princeton University Press, 1967), 222.

25. Huysmans, *Là-bas,* pt. 1, 11.

26. Hall, *Secret Teachings of All Ages,* 158.

27. Huysmans, *Là-bas,* pt. 1, 30.

28. Ibid., pt. 1, 48.

29. Ibid., pt. 1, 117.

30. J.-K. Huysmans, preface to *Le Satanisme et la magie,* by Jules Bois (Paris: Chailley, 1895), xvi-xvii.

31. Huysmans, *Là-bas,* pt. 1, 191.

32. Qtd. in Durand, *Les Structures anthropologiques de l'imaginaire,* 302-3.

33. Durand, *Les Structures anthropologiques de l'imaginaire*, 293.

34. Huysmans, *Là-bas*, pt. 1, 45.

35. Hall, *Secret Teachings of All Ages*, 156.

36. Huysmans, *Là-bas*, pt. 1, 19.

37. Ibid., pt. 1, 216.

38. J.-M. Wittmann, "Notes sur un personnage 'diabolique': Hyacinthe Chantelouve dans *Là-bas* de Huysmans," *Les Lettres Romanes* 49, nos. 3-4 (1979): 279.

39. Huysmans, *Là-bas*, pt. 1, 182.

40. Ibid.

41. The phrase is used by the shabby but grandiloquent mythomaniac Monsieur de Bougrelon, hero of Jean Lorrain's eponymous 1901 novel. Escorting two French tourists through a fashion exhibit in an Amsterdam museum, Bougrelon is similarly aroused by a combination of superannuated dresses and their absent female wearers.

42. Huysmans, *Là-bas*, pt. 1, 186.

43. Wittmann, "Notes sur un personnage 'diabolique,'" 286.

44. Ibid.

45. Huysmans, *Là-bas*, pt. 2, 109.

46. Ibid.

47. Ibid.

48. Ibid., pt. 2, 35.

49. Ibid., pt. 2, 83.

50. Wittmann, "Notes sur un personnage 'diabolique,'" 281.

51. Janine Chasseguet-Smirgel, "The Devil Religion: Some Reflections on the Historical and Social Meanings of the Perversions," *Journal of Clinical Psychoanalysis* 8, no. 3 (1999): 393.

52. Françoise Gaillard sees the same impulse guiding des Esseintes's project to convert "natural" floral scents into alcoholic distillates: "Ce projet de parvenir à une contrefaçon idéale du monde à l'aide d'une matière totalement maîtrisable, vise en fait à retrouver par-delà le divers naturel, une *unicité perdue*, à opposer au chaos du monde le grand *Un* et cela au prix de la destruction d'un réel dévalué, un réel qui a perdu son sens en sacrifiant l'uni à l'attrait du divers" ("*A rebours* ou l'inversion de signes," in *L'Esprit de décadence* [Nantes: Minard, 1980], 139). [This desire to create an ideal counterfeit of the world, using matter that can be completely controlled, intends the recovery of a *lost unity* that exists beyond the diversity of nature. It opposes to the chaos of the world a *Oneness* attained by destroying a devalued reality, whose meaning has been lost by sacrificing unity to the attraction of the diverse.]

53. Chasseguet-Smirgel, "Devil Religion," 385.

54. Ibid., 394.

55. Ibid., 389.

56. Huysmans, *Là-bas*, pt. 2, 36.

57. Qtd. in Chasseguet-Smirgel, "Devil Religion," 395. Italics in original.

58. Jean Koralewski, "Les Aigles," *Revue Française de Psychanalyse* 4 (1988): 1051.

59. Huysmans, *Là-bas*, pt. 2, 235.

60. Bancquart, "Huysmans, l'insatiable anorexique," 17.

61. Jung, *Alchemical Studies*, 329.

62. Mircea Eliade, *The Forge and the Crucible: The Origins and Structures of Alchemy*, trans. Stephen Corrin (New York: Harper and Row, 1971), 151.

63. Huysmans, *Là-bas*, pt. 2, 136.

64. Ibid., pt. 2, 144.

65. Ibid., pt. 2, 132.

66. Hall, *Secret Teachings of All Ages*, 159.

67. Huysmans, *Là-bas*, pt. 1, 18.

68. Ibid., pt. 1, 19.

69. Ibid.

70. Ibid., pt. 2, 56.

71. Huysmans, *Sainte Lydwine de Schiedam*, pt. 2, 126.

72. Ibid., pt. 2, 127.

References

Bancquart, Marie-Claire. "Huysmans, l'insatiable anorexique." *Bulletin de la Société J.-K. Huysmans*. 93 (June 2000): 1-22.

Chasseguet-Smirgel, Janine. "The Devil Religion: Some Reflections on the Historical and Social Meanings of the Perversions." *Journal of Clinical Psychoanalysis* 8, no. 3 (1999): 382-400.

Colonna, Marie-Laure. "L'Attitude alchimique." *Cahiers Jungiens de Psychanalyse* 88 (Spring 1997): 9-20.

Descottignies, Jean. "*Là-bas* ou la phase démoniaque de l'écriture." *Revue des Sciences Humaines* 43, nos. 170-71 (April-September 1978): 69-79.

Durand. Gilbert. *Les Structures anthropologiques de l'imaginaire.* Paris: Bordas, 1969.

Eliade, Mircea. *The Forge and the Crucible: The Origins and Structures of Alchemy.* Translated by Stephen Corrin. New York: Harper and Row, 1971.

Gaillard, Françoise. "*A rebours* ou l'inversion des signes." In *L'Esprit de décadence.* Nantes: Minard, 1980.

Hall, Manly. *The Secret Teachings of All Ages.* Los Angeles: Philosophical Research Association, 1977.

Huysmans, J.-K. *A rebours.* In vol. 7 of *Œuvres complètes.* Geneva: Slatkine, 1972.

———. *Interviews.* Edited by Jean-Marie Seillan. Paris: Champion, 2002.

———. *Là-bas.* In vol. 12 of *Œuvres complètes.* Geneva: Slatkine, 1972.

———. *Lettres à Arij Prins.* Edited by Louis Gillet. Geneva: Droz, 1977.

———. *Marthe.* Paris: Le Cercle du Livre, 1955.

———. Preface to *Le Satanisme et la magie,* by Jules Bois. Paris: Chailley, 1895.

———. *La Retraite de Monsieur Bougran.* In *"Un Dilemme" précédé de "Sac au dos" et suivi de "La Retraite de Monsieur Bougran."* Toulouse: Editions Ombres, 1993.

———. *Sainte Lydwine de Schiedam.* In vol. 15 of *Œuvres complètes.* Geneva: Slatkine, 1972.

———. *Les Sœurs Vatard.* In vol. 2 of *Œuvres complètes.* Geneva: Slatkine, 1972.

Jung, C. G. *Alchemical Studies.* Translated by R. F. C. Hull. In vol. 13 of *The Collected Works of C. G. Jung.* Princeton, NJ: Princeton University Press, 1967.

Koralewski, Jean. "Les Aigles." *Revue Française de Psychanalyse* 4 (1998): 1049-52.

Leavy, Stanley. *In the Image of God.* New Haven, CT: Yale University Press, 1988.

Lewis, Christopher Alan. "Oral Pessimism and Depressive Symptoms." *Journal of Psychology* 127, no. 3 (1992): 335-43.

Lipton, Edgar. "On Ventriloquism." *Psychoanalytic Study of the Child* 38 (1983): 601-16.

Livi, François, *J.-K. Huysmans: "A rebours" et l'esprit décadent.* Paris: Nizet, 1972.

Lloyd, Christopher. "*A vau-l'eau*: Le monde indigeste du naturalisme." *Bulletin de la Sociéte J.-K. Huysmans* 19, no. 71 (1980): 44-57.

Maupassant, Guy de. *Sur l'eau.* Paris: Albin Michel, 1888.

Modenesi, Marco. "Le héros à table: *A vau-l'eau* ou le piège gastronomique." *Etudes Françaises* 23, no. 3 (1988): 77-88.

Mrosovsky, Kitty. Introduction to *The Temptation of Saint Anthony,* by Gustave Flaubert. London: Penguin Books, 1983.

Mugnier, Abbé. *J.-K. Huysmans à La Trappe.* Paris: Le Divan, 1927.

Olrik, Hilde. "Marthe: Une Prostituée au XIXème siècle." *Revue des Sciences Humaines* 43, nos. 170-71 (1978): 273-83.

Ortoleva, Madeleine. *Joris-Karl Huysmans: Romancier du salut.* Sherbrooke, QC: Naaman, 1981.

Pallasmaa, Juhani. "Stairways of the Mind." *International Forum on Psychoanaly-Paracelsus. Selected Writings.* Princeton, NJ: Princeton University Press, 1969.

Wittmann, J.-M. "Notes sur un personnage 'diabolique': Hyacinthe Chantelouve dans *Là-bas de Huysmans." Les Lettres Romanes* 49, nos. 3-4 (1979): 279-86.

FURTHER READING

Criticism

Antosh, Ruth B. "The Role of Paintings in Three Novels by J.-K. Huysmans." *Nineteenth-Century French Studies* 12-13, nos. 4-1 (summer-fall 1984): 131-46.

> Examines Huysmans' use of certain paintings in three of his novels, *Marthe, Against the Grain,* and *Là-bas,* focusing not on the works of art themselves but on what they tell us about the author's views on the relationship between literature and painting.

Baldick, Robert. Introduction to *Down There (La Bas): A Study in Satanism,* by J.-K. Huysmans, translated by Keene Wallis, pp. vii-xxviii. Evanston, Ill.: University Books, 1958.

> Discusses the historical figures and events, as well as details from his own life, that Huysmans drew upon in writing *Là-bas.*

Carter, A. E. "J.-K. Huysmans and the Middle Ages." In *Medieval Studies in Honor of Robert White Linker: By His Colleagues and Friends,* edited by Brian Dutton, J. Woodrow Hassell, Jr., and John E. Keller, pp. 17-53. Valencia, Spain: Editorial Castalia, 1973.

> Critiques *Là-bas,* claiming that in the composite figure of Durtal-Gilles de Rais, "Huysmans was sketching a portrait of himself," and laments how Huysmans' "horrible fascination" with the black arts "distorts his judgment" in the novel at various points.

Ridge, George Ross. "The Decadent." In *Joris-Karl Huysmans,* pp. 60-80. New York: Twayne Publishers, 1968.

> Summarizes the characters and central themes of *Là-bas,* concluding that although the novel "is not the very summation of Decadence," it is nonetheless "a powerful and important" work.

Ziegler, Robert. "From Prostitution to Prayer: The Writer and His Public in J.-K. Huysmans." *French Review* 67, no. 1 (October 1993): 37-46.

> Traces Huysmans' evolving attitudes toward the reader and the function of his art in *Marthe, En Route,* and *Là-bas.*

Zielonka, Anthony. "Huysmans and Grünewald: The Discovery of 'Spiritual Naturalism.'" *Nineteenth-Century French Studies* 18, nos. 1-2 (fall 1989): 212-30.

> Analyzes the manner in which Huysmans responded to the crucifixion paintings of Matthaeus Grünewald in *Là-bas* and in his work of art criticism, *Trois primitifs.*

Additional coverage of Huysmans' life and career is contained in the following sources published by Gale: *Contemporary Authors,* **Vols. 104, 165;** *Dictionary of Literary Biography,* **Vol. 123;** *European Writers,* **Vol. 7;** *Guide to French Literature: 1789 to the Present; Literary Movements for Students,* **Vol. 2;** *Literature Resource Center; Reference Guide to World Literature,* **Eds. 2, 3; and** *Twentieth-Century Literary Criticism,* **Vols. 7, 69.**

Pedro Salinas
1891?-1951

(Full name Pedro Salinas y Serrano) Spanish poet, playwright, novelist, critic, essayist, and translator.

The following entry provides an overview of Salinas's life and works. For additional information on his career, see *TCLC,* Volume 17.

INTRODUCTION

Pedro Salinas is considered one of the most important Spanish poets of the twentieth century. He is often remembered as a senior member of the influential group of poets known as the "Generation of 1927"—including such other Spanish literary figures as Jorge Guillén, Luis Cernuda, Rafael Alberti, and Federico García Lorca—although his versatile writings defy categorization or adherence to a specific poetic movement or school of thought. In addition to poetry, Salinas wrote novels, plays, and essays, and was a respected literary critic. In many of his various works, he explored themes related to the poet's creative process, as well as the tension between reality and illusion and the conflict between artistic perception and the external, material world. While Salinas has received critical acclaim for his literary criticism and experimental dramatic work, most scholars favor his poetry, particularly his meditations on love in the volumes *La voz a ti debida* (1933; *My Voice Because of You*) and *Razón de amor* (1936). For some critics, Salinas's work not only represents a significant aspect of early twentieth-century Spanish literature but also anticipates the direction of Western poetry in the later twentieth century, bridging the modern and postmodern eras of literature. According to critic John Devlin, Salinas "is one of the greatest poets of the twentieth century and of Spain's *post modernista* renaissance."

BIOGRAPHICAL INFORMATION

Salinas was born on November 27, 1891, in Madrid, although some sources indicate he was born in 1892. His father, Pedro Salinas Elmas, the proprietor of a small general store, died prematurely in 1899. Following his father's death Salinas led a sheltered life, and his mother, Soledad Serrano Fernández de Salinas, limited his time with other children. Salinas suffered from poor health as a child and spent much of his time alone. Rather than playing with other children, he developed his imaginative and creative abilities.

In 1897 Salinas began his education at the Colegio Hispano-Francés, where he studied French in addition to a basic curriculum. He graduated in 1903 and then earned a secondary degree from the Instituto San Isidro in 1908. Salinas briefly studied law at the Central University in Madrid but changed his course of studies, graduating with a Licentiate in Philosophy and Letters in 1913. During his time at college, Salinas began developing an interest in writing and literature. He spent much of his time reading at the library and became acquainted with Enrique Díez-Canedo, a modernist poet affiliated with the so-called "Generation of 1898."

In 1911 several of Salinas's poems were published in the literary magazine *Prometeo,* and the following year he studied art history in Paris. Soon after, Salinas translated several works of French poetry, began working on his doctoral dissertation, and taught Spanish literature at the Sorbonne from 1914 to 1917. At the Sorbonne he met Mathilde Pomés and Jean Cassou, as well as the symbolist poet Paul Valéry. In 1915 Salinas married Margarita Bonmatí, whom he had met in the small Mediterranean village of Santa Pola, and the following year completed his doctoral thesis. Salinas returned to Spain and in 1919 accepted a professorship at the University of Seville, where he taught until 1928. During this time he formed lasting friendships with two important writers of his generation, Jorge Guillén and Luis Cernuda.

While teaching at the University of Seville Salinas was involved with a number of literary projects. He collaborated with several literary magazines, including *España, La Pluma,* and *Revista de Occidente,* and translated works by Alfred de Musset and Marcel Proust. During this time Salinas also completed his first novel, *Víspera del gozo (Prelude to Pleasure),* in 1926 and began writing the poems that comprise his first important poetic phase, collected in *Presagios* (1923), *Seguro azar* (1929; *Certain Chance*), and *Fábula y signo* (1931). Salinas left the University of Seville in 1928 and accepted a research position at the Centro de Estudios Históricos in Madrid, where he also headed a summer program teaching foreign-exchange students. In 1930 he accepted a professorship at the Central School for Languages, where he remained until 1936.

In 1933, with the publication of *My Voice Because of You,* Salinas entered his second poetic phase, distinguished by its thematic focus on the subject of love. That same year he initiated the International Summer

University, which was supported by the Second Spanish Republican government. In 1936, however, with the beginning of the Spanish Civil War, Salinas was forced to abandon the project and escape to the United States. He accepted a position at Wellesley College in Massachusetts in the fall of 1936, and the following spring served as a visiting professor at Johns Hopkins University in Baltimore, where he occupied the Turnbull Chair of Poetry. During this time Salinas produced two more volumes of poetry, *Razón de amor* and *Largo lamento,* which was completed in 1938 but not published until its inclusion in the 1971 edition of Salinas's *Poesías completas.* These collections, together with *My Voice Because of You,* form a trilogy outlining Salinas's spiritual vision of the various stages of love.

Salinas's years of exile in the United States, between 1936 and 1951, were productive, though sometimes lonely and isolating for the poet, who deeply missed his friends and native country. He published numerous essays and literary criticism, including *Reality and the Poet in Spanish Poetry* (1940), which was based on his lectures at Johns Hopkins. Salinas also turned to writing drama and published fourteen plays, including *La fuenta del Arcángel, El precio,* and *El director,* collected in *Teatro completo* (1957), many of which reflect the author's nostalgia for Spain.

Ten years after moving to the United States, Salinas published his next collection of poetry, titled *El contemplado: Tema con variaciones* (1946; *Sea of San Juan: A Contemplation*). These poems were composed between 1943 and 1946, while Salinas was teaching at the University of Puerto Rico in Río Piedras. After returning to Johns Hopkins, he wrote two more volumes of poetry, *Todo más claro y otros poemas,* published in 1949, and *Confianza,* which was issued posthumously in 1955, as well as a novel, *La bomba increíble,* which was published in 1950. In the last months of his life, after being diagnosed with bone cancer, Salinas lived in Boston, and continued to write until he lost the use of his right arm. Salinas died on December 4, 1951, in Massachusetts, and his body was taken to Puerto Rico, where he was interred in a cemetery in San Juan.

MAJOR WORKS

The volumes representing Salinas's first poetic phase, *Presagios, Certain Chance,* and *Fábula y signo,* are experimental works that form a unit, and which put forth Salinas's views on the role of poetry for both the poet and humankind. In *Presagios,* Salinas examines the relationship between the inner reality of the poet and that of the external world. The speaker of the poems recognizes the superficiality and volatility of the material world, which tempts him to retreat fully into the inner reality, but at the same time acknowledges that in order to engage in art, he must connect with the external world. Stylistically, the volume borrows forms from traditional Spanish literature, particularly those employed by the poets of Spain's Golden Age, including Pedro Calderón de la Barca and Fray Luis de León. In many of the poems, however, Salinas purposely avoided relying on the baroque influences of that period, such as the use of complex imagery and metaphor.

In his next volume, *Certain Chance,* Salinas introduces the idea of the "transrealidad," or "transreality," described as matter transformed by the poet's imagination, which eventually enters the collective imagination. This idea is explored most notably in the poem "Vocación" ("Vocation"). In other poems in the collection, including "Navacerrada, abril" ("Navacerrada, April"), "35 bujías" ("35 Candle Power"), and "Cinematógrafo" ("Movie Theater"), Salinas contemplates technological advancements and modern inventions of the 1920s, such as the automobile, the cinema, and the light bulb.

The third poetic volume, *Fábula y signo,* revisits ideas presented in the first two works, including the interaction between reality and illusion and the nature of the creative process. As in *Certain Chance,* several of the poems in the volume, such as "Radiator y fogata" and "El teléfono," focus on modern machines and technology. According to some critics, the material world in *Fábula y signo* is less stable or exact than that depicted in Salinas's previous two collections; it is a world in which the external object is intrinsically transformed by the poet's intuitive process and given new life in his imagination. Andrew P. Debicki has declared that Salinas's first three books of poetry make "us experience, again and again, ways in which elements from the world around us both are and are not what they seem, both do and do not explain patterns and correspondences in our lives and our history. And he highlights the unique power of poetic language to reach beyond clear logical formulations, and to embody, while reflecting upon its own process, the contradictions inherent in a life that is also dream."

Salinas's second poetic trilogy—*My Voice Because of You, Razón de amor,* and *Largo lamento*—is regarded by many critics as the pinnacle of his career as a poet. Along with the poetry of his contemporaries, these works are credited with initiating a modern revival of traditional love themes in Spanish literature. In *My Voice Because of You,* Salinas traces four stages of a romantic relationship, beginning with the discovery of love, followed by the culmination of the experience and, eventually, estrangement and separation. In the fourth section of the collection, the poet-speaker examines his grief and finds new meaning in the experience by revising his definition of love to encompass greater forces. In this volume the poet-speaker's beloved is characterized as a muse, capable of wielding both creative and destructive energy.

Personal sacrifice for the greater good and salvation are important themes in the second volume of the trilogy, *Razón de amor*. While the poet-speaker once again struggles with his grief over the loss of his beloved, he ultimately sacrifices his own happiness, thus preparing the way for a universal harmony that can be experienced by all.

Salinas focuses on similar ideas of love in *Largo lamento*. The estrangement between the two lovers, however, is emphasized in this collection, leaving the poet-speaker weary and isolated. For some scholars, *Largo lamento* is a transitional work, anticipating some of the themes in Salinas's later writings. Philip G. McLaughlin, who has described *Largo lamento* as the "swansong of love for Salinas" and an "elegiac response to the failure of love," argues that it is "an important work for our overall understanding of Salinas's poetry by virtue of its pivotal position between the love poetry of the thirties and the broader concerns of later years."

Although Salinas is chiefly remembered as a poet, his plays have received increasing critical attention in recent years. Noting the influence of the Italian playwright Luigi Pirandello on Salinas's theater, Wilma Newberry has argued that "these imaginative, fanciful, individualistic, short dramatic pieces are very delightful to read. But they are more than lyrical stories in the form of plays."

Self-discovery, the interplay between fantasy and reality, and the search for freedom and redemption are important themes in many of Salinas's dramatic works. For example, *La fuente del Arcángel,* set in Andalusia, Spain, fuses reality and illusion and explores the multiplicity of human personality. Claribel, who has previously led a sheltered life, is transformed when a magician briefly changes her into the character of a courtesan. She is spirited away, at the end of the play, by an archangel figure from a fountain, rumored to be the pagan god Eros.

Many scholars have also noted metafictional tendencies in Salinas's plays, which often employ a poet-protagonist who derives fulfillment and joy from the act of creation. In *El precio,* the protagonist of the play, Jáuregui, is an author searching for a "lost" female character, Melisa, who has physically manifested and eluded her creator. To have a complete life, however, Melisa must pay the price of death, after which she will achieve immortality in the author's literary work. *El director* depicts the interactions between a young woman, known as the Typist, and a dual divinity figure called the Director-Gerente, or Director, who demonstrates both good and evil qualities. The central action of the play deals with the themes of identity and self-fulfillment, as the Director brings happiness to the Typist but fails to convince her that the evil Gerente is an essential part of his being. Her refusal to see this truth about him, as well as the meaning of human happiness, leads to a tragic ending in which she recognizes the unity of his character too late.

Susan G. Polansky has observed that the "pivotal role of poet heroes in pursuit of a redemptive unification with kindred figures provides Salinas's dramatic corpus with a structural unity. As key supports of the framework of the plays, these characters stand at the core of his organization of his *fabulas* to embody spiritual and social attributes exalted by Salinas."

CRITICAL RECEPTION

Commentators generally agree that Salinas, as a leading member of the Generation of 1927, helped shape the development of Spanish literature in the twentieth century. While his work garnered respect throughout his life, most critics consider the period from 1933 to 1938, during which he wrote *My Voice Because of You* and *Razón de amor,* the peak of his career as a poet and artist. But despite his renown, as some scholars have noted, Salinas's achievements were overshadowed in the latter half of the twentieth century by the imposing figure of his contemporary, Federico García Lorca. As John Devlin has contended, "Pedro Salinas has been neglected, as have many of the poets of 1927, because they fall under the shadow of Lorca, whose astounding verbal genius has had a bewitching enchantment. Salinas and the others deserve more attention, study, and love." Nevertheless, Salinas is generally remembered as one of the most important contributors to modern Spanish literature, whose unique writing style influenced future generations. Robert G. Havard has observed that "in practical terms Salinas could not invent a new language for his poetry, and had to be content with a second-hand one complete with 'gramática e historia,' but his serious efforts to free himself from some linguistic impositions, such as he considered them, resulted in a poetic style that was very much his own: one that continually questions its own reality and, paradoxically, discovers itself in the process. Indeed, it is within this concept of language and experience *in process* that we find Salinas' supreme achievement in poetry."

Many studies of Salinas's work have focused on the author's thematic concerns, especially the conflict between the external, material world and the poet's inner reality. David L. Stixrude has contended that Salinas's "rejection of the evident world spans his whole work, from *Presagios* to *Confianza*." Stixrude concludes that "the criticism of reality in terms of its conceptual definition—the words and accompanying value-associations which limit them—is the most pervasive theme in Salinas' poetry. It is frequently, necessarily, linked to a rejection of the perceived world on the one hand . . . and to a criticism of contemporary reality on the other."

Other scholars have emphasized the author's stylistic choices. Sandra Price has commented that "mythology is a stylistic constant in Salinas' poetry. It provides another strand of evidence of his conscious awareness of the importance of tradition, literary and spiritual, in the present day. His usage of it develops and changes with the poetry, maturing out of its essentially witty and humorous role in the early poetry into a vehicle for the expression of central concerns, poetic, personal, and social in the late collections." For Price, Salinas's use of mythology "asserts the value of the human above the technological and the materialistic."

Although he is most recognized as a poet, Salinas has received increasing praise for the plays he wrote late in his career. In discussing his dramatic work, critics often note the similarity of themes in both his poetry and his plays, especially issues related to reality, identity, and self-fulfillment. Stephanie L. Orringer has explored the metafictional element and theme of "self-authentication" in the works, noting the various ways that Salinas's dramatic protagonists, either through their art or through interactions with other characters, "author their own essential beings." In a similar manner, Susan G. Polansky has asserted that by employing his protagonists to "shape his creations of 'reality in fable form,'" Salinas constructs a body of drama that reflects his unique blending of contemporaneous currents of realism and antirealism in the modern theater. On the one hand, Salinas shows with realism ordinary people and commonplace settings to reflect truths about human life. On the other hand, he reaches for a timeless perspective and probes beyond everyday routine to enter the world of hopes, dreams, and visions and to explore significant intangibles of existence."

Whether as a poet or a playwright, or as a critic, translator, and novelist, Salinas occupies an important place in the history of Spanish literature. In many respects, as Vialla Hartfield-Méndez has suggested, his work transcends the modernist forms of European writing and anticipates the postmodern in its concern with authorship, language, reality, and identity. "[In] spite of his strong symbolist legacy, or perhaps because of it," Hartfield-Méndez declares, "Salinas came to question its essential tenets in his work, anticipating early on some of the postmodernist tendencies that were to surface in the second half of the century." Ultimately, as John Devlin has maintained, Salinas will be remembered for the force of his artistic vision, for his ceaseless exploration of reality, and his meditations on the theme of love.

PRINCIPAL WORKS

Presagios (poetry) 1923
Víspera del gozo [*Prelude to Pleasure*] (novel) 1926
Seguro azar [*Certain Chance*] (poetry) 1929

Fábula y signo (poetry) 1931
La voz a ti debida [*My Voice Because of You*] (poetry) 1933
Razón de amor (poetry) 1936
Lost Angel, and Other Poems (poetry) 1938
Reality and the Poet in Spanish Poetry (lectures) 1940
Truth of Two, and Other Poems (poetry) 1940
Literatura española, siglo XX (criticism) 1941
El contemplado: Tema con variaciones [*Sea of San Juan: A Contemplation*] (poetry) 1946
Zero (poetry) 1947
El defensor (essays) 1948
Todo más claro y otros poemas (poetry) 1949
La bomba increíble (novel) 1950
El desnudo impeccable y otras narraciones (short stories) 1951
Teatro: La cabeza de Medusa, La estratoesfera, La isla del teatro (plays) 1952
Poemas escogidos (poetry) 1953
Confianza (poetry) 1955
Poesías completas (poetry) 1955; enlarged editions, 1971 and 1975
Teatro completo (plays) 1957
Volverse sombra y otros poemas (poetry) 1957
Ensayos de literatura hispánica (essays) 1958
La responsabilidad del escritor (essays) 1961
*Largo lamento (poetry) 1971
To Live in Pronouns (poetry) 1974
Narrativa completa (novel and short stories) 1976
Ensayos completos (essays) 1983
Cartas de amor a Margarita, 1912-1915 (letters) 1984
Correspondencia 1923-1951 (letters) 1992
Translation of the Love Poetry of Pedro Salinas, 1892-1951 (poetry) 2000

*This work was first published in the 1971 edition of *Poesías completas*.

CRITICISM

Wilma Newberry (essay date spring 1971)

SOURCE: Newberry, Wilma. "Pirandellism in the Plays of Pedro Salinas." *Symposium* 25, no. 1 (spring 1971): 59-69.

[*In the following essay, Newberry discusses the influence of the Italian dramatist Luigi Pirandello on Salinas's work as a playwright, focusing especially on the similarities of the themes and theatrical techniques of the two writers.*]

Although the poetry of Pedro Salinas has been the subject of numerous studies, very little attention has been given to his plays. Salinas as playwright is usually omitted from discussions of twentieth-century Spanish theater, or, at most, the fact that he wrote plays is mentioned. Although short articles which serve to introduce the subject appeared after three of his plays were published in 1952,[1] the first important study was not published until 1965.[2]

A playwright in exile in a country in which his native language is not spoken suffers from a handicap unknown to exiled novelists or poets. Even though some of his plays were performed by university groups,[3] it is perhaps understandable that they are not considered part of the mainstream of Spanish twentieth-century theater. However, even if we were to regard Salinas' plays merely as an extension of his poetry, they certainly deserve more attention. These imaginative, fanciful, individualistic, short dramatic pieces are very delightful to read. But they are more than lyrical stories in the form of plays, for they share at least one of the characteristics found in the Spanish theater of the twentieth century and thus form an integral part of its history. This characteristic is the imprint of Pirandello, and in the following pages I shall show how Salinas' works reflect this unmistakable sign of the epoch.

Like Pirandello, Salinas has written a play in which the center of interest is the autonomous character: *El precio*. Briefly, the story is as follows: Alicia and her father, who is a psychiatrist, are spending the summer in the country. One day when Alicia is driving she meets a girl who does not know where she is going or who she is. Alicia takes the girl home and names her Melisa. She is an exquisite poetic creature who makes Alicia very happy with her imaginative pastimes. She exists in time without knowing the meaning of yesterday and today, and sings a song which tells her story, though she does not understand it, nor can she explain how she learned it. Jáuregi, a writer, arrives in search of Melisa. He explains that he knows her completely, though he has never seen her. At ten o'clock one morning a week earlier he began to write a description of a morning: "Una mañana para ella . . . que se ajustara a su modo de ser humano, que fuese como el traje en que el mundo la envolvía, y que con ser tan inmenso, le cayese a ella justo, perfectamente, a la medida" [*Teatro Completo*] (p. 215). He wrote enthusiastically, "con todo el ardor de mi alma porque quería apartar esa mañana de las demás, detener el tiempo, pararla. Hacerla su mañana, compenetradas las dos" (p. 216). And, he says, he must have approached this goal, because through the morning she escaped from him. He explains that he created her, she was a fictional being, a poetic lie. He had her half-formed, he loved her more than anyone, and now she will remain incomplete, "y yo, igual, ella sin su pasado, que yo tengo, y yo sin su mañana, sin su otra mitad, que iba a darle, sin su vida entera" (p. 217). When Alicia brings Melisa to him she simply embraces him, saying: "A ti vuelvo . . . Ya sé quién soy . . .

Quiero vivir . . . ¡Tuya, tuya . . . !" (p. 218) and dies in his arms. Death is the price she must pay in order to continue living as a fictional character.

Like Pirandello's *Sei personaggi*, Melisa is a half-formed character who has left her author. The idea, similar to Pirandello's, is also expressed indirectly here: corporal life is worth less than the eternal life enjoyed by a fictional character. Melisa's initial appearance is especially reminiscent of the appearance of Madame Pace of *Sei personaggi* who comes to the stage lured there by the setting which has been prepared for her.

However, there are many differences between Salinas' and Pirandello's versions of the autonomous character, the main one being that in Salinas' play the conflict between character and author is lacking. Melisa is docile and places herself completely in the hands of her author. She had escaped only because the author created a situation in which she could not do otherwise. Pirandello's autonomous characters, both in his short story *La tragedia di un personaggio* and in his famous play, are characters who are said to be poorly formed or half-formed by another author, and who appeal to Pirandello in the first case and to the stage manager in the second to be given their proper vehicle of expression. They are disgruntled, frustrated entities who complain bitterly about their treatment.

The most famous Spanish autonomous character, Unamuno's Augusto Pérez, is also at odds with his author, as is Azorín's autonomous character in *El libro de Levante*.[4] André Lebois suggests this basic characteristic of all autonomous characters by entitling his article on the subject "La révolte des personnages."[5] As a matter of fact, one of the main purposes of autonomy seems to be to create a clash between art, represented by the character, and life, represented by the author, which results in a deep questioning of the nature of both.

Thus, in contrast to the other autonomous characters who confront the author, Salinas has given Melisa what seems to be a rather purposeless autonomy. However, the very contrast between the typical character who acts independently of his author and Melisa seems to underline the aspect of instinctive perfect communication which is so important in Salinas' poetry and is here transposed into theatrical terms, because his point of departure in this play could have been expected to lead him in another direction.

Several of Pirandello's themes can be found in Salinas' play *La estratoesfera*. Alvaro, a poet who is occupying one of the tables of the café called "La estratoesfera," contemplates life through the eyes of fiction. When Felipa enters the café with her blind grandfather who sells lottery tickets, the poet associates him with Oedipus and her with Antigone. While the grandfather is dozing at a table Alvaro talks to Felipa, though she understands very little of his highflown speech packed with literary allusions. A group of actors enters: César, who is playing Don Quijote in a film, Ramón, who is Sancho Panza, Luis, the Duke, and Rita, the Duchess. Noticing Felipa's agitation, Alvaro asks her to confide in him, and when she hesitates he tells her: "¡Domeña tus emociones, Felipa! Mira que tú eres progenie de Sófocles. ¡No te aplebeyes! ¿Por qué no me cuentas lo que te pasa? ¿No te fías de mí, verdad? Pero soy tu amigo . . . Te conozco de tiempo . . . Y vas a ser mucho, chiquilla . . . ¿No ves que te estoy haciendo personaje? Te estoy inventando . . . Déjame que te invente . . . Nos entendemos ¿verdad?" (p. 83). Felipa tells Alvaro that four years ago when César (whom she knew as Juan) was in her town, Toboso, he made love to her, recited to her from *Don Juan Tenorio,* promised to marry her, and then dishonored her. Alvaro approaches César, and finds it covenient to confuse fiction with reality: "Dialogo con Don Quijote de la Mancha, creación inmarcesible del Manco de Lepanto . . . Con el defensor de la honra ultrajada y la virtud escarnecida, con el amparo de los inocentes . . . Y compenetrado, como debe usted estar, con su personaje, calcúlese lo que en esta peripecia, tomada de la vida real, habría hecho el Caballero de la Triste Figura . . ." (p. 87).

César does not share Alvaro's tendency to confuse reality with fiction; nevertheless he is quite willing to speak to Felipa as Alvaro suggests, telling her that he is Juan's twin brother, that Juan's most ardent desire was to marry her, that he had gone to America, determined to earn enough to marry, and that he had died there. Thus Alvaro, with César's cooperation, has given Felipa a beautiful lie which she believes and which will give her dignity: "Es que soy otra, es que ahora me atrevería yo a ir a mi pueblo y a mirar a tós así cara a cara, sin bajarle los ojos ni al más pintao. ¡Es que me quería, no lo ha oído usté!" (p. 90). Fellip's grandfather dies in his sleep while all this is going on, probably symbolizing the end of her old life and the beginning of a new one as she goes away with Alvaro at the end of the play.

The mixture of fantasy and reality in this play is very true to the spirit of Pirandello. The hero is a poet within the play and sees everything through the veil of poetic imagination. He literally "invents" Felipa, superimposing on her real self, which is that of an ignorant village girl, that of a classical heroine. When he makes her believe that her honor is intact, he takes a step which causes fiction to be a very powerful force in the life of the girl, who will no longer be bowed down by the shame of her past. Although Salinas is much kinder to his heroine than is Pirandello, and although Pirandello's heroines are both conscious of the deception, whereas Felipa is not, this theme is reminiscent of *Vestire gli ig-* *nudi* and *Come tu mi vuoi* in which attempts are made to give dignity to a tather sordid past by covering it with the veil of fiction.

Many critics have noticed that Cervantes and Pirandello have much in common.[6] In the plays of Azorín and Grau, which show the influence of Pirandello, allusions to Cervantes are also present.[7] Salinas, by using actors who are performing in a representation of Don Quijote, also underlines the fact that Spanish tradition provides a firm precedent for the interplay of fiction and reality. As a matter of fact, the characters chosen by Salinas to represent Cervantes directly suggest the levels of reality in the Quijote, for in the second part of Cervantes' novel the Duke and Duchess create a situation in which Don Quijote can truly believe that the fantasy which he has created is truth.[8] We are also reminded of Cervantes by the fact that Felipa is from Toboso, and, in a similar way to which Alvaro "invents" Felipa don Quijote invented Dulcinea.

The invention of a character is also one of the themes in another of Salinas' plays: **El chantajista.** Lucila, one of Salinas' typical poetic heroines, is searching for her ideal mate. She writes unique and beautiful love letters and "loses" them in a cinema. Lisardo, "el chantajista," finds them. He writes to Lucila, asking her to send Eduardo, the young man to whom the letters were supposedly written, to meet him if she is interested in the return of her letters. The play opens when Lisardo arrives to find Lucila disguised as a man, waiting for him in the park. He turns down the money she offers him, stating that the price for the return of the letters is the key to Lucila's garden gate, which she gives to him.

In the second "cuadro" Lisardo appears in Lucila's garden masked and dressed as Romeo. Lucila tells him: "Yo no quiero más que a un hombre . . . A mi enamorado, a mi amante, a mi amor, a ti . . . No a tro . . . ¿Sabes por qué? Porque no hay otro . . . No hay más que uno" (p. 135), which he does not understand because he still thinks she does not know who he is. She tries to explain to him that nothing is a lie, not even his costume or mask. "También ellos tienen su verdad . . . , se les ve la verdad" (p. 135). She leaves him and reappears as Eduardo, saying that she will give Lisardo ten minutes more with Lucila, but only if he promises to tell her the truth. When he is alone he tells how much the game has confused him; he can no longer separate truth from falsehood. He does not know whether he has deceived Lucila or not, and he feels that his emotions are completely authentic though they are covered by superficial falsehood. When Lucila reappears he tries to explain all of this to her, and she then reveals the truth which is that Eduardo has just been born in him and that she had called him Eduardo when she did not know his real name. She explains when he asked to whom she had written the letters: "A ti . . . , al que ibas a ser tú . . . Es decir, a nadie, entonces . . . Ese amante de las cartas era el anhelo de un amante así . . . No existía, pero yo seguí escribiéndole, segura de que alguna vez iba a nacer . . ." (p. 141). She tells him that when he read the letters he gradually took on the features and shape of her lover, exactly as she wished him to be. He admits that while reading the letters he was longing to be Eduardo, and adds: "Tú me has hecho" (p. 142).

Although this play is very original and very much Salinas' own, it clearly belongs to the age of Pirandello; the way Salinas explains the process at the end of the play especially seems to echo the Pirandellian view. Although Lisardo cannot really have any serious doubts about his identity, he seems to doubt as he questions: "¿Quién soy yo?" (p. 138). And the remark made by Lucila that she created him makes her somewhat like the author who creates a character.

The phenomenon of a fictitious situation which becomes reality appears in Pirandello's plays, to give only one example, *Ma non è una cosa seria,* when a woman is so much changed by the experience of being a wife that the man who married her for convenience falls in love with her. Of course there are many differences between this situation and the one in the play being analyzed, but in both dramas fiction triumphs over reality and then becomes reality.

As in the case of many Spanish plays which are reminiscent of Pirandello, a Spanish precedent can also be found. In this case Benina, a servant in *Misericordia* by Galdós, invented don Romualdo to explain her absences from the house. Later don Romualdo appears, almost exactly as she had imagined him to be.

In *La fuente del Arcángel* Salinas again mixes illusion and reality in a great variety of ways. Claribel and her sister Estefanía are spending the summer vacation with their Aunt Gumersinda in Alcorada, an Andalucian town. The young ladies have led a sheltered existence, and Gumersinda has just noticed that outside the window of the room which they are occupying a nightly spectacle occurs which she considers improper for their eyes. There is a fountain with a statue of the archangel on it, and it is the custom for lovers to meet there—they hold hands and even kiss. Since it is a local superstition that the archangel protects lovers, Gumersinda wants to move the statue to the church so that they will no longer be attracted to the fountain by its presence. But when she speaks to Padre Fabián about her project, he reveals a carefully guarded secret: the statue is not really the archangel but the pagan Eros in the angel's garb.

Claribel and Estefanía had been given permission that night to go to a magician's show, and while Gumersinda is speaking to Padre Fabián a painting which is hanging on the wall becomes transparent to reveal the stage of the casino where the magician Florindo is performing. Like counterpoint we hear the conversation of Gumersinda and Fabián in which the secret is being revealed: "las cosas no son todas lo que parecen . . . Ni siquiera las personas . . ." (p. 35), and the scene in which Florindo is speaking about illusion: "Este número es ilusionismo puro . . . Porque, señoras y caballeros, todos sabemos, desde que lo afirmó en sus inmortales décimas don Pedro Calderón de la Barca,[9] que las cosas no son lo que parecen. Y mucho menos las personas . . . Todo apariencias, señoras y caballeros . . ." (p. 34). Fabián is referring to the true pagan nature of the statue which seems Christian, and Florindo is referring to a much more beautiful and spiritual aspect of illusion: "¿Quién es el caballero Florindo, que en estos momentos se honra dirigiendo la plalabra al cultísimo pueblo de Alcorada? Acaso no sea yo mismo, sino un céfiro que susurra de flor en flor, una chispa que cabrillea de ola en ola, la ilusión que palpita de alma en alma . . . ¡Ilusiones, todo ilusión! ¡Cuidado con las apariencias!" (p. 34).

Florindo's most impressive act is to turn members of the audience into characters of other epochs. Claribel volunteers and is changed into Teodora, the Byzantine courtesan. After this experience, she is no longer quite the same: "Yo no sé, pero siento como si me bailaran dentro del cuerpo tres o cuatro Claribeles juntas . . . , vamos, como si yo fuese otras cuantas más que yo . . ." (p. 39), an interesting variation on the multiplicity of personality theme.

The idea of different interpretations of a situation depending upon the point of view, found, for example in *Cosí è (se vi pare)* is also important in *La fuente del Arcángel.* Several persons contemplate the same reality of the lovers at the fountain but interpret it in different ways. Gumersinda thinks the lovers are extremely wicked, and is scandalized. Estefanía thinks it is all rather strange, does not really like to see it, and says "no es para nosotras . . ." (p. 41). Claribel invents a beautiful poetic conversation which she tells her sister she can hear. However, unlike Pirandello, Salinas permits the audience to know the truth, which is none of the truths seen by the observers: Honoria and Angelillo, whose names tell us what Salinas thinks of them, are discussing the furniture they will have in their home. This conversation brings fantasy down to a more prosaic level because Angelillo believes that Honoria's desire to have a wardrobe with two mirrors and a flower-painted basin and pitcher with which to wash their hands with perfumed soap is far above their way of life: "Y dale con la fantasía . . . ¿Pero qué te crees tú, que vamos a está lavándono la mano a ca rato . . . Mía la señorita . . ." (p. 40). Probably Salinas would like fantasy to triumph even in their lives, because he sets their wedding for the day of San Juan, traditionally the time when magic events occur in Spain.

At the end of the play the archangel comes down from the fountain, dressed as a trapeze artist, and takes Claribel away with him. The exact identity of this figure is not really clear; he seems to be a combination of many people. As Cowes explains: "La persona con que Claribel se va de Alcorada es el Arcángel y no es el Arcángel, es Eros y no es Eros, es el caballero Florindo y no es el caballero Florindo, es el mundo de la madre y no lo es."[10]

Thus, in this play various themes of Pirandello appear: the theater-within-the-theater, the deception which is caused by superficial appearance, the difference between several points of view, the multiplicity of personality, the constant interplay of reality and fantasy, and the difficulty of separating these two facets of life. In spite of the fact that we are not quite certain of the exact identity of the man, the end of the play suggests that Claribel knows and is sure of her destiny. Perhaps his identity does not matter, for the play shows the triumph of illusion over the prosiac life of Alcorada which Claribel has exchanged for what seems to be a beautiful future.

In connection with the identity problem, *La bella durmiente* must also be discussed. This is not one of Salinas' best plays, because he does not convince us that the situation is impossible enough to warrant the torment suffered by the protagonist because of an identity from which she seems to feel she cannot dissociate herself. The play takes place in an exclusive resort for celebrities who wish to spend a vacation in absolute anonymity. Soledad, which is not her real name, is spending her vacation there to escape from the unwanted fame which has accompanied her ever since she had modeled for a mattress company's saturation publicity campaign. She explains the joy she feels at being liberated from her public identity: "¡Qué gusto ser desconocida, salirse de la imagen de una que tienen los demás, dejar de ser la que se figuran los otros que es! Yo lo comparo con volver a casa después de un baile aburrido y quitarse el traje y el color y todo, y meterse en el agua y sentirse verdadera" (p. 167).

Alvaro is there to escape the public attention accorded to a millionaire, and who, by coincidence, is the owner of the mattress company for which Soledad has modeled. Alvaro and Soledad fall in love, but she feels it is necessary to explain to him who she is, as she feels soiled by what has happened to her. She especially resents the owner of the company, though she does not know him. Alvaro never reveals his identity to her, telling her only that for reasons she does not understand their marriage would be impossible. Of course Soledad's

personality and real self were never involved in her public image, nevertheless this play does seem to be Salinas' attempt to translate into his own terms the conflict presented by Pirandello in *Quando si è qualcuno,* in which a famous writer is imprisoned by the public image from which he would like to escape.

And if the identity of a living person is a problem, in *Ella y sus fuentes* Salinas shows that the search for historical truth is likely to result in an unconscious creation of fiction by the historian. Don Desiderio has devoted his life to writing the biography of Julia Riscal, a national heroine. He is proud of the accuracy of his account, having based it on documentary evidence. However, Julia shatters his whole image of her when she is permitted by the Lord to visit the earth to tell don Desiderio the truth. The truth is so elusive that it takes a miracle to uncover it.

Another theme of Pirandello's theater, illusion which attempts to conquer death, is found in Salinas' *Sobre seguro.* Here insurance men decide that their business would develop in the imaginary insurance-resistant city, Serenia, if the inhabitants were to see the benefits of insurance. Therefore, they arrange for one of the insured persons, Angel, a seventeen-years-old whose mental age is about eight, to die in a boating "accident." His body is not recovered. The father, sister, and brother believe that Angel is dead, need the money, and urge the mother to sign the receipt so that they may collect the insurance money. But she believes that as long as she does not sign he is not really dead: "Yo lo necesito vivo y aún le queda un hilo de vida, un hilo que soy yo, que quiero que viva, que no tomo dinero. Y eso es lo que no quiero vender. Si yo firmara, entonces sí que se habría muerto . . . ¿Lo entienden ustedes? Cada vez que digo 'no firmo' le siento vivir, sin verle, como le sentía en los primeros meses de su vida, dentro de mí, como un latido. No, yo le guardo su vida" (p. 293).

Up to this point the play is realistic, but after Petra is left alone the money, which had been left overnight by the insurance agents in order to tempt her to sign, comes to life to tell her, in a speech reminiscent of *Poderoso caballero es don dinero,* that no one can resist it. But then Angel returns. He is confused about what had happened to him; when he was in the boat he felt a blow, and remembers nothing more. He had spent the five days since the occurrence with a couple in the country, but then he escaped to return home. The mother decides that she and her son will go away together to a place where no one can buy him. In spite of the fantastic scene in which money talks, it seems that the return of the son was not fantasy.

Of course Salinas' play is quite different from Pirandello's *La vita che ti diedi* because the mother's faith is rewarded in the Spanish play. But at the point when she has been told that her son is dead and has no reason to doubt it, she shows the exact attitude of the mother in Pirandello's play who creates for herself the illusion that her son still lives.

Salinas wrote fourteen plays.[11] Practically all of the plays which I have not discussed also contain certain details which may be associated with Pirandello because the interplay of illusion and reality is the main substance of his theater. To give two more examples, in *La isla del tesoro* Marú rejects her attractive suitor in order to await the appearance of the man who has written a diary which she has found in a hotel room, and *Judit y el tirano* is a play in which the tyrant does not permit his subjects to see his face, as his entire personality has been invented. "Todo eso de la apariencia y la voz es histrionismo, puro teatro malo. El es un cualquiera que ha dado con esa artimaña para imponerse a la gente" (p. 308).

Salinas was a professor of literature and a literary critic. Thus it can be taken for granted that he had more than a superficial knowledge of Pirandello's plays. Also, by the time he wrote his dramatic pieces Pirandellian tendencies were found in many writers and could be said to float in the atmosphere, to use Unamuno's phrase.[12] Therefore, it would not be at all surprising to find these traits in Salinas' plays if it were not for the fact that his basic view of life is diametrically opposed to Pirandello's. Love, joy, optimism, perfect communication, and faith in the ability of the writer to clarify reality[13] are found in the poetry and plays of Pedro Salinas. Pirandello, on the other hand, usually sees only the sensual side of love; MacClintock has called him "The Perfect Pessimist";[14] his protagonists usually cannot communicate, and he seems to love chaos.[15]

Although in many ways Salinas' plays are isolated from other Spanish plays of his epoch, in at least one way they contribute a chapter to the history of Spanish theater, as they show how even a playwright who had little in common with Pirandello entered the door leading to thematic innovation which he opened. In this way, Salinas joined his fellow countrymen Unamuno, Azorín, the Machados, García Lorca, Casona, Grau, and Luca de Tena who all show either direct influence of the Italian playwright or characteristics which announce their close affinity to him.

Notes

1. For example Marta Morello-Frosch, "Teatro y crítica de Pedro Salinas," *Revista Hispánica Moderna*, XXVI (1960), 116-18. Mario Maurín, "Tema y variaciones en el teatro de Salinas," *Insula*, No. 104. Rodríguez Richart, "Sobre el teatro de Salinas," *Boletín de la Biblioteca Menéndez y Pelayo*, XXXVI, 397-427. (Despite the number of pages, this is not an important article.)

2. Hugo W. Cowes, *Relación Yo-Tú y trascendencia en la obra dramática de Pedro Salinas* (Universidad de Buenos Aires, 1965). Professor Cowes has noticed that a relationship exists between Pirandello and Salinas. Although the scope of his book does not include a thorough analysis of this aspect of Salinas' work, in a section entitled "Apéndice a *El Chantajista*" he discusses this play and four other plays which mix theatrical representation and reality: *Hamlet*, Pirandello's *Ciascuno a suo modo*, Sartre's *Kean*, and Genet's *Les Bonnes*. He also compares and contrasts Pirandello and Salinas in several footnotes.

3. Dámaso Alonso gives a very interesting report of the première of *La fuente del Arcángel* which took place at the theater of Columbia University, and was presented by a dramatic group from the Spanish Department of Barnard College. "Con Pedro Salinas," *Clavileño, September-October* 1951, 17-18. In addition, in the "Nota preliminar" to Salinas' *Teatro Completo* Juan Marichal reports that *Judit y el tirano* was done by the Compañía Cubana de Teatro Universitario. Pedro Salinas, *Teatro Completo* (Madrid: Aguilar, 1957), p. 11. All quotations from Salinas' plays are taken from this volume.

4. Furthermore, Azorín also stresses the relationship of man to countryside, as he creates his autonomous character: "El personaje central de la novela, determinado por esta atracción ineluctable de los cerritos. La personalidad moral del protagonista que se va concretando, solidificando, definiendo. Personalidad prefigurada por este paisaje o elemento primario de un paisaje." Azorín, *Obras Completas*, "El libro de Levante," Vol. V, 368.

5. André Lebois, "La révolte des personnages: de Cervantès et Calderón á Raymond Schwab," *Revue de Littérature Comparée*, 23 (1949), 482-506.

6. For example: Joseph E. Gillet, "The Autonomous Character in Spanish and European Literature," *Hispanic Review*, XXIV (1956), 179-90. And the latest example which has come to my attention is a note on the cover of Georges Piroué's *Pirandello*: "Ainsi saisie dans sa totalité, se dessine la figure d'un écrivain qui, victime de nos temps bouleversés et percevant dans sa chair même toutes nos contradictions, a su donner corps à ses rêves pitoyables et exaltants, nous les faire tenir pour plus évidents que nos branlantes convictions. Tout comme Don Quichotte, son lointain frère solitaire" (Paris: Denoël, 1967).

7. See my articles "Pirandello and Azorín," *Italica*, March, 1967, 41-60, and "A Pirandellian Trilogy by Jacinto Grau," *Forum Italicum*, December, 1967.

8. "Y todos, ó los más, derramaban pomos de aguas olorosas sobre don Quijote y sobre los Duques, de todo lo cual se admiraba don Quijote; y aquel fué el primer día que de todo conoció y creyó ser caballero andante verdadero, y no fantástico, viéndose tratar del mesmo modo que él había leído se trataban los tales caballeros en los pasados siglos." Miguel Cervantes, *El ingenioso hidalgo Don Quijote de la Mancha* (Madrid: Espasa-Calpe, 1957), VI, 235.

9. Both Azorín and Grau also included a reference to Calderón in their Pirandellian works.

10. Cowes, *Relación*, p. 39.

11. All of these plays are published in the *Teatro Completo* except "Los santos" which appears in *Cuadernos Americanos,* XIII, 3 (May-June, 1954).

12. In his article entitled "Pirandello y yo" which appeared in *La Nación* of Buenos Aires in 1923.

13. See, for example, Salinas' *El poema*: "En esta luz del poema, / todo, / desde el más nocturno beso / al cenital esplendor, / todo está mucho más claro."

14. Lander MacClintock, *the Age of Pirandello* (Bloomington: Indiana University Press, 1951), p. 175.

15. Cowes, *Relación,* in discussing *La bella durmiente,* also remarks about this difference between Salinas and Pirandello: "El destino de Soledad parece ilustrar este texto de Ortega, que supone, por la decisiva afirmación de un yo permanente, e invariable, que pugna por realizarse, y se mantiene aun en el fracaso, indestructible, una clara refutación del caos pirandeliano" (p. 142).

John Devlin (essay date winter 1972)

SOURCE: Devlin, John. "Reality and the Poet, Pedro Salinas." *Renascence* 24, no. 2 (winter 1972): 102-09.

[*In the following essay, Devlin maintains that knowledge of reality is a central theme that runs throughout Salinas's work as a poet, stating that it demonstrates that "the thrust of the creative endeavor is to know reality better and for the poet to know himself better, particularly in his relationship with reality."*]

The late, distinguished poet, Pedro Salinas, a member of Spain's famous "Generation of 1927," is one of the greatest poets of the Twentieth Century and of Spain's *post modernista* renaissance. Like all his Spanish contemporaries, he has been overshadowed, perhaps unfairly, by his friend and contemporary, García Lorca.

Any approach to the Spanish poets of 1927 must take notice of the problem of reality. *Modernismo,* at its apogee, had been a sort of hispanic escape from reality, combined with a new, very important poetic methodology. When Juan Ramón Jiménez came upon the scene, the methods of *modernismo* were united with an essentially new quest in poetry. The "ivory tower" or exotic oriental marketplace of *modernismo* were found to be insufficient. Life was seen to demand evocations over and above the description of exotic things and states—however valuable such may be in their own right.

Pedro Salinas found his early formation in the *modernista* tradition. He is, to be sure, the author of one of the most famous studies of the greatest poet of the *modernista* tradition, Rubén Darío. Yet, Salinas was one of the poets who was to move poetry far from *modernismo* into the evocative currents of our own times.

Salinas came of age in Madrid, quickly assumed prestigious positions in the Sorbonne, Seville, and, upon the onset of the Civil War, passed into important teaching posts in Middlebury, the University of Puerto Rico, Wellesley, and, above all, Johns Hopkins, where he remained until his death in 1951. Important articles and editorial assignments did not deter the poet from his own creative interior goals. During his first years at Johns Hopkins he produced a masterpiece—one of the most important works of Spanish literary criticism in our century—the Johns Hopkins lectures in English, entitled *Reality and the Poet in Spanish Literature.*

Salinas felt that the object of art is reality itself. It may serve the reading of this essay better if we announce that is our conviction that the poets of 1927 are consumed by concern for reality. Salinas was obsessed with reality; reality was his prime, if complicated, preoccupation. In the first poem of his first collection, entitled *Presagios* (*Omens* or *Tokens*), Salinas addresses himself to reality and announces a concern which will alternate and change throughout his entire creative production. The mood begins in an affirmative voice. The first poem, **"Suelo"** (**"Soil"**), reads:

> Soil, nothing more.
> Soil, nothing less.
> And let that suffice you.
> Because on the soil the feet are planted,
> on the feet body erect,
> on the body head firm,
> and there, in the lee of the forehead,
> pure idea and in the pure idea
> the tomorrow, the key
> —tomorrow—of the eternal.
> Soil. No more no less.
> And let that suffice you.[1]

This basic affirmation, however, will undergo frequent subtle and not-so-subtle transformations before many moods have passed. **"Suelo"** is, of course, the first full poem of the author's collected works. Reality will not seem so un-complex in the multiple verses to follow and the pace of **Omens** quickens as the poet plunges into his art.

Salinas's poetry has a crystalline purity and is as limpid as a clear mountain stream. Like most of his generation his poetry is a model of *depuración*—the peeling down of expression to its most absolutely essential elements. This discipline is much to be commended in the Spanish, who are notorious over-verbalizers, a defect which frequently works its way into their literary style. Some critics have commented that Salinas's poetry is rather prosaic, that there tends to be a dearth of symbolism. Nothing could be further from the truth. Personifications dominate the pages. Salinas is on familiar terms with every imaginable aspect of being outside of himself—soil, water, the sea, clouds, the day, the night. These he tries to preserve from their passing mutability by intellectualizing them. Similarly, he greets as familiar friends (thus personifying) a wide range of interior emotions—from sadness to tranquillity to joy. The fire, rage, and violence of Lorca's red-hot Andalusian style are lacking. Nonetheless, a sustained and controlled passion breathes through Salinas's lines, even though he emphasizes the more gentle, quiet, and more easily intellectualized emotions. In Lorca human love, if it can be called that, is usually sexual passion. (Two notable exceptions would be the obvious human love of the gypsy boy and girl in the "Romance Sonámbulo" and the evocation of the power of love that emerges in the last selections of *Poet in New York*.)[2] In Salinas, love is always fully human. This is the key to his work.

Salinas knew French poetry well, and was especially familiar with the symbolists. Yet he is not strikingly rooted in any direct imitation of the symbolist tradition. The Parnasse, however, with its detailed descriptions—rather than symbolist suggestion—seems to have influenced his lines. Here again Salinas differs in that the enumerated details are interior states of his own mind and soul, not exterior exquisite or imaginative objects, as is so frequently the case in the Parnasse.

Like other poets of the Generation of '27, Salinas was influenced by Góngora, the great Seventeenth Century figure. This was in the association in metaphors of objects that are most disparate in reality. One example is the title of his second collection, **Segura Azar** or **Safe Risk**. Another can be seen in the following lines from that collection where a rose is associated with white foam: "Were it not for the fragile rose / of white, white foam. . . ."

One of the most striking aspects of Salinas's imagery is the tendency to fashion enormous, cosmic symbols. For example:

> How gently you rock my child to sleep,
> enormous cradle of the world,
> cradle of the August night!

Again, Salinas personifies the entire landscape:

> These sweet syllables which you breathe in my ear
> I do not understand them, landscape,
> they are not mine.
> You whisper to me with quiet woodlands,
> in tranquil, crystalline waters,
> in trillings of bird-song.
> . . .
> But so sweet is the sound of your unlearned
> language, that in it my soul discerns the ladder
> over which descends to us secrets divine.

Beginning with the first poems and continuing through the poet's entire career, the thrust of the creative endeavor is to know reality better and for the poet to know himself better, particularly in his relationship with reality. In his strivings the poet shares with all mortals the frustration—especially heightened in the sensitive creative spirit—of longing for the revelation of the reality behind reality. It is a longing for the unattainable:

> And eager yet stupid on your borders I wait,
> hoping that you may teach me the language
> of unknown words without meaning,
> that language not mine.
> And that you may bear me to the clarity of the
> unknowable,
> gentle landscape by your unknown syllables.

Again:

> I see you not, though well
> I know you are here, behind
> a wall so lightly built. . . .

Anxiety, a kind of despair, and frustration with his limited ability to penetrate reality are not Salinas's only concern. Concommitant with these problems is an unmistakable cosmic fear. This fear seems to come in waves and is apparently rooted in strong doubt that love will ultimately prevail. At times, as in **Presagiós,** it is simply naked fear as the poet stares into the face of reality:

> Desert land, without tree
> or mountain and empty sky,
> bereft of cloud or bird;
> so quiet both, so alone,
> face to face earth and sky,
> mirror reflecting mirror,
> now there is neither far nor near
> high or low, much or little,
> in the universe,. . . .

Again:

> Because I am a coward, my brother
> my burden I bear on my shoulder,

I have a way to follow
and I shrink with fear from a door
which opens I know not when nor where
and I tremble lest I hear a voice
—whose I do not know—which may say:
"Today it cannot be, brother,
another time."

But, as frequently happens in Salinas, the universe is suddenly capable of being ordered:

But from a furrow there flies
a firstling sparrow
and all changes to suit
the pattern of his destiny.
Now the earth is once more low
and the sky up there is placed. . . .

As Salinas advanced through his mature years, one collection followed another. But, for the most part, the questions contained in the early poems continue to be evoked. Always the preoccupation is with reality and his subjective reaction to it. In Salinas, however—unlike his friend and contemporary, Jorge Guillén—the poet's attitude tends to swing back and forth like a pendulum. At times his lines ring with an affirmation of reality. At other times he recoils in terror before reality and seeks his solace in his own intellectualizing of precious moments, the better to preserve them and afford him a route of escape. In the collection *Seguro Azar* (1929), he examines the exterior world and seeks certainty in a mechanical world. He is assailed by doubt. In *Fábula y Signo* (*Fable and Sign*, 1931) the word *fábula* stands for his hopeful concept of poetic reality; the word *signo* for the logical signs under which he pursues reality. In *La Voz a ti Debida* (*The Voice for You Alone*, 1933), a title taken from Garcilaso de la Vega's *Third Egloga*, he seeks reality which seems to slip constantly through his fingers, yet he also affirms the ability of man to build a world based on love. In *Razón de Amor* (*Love's Reason*, 1936), he returns to seek reality within his own invisible intellectualized system. In *El Contemplado* (*The Contemplated One*, 1946) he seems to come close to mystic inspiration in the sea surrounding Puerto Rico. Like Alberti and Aleixandre and others of his generation, he was powerfully influenced by the sea. In *Todo Más Claro* (*Everything is Clearer*, 1949), he returns to fear—pure and simple—before the modern world. *Confianza* (*Confidence*), published posthumously, contains the same fears. But, also published posthumously, the lovely poem **"Angel Extraviado"** (**"Lost Angel"**), is the story of a struggle with "the good angel" triumphing over the movements of baser components.

It remains to insist upon a most important ingredient in Salinas's poetic production. This is the presence of his *Amada* (The Beloved), who appears everywhere in the poet's work. It does not seem unreasonable to suppose that this beloved was inspired by a great love in the poet's life, possibly his wife. She appears early in the collections, most strongly in **"La Sin Pruebas," "She Without Trace"** in *Fábula y Signo*:

When you go away, how useless
to search for the road you have taken,
to follow you!
If you have trodden on the snow
it would be like to the clouds
—their shadow—no steps, no weight
that might leave trace of you.
When you go
you direct your steps nowhere,
there is no path which then may say:
"She passed by this way."
You go not forth from the exact
simple center of yourself:
they are the illusive pathways
which stretch out to meet you.
With sweet laughter or with speech
so softly, gently
you penetrate the silence
that you wound it not, that it
feels you not:
it thinks it continues unbroken.

The presence of this "Lover" is so obvious and intense that Salinas has caused many critics to compare him to St. John of the Cross and his *Spiritual Canticle*. The spare musicality of Salinas's style, combined with the pursuit of the lover, reminds us strongly of the poems of the Sixteenth Century Saint. And from St. John we are perforce reminled of the Spanish Saint's source, the Biblical *Song of Songs,* with its constant pursuit of lovers who show themselves and then hide only to produce the frantic search all over again. Thus, Salinas's various collections tend to be connected into one continuous poem (the links, as he says, of one chain). The poet speaks to his lover and she to him. His entire collection becomes a lyric dialogue between the poet and the Beloved. The Beloved should obviously be interpreted on various levels. But she seems, above all, to be the poet's concept of reality behind reality. All that he knows of reality comes from her. At other times—and not without justification—the Beloved seems to be the poet's alter-ego, the other side of himself, just as long-tested lovers tend to merge their personalities. The *"yo"* and the *"tú"* become subject and object at the same time. The poet constantly dialogues with the Beloved. He does not describe her as the object of romantic love to enforce his masculine ego. Rather, there is a continued sharing of experience in an on-going effort to know. Love is a shared experience on the road of knowing.

Pedro Salinas died in 1951. Thus, he witnessed the onslaught of the nuclear age and all the enormous attendant perils to mankind; the huge threat to the eventual triumph of human love for which he had longed throughout his life. There can be no doubt that the spectre of nuclear holocaust haunted him and tended to deepen the pessimism of his later collections. But, if we may seek light from a source outside his poetry, his novel ***La Bomba Incredible*** (***The Incredible Bomb,*** 1949) is just that source. Not particularly a novelistic success, it nevertheless ends on a note of hope.

Unquestionably Leo Spitzer is a bit off center in his famous essay *El Conceptismo Interior de Pedro Salinas* (*The Interior Conceptism of Pedro Salinas*) if we must understand, *without qualification,* the assertion that Salinas found reality chaotic and saw order only after his own ordering. So, too, issue could be taken with Luis Cernuda who believed that Salinas's poetry was only a game of imagination. Game it may well have been but much more than that. Poetry, in ***Seguro Azar*** is creation, which, for all its joy, is ephemeral:

> I am going to create. How much mine
> is that which I am going to create!
> . . .
> Now it is finished. Behold it!
> But beware,
> the creating alienates,
> to create is to remain alone.
> . . .
> Alone with my creation.
> Separated from my own, from
> that which I made, which I invented
> that I might not be alone.
> . . .
> I wrought it with fervor, with wings
> of desire.

It is this writer's belief, based on the overwhelming evidence of the poetry (some of which has been cited) that Salinas was a man whose wrestlings with reality left him with some ultimate certainty. At times the crush of reality forced him to retreat into the tower. Frequently he sought to crystalize the passing moment through his neo Renaissance intellectualizations. Who would not? The present moment can be so passing fair. On balance, however, one sees a sincere man who faced reality on its own terms.

Salinas's poetry tends to be in the tradition of the *van-guardistas.* Their work, in turn, tends to reflect Ortega y Gasset's important and most prestigious theory expounded in his famous essay, *La Deshumanización del Arte (The Dehumanization of Art,* 1925). By "dehumanization" Ortega meant the tendency, in the production of art, to eliminate sentimentalistic scenes and the melodramatic baring of the author's heart, found especially in Nineteenth Century art forms. This is a difficult norm to apply or find in one hundred percent purity. Its quest, however, has undoubtedly had a salutary effect in various developments of modern art. But, in the last analysis, Salinas, like Lorca and Guillén and all their contemporaries, cannot, need not, and should not be fully separated from the relationship of art to life. Indeed, what artist should be fully separated from his art, how-

ever much he may wish to understate or generalize his own private emotions? Juan Marichal, the distinguished critic and Salinas's son-in-law, has made this point clear with reference to our poet. In his chapter "Pedro Salinas y los Valores Humanos de la Literatura Espanola" ("Pedro Salinas and the Human Values of Spanish Literature") in *La Voluntad de Estilo (The Disposition of Style,* 1957), Marichal insists that Salinas put his sights and those of his readers on the substantive and permanent—the human values of Spanish Literature. Furthermore, he states that the poet "aspired to make available the human values of Spanish Literature by his concern to integrate them with universal values." Thus, despite the suave dictum of the introductions to anthologies, it would be well not to link Salinas too closely to the rigorous concepts of *deshumanización.*

Although the life-long poem of Salinas's collected work can well stand by itself as a lively lyric entity, much more is suggested. The pursuit of the *Amada,* rooted as she is in the center of his own ego, suggests a constant intuition of a cosmic power with which the poet was, like all mystics, in varying degrees of awareness.

Pedro Salinas cannot be called a Christian poet in the easy, traditional sense that we would use when speaking of, for example, Charles Péguy or Paul Claudel. Yet, he certainly does not evoke what Nathan Scott in *The Broken Center* (Yale Univ. Press, 1965) has called a desacralized world. Rather, it should now be evident that he stands in what Scott describes in general terms as "a relation of reciprocity with the world, because the whole of reality is instinct with spirit and with presence, with the numinous and the Sacred." Salinas approached reality with a sense of its possessing the character of a *Thou.* Frequently he was surprised by joy as the veils momentarily lifted and his lines became alive with a consciousness of an Otherness, a sense of the Given, an awareness that there is a Reality behind reality. Just as Dante is led by Beatrice, Salinas often makes his discoveries under the inspiration of his *Amada.* It seems that throughout his life he sought—and glimpsed from time to time—the existence of a supreme cosmic power which would be, upon death, the end and fulfillment of his ardent pursuit. As Scott says: "So, in the kind of marveling astonishment with which, in a given finite reality, we behold the fullness of Being, there is already implicit a certain sense of hope, and perhaps of faith also. For, in the sense of wonder that our world elicits, there is already present a deep desire, a deep hope that in the fullness of time we *shall* know fully."

Theology is in a broken condition today due in a large part to the conviction, prevalent in so many circles, that it has nothing left to say to the modern world. It well may be, because the important interest that theology is now taking in the vital literature of our day, that poetry—such as Pedro Salinas's—can lead us back toward the precincts of Grace. Pedro Salinas has been neglected, as have many of the poets of 1927, because they fall under the shadow of Lorca, whose astounding verbal genius has had a bewitching enchantment. Salinas and the others deserve more attention, study, and love.

Notes

1. All citations are from *Lost Angel and Other Poems*, trans., Eleanor Turnbull, Baltimore, 1938.

2. See John Devlin, "Lorca's Basic Affirmation in 'Poet in New York,'" in *Studies in Honor of Samuel Waxman*, ed. H. Golden, Boston, 1969.

Robert G. Havard (essay date January 1974)

SOURCE: Havard, Robert G. "The Reality of Words in the Poetry of Pedro Salinas." *Bulletin of Hispanic Studies* 51, no. 1 (January 1974): 28-47.

[*In the following essay, Havard examines the theme of changeability in Salinas's poetry, "firstly, in the exterior sense of Salinas's attitudes through the years, and secondly, in more detail, as a dynamic concept determining both theme and the expression of theme in words."*]

"la pensée demeure incommensurable avec le langage"

Henri Bergson[1]

One of the most important and recurrent concepts in the poetry of Pedro Salinas is summarized in the following lines from *La voz a ti debida*:

Fatalmente, te mudas
sin dejar de ser tú,
en tu propia mudanza,
con la fidelidad
constante del cambiar.

([*Poesías completas*] 125)[2]

This old Petrarchan conceit about perpetual change, in addition to being a key thematic comment on the nature of the *amada*, can well be taken as an adroit piece of self-criticism by Pedro Salinas with respect to his poetic concepts and practices. The conceit, which prizes the elusive changeability of the *amada*, was as useful and pertinent for Salinas as it had been for Garcilaso, who gave it similar succinct expression, and Bécquer, who let it echo more indefinitely through his *Rimas*. But the point of changeability is not restricted solely to the *amada*. In all three poets, and never more so than in Salinas' *La voz a ti debida*, the *amada* appears as an enlarged reality; ubiquitous, multiple, physical and metaphysical, she is both the sum of exterior reality and the embodiment of the poet's sensitivity: *everything*:

'abolición / triunfal, total, de todo / lo que no es ella' (136). She incorporates even his poetry: as Bécquer's 'Poesía . . . eres tú' is already implied in the title of Salinas' major volume. Fundamentally, her prime function is to help conceptualize the poet's thought, and thus her changeability, as many other of her features, reflects a value in the poet: Salinas, as I will attempt to show, is nothing if not changeable, even inconsistent, in his attitude towards both exterior reality and, more significantly, towards words. To some large extent, his poetics, as such, may be said to focus upon this question. The present paper considers changeability in two ways: firstly, in the exterior sense of Salinas' attitudes through the years, and secondly, in more detail, as a dynamic concept determining both theme and the expression of theme in words.

Bearing in mind Salinas' point about critical appreciation, that the central problem with any poet is to discern the relation between the 'poetic world and the real world',[3] we may begin by considering Salinas' view of the real world. González Muela has drawn attention to the early poem 'Vocación' (39), suggesting that here Salinas deliberately differentiated between his own manner of viewing the world and that of his great friend and colleague Guillén.[4] The latter's celebrated openeyed vision is expressed in the first half of the poem whereas Salinas apparently chooses the opposite *vision* for himself: 'escogí: / el otro. / Cerré los ojos'. The polarization is striking and it offers a neat, though oversimplified definition of the two poets. The misleading implication here is that Salinas' choice was definitive, and that he stuck to it as doggedly as did Guillén to his. C. B. Morris developed the theme, in this and other poems, by seeing Salinas' contempt for visual impressions as 'one aspect of a literary pose already assumed at the beginning of his career and faithfully maintained thereafter';[5] and by later suggesting that 'visiones y no miradas' could be Salinas' motto.[6] A vital characteristic in Salinas' view of exterior reality is again isolated here. But at the same time it must be said that expressions and even 'miradas' which recall Guillén are found in later volumes, especially *Razón de amor,* which begins with the forceful announcement: 'Ya está la ventana abierta. / Tenía que ser así / el día' (197); while even the most visionary volume, *La voz,* as Guillén stressed,[7] and Morris later acknowledged,[8] also stems from a sensual apprehension of the *amada*'s physique: 'el tierno cuerpo rosado' (120), 'tu cuerpo limpio, exacto' (151), and 'Tu forma / corporal, / tu dulce peso rosa' (168), etc., a body that was clearly *seen*, and *felt*, as 'peso' suggests. Although, thematically, *La voz* attempts to turn away from the physical and the visible, there is awareness of the *amada*'s physical being, a celebration of sensual love, for instance at the end of the poem 'Amor, amor, catástrofe' (138), and a call for a return to 'esta corporeidad mortal y rosa' (194), when the poet's exploration beyond the physical is no longer tenable. 'Salvación por el cuerpo' of the following volume is one of several poems to indicate satisfaction with the material world, though **'Suicidio hacia arriba'** suggests that this mood was not permanent. The delight Salinas frequently takes in describing objects, both natural and mechanical, supports Guillén's opinion that: 'Este poema, "Vocación", no debe ser alzado a categoría de norma para Salinas'.[9] Yet the reader would find it difficult not to accept that **'Vocación'** partly explains an attitude that is distinctive of Salinas: the Salinas that is least like Guillén. A conclusion on this point would have to admit that Salinas is not as amenable as Guillén to fixed norms; that **'Vocación'** should not be considered an absolute manifesto; and that in contrast to what González Muela once happily described as 'la maravillosa ponderación de Guillén',[10] we find in Salinas attitudes of tantalizing flexibility, inasmuch as they often seem to be contradictory.

If Salinas' view of love, the *amada* and external reality is changeable and difficult to pin down categorically, so too is his concept of poetry and of the function of words in poetry. Reference to Guillén's comments again provides a good yardstick for appreciating this, both because of the latter's unerring consistency and because of the likelihood of mutual influence, the product of many years of intimate friendship. Not surprisingly, Salinas' ideas about poetic creation and his taste for poetry often run adjacent to Guillén's. As is well known, their thorough knowledge of the French symbolist tradition, their personal acquaintance with Paul Valéry and others, and their periods of residence in France channelled their ideas very strongly. Yet the influence of *poésie pure* was muted by their delight in the less cerebral purity of Spain: San Juan de la Cruz, Bécquer and Jiménez. To some large extent the poetry of Salinas and Guillén is a simplification, even humanization, of the French theory, as Guillén indicated: 'Pura es igual a simple, químicamente . . . poesía pura—poesía simple, prefiero yo',[11] and as Salinas, in particular, showed with the striking simplicity of his style and diction. Initially both poets have a simple and fundamental concept of poetry; they stress the notion of creation. Guillén was able to say of his generation as a whole: 'Hay que recoger, para revocar la atmósfera de aquellos años, esta voluntad de poesía como creación, de poema como quintaesenciado mundo'.[12] Earlier Salinas had suggested that the 'poet is born into a world already made' and that his object is 'the creation of a new reality within the old';[13] he admired what he called 'Adamic poetry . . . poetry of the first vision of the world that surrounds us';[14] and he emphasized 'las cosas están allí . . . la poesía tiene el deber primordial de crear'.[15] Similarly, Guillén wrote: 'Crear, término del orgullo',[16] and elegantly repeated Salinas' idea with: 'El poeta siente en su plenitud etimológica el vocablo *poesía*. (Pero esta creación será, quiéralo o no, segunda respecto a la del primer creador del Génesis. Todos los

poetas son *poètes du dimanche,* del domingo que sigue al sábado en que descansó Jehová.)'[17] For both poets, then, poetry is related to a concept of verbal purity created within a primordial atmosphere; a concept which is partly explained by Gerhard Hauptmann's definition of poetry, 'Dichten heisst, hinter Worten das Urwort erklingen lassen', referred to by C. G. Jung and translated as 'Poetry evokes out of words the resonance of the primordial word'.[18] It may be said that both Salinas and Guillén are aware of the word's primordial force. Initially, for Salinas, it appears that the poet's duty to create is based simply upon the act of *naming*: '. . . reality must be revised, confirmed, approved by the poet. And he confirms or recreates it by means of a word, by merely putting it into words. It is the poet's gift to name realities fully, to draw them out of that enormous mass of the anonymous'.[19] Frequently Salinas plays with this idea of naming objects: the poem 'Orilla' (45) gradually defines and moves deliberately towards the naming of 'mar de julio'; moods are named: 'Posesión de tu nombre, / . . . / felicidad, alma sin cuerpo. / Dentro de mí te llevo / porque digo tu nombre' (6). Numerous poems underline the poet's theme that words have a special power: **'Agua'** (31) synthesizes a person's death, **'Adiós'** (48), uttered by the *amada,* is testimony of her power, as are the orders '"Para" o "Echa a correr"' she gives in *La voz* (140). When she is lost her name is the last item to remain with the poet (*Fábula y signo,* 90). In an early Mallarméan, sonnet, 'Cerrado te quedaste libro mío' (19), Salinas deals with the theme that poetry and 'la palabra bien medida' can be a means towards understanding; and later, in *Seguro azar,* with the idea of the word's triumph over the blank page: 'contra lo blanco, en blanco, / inicial, tú, palabra' (38). The same kind of attitude again emerges in Salinas' last poetry: **'Verbo'** (330) celebrates the history of language with its 'santas palabras', 'más hermosas, / por más usadas'; **'Confianza'** (453) expresses total confidence in words; and finally, **'El poema'** (333), which explains poetic creation as a striving towards clarity, is little more than a prosaic expansion of the idea Guillén had expressed earlier in image form: 'Hacia una luz mis penas se consumen' (273).[20] Turning to Guillén's poetry, it will be agreed that the reader is always conscious here of the poet's confidence in 'la fiel plenitud de las palabras' (537). The magical and even primordial power of words is sung; especially in 'Los nombres': 'Albor. El horizonte / Entreabre sus pestañas / Y empieza a ver. ¿Qué? Nombres. / Están sobre la pátina / De las cosas' (36); in 'Más allá': '¡Qué de objetos! Nombrados / Se allanan a la mente' (30); again in 'Hacia el nombre' (302) and in 'Celinda' (259). In both Guillén and Salinas, then, there is ample evidence of the poets' belief in the power of the word, specifically the noun, and a corroboration in verse of the poetics they argued in prose. But while Guillén's consistency on this point is not doubted, Salinas, as we shall soon see, was not always content with the ritual of naming. Indeed, between his early poetry, which often indicates a strong influence of Mallarmé, and the poetry of Salinas' last period, complacent in its attitude of homage, there is found Salinas' great poetry, which is remarkable for the way it sustains a deeply inquisitive and even quarrelsome attitude towards words.

Having established certain similarities of concept between Salinas and Guillén, at least in some parts of the former's work, it would now be useful if we could situate the point of divergence we have anticipated. The question centres upon the idea of *naming realities*. For Guillén the power of naming implies an identification between word and thing, which he explains as an incarnation. The idea appears in verse: 'Encarnación en su perenne estado' (399), but is fully explained in prose: 'los materiales brutos se presentan recreados en creación, trasformados en forma, encarnados en carne verbal';[21] and: 'Poesía como arte de la poesía: forma de una encarnación. Podríamos escribir esta palabra con mayúscula: misterio de la Encarnación' (*op. cit.*, 240). The intensity and the quasi-religious hyperbole with which Guillén voices his concept is testimony to his more extreme position. Though, like Salinas, he was almost certainly influenced by Jiménez's celebrated '¡Intelijencia, dame / el nombre exacto de las cosas! / . . . Que mi palabra sea / la cosa misma', Guillén's attitude has more in common with Mallarmé's notion of the poet-*priest*. Mallarmé explained the poet's power: 'Je dis: une fleure! et, hors de l'oubli où ma voix relègue aucun contour, en tant que quelque chose d'autre que les calices sus, musicalement se lève, idée même et suave, l'absente de tous bouquets'.[22] The same important concept is explained in verse:

> Le Maître, par un oeil profond, a, sur ses pas,
> Apaisé de l'éden l'inquiète merveille
> Dont le frisson final, dans sa voix seule, éveille
> Pour la Rose et le Lys le mystère d'un nom.[23]

The magical power of the word and, specifically, the idea that it is more permanent than the thing it designates, is what Guillén expressed in 'Hacia el nombre', with its triumphant verbalized 'lila', and in 'Los nombres': 'Pero quedan los nombres'. Indeed, the major process in Guillén's poetry is to move from concrete reality to a generic, archetypal reality wherein words designate permanent rather than transient individual things. Guillén, however, has suggested that this is not Salinas' position: '¿Qué rosa inspira confianza al poeta (Salinas), según su fe? . . . ¿"L'absente de tout bouquet", como Mallarmé soñaba? No, no es la rosa-nombre, no es una quintaesencia verbal'.[24] On the one hand, Guillén's position derives from a concept of verbal concentration: 'Todo hacia la palabra se condensa' (403), and: '¡Oh concentración prodigiosa! / Todas las rosas son la rosa' (362); but Salinas, while admiring the generic force of Guillén's poetry,[25] and drawing atten-

tion to the characteristic line: 'Todo en el aire es pájaro' (85), still offers a contradictory point of view in **'¿Qué pájaros?'** (412). As though deliberately recalling Guillén's line, with its solid, cosmic and verbal unanimity, Salinas offers the alternative of perplexing multiplicity:

> ¿El pájaro? ¿Los pájaros?
> ¿Hay sólo un solo pájaro en el mundo
> que vuela con mil alas, y que canta
> con incontables trinos, siempre solo?
> ¿Son tierra y cielo espejos? ¿Es el aire
> espejeo del aire, y el gran pájaro
> único multiplica
> su soledad en apariencias miles?
> (¿Y por eso
> le llamamos los pájaros?)
>
> ¿O quizá no hay un pájaro?
> Y son ellos,
> fatal plural inmenso, como el mar,
> bandada innúmera, oleaje de alas,
> donde la vista busca y quiere el alma
> distinguir la verdad del solo pájaro,
> de su esencia sin fin, del uno hermoso?

Salinas' more sceptical, inquisitive approach is clearly in evidence here: the interrogative characterizes his attitude as surely as does the exclamation Guillén's. There are no ready solutions for Salinas: no 'pájaro-nombre' as there was no 'rosa-nombre'. Indeed, far from crystallizing concepts, Salinas' method appears to consist of withdrawing from the finite logical world into an imaginative derealized realm ('¿O quizá no hay un pájaro?') of multiple possibility.

Related to the theme of naming and of endowing essence with a name, we find a supreme instance of Salinas' sceptical and somewhat ironical approach in *El contemplado*. In refusing to name the subject of his poems, which we understand from the introduction to be 'mar de Puerto Rico', except by inventing a new name for it, 'el contemplado', Salinas is playing the game of the primordial poet, or the *poète du dimanche*, with ironical exaggeration. In **'Dulcenombre'** he delights in having conferred this new name:

> Desde que te llamo así,
> por mi nombre,
> ya nunca me eres extraño.
> . . .
> Pero tengo aquí en el alma
> tu nombre mío.
> . . .
> Si te nombro, soy tu amo
> de un segundo. ¡Qué milagro!
> . . .
> Obra, sutil, el encanto
> divino del cristianar.
> . . .
> —sacramento del nombrar—,
>
>   (289-90)

However, it is clear that the reality of *mar* is evoked by common associated denominatives ('playa', 'arenas', 'espuma', 'ola'), while the *new* name which Salinas chooses, 'el contemplado', is virtually a withdrawal or an opting-out of conferring a definitive name, for it treats the object not as a thing in itself but as an extension of subjective experience. This last point, though simple, is fundamental to what distinguishes Salinas' attitude from Guillén's. While Guillén sees objects sharply silhouetted in a spatial dimension, and while his buildings, statues and even humans ('Desnudo', 186), impress upon us the sense of autonomous form, Salinas, on the other hand, primarily refuses to grant separateness to objects and presents them as absorbed in subjective sensation; this is clearly accelerated in his best volumes where so much is contiguous to the *amada*. An example is found in **La voz** (183), when in a delightful poem Salinas attempts to define and even name the tears he sees on the *amada*'s face. He describes their texture, 'Claras, redondas, tibias', and their movement; but when it comes to crystallizing them into a single word he playfully suggests: '¿Astros?'; and then:

> ¿Son estrellas, son signos,
> son condenas o auroras?
> Ni en mirar ni en besar
> aprendí lo que eran.
> Lo que quieren se queda
> allá atrás, todo incógnito.
> Y su nombre también.

As may be expected, Salinas is not concerned here with the kind of reality that would define tears as liquid substance; but, searching for the inner reality of tears, Salinas' technique is to create an impression of multiplicity, for both their cause and meaning are complex. The typical listing of items, as possible names, is less an attempt to correlate in image form than a means of suggesting this notion of endless possibility. If their essential nature is so complex, ultimately 'todo incógnito', then it is not possible to name them properly. Here we find delicious irony in the poem's conclusion:

> (Si las llamara lágrimas,
> nadie me entendería.)

While the *naming* of 'lágrimas' is virtually necessary in order that we know what the poet is referring to, he argues that in giving us the name we no longer know what is in fact his true subject. We can surmise that the poet objects to the word 'lágrimas' for at least two reasons. Firstly, because it condenses with an illusion of singularity a subject the poet considers to be infinitely multiple and hence unfixed. This implies a second point: that in falsely condensing and translating his multiple sensation of this matter into the word 'lágrimas', a word everyone knows and whose subject everyone has experienced in his own way, Salinas is again inviting a false equation: the equation of two undoubtedly diverse experiences of the object denoted by 'lágrimas'. Now, the concept behind this argument would be clear to anyone who has read Henri Bergson. Bergson stresses the idea of two separate levels of experience, the public and private; and, when considering the problem of communication, Bergson holds that words only inadequately transmit sensations from the private to the public realm:

> En d'autres termes, nos perceptions, sensations, émotions et idées se présentent sous un double aspect: l'un net, précis, mais impersonnel; l'autre confus, infiniment mobile, et inexprimable, parce que le langage ne saurait le saisir sans en fixer la mobilité, ni l'adapter à sa forme banale sans le faire tomber dans le domaine commun . . . Nous tendons instinctivement à solidifier nos impressions, pour les exprimer par le langage. De là vient que nous confondons le sentiment même, qui est dans un perpétuel devenir, avec son objet extérieur permanent, et surtout avec le mot qui exprime cet objet . . . nos impressions sans cesse changeantes, s'enroulant autour de l'objet extérieur qui en est cause, en adoptent les contours précis et l'immobilité.[26]

We can see that in Salinas' desire to create a new name for his sea and in his reluctance to denote 'lágrimas' with their common name, he is following Bergson's theory that words are inadequate for they immobilize what is an infinitely changing subjective experience.

At this point Salinas' position is quite unlike Guillén's. Indeed, the verbal process Guillén celebrates as an incarnation results in Salinas as an *incarceration*. Now, we may wonder what Salinas had in mind when he spoke of the poet's gift as 'to name realities fully', and by so doing, 'to draw them out of that enormous mass of the anonymous'. The answer is found in the continuation of his rather perplexing argument in **Reality and the Poet**. The realities that the poet would name undergo change as they pass through the poet on to the page itself: 'The poet places himself before reality like a human body before light, in order to create something else, a shadow'; and 'shadow' is the image Salinas uses to describe 'the higher reality', the 'ultimate, impalpable category' of the spirit.[27] Again there is a clear movement here towards subjectivity. Moreover, in describing poetry as a catalytic action, it is evident that Salinas is reconnoting the term *reality*: at first 'realities' implies the things of this world, but later 'reality' indicates a spiritual experience. This may be considered a discrepancy when it is allowed that the precise naming of objects and things, as such, has nothing to do with the evocation of spiritual reality for Salinas. Consistency is found only if we appreciate that Salinas does not discriminate between objective reality and spiritual or subjective reality, since for him everything is absorbed by subjective experience. Finally, in this sense, Salinas' phrase 'to name realities fully' effectively means the evocation of innumerable qualities that express relation to subjectivity; and this, paradoxically, often results in confining objects strictly to the realm of the anonymous.

Earlier on it may have been thought that 'lágrimas' was the kind of object which inevitably begged the question of subjectivity. However, in the next poem we see that Salinas is sceptical about the reality of all kinds of words, hardly discriminating between concrete and abstract denominatives:

¿Por qué tienes nombre, tú,
día, miércoles?
¿Por qué tienes nombre, tú,
tiempo, otoñno?
Alegría, pena, siempre
¿por qué tenéis nombre: amor?
Si tú no tuvieras nombre,
yo no sabría qué era,
ni cómo, ni cuándo. Nada.

¿Sabe el mar cómo se llama,
que es el mar? ¿Saben los vientos
sus apellidos, del Sur
y del Norte, por encima
del puro soplo que son?

Si tú no tuvieras nombre,
todo sería primero,
inicial, todo inventado
por mí,
intacto hasta el beso mío.
Gozo, amor: delicia lenta
de gozar, de amar, sin nombre.

Nombre, ¡qué puñal clavado
en medio de un pecho cándido
que sería nuestro siempre
si no fuese por su nombre!

(*La voz,* 128)

Mistrusting the relationship words have with the things they designate, Salinas appeals for an abolition of words. In the desired pre-verbal, 'Adamic' state, Salinas envisages a more meaningful and certainly more intimate relationship with environment. Yet the notion of starting from scratch ('todo sería primero, / inicial, todo inventado / por mí'), which is even prior to Guillén's *poète du dimanche,* ironically implies the making of other names that will constrict, as in the case of 'el contemplado'. The point was noted by Bergson:

Pour lutter à armes égales, celles-ci (i.e. les impressions délicates et fugitives de notre conscience individuelle) devraient s'exprimer par des mots précis; mais ces mots, à peine formés, se retourneraient contre la sensation qui leur donna naissance, et inventés pour témoigner que la sensation est instable, ils lui imposeraient leur propre stabilité.

(*op. cit.,* 87)

The argument is hopelessly cyclical, and Salinas brilliantly pinpoints this in the last lines of his poem where a culminative word, 'siempre', is a deliberate repetition of a word whose reality has been questioned in the opening stanza. Suddenly both poet and reader realize that the argument of the poem is being formed out of words which are themselves mistrusted.

Salinas' veritable war with words is sustained throughout his best poetry, finding both thematic and stylistic expression; and in this way, particularly in *La voz a ti debida,* it is instrumental in constructing a remarkably cohesive volume. Fortunately Salinas' poetry has received a relatively thorough stylistic analysis, much of it based upon an early and brilliant commentary by Leo Spitzer.[28] Permitting ourselves to make only a summary conclusion of these numerous stylistic points, we should say that Salinas' best poetry clearly indicates a movement away from substantive expression with a corresponding emphasis placed upon simple words, notably, adverbs and pronouns: pronoun, *pronomen,* a word used instead of a noun. Thus, Salinas' scepticism receives as lucid expression in his lexicon as does Guillén's faith in nouns by the preponderance of substantives in his poetry.[29] Now what really concerns us at this stage is to ascertain the effectiveness of Salinas' concepts (his scepticism, his quarrelsome attitude towards words) in relation to the central theme of his work (here considered as love, and specifically, the identity of the two participants in love). It will be seen that what we have designated as Bergsonian in his attitude towards words also permeates his presentation of the love theme.

Salinas' reluctance to use definitive names is most marked when he wrestles with the problem of locating or evoking the identity of the *amada*. This is found repeatedly in *La voz*: 'Sí, por detrás de las gentes /te busco. / No en tu nombre, si lo dicen' (122); and in *Razón de amor,* where names become superfluous in the experience of love: 'Y no más nombres ya, / . . . / Los nombres se borraron / ante una luz mayor' (273). Instead, as we know, Salinas turns to the monosyllabic pronoun. In the key poem to explain his predilection for the pronoun we see that it is founded upon a concept of freedom; freedom from all kinds of restrictions, but especially names:

Para vivir no quiero
islas, palacios, torres.
¡Qué alegría más alta:
vivir en los pronombres!

Quítate ya los trajes,
las señas, los retratos;
yo no te quiero así,
disfrazada de otra,
hija siempre de algo.
Te quiero pura, libre,
irreductible: tú.
Sé que cuando te llame
entre todas las gentes
del mundo,
sólo tú serás tú.
Y cuando me preguntes
quién es el que te llama,

el que te quiere suya,
enterraré los nombres,
los rótulos, la historia.
Iré rompiendo todo
lo que encima me echaron
desde antes de nacer.
Y vuelto ya al anónimo
eterno del desnudo,
de la piedra, del mundo,
te diré:
'Yo te quiero, soy yo.'

(135)

The lucid structure of this poem gives sharp emphasis to the poet's dual subject: 'tú' and 'yo'. Action is introduced by relating these concepts to their own negative shadows; and evidently the comparison is between an intimate, private self, and a superficial, public self. Numerous items are listed to situate the self that lives in public, exterior reality: 'islas', 'palacios', 'torres', 'trajes', 'señas', 'retratos', 'nombres', 'rótulos', 'historia'; a self that lives 'entre todas las gentes / del mundo'. These are considered as paraphernalia which bar the way to the location of the real self. When it comes to evoking this latter self the poet offers a handful of qualities: 'pura, libre, / irreductible', and then 'anónimo', 'eterno' and 'desnudo'. It is suggested here that of all these meaningful qualities the most comprehensive is denoted by the adjective 'libre', which we shall consider first. In order to illustrate that the concept of freedom is at the heart of Salinas' presentation of the *amada* we may take the very first line of *La voz*, one of the most telling descriptions:

Tú vives siempre en tus actos.

Referring here to the positive self of the *amada*, the poet's concept may be understood as twofold: firstly, that of an immediate and spontaneous relationship between the *amada*'s inner self and its exterior expression in action; secondly, that by virtue of *living* in the immediacy of her actions, she thus lives in a constant state of change perpetually suspended in the present moment. The twofold concept, then, involves the authenticity of her self-expression as well as her location in time. Now, both these points are basic to Bergson's interpretation of freedom, as presented in *Essai sur les données immédiates de la conscience*. With reference to the first Bergson writes: 'Bref, nous sommes libres quand nos actes émanent de notre personnalité entière, quand ils l'expriment' (*op. cit.*, 113). Secondly, proper location in time will result inevitably from this freedom: 'Agir librement, c'est reprendre possession de soi, c'est se replacer dans la pure durée' (151). We need only to clarify that proper location in time, 'la pure durée', is Bergson's way of stating the concept of a perpetually changing and continuous present. Referring back to the disarmingly simple line, 'Tú vives siempre en tus actos', we should find that it offers a most appropriate intro-

duction to the *amada*, evoking the sense of a being *in process*, hence constantly changing, and thereby implying that her very essence is freedom. Now, if we accept that one of Salinas' main objectives is the description of the *amada*'s true identity, we find that he has indeed a most difficult task, because freedom, as Bergson says, is inexpressible in language (*op. cit.*, 145), since words will always impose restrictions. However, we may examine some points which indicate how Salinas meets this challenge.

In Bergson's philosophy, freedom, and the ability to live in 'la pure durée', is dependent upon the inner being's abolition of its concept of time as a consecutive and chronological measure. This also necessitates a new concept of space, for space as measure implies chronological time; or, as Bergson says: 'Le temps . . . n'est que le fantôme de l'espace obsédant la conscience réfléchie' (*op. cit.*, 67). Approaching *La voz a ti debida* with this in mind, we should appreciate why Salinas goes a long way towards divesting himself of spatial and temporal restrictions. In broad terms the volume is remarkable for its anonymity in these respects. The two lovers dwell in a kind of psychological limbo, freed of environment, where feelings permeate to such an extent that there is a stronger impression of simultaneity than of consecutiveness. Here it may be noted that the 'plot', as such, is deliberately obscure, frequently appearing to overlap upon itself; while Salinas' technique of using contradictory conceits (as in the play upon weight, which in one poem results in 'Amor total, quererse como masas' [161], yet which is soon transposed in another to 'La materia no pesa. / Ni tu cuerpo ni el mío' [167]), is a further means of enhancing the impression of an intuitive self in process rather than of a mind in logical development. We can see, then, that Salinas may divest himself of space and time, firstly, by stylistic measures, and secondly, by omission; that is, by refusing to locate his subject in those dimensions. This second point, however, is probably not practicable through the entire duration of a long poem, and there are occasions when Salinas locates his protagonists. In this case we almost always find them in a kind of mythical and primordial environment, wherein they are returned to a *status nascens*. This is most thoroughly evoked in the following poem:

¡Qué día sin pecado!
La espuma, hora tras hora,
infatigablemente,
fué blanca, blanca, blanca.
Inocentes materias,
los cuerpos y las rocas
—desde cenit total,
mediodía absoluto—
estaban
viviendo de la luz,
y por la luz y en ella.
Aún no se conocían

la conciencia y la sombra.
Se tendía la mano
a coger una piedra,
una nube, una flor,
un ala.
Y se las alcanzaba
a todas, porque era
antes de las distancias.
El tiempo no tenía
sospechas de ser él.

. . .

Y entonces nos dejaba
ingrávidos, flotantes
en el puro vivir
sin sucesión,
salvados de motivos,
de orígenes, de albas.
Ni volver la cabeza
ni mirar a lo lejos
aquel día supimos
tú y yo. . . .

(139-40)

Here we find an explicit exposition of Bergson's concept of 'la pure durée': 'el puro vivir / sin sucesión'. Particularly noticeable is Salinas' concern for time and space, which he evidently interprets as components of the same negative, 'era / antes de las distancias'. As in the poem dealing with pronouns, Salinas rejects chronological time, 'la historia', and returns man to a state of harmony: 'vuelto ya al anónimo / eterno del desnudo, / de la piedra, del mundo' (135). Retreating from the everyday world—'Ya no puedo encontrarte / allí en esa distancia, precisa con su nombre' (155)—Salinas resorts to a mythical environment devoid of space and time, though not duration, because this environment is adaptable to subjective processes and hence it becomes their metaphor.

However, throughout *La voz* and *Razón de amor* Salinas is aware that his concepts are thwarted by the mere fact that he voices them in words which themselves belong to a spatial and consecutive reality. This gives rise to the most ironical motifs which Salinas exploits both playfully and meaningfully. With startling irony the poet expresses amazement on discovering that his *amada* speaks a recognized 'idioma del mundo / con gramática e historia' (124). Evidently he expected a wholly new method of communication appropriate to her idiosyncratic self. Her position is temporarily saved when the poet discovers that she brings a new vitality and creative force to the existing language:

'Mañana'. La palabra
iba suelta, vacante,
ingrávida, en el aire,
tan sin alma y sin cuerpo,
tan sin color ni beso,
que la dejé pasar
por mi lado, en mi hoy.
Pero de pronto tú

dijiste: 'Yo, mañana . . .'
Y todo se pobló
de carne y de banderas.

(125-26)

But ultimately her uniqueness and her freedom from trappings can only be assured by making her prior to language:

Los verbos, indecisos,
te miraban los ojos
como los perros fieles,
trémulos. Tu mandato
iba a marcarles ya
sus rumbos, sus acciones.
¿Subir? Se estremecía
su energía ignorante.
¿Sería ir hacia arriba
'subir'? ¿E ir hacia dónde
sería 'descender'?

(133)

Here, at a most literal level, the poet is investigating the primordialism of words. But this has now been made subordinate to the *amada*'s essence; that is, in broader terms, subordinate to subjectivity. In this comparison words appear to be weak, even meaningless:

No, el pasado era nuestro:
no tenía ni nombre.
Podíamos llamarlo
a nuestro gusto: estrella,
colibrí, teorema,
en vez de así, 'pasado';
quitarle su veneno.

(133)

Here the lovers achieve emancipation from the strictures of time by destroying the word that made them aware of time. The clear implication is that words are themselves responsible for man's negative thinking, that they assign limits which imprison him. An interesting stylistic feature here is the typical and apparently haphazard listing of alternatives: 'estrella, / colibrí, teorema', then 'minas, / continentes, motores' (133). Although this can be humorous, as C. B. Morris suggests is the case elsewhere,[30] Spitzer also finds a serious intent in what he describes as 'enumeración caótica': that in reciting nouns and simultaneously denying them context, Salinas is virtually freeing them of their connotations and destroying them as denominatives. Spitzer defines this: 'Léxico donde las palabras se despojan de su sentido, es decir, *cesan de ser palabras*';[31] and this stylistic feature, finally, may be considered an extreme expression of Salinas' scepticism.

In the comparatively diluted poems of *Razón de amor* Salinas is often more comprehensive in his ideas about words. On one occasion he describes the curious reconnoting of words, desired in *La voz,* which he achieves in the *amada*'s presence:

Cuando te digo: 'alta',
no pienso en proporciones, en medidas:
incomparablemente te lo digo.
Alta la luz, el aire, el ave;
alta, tú, de otro modo.

(229)

The *amada*'s role as alchemist, here with 'alta' and subsequently with 'hermosa' and 'única', is precisely what Salinas desires of his muse: that she recharge words with new values without imposing limitations ('proporciones', 'medidas'), so that words may be as changeable and as unpredictable as the living qualities they propose to define. On another occasion, more boldly, Salinas describes the word which defines his *amada*'s essence. The poem begins:

¿Tú sabes lo que eres
de mí?
¿Sabes tú el nombre?
      No es
el que todos te llaman,
esa palabra usada
que se dicen las gentes,
si besan o si quieren,
porque ya se lo han dicho
otros que besaron.

(210)

Again we note the desire for uniqueness. As a broader literary criterion, however, this concept is contradicted in Salinas' later poetry where words are celebrated 'Cada día más hermosas, / por más usadas' (342), which restates an affinity with Guillén. The more complacent attitude of Salinas' later work is perhaps accounted for by the notion that he had, by then, in a sense, won his battle with words, whereas in poems such as the one that now concerns us we find him earnestly groping for the elusive word:

Yo no lo sé; lo digo,
se me asoma a los labios
como una aurora virgen
de la que no soy dueño.
Tú tampoco lo sabes;
lo oyes. Y lo recibe
tu oído igual que el silencio
que nos llega hasta el alma
sin saber de qué ausencias
de ruidos está hecho.
¿Son letras, son sonidos?
Es mucho más antiguo.
Lengua de paraíso,
sones primeros, vírgenes
tanteos de los labios,
cuando, antes de los números,
en el aire del mundo
se estrenaban los nombres
de los gozos primeros.

(211)

Salinas' method, with language as with reality itself, is to undermine or derealize the whole concept: '¿Son

letras, son sonidos? / Es mucho más antiguo', and then let his new paradisiacal language emerge with impalpable purity. The name which describes his *amada*'s essence is there, on his lips, partly intelligible, but still unvoiced, ineffable:

sin poderlo aprender,
sin saberlo yo mismo.

(212)

Though apparently on the point of utterance Salinas holds back at the crucial moment and thereby refuses to immobilize his subjective sensation of the *amada*. In a sense this is a development from **La voz,** where he frequently contented himself with 'tú' as a definitive, though evidently the appeal of the latter ironically lay in its lack of definition.

Salinas' means of purifying the word and his new language is by releasing it from ties with man's civilization and by hence letting it emerge like a phenomenon from the real world, chiefly from nature:

No se escribe tu nombre
donde se escribe, con lo que se escribe.
En las aguas escribe
con verde rasgo el árbol.
En el aire las máquinas
improvisan nocturnos,
tocan su seca música
de alfabeto romántico.
En los cielos abiertos
van trazando los pájaros
códigos de los vuelos.
. . .
Las estrellas se leen
con largas lentes claras
que descifran su tedio
de enigmas alejados.
Las tierras más remotas
con colores azules,
verdes, rosas, entregan
su secreto en los mapas.
. . .

(226)

Salinas' flight with words into phenomena may be seen as another, though more muted, way of stating Bécquer's insoluble equation: 'Cendal flotante de leve bruma, / rizada cinta de blanca espuma, / . . . / eso eres tú'. But also, recalling how Salinas bemoaned the way things were straitjacketed with words ('¿Sabe el mar cómo se llama, / que es el mar?'), the technique of making nature articulate appears strangely as an act of compensation. Found throughout Salinas' poetry, it is one of his favourite systems of imagery, accentuating the flux between the real and poetic worlds: 'El mar . . . / Escribe blanca espuma' (49), 'el cielo monosílabo' (115), 'Alfabetos de la espuma' (129), 'mares, cielos, azules / con espumas y brisas, / júbilos monosílabos / repiten sin parar' (137), 'Las olas / —más, más, más, más—van diciendo / en la arena, monosílabas' (306-07), and it is apparent that the language of nature is akin to Salinas' own 'monosilabismo', as Spitzer termed it.[32] A significant example of nature's articulation is found in a very early poem:

Estos dulces vocablos con que me estás hablando
no los entiendo, paisaje,
no son los míos.

(16)

The 'incógnitas palabras' of the landscape are a fatal attraction for Salinas, who concludes the poem with a general statement of poetic aspiration:

Y que me lleves a la claridad de lo incognoscible,
paisaje dulce, por vocablos desconocidos.

Here we see that Salinas has a rather special interpretation of clarity. We should define it as intuitive illumination: 'Iluminación, todo iluminaciones. Que no es lo mismo que claridad, esa claridad que desean tantos honrados lectores de poesía'.[33]

The metaphor of articulate phenomena is transmitted to the *amada* when, for instance, Salinas describes her ineffable speech: 'tú respondas / con estrellas equívocas' (164). Finally, recalling a conversation with the *amada*, he describes their sublime use of words and offers the most literal definition of the kind of language he desires:

Palabras sueltas, palabras,
deleite en incoherencias,
no eran ya signo de cosas,
eran voces puras, voces
de su servir olvidadas.

(241)

Evidently, when words are released from their prime function of designating things, incoherence results. Though this in itself can hardly be acceptable as a poetic norm, it may be argued that Salinas' position is not unlike Bécquer's when the latter complained about his 'mezquino idioma' and hoped for a miraculous transmutation of language: 'con palabras que fuesen a un tiempo / suspiros y risas, colores y notas'. But whereas Bécquer relies heavily upon image correlatives, Salinas' means of approaching the indefinable essence summarized in the pronoun 'tú' is by giving the texture of his expression a corresponding quality of impalpability. Virtually divesting himself of poetic form and shunning or undermining denominatives, Salinas escapes into a world of less material definition; and in this sense, texture rather than meaning of language becomes the key correlative. Meaning is strangely of only doubtful assistance; for in their tendency to situate, define and confine, words work in opposition to the essence of 'tú'.

The desire that words be unpredictable, changeable, and hence even incoherent, is an ironical though rational extension of the poet's argument. In practical terms Salinas could not invent a new language for his poetry, and had to be content with a second-hand one complete with 'gramática e historia', but his serious efforts to free himself from some linguistic impositions, such as he considered them, resulted in a poetic style that was very much his own: one that continually questions its own reality and, paradoxically, discovers itself in the process. Indeed, it is within this concept of language and experience *in process* that we find Salinas' supreme achievement in poetry. Here we see that he fully appreciated Bergson's point that 'les états de conscience sont des progrès, et non pas des choses; qui si nous les désignons chacun par un seul mot, c'est pour la commodité du langage; qu'ils vivent, et que, vivant, ils changent sans cesse' (*op. cit.,* 129).

Notes

1. Henri Bergson, *Essai sur les données immédiates de la conscience* (1889), in *Œuvres* (Paris 1959), 109.

2. Numbers in parenthesis indicate the page of reference in Pedro Salinas, *Poesías completas,* second edition (Madrid 1956).

3. Pedro Salinas, *Reality and the Poet in Spanish Poetry* (Baltimore 1940), 3.

4. J. González Muela makes this point in both 'Poesía y amistad: Jorge Guillén y Pedro Salinas', *BHS,* XXXV (1958), 28, and in his introduction to Pedro Salinas, *La voz a ti debida, Razón de amor* (Madrid 1969), 29.

5. C. B. Morris, '"Visión" and "mirada" in the poetry of Salinas, Guillén and Dámaso Alonso', *BHS,* XXXVIII (1961), 103.

6. C. B. Morris, *A Generation of Spanish Poets* (Cambridge 1969), 43.

7. Jorge Guillén, prologue to Pedro Salinas, *Poemas escogidos* (Madrid 1953), 12-13.

8. C. B. Morris, 'Pedro Salinas and Marcel Proust', *RLC,* XLIV (1970), 211.

9. Jorge Guillén, prologue to Alma de Zubizarreta, *Pedro Salinas: El diálogo creador* (Madrid 1969), 10.

10. J. González Muela, *La realidad y Jorge Guillén* (Madrid 1962), 23.

11. See Fernando Vela, 'La poesía pura', *RO,* XIV (1926), 234.

12. Jorge Guillén, *Lenguaje y poesía* (Madrid 1962), 243.

13. *Reality and the Poet,* 3-4.

14. *Ibid.,* 29.

15. Pedro Salinas, *Literatura española siglo XX* (Mexico 1949), 191.

16. *Lenguaje y poesía,* 244.

17. *Ibid.,* 243.

18. See *The Collected Works of C. G. Jung,* translated by R. F. C. Hull, XV (London 1966), 80.

19. *Reality and the Poet,* 4.

20. Numbers in parenthesis indicate the page of reference in Jorge Guillén, *Aire nuestro* (Milan 1968).

21. *Lenguaje y poesía,* 247.

22. Stéphane Mallarmé, 'Variations sur un sujet', *Œuvres complètes* (Tours 1951), 368.

23. 'Toast Funèbre', *Œuvres complètes,* 55.

24. Prologue to Pedro Salinas, *Poemas escogidos,* 11.

25. *Literatura española siglo XX,* 191.

26. Henri Bergson, *Œuvres,* 85-86.

27. *Reality and the Poet,* 5-6.

28. Leo Spitzer, 'El conceptismo interior de Pedro Salinas', *RHM,* VII (1941). Some of Spitzer's stylistic points are taken up by C. Feal Deibe, *La poesía de Pedro Salinas* (Madrid 1965), but are most thoroughly explored by Elsa Dehennin, *Passion d'absolu et tension expressive dans l'oeuvre poétique de Pedro Salinas* (Ghent 1957).

29. The substantive force of Guillén's poetry was noted for instance by F. A. Pleak, *The Poetry of Jorge Guillén* (Princeton 1942), 68, and by J. Casalduero, *Jorge Guillén, Cántico* (Santiago de Chile 1946), 50-51.

30. *A Generation of Spanish Poets,* 117.

31. 'El conceptismo interior', 41.

32. 'El conceptismo interior', 52.

33. Pedro Salinas, 'Poética', in Gerardo Diego, *Poesía española contemporánea (1901-1934),* 'nueva edición completa' (Madrid 1959), 318.

Sandra Price (essay date January 1984)

SOURCE: Price, Sandra. "'Verdad de mitos': Some Aspects of the Use of Classical Mythology in the Poetry of Pedro Salinas." *Forum for Modern Language Studies* 20, no. 1 (January 1984): 342-59.

[*In the following essay, Price studies the ways in which Salinas employs mythology in his "poems on the city and its inventions," showing that "the eventual failure of the city to accommodate a mythical viewpoint" fore-shadows the poet's "renewed interest in the natural world as a poetic theme in much of his later poetry."*]

The use of mythology in the poetry of Pedro Salinas has been explored in recent years by two critics. Francesco Guazzelli takes as his starting point the poem **"Atalanta"**, and relates it to other poems of the same collection (**Seguro azar**) which also make reference to a mythical female character. He extends his comments to a consideration of the mythical background against which the entire male-female relationship in Salinas' poetry must be viewed.[1]

John Crispin, on the other hand, turns his attention to the poetry following **Razón de amor,** concentrating on **Todo más claro.** He examines Salinas' rejection of the false myths of modern society (the myths of youth, of the "American way of life", and of romantic love) which come into conflict with the eternal values represented by classical and biblical myth, which permits a collective interpretation of life as continuity and as a creative cycle.[2]

My intention is to complement Crispin's article in particular by examining the ways in which mythology is used in Salinas' poems on the city and its inventions, from his earliest works to those written in exile in the United States. I hope also to demonstrate that the eventual failure of the city to accommodate a mythical viewpoint contributes to Salinas' renewed interest in the natural world as a poetic theme in much of his later poetry.

In contrast to Crispin's examination of mythical themes and archetypal structures, I have elected to refer principally to individual myths and to named figures. I discuss only those figures drawn from classical mythology. Salinas' use of other mythologies, chiefly the biblical, demands more detailed study than is possible in the space of this article and is therefore omitted.

Another significant area of mythical reference which lies beyond the scope of my study is the depiction of the *Amada* as mythical being (the nymph, the muse, the goddess) and as Venus Aphrodite. I hope to return to this subject at a later date.

Any study of Salinas' use of an existing frame of reference or literary tradition may usefully begin in his critical works. It is difficult to divide Salinas the poet from Salinas the critic, for the same themes and preoccupations occur time and again in both poetry and prose, the one shedding light on the other. We find similar phraseology in both, as key themes are repeated. Attitudes implicit in the poetry may be made clear in the prose and are often given a theoretical context. Despite this, the two may on occasion contradict each other, just as two of Salinas' poems will often appear to contain opposing attitudes. It is in part Salinas' willingness to reappraise an opinion, to examine possible alternative stances, that makes his poetry so appealing, particularly when he is writing of that most changeable and irrational subject, human emotion. In our study of his use of mythology we will find both changes of attitude and conflicts of viewpoint between poetry and prose.

What then does Salinas the critic have to say about mythology? The first place to look must be in his book *La poesía de Rubén Darío*,[3] for the Nicaraguan poet so often inhabits a world of myth in his own poetry. In this work Salinas puts forward the not uncommon view of myth as an extension of human emotions and characteristics: "los dioses, los seres míticos, son, entre otras cosas, símbolos corporeizados de las cualidades humanas alzadas a su mayor potencia" (87). As such, the gods become not merely reflections of the human, but also "los blancos de los deseos y afanes de los hombres". Their value is that of a positive example.

Mythology provides Darío with "un mundo de traslación", with an escape from the world of "la pasión humana" to which he was so strongly drawn. The poet leaves behind "la actualidad del individuo que la siente con la fatal limitación del hombre" in order to gain access to "la eternidad del dios que la represente sin límites". This aspect of myth as the casting off of the limitations of time and of personality is one which appeals to Salinas, in his desire to superimpose what he refers to as a "tercera realidad" or as the "más allá" onto restricted "ordinary" life.

Having stressed the value of myth, Salinas moves on in **PRD** [*La poesía de Rubén Diarío*] to examine briefly the rise and fall of the role of mythology in art, reminding us that "es muy difícil entender buena parte, y de lo mejor, de la lírica clásica, sin dominio de ese mundo mitológico" (85). As it is chiefly through literature that such a knowledge is passed on, Salinas laments the apparent refusal of the twentieth century to continue the transmission:

> el siglo XIX, con los románticos, empieza a derrocar esa mítica, y el nuestro la ha relegado ya a la guardarropía, considerando que esas clásicas fabulaciones son mentiras tediosas, inadmisibles para el sentido crítico moderno.

It is indeed in the years following Darío and the *modernista* period that Spanish poets react most violently against the use of mythology in literature, considering it a part of the sterile past from which they must liberate themselves. Both *ultraístas* and *creacionistas* advocate rejection of myth. Jorge Luis Borges writes in 1920:

> queremos ver con los ojos nuevos. Por eso olvidamos la fastuosa fantasmagoría mitológica, que en toda hembra lúbrica quiere visualizar una faunesa y ante las for-

midables selvas del mar, inevitablemente nos sugiere, con lívida sonrisa encubridora, la visión lamentable de Afrodita surgiendo de un Mediterráneo de añil ante un coro de obligados tritones.[4]

At much the same time, Vicente Huidobro warns against both classical mythology and the danger of replacing it with a new, modern mythology of technology:

> Ignoro si otros poetas, al igual que yo, tienen horror a los términos mitológicos, y si también rehuyen los versos con Minervas y Ledas.
>
> Creo que ciertos poetas actuales están creando una mitología, la mitología de la máquina. Ella es tan antipática como la otra.[5]

The *futurista* poets do replace the classical god with the aviator, the motorist and the sportsman. The *creacionista* takes upon himself the role of creator and thus has no place for a realm of superior, timeless beings. As Gerardo Diego says,

> Paso a paso
>   se asciende hasta el Parnaso.
> Yo no quiero las alas de Pegaso.[6]

The *ultraísta,* too, seeks his "ultra" in the city or in a natural landscape transformed by the presence of speeding cars or telegraph wires into a mechanical paradise of modernity.

Each of these literary movements values the transitory above the permanent—age-old figures and the values they perpetuate appear irrelevant to contemporary life.

However, Rafael Cansinos-Asséns, the *ultraístas*' mentor and theorist, takes a different, perhaps more objective, view. He is one of the first to single out Góngora and Mallarmé as joint precursors of the Spanish avant-garde, and to indicate that these poets, as much as the *modernistas,* make extensive use of mythology, and do so in a way that is neither stifling nor retrograde:

> los poetas novísimos hallan sus arquetipos en la poesia mítica, y en Góngora y Mallarmé, por cuya obra circula la olímpica sangre pindárica.[7]

This realisation prevails into the following decade, the twenties, of which the debt to Góngora is to become such a major feature. Yet it is for his brilliant, *culto* language and, above all, for his use of metaphor that Góngora is revered.[8] His mythological subject matter is neither here nor there for the poets who so flamboyantly defend him against the cultural Establishment of the period.

In the poetry of the middle to late 1920s we do not find a great many mythological references, but neither do we meet the iconoclastic attitudes of Borges and Huidobro. Certain mythical figures do occur in individual poets, yet a tendency still prevails to create new, popular gods in the bullfighter, the gypsy or the cinema star. It is notable that those poets whose work has best stood the test of time are precisely those who do not reject the past, who do not insist upon being "modern" at the expense of all literary heritage. Jorge Guillén, for example, perhaps as a result of his affection for the poetry of Paul Valéry, does explore mythological themes, notably that of Venus as the eternal figure of woman and love, and that of Narcissus as the Self. This last is present in the works of Manuel Altolaguirre and Emilio Prados also. Federico García Lorca refers to Venus in his early works and includes reworked elements of classical myth in his *Romancero gitano.*[9]

Luis Cernuda stands as one of the few poets for whom myth was of major importance. In his work the Romantic cult of the lost paradise of pagan gods, equated with the childhood of the individual, gains new validity. Cernuda's innate nostalgia is fired by his reading and translation of the German poet, Hölderlin. In the prose work, *Ocnos,* Cernuda expresses the attraction held by mythology for him:

> Bien temprano en la vida, antes que leyeses versos algunos, cayó en tus manos un libro de mitología. Aquellas páginas te revelaron un mundo donde la poesía, vivificándolo como la llama al leño, trasmutaba lo real. ¡Qué triste te apareció entonces tu propia religión![10]

Again we find the idea of mythology as transformation of reality and, perhaps more importantly, as closely linked with poetry. We shall return to both these concepts in our discussion of Salinas' poetry.

Salinas himself rejects nothing from his literary heritage, embracing no single artistic school and casting aside no cultural legacy. He is as at home in the mythical atmosphere of the Golden Age lyric as he is in the avant-garde's mechanistic world. Not only is he willing to draw on both the classical and the modern in his own verse, but he refuses to recognise any gulf between them. For him the machine does not replace the god, but is rather an extension of the same myth, equally mysterious and fascinating. It is in this that he differs from the *futuristas,* of whom he says: "no m'interessa el futurisme passat de moda de Marinetti",[11] for they attempt to exalt all modernity as essentially mancontrolled and rejoice in its physical power alone. Salinas stresses the continuity of the mythical: "el mundo hoy es un fabuloso despliegue de mitos realizados".[12] This fusion of the classical with the modern is central to Salinas' use of mythology and will be discussed fully in due course.

Salinas' continuing interest in myth is evident throughout his poetry, from start to finish. It will be helpful to illustrate this with a look at his use of the general term "mito" before moving on to examine individual figures as they occur.

In the poem **"Atalanta"** (*SA* [*Seguro azar*] 154) we find myth defined as an "ascensor antiguo".[13] The poem describes the desired transformation of a female character, rooted in the everyday and the limited, into the mythical Atalanta. The mortal is elevated to the eternal:

> el mito, ascensor antiguo,
> que te sube, allá, a la fábula.[14]

This reflects the attitude expressed in **PRD,** that myth is an extension and amplification of human desires. Atalanta, as Guazzelli indicates in his article, is associated with the sensual freedom repressed in the earlier parts of the poem.[15] It represents the stripping away of the superficial to allow revelation of the essential.[16] Salinas already associates the inclusion of a mythological level of interpretation with physical ascent, a fact on which we will have occasion to comment in our analysis of other poems. **"Atalanta"**, too, provides an early example of the fusion of the modern, "ascensor", with the traditional.

The same idea of myth as expression of the essential remains in a very much later poem, **"Primavera diaria"** (*ElC* [*El Contemplado*] 614-615). Here light is said to create on the sea "su verdad de mitos", thus giving the illumination of true understanding to the onlooker. The association with light will also occur frequently in the mythological poems.

A third example of the term "mito" occurs in the long poem **"Cero"**, (*TMC* [*Todo más claro*] 767-782), written at most a year later than *El Contemplado.* Here the dome of a temple on which are depicted classical gods becomes a spiritual oasis in the modern world, providing artistic and emotional nourishment:

> suave concavidad, nido de dioses.
> Poseidón, Venus, Iris, sus siluetas
> en su seno se posan. A esta crátera
> ojos siempre sedientos, a abrevarse
> vienen de agua de mito, inagotable.

The continuing presence of a mythical tradition, passed on through art, gives modern man a sense of his own place in a tradition. He is made aware of his responsibility to generations past and to those as yet unborn. The destruction of this temple brings past, present and future to ruins because contemporary society abandons those values inherent in the great myths. Man no longer aspires to mythical greatness, but creates his own clay-footed, false gods. This is a central theme of Salinas' late poetry, and one to which much of this article is to be devoted.

Bearing in mind these general usages of the term "mito", let us move on to look at the ways in which mythical figures are used by Salinas. I propose to divide my discussion into two sections, corresponding to the two chief areas in which Salinas seeks to discover mythological significance: myth in the modern world and myth in the natural world.

MYTH IN THE MODERN WORLD

Paul Ginestier, in his book *The Poet and the Machine*, stresses the need for the modern poet to explore the mythical possibilities of the twentieth century and to establish a relationship with his times, be it of criticism or compliance:

> The poet [. . .] will not attain to the poetic myth if he has not "realised" his position [. . .] modern poetry, if it is to exist and flourish, must consider the mythological greatness of a new, exterior world, so rich in possibilities, so susceptible of an unfolding of extraordinary forces.[17]

Optimistically, Lilian Feder, in *Ancient Myth in Modern Poetry,* believes that the timeless qualities of myth are such that it will inevitably adapt itself to successive cultures:

> myth [. . .] survives because it functions in the present, revealing a remarkable capacity to evolve and adapt to the intellectual and aesthetic requirements of the twentieth century.[18]

Salinas' prose would indicate that he holds much the same opinion, but this is not always the case in the poetry. However, he most certainly would agree with Ginestier that the poet's prime task is to come to terms with his surroundings. In *Reality and the Poet in Spanish Literature,* Salinas expounds the belief that "the first thing that characterises a poet is his way of perceiving reality, in short, his attitude towards the world".[19] It is in the modern city and its inventions that the greatest challenge to the poet lies, for it is often there that the gulf between poetry and the external world seems greatest.

However, in Salinas' early poetry, particularly in *Seguro azar* and *Fábula y signo,* we find an easy relationship between the poet and his technological surroundings, a relationship often expressed in mythological terms and images. The tone of these poems is essentially playful, witty and humorous. Classical and modern images are juxtaposed gleefully, creating connections only possible in the verse. Ricardo Gullón has described this technique with reference to *Fábula y signo*:

> los objetos viven como partes de un mito forjado por el hombre, como elementos estimulantes de su imaginación, leña para su capacidad de encender fantásticas iluminaciones. La fábula y el signo existen en el poeta, y no tienen otra esencia que la obtenida a través de la poesía y en la poesía.[20]

The most outstanding example of this technique is perhaps **"Radiador y fogata"** (*FS* [*Fábula y signo*] 181). The visible flame of the "fogata" is contrasted with the invisible heat of the "radiador":

> Paralelos
> tubos son tu cuerpo. Nueva
> criatura, deliciosa
> hija del agua, sirena
> callada de los inviernos
> que va por los radiadores
> sin ruido, tan recatada
> que solo la están sintiendo
> con amores verticales,
> los donceles cristalinos,
> Mercurios, en los termómetros.

A "nueva criature" has indeed been created, for this modern siren lacks the essential feature of her classical antecedent: the voice. This lack is stressed: "callada", "sin ruido", "recatada". Yet this silence is as effective as the voice of the Greek siren, as it lures the unsuspecting cold of winter to its death. The inspiration of the metaphor is perhaps the connection of both siren and radiator with water. Emphasis of the water element in this way is also effective as it contrasts with the opposing element, fire, in the "fogata". The basis is essentially witty and intellectual, requiring the reader to fill in the gaps in what is said from his own knowledge.

The second mythological reference of the same poem, **"Mercurios"**, also relies on an intellectual basis—the play on words between Mercury, the messenger of the gods, and mercury, the liquid metal. Again, myth is associated with ascent, "con amores verticales", as Mercury is a traditional representation of the intellect, mediating between man's mind and divine wisdom.

The results of this juxtaposition of traditional and modern are described by Vicente Cabrera:

> se crea una tensión lingüística que sorprende. Se poetizan simultáneamente las imágenes por la pérdida de afectación de la tradicional (sirena) y por la ganancia poética y expresiva de la moderna (termómetro). Esta tensión lingüística produce a su vez otra: la tensión intelectual ye sensible en el lector.[21]

Another early poem, **"35 bujías"** (*SA* 136), uses a similar technique, also relying on the reader to bring to the poem a knowledge of classical literature. I quote the poem in full:

> Sí. Cuando quiera yo
> la soltaré. Está presa
> aquí arriba, invisible.
> Yo la veo en su claro
> castillo de cristal, y la vigilan
> —cien mil lanzas—los rayos
> —cien mil rayos—del sol. Pero de noche,
> cerradas las ventanas
> para que no la vean
> —guiñadoras espías—las estrellas,
> la soltaré. (Apretar un botón.)
> Caerá toda de arriba
> a besarme, a envolverme
> de bendición, de claro, de amor, pura.

En el cuarto ella y yo no más, amantes
eternos, ella mi iluminadora
musa dócil en contra
de secretos en masa de la noche
—afuera—
descifraremos formas leves, signos,
persequidos en mares de blancura
por mí, por ella, artificial princesa,
amada eléctrica.

The juxtaposition of the mythical, or traditional, "musa", and the modern, the light bulb, is again unexpected, yet is shown to be as apt as it is witty. This light bulb is not merely the physical source of the light by which Salinas writes, but is also the inspiration and the subject matter of the poem. To Salinas' mind, the wonder of electricity is as fitting a topic for poetry as is any classical theme. Borges uses the same image in "Al margen de la moderna lírica", referring to "esta única noche deslumbrada, cuyos dioses magníficos son los augustos reverberos de luces aúreas, semejantes a genios salomónicos, prisioneros en copas de cristal".

Salinas' poem goes beyond this metaphorical description to become a continuation of the classical appeal to, and acknowledgment of debt to, the Muse. Nor has this electric muse lost the beauty and mystery of her antecedents: she is a fairy-tale princess in a glass castle, generous, pure and loving. Yet she differs from her classical form, just as the "sirena callada" does. The muse is not entirely free, "está presa / aquí arriba", jealously guarded by the poet from rivals for her attentions, the "guiñadoras espías". She is set free only in seclusion and after dark, "de noche, / cerradas las ventanas / para que no la vean". In fact, she is poetic inspiration held in check by the poet, who exercises the ultimate control over whether to write or not. Salinas stresses his opinion that writing is a combination of both inspiration and personal effort, an idea with which he introduces his first book of poetry, ***Presagios***:

Forjé un eslabón un día,
otro día forjé otro
y otro.
De pronto se me juntaron
—era la cadena—todos.

(51)

The phrase "apretar un botón" is thus surely used tongue-in-cheek, for no poem is created instantaneously.[22]

Again, linguistic "tensión" is the result, as the muse is purely a product of the poet's imagination. The traditional relationship between poet and Muse has been turned on its head. She is indeed "artificial", in all the senses of the word.

These poems depict an easy, creative relationship with surrounding objects, even those apparently furthest from the traditional world of poetry. Myth is discovered wherever man chooses to look for it and is enriched by new associations and possibilities.

In later collections of poetry, however, problems appear. Salinas now finds himself in the United States, confronted with city life and modernity on a scale inconceivable in the Spain he has left behind. No space seems left for poetry, and thus for myth, in the city from whence "the nymphs are departed".[23] Salinas reacts to this in his poetry by using more mythological references than ever before, in his desire to reassert the values contained in cultural tradition. At times he succeeds, but often the attempt is frustrated.

To look first at the successes, we are returned to Salinas' description of the city as "un fabuloso despliegue de mitos realizados". In the same essay he cites the example of the humble cigarette lighter as an extension of myth, saying of it, "no podemos por menos de recorder a Prometeo y su exasperada lucha por la posesión del fuego". The same illustration is given poetic form in **"Los puentes"** (*LL* [***Largo lamento***] 463-468):

la breve máquina
de plata en que tramite
después de tantos siglos afanosos
su ambiciosa tarea Prometeo
a unos esbeltos dedos de mujer.

A mythical interpretation is still possible, but the dangers of it becoming incongruous are evident. As Marx says:

All mythology overcomes and dominates and shapes the forces of nature in the imagination and by the imagination; it therefore vanishes with the advent of real mastery over them.[24]

This reminds us perhaps of the *futurista, ultraísta* and *creacionista* rejection of myth at precisely the time at which man's mastery over the elements, over power and light, is becoming apparent.

However, Salinas still sees hope for mythology in fusion with modernity where human emotions are concerned. In the poem **"Error de cálculo"** (*TMC* 740-745) two lovers meet in a crowded cafe, in order to analyse, or "calculate", their love, in a place free of tradition: "exenta de romanzas, / de cisnes e ilusiones". Yet these very same elements force themselves back into the poet's mind: "sin querer me acuerdo / del lago y de los cisnes de que huimos". The turning point comes when a mythical, archetypal, interpretation reveals itself:

De una mesa de al lado se levanta
una pareja; son Venus y Apolo
con disfraz de Abelardo y Eloisa,

y para más disimular vestidos
al modo de París.

The modern lovers, like it or not, form a link in a chain of other couples, who have come down to use through tradition, literature and art. Our view of love is conditioned by our awareness of these past lovers:

Son precisamente los poetas del amor y los héroes del amor los que han contribuido a que el sentimiento amoroso, siempre existente, sea hoy mucho más rico en matices, en horizontes y en profundidades'.[25]

The discovery of this continuity, like the sight of the gods in "Cero", is at the same time comforting and awe-inspiring, almost fearful:

y este insólito
descubrimiento me hace
agachar la cabeza porque siento
que voy a darme con el techo antiguo:
con nuestros padres.[26]

Having gained this new perspective, the lovers leave the cafe, accepting their place in the tradition and, as a consequence, their own mortality. Realising that cold calculation is impossible and unprofitable, they embrace "lo incalculable",[27] physical love and its intensification of the awareness of mortality. Again this is expressed in terms of myth, as the lovers get into a taxi:

y pagando su óbolo a Caronte
entramos en la barca
que surca la laguna de la noche
sin prisa. Al otro lado
una alcoba, en la costa de la muerte,
nos abrirá el gran hueco
donde todos los cálculos se abisman.

So, myth can be a positive lesson, adding to a sense of continuity and giving a feeling of belonging in a society which appears to live increasingly in the present moment, an attitude taken to its logical limits in the destruction of "Cero".

All too often it is this negative aspect which comes to the surface, reversing the human values and aspirations implicit in myth. Materialistic concerns adopt and invert the mythical.

Money has become a god, with the power of life and death over its subjects:

Las bandadas diarias de las cifras,
cotizaciones de la bolsa, diosas,
dueñas de los destinos.

(*TMC* 736)

In "Hombre en la orilla" (*TMC* 681-693), the illusion of eternal life is guaranteed, again by money, by the Phoenix insurance company and its ironically named salesman, Robert Freeman. The immortal bird is but an image for the power of finance.[28]

The continuity of love revealed in "Error de cálculo" all too often becomes submerged by these materialistic concerns and the feelings of isolation to which they give rise. Alienation replaces fellow feeling and human contact. Artificial, stereotyped female beauty usurps the place of the eternal goddess of beauty:

—mitología en los escaparates
a cuyos pies las almas sin amante
rezan por un momento cuando pasan
y cosechan sus sueños de la noche—.

(*TMC* 736)

The disillusioned, saddened tone of these poems is often softened by notes of humour, irony and the occasional glimpse of hope. Yet it comes to the surface in the later, apocalyptic sections of "Hombre en la orilla"[29] and, more significantly from the point of view of myth, in "Nocturno de los avisos" (*TMC* 717-720).

In this poem, mythology is a central element of the communication of an artistic and social standpoint. The poet attempts to impose upon the city a mythological level of interpretation, of the kind found so creative in the early poetry. Yet the urban landscape resists the operation and the attempt results in incongruity and disillusionment. Crispin sees the technique of juxtaposition and confrontation as characteristic of *Todo más claro* as a whole:

La estructura de *Todo más claro* . . . se plantea mediante la contraposición de los verdaderos mitos (los que tuvieron vigencia en el pasado, incluyendo los mitos judeo-cristianos del paraíso perdido, de la resurrección y vida eterna) y los falsos mitos que han venido a sustituirlos en la cultura contemporánea.[30]

In "Nocturno de los avisos", a street (to which the poem is addressed), is compared to a river, moving relentlessly through a quasi-pastoral scene, undistracted by the human activity on its pavements:

Todos acatan, hasta el más rebelde,
tus riguroses normas paralelas:
aceras, el arroyo,
los rieles de tranvía,
tus orillas, altísimos ribazos
sembrados de ventanas, hierba espesa,
que a la noche rebrilla
con gotas del eléctrico rocío.

The comparison feels strained and the two elements pull apart, rather than fusing into a new, composite reality. This is perhaps because the terms of each metaphor are baldly stated and strongly divided by punctuation: "aceras, el arroyo" and "ventanas, hierba espesa".[31]

Despite this, the poet hopes to discover an objective in the street, clinging on to the traditional image of the river as the individual life leading to fusion with all others in the eternal life of the sea. Perhaps the street will lead to Arcadia, fulfilling the promise of the pastoral opening:

¿no sería la Arcadia, y dos amantes,
a la siesta tendidos en la grama,
antes de Cristo y de los rascacielos?

What does the street reply to this questioning, when at night electric lights provide it with a voice? The answer, contained in a cigarette advertisement, destroys the illusion with its brilliant, gaudy exaltation of nothingness, the reverse of true enlightenment:

"¡Lucky Strike, Lucky Strike!" ¡Qué refulgencia!
¿Y todo va a ser eso?
¿Un soplo entre los labios,
imitación sin canto de la música,
tránsito de humo a nada?[32]

Salinas' defence is to reject these empty values by assertion of the traditional values of myth and of poetry, putting forward an alternative vision, exalting the spiritual above and beyond the material. To do this he chooses a mythological figure which represents both the imagination and immortality: Pegasus. Once more, the city distorts the myth in another advertisement:

"White Horse. Caballo Blanco". ¿Whisky? No.
Sublimación, Pegaso.
Dócil sirviente antiguo de las musas,
ofreciendo su grupa de botella,
al que encuentre el estribo que le suba.
¿Cambiaré el humo aquel por tu poema?

In the emphatic "¿Whisky? No." the poet rejects both the prosaic interpretation of the symbol and the temptation to take refuge in alcohol. Reliance on either will lead to downfall as surely as did Bellerophon's attempted ascent to the skies on Pegasus. Instead, the true Pegasus, creator of Hippocrene, the spring of the Muses, and thus of poetic inspiration, is sought. But little remains of that Pegasus, subsumed into the generic "White Horse", the myth prostituted to the god of commercialism.

Doubt assails the poet now that the fount of poetry appears to have dried up in this flashing, glaring wilderness. He feels lost and overwhelmed, groping for guidance. Once again, he turns to myth for salvation:

y el aire se me vuelve laberinto,
sin más hilo posible que aquí abajo:
el hilo de un tranvía sin Ariadna.
¡Qué fácil, sí, perderse en una recta!

This is reminiscent of Jorge Guillén's appeal in a similar moment of doubt:

¿No habré de merecer, si aún vacilo,
la penumbra de un rayo o su vislumbre?
Ariadna, Ariadna, por favor, tu hilo.[33]

It reminds us too of W. H. Auden's lines, quoted by Lilian Feder, on that mecca of materialism, the casino:

But here no nymph comes naked to the youngest shepherd;
The fountain is deserted; the laurel will not grow;
The labyrinth is safe but endless, and broken
Is Ariadne's thread.[34]

Feder comments on this that "the failure of myth to ring true indicates a failure of imagination and a failure of love". These are the central failures in Salinas' vision of New York. The absence of Ariadne is the absence of any guiding principle, of any reason for the frantic human activity. She represents traditionally the soul, lost in the metropolis.

The city lights are not merely uninformative, but actively misleading, their "luz" becomes "oscuridad". This idea is expressed on a mythical level in these terms:

Lo malo son las luces, las hechizas
luces, las ignorantes pitonisas
que responden con voces oscuras
a las oscuras voces que pedían.

This is a reference to the Delphic oracle. Pythia, the voice of truth and prophecy (albeit often in an ambiguous manner), becomes the voice of darkness. She is the priestess of Apollo, the god of light, truth, eloquence and poetry. All of these attributes have now been stripped away.

Reaching the end of the street, the poet looks back at the final advertisement, for toothpaste this time:

El dentífrico salva:
meditación, mañana tras mañana,
al verse en el espejo el esqueleto;
cuidarlo bien. Los huesos nunca engañan,
y ellos han de heredar lo que dejemos.
Ellos, puro resumen de Afrodita
poso final del sueño.

This "memento mori" and its stark vision of death contrast sharply with the desired ending to the street, the peaceful sleep of the lovers in Arcadia.

The poet now abandons his journey and its unfruitful hopes to await the time when the artificial lights go out and he is left with the stars, the "publicidad de dios", which do provide for the needs of the soul, "con ángeles sirviendo / al alma, que los pague sin moneda". Often Salinas uses biblical myth in conjunction with the classical. He appears to value both equally as metaphors for spiritual values. As Juan Ramón Jiménez says, "no hay que olvidar que teolojía es mitolojía y mitolojía es teolojía".[35] Here Salinas associates a Christian heaven with the stars and the myths they represent. Two of the myths central to **"Nocturno de los avisos"**, Pegasus and Ariadne, are figures who become constellations in their respective myths, attaining immortality in ascent once more.[36] The sky seems to be the only place where myth can still subsist.

Thus criticism of the inverted values of modern urban life is made all the sharper by the series of attempts to integrate myth into the world. The lack of continuity, of a sense of purpose, is revealed in the failure to incorporate the past and to permit a poetic, spiritual interpretation of life. The poet is left feeling alienated, rejected:

> The spiritual problems of the poet in contemporary society arise in part out of the lack of myths which can be felt warmly, envisaged in concrete and contemporary imagery, and shared with a wide body of responsive readers.[37]

Myth will always return, but is forced to do so in a form which becomes a travesty of what it should be. Salinas views this as the natural consequence of previous decades' attempts to remove it altogether:

> el mito se venga, burlonamente, y los hijos y nietos de esos hombres que rechazan a Hércules, a Venus . . . se sumen diariamente en las columnas de muñequitos o *comics,* de los diarios donde Popeye, el Superhombre o Blondie, usurpan bochornosamente el oficio augusto del mito, ofreciendo a la necesidad de imaginar del hombre la papilla más baja, la bazofia de más vergonzosa calidad, que jamás se le ha tendido.[38]

Myth represents the need to imagine, to escape, like Darío, from personal limitation. A society which attempts to stifle such a natural impulse will inevitably come to grief, as **"Cero"** and Salinas' novel, or "fabulación", *La bomba increíble,* show.[39]

There is a central lack, or absence in man's spiritual life, a gap which the poet has always tried to fill with myth. In 1948, around the period at which Salinas is writing these poems, W. H. Auden writes of the need for myth in

> a society in which men are no longer supported by tradition without being aware of it, and in which, therefore, every individual who wishes to bring order and coherence into the stream of sensations, emotions, and ideas entering his consciousness, from without and within, is forced to do deliberately for himself what in previous ages has been done for him by family, custom, church, and state, namely the choice of the principles and presuppositions in terms of which he can make sense of his experience.[40]

Auden's stress on myth as a part of a wider tradition, and on the importance of this tradition as a spiritual and emotional life-line, is in tune with Salinas' views on tradition, so amply expressed in his prose work, *Jorge Manrique o tradición y originalidad,* and summed up in the belief that "en historia espiritual la tradición es la habitación natural del poeta".[41]

Salinas' reaction to the failure of a traditional, mythological interpretation of the city is to seek an alternative, and it is in this late period that we find him turning back to nature as a refuge.

MYTH IN THE NATURAL WORLD

The collection *Confianza* sees a return to the theme of nature, to a world in which myth survives intact.

One entire poem, **"Las ninfas"** (*C* [*Confianza*] 806-808), is, as its title suggests, devoted to a mythological figure. The pastoral elements distorted in **"Nocturno de los avisos"** reappear, alongside Salinas' constant themes of the mirror image as revelatory, of the desire for the eternal in the present and of the transcendence of the purely physical. We are truly in the realms of Góngora, Garcilaso and of Mallarmé's "Ces nymphes, je les veux perpétuer".[42]

Salinas' nymph appears in harmony with her surroundings, not fighting against them for her very continued existence:

> De pronto surge, clara y sin origen,
> ninfa, sorpresa.
>
> Su aparición ningún encanto rompe,
> todos se aumentan.

All of nature pays homage to this divine creature, and "todo es reverencia". The world appears to hold its breath as she stands poised on the river bank, in perfect communion with the water below: "Nada le da al arroyo todavía / y ya se besan". Is this reflection not the supreme beauty, asks the poet, for "¡Es más que ella!"? The dilemma "entre su más y entre su menos" can only be resolved by divine intervention, by a mythical solution:

> Un celeste misterio cae, de pronto
> y se la lleva
>
> por designio de dioses, en la nube,
> al cielo, entera.

As so often, she is then immortalised as a constellation, "dibujada / virgen de estrellas". Nature is shown to have remained open to the revelation of a mythological, poetic dimension.

A similarly fruitful revelation of myth in nature runs through the collection *El Contemplado.* The sea immediately suggests mythical themes to Salinas, just as it did to Darío:

> esta superficia marina, inmediata provocadora para la imaginación de mitos gloriosos, de fábulas en las que todo se envuelve en belleza.
>
> (*PRD* 171)

Several critics have commented on this aspect of *El Contemplado.* Elsa Dehennin, for example, has this to say:

Ce n'est pas un pur hasard que Salinas se soit inspiré de la mythologie . . . l'appareil métaphorique a une valeur fonctionelle: il traduit un mouvement spiritualisé et affectif de la mer et l'enveloppe, en même temps, d'un halo fabuleux . . . Les concepts mythologiques créent, en outre, un climat de religiosité fabuleuse.[43]

María Teresa Babín stresses the mixture of classical and Golden Age echoes as myth is incorporated

con asombro, sensual complacencia, y las esquirlas de una literatura de fuentes grecoromanas a través del espejo gongorino en que la generación de Salinas adquirió el artificio de alusiones y elusiones emanantes de "el suelo undoso de las mitologías".[44]

Bearing in mind what we have found in *Todo más claro*, it is not unexpected that Salinas values in the sea the absence of human concerns which exclude the mythical from the city:

Vuelve el mar a su tiempo el inocente,
    ignorante de quillas,

sin carga de mortales.

(632)[45]

Instead, "un gran hervir de cuerpos en proyecto / alumbra la marina". Nymphs, goddesses, sea creatures all appear "por numen secreto convocadas".

The revelation of these is equated with that of truth and with genuine illumination: "y ella le cubre su verdad de mitos: / la luz, eterna magia". Again, there is an evident contrast with **"Nocturno de los avisos"** and the false lights of the city. The constant motion of the sea, which creates these effects of light, and thus precipitates the vision of myth, is equated also with poetic creation. The sea, like the poet, is forced into creative movement by "el más que en el alma tienes" (636). This motion culminates in the revelation of the present moment, "el presente, que tanto se ha negado, / hoy, aquí, ya, se entrega" (627), containing within it a consciousness of the continuity of the past and of one's personal duty to continue the chain of existence into the future: "soy un momento / de esa larga mirada que te ojea, / desde ayer, desde hoy, desde mañana" (649). This is the same awareness as that, gained through mythology, of the lovers in **"Error de cálculo"**. In *El Contemplado* the realisation of this continuity is again expressed in terms of mythology, in the poem **"Renacimiento de Venus"** (627-628). The soul, no longer lost in its labyrinth, rises to the surface, depicted as Venus rising from the sea-foam:

Radiante mediodía. En él, el alma
    se reconoce: esencia.

Segunda, y la mejor, surge del mar
    la Venus verdadera.[46]

Again Salinas has made over a myth in keeping with his own preoccupations, as is noted by Matos Paoli in an article on the collection:

el poeta [. . .] crea otro mito puertorriqueño utilizando para ello los viejos ingredientes de la mitología griega. Salinas no hace referencia a una Venus carnal, diosa del amor erótico, sino a un prístino ser venusiano, toda desnudez esencial, que gravita en alas sobre las ondas, hija aerea de la poesía y del ensueño.[47]

Again, myth is linked to poetry and a poetic vision, transcending individual limitations.

Perhaps the most "mythological" poem of *El Contemplado* is **"Las ínsulas extrañas"** (624-626), the title taken of course from San Juan de la Cruz's *Cántico espiritual*.[48] The islands, "¡felices inmortales!", are equated, in their descent from the high rocks down to their continued presence beneath the sea, with the life cycle of nymphs from birth ("altas cunas, los riscos"), through adolescence ("breve sueño feliz") and into eternal life in the "Arcadia que abajo se eterniza". Mythical figures which we have encountered before reappear. The nymphs/islands are "Venus verdes, tendiéndose en la umbría". They again discover themselves in reflections in water: "espejo, en él se encuentran, sorprendidas". Again they hesitate on the borders between physical and immortal life: "se detienen las islas, asombradas, / al llegar a los bordes de su vida". The discovery of the sea is equated with the realisation of the possibility of continuing life: "empieza aquí / un mundo sin otoño y sin ceniza". The physical decay of death visualised in **"Nocturno de los avisos"** has no place here, nor has the feeling of isolation for now "no hay soledad, es todo compañía". The siren reappears, equated with the angel, in another fusion of the biblical and the mythical, and now found in her true element, the sea. Yet the death to which this siren lures her prey is not destruction but immortality: "Si la tierra se acaba algo se empieza; / las olas que sin pausa se lo afirman, / angélicas sirenas, les convencen". The poem ends on a triumphant note, as the Arcadia sought in **"Nocturno de los avisos"** is now attained:

Y ese verdor que el agua transparenta
es de Arcadia que abajo se eterniza:
en los hondos del mar viven, salvadas,
almas verdes, las almas de las islas.

The poem, as much in its language as in its themes, has much in common with Góngora's transformation of an everyday scene into something magical by means of myth and metaphor.[49] In *Reality and the Poet in Spanish Literature* Salinas analyses a passage of the *Soledad Primera* ("De Alcides le llevó luego a las plantas"), seeing as Góngora's main achievement the enrichment and adaptation of the myth of Phaeton's sisters as poplar trees, reflected in water and in the light of fireworks:

Góngora makes over the myth, changes the plants into maidens and presents them as bending over the water, combing their hair in the mysterios light of the fireworks. Out of the few trees he draws a vision of incomparable charm, transforming them into a group of girls in graceful occupation and posture. And from the word poplars we get to mythology, Phaeton, shining mirrors, the reflection of coloured lights in running water.

(p. 143)

This is not unlike Salinas' own picture of the islands as nymphs braiding their hair over the running stream in **"Las ínsulas extrañas"**.

Myth is revealed then, particularly in **El Contemplado,** to be both artistically satisfying and, at the same time, a significant part of the expression of a view of the world. Whilst in some of his prose works, Salinas appears to have hope for the future of contemporary society and its creative potential, this attitude is qualified in the poetry by the stress placed on the necessity to regain contact with the past, with the natural world and with one's own imaginative and creative faculties.

In conclusion, mythology is a stylistic constant in Salinas' poetry. It provides another strand of evidence of his conscious awareness of the importance of tradition, literary and spiritual, in the present day. His usage of it develops and changes with the poetry, maturing out of its essentially witty and humorous role in the early poetry into a vehicle for the expression of central concerns, poetic, personal, and social in the late collections. It comes to give poetic expression to a whole attitude of mind, a whole stance before external reality. Through the mythological, Salinas asserts the value of the human above the technological and the materialistic.

Notes

1. *"Atalanta di Pedro Salinas. L'evasione ne mito"*, *Linguistica e letteratura* 1 (1976), 331-352.

2. "Metáfora y mito en la generación de 1927: el caso de Pedro Salinas", *Journal of Spanish Studies. Twentieth Century* 6 (1978), 107-122.

3. Buenos Aires, 1948. This work is henceforth abbreviated as *PRD*.

4. "Al margen de la moderna lírica", *Grecia* 30 (1920), 15, quoted in Anthony Leo Geist, *La poética de la generación de 27 y las revistas literarias: de la vanguardia al compromiso* (1918-1936) (Barcelona, 1980), p.41.

5. *Obras completas,* 2 vols (Santiago, 1976), II, 744.

6. *Poesía de creación* (Barcelona, 1974), p.81.

7. "La nueva lírica", *Cosmopolis* 1, no.5 (1919), 72-80.

8. It is also this aspect of the generation's writings that is most strongly criticised by Ortega y Gasset and Antonio Machado, amongst others.

9. Of "Preciosa y el aire" he says in a 1926 letter to Jorge Guillén: "es un romance gitano, que es un *mito* inventado por mí. En esta parte del romancero procuro armonizar lo *mitológico gitano* con lo puramente vulgar de los días presentes, y el resultado es extraño, pero creo que de belleza nueva". *Obras completas,* 2 vols (Madrid, 1980), I, 1259.

10. Second edition (Madrid, 1979), p.17. For a full analysis of this theme, see Jose Luis Cano, "La poesía de Luis Cernuda: en busca de un paraíso", in *La poesía de la generación del 27* (Madrid, 1973), pp.189-202.

11. J. Cabre i Oliva, "Parlant amb Pedro Salinas", *Mirador,* 21 diciembre de 1933, p.10.

12. "El poeta y las fases de la realidad", *Insula* 46 (1959), 1, 3, 11 (p.3).

13. All references are to Pedro Salinas, *Poesías completas* (Barcelona, 1975). I give the page reference from this edition, preceded by the name of the collection, abbreviated as follows: *P, Presagios; SA, Seguro azar; FS, Fábula y signo; V, La voz a ti debida*; RA, *Razón de amor; LL, Largo lamento; ElC, El Contemplado; TMC, Todo más claro*; C, Confianza.

14. The term "fábula" is also of significance in Salinas's work, and is at times equated with "mito". Here, the "fábula" is the result of the "mythologising" process, the "mito".

15. "La sorpresa deriva de questa connotazione di animalità femminile che il mito pare non giustificare nella sua tradizione letteraria." Guazzelli, p.340.

16. Rupert C. Allen also discusses this poem, in Chapter Six of his book *Symbolic Experience: A Study of Poems by Pedro Salinas* (Alabama, 1982).

17. Chapel Hill, 1961, p.18.

18. Princeton, 1971, pp.3-4.

19. Baltimore, 1966, p.4.

20. "La poesía de Pedro Salinas", in *Pedro Salinas,* edited by Andrew P. Debicki, El escritor y la crítica (Madrid, 1976), pp.85-98 (pp.85-86).

21. *Tres poetas a la luz de la metáfora* (Madrid, 1975), p.104.

22. For a detailed analysis of the theme of inspiration in the generation of 1927, see Biruté Ciplijauskaite, *El poeta y la poesía* (Madrid, 1966), Chapter 4.

23. This quotation from T. S. Eliot's *The Wasteland* is used so aptly in reference to "Nocturno de los avisos" by Manuel Durán in his "Pedro Salinas y su 'Nocturno de los avisos'", in Debicki's *Pedro Salinas*, p.165. Durán, however, does not make any other comments on the use of mythology in the poem.

24. Karl Marx, *Grundrisse,* quoted in Peter France, "Myth and Modernity: Racine's *Phèdre*", in *Myth and Legend in French Literature,* edited by Keith Aspley, David Bellos and Peter Sharratt (London, 1982), pp.227-242 (p.227).

25. "El poeta y las fases de la realidad", p.1.

26. There is of course also a reference to the biblical myth of the Garden of Eden here. Adam and Eve, too, form a link in the chain.

27. Salinas' negative view of the city in "Civitas Dei" (*ElC* 640-646) is expressed in similar terms: "Lo exacto triunfa de lo incalculable las palabras vencidas".

28. Salinas appears to have nurtured a dislike of the insurance trade. See his play *Sobre seguro* on the subject.

29. Crispin discusses the concluding sections of this poem as a parody of the Last Judgment (p.112).

30. P.111.

31. This contrasts with the use of the same metaphor in "Hombre en la orilla", where the juxtaposition is more successful.

32. The last line is an allusion to the closing line of Góngora's sonnet "Mientras por competir con tu cabello": "en tierra, en humo, en polvo, en sombra, en nada".

33. *Cántico* (Barcelona, 1974), p.265.

34. Feder, p.146.

35. Ricardo Gullón, *Conversaciones con Juan Ramón Jiménez* (Madrid, 1958), p.83.

36. In *PRD,* Salinas refers to Venus in her heavenly form thus: "Venus, diosa patrona del amor, emblema del placer carnal, purifica su ser, cuando se le mira en lo alto del cielo, vuelta estrella" (p.56).

37. *Princeton Encyclopedia of Poetry and Poetics,* edited by A. Preminger (Princeton, 1965), p.540.

38. *PRD,* p.86.

39. *Narrative completa* (Barcelona, 1976), pp.263-442.

40. Quoted by Feder, pp.26-27.

41. Buenos Aires, 1962, p.115.

42. Stéphane Mallarmé, *Poésies* (Paris, 1945), p.58. Jorge Guillén also sees the river-bank as a fitting place for the revelation of myth: "río con riberas / de historias y mitos", *Cántico,* p.28.

43. *Passion d'absolu et tension expressive dans l'oeuvre poétique de Pedro Salinas* (Ghent, 1957), p.89.

44. "Sentido y estructura de *El Contemplado*", *Sin nombre* 9 (1978), pp.44-59 (p.46).

45. This is another echo of Golden Age poetry and of the topos of criticism of sea travel for greed.

46. The theme of Venus is naturally of prime importance in Salinas' depiction of the *Amada. El Contemplado* is in many ways a continuation and development of the "tú-yo" relationship of the earlier love poetry. Many of the images, including that of Venus as desired essence, are repeated. In *PRD,* Salinas describes Venus thus: "es el amor, hecho idea, por ser mitología, y a la vez hecho cuerpo" (p.92).

47. Francisco Matos Paoli, "Visión de nuestro mar en Pedro Salinas", *Asomante,* 2 (1946), pp.75-80 (p.78)

48. "Mi Amado, las montañas, / los valles solitarios nemorosos, / las ínsulas extrañas, / los ríos sonorosos, / el silbo de los aires amorosos."

49. Salinas' earlier transformation of objects (the radiator and light bulb) through myth and metaphor is also similar to Góngora's transmutation of humble objects into objects of great beauty and grandeur.

Andrew P. Debicki (essay date March 1985)

SOURCE: Debicki, Andrew P. "The Play of Difference in the Early Poetry of Pedro Salinas." *MLN* 100, no. 2 (March 1985): 265-80.

[*In the following essay, Debicki argues that critics of Salinas's early poetry err by attempting to resolve its various meanings into a single perspective. Instead, the critic asserts, Salinas's early poems juxtapose "different and often opposing attitudes to reality," and as such they are best approached as texts "which invite us to explore various dimensions of the subjects on which they center."*]

The first three books of verse of Pedro Salinas have been puzzling critics for many years. There is general agreement that all of them involve a questioning of external reality, a series of attempts to examine poetically the appearance of things and to seek behind it some essential values. But critics have offered radically different interpretations of this search. Angel del Río described Salinas' first book, *Presagios,* as a record of the poet's failure to capture reality's elusive essence in words; he then characterized Salinas' next volume, *Seguro azar,* as an affirmation of the exactness of the modern world. Marta Morello Frosch has seen in Salinas' portrayal of both nature and modern artifacts a lack of faith in reality; Olga Costa Viva, on the other hand, has found in it an exaltation of the real. Julian Palley has viewed Salinas' early poetry as a desperate quest to create meaning in an enigmatic universe.[1]

Attempting to transcend these conflicting views, David Stixrude has suggested that this poetry is a tensive effort to find some "solution to these oscillations between reality's allure and its deceptiveness."[2] For Stixrude, Salinas explores the paradoxical nature of external reality, balancing a fascination with its geometries against an insatisfaction with the world, based on a longing for more significant values than it can offer. But even though Stixrude avoids the danger of reducing Salinas' poetry to a simple view, his formulation doesn't account for the multiplicity of perspectives in that poetry. Like previous commentarists, Stixrude accepts a premise underlying traditional analytic criticism: that a literary work embodies and conveys a coherent set of meanings, which the critic uncovers by examining it. He therefore continues to seek a single and consistent (even if complex) outlook behind all this poetry, and to assume that every reader should obtain the same vision from Salinas' verse.

The analytic premise which has been leading critics to resolve into some single perspective Salinas' early verse is in my opinion inappropriate and distracting. If we leave it aside, we can see in this verse a fascinating play between different and often opposing attitudes to reality, the resolution of which is left to the reader. The "oscillations" which Stixrude observes confront us with contradictory views; the impact of the poems resides in these confrontations, which embody the enigmatic richness of the realities portrayed and the diverse ways in which we can view them. Salinas' poems are thus not packaged compendia of resolved meanings, but rather *texts* composed of many systems of signs, which invite us to explore various dimensions of the subjects on which they center.[3]

This becomes apparent as we examine several poems of *Presagios.* The whole book focuses on daily scenes and natural vignettes in order to explore multiple aspects of reality; its speaker juggles several perspectives and involves the reader in the same process he himself undertakes, as is evident in poem 16 (untitled, like the other works in the book):

Arena: hoy dormida en la playa
y mañana cobijada
en los senos del mar:
hoy del sol y mañana del agua.
A la mano que te oprime
le cedes blanda
y te vas con el primer viento
galán que pasa.
Arena pura y casquivana,
novia versátil y clara, te quise por mía
y te estreché contra el pecho y el alma.
Pero con olas y brisas y soles te fuiste
y me quedé sin amada,
con la frente dada al viento que me la robaba,
y la vista al mar lejano donde ella tenía
verdes amores en verde posada.[4]

Our attention is immediately called to the unusual personification of the sand, and to the metaphorical relationship between sand and beloved that it engenders. In the first part of the poem, the physical elusiveness of sand (which slips through one's hand, flies with the wind, moves from shore to sea) evokes a coquettish woman, running off with a personified wind, moving from one lover to another. In a traditional analysis of this poem, we would focus on this personification/metaphor, noting that it takes us beyond the poem's literal level and leads us to a wider vision. We would then see that the true subject of the poem is not sand, nor a flirt who tricks a man. The comparison between sand and woman, however, highlights the quality of elusiveness that they share, as well as the effect that this elusiveness has on the speaker; the poem uses its main image to dramatize the theme of fleetingness. Such a reading does go beyond the poem's literal level, making it a good example of the quest for essentials which critics have seen in *Presagios*; it underlies both my 1968 analysis of this work and Stixrude's more recent discussion of it as a portrayal of both change and durability.[5]

Such a reading, however, does not account for all aspects of the poem. To see this work as the serious embodiment of the theme of fleetingness we have to ignore the fanciful nature of the comparison sand/woman, the whimsical attitude to reality that it suggests, and the tone of excessively serious complaint by the speaker, which seems parodic—this man laments the loss of *sand* with the excess emotion of a Romantic lover! The last lines, with their evocation of the beloved/sand in an archetypal kingdom of the sea, ring hollow in this context. All these aspects make the speaker unreliable: he tries too hard to equate loss of sand and loss of love, he paints himself as too much of a Romantic, and he loses our assent when we note that his cliché declarations are not fitting to a serious love lament. Once we become aware of the speaker's limitations, our view of the poem starts to change, and we come to see its "meaning" as centered not on the theme of fleetingness as such but on the portrayal of the speaker's exaggerated efforts to define it through his metaphor.

This awareness of the speaker's unreliability undercuts the view of the poem as a serious embodiment of the theme of evanescence, making it something of a playful parody. One can account for this conflict between readings, to some extent, by speaking of the poem's use of irony, and by stressing the tension engendered between the philosophic theme on the one hand and the speaker's excess concern with a beloved (which blinds him to the larger issue) on the other. But this still leaves the traditional analytic critic in an uncomfortable position, because this tension makes it impossible to define the dominant vision of the poem. (Stixrude, for example, on seeing the "conflicting values" placed on "exactly the same perception of reality" here, is forced to go to the book as a whole for some resolution.)[6] A critic who places more emphasis on the speaker's tone would ascribe to the text a playful (or perhaps negative) vision, where one who focuses on the image would see it positively. The tension we have seen in **"Arena . . ."** explains very well why *Presagios* would engender confusion and the divergent critical interpretations which I noted at the outset of this study.

If we set aside a need to find a view which would resolve the tensions I have described, however, these divergences cease to be so problematic. The conflict in perspectives that the poem contains then becomes a creative way of immersing the reader in its subject. Portraying and calling into question the evocation of fleetingness on the one hand, and the speaker's excess romanticism on the other, **"Arena . . ."** makes us see the incompleteness of both visions, and sets up a gap that we as readers must fill. The image of sand as woman and the portrayal of the speaker operate, in this context, as "seams" in the text, as areas of indeterminacy that open the way to further readings.[7] They invite us to see the speaker as a sentimental poet, attempting unsuccessfully to define evanescence via a novel metaphor but getting trapped in the theme of lost love that he himself engendered, and taking it too seriously. This in turn makes us step back and consider the inadequacy of language, of the ways in which metaphorical expression and the clichés of a love lament undercut each other. The poem thus becomes self-referential, a commentary on its own process of expressing an experience.

Such considerations may seem irrelevant to a traditional analytic critic, concerned with defining a central theme of a poem. They would, however, be very much in keeping with the perspective of a poststructuralist or deconstructive critic, who would accept the fact that while a poem constantly strives to encompass its subject, it also is governed by the inadequacy of language to seize meanings totally, and leaves within itself gaps which render it open to further readings and extensions. And once we take into account such a deconstructive perspective, we will find in the poem other details that in-

vite us to extend our reading.[8] The speaker's statement that he held "her" against his "chest and his soul" underlines the conflict within his attitude: it juggles a literal perspective (he rubs sand against himself) and a metaphorical one (he reaches for his beloved), but cannot combine them satisfactorily, since "soul" ("alma") is ludicrously inappropriate in reference to the former. The reader, noting this and other inappropriate elements, comes to feel the inadequacy of the language used, the incompleteness of any one reading, and the creative lack of closure in the poem. By not being subject to closure, in fact, the text becomes all the more exciting: its way of engendering questions about the possibilities and limitations of metaphor, language, and perspective seems more valuable than any static portrayal of "fleetingness."

This view of **"Arena . . ."** makes the poem fit Salinas' own statements on his art; in an oft-quoted passage, he has stressed the poet's role as follows: "Reality must be revised, confirmed, approved by the poet. And he confirms or re-creates it by means of a word, by merely putting it to words."[9] This quote has been used by critics to stress Salinas' search for a deeper vision of things; to my mind, however, it principally highlights his belief in the importance of the poetic process, of the fact that poet and poem undertake an ongoing struggle with the enigmas which surround us. It points ahead, to some degree, to J. Hillis Miller's notion that poetry, in trying to name things, is constantly aware of the impossibility of defining them fully, and must reveal a consciousness of both the nature and the limitations of its quest.[10] **"Arena . . ."** exemplifies very well this dimension of poetic art, anticipating more recent attitudes to the subject.

This reading of **"Arena . . ."** suggests a reappraisal of the ways in which *Presagios* should be approached. Rather than attempting to define the book's dominant attitude to reality, we can notice how throughout it diverse outlooks are played off against each other. As we do so, we also see the book's references to verbal expression as a means of juggling those outlooks. The first five poems of the book, as John Crispin has noted, form a "kind of initial aesthetic creed" in which Salinas explores the poet's inquiry into reality and its enigmatic responses.[11] In poem 20 a personified landscape speaks to the poet in sweet words, evoking a mixture of surprise and interest; the reader becomes witness to an interplay between two creators of words, which ends with the speaker/poet serving as audience to the nature/poet:

> Estos dulces vocablos con que me estás hablando
> no los entiendo, paisaje,
> no son los míos.
> Te diriges a mí con arboledas
> suavísimas, con una ría mansa y clara
> y con trinos de ave.
> Yo aprendí otra cosa: la encina dura y seca

. . . .
Y ansioso y torpe, a tu vera me quedo
esperando que tú me enseñes el lenguaje
que no es mío, con unas incógnitas palabras
sin sentido.
Y que me lleves a la claridad de lo incognoscible,
paisaje dulce, por vocablos desconocidos.

                                        (p.74)

Although the speaker/poet awaits a deeper perception which nature may offer him, the contrast between his language and that of the landscape makes us feel, above all, his inability to arrive at a definitive vision. The poet's task is seen as an ongoing search amidst diverse perspectives, with only a distant hope that some day Reality will reveal its essence. The portrayal of speaker and landscape in a conversation in which each uses a different language highlights for us the play of different perspectives that an examination of reality entails, and stresses the role of verbal naming (and hence of poetry) in this ongoing examination.

Other poems in the book also make explicit reference to verbal naming as a way of examining reality. In poem 44, a dying woman's last word, "agua," makes a vision of water irrupt upon the scene; in poem 18, the word that two lovers speak to each other determines their fate. Language, quite clearly, is a means of examining as well as creating reality.[12] If the world that surrounds us is enigmatic and subject to diverse interpretations, language and poetry configure these interpretations and allow both the poet and the reader to take part in them. Even the literary reminiscences of Góngora, Fray Luis, Bécquer, and Juan Ramón Jiménez which Crispin has observed in *Presagios* confirm the impression that in this book Salinas involves us in a constant play of perspectives on reality and a vision of poetry's role in engendering this play within us.[13]

A first reading of *Seguro azar* and *Fábula y signo* reveals different tones and different subjects from the ones that dominate *Presagios.* Salinas' second and third book are filled with playful evocations of modern objects, and seem to take delight in the novelty and geometric precision of cars, streetcar rails, lightbulbs, movies. Yet this delight, as Stixrude has noted, is often tinged with irony; rather than simply affirm the modern world, Salinas examines it with a variety of tones and perspectives.[14] Throughout both books we feel the presence of the poetic eye, seeking clues in reality, formulating interpretations, suggesting their limits. It seems significant that *Seguro azar* begins with a poem titled **"Cuartilla,"** which portrays an effort to put into words impressions produced by reality. Stixrude, commenting on this poem, points out very well that it reveals the ambiguities of the fabulist's struggle.[15] This struggle ends, as we shall see, not in the collapse of all reality in a neatly-expressed statement, but rather in a continuing

confrontation between the mysteries of reality and the words which try to embody them in the poem. In *Fábula y signo* increasing stress is placed on the examination and transformation of reality by the poetic word. Both books, then, are more related to *Presagios* than they seem to be; they continue and extend the multifaceted vision and the play of differences that we have seen in the earlier volume, relate it to the heterogeneity of the modern mechanical world, and focus even more explicitly on the act of poetic naming as a way of confronting and examining a multivalent reality.

In **"35 bujías,"** from *Seguro azar,* the description of a lightbulb as princess leads to a poetic interplay between different interpretations of reality:

Sí. Cuando quiera yo
la soltaré. Está presa
aquí arriba, invisible.
Yo la veo en su claro
castillo de cristal, y la vigilan
—cien mil lanzas—los rayos
—cien mil rayos—del sol. Pero de noche,
cerradas las ventanas
para que no la vean
—guiñadoras espías—las estrellas,
la soltaré. (Apretar un botón.)

Caerá toda de arriba
a besarme, a enolverme
de bendición, de claro, de amor, pura.
En el cuarto ella y yo no más, amantes
eternos, ella mi iluminadora
musa dócil en contra
de secretos en masa de la noche
—afuera—
desciframos formas leves, signos,
perseguidos en mares de blancura
por mí, por ella, artificial princesa,
amada eléctrica.

                                        (p. 136)

Like **"Arena . . . ,"** this poem is based on an unusual metaphor. The correspondence created between lightbulb and princess contradicts our usual perspective, in which modern artifacts belong to a different realm than that of romance and fairy-tales. The poem insistently underlines the connection between these two disparate realms, supporting it with specific bridges between modern life and romance: the light's presence within the bulb's glass is a princess's imprisonment in a castle, the flow of light is a kiss, closed windows are protection from the enemy. It uses words which acquire different meanings depending on the plane to which they refer: "envolverme" and "iluminadora" can be fitted either into the literal realm of the lightbulb or the figurative one of the princess. The speaker's insistence on all these connections, and the contrast between the stock fairy-tale elements of one plane and the literal reality of the other, make us notice even more the far-fetched nature of the metaphor.

A traditional (or "New Critical") analysis of this poem would focus on this metaphor as a means of constructing a new and coherent vision of reality. It would adopt the common view of metaphor as a juxtaposition of two planes for the purpose of producing a new perspective, which draws on both similarities and differences between them for its meaning.[16] By juxtaposing lightbulb and princess, this poem makes us aware that modern life and chivalric romance are not totally separate from each other, and that in the former we can find elements of the latter. Transcending its two separate planes, the poem conveys the possibility of finding beauty and romance amidst our modern world. This would, for the traditional critic, become the poem's overall vision.

Such an interpretation, however, seems very incomplete. It does not take into account, for one, the humorous effect produced by so unusual a comparison. Stixrude, noting this humor, interprets the poem's ending as overtly ironic, and suggests a different interpretation, in which the main metaphor is deliberately incongruous and the poem's final meaning is an absurd vision of the mechanical world.[17] Yet this resolution seems equally unsatisfactory in its one-sidedness, since it plays down the poem's obvious delight in the correspondence created. To my mind, the poem refuses to take a single attitude to its subject; critics who try to establish such an attitude within it can only construct incomplete formulations which contradict each other.

If we resist the temptation to find a single attitude in **"35 bujías"** we can take a different approach, and bring to mind Paul de Man's definition of metaphor as a way of suspending ordinary meaning and "freez[ing] hypothesis, or fiction, into fact."[18] For de Man, metaphor does not offer a new resolution of its planes, but rather breaks the rules of reality and deliberately asserts what would normally be an "error" in order to engender perspective play, to open up an ongoing process of reading and re-reading. Following this view, we would avoid any effort to pin down a final vision in "35 bujías," and would instead explore all of the text's ramifications. By making the light like a princess, the speaker is deliberately asserting something untrue outside the poem's context. He is also revealing a superior attitude to both woman and light: both respond to his arbitrary control, both are at once idealized and made submissive and lacking in initiative. The reader, however, is invited to dissent: noting the difference between woman and light and the far-fetched nature of the metaphor, he/she stands back skeptically from the speaker's formulation.

Once we have questioned the poem's central figure and the speaker's perspective which has engendered it, we notice a whole series of specific conflicts present in the text. The speaker's fantasy at the end, in which he sees the beloved joining him in an active quest against darkness, undermines and is undermined by the compliant way in which she obeyed his command. The phrase "amada eléctrica" incorporates this conflict within the speaker's attitude. "Eléctrica" on the one hand suggests something vital, and on the other refers to the passivity of the light controlled by the speaker; "amada" both evokes the woman actively descending upon the speaker and conjures up the image of the compliant princess in the tower. Together with the companion phrase "princesa artificial," "amada eléctrica" reinforces the conflicts in the speaker's attitude and renders less integrated his vision.

The conflicts present within these phrases undercut not only the speaker but any consistent perspective of the light/princess. We have no textual clues which would help us resolve the speaker's contradictions, and cannot simply call them the errors of an unreliable narrator which we should correct. The lack of resolution with respect to the poem's main metaphor undercuts its ending, which asserts a triumphant battle against darkness on the part of speaker and light/princess. Given the poem's enigmas, any triumph seems hollow, although it may not be totally ironic. The use of the phrase "descifraremos formas leves, signos" supports this reading: it does suggest a serious striving for resolution on the one hand, but also underlines the enigmatic nature of the reality present and makes the speaker's quest a detective's futile hunting after clues on the other. And even this striving to decipher is set out as a future hypothesis and is located in "mares de blancura," which suggest further enigmas. Once we perceive the conflicts in the speaker's attitude to his main image, everything begins to unravel, creating a play of differences which put into question what to the traditional analytic critic seemed an assertion of the presence of romance in a modern setting.[19]

To my mind, this reading of the poem makes it far more compelling. Instead of giving us a simple example of romance in a modern setting, it creates a confrontation between different realities and different perspectives, inviting us to consider how electric light both can and cannot be mythified, and how a poetic recreation of the modern both can and cannot elevate its value.

A confrontation between different perspectives of modern reality and a view of poetry's role within this confrontation are also evident in **"Underwood girls"** from *Fábula y signo.* Here typewriter keys are personified as sleeping nymphs whom the speaker invites to write something more creative than the dictated text that they usually produce:

> Quietas, dormidas están,
> las treinta, redondas, blancas.
> Entre todas
> sostienen el mundo.
> Míralas, aquí en su sueño,

como nubes,
redondas, blancas, y dentro
destinos de trueno y rayo,
destinos de lluvia lenta,
de nieve, de viento, signos.
Despiértalas,
con contactos saltarines
de dedos rápidos, leves,
como a músicas antiguas.
Ellas suenan otra musica:
fantasías de metal
valses duros, al dictado.

. . . .

Que se crean que es la carta,
la fórmula, como siempre.
Tu alócate
bien los dedos, y las
raptas y las lanzas,
a las treinta, eternas ninfas
contra el mundo vacío,
blanco en blanco.

. . . .

(p. 203)

The speaker adopts a creative perspective, and fancifully envisions the possibility of making the typewriter keys produce a work more significant than the dictated letters to which they are accustomed. His attitude evokes our initial assent: we sympathize both with the outlook that personifies machines and with the effort to use them for a higher purpose. The speaker's attitude is supported by a parallel between several lines in this poem and the ending of **"Cuartilla,"** the first work in *Seguro azar,* in which the writing of a poem which captured the values of nature was described as "pluma / contra lo blanco, en blanco, / inicial, tú, palabra" (p. 107). This supports the notion that the creative use of typewriter keys represents the poet's attempt to verbally capture reality.

But several aspects of the poem undercut this interpretation. The personification of the keys as nymphs who hold, dormant, the powers of nature seems so grandiloquent, ascribes such exaggerated possibilities to the machine that it is hard to take seriously. It makes the speaker's vision seem excessively idealistic, and invites us to take an ironic attitude to it. In addition, the speaker's use of the image of roundness to connect the keys with clouds and natural powers seems like a forced effort to tie together a trivial perfection and a grand one. (Stixrude has noted the frequent use of roundness as an image of worldly perfection in these books, and the ambiguous effects it engenders.)[20] These aspects of **"Underwood girls"** undercut to some extent the poem's overt vision. Without destroying it, they bring it into question, making us on the one hand admire the speaker's quest to find transcendence in the modern, and on the other view skeptically the possibility of his carrying it off.

Similar effects are produced by **"París, abril, modelo"** from *Fábula y signo,* in which Salinas develops a cor-respondence between an ideal spring and a Paris model/mannikin (pp. 172-73). The image seems compelling in its novelty, and delights us with the way in which it brings the theme of natural beauty into our modern world and vocabulary. Yet the poem also generates tension between the theme of natural perfection and the modern image which comes to represent it. The conflict created by the double meaning of the world "modelo" (natural archetype on the one hand, petty exhibitor of clothes on the other) makes us aware of the limitations implicit in the speaker's vision, and leaves us with an ambiguous attitude to his efforts to coalesce metaphorically the natural and the modern.

"Mar distante," also from *Fábula y signo,* contains no references to modern reality. But it reveals the same ambiguity and lack of resolution among perspectives that we have seen in the poems just discussed, and immerses us even more overtly into the subject of poetry's ways of naming things:

Si no es el mar, si es su imagen,
su estampa, vuelta, en el cielo.

Si no es el mar, si es su voz
delgada,
a través del ancho mundo,
en altavoz, por los aires.
Si no es el mar, si es su nombre
en un idioma sin labios,
sin pueblo,
sin mas palabra que ésta:
mar.

Si no es el mar, si es su idea
de fuego, insondable, limpia;
y yo,
ardiendo, ahogándome en ella.

(p. 169)

The very first line begins undercutting the subject named in the title, a process that continues right to the end of the poem. A traditional reading would suggest that Salinas rejects a literal and superficial view of the sea, seeking instead a more essential definition of its value for Man, or some vision of the sea as a Platonic archetype ("su idea"). But no clear sense emerges of such a definition or vision, and the final picture of the speaker simultaneously "burning" and "drowning" in the sea is both literally impossible and a denial of simple resolutions.

The poem becomes more meaningful if we think of its subject as not a literal seascape but an image and a *sign* conjured up by the word "sea." The speaker continually rejects the literal picture of the sea and attempts to define the sign: he moves from a sound image that is still based on the sea's effect (lines 3-6) to its name, which reduces it to its linguistic representation (lines 7-11), and finally to its most absolute formulation, or "idea."

As he does so, he is denying the *object* sea, trying to reach beyond his referent in search of the essential *sign* that represents and embodies it. But this search does not produce a clear answer: at the end, he can only describe the sea as a mystery combining the normally opposite concepts of "incomprehensible" and "clean," and containing within itself the contradictory characteristics of fire and water. The speaker's attempts have immersed us in the enigmas of a term whose meanings fan out in different directions and end up overwhelming him in contradictory ways. The sign "sea," in effect, has come to mark the absence of any clear meaning, rather than a presence.[21] Seen this way the poem, far from describing the essence of the sea, is a study of the ways in which a sign both does and does not name a reality, and an invitation to the reader to consider the possibilities and the limitations of poetic language.

Once we lay aside the premise that a poem should offer an integrated perspective which in some form resolves its tensions, **Seguro azar** and **Fábula y signo** become more significant (and easier to read). No longer obligated to discern Salinas' "true" attitude to reality and the modern world, we can focus on ways in which the poems in these books counterpose diverse perspectives on their subjects and immerse us in their play of differences. When we do so, we observe the importance of the very theme of poetic naming in these books, which embody, again and again, the poet's struggle with an undefinable reality and with a language or system of signs that can but dimly reflect it, and that often marks absence more than presence.

The perspective that I have taken to Salinas' early poetry allows us to leave behind the debate regarding the "true" attitude to reality that it reveals. By laying aside the premise that a poem's meanings should be "resolved," I have been able to see in Salinas' works a constant and very compelling exploration of reality, developed in ways that allow the reader to see and explore its various (and often contradictory) dimensions.[22] I have also examined an accompanying exploration of the possibilities and limits of poetic language itself, together with an invitation to the reader join in the poem's creative process. My view of Salinas' first three books also suggests relationships between them and his later work, and a possible re-examination of his whole poetic trajectory. The open-ended nature of the texts I have examined seems to be a constant characteristic of Salinas' poetry, one that may help explain conflicts in tone and perspective in books as different as **La voz a ti debida** and **Todo más claro.** The stress on the theme of poetic naming in the early verse prefigures the role of poetry in attempting to preserve reality in **El contemplado,** as well as the subject of the poetic transformation of nature in **Todo más claro.** It also corresponds very

well to the simultaneously illusioned and skeptical attitude Salinas took to his own art. Discussing Calderón and Jorge Manrique, he wrote the following:

> Those men who demand of reality stability, permanence, eternity are all wrong. And so also are those earthly realists mistaken, who are covetous of matter in all its forms, who believe in appearances. . . . But those are in error, too, who renounce life, who withdraw from the vital duty, for fear that it may pass or that it may be a dream. And this poetic attitude of our poetry seems to end with the following lesson: accept reality with all its risk of being transitory and unreal, with all its dreamlike adventure. Only he who accepts death and dreams accepts life.[23]

In his first three books of poetry, Salinas makes us experience, again and again, ways in which elements from the world around us both are and are not what they seem, both do and do not explain patterns and correspondences in our lives and our history. And he highlights the unique power of poetic language to reach beyond clear logical formulations, and to embody, while reflecting upon its own process, the contradictions inherent in a life that is also dream.

Notes

1. See del Río, "El poeta Pedro Salinas: vida y obra," *Revista Hispánica Moderna,* 7 (1941), 14-23; Morello Frosch, "Salinas y Guillén: dos formas de esencialidad," *Revista Hispánica Moderna,* 27 (1961), 17-18; Costa Viva, *Pedro Salinas frente a la realidad* (Madrid: Alfaguara, 1969), pp. 21-40; Palley, *La luz no usada: la poesía de Pedro Salinas* (Mexico: Ed. de Andrea, 1966), pp. 9-44.

   Presagios was first published in 1924, although the edition (Madrid, Biblioteca de Indice) carries the date 1923; *Seguro azar* comes out in 1929 (Madrid, Revista de Occidente), and *Fábula y signo,* Salinas' third book of poetry, in 1931 (Madrid, Ed. Plutarco).

2. Stixrude, *The Early Poetry of Pedro Salinas* (Princeton-Madrid: Castalia, 1975), p. 11.

3. See Roland Barthes, "From Work to Text," in Josué V. Harari, ed., *Textual Strategies* (Ithaca, N.Y.: Cornell University Press, 1979), pp. 73-81. Barthes' notion of a text as a system of signs reveals an attitude very different from that of a traditional analytic critic (or "New Critic"), concerned with the organic nature of a work. Cf. Cleanth Brooks, *The Well Wrought Urn* (New York: Harcourt, Brace & Co., 1947), ch. 5.

4. Pedro Salinas, *Poesías completas,* ed. preparada por Soledad Salinas de Marichal (Barcelona: Barral Editores, 1971), p. 69. All quotations from Salinas poems will be taken from this edition, with page references given in parentheses after each quote.

5. See Debicki, *Estudios sobre poesía española contemporánea* (Madrid: Ed. Gredos, 1968), pp. 58-60, and Stixrude, pp. 50-52.

6. Stixrude, p. 52.

7. Recent deconstructive criticism has explored ways in which gaps and areas of indeterminacy within texts produce an unraveling of meanings, and invite the reader to question and extend the text. On this subject see Carol de Dobay Rifelj, "Los artífices de la deconstruccion," *Explicación de Textos Literarios,* 8 (1979-80), 6, and Douglas Atkins, *Reading Deconstruction/Deconstructive Reading* (Lexington: University Press of Kentucky, 1983), pp. 24-25.

8. On the ways in which the deconstructive critic can take into account the constantly unfolding nature of the text see Geoffrey Hartman, *Criticism in the Wilderness,* (Ithaca, N.Y.: Cornell University Press, 1980), pp. 19-41 and 265-72.

Different yet complementary insights into the ways in which texts invite diverse readings have been provided by recent "reader-response" criticism. For a general discussion, see Jonathan Culler, *The Pursuit of Signs* (Ithaca: Cornell University Press, 1981), ch. 3; salient detailed studies include Hans Robert Jauss, *Toward an Aesthetic of Reception* (Minneapolis: Univ. of Minnesota Press, 1982), ch. 2, and Stanley Fish, *Is There a Text in This Class?* (Cambridge, Mass.: Harvard University Press, 1980), especially pp. 147-80 and 339-55.

9. Salinas, *Reality and the Poet in Spanish Poetry* (Baltimore: The Johns Hopkins University Press, 1940), p. 4.

10. "Stevens' Rock and Criticism as Cure, II," *Georgia Review,* 30 (1976), 331-33.

11. Crispin, *Pedro Salinas* (New York: Twayne Publishers, 1974), pp. 41-46.

12. See Salinas, *Poesías completas,* pp. 98 and 72, respectively.

13. See Crispin, p. 41.

14. See Stixrude, pp. 63-8.

15. *Ibid.,* pp. 85-89.

16. This view is well defined by Philip Wheelwright in *Metaphor and Reality* (Bloomington: Indiana University Press, 1962), pp. 72-91; see also Salinas' own *Ensayos de literatura hispánica,* 2a. ed. (Madrid: Aguilar, 1961), p. 362.

17. Stixrude, pp. 97-98.

18. De Man, *Allegories of Reading* (New Haven: Yale University Press, 1979), pp. 150-52. For a general discussion of contemporary theories of metaphor, see Jonathan Culler, *The Pursuit of Signs,* ch. 10.

19. In *The Critical Difference,* (Baltimore: Johns Hopkins University Press, 1980), Barbara Johnson gives excellent examples of the ways in which a deconstructive perspective illuminates the play of difference in poetry. See especially pp. 4-5 and 23-29.

20. Stixrude, pp. 77-83.

21. On the sign as a mark of absence, see Johnson, pp. 45-48, and Atkins, p. 17.

22. This would support and extend Concha Zardoya's classic view of Salinas' poetry as an ongoing search for "transrealities" which lie behind the appearance of things. See Zardoya, "La 'otra' realidad de Pedro Salinas," reprinted in *Pedro Salinas,* ed. A. Debicki (Madrid: Taurus, 1976), pp. 63-84.

23. Salinas, *Reality and the Poet,* p. 63.

Philip G. McLaughlin (essay date May 1986)

SOURCE: McLaughlin, Philip G. "The Failure of Love: Transitional Experience in Pedro Salinas's *Largo lamento.*" *Revista de Estudios Hispánicos* 20, no. 2 (May 1986): 65-81.

[*In the following essay, McLaughlin focuses on Salinas's "dualistic" treatment of the death of love in* Largo lamento, *asserting that this collection is an important transitional work in the poet's canon.*]

Regarded in broad perspective, Salinas's later poetry is characterized by a vacillation or tension between optimism and pessimism. By and large, critics have tended to avoid the contradictions posed by such dualism of outlook by concentrating their attention on the pre-war cycle of love poetry or on the optimism of *El contemplado* (1946) and *Confianza* (1955). While due recognition is accorded to the troubled visions of *Todo más claro* (1949), they are often ascribed to a temporary failure of confidence on the part of the poet. Consequently, the underlying, dialectical unity of Salinas's later verse is not sufficiently emphasized. *Largo lamento* (1936-1939),[1] while not one of the major collections, is an important work for our overall understanding of Salinas's poetry by virtue of its pivotal position between the love poetry of the thirties and the broader concerns of later years.

Largo lamento has often been regarded as the swansong of love for Salinas.[2] The irrevocable finality of the beloved's decision to renounce love precipitates a crisis in the poet that prefigures much of his later development. The relationship between the poet and his beloved had never been trouble-free, with the beloved periodically drifting in and out of the poet's life. *Largo lamento* is the expected climax to the poet's fear of separation from his beloved, and, although it is not easy to distinguish the precise moment at which separation becomes the predominant theme, it is clear that in the final poems of *La voz a ti debida* (1933) the poet is becoming increasingly worried by the debilitating effects of estrangement. Attempts to reaffirm a loving commitment, based on physical proximity, meet with failure, obliging the poet, in *Razón de amor* (1936), to counter loss through nostalgic yearning.[3] In *Largo lamento* the couple are definitively disunited, a fact which explains the weary resignation of the collection. The death of love leaves the poet feeling alone and impotent, cruelly tied to a dead past and unable to perceive a meaningful future. Gone is the confident faith in orderly temporal flux as the poet, deprived of the sustaining illusion of love, struggles desperately to retain the beloved (and therefore his *razón de ser*) by concentrating his attention not on the future, but on the past.

The poet's recollections of past experience and his general response to the death of love are not clear-cut, since disillusion and misgivings concerning his experience neither reduce the burden of loss nor weaken his determination to revive the affair. Indeed, the poet's awareness of his own excesses in love increases his sadness by highlighting the painful disparity between the ideal of love and its human representation. It is through analysis and evaluation of the dualistic nature of Salinas's response, expressed through the established conventions and ironies of traditional and more recent amorous theories, that the overall importance of *Largo lamento* emerges.[4] It becomes clear that the reworking of amorous tropes traditionally associated with the final stages of a love affair give shape to his deep sense of "fracaso amoroso." The very title of the collection, taken from Bécquer's *Rima* XV, besides preparing us for the appearance of Becquerian themes, highlights the importance of *Largo lamento* as an elegiac response to the failure of love.[5]

Salinas's lamentations, expressed with wearied resignation, foreshadow his later development, since the association, in *Largo lamento,* of the death of love with the end of meaningful existence anticipates Salinas's subsequent dualism of response to the technological world. In broad terms, the poet's vacillation between optimism and pessimism in *Largo lamento,* a vacillation governed by the degree to which love is perceived in the world, sets the pattern for the conflicting views of Salinas's subsequent poetry, in which the poet's moods range from optimism, through uncertainty to defeatism. Salinas's ability to write, in an urban setting, two works which differ in mood so radically as *Todo más claro* and *Confianza,* may have much to do with the particular conditions governing his perception of the world as a setting for amorous fulfillment. On a more immediate level, the emotional repercussions described in *Largo lamento* may encourage in Salinas a jaundiced view of a society whose demands and involvements entail exclusion from the idyllic world of love. There are several indications that the disillusion of *Largo lamento* colors his subsequent response to the world; as examples of such projections of inner emotion into the perception of reality, one might point to the poet's criticism of the world at large for precisely those faults (shallowness, callousness and lack of spirituality) found in the treacherous beloved, or to his exaggeratedly hostile response to certain technological gadgets which are associated with the superficiality of the beloved (in particular the radio and telephone), or, again, to the recurring and heightened development of the very concerns which arise from the death of love. Thus the feelings of anguish and impotence which characterize *Todo más claro* may well represent, in some measure, the legacy of the anxieties which beset the poet in *Largo lamento.*

A fuller understanding of *Largo lamento* not only illuminates the complexities of the subsequent optimism/pessimism dialectic, but, moreover, gives a useful insight into one example of a generational trend towards a broad concern with society, thereby clarifying Salinas's espousal of a humanistic ideology in *El contemplado.* While no account of the generational movement in the 1930's and 1940's away from personal/aesthetic concerns towards an advocation and practice of less interiorized writing could fail to take account of the socio-political context, (the Primo de Rivera dictatorship, the troubled years of the Republic, the Civil War itself and its aftermath), it is also clear that the widening of aesthetic vision is achieved, in some instances and to varying degrees, against a background of personal crisis. The development of a wider vision in response to individual anguish in poets such as Prados, Lorca, and Cernuda is parallelled in Salinas, whose affinities with his fellow poets is reflected in the incidence of comparable themes (individual emptiness, solitude and death-fears) following disillusion in love.[6] An examination of the amorous crisis in *Largo lamento* provides a convenient framework for approaching the complex question of the inadequacy of individualistic ideology and sheds light on the therapeutic experience of *El contemplado,* a work in which the poet seeks solace through self-immersion in the concerns of wider humanity.

The decisive element in Salinas's development is that although failure in love teaches him a wider truth, that the search for self-expression in love can lead to a personal/artistic impasse, he is unable to accept such a lesson in a positive spirit and turns, resignedly, to search for alternative modes of relationship in the quest for transcendence. The grudging nature of his response—he chooses the lesser of two evils—prepares us for subsequent troubled visions, since he regards active participation in the world of men as the only alternative to thorough extinction.

THE BETRAYAL OF LOVE

A large number of poems accuse the beloved of killing love through her deception, disdain and callous aloofness, and yet the poet sustains hope by distinguishing between the beloved who responds to love and her destructive *alter ego* who is determined to devitalize the relationship. The poet develops the notion of two beloveds through the presentation of conflicting valuations of beauty, in which the beloved's earlier dynamism ("Tú vives siempre en tus actos" 219) is degraded, in *Largo lamento,* into superficial passivity ("en tus vestidos vive" 500). The juxtaposition of different notions of beauty, as in "Ruptura de las cosas" (509-514), serves not only to criticize the beloved for damaging transcendent beauty by her sartorial and cosmetic obsessions,[7] but also assumes an elegiac function in its implicit mourning of the loss of values formerly associated with the mirrors of dreams (500), now replaced by the beloved's preference for "espejos fáciles" (558). Her superficiality causes the poet to wonder whether he can still believe in the higher world apprehended through sensual experience, and explains why, in **"La memoria en las manos"** (469-471), the sleepless poet, echoing Becquerian doubts concerning the role of physical attractiveness in amorous experience, feels cheated by the beauty he perceives (471).[8]

Given Salinas's belief in the transcendent potential of erotic love (through lovemaking the couple can achieve "lo inmortal" [467]) one can understand his perception of desexualized love as a betrayal of amorous plenitude. In this sense, **"Pareja, espectro"** (451-459) is an attack on the beloved's superficial attitude which has led her to dismiss the need for erotic love and thus spiritually killed the relationship. The title's tragic association of the couple with death reveals Salinas's attitude to the type of love that now prevails as a result of the victory of false beauty over meaningful attractiveness. In a series of parallel stanzas the poet, through an unfavorable comparison of past experience with present conditions, shows how superficial beauty now dwarfs the fleeting vision of a past when meaningful beauty overcame discord (451-452), facilitated union (453-455) and palliated the destructive effects of time (453-454). Superficial beauty, by way of significant contrast, intensifies the poet's awareness of temporal flux (453) and causes the couple to go on a shopping trip for dehumanized dummies to articulate their love. It is clearly from a forced sense of gratitude that the poet in the final stanza thanks the beloved for allowing her superficial beauty to free him from its antithesis, which, divorced from its inspired origins, no longer promotes valuable responses:

> Y, sobre todo, nunca,
> nunca agradeceremos
> bastante a tu belleza
> el habernos librado
> de tu misma belleza, del terrible
> influjo que podía haber tenido
> sobre la calma de los mares, sobre Troya,
> y sobre algunos pasos míos en la tierra.
>
> (455)

False beauty now condemns the poet to contemplate inert seas in contrast to the delight in marine flux and renewal he evinces in *El contemplado.* The cumulative references to the undesirable effects of false beauty, embedded in a background of vicarious gestures of noninvolvement and spiritual death (the purchase of a catechism and radio),[9] are the signposts by which the poet leads us through to the sad conclusion that the beloved has nurtured a love that is incurably devitalized and alienating:

> Y pasamos la noche,
> tranquilos, distraídos
> de tu inmensa belleza.
> Como si tú no la llevaras
> encima, fatalmente, sin descanso.
> Como si no estuvieran esperándola
> las blancas superficies de una cama,
> o las almas,—más blancas—, de unos ángeles
> donde sueles dormir algunas veces,
> mientras que yo te miro, despierto, desde el mundo.
>
> (456)

"Pareja, espectro" with its casual and ironic presentation of a "model" love is a telling comment on the poet's predicament as an accomplice to the willful thwarting of love.

The recurring image of "sombra" in *Largo lamento* merits comment, since a proper understanding of the concept is essential to understand Salinas's irony both in **"Pareja, espectro"** and in the work as a whole. The opening of *La voz a ti debida* (219-220) depicts the beloved rescuing the poet from a shadowy existence and yet, in **"Pareja, espectro,"** the poet thanks the beloved for guiding them towards previous shadowy couples (456). The bitter irony of such gratitude is obvious when one recalls the poet's condemnation of shadowlike responses as a treacherous denial of a loving relationship:

> ¡Qué tristes nos sentiremos
> si miramos a los otros
> y queremos ser así
> lo mismo que ellos: hacemos
> traición a nuestra pareja!
> ¡Si desertamos los seres
> inconfundibles que somos
> por querer ser como son
> las sombras que nos rodean!
> ¡Cuánto nos falta por fuera!
>
> (555)

Shadows are invariably associated with devitalized existence and spiritual death[10] and yet, such is the beloved's determination, she generally succeeds in guiding the relationship into trouble-free areas of uncommitted response and, more damagingly for the poet's morale, obliges him to respond to her with a "tacto de sombra" (502) and to offer her "sombras vegetales" even though he admits bluntly that "las sombras no . . . sirven" (520). One can appreciate the frustration experienced by the poet at being forced not only to acquiesce in the beloved's desire for shallow love, but also to advance reasoned theoretical justification for such behavior. The ironic treatment of gratitude and regret in such poems as **"Volverse sombra"** (472-478) and **"Amor, mundo en peligro"** (490-494) emphasize the poet's invidious position where he is forced to renounce love to "Derrotar así su propia muerte" (470). The overall impression drawn from **Largo lamento** is that even excess in love is immensely preferable to a loveless relationship,[11] a conviction which subverts the type of regret found in **"Volverse sombra"** where what appears to be a straight-forward criticism of over-demanding sensuality is, in fact, an ironic vindication of commendable spiritual needs, since it is as normal for the soul to demand love as for the eyes to search for light. His "offence" is simply that of demanding a committed response from the beloved:

> Y por eso empezó el terrible daño
> que hacen las manos y los labios
> sobre todo las almas, cuando piden
> amor y amor, a un día y a otro día;
> necesitadas almas, como ojos
> que al abrirse, mañana tras mañana
> si no está allí la luz lloran de pena.
>
> (476)

Unfortunately, there is no viable alternative and the poet is forced to renounce integrity in a desperate attempt to rekindle love.

AGING, WEARINESS AND MEMORIES

The enervating persistence in such self-enfeebling tactics gradually erodes the poet's earlier energy to such an extent that, in **Largo lamento,** his erstwhile quest for the "máxima locura momentánea" (246-247) gives way to a desire to stabilize the affair through promises of mutual fidelity and attachment. The weariness that prompts the poet to prefer, again echoing Bécquer,[12] a passive, somnolent, and thereby accessible object of his love (463) is caused, partly at least, by the emotional stress of accommodating a truculent, game-playing beloved.[13] It is quite clear, given the predominantly negative vision of the beloved presented in **Largo lamento,** that the poet has lost patience with a callously fickle partner and that earlier hopes to discover the essential *tú* behind the smile (237) are no longer sound, given her obsession with "lo fácil" (236). Numerous references to the beloved's tormenting fickleness (466, 572-573) explain the listlessness of the poet who is wearied as a result of gallant attempts to respect her independence, leaving her the freedom to maneuver "sobre su misma dicha" (521).

At the same time, the mood of indolence and fatigue is a direct result of the beloved's departure, which destroys the poet's timeless innocence and heightens his awareness of the mortal condition and its attendant ills of aging and death.[14] Such sentiments are only to be expected in a poet who persistently associates love with Spring's rejuvenatory effects ("en su impoluto campo . . . es siempre primavera" [542]; "las almas tienen / un don de primavera" [559]). For Salinas, amorous involvement, constantly "proyectando futuros" (516), strikes at the heart of time itself. But the other side of the coin is that the death of love entails spiritual death and converts the poet into a hybrid living corpse (484), a concise self-portrait that summarizes his freakish condition as a man living a life that is not life at all.[15] The underlying belief that the death of love implies spiritual death accounts for the sense of premature aging that leads the poet to view the world as dying amid autumn and winter coldness and falling leaves.[16] Life is now a "cansancio . . . que mata" (510) whose weariness is increased by sleepless nights spent mulling over the whys and wherefores of a failed dream. Such is the burden of nostalgia that at one stage the poet, pathetically, wishes to erase all memories in order to sleep peacefully (507).[17] Such a gesture aptly demonstrates the extent of his debility, since the price to be paid for such peace is increased solitude (476) and since, furthermore, the obliteration of memory would stifle such comfort as can be gleaned from the pain of love, a bittersweet emotion preferable to a loveless but comfortable existence. There is, however, little respite for the poet's weariness, since the absence of the beloved inspires sentiments of pain and loss that can only be assuaged by the constant evocation of her memory. So involved is the poet with his beloved,

> Yo solo nada soy; vivo
> de la vida que me mandas.
>
> (537)

that he scarcely exists in his own right and compulsively seeks to rekindle love through a constant reliving of past incidents.[18] Unfortunately, memories act as an irritant reminding him not only of his sterile present, but also of the troubled nature of his experience of love. Recollections of the beloved are not entirely favorable and thus, even though some comfort is gleaned from nostalgic self-indulgence, there remains a taunting disillusion to undermine past dreams. Salinas unashamedly uses memories, in poems like **"Los puentes"** (463-468) and **"¿Por qué querer deshacer?"** (593-594), to pressurize the beloved into returning, but, once again, the tactic is futile and he concedes, in **"Como ya no me quieres desde ayer"** (515-519), that clumsy efforts to revive a moribund love are self-defeating:

> Como ya no me quieres desde ayer,
> la memoria esta noche,
> igual que mano torpe
> toda llena de ruedas diminutas,
> cuando quiere arreglar algún reló,
> repasa los recuerdos
> de cosas que yo hice
> por ganarme tu amor, y fracasaron.
>
> (515)

The reminiscence of the *mano torpe* in which, according to Bécquer,[19] the lover can betray what is valuable in love, suggests that Salinas himself equates his nostalgia with other retentive tendencies. Memories are a key factor in his *malestar*: they tire him (466) and trouble his soul "dolido de tanto recordar" (469). They also remind him of his lonely present existence that leads him to fall back on shared past experiences despite previous rejections of memory as a pale substitute for present experience, (**"'Fue' es duro como piedra"** 587).[20] The predominance of memories in *Largo lamento* captures the poet's plight living amongst the sad ruins of a dead love in a "vacío poblado de fantasmas" (501). Once again, there is no viable alternative, since the poet cannot abandon memory and its motivating persistence of desire and yet, within the nostalgia, continuing desire clashes with the memory of its past failure. Just like the decaying autumn leaves redeemed previously by the beloved's beauty, the poet, rooted to the past, is forced to "mendigar melancolías" (454).

Self-questioning

While the evocation of memories is often used as a means of criticizing the beloved, it is also true that, through them, Salinas levels accusations at himself. We should not, however, accept his protestations of regret at their face-value, since our attention is drawn as much to the beloved's callousness as to the lover's excesses. Neither should the ironic presentation of remorse cause us to underestimate the vein of genuine critical self-appraisal in *Largo lamento*. Even the characteristic linking of admissions of guilt with references to mitigating circumstances (as in **"Volverse sombra"**), while partly undermining the sincerity of the poet's regret, should be interpreted, nevertheless, in terms of his dissatisfaction: he prefers a tarnished present experience of love to its memory. The poet realises that amorous experience has subjugated rather than liberated the beloved (**"¿Te acuerdas del laberinto?"** 565-567) and he is aware of the disparity of such an interpretation of love with the passionate ideal, evoked in **"El aire ya es apenas respirable,"** where intense erotic involvement highlights essential differences and proclaims love to be a union between free souls (533). The poet has betrayed

such liberating ideals and, while reviving the traditional theme of the morally blinding effects of physical love, he blames the attractiveness of the beloved for prompting selfishness. Just as Bécquer evokes the *mano torpe* of a savage to stress the debasement of an ideal of love, so Salinas regrets having loved "torpemente" (497) at having blinded himself, through the "complicidad de muchos besos" (472), to the demeaning nature of a love articulated by grasping hands (523).[21] Salinas is concerned, in **"Volverse sombra,"** to present himself not as a unique individual, but as a member of a race that inexorably spoils love—it is the "pecho de un hombre . . . que lo ahoga" (452). He laments not so much the destructive power of erotic love as the tendency of men to fall into the trap it lays by inevitably seeking to possess the object of attraction (472-473). Such an attitude is in keeping with the poet's depiction of the world as a "gran pecado" (425) into which the couple are flung (435) and partly explains his subsequent dissatisfaction at being forced to enter such a world without the saving grace of the beloved's presence.

The essential immobility of Salinas's situation is again evident in his treatment of regret, since whilst unashamedly accepting blame for his unjust behavior and his attacks on the beloved's free-will (566), he is aware that not only is such tarnished love preferable to none at all, but also that, paradoxically, a love devoid of "excesses" is not human love. Although he may occasionally advocate a tranquil love in which sensual elements are replaced by innocent, undemanding contemplation "que por ser tan pura / no puede romper nada" (494),[22] he is aware that such an approach is self-defeating if it is maintained indefinitely since it tends to destroy love itself. The conviction that the bypassing of involvement to reduce excesses in love entails a Pyrrhic victory is the underlying concept behind **"La rosa pura"** (479-480) where the poet's intention to suppress the claims of reflexive consciousness in favor of an idyllic, undemanding love is offset by the realization that such an approach denies his very humanity: if he thoughtlessly desires the rose, he ceases to be human and returns to the world of shadows. One can see that although the poet draws on a Dantesque *mezzo del cammin* line of argument,[23] his approach is a more modern and secular one, where amorous love is not considered inferior to transcendent love but the gateway to it. Thus, the poet's palinodes, while recalling Petrarch's rejection of his "giovenile errore" and his "perduti giorni,"[24] offer little spiritual consolation, since his recantation lacks conviction of the rightness of renouncing amorous love. In a sense, Salinas inverts the *mezzo del cammin* convention, since regret concerning the betrayal of amorous ideals exacerbates dissatisfaction with his human condition and anticipates his later, ambivalent view of the suitability of the world as a nurturing ground for love. The situation is a closed and self-perpetuating one. The poet feels trapped in a world that corrupts love and yet cannot escape because human love is the highest fulfillment available.

RESIGNATION AND RENEWAL

The pervasive mood of *Largo lamento* is one of impotence and inertia; the poet meets insuperable barriers to transcendence. He is unable to detach himself from the often disillusioning experience of past love, yet derives little comfort from the nostalgic sifting of memories. He fails to give a meaningful structure to his present existence and fears a future devoid of love. His world has collapsed, a fact that leads him to dismiss his present as one of "vanas apariencias" (527).[25] The notion of a painful void is applied to the period between the beloved's departure and her hoped-for return. The debilitating effects of love's decline are recorded both in the relatively impoverished thematic content of the collection and its stylistic simplicity as compared with the more rhetorical manner and conceptist approach of Salinas's earlier love poetry. The change in poetic register is understandable since the poet earlier consecrated his beloved as Muse; hence her departure heralds the appearance of a more simple direct style as if the poet lacked the inspiration to repeat earlier feats of expressive concentration. Now the poetic language becomes more matter-of-fact, with a marked tendency to reiterate key images such as *sombra, espectro* and *muerte*. The flat, discursive diction provides an appropriate vehicle for the limited themes dealt with in the collection. In poem after poem, the poet returns to the same concerns, without any noticeable progression in mood or perception of his situation. Indeed, amelioration is impossible since emphasis on feelings of spiritual impoverishment reveals the extent to which life continues to be equated with love. The beloved's withdrawal is not accepted with good grace but is deemed an inexcusable "traición . . . a todo lo que fue paraíso" (661).[26]

The poet has reached a personal and artistic impasse:

> Yo estaba solo, solo.
> Solo con mi silencio;
> solo, si lo rompía,
> también, con mis palabras.

> (458)

The psychological repercussions of this enforced sterility will be projected on to Salinas's subsequent world-view and poetics and will provide the driving force behind much of the conflict from which the later poetry draws its energy. In this respect, his reaction to the parting advice in **"La falsa compañera"** (457-459) is significant:

> Aún volvió la cabeza;
> y me dijo, al marcharse
> que yo era sólo un hombre,
> que buscara a los míos.

> Y empecé, cuesta arriba,
> despacio, mi retorno
> al triste techo oscuro
> de mí mismo: a mi alma.

> (459)

The need to search for self-knowledge in brotherhood is accepted with resigned disillusion, since involvement with one's fellow-men represents a loss of status and, in this sense, fraternal sentiments are a constant reminder of a fall from grace. An understanding of such motives can clarify our understanding of the troubled visions of *Todo más claro* and the redemptive pantheism of *El contemplado*.

Furthermore, the persistent faith in the ideal of love which emerges afresh in *Confianza* may well account for the coetaneous optimism of the later work. Besides anticipating the difficult-to-reconcile dualism of Salinas's later work, the experience of *Largo lamento* also teaches us that the twin perspectives cannot be separated, since they have the same origin insofar as the poet's response to the world represents a direct counterpart of his mood. Within such a framework, the contradictory responses of *Todo más claro* and *Confianza* can be seen as complementary visions of the same society: whereas, in *Todo más claro*, the death of love leads the poet to envisage the defeat of art and humanity by forces inimical to love, in *Confianza*, the poet's restored optimism concerning amorous love vanquishes death and restores the poet's vision of meaningful earthly existence. While, in *Todo más claro*, the poet's function is to mourn what is lost, in *Confianza*, poems such as **"Los otros"** (818-820) and **"Los signos"** (830-831) attest the poet's rediscovery of his role as a creative artist. If such optimism is to be understood as more than the obverse of the negative vision of *Todo más claro*, one must give due weight to the psychological repercussions of the poet's amorous failure, the overcoming of whose effects, in *Confianza*, usher in a fulfilling existence in which preoccupations with autumn and death are succeeded by thoughts of spring and life, and temporal flux becomes, once again, a source of regenerative potential (**"Confianza"** 840-842). In the last resort, the joy in life expressed in *Confianza* is fuller and better-founded for having known, if only as a transitional experience, the disillusion and loss of *Largo lamento*.

Notes

1. All page references are to Pedro Salinas, *Poesías completas* (Barcelona, 1975). For information concerning the late and staggered publication of *Largo lamento,* see the preliminary note to this edition (31-36).

2. Alma de Zubizarreta, *Pedro Salinas: el diálogo creador* (Madrid, 1969) 173-203. D.L. Stixrude, "The Final Lament of Pedro Salinas," *Revista ca-*

nadiense de estudios hispánicos 2 (1978): 122-141, and "El 'Largo lamento' de Pedro Salinas," *Papeles de Son Armadans* 232 (1975): 3-36, also discusses *Largo lamento* as a response to the failure of love.

3. Other critics have commented on the troublesome nature of the relationship between the poet and his beloved, characterized, as it is, by a gradual movement towards devitalized love. Certainly, the poet's happiness is undermined, in *La voz a ti debida,* by fears concerning the beloved's absence and indifference. In *Razón de amor,* the presence of currents of melancholy, doubt, resignation and nostalgia anticipates the poet's response to amorous failure evinced in *Largo lamento.* For a discussion of the gradual build-up of tensions within the relationship, see R.G. Havard, "Pedro Salinas and Courtly Love. The 'amada' in *La voz a ti debida*: woman, muse and symbol," *Bulletin of Hispanic Studies* LVI (1979): 123-144; and Sara E. Schyfter, "The Rebellious Beloved in 'La voz a ti debida,'" *Hispanófila* 68 (1980): 57-71.

4. Numerous critics have drawn attention to Salinas's reworking of Courtly Love and Becquerian notions. Concerning Becquerian resonances in Salinas, see S. Gilman, "El proemio a 'La voz a ti debida,'" *Asomante* 19 (1963): 7-15. On Salinas's debt to Courtly Love conventions, see R.G. Havard, and Carlos Feal Deibe, "THOU WONDER AND THOU BEAUTY, AND THOU TERROR: La poesía amorosa de Pedro Salinas," *Modern Language Notes* 94 (1979): 283-301. Numerous critics have discussed the influence of modern theories of love on Salinas and have analyzed the poet's changing view of love in terms of the theories of such thinkers as Max Scheler, Martin Buber and Teilhard de Chardin. See, in particular, Zubizarreta for a discussion of the influence of Buber. Carlos Feal Deibe, *La poesía de Pedro Salinas* (Madrid, 1965) 153-161, examines the influence of Scheler, as does Julieta Gómez Paz, "El amor en la poesía de Pedro Salinas," *Buenos Aires Literaria* 13 (1953): 55-68. Juan Marichal, "Pedro Salinas: La voz a la confidencia debida," *Revista de Occidente* 2a época, 26 (1965): 155-170, considers Salinas's development in terms of the theories of Teilhard de Chardin.

5. For an understanding of conventional responses to amorous failure, see Petrarch's *Canzoniere,* and Gustavo Adolfo Bécquer's *Rimas* (especially *Rimas* XXX-LXXVI).

6. Amorous failure, while not the only cause of the *malestar* affecting certain of Salinas's fellow-poets, is, nevertheless, a prevalent feature of the mid-life crisis that was to change the nature of their poetry during the 1930's and early 1940's. The response to crisis is, initially, one of intro-

spection and reappraisal, leading to a widening of concerns from the personal to the collective. Critics who discuss the role of personal crisis in precipitating new directions of individual poets include Derek Harris, *Luis Cernuda. A Study of the Poetry* (London, 1973); Manuel Duran and Margery Safir, *Earth Tones: The Poetry of Pablo Neruda* (Bloomington, Indiana, 1981); P.J. Ellis, *The Poetry of Emilio Prados: A Progression Towards Fertility* (Cardiff, 1981); Derek Harris, *García Lorca: Poeta en Nueva York* (London, 1978).

7. Numerous poems reveal the beloved's obsession with external beauty aids. In "¡Qué olvidadas están ya las sortijas!" (498-501), the poet ironically recalls the couple's frequent shopping trips for new clothes. In "El aire ya es apenas respirable" (530-534) the beloved prefers to avoid troublesome sentiments "probando . . . vestidos . . . que calman" (531). Indeed, so misled is the beloved that in "Deja ya, deja ya por un momento" (572), the poet advises her to renounce cosmetic concerns for more spiritually beneficial pursuits.

8. The theme of the contrast of the power of beauty with the lack of spiritual communion in the context of a "fracaso amoroso" is a favorite one of Bécquer. See *Rimas* XIV, LXXXIV, and LXXXVI.

9. Stixrude, "El 'Largo lamento,'" 16, argues that love is reduced to a catechism that has repressed any trace of vitality with its doctrinaire insistence on spirituality. The purchase of a radio is clearly ironic, since elsewhere the poet claims the radio is peopled by spectres (352), a conviction that accounts for his criticism of the beloved for betraying her integrity "oyendo anuncios de abstracciones por la radio" (486).

10. For Bécquer the absence of love entails a shadowy existence (*Rimas* LXX and LXXIII).

11. The poet even goes so far as to embrace suffering as comforting proof of love's existence (319). Salinas's conviction that the joys of love are inseparable from suffering is a traditional one, recalling Petrarch's definition of love as a "dolce affano" (*Rima* LXI) and Bécquer's attachment to the pain of love as comforting proof of meaningful existence (*Rimas* LXIV and LXVIII). For both Salinas ("Volverse sombra") and Bécquer (*Rima* XLVIII), the willful destruction of love implies spiritual suicide.

12. *Rima* XXVII. Bécquer's weariness also stems, in part, from the struggle to further his love (*Rima* LXXXVI).

13. See R.G. Havard for a discussion of the warlike relationship that often prevails between the poet and his beloved.

14. Bécquer's response to amorous failure also entails weariness, premature aging and a sense of the destructive transience of life (see *Rimas* XLIII, LVII and LXXVI).

15. This self-portrait recalls a similar one in Bécquer's poetry (*Rima* XLV).

16. In "Los puentes" (463), Salinas is resignedly coping with a cold January evening, and in "Volverse sombra" the setting is, once again, a cold snowy one. In "Muerte del sueño" (483-484), the death of love precipitates autumn decay. Bécquer also exists in a cold, inhospitable winter world of decay (see *Rimas* LXXIII, LII, LX, LXX).

17. One recalls, in Bécquer's poetry, similar frustrated desires to erase memory (*Rimas* LII and LXIII).

18. Concerning Salinas's dependence, see "Paz, sí, de pronto, paz" (546-548), "Canción de la vida total" (568-71) and "¿Es de acero, de mármol, di?" (597-598). Although Salinas's self-effacement derives from traditional courtly love concepts it does indicate a dangerous degree of servility. It is interesting to note that modern theoreticians of love warn of the need to retain self-integrity in love, since amorous plenitude depends on personal independence. See Martin Buber, *I and Thou*, translated by R.G. Smith with a Prologue by W. Kaufmann (Edinburgh, 1970) 62, and Max Scheler, *The Nature of Sympathy* translated by Peter Heath with an Introduction by W. Stark (London, 1954) 70-71.

19. *Rima* L.

20. Bécquer also claims that the only valid memory is ironically non-memory (*Rima* LVIII). Martin Buber, 63-73, argues that love is a present experience and should not be stifled by memories.

21. Scheler 157, warns that sensual pleasure can trap man in selfish atitudes.

22. Salinas's emphasis on contemplation recalls Bécquer's reminder that although kisses burn, the soul can avoid such dangers through contemplation (*Rima* XX).

23. "Nel mezzo del cammin di nostra vita / mi ritrovai per una selva oscura / che la diritta via era smarrita" (Dante, *La Divina Commedia, Inferno*, Book I, 1-3). The convention was taken up by Garcilaso de la Vega (Sonnet VI) and, more recently, by Luis Cernuda ("La visita de Dios" *Las nubes* [1937-1946]).

24. See Petrarch's *Rima* LXII and *Rima* I respectively.

25. Failure in love also strips Bécquer's existence of meaning (see *Rimas* XXXVIII and LVI).

26. See Bécquer's *Rima* XLVI for similar accusations of treachery.

Stephanie L. Orringer (essay date 1995)

SOURCE: Orringer, Stephanie L. "The Author's Search for Authentic Being." In *Pedro Salinas' Theater of Self-Authentication*, pp. 9-30. New York: Peter Lang, 1995.

[*In the following essay, Orringer emphasizes the metafictional aspect of four plays by Salinas—El precio, La estratoesfera, El parecido, and El chantajista—focusing on the theme of identity or authenticity and reconstructing the action of each work, as the protagonists, either through their art or through interactions with other characters, "author their own essential beings."*]

In *metafiction* the awareness of the creative process becomes a component of fiction. In four of Salinas' plays, the conscious unfolding of that process enables the author to realize his essential being. In *El precio* and *La estratoesfera,* an authorial figure, easily identifiable as Salinas' *alter ego,* authenticates himself by making it possible for his characters to attain their own identities. On the other hand, in *El parecido* and *El chantajista,* interaction with other characters enables protagonists to author their own essential beings.

SELF-AUTHORSHIP THROUGH CHARACTER
AUTHENTICATION

El precio and *La estratoesfera* have much in common: each features a literary creator who manipulates the protagonist and thus shows awareness of handling a fiction as such. Further, in fictionalizing, the author-figure discovers a truth about living, and achieves identity in the process.

Jáuregui of *El precio* is a novelist by profession, who arrives on the scene in search of his character Melisa. As Zubizarreta has suggested (352-53), it is no coincidence that Salinas' author is named Miguel and has a Basque surname: just as in the novel *Niebla* (*Mist*) by a more famous Basque novelist, Miguel de Unamuno, Jáuregui claims omniscient knowledge of his character. As an author, he approaches his goal of eternalizing a moment in time, "of separating that morning from the rest, [of] stopping time" (*Teatro* [*Teatro completo*] 286). He himself thereby becomes godlike. He wishes to "describe a unique morning," suitable for his character Melisa to become real. By describing the first morning of creation, he will have succeeded in arriving at a universal situation (286). To allow her to materialize, her author must select the apt temporal circumstance. He would discover the first morning of a human being who has suddenly acquired awareness of her surroundings (286). Melisa's hostess Alicia confirms to Jáuregui that on just such a morning Melisa first appeared to her (286).

The writer, Jáuregui, receives further evidence of having approached his goal: his creature has escaped from his grasp. However, the audience is not permitted to learn of this character-author relationship until the end of the drama (cf Moraleda, "Intro" 15-16). As a result, Jáuregui discovers he cannot live without his fictional creature. When she departed, he says, the morning "escaped from me, went away from me, . . . and . . . stood still for a while" (286). In a reversal of Unamuno and Pirandello, where characters search for their authors, Salinas' writer seeks his character. Only by locating her can he become himself. He feels "a strange terror" that she does not accompany him through no fault or action of his. "She has slipped my mind and I do not see her" (298). Yet along with the audience, Alicia's father, a psychiatrist, knows that the author held Melisa firmly in his mind while he was composing the first part of his novel.

Jáuregui describes his own relationship to his creature in terms of bringing her to life, giving her identity. Clearly the implied playwright is allegorizing the creative process of characterization. When Melisa escaped from her novelist Jáuregui, she was as yet unable to exert influence on him. No interaction existed between the two of them. As Jáuregui puts it, his character was present, but simply "in lifeless words." Melisa lacked awareness. She had no "soul"; hence, she could not "animate her author to continue to give her life" (287). In short, author and character are mutually dependent for their identities: neither can exist nor achieve selfhood without the other. Here *in nuce* is the plot of Unamuno's *Niebla*, but with the author-character dispute resolved. Augusto Pérez claims his autonomy and the right to determine his own existence and destiny without regard to his author Unamuno. The novelistic creature, Augusto, in his own view, has immortalized Unamuno, the creator. The Author-God Unamuno, of course, disagrees. He insists that it is his right to let Augusto live or die, because a creature of fiction is immortal only thanks to his creator. Unamuno reminds Augusto, "You do not exist outside of me" (667). Augusto replies, "It is you who do not exist outside of me and the other characters whom you think you have invented" (667). Augusto will not let himself be subjected to his author's whim because "even fictional characters have their own internal logic" (667).

Analogously, Melisa's creator Jáuregui had endowed her with enough independence to assert herself vis-à-vis her author. She "threw herself into living" the very morning of her creation. Jáuregui had put into her *persona* "all the fire of life that he had to give" (*Teatro* 287). When she realized that she was experiencing her own special morning, she picked herself up out of the pages of Jáuregui's novel and walked away (287). The playwright mocks himself through the words of the skeptical psychiatrist, who voices the opinion of the audience that the novelist has gone beyond the bounds of poetry. Jáuregui assumes the rôle of Augusto Pérez here when he excitedly exclaims, "There is nothing which is outside poetry [i.e., art]. Everyone, you and I, . . . all of us are in poetry. . . . And the Earth, and this room, and the words that are sounding now. . . . For we are all inside it . . . as in the air even though we do see it" (287). This idea comes straight out of *Niebla* (667), where Augusto tells the Author-God Unamuno that his own fictitious characters, don Avito Carrascal and don Fulgencio Entrambosmares, would share Augusto's opinion that the author cannot exist independently of them, his creatures.

Jáuregui, in tones reminiscent of Unamuno, announces that he created Melisa and that she is indeed a fictional being. In short, she is a "poetic lie" (*Teatro* 287). Like Unamuno, Jáuregui recognizes that his creature forms part of him. But he differs from Unamuno in his Pygmalion-like relationship to his creature: he loved her as he "loved no one else" (288). Jáuregui sees both himself and Melisa as inauthentic. He is incomplete without that beloved portion of himself. When she left him, he had only had his offspring "half-formed." Therefore, he, too, is only "half-formed," in the sense that without her he lacks authenticity, while she is incomplete because she has no past. Jáuregui possesses her past, and he was going to give her wholeness of being by endowing her with memories upon which to draw for her present experience in order to make her life complete. By thus making her a well-motivated character, he would have enabled her to "ring true" to herself. Nevertheless, he never had a chance to accomplish this personalization of her. "I cannot give [her other half] to her, because only by feeling it in . . . her yesterday could she know how to continue living" (288). Moreover, while Melisa lacks her past, her author Jáuregui lacks the ability to fashion her future in her absence (288). This, then, also accounts for his own feeling of incompleteness and inadequacy.

Jáuregui says that he cannot finish creating Melisa, because he has forgotten the missing half of her. This is an allegory of metafiction in which the author depicts his dependence upon his literary creation. If he has lost sight of the "inner logic" of the character he is creating, to employ Augusto Pérez's term (Unamuno 667), creation cannot proceed. Jáuregui seemingly is aware that his discourse sounds like madness, but he persists in calling it "amnesia and something more" (*Teatro* 288). In this case he refers to his own lack of memory in the sense of anamnesis: he must un-forget what he has repressed so as to learn who she is.

In view of what has been said until now, it is easy to understand the meaning of Melisa's return to Jáuregui at the end of the play. Melisa, hanging onto Jáuregui's neck, states that, upon returning to him, she now knows who she is: "I have come back to *you*. . . . Now I know who I am. . . . I want to live . . . yours, yours . . . !" (288). Comparing these words of Melisa to like words of Augusto Pérez shows the difference between Unamuno and Salinas on the author-character relationship. Melisa wishes to be possessed by her author, whereas Augusto wants to be independent. Augusto, informed that his Author-God is about to execute him, says, "Now that you want to kill me, I want to live, live, live." But he insists on being "myself, myself, myself" (669). Augusto wants independence. Melisa wants completeness. To achieve a full, complete life, she must pay a price—the death of her body, so that she can live on eternally in the literary work (*Teatro* 288). Antonio Gila notes the importance of Salinas' titles (12-13) since they preserve an "indirect relationship to the theme of the work." However, in *El precio* the relationship is direct, for the price paid offers Melisa and her author authentic being. Immediately before the curtain falls, Jáuregui displays unmitigated joy, signaled in the stage direction by a "radiant face": he, too, has achieved immortality through her bodily death. Now he can be complete.

Time stopped immortalizes and therefore authenticates. In Salinas' poem **"Pasajero en el museo"** (*Todo* 645) appears the apposite line, "The life which is stopped is what is immortal." The life portrayed then willingly "accepts its frame" (*Todo* 646).[1] In this poem, of course, Salinas refers to portraits framed and hung in a museum. Artistic license, however, should be applied to refer to any creative work; even a novel or play and its creatures live within the temporal and spatial framework of the manuscript. Little wonder, therefore, that Salinas divides his one-act play into two "frames" ("cuadros"). In any case, with the acceptance of its artistic limitations, "happiness is assured" in the artwork (*Todo* 645). More significantly, the poet Salinas has carefully and determinedly expressed his own beliefs: "Renunciation of earthly life" brings "salvation" in the form of continued living and willingness to continue living. "Yes, your salvation was renunciation / of what there is on this side of the picture-frames; / living, to keep on, to want to keep on living . . ." (647). The poet refers to the picture captured in time and preserved forever, within a determined frame, this time in a museum for all to appreciate. A life, that of the portrait, has been preserved within its own time. Its life has been "stopped permanently in an instant" and is "sufficient unto itself" (645).

The form of *El precio* suits its substance. In one of the few plays in which Salinas lets character come across through dialogue and action, Melisa reveals her authentication directly through words and deeds. It is true that she is eventually recognized as a "fictional entity," to employ Unamuno's terms. But that disclosure does not occur until the last scene with the appearance of her au-

thor, and is developed with her reaction to him. She is a "fable" brought to life in Salinas' sense of an artistic rendering of true being. Moreover, from her very first words, we understand that she poeticizes her surroundings. After she has allowed the fountain to play over her cheek, she tells Alicia that the water has "kissed" her (*Teatro* 269). Throughout the play, it is her fey, otherworldly behavior and conversation which reveal her personality. Her light, dancing movements in the everyday world are not quite those of the persons around her.[2] Her speech is often disjointed, or at the least unrelated to events and persons which the audience recognizes. Salinas' stage directions call for an actress who is tall and slim, with flowing hair, and mannerisms revealing "a certain arrhythmia, at times fast, at times slow" (268). Her speech must display the same whimsical patterns. She must convey "spiritual beauty" in contrast with her earthy companion Alicia, "more sensually beautiful" (268). From the opening scene, the audience is to understand that Melisa is "different," but delightful (268).

Her problem seems to be that she floats free, unbound, lacking an anchor to her authentic reality. Past or future time holds no meaning for her. She lives outside time in her own world of fantasy. Her song shows this atemporality: "Here I await you / in my now, island in which you have kept me, / happy, world, forgotten / by future and past, / world of this moment" (276). Melisa has lived on a "fantasy island" similar to Prospero's, to which workaday rules do not apply. This free-floating, imaginary region may in turn denote a lack of known geographical bounds, or conversely, may show her limited spatial orientation. Accordingly, she refuses to walk as the rest of us do, with feet planted on the ground. Rather, she dances on her toes, poetizing movement. Alicia wonders if she is "afraid of the ground" (269). We may ask if she is frightened to discover reality. She inhabits a happy world without yesterday and tomorrow. Further, she sings to a special person, "thou," to whom she must eventually return and to whom she belongs: "Once again what I owe you will have to be yours" (277). Melisa's "creditor" is Jáuregui, and it is he who can provide her with the spatio-temporal mooring she lacks in order to be authentic. She, in turn, will abandon her body.

Her song furnishes the link of a vague memory to her creator, key to her true identity. She does not remember who composed the song, but only that it was not she herself (277). She dreamed that she was singing it and on awakening found that she was. Hence, once again she is translating existence into fantasy. With an obvious evocation of a well-known poem, Fray Luis de León's "Vida retirada" ("Ode to the Secluded Life"),[3] she likens herself to the bird who neither "invents" nor "understands" his own song, but knows it from within himself. Her own creative process consists, she tells

Alicia, of first dreaming, then singing what she has dreamed, and afterwards of poeticizing or "fabulizing" the dream-song (277). Continuing her fantasizing, she explains that she needs no toys, as the world provides them all around her, beginning with the birds themselves.

Melisa's very name, well chosen by Salinas, sums up her personality as sketched up to now. A very unusual name in the Spanish-speaking world, Melisa comes from the Greek *mélissa,* honeybee. This insect tends to communicate by dancing on a vertical surface while oriented by its perception of light (Michener 758-59). Rubén Darío (495), subject of one of Salinas' monographs, speaks in the poem "Coloquio de los centauros" ("Coloquy of the Centaurs") of "Greek bees" caught in the mane of the wise centaur Chiron. These winged creatures symbolize poetic inspiration. Naming, Salinas has emphasized, gives a concrete identity to the person. Melisa has been found wandering with no clues to her identity. Alicia offers her a name (273), a start for the quest for Melisa's identity.

Alicia's name itself holds significance for Salinas' vision of authentication. She is enthralled with the fantasies of her new-found friend Melisa, with her knack for disclosing new facets to the world around her. Hence, Alicia, in Melisa's presence, is like an Alice in Wonderland (cf Moraleda, "Introducción" 15). For each individual, in Salinas' opinion, there exists a unique soulmate.[4] Here, then, is Salinas' reaffirmation of the uniqueness of each essential being. This time the meeting of the souls seems to be without sexual or romantic nuances. Alicia does not find Melisa strange, but delightful. Having discovered her, Alicia believes that she "belongs to her" (268). This is a phrase which she repeats as she tells Melisa that she loves her, that she "seems to be hers" (277).

Other clues to Melisa's identity come through descriptions of missing women, and through the interaction of the people seeking these women. A psychiatrist's notification of the authorities that he has found a young female amnesiac serves to speed up the action that follows. Both the police inspector, who is seeking a murder suspect, and Prudencio, who is looking for his missing wife, are catalytical. The dénouement comes quickly with the second tableau and the arrival of the author Jáuregui himself. His identity spans two worlds: the outside one of appearances and the inner one of essences. He is accepted as a writer of renown, a member of the Royal Academy. But inwardly unfulfilled, he is looking for Melisa. She recognizes her author as omnipotent when brought face to face with him, and thereby rejoices in her bodily death. In all ways, Salinas has appropriately subtitled his one-act drama "a fantasy," because he has taken the external sphere of appearances and integrated it with fable, thereby earning for *El precio* his own label "fabulized reality."

As in *El precio,* in *La estratoesfera* the moving force is a writer. He is the Bohemian poet Alvaro de Tarteso, who concocts the "fiction" or "fable" which will restore honor to the peasant-girl Felipa.[5] He is to become author of a play within the play and thereby to acquire his identity. His irresponsibility evolves into a sense of accountability. Salinas situates him in an improbable setting conducive to "fabulizing" reality. The name of a neighborhood Madrid tavern, *The Stratosphere,* implies something highfalutin: it conjures up images of an elevated ambiance, which it lacks. Alvaro resembles Melisa at the beginning in his flights of fancy, and he eventually achieves authenticity by coming down to earth as she does. In the first scene of the play, he immediately mythicizes an otherwise sordid scenario. He metamorphoses the blind vendor of lottery tickets into the most famous of classical blind men Oedipus (194). In the Sophoclean mode he renames Felipa, the blind man's granddaughter, Antigone (197). Alvaro parades his learning as he puns on Felipa's words of protest, "I am a minor," for he responds, "Minor? You're major!" (197). Continuing his practice of making classical allusions, he calls Felipa a "Pythagorean damsel" as she calculates her grandfather's earnings from his sales (195). Salinas would have his audience constantly aware of Alvaro as the creator of fable when he directs the actor playing him to declaim "in an emphatic and consciously literary tone" (195). Such self-aware literariness explicitly points to Salinas' recourse to metafiction. Alvaro refers to Felipa's work-worn hands as "pearly fingers," and to his own artistic hands as "unworthy and mortal" (196). He refuses a lottery ticket since he "plays other games." Using a metaphor borrowed from Ultraist poets, he plays the "multicolored roulette of rhyme" or the Modernist "marble dice of the stanza." He is recklessly impervious to the "harm" which his high-flown irony may be doing to Felipa, who, in anguish, insists that he be silent (197).

His name offers a clue to what Alvaro must do to overcome his frivolity and pursue his identity. Dialogue with Felipa enables the audience, through a process of literary associations, to determine how Alvaro must poeticize the situation to authenticate himself and the other characters. He identifies himself with Don Alvaro, the hero of *Don Alvaro o la fuerza del sino (Don Alvaro or the Force of Destiny),* the Romantic drama by the Duke of Rivas. Alvaro de Tarteso is a pseudonym which he has invented for himself (204), probably to ease his own search for identity and to allow others to recognize him in his fictitious but self-authenticating rôle. When Felipa informs him of her dishonor, he continues resorting to fiction, denying her workaday situation and translating it into poetic terms: "A blot on *your* honor? My homonym [Don Alvaro] once said it: 'Pure as the breath of angels surrounding the throne of the Most High'" (203). In other words, he will enlist the aid of the "force of destiny" to improve her situation.

This figurative speech is literalization, which includes the "roulette of rhyme." Alvaro, moreover, refers to the Don Alvaro legend when he remarks that Felipa may have been "predestined" to be dishonored (as Doña Leonor had been in Rivas' play). However, he will "invent" her as a literary figure (202). Alvaro continues fictionalizing his perception of her, ennobling her at every step, as Don Quixote did the peasant woman Aldonza Lorenzo. Like Dulcinea, Felipa happens to come from the village in La Mancha called El Toboso (202). First Alvaro adjures, "Do not debase yourself." After all, she is, he says, one of Sophocles' progeny. (He has, we recall, likened her to Antigone.) Felipa recognizes his rôle as author, since his speech resembles the kind of discourse used by novelists who write serials for publication in the newspaper (202).

Salinas' Alvaro becomes the "force of destiny" to guide Felipa to the restoration of her honor, identifying himself as her "future" (211). He is her Don Quixote, making her a Dulcinea by elevating her from her abject state. By offering her his hand, he provides her with a future life, material and spiritual. This heroism, or self-authentication on his part, comes about by convincing César, the actor who had dishonored Felipa, to participate with him in the literary fiction he has created to vindicate her. Alvaro is consciously shifting rôles. Stage directions indicate that he even changes his tone of voice (211). First he plays an actor in Felipa's drama, then the omnipotent author who solves her problem. He has all along seemed to be a Bohemian poet, a Don Juan. But this is now clearly a disguise, because he is actually concerned about Felipa's identity and his own. Afterwards, he takes on the rôle of her protector, but this rôle is no deception.

Alvaro's rival César, his counterfigure, is a movie actor without authentic being. César, not Alvaro, is a Don Juan in actual fact, because he has seduced and abandoned Felipa. Further, although César is attempting to play Don Quixote, it is Alvaro himself who succeeds in this rôle by succoring the unfortunate Felipa. In a toast to the essential man Don Alonso Quijano, lying behind the visionary Don Quixote, Alvaro shows his disdain for "farce" and his preference for authenticity. César finally admits, perhaps ceremoniously, his own unworthiness to play the Manchegan hero (201). This admission, as well as the toast provoking it, may well serve to foreshadow the authentications to come of both rivals and of Felipa.

Through his alter ego Alvaro, Salinas seem to invite movie-actors like César to engage in "cleaning up their acts" as actors. Cinema, it seems to Salinas, falsifies the novelistic texts on which it is based. Live theater, on the other hand, stays faithful to the original script.[6] Likewise, in *La estratoesfera,* a minor character asserts that it is hard to understand how "real figures can ap-

pear on a bit of white material and sing and dance without ever truly being there because they have no bulk" (200). These notions hark back to an early Salinas poem, **"Far West,"** on ontological implications of cinema (*Seguro azar* 121). Here the poetic voice accents the bodilessness of the images represented on the screen, that is, their lack of existence in time and space. Nothing can lay claim to an identity on the screen, but is a mere portrait of something intangible. In *La estratoesfera* César tries to take on the movie rôle of Don Quixote, but Alvaro calls him an "apocryphal" being, implying his lack of authenticity in his actor's rôle. In Alvaro's view, he is unworthy of playing the noble Manchegan knight (*Teatro* 201). He seems instead to Alvaro to be a kind of "Avellaneda of the silver screen" (202), in other words, that unidentified character of Spanish letters who wrote a sequel to *Don Quixote* and thereby inspired an indignant Cervantes to attack him in its second part (1615).

César undergoes a transformation from an "Iberian Valentino" (205) into a genuine actor on a living stage. He submits to stage directions provided this time by Alvaro, eager to redeem Felipa. For this play within the play, Alvaro, transformed into a playwright, hopes that César will truly take on the ennobling qualities of his character Don Quixote (205-206), "defender of outraged honor and ridiculed virtue," to employ Alvaro's quixotic bombast. Moreover, he reminds César to respond to whatever in this true-to-life situation lends itself to poetizing (206). Although César hesitates at first by affirming the separation of the two worlds, the one of literary fantasy and the other of the "prose of this world" (206), he eventually recants, accepting the rôle assigned to authenticate him. He does so threatened by Alvaro's quixotic gesture to kill him if he does not engage in such a fiction. Accordingly, César, instructed by Alvaro, restores Felipa's honor by inventing for her his own identical twin who has died before being able to wed her. Meanwhile, Alvaro jokingly communes with the audience by indicating to it that he, as author, is aware of ennobling the rather unsavory love affair underlying this play within a play. Hence, both the internal and the external play end on a note of metafiction. Felipa, by playing her own fictitious rôle to its conclusion, has become someone new. "I am no longer myself, I am someone else" (208). This is her true identity, acquired through the mediation of fiction.

Self-Authorship through Character Interaction

In the two plays just analyzed, the author-figure, like Salinas, has an artistic vocation and can, therefore, reflect with some expertise on the creative process. However, this is not the case in *El chantajista* and *El parecido,* where characters not belonging to the profession of writing, also devote themselves to fictional creativity.

In the first, the medium of artistic expression is correspondence; in the second, it is merely provocative memories which afford certain esthetic enjoyment.

Reality is made "fable" in *El chantajista.* Lucila creates out of yearning and imagination a fictitious lover to whom she writes love-letters. Like Don Quixote corresponding with Dulcinea del Toboso, as interpreted in a Salinas essay (**"La mejor carta"** 111), she writes to "the shadow of a person who never truly came into being but was a figment of her imagination." According to Salinas, Don Quixote gave a definite existence, through his billet-doux, to "an illusion of impossible beauty and doubtful existence" ([*Ensayos de literatura hispánica*] 120). Dulcinea, therefore, "exists united to Don Quixote, only within him"; and "from loving" this illusion so much, "he has made her love him." His desire that Dulcinea exist has made her exist (126). Lucila has left her letters in a theater in hopes of attracting a responsive, ideal mate. Lisardo, upon finding them, believes that their addressee had forgotten them there. He decides to turn Lucila's fiction to his own advantage.

The resultant play within a play invented by Lisardo authenticates both the author and Lucila. He has taken her fiction and made it his. Lucila has bewitched him with her correspondence, so that he is impelled to meet her. Hence, he resolves to blackmail the addressee (Lucila, disguised as a non-existent person Eduardo). Because Lisardo feels that lovers dare write much more in letters than they can express orally, he finds it romantic to love by letter. To give the tale even more elegance, he decides to recount the story of the two star-crossed correspondents in third person to a child rather than quoting from the letters written in the familiar second person (*Teatro* 293). Therefore, "past reality is felt as if it were still occurring in the present" (294); a fiction embellishes the prosaic world. The playwright encourages this fantasizing in the stage directions by suggesting that several scenes of *El chantajista* be "produced in a dream-sequence without any realistic touches" (299-306). These scenes unfold in "semi-shadow," illumined only by moonlight. Lisardo appears in them disguised with a mask (133) as if to stress his false identity. "I in the shadow as my rôle demands, hiding myself, pretending" (298). Lisardo's disguise is intended to prevent Lucila from recognizing him, yet is a whim inspired by one of Lucila's letters in which she spoke of a similar situation (299). She has, therefore, created his new persona, which gives him the identity he has ultimately been pursuing—that of her lover. At the same time, she is eagerly trying to authenticate herself by finding in him the lover she has been seeking. At this point in the play (sc. 2), authenticity lies almost within grasp of both protagonists. Self-fulfillment is about to bear them both aloft as they discover their own and each other's essence. Heart's desires are about to be realized. The world surrounding the two lovers intrudes upon them in the shape of a little girl with her kite. She symbolizes the happy freedom of childhood, skipping through green meadows and white clouds. The urchin who unpleasantly surprises her by snatching away her kite may symbolically correspond to Lisardo, who has stolen Lucila's love-letters away from her and plans blackmail. The multicolored kite itself may dignify dreams of the lovers' authentication, almost within reach. The child thief may be the agent sent to destroy these dreams and to return the dreamers, unfulfilled, to the everyday world. Salinas, in his article on Don Quixote's love-letter to Dulcinea, compares the "gratuitous letter to an inflated balloon which in pure play is let loose so that we may watch it ascend heavenward."[7]

Lisardo's and Lucila's rôle-playing in each other's fiction will eventually enable them to reveal their essential selves to each other. Meanwhile, in a series of cloak-and-dagger scenes, they play games to achieve their final encounter, undisguised. In order to arrange this meeting with the "incomparable" letter-writer (296), Lisardo blackmails Eduardo for the key to Lucila's home. But the idea of blackmail causes him shame, does violence to his identity. He calls himself an "ex-gentleman," to use his own self-deprecating expression. He wants to end the charade to turn from fiction to the everyday sphere (295). Lucila, on the other hand, prefers to retain her fictional self until she can determine that Lisardo is indeed the lover she invented in her letters. In other words, she will not relinquish her disguise until the point that she can truly claim her identity as a beloved.

The letters themselves serve as catalytic agents to precipitate the dénouement of this play, bringing the two lovers together and enabling them to authenticate themselves then and there. Having come across these letters has caused Lisardo to go astray by resorting to blackmail. On the other hand, recall that Lucila, author of the letters, has taken the initiative in composing them and arranging for their discovery in the theater. The letters are far from being impersonal objects: they show the very "essence" of the writer herself. As Salinas suggests in his essay *El defensor* (49), "Paradoxically, a letter, subjective as it may be, is an abstraction of the person [i.e., its author]. The latter does not live in what he is as a whole human being, but in what he says." A letter, therefore, presupposes and even requires a second person, its recipient. "Behold the minimum social circle of the letter: two people. It is the number of perfect intimacy. The most akin to the number of love" (26). Letters, Salinas adds, allow the author not only to yield to the pleasure of personal identity, but also to conceive of their addressee as he wishes.[8]

Lucila the letter-writer directly motivates the forward action of the drama, which eventually leads to a happy solution for both protagonists. Her impersonation of

Eduardo shows that she has been creating a plot, even if it is Lisardo who sets that plot in motion through discovering the letters and through devising his subsequent blackmail scheme. Luck, moreover, "the greatest companion of all great acts," has guided his behavior (*Teatro* 292). With the aid of good fortune, added to Lucila's letters, he achieves self-authentication: "I am me and I am not me. . . . Luck has found me" (292), or given Lisardo an identity. This self-same situation is described in Salinas' poem **"Triunfo suyo"** (**"His triumph"**), which closes the anthology *Seguro azar* (*Sure Chance*). Here, the force of destiny or "sure chance" seems to give the individual feigned control over his own situation, but in the last analysis, disguises and masks come off as the true force of fate triumphs despite all appearances: "I am going to see it face to face, / because it is now doffing, / because now it is tugging / on heavens, on joys, / on disguises, on epochs, / on words, on light masks / that I put on it" (162).

Lucila confesses that her letters were destined for an unknown lover, and that she was sure he would be born sometime out of the very act of her writing to him (*Teatro* 305). He has just arrived in the person of Lisardo. She attempted a great gamble by leaving her letters in the theater. She won because Lisardo found them and, upon reading them, took on the very form of the lover she desired so fervently. Lisardo invested her letters with his own being, filled their emptiness with his body (305). Speaking to Lucila, he confesses, "When reading what you wrote to your lover in the letters, I wanted nothing except to be he." When Lisardo suggests that by writing she has created him, she responds, "It is love that makes the lover. He made me first. . . . And since he left me by myself, . . . I had to look for you . . . to make you" (306). Because they proclaim themselves true lovers, they become authentic, authenticating as well the letters themselves, now truly addressed to Lisardo, lover of Lucila. Accordingly, the play ends with the spotlight illumining the letters and proving that they had been meant for Lisardo.

As with Lisardo and Lucila, self-authentication for the protagonists Roberto and Julia of *El parecido* depends on their relationship to one another. Both define themselves within the framework of their marriage. People outside, specifically men, threaten the relationship and, hence, the identity of each. The action of authentication unfolds simply in dialogue between husband and wife always seated at the same restaurant table, with only brief interruptions from the waiter to lend credibility to the setting. Conversely, the intervention of a stranger seated behind them lends an air of unreality to their search for identity, for the waiter denies his presence. The couple's conversation, at times intense, suggests in itself inner drama, bearing out Ruiz Ramón's contention (*Historia* 285) that Pedro Salinas' one-act plays usually contain more "dramatic dialogue" than action.

The playwright counts on the "dynamism and tension" of words to provide the necessary dramatic impact. The protagonists' perception of the stranger seated at a distant table evokes Proustian recall, in the sense that awareness of the most trivial details of his person provokes a novelistic abundance of memories. The couple's embellishment of their memories amounts to a self-affirming fictionalization of the prosaic world.

The relationship of fiction to self-affirmation emerges as a dramatic possibility at the very opening of the curtain. The playwright suggests this possibility in two ways: by hinting that he could well have derived his protagonists straight from a soap-opera, and by having them speak in affected styles. The disembodied voice of a radio announcer closes the day's episode of a passionate soap opera by posing the usual hackneyed series of questions concerning the fate of two lovers. The radio can be used to replace diners' conversation, the waiter tells the protagonists (*Teatro* 27). The husband Roberto requests that the radio be turned off: only with no distractions can he and Julia affirm their identities. She points out that they have come to the restaurant with "something to talk about" while Roberto asserts that she is his "Muse of conversation" (28). He admittedly feels inspired to converse (hence, to authenticate himself) in her company. Further, the soap opera at the outset has alerted the audience to certain issues involved in the authentication process before the protagonists have even revealed them. As a matter of fact, the style in which they have communicated with one another at the beginning smacks of soap-opera affectedness: celebrating their wedding anniversary, the husband Roberto compliments his wife Julia in proparoxytones to her amusement. She notes that he serves up prosaic allusions—"roastbeef"—with poetic flights of fancy—"humbly awaiting its ascent to her precious mouth" (151).

In that process of authentication the rôle of the stranger (*el Incógnito*) has been that of a catalyst to the thoughts and reactions of Julia and Roberto. They assign him various identities. This situation resembles one described in Salinas' poem **"Vida segunda"** (**"Second Life"**) (*Fábula y signo* 188): "You escaped from memory. / You were already there, without your limits, / lost in unmemory. / And I had to invent you." The protagonists themselves invest the stranger with meaning, sometimes pleasant, sometimes vaguely sinister. On the one hand, he might be the diabolical elevator companion, capable of enticing Julia away from her husband; on the other hand, he could be the taxi driver who purposely keeps her away from temptation. The impression of his presence there behind the married couple, whoever he may be, serves to stoke their memories. Both protagonists deny that they are looking at anyone, and that his face reminds them of anyone. They refer to him as "nobody" (*Teatro* 29). For Julia, however, "that face is on the very tip of my memory" (29); for Roberto, the stranger has been "something like an apparition" (34). If the stranger does not exist at all, as the waiter claims, then the reality of their experience is also questionable. "Fable" (imaginings) has become reality, a key to identity, as both relive past experiences in narrating them in the presence of the audience.

The spouses must share their memories with each other. Otherwise, neither can become complete, authentic. Each lightly mocks the embroiderings on the recollections offered by the other. "Material for novels!" is what Roberto calls Julia's musings (31); she calls his a "little novel," resembling *Paul et Virginie*, though taking place on a less fabled isle, Manhattan (33). Amidst reminiscences, each pulls the other back to the mundane world because each needs the other's company in the immediate present. The past experiences narrated by each one necessarily excluded the other. For this reason, a certain instinctive rejection of the spouse's memories takes place despite the need to hear them for the sake of mutual understanding and personal authenticity.

Part of Julia's personality consists of an ability to foretell events. She turns this talent to her own advantage for attaining identity. At the same time, she convinces Roberto that his personal memories are as valid as hers, for they reaffirm *his* being just as hers do for her. In Spanish, the word *sí* signifies the positive response "yes"; its homonym *si* means the hypothetical conjunction "if." At once conditional and affirmative, these two phonemes, set together, symbolize for the implied playwright "all those things which might have been able to happen" (31). Salinas' stage directions call for the actress playing Julia to stress the word *sí* (31). In his poetry the word *sí* is the affirmation of all possibilities.[9] In the poem **"Lo nunca igual"** (**"Never the Same,"** *Fábula* 174), the poetic voice points out that the perception of each moment is unique. Interpreting the moment determines its essence in itself together with its meaning for the person experiencing it. The uniqueness of each moment as the person lives it constitutes a personal affirmation. Julia, therefore, tells Roberto, if (*si*) she and he had not made the choices that they did from among all their many possibilities, they would not be in the affirmative flush of celebrating their fifteenth anniversary (*Teatro* 31). Analogously, when a living person did not exist to confirm Roberto's fears of separation from his beloved Julia, he invented a seducer, who in fact personified his fears. He thereby affirmed himself, as well as his love for her. Fiction mediated his self-affirmation (33-34).

Julia, on the other hand, finds memories hard to grasp and has had to cover her eyes in order to see inwardly. Nevertheless, her last remembered anecdote comes almost in spite of herself; as Roberto notes, she seems to

want to "suppress its reality" (36). That would mean denying a lived experience that helped authenticate her. Roberto himself is so in harmony with his wife, on whom he depends for his own affirmation, that he reacts strongly to her story: he feels a "long-delayed shiver" of apprehension, for now he understands how close he came to losing her . . . and himself. His being with her now, sharing the celebration of more than fifteen years of married life, seems more than a fiction. It is a "miracle" that he is still alive, authenticated, having escaped mortal danger (40).

Salinas as playwright uses a theatrical device to emphasize how attuned Julia and Roberto are to one another. It is "pure coincidence"—in the words of the poet Salinas, "sure chance"—that even the buttons on their jackets are the same. It takes the stranger to point out the coincidence to them on offering them the tangible evidence of a button fallen from someone's clothing. If the protagonists have been blind before, unable to "see what is put before their eyes" (35), they are now made aware of both their physical surroundings and their own inner world through a combination of memory and the fictionalizing of it.

Until now Roberto and Julia have accepted the stranger as a catalyst for reminiscing. They have been unwilling to verify his true identity. However, in a reversal of the opening scenes of the play, Roberto acts like an automaton, according to stage directions, while the stranger is to behave "naturally" though implying through attitude and voice tone that there is still something strange about him (40). It has been the waiter, we have seen, who has denied the stranger any corporality. The mound of ashes he has left behind in his ashtray still does not make him real for the waiter (41-42). What symbolism may the ashes hold? Memories are ephemeral, and the stranger has not really existed except as an object of a passing perception. Still, in *El parecido* the protagonists' perception of him has served to affirm the essential being both of Julia and of Roberto. The word *incógnito*, after all, might more accurately translate into English as "unknown," in some contexts, even as "hidden." Although neither Roberto nor Julia may ever truly know the other, both have certainly understood their own inner worlds. They have discovered and analyzed their emotions and reactions to past situations and thus have authenticated themselves.

The four plays here analyzed all show the authorial figures' awareness of employing metafiction in their search for their essential beings. In *El precio* and *La estratoesfera* the author-character facilitates his character's self-affirmation and simultaneously affirms himself. Letters in *El chantajista* and reminiscences in *El parecido* are the media through which protagonists author their own and their beloveds' attainment of identity. In the process, all these characters discover truths about existence: to achieve immortality for himself and his fictional character, a writer must situate his creature in a convincing spatio-temporal setting within the literary work (*El precio, La estratoesfera*); for self-fulfillment, the individual must design fictions in such a way as to affirm the beloved through them (*El chantajista, El parecido*).

Notes

1. Cf Materna (119, n 57), where four lines from this poem are discussed.

2. Hugo Cowes finds that Melisa does not "act like a human being . . . but always has an aura of unreality in her speech and mode of walking" (*Relación* 93).

3. Cf Fray Luis de Leôn (69): "Despiértenme las aves / con su cantar sabroso no aprendido" ("May birds wake me up, / with their sweet, untutored song").

4. In *La voz a ti debida* (243) the poet, speaking in first person, reduces all cosmic being to the essential pronoun, the irreducible Thou, which enables him to unite with his beloved.

5. For Cowes (47), all the dramatic movement has been motivated by the actions of Alvaro.

6. *La responsabilidad del escritor* (84). A group of workers in *La estratoesfera* offers a socialist interpretation of *Don Quixote,* available to everyone through the medium of the movies (79-80).

7. *Teatro* (107); cf "Fecha cualquiera," *Seguro azar* (114). Moraleda (*Teatro de P. S.* 109) notes that Lucila, like the little girl, pursues a fantasy, that of a man's love. Cowes (79) only sees the little girl and her kite as a "fumdamental symbol," but does not explain of what.

8. *El defensor* (23). Salinas may well have chosen for *El chantajista* a female author because he finds that a woman has a "special aptitude for intimate letter-writing as proven so repeatedly from the Middle Ages to today. This aptitude must correspond to some particularly feminine psychological trait": *El defensor* (52).

9. Fifteen poems included in his *Poesías completas* start with *sí* or *si*. Of these poems, perhaps most significant are the six included in the anthology *Fábula y signo* (*Fable and Sign*). "Mar distante" ("Distant sea": 169) repeats the theme of possibilities in each of its four strophes. The world of things seems to be interchangeable with each of its many facets: sea = its image = its name = its very idea. In the poem "Muertes" ("Deaths" 177-178), the poetic voice explains the fading from memory of the beloved's physical attributes while thinking that it would be necessary to ask who she was if she were now nearby.

Bibliography

I. PRIMARY SOURCES

Salinas, Pedro. *El defensor.* Bogotá: Universidad Nacional, 1948.

————. "Don Quijote en presente." In *Ensayos de literatura hispánica.* Ed. Juan Marichal. Madrid: Aguilar, 1961. Pp. 75-87.

————. *Fábula y signo.* In *Poesías completas.* Pp. 163-214.

————. "La mejor carta de amores de la literatura española." In *Ensayos de literatura hispánica.* Pp. 111-26.

————. *La responsabilidad del escritor.* Barcelona: Seix-Barral, 1961.

————. *Seguro azar.* In *Poesías completas.* Pp. 105-62.

————. *Teatro completo.* Ed. Pilar Moraleda. Seville: Ediciones Alfar, 1992.

————. *Todo más claro.* In *Poesías completas.* Pp. 591-722.

————. *La voz a ti debida.* In *Poesías completas.* Pp. 215-329.

II. OTHER WORKS CONSULTED

Cowes, Hugo W. "Realidad y superrealidad en *Los Santos* de Pedro Salinas." *Cuadernos Americanos,* 32, 3 (May-June 1973): 262-77.

Darío, Rubén. "Coloquio de los centauros." *Prosas profanas.* In *Obras Completas.* Madrid: Afrodisio Aguado, 1953. V: 794-803.

Gila, Antonio. "*El chantajista* y el teatro de Salinas." *Duquesne Hispanic Review,* 6 (Autumn 1967): 9-21.

Materna, Linda S. "Poetry and Realism in Modern Spanish Theater: Pedro Salinas and Other Dramatists of the Generation of 1927." Unpubl. Ph.D. Diss., U. Wisc., 1980.

Michener, Charles D. and Mary. "Bee." *Collier's Encyclopedia.* New York: Crowell, Collier and Macmillan, 1967. III: 758-69.

Moraleda, Pilar. "Introducción." In *Teatro completo* by Pedro Salinas. Pp. 9-21.

————. *El teatro de Pedro Salinas.* Madrid: Ediciones Pegaso, 1985.

Ruiz Ramón, Francisco. *Historia del teatro español. Siglo XX.* 2d ed. Madrid: Cátedra, 1975.

Unamuno, Miguel de. *Niebla.* In *Obras completas,* II. Pp. 540-682.

Zubizarreta, Alma de. *Pedro Salinas: El diálogo creador.* Madrid: Gredos, 1969.

Vialla Hartfield-Méndez (essay date summer 1999)

SOURCE: Hartfield-Méndez, Vialla. "Mirrors and Pedro Salinas' Doubled 'You.'" *Bulletin of Hispanic Studies* 76, no. 3 (summer 1999): 415-31.

[*In the following essay, Hartfield-Méndez investigates Salinas's use of mirror images in his poetry, contending that they not only inform male-female relationships in the poems but act in such a way "as to go beyond the nature of these relationships to the nature of language and even reality itself."*]

> And certainly the glass *was* beginning to melt away, just like a bright silvery mist.
>
> Lewis Carrol, *Through the Looking-Glass*

The mirror, together with other specular devices, has long held symbolic meaning in Western culture and literature. It also early on came to stand as a metaphor for language, or certain aspects of language, a function that has been exploited with a great deal of subtlety in the twentieth century.[1] This is the case in the writings of Pedro Salinas, whose specular images most frequently occur when a man is looking at a woman, though the situation is sometimes reversed. I have earlier argued, in a somewhat different context, that female split identities can be observed in Salinas' mirrors, and that his specular images are often related to treacherous memory, thus frequently indicating a disillusion in the search for a mutual transcendence for lovers.[2] Moreover, I will argue here, Salinas' exploration of male-female relationships also involves mirror images in such a way as to go beyond the nature of these relationships to the nature of language and even of reality itself. Indeed, the special reciprocal relationship that mirrors and language have in Salinas' work reveals a profound ambiguity about both. As we explore his equivocal view of these two reflexive devices—the mirror and language—it becomes clear that, while Salinas fully participated in a symbolist-modernist *Weltanschauung*, he also patently anticipated what is now considered the postmodern.

Among Hispanists, Andrew Debicki has perhaps most successfully recast the traditional divisions of Hispanic letters in European and American terms, referring to a 'modernity' in Spanish letters that loosely corresponds to a more general concept of modernism than the somewhat narrowly defined Latin-American *modernista* movement. Departing from Marjorie Perloff's view that in Anglo-American modernism there are two antithetical tendencies, one stemming from symbolism, the other 'anti-Symbolist' in its 'indeterminancy or "undecidability"' (Perloff's phrase), Debicki maintains that a similar 'strand of indeterminacy' runs through Spanish poetics of the early twentieth century.[3] Salinas is cited by Debicki as representative of this tendency to

undermine confidence in language's ultimate powers to convey experience. As he points out, the critic and observer in Salinas often propounded language's capabilities, the best example of this stance being his *El defensor,* a series of essays in defence of the acts of writing and reading.[4] Nevertheless, Debicki observes, 'many of Salinas's actual poems convey, above all, the impossibility of this quest [for ultimate meanings] and the undecidable nature of what we see, experience and seek'.[5] While stopping short of declaring Salinas' poetry 'indeterminate', Robert Havard has also observed a central preoccupation with language, along with an 'often antagonistic attitude towards language', stating that 'Salinas's whole purpose is to destabilize language, in its lexicon, its syntax, and in its rhetorical resources'.[6] A close study of Salinas' treatment of the mirror helps to elucidate this writer's relationship to language, and reveals that specular devices play a much larger role in his poetics of language than critics have heretofore observed. Furthermore, this image appears in his earliest works and continues throughout his literary production. But before we engage in a systematic explication of the Salinian mirror images, a prior consideration of the speculum as a semantic presence will greatly aid our understanding of the mirror's central position in Salinas' articulation of the pitfalls of language.

The mirror's ability to function as a literary sign has been seriously questioned, most notably by Umberto Eco, in his *Semiotics and the Philosophy of Language.* This may be due, in part, to a form of logocentrism, that is, the privileging of spoken and written language over other forms of communication, a process arising from what Albert Borgmann, following Richard Rorty, calls the 'linguistic turn' that philosophy took with the publication of Wittgenstein's *Tractatus Logico-Philosophicus* in 1921.[7] This precludes granting to any object the power to communicate or express reality, a process which is usurped by a discussion of the language used to present that object. While he makes no specific reference to such a 'linguistic turn', it is within this milieu that Eco argues that the mirror, and whatever may occur in the catoptric process, can only be considered a '(pseudo-)semantics'.[8] Other critics have taken issue with Eco, some more emphatically than others. Jenijoy La Belle, in *Herself Beheld. The Literature of the Looking-Glass,* offers the most thorough rebuttal of the assumption that the mirror image is not a sign, preferring to see the catoptric and the linguistic as inextricably intertwined. Eco maintains that 'the mirror image *cannot be interpreted.* At most the object to which it refers can be interpreted [. . .]' [his emphasis].[9] La Belle counters with the argument that the mirror does indeed have a 'differential' property that can be perceived when one focuses on the psychological interaction with the mirror, a property that allows for interpretation, both of the mirror image *and* the object to which it refers.

In her analysis of women in literature looking at themselves in mirrors, La Belle observes a phenomenon that she calls the 'oxymoronic mirror', where the specular image is a

> signifier necessarily different from its signified—and yet a signifier with a peculiarly (perhaps even uniquely) intimate, direct, and complete relationship with the signified.[10]

The mirror image is 'at once the self (at least in the visual sense) and not the self; that is, at once self and other.[11] It is this oxymoronic nature that, La Belle contends, 'provides mirroring with the differential nature of the lingual sign'.[12] In numerous texts, this critic observes 'competing semiotic modes of self-realization: writing and mirroring'.[13] Thus, while she recognizes that the intertwining of the catoptric and the linguistic occurs 'when the experience of mirroring is communicated to us through a text', she maintains that this also occurs 'at a more fundamental level when one recognizes one's own reflection'.[14] Hence the mirror's competition with lingual signs in certain literary texts that present self-reflexive situations.

La Belle's study is generally focused on women looking at themselves in mirrors. When the third, and male, party is introduced (as is the case in so many Salinian texts), we find that the intermingling of the catoptric and the semiotic becomes even more complex, and paradoxically, more perspicuous. In a consideration of this writer's poetry, Jonathan Mayhew has also taken some exception to Eco's argument that the mirror image cannot function as a sign, asserting that Salinas does indeed 'posit a semiotics of the mirror'.[15] Mayhew's observations regarding the Salinian mirror are along the lines of La Belle's argument: that the reflection in certain texts is not merely mimetic but in fact it fundamentally changes the referent, and that even its mimetic characteristics create ambiguity. Mayhew's study confines itself to Salinas' poetry. Yet in his prose works, as well as in his theatre, we can also observe one being looking at the reflection of the other in the mirror, using the mirror in the realization of the other, in a strikingly semiotic manner, then facing the consequences of this act.[16] Thus, while the mirror is crucial to any interpretation of Salinas' treatment of the man/woman relationship, it is just as fundamental to any interpretation of his views of language and of reality.

As early as 1914 and 1915, in love letters to his then fiancée Margarita Bonmatí, the mirror image appears metaphorically. For the young writer, he and Margarita are mutually illuminating and reflective: 'Vida, los dos somos luz y espejo. Yo espejo para tu luz y tú, alma, espejo para la mía'.[17] This and other similar references in the letters anticipate certain images in Salinas' later love poetry and in his theatrical and narrative projections of the male/female relationship. The mirror images form an integral part of the way in which Salinas perceives and projects the female *persona,* the male *persona,* and especially the relationship between the two. Narrative, theatrical and poetic pieces written throughout his career point to a dual function of the speculum. On the one hand, mirrors are a possible tool in a metaphysical quest for the essence of woman, of man, or of a world beyond the parameters of the individual human soul accessible to the man and woman together. On the other hand, there is ample evidence that the mirror fails as a transcending device and thus becomes a symbol of disillusion and error: disillusion in the process of mutual knowledge in the male/female relationship, in the process of self-knowledge through that relationship, and ultimately in the search for transcendence through language, or the expression of such a relationship.[18]

One of the most salient characteristics of Salinas' poetry is his insistence on the use of pronouns, especially the *yo* and the *tú*. A frequently cited passage from *La voz a ti debida* points to this obsession: '¡Qué alegría más alta: / vivir en los pronombres!'.[19] Numerous interpretations of Salinas' pronouns have been put forth, most of which have to do with a search for some sort of transcendence.[20] J. M. Aguirre, referring to Bergson's postulation of the existence of a fundamental 'I' set in opposition to a conventional, mundane and material 'I', has argued that *La voz a ti debida* presents the case of the poet's fundamental 'I' searching for communication with the fundamental 'I' of the beloved.[21] Yet there are many instances in Salinas' work of a divided *yo,* or *tú,* that is very aware of its own division—instances in which later psychoanalytical approaches prove to be more pertinent.

The idea of *aware* divided selves, of one self that observes the other, is of course Freudian in origin, and has been developed further by various psychoanalysts and theorists. Best known among these is perhaps Jacques Lacan, whose theories regarding the *stade du miroir* and the construct of self through reflection in another, are related to the ontological questions of self-knowledge and knowledge of the other. Crucial to Lacan's notion of a developmental 'mirror phase' is the idea that the child at once discovers himself and sees himself as other in the mirror.[22] D. W. Winnicott and Heinz Kohut go beyond the actual mirror to other ways of self-reflection. As Wendy Lesser points out, for both these theorists, it is the mother or a similar substitute figure who initially 'offers the mirroring function that Lacan attributes to the mirror itself'.[23] Departing from this premise, Lesser argues that such a concept of mirroring opens up the process, so that, instead of the closed prospect offered by the cold inanimate mirror there is a sense of mutuality and of a self contained within another being.[24] Thus, for Lesser, when men look at women through art, there is a sense of completion of themselves, a discovery of their other selves. This frequently manifests itself explicitly in the image of the woman-as-mirror (an image that occurs in Salinas' texts). This is a mirror 'in which the portrait one gets back is not the self one expects, but the lost self for which one searches'.[25] There is the sense of a self regarding itself, being truly self-aware and simultaneously aware of a lack, a gap into which another being can step and act as a mirror where one can find, as it were, the rest of oneself. Even in Lacan's explication of the mirror stage, this lack, or gap, is intuited, since, as Carmen Chaves Tesser notes, '[t]he mirror stage is also the point at which language begins to fill voids'.[26] When one is at once self-aware and aware of a space which another being can fill, the articulation of that space is through language. At the same time, language is also the medium through which that space may be filled—the expression of the recognition and/or creation of the other.[27]

And yet in Salinas' work, we are confronted, not only with self-contemplation and division of the 'I', but also the complicated relationship of self to the other. The distinction between self and other has also been explored by Tzvetan Todorov, who in turn refers to Martin Buber's concept of *I-Thou*, according to which, '[t]here is no *I* taken in itself, but only the *I* of the primary word *I-Thou* and the *I* of the primary word *I-It*. When a man says *I*, he refers to one or the other of these'. Todorov adds: 'Further, the *I* and the *Thou*—that is, the self and the other—designate the two participants in the act of discourse; the one who speaks and the one addressed'.[28] The creation, or acknowledgement, of the other—of a *tú*, as in Salinas' poetry—thus presupposes the relationship of the self, or the *yo*, to that other. If we continue Todorov's line of thought, it follows that the literary creation of the other also arranges the self and the other in an active (speaker)/passive (listener) relationship. Thus, we can argue, the *I* of a narrative or poem or theatrical speech simultaneously speaks *to* the other and speaks the other *into being*. This may seem almost tautological, and yet it is fundamental to a clear understanding of the *yo-tú* relationships found in Salinas' work. Not surprisingly, especially given that much of his poetry evokes an apparently real love affair, in most of these relationships the speaker/listener dichotomy is also male/female. It will also be clear by now that the dichotomy 'self/other' exists in two domains: first, there is the self and the other as two distinct beings, two different people in relationship (even though the 'other' may be a construct of the 'self'); and within that relationship, both entities, the self and the other, may become divided, so that we have the self (or I) and its other 'self', and the other and its other 'self'. That is, both the *yo* and the *tú* can have other 'selves' unilaterally.

In his 1914-15 letters to Margarita, Pedro Salinas had already conceived of the divided self as both masculine and feminine. Each is light and mirror, source and reflection. And each sees another self reflected in the other's mirror. In these early letters, Salinas celebrates the separation within each individual self because he wants it to mean union with the other being and thereby access to their higher 'true' selves. However, he quickly begins to recognize the pitfalls of this division of self and is suspicious of the veracity of the reflected selves. Interestingly, the references to a division of the masculine self disappear almost entirely, allowing for a concentration on a doubled feminine *tú*. This reflects a deliberate *I-Thou* construct in which the emphasis is on the *Thou*, yet in which definition of self is in the other.

Keeping in mind the implication of the *yo* in the construct of the *tú*, let us examine this feminine *tú* and her experience with the mirror in Salinas' work. La Belle identifies a particularly feminine tendency in literature toward a psychological dependence on the mirror and observes two internal processes. The first is an identification of the reflection in the mirror with the self, leading to the definition of self (sometimes exclusively) through that intangible image. In the second process the differences between the two images are emphasized, in some cases to such a degree that the woman does not recognize her own reflection and refuses to own it. There is a 'destabilization of identity'; the act of looking into a speculum actually produces a division of the self.[29] In Salinas' work, the poetic male *yo*, or other male characters tend to observe and even create the feminine split identities by placing literal and figurative mirrors before the women. The resulting doubled selves are a barrier to communication between the sexes, a barrier that is clearly evident in a poem from **Razón de amor** in which the poet addresses a *tú* who vacillates between her selves: the self that responds to his love, and is in fact identified with the emotion *amor*; and the other more cautious self. The poet exclaims:

> ¡Qué vaivén entre una y otra!
> A los espejos del mundo,
> al silencio, a los azares,
> preguntabas
> cuál sería la mejor.
>
> (*Poesías*, 363)

The *espejos* are a place where the beloved must choose between one and the other, a place which assumes the division of herself. The suitor's frustration stems from his inability to be with both simultaneously:

> Cuando estabais separadas,
> como la flor de su flor,
> ¡qué lejos de ti tenía
> que ir a buscarte el querer!
>
> (*Poesías*, 363)

A resolution of the conflict occurs when the beloved's two selves look at each other, as in a mirror, and are focused into one being:

> Cara a cara te miraste,
> tu mirada en ti te vio:
> eras ya la que querías.

(Poesías, 363)

Yet the poem ends ambiguously, as Salinas intended. In the poet's earlier description, the woman's self is separate from her other self, the one that loves, and that other self's identity is 'amor', a masculine noun in Spanish. The self that loves is the self that responds to her lover's demands and is indistinguishable from his masculine perspective. In the end, when the doubled *tú* seems to be refocused into one, the poem takes a turn from resolution to a sense that one being has overcome and eclipsed the other:

> Y esta paz de ser entero
> no sabe el alma quién la ganó:
> o es que tu amor se parece
> a ti, de tanto quererte,
> o es que tú,
> de tanto estarle queriendo,
> eres ya igual que tu amor.

(Poesías, 364)

The use of a mirror by the male *yo* is even more patent in an early poem from ***Presagios***. It is not the woman but her lover who observes her image in the mirror, and who therefore *a priori* doubles the *you*:

> ¡Cuánto rato te he mirado
> sin mirarte a ti, en la imagen
> exacta e inaccesible
> que te traiciona el espejo!

(Poesías, 60)

The flesh-and-blood woman urges him to kiss her, but the mirror woman interposes herself:

> y mientras te beso pienso
> en lo frío que serán
> tus labios en el espejo.

(Poesías, 60)

The probable frigidity of her lips in the mirror makes it impossible for him to be satisfied that the woman is truthful when she says, 'Toda el alma para ti'. He experiences an emptiness that can be filled only by 'ese alma / que no me das'. But the essence of herself that she is not surrendering to him (notwithstanding her protestation to the contrary) is in the mirror, the poet says. Or is it? The last three lines reveal both a 'true' self and a disguise:

> El alma que se recata
> con disfraz de claridades
> en tu forma del espejo.

(Poesías, 60)

It is in the context of his discussion of this poem that Mayhew makes his observation, cited earlier, that Salinas posits 'a semiotics of the mirror', since 'the reflection does not merely copy the referent, but rather simultaneously adds to and subtracts from it'.[30] The mirror thus becomes ambiguous and paradoxical, rather than a mere mimetic device. According to Mayhew, the conclusion 'willfully introduces obstacles to the mimetic directness of the mirror image'.[31] Mayhew's commentary is centred on Salinas' 'poetics of self-consciousness' and the poet's deliberate foregrounding of the medium of expression 'at the expense of the reality represented'.[32] Yet Salinas' intentional focus on the mirror, and therefore the medium of language, does have consequences in the poet's relationship with the *tú*, which are not considered in Mayhew's comments. If we focus on the nature of the *tú*, given the equivocal characteristics of the Salinian mirror, we can see that the result is a disconcerting doubling of the *tú* that alternates between, and exists in, both the real woman and her reflection. Salinas' intent is not so much to reject the living reality of the woman as it is to explore the repercussions of the poetic medium in his relationship with her.

In the last lines of another poem from the same book, the poet clearly recognizes the danger in seeking out images of the woman in a speculum. There is a clear 'amenaza / de romperte en dos pedazos / —vida o muerte, tierra o cielo— / bruscamente, irreparable' *(Poesías,* 64). Once having separated the *tú* into something like a Bergsonian fundamental 'I' and superficial 'I', the doubling may be irrevocable. At the very least, it becomes another obstacle to the union of the *yo* and the *tú*. Salinas expresses a similar fundamental fear in ***La voz a ti debida***:

> . . . Mejor no amarse
> mirándose en espejos complacidos
> deshaciendo
> esa gran unidad en juegos vanos.

(Poesías, 281)

Here the fear is not so much that the *tú* will be irreversibly doubled and therefore inaccessible, but that the union of the lovers can be annulled by the mirror's power to separate. Thus, even when the lovers seem to have found their other selves in each other, thereby forming a new being that transcends themselves and the mundane, there is still the constant threat that the new being will be rent asunder.

There are also numerous parallels in Salinas' short narratives and theatre where, as in the poetry we have seen, the woman's reflection in a mirror is manipulated by the man. The central motif of the short drama ***La bella durmiente*** is the female protagonist's loss of herself in a mirror owned by her would-be suitor. The two characters meet at a mountain retreat under the assumed names of Soledad and Álvaro. They begin to talk and to fall in love, but their past will prevent a happy ending. Soledad works as a model for the Rolán mattress company, for which she created a 'Sleeping Beauty' character as part of an advertising campaign. She feels that she has lost her own identity and blames its destruction on the company. Álvaro, as it turns out, is the owner of the company, and thereby the owner of the 'Sleeping Beauty' image. Soledad, never cognisant of this, tells her story to Álvaro in all confidence. In her description of the loss of identity, she speaks of a moment which occurred while she was dressed as Sleeping Beauty, when someone held a mirror for her: 'yo me incliné sobre su círculo y me hundí desde entonces para siempre en él. La vi a ella, no a mí'.[33] The radical disjunction of her two selves is indeed irreparable, as the poet Salinas had earlier comprehended that it could be. Soledad's autonomous self is lost in a mirror image belonging to Álvaro. Before hearing her story, he had proposed to her. At the end of her story, she explains why she can never marry:

> Ese nombre me ha vaciado de mí misma. ¿Siente usted ahora por qué le dije que no tenía en mí mujer con quién casarse? La ha absorbido toda . . . el nombre ese. Rolán . . .
>
> (*Teatro*, 189)

The possibility of relationship or even the most basic communication is denied. Once Soledad has told him her story, he cannot even acknowledge that he is the owner of the Rolán company, the man who has already 'absorbed' her entire identity.[34]

Soledad's tragedy lies in her inability either to return to herself, or go forward into a mutually reflective relationship with Álvaro. Not all of Salinas' female characters are so paralysed, however. On occasion, the woman takes the mirror into her own hands, holding it for herself, creating her own self image. Paradoxically, this action on the part of the woman removes her even further from the male/female relationship, as she turns from her lover to her mirror. It also upsets the active/passive arrangement of the discourse. In Salinas' work, when the male *yo* extends a mirror to the female *tú*, this action is part and parcel of the creation of the female other, which depends upon the passive acceptance by the woman of the image that she finds there. When that acquiescence disappears, so does the relationship of self/other that the male *yo* has been creating. La Belle has found numerous examples of 'how the male/female bond breaks down as the mirror/female bond becomes stronger', and she offers an explanation:

> Since the mirror image is both self and other, it becomes possible to conceive of a relationship with the glass having a degree of intimacy more intense than any relationship a woman can have with a lover.[35]

The clearest literary examples of this counterbalance that La Belle finds are in D. H. Lawrence's portrayals of women with their mirrors, texts in which Lawrence consistently urges the woman to forgo acts of self-reflection in front of her mirror in order to, in La Belle's words, 'forget the ego and dissolve into the greater male/female unity'.[36] Lawrence and Salinas coincide in the search for unity and in the view that a woman's deliberate use of her own mirror disrupts that unity.

'Livia Schubert, incompleta', an early short story from *Víspera del gozo* illustrates the way this transpires in Salinas' literary evocations of relationship. Livia is asleep on the bed after an afternoon of love. Her lover, the narrator, observes her. He sees himself on her sleeping face, but knows that upon awakening she will remove every vestige of him. Finally,

> se quedará ante el espejo, yo deshecho, rehecha ella, convertida lo que era hace un instante, rica y tumultuosa, vida en mis brazos, en una biografía correctísima, sin una imperfección.[37]

As the story progresses, Livia's actions correspond to her lover's figurative expectations. Her final act is to leave on a train with the clear intention of never returning.

The woman's deliberate use of the mirror in a solitary fashion that removes her from the mutual relationship has similar connotations in Salinas' poetry. In his trilogy of love poems (*La voz a ti debida, Razón de amor* and *Largo lamento*) there is a discernible progression from a mutual, transcendental relationship to the lovers' separation and the poet's disillusionment—with love and with the act of writing. Repeated references to mirrors in *Razón de amor* and *Largo lamento* evoke a nostalgia for the earlier relationship. In an especially poignant passage in *Largo lamento,* the speculum conveys the pain of the lovers' separation:

> ¡Qué olvidado el espejo, sí el espejo,
> en donde nos miramos una tarde
> [. . .]
> un deseo común nos subió al alma!:
> no salir nunca de él, allí quedarnos
> igual que en una tumba,
> mas una tumba de vivir,
> [. . .]
> Tú te marchaste de él: era mi vida.
> Y mientras yo contemplo en su vacío
> poblado de fantasmas de reflejos,
> la soledad que es siempre
> mi cara si la veo sin la tuya,
> tú, antes de ir a algún baile,
> en otro espejo, sola, te miras a ti misma
> con los ojos que un día prometieron
> que sólo te verías en los míos.
>
> (*Poesías*, 500-01)

First, the lovers had contemplated themselves together in a mirror that became a tomb—an ominous prison from which the *tú* escaped. The poetic *yo* is left with an empty mirror, or, more correctly, a mirror in which the reflected beings are ghosts from the tomb, while the feminine *yo* turns to her own solitary reflected image, refusing to see herself in the man's eyes. The poem's subtle shift from an external mirror to the poet's eyes reveals the reason for the woman's flight from a 'tumba de vivir'. Her identity is in her mirrored image, and it is impossible for her to be both the identity that her lover reflects back to her (and in a real sense creates for her) and the identity that her own mirror reflects back (that is, her own construct of herself). This fatalistic outcome had been foreshadowed in *La voz a ti debida*, the first book of the trilogy:

> Y al verte en el amor
> que yo te tiendo siempre
> como un espejo ardiendo,
> tú reconocerás
> un rostro serio, grave,
> una desconocida
> alta, pálida y triste,
> que es mi amada [. . .]

(***Poesías***, 236-37)

Thus, the attempt at a union of two individuals is thwarted. When the male *yo* extends a mirror to the woman, it is an act fraught with the danger that she will lose herself in that speculum owned by the man, or that she will be irremediably fractured into two pieces. If she then returns to her own mirror image she is twice lost to him. The poem from *Largo lamento* is one of the few texts in which the poet or male *yo* contemplates himself in the mirror. Notably, what is left for the poet, in the absence of the beloved, is a doubling of his own *yo*, so that what fills the semantic void ('vacío') of the mirror is not the expected image of himself in relationship with her, but rather 'soledad', an image which of course finds resonance in the character Soledad in *La bella durmiente*; it turns out that the male active partner/speaker is in fact vulnerable to the same dilemma of isolation and paralysis that the female (passive partner/listener) protagonist of this drama faces.

In Salinas' work only rarely does the woman offer a mirror to the man. Yet when this does occur, the result is just as disconcerting for their relationship and identities. In **'La gloria y la niebla'**, a short story written late in his life, Salinas explores this inversion of roles. Lena, an American woman, while on vacation in Mexico, falls in love with Luis, a Spaniard in exile in that country. Luis is a budding writer. Lena is the product of a prudish environment that fears the stereotypical Latin passion that Luis represents. As a result, she disguises her authentic attraction to Luis in the form of intense admiration for his writing. Their long-distance courtship is conducted through letters. Lena's letters create a third entity, an idealized, literary Luis. Her letters insist repeatedly that Luis think 'más que en sus propias personas de amantes, en el gran tercero en concordia, el Luis soñado, ideal'.[38] Luis resists: '¿Por qué

tenderme siempre ese espejo, azogado por tu generosidad, para que yo me vea embellecido, quizá imposible?' (***Narrativa*** [***Narrativa completa***], 119).

Finally, it becomes clear for both that they must see each other and 'pararle los pies, o las alas, a un sueño que iba muy de prisa' (***Narrativa***, 120). They agree to meet and marry in San Francisco. Their first afternoon together is spent exploring the city. A thick fog overtakes them in the park. Eventually, they stumble upon a large monument and manage to decipher the name Edgard [*sic*] Allan Poe. For Lena, this is an omen: Luis will be as famous as Poe one day. On a sudden impulse, Luis succumbs to Lena's insistence on his future of glory, and decides to climb the statue. Blinded by the fog, Luis is unable to see that there is in fact no statue at the top of the base. Groping to find it, he falls to his death, recognizing in his last moments the great error that they have committed.

Robert Spires has analysed this story in the context of a conflict between 'una realidad concreta de hoy frente a una realidad inventada e intemporal' and notes that it is Luis who first gives Lena access to this other invented world, with his 'habilidad de crear una realidad a base de signos de sugestión'.[39] In the first part of the story, Luis, who is acting as a guide for Lena and her friend Florence, accompanies them to the indigenous ruins near Mexico City. When they stop to have dinner at a seventeenth-century palace converted into a restaurant, Luis describes in great detail the private regions of the palace that are off limits to the tourists, even though he has never entered them. This affects Lena profoundly, and is the beginning of her obsession with Luis. Spires interprets Lena's growing creation of Luis as a great and famous writer as her impulse to concretize everything, resisting that 'invented and atemporal reality', and yet her creation of Luis may also be read as precisely her own invention of reality, set in opposition to concrete evidence—an invention tainted, it is true, by her materialistic and puritan manner of being that rejects sexual impulses and substitutes the idea of glory in their place, as Spires observes,[40] but an invention, nevertheless.

Throughout most of Salinas' work, the man creates another self for the woman, frequently by offering her a literal mirror. In this story, he has turned the tables. Lena's letters, her written word, are the figurative mirror that creates a new self for Luis, just as the poet's written word was the mirror for the woman. Luis at first resists this literary and specular self. When he does embrace it, the result is death for both his selves.[41]

Salinas repeatedly turns to specular devices to explore the male/female relationship. Early on, the mirror symbol suggests the possibility of transcendence of the individual selves when they find the completion of themselves in the other. Yet, ultimately, the mirror is a sign of the impossibility of such transcendence. Consistently in Salinas, identity is split, or doubled, in the speculum. When male and female *personae* are in relationship, one offers a mirror to the other, most frequently the man to the woman. Repeatedly this action results in a fracturing of the other's self in the mirror, and finally in a disintegration of the *yo-tú* relationship. Since, as we have seen, the self-definition of the *yo* is bound up in that relationship, the implications for this self are ominous. The situation of one being observing, or even creating, another in a speculum allows the mirror to take on semiotic characteristics that are even more clearly apparent than when one being interacts with the mirror in self-reflection. The aborted mutuality of Salinas' mirrors; their dynamic potential for realizing the other, or for encountering the 'other' of the other; their differential nature present in the radical disjunctures of self that occur in them: all these elements contribute to their function within a semiotic structure. Clearly, these mirrors operate at the symbolic level as well: they are themselves symbols for a literarization of the other human being, and ultimately for literature. It is their peculiar semiotic quality, however, that allows their function in the symbolic realm to be so compelling. It is precisely their differential, semiotic nature that creates a distrust toward the catoptric, in the writer and in the reader; and the distrust of the mirror becomes a distrust of language. In an essayistic 'defence' of language, Salinas goes to great lengths to insist on language's ability to allow man to know himself and his surroundings. Yet he prefaces his arguments with a caveat:

> las palabras poseen doble potencia: una letal, y otra vivificante. Un secreto poder de muerte, parejo con otro poder de vida; que contienen, inseparables, dos realidades contrarias: la verdad y la mentira, y por eso, ofrecen a los hombres lo mismo la ocasión de engañar que la de aclarar, igual la capacidad de confundir y extraviar, que la de iluminar y encaminar.

(***El defensor*** 284-85)

This double-edged power of the word is played out in the specular images of his narrative, theatre and poetry. The mirrors in which the poet Salinas sees another *you* are essentially his creation of her in words. And just as Lena's word mirror has the intention of union and the effect of disunion, so the poet's words have the intention of transcendence and the effect of disillusion.

Having established the connection between mirrors and language, we can see, as a consequence of the mistrust of the catoptric, an undermining of the expectation that language embodies meaning and can distil the essence of experience—or even function as a tool in *creating* realities. This is most poignantly intuited in Salinian texts that set men and women in relationships where one is 'creating' the other, either directly through words or in literal or metaphorical mirrors. When language no

longer illuminates and guides, it betrays and stymies. In the place of Poe's symbolism, a *vacío* or emptiness gapes, tricking a would-be writer into falling to his death.

This pervasive element of distrust of language is related to Salinas' 'antagonistic attitude' toward language that Havard observes, and to the indeterminacy that Debicki sees in an early poem, influenced by the avant-garde movement, '35 bujías'.[42] It is also one of the hallmarks of what has come to be known as postmodernism. Matei Calinescu has posited the question of whether the insistent use of the technique of *palinode*, or retraction of one's position, might be considered a defining characteristic of a certain direction in postmodernism. The effect of palinode as it appears in postmodernism is that a text doubles back upon itself, refuting or at least calling into question its own earlier assertions. In this respect, we can see a certain anticipation of the postmodern in Salinas' semiotic mirrors. These at first seem to offer various possibilities: that a lover can find the true self of his beloved in the speculum; that he can create an image for her that she will adopt, thereby opening communication between them; that together in the mirror they can transcend their circumstances; and even that the two protagonists can be mutually reflective, turning from other mirrors to become a mirror for each other. Nevertheless, no sooner has Salinas proposed these scenarios than he retracts them, questions them, or negates them outright, always paradoxically or ironically, allowing the inherent dangers of doubling the you in the mirror to manifest themselves. Furthermore, just as the mirror takes on semiotic attributes in Salinas' work, language becomes specular, taking on the equivocal nature of his mirrors, and acting as a mirroring device whose meanings are as slippery as the quicksilver that his silvered glasses suggest. Thus, in spite of his strong symbolist legacy, or perhaps because of it, Salinas came to question its essential tenets in his work, anticipating early on some of the postmodernist tendencies that were to surface in the second half of the century.

Notes

1. For example, John Lyons and Stephen Nichols recognize this metaphorical function of the mirror in the title of a collection of essays about mimesis: *Mimesis. From Mirror to Method, Augustine to Descartes,* where 'mirror' refers to the idea of literature as 'an imitation of some reality outside itself' present since antiquity (*Mimesis. From Mirror to Method, Augustine to Descartes,* ed. John Lyons and Stephen Nichols [Hanover/London: Univ. Press of New England, 1982], 1).

2. Vialla Hartfield-Méndez, *Woman and the Infinite: Epiphanic Moments in Pedro Salinas's Art* (Lewisburg: Bucknell U. P./London: Associated University Presses, 1996).

3. Marjorie Perloff, *The Poetics of Indeterminacy: Rimbaud to Cage* (Princeton: Princeton U. P.,

1981), vii; Andrew Debicki, *Spanish Poetry of the Twentieth Century: Modernity and Beyond* (Lexington: Univ. Press of Kentucky, 1994), 30. It should be noted that Debicki considers this early 'indeterminacy' as clearly secondary to the dominant modernism rooted in symbolism.

4. Pedro Salinas, *El defensor,* ed. and intro. by Juan Marichal, first published 1954 (Madrid: Alianza, 1967). Further references to this work are indicated by page number in the text.

5. Debicki, *Spanish Poetry of the Twentieth Century,* 38.

6. Robert G. Havard, *From Romanticism to Surrealism: Seven Spanish Poets* (Totowa, New Jersey: Barnes and Noble Books, 1988), 177, 182.

7. Albert Borgmann, *The Philosophy of Language. Historical Foundations and Contemporary Issues* (The Hague: Martinus Nijhoff, 1974), 91. As Borgmann puts it, this linguistic turn 'implies that fruitful talk about reality is possible only if first of all we concern ourselves with the language in which that reality is accessible to us' (91).

8. Umberto Eco, *Semiotics and the Philosophy of Language.* Advances in Semiotics Series (Bloomington: Indiana U. P., 1984), 213. This is so, he argues, because, even if 'the mirror "names" (and this is clearly a metaphor), it only names a concrete object, it names one at a time, and it always names only the object standing in front of it' (211). Thus the mirror remains in the realm of relation between *tokens,* unable to refer to a relation between *types,* a move that Eco considers *sine qua non* for an object to be considered semiotic, or a sign (215).

9. *Ibid.,* 216.

10. Jenijoy La Belle, *Herself Beheld: The Literature of the Looking Glass* (Ithaca: Cornell U. P., 1988), 41-42.

11. Kathleen Woodward, in an article on ageism, perceives this equivocal nature of the mirror in our rejection of the mimetic function of the speculum in old age. Woodward observes, 'As we age we increasingly separate ourselves—what we take to be ourselves—from our bodies. We believe our real selves, that is our youthful selves, are hidden inside our bodies, not commensurate with them' (55). Thus, Woodward proposes a kind of Lacanian 'mirror stage' that occurs at the opposite end of the spectrum from infancy—old age. Characteristic of this later 'mirror stage' is a *resistance* to the specular image, which paradoxically has the effect of evoking the presence of the other, just as the Lacanian 'mirror stage' of infancy evokes the presence of the other in the formation of the 'I'

(Kathleen Woodward, 'Instant Repulsion: Decrepitude, the Mirror Stage, and the Literary Imagination', *The Kenyon Review,* V [1983], No. 4, 43-66).

12. La Belle, *Herself Beheld: The Literature of the Looking Glass,* 153.

13. *Ibid.,* 159.

14. *Ibid.,* 153.

15. Jonathan Mayhew, *The Poetics of Self-Consciousness: Twentieth-Century Spanish Poetry* (Lewisburg: Bucknell U. P./London and Toronto: Associated University Presses, 1994), 45.

16. Few critics have commented on the presence of mirror imagery in Salinas' work. Mayhew's chapter on Salinas in his *Poetics of Self-Consciousness* is a notable exception. See also David L. Stixrude's *The Early Poetry of Pedro Salinas* (Madrid: Castalia, 1975), which includes a brief mention of mirror images within the context of Stixrude's argument for a broad interpretation of the poet's deep existential dissatisfaction; and Rupert C. Allen's *Symbolic Experience: A Study of Poems by Pedro Salinas* (University, Alabama: Univ. of Alabama Press, 1986), in which the mirror is interpreted as 'divinatory' in the sense that it 'readily activates the projection of unconscious contents' (43). Additionally, several of the mirror images treated here also appear in my study *Woman and the Infinite,* though, as mentioned earlier, in different contexts.

17. Pedro Salinas, *Cartas de amor a Margarita, 1912-1915,* ed. Solita Salinas de Marichal (Madrid: Alianza, 1984), 159.

18. In Salinas' early and late poetry there are references to a unilateral relationship between the poet and the mirror, yet the most significant development of the specular theme is in the context of the love relationship.

19. Pedro Salinas, *Poesías completas,* ed. Soledad Salinas de Marichal (Barcelona: Barral Editores, 1971), 243. All further references to Salinas' poetry are to this edition, and are indicated by page number in the text.

20. I cite a few represe[..]tative views: Elsa Dehennin, in the first book-length study on Salinas, proposed that the pronouns substitute for more carnal language and thus are transcending devices. See *Passion d'absolu et tension expressive dans l'oeuvre poetique de Pedro Salinas* (Gent: Romanica Gandensia, 1957), 45. Salinas' close friend, fellow poet and life-long confidant Jorge Guillén suggests that the pronouns allude to the essence of things (see 'Poesía de Pedro Salinas', *Buenos Aires Literaria* [13 October 1953], 32-53). Carlos

Feal Deibe sees the pronouns as an escape from names, which he considers corporeal, into the realm of the soul (see *La poesía de Pedro Salinas* [Madrid: Gredos, 1965], 151). And C. B. Morris notes the freedom of anonymity in Salinas' use of pronouns in *Una generación de poetas españoles (1920-1936)* (Madrid: Gredos, 1988).

21. J. M. Aguirre, 'La voz a ti debida: Salinas y Bergson', *Revue de Littérature Comparée,* LII (1978), 98-118, at p. 101.

22. Jacques Lacan, *The Language of the Self. The Function of Language in Psychoanalysis,* trans., with notes and commentary, by Anthony Wilden (Baltimore/London: Johns Hopkins U. P., 1968), 160.

23. Wendy Lesser, *His Other Half. Men Looking at Women through Art* (Cambridge, MA/London: Harvard U. P., 1991), 16.

24. *Ibid.,* 17-19.

25. *Ibid.,* 11.

26. Carmen Chaves Tesser, 'Post-Structuralist Theory Mirrored in Helen Parente Cunha's *Woman Between Mirrors*', *Hispania* (USA), LXXIV (1991), No. 3, 594-97, at p. 595.

27. Ruth Katz Crispin has written an explication of Salinas' *La voz a ti debida* in Lacanian terms, according to which the trajectory of this book is comprised of an intent to communicate with the other, in order to 'lograr una confirmación más auténtica de su propio yo' (see 'Interpretando a Salinas a través de Lacan: el lenguaje y la identidad en *La voz a ti debida*', *Texto Crítico,* XVI [1990], Nos. 42-43, 37-52, at p. 37). According to Crispin, in *La voz a ti debida,* this 'interrogation' of the beloved is combined with 'la apremiante cuestión ontológica de la muerte y a la confrontación inconsciente pero esencial con la misma tradición poética', a confrontation that Crispin regards as resolved at the end of the book—that is that Salinas sees himself, not so much in competition with earlier poets, but as an essential link in the endless chain of the poetic tradition. The present study observes a confrontation, not only with the poetic tradition, but with the nature of language itself, a conflict that is not necessarily resolved.

28. Tzvetan Todorov, *The Fantastic: A Structural Approach to a Literary Genre,* trans. Richard Howard (Cleveland/London: Case Western Reserve Press, 1973), 155.

29. La Belle, *Herself Beheld: The Literature of the Looking Glass,* 112.

30. Mayhew, *The Poetics of Self-Consciousness,* 45.

31. *Ibid.,* 47.

32. *Ibid.,* 50.

33. Pedro Salinas, *Teatro completo* (Madrid: Aguilar, 1957), 185. Further references to Salinas' theatrical pieces are from this collection, and are indicated by page number in the text.

34. Salinas thus turns on its head the traditional Sleeping Beauty myth, according to which the Prince Charming who is her true love is the only possible agent of Beauty's release into life from her death sleep. In this case, the predicament that Salinas creates for his characters is oxymoronic in the way that La Belle takes the mirror to be: Soledad is for Álvaro at once her self and not her self; the 'true' Soledad bares her soul for him, but is prevented from being in relationship by the 'other' that his mirror has created for her. The kiss of her Prince Charming has become the source of her solitude.

35. La Belle, *Herself Beheld: The Literature of the Looking Glass,* 67, 69.

36. *Ibid.,* 71.

37. Pedro Salinas, *Prelude to Pleasure,* a bilingual edition of *Víspera del gozo,* trans. and intro. Noël Valis (Lewisburg: Bucknell U. P./London and Toronto: Associated University Presses, 1993), 94.

38. Pedro Salinas, *Narrativa completa,* ed. Soledad Salinas de Marichal (Barcelona: Barral, 1976), 119. Further references to this story are to this edition and are indicated by page number in the text.

39. Robert C. Spires, 'Realidad prosaica e imaginación transcendente en dos cuentos de Pedro Salinas', in *Pedro Salinas,* ed. Andrew P. Debicki. El Escritor y la Crítica (Madrid: Taurus, 1976), 249-57, at p. 253.

40. *Ibid.,* 255.

41. Poe's influence on Salinas has not been fully explored. The Spanish poet lived in Baltimore, site of Poe's death and burial, for a number of years while teaching at Johns Hopkins University and was well aware of the American writer's influence on other Hispanic writers, including Darío and the other *modernistas.* For our purposes here, it is of considerable interest that Poe also explored the question of doubleness, or of a divided self in his stories of the detective Dupin; and certainly, the almost other-worldly aura of mystery in this story created by the fog, which is in itself a perfectly explainable natural phenomenon, yet in combination with human interpretations and actions has disastrous consequences, evokes similar scenarios in Poe.

42. Debicki, *Spanish Poetry of the Twentieth Century,* 36-38.

Susan G. Polansky (essay date 2006)

SOURCE: Polansky, Susan G. "Poet and Plot: Salinas's 'Fabula' of Confinement-to-Freedom." In *The Poet as Hero: Pedro Salinas and His Theater,* pp. 141-65. Newark, Del.: Juan de la Cuesta, 2006.

[*In the following essay, Polansky traces a "fundamental action" that runs throughout and unites Salinas's fourteen plays: "the movement by a character or characters out of confining isolation toward liberating contact with another or others."*]

Es inútil tratar de convertirla [la poesía] en un ave doméstica, subyugada, confinada, pronto a servir en cualquier momento, transformándose en el plato familiar de cada día. No admite jaulas ni corrales.

Salinas, **"Prólogo a una traducción de sus poemas,"** *Ensayos completos III* 430

It is useless to try to turn it [poetry] into a domestic bird, subdued, confined, ready to serve at any moment, by changing it into an ordinary, everyday dish. It does not allow cages or corrals.

In the preface to **Reality and the Poet in Spanish Poetry,** Guillén wrote of Salinas's dramatic works, "For him they were 'reality in fable form' (xxi)." Guillén then concurred, "Precisely: an action situated on a normal level, so to speak, rises little by little, leaving behind the first level, until it reaches the heights of fantasy (xxi)." These words serve as a point of departure for offering a preliminary account of the structure of the dramatic works as a guide to poetic action. It can be established that each of Salinas's fourteen plays conforms to a basic *fabula,* or fundamental story-line, and that his dramatic corpus stands as a unified body. At the same time, every play might be considered a representation of a particular configuration of narratable events into a plot, in Russian formalist terminology *sjuzet,* the arrangement of the "narration" which includes omissions, changes in sequencing, flashbacks, incidental comments, etc. that do not contribute directly to the dynamic chain of events (Elam 119). A particular story could be communicated through any number of plots. Each different arrangement of the same story elements would result in a new plot. An overview of Salinas's fourteen different plot lines will show that each constitutes a kind of variation of the same fundamental action, that is, the movement by a character or characters out of confining isolation toward liberating contact with another or others. His protagonists, initiators of the process, are the key contributing factor to this basic unity. Employing these figures to shape his creations of "reality in fable form," Salinas constructs a body of drama that reflects his unique blending of contemporaneous currents of realism and antirealism in the modern theater. On the one hand, Salinas shows with realism ordinary people and commonplace settings to reflect truths about human life. On the other hand, he reaches for a timeless perspective and probes beyond everyday routine to enter the world of hopes, dreams, and visions and to explore significant intangibles of existence. Moreover, Salinas's artistic blending combines this universal, humanistic outlook with immediate circumstances that touch him personally and profoundly.

Persistently adhering to the unifying, underlying confinement-to-freedom framework, Salinas joins his characters in a variety of thematic spheres. Most often, he sets their pursuits in a predominantly romantic context, for example, in **La isla del tesoro, La fuente del arcángel,** and **El chantajista.** In other plays, he casts his freedom seekers in a political context (**Caín o una gloria científica, Los santos**), the business world (**Sobre seguro**), or in a sphere involving artistic endeavor or intellectual and existential pursuit (**Ella y sus fuentes, El precio**). In some of his works, he blends the romantic with other contexts, for example, the political (**Judit y el tirano**), the commercial (**La Bella Durmiente, La Cabeza de Medusa**), or the existential (**El Director**). Spatially and geographically, he locates them in environs which suggest contemporary yet universal contexts: in a restaurant (**El parecido**), a mountain resort (**La Bella Durmiente, El Director**), a café ("**La Estratoesfera**"), a park and garden (**El chantajista**), a hotel room (**La isla del tesoro**), a boutique shop (**La Cabeza de Medusa**). The majority of the plays take place in imaginary countries in urban or rural locations, but even the works with specific local color such as **La fuente del arcángel,** "**La Estratoesfera,**" and **Los santos** transcend immediate surroundings to project a universality connected to the fundamental action.

Salinas also employs variety in his choice of characters and key character combinations. Although the majority of works depict the pairing of a male and female in a developing amorous relationship, there also exist prominent interactions among groupings such as mother and son (**Sobre seguro**), brothers (**Caín o una gloria científica**), writer and invented character (**Ella y sus fuentes, El precio**), fellow prisoners (**Los santos**), employer and employee (**La Cabeza de Medusa**), and divinity and worshiper (**El Director**). His characterizations typify what Scanlan has categorized as the four chief macroconflicts in modern drama: male versus female, the individual versus social injustice, human consciousness versus the mystery of life, and personal dream versus the real world (136-42). Salinas projects these struggles in a variety of formulations and combinations, all initiated and driven by his poet heroes' quests for freedom. In his frequent male-female pairings, Salinas emphasizes the search of the protagonists for outlet for their individuality and creativity, for example, in **La fu-**

ente del arcángel (Florindo-Claribel), **"La Estratoesfera"** (Alvaro-Felipa), **"La isla del tesoro"** (the journal writer-Marú), *El chantajista* (Lisardo-Lucila), and *El precio* (Jáuregui-Melisa). In some of the male-female conflicts, Salinas highlights the characters' search for emancipation from the social context [*Judit y el tirano* (Andrés-Judit), *La Bella Durmiente* (Carlos-Soledad)], the desire to penetrate the mysteries of life [*El parecido* (Roberto-Julia), *El director* (Gerente-Mecanógrafa)], or the confrontation of personal dreams with the "real" world [*Sobre seguro* (Angel-Petra), *Ella y sus fuentes* (Merlín-Julia), *La Cabeza de Medusa* (Andrenio-Lucila)]. In the conflicts of *Caín o una gloria científica* and *Los santos*, Salinas also incorporates male-female interactions while focusing on the heroic characters' expression of humanity and truth as they struggle with sociopolitical pressures.

Salinas's plays move horizontally, with a causal structure propelled principally by the aspirations and movements of dominating poet characters. The motivational force of these characters in the emancipation process forges connections and advances toward a fulfillment. After surveying the fundamental *fabula* and its two variations, confinement-to-freedom with felicitous outcome or with tragic resolution, this chapter will examine the structural components of Salinas's plot creations to show the essential motivating force of the poet heroes in the action.

"REALITY IN FABLE FORM": THE FABULA OF
CONFINEMENT-TO-FREEDOM

The structure common to the diverse plot lines of the fourteen plays, the *fabula* of confinement-to-freedom, is a dynamic progression of actions and events involving poet heroes as chief agents. In general terms, it appears that initially, characters function apart from one another or in solitude with an unenlightened view of their circumstances. The fundamental redemptive action begins when the guiding "poet" successfully sets forth to the character or characters to be transformed a vision that prods their self-discovery and desire for freedom. The process develops as the evolving character or characters show a predisposition to enter the orbit of the leader character. The union is realized when the one comes to define himself or herself through the lens of the poet. Their vital connection often stands in sharp contrast to the negativity and confinement in relationships other than their own. The plays end in one of two ways. Either the redeemed characters "exit" from the plays together, in an auspicious poetic union, or they are separated, usually through the death of one of the characters, after the experience of a climactic, liberating revelation. Eight plays conclude in the more optimistic and open-ended manner. The other six culminate in a transformation possessing tragic overtones. All demonstrate the crucial impetus of the poet hero in the redemptive process.

In the first group, the primary poet figures exhibit an influential confidence in their own identities and the emerging identities of their counterparts. Exercising an energetic independence that enables them to open relationships with those so far confined, these poets are able to combat the circumstances threatening to their liberating unions. Before they initiate the action of redemption with their chosen kindred spirits, they have already experienced a spiritual emancipation from the sorts of repressive, divisive obstacles they will encounter freeing others. Their successful interactions and ultimate unions take place outside the oppressive milieu that therefore can only touch them slightly. At the conclusion of these plays, the united characters exit transformed and free to pursue together their happiness in keeping with the original stance of the poet initiator. This happy open-endedness shows that even the structure of these plays suggests the outcome of transcendence.

In the second group, the main poet characters are extremely preoccupied with self identity and with the identity of their kindred characters, but successful affirmation along with liberation from confinement is tragic because one or both characters have been impeded by obstacles that must be faced through painful struggle. Ultimately, they are compromised or remain trapped in a highly limiting, spiritually oppressive environment that outlives the success of their discovery process. The communicating characters achieve a liberating understanding and measure of fulfillment, but identity problems and the related overburdening circumstances determine the unhappy conclusions of these plays.

A typology of the plays based on the outcome of the confinement-to-freedom process points to the following two groupings:

Freedom and Felicitous Outcome

La fuente del arcángel	comedia
"La Estratoesfera"	escenas de taberna en un acto
La isla del tesoro	comedia
Ella y sus fuentes	comedia
El chantajista	fantasía en un acto y dos cuadros
El parecido	comedia
Sobre seguro	comedia
Los santos	

Freedom and Tragic Outcome

La Bella Durmiente	comedia
Judit y el tirano	drama en tres actos
La Cabeza de Medusa	comedia
El precio	fantasía en un acto y dos cuadros
Caín o una gloria científica	comedia
El director	misterio en tres actos

While all the works except *Los santos* bear subtitles, these denominations do not demarcate the two variations, though they indicate each play's broad dramatic form or structure. Salinas's earliest play, *El director,* a mystery in three acts, with its enigmatic Divinity figure, its puzzled, soul-searching creatures, and symbolic touches, shares features of the allegorical *autos* or eucharistic plays of Spanish Golden Age theater. *"La Estratoesfera,"* subtitled "tavern scenes in one act," approximates the *sainete*-like, slice-of-life exchanges Salinas admired in the works of Carlos Arniches. His final two compositions, *El precio* and *El chantajista,* "fantasies" in one act and two scenes, both represent dreamlike, metatextual creations by poet characters in search of counterparts; but these works stand in different groups because the *fabula* of confinement-to-freedom concludes painfully in one and blissfully in the other. His other full-length work, *Judit y el tirano,* as well as the majority of the shorter pieces, carry more the generic subtitles of *drama* or *comedia.* Different from the English word "comedy," the term *comedia* reflects a broader scope and the more traditional Spanish definition of play or dramatic work. Salinas's plays contain both humorous and serious elements. The subtitles mark the works' theatrical shape and composition, but do not signal the nature of the resolutions of the plays. An overview of the two variations will illustrate their key similarities and differences.

Freedom and Felicitous Outcome

With the exception of *Los santos,* in each play of this first group, the redemptive communication develops essentially between two characters, a male and a female. The man successfully seeks and guides the woman in *La fuente del arcángel* and *"La Estratoesfera"*; the woman pursues and breaks the confinement of the man in *La isla del tesoro* and *Ella y sus fuentes*; and in *El chantajista, El parecido,* and *Sobre seguro,* there occurs between the male and female a more mutual, interactive liberation process. In *Los santos,* there is no single poet figure. Instead, Salinas augments the basic couple construction to focus on the transcendence of the six principal characters in concert with their saintly counterparts. These plays all develop according to the same pattern: characters emerge from isolation or constricting surroundings. Often, Salinas contrasts the evolving successful relationship with other deficient relationships. The following situations illustrate the fundamental movement and transformation out of oppressive circumstances toward emancipation.

In *La fuente del arcángel* and *"La Estratoesfera,"* both Claribel and Felipa escape from extremely cloistered lives. Claribel boards ten months a year at a convent school, and for the remaining two months vacations at the home of her aunt Gumersinda, who carefully arranges and inspects every activity in which Claribel and her sister participate. Felipa, after having to leave her town in disgrace, is the constant companion of her blind grandfather, with whom she sells lottery tickets.

Each young woman finds newer, richer meaning for her life with the aid of a young man, a poet character, who charms her out of her rigid, sterile environment. Florindo the magician (and later, the come-to-life Eros statue of the fountain) communicates with Claribel, awakening within her the imaginative spirit that is longing to emerge. Alvaro the poet restores Felipa's sense of honor and opens for her a happier future. In both plays, Salinas incorporates the physical gesture of hand holding to mark the unions. At the conclusion of *La fuente del arcángel,* Claribel, transformed into the Byzantine empress Teodora, now believing in the authenticity of illusion sees some of the falseness of her sheltered existence. In the final scene, she exits hand in hand with the Archangel-turned-Eros figure (*Teatro completo* 241). *"La Estratoesfera"* ends with a similar transformation. Leaving her past experiences behind, Felipa smiles and gives her hand to Alvaro as they move toward the door (*Teatro completo* 211).

Salinas even utilizes the stage design in these two plays to complement his plot development, focusing on isolation versus liberating communication. He creates in *La fuente del arcangel* a set with three divisions: the parlor in the home of Gumersinda, the stage for Florindo's performance, seen through a picture on a wall of the parlor, and, just outside the house, the main square of the town, in which the fountain of the Arcángel is located. Claribel functions as the only character in the family capable of linking with Florindo and the Arcángel, and therefore inhabits all three environments. Gumersinda remains enclosed within the parlor setting. Estefanía and Sergio attend the magic show but return home to stay there. *"La Estratoesfera"* is furnished with at least five separate tables. One group of customers, Julián and his friends, remains forever isolated in the play, because they never interact with any of the characters at the other tables. In addition to portraying their withdrawal from everyone else, Salinas satirizes the inability of these few men to communicate with each other. They argue incessantly, and their discussions about social justice are filled with meaningless jargon and malapropisms. Only the patrons who move away from their tables to visit others achieve some degree of meaningful communication. Alvaro, the most mobile character, is the one who communicates most effectively, and who, in turn, influences Felipa, César, and even Luis, to reach beyond their narrow spheres.

In *La isla del tesoro* and *Ella y sus fuentes,* the female protagonists Marú and Julia share the goal of identity clarification with relation to a particular individual, the writer of the mysterious notebook, and Desiderio Merlín, respectively. Their pursuit of successful interaction with these men constitutes the driving force behind the action of each play. Once Marú finds the notebook and discovers its contents, she feels compelled to know the identity of this person whose ideas so perfectly match her own, and with whom she feels destined to share her life. Once Julia learns that she is being so grossly misinterpreted by someone reputed to be an expert about her and her life, she feels driven to make Merlín see his errors. Both women accomplish their aims, and at the end of each play, Salinas links the characters in a poetic, spiritual union. In *La isla del tesoro,* Marú, certain that the young man will read her newspaper advertisement the following morning, confidently awaits his reply. In *Ella y sus fuentes,* even though Julia cannot change her image within the national heritage, she does bring the truth to Merlín, and finds a way for him to remain by the truth. Merlín chooses to die, to follow Julia to the afterlife, and an idealized connection in the world beyond. Salinas's concluding portrayal of them, as well as his concluding representation of Marú awaiting her young man, thus suggest a transcendent union between each pair.

The formation of these ties underlines the breakdown or falseness of other interactions in the two plays. In *La isla del tesoro,* the relationship between Marú and Severino proves to be extremely weak and confining to Marú, as well as devoid of any special magnetism like that which exists between Marú and the mysterious writer. In fact, their differing interpretations of what constitutes true communication lie at the heart of their fragile match. Severino demands a rational explanation about the notebook and insists on remaining within the bonds of conventionality, but Marú sees a valid place for the inexplicable and for free imagination, which, to her, in no way hamper communication, and, in fact, allow for a necessary limitlessness in the interpretation of events.

In *Ella y sus fuentes,* the reason Julia, dead for one hundred years, is granted permission to return to earth for a short while, is to correct an error that has been communicated widely during the century, perpetuated through cold, rigid, written sources, to which Merlín is bound. Merlín discounts too much the validity of more colorful human sources and of the oral tradition, those more imaginative sources that could possibly tell more than dry documents. The interview with the one surviving man who said that he knew Julia, and certainly the appearance of Julia herself, prove to be more liberating forms of communication than all of Merlín's written research.

The female protagonists lead the action in *El chantajista, El parecido,* and *Sobre seguro,* though in these works there is much more developed reciprocity on the part of the male principals than in *La isla del tesoro* and *Ella y sus fuentes.* In *El chantajista,* Lucila's planting of the love letters activates Lisardo to co-create a relationship that draws them out of their respective states of isolation. In *El parecido,* once the Incógnito piques Julia's curiosity and she arouses Roberto's pre-occupation with the identity of the Incógnito and the initiation of the confessions about the past, Roberto takes as great a part as she does in unlocking his sentiments and increasing their intimacy. In *Sobre seguro,* the initial view of the mother-son relationship focuses on the fierce attachment of Petra to her missing son, but is soon broadened to include Angel's return and a look at their transcendence beyond the oppresive worlds of family and insurance.

The individuals in each of these three plays emerge from relative isolation or from a frustrating environment to attain fulfillment as part of a pair. At the end of each play, Salinas points to the continuation of their transformed status. Lisardo and Lucila fall in love to escape loneliness, and after a series of mysterious encounters, explain their charades, uncover their true feelings, and look ahead to a promising future. Lucila, in the final moments of the play, recaps her movement out of solitude:

> El amor es el que hace al amante. El me hizo a mí, primero . . . Y como me dejó sola yo tuve que buscarte . . . , que hacerte (Sacando las cartas.) así . . . , Lisardo. Te he engañado para la verdad.
>
> (*Teatro completo* 306)

> Love is what makes the lover. It made me, first . . . And since it left me alone I had to look for you . . . , and make you (Taking out the letters.) like this . . . , Lisardo. I have deceived you in order to arrive at the truth.

The couple shares the contents of one of the letters to begin their idyllic alliance. In *El parecido,* Roberto and Julia leave the restaurant freed from harboring secrets from their pasts and having undergone a kind of renewal. Trying to discover the identity of the Incógnito intensifies their mutual understanding, elicits significant personal confession, and brings them to harmony.

A confinement-to-freedom process is also evident in *Sobre seguro,* in the bonding between Petra and Angel. Although the insurance men and the other family members presume he is dead, Petra refuses to accept his death. The scene in which the others try to convince her to sign the paper in order to receive the insurance money contains the best examples of their failure to reach her. Petra makes her position perfectly clear to them, but they are utterly ineffective with her and cannot speak her language. When one of the men attempts to explain the situation, she laments to her husband:

> ¿Qué dicen? ¿Qué es eso? ¿Por qué me hablan tantas y tantas palabras y no se entiende nada?
>
> (*Teatro completo* 152)

> What are they saying? What is that? Why are they speaking so many words to me and nothing is comprehensible?

In the scene of Angel's return, Salinas emphasizes the exclusivity of the mother-son relationship from which everyone else is distanced. Angel looks to Petra for love, protection, and guidance. After destroying the insurance money, they escape together, hand in hand, "los dos solos" (alone together; *Teatro completo* 162). Their union is the enduring, authentic spiritual interaction upheld in the play, and it provides stark contrast with Petra's lack of rapport with the rest of the family and with the insurance agents.

In *Los santos,* Salinas expands the first basic plot variation beyond the male-female pairings to represent solidarity among an archetypical body of three men and three women. A generous act by the prisoners to save one of their group provokes the miraculous force of the saint statues. The icons represent poetic counterparts to five of the characters whom they replace and save. This play, with its six interacting characters against the backdrop of a historical event, is the most compelling among the eight plays that represent the movement from confinement to freedom with a happy outcome. While underlining the catastrophic effects of disconnection, Salinas expresses his hope for a sustained union among divided peoples, regardless of position or politics. All eight plays end on a positive note, suggesting ongoing relationships among characters. In *Los santos,* Salinas most forcefully shows the redeeming value of genuine fellowship contrasted with the consequences of its desintegration.

FREEDOM AND TRAGIC OUTCOME

In the other six plays, Salinas also demonstrates how certain characters emerge from isolation to share a liberating connection with others. Likewise usually the communication occurs between a pair, though the male-female coupling prevalent in the first group of plays is by no means the general rule for this group. In two of the plays, *La Bella Durmiente* and *Judit y el tirano,* Salinas develops the relationship between a single man and woman. In *La Cabeza de Medusa,* the principal communication exists between one male character, Andrenio, and three women, although perhaps viewable as one (Cowes, "Relación . . ."; Maurín). In *El precio,* in addition to the bond between the writer Jáuregui and his character Melisa, a strong link develops between Melisa and Alicia. In *Caín o una gloria científica,* the primary bond is between two brothers. In *El director,* the key interaction is between a female, the "Mecanógrafa" (Typist) and the "double male divinity" figure, the "Director-Gerente" (Director), with numerous subplots involving one man and one woman, or two women. While Salinas exhibits more variety in combining his communicating characters in these six plays, what really sets this group apart to form the second variation of his basic plot is the outcome: the redemptive process culminates in tragedy.

The characters strive toward and achieve some measure of freedom, but in all six plays, for one of two reasons, their escape from confinement is curtailed. One reason, found in *Caín o una gloria científica* and *Judit y el tirano,* is that a character cannot disengage himself or herself sufficiently from external circumstances in which restrictions persist. The other cause of separation, present in *La Cabeza de Medusa, La Bella Durmiente, El director,* and *El precio,* is that there remains a lingering disconnect in the relationship of the characters involved in the transformation process. This group of plays contains the same movement toward emancipation found in the first eight plays, but with obstacles enduring.

Both in *Caín o una gloria científica* and *Judit y el tirano,* a pair of characters gains essential, mutual understanding, only to be separated by the circumstances that have drawn them close together. Abel, unable to cope alone with the dilemma concerning his nuclear research, engages his brother Clemente. With total commitment, Clemente accepts a full share of the burden, but in doing so, is forced to kill Abel. The total absence of understanding between Abel and his superiors tests the relationship of the brothers and proves their unity in the quest for redemption, but paradoxically separates them with the death of Abel, and leaves open the question of the fate of mankind.

Similarly, in *Judit y el tirano,* the Regente, a completely solitary figure, seeks to emerge from isolation with the help of Judit. She gives him the courage to re-enter the world and engage in life outside his office, to leave behind the reclusive existence in which he communicates with his people only as a faceless entity. The circumstances of his past are too powerful to overcome, and they cause the tragic separation of Judit and the Regente. The Regente's police kill him because they see him as a man who threatens the life of the official Regente. Salinas underscores the irony of this apt description of what he has become. The police do not recognize him to be the Regente himself, because of the previous, secret, inhuman manner of interaction with his people. The liberating connection between the new man and Judit cannot overcome the forces of his former life.

In the four remaining plays, successful sharing among characters is likewise interrupted, but this time it is due to some deficiency within the relationship itself. The characters are transformed in their achievement of some significant communication, but ultimately separate because one of them is unable to transcend certain self-imposed boundaries, or because one of the characters feels compelled to hold back from the relationship a part of himself or herself.

In *La Cabeza de Medusa,* Andrenio ventures from the shelter of his upbringing to attain a deeper knowledge about life from Lucila and the visitors to her shop. Andrenio is sadly ill-equipped, however, to participate in life, and merely absorbs everything before him as a passive listener. He follows the instructions of his father to the letter: to get to know life by observing it from the outside, objectively, and by not getting carried away in its whirlwind (*Teatro completo* 122). Seeing the disillusion present in life, yet unprepared to cope with it, Andrenio chooses death as the only real solution for himself. The consummation of Andrenio's liberating understanding of those he observes is marked by his exclamation that everything is clear, and his sudden death (*Teatro completo* 136).

In *La Bella Durmiente, El director,* and *El precio,* an unhappy escape from confinement for the central characters is most directly related to the clarification of the identity of one of them. In *La Bella Durmiente,* Carlos Rolán and Soledad, the famous model of his mattress advertisements, each ignorant of the other's identity, flee from the superficial relationships they have with people in their public lives. They fall in love at the mountain retreat, **"La Cima Incógnita" ("The Hidden Summit")**. Their candid self-expression of feelings for one another holds promise of a happy future together, but after the full confession of Soledad, Carlos feels he must maintain the lock on the secret of his identity in order to preserve any of Soledad's affection. Believing that he pities her more than he loves her, Soledad misinterprets the reason for the impossibility of their marriage. Carlos prefers to stay trapped in his past rather than allow emergence of the truth, which he believes would totally destroy their relationship. Either way, they are destined to separate, but now Carlos believes that at least he can carry within him a union of their sufferings.

In *El director,* the separation of the divinity figure from the typist and the rest of the people he oversees is also tied to the problem of his identity. The director is able to transform the typist and to draw her close to him by explaining how he brings happiness to others, but he fails to convince her that the "evil" Gerente is an integral part of his being. Her close-minded refusal to believe the truth about him and the meaning of happiness leads to the tragic conclusion in which she sees the unity of his two parts too late.

In *El precio,* although Melisa exerts a strong influence over Alicia and successfully injects more poetry into the life of her new friend, a bothersome insecurity plagues their relationship. All the while Melisa gropes for her identity, Alicia fears that its discovery will mean Melisa's departure. The union of the girls necessarily dissolves when Jáuregui appears and the mystery is solved. Through her interaction with Melisa, book char-

acter come to life, Alicia undergoes a significant transformation, but their connection is severed when Melisa must pay for her survival in a literary medium with her physical life.

The preceding review of the design of the *fabula* of confinement-to-freedom has introduced both the diversity and unity across the plays. Whether, as in the second group of plays, the characters find freedom but also tragic separation, or, as in the first group, their transformation perpetuates a happy union, Salinas traces the same development in their relationship. The characters seek to escape the emptiness and restrictiveness of an isolated existence, and whether or not they are able to sustain union with others, all experience, due to the impetus of the idealist characters, a close and emancipating contact with another figure or figures, which Salinas has set forth as an aim to be pursued.

The chief difference between the two groups may be understood in terms of the intention and purpose of the actions in which the poet figures engage. In both variations, the poet agents perform with success their intended actions of bonding with and transforming certain coagents or patients; that is, they initiate and advance the process. Also in both groups, to some extent, the coherent sequences of distinct actions and interactions governed by the desired ends or purposes of the leading characters are achieved; in other words, the agents realize linkage and transcendence. The separating feature is found in the macro-purpose or long-term outcome of the actions. "The dynamism of the drama derives from the suspension—and thus projection into the future—of the purpose-success/purpose-failure of the sequence, so that every distinct act is replete with the possible global result: '[The drama's] basic abstraction is the act, which springs from the past, but is directed towards the future, and is always great with things to come (Langer 306)'" (Elam 124). In both variations, Salinas elevates the spiritual force of the poet liberator. Social circumstances and identity issues impact upon the global results.

The macro-purpose and resulting success of the *fabula* of confinement-to-freedom signify rupture with the depersonalizing, restrictive forces of modern life which provoke human division by causing spiritual blindness, deterring creative invention, and impelling conformity with the dull and commonplace. In casting his poet activists both as boundary-breakers and bridge-builders, Salinas endows these liberators with creative capacities to rework old blueprints and design new ones. He envisions new constructions, erected with poetic purpose. As the poet attempts to inhabit a concrete social realm, his or her inner animating force upholds an identity of independence, an identity celebrating its opposition to obstacles in the material sphere. The ultimate success depends on the degree to which the force of their identity of independence overpowers the opposing forces met in the social realm.

The grouping of Salinas's plays according to their fe-licitous or tragic outcomes does not diminish the hero-ism of the poet. Both variations evidence the poet's strong spiritual stance, humanistic outlook, and funda-mental idealism. Moreover, many actions of Salinas's characters have autobiographical significance and sug-gest the circumstances and world-view of Salinas the poet. While the first group celebrates the promise in hu-man relationships, the latter group underscores the enor-mous tensions and pressures in the confrontation with modernity. In both variations, Salinas accentuates the search for liberation and the crucial importance of the poet's mission, and there is a persistent, optimistic affir-mation of the poet's enterprise.

THE POET IN THE PLOT

Functioning as crucial links, the directive role of Sali-nas's poet heroes is connected to the key narrative events of the *fabula* of confinement-to-freedom. Their actions advance the narrative logic and constitute major story events. Translating Barthes's term *noyau*, Chat-man describes these events as "kernels . . . narrative moments that give rise to cruxes in the direction taken by events" (53). "Kernels cannot be deleted without de-stroying the narrative logic" (Chatman 53). This termi-nology, though applied primarily to analysis of the genre of narrative, lends itself as well to discussion of the structure of fundamental story events in the drama. The actions of the poet figures configure the logical sequence of consequential events and form the nucleus of the playwright's "narrative." In addition to constituting the *kernels*, their movements often give rise to minor plot events that Chatman, interpreting the French structural-ist term *catalyse*, calls *satellites* (Chatman 54-55). *Sat-ellites* are elaborations that enrich and flesh out the skeletal narrative. A further look at story construction in Salinas's plays will illustrate in more detail this struc-tural significance of his poet heroes, whose sharing of self and circumstance determines the propitiousness and permanence of the emancipation attained.

A convenient organization for examining the form of their action in the confinement-redemption *fabula* de-rives from Smiley's *Playwriting The Structure of Action* and his discussion of the structure of story and action in drama. His typology of ten basic story elements—bal-ance, disturbance, protagonist, plan, obstacles, compli-cations, sub-story, crisis, climax, and resolution—is not intended to be formulaic, but does suggest the means for construction of a story and a method for a play-wright to organize actions, characters, and thoughts (Smiley 53-61). The components enforce no pattern, and a playwright may use them or not, or use some of them. A sub-story, for example, may be absent, as could almost any other element, except crisis and climax (Smiley 61). Though a fully developed story is not ab-solutely necessary for every play, most sets of dramatic

materials are better organized for having one. The story construction across Salinas's fourteen dramatic works is solid, and the following presentation of the happenings in his plays will show that he is a purposeful story builder. Even into the short pieces, Salinas incorporates most, if not all of the basic elements. Though inclusion of these story components does not automatically create story, in Salinas's case, their representation and combi-nation produced vivid illustrations of the basic *fabula* in its two principal variations. A survey of the components in Salinas's plays will highlight the core movements of the poet heroes and will help differentiate the two groupings—freedom with happy outcome and freedom with tragic overtones. Distinguishing features of the two groups appear especially in Salinas's composition of obstacles, complications, crises, climaxes, and reso-lutions. The following overview of the key story com-ponents in the plays will clarify the differentiation, mark the dominance of the poet figures in the dramatic struc-ture, and precede comprehensive attention to one work of each variation—*El chantajista* and *Caín o una glo-ria científica*. A close look at these two compositions will further elucidate their dramatic structure and sharpen the definition of *kernel* and *satellite* dramatic moments hinging on the actions of the poet figures, the crucial initiators and promoters of communication.

Throughout his plays, the structural dominance of Sali-nas's poet characters and their actions stands firm. In his design of story elements, from initial balance through to resolution, Salinas sustains their anchoring function. A view of the role of the poet characters in the balance or opening situation of the plays reveals that they are essential to the establishment of an initial dynamic stability that leads into the central actions. They are an integral part of a tense equilibrium between contrasting forces that holds the potential for subse-quent conflict. In *Ella y sus fuentes*, for example, the guiding force Julia Riscal is key inspiration to the biog-rapher Desiderio Merlín, who is claiming to dispute the lies and exaggerations of other studies in his definitive work of her life and deeds. In *La Bella Durmiente*, Soledad and Alvaro have just returned from an idyllic walk they have both enjoyed. Her simple and sincere bearing has captured his interest and piqued his curios-ity about her. While cherishing her privacy, she points to the tension between their position of retreat and their other lives outside the resort.

When the story yields to a first disturbance, an event that upsets the balanced situation and initiates the ac-tion, the poet characters are again crucial factors. They either effect or inspire an agitation in the world of the participants in the play. Such disturbances take place in both variations, and often constitute a first step by the poet hero on his or her idealistic course. For instance, early stable circumstances are agitated when Julia Riscal appears to the confident Merlín, and when the drawing of Judit's lot makes her the assassin of the tyrant. The initial disturbance represents a kind of specialized complication in the story. Later complications in the story structure present new obstacles to the protagonists, and figure more significantly in the distinction between the two variations.

As protagonists, poet characters are clearly focal because they cause or receive most of the action, they are most affected when the disturbance causes imbalance— even when they themselves cause the upset, and usually it is they who set about to restore order in the situation. Smiley differentiates between main characters that are volitional and force the action and those who are less volitional. The latter are central but more victimized by opposing characters or forces (55). Even though powerful obstacles thwart their attempts to retain a joyous emancipation, Salinas's primary poet heroes of the second variation are no less volitional than their more successful counterparts. In the six plays with tragic outcomes, they are greatly, if not most affected by the misfortune. Soledad the Sleeping Beauty, Judit the tyrant slayer, Lucila the proprietress of La Cabeza de Medusa, Alicia the autonomous character of author Jáuregui, Abel the physicist and glory of science, and the Regente, divinity figure of *El director,* all suffer the oppression of an overwhelming power. It is they, nevertheless, who chiefly propel the action and advance it to resolution. Less volitional are the proximate poets, or characters transformed by the main poets. These are often co-protagonists or complementary central figures whose function bolsters the position and authority of the guiding poet heroes. Drawn into the action and carried along by the principal poets, their circumstances and fate, whether favorable or ill, converge with those of their guiders and mirror them. In good fortune, Claribel thus accompanies the Florindo/Eros/Archangel figure of *La fuente del arcángel,* and Felipa follows Alvaro in *"La Estratoesfera."* Likewise, in somber conclusion, Andrés the tyrant both comes to life and dies with Judit, and the typist sees happiness fulfilled and doomed in her association with the divinity figure.

Normally, when the protagonist begins the activity of reestablishing the balance, he or she has a plan. While founded upon creative inspiration and idealistic motivation, the plans of Salinas's poet heroes are most often conscious and carefully formulated. Also, the plans frequently involve a goal or stake (a person, place, or thing desired by the protagonist and usually wanted also by his opposition; Smiley 55). In *Ella y sus fuentes,* Julia's plan is to communicate to Merlín the truth about her identity. Merlín, initially Julia's opposition, is also desirous of this same goal. In *La isla del tesoro,* Marú's plan is to find the journal writer, or creator of the treasure. Her oppositions are, on the one hand, members of the hotel staff who want to keep secret his existence, and, on the other hand, her fiancé Severio, who

cannot reach her in the same way as the mystery notebook writer. The plans of Judit are more complicated and changing because when she is about to execute her plan to kill the apersonal, faceless tyrant, she discovers the man. Salinas incorporates a number of key speeches to elaborate her adaptations, establish the credibility of her actions and uphold her axial position.

As protagonists attempt to restore balance by carrying out their plans, they meet with obstacles or factors that oppose or impede their progress. An obstacle generates the most tension and is strongest when it imposes two conditions upon the protagonist: it aims a threat toward the protagonist and it causes conflict when the protagonist tries to remove it. Consequently, the obstacle will lead to a major or minor climax in the story. For Smiley, the plays with the best stories are those which combine use of four kinds of obstacles: physical obstructions; antagonists, or other characters in the play who oppose the protagonist; obstructions within the personality of the protagonist himself or herself; and mystic forces, or elements such as accidents, god figures, or moral and ethical codes (56). Into many of his works, into the plans of his poet characters, Salinas incorporates all four types of obstacles. In *Los santos,* for example, the prisoners must contend with their confinement in the church basement, with the enemy soldiers, with their own fears, and with the accidents of war that have brought them to confront death. In *Sobre seguro,* Petra experiences threat and conflict from the insurance agents, from her persistent refusal to accept the death of Angel, and from the insurance money, both in its realistic containment in an envelope and in her vision of its colorful personification.

Complications may appear at any point in a story in the form of "characters, circumstances, events, mistakes, misunderstandings, and best of all-discoveries" (Smiley 56-57). They set new obstacles for the protagonists, and provoke a change in the course of the action. They can be positive or negative forces for any of the conflicting aspects of the play. These elements in Salinas's plays are numerous, and while aiding or hampering progress, they showcase the creative genius of the confronted poet characters. In *El precio,* when the inspector of police arrives to connect Melisa with an unsolved murder, she totally dominates the conversation with lyrical explanation about buried jewels and surprising fruits that strangely coincide with details of the case but soar beyond the scope of the everyday world and exemplify her imaginative flight (*Teatro completo* 274-75).

Builders of tension and surprise, the obstacles and complications encountered by the poet characters also help mark the distinction between the two variations of Salinas's *fabula* of confinement-to-freedom. In the plays of felicitous conclusion, these factors exert vitally positive force. Whether or not they augment a work's humor, they solidify the dominance of the poet's vision. In **"La Estratoesfera,"** for instance, the death of Felipa's grandfather generates an expression of feeling by her that proves she has been transformed by the poet's influence (**Teatro completo** 210-11). In **Sobre seguro,** the reappearance of Angel and his attraction to the insurance money moves Petra to share her vision of their retreat to "la casa clara" (the bright house; **Teatro completo** 160). Obstacles and complications built into the works of tragic outcome carry chiefly negative force. They contribute to the continuation of an anti-poetic environment that survives beyond the interrupted success of the redeemed poet characters. When, in **Judit y el tirano,** the secret police who have never seen the tyrant face-to-face hear him say he has killed the "other," they do not understand that he has been liberated from his former guise. Their actions, ultimately provoked by Judit and her weapon, end the life of the tyrant, terminate the relationship of the protagonists, and perpetuate the system that has separated them.

An element to mirror the main story of a play or contrast with it is the sub-story, or secondary story. In his twelve one-act plays, by ascribing to tenets of unity, brevity, and economy, Salinas retains focus on the central figures, and does not compose sub-stories with any intricacy. At times, to highlight or reflect the position of the protagonists, he includes a scene or fragments of scenes that appear as a vivid flash or series of flashes. In **La Cabeza de Medusa,** the episodes involving Gloria and Rosaura are more extended segments, and possibly viewable as sub-stories to the extent that they may be representations of earlier moments in the life of protagonist Lucila, but they are not really subordinate to the main story. Their inclusion is central to the bonding between Lucila and Andrenio. In **La fuente del arcángel,** the scene of lovers Honoria and Angelillo at the fountain echoes briefly Claribel's growing connection to the fountain figure. In the three-act **El director,** Salinas weaves into the central relationship of the typist and the director a more detailed subordinate story of the minor characters in search of happiness. The pursuits of Juan, Juana, Inocencio, and Esperanza intertwine with the quests of the Typist and Director. They reach crisis and climax just before the major climax in the main story to thus complement it and affect it.

Crisis is a story component that demonstrates the concentrated activity of the poet protagonists and forces significant change. Crises, or turns in the action that mark conflict during which the outcome is uncertain, may be scenes of progressively heightened struggle. They may transpire throughout a play until the occurrence of a major crisis scene, followed by a culminating moment that settles the conflict either intermediately or permanently. Related structurally to obstacles and complications, crises, like these components, also serve to distinguish between the two variations of Salinas's

fabula of confinement-to-freedom. The major crises of the works of happy conclusion portray the primary and proximate poet characters in triumphant acts of unmasking and co-discovery. As the ensuing climaxes indicate, once these characters reveal their true identities, any threats to their union dissolve. Accordingly, after the prisoners share their sufferings, the saint statues come to life to save them in **Los santos.** Similarly, in **La fuente del arcángel,** after Florindo awakens Claribel to the power of illusion, the fountain figure comes to life to emancipate her.

The crises in the works of tragic conclusion generally depict more violent conflict and change. In the freedom-seeking process, the major crises of uncovering or co-disclosure by poet heroes and their counterparts push them to face a final opponent who endeavors to interrupt their success. This final opponent may be one of the poet characters themselves, forced by constricting circumstances to withhold definitive identification, as occurs in **La Bella Durmiente,** or driven by misunderstanding to eliminate an enemy to their unity, as in the case of the typist who kills the director. Or the fatal force may be one other than a protagonist, a power of the oppressive system, such as the secret police who confront the tyrant in **Judit y el tirano,** or "¡la vida!" (life!; 137) in **La Cabeza de Medusa.**

The climax, or result of a crisis, is the point at which a conflict is settled. In all his plays, Salinas creates a series of minor climaxes to lead to a major climax in which the final outcome is determined. Across his two groups of plays, the conclusive climactic moments constitute a key distinguishing element. In the works of the first variation, the final climaxes show the protagonists having won their goal or "stake" of freedom. They join together to realize a transcendant union beyond any contact they have experienced with an everyday, mundane, constricting milieu before this moment. They are about to take a victorious first step toward an idyllic fulfillment. Salinas thus constructs final climaxes in which transformed characters respond to the beckoning of the primary poet figures: Claribel takes the hand of Florindo; Claribel accepts the invitation of the fountain figure; Desiderio Merlín joins Julia Riscal; Angel leaves with Petra. Or Salinas depicts the promise of a felicitous alliance resulting from the impetus of potent poetic entities. In **La isla del tesoro,** for example, Marú advertises to find her ideal mate, the notebook writer; in **El parecido,** the *Incógnito* encourages the unity of Julia and Roberto; and in **Los santos,** the animated statues redeem the prisoners. These climaxes of the first variation portray optimistic moments of decision or discovery, and in the case of **Los santos,** a happy reversal of fortune.

In contrast, the final climaxes of the six plays with tragic outcome all depict reversals of circumstance that interrupt the transformation of poet characters and separate them from their idealistic course. Close to or as part of the major climax, Salinas portrays them claiming or about to claim their "stake" of redemption, but inserts an ultimate clash with their definition of self or with outside forces. Salinas upholds these characters as moral and spiritual champions, but in their search for wholeness and emancipation grounded in truth and happiness, he does not discount the hostility of their social context. By way of illustration, one can witness the parting of Soledad and Alvaro in **La Bella Durmiente,** the defeat of Judit and the tyrant, the separation of Melisa and Alicia in **El precio,** and the typist's erring elimination of the director.

After the final climax, the resolution of a play sets the situation of the characters and restores a kind of balance to the work. Like the crises and climaxes from which they follow, the resolutions of Salinas's dramatic works differ. Underscoring the idealisim and positive expectations of the poet protagonists, the resolutions of the works of the first variation tend to indicate the fortune of these characters without providing an absolute close. In contrast, the final circumstances of the more tragic works set the destiny of the characters more firmly, usually with a death (for example, of the tyrant, Melisa, Andrenio, Abel, and the director) or some definitive separation (Alvaro and Soledad).

If the plays do not end with close focus on the poet protagonists themselves, then whatever the outcome, the final scene measures their effects or contains an assessment of the relationship by others. A journalist in **Ella y sus fuentes** thus reports the coincidental death of Merlín near the statue of Julia Riscal; and at the conclusion of **La fuente del arcángel,** the family's discovery of the pieces of the Eros/Archangel statue is connected to the disappearance of Claribel.

The pivotal role of poet heroes in pursuit of a redemptive unification with kindred figures provides Salinas's dramatic corpus with a structural unity. As key supports of the framework of the plays, these characters stand at the core of his organization of his *fabulas* to embody spiritual and social attributes exalted by Salinas. Whether the plays end happily or unhappily, whether Salinas allows that the ideal may or may not be immanently achievable or sustainable, he upholds the quixotic virtue of patience he had praised in his essay **"Lo que debemos a don Quijote"** (**"What We Owe Don Quixote"**; **Ensayos de literatura hispánica** 101). This patience is the resolve to continue. The happy conclusions exhibit with sunny optimism the virtues advocated by the poet. The unhappy outcomes do not suggest the passive acceptance of defeat, but rather they imply the necessity of converting failure into a stage or step toward a desired future triumph.

Bibliography

Chatman, Seymour. *Story and Discourse Narrative Structure in Fiction and Film,* Ithaca and London: Cornell University Press, 1978.

Elam, Kier. *The Semiotics of Theatre and Drama.* London and New York: Methuen, 1980.

Salinas, Pedro. *Ensayos completos,* I, II, and III, Madrid: Taurus, 1981.

———. *Ensayos de la literatura hispánica. Del Cantar de Mío Cid a García Lorca.* Edición y Prólogo de Juan Marichal. Madrid: Aguilar, 1961.

———. *Reality and the Poet in Spanish Poetry,* translated by Edith Fishtine Helman, with an Introduction by Jorge Guillén, translated by Elias L. Rivers, Baltimore: Johns Hopkins UP, 1940, 1966.

———. *Los santos. Cuadernos americanos.* (México) 13 3(1954):265-91.

———. *Los santos. Estreno* 7,2(1981): 12.

———. *Teatro Completo.* Ed. Juan Marichal. Madrid: Aguilar, 1957.

———. *Teatro Completo.* Edición crítica e introducción de Pilar Moraleda García. Sevilla: Alfar, 1992.

Scanlan, David. *Reading Drama.* Mountain View, CA: Mayfield Publishing Co., 1988.

Smiley, Sam. *Playwriting The Structure of Action.* Englewood Cliffs, NJ: Prentice Hall, 1971.

FURTHER READING

Bibliography

Stixrude, David L. "Critical Reception of the Poetry of Pedro Salinas: 1969-1989." *Anales de la Literatura Española Contemporánea* 16, nos. 1-2 (1991): 129-48.

    Offers a brief compendium of critical writings on Salinas's poetry published between 1969 and 1989.

Biography

Newman, Jean Cross. *Pedro Salinas and His Circumstance,* San Juan, Puerto Rico: Inter American University Press, 1983, 274 p.

    Biography of Salinas that seeks "to piece together the mosaic" of his life, based on the testimony of his friends and colleagues as well as his correspondence and other writings.

Criticism

Bermúdez, Silvia. "The Ideology of Gender in Pedro Salinas' *La voz a ti debida.*" *Revista Hispánica Moderna* 48, no. 2 (December 1995): 321-34.

Highlights the tension between "the operating mechanisms of the voice" and the "ideology of gender" in Salinas's *My Voice Because of You*, suggesting "the ways in which questions of gender may complicate the presence of a poetic male voice within the dynamics of traditional love poetry."

Crispin, John. *Pedro Salinas,* New York: Twayne Publishers, Inc., 1974, 180 p.
Book-length study of Salinas that attempts to show his "entire creative production as an integral whole."

Garrison, David Lee. "Translator's Introduction." In *Certain Chance: Poems by Pedro Salinas,* by Pedro Salinas, translated by David Lee Garrison, pp. 31-7. Lewisburg, Pa.: Bucknell University Press, 2000.
Briefly explicates a number of the poems in *Certain Chance,* claiming that the book "is a kind of dialogue in which the poet speaks to things and people as he searches for their true essence."

Havard, Robert G. "Pedro Salinas and Courtly Love: The 'amada' in *La voz a ti debida*: Woman, Muse and Symbol." *Bulletin of Hispanic Studies* 56, no. 2 (April 1979): 123-44.
Examines the role of courtly love and the *amada* in Salinas's *My Voice Because of You.*

Helman, Edith. "A Way of Seeing: 'Nube en la mano' by Pedro Salinas." *Hispanic Review* 45, no. 4 (autumn 1977): 359-84.
Studies Salinas's late poem "Nube en la mano," tracing "the transforming process the poem undergoes from its generating idea in manuscript to its final printed form."

Materna, Linda S. "The Dialogue of Pedro Salinas' *La fuente del Arcángel*: A Dialectic of Poetry and Realism." *Hispanic Review* 54, no. 3 (summer 1986): 297-312.
Analyzes Salinas's "synthesis of poetry and Realism" in his play *La fuente del Arcángel.*

Mayhew, Jonathan. "'Cuartilla': Pedro Salinas and the Semiotics of Poetry." *Anales de la Literatura Española Contemporánea* 16, nos. 1-2 (1991): 119-27.

Proposes a "metasemiotic reading" of Salinas's poem "Cuartilla," from the collection *Certain Chance,* as a "test case" for re-evaluating Michael Riffaterre's theories on the semiotics of poetry set forth in his book, *Semiotics of Poetry.*

Pao, Maria T. "Making Time with Pedro Salinas: *Víspera del gozo* (1926)." *Hispanic Review* 74, no. 4 (autumn 2006): 437-59.
Discusses the influence of Albert Einstein and Marcel Proust on Salinas's depiction of time in his prose narrative *Prelude to Pleasure.*

Polansky, Susan G. "Communication and the 'Poet Figures': The Essence of the Dramatic Works of Pedro Salinas." *Hispania* 70, no. 3 (September 1987): 437-46.
Maintains that regardless of the specific thematic content of Salinas's plays, the theme of communication "stands as an essential unifying element."

———. "Mail and Blackmail: Pedro Salinas's *Cartas de amor a Margarita* and *El chantajista*." *Hispania* 78, no. 1 (March 1995): 43-52.
Calls Salinas's play *El chantajista* "a particularly vivid, autobiographical work," arguing that Salinas intentionally recreated in this work personal experiences conveyed in his collection of love letters entitled *Cartas de amor a Margarita, 1912-1915.*

Stixrude, David L. *The Early Poetry of Pedro Salinas,* N.J.: Princeton, 1975, 166 p.
Book-length study that investigates what the critic regards as the unifying theme in Salinas's early poetry, namely "the poet's dissatisfaction with outer reality" and his "intense desire to discover what is essential" in human life, as presented in such early works as *Fábula y signo, Certain Chance,* and *Presagios.*

———. "The Final Lament of Pedro Salinas." *Revista Canadiense de Estudios Hispánicos* 2, no. 2 (winter 1978): 122-41.
Explicates each of the twenty-five poems left out of the 1971 edition of Salinas's *Largo lamento* but included in his *Poesías completas* in 1975.

Additional coverage of Salinas's life and career is contained in the following sources published by Gale: *Contemporary Authors,* **Vol. 117;** *Dictionary of Literary Biography,* **Vol. 134;** *Encyclopedia of World Literature in the 20th Century,* **Ed. 3;** *Literature Resource Center***; and** *Twentieth-Century Literary Criticism,* **Vol. 17.**

How to Use This Index

The main references

Calvino, Italo
1923-1985 .... CLC 5, 8, 11, 22, 33, 39,
73; SSC 3, 48

---

list all author entries in the following Gale Literary Criticism series:

AAL = *Asian American Literature*
BG = *The Beat Generation: A Gale Critical Companion*
BLC = *Black Literature Criticism*
BLCS = *Black Literature Criticism Supplement*
CLC = *Contemporary Literary Criticism*
CLR = *Children's Literature Review*
CMLC = *Classical and Medieval Literature Criticism*
DC = *Drama Criticism*
FL = *Feminism in Literature: A Gale Critical Companion*
GL = *Gothic Literature: A Gale Critical Companion*
HLC = *Hispanic Literature Criticism*
HLCS = *Hispanic Literature Criticism Supplement*
HR = *Harlem Renaissance: A Gale Critical Companion*
LC = *Literature Criticism from 1400 to 1800*
NCLC = *Nineteenth-Century Literature Criticism*
NNAL = *Native North American Literature*
PC = *Poetry Criticism*
SSC = *Short Story Criticism*
TCLC = *Twentieth-Century Literary Criticism*
WLC = *World Literature Criticism, 1500 to the Present*
WLCS = *World Literature Criticism Supplement*

The cross-references

See also CA 85-88, 116; CANR 23, 61;
DAM NOV; DLB 196; EW 13; MTCW 1, 2;
RGSF 2; RGWL 2; SFW 4; SSFS 12

---

list all author entries in the following Gale biographical and literary sources:

AAYA = *Authors & Artists for Young Adults*
AFAW = *African American Writers*
AFW = *African Writers*
AITN = *Authors in the News*
AMW = *American Writers*
AMWR = *American Writers Retrospective Supplement*
AMWS = *American Writers Supplement*
ANW = *American Nature Writers*
AW = *Ancient Writers*
BEST = *Bestsellers*
BPFB = *Beacham's Encyclopedia of Popular Fiction: Biography and Resources*
BRW = *British Writers*
BRWS = *British Writers Supplement*
BW = *Black Writers*
BYA = *Beacham's Guide to Literature for Young Adults*
CA = *Contemporary Authors*
CAAS = *Contemporary Authors Autobiography Series*
CABS = *Contemporary Authors Bibliographical Series*
CAD = *Contemporary American Dramatists*
CANR = *Contemporary Authors New Revision Series*
CAP = *Contemporary Authors Permanent Series*
CBD = *Contemporary British Dramatists*
CCA = *Contemporary Canadian Authors*
CD = *Contemporary Dramatists*
CDALB = *Concise Dictionary of American Literary Biography*

CDALBS = Concise Dictionary of American Literary Biography Supplement
CDBLB = Concise Dictionary of British Literary Biography
CMW = St. James Guide to Crime & Mystery Writers
CN = Contemporary Novelists
CP = Contemporary Poets
CPW = Contemporary Popular Writers
CSW = Contemporary Southern Writers
CWD = Contemporary Women Dramatists
CWP = Contemporary Women Poets
CWRI = St. James Guide to Children's Writers
CWW = Contemporary World Writers
DA = DISCovering Authors
DA3 = DISCovering Authors 3.0
DAB = DISCovering Authors: British Edition
DAC = DISCovering Authors: Canadian Edition
DAM = DISCovering Authors: Modules
    DRAM: Dramatists Module; **MST:** Most-studied Authors Module;
    MULT: Multicultural Authors Module; **NOV:** Novelists Module;
    POET: Poets Module; **POP:** Popular Fiction and Genre Authors Module
DFS = Drama for Students
DLB = Dictionary of Literary Biography
DLBD = Dictionary of Literary Biography Documentary Series
DLBY = Dictionary of Literary Biography Yearbook
DNFS = Literature of Developing Nations for Students
EFS = Epics for Students
EXPN = Exploring Novels
EXPP = Exploring Poetry
EXPS = Exploring Short Stories
EW = European Writers
FANT = St. James Guide to Fantasy Writers
FW = Feminist Writers
GFL = Guide to French Literature, Beginnings to 1789, 1798 to the Present
GLL = Gay and Lesbian Literature
HGG = St. James Guide to Horror, Ghost & Gothic Writers
HW = Hispanic Writers
IDFW = International Dictionary of Films and Filmmakers: Writers and Production Artists
IDTP = International Dictionary of Theatre: Playwrights
LAIT = Literature and Its Times
LAW = Latin American Writers
JRDA = Junior DISCovering Authors
MAICYA = Major Authors and Illustrators for Children and Young Adults
MAICYAS = Major Authors and Illustrators for Children and Young Adults Supplement
MAWW = Modern American Women Writers
MJW = Modern Japanese Writers
MTCW = Major 20th-Century Writers
NCFS = Nonfiction Classics for Students
NFS = Novels for Students
PAB = Poets: American and British
PFS = Poetry for Students
RGAL = Reference Guide to American Literature
RGEL = Reference Guide to English Literature
RGSF = Reference Guide to Short Fiction
RGWL = Reference Guide to World Literature
RHW = Twentieth-Century Romance and Historical Writers
SAAS = Something about the Author Autobiography Series
SATA = Something about the Author
SFW = St. James Guide to Science Fiction Writers
SSFS = Short Stories for Students
TCWW = Twentieth-Century Western Writers
WLIT = World Literature and Its Times
WP = World Poets
YABC = Yesterday's Authors of Books for Children
YAW = St. James Guide to Young Adult Writers

Literary Criticism Series
Cumulative Author Index

Alexander, Lloyd 1924-2007 .... **CLC 35**
See also AAYA 1, 27; BPFB 1; BYA 5, 6,
7, 9, 10, 11; CA 1-4R; 260; CANR 1, 24,
38, 55, 113; CLR 1, 5, 48; CWRI 5; DLB
52; FANT; JRDA; MAICYA 1, 2; MAIC-
YAS 1; MTCW 1; SAAS 19; SATA 3, 49,
81, 129, 135; SATA-Obit 182; SUFW;
TUS; WYA; YAW

Alexander, Lloyd Chudley
See Alexander, Lloyd

Alexander, Meena 1951- .... **CLC 121**
See also CA 115; CANR 38, 70, 146; CP 5,
6, 7; CWP; DLB 323; FW

Alexander, Samuel 1859-1938 .... **TCLC 77**

Alexeiev, Konstantin
See Stanislavsky, Constantin

Alexeyev, Constantin Sergeivich
See Stanislavsky, Constantin

Alexeyev, Konstantin Sergeyevich
See Stanislavsky, Constantin

Alexie, Sherman 1966- .... **CLC 96, 154;**
NNAL; PC 53; SSC 107
See also AAYA 28; BYA 15; CA 138;
CANR 65, 95, 133, 174; CN 7; DA3;
DAM MULT; DLB 175, 206, 278; LATS
1:2; MTCW 2; MTFW 2005; NFS 17;
SSFS 18

Alexie, Sherman Joseph, Jr.
See Alexie, Sherman

al-Farabi 870(?)-950 .... **CMLC 58**
See also DLB 115

Alfau, Felipe 1902-1999 .... **CLC 66**
See also CA 137

Alfieri, Vittorio 1749-1803 .... **NCLC 101**
See also EW 4; RGWL 2, 3; WLIT 7

Alfonso X 1221-1284 .... **CMLC 78**

Alfred, Jean Gaston
See Ponge, Francis

Alger, Horatio, Jr. 1832-1899 .... **NCLC 8, 83**
See also CLR 87; DLB 42; LAIT 2; RGAL
4; SATA 16; TUS

Al-Ghazali, Muhammad ibn Muhammad
1058-1111 .... **CMLC 50**
See also DLB 115

Algren, Nelson 1909-1981 ..... **CLC 4, 10, 33;**
SSC 33
See also AMWS 9; BPFB 1; CA 13-16R;
103; CANR 20, 61; CDALB 1941-1968;
CN 1, 2; DLB 9; DLBY 1981, 1982,
2000; EWL 3; MAL 5; MTCW 1, 2;
MTFW 2005; RGAL 4; RGSF 2

al-Hamadhani 967-1007 .... **CMLC 93**
See also WLIT 6

al-Hariri, al-Qasim ibn 'Ali Abu
Muhammad al-Basri
1054-1122 .... **CMLC 63**
See also RGWL 3

Ali, Ahmed 1908-1998 .... **CLC 69**
See also CA 25-28R; CANR 15, 34; CN 1,
2, 3, 4, 5; DLB 323; EWL 3

Ali, Tariq 1943- .... **CLC 173**
See also CA 25-28R; CANR 10, 99, 161

Alighieri, Dante
See Dante
See also WLIT 7

al-Kindi, Abu Yusuf Ya'qub ibn Ishaq c.
801-c. 873 .... **CMLC 80**

Allan, John B.
See Westlake, Donald E.

Allan, Sidney
See Hartmann, Sadakichi

Allan, Sydney
See Hartmann, Sadakichi

Allard, Janet .... **CLC 59**
Allen, Edward 1948- .... **CLC 59**
Allen, Fred 1894-1956 .... **TCLC 87**
Allen, Paula Gunn 1939-2008 . **CLC 84, 202;**
NNAL
See also AMWS 4; CA 112; 143; 272;
CANR 63, 130; CWP; DA3; DAM

MULT; DLB 175; FW; MTCW 2; MTFW
2005; RGAL 4; TCWW 2

Allen, Roland
See Ayckbourn, Alan

Allen, Sarah A.
See Hopkins, Pauline Elizabeth

Allen, Sidney H.
See Hartmann, Sadakichi

Allen, Woody 1935- .... **CLC 16, 52, 195**
See also AAYA 10, 51; AMWS 15; CA 33-
36R; CANR 27, 38, 63, 128, 172; DAM
POP; DLB 44; MTCW 1; SSFS 21

Allende, Isabel 1942- ... **CLC 39, 57, 97, 170;**
HLC 1; SSC 65; WLCS
See also AAYA 18, 70; CA 125; 130; CANR
51, 74, 129, 165; CDWLB 3; CLR 99;
CWW 2; DA3; DAM MULT, NOV; DLB
145; DNFS 1; EWL 3; FL 1:5; FW; HW
1, 2; INT CA-130; LAIT 5; LAWS 1;
LMFS 2; MTCW 1, 2; MTFW 2005;
NCFS 1; NFS 6, 18; RGSF 2; RGWL 3;
SATA 163; SSFS 11, 16; WLIT 1

Alleyn, Ellen
See Rossetti, Christina

Alleyne, Carla D. .... **CLC 65**

Allingham, Margery (Louise)
1904-1966 .... **CLC 19**
See also CA 5-8R; 25-28R; CANR 4, 58;
CMW 4; DLB 77; MSW; MTCW 1, 2

Allingham, William 1824-1889 ...... **NCLC 25**
See also DLB 35; RGEL 2

Allison, Dorothy E. 1949- .... **CLC 78, 153**
See also AAYA 53; CA 140; CANR 66, 107;
CN 7; CSW; DA3; FW; MTCW 2; MTFW
2005; NFS 11; RGAL 4

Alloula, Malek .... **CLC 65**

Allston, Washington 1779-1843 .... **NCLC 2**
See also DLB 1, 235

Almedingen, E. M. .... **CLC 12**
See Almedingen, Martha Edith von
See also SATA 3

Almedingen, Martha Edith von 1898-1971
See Almedingen, E. M.
See also CA 1-4R; CANR 1

Almodovar, Pedro 1949(?)- .... **CLC 114, 229;**
HLCS 1
See also CA 133; CANR 72, 151; HW 2

Almqvist, Carl Jonas Love
1793-1866 .... **NCLC 42**

al-Mutanabbi, Ahmad ibn al-Husayn Abu
al-Tayyib al-Jufi al-Kindi
915-965 .... **CMLC 66**
See Mutanabbi, Al-
See also RGWL 3

Alonso, Damaso 1898-1990 .... **CLC 14**
See also CA 110; 131; 130; CANR 72; DLB
108; EWL 3; HW 1, 2

Alov
See Gogol, Nikolai (Vasilyevich)

al'Sadaawi, Nawal
See El Saadawi, Nawal
See also FW

al-Shaykh, Hanan 1945- .... **CLC 218**
See Shaykh, al- Hanan
See also CA 135; CANR 111; WLIT 6

Al Siddik
See Rolfe, Frederick (William Serafino Aus-
tin Lewis Mary)
See also GLL 1; RGEL 2

Alta 1942- .... **CLC 19**
See also CA 57-60

Alter, Robert B. 1935- .... **CLC 34**
See also CA 49-52; CANR 1, 47, 100, 160

Alter, Robert Bernard
See Alter, Robert B.

Alther, Lisa 1944- .... **CLC 7, 41**
See also BPFB 1; CA 65-68; CAAS 30;
CANR 12, 30, 51, 180; CN 4, 5, 6, 7;
CSW; GLL 2; MTCW 1

Althusser, L.
See Althusser, Louis

Althusser, Louis 1918-1990 .... **CLC 106**
See also CA 131; 132; CANR 102; DLB
242

Altman, Robert 1925-2006 .... **CLC 16, 116,**
242
See also CA 73-76; 254; CANR 43

Alurista .... **HLCS 1; PC 34**
See Urista (Heredia), Alberto (Baltazar)
See also CA 45-48R; DLB 82; LLW

Alvarez, A. 1929- .... **CLC 5, 13**
See also CA 1-4R; CANR 3, 33, 63, 101,
134; CN 3, 4, 5, 6; CP 1, 2, 3, 4, 5, 6, 7;
DLB 14, 40; MTFW 2005

Alvarez, Alejandro Rodriguez 1903-1965
See Casona, Alejandro
See also CA 131; 93-96; HW 1

Alvarez, Julia 1950- .... **CLC 93; HLCS 1**
See also AAYA 25; AMWS 7; CA 147;
CANR 69, 101, 133, 166; DA3; DLB 282;
LATS 1:2; LLW; MTCW 2; MTFW 2005;
NFS 5, 9; SATA 129; WLIT 1

Alvaro, Corrado 1896-1956 .... **TCLC 60**
See also CA 163; DLB 264; EWL 3

Amado, Jorge 1912-2001 ... **CLC 13, 40, 106,**
232; HLC 1
See also CA 77-80; 201; CANR 35, 74, 135;
CWW 2; DAM MULT; DLB 113,
307; EWL 3; HW 2; LAW; LAWS 1;
MTCW 1, 2; MTFW 2005; RGWL 2, 3;
TWA; WLIT 1

Ambler, Eric 1909-1998 .... **CLC 4, 6, 9**
See also BRWS 4; CA 9-12R; 171; CANR
7, 38, 74; CMW 4; CN 1, 2, 3, 4, 5, 6;
DLB 77; MSW; MTCW 1, 2; TEA

Ambrose c. 339-c. 397 .... **CMLC 103**

Ambrose, Stephen E. 1936-2002 ...... **CLC 145**
See also AAYA 44; CA 1-4R; 209; CANR
3, 43, 57, 83, 105; MTFW 2005; NCFS 2;
SATA 40, 138

Amichai, Yehuda 1924-2000 .. **CLC 9, 22, 57,**
116; PC 38
See also CA 85-88; 189; CANR 46, 60, 99,
132; CWW 2; EWL 3; MTCW 1, 2;
MTFW 2005; PFS 24; RGHL; WLIT 6

Amichai, Yehudah
See Amichai, Yehuda

Amiel, Henri Frederic 1821-1881 .... **NCLC 4**
See also DLB 217

Amis, Kingsley 1922-1995 . **CLC 1, 2, 3, 5, 8,**
13, 40, 44, 129
See also AAYA 77; AITN 2; BPFB 1;
BRWS 2; CA 9-12R; 150; CANR 8, 28,
54; CDBLB 1945-1960; CN 1, 2, 3, 4, 5,
6; CP 1, 2, 3, 4; DA; DA3; DAB; DAC;
DAM MST, NOV; DLB 15, 27, 100, 139,
326; DLBY 1996; EWL 3; HGG; INT
CANR-8; MTCW 1, 2; MTFW 2005;
RGEL 2; RGSF 2; SFW 4

Amis, Martin 1949- ... **CLC 4, 9, 38, 62, 101,**
213; SSC 112
See also BEST 90:3; BRWS 4; CA 65-68;
CANR 8, 27, 54, 73, 95, 132, 166; CN 5,
6, 7; DA3; DLB 14, 194; EWL 3; INT
CANR-27; MTCW 2; MTFW 2005

Amis, Martin Louis
See Amis, Martin

Ammianus Marcellinus c. 330-c.
395 .... **CMLC 60**
See also AW 2; DLB 211

Ammons, A.R. 1926-2001 .. **CLC 2, 3, 5, 8, 9,**
25, 57, 108; PC 16
See also AITN 1; AMWS 7; CA 9-12R;
193; CANR 6, 36, 51, 73, 107, 156; CP 1,
2, 3, 4, 5, 6, 7; CSW; DAM POET; DLB
5, 165, 342; EWL 3; MAL 5; MTCW 1,
2; PFS 19; RGAL 4; TCLE 1:1

Ammons, Archie Randolph
See Ammons, A.R.

Apple, Max (Isaac) 1941- .... **CLC 9, 33; SSC 50**
See also AMWS 17; CA 81-84; CANR 19, 54; DLB 130

Appleman, Philip (Dean) 1926- .... **CLC 51**
See also CA 13-16R; CAAS 18; CANR 6, 29, 56

Appleton, Lawrence
See Lovecraft, H. P.

Apteryx
See Eliot, T(homas) S(tearns)

Apuleius, (Lucius Madaurensis) c. 125-c. 164 .... **CMLC 1, 84**
See also AW 2; CDWLB 1; DLB 211; RGWL 2, 3; SUFW; WLIT 8

Aquin, Hubert 1929-1977 .... **CLC 15**
See also CA 105; DLB 53; EWL 3

Aquinas, Thomas 1224(?)-1274 ..... **CMLC 33**
See also DLB 115; EW 1; TWA

Aragon, Louis 1897-1982 .... **CLC 3, 22; TCLC 123**
See also CA 69-72; 108; CANR 28, 71; DAM NOV, POET; DLB 72, 258; EW 11; EWL 3; GFL 1789 to the Present; GLL 2; LMFS 2; MTCW 1, 2; RGWL 2, 3

Arany, Janos 1817-1882 .... **NCLC 34**

Aranyos, Kakay 1847-1910
See Mikszath, Kalman

Aratus of Soli c. 315B.C.-c. 240B.C. .... **CMLC 64**
See also DLB 176

Arbuthnot, John 1667-1735 .... **LC 1**
See also DLB 101

Archer, Herbert Winslow
See Mencken, H(enry) L(ouis)

Archer, Jeffrey 1940- .... **CLC 28**
See also AAYA 16; BEST 89:3; BPFB 1; CA 77-80; CANR 22, 52, 95, 136; CPW; DA3; DAM POP; INT CANR-22; MTFW 2005

Archer, Jeffrey Howard
See Archer, Jeffrey

Archer, Jules 1915- .... **CLC 12**
See also CA 9-12R; CANR 6, 69; SAAS 5; SATA 4, 85

Archer, Lee
See Ellison, Harlan

Archilochus c. 7th cent. B.C.- .... **CMLC 44**
See also DLB 176

Ard, William
See Jakes, John

Arden, John 1930- .... **CLC 6, 13, 15**
See also BRWS 2; CA 13-16R; CAAS 4; CANR 31, 65, 67, 124; CBD; CD 5, 6; DAM DRAM; DFS 9; DLB 13, 245; EWL 3; MTCW 1

Arenas, Reinaldo 1943-1990 .. **CLC 41; HLC 1; TCLC 191**
See also CA 124; 128; 133; CANR 73, 106; DAM MULT; DLB 145; EWL 3; GLL 2; HW 1; LAW; LAWS 1; MTCW 2; MTFW 2005; RGSF 2; RGWL 3; WLIT 1

Arendt, Hannah 1906-1975 .... **CLC 66, 98; TCLC 193**
See also CA 17-20R; 61-64; CANR 26, 60, 172; DLB 242; MTCW 1, 2

Aretino, Pietro 1492-1556 .... **LC 12**
See also RGWL 2, 3

Arghezi, Tudor .... **CLC 80**
See Theodorescu, Ion N.
See also CA 167; CDWLB 4; DLB 220; EWL 3

Arguedas, Jose Maria 1911-1969 .... **CLC 10, 18; HLCS 1; TCLC 147**
See also CA 89-92; CANR 73; DLB 113; EWL 3; HW 1; LAW; RGWL 2, 3; WLIT 1

Argueta, Manlio 1936- .... **CLC 31**
See also CA 131; CANR 73; CWW 2; DLB 145; EWL 3; HW 1; RGWL 3

Arias, Ron 1941- .... **HLC 1**
See also CA 131; CANR 81, 136; DAM MULT; DLB 82; HW 1, 2; MTCW 2; MTFW 2005

Ariosto, Lodovico
See Ariosto, Ludovico
See also WLIT 7

Ariosto, Ludovico 1474-1533 ... **LC 6, 87; PC 42**
See Ariosto, Lodovico
See also EW 2; RGWL 2, 3

Aristides
See Epstein, Joseph

Aristophanes 450B.C.-385B.C. .... **CMLC 4, 51; DC 2; WLCS**
See also AW 1; CDWLB 1; DA; DA3; DAB; DAC; DAM DRAM, MST; DFS 10; DLB 176; LMFS 1; RGWL 2, 3; TWA; WLIT 8

Aristotle 384B.C.-322B.C. .... **CMLC 31; WLCS**
See also AW 1; CDWLB 1; DA; DA3; DAB; DAC; DAM MST; DLB 176; RGWL 2, 3; TWA; WLIT 8

Arlt, Roberto (Godofredo Christophersen) 1900-1942 .... **HLC 1; TCLC 29**
See also CA 123; 131; CANR 67; DAM MULT; DLB 305; EWL 3; HW 1, 2; IDTP; LAW

Armah, Ayi Kwei 1939- . **BLC 1:1, 2:1; CLC 5, 33, 136**
See also AFW; BRWS 10; BW 1; CA 61-64; CANR 21, 64; CDWLB 3; CN 1, 2, 3, 4, 5, 6, 7; DAM MULT, POET; DLB 117; EWL 3; MTCW 1; WLIT 2

Armatrading, Joan 1950- .... **CLC 17**
See also CA 114; 186

Armin, Robert 1568(?)-1615(?) .... **LC 120**

Armitage, Frank
See Carpenter, John (Howard)

Armstrong, Jeannette (C.) 1948- .... **NNAL**
See also CA 149; CCA 1; CN 6, 7; DAC; DLB 334; SATA 102

Arnette, Robert
See Silverberg, Robert

Arnim, Achim von (Ludwig Joachim von Arnim) 1781-1831 .. **NCLC 5, 159; SSC 29**
See also DLB 90

Arnim, Bettina von 1785-1859 ...... **NCLC 38, 123**
See also DLB 90; RGWL 2, 3

Arnold, Matthew 1822-1888 ..... **NCLC 6, 29, 89, 126; PC 5; WLC 1**
See also BRW 5; CDBLB 1832-1890; DA; DAB; DAC; DAM MST, POET; DLB 32, 57; EXPP; PAB; PFS 2; TEA; WP

Arnold, Thomas 1795-1842 .... **NCLC 18**
See also DLB 55

Arnow, Harriette (Louisa) Simpson 1908-1986 ...... **CLC 2, 7, 18; TCLC 196**
See also BPFB 1; CA 9-12R; 118; CANR 14; CN 2, 3, 4; DLB 6; FW; MTCW 1, 2; RHW; SATA 42; SATA-Obit 47

Arouet, Francois-Marie
See Voltaire

Arp, Hans
See Arp, Jean

Arp, Jean 1887-1966 .... **CLC 5; TCLC 115**
See also CA 81-84; 25-28R; CANR 42, 77; EW 10

Arrabal
See Arrabal, Fernando

Arrabal (Teran), Fernando
See Arrabal, Fernando
See also CWW 2

Arrabal, Fernando 1932- ... **CLC 2, 9, 18, 58**
See Arrabal (Teran), Fernando
See also CA 9-12R; CANR 15; DLB 321; EWL 3; LMFS 2

Arreola, Juan Jose 1918-2001 .... **CLC 147; HLC 1; SSC 38**
See also CA 113; 131; 200; CANR 81; CWW 2; DAM MULT; DLB 113; DNFS 2; EWL 3; HW 1, 2; LAW; RGSF 2

Arrian c. 89(?)-c. 155(?) .... **CMLC 43**
See also DLB 176

Arrick, Fran .... **CLC 30**
See Gaberman, Judie Angell
See also BYA 6

Arrley, Richmond
See Delany, Samuel R., Jr.

Artaud, Antonin (Marie Joseph) 1896-1948 .... **DC 14; TCLC 3, 36**
See also CA 104; 149; DA3; DAM DRAM; DFS 22; DLB 258, 321; EW 11; EWL 3; GFL 1789 to the Present; MTCW 2; MTFW 2005; RGWL 2, 3

Arthur, Ruth M(abel) 1905-1979 ..... **CLC 12**
See also CA 9-12R; 85-88; CANR 4; CWRI 5; SATA 7, 26

Artsybashev, Mikhail (Petrovich) 1878-1927 .... **TCLC 31**
See also CA 170; DLB 295

Arundel, Honor (Morfydd) 1919-1973 .... **CLC 17**
See also CA 21-22; 41-44R; CAP 2; CLR 35; CWRI 5; SATA 4; SATA-Obit 24

Arzner, Dorothy 1900-1979 .... **CLC 98**

Asch, Sholem 1880-1957 .... **TCLC 3**
See also CA 105; DLB 333; EWL 3; GLL 2; RGHL

Ascham, Roger 1516(?)-1568 .... **LC 101**
See also DLB 236

Ash, Shalom
See Asch, Sholem

Ashbery, John 1927- ... **CLC 2, 3, 4, 6, 9, 13, 15, 25, 41, 77, 125, 221; PC 26**
See also AMWS 3; CA 5-8R; CANR 9, 37, 66, 102, 132, 170; CP 1, 2, 3, 4, 5, 6, 7; DA3; DAM POET; DLB 5, 165; DLBY 1981; EWL 3; GLL 1; INT CANR-9; MAL 5; MTCW 1, 2; MTFW 2005; PAB; PFS 11, 28; RGAL 4; TCLE 1:1; WP

Ashbery, John Lawrence
See Ashbery, John

Ashbridge, Elizabeth 1713-1755 .... **LC 147**
See also DLB 200

Ashdown, Clifford
See Freeman, R(ichard) Austin

Ashe, Gordon
See Creasey, John

Ashton-Warner, Sylvia (Constance) 1908-1984 .... **CLC 19**
See also CA 69-72; 112; CANR 29; CN 1, 2, 3; MTCW 1, 2

Asimov, Isaac 1920-1992 ..... **CLC 1, 3, 9, 19, 26, 76, 92**
See also AAYA 13; BEST 90:2; BPFB 1; BYA 4, 6, 7, 9; CA 1-4R; 137; CANR 2, 19, 36, 60, 125; CLR 12, 79; CMW 4; CN 1, 2, 3, 4, 5; CPW; DA3; DAM POP; DLB 8; DLBY 1992; INT CANR-19; JRDA; LAIT 5; LMFS 2; MAICYA 1, 2; MAL 5; MTCW 1, 2; MTFW 2005; RGAL 4; SATA 1, 26, 74; SCFW 1, 2; SFW 4; SSFS 17; TUS; YAW

Askew, Anne 1521(?)-1546 .... **LC 81**
See also DLB 136

Assis, Joaquim Maria Machado de
See Machado de Assis, Joaquim Maria

Astell, Mary 1666-1731 .... **LC 68**
See also DLB 252, 336; FW

Bacovia, George 1881-1957 .... **TCLC 24**
   See Vasiliu, Gheorghe
   See also CDWLB 4; DLB 220; EWL 3
Badanes, Jerome 1937-1995 .... **CLC 59**
   See also CA 234
Bage, Robert 1728-1801 .... **NCLC 182**
   See also DLB 39; RGEL 2
Bagehot, Walter 1826-1877 .... **NCLC 10**
   See also DLB 55
Bagnold, Enid 1889-1981 .... **CLC 25**
   See also AAYA 75; BYA 2; CA 5-8R; 103;
   CANR 5, 40; CBD; CN 2; CWD; CWRI
   5; DAM DRAM; DLB 13, 160, 191, 245;
   FW; MAICYA 1, 2; RGEL 2; SATA 1, 25
Bagritsky, Eduard .... **TCLC 60**
   See Dzyubin, Eduard Georgievich
Bagrjana, Elisaveta
   See Belcheva, Elisaveta Lyubomirova
Bagryana, Elisaveta .... **CLC 10**
   See Belcheva, Elisaveta Lyubomirova
   See also CA 178; CDWLB 4; DLB 147;
   EWL 3
Bailey, Paul 1937- .... **CLC 45**
   See also CA 21-24R; CANR 16, 62, 124;
   CN 1, 2, 3, 4, 5, 6, 7; DLB 14, 271; GLL
   2
Baillie, Joanna 1762-1851 ...... **NCLC 71, 151**
   See also DLB 93, 344; GL 2; RGEL 2
Bainbridge, Beryl 1934- ...... **CLC 4, 5, 8, 10,**
   14, 18, 22, 62, 130
   See also BRWS 6; CA 21-24R; CANR 24,
   55, 75, 88, 128; CN 2, 3, 4, 5, 6, 7; DAM
   NOV; DLB 14, 231; EWL 3; MTCW 1,
   2; MTFW 2005
Baker, Carlos (Heard)
   1909-1987 .... **TCLC 119**
   See also CA 5-8R; 122; CANR 3, 63; DLB
   103
Baker, Elliott 1922-2007 .... **CLC 8**
   See also CA 45-48; 257; CANR 2, 63; CN
   1, 2, 3, 4, 5, 6, 7
Baker, Elliott Joseph
   See Baker, Elliott
Baker, Jean H. .... **TCLC 3, 10**
   See Russell, George William
Baker, Nicholson 1957- .... **CLC 61, 165**
   See also AMWS 13; CA 135; CANR 63,
   120, 138; CN 6; CPW; DA3; DAM POP;
   DLB 227; MTFW 2005
Baker, Ray Stannard 1870-1946 .... **TCLC 47**
   See also CA 118
Baker, Russell 1925- .... **CLC 31**
   See also BEST 89:4; CA 57-60; CANR 11,
   41, 59, 137; MTCW 1, 2; MTFW 2005
Bakhtin, M.
   See Bakhtin, Mikhail Mikhailovich
Bakhtin, M. M.
   See Bakhtin, Mikhail Mikhailovich
Bakhtin, Mikhail
   See Bakhtin, Mikhail Mikhailovich
Bakhtin, Mikhail Mikhailovich
   1895-1975 .... **CLC 83; TCLC 160**
   See also CA 128; 113; DLB 242; EWL 3
Bakshi, Ralph 1938(?)- .... **CLC 26**
   See also CA 112; 138; IDFW 3
Bakunin, Mikhail (Alexandrovich)
   1814-1876 .... **NCLC 25, 58**
   See also DLB 277
Bal, Mieke (Maria Gertrudis)
   1946- .... **CLC 252**
   See also CA 156; CANR 99
Baldwin, James 1924-1987 ...... **BLC 1:1, 2:1;**
   CLC 1, 2, 3, 4, 5, 8, 13, 15, 17, 42, 50,
   67, 90, 127; DC 1; SSC 10, 33, 98;
   WLC 1
   See also AAYA 4, 34; AFAW 1, 2; AMWR
   2; AMWS 1; BPFB 1; BW 1; CA 1-4R;
   124; CABS 1; CAD; CANR 3, 24;
   CDALB 1941-1968; CN 1, 2, 3, 4; CPW;

DA; DA3; DAB; DAC; DAM MST,
MULT, NOV, POP; DFS 11, 15; DLB 2,
7, 33, 249, 278; DLBY 1987; EWL 3;
EXPS; LAIT 5; MAL 5; MTCW 1, 2;
MTFW 2005; NCFS 4; NFS 4; RGAL 4;
RGSF 2; SATA 9; SATA-Obit 54; SSFS
2, 18; TUS
Baldwin, William c. 1515-1563 .... **LC 113**
   See also DLB 132
Bale, John 1495-1563 .... **LC 62**
   See also DLB 132; RGEL 2; TEA
Ball, Hugo 1886-1927 .... **TCLC 104**
Ballard, J.G. 1930- .... **CLC 3, 6, 14, 36, 137;**
   SSC 1, 53
   See also AAYA 3, 52; BRWS 5; CA 5-8R;
   CANR 15, 39, 65, 107, 133; CN 1, 2, 3,
   4, 5, 6, 7; DA3; DAM NOV, POP; DLB
   14, 207, 261, 319; EWL 3; HGG; MTCW
   1, 2; MTFW 2005; NFS 8; RGEL 2;
   RGSF 2; SATA 93; SCFW 1, 2; SFW 4
Balmont, Konstantin (Dmitriyevich)
   1867-1943 .... **TCLC 11**
   See also CA 109; 155; DLB 295; EWL 3
Baltausis, Vincas 1847-1910
   See Mikszath, Kalman
Balzac, Honore de 1799-1850 ... **NCLC 5, 35,**
   53, 153; SSC 5, 59, 102; WLC 1
   See also DA; DA3; DAB; DAC; DAM
   MST, NOV; DLB 119; EW 5; GFL 1789
   to the Present; LMFS 1; RGSF 2; RGWL
   2, 3; SSFS 10; SUFW; TWA
Bambara, Toni Cade 1939-1995 ..... **BLC 1:1,**
   2:1; CLC 19, 88; SSC 35, 107; TCLC
   116; WLCS
   See also AAYA 5, 49; AFAW 2; AMWS 11;
   BW 2, 3; BYA 12, 14; CA 29-32R; 150;
   CANR 24, 49, 81; CDALBS; DA; DA3;
   DAC; DAM MST, MULT; DLB 38, 218;
   EXPS; MAL 5; MTCW 1, 2; MTFW
   2005; RGAL 4; RGSF 2; SATA 112; SSFS
   4, 7, 12, 21
Bamdad, A.
   See Shamlu, Ahmad
Bamdad, Alef
   See Shamlu, Ahmad
Banat, D. R.
   See Bradbury, Ray
Bancroft, Laura
   See Baum, L(yman) Frank
Banim, John 1798-1842 .... **NCLC 13**
   See also DLB 116, 158, 159; RGEL 2
Banim, Michael 1796-1874 .... **NCLC 13**
   See also DLB 158, 159
Banjo, The
   See Paterson, A(ndrew) B(arton)
Banks, Iain 1954- .... **CLC 34**
   See also BRWS 11; CA 123; 128; CANR
   61, 106, 180; DLB 194, 261; EWL 3;
   HGG; INT CA-128; MTFW 2005; SFW 4
Banks, Iain M.
   See Banks, Iain
Banks, Iain Menzies
   See Banks, Iain
Banks, Lynne Reid .... **CLC 23**
   See Reid Banks, Lynne
   See also AAYA 6; BYA 7; CN 4, 5, 6
Banks, Russell 1940- . **CLC 37, 72, 187; SSC**
   42
   See also AAYA 45; AMWS 5; CA 65-68;
   CAAS 15; CANR 19, 52, 73, 118; CN 4,
   5, 6, 7; DLB 130, 278; EWL 3; MAL 5;
   MTCW 2; MTFW 2005; NFS 13
Banks, Russell Earl
   See Banks, Russell
Banville, John 1945- .... **CLC 46, 118, 224**
   See also CA 117; 128; CANR 104, 150,
   176; CN 4, 5, 6, 7; DLB 14, 271, 326;
   INT CA-128

Banville, Theodore (Faullain) de
   1832-1891 .... **NCLC 9**
   See also DLB 217; GFL 1789 to the Present
Baraka, Amiri 1934- .. **BLC 1:1, 2:1; CLC 1,**
   2, 3, 5, 10, 14, 33, 115, 213; DC 6; PC
   4; WLCS
   See Jones, LeRoi
   See also AAYA 63; AFAW 1, 2; AMWS 2;
   BW 2, 3; CA 21-24R; CABS 3; CAD;
   CANR 27, 38, 61, 133, 172; CD 3, 5, 6;
   CDALB 1941-1968; CP 4, 5, 6, 7; CPW;
   DA; DA3; DAC; DAM MST, MULT,
   POET, POP; DFS 3, 11, 16; DLB 5, 7,
   16, 38; DLBD 8; EWL 3; MAL 5; MTCW
   1, 2; MTFW 2005; PFS 9; RGAL 4;
   TCLE 1:1; TUS; WP
Baratynsky, Evgenii Abramovich
   1800-1844 .... **NCLC 103**
   See also DLB 205
Barbauld, Anna Laetitia
   1743-1825 .... **NCLC 50, 185**
   See also DLB 107, 109, 142, 158, 336;
   RGEL 2
Barbellion, W. N. P. .... **TCLC 24**
   See Cummings, Bruce F(rederick)
Barber, Benjamin R. 1939- .... **CLC 141**
   See also CA 29-32R; CANR 12, 32, 64, 119
Barbera, Jack (Vincent) 1945- .... **CLC 44**
   See also CA 110; CANR 45
Barbey d'Aurevilly, Jules-Amedee
   1808-1889 .... **NCLC 1; SSC 17**
   See also DLB 119; GFL 1789 to the Present
Barbour, John c. 1316-1395 .... **CMLC 33**
   See also DLB 146
Barbusse, Henri 1873-1935 .... **TCLC 5**
   See also CA 105; 154; DLB 65; EWL 3;
   RGWL 2, 3
Barclay, Alexander c. 1475-1552 .... **LC 109**
   See also DLB 132
Barclay, Bill
   See Moorcock, Michael
Barclay, William Ewert
   See Moorcock, Michael
Barea, Arturo 1897-1957 .... **TCLC 14**
   See also CA 111; 201
Barfoot, Joan 1946- .... **CLC 18**
   See also CA 105; CANR 141, 179
Barham, Richard Harris
   1788-1845 .... **NCLC 77**
   See also DLB 159
Baring, Maurice 1874-1945 .... **TCLC 8**
   See also CA 105; 168; DLB 34; HGG
Baring-Gould, Sabine 1834-1924 ... **TCLC 88**
   See also DLB 156, 190
Barker, Clive 1952- .... **CLC 52, 205; SSC 53**
   See also AAYA 10, 54; BEST 90:3; BPFB
   1; CA 121; 129; CANR 71, 111, 133;
   CPW; DA3; DAM POP; DLB 261; HGG;
   INT CA-129; MTCW 1, 2; MTFW 2005;
   SUFW 2
Barker, George Granville
   1913-1991 .... **CLC 8, 48; PC 77**
   See also CA 9-12R; 135; CANR 7, 38; CP
   1, 2, 3, 4, 5; DAM POET; DLB 20; EWL
   3; MTCW 1
Barker, Harley Granville
   See Granville-Barker, Harley
   See also DLB 10
Barker, Howard 1946- .... **CLC 37**
   See also CA 102; CBD; CD 5, 6; DLB 13,
   233
Barker, Jane 1652-1732 .... **LC 42, 82; PC 91**
   See also DLB 39, 131
Barker, Pat 1943- .... **CLC 32, 94, 146**
   See also BRWS 4; CA 117; 122; CANR 50,
   101, 148; CN 6, 7; DLB 271, 326; INT
   CA-122
Barker, Patricia
   See Barker, Pat

Beattie, James 1735-1803 .... **NCLC 25**
See also DLB 109

Beauchamp, Kathleen Mansfield 1888-1923
See Mansfield, Katherine
See also CA 104; 134; DA; DA3; DAC;
DAM MST; MTCW 2; TEA

Beaumarchais, Pierre-Augustin Caron de
1732-1799 .... **DC 4; LC 61**
See also DAM DRAM; DFS 14, 16; DLB
313; EW 4; GFL Beginnings to 1789;
RGWL 2, 3

Beaumont, Francis 1584(?)-1616 .. **DC 6; LC 33**
See also BRW 2; CDBLB Before 1660;
DLB 58; TEA

Beauvoir, Simone de 1908-1986 .... **CLC 1, 2, 4, 8, 14, 31, 44, 50, 71, 124; SSC 35; WLC 1**
See also BPFB 1; CA 9-12R; 118; CANR
28, 61; DA; DA3; DAB; DAC; DAM
MST, NOV; DLB 72; DLBY 1986; EW
12; EWL 3; FL 1:5; FW; GFL 1789 to the
Present; LMFS 2; MTCW 1, 2; MTFW
2005; RGSF 2; RGWL 2, 3; TWA

Beauvoir, Simone Lucie Ernestine Marie Bertrand de
See Beauvoir, Simone de

Becker, Carl (Lotus) 1873-1945 ..... **TCLC 63**
See also CA 157; DLB 17

Becker, Jurek 1937-1997 .... **CLC 7, 19**
See also CA 85-88; 157; CANR 60, 117;
CWW 2; DLB 75, 299; EWL 3; RGHL

Becker, Walter 1950- .... **CLC 26**

Becket, Thomas a 1118(?)-1170 .... **CMLC 83**

Beckett, Samuel 1906-1989 ... **CLC 1, 2, 3, 4, 6, 9, 10, 11, 14, 18, 29, 57, 59, 83; DC 22; SSC 16, 74; TCLC 145; WLC 1**
See also BRWC 2; BRWR 1; BRWS 1; CA
5-8R; 130; CANR 33, 61; CDBLB
1945-1960; CN 1, 2, 3, 4; CP 1, 2, 3, 4;
DA; DA3; DAB; DAC; DAM DRAM,
MST, NOV; DFS 2, 7, 18; DLB 13, 15,
233, 319, 321; DLBY 1990; EWL 3;
GFL 1789 to the Present; LATS 1:2;
LMFS 2; MTCW 1, 2; MTFW 2005;
RGSF 2; RGWL 2, 3; SSFS 15; TEA;
WLIT 4

Beckford, William 1760-1844 .... **NCLC 16**
See also BRW 3; DLB 39, 213; GL 2; HGG;
LMFS 1; SUFW

Beckham, Barry (Earl) 1944- .... **BLC 1:1**
See also BW 1; CA 29-32R; CANR 26, 62;
CN 1, 2, 3, 4, 5, 6; DAM MULT; DLB 33

Beckman, Gunnel 1910- .... **CLC 26**
See also CA 33-36R; CANR 15, 114; CLR
25; MAICYA 1, 2; SAAS 9; SATA 6

Becque, Henri 1837-1899 .... **DC 21; NCLC 3**
See also DLB 192; GFL 1789 to the Present

Becquer, Gustavo Adolfo
1836-1870 .... **HLCS 1; NCLC 106**
See also DAM MULT

Beddoes, Thomas Lovell 1803-1849 .. **DC 15; NCLC 3, 154**
See also BRWS 11; DLB 96

Bede c. 673-735 .... **CMLC 20**
See also DLB 146; TEA

Bedford, Denton R. 1907-(?) .... **NNAL**

Bedford, Donald F.
See Fearing, Kenneth (Flexner)

Beecher, Catharine Esther
1800-1878 .... **NCLC 30**
See also DLB 1, 243

Beecher, John 1904-1980 .... **CLC 6**
See also AITN 1; CA 5-8R; 105; CANR 8;
CP 1, 2, 3

Beer, Johann 1655-1700 .... **LC 5**
See also DLB 168

Beer, Patricia 1924- .... **CLC 58**
See also CA 61-64; 183; CANR 13, 46; CP
1, 2, 3, 4, 5, 6; CWP; DLB 40; FW

Beerbohm, Max
See Beerbohm, (Henry) Max(imilian)

Beerbohm, (Henry) Max(imilian)
1872-1956 .... **TCLC 1, 24**
See also BRWS 2; CA 104; 154; CANR 79;
DLB 34, 100; FANT; MTCW 2

Beer-Hofmann, Richard
1866-1945 .... **TCLC 60**
See also CA 160; DLB 81

Beg, Shemus
See Stephens, James

Begiebing, Robert J(ohn) 1946- .... **CLC 70**
See also CA 122; CANR 40, 88

Begley, Louis 1933- .... **CLC 197**
See also CA 140; CANR 98, 176; DLB 299;
RGHL; TCLE 1:1

Behan, Brendan (Francis)
1923-1964 .... **CLC 1, 8, 11, 15, 79**
See also BRWS 2; CA 73-76; CANR 33,
121; CBD; CDBLB 1945-1960; DAM
DRAM; DFS 7; DLB 13, 233; EWL 3;
MTCW 1, 2

Behn, Aphra 1640(?)-1689 .. **DC 4; LC 1, 30, 42, 135; PC 13, 88; WLC 1**
See also BRWS 3; DA; DA3; DAB; DAC;
DAM DRAM, MST, NOV, POET; DFS
16, 24; DLB 39, 80, 131; FW; TEA;
WLIT 3

Behrman, S(amuel) N(athaniel)
1893-1973 .... **CLC 40**
See also CA 13-16; 45-48; CAD; CAP 1;
DLB 7, 44; IDFW 3; MAL 5; RGAL 4

Bekederemo, J. P. Clark
See Clark Bekederemo, J.P.
See also CD 6

Belasco, David 1853-1931 .... **TCLC 3**
See also CA 104; 168; DLB 7; MAL 5;
RGAL 4

Belcheva, Elisaveta Lyubomirova
1893-1991 .... **CLC 10**
See Bagryana, Elisaveta

Beldone, Phil "Cheech"
See Ellison, Harlan

Beleno
See Azuela, Mariano

Belinski, Vissarion Grigoryevich
1811-1848 .... **NCLC 5**
See also DLB 198

Belitt, Ben 1911- .... **CLC 22**
See also CA 13-16R; CAAS 4; CANR 7,
77; CP 1, 2, 3, 4, 5, 6; DLB 5

Belknap, Jeremy 1744-1798 .... **LC 115**
See also DLB 30, 37

Bell, Gertrude (Margaret Lowthian)
1868-1926 .... **TCLC 67**
See also CA 167; CANR 110; DLB 174

Bell, J. Freeman
See Zangwill, Israel

Bell, James Madison 1826-1902 ..... **BLC 1:1; TCLC 43**
See also BW 1; CA 122; 124; DAM MULT;
DLB 50

Bell, Madison Smartt 1957- ..... **CLC 41, 102, 223**
See also AMWS 10; BPFB 1; CA 111; 183;
CAAE 183; CANR 28, 54, 73, 134, 176;
CN 5, 6, 7; CSW; DLB 218, 278; MTCW
2; MTFW 2005

Bell, Marvin (Hartley) 1937- ...... **CLC 8, 31; PC 79**
See also CA 21-24R; CAAS 14; CANR 59,
102; CP 1, 2, 3, 4, 5, 6, 7; DAM POET;
DLB 5; MAL 5; MTCW 1; PFS 25

Bell, W. L. D.
See Mencken, H(enry) L(ouis)

Bellamy, Atwood C.
See Mencken, H(enry) L(ouis)

Bellamy, Edward 1850-1898 ..... **NCLC 4, 86, 147**
See also DLB 12; NFS 15; RGAL 4; SFW 4

Belli, Gioconda 1948- .... **HLCS 1**
See also CA 152; CANR 143; CWW 2;
DLB 290; EWL 3; RGWL 3

Bellin, Edward J.
See Kuttner, Henry

Bello, Andres 1781-1865 .... **NCLC 131**
See also LAW

Belloc, (Joseph) Hilaire (Pierre Sebastien Rene Swanton) 1870-1953 .... **PC 24; TCLC 7, 18**
See also CA 106; 152; CLR 102; CWRI 5;
DAM POET; DLB 19, 100, 141, 174;
EWL 3; MTCW 2; MTFW 2005; SATA
112; WCH; YABC 1

Belloc, Joseph Peter Rene Hilaire
See Belloc, (Joseph) Hilaire (Pierre Sebastien Rene Swanton)

Belloc, Joseph Pierre Hilaire
See Belloc, (Joseph) Hilaire (Pierre Sebastien Rene Swanton)

Belloc, M. A.
See Lowndes, Marie Adelaide (Belloc)

Belloc-Lowndes, Mrs.
See Lowndes, Marie Adelaide (Belloc)

Bellow, Saul 1915-2005 ...... **CLC 1, 2, 3, 6, 8, 10, 13, 15, 25, 33, 34, 63, 79, 190, 200; SSC 14, 101; WLC 1**
See also AITN 2; AMW; AMWC 2; AMWR
2; BEST 89:3; BPFB 1; CA 5-8R; 238;
CABS 1; CANR 29, 53, 95, 132; CDALB
1941-1968; CN 1, 2, 3, 4, 5, 6, 7; DA;
DA3; DAB; DAC; DAM MST, NOV,
POP; DLB 2, 28, 299, 329; DLBD 3;
DLBY 1982; EWL 3; MAL 5; MTCW 1,
2; MTFW 2005; NFS 4, 14, 26; RGAL 4;
RGHL; RGSF 2; SSFS 12, 22; TUS

Belser, Reimond Karel Maria de 1929-
See Ruyslinck, Ward
See also CA 152

Bely, Andrey .... **PC 11; TCLC 7**
See Bugayev, Boris Nikolayevich
See also DLB 295; EW 9; EWL 3

Belyi, Andrei
See Bugayev, Boris Nikolayevich
See also RGWL 2, 3

Bembo, Pietro 1470-1547 .... **LC 79**
See also RGWL 2, 3

Benary, Margot
See Benary-Isbert, Margot

Benary-Isbert, Margot 1889-1979 .... **CLC 12**
See also CA 5-8R; 89-92; CANR 4, 72;
CLR 12; MAICYA 1, 2; SATA 2; SATA-
Obit 21

Benavente (y Martinez), Jacinto
1866-1954 .... **DC 26; HLCS 1; TCLC 3**
See also CA 106; 131; CANR 81; DAM
DRAM, MULT; DLB 329; EWL 3; GLL
2; HW 1, 2; MTCW 1, 2

Benchley, Peter 1940-2006 .... **CLC 4, 8**
See also AAYA 14; AITN 2; BPFB 1; CA
17-20R; 248; CANR 12, 35, 66, 115;
CPW; DAM NOV, POP; HGG; MTCW 1,
2; MTFW 2005; SATA 3, 89, 164

Benchley, Peter Bradford
See Benchley, Peter

Benchley, Robert (Charles)
1889-1945 .... **TCLC 1, 55**
See also CA 105; 153; DLB 11; MAL 5;
RGAL 4

Benda, Julien 1867-1956 .... **TCLC 60**
See also CA 120; 154; GFL 1789 to the
Present

Buck, Pearl S(ydenstricker)
1892-1973 .... **CLC 7, 11, 18, 127**
See also AAYA 42; AITN 1; AMWS 2;
BPFB 1; CA 1-4R; 41-44R; CANR 1, 34;
CDALBS; CN 1; DA; DA3; DAB; DAC;
DAM MST, NOV; DLB 9, 102, 329; EWL
3; LAIT 3; MAL 5; MTCW 1, 2; MTFW
2005; NFS 25; RGAL 4; RHW; SATA 1,
25; TUS

Buckler, Ernest 1908-1984 .... **CLC 13**
See also CA 11-12; 114; CAP 1; CCA 1;
CN 1, 2, 3; DAC; DAM MST; DLB 68;
SATA 47

Buckley, Christopher 1952- .... **CLC 165**
See also CA 139; CANR 119, 180

Buckley, Christopher Taylor
See Buckley, Christopher

Buckley, Vincent (Thomas)
1925-1988 .... **CLC 57**
See also CA 101; CP 1, 2, 3, 4; DLB 289

Buckley, William F., Jr. 1925-2008 ... **CLC 7,
18, 37**
See also AITN 1; BPFB 1; CA 1-4R; 269;
CANR 1, 24, 53, 93, 133; CMW 4; CPW;
DA3; DAM POP; DLB 137; DLBY 1980;
INT CANR-24; MTCW 1, 2; MTFW
2005; TUS

Buckley, William Frank
See Buckley, William F., Jr.

Buckley, William Frank, Jr.
See Buckley, William F., Jr.

Buechner, Frederick 1926- ..... **CLC 2, 4, 6, 9**
See also AMWS 12; BPFB 1; CA 13-16R;
CANR 11, 39, 64, 114, 138; CN 1, 2, 3,
4, 5, 6, 7; DAM NOV; DLBY 1980; INT
CANR-11; MAL 5; MTCW 1, 2; MTFW
2005; TCLE 1:1

Buell, John (Edward) 1927- .... **CLC 10**
See also CA 1-4R; CANR 71; DLB 53

Buero Vallejo, Antonio 1916-2000 ... **CLC 15,
46, 139, 226; DC 18**
See also CA 106; 189; CANR 24, 49, 75;
CWW 2; DFS 11; EWL 3; HW 1; MTCW
1, 2

Bufalino, Gesualdo 1920-1996 .... **CLC 74**
See also CA 209; CWW 2; DLB 196

Bugayev, Boris Nikolayevich
1880-1934 .... **PC 11; TCLC 7**
See Bely, Andrey; Belyi, Andrei
See also CA 104; 165; MTCW 2; MTFW
2005

Bukowski, Charles 1920-1994 ... **CLC 2, 5, 9,
41, 82, 108; PC 18; SSC 45**
See also CA 17-20R; 144; CANR 40, 62,
105, 180; CN 4, 5; CP 1, 2, 3, 4, 5; CPW;
DA3; DAM NOV, POET; DLB 5, 130,
169; EWL 3; MAL 5; MTCW 1, 2;
MTFW 2005; PFS 28

Bulgakov, Mikhail 1891-1940 .... **SSC 18;
TCLC 2, 16, 159**
See also AAYA 74; BPFB 1; CA 105; 152;
DAM DRAM, NOV; DLB 272; EWL 3;
MTCW 2; MTFW 2005; NFS 8; RGSF 2;
RGWL 2, 3; SFW 4; TWA

Bulgakov, Mikhail Afanasevich
See Bulgakov, Mikhail

Bulgya, Alexander Alexandrovich
1901-1956 .... **TCLC 53**
See Fadeev, Aleksandr Aleksandrovich;
Fadeev, Alexandr Alexandrovich; Fadeyev,
Alexander
See also CA 117; 181

Bullins, Ed 1935- ...... **BLC 1:1; CLC 1, 5, 7;
DC 6**
See also BW 2, 3; CA 49-52; CAAS 16;
CAD; CANR 24, 46, 73, 134; CD 5, 6;
DAM DRAM, MULT; DLB 7, 38, 249;
EWL 3; MAL 5; MTCW 1, 2; MTFW
2005; RGAL 4

Bulosan, Carlos 1911-1956 .... **AAL**
See also CA 216; DLB 312; RGAL 4

**Bulwer-Lytton, Edward (George Earle
Lytton)** 1803-1873 .... **NCLC 1, 45**
See also DLB 21; RGEL 2; SFW 4; SUFW
1; TEA

Bunin, Ivan
See Bunin, Ivan Alexeyevich

Bunin, Ivan Alekseevich
See Bunin, Ivan Alexeyevich

Bunin, Ivan Alexeyevich 1870-1953 ... **SSC 5;
TCLC 6**
See also CA 104; DLB 317, 329; EWL 3;
RGSF 2; RGWL 2, 3; TWA

Bunting, Basil 1900-1985 ...... **CLC 10, 39, 47**
See also BRWS 7; CA 53-56; 115; CANR
7; CP 1, 2, 3, 4; DAM POET; DLB 20;
EWL 3; RGEL 2

Bunuel, Luis 1900-1983 ... **CLC 16, 80; HLC
1**
See also CA 101; 110; CANR 32, 77; DAM
MULT; HW 1

Bunyan, John 1628-1688 .. **LC 4, 69; WLC 1**
See also BRW 2; BYA 5; CDBLB 1660-
1789; CLR 124; DA; DAB; DAC; DAM
MST; DLB 39; RGEL 2; TEA; WCH;
WLIT 3

Buravsky, Alexandr .... **CLC 59**

Burchill, Julie 1959- .... **CLC 238**
See also CA 135; CANR 115, 116

Burckhardt, Jacob (Christoph)
1818-1897 .... **NCLC 49**
See also EW 6

Burford, Eleanor
See Hibbert, Eleanor Alice Burford

Burgess, Anthony 1917-1993 . **CLC 1, 2, 4, 5,
8, 10, 13, 15, 22, 40, 62, 81, 94**
See also AAYA 25; AITN 1; BRWS 1; CA
1-4R; 143; CANR 2, 46; CDBLB 1960 to
Present; CN 1, 2, 3, 4, 5; DA3; DAB;
DAC; DAM NOV; DLB 14, 194, 261;
DLBY 1998; EWL 3; MTCW 1, 2; MTFW
2005; NFS 15; RGEL 2; RHW; SFW 4;
TEA; YAW

Buridan, John c. 1295-c. 1358 ...... **CMLC 97**

Burke, Edmund 1729(?)-1797 .... **LC 7, 36,
146; WLC 1**
See also BRW 3; DA; DA3; DAB; DAC;
DAM MST; DLB 104, 252, 336; RGEL
2; TEA

Burke, Kenneth (Duva) 1897-1993 ... **CLC 2,
24**
See also AMW; CA 5-8R; 143; CANR 39,
74, 136; CN 1, 2; CP 1, 2, 3, 4, 5; DLB
45, 63; EWL 3; MAL 5; MTCW 1, 2;
MTFW 2005; RGAL 4

Burke, Leda
See Garnett, David

Burke, Ralph
See Silverberg, Robert

Burke, Thomas 1886-1945 .... **TCLC 63**
See also CA 113; 155; CMW 4; DLB 197

Burney, Fanny 1752-1840 .... **NCLC 12, 54,
107**
See also BRWS 3; DLB 39; FL 1:2; NFS
16; RGEL 2; TEA

Burney, Frances
See Burney, Fanny

Burns, Robert 1759-1796 ... **LC 3, 29, 40; PC
6; WLC 1**
See also AAYA 51; BRW 3; CDBLB 1789-
1832; DA; DA3; DAB; DAC; DAM MST,
POET; DLB 109; EXPP; PAB; RGEL 2;
TEA; WP

Burns, Tex
See L'Amour, Louis

Burnshaw, Stanley 1906-2005 ..... **CLC 3, 13,
44**
See also CA 9-12R; 243; CP 1, 2, 3, 4, 5, 6,
7; DLB 48; DLBY 1997

Burr, Anne 1937- .... **CLC 6**
See also CA 25-28R

Burroughs, Edgar Rice 1875-1950 . **TCLC 2,
32**
See also AAYA 11; BPFB 1; BYA 4, 9; CA
104; 132; CANR 131; DA3; DAM NOV;
DLB 8; FANT; MTCW 1, 2; MTFW
2005; RGAL 4; SATA 41; SCFW 1, 2;
SFW 4; TCWW 1, 2; TUS; YAW

Burroughs, William S. 1914-1997 . **CLC 1, 2,
5, 15, 22, 42, 75, 109; TCLC 121; WLC
1**
See Lee, William; Lee, Willy
See also AAYA 60; AITN 2; AMWS 3; BG
1:2; BPFB 1; CA 9-12R; 160; CANR 20,
52, 104; CN 1, 2, 3, 4, 5, 6; CPW; DA;
DA3; DAB; DAC; DAM MST, NOV,
POP; DLB 2, 8, 16, 152, 237; DLBY
1981, 1997; EWL 3; HGG; LMFS 2;
MAL 5; MTCW 1, 2; MTFW 2005;
RGAL 4; SFW 4

Burroughs, William Seward
See Burroughs, William S.

Burton, Sir Richard F(rancis)
1821-1890 .... **NCLC 42**
See also DLB 55, 166, 184; SSFS 21

Burton, Robert 1577-1640 .... **LC 74**
See also DLB 151; RGEL 2

Buruma, Ian 1951- .... **CLC 163**
See also CA 128; CANR 65, 141

Busch, Frederick 1941-2006 .. **CLC 7, 10, 18,
47, 166**
See also CA 33-36R; 248; CAAS 1; CANR
45, 73, 92, 157; CN 1, 2, 3, 4, 5, 6, 7;
DLB 6, 218

Busch, Frederick Matthew
See Busch, Frederick

Bush, Barney (Furman) 1946- .... **NNAL**
See also CA 145

Bush, Ronald 1946- .... **CLC 34**
See also CA 136

Busia, Abena, P. A. 1953- .... **BLC 2:1**

Bustos, F(rancisco)
See Borges, Jorge Luis

Bustos Domecq, H(onorio)
See Bioy Casares, Adolfo; Borges, Jorge
Luis

Butler, Octavia E. 1947-2006 .... **BLC 2:1;
BLCS; CLC 38, 121, 230, 240**
See also AAYA 18, 48; AFAW 2; AMWS
13; BPFB 1; BW 2, 3; CA 73-76; 248;
CANR 12, 24, 38, 73, 145, 240; CLR 65;
CN 7; CPW; DA3; DAM MULT, POP;
DLB 33; LATS 1:2; MTCW 1, 2; MTFW
2005; NFS 8, 21; SATA 84; SCFW 2;
SFW 4; SSFS 6; TCLE 1:1; YAW

Butler, Octavia Estelle
See Butler, Octavia E.

Butler, Robert Olen, (Jr.) 1945- ...... **CLC 81,
162**
See also AMWS 12; BPFB 1; CA 112;
CANR 66, 138; CN 7; CSW; DAM POP;
DLB 173, 335; INT CA-112; MAL 5;
MTCW 2; MTFW 2005; SSFS 11, 22

Butler, Samuel 1612-1680 .... **LC 16, 43**
See also DLB 101, 126; RGEL 2

Butler, Samuel 1835-1902 .... **TCLC 1, 33;
WLC 1**
See also BRWS 2; CA 143; CDBLB 1890-
1914; DA; DA3; DAB; DAC; DAM MST,
NOV; DLB 18, 57, 174; RGEL 2; SFW 4;
TEA

Butler, Walter C.
See Faust, Frederick (Schiller)

Butor, Michel (Marie Francois)
1926- .... **CLC 1, 3, 8, 11, 15, 161**
See also CA 9-12R; CANR 33, 66; CWW
2; DLB 83; EW 13; EWL 3; GFL 1789 to
the Present; MTCW 1, 2; MTFW 2005

Butts, Mary 1890(?)-1937 .... **TCLC 77**
See also CA 148; DLB 240

Buxton, Ralph
See Silverstein, Alvin; Silverstein, Virginia
B(arbara Opshelor)

Buzo, Alex
See Buzo, Alexander (John)
See also DLB 289

Buzo, Alexander (John) 1944- .... **CLC 61**
See also CA 97-100; CANR 17, 39, 69; CD
5, 6

Buzzati, Dino 1906-1972 .... **CLC 36**
See also CA 160; 33-36R; DLB 177; RGWL
2, 3; SFW 4

Byars, Betsy 1928- .... **CLC 35**
See also AAYA 19; BYA 3; CA 33-36R,
183; CAAE 183; CANR 18, 36, 57, 102,
148; CLR 1, 16, 72; DLB 52; INT CANR-
18; JRDA; MAICYA 1, 2; MAICYAS 1;
MTCW 1; SAAS 1; SATA 4, 46, 80, 163;
SATA-Essay 108; WYA; YAW

Byars, Betsy Cromer
See Byars, Betsy

Byatt, Antonia Susan Drabble
See Byatt, A.S.

Byatt, A.S. 1936- .... **CLC 19, 65, 136, 223;
SSC 91**
See also BPFB 1; BRWC 2; BRWS 4; CA
13-16R; CANR 13, 33, 50, 75, 96, 133;
CN 1, 2, 3, 4, 5, 6; DA3; DAM NOV,
POP; DLB 14, 194, 319, 326; EWL 3;
MTCW 1, 2; MTFW 2005; RGSF 2;
RHW; SSFS 26; TEA

Byrd, William II 1674-1744 .... **LC 112**
See also DLB 24, 140; RGAL 4

Byrne, David 1952- .... **CLC 26**
See also CA 127

Byrne, John Keyes 1926-
See Leonard, Hugh
See also CA 102; CANR 78, 140; INT CA-
102

Byron, George Gordon (Noel)
1788-1824 ..... **DC 24; NCLC 2, 12, 109,
149; PC 16; WLC 1**
See also AAYA 64; BRW 4; BRWC 2; CD-
BLB 1789-1832; DA; DA3; DAB; DAC;
DAM MST, POET; DLB 96, 110; EXPP;
LMFS 1; PAB; PFS 1, 14; RGEL 2; TEA;
WLIT 3; WP

Byron, Robert 1905-1941 .... **TCLC 67**
See also CA 160; DLB 195

C. 3. 3.
See Wilde, Oscar

Caballero, Fernan 1796-1877 .... **NCLC 10**

Cabell, Branch
See Cabell, James Branch

Cabell, James Branch 1879-1958 .... **TCLC 6**
See also CA 105; 152; DLB 9, 78; FANT;
MAL 5; MTCW 2; RGAL 4; SUFW 1

Cabeza de Vaca, Alvar Nunez
1490-1557(?) .... **LC 61**

Cable, George Washington
1844-1925 .... **SSC 4; TCLC 4**
See also CA 104; 155; DLB 12, 74; DLBD
13; RGAL 4; TUS

Cabral de Melo Neto, Joao
1920-1999 .... **CLC 76**
See Melo Neto, Joao Cabral de
See also CA 151; DAM MULT; DLB 307;
LAW; LAWS 1

Cabrera Infante, G. 1929-2005 ... **CLC 5, 25,
45, 120; HLC 1; SSC 39**
See also CA 85-88; 236; CANR 29, 65, 110;
CDWLB 3; CWW 2; DA3; DAM MULT;
DLB 113; EWL 3; HW 1, 2; LAW; LAWS
1; MTCW 1, 2; MTFW 2005; RGSF 2;
WLIT 1

Cabrera Infante, Guillermo
See Cabrera Infante, G.

Cade, Toni
See Bambara, Toni Cade

Cadmus and Harmonia
See Buchan, John

Caedmon fl. 658-680 .... **CMLC 7**
See also DLB 146

Caeiro, Alberto
See Pessoa, Fernando (Antonio Nogueira)

Caesar, Julius .... **CMLC 47**
See Julius Caesar
See also AW 1; RGWL 2, 3; WLIT 8

Cage, John (Milton), (Jr.)
1912-1992 .... **CLC 41; PC 58**
See also CA 13-16R; 169; CANR 9, 78;
DLB 193; INT CANR-9; TCLE 1:1

Cahan, Abraham 1860-1951 .... **TCLC 71**
See also CA 108; 154; DLB 9, 25, 28; MAL
5; RGAL 4

Cain, G.
See Cabrera Infante, G.

Cain, Guillermo
See Cabrera Infante, G.

Cain, James M(allahan) 1892-1977 .. **CLC 3,
11, 28**
See also AITN 1; BPFB 1; CA 17-20R; 73-
76; CANR 8, 34, 61; CMW 4; CN 1, 2;
DLB 226; EWL 3; MAL 5; MSW; MTCW
1; RGAL 4

Caine, Hall 1853-1931 .... **TCLC 97**
See also RHW

Caine, Mark
See Raphael, Frederic (Michael)

Calasso, Roberto 1941- .... **CLC 81**
See also CA 143; CANR 89

Calderon de la Barca, Pedro
1600-1681 . **DC 3; HLCS 1; LC 23, 136**
See also DFS 23; EW 2; RGWL 2, 3; TWA

Caldwell, Erskine 1903-1987 ... **CLC 1, 8, 14,
50, 60; SSC 19; TCLC 117**
See also AITN 1; AMW; BPFB 1; CA 1-4R;
121; CAAS 1; CANR 2, 33; CN 1, 2, 3,
4; DA3; DAM NOV; DLB 9, 86; EWL 3;
MAL 5; MTCW 1, 2; MTFW 2005;
RGAL 4; RGSF 2; TUS

Caldwell, (Janet Miriam) Taylor (Holland)
1900-1985 .... **CLC 2, 28, 39**
See also BPFB 1; CA 5-8R; 116; CANR 5;
DA3; DAM NOV, POP; DLBD 17;
MTCW 2; RHW

Calhoun, John Caldwell
1782-1850 .... **NCLC 15**
See also DLB 3, 248

Calisher, Hortense 1911- ..... **CLC 2, 4, 8, 38,
134; SSC 15**
See also CA 1-4R; CANR 1, 22, 117; CN
1, 2, 3, 4, 5, 6, 7; DA3; DAM NOV; DLB
2, 218; INT CANR-22; MAL 5; MTCW
1, 2; MTFW 2005; RGAL 4; RGSF 2

Callaghan, Morley Edward
1903-1990 ..... **CLC 3, 14, 41, 65; TCLC
145**
See also CA 9-12R; 132; CANR 33, 73;
CN 1, 2, 3, 4; DAC; DAM MST; DLB
68; EWL 3; MTCW 1, 2; MTFW 2005;
RGEL 2; RGSF 2; SSFS 19

Callimachus c. 305B.C.-c.
240B.C. .... **CMLC 18**
See also AW 1; DLB 176; RGWL 2, 3

Calvin, Jean
See Calvin, John
See also DLB 327; GFL Beginnings to 1789

Calvin, John 1509-1564 .... **LC 37**
See Calvin, Jean

Calvino, Italo 1923-1985 .... **CLC 5, 8, 11, 22,
33, 39, 73; SSC 3, 48; TCLC 183**
See also AAYA 58; CA 85-88; 116; CANR
23, 61, 132; DAM NOV; DLB 196; EW
13; EWL 3; MTCW 1, 2; MTFW 2005;
RGHL; RGSF 2; RGWL 2, 3; SFW 4;
SSFS 12; WLIT 7

Camara Laye
See Laye, Camara
See also EWL 3

Camden, William 1551-1623 .... **LC 77**
See also DLB 172

Cameron, Carey 1952- .... **CLC 59**
See also CA 135

Cameron, Peter 1959- .... **CLC 44**
See also AMWS 12; CA 125; CANR 50,
117; DLB 234; GLL 2

Camoens, Luis Vaz de 1524(?)-1580
See Camoes, Luis de
See also EW 2

Camoes, Luis de 1524(?)-1580 . **HLCS 1; LC
62; PC 31**
See Camoens, Luis Vaz de
See also DLB 287; RGWL 2, 3

Camp, Madeleine L'Engle
See L'Engle, Madeleine

Campana, Dino 1885-1932 .... **TCLC 20**
See also CA 117; 246; DLB 114; EWL 3

Campanella, Tommaso 1568-1639 .... **LC 32**
See also RGWL 2, 3

Campbell, Bebe Moore 1950-2006 . **BLC 2:1;
CLC 246**
See also AAYA 26; BW 2, 3; CA 139; 254;
CANR 81, 134; DLB 227; MTCW 2;
MTFW 2005

Campbell, John Ramsey
See Campbell, Ramsey

Campbell, John W(ood, Jr.)
1910-1971 .... **CLC 32**
See also CA 21-22; 29-32R; CANR 34;
CAP 2; DLB 8; MTCW 1; SCFW 1, 2;
SFW 4

Campbell, Joseph 1904-1987 .... **CLC 69;
TCLC 140**
See also AAYA 3, 66; BEST 89:2; CA 1-4R;
124; CANR 3, 28, 61, 107; DA3; MTCW
1, 2

Campbell, Maria 1940- .... **CLC 85; NNAL**
See also CA 102; CANR 54; CCA 1; DAC

Campbell, Ramsey 1946- ... **CLC 42; SSC 19**
See also AAYA 51; CA 57-60, 228; CAAE
228; CANR 7, 102, 171; DLB 261; HGG;
INT CANR-7; SUFW 1, 2

Campbell, (Ignatius) Roy (Dunnachie)
1901-1957 .... **TCLC 5**
See also AFW; CA 104; 155; DLB 20, 225;
EWL 3; MTCW 2; RGEL 2

Campbell, Thomas 1777-1844 .... **NCLC 19**
See also DLB 93, 144; RGEL 2

Campbell, Wilfred .... **TCLC 9**
See Campbell, William

Campbell, William 1858(?)-1918
See Campbell, Wilfred
See also CA 106; DLB 92

Campbell, William Edward March
1893-1954
See March, William
See also CA 108

Campion, Jane 1954- .... **CLC 95, 229**
See also AAYA 33; CA 138; CANR 87

Campion, Thomas 1567-1620 . **LC 78; PC 87**
See also CDBLB Before 1660; DAM POET;
DLB 58, 172; RGEL 2

Casanova, Giacomo
See Casanova de Seingalt, Giovanni Jacopo
See also WLIT 7
Casanova, Giovanni Giacomo
See Casanova de Seingalt, Giovanni Jacopo
Casanova de Seingalt, Giovanni Jacopo
1725-1798 .... **LC 13, 151**
See Casanova, Giacomo
Casares, Adolfo Bioy
See Bioy Casares, Adolfo
See also RGSF 2
Casas, Bartolome de las 1474-1566
See Las Casas, Bartolome de
See also WLIT 1
Case, John
See Hougan, Carolyn
Casely-Hayford, J(oseph) E(phraim)
1866-1903 .... **BLC 1:1; TCLC 24**
See also BW 2; CA 123; 152; DAM MULT
Casey, John (Dudley) 1939- .... **CLC 59**
See also BEST 90:2; CA 69-72; CANR 23, 100
Casey, Michael 1947- .... **CLC 2**
See also CA 65-68; CANR 109; CP 2, 3; DLB 5
Casey, Patrick
See Thurman, Wallace (Henry)
Casey, Warren (Peter) 1935-1988 .... **CLC 12**
See also CA 101; 127; INT CA-101
Casona, Alejandro . **CLC 49; DC 32; TCLC 199**
See Alvarez, Alejandro Rodriguez
See also EWL 3
Cassavetes, John 1929-1989 .... **CLC 20**
See also CA 85-88; 127; CANR 82
Cassian, Nina 1924- .... **PC 17**
See also CWP; CWW 2
Cassill, R(onald) V(erlin)
1919-2002 .... **CLC 4, 23**
See also CA 9-12R; 208; CAAS 1; CANR 7, 45; CN 1, 2, 3, 4, 5, 6, 7; DLB 6, 218; DLBY 2002
Cassiodorus, Flavius Magnus c. 490(?)-c.
583(?) .... **CMLC 43**
Cassirer, Ernst 1874-1945 .... **TCLC 61**
See also CA 157
Cassity, (Allen) Turner 1929- .... **CLC 6, 42**
See also CA 17-20R; 223; CAAE 223; CAAS 8; CANR 11; CSW; DLB 105
Cassius Dio c. 155-c. 229 .... **CMLC 99**
See also DLB 176
Castaneda, Carlos (Cesar Aranha)
1931(?)-1998 .... **CLC 12, 119**
See also CA 25-28R; CANR 32, 66, 105; DNFS 1; HW 1; MTCW 1
Castedo, Elena 1937- .... **CLC 65**
See also CA 132
Castedo-Ellerman, Elena
See Castedo, Elena
Castellanos, Rosario 1925-1974 .... **CLC 66; HLC 1; SSC 39, 68**
See also CA 131; 53-56; CANR 58; CDWLB 3; DAM MULT; DLB 113, 290; EWL 3; FW; HW 1; LAW; MTCW 2; MTFW 2005; RGSF 2; RGWL 2, 3
Castelvetro, Lodovico 1505-1571 .... **LC 12**
Castiglione, Baldassare 1478-1529 ...... **LC 12**
See Castiglione, Baldesar
See also LMFS 1; RGWL 2, 3
Castiglione, Baldesar
See Castiglione, Baldassare
See also EW 2; WLIT 7
Castillo, Ana 1953- .... **CLC 151**
See also AAYA 42; CA 131; CANR 51, 86, 128, 172; CWP; DLB 122, 227; DNFS 2; FW; HW 1; LLW; PFS 21
Castillo, Ana Hernandez Del
See Castillo, Ana

Castle, Robert
See Hamilton, Edmond
Castro (Ruz), Fidel 1926(?)- .... **HLC 1**
See also CA 110; 129; CANR 81; DAM MULT; HW 2
Castro, Guillen de 1569-1631 .... **LC 19**
Castro, Rosalia de 1837-1885 ... **NCLC 3, 78; PC 41**
See also DAM MULT
Cather, Willa (Sibert) 1873-1947 . **SSC 2, 50, 114; TCLC 1, 11, 31, 99, 132, 152; WLC 1**
See also AAYA 24; AMW; AMWC 1; AMWR 1; BPFB 1; CA 104; 128; CDALB 1865-1917; CLR 98; DA; DA3; DAB; DAC; DAM MST, NOV; DLB 9, 54, 78, 256; DLBD 1; EWL 3; EXPN; EXPS; FL 1:5; LAIT 3; LATS 1:1; MAL 5; MBL; MTCW 1, 2; MTFW 2005; NFS 2, 19; RGAL 4; RGSF 2; RHW; SATA 30; SSFS 2, 7, 16; TCWW 1, 2; TUS
Catherine II
See Catherine the Great
See also DLB 150
Catherine, Saint 1347-1380 ..... **CMLC 27, 95**
Catherine the Great 1729-1796 .... **LC 69**
See Catherine II
Cato, Marcus Porcius
234B.C.-149B.C. .... **CMLC 21**
See Cato the Elder
Cato, Marcus Porcius, the Elder
See Cato, Marcus Porcius
Cato the Elder
See Cato, Marcus Porcius
See also DLB 211
Catton, (Charles) Bruce 1899-1978 . **CLC 35**
See also AITN 1; CA 5-8R; 81-84; CANR 7, 74; DLB 17; MTCW 2; MTFW 2005; SATA 2; SATA-Obit 24
Catullus c. 84B.C.-54B.C. .... **CMLC 18**
See also AW 2; CDWLB 1; DLB 211; RGWL 2, 3; WLIT 8
Cauldwell, Frank
See King, Francis (Henry)
Caunitz, William J. 1933-1996 .... **CLC 34**
See also BEST 89:3; CA 125; 130; 152; CANR 73; INT CA-130
Causley, Charles (Stanley)
1917-2003 .... **CLC 7**
See also CA 9-12R; 223; CANR 5, 35, 94; CLR 30; CP 1, 2, 3, 4, 5; CWRI 5; DLB 27; MTCW 1; SATA 3, 66; SATA-Obit 149
Caute, (John) David 1936- .... **CLC 29**
See also CA 1-4R; CAAS 4; CANR 1, 33, 64, 120; CBD; CD 5, 6; CN 1, 2, 3, 4, 5, 6, 7; DAM NOV; DLB 14, 231
Cavafy, C(onstantine) P(eter) .... **PC 36; TCLC 2, 7**
See Kavafis, Konstantinos Petrou
See also CA 148; DA3; DAM POET; EW 8; EWL 3; MTCW 2; PFS 19; RGWL 2, 3; WP
Cavalcanti, Guido c. 1250-c.
1300 .... **CMLC 54**
See also RGWL 2, 3; WLIT 7
Cavallo, Evelyn
See Spark, Muriel
Cavanna, Betty .... **CLC 12**
See Harrison, Elizabeth (Allen) Cavanna
See also JRDA; MAICYA 1; SAAS 4; SATA 1, 30
Cavendish, Margaret Lucas
1623-1673 .... **LC 30, 132**
See also DLB 131, 252, 281; RGEL 2
Caxton, William 1421(?)-1491(?) .... **LC 17**
See also DLB 170
Cayer, D. M.
See Duffy, Maureen (Patricia)

Cayrol, Jean 1911-2005 .... **CLC 11**
See also CA 89-92; 236; DLB 83; EWL 3
Cela (y Trulock), Camilo Jose
See Cela, Camilo Jose
See also CWW 2
Cela, Camilo Jose 1916-2002 .... **CLC 4, 13, 59, 122; HLC 1; SSC 71**
See Cela (y Trulock), Camilo Jose
See also BEST 90:2; CA 21-24R; 206; CAAS 10; CANR 21, 32, 76, 139; DAM MULT; DLB 322; DLBY 1989; EW 13; EWL 3; HW 1; MTCW 1, 2; MTFW 2005; RGSF 2; RGWL 2, 3
Celan, Paul .... **CLC 10, 19, 53, 82; PC 10**
See Antschel, Paul
See also CDWLB 2; DLB 69; EWL 3; RGHL; RGWL 2, 3
Celine, Louis-Ferdinand .. **CLC 1, 3, 4, 7, 9, 15, 47, 124**
See Destouches, Louis-Ferdinand
See also DLB 72; EW 11; EWL 3; GFL 1789 to the Present; RGWL 2, 3
Cellini, Benvenuto 1500-1571 .... **LC 7**
See also WLIT 7
Cendrars, Blaise .... **CLC 18, 106**
See Sauser-Hall, Frederic
See also DLB 258; EWL 3; GFL 1789 to the Present; RGWL 2, 3; WP
Centlivre, Susanna 1669(?)-1723 .... **DC 25; LC 65**
See also DLB 84; RGEL 2
Cernuda (y Bidon), Luis
1902-1963 .... **CLC 54; PC 62**
See also CA 131; 89-92; DAM POET; DLB 134; EWL 3; GLL 1; HW 1; RGWL 2, 3
Cervantes, Lorna Dee 1954- ..... **HLCS 1; PC 35**
See also CA 131; CANR 80; CP 7; CWP; DLB 82; EXPP; HW 1; LLW
Cervantes (Saavedra), Miguel de
1547-1616 .... **HLCS; LC 6, 23, 93; SSC 12, 108; WLC 1**
See also AAYA 56; BYA 1, 14; DA; DAB; DAC; DAM MST, NOV; EW 2; LAIT 1; LATS 1:1; LMFS 1; NFS 8; RGSF 2; RGWL 2, 3; TWA
Cesaire, Aime
See Cesaire, Aime
Cesaire, Aime 1913-2008 .... **BLC 1:1; CLC 19, 32, 112; DC 22; PC 25**
See also BW 2, 3; CA 65-68; 271; CANR 24, 43, 81; CWW 2; DA3; DAM MULT, POET; DLB 321; EWL 3; GFL 1789 to the Present; MTCW 1, 2; MTFW 2005; WP
Cesaire, Aime Fernand
See Cesaire, Aime
Chaadaev, Petr Iakovlevich
1794-1856 .... **NCLC 197**
See also DLB 198
Chabon, Michael 1963- ... **CLC 55, 149; SSC 59**
See also AAYA 45; AMWS 11; CA 139; CANR 57, 96, 127, 138; DLB 278; MAL 5; MTFW 2005; NFS 25; SATA 145
Chabrol, Claude 1930- .... **CLC 16**
See also CA 110
Chairil Anwar
See Anwar, Chairil
See also EWL 3
Challans, Mary 1905-1983
See Renault, Mary
See also CA 81-84; 111; CANR 74; DA3; MTCW 2; MTFW 2005; SATA 23; SATA-Obit 36; TEA
Challis, George
See Faust, Frederick (Schiller)

Ch'ien, Chung-shu 1910-1998 .... **CLC 22**
See Qian Zhongshu
See also CA 130; CANR 73; MTCW 1, 2

Chikamatsu Monzaemon 1653-1724 ... **LC 66**
See also RGWL 2, 3

Child, Francis James 1825-1896 . **NCLC 173**
See also DLB 1, 64, 235

Child, L. Maria
See Child, Lydia Maria

Child, Lydia Maria 1802-1880 .. **NCLC 6, 73**
See also DLB 1, 74, 243; RGAL 4; SATA 67

Child, Mrs.
See Child, Lydia Maria

Child, Philip 1898-1978 .... **CLC 19, 68**
See also CA 13-14; CAP 1; CP 1; DLB 68; RHW; SATA 47

Childers, (Robert) Erskine
1870-1922 .... **TCLC 65**
See also CA 113; 153; DLB 70

Childress, Alice 1920-1994 .... **BLC 1:1; CLC 12, 15, 86, 96; DC 4; TCLC 116**
See also AAYA 8; BW 2, 3; BYA 2; CA 45-48; 146; CAD; CANR 3, 27, 50, 74; CLR 14; CWD; DA3; DAM DRAM, MULT, NOV; DFS 2, 8, 14; DLB 7, 38, 249; JRDA; LAIT 5; MAICYA 1, 2; MAICYAS 1; MAL 5; MTCW 1, 2; MTFW 2005; RGAL 4; SATA 7, 48, 81; TUS; WYA; YAW

Chin, Frank (Chew, Jr.) 1940- .... **AAL; CLC 135; DC 7**
See also CA 33-36R; CAD; CANR 71; CD 5, 6; DAM MULT; DLB 206, 312; LAIT 5; RGAL 4

Chin, Marilyn (Mei Ling) 1955- .... **PC 40**
See also CA 129; CANR 70, 113; CWP; DLB 312; PFS 28

Chislett, (Margaret) Anne 1943- ...... **CLC 34**
See also CA 151

Chitty, Thomas Willes 1926- .... **CLC 11**
See Hinde, Thomas
See also CA 5-8R; CN 7

Chivers, Thomas Holley
1809-1858 .... **NCLC 49**
See also DLB 3, 248; RGAL 4

Choi, Susan 1969- .... **CLC 119**
See also CA 223

Chomette, Rene Lucien 1898-1981
See Clair, Rene
See also CA 103

Chomsky, Avram Noam
See Chomsky, Noam

Chomsky, Noam 1928- .... **CLC 132**
See also CA 17-20R; CANR 28, 62, 110, 132, 179; DA3; DLB 246; MTCW 1, 2; MTFW 2005

Chona, Maria 1845(?)-1936 .... **NNAL**
See also CA 144

Chopin, Kate ... **SSC 8, 68, 110; TCLC 127; WLCS**
See Chopin, Katherine
See also AAYA 33; AMWR 2; AMWS 1; BYA 11, 15; CDALB 1865-1917; DA; DAB; DLB 12, 78; EXPN; EXPS; FL 1:3; FW; LAIT 3; MAL 5; MBL; NFS 3; RGAL 4; RGSF 2; SSFS 2, 13, 17, 26; TUS

Chopin, Katherine 1851-1904
See Chopin, Kate
See also CA 104; 122; DA3; DAC; DAM MST, NOV

Chretien de Troyes c. 12th cent. - . **CMLC 10**
See also DLB 208; EW 1; RGWL 2, 3; TWA

Christie
See Ichikawa, Kon

Christie, Agatha (Mary Clarissa)
1890-1976 .. **CLC 1, 6, 8, 12, 39, 48, 110**
See also AAYA 9; AITN 1, 2; BPFB 1; BRWS 2; CA 17-20R; 61-64; CANR 10, 37, 108; CBD; CDBLB 1914-1945; CMW 4; CN 1, 2; CPW; CWD; DA3; DAB; DAC; DAM NOV; DFS 2; DLB 13, 77, 245; MSW; MTCW 1, 2; MTFW 2005; NFS 8; RGEL 2; RHW; SATA 36; TEA; YAW

Christie, Philippa .... **CLC 21**
See Pearce, Philippa
See also BYA 5; CANR 109; CLR 9; DLB 161; MAICYA 1; SATA 1, 67, 129

Christine de Pisan
See Christine de Pizan
See also FW

Christine de Pizan 1365(?)-1431(?) ...... **LC 9, 130; PC 68**
See Christine de Pisan; de Pizan, Christine
See also DLB 208; FL 1:1; RGWL 2, 3

Chuang-Tzu c. 369B.C.-c.
286B.C. .... **CMLC 57**

Chubb, Elmer
See Masters, Edgar Lee

Chulkov, Mikhail Dmitrievich
1743-1792 .... **LC 2**
See also DLB 150

Churchill, Caryl 1938- .... **CLC 31, 55, 157; DC 5**
See Churchill, Chick
See also BRWS 4; CA 102; CANR 22, 46, 108; CBD; CD 6; CWD; DFS 25; DLB 13, 310; EWL 3; FW; MTCW 1; RGEL 2

Churchill, Charles 1731-1764 .... **LC 3**
See also DLB 109; RGEL 2

Churchill, Chick
See Churchill, Caryl
See also CD 5

Churchill, Sir Winston (Leonard Spencer)
1874-1965 .... **TCLC 113**
See also BRW 6; CA 97-100; CDBLB 1890-1914; DA3; DLB 100, 329; DLBD 16; LAIT 4; MTCW 1, 2

Chute, Carolyn 1947- .... **CLC 39**
See also CA 123; CANR 135; CN 7

Ciardi, John (Anthony) 1916-1986 . **CLC 10, 40, 44, 129; PC 69**
See also CA 5-8R; 118; CAAS 2; CANR 5, 33; CLR 19; CP 1, 2, 3, 4; CWRI 5; DAM POET; DLB 5; DLBY 1986; INT CANR-5; MAICYA 1, 2; MAL 5; MTCW 1, 2; MTFW 2005; RGAL 4; SAAS 26; SATA 1, 65; SATA-Obit 46

Cibber, Colley 1671-1757 .... **LC 66**
See also DLB 84; RGEL 2

Cicero, Marcus Tullius
106B.C.-43B.C. .... **CMLC 3, 81**
See also AW 1; CDWLB 1; DLB 211; RGWL 2, 3; WLIT 8

Cimino, Michael 1943- .... **CLC 16**
See also CA 105

Cioran, E(mil) M. 1911-1995 .... **CLC 64**
See also CA 25-28R; 149; CANR 91; DLB 220; EWL 3

Cisneros, Sandra 1954- .... **CLC 69, 118, 193; HLC 1; PC 52; SSC 32, 72**
See also AAYA 9, 53; AMWS 7; CA 131; CANR 64, 118; CLR 123; CN 7; CWP; DA3; DAM MULT; DLB 122, 152; EWL 3; EXPN; FL 1:5; FW; HW 1, 2; LAIT 5; LATS 1:2; LLW; MAICYA 2; MAL 5; MTCW 2; MTFW 2005; NFS 2; PFS 19; RGAL 4; RGSF 2; SSFS 3, 13; WLIT 1; YAW

Cixous, Helene 1937- .... **CLC 92, 253**
See also CA 126; CANR 55, 123; CWW 2; DLB 83, 242; EWL 3; FL 1:5; FW; GLL 2; MTCW 1, 2; MTFW 2005; TWA

Clair, Rene .... **CLC 20**
See Chomette, Rene Lucien

Clampitt, Amy 1920-1994 .... **CLC 32; PC 19**
See also AMWS 9; CA 110; 146; CANR 29, 79; CP 4, 5; DLB 105; MAL 5; PFS 27

Clancy, Thomas L., Jr. 1947-
See Clancy, Tom
See also CA 125; 131; CANR 62, 105; DA3; INT CA-131; MTCW 1, 2; MTFW 2005

Clancy, Tom .... **CLC 45, 112**
See Clancy, Thomas L., Jr.
See also AAYA 9, 51; BEST 89:1, 90:1; BPFB 1; BYA 10, 11; CANR 132; CMW 4; CPW; DAM NOV, POP; DLB 227

Clare, John 1793-1864 .. **NCLC 9, 86; PC 23**
See also BRWS 11; DAB; DAM POET; DLB 55, 96; RGEL 2

Clarin
See Alas (y Urena), Leopoldo (Enrique Garcia)

Clark, Al C.
See Goines, Donald

Clark, Brian (Robert)
See Clark, (Robert) Brian
See also CD 6

Clark, (Robert) Brian 1932- .... **CLC 29**
See Clark, Brian (Robert)
See also CA 41-44R; CANR 67; CBD; CD 5

Clark, Curt
See Westlake, Donald E.

Clark, Eleanor 1913-1996 .... **CLC 5, 19**
See also CA 9-12R; 151; CANR 41; CN 1, 2, 3, 4, 5, 6; DLB 6

Clark, J. P.
See Clark Bekederemo, J.P.
See also CDWLB 3; DLB 117

Clark, John Pepper
See Clark Bekederemo, J.P.
See also AFW; CD 5; CP 1, 2, 3, 4, 5, 6, 7; RGEL 2

Clark, Kenneth (Mackenzie)
1903-1983 .... **TCLC 147**
See also CA 93-96; 109; CANR 36; MTCW 1, 2; MTFW 2005

Clark, M. R.
See Clark, Mavis Thorpe

Clark, Mavis Thorpe 1909-1999 ...... **CLC 12**
See also CA 57-60; CANR 8, 37, 107; CLR 30; CWRI 5; MAICYA 1, 2; SAAS 5; SATA 8, 74

Clark, Walter Van Tilburg
1909-1971 .... **CLC 28**
See also CA 9-12R; 33-36R; CANR 63, 113; CN 1; DLB 9, 206; LAIT 2; MAL 5; RGAL 4; SATA 8; TCWW 1, 2

Clark Bekederemo, J.P. 1935- .... **BLC 1:1; CLC 38; DC 5**
See Bekederemo, J. P. Clark; Clark, J. P.; Clark, John Pepper
See also BW 1; CA 65-68; CANR 16, 72; DAM DRAM, MULT; DFS 13; EWL 3; MTCW 2; MTFW 2005

Clarke, Arthur
See Clarke, Arthur C.

Clarke, Arthur C. 1917-2008 .. **CLC 1, 4, 13, 18, 35, 136; SSC 3**
See also AAYA 4, 33; BPFB 1; BYA 13; CA 1-4R; 270; CANR 2, 28, 55, 74, 130; CLR 119; CN 1, 2, 3, 4, 5, 6, 7; CPW; DA3; DAM POP; DLB 261; JRDA; LAIT 5; MAICYA 1, 2; MTCW 1, 2; MTFW 2005; SATA 13, 70, 115; SATA-Obit 191; SCFW 1, 2; SFW 4; SSFS 4, 18; TCLE 1:1; YAW

Clarke, Arthur Charles
See Clarke, Arthur C.

Clarke, Austin 1896-1974 .... **CLC 6, 9**
See also CA 29-32; 49-52; CAP 2; CP 1, 2;
DAM POET; DLB 10, 20; EWL 3; RGEL
2

Clarke, Austin C. 1934- .... **BLC 1:1; CLC 8,
53; SSC 45, 116**
See also BW 1; CA 25-28R; CAAS 16;
CANR 14, 32, 68, 140; CN 1, 2, 3, 4, 5,
6, 7; DAC; DAM MULT; DLB 53, 125;
DNFS 2; MTCW 2; MTFW 2005; RGSF
2

Clarke, Gillian 1937- .... **CLC 61**
See also CA 106; CP 3, 4, 5, 6, 7; CWP;
DLB 40

Clarke, Marcus (Andrew Hislop)
1846-1881 .... **NCLC 19; SSC 94**
See also DLB 230; RGEL 2; RGSF 2

Clarke, Shirley 1925-1997 .... **CLC 16**
See also CA 189

Clash, The
See Headon, (Nicky) Topper; Jones, Mick;
Simonon, Paul; Strummer, Joe

Claudel, Paul (Louis Charles Marie)
1868-1955 .... **TCLC 2, 10**
See also CA 104; 165; DLB 192, 258, 321;
EW 8; EWL 3; GFL 1789 to the Present;
RGWL 2, 3; TWA

Claudian 370(?)-404(?) .... **CMLC 46**
See also RGWL 2, 3

Claudius, Matthias 1740-1815 .... **NCLC 75**
See also DLB 97

Clavell, James 1925-1994 .... **CLC 6, 25, 87**
See also BPFB 1; CA 25-28R; 146; CANR
26, 48; CN 5; CPW; DA3; DAM NOV,
POP; MTCW 1, 2; MTFW 2005; NFS 10;
RHW

Clayman, Gregory .... **CLC 65**

Cleage, Pearl 1948- .... **DC 32**
See also BW 2; CA 41-44R; CANR 27, 148,
177; DFS 14, 16; DLB 228; NFS 17

Cleage, Pearl Michelle
See Cleage, Pearl

Cleaver, (Leroy) Eldridge
1935-1998 .... **BLC 1:1; CLC 30, 119**
See also BW 1, 3; CA 21-24R; 167; CANR
16, 75; DA3; DAM MULT; MTCW 2;
YAW

Cleese, John (Marwood) 1939- .... **CLC 21**
See Monty Python
See also CA 112; 116; CANR 35; MTCW 1

Cleishbotham, Jebediah
See Scott, Sir Walter

Cleland, John 1710-1789 .... **LC 2, 48**
See also DLB 39; RGEL 2

Clemens, Samuel Langhorne 1835-1910
See Twain, Mark
See also CA 104; 135; CDALB 1865-1917;
DA; DA3; DAB; DAC; DAM MST, NOV;
DLB 12, 23, 64, 74, 186, 189; JRDA;
LMFS 1; MAICYA 1, 2; NCFS 4; NFS
20; SATA 100; YABC 2

Clement of Alexandria
150(?)-215(?) .... **CMLC 41**

Cleophil
See Congreve, William

Clerihew, E.
See Bentley, E(dmund) C(lerihew)

Clerk, N. W.
See Lewis, C.S.

Cleveland, John 1613-1658 .... **LC 106**
See also DLB 126; RGEL 2

Cliff, Jimmy .... **CLC 21**
See Chambers, James
See also CA 193

Cliff, Michelle 1946- .... **BLCS; CLC 120**
See also BW 2; CA 116; CANR 39, 72; CD-
WLB 3; DLB 157; FW; GLL 2

Clifford, Lady Anne 1590-1676 .... **LC 76**
See also DLB 151

Clifton, Lucille 1936- ..... **BLC 1:1, 2:1; CLC
19, 66, 162; PC 17**
See also AFAW 2; BW 2, 3; CA 49-52;
CANR 2, 24, 42, 76, 97, 138; CLR 5; CP
2, 3, 4, 5, 6, 7; CSW; CWP; CWRI 5;
DA3; DAM MULT, POET; DLB 5, 41;
EXPP; MAICYA 1, 2; MTCW 1, 2;
MTFW 2005; PFS 1, 14; SATA 20, 69,
128; WP

Clinton, Dirk
See Silverberg, Robert

Clough, Arthur Hugh 1819-1861 .. **NCLC 27,
163**
See also BRW 5; DLB 32; RGEL 2

Clutha, Janet Paterson Frame
See Frame, Janet

Clyne, Terence
See Blatty, William Peter

Cobalt, Martin
See Mayne, William (James Carter)

Cobb, Irvin S(hrewsbury)
1876-1944 .... **TCLC 77**
See also CA 175; DLB 11, 25, 86

Cobbett, William 1763-1835 .... **NCLC 49**
See also DLB 43, 107, 158; RGEL 2

Coburn, D(onald) L(ee) 1938- .... **CLC 10**
See also CA 89-92; DFS 23

Cocteau, Jean 1889-1963 ... **CLC 1, 8, 15, 16,
43; DC 17; TCLC 119; WLC 2**
See also AAYA 74; CA 25-28; CANR 40;
CAP 2; DA; DA3; DAB; DAC; DAM
DRAM, MST, NOV; DFS 24; DLB 65,
258, 321; EW 10; EWL 3; GFL 1789 to
the Present; MTCW 1, 2; RGWL 2, 3;
TWA

Cocteau, Jean Maurice Eugene Clement
See Cocteau, Jean

Codrescu, Andrei 1946- .... **CLC 46, 121**
See also CA 33-36R; CAAS 19; CANR 13,
34, 53, 76, 125; CN 7; DA3; DAM POET;
MAL 5; MTCW 2; MTFW 2005

Coe, Max
See Bourne, Randolph S(illiman)

Coe, Tucker
See Westlake, Donald E.

Coelho, Paulo 1947- .... **CLC 258**
See also CA 152; CANR 80, 93, 155

Coen, Ethan 1958- .... **CLC 108**
See also AAYA 54; CA 126; CANR 85

Coen, Joel 1955- .... **CLC 108**
See also AAYA 54; CA 126; CANR 119

The Coen Brothers
See Coen, Ethan; Coen, Joel

Coetzee, J.M. 1940- ...... **CLC 23, 33, 66, 117,
161, 162**
See also AAYA 37; AFW; BRWS 6; CA 77-
80; CANR 41, 54, 74, 114, 133, 180; CN
4, 5, 6, 7; DA3; DAM NOV; DLB 225,
326, 329; EWL 3; LMFS 2; MTCW 1, 2;
MTFW 2005; NFS 21; WLIT 2; WWE 1

Coetzee, John Maxwell
See Coetzee, J.M.

Coffey, Brian
See Koontz, Dean R.

Coffin, Robert P(eter) Tristram
1892-1955 .... **TCLC 95**
See also CA 123; 169; DLB 45

Cohan, George M. 1878-1942 .... **TCLC 60**
See also CA 157; DLB 249; RGAL 4

Cohan, George Michael
See Cohan, George M.

Cohen, Arthur A(llen) 1928-1986 ...... **CLC 7,
31**
See also CA 1-4R; 120; CANR 1, 17, 42;
DLB 28; RGHL

Cohen, Leonard 1934- .... **CLC 3, 38, 260**
See also CA 21-24R; CANR 14, 69; CN 1,
2, 3, 4, 5, 6; CP 1, 2, 3, 4, 5, 6, 7; DAC;
DAM MST; DLB 53; EWL 3; MTCW 1

Cohen, Leonard Norman
See Cohen, Leonard

Cohen, Matt(hew) 1942-1999 .... **CLC 19**
See also CA 61-64; 187; CAAS 18; CANR
40; CN 1, 2, 3, 4, 5, 6; DAC; DLB 53

Cohen-Solal, Annie 1948- .... **CLC 50**
See also CA 239

Colegate, Isabel 1931- .... **CLC 36**
See also CA 17-20R; CANR 8, 22, 74; CN
4, 5, 6, 7; DLB 14, 231; INT CANR-22;
MTCW 1

Coleman, Emmett
See Reed, Ishmael

Coleridge, Hartley 1796-1849 .... **NCLC 90**
See also DLB 96

Coleridge, M. E.
See Coleridge, Mary E(lizabeth)

Coleridge, Mary E(lizabeth)
1861-1907 .... **TCLC 73**
See also CA 116; 166; DLB 19, 98

Coleridge, Samuel Taylor
1772-1834 ..... **NCLC 9, 54, 99, 111, 177,
197; PC 11, 39, 67; WLC 2**
See also AAYA 66; BRW 4; BRWR 2; BYA
4; CDBLB 1789-1832; DA; DA3; DAB;
DAC; DAM MST, POET; DLB 93, 107;
EXPP; LATS 1:1; LMFS 1; PAB; PFS 4,
5; RGEL 2; TEA; WLIT 3; WP

Coleridge, Sara 1802-1852 .... **NCLC 31**
See also DLB 199

Coles, Don 1928- .... **CLC 46**
See also CA 115; CANR 38; CP 5, 6, 7

Coles, Robert (Martin) 1929- .... **CLC 108**
See also CA 45-48; CANR 3, 32, 66, 70,
135; INT CANR-32; SATA 23

Colette, (Sidonie-Gabrielle)
1873-1954 .. **SSC 10, 93; TCLC 1, 5, 16**
See Willy, Colette
See also CA 104; 131; DA3; DAM NOV;
DLB 65; EW 9; EWL 3; GFL 1789 to the
Present; MTCW 1, 2; MTFW 2005;
RGWL 2, 3; TWA

Collett, (Jacobine) Camilla (Wergeland)
1813-1895 .... **NCLC 22**

Collier, Christopher 1930- .... **CLC 30**
See also AAYA 13; BYA 2; CA 33-36R;
CANR 13, 33, 102; CLR 126; JRDA;
MAICYA 1, 2; SATA 16, 70; WYA; YAW
1

Collier, James Lincoln 1928- .... **CLC 30**
See also AAYA 13; BYA 2; CA 9-12R;
CANR 4, 33, 60, 102; CLR 3, 126; DAM
POP; JRDA; MAICYA 1, 2; SAAS 21;
SATA 8, 70, 166; WYA; YAW 1

Collier, Jeremy 1650-1726 .... **LC 6, 157**
See also DLB 336

Collier, John 1901-1980 . **SSC 19; TCLC 127**
See also CA 65-68; 97-100; CANR 10; CN
1, 2; DLB 77, 255; FANT; SUFW 1

Collier, Mary 1690-1762 .... **LC 86**
See also DLB 95

Collingwood, R(obin) G(eorge)
1889(?)-1943 .... **TCLC 67**
See also CA 117; 155; DLB 262

Collins, Billy 1941- .... **PC 68**
See also AAYA 64; CA 151; CANR 92; CP
7; MTFW 2005; PFS 18

Collins, Hunt
See Hunter, Evan

Collins, Linda 1931- .... **CLC 44**
See also CA 125

Collins, Merle 1950- .... **BLC 2:1**
See also BW 3; CA 175; DLB 157

Collins, Tom
See Furphy, Joseph
See also RGEL 2

Crews, Harry 1935- .... **CLC 6, 23, 49**
See also AITN 1; AMWS 11; BPFB 1; CA 25-28R; CANR 20, 57; CN 3, 4, 5, 6, 7; CSW; DA3; DLB 6, 143, 185; MTCW 1, 2; MTFW 2005; RGAL 4

Crichton, Michael 1942- .... **CLC 2, 6, 54, 90, 242**
See also AAYA 10, 49; AITN 2; BPFB 1; CA 25-28R; CANR 13, 40, 54, 76, 127, 179; CMW 4; CN 2, 3, 6, 7; CPW; DA3; DAM NOV, POP; DLB 292; DLBY 1981; INT CANR-13; JRDA; MTCW 1, 2; MTFW 2005; SATA 9, 88; SFW 4; YAW

Crispin, Edmund .... **CLC 22**
See Montgomery, (Robert) Bruce
See also DLB 87; MSW

Cristina of Sweden 1626-1689 .... **LC 124**

Cristofer, Michael 1945(?)- .... **CLC 28**
See also CA 110; 152; CAD; CANR 150; CD 5, 6; DAM DRAM; DFS 15; DLB 7

Cristofer, Michael Ivan
See Cristofer, Michael

Criton
See Alain

Croce, Benedetto 1866-1952 .... **TCLC 37**
See also CA 120; 155; EW 8; EWL 3; WLIT 7

Crockett, David 1786-1836 .... **NCLC 8**
See also DLB 3, 11, 183, 248

Crockett, Davy
See Crockett, David

Crofts, Freeman Wills 1879-1957 .. **TCLC 55**
See also CA 115; 195; CMW 4; DLB 77; MSW

Croker, John Wilson 1780-1857 .... **NCLC 10**
See also DLB 110

Crommelynck, Fernand 1885-1970 .. **CLC 75**
See also CA 189; 89-92; EWL 3

Cromwell, Oliver 1599-1658 .... **LC 43**

Cronenberg, David 1943- .... **CLC 143**
See also CA 138; CCA 1

Cronin, A(rchibald) J(oseph) 1896-1981 .... **CLC 32**
See also BPFB 1; CA 1-4R; 102; CANR 5; CN 2; DLB 191; SATA 47; SATA-Obit 25

Cross, Amanda
See Heilbrun, Carolyn G(old)
See also BPFB 1; CMW; CPW; DLB 306; MSW

Crothers, Rachel 1878-1958 .... **TCLC 19**
See also CA 113; 194; CAD; CWD; DLB 7, 266; RGAL 4

Croves, Hal
See Traven, B.

Crow Dog, Mary (?)- .... **CLC 93; NNAL**
See also CA 154

Crowfield, Christopher
See Stowe, Harriet (Elizabeth) Beecher

Crowley, Aleister .... **TCLC 7**
See Crowley, Edward Alexander
See also GLL 1

Crowley, Edward Alexander 1875-1947
See Crowley, Aleister
See also CA 104; HGG

Crowley, John 1942- .... **CLC 57**
See also AAYA 57; BPFB 1; CA 61-64; CANR 43, 98, 138, 177; DLBY 1982; FANT; MTFW 2005; SATA 65, 140; SFW 4; SUFW 2

Crowne, John 1641-1712 .... **LC 104**
See also DLB 80; RGEL 2

Crud
See Crumb, R.

Crumarums
See Crumb, R.

Crumb, R. 1943- .... **CLC 17**
See also CA 106; CANR 107, 150

Crumb, Robert
See Crumb, R.

Crumbum
See Crumb, R.

Crumski
See Crumb, R.

Crum the Bum
See Crumb, R.

Crunk
See Crumb, R.

Crustt
See Crumb, R.

Crutchfield, Les
See Trumbo, Dalton

Cruz, Victor Hernandez 1949- ... **HLC 1; PC 37**
See also BW 2; CA 65-68, 271; CAAE 271; CAAS 17; CANR 14, 32, 74, 132; CP 1, 2, 3, 4, 5, 6, 7; DAM MULT, POET; DLB 41; DNFS 1; EXPP; HW 1, 2; LLW; MTCW 2; MTFW 2005; PFS 16; WP

Cryer, Gretchen (Kiger) 1935- .... **CLC 21**
See also CA 114; 123

Csath, Geza .... **TCLC 13**
See Brenner, Jozef
See also CA 111

Cudlip, David R(ockwell) 1933- .... **CLC 34**
See also CA 177

Cullen, Countee 1903-1946 ..... **BLC 1:1; HR 1:2; PC 20; TCLC 4, 37; WLCS**
See also AAYA 78; AFAW 2; AMWS 4; BW 1; CA 108; 124; CDALB 1917-1929; DA; DA3; DAC; DAM MST, MULT, POET; DLB 4, 48, 51; EWL 3; EXPP; LMFS 2; MAL 5; MTCW 1, 2; MTFW 2005; PFS 3; RGAL 4; SATA 18; WP

Culleton, Beatrice 1949- .... **NNAL**
See also CA 120; CANR 83; DAC

Cum, R.
See Crumb, R.

Cumberland, Richard 1732-1811 .... **NCLC 167**
See also DLB 89; RGEL 2

Cummings, Bruce F(rederick) 1889-1919
See Barbellion, W. N. P.
See also CA 123

Cummings, E(dward) E(stlin) 1894-1962 .. **CLC 1, 3, 8, 12, 15, 68; PC 5; TCLC 137; WLC 2**
See also AAYA 41; AMW; CA 73-76; CANR 31; CDALB 1929-1941; DA; DA3; DAB; DAC; DAM MST, POET; DLB 4, 48; EWL 3; EXPP; MAL 5; MTCW 1, 2; MTFW 2005; PAB; PFS 1, 3, 12, 13, 19; RGAL 4; TUS; WP

Cummins, Maria Susanna 1827-1866 .... **NCLC 139**
See also DLB 42; YABC 1

Cunha, Euclides (Rodrigues Pimenta) da 1866-1909 .... **TCLC 24**
See also CA 123; 219; DLB 307; LAW; WLIT 1

Cunningham, E. V.
See Fast, Howard

Cunningham, J(ames) V(incent) 1911-1985 .... **CLC 3, 31**
See also CA 1-4R; 115; CANR 1, 72; CP 1, 2, 3, 4; DLB 5

Cunningham, Julia (Woolfolk) 1916- .... **CLC 12**
See also CA 9-12R; CANR 4, 19, 36; CWRI 5; JRDA; MAICYA 1, 2; SAAS 2; SATA 1, 26, 132

Cunningham, Michael 1952- .... **CLC 34, 243**
See also AMWS 15; CA 136; CANR 96, 160; CN 7; DLB 292; GLL 2; MTFW 2005; NFS 23

Cunninghame Graham, R. B.
See Cunninghame Graham, Robert (Gallnigad) Bontine

Cunninghame Graham, Robert (Gallnigad) Bontine 1852-1936 .... **TCLC 19**
See Graham, R(obert) B(ontine) Cunninghame
See also CA 119; 184

Curnow, (Thomas) Allen (Monro) 1911-2001 .... **PC 48**
See also CA 69-72; 202; CANR 48, 99; CP 1, 2, 3, 4, 5, 6, 7; EWL 3; RGEL 2

Currie, Ellen 19(?)- .... **CLC 44**

Curtin, Philip
See Lowndes, Marie Adelaide (Belloc)

Curtin, Phillip
See Lowndes, Marie Adelaide (Belloc)

Curtis, Price
See Ellison, Harlan

Cusanus, Nicolaus 1401-1464 .... **LC 80**
See Nicholas of Cusa

Cutrate, Joe
See Spiegelman, Art

Cynewulf c. 770- .... **CMLC 23**
See also DLB 146; RGEL 2

Cyrano de Bergerac, Savinien de 1619-1655 .... **LC 65**
See also DLB 268; GFL Beginnings to 1789; RGWL 2, 3

Cyril of Alexandria c. 375-c. 430 . **CMLC 59**

Czaczkes, Shmuel Yosef Halevi
See Agnon, S(hmuel) Y(osef Halevi)

Dabrowska, Maria (Szumska) 1889-1965 .... **CLC 15**
See also CA 106; CDWLB 4; DLB 215; EWL 3

Dabydeen, David 1955- .... **CLC 34**
See also BW 1; CA 125; CANR 56, 92; CN 6, 7; CP 5, 6, 7

Dacey, Philip 1939- .... **CLC 51**
See also CA 37-40R, 231; CAAE 231; CAAS 17; CANR 14, 32, 64; CP 4, 5, 6, 7; DLB 105

Dacre, Charlotte c. 1772-1825(?) . **NCLC 151**

Dafydd ap Gwilym c. 1320-c. 1380 ..... **PC 56**

Dagerman, Stig (Halvard) 1923-1954 .... **TCLC 17**
See also CA 117; 155; DLB 259; EWL 3

D'Aguiar, Fred 1960- ..... **BLC 2:1; CLC 145**
See also CA 148; CANR 83, 101; CN 7; CP 5, 6, 7; DLB 157; EWL 3

Dahl, Roald 1916-1990 ...... **CLC 1, 6, 18, 79; TCLC 173**
See also AAYA 15; BPFB 1; BRWS 4; BYA 5; CA 1-4R; 133; CANR 6, 32, 37, 62; CLR 1, 7, 41, 111; CN 1, 2, 3, 4; CPW; DA3; DAB; DAC; DAM MST, NOV, POP; DLB 139, 255; HGG; JRDA; MAICYA 1, 2; MTCW 1, 2; MTFW 2005; RGSF 2; SATA 1, 26, 73; SATA-Obit 65; SSFS 4; TEA; YAW

Dahlberg, Edward 1900-1977 . **CLC 1, 7, 14; TCLC 208**
See also CA 9-12R; 69-72; CANR 31, 62; CN 1, 2; DLB 48; MAL 5; MTCW 1; RGAL 4

Daitch, Susan 1954- .... **CLC 103**
See also CA 161

Dale, Colin .... **TCLC 18**
See Lawrence, T(homas) E(dward)

Dale, George E.
See Asimov, Isaac

d'Alembert, Jean Le Rond 1717-1783 .... **LC 126**

Dalton, Roque 1935-1975(?) ..... **HLCS 1; PC 36**
See also CA 176; DLB 283; HW 2

Daly, Elizabeth 1878-1967 .... **CLC 52**
See also CA 23-24; 25-28R; CANR 60; CAP 2; CMW 4

de Brissac, Malcolm
See Dickinson, Peter (Malcolm de Brissac)
de Campos, Alvaro
See Pessoa, Fernando (Antonio Nogueira)
de Chardin, Pierre Teilhard
See Teilhard de Chardin, (Marie Joseph) Pierre
de Crenne, Helisenne c. 1510-c. 1560 .... **LC 113**
Dee, John 1527-1608 .... **LC 20**
See also DLB 136, 213
Deer, Sandra 1940- .... **CLC 45**
See also CA 186
De Ferrari, Gabriella 1941- .... **CLC 65**
See also CA 146
de Filippo, Eduardo 1900-1984 ... **TCLC 127**
See also CA 132; 114; EWL 3; MTCW 1; RGWL 2, 3
Defoe, Daniel 1660(?)-1731 .... **LC 1, 42, 108; WLC 2**
See also AAYA 27; BRW 3; BRWR 1; BYA 4; CDBLB 1660-1789; CLR 61; DA; DA3; DAB; DAC; DAM MST, NOV; DLB 39, 95, 101, 336; JRDA; LAIT 1; LMFS 1; MAICYA 1, 2; NFS 9, 13; RGEL 2; SATA 22; TEA; WCH; WLIT 3
de Gouges, Olympe
See de Gouges, Olympe
de Gouges, Olympe 1748-1793 .... **LC 127**
See also DLB 313
de Gourmont, Remy(-Marie-Charles)
See Gourmont, Remy(-Marie-Charles) de
de Gournay, Marie le Jars 1566-1645 .... **LC 98**
See also DLB 327; FW
de Hartog, Jan 1914-2002 .... **CLC 19**
See also CA 1-4R; 210; CANR 1; DFS 12
de Hostos, E. M.
See Hostos (y Bonilla), Eugenio Maria de
de Hostos, Eugenio M.
See Hostos (y Bonilla), Eugenio Maria de
Deighton, Len .... **CLC 4, 7, 22, 46**
See Deighton, Leonard Cyril
See also AAYA 6; BEST 89:2; BPFB 1; CD-BLB 1960 to Present; CMW 4; CN 1, 2, 3, 4, 5, 6, 7; CPW; DLB 87
Deighton, Leonard Cyril 1929-
See Deighton, Len
See also AAYA 57; CA 9-12R; CANR 19, 33, 68; DA3; DAM NOV, POP; MTCW 1, 2; MTFW 2005
Dekker, Thomas 1572(?)-1632 ..... **DC 12; LC 22**
See also CDBLB Before 1660; DAM DRAM; DLB 62, 172; LMFS 1; RGEL 2
de Laclos, Pierre Ambroise Franois
See Laclos, Pierre-Ambroise Francois
Delacroix, (Ferdinand-Victor-)Eugene 1798-1863 .... **NCLC 133**
See also EW 5
Delafield, E. M. .... **TCLC 61**
See Dashwood, Edmee Elizabeth Monica de la Pasture
See also DLB 34; RHW
de la Mare, Walter (John) 1873-1956 ..... **PC 77; SSC 14; TCLC 4, 53; WLC 2**
See also CA 163; CDBLB 1914-1945; CLR 23; CWRI 5; DA3; DAB; DAC; DAM MST, POET; DLB 19, 153, 162, 255, 284; EWL 3; EXPP; HGG; MAICYA 1, 2; MTCW 2; MTFW 2005; RGEL 2; RGSF 2; SATA 16; SUFW 1; TEA; WCH
de Lamartine, Alphonse (Marie Louis Prat)
See Lamartine, Alphonse (Marie Louis Prat) de
Delaney, Franey
See O'Hara, John (Henry)

Delaney, Shelagh 1939- .... **CLC 29**
See also CA 17-20R; CANR 30, 67; CBD; CD 5, 6; CDBLB 1960 to Present; CWD; DAM DRAM; DFS 7; DLB 13; MTCW 1
Delany, Martin Robison 1812-1885 .... **NCLC 93**
See also DLB 50; RGAL 4
Delany, Mary (Granville Pendarves) 1700-1788 .... **LC 12**
Delany, Samuel R., Jr. 1942- .... **BLC 1:1; CLC 8, 14, 38, 141**
See also AAYA 24; AFAW 2; BPFB 1; BW 2, 3; CA 81-84; CANR 27, 43, 116, 172; CN 2, 3, 4, 5, 6, 7; DAM MULT; DLB 8, 33; FANT; MAL 5; MTCW 1, 2; RGAL 4; SATA 92; SCFW 1, 2; SFW 4; SUFW 2
Delany, Samuel Ray
See Delany, Samuel R., Jr.
de la Parra, (Ana) Teresa (Sonojo) 1890(?)-1936 .... **TCLC 185**
See Parra, Ana Teresa de la
See also CA 178; HW 2
De La Ramee, Marie Louise 1839-1908
See Ouida
See also CA 204; SATA 20
de la Roche, Mazo 1879-1961 .... **CLC 14**
See also CA 85-88; CANR 30; DLB 68; RGEL 2; RHW; SATA 64
De La Salle, Innocent
See Hartmann, Sadakichi
de Laureamont, Comte
See Lautreamont
Delbanco, Nicholas 1942- ..... **CLC 6, 13, 167**
See also CA 17-20R; 189; CAAE 189; CAAS 2; CANR 29, 55, 116, 150; CN 7; DLB 6, 234
Delbanco, Nicholas Franklin
See Delbanco, Nicholas
del Castillo, Michel 1933- .... **CLC 38**
See also CA 109; CANR 77
Deledda, Grazia (Cosima) 1875(?)-1936 .... **TCLC 23**
See also CA 123; 205; DLB 264, 329; EWL 3; RGWL 2, 3; WLIT 7
Deleuze, Gilles 1925-1995 .... **TCLC 116**
See also DLB 296
Delgado, Abelardo (Lalo) B(arrientos) 1930-2004 .... **HLC 1**
See also CA 131; 230; CAAS 15; CANR 90; DAM MST, MULT; DLB 82; HW 1, 2
Delibes, Miguel .... **CLC 8, 18**
See Delibes Setien, Miguel
See also DLB 322; EWL 3
Delibes Setien, Miguel 1920-
See Delibes, Miguel
See also CA 45-48; CANR 1, 32; CWW 2; HW 1; MTCW 1
DeLillo, Don 1936- ..... **CLC 8, 10, 13, 27, 39, 54, 76, 143, 210, 213**
See also AMWC 2; AMWS 6; BEST 89:1; BPFB 1; CA 81-84; CANR 21, 76, 92, 133, 173; CN 3, 4, 5, 6, 7; CPW; DA3; DAM NOV, POP; DLB 6, 173; EWL 3; MAL 5; MTCW 1, 2; MTFW 2005; RGAL 4; TUS
de Lisser, H. G.
See De Lisser, H(erbert) G(eorge)
See also DLB 117
De Lisser, H(erbert) G(eorge) 1878-1944 .... **TCLC 12**
See de Lisser, H. G.
See also BW 2; CA 109; 152
Deloire, Pierre
See Peguy, Charles (Pierre)
Deloney, Thomas 1543(?)-1600 .... **LC 41; PC 79**
See also DLB 167; RGEL 2

Deloria, Ella (Cara) 1889-1971(?) ..... **NNAL**
See also CA 152; DAM MULT; DLB 175
Deloria, Vine, Jr. 1933-2005 .... **CLC 21, 122; NNAL**
See also CA 53-56; 245; CANR 5, 20, 48, 98; DAM MULT; DLB 175; MTCW 1; SATA 21; SATA-Obit 171
Deloria, Vine Victor, Jr.
See Deloria, Vine, Jr.
del Valle-Inclan, Ramon (Maria)
See Valle-Inclan, Ramon (Maria) del
See also DLB 322
Del Vecchio, John M(ichael) 1947- .. **CLC 29**
See also CA 110; DLBD 9
de Man, Paul (Adolph Michel) 1919-1983 .... **CLC 55**
See also CA 128; 111; CANR 61; DLB 67; MTCW 1, 2
DeMarinis, Rick 1934- .... **CLC 54**
See also CA 57-60, 184; CAAE 184; CAAS 24; CANR 9, 25, 50, 160; DLB 218; TCWW 2
de Maupassant, (Henri Rene Albert) Guy
See Maupassant, (Henri Rene Albert) Guy de
Dembry, R. Emmet
See Murfree, Mary Noailles
Demby, William 1922- ...... **BLC 1:1; CLC 53**
See also BW 1, 3; CA 81-84; CANR 81; DAM MULT; DLB 33
de Menton, Francisco
See Chin, Frank (Chew, Jr.)
Demetrius of Phalerum c. 307B.C.- .... **CMLC 34**
Demijohn, Thom
See Disch, Thomas M.
De Mille, James 1833-1880 .... **NCLC 123**
See also DLB 99, 251
Deming, Richard 1915-1983
See Queen, Ellery
See also CA 9-12R; CANR 3, 94; SATA 24
Democritus c. 460B.C.-c. 370B.C. . **CMLC 47**
de Montaigne, Michel (Eyquem)
See Montaigne, Michel (Eyquem) de
de Montherlant, Henry (Milon)
See Montherlant, Henry (Milon) de
Demosthenes 384B.C.-322B.C. ...... **CMLC 13**
See also AW 1; DLB 176; RGWL 2, 3; WLIT 8
de Musset, (Louis Charles) Alfred
See Musset, Alfred de
de Natale, Francine
See Malzberg, Barry N(athaniel)
de Navarre, Marguerite 1492-1549 ... **LC 61; SSC 85**
See Marguerite d'Angouleme; Marguerite de Navarre
See also DLB 327
Denby, Edwin (Orr) 1903-1983 .... **CLC 48**
See also CA 138; 110; CP 1
de Nerval, Gerard
See Nerval, Gerard de
Denham, John 1615-1669 .... **LC 73**
See also DLB 58, 126; RGEL 2
Denis, Julio
See Cortazar, Julio
Denmark, Harrison
See Zelazny, Roger
Dennis, John 1658-1734 .... **LC 11, 154**
See also DLB 101; RGEL 2
Dennis, Nigel (Forbes) 1912-1989 ...... **CLC 8**
See also CA 25-28R; 129; CN 1, 2, 3, 4; DLB 13, 15, 233; EWL 3; MTCW 1
Dent, Lester 1904-1959 .... **TCLC 72**
See also CA 112; 161; CMW 4; DLB 306; SFW 4
De Palma, Brian 1940- .... **CLC 20, 247**
See also CA 109

De Palma, Brian Russell
See De Palma, Brian
de Pizan, Christine
See Christine de Pizan
See also FL 1:1
De Quincey, Thomas 1785-1859 ..... NCLC 4, 87, 198
See also BRW 4; CDBLB 1789-1832; DLB 110, 144; RGEL 2
Deren, Eleanora 1908(?)-1961
See Deren, Maya
See also CA 192; 111
Deren, Maya .... CLC 16, 102
See Deren, Eleanora
Derleth, August (William)
1909-1971 .... CLC 31
See also BPFB 1; BYA 9, 10; CA 1-4R; 29-32R; CANR 4; CMW 4; CN 1; DLB 9; DLBD 17; HGG; SATA 5; SUFW 1
Der Nister 1884-1950 .... TCLC 56
See Nister, Der
de Routisie, Albert
See Aragon, Louis
Derrida, Jacques 1930-2004 ...... CLC 24, 87, 225
See also CA 124; 127; 232; CANR 76, 98, 133; DLB 242; EWL 3; LMFS 2; MTCW 2; TWA
Derry Down Derry
See Lear, Edward
Dersonnes, Jacques
See Simenon, Georges (Jacques Christian)
Der Stricker c. 1190-c. 1250 .... CMLC 75
See also DLB 138
Desai, Anita 1937- .... CLC 19, 37, 97, 175
See also BRWS 5; CA 81-84; CANR 33, 53, 95, 133; CN 1, 2, 3, 4, 5, 6, 7; CWRI 5; DA3; DAB; DAM NOV; DLB 271, 323; DNFS 2; EWL 3; FW; MTCW 1, 2; MTFW 2005; SATA 63, 126
Desai, Kiran 1971- .... CLC 119
See also BYA 16; CA 171; CANR 127
de Saint-Luc, Jean
See Glassco, John
de Saint Roman, Arnaud
See Aragon, Louis
Desbordes-Valmore, Marceline
1786-1859 .... NCLC 97
See also DLB 217
Descartes, Rene 1596-1650 .... LC 20, 35, 150
See also DLB 268; EW 3; GFL Beginnings to 1789
Deschamps, Eustache 1340(?)-1404 .. LC 103
See also DLB 208
De Sica, Vittorio 1901(?)-1974 .... CLC 20
See also CA 117
Desnos, Robert 1900-1945 .... TCLC 22
See also CA 121; 151; CANR 107; DLB 258; EWL 3; LMFS 2
Destouches, Louis-Ferdinand
1894-1961 .... CLC 9, 15
See Celine, Louis-Ferdinand
See also CA 85-88; CANR 28; MTCW 1
de Tolignac, Gaston
See Griffith, D.W.
Deutsch, Babette 1895-1982 .... CLC 18
See also BYA 3; CA 1-4R; 108; CANR 4, 79; CP 1, 2, 3; DLB 45; SATA 1; SATA-Obit 33
Devenant, William 1606-1649 .... LC 13
Devkota, Laxmiprasad 1909-1959 . TCLC 23
See also CA 123
De Voto, Bernard (Augustine)
1897-1955 .... TCLC 29
See also CA 113; 160; DLB 9, 256; MAL 5; TCWW 1, 2

De Vries, Peter 1910-1993 ..... CLC 1, 2, 3, 7, 10, 28, 46
See also CA 17-20R; 142; CANR 41; CN 1, 2, 3, 4, 5; DAM NOV; DLB 6; DLBY 1982; MAL 5; MTCW 1, 2; MTFW 2005
Dewey, John 1859-1952 .... TCLC 95
See also CA 114; 170; CANR 144; DLB 246, 270; RGAL 4
Dexter, John
See Bradley, Marion Zimmer
See also GLL 1
Dexter, Martin
See Faust, Frederick (Schiller)
Dexter, Pete 1943- .... CLC 34, 55
See also BEST 89:2; CA 127; 131; CANR 129; CPW; DAM POP; INT CA-131; MAL 5; MTCW 1; MTFW 2005
Diamano, Silmang
See Senghor, Leopold Sedar
Diamant, Anita 1951- .... CLC 239
See also CA 145; CANR 126
Diamond, Neil 1941- .... CLC 30
See also CA 108
Diaz, Junot 1968- .... CLC 258
See also BYA 12; CA 161; CANR 119, 183; LLW; SSFS 20
Diaz del Castillo, Bernal c.
1496-1584 .... HLCS 1; LC 31
See also DLB 318; LAW
di Bassetto, Corno
See Shaw, George Bernard
Dick, Philip K. 1928-1982 ... CLC 10, 30, 72; SSC 57
See also AAYA 24; BPFB 1; BYA 11; CA 49-52; 106; CANR 2, 16, 132; CN 2, 3; CPW; DA3; DAM NOV, POP; DLB 8; MTCW 1, 2; MTFW 2005; NFS 5, 26; SCFW 1, 2; SFW 4
Dick, Philip Kindred
See Dick, Philip K.
Dickens, Charles (John Huffam)
1812-1870 .... NCLC 3, 8, 18, 26, 37, 50, 86, 105, 113, 161, 187; SSC 17, 49, 88; WLC 2
See also AAYA 23; BRW 5; BRWC 1, 2; BYA 1, 2, 3, 13, 14; CDBLB 1832-1890; CLR 95; CMW 4; DA; DA3; DAB; DAC; DAM MST, NOV; DLB 21, 55, 70, 159, 166; EXPN; GL 2; HGG; JRDA; LAIT 1, 2; LATS 1:1; LMFS 1; MAICYA 1, 2; NFS 4, 5, 10, 14, 20, 25; RGEL 2; RGSF 2; SATA 15; SUFW 1; TEA; WCH; WLIT 4; WYA
Dickey, James (Lafayette)
1923-1997 .... CLC 1, 2, 4, 7, 10, 15, 47, 109; PC 40; TCLC 151
See also AAYA 50; AITN 1, 2; AMWS 4; BPFB 1; CA 9-12R; 156; CABS 2; CANR 10, 48, 61, 105; CDALB 1968-1988; CP 1, 2, 3, 4, 5, 6; CPW; CSW; DA3; DAM NOV, POET, POP; DLB 5, 193, 342; DLBD 7; DLBY 1982, 1993, 1996, 1997, 1998; EWL 3; INT CANR-10; MAL 5; MTCW 1, 2; NFS 9; PFS 6, 11; RGAL 4; TUS
Dickey, William 1928-1994 .... CLC 3, 28
See also CA 9-12R; 145; CANR 24, 79; CP 1, 2, 3, 4; DLB 5
Dickinson, Charles 1951- .... CLC 49
See also CA 128; CANR 141
Dickinson, Emily (Elizabeth)
1830-1886 ..... NCLC 21, 77, 171; PC 1; WLC 2
See also AAYA 22; AMW; AMWR 1; CDALB 1865-1917; DA; DA3; DAB; DAC; DAM MST, POET; DLB 1, 243; EXPP; FL 1:3; MBL; PAB; PFS 1, 2, 3, 4, 5, 6, 8, 10, 11, 13, 16, 28; RGAL 4; SATA 29; TUS; WP; WYA

Dickinson, Mrs. Herbert Ward
See Phelps, Elizabeth Stuart
Dickinson, Peter (Malcolm de Brissac)
1927- .... CLC 12, 35
See also AAYA 9, 49; BYA 5; CA 41-44R; CANR 31, 58, 88, 134; CLR 29, 125; CMW 4; DLB 87, 161, 276; JRDA; MAICYA 1, 2; SATA 5, 62, 95, 150; SFW 4; WYA; YAW
Dickson, Carr
See Carr, John Dickson
Dickson, Carter
See Carr, John Dickson
Diderot, Denis 1713-1784 .... LC 26, 126
See also DLB 313; EW 4; GFL Beginnings to 1789; LMFS 1; RGWL 2, 3
Didion, Joan 1934- . CLC 1, 3, 8, 14, 32, 129
See also AITN 1; AMWS 4; CA 5-8R; CANR 14, 52, 76, 125, 174; CDALB 1968-1988; CN 2, 3, 4, 5, 6, 7; DA3; DAM NOV; DLB 2, 173, 185; DLBY 1981, 1986; EWL 3; MAL 5; MBL; MTCW 1, 2; MTFW 2005; NFS 3; RGAL 4; TCLE 1:1; TCWW 2; TUS
di Donato, Pietro 1911-1992 .... TCLC 159
See also CA 101; 136; DLB 9
Dietrich, Robert
See Hunt, E. Howard
Difusa, Pati
See Almodovar, Pedro
Dillard, Annie 1945- .... CLC 9, 60, 115, 216
See also AAYA 6, 43; AMWS 6; ANW; CA 49-52; CANR 3, 43, 62, 90, 125; DA3; DAM NOV; DLB 275, 278; DLBY 1980; LAIT 4, 5; MAL 5; MTCW 1, 2; MTFW 2005; NCFS 1; RGAL 4; SATA 10, 140; TCLE 1:1; TUS
Dillard, R(ichard) H(enry) W(ilde)
1937- .... CLC 5
See also CA 21-24R; CAAS 7; CANR 10; CP 2, 3, 4, 5, 6, 7; CSW; DLB 5, 244
Dillon, Eilis 1920-1994 .... CLC 17
See also CA 9-12R, 182; 147; CAAE 182; CAAS 3; CANR 4, 38, 78; CLR 26; MAICYA 1, 2; MAICYAS 1; SATA 2, 74; SATA-Essay 105; SATA-Obit 83; YAW
Dimont, Penelope
See Mortimer, Penelope (Ruth)
Dinesen, Isak ..... CLC 10, 29, 95; SSC 7, 75
See Blixen, Karen (Christentze Dinesen)
See also EW 10; EWL 3; EXPS; FW; GL 2; HGG; LAIT 3; MTCW 1; NCFS 2; NFS 9; RGSF 2; RGWL 2, 3; SSFS 3, 6, 13; WLIT 2
Ding Ling .... CLC 68
See Chiang, Pin-chin
See also DLB 328; RGWL 3
Diodorus Siculus c. 90B.C.-c.
31B.C. .... CMLC 88
Diphusa, Patty
See Almodovar, Pedro
Disch, Thomas M. 1940- .... CLC 7, 36
See Disch, Tom
See also AAYA 17; BPFB 1; CA 21-24R; CAAS 4; CANR 17, 36, 54, 89; CLR 18; CP 5, 6, 7; DA3; DLB 8; HGG; MAICYA 1, 2; MTCW 1, 2; MTFW 2005; SAAS 15; SATA 92; SCFW 1, 2; SFW 4; SUFW 2
Disch, Thomas Michael
See Disch, Thomas M.
Disch, Tom
See Disch, Thomas M.
See also DLB 282
d'Isly, Georges
See Simenon, Georges (Jacques Christian)
Disraeli, Benjamin 1804-1881 ... NCLC 2, 39, 79
See also BRW 4; DLB 21, 55; RGEL 2

Ditcum, Steve
See Crumb, R.

Dixon, Paige
See Corcoran, Barbara (Asenath)

Dixon, Stephen 1936- .... **CLC 52; SSC 16**
See also AMWS 12; CA 89-92; CANR 17,
40, 54, 91, 175; CN 4, 5, 6, 7; DLB 130;
MAL 5

Dixon, Thomas, Jr. 1864-1946 ..... **TCLC 163**
See also RHW

Djebar, Assia 1936- .... **BLC 2:1; CLC 182;
SSC 114**
See also CA 188; CANR 169; EWL 3;
RGWL 3; WLIT 2

Doak, Annie
See Dillard, Annie

Dobell, Sydney Thompson
1824-1874 .... **NCLC 43**
See also DLB 32; RGEL 2

Doblin, Alfred .... **TCLC 13**
See Doeblin, Alfred
See also CDWLB 2; EWL 3; RGWL 2, 3

Dobroliubov, Nikolai Aleksandrovich
See Dobrolyubov, Nikolai Alexandrovich
See also DLB 277

Dobrolyubov, Nikolai Alexandrovich
1836-1861 .... **NCLC 5**
See Dobroliubov, Nikolai Aleksandrovich

Dobson, Austin 1840-1921 .... **TCLC 79**
See also DLB 35, 144

Dobyns, Stephen 1941- .... **CLC 37, 233**
See also AMWS 13; CA 45-48; CANR 2,
18, 99; CMW 4; CP 4, 5, 6, 7; PFS 23

Doctorow, Edgar Laurence
See Doctorow, E.L.

Doctorow, E.L. 1931- . **CLC 6, 11, 15, 18, 37,
44, 65, 113, 214**
See also AAYA 22; AITN 2; AMWS 4;
BEST 89:3; BPFB 1; CA 45-48; CANR
2, 33, 51, 76, 97, 133, 170; CDALB 1968-
1988; CN 3, 4, 5, 6, 7; CPW; DA3; DAM
NOV, POP; DLB 2, 28, 173; DLBY 1980;
EWL 3; LAIT 3; MAL 5; MTCW 1, 2;
MTFW 2005; NFS 6; RGAL 4; RGHL;
RHW; TCLE 1:1; TCWW 1, 2; TUS

Dodgson, Charles L(utwidge) 1832-1898
See Carroll, Lewis
See also CLR 2; DA; DA3; DAB; DAC;
DAM MST, NOV, POET; MAICYA 1, 2;
SATA 100; YABC 2

Dodsley, Robert 1703-1764 .... **LC 97**
See also DLB 95; RGEL 2

Dodson, Owen (Vincent)
1914-1983 .... **BLC 1:1; CLC 79**
See also BW 1; CA 65-68; 110; CANR 24;
DAM MULT; DLB 76

Doeblin, Alfred 1878-1957 .... **TCLC 13**
See Doblin, Alfred
See also CA 110; 141; DLB 66

Doerr, Harriet 1910-2002 .... **CLC 34**
See also CA 117; 122; 213; CANR 47; INT
CA-122; LATS 1:2

Domecq, H(onorio) Bustos
See Bioy Casares, Adolfo; Borges, Jorge
Luis

Domini, Rey
See Lorde, Audre
See also GLL 1

Dominique
See Proust, (Valentin-Louis-George-Eugene)
Marcel

Don, A
See Stephen, Sir Leslie

Donaldson, Stephen R. 1947- ... **CLC 46, 138**
See also AAYA 36; BPFB 1; CA 89-92;
CANR 13, 55, 99; CPW; DAM POP;
FANT; INT CANR-13; SATA 121; SFW
4; SUFW 1, 2

Donleavy, J(ames) P(atrick) 1926- .... **CLC 1,
4, 6, 10, 45**
See also AITN 2; BPFB 1; CA 9-12R;
CANR 24, 49, 62, 80, 124; CBD; CD 5,
6; CN 1, 2, 3, 4, 5, 6, 7; DLB 6, 173; INT
CANR-24; MAL 5; MTCW 1, 2; MTFW
2005; RGAL 4

Donnadieu, Marguerite
See Duras, Marguerite

Donne, John 1572-1631 ... **LC 10, 24, 91; PC
1, 43; WLC 2**
See also AAYA 67; BRW 1; BRWC 1;
BRWR 2; CDBLB Before 1660; DA;
DAB; DAC; DAM MST, POET; DLB
121, 151; EXPP; PAB; PFS 2, 11; RGEL
3; TEA; WLIT 3; WP

Donnell, David 1939(?)- .... **CLC 34**
See also CA 197

Donoghue, Denis 1928- .... **CLC 209**
See also CA 17-20R; CANR 16, 102

Donoghue, Emma 1969- .... **CLC 239**
See also CA 155; CANR 103, 152; DLB
267; GLL 2; SATA 101

Donoghue, P.S.
See Hunt, E. Howard

Donoso (Yanez), Jose 1924-1996 ... **CLC 4, 8,
11, 32, 99; HLC 1; SSC 34; TCLC 133**
See also CA 81-84; 155; CANR 32, 73; CD-
WLB 3; CWW 2; DAM MULT; DLB 113;
EWL 3; HW 1, 2; LAW; LAWS 1; MTCW
1, 2; MTFW 2005; RGSF 2; WLIT 1

Donovan, John 1928-1992 .... **CLC 35**
See also AAYA 20; CA 97-100; 137; CLR
3; MAICYA 1, 2; SATA 72; SATA-Brief
29; YAW

Don Roberto
See Cunninghame Graham, Robert
(Gallnigad) Bontine

Doolittle, Hilda 1886-1961 . **CLC 3, 8, 14, 31,
34, 73; PC 5; WLC 3**
See H. D.
See also AAYA 66; AMWS 1; CA 97-100;
CANR 35, 131; DA; DAC; DAM MST,
POET; DLB 4, 45; EWL 3; FW; GLL 1;
LMFS 2; MAL 5; MBL; MTCW 1, 2;
MTFW 2005; PFS 6, 28; RGAL 4

Doppo, Kunikida .... **TCLC 99**
See Kunikida Doppo

Dorfman, Ariel 1942- .... **CLC 48, 77, 189;
HLC 1**
See also CA 124; 130; CANR 67, 70, 135;
CWW 2; DAM MULT; DFS 4; EWL 3;
HW 1, 2; INT CA-130; WLIT 1

Dorn, Edward (Merton)
1929-1999 .... **CLC 10, 18**
See also CA 93-96; 187; CANR 42, 79; CP
1, 2, 3, 4, 5, 6, 7; DLB 5; INT CA-93-96;
WP

Dor-Ner, Zvi .... **CLC 70**

Dorris, Michael 1945-1997 .... **CLC 109;
NNAL**
See also AAYA 20; BEST 90:1; BYA 12;
CA 102; 157; CANR 19, 46, 75; CLR 58;
DA3; DAM MULT, NOV; DLB 175;
LAIT 5; MTCW 2; MTFW 2005; NFS 3;
RGAL 4; SATA 75; SATA-Obit 94;
TCWW 2; YAW

Dorris, Michael A.
See Dorris, Michael

Dorsan, Luc
See Simenon, Georges (Jacques Christian)

Dorsange, Jean
See Simenon, Georges (Jacques Christian)

Dorset
See Sackville, Thomas

Dos Passos, John (Roderigo)
1896-1970 ... **CLC 1, 4, 8, 11, 15, 25, 34,
82; WLC 2**
See also AMW; BPFB 1; CA 1-4R; 29-32R;
CANR 3; CDALB 1929-1941; DA; DA3;
DAB; DAC; DAM MST, NOV; DLB 4,

9, 274, 316; DLBD 1, 15; DLBY 1996;
EWL 3; MAL 5; MTCW 1, 2; MTFW
2005; NFS 14; RGAL 4; TUS

Dossage, Jean
See Simenon, Georges (Jacques Christian)

Dostoevsky, Fedor Mikhailovich
1821-1881 ... **NCLC 2, 7, 21, 33, 43, 119,
167, 202; SSC 2, 33, 44; WLC 2**
See Dostoevsky, Fyodor
See also AAYA 40; DA; DA3; DAB; DAC;
DAM MST, NOV; EW 7; EXPN; NFS 3,
8; RGSF 2; RGWL 2, 3; SSFS 8; TWA

Dostoevsky, Fyodor
See Dostoevsky, Fedor Mikhailovich
See also DLB 238; LATS 1:1; LMFS 1, 2

Doty, Mark 1953(?)- .... **CLC 176; PC 53**
See also AMWS 11; CA 161, 183; CAAE
183; CANR 110, 173; CP 7; PFS 28

Doty, Mark A.
See Doty, Mark

Doty, Mark Alan
See Doty, Mark

Doty, M.R.
See Doty, Mark

Doughty, Charles M(ontagu)
1843-1926 .... **TCLC 27**
See also CA 115; 178; DLB 19, 57, 174

Douglas, Ellen 1921- .... **CLC 73**
See also CA 115; CANR 41, 83; CN 5, 6,
7; CSW; DLB 292

Douglas, Gavin 1475(?)-1522 .... **LC 20**
See also DLB 132; RGEL 2

Douglas, George
See Brown, George Douglas
See also RGEL 2

Douglas, Keith (Castellain)
1920-1944 .... **TCLC 40**
See also BRW 7; CA 160; DLB 27; EWL
3; PAB; RGEL 2

Douglas, Leonard
See Bradbury, Ray

Douglas, Michael
See Crichton, Michael

Douglas, (George) Norman
1868-1952 .... **TCLC 68**
See also BRW 6; CA 119; 157; DLB 34,
195; RGEL 2

Douglas, William
See Brown, George Douglas

Douglass, Frederick 1817(?)-1895 .. **BLC 1:1;
NCLC 7, 55, 141; WLC 2**
See also AAYA 48; AFAW 1, 2; AMWC 1;
AMWS 3; CDALB 1640-1865; DA; DA3;
DAC; DAM MST, MULT; DLB 1, 43, 50,
79, 243; FW; LAIT 2; NCFS 2; RGAL 4;
SATA 29

Dourado, (Waldomiro Freitas) Autran
1926- .... **CLC 23, 60**
See also CA 25-28R; 179; CANR 34, 81;
DLB 145; 307; HW 2

Dourado, Waldomiro Freitas Autran
See Dourado, (Waldomiro Freitas) Autran

Dove, Rita 1952- . **BLC 2:1; BLCS; CLC 50,
81; PC 6**
See also AAYA 46; AMWS 4; BW 2; CA
109; CAAS 19; CANR 27, 42, 68, 76, 97,
132; CDALBS; CP 5, 6, 7; CSW; CWP;
DA3; DAM MULT, POET; DLB 120;
EWL 3; EXPP; MAL 5; MTCW 2; MTFW
2005; PFS 1, 15; RGAL 4

Dove, Rita Frances
See Dove, Rita

Doveglion
See Villa, Jose Garcia

Dowell, Coleman 1925-1985 .... **CLC 60**
See also CA 25-28R; 117; CANR 10; DLB
130; GLL 2

Downing, Major Jack
See Smith, Seba

Dowson, Ernest (Christopher)
1867-1900 .... **TCLC 4**
See also CA 105; 150; DLB 19, 135; RGEL
2

Doyle, A. Conan
See Doyle, Sir Arthur Conan

Doyle, Sir Arthur Conan
1859-1930 ..... **SSC 12, 83, 95; TCLC 7;
WLC 2**
See Conan Doyle, Arthur
See also AAYA 14; BRWS 2; CA 104; 122;
CANR 131; CDBLB 1890-1914; CLR
106; CMW 4; DA; DA3; DAB; DAC;
DAM MST, NOV; DLB 18, 70, 156, 178;
EXPS; HGG; LAIT 2; MSW; MTCW 1,
2; MTFW 2005; RGEL 2; RGSF 2; RHW;
SATA 24; SCFW 1, 2; SFW 4; SSFS 2;
TEA; WCH; WLIT 4; WYA; YAW

Doyle, Conan
See Doyle, Sir Arthur Conan

Doyle, John
See Graves, Robert

Doyle, Roddy 1958- .... **CLC 81, 178**
See also AAYA 14; BRWS 5; CA 143;
CANR 73, 128, 168; CN 6, 7; DA3; DLB
194, 326; MTCW 2; MTFW 2005

Doyle, Sir A. Conan
See Doyle, Sir Arthur Conan

Dr. A
See Asimov, Isaac; Silverstein, Alvin; Silverstein, Virginia B(arbara Opshelor)

Drabble, Margaret 1939- ...... **CLC 2, 3, 5, 8,
10, 22, 53, 129**
See also BRWS 4; CA 13-16R; CANR 18,
35, 63, 112, 131, 174; CDBLB 1960 to
Present; CN 1, 2, 3, 4, 5, 6, 7; CPW; DA3;
DAB; DAC; DAM MST, NOV, POP;
DLB 14, 155, 231; EWL 3; FW; MTCW
1, 2; MTFW 2005; RGEL 2; SATA 48;
TEA

Drakulic, Slavenka 1949- .... **CLC 173**
See also CA 144; CANR 92

Drakulic-Ilic, Slavenka
See Drakulic, Slavenka

Drapier, M. B.
See Swift, Jonathan

Drayham, James
See Mencken, H(enry) L(ouis)

Drayton, Michael 1563-1631 .... **LC 8**
See also DAM POET; DLB 121; RGEL 2

Dreadstone, Carl
See Campbell, Ramsey

Dreiser, Theodore 1871-1945 .... **SSC 30, 114;
TCLC 10, 18, 35, 83; WLC 2**
See also AMW; AMWC 2; AMWR 2; BYA
15, 16; CA 106; 132; CDALB 1865-1917;
DA; DA3; DAC; DAM MST, NOV; DLB
9, 12, 102, 137; DLBD 1; EWL 3; LAIT
2; LMFS 2; MAL 5; MTCW 1, 2; MTFW
2005; NFS 8, 17; RGAL 4; TUS

Dreiser, Theodore Herman Albert
See Dreiser, Theodore

Drexler, Rosalyn 1926- .... **CLC 2, 6**
See also CA 81-84; CAD; CANR 68, 124;
CD 5, 6; CWD; MAL 5

Dreyer, Carl Theodor 1889-1968 ...... **CLC 16**
See also CA 116

Drieu la Rochelle, Pierre
1893-1945 .... **TCLC 21**
See also CA 117; 250; DLB 72; EWL 3;
GFL 1789 to the Present

Drieu la Rochelle, Pierre-Eugene 1893-1945
See Drieu la Rochelle, Pierre

Drinkwater, John 1882-1937 .... **TCLC 57**
See also CA 109; 149; DLB 10, 19, 149;
RGEL 2

Drop Shot
See Cable, George Washington

Droste-Hulshoff, Annette Freiin von
1797-1848 .... **NCLC 3, 133**
See also CDWLB 2; DLB 133; RGSF 2;
RGWL 2, 3

Drummond, Walter
See Silverberg, Robert

Drummond, William Henry
1854-1907 .... **TCLC 25**
See also CA 160; DLB 92

Drummond de Andrade, Carlos
1902-1987 .... **CLC 18; TCLC 139**
See Andrade, Carlos Drummond de
See also CA 132; 123; DLB 307; LAW

Drummond of Hawthornden, William
1585-1649 .... **LC 83**
See also DLB 121, 213; RGEL 2

Drury, Allen (Stuart) 1918-1998 .... **CLC 37**
See also CA 57-60; 170; CANR 18, 52; CN
1, 2, 3, 4, 5, 6; INT CANR-18

Druse, Eleanor
See King, Stephen

Dryden, John 1631-1700 ..... **DC 3; LC 3, 21,
115; PC 25; WLC 2**
See also BRW 2; CDBLB 1660-1789; DA;
DAB; DAC; DAM DRAM, MST, POET;
DLB 80, 101, 131; EXPP; IDTP; LMFS
1; RGEL 2; TEA; WLIT 3

du Bellay, Joachim 1524-1560 .... **LC 92**
See also DLB 327; GFL Beginnings to
1789; RGWL 2, 3

Duberman, Martin 1930- .... **CLC 8**
See also CA 1-4R; CAD; CANR 2, 63, 137,
174; CD 5, 6

Dubie, Norman (Evans) 1945- .... **CLC 36**
See also CA 69-72; CANR 12, 115; CP 3,
4, 5, 6, 7; DLB 120; PFS 12

Du Bois, W(illiam) E(dward) B(urghardt)
1868-1963 .. **BLC 1:1; CLC 1, 2, 13, 64,
96; HR 1:2; TCLC 169; WLC 2**
See also AAYA 40; AFAW 1, 2; AMWC 1;
AMWS 2; BW 1, 3; CA 85-88; CANR
34, 82, 132; CDALB 1865-1917; DA;
DA3; DAC; DAM MST, MULT, NOV;
DLB 47, 50, 91, 246, 284; EWL 3; EXPP;
LAIT 2; LMFS 2; MAL 5; MTCW 1, 2;
MTFW 2005; NCFS 1; PFS 13; RGAL 4;
SATA 42

Dubus, Andre 1936-1999 ..... **CLC 13, 36, 97;
SSC 15**
See also AMWS 7; CA 21-24R; 177; CANR
17; CN 5, 6; CSW; DLB 130; INT CANR-
17; RGAL 4; SSFS 10; TCLE 1:1

Duca Minimo
See D'Annunzio, Gabriele

Ducharme, Rejean 1941- .... **CLC 74**
See also CA 165; DLB 60

du Chatelet, Emilie 1706-1749 .... **LC 96**
See Chatelet, Gabrielle-Emilie Du

Duchen, Claire .... **CLC 65**

Duck, Stephen 1705(?)-1756 .... **PC 89**
See also DLB 95; RGEL 2

Duclos, Charles Pinot- 1704-1772 .... **LC 1**
See also GFL Beginnings to 1789

Ducornet, Erica 1943-
See Ducornet, Rikki
See also CA 37-40R; CANR 14, 34, 54, 82;
SATA 7

Ducornet, Rikki .... **CLC 232**
See Ducornet, Erica

Dudek, Louis 1918-2001 .... **CLC 11, 19**
See also CA 45-48; 215; CAAS 14; CANR
1; CP 1, 2, 3, 4, 5, 6, 7; DLB 88

Duerrenmatt, Friedrich 1921-1990 ... **CLC 1,
4, 8, 11, 15, 43, 102**
See Durrenmatt, Friedrich
See also CA 17-20R; CANR 33; CMW 4;
DAM DRAM; DLB 69, 124; MTCW 1, 2

Duffy, Bruce 1953(?)- .... **CLC 50**
See also CA 172

Duffy, Maureen (Patricia) 1933- ...... **CLC 37**
See also CA 25-28R; CANR 33, 68; CBD;
CN 1, 2, 3, 4, 5, 6, 7; CP 5, 6, 7; CWD;
CWP; DFS 15; DLB 14, 310; FW; MTCW
1

Du Fu
See Tu Fu
See also RGWL 2, 3

Dugan, Alan 1923-2003 .... **CLC 2, 6**
See also CA 81-84; 220; CANR 119; CP 1,
2, 3, 4, 5, 6, 7; DLB 5; MAL 5; PFS 10

du Gard, Roger Martin
See Martin du Gard, Roger

Duhamel, Georges 1884-1966 .... **CLC 8**
See also CA 81-84; 25-28R; CANR 35;
DLB 65; EWL 3; GFL 1789 to the
Present; MTCW 1

du Hault, Jean
See Grindel, Eugene

Dujardin, Edouard (Emile Louis)
1861-1949 .... **TCLC 13**
See also CA 109; DLB 123

Duke, Raoul
See Thompson, Hunter S.

Dulles, John Foster 1888-1959 .... **TCLC 72**
See also CA 115; 149

Dumas, Alexandre (pere)
1802-1870 .... **NCLC 11, 71; WLC 2**
See also AAYA 22; BYA 3; CLR 134; DA;
DA3; DAB; DAC; DAM MST, NOV;
DLB 119, 192; EW 6; GFL 1789 to the
Present; LAIT 1, 2; NFS 14, 19; RGWL
2, 3; SATA 18; TWA; WCH

Dumas, Alexandre (fils) 1824-1895 ...... **DC 1;
NCLC 9**
See also DLB 192; GFL 1789 to the Present;
RGWL 2, 3

Dumas, Claudine
See Malzberg, Barry N(athaniel)

Dumas, Henry L. 1934-1968 . **BLC 2:1; CLC
6, 62; SSC 107**
See also BW 1; CA 85-88; DLB 41; RGAL
4

du Maurier, Daphne 1907-1989 .. **CLC 6, 11,
59; SSC 18; TCLC 209**
See also AAYA 37; BPFB 1; BRWS 3; CA
5-8R; 128; CANR 6, 55; CMW 4; CN 1,
2, 3, 4; CPW; DA3; DAB; DAC; DAM
MST, POP; DLB 191; GL 2; HGG; LAIT
3; MSW; MTCW 1, 2; NFS 12; RGEL 2;
RGSF 2; RHW; SATA 27; SATA-Obit 60;
SSFS 14, 16; TEA

Du Maurier, George 1834-1896 ..... **NCLC 86**
See also DLB 153, 178; RGEL 2

Dunbar, Paul Laurence
1872-1906 .... **BLC 1:1; PC 5; SSC 8;
TCLC 2, 12; WLC 2**
See also AAYA 75; AFAW 1, 2; AMWS 2;
BW 1, 3; CA 104; 124; CANR 79;
CDALB 1865-1917; DA; DA3; DAC;
DAM MST, MULT, POET; DLB 50, 54,
78; EXPP; MAL 5; RGAL 4; SATA 34

Dunbar, William 1460(?)-1520(?) .... **LC 20;
PC 67**
See also BRWS 8; DLB 132, 146; RGEL 2

Dunbar-Nelson, Alice .... **HR 1:2**
See Nelson, Alice Ruth Moore Dunbar

Duncan, Dora Angela
See Duncan, Isadora

Duncan, Isadora 1877(?)-1927 .... **TCLC 68**
See also CA 118; 149

Duncan, Lois 1934- .... **CLC 26**
See also AAYA 4, 34; BYA 6, 8; CA 1-4R;
CANR 2, 23, 36, 111; CLR 29, 129;
JRDA; MAICYA 1, 2; MAICYAS 1;
MTFW 2005; SAAS 2; SATA 1, 36, 75,
133, 141; SATA-Essay 141; WYA; YAW

Fuller, Henry Blake 1857-1929 .... **TCLC 103**
See also CA 108; 177; DLB 12; RGAL 4
Fuller, John (Leopold) 1937- .... **CLC 62**
See also CA 21-24R; CANR 9, 44; CP 1, 2, 3, 4, 5, 6, 7; DLB 40
Fuller, Margaret
See Ossoli, Sarah Margaret (Fuller)
See also AMWS 2; DLB 183, 223, 239; FL 1:3
Fuller, Roy (Broadbent) 1912-1991 ... **CLC 4, 28**
See also BRWS 7; CA 5-8R; 135; CAAS 10; CANR 53, 83; CN 1, 2, 3, 4, 5; CP 1, 2, 3, 4, 5; CWRI 5; DLB 15, 20; EWL 3; RGEL 2; SATA 87
Fuller, Sarah Margaret
See Ossoli, Sarah Margaret (Fuller)
Fuller, Sarah Margaret
See Ossoli, Sarah Margaret (Fuller)
Fuller, Thomas 1608-1661 .... **LC 111**
See also DLB 151
Fulton, Alice 1952- .... **CLC 52**
See also CA 116; CANR 57, 88; CP 5, 6, 7; CWP; DLB 193; PFS 25
Furphy, Joseph 1843-1912 .... **TCLC 25**
See Collins, Tom
See also CA 163; DLB 230; EWL 3; RGEL 2
Furst, Alan 1941- .... **CLC 255**
See also CA 69-72; CANR 12, 34, 59, 102, 159; DLBY 01
Fuson, Robert H(enderson) 1927- .... **CLC 70**
See also CA 89-92; CANR 103
Fussell, Paul 1924- .... **CLC 74**
See also BEST 90:1; CA 17-20R; CANR 8, 21, 35, 69, 135; INT CANR-21; MTCW 1, 2; MTFW 2005
Futabatei, Shimei 1864-1909 .... **TCLC 44**
See Futabatei Shimei
See also CA 162; MJW
Futabatei Shimei
See Futabatei, Shimei
See also DLB 180; EWL 3
Futrelle, Jacques 1875-1912 .... **TCLC 19**
See also CA 113; 155; CMW 4
Gaboriau, Emile 1835-1873 .... **NCLC 14**
See also CMW 4; MSW
Gadda, Carlo Emilio 1893-1973 ...... **CLC 11; TCLC 144**
See also CA 89-92; DLB 177; EWL 3; WLIT 7
Gaddis, William 1922-1998 ... **CLC 1, 3, 6, 8, 10, 19, 43, 86**
See also AMWS 4; BPFB 1; CA 17-20R; 172; CANR 21, 48, 148; CN 1, 2, 3, 4, 5, 6; DLB 2, 278; EWL 3; MAL 5; MTCW 1, 2; MTFW 2005; RGAL 4
Gage, Walter
See Inge, William (Motter)
Gaiman, Neil 1960- .... **CLC 195**
See also AAYA 19, 42; CA 133; CANR 81, 129; CLR 109; DLB 261; HGG; MTFW 2005; SATA 85, 146; SFW 4; SUFW 2
Gaiman, Neil Richard
See Gaiman, Neil
Gaines, Ernest J. 1933- ..... **BLC 1:2; CLC 3, 11, 18, 86, 181; SSC 68**
See also AAYA 18; AFAW 1, 2; AITN 1; BPFB 2; BW 2, 3; BYA 6; CA 9-12R; CANR 6, 24, 42, 75, 126; CDALB 1968-1988; CLR 62; CN 1, 2, 3, 4, 5, 6, 7; CSW; DA3; DAM MULT; DLB 2, 33, 152; DLBY 1980; EWL 3; EXPN; LAIT 5; LATS 1:2; MAL 5; MTCW 1, 2; MTFW 2005; NFS 5, 7, 16; RGAL 4; RGSF 2; RHW; SATA 86; SSFS 5; YAW
Gaitskill, Mary 1954- .... **CLC 69**
See also CA 128; CANR 61, 152; DLB 244; TCLE 1:1

Gaitskill, Mary Lawrence
See Gaitskill, Mary
Gaius Suetonius Tranquillus
See Suetonius
Galdos, Benito Perez
See Perez Galdos, Benito
See also EW 7
Gale, Zona 1874-1938 .... **DC 30; TCLC 7**
See also CA 105; 153; CANR 84; DAM DRAM; DFS 17; DLB 9, 78, 228; RGAL 4
Galeano, Eduardo 1940- ... **CLC 72; HLCS 1**
See also CA 29-32R; CANR 13, 32, 100, 163; HW 1
Galeano, Eduardo Hughes
See Galeano, Eduardo
Galiano, Juan Valera y Alcala
See Valera y Alcala-Galiano, Juan
Galilei, Galileo 1564-1642 .... **LC 45**
Gallagher, Tess 1943- .... **CLC 18, 63; PC 9**
See also CA 106; CP 3, 4, 5, 6, 7; CWP; DAM POET; DLB 120, 212, 244; PFS 16
Gallant, Mavis 1922- ..... **CLC 7, 18, 38, 172; SSC 5, 78**
See also CA 69-72; CANR 29, 69, 117; CCA 1; CN 1, 2, 3, 4, 5, 6, 7; DAC; DAM MST; DLB 53; EWL 3; MTCW 1, 2; MTFW 2005; RGEL 2; RGSF 2
Gallant, Roy A(rthur) 1924- .... **CLC 17**
See also CA 5-8R; CANR 4, 29, 54, 117; CLR 30; MAICYA 1, 2; SATA 4, 68, 110
Gallico, Paul (William) 1897-1976 ..... **CLC 2**
See also AITN 1; CA 5-8R; 69-72; CANR 23; CN 1, 2; DLB 9, 171; FANT; MAICYA 1, 2; SATA 13
Gallo, Max Louis 1932- .... **CLC 95**
See also CA 85-88
Gallois, Lucien
See Desnos, Robert
Gallup, Ralph
See Whitemore, Hugh (John)
Galsworthy, John 1867-1933 .... **SSC 22; TCLC 1, 45; WLC 2**
See also BRW 6; CA 104; 141; CANR 75; CDBLB 1890-1914; DA; DA3; DAB; DAC; DAM DRAM, MST, NOV; DLB 10, 34, 98, 162, 330; DLBD 16; EWL 3; MTCW 2; RGEL 2; SSFS 3; TEA
Galt, John 1779-1839 .... **NCLC 1, 110**
See also DLB 99, 116, 159; RGEL 2; RGSF 2
Galvin, James 1951- .... **CLC 38**
See also CA 108; CANR 26
Gamboa, Federico 1864-1939 .... **TCLC 36**
See also CA 167; HW 2; LAW
Gandhi, M. K.
See Gandhi, Mohandas Karamchand
Gandhi, Mahatma
See Gandhi, Mohandas Karamchand
Gandhi, Mohandas Karamchand 1869-1948 .... **TCLC 59**
See also CA 121; 132; DA3; DAM MULT; DLB 323; MTCW 1, 2
Gann, Ernest Kellogg 1910-1991 ..... **CLC 23**
See also AITN 1; BPFB 2; CA 1-4R; 136; CANR 1, 83; RHW
Gao Xingjian 1940- .... **CLC 167**
See Xingjian, Gao
See also MTFW 2005
Garber, Eric 1943(?)-
See Holleran, Andrew
See also CANR 89, 162
Garber, Esther
See Lee, Tanith
Garcia, Cristina 1958- .... **CLC 76**
See also AMWS 11; CA 141; CANR 73, 130, 172; CN 7; DLB 292; DNFS 1; EWL 3; HW 2; LLW; MTFW 2005

Garcia Lorca, Federico 1898-1936 ...... **DC 2; HLC 2; PC 3; TCLC 1, 7, 49, 181, 197; WLC 2**
See Lorca, Federico Garcia
See also AAYA 46; CA 104; 131; CANR 81; DA; DA3; DAB; DAC; DAM DRAM, MST, MULT, POET; DFS 4, 10; DLB 108; EWL 3; HW 1, 2; LATS 1:2; MTCW 1, 2; MTFW 2005; TWA
Garcia Marquez, Gabriel 1928- .... **CLC 2, 3, 8, 10, 15, 27, 47, 55, 68, 170, 254; HLC 1; SSC 8, 83; WLC 3**
See also AAYA 3, 33; BEST 89:1, 90:4; BPFB 2; BYA 12, 16; CA 33-36R; CANR 10, 28, 50, 75, 82, 128; CDWLB 3; CPW; CWW 2; DA; DA3; DAB; DAC; DAM MST, MULT, NOV, POP; DLB 113, 330; DNFS 1, 2; EWL 3; EXPN; EXPS; HW 1, 2; LAIT 2; LATS 1:2; LAW; LAWS 1; LMFS 2; MTCW 1, 2; MTFW 2005; NCFS 3; NFS 1, 5, 10; RGSF 2; RGWL 2, 3; SSFS 1, 6, 16, 21; TWA; WLIT 1
Garcia Marquez, Gabriel Jose
See Garcia Marquez, Gabriel
Garcilaso de la Vega, El Inca 1539-1616 .... **HLCS 1; LC 127**
See also DLB 318; LAW
Gard, Janice
See Latham, Jean Lee
Gard, Roger Martin du
See Martin du Gard, Roger
Gardam, Jane 1928- .... **CLC 43**
See also CA 49-52; CANR 2, 18, 33, 54, 106, 167; CLR 12; DLB 14, 161, 231; MAICYA 1, 2; MTCW 1; SAAS 9; SATA 39, 76, 130; SATA-Brief 28; YAW
Gardam, Jane Mary
See Gardam, Jane
Gardner, Herb(ert George) 1934-2003 .... **CLC 44**
See also CA 149; 220; CAD; CANR 119; CD 5, 6; DFS 18, 20
Gardner, John, Jr. 1933-1982 ... **CLC 2, 3, 5, 7, 8, 10, 18, 28, 34; SSC 7; TCLC 195**
See also AAYA 45; AITN 1; AMWS 6; BPFB 2; CA 65-68; 107; CANR 33, 73; CDALBS; CN 2, 3; CPW; DA3; DAM NOV, POP; DLB 2; DLBY 1982; EWL 3; FANT; LATS 1:2; MAL 5; MTCW 1, 2; MTFW 2005; NFS 3; RGAL 4; RGSF 2; SATA 40; SATA-Obit 31; SSFS 8
Gardner, John 1926-2007 .... **CLC 30**
See also CA 103; 263; CANR 15, 69, 127, 183; CMW 4; CPW; DAM POP; MTCW 1
Gardner, John Edmund
See Gardner, John
Gardner, Miriam
See Bradley, Marion Zimmer
See also GLL 1
Gardner, Noel
See Kuttner, Henry
Gardons, S. S.
See Snodgrass, W.D.
Garfield, Leon 1921-1996 .... **CLC 12**
See also AAYA 8, 69; BYA 1, 3; CA 17-20R; 152; CANR 38, 41, 78; CLR 21; DLB 161; JRDA; MAICYA 1, 2; MAICYAS 1; SATA 1, 32, 76; SATA-Obit 90; TEA; WYA; YAW
Garland, (Hannibal) Hamlin 1860-1940 .... **SSC 18; TCLC 3**
See also CA 104; DLB 12, 71, 78, 186; MAL 5; RGAL 4; RGSF 2; TCWW 1, 2
Garneau, (Hector de) Saint-Denys 1912-1943 .... **TCLC 13**
See also CA 111; DLB 88

Godwin, Gail 1937- ...... **CLC 5, 8, 22, 31, 69, 125**
See also BPFB 2; CA 29-32R; CANR 15, 43, 69, 132; CN 3, 4, 5, 6, 7; CPW; CSW; DA3; DAM POP; DLB 6, 234; INT CANR-15; MAL 5; MTCW 1, 2; MTFW 2005

Godwin, Gail Kathleen
See Godwin, Gail

Godwin, William 1756-1836 .. **NCLC 14, 130**
See also CDBLB 1789-1832; CMW 4; DLB 39, 104, 142, 158, 163, 262, 336; GL 2; HGG; RGEL 2

Goebbels, Josef
See Goebbels, (Paul) Joseph

Goebbels, (Paul) Joseph
1897-1945 .... **TCLC 68**
See also CA 115; 148

Goebbels, Joseph Paul
See Goebbels, (Paul) Joseph

Goethe, Johann Wolfgang von
1749-1832 . **DC 20; NCLC 4, 22, 34, 90, 154; PC 5; SSC 38; WLC 3**
See also CDWLB 2; DA; DA3; DAB; DAC; DAM DRAM, MST, POET; DLB 94; EW 5; GL 2; LATS 1; LMFS 1:1; RGWL 2, 3; TWA

Gogarty, Oliver St. John
1878-1957 .... **TCLC 15**
See also CA 109; 150; DLB 15, 19; RGEL 2

Gogol, Nikolai (Vasilyevich)
1809-1852 .... **DC 1; NCLC 5, 15, 31, 162; SSC 4, 29, 52; WLC 3**
See also DA; DAB; DAC; DAM DRAM, MST; DFS 12; DLB 198; EW 6; EXPS; RGSF 2; RGWL 2, 3; SSFS 7; TWA

Goines, Donald 1937(?)-1974 .... **BLC 1:2; CLC 80**
See also AITN 1; BW 1, 3; CA 124; 114; CANR 82; CMW 4; DA3; DAM MULT, POP; DLB 33

Gold, Herbert 1924- ... **CLC 4, 7, 14, 42, 152**
See also CA 9-12R; CANR 17, 45, 125; CN 1, 2, 3, 4, 5, 6, 7; DLB 2; DLBY 1981; MAL 5

Goldbarth, Albert 1948- .... **CLC 5, 38**
See also AMWS 12; CA 53-56; CANR 6, 40; CP 3, 4, 5, 6, 7; DLB 120

Goldberg, Anatol 1910-1982 .... **CLC 34**
See also CA 131; 117

Goldemberg, Isaac 1945- .... **CLC 52**
See also CA 69-72; CAAS 12; CANR 11, 32; EWL 3; HW 1; WLIT 1

Golding, Arthur 1536-1606 .... **LC 101**
See also DLB 136

Golding, William 1911-1993 . **CLC 1, 2, 3, 8, 10, 17, 27, 58, 81; WLC 3**
See also AAYA 5, 44; BPFB 2; BRWR 1; BRWS 1; BYA 2; CA 5-8R; 141; CANR 13, 33, 54; CD 5; CDBLB 1945-1960; CLR 94, 130; CN 1, 2, 3, 4; DA; DA3; DAB; DAC; DAM MST, NOV; DLB 15, 100, 255, 326, 330; EWL 3; EXPN; HGG; LAIT 4; MTCW 1, 2; MTFW 2005; NFS 2; RGEL 2; RHW; SFW 4; TEA; WLIT 4; YAW

Golding, William Gerald
See Golding, William

Goldman, Emma 1869-1940 .... **TCLC 13**
See also CA 110; 150; DLB 221; FW; RGAL 4; TUS

Goldman, Francisco 1954- .... **CLC 76**
See also CA 162

Goldman, William 1931- .... **CLC 1, 48**
See also BPFB 2; CA 9-12R; CANR 29, 69, 106; CN 1, 2, 3, 4, 5, 6, 7; DLB 44; FANT; IDFW 3, 4

Goldman, William W.
See Goldman, William

Goldmann, Lucien 1913-1970 .... **CLC 24**
See also CA 25-28; CAP 2

Goldoni, Carlo 1707-1793 .... **LC 4, 152**
See also DAM DRAM; EW 4; RGWL 2, 3; WLIT 7

Goldsberry, Steven 1949- .... **CLC 34**
See also CA 131

Goldsmith, Oliver 1730(?)-1774 .... **DC 8; LC 2, 48, 122; PC 77; WLC 3**
See also BRW 3; CDBLB 1660-1789; DA; DAB; DAC; DAM DRAM, MST, NOV, POET; DFS 1; DLB 39, 89, 104, 109, 142, 336; IDTP; RGEL 2; SATA 26; TEA; WLIT 3

Goldsmith, Peter
See Priestley, J(ohn) B(oynton)

Goldstein, Rebecca 1950- .... **CLC 239**
See also CA 144; CANR 99, 165; TCLE 1:1

Goldstein, Rebecca Newberger
See Goldstein, Rebecca

Gombrowicz, Witold 1904-1969 .... **CLC 4, 7, 11, 49**
See also CA 19-20; 25-28R; CANR 105; CAP 2; CDWLB 4; DAM DRAM; DLB 215; EW 12; EWL 3; RGWL 2, 3; TWA

Gomez de Avellaneda, Gertrudis
1814-1873 .... **NCLC 111**
See also LAW

Gomez de la Serna, Ramon
1888-1963 .... **CLC 9**
See also CA 153; 116; CANR 79; EWL 3; HW 1, 2

Goncharov, Ivan Alexandrovich
1812-1891 .... **NCLC 1, 63**
See also DLB 238; EW 6; RGWL 2, 3

Goncourt, Edmond (Louis Antoine Huot) de
1822-1896 .... **NCLC 7**
See also DLB 123; EW 7; GFL 1789 to the Present; RGWL 2, 3

Goncourt, Jules (Alfred Huot) de
1830-1870 .... **NCLC 7**
See also DLB 123; EW 7; GFL 1789 to the Present; RGWL 2, 3

Gongora (y Argote), Luis de
1561-1627 .... **LC 72**
See also RGWL 2, 3

Gontier, Fernande 19(?)- .... **CLC 50**

Gonzalez Martinez, Enrique
See Gonzalez Martinez, Enrique
See also DLB 290

Gonzalez Martinez, Enrique
1871-1952 .... **TCLC 72**
See Gonzalez Martinez, Enrique
See also CA 166; CANR 81; EWL 3; HW 1, 2

Goodison, Lorna 1947- .... **BLC 2:2; PC 36**
See also CA 142; CANR 88; CP 5, 6, 7; CWP; DLB 157; EWL 3; PFS 25

Goodman, Allegra 1967- .... **CLC 241**
See also CA 204; CANR 162; DLB 244

Goodman, Paul 1911-1972 ..... **CLC 1, 2, 4, 7**
See also CA 19-20; 37-40R; CAD; CANR 34; CAP 2; CN 1; DLB 130, 246; MAL 5; MTCW 1; RGAL 4

Goodweather, Hartley
See King, Thomas

GoodWeather, Hartley
See King, Thomas

Googe, Barnabe 1540-1594 .... **LC 94**
See also DLB 132; RGEL 2

Gordimer, Nadine 1923- ...... **CLC 3, 5, 7, 10, 18, 33, 51, 70, 123, 160, 161, 263; SSC 17, 80; WLCS**
See also AAYA 39; AFW; BRWS 2; CA 5-8R; CANR 3, 28, 56, 88, 131; CN 1, 2, 3, 4, 5, 6, 7; DA; DA3; DAB; DAC; DAM MST, NOV; DLB 225, 326, 330; EWL 3; EXPS; INT CANR-28; LATS 1:2; MTCW 1, 2; MTFW 2005; NFS 4; RGEL 2; RGSF 2; SSFS 2, 14, 19; TWA; WLIT 2; YAW

Gordon, Adam Lindsay
1833-1870 .... **NCLC 21**
See also DLB 230

Gordon, Caroline 1895-1981 . **CLC 6, 13, 29, 83; SSC 15**
See also AMW; CA 11-12; 103; CANR 36; CAP 1; CN 1, 2; DLB 4, 9, 102; DLBD 17; DLBY 1981; EWL 3; MAL 5; MTCW 1, 2; MTFW 2005; RGAL 4; RGSF 2

Gordon, Charles William 1860-1937
See Connor, Ralph
See also CA 109

Gordon, Mary 1949- .. **CLC 13, 22, 128, 216; SSC 59**
See also AMWS 4; BPFB 2; CA 102; CANR 44, 92, 154, 179; CN 4, 5, 6, 7; DLB 6; DLBY 1981; FW; INT CA-102; MAL 5; MTCW 1

Gordon, Mary Catherine
See Gordon, Mary

Gordon, N. J.
See Bosman, Herman Charles

Gordon, Sol 1923- .... **CLC 26**
See also CA 53-56; CANR 4; SATA 11

Gordone, Charles 1925-1995 .... **BLC 2:2; CLC 1, 4; DC 8**
See also BW 1, 3; CA 93-96; 180; 150; CAAE 180; CAD; CANR 55; DAM DRAM; DLB 7; INT CA-93-96; MTCW 1

Gore, Catherine 1800-1861 .... **NCLC 65**
See also DLB 116, 344; RGEL 2

Gorenko, Anna Andreevna
See Akhmatova, Anna

Gorky, Maxim .... **SSC 28; TCLC 8; WLC 3**
See Peshkov, Alexei Maximovich
See also DAB; DFS 9; DLB 295; EW 8; EWL 3; TWA

Goryan, Sirak
See Saroyan, William

Gosse, Edmund (William)
1849-1928 .... **TCLC 28**
See also CA 117; DLB 57, 144, 184; RGEL 2

Gotlieb, Phyllis (Fay Bloom) 1926- .. **CLC 18**
See also CA 13-16R; CANR 7, 135; CN 7; CP 1, 2, 3, 4; DLB 88, 251; SFW 4

Gottesman, S. D.
See Kornbluth, C(yril) M.; Pohl, Frederik

Gottfried von Strassburg fl. c.
1170-1215 .... **CMLC 10, 96**
See also CDWLB 2; DLB 138; EW 1; RGWL 2, 3

Gotthelf, Jeremias 1797-1854 .... **NCLC 117**
See also DLB 133; RGWL 2, 3

Gottschalk, Laura Riding
See Jackson, Laura (Riding)

Gould, Lois 1932(?)-2002 .... **CLC 4, 10**
See also CA 77-80; 208; CANR 29; MTCW 1

Gould, Stephen Jay 1941-2002 .... **CLC 163**
See also AAYA 26; BEST 90:2; CA 77-80; 205; CANR 10, 27, 56, 75, 125; CPW; INT CANR-27; MTCW 1, 2; MTFW 2005

Gourmont, Remy(-Marie-Charles) de
1858-1915 .... **TCLC 17**
See also CA 109; 150; GFL 1789 to the Present; MTCW 2

Gournay, Marie le Jars de
See de Gournay, Marie le Jars

Govier, Katherine 1948- .... **CLC 51**
See also CA 101; CANR 18, 40, 128; CCA 1

Gower, John c. 1330-1408 .... **LC 76; PC 59**
See also BRW 1; DLB 146; RGEL 2

Greene, Robert 1558-1592 .... **LC 41**
See also BRWS 8; DLB 62, 167; IDTP;
RGEL 2; TEA

Greer, Germaine 1939- .... **CLC 131**
See also AITN 1; CA 81-84; CANR 33, 70,
115, 133; FW; MTCW 1, 2; MTFW 2005

Greer, Richard
See Silverberg, Robert

Gregor, Arthur 1923- .... **CLC 9**
See also CA 25-28R; CAAS 10; CANR 11;
CP 1, 2, 3, 4, 5, 6, 7; SATA 36

Gregor, Lee
See Pohl, Frederik

Gregory, Lady Isabella Augusta (Persse)
1852-1932 .... **TCLC 1, 176**
See also BRW 6; CA 104; 184; DLB 10;
IDTP; RGEL 2

Gregory, J. Dennis
See Williams, John A(lfred)

Gregory of Nazianzus, St.
329-389 .... **CMLC 82**

Grekova, I. .... **CLC 59**
See Ventsel, Elena Sergeevna
See also CWW 2

Grendon, Stephen
See Derleth, August (William)

Grenville, Kate 1950- .... **CLC 61**
See also CA 118; CANR 53, 93, 156; CN
7; DLB 325

Grenville, Pelham
See Wodehouse, P(elham) G(renville)

Greve, Felix Paul (Berthold Friedrich)
1879-1948
See Grove, Frederick Philip
See also CA 104; 141, 175; CANR 79;
DAC; DAM MST

Greville, Fulke 1554-1628 .... **LC 79**
See also BRWS 11; DLB 62, 172; RGEL 2

Grey, Lady Jane 1537-1554 .... **LC 93**
See also DLB 132

Grey, Zane 1872-1939 .... **TCLC 6**
See also BPFB 2; CA 104; 132; DA3; DAM
POP; DLB 9, 212; MTCW 1, 2; MTFW
2005; RGAL 4; TCWW 1, 2; TUS

Griboedov, Aleksandr Sergeevich
1795(?)-1829 .... **NCLC 129**
See also DLB 205; RGWL 2, 3

Grieg, (Johan) Nordahl (Brun)
1902-1943 .... **TCLC 10**
See also CA 107; 189; EWL 3

Grieve, C(hristopher) M(urray)
1892-1978 .... **CLC 11, 19**
See MacDiarmid, Hugh; Pteleon
See also CA 5-8R; 85-88; CANR 33, 107;
DAM POET; MTCW 1; RGEL 2

Griffin, Gerald 1803-1840 .... **NCLC 7**
See also DLB 159; RGEL 2

Griffin, John Howard 1920-1980 ..... **CLC 68**
See also AITN 1; CA 1-4R; 101; CANR 2

Griffin, Peter 1942- .... **CLC 39**
See also CA 136

Griffith, David Lewelyn Wark
See Griffith, D.W.

Griffith, D.W. 1875(?)-1948 .... **TCLC 68**
See also AAYA 78; CA 119; 150; CANR 80

Griffith, Lawrence
See Griffith, D.W.

Griffiths, Trevor 1935- .... **CLC 13, 52**
See also CA 97-100; CANR 45; CBD; CD
5, 6; DLB 13, 245

Griggs, Sutton (Elbert)
1872-1930 .... **TCLC 77**
See also CA 123; 186; DLB 50

Grigson, Geoffrey (Edward Harvey)
1905-1985 .... **CLC 7, 39**
See also CA 25-28R; 118; CANR 20, 33;
CP 1, 2, 3, 4; DLB 27; MTCW 1, 2

Grile, Dod
See Bierce, Ambrose (Gwinett)

Grillparzer, Franz 1791-1872 .... **DC 14;
NCLC 1, 102; SSC 37**
See also CDWLB 2; DLB 133; EW 5;
RGWL 2, 3; TWA

Grimble, Reverend Charles James
See Eliot, T(homas) S(tearns)

Grimke, Angelina (Emily) Weld
1880-1958 .... **HR 1:2**
See Weld, Angelina (Emily) Grimke
See also BW 1; CA 124; DAM POET; DLB
50, 54

Grimke, Charlotte L(ottie) Forten
1837(?)-1914
See Forten, Charlotte L.
See also BW 1; CA 117; 124; DAM MULT,
POET

Grimm, Jacob Ludwig Karl
1785-1863 .... **NCLC 3, 77; SSC 36**
See Grimm Brothers
See also CLR 112; DLB 90; MAICYA 1, 2;
RGSF 2; RGWL 2, 3; SATA 22; WCH

Grimm, Wilhelm Karl 1786-1859 .. **NCLC 3,
77; SSC 36**
See Grimm Brothers
See also CDWLB 2; CLR 112; DLB 90;
MAICYA 1, 2; RGSF 2; RGWL 2, 3;
SATA 22; WCH

Grimm and Grim
See Grimm, Jacob Ludwig Karl; Grimm,
Wilhelm Karl

Grimm Brothers .... **SSC 88**
See Grimm, Jacob Ludwig Karl; Grimm,
Wilhelm Karl
See also CLR 112

Grimmelshausen, Hans Jakob Christoffel
von
See Grimmelshausen, Johann Jakob Christoffel von
See also RGWL 2, 3

Grimmelshausen, Johann Jakob Christoffel
von 1621-1676 .... **LC 6**
See Grimmelshausen, Hans Jakob Christof-
fel von
See also CDWLB 2; DLB 168

Grindel, Eugene 1895-1952 .... **PC 38; TCLC
7, 41**
See also CA 104; 193; EWL 3; GFL 1789
to the Present; LMFS 2; RGWL 2, 3

Grisham, John 1955- .... **CLC 84**
See also AAYA 14, 47; BPFB 2; CA 138;
CANR 47, 69, 114, 133; CMW 4; CN 6,
7; CPW; CSW; DA3; DAM POP; MSW;
MTCW 2; MTFW 2005

Grosseteste, Robert 1175(?)-1253 . **CMLC 62**
See also DLB 115

Grossman, David 1954- .... **CLC 67, 231**
See also CA 138; CANR 114, 175; CWW
2; DLB 299; EWL 3; RGHL; WLIT 6

Grossman, Vasilii Semenovich
See Grossman, Vasily (Semenovich)
See also DLB 272

Grossman, Vasily (Semenovich)
1905-1964 .... **CLC 41**
See Grossman, Vasilii Semenovich
See also CA 124; 130; MTCW 1; RGHL

Grove, Frederick Philip .... **TCLC 4**
See Greve, Felix Paul (Berthold Friedrich)
See also DLB 92; RGEL 2; TCWW 1, 2

Grubb
See Crumb, R.

Grumbach, Doris 1918- .... **CLC 13, 22, 64**
See also CA 5-8R; CAAS 2; CANR 9, 42,
70, 127; CN 6, 7; INT CANR-9; MTCW
2; MTFW 2005

Grundtvig, Nikolai Frederik Severin
1783-1872 .... **NCLC 1, 158**
See also DLB 300

Grunge
See Crumb, R.

Grunwald, Lisa 1959- .... **CLC 44**
See also CA 120; CANR 148

Gryphius, Andreas 1616-1664 .... **LC 89**
See also CDWLB 2; DLB 164; RGWL 2, 3

Guare, John 1938- .... **CLC 8, 14, 29, 67; DC
20**
See also CA 73-76; CAD; CANR 21, 69,
118; CD 5, 6; DAM DRAM; DFS 8, 13;
DLB 7, 249; EWL 3; MAL 5; MTCW 1,
2; RGAL 4

Guarini, Battista 1538-1612 .... **LC 102**
See also DLB 339

Gubar, Susan 1944- .... **CLC 145**
See also CA 108; CANR 45, 70, 139, 179;
FW; MTCW 1; RGAL 4

Gubar, Susan David
See Gubar, Susan

Gudjonsson, Halldor Kiljan 1902-1998
See Halldor Laxness
See also CA 103; 164

Guenter, Erich
See Eich, Gunter

Guest, Barbara 1920-2006 ... **CLC 34; PC 55**
See also BG 1:2; CA 25-28R; 248; CANR
11, 44, 84; CP 1, 2, 3, 4, 5, 6, 7; CWP;
DLB 5, 193

Guest, Edgar A(lbert) 1881-1959 ... **TCLC 95**
See also CA 112; 168

Guest, Judith 1936- .... **CLC 8, 30**
See also AAYA 7, 66; CA 77-80; CANR
15, 75, 138; DA3; DAM NOV, POP;
EXPN; INT CANR-15; LAIT 5; MTCW
1, 2; MTFW 2005; NFS 1

Guevara, Che .... **CLC 87; HLC 1**
See Guevara (Serna), Ernesto

Guevara (Serna), Ernesto
1928-1967 .... **CLC 87; HLC 1**
See Guevara, Che
See also CA 127; 111; CANR 56; DAM
MULT; HW 1

Guicciardini, Francesco 1483-1540 ..... **LC 49**

Guido delle Colonne c. 1215-c.
1290 .... **CMLC 90**

Guild, Nicholas M. 1944- .... **CLC 33**
See also CA 93-96

Guillemin, Jacques
See Sartre, Jean-Paul

Guillen, Jorge 1893-1984 . **CLC 11; HLCS 1;
PC 35**
See also CA 89-92; 112; DAM MULT,
POET; DLB 108; EWL 3; HW 1; RGWL
2, 3

Guillen, Nicolas (Cristobal)
1902-1989 .... **BLC 1:2; CLC 48, 79;
HLC 1; PC 23**
See also BW 2; CA 116; 125; 129; CANR
84; DAM MST, MULT, POET; DLB 283;
EWL 3; HW 1; LAW; RGWL 2, 3; WP

Guillen y Alvarez, Jorge
See Guillen, Jorge

Guillevic, (Eugene) 1907-1997 .... **CLC 33**
See also CA 93-96; CWW 2

Guillois
See Desnos, Robert

Guillois, Valentin
See Desnos, Robert

Guimaraes Rosa, Joao 1908-1967 .... **HLCS 2**
See Rosa, Joao Guimaraes
See also CA 175; LAW; RGSF 2; RGWL 2,
3

Guiney, Louise Imogen
1861-1920 .... **TCLC 41**
See also CA 160; DLB 54; RGAL 4

Guinizelli, Guido c. 1230-1276 ...... **CMLC 49**
See Guinizzelli, Guido

Guinizzelli, Guido
See Guinizelli, Guido
See also WLIT 7

Hamburger, Michael 1924-2007 ... **CLC 5, 14**
See also CA 5-8R, 196; 261; CAAE 196;
CAAS 4; CANR 2, 47; CP 1, 2, 3, 4, 5, 6,
7; DLB 27

Hamburger, Michael Peter Leopold
See Hamburger, Michael

Hamill, Pete 1935- .... **CLC 10, 261**
See also CA 25-28R; CANR 18, 71, 127,
180

Hamill, William Peter
See Hamill, Pete

Hamilton, Alexander 1712-1756 .... **LC 150**
See also DLB 31

Hamilton, Alexander
1755(?)-1804 .... **NCLC 49**
See also DLB 37

Hamilton, Clive
See Lewis, C.S.

Hamilton, Edmond 1904-1977 .... **CLC 1**
See also CA 1-4R; CANR 3, 84; DLB 8;
SATA 118; SFW 4

Hamilton, Elizabeth 1758-1816 ... **NCLC 153**
See also DLB 116, 158

Hamilton, Eugene (Jacob) Lee
See Lee-Hamilton, Eugene (Jacob)

Hamilton, Franklin
See Silverberg, Robert

Hamilton, Gail
See Corcoran, Barbara (Asenath)

Hamilton, (Robert) Ian 1938-2001 . **CLC 191**
See also CA 106; 203; CANR 41, 67; CP 1,
2, 3, 4, 5, 6, 7; DLB 40, 155

Hamilton, Jane 1957- .... **CLC 179**
See also CA 147; CANR 85, 128; CN 7;
MTFW 2005

Hamilton, Mollie
See Kaye, M.M.

Hamilton, (Anthony Walter) Patrick
1904-1962 .... **CLC 51**
See also CA 176; 113; DLB 10, 191

Hamilton, Virginia 1936-2002 .... **CLC 26**
See also AAYA 2, 21; BW 2, 3; BYA 1, 2,
8; CA 25-28R; 206; CANR 20, 37, 73,
126; CLR 1, 11, 40, 127; DAM MULT;
DLB 33, 52; DLBY 2001; INT CANR-
20; JRDA; LAIT 5; MAICYA 1, 2; MAI-
CYAS 1; MTCW 1, 2; MTFW 2005;
SATA 4, 56, 79, 123; SATA-Obit 132;
WYA; YAW

Hammett, (Samuel) Dashiell
1894-1961 .... **CLC 3, 5, 10, 19, 47; SSC
17; TCLC 187**
See also AAYA 59; AITN 1; AMWS 4;
BPFB 2; CA 81-84; CANR 42; CDALB
1929-1941; CMW 4; DA3; DLB 226, 280;
DLBD 6; DLBY 1996; EWL 3; LAIT 3;
MAL 5; MSW; MTCW 1, 2; MTFW
2005; NFS 21; RGAL 4; RGSF 2; TUS

Hammon, Jupiter 1720(?)-1800(?) . **BLC 1:2;
NCLC 5; PC 16**
See also DAM MULT, POET; DLB 31, 50

Hammond, Keith
See Kuttner, Henry

Hamner, Earl (Henry), Jr. 1923- ...... **CLC 12**
See also AITN 2; CA 73-76; DLB 6

Hampton, Christopher 1946- .... **CLC 4**
See also CA 25-28R; CD 5, 6; DLB 13;
MTCW 1

Hampton, Christopher James
See Hampton, Christopher

Hamsun, Knut ..... **TCLC 2, 14, 49, 151, 203**
See Pedersen, Knut
See also DLB 297, 330; EW 8; EWL 3;
RGWL 2, 3

Handke, Peter 1942- .... **CLC 5, 8, 10, 15, 38,
134; DC 17**
See also CA 77-80; CANR 33, 75, 104, 133,
180; CWW 2; DAM DRAM, NOV; DLB
85, 124; EWL 3; MTCW 1, 2; MTFW
2005; TWA

Handy, W(illiam) C(hristopher)
1873-1958 .... **TCLC 97**
See also BW 3; CA 121; 167

Hanley, James 1901-1985 ..... **CLC 3, 5, 8, 13**
See also CA 73-76; 117; CANR 36; CBD;
CN 1, 2, 3; DLB 191; EWL 3; MTCW 1;
RGEL 2

Hannah, Barry 1942- .. **CLC 23, 38, 90; SSC
94**
See also BPFB 2; CA 108; 110; CANR 43,
68, 113; CN 4, 5, 6, 7; CSW; DLB 6, 234;
INT CA-110; MTCW 1; RGSF 2

Hannon, Ezra
See Hunter, Evan

Hansberry, Lorraine (Vivian)
1930-1965 ... **BLC 1:2, 2:2; CLC 17, 62;
DC 2; TCLC 192**
See also AAYA 25; AFAW 1, 2; AMWS 4;
BW 1, 3; CA 109; 25-28R; CABS 3;
CAD; CANR 58; CDALB 1941-1968;
CWD; DA; DA3; DAB; DAC; DAM
DRAM, MST, MULT; DFS 2; DLB 7, 38;
EWL 3; FL 1:6; FW; LAIT 4; MAL 5;
MTCW 1, 2; MTFW 2005; RGAL 4; TUS

Hansen, Joseph 1923-2004 .... **CLC 38**
See Brock, Rose; Colton, James
See also BPFB 2; CA 29-32R; 233; CAAS
17; CANR 16, 44, 66, 125; CMW 4; DLB
226; GLL 1; INT CANR-16

Hansen, Karen V. 1955- .... **CLC 65**
See also CA 149; CANR 102

Hansen, Martin A(lfred)
1909-1955 .... **TCLC 32**
See also CA 167; DLB 214; EWL 3

Hanson, Kenneth O(stlin) 1922- .... **CLC 13**
See also CA 53-56; CANR 7; CP 1, 2, 3, 4,
5

Hardwick, Elizabeth 1916-2007 .... **CLC 13**
See also AMWS 3; CA 5-8R; 267; CANR
3, 32, 70, 100, 139; CN 4, 5, 6; CSW;
DA3; DAM NOV; DLB 6; MBL; MTCW
1, 2; MTFW 2005; TCLE 1:1

Hardwick, Elizabeth Bruce
See Hardwick, Elizabeth

Hardwick, Elizabeth Bruce
See Hardwick, Elizabeth

Hardy, Thomas 1840-1928 . **PC 8; SSC 2, 60,
113; TCLC 4, 10, 18, 32, 48, 53, 72,
143, 153; WLC 3**
See also AAYA 69; BRW 6; BRWC 1, 2;
BRWR 1; CA 104; 123; CDBLB 1890-
1914; DA; DA3; DAB; DAC; DAM MST,
NOV, POET; DLB 18, 19, 135, 284; EWL
3; EXPN; EXPP; LAIT 2; MTCW 1, 2;
MTFW 2005; NFS 3, 11, 15, 19; PFS 3,
4, 18; RGEL 2; RGSF 2; TEA; WLIT 4

Hare, David 1947- . **CLC 29, 58, 136; DC 26**
See also BRWS 4; CA 97-100; CANR 39,
91; CBD; CD 5, 6; DFS 4, 7, 16; DLB
13, 310; MTCW 1; TEA

Harewood, John
See Van Druten, John (William)

Harford, Henry
See Hudson, W(illiam) H(enry)

Hargrave, Leonie
See Disch, Thomas M.

**Hariri, Al- al-Qasim ibn 'Ali Abu
Muhammad al-Basri**
See al-Hariri, al-Qasim ibn 'Ali Abu Mu-
hammad al-Basri

Harjo, Joy 1951- ..... **CLC 83; NNAL; PC 27**
See also AMWS 12; CA 114; CANR 35,
67, 91, 129; CP 6, 7; CWP; DAM MULT;
DLB 120, 175, 342; EWL 3; MTCW 2;
MTFW 2005; PFS 15; RGAL 4

Harlan, Louis R(udolph) 1922- .... **CLC 34**
See also CA 21-24R; CANR 25, 55, 80

Harling, Robert 1951(?)- .... **CLC 53**
See also CA 147

Harmon, William (Ruth) 1938- .... **CLC 38**
See also CA 33-36R; CANR 14, 32, 35;
SATA 65

Harper, F. E. W.
See Harper, Frances Ellen Watkins

Harper, Frances E. W.
See Harper, Frances Ellen Watkins

Harper, Frances E. Watkins
See Harper, Frances Ellen Watkins

Harper, Frances Ellen
See Harper, Frances Ellen Watkins

Harper, Frances Ellen Watkins
1825-1911 .. **BLC 1:2; PC 21; TCLC 14**
See also AFAW 1, 2; BW 1, 3; CA 111; 125;
CANR 79; DAM MULT, POET; DLB 50,
221; MBL; RGAL 4

Harper, Michael S(teven) 1938- ..... **BLC 2:2;
CLC 7, 22**
See also AFAW 2; BW 1; CA 33-36R; 224;
CAAE 224; CANR 24, 108; CP 2, 3, 4, 5,
6, 7; DLB 41; RGAL 4; TCLE 1:1

Harper, Mrs. F. E. W.
See Harper, Frances Ellen Watkins

Harpur, Charles 1813-1868 .... **NCLC 114**
See also DLB 230; RGEL 2

Harris, Christie
See Harris, Christie (Lucy) Irwin

Harris, Christie (Lucy) Irwin
1907-2002 .... **CLC 12**
See also CA 5-8R; CANR 6, 83; CLR 47;
DLB 88; JRDA; MAICYA 1, 2; SAAS 10;
SATA 6, 74; SATA-Essay 116

Harris, Frank 1856-1931 .... **TCLC 24**
See also CA 109; 150; CANR 80; DLB 156,
197; RGEL 2

Harris, George Washington
1814-1869 .... **NCLC 23, 165**
See also DLB 3, 11, 248; RGAL 4

Harris, Joel Chandler 1848-1908 ..... **SSC 19,
103; TCLC 2**
See also CA 104; 137; CANR 80; CLR 49,
128; DLB 11, 23, 42, 78, 91; LAIT 2;
MAICYA 1, 2; RGSF 2; SATA 100; WCH;
YABC 1

**Harris, John (Wyndham Parkes Lucas)
Beynon** 1903-1969
See Wyndham, John
See also CA 102; 89-92; CANR 84; SATA
118; SFW 4

Harris, MacDonald .... **CLC 9**
See Heiney, Donald (William)

Harris, Mark 1922-2007 .... **CLC 19**
See also CA 5-8R; 260; CAAS 3; CANR 2,
55, 83; CN 1, 2, 3, 4, 5, 6, 7; DLB 2;
DLBY 1980

Harris, Norman .... **CLC 65**

Harris, (Theodore) Wilson 1921- ... **BLC 2:2;
CLC 25, 159**
See also BRWS 5; BW 2, 3; CA 65-68;
CAAS 16; CANR 11, 27, 69, 114; CD-
WLB 3; CN 1, 2, 3, 4, 5, 6, 7; CP 1, 2, 3,
4, 5, 6, 7; DLB 117; EWL 3; MTCW 1;
RGEL 2

Harrison, Barbara Grizzuti
1934-2002 .... **CLC 144**
See also CA 77-80; 205; CANR 15, 48; INT
CANR-15

Hecht, Anthony (Evan) 1923-2004 .... **CLC 8, 13, 19; PC 70**
See also AMWS 10; CA 9-12R; 232; CANR 6, 108; CP 1, 2, 3, 4, 5, 6, 7; DAM POET; DLB 5, 169; EWL 3; PFS 6; WP

Hecht, Ben 1894-1964 ..... **CLC 8; TCLC 101**
See also CA 85-88; DFS 9; DLB 7, 9, 25, 26, 28, 86; FANT; IDFW 3, 4; RGAL 4

Hedayat, Sadeq 1903-1951 .... **TCLC 21**
See also CA 120; EWL 3; RGSF 2

Hegel, Georg Wilhelm Friedrich
1770-1831 .... **NCLC 46, 151**
See also DLB 90; TWA

Heidegger, Martin 1889-1976 .... **CLC 24**
See also CA 81-84; CANR 34; DLB 296; MTCW 1, 2; MTFW 2005

Heidenstam, (Carl Gustaf) Verner von
1859-1940 .... **TCLC 5**
See also CA 104; DLB 330

Heidi Louise
See Erdrich, Louise

Heifner, Jack 1946- .... **CLC 11**
See also CA 105; CANR 47

Heijermans, Herman 1864-1924 .... **TCLC 24**
See also CA 123; EWL 3

Heilbrun, Carolyn G(old)
1926-2003 .... **CLC 25, 173**
See Cross, Amanda
See also CA 45-48; 220; CANR 1, 28, 58, 94; FW

Hein, Christoph 1944- .... **CLC 154**
See also CA 158; CANR 108; CDWLB 2; CWW 2; DLB 124

Heine, Heinrich 1797-1856 .... **NCLC 4, 54, 147; PC 25**
See also CDWLB 2; DLB 90; EW 5; RGWL 2, 3; TWA

Heinemann, Larry 1944- .... **CLC 50**
See also CA 110; CAAS 21; CANR 31, 81, 156; DLBD 9; INT CANR-31

Heinemann, Larry Curtiss
See Heinemann, Larry

Heiney, Donald (William) 1921-1993
See Harris, MacDonald
See also CA 1-4R; 142; CANR 3, 58; FANT

Heinlein, Robert A. 1907-1988 .. **CLC 1, 3, 8, 14, 26, 55; SSC 55**
See also AAYA 17; BPFB 2; BYA 4, 13; CA 1-4R; 125; CANR 1, 20, 53; CLR 75; CN 1, 2, 3, 4; CPW; DA3; DAM POP; DLB 8; EXPS; JRDA; LAIT 5; LMFS 2; MAICYA 1, 2; MTCW 1, 2; MTFW 2005; RGAL 4; SATA 9, 69; SATA-Obit 56; SCFW 1, 2; SFW 4; SSFS 7; YAW

Heldris of Cornwall fl. 13th cent.
- .... **CMLC 97**

Helforth, John
See Doolittle, Hilda

Heliodorus fl. 3rd cent. - .... **CMLC 52**
See also WLIT 8

Hellenhofferu, Vojtech Kapristian z
See Hasek, Jaroslav (Matej Frantisek)

Heller, Joseph 1923-1999 . **CLC 1, 3, 5, 8, 11, 36, 63; TCLC 131, 151; WLC 3**
See also AAYA 24; AITN 1; AMWS 4; BPFB 2; BYA 1; CA 5-8R; 187; CABS 1; CANR 8, 42, 66, 126; CN 1, 2, 3, 4, 5, 6; CPW; DA; DA3; DAB; DAC; DAM MST, NOV, POP; DLB 2, 28, 227; DLBY 1980, 2002; EWL 3; EXPN; INT CANR-8; LAIT 4; MAL 5; MTCW 1, 2; MTFW 2005; NFS 1; RGAL 4; TUS; YAW

Hellman, Lillian 1905-1984 . **CLC 2, 4, 8, 14, 18, 34, 44, 52; DC 1; TCLC 119**
See also AAYA 47; AITN 1, 2; AMWS 1; CA 13-16R; 112; CAD; CANR 33; CWD; DA3; DAM DRAM; DFS 1, 3, 14; DLB

7, 228; DLBY 1984; EWL 3; FL 1:6; FW; LAIT 3; MAL 5; MBL; MTCW 1, 2; MTFW 2005; RGAL 4; TUS

Helprin, Mark 1947- .... **CLC 7, 10, 22, 32**
See also CA 81-84; CANR 47, 64, 124; CDALBS; CN 7; CPW; DA3; DAM NOV, POP; DLB 335; DLBY 1985; FANT; MAL 5; MTCW 1, 2; MTFW 2005; SSFS 25; SUFW 2

Helvetius, Claude-Adrien 1715-1771 .. **LC 26**
See also DLB 313

Helyar, Jane Penelope Josephine 1933-
See Poole, Josephine
See also CA 21-24R; CANR 10, 26; CWRI 5; SATA 82, 138; SATA-Essay 138

Hemans, Felicia 1793-1835 ...... **NCLC 29, 71**
See also DLB 96; RGEL 2

Hemingway, Ernest (Miller)
1899-1961 .... **CLC 1, 3, 6, 8, 10, 13, 19, 30, 34, 39, 41, 44, 50, 61, 80; SSC 1, 25, 36, 40, 63; TCLC 115, 203; WLC 3**
See also AAYA 19; AMW; AMWC 1; AMWR 1; BPFB 2; BYA 2, 3, 13, 15; CA 77-80; CANR 34; CDALB 1917-1929; DA; DA3; DAB; DAC; DAM MST, NOV; DLB 4, 9, 102, 210, 308, 316, 330; DLBD 1, 15, 16; DLBY 1981, 1987, 1996, 1998; EWL 3; EXPN; EXPS; LAIT 3, 4; LATS 1:1; MAL 5; MTCW 1, 2; MTFW 2005; NFS 1, 5, 6, 14; RGAL 4; RGSF 2; SSFS 17; TUS; WYA

Hempel, Amy 1951- .... **CLC 39**
See also CA 118; 137; CANR 70, 166; DA3; DLB 218; EXPS; MTCW 2; MTFW 2005; SSFS 2

Henderson, F. C.
See Mencken, H(enry) L(ouis)

Henderson, Sylvia
See Ashton-Warner, Sylvia (Constance)

Henderson, Zenna (Chlarson)
1917-1983 .... **SSC 29**
See also CA 1-4R; 133; CANR 1, 84; DLB 8; SATA 5; SFW 4

Henkin, Joshua 1964- .... **CLC 119**
See also CA 161

Henley, Beth .... **CLC 23, 255; DC 6, 14**
See Henley, Elizabeth Becker
See also AAYA 70; CABS 3; CAD; CD 5, 6; CSW; CWD; DFS 2, 21; DLBY 1986; FW

Henley, Elizabeth Becker 1952-
See Henley, Beth
See also CA 107; CANR 32, 73, 140; DA3; DAM DRAM, MST; MTCW 1, 2; MTFW 2005

Henley, William Ernest 1849-1903 .. **TCLC 8**
See also CA 105; 234; DLB 19; RGEL 2

Hennissart, Martha 1929-
See Lathen, Emma
See also CA 85-88; CANR 64

Henry VIII 1491-1547 .... **LC 10**
See also DLB 132

Henry, O. .... **SSC 5, 49, 114; TCLC 1, 19; WLC 3**
See Porter, William Sydney
See also AAYA 41; AMWS 2; EXPS; MAL 5; RGAL 4; RGSF 2; SSFS 2, 18; TCWW 1, 2

Henry, Patrick 1736-1799 .... **LC 25**
See also LAIT 1

Henryson, Robert 1430(?)-1506(?) ..... **LC 20, 110; PC 65**
See also BRWS 7; DLB 146; RGEL 2

Henschke, Alfred
See Klabund

Henson, Lance 1944- .... **NNAL**
See also CA 146; DLB 175

Hentoff, Nat(han Irving) 1925- .... **CLC 26**
See also AAYA 4, 42; BYA 6; CA 1-4R; CAAS 6; CANR 5, 25, 77, 114; CLR 1, 52; INT CANR-25; JRDA; MAICYA 1, 2; SATA 42, 69, 133; SATA-Brief 27; WYA; YAW

Heppenstall, (John) Rayner
1911-1981 .... **CLC 10**
See also CA 1-4R; 103; CANR 29; CN 1, 2; CP 1, 2, 3; EWL 3

Heraclitus c. 540B.C.-c. 450B.C. ... **CMLC 22**
See also DLB 176

Herbert, Frank 1920-1986 ... **CLC 12, 23, 35, 44, 85**
See also AAYA 21; BPFB 2; BYA 4, 14; CA 53-56; 118; CANR 5, 43; CDALBS; CPW; DAM POP; DLB 8; INT CANR-5; LAIT 5; MTCW 1, 2; MTFW 2005; NFS 17; SATA 9, 37; SATA-Obit 47; SCFW 1, 2; SFW 4; YAW

Herbert, George 1593-1633 . **LC 24, 121; PC 4**
See also BRW 2; BRWR 2; CDBLB Before 1660; DAB; DAM POET; DLB 126; EXPP; PFS 25; RGEL 2; TEA; WP

Herbert, Zbigniew 1924-1998 ..... **CLC 9, 43; PC 50; TCLC 168**
See also CA 89-92; 169; CANR 36, 74, 177; CDWLB 4; CWW 2; DAM POET; DLB 232; EWL 3; MTCW 1; PFS 22

Herbst, Josephine (Frey)
1897-1969 .... **CLC 34**
See also CA 5-8R; 25-28R; DLB 9

Herder, Johann Gottfried von
1744-1803 .... **NCLC 8, 186**
See also DLB 97; EW 4; TWA

Heredia, Jose Maria 1803-1839 .... **HLCS 2**
See also LAW

Hergesheimer, Joseph 1880-1954 ... **TCLC 11**
See also CA 109; 194; DLB 102, 9; RGAL 4

Herlihy, James Leo 1927-1993 .... **CLC 6**
See also CA 1-4R; 143; CAD; CANR 2; CN 1, 2, 3, 4, 5

Herman, William
See Bierce, Ambrose (Gwinett)

Hermogenes fl. c. 175- .... **CMLC 6**

Hernandez, Jose 1834-1886 .... **NCLC 17**
See also LAW; RGWL 2, 3; WLIT 1

Herodotus c. 484B.C.-c. 420B.C. ... **CMLC 17**
See also AW 1; CDWLB 1; DLB 176; RGWL 2, 3; TWA; WLIT 8

Herr, Michael 1940(?)- .... **CLC 231**
See also CA 89-92; CANR 68, 142; DLB 185; MTCW 1

Herrick, Robert 1591-1674 .. **LC 13, 145; PC 9**
See also BRW 2; BRWC 2; DA; DAB; DAC; DAM MST, POP; DLB 126; EXPP; PFS 13; RGAL 4; RGEL 2; TEA; WP

Herring, Guilles
See Somerville, Edith Oenone

Herriot, James 1916-1995 .... **CLC 12**
See Wight, James Alfred
See also AAYA 1, 54; BPFB 2; CA 148; CANR 40; CLR 80; CPW; DAM POP; LAIT 3; MAICYA 2; MAICYAS 1; MTCW 2; SATA 86, 135; TEA; YAW

Herris, Violet
See Hunt, Violet

Herrmann, Dorothy 1941- .... **CLC 44**
See also CA 107

Herrmann, Taffy
See Herrmann, Dorothy

Hersey, John 1914-1993 .. **CLC 1, 2, 7, 9, 40, 81, 97**
See also AAYA 29; BPFB 2; CA 17-20R; 140; CANR 33; CDALBS; CN 1, 2, 3, 4, 5; CPW; DAM POP; DLB 6, 185, 278, 299; MAL 5; MTCW 1, 2; MTFW 2005; RGHL; SATA 25; SATA-Obit 76; TUS

Hoch, Edward D. 1930-2008
See Queen, Ellery
See also CA 29-32R; CANR 11, 27, 51, 97;
CMW 4; DLB 306; SFW 4

Hochhuth, Rolf 1931- .... **CLC 4, 11, 18**
See also CA 5-8R; CANR 33, 75, 136;
CWW 2; DAM DRAM; DLB 124; EWL
3; MTCW 1, 2; MTFW 2005; RGHL

Hochman, Sandra 1936- .... **CLC 3, 8**
See also CA 5-8R; CP 1, 2, 3, 4, 5; DLB 5

Hochwaelder, Fritz 1911-1986 .... **CLC 36**
See Hochwalder, Fritz
See also CA 29-32R; 120; CANR 42; DAM
DRAM; MTCW 1; RGWL 3

Hochwalder, Fritz
See Hochwaelder, Fritz
See also EWL 3; RGWL 2

Hocking, Mary (Eunice) 1921- .... **CLC 13**
See also CA 101; CANR 18, 40

Hodge, Merle 1944- .... **BLC 2:2**
See also EWL 3

Hodgins, Jack 1938- .... **CLC 23**
See also CA 93-96; CN 4, 5, 6, 7; DLB 60

Hodgson, William Hope
1877(?)-1918 .... **TCLC 13**
See also CA 111; 164; CMW 4; DLB 70,
153, 156, 178; HGG; MTCW 2; SFW 4;
SUFW 1

Hoeg, Peter 1957- .... **CLC 95, 156**
See also CA 151; CANR 75; CMW 4; DA3;
DLB 214; EWL 3; MTCW 2; MTFW
2005; NFS 17; RGWL 3; SSFS 18

Hoffman, Alice 1952- .... **CLC 51**
See also AAYA 37; AMWS 10; CA 77-80;
CANR 34, 66, 100, 138, 170; CN 4, 5, 6,
7; CPW; DAM NOV; DLB 292; MAL 5;
MTCW 1, 2; MTFW 2005; TCLE 1:1

Hoffman, Daniel (Gerard) 1923- . **CLC 6, 13, 23**
See also CA 1-4R; CANR 4, 142; CP 1, 2,
3, 4, 5, 6, 7; DLB 5; TCLE 1:1

Hoffman, Eva 1945- .... **CLC 182**
See also AMWS 16; CA 132; CANR 146

Hoffman, Stanley 1944- .... **CLC 5**
See also CA 77-80

Hoffman, William 1925- .... **CLC 141**
See also CA 21-24R; CANR 9, 103; CSW;
DLB 234; TCLE 1:1

Hoffman, William M.
See Hoffman, William M(oses)
See also CAD; CD 5, 6

Hoffman, William M(oses) 1939- ..... **CLC 40**
See Hoffman, William M.
See also CA 57-60; CANR 11, 71

Hoffmann, E(rnst) T(heodor) A(madeus)
1776-1822 ..... **NCLC 2, 183; SSC 13, 92**
See also CDWLB 2; CLR 133; DLB 90;
EW 5; GL 2; RGSF 2; RGWL 2, 3; SATA
27; SUFW 1; WCH

Hofmann, Gert 1931-1993 .... **CLC 54**
See also CA 128; CANR 145; EWL 3;
RGHL

Hofmannsthal, Hugo von 1874-1929 ... **DC 4;
TCLC 11**
See also CA 106; 153; CDWLB 2; DAM
DRAM; DFS 17; DLB 81, 118; EW 9;
EWL 3; RGWL 2, 3

Hogan, Linda 1947- ..... **CLC 73; NNAL; PC
35**
See also AMWS 4; ANW; BYA 12; CA 120,
226; CAAE 226; CANR 45, 73, 129;
CWP; DAM MULT; DLB 175; SATA
132; TCWW 2

Hogarth, Charles
See Creasey, John

Hogarth, Emmett
See Polonsky, Abraham (Lincoln)

Hogarth, William 1697-1764 .... **LC 112**
See also AAYA 56

Hogg, James 1770-1835 .... **NCLC 4, 109**
See also BRWS 10; DLB 93, 116, 159; GL
2; HGG; RGEL 2; SUFW 1

Holbach, Paul-Henri Thiry
1723-1789 .... **LC 14**
See also DLB 313

Holberg, Ludvig 1684-1754 .... **LC 6**
See also DLB 300; RGWL 2, 3

Holcroft, Thomas 1745-1809 .... **NCLC 85**
See also DLB 39, 89, 158; RGEL 2

Holden, Ursula 1921- .... **CLC 18**
See also CA 101; CAAS 8; CANR 22

Holderlin, (Johann Christian) Friedrich
1770-1843 .... **NCLC 16, 187; PC 4**
See also CDWLB 2; DLB 90; EW 5; RGWL
2, 3

Holding, James (Clark Carlisle, Jr.)
1907-1997
See Queen, Ellery
See also CA 25-28R; SATA 3

Holdstock, Robert 1948- .... **CLC 39**
See also CA 131; CANR 81; DLB 261;
FANT; HGG; SFW 4; SUFW 2

Holdstock, Robert P.
See Holdstock, Robert

Holinshed, Raphael fl. 1580- .... **LC 69**
See also DLB 167; RGEL 2

Holland, Isabelle (Christian)
1920-2002 .... **CLC 21**
See also AAYA 11, 64; CA 21-24R; 205;
CAAE 181; CANR 10, 25, 47; CLR 57;
CWRI 5; JRDA; LAIT 4; MAICYA 1, 2;
SATA 8, 70; SATA-Essay 103; SATA-Obit
132; WYA

Holland, Marcus
See Caldwell, (Janet Miriam) Taylor
(Holland)

Hollander, John 1929- .... **CLC 2, 5, 8, 14**
See also CA 1-4R; CANR 1, 52, 136; CP 1,
2, 3, 4, 5, 6, 7; DLB 5; MAL 5; SATA 13

Hollander, Paul
See Silverberg, Robert

Holleran, Andrew .... **CLC 38**
See Garber, Eric
See also CA 144; GLL 1

Holley, Marietta 1836(?)-1926 .... **TCLC 99**
See also CA 118; DLB 11; FL 1:3

Hollinghurst, Alan 1954- .... **CLC 55, 91**
See also BRWS 10; CA 114; CN 5, 6, 7;
DLB 207, 326; GLL 1

Hollis, Jim
See Summers, Hollis (Spurgeon, Jr.)

Holly, Buddy 1936-1959 .... **TCLC 65**
See also CA 213

Holmes, Gordon
See Shiel, M(atthew) P(hipps)

Holmes, John
See Souster, (Holmes) Raymond

Holmes, John Clellon 1926-1988 ...... **CLC 56**
See also BG 1:2; CA 9-12R; 125; CANR 4;
CN 1, 2, 3, 4; DLB 16, 237

Holmes, Oliver Wendell, Jr.
1841-1935 .... **TCLC 77**
See also CA 114; 186

Holmes, Oliver Wendell
1809-1894 .... **NCLC 14, 81; PC 71**
See also AMWS 1; CDALB 1640-1865;
DLB 1, 189, 235; EXPP; PFS 24; RGAL
4; SATA 34

Holmes, Raymond
See Souster, (Holmes) Raymond

Holt, Victoria
See Hibbert, Eleanor Alice Burford
See also BPFB 2

Holub, Miroslav 1923-1998 .... **CLC 4**
See also CA 21-24R; 169; CANR 10; CD-
WLB 4; CWW 2; DLB 232; EWL 3;
RGWL 3

Holz, Detlev
See Benjamin, Walter

Homer c. 8th cent. B.C.- .... **CMLC 1, 16, 61;
PC 23; WLCS**
See also AW 1; CDWLB 1; DA; DA3;
DAB; DAC; DAM MST, POET; DLB
176; EFS 1; LAIT 1; LMFS 1; RGWL 2,
3; TWA; WLIT 8; WP

Hong, Maxine Ting Ting
See Kingston, Maxine Hong

Hongo, Garrett Kaoru 1951- .... **PC 23**
See also CA 133; CAAS 22; CP 5, 6, 7;
DLB 120, 312; EWL 3; EXPP; PFS 25;
RGAL 4

Honig, Edwin 1919- .... **CLC 33**
See also CA 5-8R; CAAS 8; CANR 4, 45,
144; CP 1, 2, 3, 4, 5, 6, 7; DLB 5

Hood, Hugh (John Blagdon) 1928- . **CLC 15,
28; SSC 42**
See also CA 49-52; CAAS 17; CANR 1,
33, 87; CN 1, 2, 3, 4, 5, 6, 7; DLB 53;
RGSF 2

Hood, Thomas 1799-1845 .... **NCLC 16**
See also BRW 4; DLB 96; RGEL 2

Hooker, (Peter) Jeremy 1941- .... **CLC 43**
See also CA 77-80; CANR 22; CP 2, 3, 4,
5, 6, 7; DLB 40

Hooker, Richard 1554-1600 .... **LC 95**
See also BRW 1; DLB 132; RGEL 2

Hooker, Thomas 1586-1647 .... **LC 137**
See also DLB 24

hooks, bell 1952(?)- .... **BLCS; CLC 94**
See also BW 2; CA 143; CANR 87, 126;
DLB 246; MTCW 2; MTFW 2005; SATA
115, 170

Hooper, Johnson Jones
1815-1862 .... **NCLC 177**
See also DLB 3, 11, 248; RGAL 4

Hope, A(lec) D(erwent) 1907-2000 .... **CLC 3,
51; PC 56**
See also BRWS 7; CA 21-24R; 188; CANR
33, 74; CP 1, 2, 3, 4, 5; DLB 289; EWL
3; MTCW 1, 2; MTFW 2005; PFS 8;
RGEL 2

Hope, Anthony 1863-1933 .... **TCLC 83**
See also CA 157; DLB 153, 156; RGEL 2;
RHW

Hope, Brian
See Creasey, John

Hope, Christopher 1944- .... **CLC 52**
See also AFW; CA 106; CANR 47, 101,
177; CN 4, 5, 6, 7; DLB 225; SATA 62

Hope, Christopher David Tully
See Hope, Christopher

Hopkins, Gerard Manley
1844-1889 .... **NCLC 17, 189; PC 15;
WLC 3**
See also BRW 5; BRWR 2; CDBLB 1890-
1914; DA; DA3; DAB; DAC; DAM MST,
POET; DLB 35, 57; EXPP; PAB; PFS 26;
RGEL 2; TEA; WP

Hopkins, John (Richard) 1931-1998 .. **CLC 4**
See also CA 85-88; 169; CBD; CD 5, 6

Hopkins, Pauline Elizabeth
1859-1930 .... **BLC 1:2; TCLC 28**
See also AFAW 2; BW 2, 3; CA 141; CANR
82; DAM MULT; DLB 50

Hopkinson, Francis 1737-1791 .... **LC 25**
See also DLB 31; RGAL 4

Hopley-Woolrich, Cornell George 1903-1968
See Woolrich, Cornell
See also CA 13-14; CANR 58, 156; CAP 1;
CMW 4; DLB 226; MTCW 2

Horace 65B.C.-8B.C. .... **CMLC 39; PC 46**
See also AW 2; CDWLB 1; DLB 211;
RGWL 2, 3; WLIT 8

Horatio
See Proust, (Valentin-Louis-George-Eugene)
Marcel

Hulme, Keri 1947- .... **CLC 39, 130**
See also CA 125; CANR 69; CN 4, 5, 6, 7;
CP 6, 7; CWP; DLB 326; EWL 3; FW;
INT CA-125; NFS 24

Hulme, T(homas) E(rnest)
1883-1917 .... **TCLC 21**
See also BRWS 6; CA 117; 203; DLB 19

Humboldt, Alexander von
1769-1859 .... **NCLC 170**
See also DLB 90

Humboldt, Wilhelm von
1767-1835 .... **NCLC 134**
See also DLB 90

Hume, David 1711-1776 .. **LC 7, 56, 156, 157**
See also BRWS 3; DLB 104, 252, 336;
LMFS 1; TEA

Humphrey, William 1924-1997 .... **CLC 45**
See also AMWS 9; CA 77-80; 160; CANR
68; CN 1, 2, 3, 4, 5, 6; CSW; DLB 6, 212,
234, 278; TCWW 1, 2

Humphreys, Emyr Owen 1919- .... **CLC 47**
See also CA 5-8R; CANR 3, 24; CN 1, 2,
3, 4, 5, 6, 7; DLB 15

Humphreys, Josephine 1945- ..... **CLC 34, 57**
See also CA 121; 127; CANR 97; CSW;
DLB 292; INT CA-127

Huneker, James Gibbons
1860-1921 .... **TCLC 65**
See also CA 193; DLB 71; RGAL 4

Hungerford, Hesba Fay
See Brinsmead, H(esba) F(ay)

Hungerford, Pixie
See Brinsmead, H(esba) F(ay)

Hunt, E. Howard 1918-2007 .... **CLC 3**
See also AITN 1; CA 45-48; 256; CANR 2,
47, 103, 160; CMW 4

Hunt, Everette Howard, Jr.
See Hunt, E. Howard

Hunt, Francesca
See Holland, Isabelle (Christian)

Hunt, Howard
See Hunt, E. Howard

Hunt, Kyle
See Creasey, John

Hunt, (James Henry) Leigh
1784-1859 .... **NCLC 1, 70; PC 73**
See also DAM POET; DLB 96, 110, 144;
RGEL 2; TEA

Hunt, Marsha 1946- .... **CLC 70**
See also BW 2, 3; CA 143; CANR 79

Hunt, Violet 1866(?)-1942 .... **TCLC 53**
See also CA 184; DLB 162, 197

Hunter, E. Waldo
See Sturgeon, Theodore (Hamilton)

Hunter, Evan 1926-2005 .... **CLC 11, 31**
See McBain, Ed
See also AAYA 39; BPFB 2; CA 5-8R; 241;
CANR 5, 38, 62, 97, 149; CMW 4; CN 1,
2, 3, 4, 5, 6, 7; CPW; DAM POP; DLB
306; DLBY 1982; INT CANR-5; MSW;
MTCW 1; SATA 25; SATA-Obit 167;
SFW 4

Hunter, Kristin
See Lattany, Kristin (Elaine Eggleston)
Hunter
See also CN 1, 2, 3, 4, 5, 6

Hunter, Mary
See Austin, Mary (Hunter)

Hunter, Mollie 1922- .... **CLC 21**
See McIlwraith, Maureen Mollie Hunter
See also AAYA 13, 71; BYA 6; CANR 37,
78; CLR 25; DLB 161; JRDA; MAICYA
1, 2; SAAS 7; SATA 54, 106, 139; SATA-
Essay 139; WYA; YAW

Hunter, Robert (?)-1734 .... **LC 7**

Hurston, Zora Neale 1891-1960 ..... **BLC 1:2;**
CLC 7, 30, 61; DC 12; HR 1:2; SSC 4,
80; TCLC 121, 131; WLCS
See also AAYA 15, 71; AFAW 1, 2; AMWS
6; BW 1, 3; BYA 12; CA 85-88; CANR
61; CDALBS; DA; DA3; DAC; DAM
MST, MULT, NOV; DFS 6; DLB 51, 86;
EWL 3; EXPN; EXPS; FL 1:6; FW; LAIT
3; LATS 1:1; LMFS 2; MAL 5; MBL;
MTCW 1, 2; MTFW 2005; NFS 3; RGAL
4; RGSF 2; SSFS 1, 6, 11, 19, 21; TUS;
YAW

Husserl, E. G.
See Husserl, Edmund (Gustav Albrecht)

Husserl, Edmund (Gustav Albrecht)
1859-1938 .... **TCLC 100**
See also CA 116; 133; DLB 296

Huston, John (Marcellus)
1906-1987 .... **CLC 20**
See also CA 73-76; 123; CANR 34; DLB
26

Hustvedt, Siri 1955- .... **CLC 76**
See also CA 137; CANR 149

Hutcheson, Francis 1694-1746 .... **LC 157**
See also DLB 252

Hutchinson, Lucy 1620-1675 .... **LC 149**

Hutten, Ulrich von 1488-1523 .... **LC 16**
See also DLB 179

Huxley, Aldous (Leonard)
1894-1963 .... **CLC 1, 3, 4, 5, 8, 11, 18,**
35, 79; SSC 39; WLC 3
See also AAYA 11; BPFB 2; BRW 7; CA
85-88; CANR 44, 99; CDBLB 1914-1945;
DA; DA3; DAB; DAC; DAM MST, NOV;
DLB 36, 100, 162, 195, 255; EWL 3;
EXPN; LAIT 5; LMFS 2; MTCW 1, 2;
MTFW 2005; NFS 6; RGEL 2; SATA 63;
SCFW 1, 2; SFW 4; TEA; YAW

Huxley, T(homas) H(enry)
1825-1895 .... **NCLC 67**
See also DLB 57; TEA

Huygens, Constantijn 1596-1687 .... **LC 114**
See also RGWL 2, 3

Huysmans, Joris-Karl 1848-1907 ... **TCLC 7,**
69, 212
See also CA 104; 165; DLB 123; EW 7;
GFL 1789 to the Present; LMFS 2; RGWL
2, 3

Hwang, David Henry 1957- .... **CLC 55, 196;**
DC 4, 23
See also CA 127; 132; CAD; CANR 76,
124; CD 5, 6; DA3; DAM DRAM; DFS
11, 18; DLB 212, 228, 312; INT CA-132;
MAL 5; MTCW 2; MTFW 2005; RGAL
4

Hyde, Anthony 1946- .... **CLC 42**
See Chase, Nicholas
See also CA 136; CCA 1

Hyde, Margaret O(ldroyd) 1917- ..... **CLC 21**
See also CA 1-4R; CANR 1, 36, 137; CLR
23; JRDA; MAICYA 1, 2; SAAS 8; SATA
1, 42, 76, 139

Hynes, James 1956(?)- .... **CLC 65**
See also CA 164; CANR 105

Hypatia c. 370-415 .... **CMLC 35**

Ian, Janis 1951- .... **CLC 21**
See also CA 105; 187

Ibanez, Vicente Blasco
See Blasco Ibanez, Vicente
See also DLB 322

Ibarbourou, Juana de
1895(?)-1979 .... **HLCS 2**
See also DLB 290; HW 1; LAW

Ibarguengoitia, Jorge 1928-1983 ..... **CLC 37;**
TCLC 148
See also CA 124; 113; EWL 3; HW 1

Ibn Arabi 1165-1240 .... **CMLC 105**

Ibn Battuta, Abu Abdalla
1304-1368(?) .... **CMLC 57**
See also WLIT 2

Ibn Hazm 994-1064 .... **CMLC 64**

Ibn Zaydun 1003-1070 .... **CMLC 89**

Ibsen, Henrik (Johan) 1828-1906 .. **DC 2, 30;**
TCLC 2, 8, 16, 37, 52; WLC 3
See also AAYA 46; CA 104; 141; DA; DA3;
DAB; DAC; DAM DRAM, MST; DFS 1,
6, 8, 10, 11, 15, 16, 25; EW 7; LAIT 2;
LATS 1:1; MTFW 2005; RGWL 2, 3

Ibuse, Masuji 1898-1993 .... **CLC 22**
See Ibuse Masuji
See also CA 127; 141; MJW; RGWL 3

Ibuse Masuji
See Ibuse, Masuji
See also CWW 2; DLB 180; EWL 3

Ichikawa, Kon 1915-2008 .... **CLC 20**
See also CA 121; 269

Ichiyo, Higuchi 1872-1896 .... **NCLC 49**
See also MJW

Idle, Eric 1943- .... **CLC 21**
See Monty Python
See also CA 116; CANR 35, 91, 148

Idris, Yusuf 1927-1991 .... **SSC 74**
See also AFW; EWL 3; RGSF 2, 3; RGWL
3; WLIT 2

Ignatieff, Michael 1947- .... **CLC 236**
See also CA 144; CANR 88, 156; CN 6, 7;
DLB 267

Ignatieff, Michael Grant
See Ignatieff, Michael

Ignatow, David 1914-1997 .... **CLC 4, 7, 14,**
40; PC 34
See also CA 9-12R; 162; CAAS 3; CANR
31, 57, 96; CP 1, 2, 3, 4, 5, 6; DLB 5;
EWL 3; MAL 5

Ignotus
See Strachey, (Giles) Lytton

Ihimaera, Witi (Tame) 1944- .... **CLC 46**
See also CA 77-80; CANR 130; CN 2, 3, 4,
5, 6, 7; RGSF 2; SATA 148

Il'f, Il'ia
See Fainzilberg, Ilya Arnoldovich
See also DLB 272

Ilf, Ilya
See Fainzilberg, Ilya Arnoldovich

Illyes, Gyula 1902-1983 .... **PC 16**
See also CA 114; 109; CDWLB 4; DLB
215; EWL 3; RGWL 2, 3

Imalayen, Fatima-Zohra
See Djebar, Assia

Immermann, Karl (Lebrecht)
1796-1840 .... **NCLC 4, 49**
See also DLB 133

Ince, Thomas H. 1882-1924 .... **TCLC 89**
See also IDFW 3, 4

Inchbald, Elizabeth 1753-1821 ...... **NCLC 62**
See also DLB 39, 89; RGEL 2

Inclan, Ramon (Maria) del Valle
See Valle-Inclan, Ramon (Maria) del

Infante, G(uillermo) Cabrera
See Cabrera Infante, G.

Ingalls, Rachel 1940- .... **CLC 42**
See also CA 123; 127; CANR 154

Ingalls, Rachel Holmes
See Ingalls, Rachel

Ingamells, Reginald Charles
See Ingamells, Rex

Ingamells, Rex 1913-1955 .... **TCLC 35**
See also CA 167; DLB 260

Inge, William (Motter) 1913-1973 ..... **CLC 1,**
8, 19
See also CA 9-12R; CAD; CDALB 1941-
1968; DA3; DAM DRAM; DFS 1, 3, 5,
8; DLB 7, 249; EWL 3; MAL 5; MTCW
1, 2; MTFW 2005; RGAL 4; TUS

Ingelow, Jean 1820-1897 .... **NCLC 39, 107**
See also DLB 35, 163; FANT; SATA 33
Ingram, Willis J.
See Harris, Mark
Innaurato, Albert (F.) 1948(?)- ... **CLC 21, 60**
See also CA 115; 122; CAD; CANR 78;
CD 5, 6; INT CA-122
Innes, Michael
See Stewart, J(ohn) I(nnes) M(ackintosh)
See also DLB 276; MSW
Innis, Harold Adams 1894-1952 .... **TCLC 77**
See also CA 181; DLB 88
Insluis, Alanus de
See Alain de Lille
Iola
See Wells-Barnett, Ida B(ell)
Ionesco, Eugene 1912-1994 ... **CLC 1, 4, 6, 9,**
11, 15, 41, 86; DC 12; WLC 3
See also CA 9-12R; 144; CANR 55, 132;
CWW 2; DA; DA3; DAC; DAM
DRAM, MST; DFS 4, 9, 25; DLB 321;
EW 13; EWL 3; GFL 1789 to the Present;
LMFS 2; MTCW 1, 2; MTFW 2005;
RGWL 2, 3; SATA 7; SATA-Obit 79;
TWA
Iqbal, Muhammad 1877-1938 .... **TCLC 28**
See also CA 215; EWL 3
Ireland, Patrick
See O'Doherty, Brian
Irenaeus St. 130- .... **CMLC 42**
Irigaray, Luce 1930- .... **CLC 164**
See also CA 154; CANR 121; FW
Iron, Ralph
See Schreiner, Olive (Emilie Albertina)
Irving, John 1942- . **CLC 13, 23, 38, 112, 175**
See also AAYA 8, 62; AMWS 6; BEST
89:3; BPFB 2; CA 25-28R; CANR 28, 73,
112, 133; CN 3, 4, 5, 6, 7; CPW; DA3;
DAM NOV, POP; DLB 6, 278; DLBY
1982; EWL 3; MAL 5; MTCW 1, 2;
MTFW 2005; NFS 12, 14; RGAL 4; TUS
Irving, John Winslow
See Irving, John
Irving, Washington 1783-1859 . **NCLC 2, 19,**
95; SSC 2, 37, 104; WLC 3
See also AAYA 56; AMW; CDALB 1640-
1865; CLR 97; DA; DA3; DAB; DAC;
DAM MST; DLB 3, 11, 30, 59, 73, 74,
183, 186, 250, 254; EXPS; GL 2; LAIT
1; RGAL 4; RGSF 2; SSFS 1, 8, 16;
SUFW 1; TUS; WCH; YABC 2
Irwin, P. K.
See Page, P(atricia) K(athleen)
Isaacs, Jorge Ricardo 1837-1895 ... **NCLC 70**
See also LAW
Isaacs, Susan 1943- .... **CLC 32**
See also BEST 89:1; BPFB 2; CA 89-92;
CANR 20, 41, 65, 112, 134, 165; CPW;
DA3; DAM POP; INT CANR-20; MTCW
1, 2; MTFW 2005
Isherwood, Christopher 1904-1986 ... **CLC 1,**
9, 11, 14, 44; SSC 56
See also AMWS 14; BRW 7; CA 13-16R;
117; CANR 35, 97, 133; CN 1, 2, 3; DA3;
DAM DRAM, NOV; DLB 15, 195; DLBY
1986; EWL 3; IDTP; MTCW 1, 2; MTFW
2005; RGAL 4; RGEL 2; TUS; WLIT 4
Ishiguro, Kazuo 1954- . **CLC 27, 56, 59, 110,**
219
See also AAYA 58; BEST 90:2; BPFB 2;
BRWS 4; CA 120; CANR 49, 95, 133;
CN 5, 6, 7; DA3; DAM NOV; DLB 194,
326; EWL 3; MTCW 1, 2; MTFW 2005;
NFS 13; WLIT 4; WWE 1
Ishikawa, Hakuhin
See Ishikawa, Takuboku

Ishikawa, Takuboku 1886(?)-1912 ..... **PC 10;**
TCLC 15
See Ishikawa Takuboku
See also CA 113; 153; DAM POET
Isidore of Seville c. 560-636 .... **CMLC 101**
Iskander, Fazil (Abdulovich) 1929- .. **CLC 47**
See Iskander, Fazil' Abdulevich
See also CA 102; EWL 3
Iskander, Fazil' Abdulevich
See Iskander, Fazil (Abdulovich)
See also DLB 302
Isler, Alan (David) 1934- .... **CLC 91**
See also CA 156; CANR 105
Ivan IV 1530-1584 .... **LC 17**
Ivanov, V.I.
See Ivanov, Vyacheslav
Ivanov, Vyacheslav 1866-1949 .... **TCLC 33**
See also CA 122; EWL 3
Ivanov, Vyacheslav Ivanovich
See Ivanov, Vyacheslav
Ivask, Ivar Vidrik 1927-1992 .... **CLC 14**
See also CA 37-40R; 139; CANR 24
Ives, Morgan
See Bradley, Marion Zimmer
See also GLL 1
Izumi Shikibu c. 973-c. 1034 .... **CMLC 33**
J. R. S.
See Gogarty, Oliver St. John
Jabran, Kahlil
See Gibran, Kahlil
Jabran, Khalil
See Gibran, Kahlil
Jackson, Daniel
See Wingrove, David
Jackson, Helen Hunt 1830-1885 .... **NCLC 90**
See also DLB 42, 47, 186, 189; RGAL 4
Jackson, Jesse 1908-1983 .... **CLC 12**
See also BW 1; CA 25-28R; 109; CANR
27; CLR 28; CWRI 5; MAICYA 1, 2;
SATA 2, 29; SATA-Obit 48
Jackson, Laura (Riding) 1901-1991 .... **PC 44**
See Riding, Laura
See also CA 65-68; 135; CANR 28, 89;
DLB 48
Jackson, Sam
See Trumbo, Dalton
Jackson, Sara
See Wingrove, David
Jackson, Shirley 1919-1965 . **CLC 11, 60, 87;**
SSC 9, 39; TCLC 187; WLC 3
See also AAYA 9; AMWS 9; BPFB 2; CA
1-4R; 25-28R; CANR 4, 52; CDALB
1941-1968; DA; DA3; DAC; DAM MST;
DLB 6, 234; EXPS; HGG; LAIT 4; MAL
5; MTCW 2; MTFW 2005; RGAL 4;
RGSF 2; SATA 2; SSFS 1; SUFW 1, 2
Jacob, (Cyprien-)Max 1876-1944 .... **TCLC 6**
See also CA 104; 193; DLB 258; EWL 3;
GFL 1789 to the Present; GLL 2; RGWL
2, 3
Jacobs, Harriet A(nn)
1813(?)-1897 .... **NCLC 67, 162**
See also AFAW 1, 2; DLB 239; FL 1:3; FW;
LAIT 2; RGAL 4
Jacobs, Jim 1942- .... **CLC 12**
See also CA 97-100; INT CA-97-100
Jacobs, W(illiam) W(ymark)
1863-1943 .... **SSC 73; TCLC 22**
See also CA 121; 167; DLB 135; EXPS;
HGG; RGEL 2; RGSF 2; SSFS 2; SUFW
1
Jacobsen, Jens Peter 1847-1885 .... **NCLC 34**
Jacobsen, Josephine (Winder)
1908-2003 .... **CLC 48, 102; PC 62**
See also CA 33-36R; 218; CAAS 18; CANR
23, 48; CCA 1; CP 2, 3, 4, 5, 6, 7; DLB
244; PFS 23; TCLE 1:1

Jacobson, Dan 1929- ...... **CLC 4, 14; SSC 91**
See also AFW; CA 1-4R; CANR 2, 25, 66,
170; CN 1, 2, 3, 4, 5, 6, 7; DLB 14, 207,
225, 319; EWL 3; MTCW 1; RGSF 2
Jacopone da Todi 1236-1306 .... **CMLC 95**
Jacqueline
See Carpentier (y Valmont), Alejo
Jacques de Vitry c. 1160-1240 ...... **CMLC 63**
See also DLB 208
Jagger, Michael Philip
See Jagger, Mick
Jagger, Mick 1943- .... **CLC 17**
See also CA 239
Jahiz, al- c. 780-c. 869 .... **CMLC 25**
See also DLB 311
Jakes, John 1932- .... **CLC 29**
See also AAYA 32; BEST 89:4; BPFB 2;
CA 57-60, 214; CAAE 214; CANR 10,
43, 66, 111, 142, 171; CPW; CSW; DA3;
DAM NOV, POP; DLB 278; DLBY 1983;
FANT; INT CANR-10; MTCW 1, 2;
MTFW 2005; RHW; SATA 62; SFW 4;
TCWW 1, 2
Jakes, John William
See Jakes, John
James I 1394-1437 .... **LC 20**
See also RGEL 2
James, Andrew
See Kirkup, James
James, C(yril) L(ionel) R(obert)
1901-1989 .... **BLCS; CLC 33**
See also BW 2; CA 117; 125; 128; CANR
62; CN 1, 2, 3, 4; DLB 125; MTCW 1
James, Daniel (Lewis) 1911-1988
See Santiago, Danny
See also CA 174; 125
James, Dynely
See Mayne, William (James Carter)
James, Henry Sr. 1811-1882 .... **NCLC 53**
James, Henry 1843-1916 .... **SSC 8, 32, 47,**
108; TCLC 2, 11, 24, 40, 47, 64, 171;
WLC 3
See also AMW; AMWC 1; AMWR 1; BPFB
2; BRW 6; CA 104; 132; CDALB 1865-
1917; DA; DA3; DAB; DAC; DAM MST,
NOV; DLB 12, 71, 74, 189; DLBD 13;
EWL 3; EXPS; GL 2; HGG; LAIT 2;
MAL 5; MTCW 1, 2; MTFW 2005; NFS
12, 16, 19; RGAL 4; RGEL 2; RGSF 2;
SSFS 9; SUFW 1; TUS
James, M. R. .... **SSC 93**
See James, Montague (Rhodes)
See also DLB 156, 201
James, Mary
See Meaker, Marijane
James, Montague (Rhodes)
1862-1936 .... **SSC 16; TCLC 6**
See James, M. R.
See also CA 104; 203; HGG; RGEL 2;
RGSF 2; SUFW 1
James, P. D. .... **CLC 18, 46, 122, 226**
See White, Phyllis Dorothy James
See also BEST 90:2; BPFB 2; BRWS 4;
CDBLB 1960 to Present; CN 4, 5, 6; DLB
87, 276; DLBD 17; MSW
James, Philip
See Moorcock, Michael
James, Samuel
See Stephens, James
James, Seumas
See Stephens, James
James, Stephen
See Stephens, James
James, William 1842-1910 .... **TCLC 15, 32**
See also AMW; CA 109; 193; DLB 270,
284; MAL 5; NCFS 5; RGAL 4
Jameson, Anna 1794-1860 .... **NCLC 43**
See also DLB 99, 166

Jameson, Fredric 1934- .... **CLC 142**
 See also CA 196; CANR 169; DLB 67;
 LMFS 2
Jameson, Fredric R.
 See Jameson, Fredric
James VI of Scotland 1566-1625 .... **LC 109**
 See also DLB 151, 172
Jami, Nur al-Din 'Abd al-Rahman
 1414-1492 .... **LC 9**
Jammes, Francis 1868-1938 .... **TCLC 75**
 See also CA 198; EWL 3; GFL 1789 to the
 Present
Jandl, Ernst 1925-2000 .... **CLC 34**
 See also CA 200; EWL 3
Janowitz, Tama 1957- .... **CLC 43, 145**
 See also CA 106; CANR 52, 89, 129; CN
 5, 6, 7; CPW; DAM POP; DLB 292;
 MTFW 2005
Jansson, Tove (Marika) 1914-2001 ... **SSC 96**
 See also CA 17-20R; 196; CANR 38, 118;
 CLR 2, 125; CWW 2; DLB 257; EWL 3;
 MAICYA 1, 2; RGSF 2; SATA 3, 41
Japrisot, Sebastien 1931- .... **CLC 90**
 See Rossi, Jean-Baptiste
 See also CMW 4; NFS 18
Jarrell, Randall 1914-1965 .... **CLC 1, 2, 6, 9,
 13, 49; PC 41; TCLC 177**
 See also AMW; BYA 5; CA 5-8R; 25-28R;
 CABS 2; CANR 6, 34; CDALB 1941-
 1968; CLR 6, 111; CWRI 5; DAM POET;
 DLB 48, 52; EWL 3; EXPP; MAICYA 1,
 2; MAL 5; MTCW 1, 2; PAB; PFS 2;
 RGAL 4; SATA 7
Jarry, Alfred 1873-1907 .... **SSC 20; TCLC 2,
 14, 147**
 See also CA 104; 153; DA3; DAM DRAM;
 DFS 8; DLB 192, 258; EW 9; EWL 3;
 GFL 1789 to the Present; RGWL 2, 3;
 TWA
Jarvis, E.K.
 See Ellison, Harlan; Silverberg, Robert
Jawien, Andrzej
 See John Paul II, Pope
Jaynes, Roderick
 See Coen, Ethan
Jeake, Samuel, Jr.
 See Aiken, Conrad (Potter)
Jean Paul 1763-1825 .... **NCLC 7**
Jefferies, (John) Richard
 1848-1887 .... **NCLC 47**
 See also DLB 98, 141; RGEL 2; SATA 16;
 SFW 4
Jeffers, John Robinson
 See Jeffers, Robinson
Jeffers, Robinson 1887-1962 .... **CLC 2, 3, 11,
 15, 54; PC 17; WLC 3**
 See also AMWS 2; CA 85-88; CANR 35;
 CDALB 1917-1929; DA; DAC; DAM
 MST, POET; DLB 45, 212, 342; EWL 3;
 MAL 5; MTCW 1, 2; MTFW 2005; PAB;
 PFS 3, 4; RGAL 4
Jefferson, Janet
 See Mencken, H(enry) L(ouis)
Jefferson, Thomas 1743-1826 . **NCLC 11, 103**
 See also AAYA 54; ANW; CDALB 1640-
 1865; DA3; DLB 31, 183; LAIT 1; RGAL
 4
Jeffrey, Francis 1773-1850 .... **NCLC 33**
 See Francis, Lord Jeffrey
Jelakowitch, Ivan
 See Heijermans, Herman
Jelinek, Elfriede 1946- .... **CLC 169**
 See also AAYA 68; CA 154; CANR 169;
 DLB 85, 330; FW
Jellicoe, (Patricia) Ann 1927- .... **CLC 27**
 See also CA 85-88; CBD; CD 5, 6; CWD;
 CWRI 5; DLB 13, 233; FW
Jelloun, Tahar ben
 See Ben Jelloun, Tahar

Jemyma
 See Holley, Marietta
Jen, Gish .... **AAL; CLC 70, 198, 260**
 See Jen, Lillian
 See also AMWC 2; CN 7; DLB 312
Jen, Lillian 1955-
 See Jen, Gish
 See also CA 135; CANR 89, 130
Jenkins, (John) Robin 1912- .... **CLC 52**
 See also CA 1-4R; CANR 1, 135; CN 1, 2,
 3, 4, 5, 6, 7; DLB 14, 271
Jennings, Elizabeth (Joan)
 1926-2001 .... **CLC 5, 14, 131**
 See also BRWS 5; CA 61-64; 200; CAAS
 5; CANR 8, 39, 66, 127; CP 1, 2, 3, 4, 5,
 6, 7; CWP; DLB 27; EWL 3; MTCW 1;
 SATA 66
Jennings, Waylon 1937-2002 .... **CLC 21**
Jensen, Johannes V(ilhelm)
 1873-1950 .... **TCLC 41**
 See also CA 170; DLB 214, 330; EWL 3;
 RGWL 3
Jensen, Laura (Linnea) 1948- .... **CLC 37**
 See also CA 103
Jerome, Saint 345-420 .... **CMLC 30**
 See also RGWL 3
Jerome, Jerome K(lapka)
 1859-1927 .... **TCLC 23**
 See also CA 119; 177; DLB 10, 34, 135;
 RGEL 2
Jerrold, Douglas William
 1803-1857 .... **NCLC 2**
 See also DLB 158, 159, 344; RGEL 2
Jewett, (Theodora) Sarah Orne
 1849-1909 . **SSC 6, 44, 110; TCLC 1, 22**
 See also AAYA 76; AMW; AMWC 2;
 AMWR 2; CA 108; 127; CANR 71; DLB
 12, 74, 221; EXPS; FL 1:3; FW; MAL 5;
 MBL; NFS 15; RGAL 4; RGSF 2; SATA
 15; SSFS 4
Jewsbury, Geraldine (Endsor)
 1812-1880 .... **NCLC 22**
 See also DLB 21
Jhabvala, Ruth Prawer 1927- . **CLC 4, 8, 29,
 94, 138; SSC 91**
 See also BRWS 5; CA 1-4R; CANR 2, 29,
 51, 74, 91, 128; CN 1, 2, 3, 4, 5, 6, 7;
 DAB; DAM NOV; DLB 139, 194, 323,
 326; EWL 3; IDFW 3, 4; INT CANR-29;
 MTCW 1, 2; MTFW 2005; RGSF 2;
 RGWL 2; RHW; TEA
Jibran, Kahlil
 See Gibran, Kahlil
Jibran, Khalil
 See Gibran, Kahlil
Jiles, Paulette 1943- .... **CLC 13, 58**
 See also CA 101; CANR 70, 124, 170; CP
 5; CWP
Jimenez (Mantecon), Juan Ramon
 1881-1958 .... **HLC 1; PC 7; TCLC 4,
 183**
 See also CA 104; 131; CANR 74; DAM
 MULT, POET; DLB 134, 330; EW 9;
 EWL 3; HW 1; MTCW 1, 2; MTFW
 2005; RGWL 2, 3
Jimenez, Ramon
 See Jimenez (Mantecon), Juan Ramon
Jimenez Mantecon, Juan
 See Jimenez (Mantecon), Juan Ramon
Jin, Ba 1904-2005
 See Pa Chin
 See also CA 244; CWW 2; DLB 328
Jin, Xuefei
 See Ha Jin
Jodelle, Etienne 1532-1573 .... **LC 119**
 See also DLB 327; GFL Beginnings to 1789
Joel, Billy .... **CLC 26**
 See Joel, William Martin

Joel, William Martin 1949-
 See Joel, Billy
 See also CA 108
John, St.
 See John of Damascus, St.
John of Damascus, St. c.
 675-749 .... **CMLC 27, 95**
John of Salisbury c. 1115-1180 ..... **CMLC 63**
John of the Cross, St. 1542-1591 .... **LC 18,
 146**
 See also RGWL 2, 3
John Paul II, Pope 1920-2005 .... **CLC 128**
 See also CA 106; 133; 238
Johnson, B(ryan) S(tanley William)
 1933-1973 .... **CLC 6, 9**
 See also CA 9-12R; 53-56; CANR 9; CN 1;
 CP 1, 2; DLB 14, 40; EWL 3; RGEL 2
Johnson, Benjamin F., of Boone
 See Riley, James Whitcomb
Johnson, Charles (Richard) 1948- . **BLC 1:2,
 2:2; CLC 7, 51, 65, 163**
 See also AFAW 2; AMWS 6; BW 2, 3; CA
 116; CAAS 18; CANR 42, 66, 82, 129;
 CN 5, 6, 7; DAM MULT; DLB 33, 278;
 MAL 5; MTCW 2; MTFW 2005; RGAL
 4; SSFS 16
Johnson, Charles S(purgeon)
 1893-1956 .... **HR 1:3**
 See also BW 1, 3; CA 125; CANR 82; DLB
 51, 91
Johnson, Denis 1949- . **CLC 52, 160; SSC 56**
 See also CA 117; 121; CANR 71, 99, 178;
 CN 4, 5, 6, 7; DLB 120
Johnson, Diane 1934- ...... **CLC 5, 13, 48, 244**
 See also BPFB 2; CA 41-44R; CANR 17,
 40, 62, 95, 155; CN 4, 5, 6, 7; DLBY
 1980; INT CANR-17; MTCW 1
Johnson, E(mily) Pauline 1861-1913 . **NNAL**
 See also CA 150; CCA 1; DAC; DAM
 MULT; DLB 92, 175; TCWW 2
Johnson, Eyvind (Olof Verner)
 1900-1976 .... **CLC 14**
 See also CA 73-76; 69-72; CANR 34, 101;
 DLB 259, 330; EW 12; EWL 3
Johnson, Fenton 1888-1958 .... **BLC 1:2**
 See also BW 1; CA 118; 124; DAM MULT;
 DLB 45, 50
Johnson, Georgia Douglas (Camp)
 1880-1966 .... **HR 1:3**
 See also BW 1; CA 125; DLB 51, 249; WP
Johnson, Helene 1907-1995 .... **HR 1:3**
 See also CA 181; DLB 51; WP
Johnson, J. R.
 See James, C(yril) L(ionel) R(obert)
Johnson, James Weldon
 1871-1938 .... **BLC 1:2; HR 1:3; PC 24;
 TCLC 3, 19, 175**
 See also AAYA 73; AFAW 1, 2; BW 1, 3;
 CA 104; 125; CANR 82; CDALB 1917-
 1929; CLR 32; DA3; DAM MULT, POET;
 DLB 51; EWL 3; EXPP; LMFS 2; MAL
 5; MTCW 1, 2; MTFW 2005; NFS 22;
 PFS 1; RGAL 4; SATA 31; TUS
Johnson, Joyce 1935- .... **CLC 58**
 See also BG 1:3; CA 125; 129; CANR 102
Johnson, Judith (Emlyn) 1936- .... **CLC 7, 15**
 See Sherwin, Judith Johnson
 See also CA 25-28R; 153; CANR 34; CP 6,
 7
Johnson, Lionel (Pigot)
 1867-1902 .... **TCLC 19**
 See also CA 117; 209; DLB 19; RGEL 2
Johnson, Marguerite Annie
 See Angelou, Maya
Johnson, Mel
 See Malzberg, Barry N(athaniel)

Johnson, Pamela Hansford
1912-1981 .... **CLC 1, 7, 27**
See also CA 1-4R; 104; CANR 2, 28; CN 1, 2, 3; DLB 15; MTCW 1, 2; MTFW 2005; RGEL 2

Johnson, Paul 1928- .... **CLC 147**
See also BEST 89:4; CA 17-20R; CANR 34, 62, 100, 155

Johnson, Paul Bede
See Johnson, Paul

Johnson, Robert .... **CLC 70**

Johnson, Robert 1911(?)-1938 .... **TCLC 69**
See also BW 3; CA 174

Johnson, Samuel 1709-1784 . **LC 15, 52, 128; PC 81; WLC 3**
See also BRW 3; BRWR 1; CDBLB 1660-1789; DA; DAB; DAC; DAM MST; DLB 39, 95, 104, 142, 213; LMFS 1; RGEL 2; TEA

Johnson, Uwe 1934-1984 .. **CLC 5, 10, 15, 40**
See also CA 1-4R; 112; CANR 1, 39; CD-WLB 2; DLB 75; EWL 3; MTCW 1; RGWL 2, 3

Johnston, Basil H. 1929- .... **NNAL**
See also CA 69-72; CANR 11, 28, 66; DAC; DAM MULT; DLB 60

Johnston, George (Benson) 1913- .... **CLC 51**
See also CA 1-4R; CANR 5, 20; CP 1, 2, 3, 4, 5, 6, 7; DLB 88

Johnston, Jennifer (Prudence)
1930- .... **CLC 7, 150, 228**
See also CA 85-88; CANR 92; CN 4, 5, 6, 7; DLB 14

Joinville, Jean de 1224(?)-1317 ..... **CMLC 38**

Jolley, Elizabeth 1923-2007 ..... **CLC 46, 256, 260; SSC 19**
See also CA 127; 257; CAAS 13; CANR 59; CN 4, 5, 6, 7; DLB 325; EWL 3; RGSF 2

Jolley, Monica Elizabeth
See Jolley, Elizabeth

Jones, Arthur Llewellyn 1863-1947
See Machen, Arthur
See also CA 104; 179; HGG

Jones, D(ouglas) G(ordon) 1929- ..... **CLC 10**
See also CA 29-32R; CANR 13, 90; CP 1, 2, 3, 4, 5, 6, 7; DLB 53

Jones, David (Michael) 1895-1974 .... **CLC 2, 4, 7, 13, 42**
See also BRW 6; BRWS 7; CA 9-12R; 53-56; CANR 28; CDBLB 1945-1960; CP 1, 2; DLB 20, 100; EWL 3; MTCW 1; PAB; RGEL 2

Jones, David Robert 1947-
See Bowie, David
See also CA 103; CANR 104

Jones, Diana Wynne 1934- .... **CLC 26**
See also AAYA 12; BYA 6, 7, 9, 11, 13, 16; CA 49-52; CANR 4, 26, 56, 120, 167; CLR 23, 120; DLB 161; FANT; JRDA; MAICYA 1, 2; MTFW 2005; SAAS 7; SATA 9, 70, 108, 160; SFW 4; SUFW 2; YAW

Jones, Edward P. 1950- .. **BLC 2:2; CLC 76, 223**
See also AAYA 71; BW 2, 3; CA 142; CANR 79, 134; CSW; MTFW 2005; NFS 26

Jones, Everett LeRoi
See Baraka, Amiri

Jones, Gayl 1949- ... **BLC 1:2; CLC 6, 9, 131**
See also AFAW 1, 2; BW 2, 3; CA 77-80; CANR 27, 66, 122; CN 4, 5, 6, 7; CSW; DA3; DAM MULT; DLB 33, 278; MAL 5; MTCW 1, 2; MTFW 2005; RGAL 4

Jones, James 1921-1977 ...... **CLC 1, 3, 10, 39**
See also AITN 1, 2; AMWS 11; BPFB 2; CA 1-4R; 69-72; CANR 6; CN 1, 2; DLB 2, 143; DLBD 17; DLBY 1998; EWL 3; MAL 5; MTCW 1; RGAL 4

Jones, John J.
See Lovecraft, H. P.

Jones, LeRoi .... **CLC 1, 2, 3, 5, 10, 14**
See Baraka, Amiri
See also CN 1, 2; CP 1, 2, 3; MTCW 2

Jones, Louis B. 1953- .... **CLC 65**
See also CA 141; CANR 73

Jones, Madison 1925- .... **CLC 4**
See also CA 13-16R; CAAS 11; CANR 7, 54, 83, 158; CN 1, 2, 3, 4, 5, 6, 7; CSW; DLB 152

Jones, Madison Percy, Jr.
See Jones, Madison

Jones, Mervyn 1922- .... **CLC 10, 52**
See also CA 45-48; CAAS 5; CANR 1, 91; CN 1, 2, 3, 4, 5, 6, 7; MTCW 1

Jones, Mick 1956(?)- .... **CLC 30**

Jones, Nettie (Pearl) 1941- .... **CLC 34**
See also BW 2; CA 137; CAAS 20; CANR 88

Jones, Peter 1802-1856 .... **NNAL**

Jones, Preston 1936-1979 .... **CLC 10**
See also CA 73-76; 89-92; DLB 7

Jones, Robert F(rancis) 1934-2003 .... **CLC 7**
See also CA 49-52; CANR 2, 61, 118

Jones, Rod 1953- .... **CLC 50**
See also CA 128

Jones, Terence Graham Parry
1942- .... **CLC 21**
See Jones, Terry; Monty Python
See also CA 112; 116; CANR 35, 93, 173; INT CA-116; SATA 127

Jones, Terry
See Jones, Terence Graham Parry
See also SATA 67; SATA-Brief 51

Jones, Thom (Douglas) 1945(?)- ..... **CLC 81; SSC 56**
See also CA 157; CANR 88; DLB 244; SSFS 23

Jong, Erica 1942- .... **CLC 4, 6, 8, 18, 83**
See also AITN 1; AMWS 5; BEST 90:2; BPFB 2; CA 73-76; CANR 26, 52, 75, 132, 166; CN 3, 4, 5, 6, 7; CP 2, 3, 4, 5, 6, 7; CPW; DA3; DAM NOV, POP; DLB 2, 5, 28, 152; FW; INT CANR-26; MAL 5; MTCW 1, 2; MTFW 2005

Jonson, Ben(jamin) 1572(?)-1637 . **DC 4; LC 6, 33, 110; PC 17; WLC 3**
See also BRW 1; BRWC 1; BRWR 1; CD-BLB Before 1660; DA; DAB; DAC; DAM DRAM, MST, POET; DFS 4, 10; DLB 62, 121; LMFS 1; PFS 23; RGEL 2; TEA; WLIT 3

Jordan, June 1936-2002 .. **BLCS; CLC 5, 11, 23, 114, 230; PC 38**
See also AAYA 2, 66; AFAW 1, 2; BW 2, 3; CA 33-36R; 206; CANR 25, 70, 114, 154; CLR 10; CP 3, 4, 5, 6, 7; CWP; DAM MULT, POET; DLB 38; GLL 2; LAIT 5; MAICYA 1, 2; MTCW 1; SATA 4, 136; YAW

Jordan, June Meyer
See Jordan, June

Jordan, Neil 1950- .... **CLC 110**
See also CA 124; 130; CANR 54, 154; CN 4, 5, 6, 7; GLL 2; INT CA-130

Jordan, Neil Patrick
See Jordan, Neil

Jordan, Pat(rick M.) 1941- .... **CLC 37**
See also CA 33-36R; CANR 121

Jorgensen, Ivar
See Ellison, Harlan

Jorgenson, Ivar
See Silverberg, Robert

Joseph, George Ghevarughese .... **CLC 70**

Josephson, Mary
See O'Doherty, Brian

Josephus, Flavius c. 37-100 ..... **CMLC 13, 93**
See also AW 2; DLB 176; WLIT 8

Josiah Allen's Wife
See Holley, Marietta

Josipovici, Gabriel 1940- ...... **CLC 6, 43, 153**
See also CA 37-40R; 224; CAAE 224; CAAS 8; CANR 47, 84; CN 3, 4, 5, 6, 7; DLB 14, 319

Josipovici, Gabriel David
See Josipovici, Gabriel

Joubert, Joseph 1754-1824 .... **NCLC 9**

Jouve, Pierre Jean 1887-1976 .... **CLC 47**
See also CA 252; 65-68; DLB 258; EWL 3

Jovine, Francesco 1902-1950 .... **TCLC 79**
See also DLB 264; EWL 3

Joyaux, Julia
See Kristeva, Julia

Joyce, James (Augustine Aloysius)
1882-1941 .... **DC 16; PC 22; SSC 3, 26, 44, 64; TCLC 3, 8, 16, 35, 52, 159; WLC 3**
See also AAYA 42; BRW 7; BRWC 1; BRWR 1; BYA 11, 13; CA 104; 126; CD-BLB 1914-1945; DA; DA3; DAB; DAC; DAM MST, NOV, POET; DLB 10, 19, 36, 162, 247; EWL 3; EXPN; EXPS; LAIT 3; LMFS 1, 2; MTCW 1, 2; MTFW 2005; NFS 7, 26; RGSF 2; SSFS 1, 19; TEA; WLIT 4

Jozsef, Attila 1905-1937 .... **TCLC 22**
See also CA 116; 230; CDWLB 4; DLB 215; EWL 3

Juana Ines de la Cruz, Sor
1651(?)-1695 ... **HLCS 1; LC 5, 136; PC 24**
See also DLB 305; FW; LAW; RGWL 2, 3; WLIT 1

Juana Inez de La Cruz, Sor
See Juana Ines de la Cruz, Sor

Juan Manuel, Don 1282-1348 .... **CMLC 88**

Judd, Cyril
See Kornbluth, C(yril) M.; Pohl, Frederik

Juenger, Ernst 1895-1998 .... **CLC 125**
See Junger, Ernst
See also CA 101; 167; CANR 21, 47, 106; DLB 56

Julian of Norwich 1342(?)-1416(?) . **LC 6, 52**
See also BRWS 12; DLB 146; LMFS 1

Julius Caesar 100B.C.-44B.C.
See Caesar, Julius
See also CDWLB 1; DLB 211

Jung, Patricia B.
See Hope, Christopher

Junger, Ernst
See Juenger, Ernst
See also CDWLB 2; EWL 3; RGWL 2, 3

Junger, Sebastian 1962- .... **CLC 109**
See also AAYA 28; CA 165; CANR 130, 171; MTFW 2005

Juniper, Alex
See Hospital, Janette Turner

Junius
See Luxemburg, Rosa

Junzaburo, Nishiwaki
See Nishiwaki, Junzaburo
See also EWL 3

Just, Ward 1935- .... **CLC 4, 27**
See also CA 25-28R; CANR 32, 87; CN 6, 7; DLB 335; INT CANR-32

Just, Ward Swift
See Just, Ward

Justice, Donald 1925-2004 ... **CLC 6, 19, 102; PC 64**
See also AMWS 7; CA 5-8R; 230; CANR 26, 54, 74, 121, 122, 169; CP 1, 2, 3, 4, 5, 6, 7; CSW; DAM POET; DLBY 1983; EWL 3; INT CANR-26; MAL 5; MTCW 2; PFS 14; TCLE 1:1
Justice, Donald Rodney
See Justice, Donald
Juvenal c. 60-c. 130 .... **CMLC 8**
See also AW 2; CDWLB 1; DLB 211; RGWL 2, 3; WLIT 8
Juvenis
See Bourne, Randolph S(illiman)
K., Alice
See Knapp, Caroline
Kabakov, Sasha .... **CLC 59**
Kabir 1398(?)-1448(?) .... **LC 109; PC 56**
See also RGWL 2, 3
Kacew, Romain 1914-1980
See Gary, Romain
See also CA 108; 102
Kadare, Ismail 1936- .... **CLC 52, 190**
See also CA 161; CANR 165; EWL 3; RGWL 3
Kadohata, Cynthia 1956(?)- ..... **CLC 59, 122**
See also AAYA 71; CA 140; CANR 124; CLR 121; SATA 155, 180
Kafka, Franz 1883-1924 ... **SSC 5, 29, 35, 60; TCLC 2, 6, 13, 29, 47, 53, 112, 179; WLC 3**
See also AAYA 31; BPFB 2; CA 105; 126; CDWLB 2; DA; DA3; DAB; DAC; DAM MST, NOV; DLB 81; EW 9; EWL 3; EXPS; LATS 1:1; LMFS 2; MTCW 1, 2; MTFW 2005; NFS 7; RGSF 2; RGWL 2, 3; SFW 4; SSFS 3, 7, 12; TWA
Kafu
See Nagai, Sokichi
See also MJW
Kahanovitch, Pinchas
See Der Nister
Kahanovitsch, Pinkhes
See Der Nister
Kahanovitsh, Pinkhes
See Der Nister
Kahn, Roger 1927- .... **CLC 30**
See also CA 25-28R; CANR 44, 69, 152; DLB 171; SATA 37
Kain, Saul
See Sassoon, Siegfried (Lorraine)
Kaiser, Georg 1878-1945 .... **TCLC 9**
See also CA 106; 190; CDWLB 2; DLB 124; EWL 3; LMFS 2; RGWL 2, 3
Kaledin, Sergei .... **CLC 59**
Kaletski, Alexander 1946- .... **CLC 39**
See also CA 118; 143
Kalidasa fl. c. 400-455 .... **CMLC 9; PC 22**
See also RGWL 2, 3
Kallman, Chester (Simon) 1921-1975 .... **CLC 2**
See also CA 45-48; 53-56; CANR 3; CP 1, 2
Kaminsky, Melvin .... **CLC 12, 217**
See Brooks, Mel
See also AAYA 13, 48; DLB 26
Kaminsky, Stuart M. 1934- .... **CLC 59**
See also CA 73-76; CANR 29, 53, 89, 161; CMW 4
Kaminsky, Stuart Melvin
See Kaminsky, Stuart M.
Kamo no Chomei 1153(?)-1216 .... **CMLC 66**
See also DLB 203
Kamo no Nagaakira
See Kamo no Chomei
Kandinsky, Wassily 1866-1944 .... **TCLC 92**
See also AAYA 64; CA 118; 155
Kane, Francis
See Robbins, Harold

Kane, Henry 1918-
See Queen, Ellery
See also CA 156; CMW 4
Kane, Paul
See Simon, Paul
Kane, Sarah 1971-1999 .... **DC 31**
See also BRWS 8; CA 190; CD 5, 6; DLB 310
Kanin, Garson 1912-1999 .... **CLC 22**
See also AITN 1; CA 5-8R; 177; CAD; CANR 7, 78; DLB 7; IDFW 3, 4
Kaniuk, Yoram 1930- .... **CLC 19**
See also CA 134; DLB 299; RGHL
Kant, Immanuel 1724-1804 ..... **NCLC 27, 67**
See also DLB 94
Kantor, MacKinlay 1904-1977 .... **CLC 7**
See also CA 61-64; 73-76; CANR 60, 63; CN 1, 2; DLB 9, 102; MAL 5; MTCW 2; RHW; TCWW 1, 2
Kanze Motokiyo
See Zeami
Kaplan, David Michael 1946- .... **CLC 50**
See also CA 187
Kaplan, James 1951- .... **CLC 59**
See also CA 135; CANR 121
Karadzic, Vuk Stefanovic 1787-1864 .... **NCLC 115**
See also CDWLB 4; DLB 147
Karageorge, Michael
See Anderson, Poul
Karamzin, Nikolai Mikhailovich 1766-1826 .... **NCLC 3, 173**
See also DLB 150; RGSF 2
Karapanou, Margarita 1946- .... **CLC 13**
See also CA 101
Karinthy, Frigyes 1887-1938 .... **TCLC 47**
See also CA 170; DLB 215; EWL 3
Karl, Frederick R(obert) 1927-2004 .... **CLC 34**
See also CA 5-8R; 226; CANR 3, 44, 143
Karr, Mary 1955- .... **CLC 188**
See also AMWS 11; CA 151; CANR 100; MTFW 2005; NCFS 5
Kastel, Warren
See Silverberg, Robert
Kataev, Evgeny Petrovich 1903-1942
See Petrov, Evgeny
See also CA 120
Kataphusin
See Ruskin, John
Katz, Steve 1935- .... **CLC 47**
See also CA 25-28R; CAAS 14, 64; CANR 12; CN 4, 5, 6, 7; DLBY 1983
Kauffman, Janet 1945- .... **CLC 42**
See also CA 117; CANR 43, 84; DLB 218; DLBY 1986
Kaufman, Bob (Garnell) 1925-1986 .... **CLC 49; PC 74**
See also BG 1:3; BW 1; CA 41-44R; 118; CANR 22; CP 1; DLB 16, 41
Kaufman, George S. 1889-1961 ...... **CLC 38; DC 17**
See also CA 108; 93-96; DAM DRAM; DFS 1, 10; DLB 7; INT CA-108; MTCW 2; MTFW 2005; RGAL 4; TUS
Kaufman, Moises 1964- .... **DC 26**
See also CA 211; DFS 22; MTFW 2005
Kaufman, Sue .... **CLC 3, 8**
See Barondess, Sue K(aufman)
Kavafis, Konstantinos Petrou 1863-1933
See Cavafy, C(onstantine) P(eter)
See also CA 104
Kavan, Anna 1901-1968 .... **CLC 5, 13, 82**
See also BRWS 7; CA 5-8R; CANR 6, 57; DLB 255; MTCW 1; RGEL 2; SFW 4
Kavanagh, Dan
See Barnes, Julian

Kavanagh, Julie 1952- .... **CLC 119**
See also CA 163
Kavanagh, Patrick (Joseph) 1904-1967 .... **CLC 22; PC 33**
See also BRWS 7; CA 123; 25-28R; DLB 15, 20; EWL 3; MTCW 1; RGEL 2
Kawabata, Yasunari 1899-1972 ..... **CLC 2, 5, 9, 18, 107; SSC 17**
See Kawabata Yasunari
See also CA 93-96; 33-36R; CANR 88; DAM MULT; DLB 330; MJW; MTCW 2; MTFW 2005; RGSF 2; RGWL 2, 3
Kawabata Yasunari
See Kawabata, Yasunari
See also DLB 180; EWL 3
Kaye, Mary Margaret
See Kaye, M.M.
Kaye, M.M. 1908-2004 .... **CLC 28**
See also CA 89-92; 223; CANR 24, 60, 102, 142; MTCW 1, 2; MTFW 2005; RHW; SATA 62; SATA-Obit 152
Kaye, Mollie
See Kaye, M.M.
Kaye-Smith, Sheila 1887-1956 .... **TCLC 20**
See also CA 118; 203; DLB 36
Kaymor, Patrice Maguilene
See Senghor, Leopold Sedar
Kazakov, Iurii Pavlovich
See Kazakov, Yuri Pavlovich
See also DLB 302
Kazakov, Yuri Pavlovich 1927-1982 . **SSC 43**
See Kazakov, Iurii Pavlovich; Kazakov, Yury
See also CA 5-8R; CANR 36; MTCW 1; RGSF 2
Kazakov, Yury
See Kazakov, Yuri Pavlovich
See also EWL 3
Kazan, Elia 1909-2003 .... **CLC 6, 16, 63**
See also CA 21-24R; 220; CANR 32, 78
Kazantzakis, Nikos 1883(?)-1957 .... **TCLC 2, 5, 33, 181**
See also BPFB 2; CA 105; 132; DA3; EW 9; EWL 3; MTCW 1, 2; MTFW 2005; RGWL 2, 3
Kazin, Alfred 1915-1998 ..... **CLC 34, 38, 119**
See also AMWS 8; CA 1-4R; CAAS 7; CANR 1, 45, 79; DLB 67; EWL 3
Keane, Mary Nesta (Skrine) 1904-1996
See Keane, Molly
See also CA 108; 114; 151; RHW
Keane, Molly .... **CLC 31**
See Keane, Mary Nesta (Skrine)
See also CN 5, 6; INT CA-114; TCLE 1:1
Keates, Jonathan 1946(?)- .... **CLC 34**
See also CA 163; CANR 126
Keaton, Buster 1895-1966 .... **CLC 20**
See also CA 194
Keats, John 1795-1821 ...... **NCLC 8, 73, 121; PC 1; WLC 3**
See also AAYA 58; BRW 4; BRWR 1; CDBLB 1789-1832; DA; DA3; DAB; DAC; DAM MST, POET; DLB 96, 110; EXPP; LMFS 1; PAB; PFS 1, 2, 3, 9, 17; RGEL 2; TEA; WLIT 3; WP
Keble, John 1792-1866 .... **NCLC 87**
See also DLB 32, 55; RGEL 2
Keene, Donald 1922- .... **CLC 34**
See also CA 1-4R; CANR 5, 119
Keillor, Garrison 1942- ..... **CLC 40, 115, 222**
See also AAYA 2, 62; AMWS 16; BEST 89:3; BPFB 2; CA 111; 117; CANR 36, 59, 124, 180; CPW; DA3; DAM POP; DLBY 1987; EWL 3; MTCW 1, 2; MTFW 2005; SATA 58; TUS
Keith, Carlos
See Lewton, Val
Keith, Michael
See Hubbard, L. Ron

Kincaid, Jamaica 1949- . **BLC 1:2, 2:2; CLC 43, 68, 137, 234; SSC 72**
See also AAYA 13, 56; AFAW 2; AMWS 7; BRWS 7; BW 2, 3; CA 125; CANR 47, 59, 95, 133; CDALBS; CDWLB 3; CLR 63; CN 4, 5, 6, 7; DA3; DAM MULT, NOV; DLB 157, 227; DNFS 1; EWL 3; EXPS; FW; LATS 1:2; LMFS 2; MAL 5; MTCW 2; MTFW 2005; NCFS 1; NFS 3; SSFS 5, 7; TUS; WWE 1; YAW

King, Francis (Henry) 1923- .... **CLC 8, 53, 145**
See also CA 1-4R; CANR 1, 33, 86; CN 1, 2, 3, 4, 5, 6, 7; DAM NOV; DLB 15, 139; MTCW 1

King, Kennedy
See Brown, George Douglas

King, Martin Luther, Jr.
1929-1968 ... **BLC 1:2; CLC 83; WLCS**
See also BW 2, 3; CA 25-28; CANR 27, 44; CAP 2; DA; DA3; DAB; DAC; DAM MST, MULT; LAIT 5; LATS 1:2; MTCW 1, 2; MTFW 2005; SATA 14

King, Stephen 1947- .... **CLC 12, 26, 37, 61, 113, 228, 244; SSC 17, 55**
See also AAYA 1, 17; AMWS 5; BEST 90:1; BPFB 2; CA 61-64; CANR 1, 30, 52, 76, 119, 134, 168; CLR 124; CN 7; CPW; DA3; DAM NOV, POP; DLB 143; DLBY 1980; HGG; JRDA; LAIT 5; MTCW 1, 2; MTFW 2005; RGAL 4; SATA 9, 55, 161; SUFW 1, 2; WYAS 1; YAW

King, Stephen Edwin
See King, Stephen

King, Steve
See King, Stephen

King, Thomas 1943- .... **CLC 89, 171; NNAL**
See also CA 144; CANR 95, 175; CCA 1; CN 6, 7; DAC; DAM MULT; DLB 175, 334; SATA 96

King, Thomas Hunt
See King, Thomas

Kingman, Lee .... **CLC 17**
See Natti, (Mary) Lee
See also CWRI 5; SAAS 3; SATA 1, 67

Kingsley, Charles 1819-1875 .... **NCLC 35**
See also CLR 77; DLB 21, 32, 163, 178, 190; FANT; MAICYA 2; MAICYAS 1; RGEL 2; WCH; YABC 2

Kingsley, Henry 1830-1876 .... **NCLC 107**
See also DLB 21, 230; RGEL 2

Kingsley, Sidney 1906-1995 .... **CLC 44**
See also CA 85-88; 147; CAD; DFS 14, 19; DLB 7; MAL 5; RGAL 4

Kingsolver, Barbara 1955- .... **CLC 55, 81, 130, 216**
See also AAYA 15; AMWS 7; CA 129; 134; CANR 60, 96, 133, 179; CDALBS; CN 7; CPW; CSW; DA3; DAM POP; DLB 206; INT CA-134; LAIT 5; MTCW 2; MTFW 2005; NFS 5, 10, 12, 24; RGAL 4; TCLE 1:1

Kingston, Maxine Hong 1940- .... **AAL; CLC 12, 19, 58, 121; WLCS**
See also AAYA 8, 55; AMWS 5; BPFB 2; CA 69-72; CANR 13, 38, 74, 87, 128; CDALBS; CN 6, 7; DA3; DAM MULT, NOV; DLB 173, 212, 312; DLBY 1980; EWL 3; FL 1:6; FW; INT CANR-13; LAIT 5; MAL 5; MBL; MTCW 1, 2; MTFW 2005; NFS 6; RGAL 4; SATA 53; SSFS 3; TCWW 2

Kingston, Maxine Ting Ting Hong
See Kingston, Maxine Hong

Kinnell, Galway 1927- ..... **CLC 1, 2, 3, 5, 13, 29, 129; PC 26**
See also AMWS 3; CA 9-12R; CANR 10, 34, 66, 116, 138, 175; CP 1, 2, 3, 4, 5, 6, 7; DLB 5, 342; DLBY 1987; EWL 3; INT

CANR-34; MAL 5; MTCW 1, 2; MTFW 2005; PAB; PFS 9, 26; RGAL 4; TCLE 1:1; WP

Kinsella, Thomas 1928- .... **CLC 4, 19, 138; PC 69**
See also BRWS 5; CA 17-20R; CANR 15, 122; CP 1, 2, 3, 4, 5, 6, 7; DLB 27; EWL 3; MTCW 1, 2; MTFW 2005; RGAL 2; TEA

Kinsella, W.P. 1935- .... **CLC 27, 43, 166**
See also AAYA 7, 60; BPFB 2; CA 97-100, 222; CAAE 222; CAAS 7; CANR 21, 35, 66, 75, 129; CN 4, 5, 6, 7; CPW; DAC; DAM NOV, POP; FANT; INT CANR-21; LAIT 5; MTCW 1, 2; MTFW 2005; NFS 15; RGSF 2

Kinsey, Alfred C(harles)
1894-1956 .... **TCLC 91**
See also CA 115; 170; MTCW 2

Kipling, (Joseph) Rudyard 1865-1936 . **PC 3, 91; SSC 5, 54, 110; TCLC 8, 17, 167; WLC 3**
See also AAYA 32; BRW 6; BRWC 1, 2; BYA 4; CA 105; 120; CANR 33; CDBLB 1890-1914; CLR 39, 65; CWRI 5; DA; DA3; DAB; DAC; DAM MST, POET; DLB 19, 34, 141, 156, 330; EWL 3; EXPS; FANT; LAIT 3; LMFS 1; MAICYA 1, 2; MTCW 1, 2; MTFW 2005; NFS 21; PFS 22; RGEL 2; RGSF 2; SATA 100; SFW 4; SSFS 8, 21, 22; SUFW 1; TEA; WCH; WLIT 4; YABC 2

Kircher, Athanasius 1602-1680 .... **LC 121**
See also DLB 164

Kirk, Russell (Amos) 1918-1994 .. **TCLC 119**
See also AITN 1; CA 1-4R; 145; CAAS 9; CANR 1, 20, 60; HGG; INT CANR-20; MTCW 1, 2

Kirkham, Dinah
See Card, Orson Scott

Kirkland, Caroline M. 1801-1864 . **NCLC 85**
See also DLB 3, 73, 74, 250, 254; DLBD 13

Kirkup, James 1918- .... **CLC 1**
See also CA 1-4R; CAAS 4; CANR 2; CP 1, 2, 3, 4, 5, 6, 7; DLB 27; SATA 12

Kirkwood, James 1930(?)-1989 .... **CLC 9**
See also AITN 2; CA 1-4R; 128; CANR 6, 40; GLL 2

Kirsch, Sarah 1935- .... **CLC 176**
See also CA 178; CWW 2; DLB 75; EWL 3

Kirshner, Sidney
See Kingsley, Sidney

Kis, Danilo 1935-1989 .... **CLC 57**
See also CA 109; 118; 129; CANR 61; CDWLB 4; DLB 181; EWL 3; MTCW 1; RGSF 2; RGWL 2, 3

Kissinger, Henry A(lfred) 1923- ..... **CLC 137**
See also CA 1-4R; CANR 2, 33, 66, 109; MTCW 1

Kittel, Frederick August
See Wilson, August

Kivi, Aleksis 1834-1872 .... **NCLC 30**

Kizer, Carolyn 1925- ..... **CLC 15, 39, 80; PC 66**
See also CA 65-68; CAAS 5; CANR 24, 70, 134; CP 1, 2, 3, 4, 5, 6, 7; CWP; DAM POET; DLB 5, 169; EWL 3; MAL 5; MTCW 2; MTFW 2005; PFS 18; TCLE 1:1

Klabund 1890-1928 .... **TCLC 44**
See also CA 162; DLB 66

Klappert, Peter 1942- .... **CLC 57**
See also CA 33-36R; CSW; DLB 5

Klausner, Amos
See Oz, Amos

Klein, A(braham) M(oses)
1909-1972 .... **CLC 19**
See also CA 101; 37-40R; CP 1; DAB; DAC; DAM MST; DLB 68; EWL 3; RGEL 2; RGHL

Klein, Joe
See Klein, Joseph

Klein, Joseph 1946- .... **CLC 154**
See also CA 85-88; CANR 55, 164

Klein, Norma 1938-1989 .... **CLC 30**
See also AAYA 2, 35; BPFB 2; BYA 6, 7, 8; CA 41-44R; 128; CANR 15, 37; CLR 2, 19; INT CANR-15; JRDA; MAICYA 1, 2; SAAS 1; SATA 7, 57; WYA; YAW

Klein, T.E.D. 1947- .... **CLC 34**
See also CA 119; CANR 44, 75, 167; HGG

Klein, Theodore Eibon Donald
See Klein, T.E.D.

Kleist, Heinrich von 1777-1811 .... **DC 29; NCLC 2, 37; SSC 22**
See also CDWLB 2; DAM DRAM; DLB 90; EW 5; RGSF 2; RGWL 2, 3

Klima, Ivan 1931- .... **CLC 56, 172**
See also CA 25-28R; CANR 17, 50, 91; CDWLB 4; CWW 2; DAM NOV; DLB 232; EWL 3; RGWL 3

Klimentev, Andrei Platonovich
See Klimentov, Andrei Platonovich

Klimentov, Andrei Platonovich
1899-1951 .... **SSC 42; TCLC 14**
See Platonov, Andrei Platonovich; Platonov, Andrey Platonovich
See also CA 108; 232

Klinger, Friedrich Maximilian von
1752-1831 .... **NCLC 1**
See also DLB 94

Klingsor the Magician
See Hartmann, Sadakichi

Klopstock, Friedrich Gottlieb
1724-1803 .... **NCLC 11**
See also DLB 97; EW 4; RGWL 2, 3

Kluge, Alexander 1932- .... **SSC 61**
See also CA 81-84; CANR 163; DLB 75

Knapp, Caroline 1959-2002 .... **CLC 99**
See also CA 154; 207

Knebel, Fletcher 1911-1993 .... **CLC 14**
See also AITN 1; CA 1-4R; 140; CAAS 3; CANR 1, 36; CN 1, 2, 3, 4, 5; SATA 36; SATA-Obit 75

Knickerbocker, Diedrich
See Irving, Washington

Knight, Etheridge 1931-1991 .... **BLC 1:2; CLC 40; PC 14**
See also BW 1, 3; CA 21-24R; 133; CANR 23, 82; CP 1, 2, 3, 4, 5; DAM POET; DLB 41; MTCW 2; MTFW 2005; RGAL 4; TCLE 1:1

Knight, Sarah Kemble 1666-1727 .... **LC 7**
See also DLB 24, 200

Knister, Raymond 1899-1932 .... **TCLC 56**
See also CA 186; DLB 68; RGEL 2

Knowles, John 1926-2001 ... **CLC 1, 4, 10, 26**
See also AAYA 10, 72; AMWS 12; BPFB 2; BYA 3; CA 17-20R; 203; CANR 40, 74, 76, 132; CDALB 1968-1988; CLR 98; CN 1, 2, 3, 4, 5, 6, 7; DA; DAC; DAM MST, NOV; DLB 6; EXPN; MTCW 1, 2; MTFW 2005; NFS 2; RGAL 4; SATA 8, 89; SATA-Obit 134; YAW

Knox, Calvin M.
See Silverberg, Robert

Knox, John c. 1505-1572 .... **LC 37**
See also DLB 132

Knye, Cassandra
See Disch, Thomas M.

Koch, C(hristopher) J(ohn) 1932- .... **CLC 42**
See also CA 127; CANR 84; CN 3, 4, 5, 6, 7; DLB 289

Kunze, Reiner 1933- .... **CLC 10**
See also CA 93-96; CWW 2; DLB 75; EWL 3

Kuprin, Aleksander Ivanovich
1870-1938 .... **TCLC 5**
See Kuprin, Aleksandr Ivanovich; Kuprin, Alexandr Ivanovich
See also CA 104; 182

Kuprin, Aleksandr Ivanovich
See Kuprin, Aleksander Ivanovich
See also DLB 295

Kuprin, Alexandr Ivanovich
See Kuprin, Aleksander Ivanovich
See also EWL 3

Kureishi, Hanif 1954- .. **CLC 64, 135; DC 26**
See also BRWS 11; CA 139; CANR 113; CBD; CD 5, 6; CN 6, 7; DLB 194, 245; GLL 2; IDFW 4; WLIT 4; WWE 1

Kurosawa, Akira 1910-1998 ..... **CLC 16, 119**
See also AAYA 11, 64; CA 101; 170; CANR 46; DAM MULT

Kushner, Tony 1956- .... **CLC 81, 203; DC 10**
See also AAYA 61; AMWS 9; CA 144; CAD; CANR 74, 130; CD 5, 6; DA3; DAM DRAM; DFS 5; DLB 228; EWL 3; GLL 1; LAIT 5; MAL 5; MTCW 2; MTFW 2005; RGAL 4; RGHL; SATA 160

Kuttner, Henry 1915-1958 .... **TCLC 10**
See also CA 107; 157; DLB 8; FANT; SCFW 1, 2; SFW 4

Kutty, Madhavi
See Das, Kamala

Kuzma, Greg 1944- .... **CLC 7**
See also CA 33-36R; CANR 70

Kuzmin, Mikhail (Alekseevich)
1872(?)-1936 .... **TCLC 40**
See also CA 170; DLB 295; EWL 3

Kyd, Thomas 1558-1594 .. **DC 3; LC 22, 125**
See also BRW 1; DAM DRAM; DFS 21; DLB 62; IDTP; LMFS 1; RGEL 2; TEA; WLIT 3

Kyprianos, Iossif
See Samarakis, Antonis

L. S.
See Stephen, Sir Leslie

Labe, Louise 1521-1566 .... **LC 120**
See also DLB 327

Labrunie, Gerard
See Nerval, Gerard de

La Bruyere, Jean de 1645-1696 .... **LC 17**
See also DLB 268; EW 3; GFL Beginnings to 1789

LaBute, Neil 1963- .... **CLC 225**
See also CA 240

Lacan, Jacques (Marie Emile)
1901-1981 .... **CLC 75**
See also CA 121; 104; DLB 296; EWL 3; TWA

Laclos, Pierre-Ambroise Francois
1741-1803 .... **NCLC 4, 87**
See also DLB 313; EW 4; GFL Beginnings to 1789; RGWL 2, 3

Lacolere, Francois
See Aragon, Louis

La Colere, Francois
See Aragon, Louis

La Deshabilleuse
See Simenon, Georges (Jacques Christian)

Lady Gregory
See Gregory, Lady Isabella Augusta (Persse)

Lady of Quality, A
See Bagnold, Enid

La Fayette, Marie-(Madelaine Pioche de la Vergne) 1634-1693 .... **LC 2, 144**
See Lafayette, Marie-Madeleine
See also GFL Beginnings to 1789; RGWL 2, 3

Lafayette, Marie-Madeleine
See La Fayette, Marie-(Madelaine Pioche de la Vergne)
See also DLB 268

Lafayette, Rene
See Hubbard, L. Ron

La Flesche, Francis 1857(?)-1932 ...... **NNAL**
See also CA 144; CANR 83; DLB 175

La Fontaine, Jean de 1621-1695 .... **LC 50**
See also DLB 268; EW 3; GFL Beginnings to 1789; MAICYA 1, 2; RGWL 2, 3; SATA 18

LaForet, Carmen 1921-2004 .... **CLC 219**
See also CA 246; CWW 2; DLB 322; EWL 3

LaForet Diaz, Carmen
See LaForet, Carmen

Laforgue, Jules 1860-1887 . **NCLC 5, 53; PC 14; SSC 20**
See also DLB 217; EW 7; GFL 1789 to the Present; RGWL 2, 3

Lagerkvist, Paer (Fabian)
1891-1974 ..... **CLC 7, 10, 13, 54; TCLC 144**
See Lagerkvist, Par
See also CA 85-88; 49-52; DA3; DAM DRAM, NOV; MTCW 1, 2; MTFW 2005; TWA

Lagerkvist, Par .... **SSC 12**
See Lagerkvist, Paer (Fabian)
See also DLB 259, 331; EW 10; EWL 3; RGSF 2; RGWL 2, 3

Lagerloef, Selma (Ottiliana Lovisa)
.... **TCLC 4, 36**
See Lagerlof, Selma (Ottiliana Lovisa)
See also CA 108; MTCW 2

Lagerlof, Selma (Ottiliana Lovisa)
1858-1940
See Lagerloef, Selma (Ottiliana Lovisa)
See also CA 188; CLR 7; DLB 259, 331; RGWL 2, 3; SATA 15; SSFS 18

La Guma, Alex 1925-1985 .. **BLCS; CLC 19; TCLC 140**
See also AFW; BW 1, 3; CA 49-52; 118; CANR 25, 81; CDWLB 3; CN 1, 2, 3; CP 1; DAM NOV; DLB 117, 225; EWL 3; MTCW 1, 2; MTFW 2005; WLIT 2; WWE 1

Lahiri, Jhumpa 1967- .... **SSC 96**
See also AAYA 56; CA 193; CANR 134; DLB 323; MTFW 2005; SSFS 19

Laidlaw, A. K.
See Grieve, C(hristopher) M(urray)

Lainez, Manuel Mujica
See Mujica Lainez, Manuel
See also HW 1

Laing, R(onald) D(avid) 1927-1989 . **CLC 95**
See also CA 107; 129; CANR 34; MTCW 1

Laishley, Alex
See Booth, Martin

Lamartine, Alphonse (Marie Louis Prat) de
1790-1869 .... **NCLC 11, 190; PC 16**
See also DAM POET; DLB 217; GFL 1789 to the Present; RGWL 2, 3

Lamb, Charles 1775-1834 ..... **NCLC 10, 113; SSC 112; WLC 3**
See also BRW 4; CDBLB 1789-1832; DA; DAB; DAC; DAM MST; DLB 93, 107, 163; RGEL 2; SATA 17; TEA

Lamb, Lady Caroline 1785-1828 ... **NCLC 38**
See also DLB 116

Lamb, Mary Ann 1764-1847 ...... **NCLC 125; SSC 112**
See also DLB 163; SATA 17

Lame Deer 1903(?)-1976 .... **NNAL**
See also CA 69-72

Lamming, George (William)
1927- . **BLC 1:2, 2:2; CLC 2, 4, 66, 144**
See also BW 2, 3; CA 85-88; CANR 26, 76; CDWLB 3; CN 1, 2, 3, 4, 5, 6, 7; CP 1; DAM MULT; DLB 125; EWL 3; MTCW 1, 2; MTFW 2005; NFS 15; RGEL 2

L'Amour, Louis 1908-1988 .... **CLC 25, 55**
See also AAYA 16; AITN 2; BEST 89:2; BPFB 2; CA 1-4R; CANR 3, 25, 40; CPW; DA3; DAM NOV, POP; DLB 206; DLBY 1980; MTCW 1, 2; MTFW 2005; RGAL 4; TCWW 1, 2

Lampedusa, Giuseppe (Tomasi) di
.... **TCLC 13**
See Tomasi di Lampedusa, Giuseppe
See also CA 164; EW 11; MTCW 2; MTFW 2005; RGWL 2, 3

Lampman, Archibald 1861-1899 .. **NCLC 25, 194**
See also DLB 92; RGEL 2; TWA

Lancaster, Bruce 1896-1963 .... **CLC 36**
See also CA 9-10; CANR 70; CAP 1; SATA 9

Lanchester, John 1962- .... **CLC 99**
See also CA 194; DLB 267

Landau, Mark Alexandrovich
See Aldanov, Mark (Alexandrovich)

Landau-Aldanov, Mark Alexandrovich
See Aldanov, Mark (Alexandrovich)

Landis, Jerry
See Simon, Paul

Landis, John 1950- .... **CLC 26**
See also CA 112; 122; CANR 128

Landolfi, Tommaso 1908-1979 .... **CLC 11, 49**
See also CA 127; 117; DLB 177; EWL 3

Landon, Letitia Elizabeth
1802-1838 .... **NCLC 15**
See also DLB 96

Landor, Walter Savage
1775-1864 .... **NCLC 14**
See also BRW 4; DLB 93, 107; RGEL 2

Landwirth, Heinz
See Lind, Jakov

Lane, Patrick 1939- .... **CLC 25**
See also CA 97-100; CANR 54; CP 3, 4, 5, 6, 7; DAM POET; DLB 53; INT CA-97-100

Lane, Rose Wilder 1887-1968 ...... **TCLC 177**
See also CA 102; CANR 63; SATA 29; SATA-Brief 28; TCWW 2

Lang, Andrew 1844-1912 .... **TCLC 16**
See also CA 114; 137; CANR 85; CLR 101; DLB 98, 141, 184; FANT; MAICYA 1, 2; RGEL 2; SATA 16; WCH

Lang, Fritz 1890-1976 .... **CLC 20, 103**
See also AAYA 65; CA 77-80; 69-72; CANR 30

Lange, John
See Crichton, Michael

Langer, Elinor 1939- .... **CLC 34**
See also CA 121

Langland, William 1332(?)-1400(?) .... **LC 19, 120**
See also BRW 1; DA; DAB; DAC; DAM MST, POET; DLB 146; RGEL 2; TEA; WLIT 3

Langstaff, Launcelot
See Irving, Washington

Lanier, Sidney 1842-1881 . **NCLC 6, 118; PC 50**
See also AMWS 1; DAM POET; DLB 64; DLBD 13; EXPP; MAICYA 1; PFS 14; RGAL 4; SATA 18

Lanyer, Aemilia 1569-1645 .... **LC 10, 30, 83; PC 60**
See also DLB 121

Lao-Tzu
See Lao Tzu

Lilar, Francoise
　　See Mallet-Joris, Francoise
Liliencron, Detlev
　　See Liliencron, Detlev von
Liliencron, Detlev von 1844-1909 .. **TCLC 18**
　　See also CA 117
Liliencron, Friedrich Adolf Axel Detlev von
　　See Liliencron, Detlev von
Liliencron, Friedrich Detlev von
　　See Liliencron, Detlev von
Lille, Alain de
　　See Alain de Lille
Lillo, George 1691-1739 .... **LC 131**
　　See also DLB 84; RGEL 2
Lilly, William 1602-1681 .... **LC 27**
Lima, Jose Lezama
　　See Lezama Lima, Jose
Lima Barreto, Afonso Henrique de
　　1881-1922 .... **TCLC 23**
　　See Lima Barreto, Afonso Henriques de
　　See also CA 117; 181; LAW
Lima Barreto, Afonso Henriques de
　　See Lima Barreto, Afonso Henrique de
　　See also DLB 307
Limonov, Eduard
　　See Limonov, Edward
　　See also DLB 317
Limonov, Edward 1944- .... **CLC 67**
　　See Limonov, Eduard
　　See also CA 137
Lin, Frank
　　See Atherton, Gertrude (Franklin Horn)
Lin, Yutang 1895-1976 .... **TCLC 149**
　　See also CA 45-48; 65-68; CANR 2; RGAL
　　4
Lincoln, Abraham 1809-1865 .... **NCLC 18,
　　201**
　　See also LAIT 2
Lind, Jakov 1927-2007 ... **CLC 1, 2, 4, 27, 82**
　　See also CA 9-12R; 257; CAAS 4; CANR
　　7; DLB 299; EWL 3; RGHL
Lindbergh, Anne Morrow
　　1906-2001 .... **CLC 82**
　　See also BPFB 2; CA 17-20R; 193; CANR
　　16, 73; DAM NOV; MTCW 1, 2; MTFW
　　2005; SATA 33; SATA-Obit 125; TUS
Lindsay, David 1878(?)-1945 .... **TCLC 15**
　　See also CA 113; 187; DLB 255; FANT;
　　SFW 4; SUFW 1
Lindsay, (Nicholas) Vachel
　　1879-1931 .... **PC 23; TCLC 17; WLC 4**
　　See also AMWS 1; CA 114; 135; CANR
　　79; CDALB 1865-1917; DA; DA3; DAC;
　　DAM MST, POET; DLB 54; EWL 3;
　　EXPP; MAL 5; RGAL 4; SATA 40; WP
Linke-Poot
　　See Doeblin, Alfred
Linney, Romulus 1930- .... **CLC 51**
　　See also CA 1-4R; CAD; CANR 40, 44,
　　79; CD 5, 6; CSW; RGAL 4
Linton, Eliza Lynn 1822-1898 .... **NCLC 41**
　　See also DLB 18
Li Po 701-763 .... **CMLC 2, 86; PC 29**
　　See also PFS 20; WP
Lippard, George 1822-1854 .... **NCLC 198**
　　See also DLB 202
Lipsius, Justus 1547-1606 .... **LC 16**
Lipsyte, Robert 1938- .... **CLC 21**
　　See also AAYA 7, 45; CA 17-20R; CANR
　　8, 57, 146; CLR 23, 76; DA; DAC; DAM
　　MST, NOV; JRDA; LAIT 5; MAICYA 1,
　　2; SATA 5, 68, 113, 161; WYA; YAW
Lipsyte, Robert Michael
　　See Lipsyte, Robert
Lish, Gordon 1934- .... **CLC 45; SSC 18**
　　See also CA 113; 117; CANR 79, 151; DLB
　　130; INT CA-117

Lish, Gordon Jay
　　See Lish, Gordon
Lispector, Clarice 1925(?)-1977 .... **CLC 43;
　　HLCS 2; SSC 34, 96**
　　See also CA 139; 116; CANR 71; CDWLB
　　3; DLB 113, 307; DNFS 1; EWL 3; FW;
　　HW 2; LAW; RGSF 2; RGWL 2, 3; WLIT
　　1
Liszt, Franz 1811-1886 .... **NCLC 199**
Littell, Robert 1935(?)- .... **CLC 42**
　　See also CA 109; 112; CANR 64, 115, 162;
　　CMW 4
Little, Malcolm 1925-1965
　　See Malcolm X
　　See also BW 1, 3; CA 125; 111; CANR 82;
　　DA; DA3; DAB; DAC; DAM MST,
　　MULT; MTCW 1, 2; MTFW 2005
Littlewit, Humphrey Gent.
　　See Lovecraft, H. P.
Litwos
　　See Sienkiewicz, Henryk (Adam Alexander
　　Pius)
Liu, E. 1857-1909 .... **TCLC 15**
　　See also CA 115; 190; DLB 328
Lively, Penelope 1933- .... **CLC 32, 50**
　　See also BPFB 2; CA 41-44R; CANR 29,
　　67, 79, 131, 172; CLR 7; CN 5, 6, 7;
　　CWRI 5; DAM NOV; DLB 14, 161, 207,
　　326; FANT; JRDA; MAICYA 1, 2;
　　MTCW 1, 2; MTFW 2005; SATA 7, 60,
　　101, 164; TEA
Lively, Penelope Margaret
　　See Lively, Penelope
Livesay, Dorothy (Kathleen)
　　1909-1996 .... **CLC 4, 15, 79**
　　See also AITN 2; CA 25-28R; CAAS 8;
　　CANR 36, 67; CP 1, 2, 3, 4, 5; DAC;
　　DAM MST, POET; DLB 68; FW; MTCW
　　1; RGEL 2; TWA
Livius Andronicus c. 284B.C.-c.
　　204B.C. .... **CMLC 102**
Livy c. 59B.C.-c. 12 .... **CMLC 11**
　　See also AW 2; CDWLB 1; DLB 211;
　　RGWL 2, 3; WLIT 8
Lizardi, Jose Joaquin Fernandez de
　　1776-1827 .... **NCLC 30**
　　See also LAW
Llewellyn, Richard
　　See Llewellyn Lloyd, Richard Dafydd Viv-
　　ian
　　See also DLB 15
Llewellyn Lloyd, Richard Dafydd Vivian
　　1906-1983 .... **CLC 7, 80**
　　See Llewellyn, Richard
　　See also CA 53-56; 111; CANR 7, 71;
　　SATA 11; SATA-Obit 37
Llosa, Jorge Mario Pedro Vargas
　　See Vargas Llosa, Mario
　　See also RGWL 3
Llosa, Mario Vargas
　　See Vargas Llosa, Mario
Lloyd, Manda
　　See Mander, (Mary) Jane
Lloyd Webber, Andrew 1948-
　　See Webber, Andrew Lloyd
　　See also AAYA 1, 38; CA 116; 149; DAM
　　DRAM; SATA 56
Llull, Ramon c. 1235-c. 1316 .... **CMLC 12**
Lobb, Ebenezer
　　See Upward, Allen
Locke, Alain (Le Roy)
　　1886-1954 .... **BLCS; HR 1:3; TCLC 43**
　　See also AMWS 14; BW 1, 3; CA 106; 124;
　　CANR 79; DLB 51; LMFS 2; MAL 5;
　　RGAL 4
Locke, John 1632-1704 .... **LC 7, 35, 135**
　　See also DLB 31, 101, 213, 252; RGEL 2;
　　WLIT 3

Locke-Elliott, Sumner
　　See Elliott, Sumner Locke
Lockhart, John Gibson 1794-1854 .. **NCLC 6**
　　See also DLB 110, 116, 144
Lockridge, Ross (Franklin), Jr.
　　1914-1948 .... **TCLC 111**
　　See also CA 108; 145; CANR 79; DLB 143;
　　DLBY 1980; MAL 5; RGAL 4; RHW
Lockwood, Robert
　　See Johnson, Robert
Lodge, David 1935- .... **CLC 36, 141**
　　See also BEST 90:1; BRWS 4; CA 17-20R;
　　CANR 19, 53, 92, 139; CN 1, 2, 3, 4, 5,
　　6, 7; CPW; DAM POP; DLB 14, 194;
　　EWL 3; INT CANR-19; MTCW 1, 2;
　　MTFW 2005
Lodge, Thomas 1558-1625 .... **LC 41**
　　See also DLB 172; RGEL 2
Loewinsohn, Ron(ald William)
　　1937- .... **CLC 52**
　　See also CA 25-28R; CANR 71; CP 1, 2, 3,
　　4
Logan, Jake
　　See Smith, Martin Cruz
Logan, John (Burton) 1923-1987 .... **CLC 5**
　　See also CA 77-80; 124; CANR 45; CP 1,
　　2, 3, 4; DLB 5
Lo Kuan-chung 1330(?)-1400(?) .... **LC 12**
Lomax, Pearl
　　See Cleage, Pearl
Lomax, Pearl Cleage
　　See Cleage, Pearl
Lombard, Nap
　　See Johnson, Pamela Hansford
Lombard, Peter 1100(?)-1160(?) ... **CMLC 72**
Lombino, Salvatore
　　See Hunter, Evan
London, Jack 1876-1916 .. **SSC 4, 49; TCLC
　　9, 15, 39; WLC 4**
　　See London, John Griffith
　　See also AAYA 13; AITN 2; AMW; BPFB
　　2; BYA 4, 13; CDALB 1865-1917; CLR
　　108; DLB 8, 12, 78, 212; EWL 3; EXPS;
　　LAIT 3; MAL 5; NFS 8; RGAL 4; RGSF
　　2; SATA 18; SFW 4; SSFS 7; TCWW 1,
　　2; TUS; WYA; YAW
London, John Griffith 1876-1916
　　See London, Jack
　　See also AAYA 75; CA 110; 119; CANR
　　73; DA; DA3; DAB; DAC; DAM MST,
　　NOV; JRDA; MAICYA 1, 2; MTCW 1,
　　2; MTFW 2005; NFS 19
Long, Emmett
　　See Leonard, Elmore
Longbaugh, Harry
　　See Goldman, William
Longfellow, Henry Wadsworth
　　1807-1882 .... **NCLC 2, 45, 101, 103; PC
　　30; WLCS**
　　See also AMW; AMWR 2; CDALB 1640-
　　1865; CLR 99; DA; DA3; DAC;
　　DAM MST, POET; DLB 1, 59, 235;
　　EXPP; PAB; PFS 2, 7, 17; RGAL 4;
　　SATA 19; TUS; WP
Longinus c. 1st cent. - .... **CMLC 27**
　　See also AW 2; DLB 176
Longley, Michael 1939- .... **CLC 29**
　　See also BRWS 8; CA 102; CP 1, 2, 3, 4, 5,
　　6, 7; DLB 40
Longstreet, Augustus Baldwin
　　1790-1870 .... **NCLC 159**
　　See also DLB 3, 11, 74, 248; RGAL 4
Longus fl. c. 2nd cent. - .... **CMLC 7**
Longway, A. Hugh
　　See Lang, Andrew
Lonnbohm, Armas Eino Leopold 1878-1926
　　See Leino, Eino
　　See also CA 123

Mantel, Hilary Mary
See Mantel, Hilary
Manton, Peter
See Creasey, John
Man Without a Spleen, A
See Chekhov, Anton (Pavlovich)
Manzano, Juan Franciso
1797(?)-1854 .... **NCLC 155**
Manzoni, Alessandro 1785-1873 ... **NCLC 29, 98**
See also EW 5; RGWL 2, 3; TWA; WLIT 7
Map, Walter 1140-1209 .... **CMLC 32**
Mapu, Abraham (ben Jekutiel)
1808-1867 .... **NCLC 18**
Mara, Sally
See Queneau, Raymond
Maracle, Lee 1950- .... **NNAL**
See also CA 149
Marat, Jean Paul 1743-1793 .... **LC 10**
Marcel, Gabriel Honore 1889-1973 . **CLC 15**
See also CA 102; 45-48; EWL 3; MTCW 1, 2
March, William .... **TCLC 96**
See Campbell, William Edward March
See also CA 216; DLB 9, 86, 316; MAL 5
Marchbanks, Samuel
See Davies, Robertson
See also CCA 1
Marchi, Giacomo
See Bassani, Giorgio
Marcus Aurelius
See Aurelius, Marcus
See also AW 2
Marcuse, Herbert 1898-1979 .... **TCLC 207**
See also CA 188; 89-92; DLB 242
Marguerite
See de Navarre, Marguerite
Marguerite d'Angouleme
See de Navarre, Marguerite
See also GFL Beginnings to 1789
Marguerite de Navarre
See de Navarre, Marguerite
See also RGWL 2, 3
Margulies, Donald 1954- .... **CLC 76**
See also AAYA 57; CA 200; CD 6; DFS 13; DLB 228
Marias, Javier 1951- .... **CLC 239**
See also CA 167; CANR 109, 139; DLB 322; HW 2; MTFW 2005
Marie de France c. 12th cent. - ..... **CMLC 8; PC 22**
See also DLB 208; FW; RGWL 2, 3
Marie de l'Incarnation 1599-1672 ...... **LC 10**
Marier, Captain Victor
See Griffith, D.W.
Mariner, Scott
See Pohl, Frederik
Marinetti, Filippo Tommaso
1876-1944 .... **TCLC 10**
See also CA 107; DLB 114, 264; EW 9; EWL 3; WLIT 7
Marivaux, Pierre Carlet de Chamblain de
1688-1763 .... **DC 7; LC 4, 123**
See also DLB 314; GFL Beginnings to 1789; RGWL 2, 3; TWA
Markandaya, Kamala .... **CLC 8, 38**
See Taylor, Kamala
See also BYA 13; CN 1, 2, 3, 4, 5, 6, 7; DLB 323; EWL 3
Markfield, Wallace (Arthur)
1926-2002 .... **CLC 8**
See also CA 69-72; 208; CAAS 3; CN 1, 2, 3, 4, 5, 6, 7; DLB 2, 28; DLBY 2002
Markham, Edwin 1852-1940 .... **TCLC 47**
See also CA 160; DLB 54, 186; MAL 5; RGAL 4
Markham, Robert
See Amis, Kingsley

Marks, J.
See Highwater, Jamake (Mamake)
Marks-Highwater, J.
See Highwater, Jamake (Mamake)
Markson, David M. 1927- .... **CLC 67**
See also AMWS 17; CA 49-52; CANR 1, 91, 158; CN 5, 6
Markson, David Merrill
See Markson, David M.
Marlatt, Daphne (Buckle) 1942- .... **CLC 168**
See also CA 25-28R; CANR 17, 39; CN 6, 7; CP 4, 5, 6, 7; CWP; DLB 60; FW
Marley, Bob .... **CLC 17**
See Marley, Robert Nesta
Marley, Robert Nesta 1945-1981
See Marley, Bob
See also CA 107; 103
Marlowe, Christopher 1564-1593 . **DC 1; LC 22, 47, 117; PC 57; WLC 4**
See also BRW 1; BRWR 1; CDBLB Before 1660; DA; DA3; DAB; DAC; DAM DRAM, MST; DFS 1, 5, 13, 21; DLB 62; EXPP; LMFS 1; PFS 22; RGEL 2; TEA; WLIT 3
Marlowe, Stephen 1928-2008 .... **CLC 70**
See Queen, Ellery
See also CA 13-16R; 269; CANR 6, 55; CMW 4; SFW 4
Marmion, Shakerley 1603-1639 .... **LC 89**
See also DLB 58; RGEL 2
Marmontel, Jean-Francois 1723-1799 .. **LC 2**
See also DLB 314
Maron, Monika 1941- .... **CLC 165**
See also CA 201
Marot, Clement c. 1496-1544 .... **LC 133**
See also DLB 327; GFL Beginnings to 1789
Marquand, John P(hillips)
1893-1960 .... **CLC 2, 10**
See also AMW; BPFB 2; CA 85-88; CANR 73; CMW 4; DLB 9, 102; EWL 3; MAL 5; MTCW 2; RGAL 4
Marques, Rene 1919-1979 .. **CLC 96; HLC 2**
See also CA 97-100; 85-88; CANR 78; DAM MULT; DLB 305; EWL 3; HW 1, 2; LAW; RGSF 2
Marquez, Gabriel Garcia
See Garcia Marquez, Gabriel
Marquis, Don(ald Robert Perry)
1878-1937 .... **TCLC 7**
See also CA 104; 166; DLB 11, 25; MAL 5; RGAL 4
Marquis de Sade
See Sade, Donatien Alphonse Francois
Marric, J. J.
See Creasey, John
See also MSW
Marryat, Frederick 1792-1848 .... **NCLC 3**
See also DLB 21, 163; RGEL 2; WCH
Marsden, James
See Creasey, John
Marsh, Edward 1872-1953 .... **TCLC 99**
Marsh, (Edith) Ngaio 1895-1982 .. **CLC 7, 53**
See also CA 9-12R; CANR 6, 58; CMW 4; CN 1, 2, 3; CPW; DAM POP; DLB 77; MSW; MTCW 1, 2; RGEL 2; TEA
Marshall, Allen
See Westlake, Donald E.
Marshall, Garry 1934- .... **CLC 17**
See also AAYA 3; CA 111; SATA 60
Marshall, Paule 1929- .... **BLC 1:3, 2:3; CLC 27, 72, 253; SSC 3**
See also AFAW 1, 2; AMWS 11; BPFB 2; BW 2, 3; CA 77-80; CANR 25, 73, 129; CN 1, 2, 3, 4, 5, 6, 7; DA3; DAM MULT; DLB 33, 157, 227; EWL 3; LATS 1:2; MAL 5; MTCW 1, 2; MTFW 2005; RGAL 4; SSFS 15
Marshallik
See Zangwill, Israel

Marsten, Richard
See Hunter, Evan
Marston, John 1576-1634 .... **LC 33**
See also BRW 2; DAM DRAM; DLB 58, 172; RGEL 2
Martel, Yann 1963- .... **CLC 192**
See also AAYA 67; CA 146; CANR 114; DLB 326, 334; MTFW 2005; NFS 27
Martens, Adolphe-Adhemar
See Ghelderode, Michel de
Martha, Henry
See Harris, Mark
Marti, Jose .... **PC 76**
See Marti (y Perez), Jose (Julian)
See also DLB 290
Marti (y Perez), Jose (Julian)
1853-1895 .... **HLC 2; NCLC 63**
See Marti, Jose
See also DAM MULT; HW 2; LAW; RGWL 2, 3; WLIT 1
Martial c. 40-c. 104 .... **CMLC 35; PC 10**
See also AW 2; CDWLB 1; DLB 211; RGWL 2, 3
Martin, Ken
See Hubbard, L. Ron
Martin, Richard
See Creasey, John
Martin, Steve 1945- .... **CLC 30, 217**
See also AAYA 53; CA 97-100; CANR 30, 100, 140; DFS 19; MTCW 1; MTFW 2005
Martin, Valerie 1948- .... **CLC 89**
See also BEST 90:2; CA 85-88; CANR 49, 89, 165
Martin, Violet Florence 1862-1915 .. **SSC 56; TCLC 51**
Martin, Webber
See Silverberg, Robert
Martindale, Patrick Victor
See White, Patrick (Victor Martindale)
Martin du Gard, Roger
1881-1958 .... **TCLC 24**
See also CA 118; CANR 94; DLB 65, 331; EWL 3; GFL 1789 to the Present; RGWL 2, 3
Martineau, Harriet 1802-1876 ...... **NCLC 26, 137**
See also DLB 21, 55, 159, 163, 166, 190; FW; RGEL 2; YABC 2
Martines, Julia
See O'Faolain, Julia
Martinez, Enrique Gonzalez
See Gonzalez Martinez, Enrique
Martinez, Jacinto Benavente y
See Benavente (y Martinez), Jacinto
Martinez de la Rosa, Francisco de Paula
1787-1862 .... **NCLC 102**
See also TWA
Martinez Ruiz, Jose 1873-1967
See Azorin; Ruiz, Jose Martinez
See also CA 93-96; HW 1
Martinez Sierra, Gregorio
See Martinez Sierra, Maria
Martinez Sierra, Gregorio
1881-1947 .... **TCLC 6**
See also CA 115; EWL 3
Martinez Sierra, Maria 1874-1974 .. **TCLC 6**
See also CA 250; 115; EWL 3
Martinsen, Martin
See Follett, Ken
Martinson, Harry (Edmund)
1904-1978 .... **CLC 14**
See also CA 77-80; CANR 34, 130; DLB 259, 331; EWL 3
Martyn, Edward 1859-1923 .... **TCLC 131**
See also CA 179; DLB 10; RGEL 2
Marut, Ret
See Traven, B.

McNeile, Herman Cyril 1888-1937
See Sapper
See also CA 184; CMW 4; DLB 77

McNickle, (William) D'Arcy
1904-1977 .... **CLC 89; NNAL**
See also CA 9-12R; 85-88; CANR 5, 45;
DAM MULT; DLB 175, 212; RGAL 4;
SATA-Obit 22; TCWW 1, 2

McPhee, John 1931- .... **CLC 36**
See also AAYA 61; AMWS 3; ANW; BEST
90:1; CA 65-68; CANR 20, 46, 64, 69,
121, 165; CPW; DLB 185, 275; MTCW
1, 2; MTFW 2005; TUS

McPhee, John Angus
See McPhee, John

McPherson, James Alan 1943- . **BLCS; CLC
19, 77; SSC 95**
See also BW 1, 3; CA 25-28R; 273; CAAE
273; CAAS 17; CANR 24, 74, 140; CN
3, 4, 5, 6; CSW; DLB 38, 244; EWL 3;
MTCW 1, 2; MTFW 2005; RGAL 4;
RGSF 2; SSFS 23

McPherson, William (Alexander)
1933- .... **CLC 34**
See also CA 69-72; CANR 28; INT
CANR-28

McTaggart, J. McT. Ellis
See McTaggart, John McTaggart Ellis

McTaggart, John McTaggart Ellis
1866-1925 .... **TCLC 105**
See also CA 120; DLB 262

Mda, Zakes 1948- .... **BLC 2:3; CLC 262**
See also CA 205; CANR 151; CD 5, 6;
DLB 225

Mda, Zanemvula
See Mda, Zakes

Mda, Zanemvula Kizito Gatyeni
See Mda, Zakes

Mead, George Herbert 1863-1931 . **TCLC 89**
See also CA 212; DLB 270

Mead, Margaret 1901-1978 .... **CLC 37**
See also AITN 1; CA 1-4R; 81-84; CANR
4; DA3; FW; MTCW 1, 2; SATA-Obit 20

Meaker, M. J.
See Meaker, Marijane

Meaker, Marijane 1927- .... **CLC 12, 35**
See also AAYA 2, 23; BYA 1, 7, 8; CA 107;
CANR 37, 63, 145, 180; CLR 29; GLL 2;
INT CA-107; JRDA; MAICYA 1, 2; MAI-
CYAS 1; MTCW 1; SAAS 1; SATA 20,
61, 99, 160; SATA-Essay 111; WYA;
YAW

Meaker, Marijane Agnes
See Meaker, Marijane

Mechthild von Magdeburg c. 1207-c.
1282 .... **CMLC 91**
See also DLB 138

Medoff, Mark (Howard) 1940- .... **CLC 6, 23**
See also AITN 1; CA 53-56; CAD; CANR
5; CD 5, 6; DAM DRAM; DFS 4; DLB
7; INT CANR-5

Medvedev, P. N.
See Bakhtin, Mikhail Mikhailovich

Meged, Aharon
See Megged, Aharon

Meged, Aron
See Megged, Aharon

Megged, Aharon 1920- .... **CLC 9**
See also CA 49-52; CAAS 13; CANR 1,
140; EWL 3; RGHL

Mehta, Deepa 1950- .... **CLC 208**

Mehta, Gita 1943- .... **CLC 179**
See also CA 225; CN 7; DNFS 2

Mehta, Ved 1934- .... **CLC 37**
See also CA 1-4R, 212; CAAE 212; CANR
2, 23, 69; DLB 323; MTCW 1; MTFW
2005

Melanchthon, Philipp 1497-1560 .... **LC 90**
See also DLB 179

Melanter
See Blackmore, R(ichard) D(oddridge)

Meleager c. 140B.C.-c. 70B.C. ...... **CMLC 53**

Melies, Georges 1861-1938 .... **TCLC 81**

Melikow, Loris
See Hofmannsthal, Hugo von

Melmoth, Sebastian
See Wilde, Oscar

Melo Neto, Joao Cabral de
See Cabral de Melo Neto, Joao
See also CWW 2; EWL 3

Meltzer, Milton 1915- .... **CLC 26**
See also AAYA 8, 45; BYA 2, 6; CA 13-
16R; CANR 38, 92, 107; CLR 13; DLB
61; JRDA; MAICYA 1, 2; SAAS 1; SATA
1, 50, 80, 128; SATA-Essay 124; WYA;
YAW

Melville, Herman 1819-1891 ..... **NCLC 3, 12,
29, 45, 49, 91, 93, 123, 157, 181, 193;
PC 82; SSC 1, 17, 46, 95; WLC 4**
See also AAYA 25; AMW; AMWR 1;
CDALB 1640-1865; DA; DA3; DAB;
DAC; DAM MST, NOV; DLB 3, 74, 250,
254; EXPN; EXPS; GL 3; LAIT 1, 2; NFS
7, 9; RGAL 4; RGSF 2; SATA 59; SSFS
3; TUS

Members, Mark
See Powell, Anthony

Membreno, Alejandro .... **CLC 59**

Menand, Louis 1952- .... **CLC 208**
See also CA 200

Menander c. 342B.C.-c. 293B.C. .... **CMLC 9,
51, 101; DC 3**
See also AW 1; CDWLB 1; DAM DRAM;
DLB 176; LMFS 1; RGWL 2, 3

Menchu, Rigoberta 1959- .. **CLC 160; HLCS
2**
See also CA 175; CANR 135; DNFS 1;
WLIT 1

Mencken, H(enry) L(ouis)
1880-1956 .... **TCLC 13**
See also AMW; CA 105; 125; CDALB
1917-1929; DLB 11, 29, 63, 137, 222;
EWL 3; MAL 5; MTCW 1, 2; MTFW
2005; NCFS 4; RGAL 4; TUS

Mendelsohn, Jane 1965- .... **CLC 99**
See also CA 154; CANR 94

Mendelssohn, Moses 1729-1786 .... **LC 142**
See also DLB 97

Mendoza, Inigo Lopez de
See Santillana, Inigo Lopez de Mendoza,
Marques de

Menton, Francisco de
See Chin, Frank (Chew, Jr.)

Mercer, David 1928-1980 .... **CLC 5**
See also CA 9-12R; 102; CANR 23; CBD;
DAM DRAM; DLB 13, 310; MTCW 1;
RGEL 2

Merchant, Paul
See Ellison, Harlan

Meredith, George 1828-1909 .. **PC 60; TCLC
17, 43**
See also CA 117; 153; CANR 80; CDBLB
1832-1890; DAM POET; DLB 18, 35, 57,
159; RGEL 2; TEA

Meredith, William 1919-2007 ...... **CLC 4, 13,
22, 55; PC 28**
See also CA 9-12R; 260; CAAS 14; CANR
6, 40, 129; CP 1, 2, 3, 4, 5, 6, 7; DAM
POET; DLB 5; MAL 5

Meredith, William Morris
See Meredith, William

Merezhkovsky, Dmitrii Sergeevich
See Merezhkovsky, Dmitry Sergeyevich
See also DLB 295

Merezhkovsky, Dmitry Sergeevich
See Merezhkovsky, Dmitry Sergeyevich
See also EWL 3

Merezhkovsky, Dmitry Sergeyevich
1865-1941 .... **TCLC 29**
See Merezhkovsky, Dmitrii Sergeevich;
Merezhkovsky, Dmitry Sergeevich
See also CA 169

Merimee, Prosper 1803-1870 ... **NCLC 6, 65;
SSC 7, 77**
See also DLB 119, 192; EW 6; EXPS; GFL
1789 to the Present; RGSF 2; RGWL 2,
3; SSFS 8; SUFW

Merkin, Daphne 1954- .... **CLC 44**
See also CA 123

Merleau-Ponty, Maurice
1908-1961 .... **TCLC 156**
See also CA 114; 89-92; DLB 296; GFL
1789 to the Present

Merlin, Arthur
See Blish, James (Benjamin)

Mernissi, Fatima 1940- .... **CLC 171**
See also CA 152; FW

Merrill, James 1926-1995 ...... **CLC 2, 3, 6, 8,
13, 18, 34, 91; PC 28; TCLC 173**
See also AMWS 3; CA 13-16R; 147; CANR
10, 49, 63, 108; CP 1, 2, 3, 4; DA3; DAM
POET; DLB 5, 165; DLBY 1985; EWL 3;
INT CANR-10; MAL 5; MTCW 1, 2;
MTFW 2005; PAB; PFS 23; RGAL 4

Merrill, James Ingram
See Merrill, James

Merriman, Alex
See Silverberg, Robert

Merriman, Brian 1747-1805 .... **NCLC 70**

Merritt, E. B.
See Waddington, Miriam

Merton, Thomas (James)
1915-1968 . **CLC 1, 3, 11, 34, 83; PC 10**
See also AAYA 61; AMWS 8; CA 5-8R;
25-28R; CANR 22, 53, 111, 131; DA3;
DLB 48; DLBY 1981; MAL 5; MTCW 1,
2; MTFW 2005

Merwin, W.S. 1927- ..... **CLC 1, 2, 3, 5, 8, 13,
18, 45, 88; PC 45**
See also AMWS 3; CA 13-16R; CANR 15,
51, 112, 140; CP 1, 2, 3, 4, 5, 6, 7; DA3;
DAM POET; DLB 5, 169, 342; EWL 3;
INT CANR-15; MAL 5; MTCW 1, 2;
MTFW 2005; PAB; PFS 5, 15; RGAL 4

Metastasio, Pietro 1698-1782 .... **LC 115**
See also RGWL 2, 3

Metcalf, John 1938- .... **CLC 37; SSC 43**
See also CA 113; CN 4, 5, 6, 7; DLB 60;
RGSF 2; TWA

Metcalf, Suzanne
See Baum, L(yman) Frank

Mew, Charlotte (Mary) 1870-1928 .. **TCLC 8**
See also CA 105; 189; DLB 19, 135; RGEL
2

Mewshaw, Michael 1943- .... **CLC 9**
See also CA 53-56; CANR 7, 47, 147;
DLBY 1980

Meyer, Conrad Ferdinand
1825-1898 .... **NCLC 81; SSC 30**
See also DLB 129; EW; RGWL 2, 3

Meyer, Gustav 1868-1932
See Meyrink, Gustav
See also CA 117; 190

Meyer, June
See Jordan, June

Meyer, Lynn
See Slavitt, David R.

Meyers, Jeffrey 1939- .... **CLC 39**
See also CA 73-76, 186; CAAE 186; CANR
54, 102, 159; DLB 111

**Meynell, Alice (Christina Gertrude
Thompson)** 1847-1922 .... **TCLC 6**
See also CA 104; 177; DLB 19, 98; RGEL
2

Meyrink, Gustav .... **TCLC 21**
See Meyer, Gustav
See also DLB 81; EWL 3

Mhlophe, Gcina 1960- .... **BLC 2:3**

Michaels, Leonard 1933-2003 ..... **CLC 6, 25; SSC 16**
See also AMWS 16; CA 61-64; 216; CANR 21, 62, 119, 179; CN 3, 45, 6, 7; DLB 130; MTCW 1; TCLE 1:2

Michaux, Henri 1899-1984 .... **CLC 8, 19**
See also CA 85-88; 114; DLB 258; EWL 3; GFL 1789 to the Present; RGWL 2, 3

Micheaux, Oscar (Devereaux)
1884-1951 .... **TCLC 76**
See also BW 3; CA 174; DLB 50; TCWW 2

Michelangelo 1475-1564 .... **LC 12**
See also AAYA 43

Michelet, Jules 1798-1874 .... **NCLC 31**
See also EW 5; GFL 1789 to the Present

Michels, Robert 1876-1936 .... **TCLC 88**
See also CA 212

Michener, James A. 1907(?)-1997 . **CLC 1, 5, 11, 29, 60, 109**
See also AAYA 27; AITN 1; BEST 90:1; BPFB 2; CA 5-8R; 161; CANR 21, 45, 68; CN 1, 2, 3, 4, 5, 6; CPW; DA3; DAM NOV, POP; DLB 6; MAL 5; MTCW 1, 2; MTFW 2005; RHW; TCWW 1, 2

Mickiewicz, Adam 1798-1855 . **NCLC 3, 101; PC 38**
See also EW 5; RGWL 2, 3

Middleton, (John) Christopher
1926- .... **CLC 13**
See also CA 13-16R; CANR 29, 54, 117; CP 1, 2, 3, 4, 5, 6, 7; DLB 40

Middleton, Richard (Barham)
1882-1911 .... **TCLC 56**
See also CA 187; DLB 156; HGG

Middleton, Stanley 1919- .... **CLC 7, 38**
See also CA 25-28R; CAAS 23; CANR 21, 46, 81, 157; CN 1, 2, 3, 4, 5, 6, 7; DLB 14, 326

Middleton, Thomas 1580-1627 ...... **DC 5; LC 33, 123**
See also BRW 2; DAM DRAM, MST; DFS 18, 22; DLB 58; RGEL 2

Mieville, China 1972(?)- .... **CLC 235**
See also AAYA 52; CA 196; CANR 138; MTFW 2005

Migueis, Jose Rodrigues 1901-1980 . **CLC 10**
See also DLB 287

Mikszath, Kalman 1847-1910 .... **TCLC 31**
See also CA 170

Miles, Jack .... **CLC 100**
See also CA 200

Miles, John Russiano
See Miles, Jack

Miles, Josephine (Louise)
1911-1985 .... **CLC 1, 2, 14, 34, 39**
See also CA 1-4R; 116; CANR 2, 55; CP 1, 2, 3, 4; DAM POET; DLB 48; MAL 5; TCLE 1:2

Militant
See Sandburg, Carl (August)

Mill, Harriet (Hardy) Taylor
1807-1858 .... **NCLC 102**
See also FW

Mill, John Stuart 1806-1873 ... **NCLC 11, 58, 179**
See also CDBLB 1832-1890; DLB 55, 190, 262; FW 1; RGEL 2; TEA

Millar, Kenneth 1915-1983 .... **CLC 14**
See Macdonald, Ross
See also CA 9-12R; 110; CANR 16, 63, 107; CMW 4; CPW; DA3; DAM POP; DLB 2, 226; DLBD 6; DLBY 1983; MTCW 1, 2; MTFW 2005

Millay, E. Vincent
See Millay, Edna St. Vincent

Millay, Edna St. Vincent 1892-1950 ..... **PC 6, 61; TCLC 4, 49, 169; WLCS**
See Boyd, Nancy
See also AMW; CA 104; 130; CDALB 1917-1929; DA; DA3; DAB; DAC; DAM MST, POET; DLB 45, 249; EWL 3; EXPP; FL 1:6; MAL 5; MBL; MTCW 1, 2; MTFW 2005; PAB; PFS 3, 17; RGAL 4; TUS; WP

Miller, Arthur 1915-2005 ..... **CLC 1, 2, 6, 10, 15, 26, 47, 78, 179; DC 1, 31; WLC 4**
See also AAYA 15; AITN 1; AMW; AMWC 1; CA 1-4R; 236; CABS 3; CAD; CANR 2, 30, 54, 76, 132; CD 5, 6; CDALB 1941-1968; DA; DA3; DAB; DAC; DAM DRAM, MST; DFS 1, 3, 8; DLB 7, 266; EWL 3; LAIT 1, 4; LATS 1:2; MAL 5; MTCW 1, 2; MTFW 2005; RGAL 4; RGHL; TUS; WYAS 1

Miller, Henry (Valentine)
1891-1980 ... **CLC 1, 2, 4, 9, 14, 43, 84; WLC 4**
See also AMW; BPFB 2; CA 9-12R; 97-100; CANR 33, 64; CDALB 1929-1941; CN 1, 2; DA; DA3; DAB; DAC; DAM MST, NOV; DLB 4, 9; DLBY 1980; EWL 3; MAL 5; MTCW 1, 2; MTFW 2005; RGAL 4; TUS

Miller, Hugh 1802-1856 .... **NCLC 143**
See also DLB 190

Miller, Jason 1939(?)-2001 .... **CLC 2**
See also AITN 1; CA 73-76; 197; CAD; CANR 130; DFS 12; DLB 7

Miller, Sue 1943- .... **CLC 44**
See also AMWS 12; BEST 90:3; CA 139; CANR 59, 91, 128; DA3; DAM POP; DLB 143

Miller, Walter M(ichael, Jr.)
1923-1996 .... **CLC 4, 30**
See also BPFB 2; CA 85-88; CANR 108; DLB 8; SCFW 1, 2; SFW 4

Millett, Kate 1934- .... **CLC 67**
See also AITN 1; CA 73-76; CANR 32, 53, 76, 110; DA3; DLB 246; FW; GLL 1; MTCW 1, 2; MTFW 2005

Millhauser, Steven 1943- ... **CLC 21, 54, 109; SSC 57**
See also AAYA 76; CA 110; 111; CANR 63, 114, 133; CN 6, 7; DA3; DLB 2; FANT; INT CA-111; MAL 5; MTCW 2; MTFW 2005

Millhauser, Steven Lewis
See Millhauser, Steven

Millin, Sarah Gertrude 1889-1968 ... **CLC 49**
See also CA 102; 93-96; DLB 225; EWL 3

Milne, A. A. 1882-1956 .... **TCLC 6, 88**
See also BRWS 5; CA 104; 133; CLR 1, 26, 108; CMW 4; CWRI 5; DA3; DAB; DAC; DAM MST; DLB 10, 77, 100, 160; FANT; MAICYA 1, 2; MTCW 1, 2; MTFW 2005; RGEL 2; SATA 100; WCH; YABC 1

Milne, Alan Alexander
See Milne, A. A.

Milner, Ron(ald) 1938-2004 .. **BLC 1:3; CLC 56**
See also AITN 1; BW 1; CA 73-76; 230; CAD; CANR 24, 81; CD 5, 6; DAM MULT; DLB 38; MAL 5; MTCW 1

Milnes, Richard Monckton
1809-1885 .... **NCLC 61**
See also DLB 32, 184

Milosz, Czeslaw 1911-2004 .... **CLC 5, 11, 22, 31, 56, 82, 253; PC 8; WLCS**
See also AAYA 62; CA 81-84; 230; CANR 23, 51, 91, 126; CDWLB 4; CWW 2; DA3; DAM MST, POET; DLB 215, 331; EW 13; EWL 3; MTCW 1, 2; MTFW 2005; PFS 16; RGHL; RGWL 2, 3

Milton, John 1608-1674 ..... **LC 9, 43, 92; PC 19, 29; WLC 4**
See also AAYA 65; BRW 2; BRWR 2; CD-BLB 1660-1789; DA; DA3; DAB; DAC; DAM MST, POET; DLB 131, 151, 281; EFS 1; EXPP; LAIT 1; PAB; PFS 3, 17; RGEL 2; TEA; WLIT 3; WP

Min, Anchee 1957- .... **CLC 86**
See also CA 146; CANR 94, 137; MTFW 2005

Minehaha, Cornelius
See Wedekind, Frank

Miner, Valerie 1947- .... **CLC 40**
See also CA 97-100; CANR 59, 177; FW; GLL 2

Minimo, Duca
See D'Annunzio, Gabriele

Minot, Susan (Anderson) 1956- ...... **CLC 44, 159**
See also AMWS 6; CA 134; CANR 118; CN 6, 7

Minus, Ed 1938- .... **CLC 39**
See also CA 185

Mirabai 1498(?)-1550(?) .... **LC 143; PC 48**
See also PFS 24

Miranda, Javier
See Bioy Casares, Adolfo
See also CWW 2

Mirbeau, Octave 1848-1917 .... **TCLC 55**
See also CA 216; DLB 123, 192; GFL 1789 to the Present

Mirikitani, Janice 1942- .... **AAL**
See also CA 211; DLB 312; RGAL 4

Mirk, John (?)-c. 1414 .... **LC 105**
See also DLB 146

Miro (Ferrer), Gabriel (Francisco Victor)
1879-1930 .... **TCLC 5**
See also CA 104; 185; DLB 322; EWL 3

Misharin, Alexandr .... **CLC 59**

Mishima, Yukio ... **CLC 2, 4, 6, 9, 27; DC 1; SSC 4; TCLC 161; WLC 4**
See Hiraoka, Kimitake
See also AAYA 50; BPFB 2; DLB 182; EWL 3; GLL 1; MJW; RGSF 2; RGWL 2, 3; SSFS 5, 12

Mistral, Frederic 1830-1914 .... **TCLC 51**
See also CA 122; 213; DLB 331; GFL 1789 to the Present

Mistral, Gabriela
See Godoy Alcayaga, Lucila
See also DLB 283, 331; DNFS 1; EWL 3; LAW; RGWL 2, 3; WP

Mistry, Rohinton 1952- ... **CLC 71, 196; SSC 73**
See also BRWS 10; CA 141; CANR 86, 114; CCA 1; CN 6, 7; DAC; DLB 334; SSFS 6

Mitchell, Clyde
See Ellison, Harlan; Silverberg, Robert

Mitchell, Emerson Blackhorse Barney
1945- .... **NNAL**
See also CA 45-48

Mitchell, James Leslie 1901-1935
See Gibbon, Lewis Grassic
See also CA 104; 188; DLB 15

Mitchell, Joni 1943- .... **CLC 12**
See also CA 112; CCA 1

Mitchell, Joseph (Quincy)
1908-1996 .... **CLC 98**
See also CA 77-80; 152; CANR 69; CN 1, 2, 3, 4, 5, 6; CSW; DLB 185; DLBY 1996

Mitchell, Margaret (Munnerlyn)
1900-1949 .... **TCLC 11, 170**
See also AAYA 23; BPFB 2; BYA 1; CA 109; 125; CANR 55, 94; CDALBS; DA3; DAM NOV, POP; DLB 9; LAIT 2; MAL 5; MTCW 1, 2; MTFW 2005; NFS 9; RGAL 4; RHW; TUS; WYAS 1; YAW

Morand, Paul 1888-1976 .... **CLC 41; SSC 22**
See also CA 184; 69-72; DLB 65; EWL 3
Morante, Elsa 1918-1985 .... **CLC 8, 47**
See also CA 85-88; 117; CANR 35; DLB
177; EWL 3; MTCW 1, 2; MTFW 2005;
RGHL; RGWL 2, 3; WLIT 7
Moravia, Alberto .... **CLC 2, 7, 11, 27, 46;
SSC 26**
See Pincherle, Alberto
See also DLB 177; EW 12; EWL 3; MTCW
2; RGSF 2; RGWL 2, 3; WLIT 7
Morck, Paul
See Rolvaag, O.E.
More, Hannah 1745-1833 ...... **NCLC 27, 141**
See also DLB 107, 109, 116, 158; RGEL 2
More, Henry 1614-1687 .... **LC 9**
See also DLB 126, 252
More, Sir Thomas 1478(?)-1535 ... **LC 10, 32,
140**
See also BRWC 1; BRWS 7; DLB 136, 281;
LMFS 1; RGEL 2; TEA
Moreas, Jean .... **TCLC 18**
See Papadiamantopoulos, Johannes
See also GFL 1789 to the Present
Moreton, Andrew Esq.
See Defoe, Daniel
Moreton, Lee
See Boucicault, Dion
Morgan, Berry 1919-2002 .... **CLC 6**
See also CA 49-52; 208; DLB 6
Morgan, Claire
See Highsmith, Patricia
See also GLL 1
Morgan, Edwin 1920- .... **CLC 31**
See also BRWS 9; CA 5-8R; CANR 3, 43,
90; CP 1, 2, 3, 4, 5, 6, 7; DLB 27
Morgan, Edwin George
See Morgan, Edwin
Morgan, (George) Frederick
1922-2004 .... **CLC 23**
See also CA 17-20R; 224; CANR 21, 144;
CP 2, 3, 4, 5, 6, 7
Morgan, Harriet
See Mencken, H(enry) L(ouis)
Morgan, Jane
See Cooper, James Fenimore
Morgan, Janet 1945- .... **CLC 39**
See also CA 65-68
Morgan, Lady 1776(?)-1859 .... **NCLC 29**
See also DLB 116, 158; RGEL 2
Morgan, Robin (Evonne) 1941- .... **CLC 2**
See also CA 69-72; CANR 29, 68; FW;
GLL 2; MTCW 1; SATA 80
Morgan, Scott
See Kuttner, Henry
Morgan, Seth 1949(?)-1990 .... **CLC 65**
See also CA 185; DLB 34
**Morgenstern, Christian (Otto Josef
Wolfgang)** 1871-1914 .... **TCLC 8**
See also CA 105; 191; EWL 3
Morgenstern, S.
See Goldman, William
Mori, Rintaro
See Mori Ogai
See also CA 110
Mori, Toshio 1910-1980 .... **AAL; SSC 83**
See also CA 116; 244; DLB 312; RGSF 2
Moricz, Zsigmond 1879-1942 .... **TCLC 33**
See also CA 165; DLB 215; EWL 3
Morike, Eduard (Friedrich)
1804-1875 .... **NCLC 10, 201**
See also DLB 133; RGWL 2, 3
Mori Ogai 1862-1922 .... **TCLC 14**
See Ogai
See also CA 164; DLB 180; EWL 3; RGWL
3; TWA
Moritz, Karl Philipp 1756-1793 .... **LC 2**
See also DLB 94

Morland, Peter Henry
See Faust, Frederick (Schiller)
Morley, Christopher (Darlington)
1890-1957 .... **TCLC 87**
See also CA 112; 213; DLB 9; MAL 5;
RGAL 4
Morren, Theophil
See Hofmannsthal, Hugo von
Morris, Bill 1952- .... **CLC 76**
See also CA 225
Morris, Julian
See West, Morris L(anglo)
Morris, Steveland Judkins (?)-
See Wonder, Stevie
Morris, William 1834-1896 . **NCLC 4; PC 55**
See also BRW 5; CDBLB 1832-1890; DLB
18, 35, 57, 156, 178, 184; FANT; RGEL
2; SFW 4; SUFW
Morris, Wright (Marion) 1910-1998 . **CLC 1,
3, 7, 18, 37; TCLC 107**
See also AMW; CA 9-12R; 167; CANR 21,
81; CN 1, 2, 3, 4, 5, 6; DLB 2, 206, 218;
DLBY 1981; EWL 3; MAL 5; MTCW 1,
2; MTFW 2005; RGAL 4; TCWW 1, 2
Morrison, Arthur 1863-1945 .... **SSC 40;
TCLC 72**
See also CA 120; 157; CMW 4; DLB 70,
135, 197; RGEL 2
Morrison, Chloe Anthony Wofford
See Morrison, Toni
Morrison, James Douglas 1943-1971
See Morrison, Jim
See also CA 73-76; CANR 40
Morrison, Jim .... **CLC 17**
See Morrison, James Douglas
Morrison, John Gordon 1904-1998 ... **SSC 93**
See also CA 103; CANR 92; DLB 260
Morrison, Toni 1931- . **BLC 1:3, 2:3; CLC 4,
10, 22, 55, 81, 87, 173, 194; WLC 4**
See also AAYA 1, 22, 61; AFAW 1, 2;
AMWC 1; AMWS 3; BPFB 2; BW 2, 3;
CA 29-32R; CANR 27, 42, 67, 113, 124;
CDALB 1968-1988; CLR 99; CN 3, 4, 5,
6, 7; CPW; DA; DA3; DAB; DAC; DAM
MST, MULT, NOV, POP; DLB 6, 33, 143,
331; DLBY 1981; EWL 3; EXPN; FL 1:6;
FW; GL 3; LAIT 2, 4; LATS 1:2; LMFS
2; MAL 5; MBL; MTCW 1, 2; MTFW
2005; NFS 1, 6, 8, 14; RGAL 4; RHW;
SATA 57, 144; SSFS 5; TCLE 1:2; TUS;
YAW
Morrison, Van 1945- .... **CLC 21**
See also CA 116; 168
Morrissy, Mary 1957- .... **CLC 99**
See also CA 205; DLB 267
Mortimer, John 1923- .... **CLC 28, 43**
See also CA 13-16R; CANR 21, 69, 109,
172; CBD; CD 5, 6; CDBLB 1960 to
Present; CMW 4; CN 5, 6, 7; CPW; DA3;
DAM DRAM, POP; DLB 13, 245, 271;
INT CANR-21; MSW; MTCW 1, 2;
MTFW 2005; RGEL 2
Mortimer, John Clifford
See Mortimer, John
Mortimer, Penelope (Ruth)
1918-1999 .... **CLC 5**
See also CA 57-60; 187; CANR 45, 88; CN
1, 2, 3, 4, 5, 6
Mortimer, Sir John
See Mortimer, John
Morton, Anthony
See Creasey, John
Morton, Thomas 1579(?)-1647(?) .... **LC 72**
See also DLB 24; RGEL 2
Mosca, Gaetano 1858-1941 .... **TCLC 75**
Moses, Daniel David 1952- .... **NNAL**
See also CA 186; CANR 160; DLB 334
Mosher, Howard Frank 1943- .... **CLC 62**
See also CA 139; CANR 65, 115

Mosley, Nicholas 1923- .... **CLC 43, 70**
See also CA 69-72; CANR 41, 60, 108, 158;
CN 1, 2, 3, 4, 5, 6, 7; DLB 14, 207
Mosley, Walter 1952- .... **BLCS; CLC 97, 184**
See also AAYA 57; AMWS 13; BPFB 2;
BW 2; CA 142; CANR 57, 92, 136, 172;
CMW 4; CN 7; CPW; DA3; DAM MULT,
POP; DLB 306; MSW; MTCW 2; MTFW
2005
Moss, Howard 1922-1987 . **CLC 7, 14, 45, 50**
See also CA 1-4R; 123; CANR 1, 44; CP 1,
2, 3, 4; DAM POET; DLB 5
Mossgiel, Rab
See Burns, Robert
Motion, Andrew 1952- .... **CLC 47**
See also BRWS 7; CA 146; CANR 90, 142;
CP 4, 5, 6, 7; DLB 40; MTFW 2005
Motion, Andrew Peter
See Motion, Andrew
Motley, Willard (Francis)
1909-1965 .... **CLC 18**
See also AMWS 17; BW 1; CA 117; 106;
CANR 88; DLB 76, 143
Motoori, Norinaga 1730-1801 .... **NCLC 45**
Mott, Michael (Charles Alston)
1930- .... **CLC 15, 34**
See also CA 5-8R; CAAS 7; CANR 7, 29
Mountain Wolf Woman 1884-1960 . **CLC 92;
NNAL**
See also CA 144; CANR 90
Moure, Erin 1955- .... **CLC 88**
See also CA 113; CP 5, 6, 7; CWP; DLB
60
Mourning Dove 1885(?)-1936 .... **NNAL**
See also CA 144; CANR 90; DAM MULT;
DLB 175, 221
Mowat, Farley 1921- .... **CLC 26**
See also AAYA 1, 50; BYA 2; CA 1-4R;
CANR 4, 24, 42, 68, 108; CLR 20; CPW;
DAC; DAM MST; DLB 68; INT CANR-
24; JRDA; MAICYA 1, 2; MTCW 1, 2;
MTFW 2005; SATA 3, 55; YAW
Mowat, Farley McGill
See Mowat, Farley
Mowatt, Anna Cora 1819-1870 ..... **NCLC 74**
See also RGAL 4
Mo Yan .... **CLC 257**
See Moye, Guan
Moye, Guan 1956(?)-
See Mo Yan
See also CA 201
Moyers, Bill 1934- .... **CLC 74**
See also AITN 2; CA 61-64; CANR 31, 52,
148
Mphahlele, Es'kia
See Mphahlele, Ezekiel
See also AFW; CDWLB 3; CN 4, 5, 6; DLB
125, 225; RGSF 2; SSFS 11
Mphahlele, Ezekiel 1919- ...... **BLC 1:3; CLC
25, 133**
See Mphahlele, Es'kia
See also BW 2, 3; CA 81-84; CANR 26,
76; CN 1, 2, 3; DA3; DAM MULT; EWL
3; MTCW 2; MTFW 2005; SATA 119
Mqhayi, S(amuel) E(dward) K(rune Loliwe)
1875-1945 .... **BLC 1:3; TCLC 25**
See also CA 153; CANR 87; DAM MULT
Mrozek, Slawomir 1930- .... **CLC 3, 13**
See also CA 13-16R; CAAS 10; CANR 29;
CDWLB 4; CWW 2; DLB 232; EWL 3;
MTCW 1
Mrs. Belloc-Lowndes
See Lowndes, Marie Adelaide (Belloc)
Mrs. Fairstar
See Horne, Richard Henry Hengist
M'Taggart, John M'Taggart Ellis
See McTaggart, John McTaggart Ellis
Mtwa, Percy (?)- .... **CLC 47**
See also CD 6

Pearson, Jean Mary
  See Gardam, Jane
Pearson, T. R. 1956- .... **CLC 39**
  See also CA 120; 130; CANR 97, 147;
  CSW; INT CA-130
Pearson, Thomas Reid
  See Pearson, T. R.
Peck, Dale 1967- .... **CLC 81**
  See also CA 146; CANR 72, 127, 180; GLL
  2
Peck, John (Frederick) 1941- .... **CLC 3**
  See also CA 49-52; CANR 3, 100; CP 4, 5,
  6, 7
Peck, Richard 1934- .... **CLC 21**
  See also AAYA 1, 24; BYA 1, 6, 8, 11; CA
  85-88; CANR 19, 38, 129, 178; CLR 15;
  INT CANR-19; JRDA; MAICYA 1, 2;
  SAAS 2; SATA 18, 55, 97, 110, 158, 190;
  SATA-Essay 110; WYA; YAW
Peck, Richard Wayne
  See Peck, Richard
Peck, Robert Newton 1928- .... **CLC 17**
  See also AAYA 3, 43; BYA 1, 6; CA 81-84,
  182; CAAE 182; CANR 31, 63, 127; CLR
  45; DA; DAC; DAM MST; JRDA; LAIT
  3; MAICYA 1, 2; SAAS 1; SATA 21, 62,
  111, 156; SATA-Essay 108; WYA; YAW
Peckinpah, David Samuel
  See Peckinpah, Sam
Peckinpah, Sam 1925-1984 .... **CLC 20**
  See also CA 109; 114; CANR 82
Pedersen, Knut 1859-1952
  See Hamsun, Knut
  See also CA 104; 119; CANR 63; MTCW
  1, 2
Peele, George 1556-1596 .... **DC 27; LC 115**
  See also BRW 1; DLB 62, 167; RGEL 2
Peeslake, Gaffer
  See Durrell, Lawrence (George)
Peguy, Charles (Pierre)
  1873-1914 .... **TCLC 10**
  See also CA 107; 193; DLB 258; EWL 3;
  GFL 1789 to the Present
Peirce, Charles Sanders
  1839-1914 .... **TCLC 81**
  See also CA 194; DLB 270
Pelecanos, George P. 1957- .... **CLC 236**
  See also CA 138; CANR 122, 165; DLB
  306
Pelevin, Victor 1962- .... **CLC 238**
  See Pelevin, Viktor Olegovich
  See also CA 154; CANR 88, 159
Pelevin, Viktor Olegovich
  See Pelevin, Victor
  See also DLB 285
Pellicer, Carlos 1897(?)-1977 .... **HLCS 2**
  See also CA 153; 69-72; DLB 290; EWL 3;
  HW 1
Pena, Ramon del Valle y
  See Valle-Inclan, Ramon (Maria) del
Pendennis, Arthur Esquir
  See Thackeray, William Makepeace
Penn, Arthur
  See Matthews, (James) Brander
Penn, William 1644-1718 .... **LC 25**
  See also DLB 24
PEPECE
  See Prado (Calvo), Pedro
Pepys, Samuel 1633-1703 ... **LC 11, 58; WLC**
  4
  See also BRW 2; CDBLB 1660-1789; DA;
  DA3; DAB; DAC; DAM MST; DLB 101,
  213; NCFS 4; RGEL 2; TEA; WLIT 3
Percy, Thomas 1729-1811 .... **NCLC 95**
  See also DLB 104

Percy, Walker 1916-1990 .... **CLC 2, 3, 6, 8,**
  14, 18, 47, 65
  See also AMWS 3; BPFB 3; CA 1-4R; 131;
  CANR 1, 23, 64; CN 1, 2, 3, 4; CPW;
  CSW; DA3; DAM NOV, POP; DLB 2;
  DLBY 1980, 1990; EWL 3; MAL 5;
  MTCW 1, 2; MTFW 2005; RGAL 4; TUS
Percy, William Alexander
  1885-1942 .... **TCLC 84**
  See also CA 163; MTCW 2
Perec, Georges 1936-1982 .... **CLC 56, 116**
  See also CA 141; DLB 83, 299; EWL 3;
  GFL 1789 to the Present; RGHL; RGWL
  3
Pereda (y Sanchez de Porrua), Jose Maria
  de 1833-1906 .... **TCLC 16**
  See also CA 117
Pereda y Porrua, Jose Maria de
  See Pereda (y Sanchez de Porrua), Jose
  Maria de
Peregoy, George Weems
  See Mencken, H(enry) L(ouis)
Perelman, S(idney) J(oseph)
  1904-1979 .. **CLC 3, 5, 9, 15, 23, 44, 49;**
  SSC 32
  See also AITN 1, 2; BPFB 3; CA 73-76;
  89-92; CANR 18; DAM DRAM; DLB 11,
  44; MTCW 1, 2; MTFW 2005; RGAL 4
Peret, Benjamin 1899-1959 .... **PC 33; TCLC**
  20
  See also CA 117; 186; GFL 1789 to the
  Present
Peretz, Isaac Leib
  See Peretz, Isaac Loeb
  See also CA 201; DLB 333
Peretz, Isaac Loeb 1851(?)-1915 ...... **SSC 26;**
  TCLC 16
  See Peretz, Isaac Leib
  See also CA 109
Peretz, Yitzhok Leibush
  See Peretz, Isaac Loeb
Perez Galdos, Benito 1843-1920 ..... **HLCS 2;**
  TCLC 27
  See Galdos, Benito Perez
  See also CA 125; 153; EWL 3; HW 1;
  RGWL 2, 3
Peri Rossi, Cristina 1941- .. **CLC 156; HLCS**
  2
  See also CA 131; CANR 59, 81; CWW 2;
  DLB 145, 290; EWL 3; HW 1, 2
Perlata
  See Peret, Benjamin
Perloff, Marjorie G(abrielle)
  1931- .... **CLC 137**
  See also CA 57-60; CANR 7, 22, 49, 104
Perrault, Charles 1628-1703 .... **LC 2, 56**
  See also BYA 4; CLR 79, 134; DLB 268;
  GFL Beginnings to 1789; MAICYA 1, 2;
  RGWL 2, 3; SATA 25; WCH
Perry, Anne 1938- .... **CLC 126**
  See also CA 101; CANR 22, 50, 84, 150,
  177; CMW 4; CN 6, 7; CPW; DLB 276
Perry, Brighton
  See Sherwood, Robert E(mmet)
Perse, St.-John
  See Leger, (Marie-Rene Auguste) Alexis
  Saint-Leger
Perse, Saint-John
  See Leger, (Marie-Rene Auguste) Alexis
  Saint-Leger
  See also DLB 258, 331; RGWL 3
Persius 34-62 .... **CMLC 74**
  See also AW 2; DLB 211; RGWL 2, 3
Perutz, Leo(pold) 1882-1957 .... **TCLC 60**
  See also CA 147; DLB 81
Peseenz, Tulio F.
  See Lopez y Fuentes, Gregorio
Pesetsky, Bette 1932- .... **CLC 28**
  See also CA 133; DLB 130

Peshkov, Alexei Maximovich 1868-1936
  See Gorky, Maxim
  See also CA 105; 141; CANR 83; DA;
  DAC; DAM DRAM, MST, NOV; MTCW
  2; MTFW 2005
Pessoa, Fernando (Antonio Nogueira)
  1888-1935 ..... **HLC 2; PC 20; TCLC 27**
  See also CA 125; 183; DAM MULT; DLB
  287; EW 10; EWL 3; RGWL 2, 3; WP
Peterkin, Julia Mood 1880-1961 ...... **CLC 31**
  See also CA 102; DLB 9
Peters, Joan K(aren) 1945- .... **CLC 39**
  See also CA 158; CANR 109
Peters, Robert L(ouis) 1924- .... **CLC 7**
  See also CA 13-16R; CAAS 8; CP 1, 5, 6,
  7; DLB 105
Petofi, Sandor 1823-1849 .... **NCLC 21**
  See also RGWL 2, 3
Petrakis, Harry Mark 1923- .... **CLC 3**
  See also CA 9-12R; CANR 4, 30, 85, 155;
  CN 1, 2, 3, 4, 5, 6, 7
Petrarch 1304-1374 .... **CMLC 20; PC 8**
  See also DA3; DAM POET; EW 2; LMFS
  1; RGWL 2, 3; WLIT 7
Petronius c. 20-66 .... **CMLC 34**
  See also AW 2; CDWLB 1; DLB 211;
  RGWL 2, 3; WLIT 8
Petrov, Evgeny .... **TCLC 21**
  See Kataev, Evgeny Petrovich
Petry, Ann (Lane) 1908-1997 .. **CLC 1, 7, 18;**
  TCLC 112
  See also AFAW 1, 2; BPFB 3; BW 1, 3;
  BYA 2; CA 5-8R; 157; CAAS 6; CANR
  4, 46; CLR 12; CN 1, 2, 3, 4, 5, 6; DLB
  76; EWL 3; JRDA; LAIT 1; MAICYA 1,
  2; MAICYAS 1; MTCW 1; RGAL 4;
  SATA 5; SATA-Obit 94; TUS
Petursson, Halligrimur 1614-1674 .... **LC 8**
Peychinovich
  See Vazov, Ivan (Minchov)
Phaedrus c. 15B.C.-c. 50 .... **CMLC 25**
  See also DLB 211
Phelps (Ward), Elizabeth Stuart
  See Phelps, Elizabeth Stuart
  See also FW
Phelps, Elizabeth Stuart
  1844-1911 .... **TCLC 113**
  See Phelps (Ward), Elizabeth Stuart
  See also CA 242; DLB 74
Philippe de Remi c. 1247-1296 ... **CMLC 102**
Philips, Katherine 1632-1664 ..... **LC 30, 145;**
  PC 40
  See also DLB 131; RGEL 2
Philipson, Ilene J. 1950- .... **CLC 65**
  See also CA 219
Philipson, Morris H. 1926- .... **CLC 53**
  See also CA 1-4R; CANR 4
Phillips, Caryl 1958- ..... **BLCS; CLC 96, 224**
  See also BRWS 5; BW 2; CA 141; CANR
  63, 104, 140; CBD; CD 5, 6; CN 5, 6, 7;
  DA3; DAM MULT; DLB 157; EWL 3;
  MTCW 2; MTFW 2005; WLIT 4; WWE
  1
Phillips, David Graham
  1867-1911 .... **TCLC 44**
  See also CA 108; 176; DLB 9, 12, 303;
  RGAL 4
Phillips, Jack
  See Sandburg, Carl (August)
Phillips, Jayne Anne 1952- .... **CLC 15, 33,**
  139; SSC 16
  See also AAYA 57; BPFB 3; CA 101;
  CANR 24, 50, 96; CN 4, 5, 6, 7; CSW;
  DLBY 1980; INT CANR-24; MTCW 1,
  2; MTFW 2005; RGAL 4; RGSF 2; SSFS
  4
Phillips, Richard
  See Dick, Philip K.

Phillips, Robert (Schaeffer) 1938- .... **CLC 28**
See also CA 17-20R; CAAS 13; CANR 8;
DLB 105

Phillips, Ward
See Lovecraft, H. P.

Philo c. 20B.C.-c. 50 .... **CMLC 100**
See also DLB 176

Philostratus, Flavius c. 179-c.
244 .... **CMLC 62**

Piccolo, Lucio 1901-1969 .... **CLC 13**
See also CA 97-100; DLB 114; EWL 3

Pickthall, Marjorie L(owry) C(hristie)
1883-1922 .... **TCLC 21**
See also CA 107; DLB 92

Pico della Mirandola, Giovanni
1463-1494 .... **LC 15**
See also LMFS 1

Piercy, Marge 1936- .... **CLC 3, 6, 14, 18, 27,
62, 128; PC 29**
See also BPFB 3; CA 21-24R, 187; CAAE
187; CAAS 1; CANR 13, 43, 66, 111; CN
3, 4, 5, 6, 7; CP 1, 2, 3, 4, 5, 6, 7; CWP;
DLB 120, 227; EXPP; FW; MAL 5;
MTCW 1, 2; MTFW 2005; PFS 9, 22;
SFW 4

Piers, Robert
See Anthony, Piers

Pieyre de Mandiargues, Andre 1909-1991
See Mandiargues, Andre Pieyre de
See also CA 103; 136; CANR 22, 82; EWL
3; GFL 1789 to the Present

Pilnyak, Boris 1894-1938 . **SSC 48; TCLC 23**
See Vogau, Boris Andreyevich
See also EWL 3

Pinchback, Eugene
See Toomer, Jean

Pincherle, Alberto 1907-1990 ...... **CLC 11, 18**
See Moravia, Alberto
See also CA 25-28R; 132; CANR 33, 63,
142; DAM NOV; MTCW 1; MTFW 2005

Pinckney, Darryl 1953- .... **CLC 76**
See also BW 2, 3; CA 143; CANR 79

Pindar 518(?)B.C.-438(?)B.C. .... **CMLC 12;
PC 19**
See also AW 1; CDWLB 1; DLB 176;
RGWL 2

Pineda, Cecile 1942- .... **CLC 39**
See also CA 118; DLB 209

Pinero, Arthur Wing 1855-1934 .... **TCLC 32**
See also CA 110; 153; DAM DRAM; DLB
10, 344; RGEL 2

Pinero, Miguel (Antonio Gomez)
1946-1988 .... **CLC 4, 55**
See also CA 61-64; 125; CAD; CANR 29,
90; DLB 266; HW 1; LLW

Pinget, Robert 1919-1997 .... **CLC 7, 13, 37**
See also CA 85-88; 160; CWW 2; DLB 83;
EWL 3; GFL 1789 to the Present

Pink Floyd
See Barrett, (Roger) Syd; Gilmour, David;
Mason, Nick; Waters, Roger; Wright, Rick

Pinkney, Edward 1802-1828 .... **NCLC 31**
See also DLB 248

Pinkwater, D. Manus
See Pinkwater, Daniel Manus

Pinkwater, Daniel
See Pinkwater, Daniel Manus

Pinkwater, Daniel M.
See Pinkwater, Daniel Manus

Pinkwater, Daniel Manus 1941- .... **CLC 35**
See also AAYA 1, 46; BYA 9; CA 29-32R;
CANR 12, 38, 89, 143; CLR 4; CSW;
FANT; JRDA; MAICYA 1, 2; SAAS 3;
SATA 8, 46, 76, 114, 158; SFW 4; YAW

Pinkwater, Manus
See Pinkwater, Daniel Manus

Pinsky, Robert 1940- .... **CLC 9, 19, 38, 94,
121, 216; PC 27**
See also AMWS 6; CA 29-32R; CAAS 4;
CANR 58, 97, 138, 177; CP 3, 4, 5, 6, 7;
DA3; DAM POET; DLBY 1982, 1998;
MAL 5; MTCW 2; MTFW 2005; PFS 18;
RGAL 4; TCLE 1:2

Pinta, Harold
See Pinter, Harold

Pinter, Harold 1930- .. **CLC 1, 3, 6, 9, 11, 15,
27, 58, 73, 199; DC 15; WLC 4**
See also BRWR 1; BRWS 1; CA 5-8R;
CANR 33, 65, 112, 145; CBD; CD 5, 6;
CDBLB 1960 to Present; CP 1; DA; DA3;
DAB; DAC; DAM DRAM, MST; DFS 3,
5, 7, 14, 25; DLB 13, 310, 331; EWL 3;
IDFW 3, 4; LMFS 2; MTCW 1, 2; MTFW
2005; RGEL 2; RGHL; TEA

Piozzi, Hester Lynch (Thrale)
1741-1821 .... **NCLC 57**
See also DLB 104, 142

Pirandello, Luigi 1867-1936 .. **DC 5; SSC 22;
TCLC 4, 29, 172; WLC 4**
See also CA 104; 153; CANR 103; DA;
DA3; DAB; DAC; DAM DRAM, MST;
DFS 4, 9; DLB 264, 331; EW 8; EWL 3;
MTCW 2; MTFW 2005; RGSF 2; RGWL
2, 3; WLIT 7

Pirsig, Robert M(aynard) 1928- ... **CLC 4, 6,
73**
See also CA 53-56; CANR 42, 74; CPW 1;
DA3; DAM POP; MTCW 1, 2; MTFW
2005; SATA 39

Pisan, Christine de
See Christine de Pizan

Pisarev, Dmitrii Ivanovich
See Pisarev, Dmitry Ivanovich
See also DLB 277

Pisarev, Dmitry Ivanovich
1840-1868 .... **NCLC 25**
See Pisarev, Dmitrii Ivanovich

Pix, Mary (Griffith) 1666-1709 ..... **LC 8, 149**
See also DLB 80

Pixerecourt, (Rene Charles) Guilbert de
1773-1844 .... **NCLC 39**
See also DLB 192; GFL 1789 to the Present

Plaatje, Sol(omon) T(shekisho)
1878-1932 .... **BLCS; TCLC 73**
See also BW 2, 3; CA 141; CANR 79; DLB
125, 225

Plaidy, Jean
See Hibbert, Eleanor Alice Burford

Planche, James Robinson
1796-1880 .... **NCLC 42**
See also RGEL 2

Plant, Robert 1948- .... **CLC 12**

Plante, David 1940- .... **CLC 7, 23, 38**
See also CA 37-40R; CANR 12, 36, 58, 82,
152; CN 2, 3, 4, 5, 6, 7; DAM NOV;
DLBY 1983; INT CANR-12; MTCW 1

Plante, David Robert
See Plante, David

Plath, Sylvia 1932-1963 ..... **CLC 1, 2, 3, 5, 9,
11, 14, 17, 50, 51, 62, 111; PC 1, 37;
WLC 4**
See also AAYA 13; AMWR 2; AMWS 1;
BPFB 3; CA 19-20; CANR 34, 101; CAP
2; CDALB 1941-1968; DA; DA3; DAB;
DAC; DAM MST, POET; DLB 5, 6, 152;
EWL 3; EXPN; EXPP; FL 1:6; FW; LAIT
4; MAL 5; MBL; MTCW 1, 2; MTFW
2005; NFS 1; PAB; PFS 1, 15, 28; RGAL
4; SATA 96; TUS; WP; YAW

Plato c. 428B.C.-347B.C. .... **CMLC 8, 75, 98;
WLCS**
See also AW 1; CDWLB 1; DA; DA3;
DAB; DAC; DAM MST; DLB 176; LAIT
1; LATS 1:1; RGWL 2, 3; WLIT 8

Platonov, Andrei
See Klimentov, Andrei Platonovich

Platonov, Andrei Platonovich
See Klimentov, Andrei Platonovich
See also DLB 272

Platonov, Andrey Platonovich
See Klimentov, Andrei Platonovich
See also EWL 3

Platt, Kin 1911- .... **CLC 26**
See also AAYA 11; CA 17-20R; CANR 11;
JRDA; SAAS 17; SATA 21, 86; WYA

Plautus c. 254B.C.-c. 184B.C. .... **CMLC 24,
92; DC 6**
See also AW 1; CDWLB 1; DLB 211;
RGWL 2, 3; WLIT 8

Plick et Plock
See Simenon, Georges (Jacques Christian)

Plieksans, Janis
See Rainis, Janis

Plimpton, George 1927-2003 .... **CLC 36**
See also AITN 1; AMWS 16; CA 21-24R;
224; CANR 32, 70, 103, 133; DLB 185,
241; MTCW 1, 2; MTFW 2005; SATA
10; SATA-Obit 150

Pliny the Elder c. 23-79 .... **CMLC 23**
See also DLB 211

Pliny the Younger c. 61-c. 112 ...... **CMLC 62**
See also AW 2; DLB 211

Plomer, William Charles Franklin
1903-1973 .... **CLC 4, 8**
See also AFW; BRWS 11; CA 21-22; CANR
34; CAP 2; CN 1; CP 1, 2; DLB 20, 162,
191, 225; EWL 3; MTCW 1; RGEL 2;
RGSF 2; SATA 24

Plotinus 204-270 .... **CMLC 46**
See also CDWLB 1; DLB 176

Plowman, Piers
See Kavanagh, Patrick (Joseph)

Plum, J.
See Wodehouse, P(elham) G(renville)

Plumly, Stanley (Ross) 1939- .... **CLC 33**
See also CA 108; 110; CANR 97; CP 3, 4,
5, 6, 7; DLB 5, 193; INT CA-110

Plumpe, Friedrich Wilhelm
See Murnau, F.W.

Plutarch c. 46-c. 120 .... **CMLC 60**
See also AW 2; CDWLB 1; DLB 176;
RGWL 2, 3; TWA; WLIT 8

Po Chu-i 772-846 .... **CMLC 24**

Podhoretz, Norman 1930- .... **CLC 189**
See also AMWS 8; CA 9-12R; CANR 7,
78, 135, 179

Poe, Edgar Allan 1809-1849 ..... **NCLC 1, 16,
55, 78, 94, 97, 117; PC 1, 54; SSC 1,
22, 34, 35, 54, 88, 111; WLC 4**
See also AAYA 14; AMW; AMWC 1;
AMWR 2; BPFB 3; BYA 5, 11; CDALB
1640-1865; CMW 4; DA; DA3; DAB;
DAC; DAM MST, POET; DLB 3, 59, 73,
74, 248, 254; EXPP; EXPS; GL 3; HGG;
LAIT 2; LATS 1:1; LMFS 1; MSW; PAB;
PFS 1, 3, 9; RGAL 4; RGSF 2; SATA 23;
SCFW 1, 2; SFW 4; SSFS 2, 4, 7, 8, 16,
26; SUFW; TUS; WP; WYA

Poet of Titchfield Street, The
See Pound, Ezra (Weston Loomis)

Poggio Bracciolini, Gian Francesco
1380-1459 .... **LC 125**

Pohl, Frederik 1919- .... **CLC 18; SSC 25**
See also AAYA 24; CA 61-64, 188; CAAE
188; CAAS 1; CANR 11, 37, 81, 140; CN
1, 2, 3, 4, 5, 6; DLB 8; INT CANR-11;
MTCW 1, 2; MTFW 2005; SATA 24;
SCFW 1, 2; SFW 4

Poirier, Louis
See Gracq, Julien

Poitier, Sidney 1927- .... **CLC 26**
See also AAYA 60; BW 1; CA 117; CANR
94

Pokagon, Simon 1830-1899 .... **NNAL**
See also DAM MULT

Rawley, Callman 1903-2004
  See Rakosi, Carl
  See also CA 21-24R; 228; CANR 12, 32, 91

Rawlings, Marjorie Kinnan
  1896-1953 .... **TCLC 4**
  See also AAYA 20; AMWS 10; ANW; BPFB 3; BYA 3; CA 104; 137; CANR 74; CLR 63; DLB 9, 22, 102; DLBD 17; JRDA; MAICYA 1, 2; MAL 5; MTCW 2; MTFW 2005; RGAL 4; SATA 100; WCH; YABC 1; YAW

Ray, Satyajit 1921-1992 .... **CLC 16, 76**
  See also CA 114; 137; DAM MULT

Read, Herbert Edward 1893-1968 ..... **CLC 4**
  See also BRW 6; CA 85-88; 25-28R; DLB 20, 149; EWL 3; PAB; RGEL 2

Read, Piers Paul 1941- .... **CLC 4, 10, 25**
  See also CA 21-24R; CANR 38, 86, 150; CN 2, 3, 4, 5, 6, 7; DLB 14; SATA 21

Reade, Charles 1814-1884 .... **NCLC 2, 74**
  See also DLB 21; RGEL 2

Reade, Hamish
  See Gray, Simon

Reading, Peter 1946- .... **CLC 47**
  See also BRWS 8; CA 103; CANR 46, 96; CP 5, 6, 7; DLB 40

Reaney, James 1926-2008 .... **CLC 13**
  See also CA 41-44R; CAAS 15; CANR 42; CD 5, 6; CP 1, 2, 3, 4, 5, 6, 7; DAC; DAM MST; DLB 68; RGEL 2; SATA 43

Reaney, James Crerar
  See Reaney, James

Rebreanu, Liviu 1885-1944 .... **TCLC 28**
  See also CA 165; DLB 220; EWL 3

Rechy, John 1934- ..... **CLC 1, 7, 14, 18, 107; HLC 2**
  See also CA 5-8R, 195; CAAE 195; CAAS 4; CANR 6, 32, 64, 152; CN 1, 2, 3, 4, 5, 6, 7; DAM MULT; DLB 122, 278; DLBY 1982; HW 1, 2; INT CANR-6; LLW; MAL 5; RGAL 4

Rechy, John Francisco
  See Rechy, John

Redcam, Tom 1870-1933 .... **TCLC 25**

Reddin, Keith 1956- .... **CLC 67**
  See also CAD; CD 6

Redgrove, Peter (William)
  1932-2003 .... **CLC 6, 41**
  See also BRWS 6; CA 1-4R; 217; CANR 3, 39, 77; CP 1, 2, 3, 4, 5, 6, 7; DLB 40; TCLE 1:2

Redmon, Anne .... **CLC 22**
  See Nightingale, Anne Redmon
  See also DLBY 1986

Reed, Eliot
  See Ambler, Eric

Reed, Ishmael 1938- . **BLC 1:3; CLC 2, 3, 5, 6, 13, 32, 60, 174; PC 68**
  See also AFAW 1, 2; AMWS 10; BPFB 3; BW 2, 3; CA 21-24R; CANR 25, 48, 74, 128; CN 1, 2, 3, 4, 5, 6, 7; CP 1, 2, 3, 4, 5, 6, 7; CSW; DA3; DAM MULT; DLB 2, 5, 33, 169, 227; DLBD 8; EWL 3; LMFS 2; MAL 5; MSW; MTCW 1, 2; MTFW 2005; PFS 6; RGAL 4; TCWW 2

Reed, John (Silas) 1887-1920 .... **TCLC 9**
  See also CA 106; 195; MAL 5; TUS

Reed, Lou .... **CLC 21**
  See Firbank, Louis

Reese, Lizette Woodworth
  1856-1935 .... **PC 29; TCLC 181**
  See also CA 180; DLB 54

Reeve, Clara 1729-1807 .... **NCLC 19**
  See also DLB 39; RGEL 2

Reich, Wilhelm 1897-1957 .... **TCLC 57**
  See also CA 199

Reid, Christopher (John) 1949- .... **CLC 33**
  See also CA 140; CANR 89; CP 4, 5, 6, 7; DLB 40; EWL 3

Reid, Desmond
  See Moorcock, Michael

Reid Banks, Lynne 1929-
  See Banks, Lynne Reid
  See also AAYA 49; CA 1-4R; CANR 6, 22, 38, 87; CLR 24, 86; CN 1, 2, 3, 7; JRDA; MAICYA 1, 2; SATA 22, 75, 111, 165; YAW

Reilly, William K.
  See Creasey, John

Reiner, Max
  See Caldwell, (Janet Miriam) Taylor (Holland)

Reis, Ricardo
  See Pessoa, Fernando (Antonio Nogueira)

Reizenstein, Elmer Leopold
  See Rice, Elmer (Leopold)
  See also EWL 3

Remarque, Erich Maria 1898-1970 . **CLC 21**
  See also AAYA 27; BPFB 3; CA 77-80; 29-32R; CDWLB 2; DA; DA3; DAB; DAC; DAM MST, NOV; DLB 56; EWL 3; EXPN; LAIT 3; MTCW 1, 2; MTFW 2005; NFS 4; RGHL; RGWL 2, 3

Remington, Frederic S(ackrider)
  1861-1909 .... **TCLC 89**
  See also CA 108; 169; DLB 12, 186, 188; SATA 41; TCWW 2

Remizov, A.
  See Remizov, Aleksei (Mikhailovich)

Remizov, A. M.
  See Remizov, Aleksei (Mikhailovich)

Remizov, Aleksei (Mikhailovich)
  1877-1957 .... **TCLC 27**
  See Remizov, Alexey Mikhaylovich
  See also CA 125; 133; DLB 295

Remizov, Alexey Mikhaylovich
  See Remizov, Aleksei (Mikhailovich)
  See also EWL 3

Renan, Joseph Ernest 1823-1892 . **NCLC 26, 145**
  See also GFL 1789 to the Present

Renard, Jules(-Pierre) 1864-1910 .. **TCLC 17**
  See also CA 117; 202; GFL 1789 to the Present

Renart, Jean fl. 13th cent. - .... **CMLC 83**

Renault, Mary .... **CLC 3, 11, 17**
  See Challans, Mary
  See also BPFB 3; BYA 2; CN 1, 2, 3; DLBY 1983; EWL 3; GLL 1; LAIT 1; RGEL 2; RHW

Rendell, Ruth 1930- .... **CLC 28, 48**
  See Vine, Barbara
  See also BPFB 3; BRWS 9; CA 109; CANR 32, 52, 74, 127, 162; CN 5, 6, 7; CPW; DAM POP; DLB 87, 276; INT CANR-32; MSW; MTCW 1, 2; MTFW 2005

Rendell, Ruth Barbara
  See Rendell, Ruth

Renoir, Jean 1894-1979 .... **CLC 20**
  See also CA 129; 85-88

Rensie, Willis
  See Eisner, Will

Resnais, Alain 1922- .... **CLC 16**

Revard, Carter 1931- .... **NNAL**
  See also CA 144; CANR 81, 153; PFS 5

Reverdy, Pierre 1889-1960 .... **CLC 53**
  See also CA 97-100; 89-92; DLB 258; EWL 3; GFL 1789 to the Present

Rexroth, Kenneth 1905-1982 .... **CLC 1, 2, 6, 11, 22, 49, 112; PC 20**
  See also BG 1:3; CA 5-8R; 107; CANR 14, 34, 63; CDALB 1941-1968; CP 1, 2, 3; DAM POET; DLB 16, 48, 165, 212; DLBY 1982; EWL 3; INT CANR-14; MAL 5; MTCW 1, 2; MTFW 2005; RGAL 4

Reyes, Alfonso 1889-1959 .... **HLCS 2; TCLC 33**
  See also CA 131; EWL 3; HW 1; LAW

Reyes y Basoalto, Ricardo Eliecer Neftali
  See Neruda, Pablo

Reymont, Wladyslaw (Stanislaw)
  1868(?)-1925 .... **TCLC 5**
  See also CA 104; DLB 332; EWL 3

Reynolds, John Hamilton
  1794-1852 .... **NCLC 146**
  See also DLB 96

Reynolds, Jonathan 1942- .... **CLC 6, 38**
  See also CA 65-68; CANR 28, 176

Reynolds, Joshua 1723-1792 .... **LC 15**
  See also DLB 104

Reynolds, Michael S(hane)
  1937-2000 .... **CLC 44**
  See also CA 65-68; 189; CANR 9, 89, 97

Reznikoff, Charles 1894-1976 .... **CLC 9**
  See also AMWS 14; CA 33-36; 61-64; CAP 2; CP 1, 2; DLB 28, 45; RGHL; WP

Rezzori, Gregor von
  See Rezzori d'Arezzo, Gregor von

Rezzori d'Arezzo, Gregor von
  1914-1998 .... **CLC 25**
  See also CA 122; 136; 167

Rhine, Richard
  See Silverstein, Alvin; Silverstein, Virginia B(arbara Opshelor)

Rhodes, Eugene Manlove
  1869-1934 .... **TCLC 53**
  See also CA 198; DLB 256; TCWW 1, 2

R'hoone, Lord
  See Balzac, Honore de

Rhys, Jean 1890-1979 .... **CLC 2, 4, 6, 14, 19, 51, 124; SSC 21, 76**
  See also BRWS 2; CA 25-28R; 85-88; CANR 35, 62; CDBLB 1945-1960; CDWLB 3; CN 1, 2; DA3; DAM NOV; DLB 36, 117, 162; DNFS 2; EWL 3; LATS 1:1; MTCW 1, 2; MTFW 2005; NFS 19; RGEL 2; RGSF 2; RHW; TEA; WWE 1

Ribeiro, Darcy 1922-1997 .... **CLC 34**
  See also CA 33-36R; 156; EWL 3

Ribeiro, Joao Ubaldo (Osorio Pimentel)
  1941- .... **CLC 10, 67**
  See also CA 81-84; CWW 2; EWL 3

Ribman, Ronald (Burt) 1932- .... **CLC 7**
  See also CA 21-24R; CAD; CANR 46, 80; CD 5, 6

Ricci, Nino (Pio) 1959- .... **CLC 70**
  See also CA 137; CANR 130; CCA 1

Rice, Anne 1941- .... **CLC 41, 128**
  See Rampling, Anne
  See also AAYA 9, 53; AMWS 7; BEST 89:2; BPFB 3; CA 65-68; CANR 12, 36, 53, 74, 100, 133; CN 6, 7; CPW; CSW; DA3; DAM POP; DLB 292; GL 3; GLL 2; HGG; MTCW 2; MTFW 2005; SUFW 2; YAW

Rice, Elmer (Leopold) 1892-1967 ...... **CLC 7, 49**
  See Reizenstein, Elmer Leopold
  See also CA 21-22; 25-28R; CAP 2; DAM DRAM; DFS 12; DLB 4, 7; IDTP; MAL 5; MTCW 1, 2; RGAL 4

Rice, Tim(othy Miles Bindon)
  1944- .... **CLC 21**
  See also CA 103; CANR 46; DFS 7

Rich, Adrienne 1929- ..... **CLC 3, 6, 7, 11, 18, 36, 73, 76, 125; PC 5**
  See also AAYA 69; AMWR 2; AMWS 1; CA 9-12R; CANR 20, 53, 74, 128; CDALBS; CP 1, 2, 3, 4, 5, 6, 7; CSW; CWP; DA3; DAM POET; DLB 5, 67; EWL 3; EXPP; FL 1:6; FW; MAL 5; MBL; MTCW 1, 2; MTFW 2005; PAB; PFS 15; RGAL 4; RGHL; WP

Robinson, William, Jr. 1940-
See Robinson, Smokey
See also CA 116

Robison, Mary 1949- .... **CLC 42, 98**
See also CA 113; 116; CANR 87; CN 4, 5,
6, 7; DLB 130; INT CA-116; RGSF 2

Roches, Catherine des 1542-1587 ...... **LC 117**
See also DLB 327

Rochester
See Wilmot, John
See also RGEL 2

Rod, Edouard 1857-1910 .... **TCLC 52**

Roddenberry, Eugene Wesley 1921-1991
See Roddenberry, Gene
See also CA 110; 135; CANR 37; SATA 45;
SATA-Obit 69

Roddenberry, Gene .... **CLC 17**
See Roddenberry, Eugene Wesley
See also AAYA 5; SATA-Obit 69

Rodgers, Mary 1931- .... **CLC 12**
See also BYA 5; CA 49-52; CANR 8, 55,
90; CLR 20; CWRI 5; INT CANR-8;
JRDA; MAICYA 1, 2; SATA 8, 130

Rodgers, W(illiam) R(obert)
1909-1969 .... **CLC 7**
See also CA 85-88; DLB 20; RGEL 2

Rodman, Eric
See Silverberg, Robert

Rodman, Howard 1920(?)-1985 .... **CLC 65**
See also CA 118

Rodman, Maia
See Wojciechowska, Maia (Teresa)

Rodo, Jose Enrique 1871(?)-1917 .... **HLCS 2**
See also CA 178; EWL 3; HW 2; LAW

Rodolph, Utto
See Ouologuem, Yambo

Rodriguez, Claudio 1934-1999 .... **CLC 10**
See also CA 188; DLB 134

Rodriguez, Richard 1944- .... **CLC 155; HLC
2**
See also AMWS 14; CA 110; CANR 66,
116; DAM MULT; DLB 82, 256; HW 1,
2; LAIT 5; LLW; MTFW 2005; NCFS 3;
WLIT 1

Roethke, Theodore 1908-1963 ... **CLC 1, 3, 8,
11, 19, 46, 101; PC 15**
See also AMW; CA 81-84; CABS 2;
CDALB 1941-1968; DA3; DAM POET;
DLB 5, 206; EWL 3; EXPP; MAL 5;
MTCW 1, 2; PAB; PFS 3; RGAL 4; WP

Roethke, Theodore Huebner
See Roethke, Theodore

Rogers, Carl R(ansom)
1902-1987 .... **TCLC 125**
See also CA 1-4R; 121; CANR 1, 18;
MTCW 1

Rogers, Samuel 1763-1855 .... **NCLC 69**
See also DLB 93; RGEL 2

Rogers, Thomas 1927-2007 .... **CLC 57**
See also CA 89-92; 259; CANR 163; INT
CA-89-92

Rogers, Thomas Hunton
See Rogers, Thomas

Rogers, Will(iam Penn Adair)
1879-1935 .... **NNAL; TCLC 8, 71**
See also CA 105; 144; DA3; DAM MULT;
DLB 11; MTCW 2

Rogin, Gilbert 1929- .... **CLC 18**
See also CA 65-68; CANR 15

Rohan, Koda
See Koda Shigeyuki

Rohlfs, Anna Katharine Green
See Green, Anna Katharine

Rohmer, Eric .... **CLC 16**
See Scherer, Jean-Marie Maurice

Rohmer, Sax .... **TCLC 28**
See Ward, Arthur Henry Sarsfield
See also DLB 70; MSW; SUFW

Roiphe, Anne 1935- .... **CLC 3, 9**
See also CA 89-92; CANR 45, 73, 138, 170;
DLBY 1980; INT CA-89-92

Roiphe, Anne Richardson
See Roiphe, Anne

Rojas, Fernando de 1475-1541 ... **HLCS 1, 2;
LC 23**
See also DLB 286; RGWL 2, 3

Rojas, Gonzalo 1917- .... **HLCS 2**
See also CA 178; HW 2; LAWS 1

Rolaag, Ole Edvart
See Rolvaag, O.E.

Roland (de la Platiere), Marie-Jeanne
1754-1793 .... **LC 98**
See also DLB 314

Rolfe, Frederick (William Serafino Austin
Lewis Mary) 1860-1913 .... **TCLC 12**
See Al Siddik
See also CA 107; 210; DLB 34, 156; RGEL
2

Rolland, Romain 1866-1944 .... **TCLC 23**
See also CA 118; 197; DLB 65, 284, 332;
EWL 3; GFL 1789 to the Present; RGWL
2, 3

Rolle, Richard c. 1300-c. 1349 ..... **CMLC 21**
See also DLB 146; LMFS 1; RGEL 2

Rolvaag, O.E.
See Rolvaag, O.E.

Rolvaag, O.E.
See Rolvaag, O.E.

Rolvaag, O.E. 1876-1931 .... **TCLC 17, 207**
See also AAYA 75; CA 117; 171; DLB 9,
212; MAL 5; NFS 5; RGAL 4; TCWW 1,
2

Romain Arnaud, Saint
See Aragon, Louis

Romains, Jules 1885-1972 .... **CLC 7**
See also CA 85-88; CANR 34; DLB 65,
321; EWL 3; GFL 1789 to the Present;
MTCW 1

Romero, Jose Ruben 1890-1952 .... **TCLC 14**
See also CA 114; 131; EWL 3; HW 1; LAW

Ronsard, Pierre de 1524-1585 . **LC 6, 54; PC
11**
See also DLB 327; EW 2; GFL Beginnings
to 1789; RGWL 2, 3; TWA

Rooke, Leon 1934- .... **CLC 25, 34**
See also CA 25-28R; CANR 23, 53; CCA
1; CPW; DAM POP

Roosevelt, Franklin Delano
1882-1945 .... **TCLC 93**
See also CA 116; 173; LAIT 3

Roosevelt, Theodore 1858-1919 ..... **TCLC 69**
See also CA 115; 170; DLB 47, 186, 275

Roper, Margaret c. 1505-1544 .... **LC 147**

Roper, William 1498-1578 .... **LC 10**

Roquelaure, A. N.
See Rice, Anne

Rosa, Joao Guimaraes 1908-1967 ... **CLC 23;
HLCS 1**
See Guimaraes Rosa, Joao
See also CA 89-92; DLB 113, 307; EWL 3;
WLIT 1

Rose, Wendy 1948- . **CLC 85; NNAL; PC 13**
See also CA 53-56; CANR 5, 51; CWP;
DAM MULT; DLB 175; PFS 13; RGAL
4; SATA 12

Rosen, R.D. 1949- .... **CLC 39**
See also CA 77-80; CANR 62, 120, 175;
CMW 4; INT CANR-30

Rosen, Richard
See Rosen, R.D.

Rosen, Richard Dean
See Rosen, R.D.

Rosenberg, Isaac 1890-1918 .... **TCLC 12**
See also BRW 6; CA 107; 188; DLB 20,
216; EWL 3; PAB; RGEL 2

Rosenblatt, Joe .... **CLC 15**
See Rosenblatt, Joseph
See also CP 3, 4, 5, 6, 7

Rosenblatt, Joseph 1933-
See Rosenblatt, Joe
See also CA 89-92; CP 1, 2; INT CA-89-92

Rosenfeld, Samuel
See Tzara, Tristan

Rosenstock, Sami
See Tzara, Tristan

Rosenstock, Samuel
See Tzara, Tristan

Rosenthal, M(acha) L(ouis)
1917-1996 .... **CLC 28**
See also CA 1-4R; 152; CAAS 6; CANR 4,
51; CP 1, 2, 3, 4, 5, 6; DLB 5; SATA 59

Ross, Barnaby
See Dannay, Frederic; Lee, Manfred B.

Ross, Bernard L.
See Follett, Ken

Ross, J. H.
See Lawrence, T(homas) E(dward)

Ross, John Hume
See Lawrence, T(homas) E(dward)

Ross, Martin 1862-1915
See Martin, Violet Florence
See also DLB 135; GLL 2; RGEL 2; RGSF
2

Ross, (James) Sinclair 1908-1996 ... **CLC 13;
SSC 24**
See also CA 73-76; CANR 81; CN 1, 2, 3,
4, 5, 6; DAC; DAM MST; DLB 88;
RGEL 2; RGSF 2; TCWW 1, 2

Rossetti, Christina 1830-1894 ... **NCLC 2, 50,
66, 186; PC 7; WLC 5**
See also AAYA 51; BRW 5; BYA 4; CLR
115; DA; DA3; DAB; DAC; DAM MST,
POET; DLB 35, 163, 240; EXPP; FL 1:3;
LATS 1:1; MAICYA 1, 2; PFS 10, 14, 27;
RGEL 2; SATA 20; TEA; WCH

Rossetti, Christina Georgina
See Rossetti, Christina

Rossetti, Dante Gabriel 1828-1882 . **NCLC 4,
77; PC 44; WLC 5**
See also AAYA 51; BRW 5; CDBLB 1832-
1890; DA; DAB; DAC; DAM MST,
POET; DLB 35; EXPP; RGEL 2; TEA

Rossi, Cristina Peri
See Peri Rossi, Cristina

Rossi, Jean-Baptiste 1931-2003
See Japrisot, Sebastien
See also CA 201; 215

Rossner, Judith 1935-2005 .... **CLC 6, 9, 29**
See also AITN 2; BEST 90:3; BPFB 3; CA
17-20R; 242; CANR 18, 51, 73; CN 4, 5,
6, 7; DLB 6; INT CANR-18; MAL 5;
MTCW 1, 2; MTFW 2005

Rossner, Judith Perelman
See Rossner, Judith

Rostand, Edmond (Eugene Alexis)
1868-1918 .... **DC 10; TCLC 6, 37**
See also CA 104; 126; DA; DA3; DAB;
DAC; DAM DRAM, MST; DFS 1; DLB
192; LAIT 1; MTCW 1; RGWL 2, 3;
TWA

Roth, Henry 1906-1995 ..... **CLC 2, 6, 11, 104**
See also AMWS 9; CA 11-12; 149; CANR
38, 63; CAP 1; CN 1, 2, 3, 4, 5, 6; DA3;
DLB 28; EWL 3; MAL 5; MTCW 1, 2;
MTFW 2005; RGAL 4

Roth, (Moses) Joseph 1894-1939 ... **TCLC 33**
See also CA 160; DLB 85; EWL 3; RGWL
2, 3

Roth, Philip 1933- ... **CLC 1, 2, 3, 4, 6, 9, 15,
22, 31, 47, 66, 86, 119, 201; SSC 26,
102; WLC 5**
See also AAYA 67; AMWR 2; AMWS 3;
BEST 90:3; BPFB 3; CA 1-4R; CANR 1,
22, 36, 55, 89, 132, 170; CDALB 1968-

1988; CN 3, 4, 5, 6, 7; CPW 1; DA; DA3; DAB; DAC; DAM MST, NOV, POP; DLB 2, 28, 173; DLBY 1982; EWL 3; MAL 5; MTCW 1, 2; MTFW 2005; NFS 25; RGAL 4; RGHL; RGSF 2; SSFS 12, 18; TUS

Roth, Philip Milton
See Roth, Philip

Rothenberg, Jerome 1931- .... **CLC 6, 57**
See also CA 45-48; CANR 1, 106; CP 1, 2, 3, 4, 5, 6, 7; DLB 5, 193

Rotter, Pat .... **CLC 65**

Roumain, Jacques (Jean Baptiste)
1907-1944 .... **BLC 1:3; TCLC 19**
See also BW 1; CA 117; 125; DAM MULT; EWL 3

Rourke, Constance Mayfield
1885-1941 .... **TCLC 12**
See also CA 107; 200; MAL 5; YABC 1

Rousseau, Jean-Baptiste 1671-1741 ...... **LC 9**

Rousseau, Jean-Jacques 1712-1778 .... **LC 14, 36, 122; WLC 5**
See also DA; DA3; DAB; DAC; DAM MST; DLB 314; EW 4; GFL Beginnings to 1789; LMFS 1; RGWL 2, 3; TWA

Roussel, Raymond 1877-1933 .... **TCLC 20**
See also CA 117; 201; EWL 3; GFL 1789 to the Present

Rovit, Earl (Herbert) 1927- .... **CLC 7**
See also CA 5-8R; CANR 12

Rowe, Elizabeth Singer 1674-1737 ..... **LC 44**
See also DLB 39, 95

Rowe, Nicholas 1674-1718 .... **LC 8**
See also DLB 84; RGEL 2

Rowlandson, Mary 1637(?)-1678 .... **LC 66**
See also DLB 24, 200; RGAL 4

Rowley, Ames Dorrance
See Lovecraft, H. P.

Rowley, William 1585(?)-1626 ... **LC 100, 123**
See also DFS 22; DLB 58; RGEL 2

Rowling, J.K. 1965- .... **CLC 137, 217**
See also AAYA 34; BYA 11, 13, 14; CA 173; CANR 128, 157; CLR 66, 80, 112; MAICYA; MTFW 2005; SATA 109, 174; SUFW 2

Rowling, Joanne Kathleen
See Rowling, J.K.

Rowson, Susanna Haswell
1762(?)-1824 .... **NCLC 5, 69, 182**
See also AMWS 15; DLB 37, 200; RGAL 4

Roy, Arundhati 1960(?)- .... **CLC 109, 210**
See also CA 163; CANR 90, 126; CN 7; DLB 323, 326; DLBY 1997; EWL 3; LATS 1:2; MTFW 2005; NFS 22; WWE 1

Roy, Gabrielle 1909-1983 .... **CLC 10, 14**
See also CA 53-56; 110; CANR 5, 61; CCA 1; DAB; DAC; DAM MST; DLB 68; EWL 3; MTCW 1; RGWL 2, 3; SATA 104; TCLE 1:2

Royko, Mike 1932-1997 .... **CLC 109**
See also CA 89-92; 157; CANR 26, 111; CPW

Rozanov, Vasilii Vasil'evich
See Rozanov, Vassili
See also DLB 295

Rozanov, Vasily Vasilyevich
See Rozanov, Vassili
See also EWL 3

Rozanov, Vassili 1856-1919 .... **TCLC 104**
See Rozanov, Vasilii Vasil'evich; Rozanov, Vasily Vasilyevich

Rozewicz, Tadeusz 1921- ...... **CLC 9, 23, 139**
See also CA 108; CANR 36, 66; CWW 2; DA3; DAM POET; DLB 232; EWL 3; MTCW 1, 2; MTFW 2005; RGHL; RGWL 3

Ruark, Gibbons 1941- .... **CLC 3**
See also CA 33-36R; CAAS 23; CANR 14, 31, 57; DLB 120

Rubens, Bernice (Ruth) 1923-2004 . **CLC 19, 31**
See also CA 25-28R; 232; CANR 33, 65, 128; CN 1, 2, 3, 4, 5, 6, 7; DLB 14, 207, 326; MTCW 1

Rubin, Harold
See Robbins, Harold

Rudkin, (James) David 1936- .... **CLC 14**
See also CA 89-92; CBD; CD 5, 6; DLB 13

Rudnik, Raphael 1933- .... **CLC 7**
See also CA 29-32R

Ruffian, M.
See Hasek, Jaroslav (Matej Frantisek)

Ruiz, Jose Martinez .... **CLC 11**
See Martinez Ruiz, Jose

Ruiz, Juan c. 1283-c. 1350 .... **CMLC 66**

Rukeyser, Muriel 1913-1980 . **CLC 6, 10, 15, 27; PC 12**
See also AMWS 6; CA 5-8R; 93-96; CANR 26, 60; CP 1, 2, 3; DA3; DAM POET; DLB 48; EWL 3; FW; GLL 2; MAL 5; MTCW 1, 2; PFS 10; RGAL 4; SATA-Obit 22

Rule, Jane 1931-2007 .... **CLC 27**
See also CA 25-28R; 266; CAAS 18; CANR 12, 87; CN 4, 5, 6, 7; DLB 60; FW

Rule, Jane Vance
See Rule, Jane

Rulfo, Juan 1918-1986 .. **CLC 8, 80; HLC 2; SSC 25**
See also CA 85-88; 118; CANR 26; CD-WLB 3; DAM MULT; DLB 113; EWL 3; HW 1, 2; LAW; MTCW 1, 2; RGSF 2; RGWL 2, 3; WLIT 1

Rumi, Jalal al-Din 1207-1273 ...... **CMLC 20; PC 45**
See also AAYA 64; RGWL 2, 3; WLIT 6; WP

Runeberg, Johan 1804-1877 .... **NCLC 41**

Runyon, (Alfred) Damon
1884(?)-1946 .... **TCLC 10**
See also CA 107; 165; DLB 11, 86, 171; MAL 5; MTCW 2; RGAL 4

Rush, Norman 1933- .... **CLC 44**
See also CA 121; 126; CANR 130; INT CA-126

Rushdie, Salman 1947- .... **CLC 23, 31, 55, 100, 191; SSC 83; WLCS**
See also AAYA 65; BEST 89:3; BPFB 3; BRWS 4; CA 108; 111; CANR 33, 56, 108, 133; CLR 125; CN 4, 5, 6, 7; CPW 1; DA3; DAB; DAC; DAM MST, NOV, POP; DLB 194, 323, 326; EWL 3; FANT; INT CA-111; LATS 1:2; LMFS 2; MTCW 1, 2; MTFW 2005; NFS 22, 23; RGEL 2; RGSF 2; TEA; WLIT 4

Rushforth, Peter 1945-2005 .... **CLC 19**
See also CA 101; 243

Rushforth, Peter Scott
See Rushforth, Peter

Ruskin, John 1819-1900 .... **TCLC 63**
See also BRW 5; BYA 5; CA 114; 129; CD-BLB 1832-1890; DLB 55, 163, 190; RGEL 2; SATA 24; TEA; WCH

Russ, Joanna 1937- .... **CLC 15**
See also BPFB 3; CA 25-28; CANR 11, 31, 65; CN 4, 5, 6, 7; DLB 8; FW; GLL 1; MTCW 1; SCFW 1, 2; SFW 4

Russ, Richard Patrick
See O'Brian, Patrick

Russell, George William 1867-1935
See A.E.; Baker, Jean H.
See also BRWS 8; CA 104; 153; CDBLB 1890-1914; DAM POET; EWL 3; RGEL 2

Russell, Jeffrey Burton 1934- .... **CLC 70**
See also CA 25-28R; CANR 11, 28, 52, 179

Russell, (Henry) Ken(neth Alfred)
1927- .... **CLC 16**
See also CA 105

Russell, William Martin 1947-
See Russell, Willy
See also CA 164; CANR 107

Russell, Willy .... **CLC 60**
See Russell, William Martin
See also CBD; CD 5, 6; DLB 233

Russo, Richard 1949- .... **CLC 181**
See also AMWS 12; CA 127; 133; CANR 87, 114; NFS 25

Rutebeuf fl. c. 1249-1277 .... **CMLC 104**
See also DLB 208

Rutherford, Mark .... **TCLC 25**
See White, William Hale
See also DLB 18; RGEL 2

Ruysbroeck, Jan van 1293-1381 ... **CMLC 85**

Ruyslinck, Ward .... **CLC 14**
See Belser, Reimond Karel Maria de

Ryan, Cornelius (John) 1920-1974 ..... **CLC 7**
See also CA 69-72; 53-56; CANR 38

Ryan, Michael 1946- .... **CLC 65**
See also CA 49-52; CANR 109; DLBY 1982

Ryan, Tim
See Dent, Lester

Rybakov, Anatoli (Naumovich)
1911-1998 .... **CLC 23, 53**
See Rybakov, Anatolii (Naumovich)
See also CA 126; 135; 172; SATA 79; SATA-Obit 108

Rybakov, Anatolii (Naumovich)
See Rybakov, Anatoli (Naumovich)
See also DLB 302; RGHL

Ryder, Jonathan
See Ludlum, Robert

Ryga, George 1932-1987 .... **CLC 14**
See also CA 101; 124; CANR 43, 90; CCA 1; DAC; DAM MST; DLB 60

Rymer, Thomas 1643(?)-1713 .... **LC 132**
See also DLB 101, 336

S. H.
See Hartmann, Sadakichi

S. S.
See Sassoon, Siegfried (Lorraine)

Sa'adawi, al- Nawal
See El Saadawi, Nawal
See also AFW; EWL 3

Saadawi, Nawal El
See El Saadawi, Nawal
See also WLIT 2

Saadiah Gaon 882-942 .... **CMLC 97**

Saba, Umberto 1883-1957 .... **TCLC 33**
See also CA 144; CANR 79; DLB 114; EWL 3; RGWL 2, 3

Sabatini, Rafael 1875-1950 .... **TCLC 47**
See also BPFB 3; CA 162; RHW

Sabato, Ernesto 1911- ... **CLC 10, 23; HLC 2**
See also CA 97-100; CANR 32, 65; CD-WLB 3; CWW 2; DAM MULT; DLB 145; EWL 3; HW 1, 2; LAW; MTCW 1, 2; MTFW 2005

Sa-Carneiro, Mario de 1890-1916 . **TCLC 83**
See also DLB 287; EWL 3

Sacastru, Martin
See Bioy Casares, Adolfo
See also CWW 2

Sacher-Masoch, Leopold von
1836(?)-1895 .... **NCLC 31**

Sachs, Hans 1494-1576 .... **LC 95**
See also CDWLB 2; DLB 179; RGWL 2, 3

Sachs, Marilyn 1927- .... **CLC 35**
See also AAYA 2; BYA 6; CA 17-20R; CANR 13, 47, 150; CLR 2; JRDA; MAICYA 1, 2; SAAS 2; SATA 3, 68, 164; SATA-Essay 110; WYA; YAW

Sachs, Marilyn Stickle
See Sachs, Marilyn

Sachs, Nelly 1891-1970 .. **CLC 14, 98; PC 78**
See also CA 17-18; 25-28R; CANR 87; CAP 2; DLB 332; EWL 3; MTCW 2; MTFW 2005; PFS 20; RGHL; RGWL 2, 3

Sackler, Howard (Oliver)
1929-1982 .... **CLC 14**
See also CA 61-64; 108; CAD; CANR 30; DFS 15; DLB 7

Sacks, Oliver 1933- .... **CLC 67, 202**
See also CA 53-56; CANR 28, 50, 76, 146; CPW; DA3; INT CANR-28; MTCW 1, 2; MTFW 2005

Sacks, Oliver Wolf
See Sacks, Oliver

Sackville, Thomas 1536-1608 .... **LC 98**
See also DAM DRAM; DLB 62, 132; RGEL 2

Sadakichi
See Hartmann, Sadakichi

Sa'dawi, Nawal al-
See El Saadawi, Nawal
See also CWW 2

Sade, Donatien Alphonse Francois
1740-1814 .... **NCLC 3, 47**
See also DLB 314; EW 4; GFL Beginnings to 1789; RGWL 2, 3

Sade, Marquis de
See Sade, Donatien Alphonse Francois

Sadoff, Ira 1945- .... **CLC 9**
See also CA 53-56; CANR 5, 21, 109; DLB 120

Saetone
See Camus, Albert

Safire, William 1929- .... **CLC 10**
See also CA 17-20R; CANR 31, 54, 91, 148

Sagan, Carl 1934-1996 .... **CLC 30, 112**
See also AAYA 2, 62; CA 25-28R; 155; CANR 11, 36, 74; CPW; DA3; MTCW 1, 2; MTFW 2005; SATA 58; SATA-Obit 94

Sagan, Francoise .... **CLC 3, 6, 9, 17, 36**
See Quoirez, Francoise
See also CWW 2; DLB 83; EWL 3; GFL 1789 to the Present; MTCW 2

Sahgal, Nayantara (Pandit) 1927- .... **CLC 41**
See also CA 9-12R; CANR 11, 88; CN 1, 2, 3, 4, 5, 6, 7; DLB 323

Said, Edward W. 1935-2003 .... **CLC 123**
See also CA 21-24R; 220; CANR 45, 74, 107, 131; DLB 67; MTCW 2; MTFW 2005

Saikaku, Ihara 1642-1693 .... **LC 141**
See also RGWL 3

Saikaku Ihara
See Saikaku, Ihara

Saint, H(arry) F. 1941- .... **CLC 50**
See also CA 127

St. Aubin de Teran, Lisa 1953-
See Teran, Lisa St. Aubin de
See also CA 118; 126; CN 6, 7; INT CA-126

Saint Birgitta of Sweden c.
1303-1373 .... **CMLC 24**

Sainte-Beuve, Charles Augustin
1804-1869 .... **NCLC 5**
See also DLB 217; EW 6; GFL 1789 to the Present

Saint-Exupery, Antoine de
1900-1944 .... **TCLC 2, 56, 169; WLC**
See also AAYA 63; BPFB 3; BYA 3; CA 108; 132; CLR 10; DA3; DAM NOV; DLB 72; EW 12; EWL 3; GFL 1789 to the Present; LAIT 3; MAICYA 1, 2; MTCW 1, 2; MTFW 2005; RGWL 2, 3; SATA 20; TWA

Saint-Exupery, Antoine Jean Baptiste Marie Roger de
See Saint-Exupery, Antoine de

St. John, David
See Hunt, E. Howard

St. John, J. Hector
See Crevecoeur, Michel Guillaume Jean de

Saint-John Perse
See Leger, (Marie-Rene Auguste) Alexis Saint-Leger
See also EW 10; EWL 3; GFL 1789 to the Present; RGWL 2

Saintsbury, George (Edward Bateman)
1845-1933 .... **TCLC 31**
See also CA 160; DLB 57, 149

Sait Faik .... **TCLC 23**
See Abasiyanik, Sait Faik

Saki .... **SSC 12, 115; TCLC 3; WLC 5**
See Munro, H(ector) H(ugh)
See also BRWS 6; BYA 11; LAIT 2; RGEL 2; SSFS 1; SUFW

Sala, George Augustus 1828-1895 . **NCLC 46**

Saladin 1138-1193 .... **CMLC 38**

Salama, Hannu 1936- .... **CLC 18**
See also CA 244; EWL 3

Salamanca, J(ack) R(ichard) 1922- .. **CLC 4, 15**
See also CA 25-28R, 193; CAAE 193

Salas, Floyd Francis 1931- .... **HLC 2**
See also CA 119; CAAS 27; CANR 44, 75, 93; DAM MULT; DLB 82; HW 1, 2; MTCW 2; MTFW 2005

Sale, J. Kirkpatrick
See Sale, Kirkpatrick

Sale, John Kirkpatrick
See Sale, Kirkpatrick

Sale, Kirkpatrick 1937- .... **CLC 68**
See also CA 13-16R; CANR 10, 147

Salinas, Luis Omar 1937- ... **CLC 90; HLC 2**
See also AMWS 13; CA 131; CANR 81, 153; DAM MULT; DLB 82; HW 1, 2

Salinas (y Serrano), Pedro
1891(?)-1951 .... **TCLC 17, 212**
See also CA 117; DLB 134; EWL 3

Salinger, J.D. 1919- . **CLC 1, 3, 8, 12, 55, 56, 138, 243; SSC 2, 28, 65; WLC 5**
See also AAYA 2, 36; AMW; AMWC 1; BPFB 3; CA 5-8R; CANR 39, 129; CDALB 1941-1968; CLR 18; CN 1, 2, 3, 4, 5, 6, 7; CPW 1; DA; DA3; DAB; DAC; DAM MST, NOV, POP; DLB 2, 102, 173; EWL 3; EXPN; LAIT 4; MAICYA 1, 2; MAL 5; MTCW 1, 2; MTFW 2005; NFS 1; RGAL 4; RGSF 2; SATA 67; SSFS 17; TUS; WYA; YAW

Salisbury, John
See Caute, (John) David

Sallust c. 86B.C.-35B.C. .... **CMLC 68**
See also AW 2; CDWLB 1; DLB 211; RGWL 2, 3

Salter, James 1925- .. **CLC 7, 52, 59; SSC 58**
See also AMWS 9; CA 73-76; CANR 107, 160; DLB 130; SSFS 25

Saltus, Edgar (Everton) 1855-1921 . **TCLC 8**
See also CA 105; DLB 202; RGAL 4

Saltykov, Mikhail Evgrafovich
1826-1889 .... **NCLC 16**
See also DLB 238:

Saltykov-Shchedrin, N.
See Saltykov, Mikhail Evgrafovich

Samarakis, Andonis
See Samarakis, Antonis
See also EWL 3

Samarakis, Antonis 1919-2003 .... **CLC 5**
See Samarakis, Andonis
See also CA 25-28R; 224; CAAS 16; CANR 36

Sanchez, Florencio 1875-1910 .... **TCLC 37**
See also CA 153; DLB 305; EWL 3; HW 1; LAW

Sanchez, Luis Rafael 1936- .... **CLC 23**
See also CA 128; DLB 305; EWL 3; HW 1; WLIT 1

Sanchez, Sonia 1934- . **BLC 1:3, 2:3; CLC 5, 116, 215; PC 9**
See also BW 2, 3; CA 33-36R; CANR 24, 49, 74, 115; CLR 18; CP 2, 3, 4, 5, 6, 7; CSW; CWP; DA3; DAM MULT; DLB 41; DLBD 8; EWL 3; MAICYA 1, 2; MAL 5; MTCW 1, 2; MTFW 2005; PFS 26; SATA 22, 136; WP

Sancho, Ignatius 1729-1780 .... **LC 84**

Sand, George 1804-1876 .... **DC 29; NCLC 2, 42, 57, 174; WLC 5**
See also DA; DA3; DAB; DAC; DAM MST, NOV; DLB 119, 192; EW 6; FL 1:3; FW; GFL 1789 to the Present; RGWL 2, 3; TWA

Sandburg, Carl (August) 1878-1967 . **CLC 1, 4, 10, 15, 35; PC 2, 41; WLC 5**
See also AAYA 24; AMW; BYA 1, 3; CA 5-8R; 25-28R; CANR 35; CDALB 1865-1917; CLR 67; DA; DA3; DAB; DAC; DAM MST, POET; DLB 17, 54, 284; EWL 3; EXPP; LAIT 2; MAICYA 1, 2; MAL 5; MTCW 1, 2; MTFW 2005; PAB; PFS 3, 6, 12; RGAL 4; SATA 8; TUS; WCH; WP; WYA

Sandburg, Charles
See Sandburg, Carl (August)

Sandburg, Charles A.
See Sandburg, Carl (August)

Sanders, (James) Ed(ward) 1939- .... **CLC 53**
See Sanders, Edward
See also BG 1:3; CA 13-16R; CAAS 21; CANR 13, 44, 78; CP 1, 2, 3, 4, 5, 6, 7; DAM POET; DLB 16, 244

Sanders, Edward
See Sanders, (James) Ed(ward)
See also DLB 244

Sanders, Lawrence 1920-1998 .... **CLC 41**
See also BEST 89:4; BPFB 3; CA 81-84; 165; CANR 33, 62; CMW 4; CPW; DA3; DAM POP; MTCW 1

Sanders, Noah
See Blount, Roy, Jr.

Sanders, Winston P.
See Anderson, Poul

Sandoz, Mari(e Susette) 1900-1966 .. **CLC 28**
See also CA 1-4R; 25-28R; CANR 17, 64; DLB 9, 212; LAIT 2; MTCW 1, 2; SATA 5; TCWW 1, 2

Sandys, George 1578-1644 .... **LC 80**
See also DLB 24, 121

Saner, Reg(inald Anthony) 1931- .... **CLC 9**
See also CA 65-68; CP 3, 4, 5, 6, 7

Sankara 788-820 .... **CMLC 32**

Sannazaro, Jacopo 1456(?)-1530 .... **LC 8**
See also RGWL 2, 3; WLIT 7

Sansom, William 1912-1976 . **CLC 2, 6; SSC 21**
See also CA 5-8R; 65-68; CANR 42; CN 1, 2; DAM NOV; DLB 139; EWL 3; MTCW 1; RGEL 2; RGSF 2

Santayana, George 1863-1952 .... **TCLC 40**
See also AMW; CA 115; 194; DLB 54, 71, 246, 270; DLBD 13; EWL 3; MAL 5; RGAL 4; TUS

Schneider, Leonard Alfred 1925-1966
See Bruce, Lenny
See also CA 89-92

Schnitzler, Arthur 1862-1931 ..... **DC 17; SSC 15, 61; TCLC 4**
See also CA 104; CDWLB 2; DLB 81, 118; EW 8; EWL 3; RGSF 2; RGWL 2, 3

Schoenberg, Arnold Franz Walter 1874-1951 .... **TCLC 75**
See also CA 109; 188

Schonberg, Arnold
See Schoenberg, Arnold Franz Walter

Schopenhauer, Arthur 1788-1860 . **NCLC 51, 157**
See also DLB 90; EW 5

Schor, Sandra (M.) 1932(?)-1990 ..... **CLC 65**
See also CA 132

Schorer, Mark 1908-1977 .... **CLC 9**
See also CA 5-8R; 73-76; CANR 7; CN 1, 2; DLB 103

Schrader, Paul (Joseph) 1946- . **CLC 26, 212**
See also CA 37-40R; CANR 41; DLB 44

Schreber, Daniel 1842-1911 .... **TCLC 123**

Schreiner, Olive (Emilie Albertina) 1855-1920 .... **TCLC 9**
See also AFW; BRWS 2; CA 105; 154; DLB 18, 156, 190, 225; EWL 3; FW; RGEL 2; TWA; WLIT 2; WWE 1

Schulberg, Budd 1914- .... **CLC 7, 48**
See also BPFB 3; CA 25-28R; CANR 19, 87, 178; CN 1, 2, 3, 4, 5, 6, 7; DLB 6, 26, 28; DLBY 1981, 2001; MAL 5

Schulberg, Budd Wilson
See Schulberg, Budd

Schulman, Arnold
See Trumbo, Dalton

Schulz, Bruno 1892-1942 .. **SSC 13; TCLC 5, 51**
See also CA 115; 123; CANR 86; CDWLB 4; DLB 215; EWL 3; MTCW 2; MTFW 2005; RGSF 2; RGWL 2, 3

Schulz, Charles M. 1922-2000 .... **CLC 12**
See also AAYA 39; CA 9-12R; 187; CANR 6, 132; INT CANR-6; MTFW 2005; SATA 10; SATA-Obit 118

Schulz, Charles Monroe
See Schulz, Charles M.

Schumacher, E(rnst) F(riedrich) 1911-1977 .... **CLC 80**
See also CA 81-84; 73-76; CANR 34, 85

Schumann, Robert 1810-1856 ...... **NCLC 143**

Schuyler, George Samuel 1895-1977 . **HR 1:3**
See also BW 2; CA 81-84; 73-76; CANR 42; DLB 29, 51

Schuyler, James Marcus 1923-1991 .. **CLC 5, 23; PC 88**
See also CA 101; 134; CP 1, 2, 3, 4, 5; DAM POET; DLB 5, 169; EWL 3; INT CA-101; MAL 5; WP

Schwartz, Delmore (David) 1913-1966 . **CLC 2, 4, 10, 45, 87; PC 8; SSC 105**
See also AMWS 2; CA 17-18; 25-28R; CANR 35; CAP 2; DLB 28, 48; EWL 3; MAL 5; MTCW 1, 2; MTFW 2005; PAB; RGAL 4; TUS

Schwartz, Ernst
See Ozu, Yasujiro

Schwartz, John Burnham 1965- .... **CLC 59**
See also CA 132; CANR 116

Schwartz, Lynne Sharon 1939- .... **CLC 31**
See also CA 103; CANR 44, 89, 160; DLB 218; MTCW 2; MTFW 2005

Schwartz, Muriel A.
See Eliot, T(homas) S(tearns)

Schwarz-Bart, Andre 1928-2006 .... **CLC 2, 4**
See also CA 89-92; 253; CANR 109; DLB 299; RGHL

Schwarz-Bart, Simone 1938- . **BLCS; CLC 7**
See also BW 2; CA 97-100; CANR 117; EWL 3

Schwerner, Armand 1927-1999 .... **PC 42**
See also CA 9-12R; 179; CANR 50, 85; CP 2, 3, 4, 5, 6; DLB 165

Schwitters, Kurt (Hermann Edward Karl Julius) 1887-1948 .... **TCLC 95**
See also CA 158

Schwob, Marcel (Mayer Andre) 1867-1905 .... **TCLC 20**
See also CA 117; 168; DLB 123; GFL 1789 to the Present

Sciascia, Leonardo 1921-1989 .. **CLC 8, 9, 41**
See also CA 85-88; 130; CANR 35; DLB 177; EWL 3; MTCW 1; RGWL 2, 3

Scoppettone, Sandra 1936- .... **CLC 26**
See Early, Jack
See also AAYA 11, 65; BYA 8; CA 5-8R; CANR 41, 73, 157; GLL 1; MAICYA 2; MAICYAS 1; SATA 9, 92; WYA; YAW

Scorsese, Martin 1942- .... **CLC 20, 89, 207**
See also AAYA 38; CA 110; 114; CANR 46, 85

Scotland, Jay
See Jakes, John

Scott, Duncan Campbell 1862-1947 .... **TCLC 6**
See also CA 104; 153; DAC; DLB 92; RGEL 2

Scott, Evelyn 1893-1963 .... **CLC 43**
See also CA 104; 112; CANR 64; DLB 9, 48; RHW

Scott, F(rancis) R(eginald) 1899-1985 .... **CLC 22**
See also CA 101; 114; CANR 87; CP 1, 2, 3, 4; DLB 88; INT CA-101; RGEL 2

Scott, Frank
See Scott, F(rancis) R(eginald)

Scott, Joan .... **CLC 65**

Scott, Joanna 1960- .... **CLC 50**
See also AMWS 17; CA 126; CANR 53, 92, 168

Scott, Joanna Jeanne
See Scott, Joanna

Scott, Paul (Mark) 1920-1978 ...... **CLC 9, 60**
See also BRWS 1; CA 81-84; 77-80; CANR 33; CN 1, 2; DLB 14, 207, 326; EWL 3; MTCW 1; RGEL 2; RHW; WWE 1

Scott, Ridley 1937- .... **CLC 183**
See also AAYA 13, 43

Scott, Sarah 1723-1795 .... **LC 44**
See also DLB 39

Scott, Sir Walter 1771-1832 .... **NCLC 15, 69, 110; PC 13; SSC 32; WLC 5**
See also AAYA 22; BRW 4; BYA 2; CD-BLB 1789-1832; DA; DAB; DAC; DAM MST, NOV, POET; DLB 93, 107, 116, 144, 159; GL 3; HGG; LAIT 1; RGEL 2; RGSF 2; SSFS 10; SUFW 1; TEA; WLIT 3; YABC 2

Scribe, (Augustin) Eugene 1791-1861 . **DC 5; NCLC 16**
See also DAM DRAM; DLB 192; GFL 1789 to the Present; RGWL 2, 3

Scrum, R.
See Crumb, R.

Scudery, Georges de 1601-1667 .... **LC 75**
See also GFL Beginnings to 1789

Scudery, Madeleine de 1607-1701 .. **LC 2, 58**
See also DLB 268; GFL Beginnings to 1789

Scum
See Crumb, R.

Scumbag, Little Bobby
See Crumb, R.

Seabrook, John
See Hubbard, L. Ron

Seacole, Mary Jane Grant 1805-1881 .... **NCLC 147**
See also DLB 166

Sealy, I(rwin) Allan 1951- .... **CLC 55**
See also CA 136; CN 6, 7

Search, Alexander
See Pessoa, Fernando (Antonio Nogueira)

Sebald, W(infried) G(eorg) 1944-2001 .... **CLC 194**
See also BRWS 8; CA 159; 202; CANR 98; MTFW 2005; RGHL

Sebastian, Lee
See Silverberg, Robert

Sebastian Owl
See Thompson, Hunter S.

Sebestyen, Igen
See Sebestyen, Ouida

Sebestyen, Ouida 1924- .... **CLC 30**
See also AAYA 8; BYA 7; CA 107; CANR 40, 114; CLR 17; JRDA; MAICYA 1, 2; SAAS 10; SATA 39, 140; WYA; YAW

Sebold, Alice 1963(?)- .... **CLC 193**
See also AAYA 56; CA 203; MTFW 2005

Second Duke of Buckingham
See Villiers, George

Secundus, H. Scriblerus
See Fielding, Henry

Sedges, John
See Buck, Pearl S(ydenstricker)

Sedgwick, Catharine Maria 1789-1867 .... **NCLC 19, 98**
See also DLB 1, 74, 183, 239, 243, 254; FL 1:3; RGAL 4

Sedulius Scottus 9th cent. -c. 874 .. **CMLC 86**

Seebohm, Victoria
See Glendinning, Victoria

Seelye, John (Douglas) 1931- .... **CLC 7**
See also CA 97-100; CANR 70; INT CA-97-100; TCWW 1, 2

Seferiades, Giorgos Stylianou 1900-1971
See Seferis, George
See also CA 5-8R; 33-36R; CANR 5, 36; MTCW 1

Seferis, George .... **CLC 5, 11; PC 66**
See Seferiades, Giorgos Stylianou
See also DLB 332; EW 12; EWL 3; RGWL 2, 3

Segal, Erich (Wolf) 1937- .... **CLC 3, 10**
See also BEST 89:1; BPFB 3; CA 25-28R; CANR 20, 36, 65, 113; CPW; DAM POP; DLBY 1986; INT CANR-20; MTCW 1

Seger, Bob 1945- .... **CLC 35**

Seghers, Anna .... **CLC 7**
See Radvanyi, Netty
See also CDWLB 2; DLB 69; EWL 3

Seidel, Frederick 1936- .... **CLC 18**
See also CA 13-16R; CANR 8, 99, 180; CP 1, 2, 3, 4, 5, 6, 7; DLBY 1984

Seidel, Frederick Lewis
See Seidel, Frederick

Seifert, Jaroslav 1901-1986 . **CLC 34, 44, 93; PC 47**
See also CA 127; CDWLB 4; DLB 215, 332; EWL 3; MTCW 1, 2

Sei Shonagon c. 966-1017(?) ..... **CMLC 6, 89**

Sejour, Victor 1817-1874 .... **DC 10**
See also DLB 50

Sejour Marcou et Ferrand, Juan Victor
See Sejour, Victor

Selby, Hubert, Jr. 1928-2004 ..... **CLC 1, 2, 4, 8; SSC 20**
See also CA 13-16R; 226; CANR 33, 85; CN 1, 2, 3, 4, 5, 6, 7; DLB 2, 227; MAL 5

Selzer, Richard 1928- .... **CLC 74**
See also CA 65-68; CANR 14, 106

Sembene, Ousmane
See Ousmane, Sembene

Shelley, Percy Bysshe 1792-1822 .. **NCLC 18, 93, 143, 175; PC 14, 67; WLC 5**
See also AAYA 61; BRW 4; BRWR 1; CD-BLB 1789-1832; DA; DA3; DAB; DAC; DAM MST, POET; DLB 96, 110, 158; EXPP; LMFS 1; PAB; PFS 2, 27; RGEL 2; TEA; WLIT 3; WP

Shepard, James R.
See Shepard, Jim

Shepard, Jim 1956- .... **CLC 36**
See also AAYA 73; CA 137; CANR 59, 104, 160; SATA 90, 164

Shepard, Lucius 1947- .... **CLC 34**
See also CA 128; 141; CANR 81, 124, 178; HGG; SCFW 2; SFW 4; SUFW 2

Shepard, Sam 1943- .... **CLC 4, 6, 17, 34, 41, 44, 169; DC 5**
See also AAYA 1, 58; AMWS 3; CA 69-72; CABS 3; CAD; CANR 22, 120, 140; CD 5, 6; DA3; DAM DRAM; DFS 3, 6, 7, 14; DLB 7, 212, 341; EWL 3; IDFW 3, 4; MAL 5; MTCW 1, 2; MTFW 2005; RGAL 4

Shepherd, Jean (Parker)
1921-1999 .... **TCLC 177**
See also AAYA 69; AITN 2; CA 77-80; 187

Shepherd, Michael
See Ludlum, Robert

Sherburne, Zoa (Lillian Morin)
1912-1995 .... **CLC 30**
See also AAYA 13; CA 1-4R; 176; CANR 3, 37; MAICYA 1, 2; SAAS 18; SATA 3; YAW

Sheridan, Frances 1724-1766 .... **LC 7**
See also DLB 39, 84

Sheridan, Richard Brinsley
1751-1816 . **DC 1; NCLC 5, 91; WLC 5**
See also BRW 3; CDBLB 1660-1789; DA; DAB; DAC; DAM DRAM, MST; DFS 15; DLB 89; WLIT 3

Sherman, Jonathan Marc 1968- .... **CLC 55**
See also CA 230

Sherman, Martin 1941(?)- .... **CLC 19**
See also CA 116; 123; CAD; CANR 86; CD 5, 6; DFS 20; DLB 228; GLL 1; IDTP; RGHL

Sherwin, Judith Johnson
See Johnson, Judith (Emlyn)
See also CANR 85; CP 2, 3, 4, 5; CWP

Sherwood, Frances 1940- .... **CLC 81**
See also CA 146, 220; CAAE 220; CANR 158

Sherwood, Robert E(mmet)
1896-1955 .... **TCLC 3**
See also CA 104; 153; CANR 86; DAM DRAM; DFS 11, 15, 17; DLB 7, 26, 249; IDFW 3, 4; MAL 5; RGAL 4

Shestov, Lev 1866-1938 .... **TCLC 56**

Shevchenko, Taras 1814-1861 .... **NCLC 54**

Shiel, M(atthew) P(hipps)
1865-1947 .... **TCLC 8**
See Holmes, Gordon
See also CA 106; 160; DLB 153; HGG; MTCW 2; MTFW 2005; SCFW 1, 2; SFW 4; SUFW

Shields, Carol 1935-2003 .. **CLC 91, 113, 193**
See also AMWS 7; CA 81-84; 218; CANR 51, 74, 98, 133; CCA 1; CN 6, 7; CPW; DA3; DAC; DLB 334; MTCW 2; MTFW 2005; NFS 23

Shields, David 1956- .... **CLC 97**
See also CA 124; CANR 48, 99, 112, 157

Shields, David Jonathan
See Shields, David

Shiga, Naoya 1883-1971 .... **CLC 33; SSC 23; TCLC 172**
See Shiga Naoya
See also CA 101; 33-36R; MJW; RGWL 3

Shiga Naoya
See Shiga, Naoya
See also DLB 180; EWL 3; RGWL 3

Shilts, Randy 1951-1994 .... **CLC 85**
See also AAYA 19; CA 115; 127; 144; CANR 45; DA3; DLB 1; INT CA-127; MTCW 2; MTFW 2005

Shimazaki, Haruki 1872-1943
See Shimazaki Toson
See also CA 105; 134; CANR 84; RGWL 3

Shimazaki Toson .... **TCLC 5**
See Shimazaki, Haruki
See also DLB 180; EWL 3

Shirley, James 1596-1666 .... **DC 25; LC 96**
See also DLB 58; RGEL 2

Shirley Hastings, Selina
See Hastings, Selina

Sholokhov, Mikhail (Aleksandrovich)
1905-1984 .... **CLC 7, 15**
See also CA 101; 112; DLB 272, 332; EWL 3; MTCW 1, 2; MTFW 2005; RGWL 2, 3; SATA-Obit 36

Sholom Aleichem 1859-1916 .... **SSC 33; TCLC 1, 35**
See Rabinovitch, Sholem
See also DLB 333; TWA

Shone, Patric
See Hanley, James

Showalter, Elaine 1941- .... **CLC 169**
See also CA 57-60; CANR 58, 106; DLB 67; FW; GLL 2

Shreve, Susan
See Shreve, Susan Richards

Shreve, Susan Richards 1939- .... **CLC 23**
See also CA 49-52; CAAS 5; CANR 5, 38, 69, 100, 159; MAICYA 1, 2; SATA 46, 95, 152; SATA-Brief 41

Shue, Larry 1946-1985 .... **CLC 52**
See also CA 145; 117; DAM DRAM; DFS 7

Shu-Jen, Chou 1881-1936
See Lu Hsun
See also CA 104

Shulman, Alix Kates 1932- .... **CLC 2, 10**
See also CA 29-32R; CANR 43; FW; SATA 7

Shuster, Joe 1914-1992 .... **CLC 21**
See also AAYA 50

Shute, Nevil .... **CLC 30**
See Norway, Nevil Shute
See also BPFB 3; DLB 255; NFS 9; RHW; SFW 4

Shuttle, Penelope (Diane) 1947- .... **CLC 7**
See also CA 93-96; CANR 39, 84, 92, 108; CP 3, 4, 5, 6, 7; CWP; DLB 14, 40

Shvarts, Elena 1948- .... **PC 50**
See also CA 147

Sidhwa, Bapsi 1939-
See Sidhwa, Bapsy (N.)
See also CN 6, 7; DLB 323

Sidhwa, Bapsy (N.) 1938- .... **CLC 168**
See Sidhwa, Bapsi
See also CA 108; CANR 25, 57; FW

Sidney, Mary 1561-1621 .... **LC 19, 39**
See Sidney Herbert, Mary

Sidney, Sir Philip 1554-1586 .... **LC 19, 39, 131; PC 32**
See also BRW 1; BRWR 2; CDBLB Before 1660; DA; DA3; DAB; DAC; DAM MST, POET; DLB 167; EXPP; PAB; RGEL 2; TEA; WP

Sidney Herbert, Mary
See Sidney, Mary
See also DLB 167

Siegel, Jerome 1914-1996 .... **CLC 21**
See Siegel, Jerry
See also CA 116; 169; 151

Siegel, Jerry
See Siegel, Jerome
See also AAYA 50

Sienkiewicz, Henryk (Adam Alexander Pius)
1846-1916 .... **TCLC 3**
See also CA 104; 134; CANR 84; DLB 332; EWL 3; RGSF 2; RGWL 2, 3

Sierra, Gregorio Martinez
See Martinez Sierra, Gregorio

Sierra, Maria de la O'LeJarraga Martinez
See Martinez Sierra, Maria

Sigal, Clancy 1926- .... **CLC 7**
See also CA 1-4R; CANR 85; CN 1, 2, 3, 4, 5, 6, 7

Siger of Brabant 1240(?)-1284(?) . **CMLC 69**
See also DLB 115

Sigourney, Lydia H.
See Sigourney, Lydia Howard (Huntley)
See also DLB 73, 183

Sigourney, Lydia Howard (Huntley)
1791-1865 .... **NCLC 21, 87**
See Sigourney, Lydia H.; Sigourney, Lydia Huntley
See also DLB 1

Sigourney, Lydia Huntley
See Sigourney, Lydia Howard (Huntley)
See also DLB 42, 239, 243

Siguenza y Gongora, Carlos de
1645-1700 .... **HLCS 2; LC 8**
See also LAW

Sigurjonsson, Johann
See Sigurjonsson, Johann

Sigurjonsson, Johann 1880-1919 ... **TCLC 27**
See also CA 170; DLB 293; EWL 3

Sikelianos, Angelos 1884-1951 .... **PC 29; TCLC 39**
See also EWL 3; RGWL 2, 3

Silkin, Jon 1930-1997 .... **CLC 2, 6, 43**
See also CA 5-8R; CAAS 5; CANR 89; CP 1, 2, 3, 4, 5, 6; DLB 27

Silko, Leslie 1948- ...... **CLC 23, 74, 114, 211; NNAL; SSC 37, 66; WLCS**
See also AAYA 14; AMWS 4; ANW; BYA 12; CA 115; 122; CANR 45, 65, 118; CN 4, 5, 6, 7; CP 4, 5, 6, 7; CPW 1; CWP; DA; DA3; DAC; DAM MST, MULT, POP; DLB 143, 175, 256, 275; EWL 3; EXPP; EXPS; LAIT 4; MAL 5; MTCW 2; MTFW 2005; NFS 4; PFS 9, 16; RGAL 4; RGSF 2; SSFS 4, 8, 10, 11; TCWW 1, 2

Sillanpaa, Frans Eemil 1888-1964 ... **CLC 19**
See also CA 129; 93-96; DLB 332; EWL 3; MTCW 1

Sillitoe, Alan 1928- .. **CLC 1, 3, 6, 10, 19, 57, 148**
See also AITN 1; BRWS 5; CA 9-12R, 191; CAAE 191; CAAS 2; CANR 8, 26, 55, 139; CDBLB 1960 to Present; CN 1, 2, 3, 4, 5, 6; CP 1, 2, 3, 4, 5; DLB 14, 139; EWL 3; MTCW 1, 2; MTFW 2005; RGEL 2; RGSF 2; SATA 61

Silone, Ignazio 1900-1978 .... **CLC 4**
See also CA 25-28; 81-84; CANR 34; CAP 2; DLB 264; EW 12; EWL 3; MTCW 1; RGSF 2; RGWL 2, 3

Silone, Ignazione
See Silone, Ignazio

Silver, Joan Micklin 1935- .... **CLC 20**
See also CA 114; 121; INT CA-121

Silver, Nicholas
See Faust, Frederick (Schiller)

Silverberg, Robert 1935- .... **CLC 7, 140**
See also AAYA 24; BPFB 3; BYA 7, 9; CA 1-4R; 186; CAAE 186; CAAS 3; CANR 1, 20, 36, 85, 140, 175; CLR 59; CN 6, 7; CPW; DAM POP; DLB 8; INT CANR-

Slessor, Kenneth 1901-1971 .... **CLC 14**
  See also CA 102; 89-92; DLB 260; RGEL 2

Slowacki, Juliusz 1809-1849 .... **NCLC 15**
  See also RGWL 3

Smart, Christopher 1722-1771 .... **LC 3, 134; PC 13**
  See also DAM POET; DLB 109; RGEL 2

Smart, Elizabeth 1913-1986 .... **CLC 54**
  See also CA 81-84; 118; CN 4; DLB 88

Smiley, Jane 1949- ...... **CLC 53, 76, 144, 236**
  See also AAYA 66; AMWS 6; BPFB 3; CA 104; CANR 30, 50, 74, 96, 158; CN 6, 7; CPW 1; DA3; DAM POP; DLB 227, 234; EWL 3; INT CANR-30; MAL 5; MTFW 2005; SSFS 19

Smiley, Jane Graves
  See Smiley, Jane

Smith, A(rthur) J(ames) M(arshall)
  1902-1980 .... **CLC 15**
  See also CA 1-4R; 102; CANR 4; CP 1, 2, 3; DAC; DLB 88; RGEL 2

Smith, Adam 1723(?)-1790 .... **LC 36**
  See also DLB 104, 252, 336; RGEL 2

Smith, Alexander 1829-1867 .... **NCLC 59**
  See also DLB 32, 55

Smith, Anna Deavere 1950- ...... **CLC 86, 241**
  See also CA 133; CANR 103; CD 5, 6; DFS 2, 22; DLB 341

Smith, Betty (Wehner) 1904-1972 .... **CLC 19**
  See also AAYA 72; BPFB 3; BYA 3; CA 5-8R; 33-36R; DLBY 1982; LAIT 3; RGAL 4; SATA 6

Smith, Charlotte (Turner)
  1749-1806 .... **NCLC 23, 115**
  See also DLB 39, 109; RGEL 2; TEA

Smith, Clark Ashton 1893-1961 .... **CLC 43**
  See also AAYA 76; CA 143; CANR 81; FANT; HGG; MTCW 2; SCFW 1, 2; SFW 4; SUFW

Smith, Dave .... **CLC 22, 42**
  See Smith, David (Jeddie)
  See also CAAS 7; CP 3, 4, 5, 6, 7; DLB 5

Smith, David (Jeddie) 1942-
  See Smith, Dave
  See also CA 49-52; CANR 1, 59, 120; CSW; DAM POET

Smith, Iain Crichton 1928-1998 .... **CLC 64**
  See also BRWS 9; CA 21-24R; 171; CN 1, 2, 3, 4, 5, 6; CP 1, 2, 3, 4, 5, 6; DLB 40, 139, 319; RGSF 2

Smith, John 1580(?)-1631 .... **LC 9**
  See also DLB 24, 30; TUS

Smith, Johnston
  See Crane, Stephen (Townley)

Smith, Joseph, Jr. 1805-1844 .... **NCLC 53**

Smith, Kevin 1970- .... **CLC 223**
  See also AAYA 37; CA 166; CANR 131

Smith, Lee 1944- .... **CLC 25, 73, 258**
  See also CA 114; 119; CANR 46, 118, 173; CN 7; CSW; DLB 143; DLBY 1983; EWL 3; INT CA-119; RGAL 4

Smith, Martin
  See Smith, Martin Cruz

Smith, Martin Cruz 1942- .. **CLC 25; NNAL**
  See also BEST 89:4; BPFB 3; CA 85-88; CANR 6, 23, 43, 65, 119; CMW 4; CPW; DAM MULT, POP; HGG; INT CANR-23; MTCW 2; MTFW 2005; RGAL 4

Smith, Patti 1946- .... **CLC 12**
  See also CA 93-96; CANR 63, 168

Smith, Pauline (Urmson)
  1882-1959 .... **TCLC 25**
  See also DLB 225; EWL 3

Smith, Rosamond
  See Oates, Joyce Carol

Smith, Seba 1792-1868 .... **NCLC 187**
  See also DLB 1, 11, 243

Smith, Sheila Kaye
  See Kaye-Smith, Sheila

Smith, Stevie 1902-1971 .... **CLC 3, 8, 25, 44; PC 12**
  See also BRWS 2; CA 17-18; 29-32R; CANR 35; CAP 2; CP 1; DAM POET; DLB 20; EWL 3; MTCW 1, 2; PAB; PFS 3; RGEL 2; TEA

Smith, Wilbur 1933- .... **CLC 33**
  See also CA 13-16R; CANR 7, 46, 66, 134, 180; CPW; MTCW 1, 2; MTFW 2005

Smith, Wilbur Addison
  See Smith, Wilbur

Smith, William Jay 1918- .... **CLC 6**
  See also AMWS 13; CA 5-8R; CANR 44, 106; CP 1, 2, 3, 4, 5, 6, 7; CSW; CWRI 5; DLB 5; MAICYA 1, 2; SAAS 22; SATA 2, 68, 154; SATA-Essay 154; TCLE 1:2

Smith, Woodrow Wilson
  See Kuttner, Henry

Smith, Zadie 1975- .... **CLC 158**
  See also AAYA 50; CA 193; MTFW 2005

Smolenskin, Peretz 1842-1885 .... **NCLC 30**

Smollett, Tobias (George) 1721-1771 ... **LC 2, 46**
  See also BRW 3; CDBLB 1660-1789; DLB 39, 104; RGEL 2; TEA

Snodgrass, W.D. 1926- .... **CLC 2, 6, 10, 18, 68; PC 74**
  See also AMWS 6; CA 1-4R; CANR 6, 36, 65, 85; CP 1, 2, 3, 4, 5, 6, 7; DAM POET; DLB 5; MAL 5; MTCW 1, 2; MTFW 2005; RGAL 4; TCLE 1:2

Snorri Sturluson 1179-1241 .... **CMLC 56**
  See also RGWL 2, 3

Snow, C(harles) P(ercy) 1905-1980 ... **CLC 1, 4, 6, 9, 13, 19**
  See also BRW 7; CA 5-8R; 101; CANR 28; CDBLB 1945-1960; CN 1, 2; DAM NOV; DLB 15, 77; DLBD 17; EWL 3; MTCW 1, 2; MTFW 2005; RGEL 2; TEA

Snow, Frances Compton
  See Adams, Henry (Brooks)

Snyder, Gary 1930- . **CLC 1, 2, 5, 9, 32, 120; PC 21**
  See also AAYA 72; AMWS 8; ANW; BG 1:3; CA 17-20R; CANR 30, 60, 125; CP 1, 2, 3, 4, 5, 6, 7; DA3; DAM POET; DLB 5, 16, 165, 212, 237, 275, 342; EWL 3; MAL 5; MTCW 2; MTFW 2005; PFS 9, 19; RGAL 4; WP

Snyder, Zilpha Keatley 1927- .... **CLC 17**
  See also AAYA 15; BYA 1; CA 9-12R; 252; CAAE 252; CANR 38; CLR 31, 121; JRDA; MAICYA 1, 2; SAAS 2; SATA 1, 28, 75, 110, 163; SATA-Essay 112, 163; YAW

Soares, Bernardo
  See Pessoa, Fernando (Antonio Nogueira)

Sobh, A.
  See Shamlu, Ahmad

Sobh, Alef
  See Shamlu, Ahmad

Sobol, Joshua 1939- .... **CLC 60**
  See Sobol, Yehoshua
  See also CA 200; RGHL

Sobol, Yehoshua 1939-
  See Sobol, Joshua
  See also CWW 2

Socrates 470B.C.-399B.C. .... **CMLC 27**

Soderberg, Hjalmar 1869-1941 ...... **TCLC 39**
  See also DLB 259; EWL 3; RGSF 2

Soderbergh, Steven 1963- .... **CLC 154**
  See also AAYA 43; CA 243

Soderbergh, Steven Andrew
  See Soderbergh, Steven

Sodergran, Edith (Irene) 1892-1923
  See Soedergran, Edith (Irene)
  See also CA 202; DLB 259; EW 11; EWL 3; RGWL 2, 3

Soedergran, Edith (Irene)
  1892-1923 .... **TCLC 31**
  See Sodergran, Edith (Irene)

Softly, Edgar
  See Lovecraft, H. P.

Softly, Edward
  See Lovecraft, H. P.

Sokolov, Alexander V(sevolodovich) 1943-
  See Sokolov, Sasha
  See also CA 73-76

Sokolov, Raymond 1941- .... **CLC 7**
  See also CA 85-88

Sokolov, Sasha .... **CLC 59**
  See Sokolov, Alexander V(sevolodovich)
  See also CWW 2; DLB 285; EWL 3; RGWL 2, 3

Solo, Jay
  See Ellison, Harlan

Sologub, Fyodor .... **TCLC 9**
  See Teternikov, Fyodor Kuzmich
  See also EWL 3

Solomons, Ikey Esquir
  See Thackeray, William Makepeace

Solomos, Dionysios 1798-1857 .... **NCLC 15**

Solwoska, Mara
  See French, Marilyn

Solzhenitsyn, Aleksandr I.
  1918-2008 ...... **CLC 1, 2, 4, 7, 9, 10, 18, 26, 34, 78, 134, 235; SSC 32, 105; WLC 5**
  See Solzhenitsyn, Aleksandr Isayevich
  See also AAYA 49; AITN 1; BPFB 3; CA 69-72; CANR 40, 65, 116; DA; DA3; DAB; DAC; DAM MST, NOV; DLB 302, 332; EW 13; EXPS; LAIT 4; MTCW 1, 2; MTFW 2005; NFS 6; RGSF 2; RGWL 2, 3; SSFS 9; TWA

Solzhenitsyn, Aleksandr Isayevich
  See Solzhenitsyn, Aleksandr I.
  See also CWW 2; EWL 3

Somers, Jane
  See Lessing, Doris

Somerville, Edith Oenone
  1858-1949 .... **SSC 56; TCLC 51**
  See also CA 196; DLB 135; RGEL 2; RGSF 2

Somerville & Ross
  See Martin, Violet Florence; Somerville, Edith Oenone

Sommer, Scott 1951- .... **CLC 25**
  See also CA 106

Sommers, Christina Hoff 1950- ...... **CLC 197**
  See also CA 153; CANR 95

Sondheim, Stephen 1930- .. **CLC 30, 39, 147; DC 22**
  See also AAYA 11, 66; CA 103; CANR 47, 67, 125; DAM DRAM; DFS 25; LAIT 4

Sondheim, Stephen Joshua
  See Sondheim, Stephen

Sone, Monica 1919- .... **AAL**
  See also DLB 312

Song, Cathy 1955- .... **AAL; PC 21**
  See also CA 154; CANR 118; CWP; DLB 169, 312; EXPP; FW; PFS 5

Sontag, Susan 1933-2004 ... **CLC 1, 2, 10, 13, 31, 105, 195**
  See also AMWS 3; CA 17-20R; 234; CANR 25, 51, 74, 97; CN 1, 2, 3, 4, 5, 6, 7; CPW; DA3; DAM POP; DLB 2, 67; EWL 3; MAL 5; MBL; MTCW 1, 2; MTFW 2005; RGAL 4; RHW; SSFS 10

Stanislavsky, Konstantin Sergeievich
See Stanislavsky, Constantin
Stanislavsky, Konstantin Sergeivich
See Stanislavsky, Constantin
Stanislavsky, Konstantin Sergeyevich
See Stanislavsky, Constantin
Stannard, Martin 1947- .... **CLC 44**
See also CA 142; DLB 155
Stanton, Elizabeth Cady
1815-1902 .... **TCLC 73**
See also CA 171; DLB 79; FL 1:3; FW
Stanton, Maura 1946- .... **CLC 9**
See also CA 89-92; CANR 15, 123; DLB
120
Stanton, Schuyler
See Baum, L(yman) Frank
Stapledon, (William) Olaf
1886-1950 .... **TCLC 22**
See also CA 111; 162; DLB 15, 255; SCFW
1, 2; SFW 4
Starbuck, George (Edwin)
1931-1996 .... **CLC 53**
See also CA 21-24R; 153; CANR 23; CP 1,
2, 3, 4, 5, 6; DAM POET
Stark, Richard
See Westlake, Donald E.
Statius c. 45-c. 96 .... **CMLC 91**
See also AW 2; DLB 211
Staunton, Schuyler
See Baum, L(yman) Frank
Stead, Christina (Ellen) 1902-1983 ... **CLC 2,
5, 8, 32, 80**
See also BRWS 4; CA 13-16R; 109; CANR
33, 40; CN 1, 2, 3; DLB 260; EWL 3;
FW; MTCW 1, 2; MTFW 2005; NFS 27;
RGEL 2; RGSF 2; WWE 1
Stead, William Thomas
1849-1912 .... **TCLC 48**
See also BRWS 13; CA 167
Stebnitsky, M.
See Leskov, Nikolai (Semyonovich)
Steele, Richard 1672-1729 .... **LC 18, 156**
See also BRW 3; CDBLB 1660-1789; DLB
84, 101; RGEL 2; WLIT 3
Steele, Timothy (Reid) 1948- .... **CLC 45**
See also CA 93-96; CANR 16, 50, 92; CP
5, 6, 7; DLB 120, 282
Steffens, (Joseph) Lincoln
1866-1936 .... **TCLC 20**
See also CA 117; 198; DLB 303; MAL 5
Stegner, Wallace (Earle) 1909-1993 .. **CLC 9,
49, 81; SSC 27**
See also AITN 1; AMWS 4; ANW; BEST
90:3; BPFB 3; CA 1-4R; 141; CAAS 9;
CANR 1, 21, 46; CN 1, 2, 3, 4, 5; DAM
NOV; DLB 9, 206, 275; DLBY 1993;
EWL 3; MAL 5; MTCW 1, 2; MTFW
2005; RGAL 4; TCWW 1, 2; TUS
Stein, Gertrude 1874-1946 .... **DC 19; PC 18;
SSC 42, 105; TCLC 1, 6, 28, 48; WLC
5**
See also AAYA 64; AMW; AMWC 2; CA
104; 132; CANR 108; CDALB 1917-
1929; DA; DA3; DAB; DAC; DAM MST,
NOV, POET; DLB 4, 54, 86, 228; DLBD
15; EWL 3; EXPS; FL 1:6; GLL 1; MAL
5; MBL; MTCW 1, 2; MTFW 2005;
NCFS 4; NFS 27; RGAL 4; RGSF 2;
SSFS 5; TUS; WP
Steinbeck, John (Ernst) 1902-1968 ... **CLC 1,
5, 9, 13, 21, 34, 45, 75, 124; SSC 11, 37,
77; TCLC 135; WLC 5**
See also AAYA 12; AMW; BPFB 3; BYA 2,
3, 13; CA 1-4R; 25-28R; CANR 1, 35;
CDALB 1929-1941; DA; DA3; DAB;
DAC; DAM DRAM, MST, NOV; DLB 7,
9, 212, 275, 309, 332; DLBD 2; EWL 3;
EXPS; LAIT 3; MAL 5; MTCW 1, 2;

MTFW 2005; NFS 1, 5, 7, 17, 19; RGAL
4; RGSF 2; RHW; SATA 9; SSFS 3, 6,
22; TCWW 1, 2; TUS; WYA; YAW
Steinem, Gloria 1934- .... **CLC 63**
See also CA 53-56; CANR 28, 51, 139;
DLB 246; FL 1:1; FW; MTCW 1, 2;
MTFW 2005
Steiner, George 1929- .... **CLC 24, 221**
See also CA 73-76; CANR 31, 67, 108;
DAM NOV; DLB 67, 299; EWL 3;
MTCW 1, 2; MTFW 2005; RGHL; SATA
62
Steiner, K. Leslie
See Delany, Samuel R., Jr.
Steiner, Rudolf 1861-1925 .... **TCLC 13**
See also CA 107
Stendhal 1783-1842 .... **NCLC 23, 46, 178;
SSC 27; WLC 5**
See also DA; DA3; DAB; DAC; DAM
MST, NOV; DLB 119; EW 5; GFL 1789
to the Present; RGWL 2, 3; TWA
Stephen, Adeline Virginia
See Woolf, (Adeline) Virginia
Stephen, Sir Leslie 1832-1904 .... **TCLC 23**
See also BRW 5; CA 123; DLB 57, 144,
190
Stephen, Sir Leslie
See Stephen, Sir Leslie
Stephen, Virginia
See Woolf, (Adeline) Virginia
Stephens, James 1882(?)-1950 .... **SSC 50;
TCLC 4**
See also CA 104; 192; DLB 19, 153, 162;
EWL 3; FANT; RGEL 2; SUFW
Stephens, Reed
See Donaldson, Stephen R.
Stephenson, Neal 1959- .... **CLC 220**
See also AAYA 38; CA 122; CANR 88, 138;
CN 7; MTFW 2005; SFW 4
Steptoe, Lydia
See Barnes, Djuna
See also GLL 1
Sterchi, Beat 1949- .... **CLC 65**
See also CA 203
Sterling, Brett
See Bradbury, Ray; Hamilton, Edmond
Sterling, Bruce 1954- .... **CLC 72**
See also AAYA 78; CA 119; CANR 44, 135;
CN 7; MTFW 2005; SCFW 2; SFW 4
Sterling, George 1869-1926 .... **TCLC 20**
See also CA 117; 165; DLB 54
Stern, Gerald 1925- .... **CLC 40, 100**
See also AMWS 9; CA 81-84; CANR 28,
94; CP 3, 4, 5, 6, 7; DLB 105; PFS 26;
RGAL 4
Stern, Richard (Gustave) 1928- ... **CLC 4, 39**
See also CA 1-4R; CANR 1, 25, 52, 120;
CN 1, 2, 3, 4, 5, 6, 7; DLB 218; DLBY
1987; INT CANR-25
Sternberg, Josef von 1894-1969 .... **CLC 20**
See also CA 81-84
Sterne, Laurence 1713-1768 .. **LC 2, 48, 156;
WLC 5**
See also BRW 3; BRWC 1; CDBLB 1660-
1789; DA; DAB; DAC; DAM MST, NOV;
DLB 39; RGEL 2; TEA
Sternheim, (William Adolf) Carl
1878-1942 .... **TCLC 8**
See also CA 105; 193; DLB 56, 118; EWL
3; IDTP; RGWL 2, 3
Stevens, Margaret Dean
See Aldrich, Bess Streeter
Stevens, Mark 1951- .... **CLC 34**
See also CA 122

Stevens, Wallace 1879-1955 . **PC 6; TCLC 3,
12, 45; WLC 5**
See also AMW; AMWR 1; CA 104; 124;
CDALB 1929-1941; DA; DA3; DAB;
DAC; DAM MST, POET; DLB 54, 342;
EWL 3; EXPP; MAL 5; MTCW 1, 2;
PAB; PFS 13, 16; RGAL 4; TUS; WP
Stevenson, Anne (Katharine) 1933- .. **CLC 7,
33**
See also BRWS 6; CA 17-20R; CAAS 9;
CANR 9, 33, 123; CP 3, 4, 5, 6, 7; CWP;
DLB 40; MTCW 1; RHW
Stevenson, Robert Louis (Balfour)
1850-1894 ...... **NCLC 5, 14, 63, 193; PC
84; SSC 11, 51; WLC 5**
See also AAYA 24; BPFB 3; BRW 5;
BRWC 1; BRWR 1; BYA 1, 2, 4, 13; CD-
BLB 1890-1914; CLR 10, 11, 107; DA;
DA3; DAB; DAC; DAM MST, NOV;
DLB 18, 57, 141, 156, 174; DLBD 13;
GL 3; HGG; JRDA; LAIT 1, 3; MAICYA
1, 2; NFS 11, 20; RGEL 2; RGSF 2;
SATA 100; SUFW; TEA; WCH; WLIT 4;
WYA; YABC 2; YAW
Stewart, J(ohn) I(nnes) M(ackintosh)
1906-1994 .... **CLC 7, 14, 32**
See Innes, Michael
See also CA 85-88; 147; CAAS 3; CANR
47; CMW 4; CN 1, 2, 3, 4, 5; MTCW 1,
2
Stewart, Mary (Florence Elinor)
1916- .... **CLC 7, 35, 117**
See also AAYA 29, 73; BPFB 3; CA 1-4R;
CANR 1, 59, 130; CMW 4; CPW; DAB;
FANT; RHW; SATA 12; YAW
Stewart, Mary Rainbow
See Stewart, Mary (Florence Elinor)
Stifle, June
See Campbell, Maria
Stifter, Adalbert 1805-1868 ... **NCLC 41, 198;
SSC 28**
See also CDWLB 2; DLB 133; RGSF 2;
RGWL 2, 3
Still, James 1906-2001 .... **CLC 49**
See also CA 65-68; 195; CAAS 17; CANR
10, 26; CSW; DLB 9; DLBY 01; SATA
29; SATA-Obit 127
Sting 1951-
See Sumner, Gordon Matthew
See also CA 167
Stirling, Arthur
See Sinclair, Upton
Stitt, Milan 1941- .... **CLC 29**
See also CA 69-72
Stockton, Francis Richard 1834-1902
See Stockton, Frank R.
See also AAYA 68; CA 108; 137; MAICYA
1, 2; SATA 44; SFW 4
Stockton, Frank R. .... **TCLC 47**
See Stockton, Francis Richard
See also BYA 4, 13; DLB 42, 74; DLBD
13; EXPS; SATA-Brief 32; SSFS 3;
SUFW; WCH
Stoddard, Charles
See Kuttner, Henry
Stoker, Abraham 1847-1912
See Stoker, Bram
See also CA 105; 150; DA; DA3; DAC;
DAM MST, NOV; HGG; MTFW 2005;
SATA 29
Stoker, Bram . **SSC 62; TCLC 8, 144; WLC
6**
See Stoker, Abraham
See also AAYA 23; BPFB 3; BRWS 3; BYA
5; CDBLB 1890-1914; DAB; DLB 304;
GL 3; LATS 1:1; NFS 18; RGEL 2;
SUFW; TEA; WLIT 4

Summers, (Alphonsus Joseph-Mary Augustus) Montague 1880-1948 .... **TCLC 16**
See also CA 118; 163

Sumner, Gordon Matthew .... **CLC 26**
See Police, The; Sting

Sun Tzu c. 400B.C.-c. 320B.C. ...... **CMLC 56**

Surrey, Henry Howard 1517-1574 ... **LC 121; PC 59**
See also BRW 1; RGEL 2

Surtees, Robert Smith 1805-1864 .. **NCLC 14**
See also DLB 21; RGEL 2

Susann, Jacqueline 1921-1974 .... **CLC 3**
See also AITN 1; BPFB 3; CA 65-68; 53-56; MTCW 1, 2

Su Shi
See Su Shih
See also RGWL 2, 3

Su Shih 1036-1101 .... **CMLC 15**
See Su Shi

Suskind, Patrick .... **CLC 182**
See Sueskind, Patrick
See also BPFB 3; CA 145; CWW 2

Suso, Heinrich c. 1295-1366 .... **CMLC 87**

Sutcliff, Rosemary 1920-1992 .... **CLC 26**
See also AAYA 10; BYA 1, 4; CA 5-8R; 139; CANR 37; CLR 1, 37, 138; CPW; DAB; DAC; DAM MST, POP; JRDA; LATS 1:1; MAICYA 1, 2; MAICYAS 1; RHW; SATA 6, 44, 78; SATA-Obit 73; WYA; YAW

Sutherland, Efua (Theodora Morgue) 1924-1996 .... **BLC 2:3**
See also AFW; BW 1; CA 105; CWD; DLB 117; EWL 3; IDTP; SATA 25

Sutro, Alfred 1863-1933 .... **TCLC 6**
See also CA 105; 185; DLB 10; RGEL 2

Sutton, Henry
See Slavitt, David R.

Suzuki, D. T.
See Suzuki, Daisetz Teitaro

Suzuki, Daisetz T.
See Suzuki, Daisetz Teitaro

Suzuki, Daisetz Teitaro 1870-1966 .... **TCLC 109**
See also CA 121; 111; MTCW 1, 2; MTFW 2005

Suzuki, Teitaro
See Suzuki, Daisetz Teitaro

Svevo, Italo .... **SSC 25; TCLC 2, 35**
See Schmitz, Aron Hector
See also DLB 264; EW 8; EWL 3; RGWL 2, 3; WLIT 7

Swados, Elizabeth 1951- .... **CLC 12**
See also CA 97-100; CANR 49, 163; INT CA-97-100

Swados, Elizabeth A.
See Swados, Elizabeth

Swados, Harvey 1920-1972 .... **CLC 5**
See also CA 5-8R; 37-40R; CANR 6; CN 1; DLB 2, 335; MAL 5

Swados, Liz
See Swados, Elizabeth

Swan, Gladys 1934- .... **CLC 69**
See also CA 101; CANR 17, 39; TCLE 1:2

Swanson, Logan
See Matheson, Richard

Swarthout, Glendon (Fred) 1918-1992 .... **CLC 35**
See also AAYA 55; CA 1-4R; 139; CANR 1, 47; CN 1, 2, 3, 4, 5; LAIT 5; SATA 26; TCWW 1, 2; YAW

Swedenborg, Emanuel 1688-1772 ..... **LC 105**

Sweet, Sarah C.
See Jewett, (Theodora) Sarah Orne

Swenson, May 1919-1989 ...... **CLC 4, 14, 61, 106; PC 14**
See also AMWS 4; CA 5-8R; 130; CANR 36, 61, 131; CP 1, 2, 3, 4; DA; DAB; DAC; DAM MST, POET; DLB 5; EXPP; GLL 2; MAL 5; MTCW 1, 2; MTFW 2005; PFS 16; SATA 15; WP

Swift, Augustus
See Lovecraft, H. P.

Swift, Graham 1949- .... **CLC 41, 88, 233**
See also BRWC 2; BRWS 5; CA 117; 122; CANR 46, 71, 128; CN 4, 5, 6, 7; DLB 194, 326; MTCW 2; MTFW 2005; NFS 18; RGSF 2

Swift, Jonathan 1667-1745 ..... **LC 1, 42, 101; PC 9; WLC 6**
See also AAYA 41; BRW 3; BRWC 1; BRWR 1; BYA 5, 14; CDBLB 1660-1789; CLR 53; DA; DA3; DAB; DAC; DAM MST, NOV, POET; DLB 39, 95, 101; EXPN; LAIT 1; NFS 6; PFS 27; RGEL 2; SATA 19; TEA; WCH; WLIT 3

Swinburne, Algernon Charles 1837-1909 ... **PC 24; TCLC 8, 36; WLC 6**
See also BRW 5; CA 105; 140; CDBLB 1832-1890; DA; DA3; DAB; DAC; DAM MST, POET; DLB 35, 57; PAB; RGEL 2; TEA

Swinfen, Ann .... **CLC 34**
See also CA 202

Swinnerton, Frank (Arthur) 1884-1982 .... **CLC 31**
See also CA 202; 108; CN 1, 2, 3; DLB 34

Swinnerton, Frank Arthur 1884-1982 .... **CLC 31**
See also CA 108; DLB 34

Swithen, John
See King, Stephen

Sylvia
See Ashton-Warner, Sylvia (Constance)

Symmes, Robert Edward
See Duncan, Robert

Symonds, John Addington 1840-1893 .... **NCLC 34**
See also DLB 57, 144

Symons, Arthur 1865-1945 .... **TCLC 11**
See also CA 107; 189; DLB 19, 57, 149; RGEL 2

Symons, Julian (Gustave) 1912-1994 .... **CLC 2, 14, 32**
See also CA 49-52; 147; CAAS 3; CANR 3, 33, 59; CMW 4; CN 1, 2, 3, 4, 5; CP 1, 3, 4; DLB 87, 155; DLBY 1992; MSW; MTCW 1

Synge, (Edmund) J(ohn) M(illington) 1871-1909 .... **DC 2; TCLC 6, 37**
See also BRW 6; BRWR 1; CA 104; 141; CDBLB 1890-1914; DAM DRAM; DFS 18; DLB 10, 19; EWL 3; RGEL 2; TEA; WLIT 4

Syruc, J.
See Milosz, Czeslaw

Szirtes, George 1948- .... **CLC 46; PC 51**
See also CA 109; CANR 27, 61, 117; CP 4, 5, 6, 7

Szymborska, Wislawa 1923- ... **CLC 99, 190; PC 44**
See also AAYA 76; CA 154; CANR 91, 133; CDWLB 4; CWP; CWW 2; DA3; DLB 232, 332; DLBY 1996; EWL 3; MTCW 2; MTFW 2005; PFS 15, 27; RGHL; RGWL 3

T. O., Nik
See Annensky, Innokenty (Fyodorovich)

Tabori, George 1914-2007 .... **CLC 19**
See also CA 49-52; 262; CANR 4, 69; CBD; CD 5, 6; DLB 245; RGHL

Tacitus c. 55-c. 117 .... **CMLC 56**
See also AW 2; CDWLB 1; DLB 211; RGWL 2, 3; WLIT 8

Tadjo, Veronique 1955- .... **BLC 2:3**
See also EWL 3

Tagore, Rabindranath 1861-1941 .... **PC 8; SSC 48; TCLC 3, 53**
See also CA 104; 120; DA3; DAM DRAM, POET; DLB 323, 332; EWL 3; MTCW 1, 2; MTFW 2005; PFS 18; RGEL 2; RGSF 2, 3; TWA

Taine, Hippolyte Adolphe 1828-1893 .... **NCLC 15**
See also EW 7; GFL 1789 to the Present

Talayesva, Don C. 1890-(?) .... **NNAL**

Talese, Gay 1932- .... **CLC 37, 232**
See also AITN 1; AMWS 17; CA 1-4R; CANR 9, 58, 137, 177; DLB 185; INT CANR-9; MTCW 1, 2; MTFW 2005

Tallent, Elizabeth 1954- .... **CLC 45**
See also CA 117; CANR 72; DLB 130

Tallmountain, Mary 1918-1997 .... **NNAL**
See also CA 146; 161; DLB 193

Tally, Ted 1952- .... **CLC 42**
See also CA 120; 124; CAD; CANR 125; CD 5, 6; INT CA-124

Talvik, Heiti 1904-1947 .... **TCLC 87**
See also EWL 3

Tamayo y Baus, Manuel 1829-1898 .... **NCLC 1**

Tammsaare, A(nton) H(ansen) 1878-1940 .... **TCLC 27**
See also CA 164; CDWLB 4; DLB 220; EWL 3

Tam'si, Tchicaya U
See Tchicaya, Gerald Felix

Tan, Amy 1952- ..... **AAL; CLC 59, 120, 151, 257**
See also AAYA 9, 48; AMWS 10; BEST 89:3; BPFB 3; CA 136; CANR 54, 105, 132; CDALBS; CN 6, 7; CPW 1; DA3; DAM MULT, NOV, POP; DLB 173, 312; EXPN; FL 1:6; FW; LAIT 3, 5; MAL 5; MTCW 2; MTFW 2005; NFS 1, 13, 16; RGAL 4; SATA 75; SSFS 9; YAW

Tandem, Carl Felix
See Spitteler, Carl

Tandem, Felix
See Spitteler, Carl

Tanizaki, Jun'ichiro 1886-1965 ... **CLC 8, 14, 28; SSC 21**
See Tanizaki Jun'ichiro
See also CA 93-96; 25-28R; MJW; MTCW 2; MTFW 2005; RGSF 2; RGWL 2

Tanizaki Jun'ichiro
See Tanizaki, Jun'ichiro
See also DLB 180; EWL 3

Tannen, Deborah 1945- .... **CLC 206**
See also CA 118; CANR 95

Tannen, Deborah Frances
See Tannen, Deborah

Tanner, William
See Amis, Kingsley

Tante, Dilly
See Kunitz, Stanley

Tao Lao
See Storni, Alfonsina

Tapahonso, Luci 1953- .... **NNAL; PC 65**
See also CA 145; CANR 72, 127; DLB 175

Tarantino, Quentin (Jerome) 1963- .... **CLC 125, 230**
See also AAYA 58; CA 171; CANR 125

Tarassoff, Lev
See Troyat, Henri

Tarbell, Ida M(inerva) 1857-1944 . **TCLC 40**
See also CA 122; 181; DLB 47

Tardieu d'Esclavelles, Louise-Florence-Petronille
See Epinay, Louise d'

Tarkington, (Newton) Booth
1869-1946 .... **TCLC 9**
See also BPFB 3; BYA 3; CA 110; 143;
CWRI 5; DLB 9, 102; MAL 5; MTCW 2;
RGAL 4; SATA 17

Tarkovskii, Andrei Arsen'evich
See Tarkovsky, Andrei (Arsenyevich)

Tarkovsky, Andrei (Arsenyevich)
1932-1986 .... **CLC 75**
See also CA 127

Tartt, Donna 1964(?)- .... **CLC 76**
See also AAYA 56; CA 142; CANR 135;
MTFW 2005

Tasso, Torquato 1544-1595 .... **LC 5, 94**
See also EFS 2; EW 2; RGWL 2, 3; WLIT
7

Tate, (John Orley) Allen 1899-1979 .. **CLC 2,
4, 6, 9, 11, 14, 24; PC 50**
See also AMW; CA 5-8R; 85-88; CANR
32, 108; CN 1, 2; CP 1, 2; DLB 4, 45, 63;
DLBD 17; EWL 3; MAL 5; MTCW 1, 2;
MTFW 2005; RGAL 4; RHW

Tate, Ellalice
See Hibbert, Eleanor Alice Burford

Tate, James (Vincent) 1943- ..... **CLC 2, 6, 25**
See also CA 21-24R; CANR 29, 57, 114;
CP 1, 2, 3, 4, 5, 6, 7; DLB 5, 169; EWL
3; PFS 10, 15; RGAL 4; WP

Tate, Nahum 1652(?)-1715 .... **LC 109**
See also DLB 80; RGEL 2

Tauler, Johannes c. 1300-1361 ...... **CMLC 37**
See also DLB 179; LMFS 1

Tavel, Ronald 1940- .... **CLC 6**
See also CA 21-24R; CAD; CANR 33; CD
5, 6

Taviani, Paolo 1931- .... **CLC 70**
See also CA 153

Taylor, Bayard 1825-1878 .... **NCLC 89**
See also DLB 3, 189, 250, 254; RGAL 4

Taylor, C(ecil) P(hilip) 1929-1981 .... **CLC 27**
See also CA 25-28R; 105; CANR 47; CBD

Taylor, Edward 1642(?)-1729 . **LC 11; PC 63**
See also AMW; DA; DAB; DAC; DAM
MST, POET; DLB 24; EXPP; RGAL 4;
TUS

Taylor, Eleanor Ross 1920- .... **CLC 5**
See also CA 81-84; CANR 70

Taylor, Elizabeth 1912-1975 .... **CLC 2, 4, 29;
SSC 100**
See also CA 13-16R; CANR 9, 70; CN 1,
2; DLB 139; MTCW 1; RGEL 2; SATA
13

Taylor, Frederick Winslow
1856-1915 .... **TCLC 76**
See also CA 188

Taylor, Henry 1942- .... **CLC 44**
See also CA 33-36R; CAAS 7; CANR 31,
178; CP 6, 7; DLB 5; PFS 10

Taylor, Henry Splawn
See Taylor, Henry

Taylor, Kamala 1924-2004
See Markandaya, Kamala
See also CA 77-80; 227; MTFW 2005; NFS
13

Taylor, Mildred D. 1943- .... **CLC 21**
See also AAYA 10, 47; BW 1; BYA 3, 8;
CA 85-88; CANR 25, 115, 136; CLR 9,
59, 90; CSW; DLB 52; JRDA; LAIT 3;
MAICYA 1, 2; MTFW 2005; SAAS 5;
SATA 135; WYA; YAW

Taylor, Peter (Hillsman) 1917-1994 .. **CLC 1,
4, 18, 37, 44, 50, 71; SSC 10, 84**
See also AMWS 5; BPFB 3; CA 13-16R;
147; CANR 9, 50; CN 1, 2, 3, 4, 5; CSW;
DLB 218, 278; DLBY 1981, 1994; EWL
3; EXPS; INT CANR-9; MAL 5; MTCW
1, 2; MTFW 2005; RGSF 2; SSFS 9; TUS

Taylor, Robert Lewis 1912-1998 .... **CLC 14**
See also CA 1-4R; 170; CANR 3, 64; CN
1, 2; SATA 10; TCWW 1, 2

Tchekhov, Anton
See Chekhov, Anton (Pavlovich)

Tchicaya, Gerald Felix 1931-1988 .. **CLC 101**
See Tchicaya U Tam'si
See also CA 129; 125; CANR 81

Tchicaya U Tam'si
See Tchicaya, Gerald Felix
See also EWL 3

Teasdale, Sara 1884-1933 .... **PC 31; TCLC 4**
See also CA 104; 163; DLB 45; GLL 1;
PFS 14; RGAL 4; SATA 32; TUS

Tecumseh 1768-1813 .... **NNAL**
See also DAM MULT

Tegner, Esaias 1782-1846 .... **NCLC 2**

Teilhard de Chardin, (Marie Joseph) Pierre
1881-1955 .... **TCLC 9**
See also CA 105; 210; GFL 1789 to the
Present

Temple, Ann
See Mortimer, Penelope (Ruth)

Tennant, Emma 1937- .... **CLC 13, 52**
See also BRWS 9; CA 65-68; CAAS 9;
CANR 10, 38, 59, 88, 177; CN 3, 4, 5, 6,
7; DLB 14; EWL 3; SFW 4

Tenneshaw, S.M.
See Silverberg, Robert

Tenney, Tabitha Gilman
1762-1837 .... **NCLC 122**
See also DLB 37, 200

Tennyson, Alfred 1809-1892 ... **NCLC 30, 65,
115, 202; PC 6; WLC 6**
See also AAYA 50; BRW 4; CDBLB 1832-
1890; DA; DA3; DAB; DAC; DAM MST,
POET; DLB 32; EXPP; PAB; PFS 1, 2, 4,
11, 15, 19; RGEL 2; TEA; WLIT 4; WP

Teran, Lisa St. Aubin de .... **CLC 36**
See St. Aubin de Teran, Lisa

Terence c. 184B.C.-c. 159B.C. ...... **CMLC 14;
DC 7**
See also AW 1; CDWLB 1; DLB 211;
RGWL 2, 3; TWA; WLIT 8

Teresa de Jesus, St. 1515-1582 .... **LC 18, 149**

Teresa of Avila, St.
See Teresa de Jesus, St.

Terkel, Louis .... **CLC 38**
See Terkel, Studs
See also AAYA 32; AITN 1; MTCW 2; TUS

Terkel, Studs 1912-
See Terkel, Louis
See also CA 57-60; CANR 18, 45, 67, 132;
DA3; MTCW 1, 2; MTFW 2005

Terry, C. V.
See Slaughter, Frank G(ill)

Terry, Megan 1932- .... **CLC 19; DC 13**
See also CA 77-80; CABS 3; CAD; CANR
43; CD 5, 6; CWD; DFS 18; DLB 7, 249;
GLL 2

Tertullian c. 155-c. 245 .... **CMLC 29**

Tertz, Abram
See Sinyavsky, Andrei (Donatevich)
See also RGSF 2

Tesich, Steve 1943(?)-1996 .... **CLC 40, 69**
See also CA 105; 152; CAD; DLBY 1983

Tesla, Nikola 1856-1943 .... **TCLC 88**

Teternikov, Fyodor Kuzmich 1863-1927
See Sologub, Fyodor
See also CA 104

Tevis, Walter 1928-1984 .... **CLC 42**
See also CA 113; SFW 4

Tey, Josephine .... **TCLC 14**
See Mackintosh, Elizabeth
See also DLB 77; MSW

Thackeray, William Makepeace
1811-1863 ...... **NCLC 5, 14, 22, 43, 169;
WLC 6**
See also BRW 5; BRWC 2; CDBLB 1832-
1890; DA; DA3; DAB; DAC; DAM MST,
NOV; DLB 21, 55, 159, 163; NFS 13;
RGEL 2; SATA 23; TEA; WLIT 3

Thakura, Ravindranatha
See Tagore, Rabindranath

Thames, C. H.
See Marlowe, Stephen

Tharoor, Shashi 1956- .... **CLC 70**
See also CA 141; CANR 91; CN 6, 7

Thelwall, John 1764-1834 .... **NCLC 162**
See also DLB 93, 158

Thelwell, Michael Miles 1939- .... **CLC 22**
See also BW 2; CA 101

Theobald, Lewis, Jr.
See Lovecraft, H. P.

Theocritus c. 310B.C.- .... **CMLC 45**
See also AW 1; DLB 176; RGWL 2, 3

Theodorescu, Ion N. 1880-1967
See Arghezi, Tudor
See also CA 116

Theriault, Yves 1915-1983 .... **CLC 79**
See also CA 102; CANR 150; CCA 1;
DAC; DAM MST; DLB 88; EWL 3

Theroux, Alexander 1939- .... **CLC 2, 25**
See also CA 85-88; CANR 20, 63; CN 4, 5,
6, 7

Theroux, Alexander Louis
See Theroux, Alexander

Theroux, Paul 1941- .... **CLC 5, 8, 11, 15, 28,
46, 159**
See also AAYA 28; AMWS 8; BEST 89:4;
BPFB 3; CA 33-36R; CANR 20, 45, 74,
133, 179; CDALBS; CN 1, 2, 3, 4, 5, 6,
7; CP 1; CPW 1; DA3; DAM POP; DLB
2, 218; EWL 3; HGG; MAL 5; MTCW 1,
2; MTFW 2005; RGAL 4; SATA 44, 109;
TUS

Thesen, Sharon 1946- .... **CLC 56**
See also CA 163; CANR 125; CP 5, 6, 7;
CWP

Thespis fl. 6th cent. B.C.- .... **CMLC 51**
See also LMFS 1

Thevenin, Denis
See Duhamel, Georges

Thibault, Jacques Anatole Francois
1844-1924
See France, Anatole
See also CA 106; 127; DA3; DAM NOV;
MTCW 1, 2; TWA

Thiele, Colin 1920-2006 .... **CLC 17**
See also CA 29-32R; CANR 12, 28, 53,
105; CLR 27; CP 1, 2; DLB 289; MAI-
CYA 1, 2; SAAS 2; SATA 14, 72, 125;
YAW

Thiong'o, Ngugi Wa
See Ngugi wa Thiong'o

Thistlethwaite, Bel
See Wetherald, Agnes Ethelwyn

Thomas, Audrey (Callahan) 1935- .... **CLC 7,
13, 37, 107; SSC 20**
See also AITN 2; CA 21-24R; 237; CAAE
237; CAAS 19; CANR 36, 58; CN 2, 3,
4, 5, 6, 7; DLB 60; MTCW 1; RGSF 2

Thomas, Augustus 1857-1934 .... **TCLC 97**
See also MAL 5

Thomas, D.M. 1935- ..... **CLC 13, 22, 31, 132**
See also BPFB 3; BRWS 4; CA 61-64;
CAAS 11; CANR 17, 45, 75; CDBLB
1960 to Present; CN 4, 5, 6, 7; CP 1, 2, 3,
4, 5, 6, 7; DA3; DLB 40, 207, 299; HGG;
INT CANR-17; MTCW 1, 2; MTFW
2005; RGHL; SFW 4

Thomas, Dylan (Marlais) 1914-1953 .... **PC 2, 52; SSC 3, 44; TCLC 1, 8, 45, 105; WLC 6**
See also AAYA 45; BRWS 1; CA 104; 120; CANR 65; CDBLB 1945-1960; DA; DA3; DAB; DAC; DAM DRAM, MST, POET; DLB 13, 20, 139; EWL 3; EXPP; LAIT 3; MTCW 1, 2; MTFW 2005; PAB; PFS 1, 3, 8; RGEL 2; RGSF 2; SATA 60; TEA; WLIT 4; WP

Thomas, (Philip) Edward 1878-1917 . **PC 53; TCLC 10**
See also BRW 6; BRWS 3; CA 106; 153; DAM POET; DLB 19, 98, 156, 216; EWL 3; PAB; RGEL 2

Thomas, Joyce Carol 1938- .... **CLC 35**
See also AAYA 12, 54; BW 2, 3; CA 113; 116; CANR 48, 114, 135; CLR 19; DLB 33; INT CA-116; JRDA; MAICYA 1, 2; MTCW 1, 2; MTFW 2005; SAAS 7; SATA 40, 78, 123, 137; SATA-Essay 137; WYA; YAW

Thomas, Lewis 1913-1993 .... **CLC 35**
See also ANW; CA 85-88; 143; CANR 38, 60; DLB 275; MTCW 1, 2

Thomas, M. Carey 1857-1935 .... **TCLC 89**
See also FW

Thomas, Paul
See Mann, (Paul) Thomas

Thomas, Piri 1928- .... **CLC 17; HLCS 2**
See also CA 73-76; HW 1; LLW

Thomas, R(onald) S(tuart)
1913-2000 .... **CLC 6, 13, 48**
See also BRWS 12; CA 89-92; 189; CAAS 4; CANR 30; CDBLB 1960 to Present; CP 1, 2, 3, 4, 5, 6, 7; DAB; DAM POET; DLB 27; EWL 3; MTCW 1; RGEL 2

Thomas, Ross (Elmore) 1926-1995 .. **CLC 39**
See also CA 33-36R; 150; CANR 22, 63; CMW 4

Thompson, Francis (Joseph)
1859-1907 .... **TCLC 4**
See also BRW 5; CA 104; 189; CDBLB 1890-1914; DLB 19; RGEL 2; TEA

Thompson, Francis Clegg
See Mencken, H(enry) L(ouis)

Thompson, Hunter S. 1937(?)-2005 .. **CLC 9, 17, 40, 104, 229**
See also AAYA 45; BEST 89:1; BPFB 3; CA 17-20R; 236; CANR 23, 46, 74, 77, 111, 133; CPW; CSW; DA3; DAM POP; DLB 185; MTCW 1, 2; MTFW 2005; TUS

Thompson, James Myers
See Thompson, Jim (Myers)

Thompson, Jim (Myers)
1906-1977(?) .... **CLC 69**
See also BPFB 3; CA 140; CMW 4; CPW; DLB 226; MSW

Thompson, Judith (Clare Francesca)
1954- .... **CLC 39**
See also CA 143; CD 5, 6; CWD; DFS 22; DLB 334

Thomson, James 1700-1748 .... **LC 16, 29, 40**
See also BRWS 3; DAM POET; DLB 95; RGEL 2

Thomson, James 1834-1882 .... **NCLC 18**
See also DAM POET; DLB 35; RGEL 2

Thoreau, Henry David 1817-1862 .. **NCLC 7, 21, 61, 138; PC 30; WLC 6**
See also AAYA 42; AMW; ANW; BYA 3; CDALB 1640-1865; DA; DA3; DAB; DAC; DAM MST; DLB 1, 183, 223, 270, 298; LAIT 2; LMFS 1; NCFS 3; RGAL 4; TUS

Thorndike, E. L.
See Thorndike, Edward L(ee)

Thorndike, Edward L(ee)
1874-1949 .... **TCLC 107**
See also CA 121

Thornton, Hall
See Silverberg, Robert

Thorpe, Adam 1956- .... **CLC 176**
See also CA 129; CANR 92, 160; DLB 231

Thorpe, Thomas Bangs
1815-1878 .... **NCLC 183**
See also DLB 3, 11, 248; RGAL 4

Thubron, Colin 1939- .... **CLC 163**
See also CA 25-28R; CANR 12, 29, 59, 95, 171; CN 5, 6, 7; DLB 204, 231

Thubron, Colin Gerald Dryden
See Thubron, Colin

Thucydides c. 455B.C.-c. 395B.C. . **CMLC 17**
See also AW 1; DLB 176; RGWL 2, 3; WLIT 8

Thumboo, Edwin Nadason 1933- .... **PC 30**
See also CA 194; CP 1

Thurber, James (Grover)
1894-1961 .. **CLC 5, 11, 25, 125; SSC 1, 47**
See also AAYA 56; AMWS 1; BPFB 3; BYA 5; CA 73-76; CANR 17, 39; CDALB 1929-1941; CWRI 5; DA; DA3; DAB; DAC; DAM DRAM, MST, NOV; DLB 4, 11, 22, 102; EWL 3; EXPS; FANT; LAIT 3; MAICYA 1, 2; MAL 5; MTCW 1, 2; MTFW 2005; RGAL 4; RGSF 2; SATA 13; SSFS 1, 10, 19; SUFW; TUS

Thurman, Wallace (Henry)
1902-1934 .. **BLC 1:3; HR 1:3; TCLC 6**
See also BW 1, 3; CA 104; 124; CANR 81; DAM MULT; DLB 51

Tibullus c. 54B.C.-c. 18B.C. .... **CMLC 36**
See also AW 2; DLB 211; RGWL 2, 3; WLIT 8

Ticheburn, Cheviot
See Ainsworth, William Harrison

Tieck, (Johann) Ludwig
1773-1853 ..... **NCLC 5, 46; SSC 31, 100**
See also CDWLB 2; DLB 90; EW 5; IDTP; RGSF 2; RGWL 2, 3; SUFW

Tiger, Derry
See Ellison, Harlan

Tilghman, Christopher 1946- .... **CLC 65**
See also CA 159; CANR 135, 151; CSW; DLB 244

Tillich, Paul (Johannes)
1886-1965 .... **CLC 131**
See also CA 5-8R; 25-28R; CANR 33; MTCW 1, 2

Tillinghast, Richard (Williford)
1940- .... **CLC 29**
See also CA 29-32R; CAAS 23; CANR 26, 51, 96; CP 2, 3, 4, 5, 6, 7; CSW

Tillman, Lynne (?)- .... **CLC 231**
See also CA 173; CANR 144, 172

Timrod, Henry 1828-1867 .... **NCLC 25**
See also DLB 3, 248; RGAL 4

Tindall, Gillian (Elizabeth) 1938- ...... **CLC 7**
See also CA 21-24R; CANR 11, 65, 107; CN 1, 2, 3, 4, 5, 6, 7

Tiptree, James, Jr. .... **CLC 48, 50**
See Sheldon, Alice Hastings Bradley
See also DLB 8; SCFW 1, 2; SFW 4

Tirone Smith, Mary-Ann 1944- .... **CLC 39**
See also CA 118; 136; CANR 113; SATA 143

Tirso de Molina 1580(?)-1648 .... **DC 13; HLCS 2; LC 73**
See also RGWL 2, 3

Titmarsh, Michael Angelo
See Thackeray, William Makepeace

Tocqueville, Alexis (Charles Henri Maurice Clerel Comte) de 1805-1859 .. **NCLC 7, 63**
See also EW 6; GFL 1789 to the Present; TWA

Toer, Pramoedya Ananta
1925-2006 .... **CLC 186**
See also CA 197; 251; CANR 170; RGWL 3

Toffler, Alvin 1928- .... **CLC 168**
See also CA 13-16R; CANR 15, 46, 67, 183; CPW; DAM POP; MTCW 1, 2

Toibin, Colm 1955- .... **CLC 162**
See also CA 142; CANR 81, 149; CN 7; DLB 271

Tolkien, John Ronald Reuel
See Tolkien, J.R.R

Tolkien, J.R.R 1892-1973 ...... **CLC 1, 2, 3, 8, 12, 38; TCLC 137; WLC 6**
See also AAYA 10; AITN 1; BPFB 3; BRWC 2; BRWS 2; CA 17-18; 45-48; CANR 36, 134; CAP 2; CDBLB 1914-1945; CLR 56; CN 1; CPW 1; CWRI 5; DA; DA3; DAB; DAC; DAM MST, NOV, POP; DLB 15, 160, 255; EFS 2; EWL 3; FANT; JRDA; LAIT 1; LATS 1:2; LMFS 2; MAICYA 1, 2; MTCW 1, 2; MTFW 2005; NFS 8, 26; RGEL 2; SATA 2, 32, 100; SATA-Obit 24; SFW 4; SUFW; TEA; WCH; WYA; YAW

Toller, Ernst 1893-1939 .... **TCLC 10**
See also CA 107; 186; DLB 124; EWL 3; RGWL 2, 3

Tolson, M. B.
See Tolson, Melvin B(eaunorus)

Tolson, Melvin B(eaunorus)
1898(?)-1966 .... **BLC 1:3; CLC 36, 105; PC 88**
See also AFAW 1, 2; BW 1, 3; CA 124; 89-92; CANR 80; DAM MULT, POET; DLB 48, 76; MAL 5; RGAL 4

Tolstoi, Aleksei Nikolaevich
See Tolstoy, Alexey Nikolaevich

Tolstoi, Lev
See Tolstoy, Leo (Nikolaevich)
See also RGSF 2; RGWL 2, 3

Tolstoy, Aleksei Nikolaevich
See Tolstoy, Alexey Nikolaevich
See also DLB 272

Tolstoy, Alexey Nikolaevich
1882-1945 .... **TCLC 18**
See Tolstoy, Aleksei Nikolaevich
See also CA 107; 158; EWL 3; SFW 4

Tolstoy, Leo (Nikolaevich)
1828-1910 . **SSC 9, 30, 45, 54; TCLC 4, 11, 17, 28, 44, 79, 173; WLC 6**
See Tolstoi, Lev
See also AAYA 56; CA 104; 123; DA; DA3; DAB; DAC; DAM MST, NOV; DLB 238; EFS 2; EW 7; EXPS; IDTP; LAIT 2; LATS 1:1; LMFS 1; NFS 10; SATA 26; SSFS 5; TWA

Tolstoy, Count Leo
See Tolstoy, Leo (Nikolaevich)

Tomalin, Claire 1933- .... **CLC 166**
See also CA 89-92; CANR 52, 88, 165; DLB 155

Tomasi di Lampedusa, Giuseppe 1896-1957
See Lampedusa, Giuseppe (Tomasi) di
See also CA 111; DLB 177; EWL 3; WLIT 7

Tomlin, Lily 1939(?)-
See Tomlin, Mary Jean
See also CA 117

Tomlin, Mary Jean .... **CLC 17**
See Tomlin, Lily

Tomline, F. Latour
See Gilbert, W(illiam) S(chwenck)

Tomlinson, (Alfred) Charles 1927- .... **CLC 2, 4, 6, 13, 45; PC 17**
See also CA 5-8R; CANR 33; CP 1, 2, 3, 4, 5, 6, 7; DAM POET; DLB 40; TCLE 1:2

Tomlinson, H(enry) M(ajor)
1873-1958 .... **TCLC 71**
See also CA 118; 161; DLB 36, 100, 195

Tonna, Charlotte Elizabeth
1790-1846 .... **NCLC 135**
See also CA 163

Tonson, Jacob fl. 1655(?)-1736 .... **LC 86**
See also DLB 170

Toole, John Kennedy 1937-1969 ..... **CLC 19, 64**
See also BPFB 3; CA 104; DLBY 1981; MTCW 2; MTFW 2005

Toomer, Eugene
See Toomer, Jean

Toomer, Eugene Pinchback
See Toomer, Jean

Toomer, Jean 1894-1967 ... **BLC 1:3; CLC 1, 4, 13, 22; HR 1:3; PC 7; SSC 1, 45; TCLC 172; WLCS**
See also AFAW 1, 2; AMWS 3, 9; BW 1; CA 85-88; CDALB 1917-1929; DA3; DAM MULT; DLB 45, 51; EWL 3; EXPP; EXPS; LMFS 2; MAL 5; MTCW 2; MTFW 2005; NFS 11; RGAL 4; RGSF 2; SSFS 5

Toomer, Nathan Jean
See Toomer, Jean

Toomer, Nathan Pinchback
See Toomer, Jean

Torley, Luke
See Blish, James (Benjamin)

Tornimparte, Alessandra
See Ginzburg, Natalia

Torre, Raoul della
See Mencken, H(enry) L(ouis)

Torrence, Ridgely 1874-1950 .... **TCLC 97**
See also DLB 54, 249; MAL 5

Torrey, E. Fuller 1937- .... **CLC 34**
See also CA 119; CANR 71, 158

Torrey, Edwin Fuller
See Torrey, E. Fuller

Torsvan, Ben Traven
See Traven, B.

Torsvan, Benno Traven
See Traven, B.

Torsvan, Berick Traven
See Traven, B.

Torsvan, Berwick Traven
See Traven, B.

Torsvan, Bruno Traven
See Traven, B.

Torsvan, Traven
See Traven, B.

Tourneur, Cyril 1575(?)-1626 .... **LC 66**
See also BRW 2; DAM DRAM; DLB 58; RGEL 2

Tournier, Michel 1924- .... **CLC 6, 23, 36, 95, 249; SSC 88**
See also CA 49-52; CANR 3, 36, 74, 149; CWW 2; DLB 83; EWL 3; GFL 1789 to the Present; MTCW 1, 2; SATA 23

Tournier, Michel Edouard
See Tournier, Michel

Tournimparte, Alessandra
See Ginzburg, Natalia

Towers, Ivar
See Kornbluth, C(yril) M.

Towne, Robert (Burton) 1936(?)- ..... **CLC 87**
See also CA 108; DLB 44; IDFW 3, 4

Townsend, Sue .... **CLC 61**
See Townsend, Susan Lilian
See also AAYA 28; CA 119; 127; CANR 65, 107; CBD; CD 5, 6; CPW; CWD; DAB; DAC; DAM MST; DLB 271; INT CA-127; SATA 55, 93; SATA-Brief 48; YAW

Townsend, Susan Lilian 1946-
See Townsend, Sue

Townshend, Pete
See Townshend, Peter (Dennis Blandford)

Townshend, Peter (Dennis Blandford)
1945- .... **CLC 17, 42**
See also CA 107

Tozzi, Federigo 1883-1920 .... **TCLC 31**
See also CA 160; CANR 110; DLB 264; EWL 3; WLIT 7

Tracy, Don(ald Fiske) 1905-1970(?)
See Queen, Ellery
See also CA 1-4R; 176; CANR 2

Trafford, F. G.
See Riddell, Charlotte

Traherne, Thomas 1637(?)-1674 .. **LC 99; PC 70**
See also BRW 2; BRWS 11; DLB 131; PAB; RGEL 2

Traill, Catharine Parr 1802-1899 .. **NCLC 31**
See also DLB 99

Trakl, Georg 1887-1914 .... **PC 20; TCLC 5**
See also CA 104; 165; EW 10; EWL 3; LMFS 2; MTCW 2; RGWL 2, 3

Trambley, Estela Portillo .... **TCLC 163**
See Portillo Trambley, Estela
See also CA 77-80; RGAL 4

Tranquilli, Secondino
See Silone, Ignazio

Transtroemer, Tomas Gosta
See Transtromer, Tomas

Transtromer, Tomas (Gosta)
See Transtromer, Tomas
See also CWW 2

Transtromer, Tomas 1931- .... **CLC 52, 65**
See also CA 117; 129; CAAS 17; CANR 115, 172; DAM POET; DLB 257; EWL 3; PFS 21

Transtromer, Tomas Goesta
See Transtromer, Tomas

Transtromer, Tomas Gosta
See Transtromer, Tomas

Transtromer, Tomas Gosta
See Transtromer, Tomas

Traven, B. 1882(?)-1969 .... **CLC 8, 11**
See also CA 19-20; 25-28R; CAP 2; DLB 9, 56; EWL 3; MTCW 1; RGAL 4

Trediakovsky, Vasilii Kirillovich
1703-1769 .... **LC 68**
See also DLB 150

Treitel, Jonathan 1959- .... **CLC 70**
See also CA 210; DLB 267

Trelawny, Edward John
1792-1881 .... **NCLC 85**
See also DLB 110, 116, 144

Tremain, Rose 1943- .... **CLC 42**
See also CA 97-100; CANR 44, 95; CN 4, 5, 6, 7; DLB 14, 271; RGSF 2; RHW

Tremblay, Michel 1942- .... **CLC 29, 102, 225**
See also CA 116; 128; CCA 1; CWW 2; DAC; DAM MST; DLB 60; EWL 3; GLL 1; MTCW 1, 2; MTFW 2005

Trevanian .... **CLC 29**
See Whitaker, Rod

Trevisa, John c. 1342-c. 1402 .... **LC 139**
See also BRWS 9; DLB 146

Trevor, Glen
See Hilton, James

Trevor, William .. **CLC 7, 9, 14, 25, 71, 116; SSC 21, 58**
See Cox, William Trevor
See also BRWS 4; CBD; CD 5, 6; CN 1, 2, 3, 4, 5, 6, 7; DLB 14, 139; EWL 3; LATS 1:2; RGEL 2; RGSF 2; SSFS 10; TCLE 1:2

Trifonov, Iurii (Valentinovich)
See Trifonov, Yuri (Valentinovich)
See also DLB 302; RGWL 2, 3

Trifonov, Yuri (Valentinovich)
1925-1981 .... **CLC 45**
See Trifonov, Iurii (Valentinovich); Trifonov, Yury Valentinovich
See also CA 126; 103; MTCW 1

Trifonov, Yury Valentinovich
See Trifonov, Yuri (Valentinovich)
See also EWL 3

Trilling, Diana (Rubin) 1905-1996 . **CLC 129**
See also CA 5-8R; 154; CANR 10, 46; INT CANR-10; MTCW 1, 2

Trilling, Lionel 1905-1975 ..... **CLC 9, 11, 24; SSC 75**
See also AMWS 3; CA 9-12R; 61-64; CANR 10, 105; CN 1, 2; DLB 28, 63; EWL 3; INT CANR-10; MAL 5; MTCW 1, 2; RGAL 4; TUS

Trimball, W. H.
See Mencken, H(enry) L(ouis)

Tristan
See Gomez de la Serna, Ramon

Tristram
See Housman, A(lfred) E(dward)

Trogdon, William (Lewis) 1939-
See Heat-Moon, William Least
See also AAYA 66; CA 115; 119; CANR 47, 89; CPW; INT CA-119

Trollope, Anthony 1815-1882 .... **NCLC 6, 33, 101; SSC 28; WLC 6**
See also BRW 5; CDBLB 1832-1890; DA; DA3; DAB; DAC; DAM MST, NOV; DLB 21, 57, 159; RGEL 2; RGSF 2; SATA 22

Trollope, Frances 1779-1863 .... **NCLC 30**
See also DLB 21, 166

Trollope, Joanna 1943- .... **CLC 186**
See also CA 101; CANR 58, 95, 149; CN 7; CPW; DLB 207; RHW

Trotsky, Leon 1879-1940 .... **TCLC 22**
See also CA 118; 167

Trotter (Cockburn), Catharine
1679-1749 .... **LC 8**
See also DLB 84, 252

Trotter, Wilfred 1872-1939 .... **TCLC 97**

Troupe, Quincy 1943- .... **BLC 2:3**
See also BW 2; CA 113; 124; CANR 43, 90, 126; DLB 41

Trout, Kilgore
See Farmer, Philip Jose

Trow, George William Swift
See Trow, George W.S.

Trow, George W.S. 1943-2006 .... **CLC 52**
See also CA 126; 255; CANR 91

Troyat, Henri 1911-2007 .... **CLC 23**
See also CA 45-48; 258; CANR 2, 33, 67, 117; GFL 1789 to the Present; MTCW 1

Trudeau, Garry B. .... **CLC 12**
See Trudeau, G.B.
See also AAYA 10; AITN 2

Trudeau, G.B. 1948-
See Trudeau, Garry B.
See also AAYA 60; CA 81-84; CANR 31; SATA 35, 168

Truffaut, Francois 1932-1984 ... **CLC 20, 101**
See also CA 81-84; 113; CANR 34

Trumbo, Dalton 1905-1976 .... **CLC 19**
See also CA 21-24R; 69-72; CANR 10; CN 1, 2; DLB 26; IDFW 3, 4; YAW

Trumbull, John 1750-1831 .... **NCLC 30**
See also DLB 31; RGAL 4

Trundlett, Helen B.
See Eliot, T(homas) S(tearns)

Truth, Sojourner 1797(?)-1883 ...... **NCLC 94**
See also DLB 239; FW; LAIT 2

Tryon, Thomas 1926-1991 .... **CLC 3, 11**
See also AITN 1; BPFB 3; CA 29-32R; 135; CANR 32, 77; CPW; DA3; DAM POP; HGG; MTCW 1

Tryon, Tom
See Tryon, Thomas

Valery, (Ambroise) Paul (Toussaint Jules)
1871-1945 .... **PC 9; TCLC 4, 15**
See also CA 104; 122; DA3; DAM POET;
DLB 258; EW 8; EWL 3; GFL 1789 to
the Present; MTCW 1, 2; MTFW 2005;
RGWL 2, 3; TWA

Valle-Inclan, Ramon (Maria) del
1866-1936 .... **HLC 2; TCLC 5**
See del Valle-Inclan, Ramon (Maria)
See also CA 106; 153; CANR 80; DAM
MULT; DLB 134; EW 8; EWL 3; HW 2;
RGSF 2; RGWL 2, 3

Vallejo, Antonio Buero
See Buero Vallejo, Antonio

Vallejo, Cesar (Abraham)
1892-1938 .... **HLC 2; TCLC 3, 56**
See also CA 105; 153; DAM MULT; DLB
290; EWL 3; HW 1; LAW; PFS 26;
RGWL 2, 3

Valles, Jules 1832-1885 .... **NCLC 71**
See also DLB 123; GFL 1789 to the Present

Vallette, Marguerite Eymery
1860-1953 .... **TCLC 67**
See Rachilde
See also CA 182; DLB 123, 192

Valle Y Pena, Ramon del
See Valle-Inclan, Ramon (Maria) del

Van Ash, Cay 1918-1994 .... **CLC 34**
See also CA 220

Vanbrugh, Sir John 1664-1726 .... **LC 21**
See also BRW 2; DAM DRAM; DLB 80;
IDTP; RGEL 2

Van Campen, Karl
See Campbell, John W(ood, Jr.)

Vance, Gerald
See Silverberg, Robert

Vance, Jack 1916-
See Queen, Ellery; Vance, John Holbrook
See also CA 29-32R; CANR 17, 65, 154;
CMW 4; MTCW 1

Vance, John Holbrook .... **CLC 35**
See Vance, Jack
See also DLB 8; FANT; SCFW 1, 2; SFW
4; SUFW 1, 2

Van Den Bogarde, Derek Jules Gaspard
Ulric Niven 1921-1999 .... **CLC 14**
See Bogarde, Dirk
See also CA 77-80; 179

Vandenburgh, Jane .... **CLC 59**
See also CA 168

Vanderhaeghe, Guy 1951- .... **CLC 41**
See also BPFB 3; CA 113; CANR 72, 145;
CN 7; DLB 334

van der Post, Laurens (Jan)
1906-1996 .... **CLC 5**
See also AFW; CA 5-8R; 155; CANR 35;
CN 1, 2, 3, 4, 5, 6; DLB 204; RGEL 2

van de Wetering, Janwillem
1931-2008 .... **CLC 47**
See also CA 49-52; CANR 4, 62, 90; CMW
4

Van Dine, S. S. .... **TCLC 23**
See Wright, Willard Huntington
See also DLB 306; MSW

Van Doren, Carl (Clinton)
1885-1950 .... **TCLC 18**
See also CA 111; 168

Van Doren, Mark 1894-1972 .... **CLC 6, 10**
See also CA 1-4R; 37-40R; CANR 3; CN
1; CP 1; DLB 45, 284, 335; MAL 5;
MTCW 1, 2; RGAL 4

Van Druten, John (William)
1901-1957 .... **TCLC 2**
See also CA 104; 161; DLB 10; MAL 5;
RGAL 4

Van Duyn, Mona 1921-2004 .... **CLC 3, 7, 63,
116**
See also CA 9-12R; 234; CANR 7, 38, 60,
116; CP 1, 2, 3, 4, 5, 6, 7; CWP; DAM
POET; DLB 5; MAL 5; MTCW 2005;
PFS 20

Van Dyne, Edith
See Baum, L(yman) Frank

van Herk, Aritha 1954- .... **CLC 249**
See also CA 101; CANR 94; DLB 334

van Itallie, Jean-Claude 1936- .... **CLC 3**
See also CA 45-48; CAAS 2; CAD; CANR
1, 48; CD 5, 6; DLB 7

Van Loot, Cornelius Obenchain
See Roberts, Kenneth (Lewis)

van Ostaijen, Paul 1896-1928 .... **TCLC 33**
See also CA 163

Van Peebles, Melvin 1932- .... **CLC 2, 20**
See also BW 2, 3; CA 85-88; CANR 27,
67, 82; DAM MULT

van Schendel, Arthur(-Francois-Emile)
1874-1946 .... **TCLC 56**
See also EWL 3

Vansittart, Peter 1920- .... **CLC 42**
See also CA 1-4R; CANR 3, 49, 90; CN 4,
5, 6, 7; RHW

Van Vechten, Carl 1880-1964 ... **CLC 33; HR
1:3**
See also AMWS 2; CA 183; 89-92; DLB 4,
9, 51; RGAL 4

van Vogt, A(lfred) E(lton) 1912-2000 . **CLC 1**
See also BPFB 3; BYA 13, 14; CA 21-24R;
190; CANR 28; DLB 8, 251; SATA 14;
SATA-Obit 124; SCFW 1, 2; SFW 4

Vara, Madeleine
See Jackson, Laura (Riding)

Varda, Agnes 1928- .... **CLC 16**
See also CA 116; 122

Vargas Llosa, Jorge Mario Pedro
See Vargas Llosa, Mario

Vargas Llosa, Mario 1936- .. **CLC 3, 6, 9, 10,
15, 31, 42, 85, 181; HLC 2**
See Llosa, Jorge Mario Pedro Vargas
See also BPFB 3; CA 73-76; CANR 18, 32,
42, 67, 116, 140, 173; CDWLB 3; CWW
2; DA; DA3; DAB; DAC; DAM MST,
MULT, NOV; DLB 145; DNFS 2; EWL
3; HW 1, 2; LAIT 5; LATS 1:2; LAW;
LAWS 1; MTCW 1, 2; MTFW 2005;
RGWL 2; SSFS 14; TWA; WLIT 1

Varnhagen von Ense, Rahel
1771-1833 .... **NCLC 130**
See also DLB 90

Vasari, Giorgio 1511-1574 .... **LC 114**

Vasilikos, Vasiles
See Vassilikos, Vassilis

Vasiliu, George
See Bacovia, George

Vasiliu, Gheorghe
See Bacovia, George
See also CA 123; 189

Vassa, Gustavus
See Equiano, Olaudah

Vassilikos, Vassilis 1933- .... **CLC 4, 8**
See also CA 81-84; CANR 75, 149; EWL 3

Vaughan, Henry 1621-1695 .... **LC 27; PC 81**
See also BRW 2; DLB 131; PAB; RGEL 2

Vaughn, Stephanie .... **CLC 62**

Vazov, Ivan (Minchov) 1850-1921 . **TCLC 25**
See also CA 121; 167; CDWLB 4; DLB
147

Veblen, Thorstein B(unde)
1857-1929 .... **TCLC 31**
See also AMWS 1; CA 115; 165; DLB 246;
MAL 5

Vega, Lope de 1562-1635 ... **HLCS 2; LC 23,
119**
See also EW 2; RGWL 2, 3

Veldeke, Heinrich von c. 1145-c.
1190 .... **CMLC 85**

Vendler, Helen (Hennessy) 1933- ... **CLC 138**
See also CA 41-44R; CANR 25, 72, 136;
MTCW 1, 2; MTFW 2005

Venison, Alfred
See Pound, Ezra (Weston Loomis)

Ventsel, Elena Sergeevna 1907-2002
See Grekova, I.
See also CA 154

Verdi, Marie de
See Mencken, H(enry) L(ouis)

Verdu, Matilde
See Cela, Camilo Jose

Verga, Giovanni (Carmelo)
1840-1922 .... **SSC 21, 87; TCLC 3**
See also CA 104; 123; CANR 101; EW 7;
EWL 3; RGSF 2; RGWL 2, 3; WLIT 7

Vergil 70B.C.-19B.C. .. **CMLC 9, 40, 101; PC
12; WLCS**
See Virgil
See also AW 2; DA; DA3; DAB; DAC;
DAM MST, POET; EFS 1; LMFS 1

Vergil, Polydore c. 1470-1555 .... **LC 108**
See also DLB 132

Verhaeren, Emile (Adolphe Gustave)
1855-1916 .... **TCLC 12**
See also CA 109; EWL 3; GFL 1789 to the
Present

Verlaine, Paul (Marie) 1844-1896 .. **NCLC 2,
51; PC 2, 32**
See also DAM POET; DLB 217; EW 7;
GFL 1789 to the Present; LMFS 2; RGWL
2, 3; TWA

Verne, Jules (Gabriel) 1828-1905 ... **TCLC 6,
52**
See also AAYA 16; BYA 4; CA 110; 131;
CLR 88; DA3; DLB 123; GFL 1789 to
the Present; JRDA; LAIT 2; LMFS 2;
MAICYA 1, 2; MTFW 2005; RGWL 2, 3;
SATA 21; SCFW 1, 2; SFW 4; TWA;
WCH

Verus, Marcus Annius
See Aurelius, Marcus

Very, Jones 1813-1880 .... **NCLC 9; PC 86**
See also DLB 1, 243; RGAL 4

Vesaas, Tarjei 1897-1970 .... **CLC 48**
See also CA 190; 29-32R; DLB 297; EW
11; EWL 3; RGWL 3

Vialis, Gaston
See Simenon, Georges (Jacques Christian)

Vian, Boris 1920-1959(?) .... **TCLC 9**
See also CA 106; 164; CANR 111; DLB
72, 321; EWL 3; GFL 1789 to the Present;
MTCW 2; RGWL 2, 3

Viaud, (Louis Marie) Julien 1850-1923
See Loti, Pierre
See also CA 107

Vicar, Henry
See Felsen, Henry Gregor

Vicente, Gil 1465-c. 1536 .... **LC 99**
See also DLB 318; IDTP; RGWL 2, 3

Vicker, Angus
See Felsen, Henry Gregor

Vico, Giambattista .... **LC 138**
See Vico, Giovanni Battista
See also WLIT 7

Vico, Giovanni Battista 1668-1744
See Vico, Giambattista
See also EW 3

Vidal, Eugene Luther Gore
See Vidal, Gore

Vidal, Gore 1925- ...... **CLC 2, 4, 6, 8, 10, 22,
33, 72, 142**
See also AAYA 64; AITN 1; AMWS 4;
BEST 90:2; BPFB 3; CA 5-8R; CAD;
CANR 13, 45, 65, 100, 132, 167; CD 5,
6; CDALBS; CN 1, 2, 3, 4, 5, 6, 7; CPW;
DA3; DAM NOV, POP; DFS 2; DLB 6,

Waters, Mary C. .... **CLC 70**
Waters, Roger 1944- .... **CLC 35**
Watkins, Frances Ellen
  See Harper, Frances Ellen Watkins
Watkins, Gerrold
  See Malzberg, Barry N(athaniel)
Watkins, Gloria Jean
  See hooks, bell
Watkins, Paul 1964- .... **CLC 55**
  See also CA 132; CANR 62, 98
Watkins, Vernon Phillips
  1906-1967 .... **CLC 43**
  See also CA 9-10; 25-28R; CAP 1; DLB
  20; EWL 3; RGEL 2
Watson, Irving S.
  See Mencken, H(enry) L(ouis)
Watson, John H.
  See Farmer, Philip Jose
Watson, Richard F.
  See Silverberg, Robert
Watts, Ephraim
  See Horne, Richard Henry Hengist
Watts, Isaac 1674-1748 .... **LC 98**
  See also DLB 95; RGEL 2; SATA 52
Waugh, Auberon (Alexander)
  1939-2001 .... **CLC 7**
  See also CA 45-48; 192; CANR 6, 22, 92;
  CN 1, 2, 3; DLB 14, 194
Waugh, Evelyn 1903-1966 ... **CLC 1, 3, 8, 13,**
  19, 27, 44, 107; SSC 41; WLC 6
  See also AAYA 78; BPFB 3; BRW 7; CA
  85-88; 25-28R; CANR 22; CDBLB 1914-
  1945; DA; DA3; DAB; DAC; DAM MST,
  NOV, POP; DLB 15, 162, 195; EWL 3;
  MTCW 1, 2; MTFW 2005; NFS 13, 17;
  RGEL 2; RGSF 2; TEA; WLIT 4
Waugh, Evelyn Arthur St. John
  See Waugh, Evelyn
Waugh, Harriet 1944- .... **CLC 6**
  See also CA 85-88; CANR 22
Ways, C.R.
  See Blount, Roy, Jr.
Waystaff, Simon
  See Swift, Jonathan
Webb, Beatrice (Martha Potter)
  1858-1943 .... **TCLC 22**
  See also CA 117; 162; DLB 190; FW
Webb, Charles (Richard) 1939- .... **CLC 7**
  See also CA 25-28R; CANR 114
Webb, Frank J. .... **NCLC 143**
  See also DLB 50
Webb, James, Jr.
  See Webb, James
Webb, James 1946- .... **CLC 22**
  See also CA 81-84; CANR 156
Webb, James H.
  See Webb, James
Webb, James Henry
  See Webb, James
Webb, Mary Gladys (Meredith)
  1881-1927 .... **TCLC 24**
  See also CA 182; 123; DLB 34; FW; RGEL
  2
Webb, Mrs. Sidney
  See Webb, Beatrice (Martha Potter)
Webb, Phyllis 1927- .... **CLC 18**
  See also CA 104; CANR 23; CCA 1; CP 1,
  2, 3, 4, 5, 6, 7; CWP; DLB 53
Webb, Sidney (James) 1859-1947 .. **TCLC 22**
  See also CA 117; 163; DLB 190
Webber, Andrew Lloyd .... **CLC 21**
  See Lloyd Webber, Andrew
  See also DFS 7
Weber, Lenora Mattingly
  1895-1971 .... **CLC 12**
  See also CA 19-20; 29-32R; CAP 1; SATA
  2; SATA-Obit 26

Weber, Max 1864-1920 .... **TCLC 69**
  See also CA 109; 189; DLB 296
Webster, John 1580(?)-1634(?) ...... **DC 2; LC**
  33, 84, 124; WLC 6
  See also BRW 2; CDBLB Before 1660; DA;
  DAB; DAC; DAM DRAM, MST; DFS
  17, 19; DLB 58; IDTP; RGEL 2; WLIT 3
Webster, Noah 1758-1843 .... **NCLC 30**
  See also DLB 1, 37, 42, 43, 73, 243
Wedekind, Benjamin Franklin
  See Wedekind, Frank
Wedekind, Frank 1864-1918 .... **TCLC 7**
  See also CA 104; 153; CANR 121, 122;
  CDWLB 2; DAM DRAM; DLB 118; EW
  8; EWL 3; LMFS 2; RGWL 2, 3
Wehr, Demaris .... **CLC 65**
Weidman, Jerome 1913-1998 .... **CLC 7**
  See also AITN 2; CA 1-4R; 171; CAD;
  CANR 1; CD 1, 2, 3, 4, 5; DLB 28
Weil, Simone (Adolphine)
  1909-1943 .... **TCLC 23**
  See also CA 117; 159; EW 12; EWL 3; FW;
  GFL 1789 to the Present; MTCW 2
Weininger, Otto 1880-1903 .... **TCLC 84**
Weinstein, Nathan
  See West, Nathanael
Weinstein, Nathan von Wallenstein
  See West, Nathanael
Weir, Peter (Lindsay) 1944- .... **CLC 20**
  See also CA 113; 123
Weiss, Peter (Ulrich) 1916-1982 .. **CLC 3, 15,**
  51; TCLC 152
  See also CA 45-48; 106; CANR 3; DAM
  DRAM; DFS 3; DLB 69, 124; EWL 3;
  RGHL; RGWL 2, 3
Weiss, Theodore (Russell)
  1916-2003 .... **CLC 3, 8, 14**
  See also CA 9-12R; 189; 216; CAAE 189;
  CAAS 2; CANR 46, 94; CP 1, 2, 3, 4, 5,
  6, 7; DLB 5; TCLE 1:2
Welch, (Maurice) Denton
  1915-1948 .... **TCLC 22**
  See also BRWS 8, 9; CA 121; 148; RGEL
  2
Welch, James (Phillip) 1940-2003 ..... **CLC 6,**
  14, 52, 249; NNAL; PC 62
  See also CA 85-88; 219; CANR 42, 66, 107;
  CN 5, 6, 7; CP 2, 3, 4, 5, 6, 7; CPW;
  DAM MULT, POP; DLB 175, 256; LATS
  1:1; NFS 23; RGAL 4; TCWW 1, 2
Weldon, Fay 1931- . **CLC 6, 9, 11, 19, 36, 59,**
  122
  See also BRWS 4; CA 21-24R; CANR 16,
  46, 63, 97, 137; CDBLB 1960 to Present;
  CN 3, 4, 5, 6, 7; CPW; DAM POP; DLB
  14, 194, 319; EWL 3; FW; HGG; INT
  CANR-16; MTCW 1, 2; MTFW 2005;
  RGEL 2; RGSF 2
Wellek, Rene 1903-1995 .... **CLC 28**
  See also CA 5-8R; 150; CAAS 7; CANR 8;
  DLB 63; EWL 3; INT CANR-8
Weller, Michael 1942- .... **CLC 10, 53**
  See also CA 85-88; CAD; CD 5, 6
Weller, Paul 1958- .... **CLC 26**
Wellershoff, Dieter 1925- .... **CLC 46**
  See also CA 89-92; CANR 16, 37
Welles, (George) Orson 1915-1985 .. **CLC 20,**
  80
  See also AAYA 40; CA 93-96; 117
Wellman, John McDowell 1945-
  See Wellman, Mac
  See also CA 166; CD 5
Wellman, Mac .... **CLC 65**
  See Wellman, John McDowell; Wellman,
  John McDowell
  See also CAD; CD 6; RGAL 4

Wellman, Manly Wade 1903-1986 ... **CLC 49**
  See also CA 1-4R; 118; CANR 6, 16, 44;
  FANT; SATA 6; SATA-Obit 47; SFW 4;
  SUFW
Wells, Carolyn 1869(?)-1942 .... **TCLC 35**
  See also CA 113; 185; CMW 4; DLB 11
Wells, H(erbert) G(eorge) 1866-1946 . **SSC 6,**
  70; TCLC 6, 12, 19, 133; WLC 6
  See also AAYA 18; BPFB 3; BRW 6; CA
  110; 121; CDBLB 1914-1945; CLR 64,
  133; DA; DA3; DAB; DAC; DAM MST,
  NOV; DLB 34, 70, 156, 178; EWL 3;
  EXPS; HGG; LAIT 3; LMFS 2; MTCW
  1, 2; MTFW 2005; NFS 17, 20; RGEL 2;
  RGSF 2; SATA 20; SCFW 1, 2; SFW 4;
  SSFS 3; SUFW; TEA; WCH; WLIT 4;
  YAW
Wells, Rosemary 1943- .... **CLC 12**
  See also AAYA 13; BYA 7, 8; CA 85-88;
  CANR 48, 120, 179; CLR 16, 69; CWRI
  5; MAICYA 1, 2; SAAS 1; SATA 18, 69,
  114, 156; YAW
Wells-Barnett, Ida B(ell)
  1862-1931 .... **TCLC 125**
  See also CA 182; DLB 23, 221
Welsh, Irvine 1958- .... **CLC 144**
  See also CA 173; CANR 146; CN 7; DLB
  271
Welty, Eudora 1909-2001 .... **CLC 1, 2, 5, 14,**
  22, 33, 105, 220; SSC 1, 27, 51, 111;
  WLC 6
  See also AAYA 48; AMW; AMWR 1; BPFB
  3; CA 9-12R; 199; CABS 1; CANR 32,
  65, 128; CDALB 1941-1968; CN 1, 2, 3,
  4, 5, 6, 7; CSW; DA; DA3; DAB; DAC;
  DAM MST, NOV; DLB 2, 102, 143;
  DLBD 12; DLBY 1987, 2001; EWL 3;
  EXPS; HGG; LAIT 3; MAL 5; MBL;
  MTCW 1, 2; MTFW 2005; NFS 13, 15;
  RGAL 4; RGSF 2; RHW; SSFS 2, 10, 26;
  TUS
Welty, Eudora Alice
  See Welty, Eudora
Wen I-to 1899-1946 .... **TCLC 28**
  See also EWL 3
Wentworth, Robert
  See Hamilton, Edmond
Werfel, Franz (Viktor) 1890-1945 ... **TCLC 8**
  See also CA 104; 161; DLB 81, 124; EWL
  3; RGWL 2, 3
Wergeland, Henrik Arnold
  1808-1845 .... **NCLC 5**
Werner, Friedrich Ludwig Zacharias
  1768-1823 .... **NCLC 189**
  See also DLB 94
Werner, Zacharias
  See Werner, Friedrich Ludwig Zacharias
Wersba, Barbara 1932- .... **CLC 30**
  See also AAYA 2, 30; BYA 6, 12, 13; CA
  29-32R; 182; CAAE 182; CANR 16, 38;
  CLR 3, 78; DLB 52; JRDA; MAICYA 1,
  2; SAAS 2; SATA 1, 58; SATA-Essay 103;
  WYA; YAW
Wertmueller, Lina 1928- .... **CLC 16**
  See also CA 97-100; CANR 39, 78
Wescott, Glenway 1901-1987 .. **CLC 13; SSC**
  35
  See also CA 13-16R; 121; CANR 23, 70;
  CN 1, 2, 3, 4; DLB 4, 9, 102; MAL 5;
  RGAL 4
Wesker, Arnold 1932- .... **CLC 3, 5, 42**
  See also CA 1-4R; CAAS 7; CANR 1, 33;
  CBD; CD 5, 6; CDBLB 1960 to Present;
  DAB; DAM DRAM; DLB 13, 310, 319;
  EWL 3; MTCW 1; RGEL 2; TEA
Wesley, Charles 1707-1788 .... **LC 128**
  See also DLB 95; RGEL 2
Wesley, John 1703-1791 .... **LC 88**
  See also DLB 104

Wiebe, Rudy 1934- . **CLC 6, 11, 14, 138, 263**
See also CA 37-40R; CANR 42, 67, 123;
CN 1, 2, 3, 4, 5, 6, 7; DAC; DAM MST;
DLB 60; RHW; SATA 156

Wiebe, Rudy Henry
See Wiebe, Rudy

Wieland, Christoph Martin
1733-1813 .... **NCLC 17, 177**
See also DLB 97; EW 4; LMFS 1; RGWL
2, 3

Wiene, Robert 1881-1938 .... **TCLC 56**

Wieners, John 1934- .... **CLC 7**
See also BG 1:3; CA 13-16R; CP 1, 2, 3, 4,
5, 6, 7; DLB 16; WP

Wiesel, Elie 1928- ...... **CLC 3, 5, 11, 37, 165;
WLCS**
See also AAYA 7, 54; AITN 1; CA 5-8R;
CAAS 4; CANR 8, 40, 65, 125; CDALBS;
CWW 2; DA; DA3; DAB; DAC; DAM
MST, NOV; DLB 83, 299; DLBY 1987;
EWL 3; INT CANR-8; LAIT 4; MTCW
1, 2; MTFW 2005; NCFS 4; NFS 4;
RGHL; RGWL 3; SATA 56; YAW

Wiesel, Eliezer
See Wiesel, Elie

Wiggins, Marianne 1947- .... **CLC 57**
See also AAYA 70; BEST 89:3; CA 130;
CANR 60, 139, 180; CN 7; DLB 335

Wigglesworth, Michael 1631-1705 .... **LC 106**
See also DLB 24; RGAL 4

Wiggs, Susan .... **CLC 70**
See also CA 201; CANR 173

Wight, James Alfred 1916-1995
See Herriot, James
See also CA 77-80; SATA 55; SATA-Brief
44

Wilbur, Richard 1921- .. **CLC 3, 6, 9, 14, 53,
110; PC 51**
See also AAYA 72; AMWS 3; CA 1-4R;
CABS 2; CANR 2, 29, 76, 93, 139;
CDALBS; CP 1, 2, 3, 4, 5, 6, 7; DA;
DAB; DAC; DAM MST, POET; DLB 5,
169; EWL 3; EXPP; INT CANR-29;
MAL 5; MTCW 1, 2; MTFW 2005; PAB;
PFS 11, 12, 16; RGAL 4; SATA 9, 108;
WP

Wilbur, Richard Purdy
See Wilbur, Richard

Wild, Peter 1940- .... **CLC 14**
See also CA 37-40R; CP 1, 2, 3, 4, 5, 6, 7;
DLB 5

Wilde, Oscar 1854(?)-1900 ... **DC 17; SSC 11,
77; TCLC 1, 8, 23, 41, 175; WLC 6**
See also AAYA 49; BRW 5; BRWC 1, 2;
BRWR 2; BYA 15; CA 104; 119; CANR
112; CDBLB 1890-1914; CLR 114; DA;
DA3; DAB; DAC; DAM DRAM, MST,
NOV; DFS 4, 8, 9, 21; DLB 10, 19, 34,
57, 141, 156, 190, 344; EXPS; FANT; GL
3; LATS 1:1; NFS 20; RGEL 2; RGSF 2;
SATA 24; SSFS 7; SUFW; TEA; WCH;
WLIT 4

Wilde, Oscar Fingal O'Flahertie Willis
See Wilde, Oscar

Wilder, Billy .... **CLC 20**
See Wilder, Samuel
See also AAYA 66; DLB 26

Wilder, Samuel 1906-2002
See Wilder, Billy
See also CA 89-92; 205

Wilder, Stephen
See Marlowe, Stephen

Wilder, Thornton (Niven)
1897-1975 .. **CLC 1, 5, 6, 10, 15, 35, 82;
DC 1, 24; WLC 6**
See also AAYA 29; AITN 2; AMW; CA 13-
16R; 61-64; CAD; CANR 40, 132;
CDALBS; CN 1, 2; DA; DA3; DAB;
DAC; DAM DRAM, MST, NOV; DFS 1,

4, 16; DLB 4, 7, 9, 228; DLBY 1997;
EWL 3; LAIT 3; MAL 5; MTCW 1, 2;
MTFW 2005; NFS 24; RGAL 4; RHW;
WYAS 1

Wilding, Michael 1942- ...... **CLC 73; SSC 50**
See also CA 104; CANR 24, 49, 106; CN
4, 5, 6, 7; DLB 325; RGSF 2

Wiley, Richard 1944- .... **CLC 44**
See also CA 121; 129; CANR 71

Wilhelm, Kate .... **CLC 7**
See Wilhelm, Katie
See also AAYA 20; BYA 16; CAAS 5; DLB
8; INT CANR-17; SCFW 2

Wilhelm, Katie 1928-
See Wilhelm, Kate
See also CA 37-40R; CANR 17, 36, 60, 94;
MTCW 1; SFW 4

Wilkins, Mary
See Freeman, Mary E(leanor) Wilkins

Willard, Nancy 1936- .... **CLC 7, 37**
See also BYA 5; CA 89-92; CANR 10, 39,
68, 107, 152, 183; CLR 5; CP 2, 3, 4, 5;
CWP; CWRI 5; DLB 5, 52; FANT; MAI-
CYA 1, 2; MTCW 1; SATA 37, 71, 127,
191; SATA-Brief 30; SUFW; TCLE 1:2

William of Malmesbury c. 1090B.C.-c.
1140B.C. .... **CMLC 57**

William of Moerbeke c. 1215-c.
1286 .... **CMLC 91**

William of Ockham 1290-1349 ..... **CMLC 32**

Williams, Ben Ames 1889-1953 ..... **TCLC 89**
See also CA 183; DLB 102

Williams, Charles
See Collier, James Lincoln

Williams, Charles (Walter Stansby)
1886-1945 .... **TCLC 1, 11**
See also BRWS 9; CA 104; 163; DLB 100,
153, 255; FANT; RGEL 2; SUFW 1

Williams, C.K. 1936- .... **CLC 33, 56, 148**
See also CA 37-40R; CAAS 26; CANR 57,
106; CP 1, 2, 3, 4, 5, 6, 7; DAM POET;
DLB 5; MAL 5

Williams, Ella Gwendolen Rees
See Rhys, Jean

Williams, (George) Emlyn
1905-1987 .... **CLC 15**
See also CA 104; 123; CANR 36; DAM
DRAM; DLB 10, 77; IDTP; MTCW 1

Williams, Hank 1923-1953 .... **TCLC 81**
See Williams, Hiram King

Williams, Helen Maria
1761-1827 .... **NCLC 135**
See also DLB 158

Williams, Hiram Hank
See Williams, Hank

Williams, Hiram King
See Williams, Hank
See also CA 188

Williams, Hugo (Mordaunt) 1942- ... **CLC 42**
See also CA 17-20R; CANR 45, 119; CP 1,
2, 3, 4, 5, 6, 7; DLB 40

Williams, J. Walker
See Wodehouse, P(elham) G(renville)

Williams, John A(lfred) 1925- .... **BLC 1:3;
CLC 5, 13**
See also AFAW 2; BW 2, 3; CA 53-56; 195;
CAAE 195; CAAS 3; CANR 6, 26, 51,
118; CN 1, 2, 3, 4, 5, 6, 7; CSW; DAM
MULT; DLB 2, 33; EWL 3; INT CANR-6;
MAL 5; RGAL 4; SFW 4

Williams, Jonathan 1929-2008 .... **CLC 13**
See also CA 9-12R; 270; CAAS 12; CANR
8, 108; CP 1, 2, 3, 4, 5, 6, 7; DLB 5

Williams, Jonathan Chamberlain
See Williams, Jonathan

Williams, Joy 1944- .... **CLC 31**
See also CA 41-44R; CANR 22, 48, 97,
168; DLB 335; SSFS 25

Williams, Norman 1952- .... **CLC 39**
See also CA 118

Williams, Roger 1603(?)-1683 .... **LC 129**
See also DLB 24

Williams, Sherley Anne
1944-1999 .... **BLC 1:3; CLC 89**
See also AFAW 2; BW 2, 3; CA 73-76; 185;
CANR 25, 82; DAM MULT, POET; DLB
41; INT CANR-25; SATA 78; SATA-Obit
116

Williams, Shirley
See Williams, Sherley Anne

Williams, Tennessee 1911-1983 . **CLC 1, 2, 5,
7, 8, 11, 15, 19, 30, 39, 45, 71, 111; DC
4; SSC 81; WLC 6**
See also AAYA 31; AITN 1, 2; AMW;
AMWC 1; CA 5-8R; 108; CABS 3; CAD;
CANR 31, 132, 174; CDALB 1941-1968;
CN 1, 2, 3; DA; DA3; DAB; DAC; DAM
DRAM, MST; DFS 17; DLB 7, 341;
DLBD 4; DLBY 1983; EWL 3; GLL 1;
LAIT 4; LATS 1:2; MAL 5; MTCW 1, 2;
MTFW 2005; RGAL 4; TUS

Williams, Thomas (Alonzo)
1926-1990 .... **CLC 14**
See also CA 1-4R; 132; CANR 2

Williams, Thomas Lanier
See Williams, Tennessee

Williams, William C.
See Williams, William Carlos

Williams, William Carlos
1883-1963 .... **CLC 1, 2, 5, 9, 13, 22, 42,
67; PC 7; SSC 31; WLC 6**
See also AAYA 46; AMW; AMWR 1; CA
89-92; CANR 34; CDALB 1917-1929;
DA; DA3; DAB; DAC; DAM MST,
POET; DLB 4, 16, 54, 86; EWL 3; EXPP;
MAL 5; MTCW 1, 2; MTFW 2005; NCFS
4; PAB; PFS 1, 6, 11; RGAL 4; RGSF 2;
TUS; WP

Williamson, David (Keith) 1942- ..... **CLC 56**
See also CA 103; CANR 41; CD 5, 6; DLB
289

Williamson, Jack .... **CLC 29**
See Williamson, John Stewart
See also CAAS 8; DLB 8; SCFW 1, 2

Williamson, John Stewart 1908-2006
See Williamson, Jack
See also AAYA 76; CA 17-20R; 255; CANR
23, 70, 153; SFW 4

Willie, Frederick
See Lovecraft, H. P.

Willingham, Calder (Baynard, Jr.)
1922-1995 .... **CLC 5, 51**
See also CA 5-8R; 147; CANR 3; CN 1, 2,
3, 4, 5; CSW; DLB 2, 44; IDFW 3, 4;
MTCW 1

Willis, Charles
See Clarke, Arthur C.

Willis, Nathaniel Parker
1806-1867 .... **NCLC 194**
See also DLB 3, 59, 73, 74, 183, 250;
DLBD 13; RGAL 4

Willy
See Colette, (Sidonie-Gabrielle)

Willy, Colette
See Colette, (Sidonie-Gabrielle)
See also GLL 1

Wilmot, John 1647-1680 .... **LC 75; PC 66**
See Rochester
See also BRW 2; DLB 131; PAB

Wilson, A.N. 1950- .... **CLC 33**
See also BRWS 6; CA 112; 122; CANR
156; CN 4, 5, 6, 7; DLB 14, 155, 194;
MTCW 2

Wilson, Andrew Norman
See Wilson, A.N.

Wilson, Angus (Frank Johnstone)
1913-1991 . **CLC 2, 3, 5, 25, 34; SSC 21**
See also CA 5-8R; 134; CANR
21; CN 1, 2, 3, 4; DLB 15, 139, 155;
EWL 3; MTCW 1, 2; MTFW 2005; RGEL
2; RGSF 2
Wilson, August 1945-2005 .... **BLC 1:3, 2:3;**
CLC 39, 50, 63, 118, 222; DC 2, 31;
WLCS
See also AAYA 16; AFAW 2; AMWS 8; BW
2, 3; CA 115; 122; 244; CAD; CANR 42,
54, 76, 128; CD 5, 6; DA; DA3; DAB;
DAC; DAM DRAM, MST, MULT; DFS
3, 7, 15, 17, 24; DLB 228; EWL 3; LAIT
4; LATS 1:2; MAL 5; MTCW 1, 2;
MTFW 2005; RGAL 4
Wilson, Brian 1942- .... **CLC 12**
Wilson, Colin (Henry) 1931- .... **CLC 3, 14**
See also CA 1-4R; CAAS 5; CANR 1, 22,
33, 77; CMW 4; CN 1, 2, 3, 4, 5, 6; DLB
14, 194; HGG; MTCW 1; SFW 4
Wilson, Dirk
See Pohl, Frederik
Wilson, Edmund 1895-1972 .. **CLC 1, 2, 3, 8,**
24
See also AMW; CA 1-4R; 37-40R; CANR
1, 46, 110; CN 1; DLB 63; EWL 3; MAL
5; MTCW 1, 2; MTFW 2005; RGAL 4;
TUS
Wilson, Ethel Davis (Bryant)
1888(?)-1980 .... **CLC 13**
See also CA 102; CN 1, 2; DAC; DAM
POET; DLB 68; MTCW 1; RGEL 2
Wilson, Harriet
See Wilson, Harriet E. Adams
See also DLB 239
Wilson, Harriet E.
See Wilson, Harriet E. Adams
See also DLB 243
Wilson, Harriet E. Adams
1827(?)-1863(?) ...... **BLC 1:3; NCLC 78**
See Wilson, Harriet; Wilson, Harriet E.
See also DAM MULT; DLB 50
Wilson, John 1785-1854 .... **NCLC 5**
See also DLB 110
Wilson, John (Anthony) Burgess
See Burgess, Anthony
Wilson, Katharina .... **CLC 65**
Wilson, Lanford 1937- .. **CLC 7, 14, 36, 197;**
DC 19
See also CA 17-20R; CABS 3; CAD; CANR
45, 96; CD 5, 6; DAM DRAM; DFS 4, 9,
12, 16, 20; DLB 7, 341; EWL 3; MAL 5;
TUS
Wilson, Robert M. 1941- .... **CLC 7, 9**
See also CA 49-52; CAD; CANR 2, 41; CD
5, 6; MTCW 1
Wilson, Robert McLiam 1964- .... **CLC 59**
See also CA 132; DLB 267
Wilson, Sloan 1920-2003 .... **CLC 32**
See also CA 1-4R; 216; CANR 1, 44; CN
1, 2, 3, 4, 5, 6
Wilson, Snoo 1948- .... **CLC 33**
See also CA 69-72; CBD; CD 5, 6
Wilson, William S(mith) 1932- .... **CLC 49**
See also CA 81-84
Wilson, (Thomas) Woodrow
1856-1924 .... **TCLC 79**
See also CA 166; DLB 47
Winchester, Simon 1944- .... **CLC 257**
See also AAYA 66; CA 107; CANR 90, 130
Winchilsea, Anne (Kingsmill) Finch
1661-1720
See Finch, Anne
See also RGEL 2
Winckelmann, Johann Joachim
1717-1768 .... **LC 129**
See also DLB 97

Windham, Basil
See Wodehouse, P(elham) G(renville)
Wingrove, David 1954- .... **CLC 68**
See also CA 133; SFW 4
Winnemucca, Sarah 1844-1891 .... **NCLC 79;**
NNAL
See also DAM MULT; DLB 175; RGAL 4
Winstanley, Gerrard 1609-1676 .... **LC 52**
Wintergreen, Jane
See Duncan, Sara Jeannette
Winters, Arthur Yvor
See Winters, Yvor
Winters, Janet Lewis .... **CLC 41**
See Lewis, Janet
See also DLBY 1987
Winters, Yvor 1900-1968 .. **CLC 4, 8, 32; PC**
82
See also AMWS 2; CA 11-12; 25-28R; CAP
1; DLB 48; EWL 3; MAL 5; MTCW 1;
RGAL 4
Winterson, Jeanette 1959- .... **CLC 64, 158**
See also BRWS 4; CA 136; CANR 58, 116,
178; CN 5, 6, 7; CPW; DA3; DAM POP;
DLB 207, 261; FANT; FW; GLL 1;
MTCW 2; MTFW 2005; RHW; SATA 190
Winthrop, John 1588-1649 .... **LC 31, 107**
See also DLB 24, 30
Winton, Tim 1960- .... **CLC 251**
See also AAYA 34; CA 152; CANR 118;
CN 6, 7; DLB 325; SATA 98
Wirth, Louis 1897-1952 .... **TCLC 92**
See also CA 210
Wiseman, Frederick 1930- .... **CLC 20**
See also CA 159
Wister, Owen 1860-1938 ..... **SSC 100; TCLC**
21
See also BPFB 3; CA 108; 162; DLB 9, 78,
186; RGAL 4; SATA 62; TCWW 1, 2
Wither, George 1588-1667 .... **LC 96**
See also DLB 121; RGEL 2
Witkacy
See Witkiewicz, Stanislaw Ignacy
Witkiewicz, Stanislaw Ignacy
1885-1939 .... **TCLC 8**
See also CA 105; 162; CDWLB 4; DLB
215; EW 10; EWL 3; RGWL 2, 3; SFW 4
Wittgenstein, Ludwig (Josef Johann)
1889-1951 .... **TCLC 59**
See also CA 113; 164; DLB 262; MTCW 2
Wittig, Monique 1935-2003 .... **CLC 22**
See also CA 116; 135; 212; CANR 143;
CWW 2; DLB 83; EWL 3; FW; GLL 1
Wittlin, Jozef 1896-1976 .... **CLC 25**
See also CA 49-52; 65-68; CANR 3; EWL
3
Wodehouse, P(elham) G(renville)
1881-1975 .. **CLC 1, 2, 5, 10, 22; SSC 2,**
115; TCLC 108
See also AAYA 65; AITN 2; BRWS 3; CA
45-48; 57-60; CANR 3, 33; CDBLB
1914-1945; CN 1, 2; CPW 1; DA3; DAB;
DAC; DAM NOV; DLB 34, 162; EWL 3;
MTCW 1, 2; MTFW 2005; RGEL 2;
RGSF 2; SATA 22; SSFS 10
Woiwode, L.
See Woiwode, Larry (Alfred)
Woiwode, Larry (Alfred) 1941- ... **CLC 6, 10**
See also CA 73-76; CANR 16, 94; CN 3, 4,
5, 6, 7; DLB 6; INT CANR-16
Wojciechowska, Maia (Teresa)
1927-2002 .... **CLC 26**
See also AAYA 8, 46; BYA 3; CA 9-12R;
183; 209; CAAE 183; CANR 4, 41; CLR
1; JRDA; MAICYA 1, 2; SAAS 1; SATA
1, 28, 83; SATA-Essay 104; SATA-Obit
134; YAW
Wojtyla, Karol (Josef)
See John Paul II, Pope

Wojtyla, Karol (Jozef)
See John Paul II, Pope
Wolf, Christa 1929- ...... **CLC 14, 29, 58, 150,**
261
See also CA 85-88; CANR 45, 123; CD-
WLB 2; CWW 2; DLB 75; EWL 3; FW;
MTCW 1; RGWL 2, 3; SSFS 14
Wolf, Naomi 1962- .... **CLC 157**
See also CA 141; CANR 110; FW; MTFW
2005
Wolfe, Gene 1931- .... **CLC 25**
See also AAYA 35; CA 57-60; CAAS 9;
CANR 6, 32, 60, 152; CPW; DAM POP;
DLB 8; FANT; MTCW 2; MTFW 2005;
SATA 118, 165; SCFW 2; SFW 4; SUFW
2
Wolfe, Gene Rodman
See Wolfe, Gene
Wolfe, George C. 1954- .... **BLCS; CLC 49**
See also CA 149; CAD; CD 5, 6
Wolfe, Thomas (Clayton)
1900-1938 .... **SSC 33, 113; TCLC 4, 13,**
29, 61; WLC 6
See also AMW; BPFB 3; CA 104; 132;
CANR 102; CDALB 1929-1941; DA;
DA3; DAB; DAC; DAM MST, NOV;
DLB 9, 102, 229; DLBD 2, 16; DLBY
1985, 1997; EWL 3; MAL 5; MTCW 1,
2; NFS 18; RGAL 4; SSFS 18; TUS
Wolfe, Thomas Kennerly, Jr.
1931- .... **CLC 147**
See Wolfe, Tom
See also CA 13-16R; CANR 9, 33, 70, 104;
DA3; DAM POP; DLB 185; EWL 3; INT
CANR-9; MTCW 1, 2; MTFW 2005; TUS
Wolfe, Tom .... **CLC 1, 2, 9, 15, 35, 51**
See Wolfe, Thomas Kennerly, Jr.
See also AAYA 8, 67; AITN 2; AMWS 3;
BEST 89:1; BPFB 3; CN 5, 6, 7; CPW;
CSW; DLB 152; LAIT 5; RGAL 4
Wolff, Geoffrey 1937- .... **CLC 41**
See also CA 29-32R; CANR 29, 43, 78, 154
Wolff, Geoffrey Ansell
See Wolff, Geoffrey
Wolff, Sonia
See Levitin, Sonia (Wolff)
Wolff, Tobias 1945- .... **CLC 39, 64, 172; SSC**
63
See also AAYA 16; AMWS 7; BEST 90:2;
BYA 12; CA 114; 117; CAAS 22; CANR
54, 76, 96; CN 5, 6, 7; CSW; DA3; DLB
130; EWL 3; INT CA-117; MTCW 2;
MTFW 2005; RGAL 4; RGSF 2; SSFS 4,
11
Wolitzer, Hilma 1930- .... **CLC 17**
See also CA 65-68; CANR 18, 40, 172; INT
CANR-18; SATA 31; YAW
Wollstonecraft, Mary 1759-1797 .... **LC 5, 50,**
90, 147
See also BRWS 3; CDBLB 1789-1832;
DLB 39, 104, 158, 252; FL 1:1; FW;
LAIT 1; RGEL 2; TEA; WLIT 3
Wonder, Stevie 1950- .... **CLC 12**
See also CA 111
Wong, Jade Snow 1922-2006 .... **CLC 17**
See also CA 109; 249; CANR 91; SATA
112; SATA-Obit 175
Wood, Ellen Price
See Wood, Mrs. Henry
Wood, Mrs. Henry 1814-1887 ...... **NCLC 178**
See also CMW 4; DLB 18; SUFW
Wood, James 1965- .... **CLC 238**
See also CA 235
Woodberry, George Edward
1855-1930 .... **TCLC 73**
See also CA 165; DLB 71, 103
Woodcott, Keith
See Brunner, John (Kilian Houston)

Literary Criticism Series
Cumulative Topic Index

This index lists all topic entries in Gale's *Children's Literature Review* (CLR), *Classical and Medieval Literature Criticism* (CMLC), *Contemporary Literary Criticism* (CLC), *Drama Criticism* (DC), *Literature Criticism from 1400 to 1800* (LC), *Nineteenth-Century Literature Criticism* (NCLC), *Short Story Criticism* (SSC), and *Twentieth-Century Literary Criticism* (TCLC). The index also lists topic entries in the Gale Critical Companion Collection, which includes the following publications: *The Beat Generation* (BG), *Feminism in Literature* (FL), *Gothic Literature* (GL), and *Harlem Renaissance* (HR).

TCLC Cumulative Nationality Index

AMERICAN

Wilde, Oscar (Fingal O'Flahertie Wills) **1, 8, 23, 41, 175**
Yeats, William Butler **1, 11, 18, 31, 93, 116**

ISRAELI

Agnon, S(hmuel) Y(osef Halevi) **151**

ITALIAN

Alvaro, Corrado **60**
Betti, Ugo **5**
Brancati, Vitaliano **12**
Calvino, Italo **183**
Campana, Dino **20**
Carducci, Giosuè (Alessandro Giuseppe) **32**
Croce, Benedetto **37**
D'Annunzio, Gabriele **6, 40**
de Filippo, Eduardo **127**
Deledda, Grazia (Cosima) **23**
Gadda, Carlo Emilio **144**
Gentile, Giovanni **96**
Giacosa, Giuseppe **7**
Ginzburg, Natalia **156**
Jovine, Francesco **79**
Levi, Carlo **125**
Levi, Primo **109**
Malaparte, Curzio **52**
Marinetti, Filippo Tommaso **10**
Montessori, Maria **103**
Mosca, Gaetano **75**
Mussolini, Benito (Amilcare Andrea) **96**
Papini, Giovanni **22**
Pareto, Vilfredo **69**
Pascoli, Giovanni **45**
Pavese, Cesare **3**
Pirandello, Luigi **4, 29, 172**
Protolini, Vasco **124**
Saba, Umberto **33**
Tozzi, Federigo **31**
Ungaretti, Giuseppe **200**
Verga, Giovanni (Carmelo) **3**

JAMAICAN

De Lisser, H(erbert) G(eorge) **12**
Garvey, Marcus (Moziah Jr.) **41**
Mais, Roger **8**
Redcam, Tom **25**

JAPANESE

Abé, Kōbō **131**
Akutagawa Ryunosuke **16**
Dazai Osamu **11**
Endō, Shūsaku **152**
Futabatei, Shimei **44**
Hagiwara, Sakutaro **60**
Hayashi, Fumiko **27**
Ishikawa, Takuboku **15**
Kunikida, Doppo **99**
Masaoka, Shiki **18**
Mishima, Yukio **161**
Miyamoto, (Chujo) Yuriko **37**
Miyazawa, Kenji **76**
Mizoguchi, Kenji **72**
Mori Ogai **14**
Nagai, Kafu **51**
Nishida, Kitaro **83**
Noguchi, Yone **80**
Santoka, Taneda **72**
Shiga, Naoya **172**
Shimazaki Toson **5**
Suzuki, Daisetz Teitaro **109**
Yokomitsu, Riichi **47**
Yosano Akiko **59**

LATVIAN

Berlin, Isaiah **105**
Rainis, Jānis **29**

LEBANESE

Gibran, Kahlil **1, 9, 205**

LESOTHAN

Mofolo, Thomas (Mokopu) **22**

LITHUANIAN

Kreve (Mickevicius), Vincas **27**

MARTINIQUE

Fanon, Frantz **188**

MEXICAN

Azuela, Mariano **3**
Gamboa, Federico **36**
Garro, Elena **153**
Gonzalez Martinez, Enrique **72**
Ibargüengoitia, Jorge **148**
Nervo, (Jose) Amado (Ruiz de) **11**
Paz, Octavio **211**
Reyes, Alfonso **33**
Romero, José Rubén **14**
Villaurrutia, Xavier **80**

NEPALI

Devkota, Laxmiprasad **23**

NEW ZEALANDER

Mander, (Mary) Jane **31**
Mansfield, Katherine **2, 8, 39, 164**

NICARAGUAN

Darío, Rubén **4**

NIGERIAN

Okigbo, Christopher **171**
Saro-Wiwa, Ken **200**
Tutuola, Amos **188**

NORWEGIAN

Bjoernson, Bjoernstjerne (Martinius) **7, 37**
Bojer, Johan **64**
Grieg, (Johan) Nordahl (Brun) **10**
Hamsun, Knut **151, 203**
Ibsen, Henrik (Johan) **2, 8, 16, 37, 52**
Kielland, Alexander Lange **5**
Lie, Jonas (Lauritz Idemil) **5**
Obstfelder, Sigbjoern **23**
Rølvaag, O. E. **17, 207**
Skram, Amalie (Bertha) **25**
Undset, Sigrid **3, 197**

PAKISTANI

Iqbal, Muhammad **28**

PERUVIAN

Arguedas, José María **147**
Palma, Ricardo **29**
Vallejo, César (Abraham) **3, 56**

POLISH

Asch, Sholem **3**
Borowski, Tadeusz **9**
Conrad, Joseph **1, 6, 13, 25, 43, 57**
Herbert, Zbigniew **168**
Peretz, Isaac Loeb **16**
Prus, Boleslaw **48**
Przybyszewski, Stanislaw **36**
Reymont, Wladyslaw (Stanislaw) **5**
Schulz, Bruno **5, 51**
Sienkiewicz, Henryk (Adam Alexander Pius) **3**
Singer, Israel Joshua **33**
Witkiewicz, Stanislaw Ignacy **8**

PORTUGUESE

Pessoa, Fernando (António Nogueira) **27**
Sa-Carniero, Mario de **83**

PUERTO RICAN

Hostos (y Bonilla), Eugenio Maria de **24**

ROMANIAN

Bacovia, George **24**
Caragiale, Ion Luca **76**
Rebreanu, Liviu **28**

RUSSIAN

Adamov, Arthur **189**
Aldanov, Mark (Alexandrovich) **23**
Andreyev, Leonid (Nikolaevich) **3**
Annensky, Innokenty (Fyodorovich) **14**
Artsybashev, Mikhail (Petrovich) **31**
Babel, Isaak (Emmanuilovich) **2, 13, 171**
Bagritsky, Eduard **60**
Bakhtin, Mikhail **160**
Balmont, Konstantin (Dmitriyevich) **11**
Bely, Andrey **7**
Berdyaev, Nikolai (Aleksandrovich) **67**
Bergelson, David **81**
Blok, Alexander (Alexandrovich) **5**
Bryusov, Valery Yakovlevich **10**
Bulgakov, Mikhail (Afanas'evich) **2, 16, 159**
Bulgya, Alexander Alexandrovich **53**
Bunin, Ivan Alexeyevich **6**
Chekhov, Anton (Pavlovich) **3, 10, 31, 55, 96, 163**
Der Nister [Pinkhes Kahanovitsch] **56**
Eisenstein, Sergei (Mikhailovich) **57**
Esenin, Sergei (Alexandrovich) **4**
Fadeyev, Alexander **53**
Gladkov, Fyodor (Vasilyevich) **27**
Gumilev, Nikolai (Stepanovich) **60**
Gurdjieff, G(eorgei) I(vanovich) **71**
Guro, Elena **56**
Hippius, Zinaida **9**
Ilf, Ilya **21**
Ivanov, Vyacheslav Ivanovich **33**
Kahanovitsch Pinkhes **56**
Kandinsky, Wassily **92**
Khlebnikov, Velimir **20**
Khodasevich, Vladislav (Felitsianovich) **15**
Klimentov, Andrei Platonovich **14**
Korolenko, Vladimir Galaktionovich **22**
Kropotkin, Peter (Aleksieevich) **36**
Kuprin, Aleksander Ivanovich **5**
Kuzmin, Mikhail **40**
Lenin, V. I. **67**
Mandelstam, Osip (Emilievich) **2, 6**
Mayakovski, Vladimir (Vladimirovich) **4, 18**
Merezhkovsky, Dmitry Sergeyevich **29**
Nabokov, Vladimir (Vladimirovich) **108, 189**
Olesha, Yuri **136**
Pasternak, Boris **188**
Pavlov, Ivan Petrovich **91**
Petrov, Evgeny **21**
Pilnyak, Boris **23**
Prishvin, Mikhail **75**
Remizov, Aleksei (Mikhailovich) **27**
Rozanov, Vassili **104**
Shestov, Lev **56**
Sologub, Fyodor **9**
Stalin, Joseph **92**
Stanislavsky, Konstantin **167**
Tolstoy, Alexey Nikolaevich **18**
Tolstoy, Leo (Nikolaevich) **4, 11, 17, 28, 44, 79, 173**
Trotsky, Leon **22**
Tsvetaeva (Efron), Marina (Ivanovna) **7, 35**
Yezierska, Anzia **205**
Zabolotsky, Nikolai Alekseevich **52**
Zamyatin, Evgeny Ivanovich **8, 37**
Zhdanov, Andrei Alexandrovich **18**
Zoshchenko, Mikhail (Mikhailovich) **15**

SCOTTISH

Barrie, J(ames) M(atthew) **2, 164**
Brown, George Douglas **28**
Buchan, John **41**

TCLC-212 Title Index

ISBN-13: 978-0-7876-9987-1
ISBN-10: 0-7876-9987-X

90000
9 780787 699871

For Reference

Not to be taken from this room